The War Report 2014

The War Report: Armed Conflict in 2014

Edited by

Annyssa Bellal

Académie de droit international humanitaire et de droits humains à Genève
Geneva Academy of International Humanitarian Law and Human Rights
Geneva Academy

The Academy, a joint centre of

The Graduate Institute Geneva
Institut de hautes études internationales et du développement
Graduate Institute of International and Development Studies

Université de Genève
Faculté de droit

OXFORD
UNIVERSITY PRESS

OXFORD
UNIVERSITY PRESS

Great Clarendon Street, Oxford, OX2 6DP,
United Kingdom

Oxford University Press is a department of the University of Oxford.
It furthers the University's objective of excellence in research, scholarship,
and education by publishing worldwide. Oxford is a registered trade mark of
Oxford University Press in the UK and in certain other countries

First Edition published in 2015

Published in the United States of America by Oxford University Press
198 Madison Avenue, New York, NY 10016, United States of America

British Library Cataloguing in Publication Data
Data available

Library of Congress Control Number: 2015951316

ISBN 978–0–19–876606–3

DISCLAIMERS

EDITOR'S PREFACE

Human rights are never so much at threat as they are in an armed conflict. This is as true today in the bloody morass of Iraq, Syria, and Yemen and too many others, as it was in the past. Similarly, peace treaties made under threat of military defeat, even annihilation, are wont to become conveniently forgotten once strategic circumstances have changed. So it was at Runnymede in mid-June of 800 years ago.

King John, the English sovereign, had been on the throne for fifteen years; a decade and a half in which he had plumbed the depths of cruelty and depravity. The barons on whose largesse he had sought to rely, having emptied the coffers of the royal treasury, were no longer willing to accept the excesses of their monarch and had mobilized forces to resist. They seized London and with his back against the wall the king finally consented to negotiate. The result was a detailed agreement by which he agreed to respect certain rules and liberties in exchange for peace, though neither he nor the barons paid more than lip service to its contents (John secured Pope Innocent III's dismissal of the Charter as 'not only shameful and demeaning, but illegal and unjust') and England was plunged into civil war.

There is a tendency to romanticize about the Magna Carta, 'The Great Charter'.[1] Indeed, the document as we generally know it today was not even the one signed by John at Runnymede (known as the Charter of Liberties), but a text issued 100 years later by Henry III. Nonetheless, the idea it espoused that the sovereign is not omnipotent, with freedom to act in any way he or she sees fit, is an ideological underpinning of human rights. We trust our elected leaders with considerable power (rather less our self-selected leaders) but their writ is restrained by human rights, a body of international law they are not authorized to ignore or diminish.

One of the clauses of the Magna Carta that has survived into the modern era is of particular importance. It provides that:

> No free man shall be seized or imprisoned, or stripped of his rights or possessions, or outlawed or exiled, or deprived of his standing in any other way, nor will we proceed with force against him, or send others to do so, except by the lawful judgement of his equals or by the law of the land.
>
> To no one will we sell, to no one deny or delay right or justice.[2]

[1] See, e.g., the blog by Dr Dominic Selwood, 'The Cult of Magna Carta Is Historical Nonsense', *The Daily Telegraph*, 17 June 2014, at: <http://blogs.telegraph.co.uk/news/dominicselwood/100276672/the-cult-of-magna-carta-is-historical-nonsense-no-wonder-oliver-cromwell-called-it-magna-farta/>.

[2] See more at: <http://www.bl.uk/magna-carta/articles/magna-carta-an-introduction#sthash.HJvddD0g.dpuf>.

The contemporary human rights to liberty and security, to habeas corpus, to trial by jury, to the right to a fair trial, are all captured in some way by this clause.[3] As we have seen in many States that have lurched into violent failure, mass arrests, torture and abuse in detention, and enforced disappearances all carried out by the authorities and their vassals are often the presage to peaceful resistance, then insurgency, and ultimately full-scale rebellion. Some sovereigns cling to the hope that if their repression is widespread enough and sufficiently severe, they will bring their subjects to cower before their might. More often than not it is they that end up falling, albeit after awful bloodshed.

Today, detention in situations of armed conflict, especially those of a non-international character, as those schooled in international humanitarian law and international human rights law know only too well, is a hot and controversial topic. Any incarceration puts individuals at particular risk of physical, sexual, and psychological abuse; in a situation of conflict, where you have your enemy in your hands and subject to your will, the risks are greatly exaggerated. In 2015, 800 years after the Magna Carta, legal and practical challenges in implementing and complying with the basic human rights of those detained remain high, be it for States or armed groups. To what extent IHL gives States, but also armed groups, the right to detain in non-international armed conflicts is a tricky and difficult question. To what extent do armed groups have the capacity to respect habeas corpus and fair trial rights is another thorny issue. Luckily courts of law, at least some of them, remind actors of armed conflict of their responsibility. In May 2014, for instance, the Prosecutor of the ICC announced she had decided to re-open a preliminary examination about the alleged responsibility for war crimes, involving systematic detainee abuse, of the armed forces of the United Kingdom deployed in Iraq from 2003 until 2008.[4]

The third preambular paragraph of the 1948 Universal Declaration of Human Rights famously intones that 'it is essential, if man is not to be compelled to have recourse, as a last resort, to rebellion against tyranny and oppression, that human rights should be protected by the rule of law'. This axiomatic truth remains valid today. Thus, as the United Kingdom considers whether to repeal its Human Rights Act, a statute that incorporates the 1950 Convention for the Protection of Human Rights and Fundamental Freedoms into domestic law, it behoves to reflect not only on the last seventy-five years

[3] Of course, not every person was a free man. Most were 'villeins', unfree peasants who could seek justice only through the courts of their own lords; a capricious source of jurisprudence. British Library, 'Magna Carta: an introduction', undated but accessed at: <http://www.bl.uk/magna-carta/articles/magna-carta-an-introduction>.

[4] ICC, 'Prosecutor of the International Criminal Court, Fatou Bensouda, re-opens the preliminary examination of the situation in Iraq', 13 May 2014, at: <http://www.icc-cpi.int/en_menus/icc/structure%20of%20the%20court/office%20of%20the%20prosecutor/reports%20and%20statements/statement/Pages/otp-statement-iraq-13-05-2014.aspx>.

since that instrument's adoption by the Council of Europe, but also the 800 years that have elapsed since John appended his royal seal to what would later become known as the Great Charter. Such actions do not merely concern those who are the direct subject of these agreements, they also influence those who would draw inspiration—or, conversely, perverse gratification—from the decisions of a sovereign about how he may treat his subjects. Tyrants and despots watch the news too.

Dr Annyssa Bellal and Dr Stuart Casey-Maslen, June 2015

ACKNOWLEDGEMENTS

I have had the immense pleasure and privilege to assume this year's edition of the War Report. I would like to thank Professor Robert Roth, Director of the Geneva Academy of International Humanitarian Law and Human Rights, for trusting me with this endeavour and several other persons who helped me bring the book to fruition.

The *War Report 2014* would simply not have been possible without the invaluable assistance in research for the country profiles provided by Sara LaRocca and Mayank Verma, LL.M students at the Geneva Academy of International Humanitarian Law and Human Rights. Not only were they thorough and perspicacious, but always showed great enthusiasm in helping me in fulfilling the *War Report*'s mission. I wish them well for their promising careers as international lawyers.

I would also like to thank Alice Priddy and Marina Mattirolo, for their research on some of the most difficult country profiles, including Iraq, Syria, and Colombia; Natia Kalandarishvili for her research on the profile on Georgia; Georg Koeppinghoff for his research and drafting of the profile on the armed conflict in Gaza; as well as Jakob Donatz, Valentina Azarova, Sharon Weill, Bill Van Esweld, Jean-Baptiste Maillart, and Antonio Coco for their inputs on various country profiles. I thank Marie Coutin Lequin for having enlightened me on the complex DRC conflict and Gran Hewad for his thorough comments on the Afghanistan conflict. Although I have edited the *War Report 2014* entirely in my personal capacity, I would like to thank the NGO Geneva Call and its staff for their support. Last but not least, my heartfelt thanks go to Stuart Casey-Maslen, my former colleague at the Geneva Academy and constant friend. *The War Report 2014* builds up on all the work he has done for the previous editions of the book and I have benefited greatly from his immense experience and expertise. This year's Editor's preface is signed by us both as a token of my gratitude.

CONTENTS

TABLE OF CASES

African Commission on Human and Peoples' Rights

Committee against Torture

European Court of Human Rights (ECtHR)

European Court of Justice

Human Rights Committee

Inter-American Court of Human Rights (IACtHR)

Inter-American Commission of Human Rights (IAComHR)

International Court of Justice (ICJ)

CONTENTIOUS CASES

ADVISORY OPINIONS

International Criminal Court (ICC)

International Criminal Tribunal for the former Yugoslavia (ICTY)

International Criminal Tribunal for Rwanda (ICTR)

Permanent Court of International Justice (PCIJ)

Special Court for Sierra Leone

National courts

AUSTRALIA

CANADA

GREECE

HUNGARY

SLOVAKIA

SWEDEN

UNITED KINGDOM

UNITED STATES

TABLE OF TREATIES

Peace agreements and negotiations

Soft law instruments

UNITED NATIONS RESOLUTIONS

General Assembly

Human Rights Council

Security Council

European Legislation

DIRECTIVES

REGULATIONS

National Legislation

ANGOLA

AUSTRALIA

AZERBAIJAN

BOSNIA HERZEGOVINA

CANADA

CENTRAL AFRICAN REPUBLIC

COLOMBIA

USA

LIST OF ABBREVIATIONS

ABL	Administrative Boundary Line
ACLED	Armed Conflict Location & Event Data Project
ACLU	American Civil Liberties Union
ACMM	Peasant Self-Defense Forces of the Middle Magdalena
AComHPR	African Commission on Human and Peoples' Rights
ADF–NALU	Allied Democratic Forces/National Army for the Liberation of Uganda
AFISMA	African-led International Support Mission in Mali
AFP	Armed Forces of the Philippines
AFP	Agence France-Presse
AFRC	Armed Forces Revolutionary Council (Liberia)
AI	Amnesty International
AIHRC	Afghanistan Independent Human Rights Commission
ALP	Afghan Local Police
AMIB	African Union Mission in Burundi
AMIS	African Union Mission in Sudan
AMISEC	African Union Mission of Support to the Elections in the Comoros
AMISOM	African Union Mission in Somalia
ANA	Afghan National Army
ANCBS	Association of National Committees of the Blue Shield
ANP	Afghan National Police
ANSA	Armed Non-State Actor
AP	Associated Press
APRD	Popular Army for the Restoration of Democracy (CAR)
AQAP	Al-Qaeda in the Arabian Peninsula
AQIM	Al-Qaeda in the Islamic Maghreb
ASG	Abu Sayyaf Group (Philippines)
ATS	Alien Tort Statute (USA)
ATT	Arms Trade Treaty
AU	African Union

AUC	United Self-Defense Forces of Colombia
AUMF	Authorization for Use of Military Force
AzCBL	Azerbaijan Campaign to Ban Landmines
BBIED	Body-Borne Improvised Explosive Device
BGF	Border Guard Forces
BRN	Barisan Revolusi Nasional (Thailand)
BSA	Bilateral Security Agreement
BWC	Biological Weapons Convention
CAD	Comités de Autodefensa
CAFGU	Citizen Armed Force Geographical Units
CAR	Central African Republic
CCC	Center for Civilians in Conflict
CCW	Convention on Certain Conventional Weapons
CEP	Circular area probable
CERP	Commanders Emergency Response Program
CIS	Commonwealth of Independent States
C-JTF	Civilian Joint Task Force (Nigeria)
CNDP	National Congress for the Defence of the People (Congo)
COVAW	Coalition on Violence Against Women
CPA	Comprehensive Peace Agreement
CPJ	Committee to Protect Journalists
CPJP	Convention of Patriots for Justice and Peace (CAR)
CPSK	Convention patriotique du salut du Kodro
CRC	Convention on the Rights of the Child
CSDP	Common Security and Defence Policy
CSPA	Child Soldiers Prevention Act
CVO	Civilian Volunteer Organization
DDR	Disarmament, Demobilization, and Reintegration
DEA	Drug Enforcement Agency (USA)
DGSSIE	Direction Générale de Sécurisation des Services et Institutions de l'Etat
DISI	Democratic Rally (Cyprus)
DNI	Director of National Intelligence
DOD	Department of Defense
DPKO	Department of Peacekeeping Operations
DPR Korea	Democratic People's Republic of Korea

DRC	Democratic Republic of Congo
ECCC	Extraordinary Chambers in the Courts of Cambodia
ECOWAS	Economic Community of West African States
ELN	National Liberation Army (Columbia)
EOD	Explosive Ordnance Disposal
EPLF	Eritrean People's Liberation Front
EQB	Ezzeddeen al-Qassam Brigades
ERW	Explosive Remnants of War
EUFOR-RCA	European Union Force-Central African Republic
EULEX	European Union Rule of Law Mission
FACA	Forces armées centrafricaines
FAFN	Forces armées des forces nouvelles
FARC	Revolutionary Armed Forces of Colombia (Colombia)
FARDC	Forces Armées de la République Démocratique du Congo
FCO	Foreign and Commonwealth Office (UK)
FDLR	Forces Démocratiques de Libération du Rwanda
FDPC	Front démocratique du peuple centrafricain (CAR)
FRCI	Forces républicaines de Côte d'Ivoire
FSA	Free Syrian Army
GAFE	Airmobile Special Forces Group (Mexico)
GANFE	Amphibian Group of Special Forces (Mexico)
GLD	Groupes de légitime défense
GPCWD	Global Partnership on Children with Disabilities
GOA	Government of Afghanistan
HCUA	Haute Conseil pour l'unité de l'Azawad
HIG	Hezb-e-Islami Gulbuddin
HRF	Human Rights Foundation
HRL	Human Rights Law
HV	Hrvatska vojska, Croatian army
HVO	Croatian Defence Council
IAC	International Armed Conflict
IACtHR	Inter-American Court of Human Rights
IAGD	Intergovernmental Authority on Development (South Sudan)
ICBL	International Campaign to Ban Landmines
ICBS	International Committee of the Blue Shield

ICC	International Criminal Court
ICCPR	1966 International Covenant on Civil and Political Rights
ICCROM	International Centre for the Study of the Preservation and Restoration of Cultural Property
ICESCR	International Covenant on Economic, Social and Cultural Rights
ICG	International Crisis Group
ICGLR	International Conference on the Great Lakes Region
ICJ	International Court of Justice
ICJ-Kenya	Kenyan Section of the International Commission of Jurists
ICL	International Criminal Law
ICOM	International Council of Museums
ICRC	International Committee of the Red Cross
ICSR	International Centre for the Study of Radicalisation
ICT	International Crimes Tribunal of Bangladesh
ICTR	International Criminal Tribunal for Rwanda
ICTY	International Criminal Tribunal for the former Yugoslavia
IDF	Israel Defense Forces
IDP	Internally Displaced Persons
IED	Improvized Explosive Devices
IHL	International Humanitarian Law
ILC	International Law Commission
ILLE	International Law of Law Enforcement
IMLU	Independent Medico-Legal Unit
IMT	International Military Tribunal
IPC	Instituto Popular de Capacitación (Colombia)
ISA	Israel Security Agency
ISAF	International Security Assistance Force
ISIL	Islamic State of Iraq and the Levant
JCE	Joint Criminal Enterprise
JEM	Justice and Equality Movement (Sudan)
JSOC	Joint Special Operations Command
KIA	Kachin Independence Army (Myanmar)
KIO	Kachin Independence Organization (Myanmar)
LOAC	Law of Armed Conflict
LRA	Lord's Resistance Army

M23	Mouvement du 23 mars (Congo)
MBRL	Multi-Barrel Rocket Launchers
MFAA	Monuments, Fine Arts and Archives program
MICOPAX	Mission for the Consolidation of Peace in the Central African Republic
MICT	Mechanism for International Criminal Tribunals
MILF	Moro Islamic Liberation Front (Philippines)
MINURSO	UN Mission for a Referendum in Western Sahara
MINUSCA	UN Multidimensional Integrated Stabilization Mission in CAR
MINUSMA	UN Multidimensional Integrated Stabilization Mission in Mali
MLC	Mouvement de libération du Congo
MNLA	Mouvement national de libération de l'Azawad (Algeria)
MNLF	Moro National Liberation Front (Philippines)
MOJWA	Movement for Oneness and Jihad in West Africa
MONUC	UN Mission in the Democratic Republic of Congo
MONUSCO	UN Organization Stabilization Mission in the Democratic Republic of the Congo
MRT	Moldavian Republic of Transdniestria
MUJAO	Mouvement pour l'unicité et le jihad en Afrique de l'Ouest
NATO	North Atlantic Treaty Organization
NCCT	National Ceasefire Coordination Team (Myanmar)
NCP	National Congress Party (Sudan)
NDS	National Directorate of Security (Afghanistan)
NDU	National Defence University
NGO	Non-Governmental Organization
NIAC	Non-International Armed Conflict
NPA	New People's Army (Philippines)
NSAG	Non-State Armed Groups
OCHA	Office for the Coordination of Humanitarian Affairs (UN)
OHCHR	Office of the UN High Commissioner for Human Rights
OPAC	Optional Protocol to the Convention on the Rights of the Child on the involvement of children in armed conflict
OPCW	Organisation for the Prohibition of Chemical Weapons
OSCE	Organization for Security and Co-operation in Europe
OTP	Office of the Prosecutor
PA	Palestinian Authority

PAICMA	Colombian Presidential Program for Mine Action
PCIJ	Permanent Court of International Justice
PHR	Physicians for Human Rights
PIJ	Palestinian Islamic Jihad
PKK	Kurdish Worker's Party
PLO	Palestine Liberation Organisation
PNA	Palestinian National Authority
PNC	Police Nationale Congolaise
PTSD	Post-Traumatic Stress Disorder
ROK	Republic of Korea
R2P	Responsibility to Protect
RUF	Revolutionary United Front (Liberia)
RULAC	Rule of Law in armed conflicts
SADC	Southern African Development Community
SADPD	Secretariat of the African Decade of Persons with Disabilities
SAF	Sudan Armed Forces
SANDF	South African National Defence Forces
SATP	South Asia Terrorism Portal
SCSL	Special Court for Sierra Leone
SEMG	Somalia and Eritrea Monitoring Group
SLM	Sudan Liberation Movement
SLORC	State Law and Order Restoration Council (Myanmar)
SMC	Supreme Military Council (Syria)
SNHR	Syrian Network for Human Rights
SNSP	National Security System (Mexico)
SOHR	Syrian Observatory for Human Rights
SPLA	Sudan People's Liberation Army
SPLM	Sudan People's Liberation Movement
SPLM/A	Sudan People's Liberation Movement/Army
SPO	Special Police Officers
SRF	Sudan Revolutionary Front
SRSG	Special Representative of the UN Secretary-General in DRC
SSR	Security Sector Reform
TCN	Troop-Contributing Nations
TFI	Transitional Federal Institutions

TMR	Transdniestrian Moldovan Republic
UAV	Unmanned Aerial Vehicle
UCPN-Maoist	Unified Communist Party of Nepal-Maoist
UFDR	Union des forces démocratiques pour le rassemblement (CAR)
UFR	Union des forces républicaines
UIC	Union of Islamic Courts (Somalia)
UN	United Nations
UNAMA	UN Assistance Mission in Afghanistan
UNAMI	UN Assistance Mission in Iraq
UNAMID	African Union-UN Mission in Darfur
UNDOF	UN Disengagement Observer Force
UNDP	United Nations Development Programme
UNESCO	UN Educational, Scientific and Cultural Organization
UNFICYP	UN Peacekeeping Force in Cyprus
UNICEF	UN Children's Fund
UNIDROIT	Institut international pour l'unification du droit privé
UNISFA	UN Interim Security Force for Abyei
UNHCR	Office of the UN High Commissioner for Refugees
UNMISS	UN Mission in South Sudan
UNOMIG	UN Observer Mission in Georgia
UPDF	Ugandan People's Defence Force
VBIED	Vehicle-Borne Improvised Explosive Device
VDC	Center for Documentation of Violations (Syria)
VJ	Vojska Jugoslavije (Yugoslav Army)
VRS	Vojska Republike Srpska (Bosnian Serb Army)
WHO	World Health Organization
YEMEC	Yemen Mine Action Center

Introduction

This work identifies, describes, and discusses all situations of armed violence in 2014 that amounted to armed conflicts in accordance with the definitions recognized under international humanitarian law (IHL) and international criminal law (ICL). The purpose of *The War Report* is to collect information and data in the public domain and provide legal analysis under the framework of international law. The existence of an armed conflict is important because it has far-reaching implications. First and foremost, IHL governing the conduct of hostilities, which is markedly less restrictive in its prohibitions on the use of lethal force than is the international law of law enforcement, applies only in a situation of armed conflict. Notably, IHL does not prohibit the intentional use of lethal force against a member of the armed forces or a civilian 'participating directly in hostilities' (for the duration of such participation, see the 'Summary rules' sections in Part I). Second, war crimes may only be committed in connection with an armed conflict. Third, the International Committee of the Red Cross (ICRC) has a formal role in protection only in connection with armed conflicts.

No national or supranational body is authoritative in its determination or implication that a particular situation of armed violence constitutes an armed conflict; a situation threatening international peace and security is not a synonym for an armed conflict (although, unquestionably, the situations may coincide). Moreover, the existence of an armed conflict is an objective test and not a national 'decision'. Consequently, whether a State affirms that a particular situation does, or does not, amount to an armed conflict is relevant information for the purposes of determining the applicable law, but is certainly not conclusive.

Further, as explained in more detail later, however significant (and tragic) loss of life may be in any State or territory, the qualification of a situation of armed violence as an armed conflict is not simply a numbers game. Indeed, armed violence within a State may claim not only hundreds, but even thousands, of lives—and may constitute crimes against humanity[1]

[1] Crimes against humanity are those crimes that 'shock the conscience of humanity'. Under the 1998 Rome Statute of the International Criminal Court (ICC Statute), crimes against humanity occur where certain acts are undertaken as part of a widespread or systematic attack against a civilian population of which attack the perpetrator has knowledge. Such acts are murder, extermination, enslavement, forcible transfer of population, imprisonment, torture, rape, sexual slavery, enforced prostitution, forced pregnancy, enforced sterilization, sexual violence, persecution, enforced disappearance, apartheid, and other inhumane acts: Art. 7(1)(a)–(k), ICC Statute.

or even genocide[2]—without necessarily crossing the threshold into armed conflict; other factors are also pertinent, especially the extent of clashes between armed forces, or between armed forces and organized armed groups (or between such groups themselves). Thus reports detailing 'wars' based on, for example, twenty-five or 1,000 battlefield deaths annually can be valuable for political science purposes, but such categorizations do not per se have significance under international law.

Part I of this work lists and summarizes the armed conflicts that occurred in 2014 on the basis of explicit criteria that, I believe, best reflect extant international law, certain controversies and imprecision notwithstanding. Determinations that are, or are likely to be, disputed are openly acknowledged. Casualties and displacement provoked by the armed conflicts are also detailed (and sourced), accompanied by requisite caveats as to the accuracy and representativeness of the figures provided.

Casualty data are selected from all open source material that can be identified. Sources for data vary by country; each country report provides detailed information on the sources of the data used. Data sources collected include:

- the United Nations (UN) and its agencies, including the Office for the Coordination of Humanitarian Affairs (OCHA), Office of the High Commissioner for Human Rights (OHCHR), the Human Rights Council, UNICEF, reports of the UN Secretary-General to the UN Security Council, peacekeeping and assistance missions, such as the African Union–UN Mission in Darfur (UNAMID), UN Mission in South Sudan (UNMISS), UN Assistance Mission in Afghanistan (UNAMA), and UN Assistance Mission in Iraq (UNAMI);
- other international organizations, such as the World Health Organization;
- national governments reporting on the casualties occurring in other countries, such as the United States (US) Department of State and various travel warning and security briefing websites produced by other nations;
- governments of States active in conflict, including their police and/or military, such as in Colombia, the Philippines, and, internationally, the US Department of Defence;
- international non-governmental organizations, such as Amnesty International, Human Rights Watch, and the International Crisis Group;

[2] Genocide 'means any of the following acts committed with intent to destroy, in whole or in part, a national, ethnical, racial or religious group, as such:

(a) Killing members of the group;
(b) Causing serious bodily or mental harm to members of the group;
(c) Deliberately inflicting on the group conditions of life calculated to bring about its physical destruction in whole or in part;
(d) Imposing measures intended to prevent births within the group;
(e) Forcibly transferring children of the group to another group.'

Art. 6, ICC Statute; see also Art. 2, 1948 Convention on the Prevention and Punishment of the Crime of Genocide.

- NGOs such as the Violations Documentation Centre in Syria, the Syrian Observatory for Human Rights, and the Azerbaijan Campaign to Ban Landmines;
- organizations and individuals that have compiled media reports, including academics;[3]
- academic and research centres and other sources that compile or analyse reporting, including the Armed Conflict Location and Event Data Project (ACLED), the Iraq Body Count, the Bureau of Investigative Journalism, the Justice in Mexico project, and the South Asia Terrorism Portal; and
- media scanning by a specialist consultant.[4]

This list is not exhaustive but demonstrates the types and range of sources reviewed. Where alternative figures cannot reasonably be reconciled, both are given. For 2015, there remained many challenges to obtain accurate data that fit the *War Report* casualty criteria. These challenges included:

- sources focused only on civilian casualties that intentionally exclude military and militant casualties, and overall very limited data on casualties among non-State armed actors;
- sources presenting only conflict fatalities and not injuries: data on people injured remained much more difficult to obtain;
- data disaggregated by age and gender was not adequately available to enable the numbers of women and children killed and injured in conflict to be substantively analysed.

Although only one combination of data sources is chosen to represent the total conflict casualties for each conflict, country, or occupation in 2014, in cases where more than one source of casualty data is identified for a conflict or country, we have endeavoured to present all relevant datasets in the text. Whenever possible, we provide an indication of which dataset reported the most comprehensive, verified, disaggregated, or otherwise usable data.

Part II details the situations of armed conflict around the world, drawing on the work of the Rule of Law in Armed Conflicts (RULAC) project conducted since 2009 under Geneva Academy auspices.[5] The situation profiles describe in each case the qualification of the conflict, its history, the applicable rules,[6] the main parties to the conflict, the

[3] For compilations of media data, we use those that collect conflict-related casualties. However, in some cases the criteria are broader than ours and data may include casualties from other types of violence. This is noted in the country report when relevant.

[4] Media reports do not always provide sufficient detail to determine whether or not a casualty is directly related to armed conflict or other type of violence. We err on the side of excluding casualties for which the direct cause is not clear. Therefore, media reported casualties, while not verified through secondary sources, tend to provide better indications and detail about which conflict casualties may be associated when there are multiple conflicts in a country or given area.

[5] At: <http://www.rulac.org/>.

[6] Adherence by States to selected IHL and human rights treaties is included in each profile. This is not to deny or exclude the application of other treaties.

principal means and methods of warfare they used in 2014, resulting casualties, and any war crimes investigations, prosecutions, and convictions that either took place during the year or which pertained to acts committed during 2014.

Part III comprises a total of sixteen chapters, each of which addresses a thematic issue with particular relevance to 2014. The first section addresses different aspects of means and methods of warfare. In Chapter 1, Hilary Stauffer looks at the CIA Torture Report and wonders whether there was a method in the madness. In Chapter 2, Megan Burke and Loren Persi Vicentic examine gender perspectives in 2014. In Chapter 3, Sharon Weill and Valentina Azarova reflect on the *jus ad bellum*, *jus in bello*, and accountability implications of the 2014 armed conflict in Gaza. In Chapter 4, Antonio Coco and Jean-Baptiste Maillart offer a critical analysis of the conflict with the armed group 'Islamic State'. Under the rubric of protection in armed conflict, Kristin Hausler, in Chapter 5, examines how international law addresses the human tragedy faced by many refugee and asylum seekers when fleeing armed conflicts. In Chapter 6, Marina Mattirolo reviews the law and practice in 2014 of the protection of internally displaced persons in armed conflict. In Chapter 7, Alex Conte analyses the difficult and controversial question of detention in armed conflict. Chiara Redaelli looks, in Chapter 8, at the issue of the engagement of Drug Lords on protection of civilians in Colombia, Mexico, and Honduras. The right to protest in armed conflict situations is examined in Chapter 9 by Milena Costas Trascasas. In Chapter 10, Sylvie Girard wonders if the mechanisms behind youth joining 'criminal gangs' are similar to those joining violent extremist groups. The final section considers judicial enforcement of ICL and IHL in 2014. In Chapter 11, Silvia Suteu examines how 'extraordinary renditions' were dealt with by the European Court of Human Rights. In Chapter 12, Ilia-Maria Siatitsa reviews national trials of international crimes in 2014, concentrating on the issue of the prosecution of 'refugees' suspected of international crimes. Dru A. Brenner-Beck offers a thorough update and analysis of the Guantanamo War Crimes Trials in Chapter 13. In Chapter 14, Alice Priddy proposes ways to tackle impunity for sexual violence. In Chapter 15, Damien Scalia reviews important jurisprudence in the ad hoc international criminal tribunals in 2014. Finally, in Chapter 16, Valentina Cadelo examines the challenges and opportunities of transitional justice mechanisms.

Part I
Summary

Summary

In 2014, at least forty-two armed conflicts occurred on the territory of twenty-six States and territories in Afghanistan, Azerbaijan, the Central African Republic (CAR), Colombia, Cyprus, the Democratic Republic of Congo (DRC), Egypt, Eritrea, Georgia, India, Iraq, Lebanon, Libya, Mali, Moldova, Nigeria, Pakistan, Palestine, Somalia, South Sudan, Sudan, Syria, Thailand, Ukraine, Western Sahara, and Yemen.[1] Four armed conflicts ended in 2014 (in CAR, Mexico (two NIACs), and Thailand). Of course, the end of an armed conflict as defined by international law does not necessarily imply an end to armed violence, much less to the suffering of the population.

Of the forty-two conflicts, only three were active international armed conflicts: between India and Pakistan, between Israel and Syria,[2] and between Palestine and Israel. In addition, however, belligerent occupations continued in parts of ten States and territories (Azerbaijan, Cyprus, Eritrea, Georgia, Lebanon, Moldova, Palestine, Syria, Ukraine, and Western Sahara). These occupations are governed by the law of military occupation that also forms part of the law of international armed conflict.[3]

[1] On 1 January 2015, the Resolute Support mission was established by the North Atlantic Treaty Organization (NATO) in Afghanistan, in replacement of the International Security Assistance Force (ISAF), to train, advise, and assist the Afghan security forces and institutions. The following States are contributing to the mission and are, as a consequence, concerned by this armed conflict: Albania, Armenia, Australia, Austria, Azerbaijan, Belgium, Bosnia and Herzegovina, Bulgaria, Croatia, Czech Republic, Denmark, Estonia, Finland, the former Yugoslav Republic of Macedonia, Georgia, Germany, Greece, Hungary, Iceland, Ireland, Italy, Latvia, Lithuania, Luxembourg, Mongolia, Montenegro, the Netherlands, New Zealand, Norway, Poland, Portugal, Romania, Slovakia, Slovenia, Spain, Sweden, Turkey, Ukraine, the United Kingdom (UK), and the United States of America (USA).

[2] Although hostilities between Israel and Syria in 2014 amounted to at least four IACs, they are counted as one for the purpose of the global total.

[3] The Elements of Crimes established under the International Criminal Court (ICC) provide that 'the term "international armed conflict" includes military occupation': ICC, 'Elements of crimes', UN doc. PCNICC/2000/1/Add.2 (2000), n. 34. See, e.g., Cullen, A., 2008, 'The Threshold of Non-International Armed Conflict', SSRN, p. 132, at: <http://papers.ssrn.com/sol3/papers.cfm?abstract_id=2222757>.

A total of twenty-nine non-international armed conflicts took place in eighteen States: Afghanistan, CAR, Colombia, the DRC, Egypt, India, Iraq, Libya, Mali, Nigeria, Pakistan, Somalia, South Sudan, Sudan, Syria, Thailand, Ukraine, and Yemen.

The criteria used to make these determinations are detailed below, and where these criteria and/or the resulting determinations are likely to be disputed, this is acknowledged. Based on research and analysis of available sources (all of which are clearly cited and some of which are seemingly contradictory), at least 82,000 men, women, and children were killed or injured by acts committed in these conflicts. This is an extremely conservative figure, and is certainly much lower than the true number. For instance, available data for Syria only record those killed (more than 30,000), not those injured. Of the total recorded victims for conflicts in 2014, excepting the Gaza conflict, fewer than 500 were victims of international armed conflict.

What is an armed conflict?

In accordance with international humanitarian law (IHL, also called the law of armed conflict, LOAC)[4] and international criminal law (ICL) there are two categories of armed conflict: international armed conflict (IAC) and non-international armed conflict (NIAC).[5]A valuable and widely cited general definition of the two categories was

[4] Views differ as to whether international humanitarian law (IHL) is a synonym for the law of armed conflict (LOAC). Today, this is the prevailing view although it has been argued that 'Geneva' law (on the protection of those in the power of a party to conflict who are not, or no longer, participating directly in hostilities) is better termed IHL while 'Hague' law (on the conduct of hostilities) falls within the broader LOAC framework.

[5] The European Union (EU) also uses the term 'internal armed conflict' to determine, for the purposes of protection under EU law, whether a third country national or a stateless person who does not qualify as a refugee but in respect of whom substantial grounds have been shown for believing that the person concerned, if returned to his or her country of origin, or in the case of a stateless person, to his or her country of former habitual residence, would face a real risk of suffering serious harm … and is unable, or, owing to such risk, unwilling to avail himself or herself of the protection of that country'. Art. 2, EU Directive 2004/83. According to Art. 15(c) of the Directive, serious harm consists of a 'serious and individual threat to a civilian's life or person by reason of indiscriminate violence in situations of international or internal armed conflict'. In a decision in January 2014, the Court determined that an internal armed conflict exists 'if a State's armed forces confront one or more armed groups or if two or more armed groups confront each other. It is not necessary for that conflict to be categorized as 'armed conflict not of an international character' under international humanitarian law; nor is it necessary to carry out, in addition to an appraisal of the level of violence present in the territory concerned, a separate assessment of the intensity of the armed confrontations, the level of organisation of the armed forces involved or the duration of the conflict'. Court of Justice of the European Union, *Aboubacar Diakité v Commissaire général aux réfugiés et aux apatrides*, Judgment (Fourth Chamber) (Case C-285/12), 30 January 2014, §35. At: <http://curia.europa.eu/juris/document/document.jsf?text=&docid=147061&pageIndex=0&doclang=EN&mode=lst&dir=&occ=first&part=1&cid=460406>. This decision has no influence on the IHL/ICL definition of armed conflict.

advanced by the Appeals Chamber of the International Criminal Tribunal for the former Yugoslavia (ICTY) in a 1995 decision in the *Tadić* case:

> [A]n armed conflict exists whenever there is a resort to armed force between States or protracted armed violence between governmental authorities and organized armed groups or between such groups within a State.[6]

Thus, in the view of the ICTY, an IAC exists whenever there is a resort to armed force between States, while a NIAC exists when there is protracted armed violence between governmental authorities and organized armed groups, or between such groups within a State. This means that the level of violence needed to trigger an IAC differs from—i.e., is, in general, significantly lower than—that necessary to constitute a NIAC. This issue is discussed below.

Furthermore, and even though this understanding is not universally shared, it is not a case of 'either-or' in any given geographical situation. Accordingly, several different armed conflicts, comprising one or both categories, may be ongoing at the same time and in parallel in any given State. This position, sometimes called the fragmentation of conflict theory, has been supported by the International Criminal Court's (ICC's) Trial Chamber judgment in March 2014 in the *Katanga* case.[7] Such fragmentation is evidenced in a number of recent armed conflicts. For example, there were distinct NIACs in 2012 in Syria pitting Syrian armed forces (and supporting militia) against the Free Syrian Army and, separately, against Jabhat al-Nusra. In 2013, a separate NIAC broke out between the Syrian regime and the Islamic State of Iraq and Levant (ISIL)[8] and between the FSA and Hezbollah, while Israel attacked Syria from the air during the year on at least two occasions. In addition, as Israel continues, without Syrian consent, to occupy the Golan Heights, recognized as part of Syrian territory, this still amounts to a distinct military occupation governed by the rules applicable to an IAC (see section, below, 'Criteria for the existence of an international armed conflict').

[6] ICTY, *Prosecutor v Dusko Tadić (aka 'Dule')*, Decision on the Defence Motion for Interlocutory Appeal on Jurisdiction (Appeals Chamber) (Case No. IT-94-1), 2 October 1995, §70, at: <http://www.icty.org/x/cases/tadic/acdec/en/51002.htm>. See generally also International Committee of the Red Cross (ICRC), 'How is the Term "Armed Conflict" Defined in International Humanitarian Law?', ICRC Opinion Paper, March 2008, at: <http://www.icrc.org/eng/assets/files/other/opinion-paper-armed-conflict.pdf>; and Vité, S., 2009, 'Typology of Armed Conflicts in International Humanitarian Law: Legal Concepts and Actual Situations', *International Review of the Red Cross*, vol. 91, no. 873 (March 2009), pp. 69–94, at: <http://www.icrc.org/eng/assets/files/other/irrc-873-vite.pdf>.

[7] See, e.g., ICC, *Prosecutor v Germain Katanga*, Judgment (Trial Chamber II) (Case No. ICC-01/04-01/07), 7 March 2014, §1197.

[8] This armed group is also called the Islamic State of Iraq and the Levant (ISIL). It was formerly called just the Islamic State of Iraq.

In any event, the existence of an armed conflict of either category is generally limited to the areas where the parties to the conflict are conducting hostilities against each other. War crimes may, however, be committed by a member of a party to the conflict in other areas that it controls. This could concern, for example, civilians at large in the power of that party or civilians or military personnel it is detaining. According to the ICTY, in the case of Bosnia and Herzegovina:

It is sufficient that the alleged crimes were closely related to the hostilities occurring in other parts of the territories controlled by the parties to the conflict. There is no doubt that the allegations at issue here bear the required relationship. The indictment states that in 1992 Bosnian Serbs took control of the Opstina of Prijedor and established a prison camp in Omarska. It further alleges that crimes were committed against civilians inside and outside the Omarska prison camp as part of the Bosnian Serb take-over and consolidation of power in the Prijedor region, which was, in turn, part of the larger Bosnian Serb military campaign to obtain control over Bosnian territory … In light of the foregoing, we conclude that, for the purposes of applying international humanitarian law, the crimes alleged were committed in the context of an armed conflict.

Thus, consonant with the view of the ICTY, when an armed conflict is in progress, IHL generally applies throughout the territory of the State or States concerned. As a consequence, a number of fundamental rules, including those set out in Common Article 3 to the 1949 Geneva Conventions,[9] apply throughout the territory of a State engaged in an armed conflict.[10] Rules governing the conduct of hostilities are, though, limited to areas where combat is occurring.

[9] According to Common Article 3, inter alia, 'each Party to the conflict shall be bound to apply, as a minimum, the following provisions:

(1) Persons taking no active part in the hostilities, including members of armed forces who have laid down their arms and those placed *hors de combat* by sickness, wounds, detention, or any other cause, shall in all circumstances be treated humanely, without any adverse distinction founded on race, colour, religion or faith, sex, birth or wealth, or any other similar criteria.… To this end, the following acts are and shall remain prohibited at any time and in any place whatsoever with respect to the above-mentioned persons:
    (a) violence to life and person, in particular murder of all kinds, mutilation, cruel treatment and torture;
    (b) taking of hostages;
    (c) outrages upon personal dignity, in particular humiliating and degrading treatment;
    (d) the passing of sentences and the carrying out of executions without previous judgment pronounced by a regularly constituted court, affording all the judicial guarantees which are recognized as indispensable by civilized peoples.
(2) The wounded and sick shall be collected and cared for.'

(Arguably, however, even a wilful failure to collect and care for the wounded and sick would not constitute a war crime.)

[10] See, e.g., 1949 Geneva Convention IV, Arts. 35–46. See also Kolb, R. and Hyde, R., 2008, *An Introduction to the International Law of Armed Conflicts*, Hart, Oxford, pp. 94–6.

International armed conflict

CRITERIA FOR THE EXISTENCE OF AN INTERNATIONAL ARMED CONFLICT

According to Common Article 2 to the 1949 Geneva Conventions, each of the four Conventions 'shall apply to all cases of declared war or of any other armed conflict which may arise between two or more of the High Contracting Parties, even if the state of war is not recognized by one of them'.

If understood strictly, the ICTY's definition of an IAC in the *Tadić* case ('whenever there is a resort to armed force between States') is too narrow in its insistence that the armed force be *between* two or more States. It is undoubtedly true that, as Dietrich Schindler observed: 'the existence of an armed conflict within the meaning of Article 2 common to the Geneva Conventions can always be assumed when parts of the armed forces of two States clash with each other ... Any kind of use of arms between two States brings the Conventions into effect'.[11] But, consistent with *jus ad bellum* (the law governing interstate use of force), an IAC also exists whenever one State uses armed force against the territory of another State, irrespective of whether the latter State fights back. Thus, as Hans-Peter Gasser explains, 'any use of armed force by one State against the territory of another triggers the applicability of the Geneva Conventions between the two States ... It is also of no concern whether or not the party attacked resists'.[12]

The *Tadić* case appears to support the so-called 'first shot' theory, in which any use of force (or even the mere detention of foreign military personnel) is sufficient to constitute an IAC. In contrast, however, *The War Report* follows the position adopted by the International Court of Justice (ICJ) in the *Nicaragua* case whereby small-scale 'frontier incidents' (for example, where a soldier fires across an international border) do not constitute an IAC.[13]

An IAC does, though, include any situation in which one State invades another and occupies it, even if there is no armed resistance at all. This is set down in Article 2 common to the four 1949 Geneva Conventions. The precise moment at which

[11] Schindler, D., 1979, 'The Different Types of Armed Conflicts According to the Geneva Conventions and Protocols', *Recueil des cours*, Hague Academy of International law (RCADI), vol. 163, p. 131.

[12] Gasser, H.-P., 1993, 'International Humanitarian Law: An Introduction'. In *Humanity for All: The International Red Cross and Red Crescent Movement*, edited by Haug, H., Paul Haupt, Bern, pp. 510–11.

[13] ICJ, *Case Concerning Military and Paramilitary Activities in and against Nicaragua (Nicaragua v United States of America)*, Judgment (Merits), 27 June 1986, §195, at: <http://www.icj-cij.org/docket/files/70/6503.pdf>. See also Gray, C., 2008, *International Law and the Use of Force*, 3rd edn, Oxford University Press (OUP), 2008, pp. 177–83.

a belligerent occupation occurs is, though, not finally settled. According to the International Committee of the Red Cross (ICRC):

Not only is the definition of occupation vague under IHL, but other factual elements—such as the continuation of hostilities and/or the continued exercise of some degree of authority by local authorities, or by the foreign forces during and after the phase out period—may render the legal classification of a particular situation quite complex.[14]

Article 42 of the 1907 Hague Regulations reads: 'Territory is considered occupied when it is actually placed under the authority of the hostile army. The occupation extends only to the territory where such authority has been established and can be exercised.' According to Sylvain Vité, for occupation in the meaning of Article 42 to exist, 'two conditions must be fulfilled: (a) the occupier is able to exercise effective control over a territory that does not belong to it; [and] (b) its intervention has not been approved by the legitimate sovereign'.[15] Arguably, however, the threshold for the application of the 1949 Geneva Conventions is lower. According to Common Article 2:

The Convention shall also apply to all cases of partial or total occupation of the territory of a High Contracting Party, even if the said occupation meets with no armed resistance.

Of course, where one State uses armed force on the territory of another State with the latter State's consent, the two States are not engaged in an IAC. This is the case with respect to NATO's military involvement in Afghanistan, for instance. But there may be factual and legal issues concerning whether and when an occupation occurs.[16] In March

[14] ICRC, 'International Humanitarian Law And The Challenges Of Contemporary Armed Conflicts', Report to the 31st International Conference of the Red Cross and Red Crescent, Geneva, October 2011. See, e.g., Zwanenburg, M., Bothe, M., and Sassòli, M., 2012, 'Is the Law of Occupation Applicable to the Invasion Phase?', *International Review of the Red Cross*, vol. 94, no. 885 (Spring 2012), pp. 29–50.

[15] Vité, S., 'Typology of Armed Conflicts in International Humanitarian Law: Legal Concepts and Actual Situations', *International Review of the Red Cross*, p. 74.

[16] In the *Katanga* case, the ICC Trial Chamber cited with approval the ICTY trial judgment in the case against identified a non-exhaustive list of factors to take into account when determining whether an occupation was occurring:

- the occupying power must be in a position to substitute its own authority for that of the occupied authorities, which must have been rendered incapable of functioning publicly;
- the enemy's forces have surrendered, been defeated or withdrawn. In this respect, battle areas may not be considered as occupied territory. However, sporadic local resistance, even successful, does not affect the reality of occupation;
- the occupying power has a sufficient force present, or the capacity to send troops within a reasonable time to make the authority of the occupying power felt;
- a temporary administration has been established over the territory;
- the occupying power has issued and enforced directions to the civilian population.

ICC, *Prosecutor v Germain Katanga*, Judgment (Trial Chamber) (Case No. ICC-01/04-01/07), 7 March 2014, §1180, citing ICTY, *Prosecutor v Mladen Naletilic, aka 'Tuta'and Vinko Martinovic, aka 'Štela'*, Judgment (Trial Chamber) (Case No. IT-98-34-T), 31 March 2003, §217, footnotes omitted.

2014, the issue arose of whether or not the Russian Federation was occupying Ukraine, given that deposed Ukrainian President Viktor Yanukovych had seemingly authorized Russian military intervention in a letter dated 1 March.[17] However, without prejudice to the legality of his removal under Ukrainian law Mr Yanukovych did not effectively control the police or armed forces of Ukraine at the time of the letter and could not therefore be considered genuinely to represent the State. Subsequently, however, the facts on the ground demonstrated clearly that Russia had sought to annex part of Ukrainian territory (Crimea).

There may also be an IAC when one State supports an armed non-State actor (ANSA) operating in another State when that support is so significant that the foreign State is deemed to have 'overall control' over the actions of the ANSA.[18] More controversially, an IAC may also exist where there is an armed conflict 'in which peoples are fighting against colonial domination and alien occupation and against racist regimes in the exercise of their right of self-determination'.[19] The threshold of armed violence for such a conflict to occur is not settled, but is probably the same as for an IAC—that is to say, much lower than it is for a NIAC.[20]

THE GEOGRAPHICAL SCOPE OF AN INTERNATIONAL ARMED CONFLICT

The geographical scope of an IAC is potentially far broader than is the case for a NIAC (see below). Without prejudice to *jus ad bellum*, the rules of which apply in parallel to

[17] See, e.g., 'Russia Provides UN Security Council with Appeal by "Legal President" Yanukovych', 5 March 2014, at: <http://euromaidanpr.com/2014/03/05/russia-provides-un-security-council-with-appeal-by-legal-president-yanukovych/>.

[18] See, e.g., ICTY, *Prosecutor v Tadić*, Judgment (Appeals Chamber) (Case No. IT-94-1-A), 15 July 1999, §§84 and 115 *et seq.*; ICTY, *Prosecutor v Blaškić*, Judgment (Trial Chamber) (Case No. IT-95-14-T), 3 March 2000, §§149–50. See similarly the views of the Trial Chamber of the ICC in its judgment in the 2012 *Lubanga* case: ICC, *Prosecutor v Thomas Lubanga Dyilo*, Judgment (Trial Chamber) (Case No. ICC-01/04-01/06), 14 March 2012, §541. The Trial Chamber expressly approved the *Tadić* dicta on this issue. In the 2014 *Katanga* judgment, the ICC Trial Chamber further approved this position: 'Un conflit armé international existe dès lors que des hostilités armés opposent des États à travers leurs armées respectives ou à travers d'autres acteurs agissant en leur nom.' ('An international armed conflict exists whenever armed hostilities oppose states through their respective armies or through others acting on their behalf.' Unofficial translation.) ICC, *Prosecutor v. Germain Katanga*, Judgment (Trial Chamber), 7 March 2014, §§1177 *et seq.*

[19] See Art. 1(4), 1977 Additional Protocol I. The United States and a number of other States opposed this provision vociferously when it was adopted. It has never been applied in practice.

[20] This is not, though, the position of the United Kingdom, which argues that the threshold is the same as for a NIAC regulated by Common Article 3. UK Ministry of Defence, 2005, *The Manual of the Law of Armed Conflict*, OUP, §3.4.2.

any IAC, where militarily necessary States involved in an IAC may potentially target each other's armed forces anywhere.

SUMMARY IHL RULES GOVERNING INTERNATIONAL ARMED CONFLICT

The basic principles and rules of IHL applicable to the conduct of hostilities in an IAC are set out in the 1907 Hague Regulations and the 1949 Geneva Conventions and their 1977 Additional Protocols, and represent customary law applicable to all. The basis of the law of armed conflict is the rule of distinction. This rule obliges 'parties to a conflict' (in other words, the warring parties, i.e., Israel and Syria or India and Pakistan in 2013) to target only military objectives and not the civilian population, individual civilians, or civilian objects (e.g., homes, hospitals, and schools). Deliberately targeting civilians is a serious violation of IHL, as too is failing to distinguish in military operations between civilians and combatants (i.e., an indiscriminate attack), and both are war crimes under customary international law given the requisite intent (*mens rea*).[21]

Although it is understood that civilian casualties may not always be avoided in the conduct of hostilities, international law also requires that parties to a conflict take all feasible precautions in any attack to minimize civilian deaths and injuries (and damage to civilian objects). In addition, according to the rule of proportionality, attacks against lawful military objectives that may be expected to cause deaths or injuries among the civilian population, or damage to civilian objects, which jointly or severally would be 'excessive' compared to the expected 'concrete and direct' military advantage are prohibited.

Children must not be recruited into armed forces or armed groups nor allowed to take part in hostilities. Recruiting children less than fifteen years of age is a war crime. The use of indiscriminate weapons,[22] or weapons 'of a nature to cause superfluous injury or unnecessary suffering', is prohibited. In addition, among many other provisions, parties to an international conflict must respect and protect combatants who are *hors de combat*, because of sickness, wounds, detention, or any other cause. Captured combatants (primarily, members of armed forces) are to be accorded the status of prisoner of

[21] Civilians only lose their 'general protection' against hostilities if, and for such time as, they participate directly in hostilities.

[22] The ICC Statute (Art. 8(2)(a)(xx)) refers to 'inherently' indiscriminate weapons, while the ICJ, in its 1996 Nuclear Weapons Advisory Opinion, referred to 'weapons that are incapable of distinguishing between civilian and military targets'. It has sometimes been claimed that no weapons are 'inherently' indiscriminate, and certainly there is no general agreement as to which weapons might fulfil this criterion.

war, with the associated rights and obligations.[23] In providing assistance to the civilian population, women and children are to be granted preferential treatment.

SUMMARY IHL RULES GOVERNING A SITUATION OF BELLIGERENT OCCUPATION

Subject to the discussion above, during a belligerent occupation of foreign territory, applicable law is set out in the 1907 Hague Regulations (Articles 42–56), the 1949 Geneva Convention IV, the 1977 Additional Protocol I, and customary international law. The underpinning of the law of military occupation is that it is supposed to be a temporary situation which lasts until a political agreement is reached. During this period, the occupant does not enjoy sovereign rights over the territories it occupies and local law that was applicable prior to the occupation remains in force. At the same time, the occupying power is responsible for administering the local life of the population under its control, maintaining it as it was prior to the occupation as closely as possible, and for providing security (Article 43 of the Hague Regulations). In addition, international human rights law (HRL) is binding on the occupying State extraterritorially with regard to the territories it occupies.

WHEN DOES AN INTERNATIONAL ARMED CONFLICT END?

The precise duration of an international armed conflict is a difficult issue. The ICTY in the *Tadić* case suggested that IHL applies 'from the initiation of ... armed conflicts and extends beyond the cessation of hostilities until a general conclusion of peace is reached' in the case of an IAC.[24] While certain IHL obligations will clearly extend beyond the active cessation of hostilities, including those pertaining to the treatment of detainees, a notion that law of armed conflict rules governing the conduct of hostilities pertain to acts committed after the point at which active hostilities have effectively ceased is too expansive. Nonetheless, there will often be a fluctuation in regularity and extent of armed violence during a situation of armed conflict without such an oscillation amounting to an active cessation of hostilities.

A number of cases that occurred in 2014 are relevant to this issue. The IAC between Israel and Syria is one instructive example. Israel bombarded military objectives in

[23] These are set out, in particular, in 1949 Geneva Convention III.

[24] ICTY, *Prosecutor v Tadić*, Decision on the Defence Motion for Interlocutory Appeal on Jurisdiction (Appeals Chamber), 2 October 1995, §70.

Syria on a number of occasions, as described in the relevant profile in Part II. These were discrete military operations, which *The War Report* characterizes as a series of distinct IACs, each of which effectively begins and ends with the respective attack. In contrast, in the armed conflict between India and Pakistan, regular exchange of fire took place between two States that in 2003 had agreed on a ceasefire to halt cross-border fighting over Kashmir.[25] The ceasefire was followed by the greatest number of deadly clashes in the disputed region for many years (see the profile in Part II). This amounted to an IAC that effectively began in April 2014 and persisted as of writing, in May 2015.

Non-international armed conflict

CRITERIA FOR THE EXISTENCE OF A NON-INTERNATIONAL ARMED CONFLICT

In accordance with the definition in the *Tadić* case, a NIAC is a situation of regular and intense armed violence[26] between the security forces of a State, especially the army, and one or more organized non-governmental armed groups. A NIAC will also occur in a situation of intense armed violence between two or more organized armed groups within a State. Situations of 'internal disturbances and tensions', including 'riots, isolated and sporadic acts of violence', and other acts of a similar nature, are explicitly determined not to amount to armed conflicts.[27] Although not explicitly foreseen by the *Tadić* decision, a NIAC will also occur where intense armed violence occurs between two or more organized armed groups across an international border, such as between Hezbollah and the Free Syrian Army in Syria and across the border into Lebanon in 2014.

There are three cumulative requirements for a NIAC, according to the *Tadić* definition. First, there must be 'protracted armed violence'; second, violence must be conducted by government forces and at least one *organized* non-governmental armed group (or between such groups within a State or across a State's borders); and, third, the violence

[25] See, e.g., 'India, Pakistan agree on Kashmir truce', PressTV, 17 January 2013, at: <http://www.presstv.com/detail/2013/01/17/284034/india-pakistan-agree-on-kashmir-truce/>.

[26] In the trial judgment in *Tadić* and other cases, the ICTY confirmed that the specific meaning it gave to 'protracted' when qualifying armed violence was an insistence on the intensity of conflict (even though the word's meaning in ordinary parlance is one of duration, not intensity): ICTY, *Prosecutor v Tadić*, Opinion and Judgment, 7 May 1997, §562; see also ICTY, *Prosecutor v Ramush Haradinaj, Idriz Balaj, and Lahi Brahimaj*, Judgment (Trial Chamber) (Case No. IT-04-84-T), 3 April 2008, §§40 *et seq.*; ICTY, *Prosecutor v Slobodan Milosevic*, Decision on Motion for Judgment of Acquittal (Case No. IT-02-54-T), 16 June 2004, §17.

[27] Art. 1(2), 1977 Additional Protocol II; see also Art. 8(2)(d), 1998 ICC Statute.

must take place *between* the armed forces and at least one organized armed group, or between such groups. These elements are discussed in turn.

The requirement of 'protracted armed violence' means that a certain threshold of armed violence has been reached.[28] According to the ICTY:

> In an armed conflict of an internal or mixed character, these closely related criteria are used solely for the purpose, as a minimum, of distinguishing an armed conflict from banditry, unorganized and short-lived insurrections, or terrorist activities, which are not subject to international humanitarian law.[29]

Organized armed groups are those with a command-and-control structure, that typically possess and use a variety of weapons, and which control a significant logistical capacity that gives them the capability to conduct regular military operations. When engaged in regular and intense armed confrontations with armed forces or other organized armed groups, such groups are 'party' to a NIAC. These groups are sometimes called rebels, insurgents, terrorists, criminal gangs, or anti-government elements by States or other entities; such designations have no consequence for the determination of their status under international law with respect to an armed conflict. It is not, however, necessary that an armed group have a particular political or religious agenda for it to be party to a NIAC;[30] therefore, an organized armed group whose aim is purely lucrative, such as a drugs cartel or an organized crime network, can be a party to an armed conflict.[31]

The third criterion is potentially controversial. Inherent in the notion of the words 'conflict' and 'between' is, *The War Report* argues, a requirement that there be actual combat.[32] In its judgment in the *Haradinaj* case, the ICTY stated that indicative factors for an armed conflict include 'the number, duration and intensity of individual confrontations'.[33] The *San Remo Manual on the Law of Non-International Armed*

[28] As the ICRC has noted, 'the violence must reach a certain level of intensity'. ICRC, 'International Humanitarian Law and the Challenges Of Contemporary Armed Conflicts', Report for the 31st International Conference of the Red Cross and Red Crescent, 2011, p. 8.

[29] ICTY, *Prosecutor v Tadić*, Opinion and Judgment (Trial Chamber), 7 May 1997, §562.

[30] See, e.g., ICTY, *Prosecutor v Fatmir Limaj, Haradin Bala, and Isak Musliu*, Judgment (Trial Chamber) (Case No. IT-03-66-T), 30 November 2005, §170.

[31] Vité, S., 'Typology of Armed Conflicts in International Humanitarian Law: Legal Concepts and Actual Situations', *International Review of the Red Cross*, p. 78; ICRC, 'International Humanitarian Law and the Challenges of Contemporary Armed Conflicts', Report for the 31st International Conference of the Red Cross and Red Crescent, 2011, p. 11.

[32] In cases before the ICTY, the Tribunal has tended to consider the number of clashes as part of the intensity criterion: 'the seriousness of attacks and potential increase in armed clashes, their spread over territory and over a period of time'. See, e.g., ICTY, *Prosecutor v Mile Mrkšić, Miroslav Radić, and Veselin Šljivančin*, Judgment (Trial Chamber) (Case No. IT-95-13/1-T), 27 September 2007, §407, and sources cited in footnote 1592.

[33] ICTY, *Prosecutor v Haradinaj*, Judgment (Trial Chamber) (Case No. IT-04-84-T), 3 April 2008, §49.

Conflict states that NIACs are 'armed confrontations' occurring within the territory of a single State.[34] In the *Limaj* case, the ICTY Trial Chamber, in finding that an armed conflict existed in Kosovo before the end of May 1998 between the Kosovo Liberation Army and the Serb forces, stated that:

> by the end of May 1998 KLA units were constantly engaged in armed clashes with substantial Serbian forces in areas from the Kosovo–Albanian border in the west, to near Prishtina/Pristina in the east, to Prizren/Prizren and the Kosovo–Macedonian border in the south and the municipality of Mitrovice/Kosovka Mitrovica in the north. . . . The ability of the KLA to engage in such varied operations is a further indicator of its level of organisation.[35]

Thus, an armed group that constructs and emplaces (or delivers to a target) improvised explosive devices (IEDs), land mines, vehicle-borne IEDs (VBIEDs), or body-borne IEDs (BBIEDs), but which does not engage in direct 'hostilities' with the armed or security forces of a State, is *not* engaged in a NIAC. Such situations appear to fall more accurately within the notion expressed by the ICTY in the *Tadić* case and cited above of 'terrorist activities, which are not subject to international humanitarian law'.[36] As Sandesh Sivakumaran has noted, upon ratification of the 1977 Additional Protocol I, the United Kingdom entered a declaration whereby 'the term "armed conflict" of itself and in its context denotes a situation of a kind which is not constituted by the commission of ordinary crimes including acts of terrorism whether concerted or in isolation'.[37]

WHEN DOES A NON-INTERNATIONAL ARMED CONFLICT END?

More complicated than with respect to the end of an IAC is the determination of when a NIAC is effectively over. According to the *Tadić* decision, IHL applies 'in the case of internal conflicts [i.e. NIACs], [until] a peaceful settlement is achieved'.[38] This is too

[34] International Institute of Humanitarian Law, *The Manual on the Law of Non-International Armed Conflict With Commentary*, San Remo, 2006, p. 3, at: <http://www.iihl.org/iihl/Documents/The%20Manual%20on%20the%20Law%20of%20NIAC.pdf>.

[35] ICTY, *Prosecutor v Limaj, Bala, and Musliu*, Judgment (Trial Chamber) 30 November 2005, §172, footnote omitted.

[36] These situations are governed by the international law of law enforcement, including, in particular, HRL.

[37] Declaration of 28 January 1998, at: <http://www.icrc.org/ihl.nsf/NORM/0A9E03F0F2EE757CC1256402003FB6D2?OpenDocument>, cited in Sivakumaran, S., 2012, *The Law of Non-International Armed Conflict*, OUP, p. 233. Sivakumaran refers to the 'understanding' of the United Kingdom as a 'reservation', but it is more accurately termed a 'declaration' because it does not seek to modify the terms of the Protocol with respect to the United Kingdom, but rather to set out the United Kingdom's understanding of the term. See also, e.g., ICTY, *Prosecutor v Milošević*, Decision on Motion for Judgment of Acquittal (Rule 98bis Decision) (Trial Chamber) (Case No. IT-02-54-T), 16 June 2004, §26.

[38] ICTY, *Prosecutor v Tadić*, Decision on the Defence Motion for Interlocutory Appeal on Jurisdiction (Appeals Chamber), 2 October 1995, §70.

expansive, even though identifying the 'cessation of active hostilities' in armed conflicts of a non-international character is particularly difficult, since an individual attack does not amount to an armed conflict as it may under the classification of IAC.[39] Clashes between parties to a NIAC must be frequent but not necessarily daily or even weekly. Further, when an armed group that is party to such a conflict fragments or its senior commanders are killed or captured, the group may, as a consequence, no longer fulfil the criterion of organization. Establishing in fact these situations is clearly challenging, but when either criterion is no longer fulfilled, a NIAC can be said to have ended. This position has been advanced by Rogier Bartels:

> that NIACs do not necessarily end only by virtue of a peace settlement being reached, but rather by the more factual circumstance of the level of 'organisation' and 'intensity' falling below the threshold set for the application of IHL.[40]

THE GEOGRAPHICAL SCOPE OF A NON-INTERNATIONAL ARMED CONFLICT

Common Article 3 to the 1949 Geneva Conventions refers to a NIAC 'occurring in the territory of one of the High Contracting Parties'. This can be taken to mean that an armed conflict is limited to the territory of a single State or that the provisions only apply to a situation in which the territory on which an armed conflict is ongoing is governed by the authority of a State party.[41] If it is the latter, given that, as of May 2015, all United Nations (UN) member States were party to the Geneva Conventions, there is very little territory that would not be covered by the treaty provisions. Further, under customary law, there is arguably no such strict geographical limitation, at least with respect to 'spill-over' from one territory to another.

So, for example, where hostilities between the Free Syrian Army and Hezbollah take place outside Syria on the territory of neighbouring Lebanon, as well within Syrian territory, this constitutes a single armed conflict, not two distinct NIACs.

[39] As noted above, in relevant treaties 'isolated and sporadic acts of violence' explicitly do not amount to (non-international) armed conflict.

[40] Bartels, R., 'Temporal Scope of Application of IHL: When do Non-International Armed Conflicts End? Part 2', Guest Post, *Opinio Juris*, 19 February 2014, at: <http://opiniojuris.org/2014/02/19/guest-post-bartels-temporal-scope-application-ihl-non-international-armed-conflicts-end-part-2/>.

[41] For a helpful discussion of this issue, see, e.g., Jinks, D., 'The Temporal Scope of Application of International Humanitarian Law in Contemporary Conflicts', Background Paper prepared for the Informal High-Level Expert Meeting on the Reaffirmation and Development of International Humanitarian Law, Cambridge, 27–9 January 2003, Program on Humanitarian Policy and Conflict Research at Harvard University, 2003, p. 8.

This position does not, though, mean that a globalized NIAC exists as a matter of international law. Although US lawyers accept that the United States has little to no support for its stance,[42] it continues to argue that it is engaged in a global armed conflict with 'the Taliban, al-Qaeda, and associated forces'.[43] No such conflict exists under IHL/ICL, for two reasons: first, there is no longer active combat between US forces and Al-Qaeda forces in Afghanistan such as to constitute protracted armed violence and therefore an armed conflict (nor has there been for close to a decade); and, second, while a NIAC can certainly cross international borders, it is not possible under existing international law for a NIAC to be simply global. According to Sivakumaran, an armed conflict must 'have a territorial base ...; a global non-international armed conflict does not exist, at least, as a matter of law'.[44]

It is not contested here that an armed conflict may exist on 'a single territory',[45] or that, today, it may have 'a core territory plus overspill onto different territory',[46] sometimes (unhelpfully) termed a 'transnational armed conflict'. More controversial is the question of whether an armed conflict may exist across 'multiple territories' that are geographically unconnected.[47] According to one theory, where a NIAC exists on the territory of one State against a non-State armed group, and that conflict involves foreign States intervening on behalf of that State (such as by the International Security Assistance Force, ISAF, in Afghanistan), the law of armed conflict applies to any hostile act by the non-State party on the territory of any of those foreign States.[48] Thus, under this theory a single bomb attack by the Quetta Shura Taliban against the Ministry of Defence in a European State whose armed forces contributed troops to ISAF would *de jure* form part of the NIAC in Afghanistan. The attack would not violate LOAC rules on the conduct of hostilities nor would it violate the 1997 Terrorist Bombings Convention (which excludes

[42] As John Bellinger acknowledges: 'We are about the only country in the world that thinks we are in an armed conflict with Al-Qaida. We really need to get on top of this and explain to our allies why it is legal and why it is permissible under international law.' Cited in Roberts, D., 'US Drone Strikes Being Used as Alternative to Guantánamo, Lawyer Says', *Guardian*, 2 May 2013, at: <http://www.guardian.co.uk/world/2013/may/02/us-drone-strikes-guantanamo>.

[43] According to John Brennan, for example, then Assistant to the US President for Homeland Security and Counterterrorism (since March 2013, Director of the US Central Intelligence Agency): 'As a matter of international law, the United States is in an armed conflict with al-Qa'ida, the Taliban, and associated forces, in response to the 9/11 attacks.' 'The ethics and efficacy of the President's counterterrorism strategy', Remarks of John O. Brennan, Woodrow Wilson International Center for Scholars, Washington, DC, 30 April 2012, available at: <http://www.lawfareblog.com/2012/04/brennanspeech/>. In the last two years, however, the Obama Administration has been quietly dropping the reference to the Taliban. See, e.g., Chapter 1 in this *War Report*.

[44] Sivakumaran, S., *The Law of Non-International Armed Conflict*, p. 234.

[45] Indeed, the text of Common Article 3 refers to 'armed conflict not of an international character occurring in the territory of *one* of the High Contracting Parties' (author's emphasis).

[46] Sivakumaran, S., *The Law of Non-International Armed Conflict*, p. 234. [47] Ibid.

[48] Vité, S., 'Typology of Armed Conflicts in International Humanitarian Law: Legal Concepts and Actual Situations', *International Review of the Red Cross*, p. 74.

acts committed by military forces, including non-State armed groups).[49] On this understanding, it would, though, potentially not prohibit the targeted State from instantly having recourse to LOAC use of force rules, and specifically the intentional use of lethal force, against suspected terrorists belonging to the Quetta Shura Taliban on its territory (and beyond).[50]

SUMMARY RULES APPLICABLE IN A NON-INTERNATIONAL ARMED CONFLICT

IHL is applicable to all parties to the conflict, whether State or non-State armed groups. This always includes Common Article 3 to the 1949 Geneva Conventions (by virtue of their universal application under customary international law) and all other provisions of the law of armed conflict applicable to a NIAC, as well as, in certain circumstances, the 1977 Additional Protocol II.[51] States engaged in a NIAC are also bound by both applicable treaty[52] and customary human rights law. In areas in which hostilities are being actively conducted, the law of armed conflict is widely regarded as the applicable law, while outside such areas, HRL is arguably the legal framework determining lawful use of force.

There is also increasing acceptance that non-State armed groups are also bound by at least peremptory HRL norms (e.g., prohibitions on summary or arbitrary executions,

[49] Art. 19(2), 1997 International Convention for the Suppression of Terrorist Bombings, adopted by the UN General Assembly on 15 December 1997 and entered into force on 23 May 2001.

[50] Such force might be constrained by the rule in Chapter IX of the ICRC's 2009 Interpretive Guidance on the Notion of Direct Participation in Hostilities, depending on whether this rule constitutes customary international law. This is obviously also without prejudice to the rules of international law governing the interstate use of force.

[51] The scope of application of 1977 Additional Protocol II is set out in Art. 1. In its commentary on the article, the ICRC notes that the Protocol 'only applies to conflicts of a certain degree of intensity and does not have exactly the same field of application as common Article 3, which applies in all situations of non-international armed conflict'. *ICRC Commentary on the 1977 Additional Protocols to the Geneva Conventions of 1949*, p. 1348. Certain criteria are explicitly required for application of the 1977 Additional Protocol II, namely: confrontation between the armed forces of the government and opposing 'dissident' armed forces; that the dissident armed forces are under a responsible command; and that they control a part of the territory so as to enable them to 'carry out sustained and concerted military operations' and to implement the Protocol.

[52] Derogations from other human rights in accordance with the 1966 International Covenant on Civil and Political Rights may only occur in 'time of public emergency which threatens the life of the nation and the existence of which is officially proclaimed'. Any derogation must be only 'to the extent strictly required by the exigencies of the situation, provided that such measures are not inconsistent with their other obligations under international law and do not involve discrimination solely on the ground of race, colour, sex, language, religion or social origin'.

torture, and enforced disappearances).[53] They may also be bound by other customary human rights obligations, for example where they control territory. For instance, the UN Assistance Mission in Afghanistan (UNAMA) stated in February 2012 that:

> While non-State actors in Afghanistan, including non-State armed groups, cannot formally become parties to international human rights treaties, international human rights law increasingly recognizes that where non-State actors, such as the Taliban, exercise de facto control over territory, they are bound by international human rights obligations.[54]

Accordingly, based on applicable rules of the law of armed conflict, during the conduct of hostilities it is prohibited to attack any civilian taking no direct part in hostilities, or any fighter who has laid down his arms or who is *hors de combat* because of sickness, wounds, detention, or any other cause. Children must not be recruited into armed forces or armed groups, nor allowed to take part in hostilities. Recruiting children less than fifteen years of age is a war crime. It is prohibited to attack civilian objects. Civilian objects are any buildings or areas that are not lawful military objectives. Indiscriminate attacks, namely attacks that do not distinguish between military objectives and civilians and/or civilian objects, are prohibited. Use of indiscriminate weapons, or weapons 'of a nature to cause superfluous injury or unnecessary suffering', is prohibited. Violating any of these rules may constitute a war crime.

Attacks against lawful military objectives (military personnel or equipment) are prohibited if they may be expected to cause 'excessive' harm to either civilians or civilian objects, or a combination of both, in relation to the concrete and direct military advantage anticipated. All feasible precautions must be taken to avoid, and in any event to minimize, incidental loss of civilian life, injury to civilians, and damage to civilian objects.

Enforced disappearances are prohibited. Hostages shall not be taken. Arbitrary deprivation of liberty is prohibited. Anyone detained by a party to an armed conflict must be treated humanely and in accordance with their sex, age, and religious beliefs. Murder, torture, rape, bodily injury, or other cruel, humiliating, or degrading treatment is prohibited. Summary or arbitrary executions are prohibited. No one may be convicted or sentenced, except pursuant to a fair trial affording all essential judicial guarantees. This includes a defendant's right to know the charges against him/her, to understand the court proceedings, to have the opportunity to conduct a genuine defence, and to be

[53] See, e.g., 'Report of the Independent International Commission of Inquiry on the Syrian Arab Republic', UN doc. A/HRC/19/69, 22 February 2012, §106. 'In this regard, the commission notes that, at a minimum, human rights obligations constituting peremptory international law (ius cogens) bind States, individuals and non-State collective entities, including armed groups. Acts violating *ius cogens*—for instance, torture or enforced disappearances—can never be justified'.

[54] See, e.g., UNAMA, *Afghanistan: Annual Report 2011, Protection of Civilians in Armed Conflict*, Kabul, February 2012, p. iv. See also in this regard Bellal, A., Giacca, G., and Casey-Maslen, S., 2011, 'International Law and Armed Non-State Actors in Afghanistan', *International Review of the Red Cross*, vol. 93, no. 881, pp. 47–79.

able to appeal against both conviction and sentence. Everyone charged with a criminal offence shall be presumed innocent until proved guilty according to law.

Which armed conflicts occurred in 2014?

Tables 1 and 2 summarize the forty-two IACs and NIACs that took place in 2014.

Table 1 Active conflicts in 2014

Conflict no.	Location of conflict	Parties to conflict
1	India and Pakistan	India *v* Pakistan
2	Palestine	Israel v Palestine
3	Syria	Israel *v* Syria

Table 2 Belligerent occupations in 2014

Conflict no.	Location of occupation	Occupier
4	Azerbaijan	Armenia
5	Cyprus	Turkey
6	Eritrea	Ethiopia
7	Georgia	Russian Federation
8	Lebanon	Israel
9	Moldova	Russian Federation
10	Palestine	Israel
11	Syria	Israel
12	Ukraine	Russia
13	Western Sahara	Morocco

INTERNATIONAL ARMED CONFLICTS IN 2014

Only three active IACs occurred in 2014—between India and Pakistan, between Israel and Palestine and between Israel and Syria—although at least the Israel–Syria conflict is better considered as a series of brief, punctual IACs each lasting minutes or hours. The number of IACs in 2014 was thus one greater than the previous year.

The number (10) and detail of belligerent occupations in 2014 was one greater than the previous year. Indeed in late February 2014 and certainly since March 2014, the Russian Federation was occupying part of Ukraine.

Other belligerent occupations that have been alleged include the occupation by the United Kingdom of the Falkland Islands/Malvinas (Argentina claims this as sovereign territory),[55] of Tibet by China,[56] and of the State of Hawaii by the United States.[57] *The War Report* makes no determination as to whether belligerent occupation is occurring in these cases.

NON-INTERNATIONAL ARMED CONFLICTS IN 2014

A total of twenty-nine NIACs in eighteen States occurred in 2013. New conflicts broke out in CAR, Egypt, Iraq, Libya, Mali, Pakistan, Ukraine, and Yemen. Three conflicts ended during the year, however: in Mexico (2), and Thailand.

Table 3 Non-international armed conflicts in 2014

Conflict no.	Conflict location	Parties to conflict
14	Afghanistan	Afghanistan and ISAF *v* Quetta Shura Taliban
15	Afghanistan	Afghanistan and ISAF *v* Haqqani Network
16	Afghanistan	Afghanistan and ISAF v Hezb-e-Islami
17	CAR	Séléka v Anti-balaka
18	Colombia	Colombia *v* Revolutionary Armed Forces of Colombia (FARC-EP)
19	Colombia	Colombia *v* National Liberation Army (ELN)
20	DRC	DRC *v* Allied Democratic Forces/National Army for the Liberation of Uganda (ADF-NALU)
21	DRC	DRC *v* Mai-Mai
22	Egypt	Egypt vs Wilayat Sinai ('State of Sinai' or 'Province of Sinai', to November 2014 known as Ansar Beit al-Maqdis)
23	India	India *v* Naxalite Maoists
24	Iraq	Iraq *v* Islamic State of Iraq and the Levant (ISIL)/Islamic State (IS)
25	Libya	Libya and Operation Dignity forces *v* Libya Dawn/Ansar al-Sharia, Misrata brigades, Benghazi Revolutionaries Shura Council
26	Mali	Mali and France and United Nations Multidimensional Integrated Stabilization Mission in Mali (MINUSMA) *v* Al-Qaeda in the Islamic Maghreb (AQIM), Ansar Dine, and the Movement for Oneness and Jihad in West Africa (MOJWA)
27	Mali	Mali and France and (MINUSMA) *v* MNLA
28	Nigeria	Nigeria *v* Boko Haram

[55] See, e.g., 'Falkland Islands profile', *BBC*, 5 November 2013, at: <http://www.bbc.com/news/world-latin-america-18425572>.

[56] See, e.g., 'Tibet profile', *BBC*, 13 August 2013, at: <http://www.bbc.com/news/world-asia-pacific-16689779>.

[57] See, e.g., Dr. Matthew Craven, Continuity of the Hawaiian Kingdom, 'Being a portion of a Legal Brief provided for the acting Council of Regency', 12 July 2002, at: <http://www2.hawaii.edu/~hslp/journal/vol1/Craven_Opinion_(HJLP).pdf>; and Dr. David Keanu Sai, 'Legal Brief, "The Continuity of the Hawaiian State and the Legitimacy of the acting Government of the Hawaiian Kingdom"', 4 August 2013, at: <http://www.hawaiiankingdom.org/pdf/Continuity_Brief.pdf>.

29	Pakistan	Pakistan *v* Pakistan *v* Tehrik-e-Taliban Pakistan (TTP) and TTP splinter groups, Haqqani network *et al.*
30	Somalia	Somalia, Ethiopia, Kenya, Uganda, and USA *v* al-Shabaab
31	South Sudan	South Sudan and Uganda People's Defence Forces *v* Sudan People's Liberation Army (dissident faction)
32	Sudan	Sudan *v* SPLM/A-North
33	Sudan	Sudan *v* Justice and Equality Movement (JEM)
34	Syria	Syria *v* Free Syrian Army
35	Syria	Syria *v* al-Nusra
36	Syria	Syria *v* Islamic State of Iraq and the Levant (ISIL)/Islamic State (IS)
37	Syria	Free Syrian Army *v* Hezbollah
38	Thailand	Thailand *v* Barisan Revolusi Nasional independence movement (conflict ended in September 2014)
39	Ukraine	Ukraine *v* Donetsk People's Republic & Luhansk People's Republic (April 2014)
40	Yemen	Yemen *v* al-Houthi
41	Yemen	al-Houthi *v* Al-Qaeda in the Arabian Peninsula AQAP
42	Yemen	Yemen *v* AQAP

Casualties in armed conflicts in 2014

The *War Report* presents an overview of statistics based on available data on casualties as a result of armed conflict by calendar year.[58] For 2014, it is calculated that at least 171,400 were killed or injured by acts related to armed conflicts. (This marked a significant increase from the 93,500 casualties recorded in the *War Report* for 2013.) The greatest casualties in 2014 occurred in Iraq, Syria, and Afghanistan.[59]

Table 4 Casualties in armed conflicts in 2014

Conflict	Killed	Injured	Totals
Iraq	17,765	27,685	45,450
Syria	31,253	Not recorded	31,253
Afghanistan	13,887	9,691	23,578
Palestine	2,431	11,961	14,392
Ukraine	7,850	6,709	14,261
Nigeria	7,752	527	8,279
Somalia	2,958	5,000	8,031

[58] Data gathering and analysis is conducted by a team of two international experts for *The War Report*: Clémence Caraux-Pelletan and Loren Persi Vicentic.

[59] The number of casualties is likely far higher. In some cases there was a range of casualty data reported or estimated and lower total numbers were recorded in the global dataset.

Casualties are defined as individuals who have been killed or injured. Conflict-related casualties[60] are defined as those casualties occurring as the direct result of a violent act by an active participant in an armed conflict. This includes casualties resulting from:

- use of weapons such as firearms, artillery, and aerial bombing, including drone strikes;
- land mines and other victim-activated explosive remnants of war used and/or left behind in relation to armed conflict;
- torture, including physical beating; and
- sexual violence.

The conflict-fatalities recorded may also include people who have been deprived of access to medical care by force and who died as a result.

Statistics are not included on the many indirect victims of conflict, such as those who become ill or die due to increased levels of disease that often occur in the context of armed violence or because they are unable to access medical care for treatment of non-conflict-related medical issues due to violence and insecurity. It is, however, possible that indirect victims are sometimes included in sources used without being identified as such. Where data is available and relevant to the conflict 'disappeared' persons may be noted in the reporting, though these statistics are not included in the casualty totals.

For Egypt, Syria, and Yemen data on the numbers of persons injured was not available. For casualties due to conflict in Palestine, only those injuries resulting from the July–August hostilities in Gaza were included in the *War Report* global annual for 2014.

At a minimum, data gathering has sought to identify the following characteristics for each casualty recorded for the *War Report*:

- casualty outcome: as either killed or injured;
- status: civilian or member of State armed force, member of non-State armed group (see below regarding participation in hostilities);
- age: adult or child (defined as any person under the age of eighteen);
- sex: male or female;
- date the casualty occurred; and
- party to the conflict responsible for the casualty (recognizing that these data are rarely available).

Where there is uncertainty of the civilian status of casualties because of ambiguity as to the military status of the role and the direct participation of the individual in conflict,

[60] Conflict-related casualties are referred to by different names in different contexts. In India, casualty sources refer to victims of 'violent incidents' or 'terrorism-related casualties'. Victims of armed violence in Mexico are recorded as 'organized crime executions' in the media and by the Justice in Mexico project. Agence France-Presse (AFP) collects data on casualties in Iraq due to 'attacks and incidents of violence'.

the *War Report* relies on the determination made by the data source. Police, who in many situations would have a civilian status, are excluded from data on civilian casualties collected by the UN in Afghanistan.[61] In Iraq, however the UN has included data on 'civilian police' casualties among civilians.[62] Police are disaggregated from data on military forces separately from civilians in some datasets, notably in Mexico and Thailand.

Civilians participating directly in hostilities, particularly those recorded as members of opposition forces and non-State armed groups, are frequently categorized as belligerents in data sources. The *War Report* casualty data system does not seek to make a distinct determination. In some cases civilians who may have been participating directly in hostilities or the subjects of targeted killings may be recorded as civilians depending primarily on the determinations of the reporting source.

Civilians who were organized as armed local militia for protection, for example in Nigeria and Somalia against attacks by Boko Haram and Al Shabaab respectively, were likely to have primarily been reported as armed participants in the conflict. In some other instances people armed to defend themselves may have been included among civilian casualties in data. Statistics for eastern Ukraine from sources available to the UN included casualties both civilians and members of non-State armed groups, without noting participation in hostilities. As a result, only Ukrainian armed forces were disaggregated as military personnel in those data.

In some cases, the civilian status of people injured is not noted, especially when there are many injured reported cumulatively. This was the case for Palestine during the period of armed conflict and for the limited cumulative data reported by the World Health Organization (WHO) for weapon-injured persons treated in Somalia.

Casualties among peacekeeping troops are typically recorded as military casualties. Private contractors killed in Afghanistan and other countries may be recorded as security personnel or civilians depending on their role and work. Security personnel acting in a military capacity participating in hostilities are generally recorded as fighters when identified. However, civilians working in private security in a civilian capacity (such as guarding a building) are recorded as civilian. Similarly State or private prison guards and the personal guards of government officials are recorded as civilian unless noted otherwise, unlike the guards of non-State armed group leadership.

In addition to distinguishing between casualties of civilians and combatants/fighters, wherever possible, *The War Report* highlights the casualties of particular civilian

[61] UNAMA, *Afghanistan Annual Report 2014, Protection of Civilians in Armed Conflict*, Kabul, February 2014. p. 2 (footnotes).

[62] UNMAMI Monthly Updates, 'Civilian Casualties: Summary', <http://www.uniraq.org/index.php?option=com_k2&view=itemlist&task=category&id=159:civilian-casualties&Itemid=633&lang=en>.

sub-groups that may be especially targeted during armed conflicts. These sub-groups include:

- journalists who have been determined to have been killed or injured due to their work;
- human rights defenders;
- humanitarian aid workers; or
- others who have a specific role, such as government officials and tribal leaders; and
- religious leaders.

Statistics are disaggregated according to the specific armed conflict when possible. Casualty data for some countries, including that of Afghanistan, Iraq, Syria, Yemen and could not be entirely disaggregated according to each conflict occurring within the State. In these cases, casualties of all conflicts were recorded for each country, while any details that could be distinguished, such as deaths among particular armed groups, were kept distinct.

Data for conflicts in 2014 were compiled, analysed, and reported according to the time period of the conflict, or are for the entire calendar year if the conflict was ongoing throughout the year. For example, casualty data reporting for Libya started in May 2014 and started in mid-April 2014 for Ukraine, at the onset of those armed conflicts.

Part II

Situations of Armed Conflict in 2014

Situations of Armed Conflict in 2014

Armed conflict between India and Pakistan in 2014

KEY CASUALTY DATA FOR 2014

Total killed:	41	
Total injured:	93	
India military killed:	4	(Source: Media)
India military injured:	8	(Source: Media)
India civilians killed:	9	(Source: Media)
India civilians injured:	36	(Source: Media)
India unknown injured:	2	(Source: Media)
Pakistan military killed:	6	(Source: Media)
Pakistan civilians killed:	22	(Source: Media)
Pakistan civilians injured:	47	(Source: Media)
Of the total civilian casualties:		
Women deaths:	2	(Source: Media)
Women injured:	5	(Source: Media)
Child deaths:	5	(Source: Media)
Children injured:	7	(Source: Media)

CLASSIFICATION OF THE CONFLICT

India and Pakistan were involved in an international armed conflict (IAC) in 2013 until an agreement on 25 December to again cease hostilities. Cross-border firing resumed in April 2014 with military and civilian casualties reported on both sides, leading to an IAC. The intensity reached its peak in October and has subsequently continued into 2015.

SUMMARY OF APPLICABLE INTERNATIONAL LAW

Both parties to the conflict were bound by customary and conventional international humanitarian law and human rights law, including customary international humanitarian law (IHL) rules of distinction, proportionality, and precautions in attacks.

Both India and Pakistan are party to the four 1949 Geneva Conventions and to the 1966 Covenant on Civil and Political Rights. Neither State is party to the 1977 Additional Protocol I, although Pakistan is a signatory.

Neither State is party to the 1997 Anti-Personnel Mine Ban Convention or the 2008 Convention on Cluster Munitions.

Both States are party to the 1992 Chemical Weapons Convention.

Neither State is party or signatory to the 2013 Arms Trade Treaty (ATT).[1]

HISTORY OF THE CONFLICT

India and Pakistan first went to war in October 1947 after Pakistan supported a Muslim insurgency in Kashmir.[2] Under United Nations (UN) supervision, the war ended on 1 January 1949, with the establishment of a ceasefire line that left one-third of the State—comprising what Pakistan calls Azad Jammu and Kashmir as well as the Northern Areas administered by Pakistan—and two-thirds, Jammu, Ladakh, and the Kashmir Valley, administered by India.[3] The status of the territory has, though, remained in dispute ever since.[4]

In 1965, the two States went to war again after Pakistan launched a covert offensive across the ceasefire line into Indian-administered Jammu and Kashmir. India retaliated by crossing the international border at Lahore.[5] In 1971, Pakistan descended into civil war after East Pakistan demanded autonomy and later independence. India invaded East Pakistan after millions of civilians fled to India. At the end of the year, Bangladesh was created out of East Pakistan.[6]

[1] India abstained from the vote on the adoption of the ATT by the United Nations (UN) General Assembly on 2 April 2013, while Pakistan voted in favour of the resolution.

[2] 'Kashmir profile', *BBC*, 31 January 2014, at: <http://www.bbc.com/news/world-south-asia-11693674>.

[3] 'The Future of Kashmir', *BBC*, at: <http://news.bbc.co.uk/2/shared/spl/hi/south_asia/03/kashmir_future/html/default.stm>.

[4] 'The 1947–8 War', *BBC*, at: <http://news.bbc.co.uk/2/shared/spl/hi/south_asia/02/india_pakistan/timeline/html/1947_48.stm>.

[5] 'The 1965 War', *BBC*, at: <http://news.bbc.co.uk/2/shared/spl/hi/south_asia/02/india_pakistan/timeline/html/1965.stm>.

[6] 'The 1971 War', *BBC*, at: <http://news.bbc.co.uk/2/shared/spl/hi/south_asia/02/india_pakistan/timeline/html/1971.stm>.

Armed resistance to Indian rule broke out in the Kashmir valley in 1989, with some groups calling for independence and others calling for union with Pakistan. India accused Pakistan of supplying weapons to the militants. During the 1990s, with the emergence of militant Muslim groups, the movement's ideology became essentially Islamic in nature.[7] In 1972, under the terms of the Simla agreement, the ceasefire line was renamed the Line of Control (LoC).[8]

In the 1990s, the arms race between the two States escalated dramatically. In May 1998, India conducted underground nuclear tests in Rajasthan near the border with Pakistan. In response, Pakistan conducted six tests in Baluchistan. The same year, Pakistan tested its longest range missile, the 1,500km Ghauri missile, named after a twelfth century Muslim warrior who conquered part of India. Both sides were heavily criticized by the international community for the tests as fears of a nuclear confrontation grew.[9] In 1999, conflict again erupted after India launched air strikes against Pakistani-backed forces that had infiltrated Indian-administered Kashmir. Fighting built up towards a direct conflict between the two States and tens of thousands of people were reported to have fled their homes on both sides of the ceasefire line.[10]

In 2001, tension along the ceasefire line continued and in October, thirty-eight people were killed after an attack on the Kashmiri assembly in Srinagar. A month later, fourteen people were killed in an attack on the Indian Parliament in Delhi. India blamed Pakistani-backed Kashmiri militants and a dramatic build-up of troops along the Indo-Pakistan border ensued,[11] with more than one million stationed there for several months in 2002. At several points during the year the two nuclear powers looked to be on the verge of full-scale hostilities. In April 2003, however, relations began improving and in May both sides said they would restore diplomatic relations.[12] In November 2003, India and Pakistan agreed to a formal ceasefire although at the time an unnamed analyst described the accord, which

[7] 'Kashmir Insurgency', *BBC*, at: <http://news.bbc.co.uk/2/shared/spl/hi/south_asia/02/india_pakistan/timeline/html/1989.stm>.

[8] 'The Future of Kashmir', *BBC*.

[9] 'Nuclear Rivalry', *BBC*, at: <http://news.bbc.co.uk/2/shared/spl/hi/south_asia/02/india_pakistan/timeline/html/1998.stm>. The LoC runs for more than '700km of forested hills and inhospitable terrain. Defying logic in some places, it splits villages in half and bisects mountains'. Sanctuary, C., 'Contentious Line of Control', *BBC*, 4 January 2002, at: <http://news.bbc.co.uk/2/hi/south_asia/377916.stm>. Furthermore, Sanctuary reports that 'despite the painstaking process of demarcation—field commanders exchanged over 20 maps over five months before its final course was agreed on—troops on the ground have fought over differences in interpretation ever since'. Ibid.

[10] 'Kargil Conflict', *BBC*, at: <http://news.bbc.co.uk/2/shared/spl/hi/south_asia/02/india_pakistan/timeline/html/1999.stm>.

[11] 'Rising Tension', *BBC*, at: <http://news.bbc.co.uk/2/shared/spl/hi/south_asia/02/india_pakistan/timeline/html/2001.stm>.

[12] 'Threat of War', *BBC*, at: <http://news.bbc.co.uk/2/shared/spl/hi/south_asia/02/india_pakistan/timeline/html/2002_03.stm>.

restricts the States' conventional armies from attacking each other, as more 'symbolic than substantive'.[13]

In 2013, ceasefire violations, including firing of mortars and small arms fire across the LoC, increased significantly, to (depending on the source) as many as 195.[14] The 'serious hostility and military action' during the year,[15] which went considerably beyond mere 'frontier incidents', resulted in 145 casualties and amounted to an IAC. On 25 December the Indian and Pakistani Director Generals of Military Operations, meeting for the first time in fourteen years, reached an agreement effectively ending the IAC.[16]

On 25 April 2014, after a lull of almost four months along the LoC, Indian and Pakistani troops exchanged small arms and automatic weapon fire over several hours. India accused Pakistan of having initiated the fighting by resorting to unprovoked mortar shelling from across the LoC.[17]

In May 2014, General Elections were held in India bringing the Bharatiya Janta Party to power. One of the first official acts of both the newly appointed Defence Minister and Prime Minister was to visit Jammu and Kashmir. The continued ceasefire violations intensified during this period.

On 16 July 2014, one soldier of the Indian Border Security Force was killed and three others were injured in cross-border firing in RS Pura in Jammu district.[18]

On 20 and 23 July, two Pakistani civilians were reported killed in cross-firing between the Pakistani and Indian forces. On 28 August, two more civilians were killed on the Pakistani side in cross-border firing.[19]

Following the suspension of a high-level meeting in August by India, tensions escalated to their highest level in the last quarter of 2014. In the worst ceasefire violation since 2003, twenty persons were killed in cross-border firing and artillery bombing between 5 and 8 October. Thousands of civilians fled their homes as artillery shelling extended to residential areas. Both sides however claim that they have been engaged in strictly retaliatory fire to ceasefire violations.[20]

[13] Watson, P., 'India and Pakistan Agree to Cease-Fire in Kashmir', *Los Angeles Times*, 26 November 2003, at: <http://articles.latimes.com/2003/nov/26/world/fg-ceasefire26>.

[14] 'India, Pak Agree to Maintain LoC Truce', *Deccan Herald*, 25 December 2013, at: <http://www.deccanherald.com/content/376578/india-pak-agree-maintain-loc.html>.

[15] Ibid. [16] Ibid.

[17] Sharma, A., 'Pakistan Fires at Indian Posts, Violates Ceasefire', *India Express*, 25 April 2014, at: <http://indianexpress.com/article/india/india-others/pakistan-fires-at-indian-posts-violates-ceasefire/>.

[18] 'J&K: One BSF Jawan Killed in Ceasefire Violation', *NDTV*, 16 July 2014, at: <http://www.ndtv.com/india-news/j-k-one-bsf-jawan-killed-in-ceasefire-violation-589098>.

[19] 'Five More Civilians Killed in Worst India-Pakistan Fighting for Years', *World News Network*, 10 September 2014, at: <http://article.wn.com/view/2014/10/09/Five_more_civilians_killed_in_worst_IndiaPakistan_fighting_f/>.

[20] Military and security, India-Pakistan (Kashmir), *Armed Conflict Database*, retrieved on 24 March 2015, at: <https://acd.iiss.org/en/conflicts/india-pakistan--kashmir-7274?as=2630124216E54F2A93ECD0AFC454C686>.

In January 2015, nine civilians including a thirteen-year-old Pakistani girl as well as two Pakistani soldiers and one Indian soldier were reported killed.[21]

The Indian Defence Minister reported to the Upper House of the Indian Parliament that Pakistan was responsible for violating the ceasefire 685 times between July 2014 and February 2015. Of these, 126 violations occurred along the LoC and 559 along the International Border.[22]

PARTIES TO THE CONFLICT

The parties to the conflict were India and Pakistan.

India is estimated to have 1.325 million active frontline military personnel and a further 2.14 million in reserve.[23] Pakistan is estimated to have 617,000 active frontline military personnel and a further 515,000 in reserve.[24] Both States possess nuclear weapons in addition to a huge array of conventional weaponry.

CASUALTIES

A media review for calendar year 2014 identified at least 134 casualties (forty-one killed and ninety-three injured) due to cross-border fire between India and Pakistan across the LoC and the Working Boundary/International Border.[25] The vast majority of reported casualties in 2014 were civilians, with thirty-one civilians killed and eighty-three injured (two women killed and five injured and five children killed and seven injured), including three children killed and one injured in Pakistan by unexploded ordnance (UXO) remaining from cross-border mortar fire. Most child casualties reported were incurred in Pakistan with four children killed and six injured. These totals for 2014 do not include casualties due to incursions in the broader area by non-State armed groups.

[21] 'Pakistan Violates Ceasefire in Jammu, Targets 8 Indian Posts', *NDTV*, 9 February 2014, at: <http://www.ndtv.com/india-news/pakistan-violates-ceasefire-in-jammu-targets-8-indian-posts-738041>.

[22] 'Pakistan Violated Border Ceasefire 685 Times in Eight Months: Manohar Parrikar', *DNA India*, 24 February 2015, at: <http://www.dnaindia.com/india/report-pakistan-violated-border-ceasefire-685-times-in-eight-months-manohar-parrikar-2063714>.

[23] 'Indian Military Strength', *Globalfirepower.com*, last updated on 27 March 2014, at: <http://www.globalfirepower.com/country-military-strength-detail.asp?country_id=india>. The Indian Army's website contains the motto 'To be born free is an accident. To live free is a privilege. To die free is a responsibility.' At: <http://indianarmy.nic.in/Index.aspx?flag=FNzcf7eEG9ARr6J9FBR0GA==>.

[24] 'Pakistan Military Strength', *Globalfirepower.com*, last updated on 27 March 2014, at: <http://www.globalfirepower.com/country-military-strength-detail.asp?country_id=pakistan>. The Pakistani armed force's website contains the motto 'Men at their best', at: <http://www.pakistanidefence.com/>.

[25] Haider, M., 'Indian Diplomat Summoned over Loc Violation', updated 21 November 2014, <http://www.dawn.com/news/1145983/indian-diplomat-summoned-over-loc-violation>.

The month with the most casualties was October, when increasingly intense retaliatory cross-border fire from both sides regularly struck civilian settlements. Data assessed from media reporting indicated that at least twenty-six people were killed and seventy-five injured during October, with six killed and three injured in November and at least three killed in December.[26] Several casualties were also reported prior to the peak in cross-border fire in October, with at least three killed and seven injured in July and three killed and eight injured in August.

Many estimated ranges for casualties were reported in October 2014 during the peak of the cross-border fire and resulting rise in deaths and injuries. One such report stated that at least twenty people were killed and more than 100 injured.[27] Another media report found that more than thirty civilians were killed on both sides during October.[28] In December, it was reported that nineteen people were killed and over 150 injured in 2014, in what was described as 'the highest number of ceasefire violations since the truce came into force in 2003'.[29]

The border conflict in October was also referred to as 'the most intense fighting between the South Asian rivals in over a decade'.[30] Up to 410 ceasefire violations were recorded along the International Border/Working Boundary and 152 violations along LoC according to the Indian media report.[31] Similarly in Pakistani media it was reported that India fired more than 31,872 heavy mortar shells on border villages during five days in October 2014, stating that 'the number of these heavy mortar shells was much higher than the shells fired by the Indian forces during the 1971 Indo-Pak War'.[32] In December in 2013, Pakistan and India had pledged to uphold the 2003 LoC ceasefire accord 'which had been left in tatters by repeated violations that year'.[33]

[26] Other reporting indicated five deaths over 31 December. 'Five dead in New Year's Eve Clashes on India-Pakistan Border', 1 January 2015, <http://tribune.com.pk/story/815596/five-dead-in-new-years-eve-clashes-on-india-pakistan-border>; and 'Pakistan Violates Ceasefire Along Line of Control in Jammu, Jawan Injured', 31 December 2014, <http://www.ndtv.com/india-news/pakistan-violates-ceasefire-along-line-of-control-in-jammu-jawan-injured-720442>.

[27] 'Pakistan Army says Indian fire wounds four in Kashmir', 16 October 2014, <http://www.arabnews.com/news/645096>.

[28] '17-year-old Girl, Soldier Killed as Pakistani Troops Target Indian Positions along LoC in Kashmir', 8 November 2014, <http://www.deccanchronicle.com/141108/nation-current-affairs/article/17-year-old-girl-soldier-killed-pakistani-troops-target-indian>.

[29] '2014 Records 562 Ceasefire Violations in JK, Highest in 11 yrs,' 31 December 2014, <http://www.timesnow.tv/2014-records-562-ceasefire-violations-in-JK-highest-in-11-yrs/articleshow/4471788.cms>.

[30] 'Pakistan Taught "Befitting Lesson", Says Modi After Decline In Firing', 11 October 2014, <http://www.hindustantimes.com/india-news/no-let-up-in-cross-border-firing-by-pakistan-3-more-injured-overnight/article1-1273268.aspx>.

[31] '2014 Records 562 Ceasefire Violations in JK, Highest in 11 yrs', 31 December 2014.

[32] 'Govt Urged to Boldly Reply to Indian Madness', 1 December 2014, <http://nation.com.pk/national/01-Dec-2014/govt-urged-to-boldly-reply-to-indian-madness>.

[33] Haider, M., 'Indian Diplomat Summoned over Loc Violation', updated 21 November 2014, <http://www.dawn.com/news/1145983/indian-diplomat-summoned-over-loc-violation>.

DISPLACED PERSONS

Some 45,000 people were newly displaced by cross-border skirmishes between India and Pakistan in Jammu and Kashmir in October and December as well as in western Assam in May.[34]

WAR CRIMES ALLEGATIONS, INVESTIGATIONS, AND PROSECUTIONS

Neither India nor Pakistan is a State party or signatory to the 1998 Rome Statute of the International Criminal Court (ICC).

No allegations of war crimes are known to have been made against either Indian or Pakistan military personnel regarding any acts concerning the IAC in 2014.

[34] IDMC, 'Global Overview 2015', May 2015, p. 51.

Armed conflict between Israel and Palestine in 2014

KEY CASUALTY DATA FOR 2014

(From 8 July 2014 through	26	August 2014)
Total civilians killed in Gaza	2,220	(Source: OCHA)
Total injured in Gaza:	11,231	(Source: OCHA)
Civilians killed in Gaza:	1,492	(Source: OCHA)
Children killed in Gaza:	551	(Source: OCHA)
Children injured in Gaza:	3,436	(Source: OCHA)
Women killed in Gaza:	299	(Source: OCHA)
Women injured in Gaza:	3,540	(Source: OCHA)
Civilians killed in Israel:	7	(Source: Israeli Ministry of Public Security)
Children killed in Israel:	1	(Source: Israeli Ministry of Public Security)
Civilians injured in Israel:	261	(Source: Israeli Ministry of Public Security)
Israeli Defense Forces deaths:	67	(Source: Israeli Ministry of Public Security)
Israeli Defense Forces injured:	469	(Source: Israeli Ministry of Public Security)
Non-State armed group deaths in Gaza:	605	(Source: OCHA)
Unverified deaths in Gaza:	123	(Source: OCHA)

CLASSIFICATION OF THE CONFLICTS

Israel and Palestine were engaged in an international armed conflict (IAC) in 2014 not only by virtue of Israel's continued military occupation of Palestinian territory but also because Palestine, which was accorded the status of non-member observer State in the UN by the UN General Assembly on 29 November 2012, can be considered as a State under international law.[35] A unity agreement was signed between Fatah and Hamas on April 2014.[36] The international community recognizes that Hamas is part of the

[35] UN General Assembly Resolution 67/19 was adopted by 138 votes to nine, with forty-one abstentions. On April 2014, Palestine became a party to the Geneva Conventions and further acceded to thirteen international treaties, see Al-Jazeera, 'UN Accepts Palestinian Treaty Applications', 11 April 2014, at: <http://www.aljazeera.com/news/middleeast/2014/04/un-accepts-palestinian-treaty-applications-2014410225222866731.html>.

[36] 'Hamas and Fatah Unveil Palestinian Reconciliation Deal', *BBC News*, 23 April 2014, at: <http://www.bbc.com/news/world-middle-east-27128902>. For further discussion on this conflict, see in this volume, Sharon Weill and Valentina Azarova, 'Chapter 3: The 2014 Gaza War: Reflections on *Jus ad Bellum*, *Jus in Bello* and Accountability'.

Palestinian Government and forms an integral part of Palestine.[37] However, given that some of the Palestinian armed groups operating from the Gaza Strip are neither under the direct control of Hamas, nor included in the 2014 unity government, Israel's hostilities with these specific groups, notably with the Islamic Jihad, may be classified as a separate NIAC. For ease of reference, this separate NIAC will however be reported in the present section.

SUMMARY OF APPLICABLE INTERNATIONAL LAW

Both parties to the conflict were bound by customary and conventional international humanitarian law and human rights law, including customary IHL rules of distinction, proportionality, and precautions in attacks; the obligation not to recruit and use children as soldiers; and by the duty to respect and protect fundamental human rights. This includes the duty to respect the rights to life and to freedom from torture or other forms of cruel, inhuman, or degrading treatment or punishment.

Israel is party to the four 1949 Geneva Conventions but not to the 1977 Additional Protocol I. Israel is also a party to the 1966 International Covenant on Civil and Political Rights and the 1966 International Covenant on Economic, Social and Cultural Rights, since its ratification thereof on 2 April 2014.

Palestine ratified the four 1949 Geneva Conventions on 2 April 2014. Palestine acceded to the 1977 Additional Protocol II and the 2005 Additional Protocol III on 4 January 2015. Palestine has not ratified the 1966 International Covenant on Civil and Political Rights nor the 1966 International Covenant on Economic, Social and Cultural Rights. However, Palestine and Palestinian armed groups were bound domestically by customary international human rights law.

Neither State is party to the 1997 Anti-Personnel Mine Ban Convention. Palestine has acceded to the 2008 Convention on Cluster Munitions on 2 January 2015, which will enter into force for Palestine on 1 July 2015.[38] Palestine has also acceded to the 1980 Convention on Certain Conventional Weapons, including the 1980 CCW Protocol I on Non-Detectable Fragments, and the 1980 CCW Protocol III prohibiting Incendiary

[37] See for example the EU in August 2014: 'The Gaza Strip constitutes an integral part of the territory occupied in 1967 ... The situation in the Gaza Strip cannot and must not be seen separately from the broader challenges and developments on the ground that continue to make the prospect of the two-state solution increasingly difficult to attain'. <http://www.consilium.europa.eu/uedocs/cms_data/docs/pressdata/EN/foraff/144313.pdf>.

[38] 'Palestine Accedes to Convention on Cluster Munitions', *Cluster Munition Coalition*, 6 January 2015, <http://www.stopclustermunitions.org/en-gb/media/news/2015/palestine-accedes-to-convention-on-cluster-munitions.aspx>.

Weapons on 5 January 2015. Israel is also bound by the 1980 CCW Protocol I on Non-Detectable Fragments, and Protocol II (Amended), but not Protocol III.

Israel signed the Arms Trade Treaty on 18 December 2014, a week before its entry into force, but has not ratified it.

HISTORY OF THE CONFLICT[39]

The year 2014 saw the third major armed conflict in Gaza since Israel's unilateral withdrawal from the territory in 2005. Indeed, after the first Gaza War of 2008/2009 known as 'Operation Cast Lead', the second armed conflict in November 2012 called Operation 'Pillar of Cloud' (literal translation from the original Hebrew), the summer of 2014 witnessed the deadliest outbreak of violence so far with Israel's military operations known by the codename 'Operation Protective Edge'.

In 2005, Israel completed withdrawal of all its troops and settlers from inside the Gaza Strip but has retained control over the airspace, seafront, and land access—including deliveries of food and other goods—apart from the crossing with Egypt. It also controls the Gaza population registry, which is linked with that of the West Bank, and collects some taxes through the limited operation of the PA in Gaza. The Islamist Hamas movement which has functioned as the de facto local government in the Gaza Strip since 2007, explicitly rejects the Oslo Accords and its charter calls for Israel's 'nullification'.

In early 2006, Hamas won legislative elections in the Palestinian territories challenging Fatah's leadership of the Palestinian national movement. Following the elections, which were deemed free and fair by international observers,[40] Israel and the Quartet on the Middle East imposed economic sanctions against the Palestinian Authority, conditioning the lifting of sanctions on a renunciation of violence, recognition of the State of Israel, and acceptance of previous agreements. Tensions over control of Palestinian security forces soon erupted after which Hamas retained control of Gaza while its officials were ousted from government positions in the West Bank, thereby leading to a clear separation of the areas of control and influence. Israel and Egypt then imposed an economic blockade on Gaza, henceforth defined as 'hostile territory' by Israel.[41]

[39] I wish to thank Mr Georg Koeppinghoff for the extensive research and drafting he provided for this section. Mistakes and opinions expressed are however entirely my responsibility.

[40] See for instance, 'Palestinian Elections: Trip Report by Former US President Jimmy Carter', 30 January 2006, at: <http://www.cartercenter.org/news/documents/doc2287.html>.

[41] Israel Ministry of Foreign Affairs, 'Security Cabinet declares Gaza hostile territory', 19 September 2007, <http://www.mfa.gov.il/mfa/pressroom/2007/pages/security%20cabinet%20declares%20gaza%20hostile%20territory%2019-sep-2007.aspx>.

In June 2008, as part of an Egyptian-brokered ceasefire, Hamas ceased rocket attacks on Israel. After four months of calm, the conflict escalated and Israel launched Operation Cast Lead (27 December 2008–18 January 2009), justified by Israel as a response to repeated rocket and mortar fire by Palestinian armed groups.[42] Between 1,166[43] and 1,417[44] Palestinians and thirteen Israelis[45] were killed during the twenty-three-day-long operation. After the conflict, Hamas continued to govern the Gaza Strip and Israel maintained its economic blockade over the area.

The period between 2009 until the beginning of 2012 was one of relative calm in the Gaza strip. According to B'Tselem, 282 Palestinians in total were killed by Israeli security forces until the end of October 2012,[46] and the Israeli Defense Forces noted a significant decrease in rocket attacks from the Gaza Strip.[47] In September 2009, the UN special mission on the Gaza War 2008/2009 issued the Goldstone-Report, accusing both sides of war crimes and potential crimes against humanity.

The beginning of 2012 was marked by an increase in violence and tension in the Occupied Palestinian Territories and Israel. Palestinian fighters fired rockets into southern Israel, while Israeli military forces responded with strikes in the Gaza Strip. On 14 November 2012, Israel Defence Forces (IDF) launched Operation Pillar of Defence in response to an increase of rockets fired by Palestinian armed groups (not all affiliated or controlled by Hamas) following the killing, by the IDF, of Ahmed Jabari, chief of Hamas's Gaza military wing.[48] It was reported that one of the Israeli officials who negotiated the release of Gilat Shalit and was later involved in secret negotiations between the Israeli Government and Hamas went public claiming that 'on the morning that he was killed, Mr. Jabari received a draft proposal for an extended cease-fire with Israel, including mechanisms that would verify intentions and ensure compliance. This draft was agreed

[42] 'Q&A: Gaza Conflict, *BBC*, 18 January 2009, <http://news.bbc.co.uk/2/hi/middle_east/7818022.stm>.

[43] 1,166 deaths is the official figure released by the IDF. See 'The Lopsided Death Tolls in Israel-Palestinian Conflicts', *Washington Post*, 11 July 2014, <http://www.washingtonpost.com/blogs/worldviews/wp/2014/07/11/the-lopsided-death-tolls-in-israel-palestinian-conflicts>.

[44] Palestinian Centre for Human Rights. 'Confirmed figures reveal the true extent of the destruction inflicted upon the Gaza Strip; Israel's offensive resulted in 1,417 dead, including 926 civilians, 255 police officers and 236 fighters', 12 March 2009, at <http://www.pchrgaza.org/portal/en/index.php?option=com_content&id=1073:confirmed-figures-reveal-the-true-extent-of-the-destructioninflicted-upon-the-gaza-strip-israels-offensive-resulted-in-1417-dead-including-926-civilians-255-police-officers-and-236-fighters&Itemid=194>.

[45] 'The Lopsided Death Tolls in Israel-Palestinian Conflicts', *Washington Post*.

[46] B'Tselem, 'Statistics', <http://www.btselem.org/statistics/fatalities/after-cast-lead/by-date-of-event/gaza/palestinians-killed-by-israeli-security-forces>.

[47] The 2013 Report notes that rocket launchings from Gaza have decreased from 2,048 in 2008 to 569 (2009) 152 (2010), and 419 (2011). Israel Security Agency, '2013 Annual Summary', <http://www.shabak.gov.il/English/EnTerrorData/Reports/Pages/2013AnnualSummary.aspx>.

[48] Wright, R., 'Who Started the Israel-Gaza Conflict?', *The Atlantic*, 16 November 2012, <http://www.theatlantic.com/international/archive/2012/11/who-started-the-israel-gaza-conflict/265374/>.

upon by me and Hamas's deputy foreign minister, Mr Hamad, when we met last week in Egypt'.[49] The aims of the military operation, according to the Israeli Government, were to halt rocket attacks originating from the Gaza Strip and to disrupt the capabilities of militant organizations.[50] According to the Israeli Government, the operation began in response to Palestinian groups launching more than 100 rockets at Israel over a twenty-four-hour period,[51] an attack on an Israeli military patrol jeep within Israeli borders by Gaza militants, and a tunnel explosion caused by improvised explosive devices (IEDs) near Israeli soldiers on the Israeli side of the fence.[52] Palestinians blamed the Israeli Government for the escalation of violence, accusing the IDF of attacks on Gazan civilians, including a thirteen-year-old boy and four teenagers killed in Gaza, in the days leading up to the operation, and citing the blockade of the Gaza Strip, and occupation of West Bank and East Jerusalem, as the reasons for rocket attacks.[53]

During Operation Pillar of Defence, the IDF's air force struck more than 1,500 sites in the Gaza Strip, including rocket launch-pads, weapon storages, government buildings, and apartment blocks.[54] Gaza officials claimed that at least 133 Palestinians had been killed in the conflict, of whom fifty-three were civilians; they also estimated that more than 800 Palestinians were wounded in the airstrikes.[55] Eight Palestinians were executed by members of the Ezzeddeen al-Qassam Brigades for alleged collaboration with Israel.[56] During the eight-day conflict, which did not include a ground incursion phase, Hamas, the al-Qassam Brigades, and Islamic Jihad intensified their projectile fire on Israeli cities, in an operation code-named Operation Stones of Baked Clay by the al-Qassam Brigades. According to the records, more than 1,456 rockets were launched into Israel, and an additional 142 fell inside Gaza itself.[57] By the end of the operation, six Israelis had been

[49] Baskin, G., 'Israel's Shortsighted Assassination', *The New York Times*, 16 November 2012, at: <http://www.nytimes.com/2012/11/17/opinion/israels-shortsighted-assassination.html?hp&_r=0>.

[50] Lappin, Y., 'IAF Strike Kills Hamas Military Chief Jabari', *Jerusalem Post*, 14 November 2012, <http://www.jpost.com/Defense/IAF-strike-kills-Hamas-military-chief-Jabari>.

[51] Lappin, Y., 'Gaza Groups Pound Israel with over 100 Rockets', *Jerusalem Post*, 12 November 2012, <http://www.jpost.com/Defense/Gaza-groups-pound-Israel-with-over-100-rockets>.

[52] Israel Ministry of Foreign Affairs, *Operation Pillar of Defense—Selected statements*, 20 November 2012, <http://mfa.gov.il/MFA/PressRoom/2012/Pages/Operation_Pillar_of_Defense-Statements.aspx>.

[53] AFP, 'Israel Warns Hamas of "Heavy Price" For Gaza Rockets', 11 November 2012, <http://www.google.com/hostednews/afp/article/AleqMSjRUtS7PreKQztffinueg5yNepOROg?docld=CNG.eceda380b55ad442c0c0b524c5263e34.61>.

[54] 'Factbox: Gaza Targets Bombed by Israel', Gaza, *Reuters*, 21 November 2012, <http://www.reuters.com/article/2012/11/21/us-palestinians-israel-gaza-idUSBRE8AK0H920121121>.

[55] Iaccino, L., 'Israel's Operation Protective Edge: Body Count of Multiple Gaza Attacks', *International Business Times*, 9 July 2014, <http://www.ibtimes.co.uk/israels-operation-protective-edge-body-count-multiple-gaza-attacks-1456029>.

[56] 'Hamas Executes Six Suspected Informants for Israel on Gaza Street', *The Guardian*, 20 November 2012, <http://www.theguardian.com/world/2012/nov/20/hamas-executes-informants-israel-gaza>.

[57] 'Tel Aviv, 21 November 2012—Secretary-General's Remarks to the Security Council', UN Secretary-General's Statement, 21 November 2012.

killed and 240 injured.[58] The United Nations (UN) Security Council held an emergency session on the situation, but could not reach a decision.[59] On 21 November, after days of negotiation mediated by Egypt, a ceasefire was announced between Hamas and Israel.

Evolution towards the 2014 war

The ceasefire brokered by Egypt was largely respected for about nineteen months, that is, between the end of November 2012 and summer 2014. Accordingly, rocket attacks from Gaza dramatically decreased over that period, and Israel's PM Netanyahu acknowledged in March 2014 that Israel was witnessing the lowest amount of rocket attacks from Gaza for a decade.[60] The decrease in rocket attacks was facilitated by the deployment of a 600-men-force by Hamas to prevent militants in Gaza to launch rockets.[61] Similarly, the number of Palestinian deaths in Gaza caused by Israeli security forces dropped to a total of twenty for the period of November 2012 until June 2014.[62]

Yet, the ceasefire represented a 'fragile equilibrium' because of several small-scale violations of the agreement, for instance on 24 June 2013, when Israel conducted air strikes on the Gaza Strip in response to six rockets fired into Israel (no reported injuries).[63] The situation in Gaza deteriorated[64] after the overthrow of the Muslim Brotherhood in Egypt in July 2013. This heavily restricted the use of tunnels between Gaza and Egypt,[65] and Gaza became increasingly isolated and dependent upon Israel. Also, it severely weakened Hamas and inclined the organization to progressively reconcile with Fatah, which ultimately led to the reconciliation agreement of 23 April 2014[66] and the formation of a Fatah–Hamas unity government on 1 June 2014.[67]

[58] Israel Ministry of Foreign Affairs, *Israel under Fire—November 2012*, 22 November 2012, <http://mfa.gov.il/MFA/ForeignPolicy/Terrorism/Pages/Israel_under_fire-November_2012.aspx>.

[59] 'Gaza Toll Rises as UN Calls for End to the Bloodshed', *Telegraph*, 15 November 2012, <http://www.telegraph.co.uk/news/worldnews/middleeast/israel/9679500/Gaza-toll-rises-as-UN-calls-for-end-to-the-bloodshed.html>.

[60] Sterman, A., 'Netanyahu Vows "Lots of Noise in Gaza" if No Quiet for Israel's South', *Times of Israel*, 12 March 2014, <http://www.timesofisrael.com/netanyahu-vows-lots-of-noise-in-gaza-if-no-quiet-for-israels-south/>.

[61] ICG, The Next Round in Gaza, *Middle East Report N °149*, 25 March 2014, P. 6.

[62] B'Tselem, 'Statistics', <http://www.btselem.org/statistics/fatalities/after-cast-lead/by-date-of-event/gaza/palestinians-killed-by-israeli-security-forces/by-month>.

[63] ICG, Crisis Watch Database: Israel/Palestine, 1 July 2013, <http://www.crisisgroup.org/en/publication-type/crisiswatch/crisiswatch-database.aspx>.

[64] ICG Crisis Watch Database: Israel/Palestine, 2 January 2013, <http://www.crisisgroup.org/en/publication-type/crisiswatch/crisiswatch-database.aspx>.

[65] 'Egypt Floods Gaza Tunnels, Cuts Palestinian Lifeline', *Jerusalem Post*, 13 February 2013, <http://www.jpost.com/Middle-East/Egypt-floods-Gaza-tunnels-cuts-Palestinian-lifeline>.

[66] 'Profile: Hamas Palestinian Movement', *BBC News*, 11 July 2014, <http://www.bbc.com/news/world-middle-east-13331522>.

[67] Beaumont, P., 'Palestinian Unity Government of Fatah and Hamas Sworn In', *Guardian*, 2 June 2014, <http://www.theguardian.com/world/2014/jun/02/palestinian-unity-government-sworn-in-fatah-hamas>.

In July 2013, the United States launched peace talks between Palestine and Israel, which came to no conclusion after the expiration of the nine-month deadline in April 2014.[68] During that time, Israel approved several further settlement projects. On 3 November 2013, it approved the construction of 1,700 new settlements[69], on 11 November 2013 details emerged of a plan to construct 23,786 new settlement homes in East Jerusalem and West Bank (which led to the resignation of the Palestinian negotiating team on 13 November[70]), and on 5 February 2014, the construction of 558 new settlements in the West Bank was approved.[71] On 1 April 2014, Israel 'republished tenders for more than 700 housing units in East Jerusalem',[72] and Palestinian President Abbas signed applications to join 15 international treaties/conventions, including the Geneva Conventions'.[73] With respect to the failed peace talks, the PLO blamed Israel for the advancement of settlements and for not presenting a position on the borders, whereas Israel condemned President Abbas for his cooperation with Hamas and the Fatah–Hamas reconciliation agreement of 23 April 2014, which preceded the unity government.[74] As the deadline passed, some ministers in Israel's Government called for Israel to set its own borders, and annex areas of the West Bank under full Israeli control. The economy minister, Naftali Bennett, said: '[w]e will be gradually attempting to apply Israeli law on Israeli-controlled areas'.[75]

In March 2014, tensions grew between the two parties, which culminated into the first severe clashes since the ceasefire of November 2012. On 3 March, two Palestinians were killed in an Israeli airstrike. On 11 March, Israel killed three members of Islamic Jihad, which had previously fired a mortar at Israeli forces.[76] This led to the operation

[68] Beaumont, P., 'US Had Nothing to Show as Deadline for Israel-Palestine Peace Talks Passes', *Guardian*, 29 April 2014, <http://www.theguardian.com/world/2014/apr/29/israel-palestine-peace-talks-deadline-passes>.

[69] ICG, Crisis Watch Database: Israel/Palestine, 1 December 2013, <http://www.crisisgroup.org/en/publication-type/crisiswatch/crisiswatch-database.aspx>.

[70] 'Palestinian Peace Talks Delegation Resigns', *Reuters*, 13 November 2013, <http://www.reuters.com/article/2013/11/13/us-palestinians-israel-idUSBRE9AC0JE20131113>.

[71] ICG, Crisis Watch Database: Israel/Palestine, 1 March 2013, <http://www.crisisgroup.org/en/publication-type/crisiswatch/crisiswatch-database.aspx>.

[72] ICG, Crisis Watch Database: Israel/Palestine, 1 May 2014, <http://www.crisisgroup.org/en/publication-type/crisiswatch/crisiswatch-database.aspx>.

[73] Khaled Abu Toameh, 'Abbas Formally Applies to Join Int'l Bodies, "First Step Toward Joining All UN Agencies"', *Jerusalem Post*, 4 April 2014, <http://www.jpost.com/Diplomacy-and-Politics/Abbas-formally-applies-to-join-intl-bodies-first-step-toward-joining-all-UN-agencies-347283>.

[74] Beaumont, P., Black, I., and Roberts, D., 'Israel Suspends Peace Talks with Palestinians after Fatah-Hamas Deal', *Guardian*, 24 April 2014, <http://www.theguardian.com/world/2014/apr/24/middle-east-israel-halts-peace-talks-palestinians>.

[75] Beaumont, P., 'US had Nothing to Show as Deadline for Israel-Palestine Peace Talks Passes', *Guardian*, 29 April 2014, <http://www.theguardian.com/world/2014/apr/29/israel-palestine-peace-talks-deadline-passes>.

[76] ICG, Crisis Watch Database: Israel/Palestine, 1 April 2014, <http://www.crisisgroup.org/en/publication-type/crisiswatch/crisiswatch-database.aspx>.

'Breaking the Silence' of Islamic Jihad that fired the largest salve of rockets on Israel since November 2012. They claimed to have launched over 130 projectiles, half of which landed in Israel.[77] Although Hamas did not acknowledge to have actively participated in the attack, it is supposed that the attack was conducted 'apparently in coordination with Hamas',[78] or that Hamas at least lowered its effort to prevent attacks by Islamic Jihad and the other involved factions,[79] including the *Popular Resistance Committees*, and smaller factions such as *Democratic Front's National Resistance Brigades, Front for the Liberation of Palestine's Abu Ali Mustafa Brigades*, and Fatah-affiliated *Al-Aqsa Martyrs' Brigades*.[80] During the night of 12 March, Israel responded by targeting twenty-nine sites in Gaza, mostly of Islamic Jihad.[81] At the same time, tensions also grew in the West Bank, where Israel killed an eighteen-year-old on 10 March, who had thrown stones at security forces, and three Palestinians in Jenin refugee camp on 22 March in a raid against Palestinian militants.[82] Mediation by Egypt restored quiet by noon on 14 March 2014.[83]

On 15 May 2014, Israeli troops killed two Palestinian youths in West Bank that commemorated the 1948 war. Videos of the killings were later released by NGOs, which claimed that the killings were unprovoked, and the UN and the United States called for an investigation.[84] Following the formation of the unity government on 1 June, Israel announced plans for the construction of 3,300 new housing units in the West Bank.[85] On 12 June 2014, three Israeli teenagers were abducted in the West Bank. Israel's PM Netanyahu immediately attributed the kidnapping to Hamas, although Hamas officials denied any involvement of the organization[86] and Palestinian President Abbas maintained on 22 June that there was no evidence for Hamas involvement in the kidnapping.[87] Later, on 20 August Saleh el-Arouri, an exiled Hamas leader based in Turkey, claimed

[77] ICG, The Next Round in Gaza, *Middle East Report N °149*, 25 March 2014, p. i.

[78] Ibid., p. i. [79] Ibid., p. 3.

[80] 'Gaza Militants Fire Large Rocket Barrage at Israel', *The Daily Star*, 12 March 2014, <http://www.dailystar.com.lb/News/Middle-East/2014/Mar-12/250042-rocket-barrages-from-gaza-strike-israel-police.ashx>.

[81] ICG, The Next Round in Gaza, p. 2.

[82] ICG, Crisis Watch Database: Israel/Palestine, 1 April 2014, <http://www.crisisgroup.org/en/publication-type/crisiswatch/crisiswatch-database.aspx>.

[83] ICG, The Next Round in Gaza, p. i.

[84] ICG, Crisis Watch Database: Israel/Palestine, 1 June 2014, <http://www.crisisgroup.org/en/publication-type/crisiswatch/crisiswatch-database.aspx>.

[85] Judis, J., 'John Kerry's First Peace Effort in Israel and Palestine Failed, But Now He Needs to Try Again', *New Republic*, no date, <http://www.newrepublic.com/article/118630/israel-palestine-murders-cause-criss-will-john-kerry-step>.

[86] Ellis, R., and Schwarz, M., 'Mom Speaks out on 3 Abducted Teens as Israeli PM blames Hamas', *CNN*, 15 June 2015, <http://edition.cnn.com/2014/06/15/world/meast/west-bank-jewish-teens-missing/>.

[87] 'Abbas Says "No Evidence" of Hamas Involvement in Kidnapping Israelis', *Middle East Monitor*, 22 June 2014, <https://www.middleeastmonitor.com/news/middle-east/12278-abbas-says-no-evidence-of-hamas-involvement-in-kidnaping-israelis>.

responsibility for the kidnapping and murder of the three Israeli teenagers,[88] which was, however, doubted by some experts.[89] On 25 August, Khalid Meshaal, head of Hamas political wing, while acknowledging Hamas involvement stated that Hamas political leadership had no prior knowledge of the kidnapping.[90]

In reaction to the abduction on 12 June, Israel launched the same day the military operation 'Operation Brother's Keeper' in the West Bank, ostensibly aimed at obtaining the liberation of the three Israelis.[91] It has been claimed that the Israeli Government knew from the beginning of the operation that the three teenagers were already dead, and had withheld evidence and placed the press under a gag order on the incident.[92] During the operation, between 350[93] and 700[94] Palestinians were arrested, between five[95] and eleven killed, and fifty-one wounded.[96] It included measures such as the closure of the Erez Crossing (only crossing between Gaza Strip and Israel), and of the Hebron district, which prevented 750,000 Palestinians from moving between their villages and Hebron, and within the city.[97] On 30 June the bodies of the three teenagers were found dead, and anti-Arab riots broke out in the West Bank, and on 2 July a seventeen-year-old Palestinian was tortured and murdered in revenge,[98] which

[88] McCoy, T., 'The Enigmatic Hamas Leader Allegedly behind the Israeli Kidnappings that Ignited War', *Washington Post*, 10 July 2014, <http://www.washingtonpost.com/news/morning-mix/wp/2014/07/10/the-enigmatic-hamas-leader-allegedly-behind-the-israeli-kidnappings-that-ignited-war/>.

[89] Crowcroft, O., 'Hamas Official: We Were behind the Kidnapping of Three Israeli Teenagers', *Guardian*, 21 August 2014, <http://www.theguardian.com/world/2014/aug/21/hamas-kidnapping-three-israeli-teenagers-saleh-al-arouri-qassam-brigades>.

[90] Isikoff, M., 'In Personal Plea, Top Hamas Leader Calls on Obama to Stop "Holocaust" in Gaza', *Yahoo! News*, 25 August 2014, <https://news.yahoo.com/in-personal-plea--top-hamas-leader-calls-on-obama-to-stop-holocaust-in-gaza-180315615.html>.

[91] Israel Defense Forces, '200 Hamas Terrorists Arrested in Connection with Kidnapping', 17 June 2014, <http://www.idfblog.com/blog/2014/06/17/idf-searches-hamas-kidnappers/>.

[92] Judis, J. 'John Kerry's First Peace Effort in Israel and Palestine Failed, But Now He Needs to Try Again', *New Republic*, no date, <http://www.newrepublic.com/article/118630/israel-palestine-murders-cause-criss-will-john-kerry-step>. See also Goldbert, J. J., 'How Politics and Lies Triggered an Unintended War in Gaza', *Jewish Daily Forward*, 10 July 2014, <http://forward.com/articles/201764/how-politics-and-lies-triggered-an-unintended-war>. See also Sharon, A., 'Failure in Gaza', *New York Review of Books*, 25 September 2014, <http://www.nybooks.com/articles/archives/2014/sep/25/failure-gaza/>.

[93] Ahren, R., 'Is Israel's operation to find kidnapped teens a war crime?', *Times of Israel*, 23 June 2014, <http://www.timesofisrael.com/is-israels-operation-to-find-kidnapped-teens-a-war-crime/>.

[94] Human Rights Watch, 'Serious Violations in West Bank Operations', 3 July 2014, <http://www.hrw.org/news/2014/07/03/israel-serious-violations-west-bank-operations>.

[95] Ibid.

[96] According to the three weekly reports by the Palestine Center for Human Rights for the period 12 June to 2 July. Palestinian Centre for Human Rights, 'Weekly Reports 2009-2015, <http://www.pchrgaza.org/portal/en/index.php?option=com_content&view=category&id=84&Itemid=219&limitstart=30>.

[97] Amnesty International, 'Abducted Israeli Teens Must be Released, Israel Must Cease Collective Punishment of Palestinians', no date, <http://www.amnesty.ie/news/public-statementabducted-israeli-teens-must-be-released-israel-must-cease-collective-punishment>.

[98] ICG, Crisis Watch Database: Israel/Palestine, 1 August 2014, <http://www.crisisgroup.org/en/publication-type/crisiswatch/crisiswatch-database.aspx>.

in turn led to Arab rioting.[99] The same day, Israel detonated explosives in the family houses of the two suspects for the killings. Both suspects had neither been charged nor tried.[100] Overall, the operation has been considered a form of collective punishment by Human Rights NGOs such as Human Rights Watch,[101] Amnesty International,[102] and B'Tselem.[103]

Simultaneously to Operation Brother's Keeper in West Bank, rocket and mortar fire originating from Gaza strongly increased, with thirty-one rockets and two mortar shells launched in the period between 15 and 28 June, and twenty-three rockets and one mortar shell launched solely from 29 to 30 June.[104] Israel responded with air strikes, killing a Hamas operative on 29 June, and striking thirty-four targets on the night of the 30 June.[105] A spiral of violence followed, with increased rocket attacks originating from the Gaza Strip and amplified airstrikes by Israel. Between 1 and 6 July, 169 rockets and mortar shells were launched from Gaza.[106] On 4 July, Israel issued a warning that if rocket attacks persisted, a major military offensive would follow.[107] On 5 July, a Hamas official abroad, Osama Hamdan, stated that Hamas would not halt rocket fire without a removal of the blockade on Gaza.[108] On 7 July, Hamas officially assumed responsibility for recent rocket attacks, and eighty rockets were fired at Israel.[109] On 8 July 2014, 'Operation Protective Edge' officially began.[110]

[99] Crowcroft, O., 'Three Jewish Israelis Admit Kidnapping and Killing Palestinian Boy', *Guardian*, 14 July 2014, <http://www.theguardian.com/world/2014/jul/14/three-jewish-israelis-charged-kidnapping-killing-palestinian-boy>.

[100] Human Rights Watch, 'Serious Violations in West Bank Operations', 3 July 2014, <http://www.hrw.org/news/2014/07/03/israel-serious-violations-west-bank-operations>.

[101] Ibid.

[102] Amnesty International, 'Abducted Israeli Teens Must be Released, Israel Must Cease Collective Punishment of Palestinians', no date, <http://www.amnesty.ie/news/public-statementabducted-israeli-teens-must-be-released-israel-must-cease-collective-punishment>.

[103] B'Tselem, 'Human Rights Organizations: "Refrain from Collectively Punishing Palestinians"', 22 June 2014, <http://www.btselem.org/press_releases/20140622_joint_release>.

[104] Israel Security Agency, 'Monthly Summary—June 2014', <http://www.shabak.gov.il/SiteCollectionDocuments/Monthly%20summary%20%E2%80%93%20June%202014.pdf>.

[105] 'Israel Jets Strike 34 Targets in Gaza Strip', *Times of Israel*, 1 July 2014, <http://www.timesofisrael.com/palestinians-israeli-jets-strike-over-30-targets-in-gaza/>.

[106] Israel Security Agency, 'Monthly Summary—July 2014', <http://www.shabak.gov.il/SiteCollectionDocuments/ Monthly%20summary%20%E2%80%93%20July%202014%20docx.pdf>.

[107] 'Hamas "Ready For Gaza Ceasefire" if Israel Raids Stop', *BBC*, 4 July 2014, <http://www.bbc.com/news/world-middle-east-28156268>. See also: Weiss, M., 'Israel Issues Warning as Rocket Fire Maintained', *Irish Times*, 4 July 2014, <http://www.irishtimes.com/news/world/middle-east/israel-issues-warning-as-rocket-fire-maintained-1.1854537>.

[108] Sharon, I., 'Gaza Terrorists Launch Rockets at Beersheba', *Times of Israel*, 5 July 2014, <http://www.timesofisrael.com/more-rockets-hit-israel-clouding-egyptian-mediated-ceasefire-efforts/>.

[109] Israel Defense Forces, 'Operation Protective Edge—The First 10 Days', 8 July 2014, <http://www.idfblog.com/blog/2014/07/08/breaking-idf-commences-operation-protective-edge-against-hamas/>.

[110] Ho, S. and Yaakov, Y., 'Israel Hits Hamas, Islamic Jihad leaders after Rockets Land North of Tel Aviv', *Times of Israel*, 8 July 2014, <http://www.timesofisrael.com/israel-pounds-dozens-of-gaza-targets-in-major-counteroffensive/>.

'Operation Protective Edge'

The operation began with air strikes. On 16 July, after refusing an offer of a ten-year truce by Hamas and Islamic Jihad conditional on inter alia the removal of the blockade and the release of re-arrested prisoners,[111] Israel launched a ground invasion, with the stated purpose of destroying the tunnels crossing the Gaza–Israeli border.[112] Successful Hamas raids against Israeli military targets, infiltrating Israel through tunnels also showed an increased military sophistication of the group.[113]According to Israeli officials, thirty-one tunnels were destroyed.[114] On 25 July, Israel killed the leader of Islamic Jihad's military wing, Salah Abu Hassanein, and his two sons in an airstrike.[115] On 1 August, the United States and the UN announced that the parties had agreed to a seventy-two-hour humanitarian ceasefire, but disputes over the terms of the ceasefire and mutually alleged violations undermined it.[116]

On 3 August, Israel started to withdraw its troops, and an Egyptian-brokered ceasefire was announced on 5 August[117], violated on 19 August by the firing of twenty-nine Hamas rockets in twenty minutes and responding Israeli airstrikes that killed nine Palestinians in Gaza [118], including Mohammed Deif, the leader of Hamas military wing.[119] The following week, Israel killed three top Hamas commanders, and more than 1,000 rockets and mortar were launched at Israel, killing three Israelis.[120] Hamas and Israel agreed on a new ceasefire on 26 August.

[111] Okbi, Y. and Hashavua, M., 'Report: Hamas Proposes 10-Year Cease-Fire in Return for Conditions Being Met', *Jerusalem Post*, 16 July 2014, <http://www.jpost.com/Operation-Protective-Edge/What-are-Hamass-conditions-for-a-cease-fire-363011>.

[112] Rudoren, J., 'Tunnels Lead Right to the Heart of Israeli Fear', *New York Times*, 28 July 2014, <http://www.nytimes.com/2014/07/29/world/middleeast/tunnels-lead-right-to-heart-of-israeli-fear.html?&_r=0>.

[113] Groll, E., 'Video of Hamas Raid Shows Why Israel is so Freaked Out About Gaza Tunnels', 29 July 2014, <http://foreignpolicy.com/2014/07/29/video-of-hamas-raid-shows-why-israel-is-so-freaked-out-about-gaza-tunnels/>.

[114] Melman, Y., 'Analysis: Israel's Victorious Withdrawal from Gaza', *i24News*, 3 August 2014, <http://www.i24news.tv/en/news/israel/diplomacy-defense/39097-140803-analysis-israel-s-victorious-withdrawal-from-gaza>.

[115] Kershner, I. and Gordon, M. R., 'Israel Agrees to Pause in Assault on Gaza as Cease-Fire Deal is Pursued', *New York Times*, 25 July 2014, <http://www.nytimes.com/2014/07/26/world/middleeast/israel-gaza-strip.html?_r=0>.

[116] Raghavan, S., Booth, W. and Witte, G., 'How a 72-hour Truce in Gaza Fell Apart in Less than 2 Hours', *Washington Post*, 1 August 2014, <http://www.washingtonpost.com/world/israel-hamas-agree-to-72-hour-humanitarian-cease-fire/2014/08/01/059f1ff8-194e-11e4-9e3b-7f2f110c6265_story.html>.

[117] Erlanger, S. and Hubbard, B., 'Israel Exits Gaza as Truce Begins', *New York Times*, 5 August 2014, <http://www.nytimes.com/2014/08/06/world/middleeast/israel-gaza-strip-conflict.html>.

[118] Pleitgen, F., Mullen, J. and Smith-Spark, L., '29 Rockets in 20 Minutes: Israel, Hamas Ceasefire Breaks Down', *CNN*, 20 August 2014, <http://edition.cnn.com/2014/08/19/world/meast/mideast-crisis/index.html>.

[119] ICG, Crisis Watch Database: Israel/Palestine, 1 September 2014, <http://www.crisisgroup.org/en/publication-type/crisiswatch/crisiswatch-database.aspx>.

[120] Israel Security Agency, 'Monthly Summary—August 2014', <http://www.shabak.gov.il/SiteCollectionDocuments/Monthly%20summary%20%E2%80%93%20August%202014.pdf>.

During the seven weeks of 'Operation Protective Edge', Israel had conducted more than 4,760 air strikes in Gaza, and 3,488 rockets had been launched at Israel from Gaza.[121] The 2014 hostilities led to an unprecedented number of civilian casualties: at least 1,550 Palestinian civilian deaths, including 538 children (out of a total death toll of over 2,100 Palestinians),[122] and left 108,000 Palestinian homeless.[123] Palestinian attacks killed six civilians in Israel, including one child (out of a total death toll of seventy-four Israelis).[124] According to an OCHA statement on 5 August, 520,000 Palestinians in the Gaza Strip were displaced. The UN estimated that over 96,000 houses were damaged or completely destroyed by the bombing.[125] In sum, rebuilding costs were estimated at $4–6 billion over a period of twenty years.[126] In Israel, an estimated 5,000[127] to 8,000[128] citizens temporarily fled their homes due to persisting rocket fire from Gaza.

Developments after Operation Protective Edge

In late September, Hamas and Israel resumed indirect negotiations in Cairo. Egypt also brokered an agreement between Fatah and Hamas over 40,000 Hamas employees, whose salaries had not been paid anymore after the formation of the unity government.[129] Following the failure of a Jordanian-submitted draft resolution calling for the establishment of a two-State solution based on the 1967 borders, and a full withdrawal of Israel forces by the end of 2017, in January 2015, Palestine triggered the jurisdiction of the ICC with an ad hoc declaration and by acceding to the Rome Statute. This led Israel in turn to

[121] 'Gaza Conflict: Truce Holding after Israel Withdraws', *BBC*, 5 August 2014, <http://www.bbc.com/news/world-middle-east-28663576>.

[122] At least 1,550 Palestinian civilian deaths, including 538 children (out of a total death toll of over 2,100 Palestinians), and at least five civilian deaths in Israel, including one child (out of a total death toll of seventy-four Israelis. Human Rights Watch, Israel/Palestine, World Report 2015, <https://www.hrw.org/world-report/2015/country-chapters/israel-and-palestine>.

[123] Shlaim, A., 'How Israel Brought Gaza to the Brink of Humanitarian Catastrophe', *The Guardian*, 7 January 2009, <http://www.theguardian.com/world/2009/jan/07/gaza-israel-palestine>. Gisha, 'A Costly Divide: Economic Repercussions of Separating Gaza and the West Bank' February 2015, <http://gisha.org/UserFiles/File/publications/a_costly_divide/a_costly_divide_en-web.pdf>.

[124] Human Rights Watch, Israel/Palestine, World Report 2015, <https://www.hrw.org/world-report/2015/country-chapters/israel-and-palestine>.

[125] AFP, 'UN Doubles Estimate of Destroyed Gaza Homes', *Ynet News*, 19 December 2014, <http://www.ynetnews.com/articles/0,7340,L-4605408,00.html>.

[126] Asher, Z., 'The Economic Costs of the War', *CNN*, 29 August 2014, <http://money.cnn.com/2014/08/29/news/economy/gaza-rebuilding-cost/>.

[127] 'Israel, Palestinians Launch New Three-Day Truce', *Reuters*, 10 August 2014, <http://www.mobile.reuters.com/article/idUSKBN0G907R20140810?irpc=932>.

[128] Heller, A., 'Southern Israelis Cautiously Prepare to Head Home', *AP*, 6 August 2014, <http://bigstory.ap.org/article/southern-israelis-cautiously-prepare-head-home>.

[129] ICG, Crisis Watch Database: Israel/Palestine, 1 October 2014, <http://www.crisisgroup.org/en/publication-type/crisiswatch/crisiswatch-database.aspx>.

withhold Palestinian tax revenues, causing the start of another payment crisis of salaries in January.[130] It added to the severe economic crisis in Gaza after Operation Protective Edge. Only 5% of the pledged donor funds had reached Gaza by 19 February 2015.[131]

In the West Bank, the end of 2014 saw continuous incidents of clashes between Israeli Police and Palestinian protesters, causing the deaths of several Israelis and Palestinians. In particular in Jerusalem, several attacks on Israeli citizens were conducted, as well as large-scale arrests and movement restrictions on Palestinian neighbourhoods of the city, and the situation was increasingly referred to as the 'Jerusalem Intifada'. Tensions arose particularly over the access to the Holy Esplanade, which only decreased after Israel removed restrictions on Palestinian access to the al-Aqsa Mosque in December.[132]

In the context of the 17 March Israeli legislative elections, PM Netanyahu issued some controversial statements on the possibility of a two-State solution, later reversing his pre-election declaration that he would never allow the establishment of a Palestinian State.[133] On 27 March, the Israeli Government announced that it would resume the payment of Palestinian tax revenues.[134] The PLO had voted to suspend all security cooperation with Israel, but has as yet to implement this decision.[135]

PARTIES TO THE CONFLICTS

The parties to the conflict were Israel and Palestine.

However, as explained above, the conflict with the Islamic Jihad may be classified as a NIAC. The profile of this group will however be provided in this section.

Israel is estimated to have 160,000 active frontline military personnel and a further 630,000 in reserve.[136] Palestine does not possess regular armed forces. The Palestinian

[130] Rudoren, J., 'Tensions Mount as Israel Freezes Revenue Meant for Palestinians', *New York Times*, 3 January 2015, <http://www.nytimes.com/2015/01/04/world/middleeast/tensions-mount-as-israel-freezes-revenue-meant-for-palestinians.html>.

[131] 'Gaza Donations Fall Way Short of Pledges', *Aljazeera*, 19 February 2015, <http://www.aljazeera.com/news/2015/02/gaza-donations-fall-short-pledges-150218060136423.html>.

[132] ICG, Crisis Watch Database: Israel/Palestine, 1 October 2014/1 November 2014/1 December 2014/1 January 2014, <http://www.crisisgroup.org/en/publication-type/crisiswatch/crisiswatch-database.aspx>.

[133] Rudoren, J. and Shear, M., 'Israel's Netanyahu Reopens Door to Palestinian State, but White House is Unimpressed', *New York Times*, 19 March 2015, <http://www.nytimes.com/2015/03/20/world/middleeast/israel-netanyahu-elections-palestinian-state.html?_r=1>.

[134] 'Israel to Resume Tax Transfers to Palestinian Authority', *BBC*, 27 March 2015, <http://www.bbc.com/news/world-middle-east-32092236>.

[135] ICG, Crisis Watch Database: Israel/Palestine, 1 April 2015, <http://www.crisisgroup.org/en/publication-type/crisiswatch/crisiswatch-database.aspx>.

[136] 'Israel Military Strength', *Globalfirepower.com*, last updated on 1 April 2015, <http://www.globalfirepower.com/country-military-strength-detail.asp?country_id=israel>. The Israel Defence Forces' mission is '[t]o defend the existence, territorial integrity and sovereignty of the state of Israel. To protect the

National Security Forces are the paramilitary forces of the Palestinian National Authority. A number of Palestinian armed groups operate, in particular, from the Gaza Strip.

Hamas: Ezzedeen al-Qassam Brigades

Hamas was formed in late 1987 in the midst of the first Palestinian Intifada. Its roots are in the Palestinian branch of the Muslim Brotherhood.[137] The group's charter calls for an Islamic Palestinian State to be established in place of Israel and rejects all agreements made between the PLO and Israel.[138] More recently, though, Hamas publicly expressed a willingness to accept a long-term cessation of hostilities if Israel agrees to a Palestinian State based on the 1967 borders with Jerusalem as its capital.[139] Hamas's strength is concentrated in the Gaza Strip and areas of the West Bank.

Hamas has a military wing, the Ezzedeen al-Qasssam Brigades (EQB), which was established in the 1990s and has conducted attacks on Israeli locations in Israel and the Palestinian territories. Attacks on civilian targets have included rocket attacks and, from 1993 to 2008, suicide bombings.[140] Military targets included Israeli outposts and border crossings, as well as Israeli civilian targets and rival Palestinian militias in the occupied territories.

Palestinian Islamic Jihad: Al-Quds Brigade

Islamic Jihad was formed by militant Palestinians in the Gaza Strip during the 1970s. The group is committed to the creation of an Islamic State in all of historical Palestine and the destruction of Israel through attacks against Israeli military and civilian targets. It has been labelled a terrorist organization by inter alia the United States[141] and the European Union.[142] The group's central leadership resides in Syria, but the Palestinian

inhabitants of Israel and to combat all forms of terrorism which threaten the daily life', <http://www.idfblog.com/about-the-idf/idf-code-of-ethics/>.

[137] National Counterterrorism Center, *Hamas*, as of 6 April 2015, <http://www.nctc.gov/site/groups/hamas.html>.

[138] Hamas Charter 1988, available at The Jerusalem Fund, <http://www.thejerusalemfund.org/carryover/documents/charter.html?chocaid=397>.

[139] Hass, A., 'Haniyeh: Hamas Willing to Accept Palestinian State on 1967 Borders', *Haaretz*, 9 November 2008, <http://www.haaretz.com/news/haniyeh-hamas-willing-to-accept-palestinian-state-with-1967-borders-1.256915>.

[140] Blair, D., 'Attack on Israelis in Tram Queue Shows Changing Tactics of Palestinian Militants', *Telegraph*, 23 October 2014, <http://www.telegraph.co.uk/news/worldnews/middleeast/israel/11182792/Attack-on-Israelis-in-tram-queue-shows-changing-tactics-of-Palestinian-militants.html>.

[141] US Department of State: Country Reports on Terrorism 2013, 'Chapter 6. Foreign Terrorist Organizations', <http://www.state.gov/j/ct/rls/crt/2013/224829.htm>.

[142] 'Council Implementing Regulation (EU) No 790/2014 of 22 July 2014 implementing Article 2(3) of Regulation (EC) No 2580/2001 on specific restrictive measures directed against certain persons and

Islamic Jihad (PIJ) maintains small regional offices in Beirut and Teheran. PIJ receives financial assistance primarily from Iran.[143] The group's paramilitary wing—the al-Quds Brigade—has conducted numerous attacks, including large-scale rocket attacks and suicide bombings.[144] The al-Quds Brigade actively participated in the 2012 eight-day conflict against Israel.

PIJ has more recently tried to emerge 'from Hamas's shadow, positioning itself as a regional player'.[145] They were the driving force behind the March 2014 clashes, thus contrary to Hamas (which upheld the November 2012-ceasefire) demonstrating 'continuing fidelity to the principle of resistance'.[146] Moreover, following these clashes, they negotiated a ceasefire directly with Egypt without Hamas involvement, illustrating the recent struggle over influence and power in the Gaza Strip.[147]

CASUALTIES

According to preliminary figures reported by OCHA 2,220 Palestinians, including 1,492 civilians were killed in total.[148] These are the most widely cited figures and did not change significantly from the time of the end of the conflict to OCHA's end of year reporting.[149] The Human Rights Council noted the disproportionate effect on civilians and referred to the conflict in Gaza in July and August as 'the deadliest escalation in hostilities since the beginning of the Israeli occupation in 1967'.[150] OCHA reported 551 Children killed and 299 women killed during the conflict period. [151] Of the total 11,231 people recorded as injured in Gaza, 3,436 were children and another 3,540 women, according to UN accounts of reporting by the Palestinian ministry of health.[152] It was

entities with a view to combatting terrorism, and repealing Implementing Regulation (EU) No 125/2014, *Official Journal of the European Union* L 217/1, 23 July 2014, <http://eur-lex.europa.eu/legal-content/EN/TXT/HTML/?uri=CELEX:32014R0790&from=EN>.

[143] US Department of State: Country Reports on Terrorism 2013, 'Chapter 6. Foreign Terrorist Organizations', <http://www.state.gov/j/ct/rls/crt/2013/224829.htm>.

[144] Fletcher, H., 'Palestinian Islamic Jihad', *Council on Foreign Relations*, 10 April 2008, <http://www.cfr.org/israel/palestinian-islamic-jihad/p15984>.

[145] ICG, 'The Next Round in Gaza', *Middle East Report N °149*, 25 March 2014, p. 1.

[146] Ibid.

[147] 'Who's in Charge?', *The Economist*, 29 March 2014, <http://www.economist.com/news/middle-east-and-africa/21599826-decline-hamas-may-result-new-wave-chaos-whos-charge>.

[148] OCHA oPT, 'Fragmented lives Humanitarian Overview 2014,' 26 March 2015, p. 4.

[149] Some media questioned the accuracy of the number of civilian casualties counted in the data available to OCHA. See 'BBC Complaints Defends its Use of Hamas Supplied Casualty Figures', BBC Watch, 24 October 2014, <http://bbcwatch.org/tag/un-ocha/>.

[150] Human Rights Council, 'Human rights situation in Palestine and other occupied Arab territories Report of the United Nations High Commissioner for Human Rights on the implementation of Human Rights Council resolutions S-9/1 and S-12/1', 26 December 2014 (A/HRC/28/80/Add.1), para. 4.

[151] OCHA oPT, 'Fragmented lives Humanitarian Overview 2014', 26 March 2015, p. 4.

[152] Human Rights Council, 'Human rights situation in Palestine', para. 24.

not reported how many of those persons injured were actively participating in conflict at the time. [153] Research by the NGO Defense for Children International Palestine found that 547 Palestinian children were killed during Operation Protective Edge, of which 535 were killed as a direct result of actions of the Israeli military. The child fatalities included 164 children killed in drone strikes.[154] The NGO B'Tselem reported that, among the hundreds of children killed during Operation Protective Edge, one was a minor who participated in hostilities.[155]

The Israeli Defense Forces (IDF) reported sixty-seven fatalities among Israeli soldiers.[156] Seven civilians (six Israelis and one Thai national) were killed during Operation Protective Edge, including one child. Another 469 IDF soldiers and 261 Israeli civilians were reported as injured.[157] Rocket shrapnel injured thirty-seven people to varying degrees, others were injured by breaking glass, or in car accidents and other events not directly from the use of weapons.[158] The Human Rights Council cited the IDF as reporting 369 soldiers and civilians were injured during the conflict.[159] OCHA reported 2,629 Israelis injured for the entirety of 2014, and noted that 'OCHA is unable to verify neither the criteria nor the number of Palestinian and Israeli injuries resulting from the July-August hostilities in Gaza'.[160]

Four journalists were killed in Gaza during Operation Protective Edge, three were Palestinians killed during bombing and armed clashes and one Italian journalist was killed because of the accidental detonation of explosive remnant of war during the destruction process.[161]

153 OCHA oPT, 'Fragmented lives Humanitarian Overview 2014,' 26 March 2015, p. 4.

154 Defense for Children International Palestine, 'Operation Protective Edge: A War Waged on Gaza's Children', April 2015, p. 1.

155 B'Tselem 'The Israeli Information Center for Human Rights in the Occupied Territories, "Initial figures on fatalities in operation Protective Edge"', 12 August 2014, <http://www.btselem.org/gaza_strip/20140812_preliminary_data_on_fatalities>.

156 IDF, 'Operation Protective Edge General Information Since the beginning of the Operation', last updated 26 January 2015, <http://www.idfblog.com/operationgaza2014/#Genralinformation>. Other sources, including OCHA oPT recorded sixty-six Israeli military casualties, OCHA oPT, 'Fragmented lives Humanitarian Overview 2014', 26 March 2015, p. 4. The Israeli Ministry of Public Security also reported sixty-six Israeli soldiers killed.

157 Israeli Ministry of Public Security, Public Information in Emergency Crisis Situations, 'Facing New Challenges: Operation Protective Edge', p. 71, <http://mops.gov.il/Documents/Publications/InformationCenter/Innovation%20Exchange/Innovation%20Exchange%2017/Public%20Information%20in%20Emergency%20Crisis%20Situations.pdf>.

158 '50 Days of Operation Protective Edge: 842 Israeli Casualties', 26 August 2014, <http://www.israelnationalnews.com/News/News.aspx/184457#.VIBB6MnAaVI>.

159 Human Rights Council, 'Human rights situation in Palestine', para. 25.

160 OCHA oPT, 'Fragmented lives Humanitarian Overview 2014', 26 March 2015, p. 5.

161 Committee to Protect Journalists, '16 Journalists Killed in Israel and the Occupied Palestinian Territory since 1992/Motive Confirmed', <https://cpj.org/killed/mideast/israel-and-the-occupied-palestinian-territory>.

DISPLACED

In 2014, there were at least 118,200 new internal displaced persons (IDPs) in Palestine, leading to a total of 275,000 persons being internally displaced in the country as of December 2014. However, these figures are based on secondary information and surveys that use different methodologies and only reflect ad hoc occurrences of displacement. It does not reflect the full scale of displacement as no organization or mechanism monitors the number of IDPs systematically.[162]

WAR CRIMES ALLEGATIONS, INVESTIGATIONS, AND PROSECUTIONS

In August 2014, the UN Independent Commission of Inquiry on the 2014 Gaza conflict was established, following a resolution by the Human Rights Council. Its work has, however, been delayed following the resignation of the Chair of the Commission, Professor William Schabas, on 2 February 2015.[163] Palestine accepted the jurisdiction of the court by issuing a declaration to the ICC Prosecutor accepting retroactive jurisdiction from 13 June 2014 under Article 12(3) of the Rome Statute, followed by its accession to the Rome Statute, which became operative on 1 April. The ICC opened a preliminary examination on 16 January 2015 into possible war crimes committed in Palestinian territories since 13 June 2014.[164] Both sides have accused each other of having committed grave breaches of IHL, and various human rights NGOs have alleged that both sides may be responsible for the commission war crimes.

Hamas has been accused inter alia of (1) using human shields and forcing civilians to act as shields by staying in their homes despite Israeli warnings, (2) launching indiscriminate projectile (rocket and mortar) attacks against Israeli population centres, (3) using UN facilities for military purposes, and (4) executing alleged collaborators.

The UN High Commissioner for Human Rights Navi Pillay accused Hamas of violating IHL by 'locating rockets within schools and hospitals, or even launching these rockets from densely populated areas'.[165] Israel accused Hamas of forcing civilians to provide

[162] Internal Displacement Monitoring Centre (IDMC) 'Global Overview 2015', May 2015, p. 85.

[163] 'Gaza Conflict: Schabas Quits UN Inquiry over Bias Claims', *BBC*, 3 February 2015, <http://www.bbc.com/news/world-middle-east-31107988>.

[164] Lis, J., 'ICC Opens Initial Probe into Possible War Crimes in Palestinian Territories', *Haaretz*, 16 January 2015, <http://www.haaretz.com/news/diplomacy-defense/1.637518>.

[165] 'UN Official Condemns Israeli "War Crimes," US Support for Iron Dome', *Times of Israel*, 31 July 2014, <http://www.timesofisrael.com/liveblog_entry/un-official-condemns-israeli-war-crimes-us-support-for-iron-dome/>.

human shields.[166] After conducting a survey in Gaza, the Gatestone Institute also accused Hamas of forcing Palestinians to stay home even if they received Israeli warnings that their houses were about to be bombed.[167] However, this claim was dismissed as a 'myth' by reporters of the BBC,[168] *Guardian*,[169] and the *Independent*.[170] Amnesty International also concluded it had no evidence for Hamas forcing civilians to act as 'human shields'.[171]

On 26 March 2015, Amnesty International accused Hamas and other Palestinian armed groups of war crimes for launching indiscriminate rocket attacks at Israel.[172] Moreover, according to the UN Relief and Works Agency for Palestine Refugees in the Near East, and the UN Board of Inquiry report summary released in April 2015, a number of UN schools that had been closed were used by Palestinian armed groups for such attacks to provide room for weapon storage.[173]

Hamas executed between thirty and forty alleged collaborators during the seven-week Operation Protective Edge. Amnesty International[174] and Human Rights Watch have condemned these 'extrajudicial killings'.[175] Referring to these acts, Shurat HaDin civil rights group asked the International Criminal Court to indict Hamas leader Khaled Mashaal on war crimes.[176]

[166] Lynfield, B., 'Israel-Gaza Conflict: Netanyahu Says Hamas Using Rising Death Toll to Make Israel Look Bad', *Independent*, 20 July 2014, <http://www.independent.co.uk/news/world/middle-east/israelgaza-conflict-netanyahu-says-hamas-using-rising-death-toll-to-make-israel-look-bad-9617583.html>.

[167] Zahran, M., 'Gazans Speak Out: Hamas War Crimes', *Gatestone Institute*, 19 September 2014, <http://www.gatestoneinstitute.org/4706/gazan-hamas-war-crimes>.

[168] Bowen, J., 'Jeremy Bowen's Gaza Notebook: I saw no evidence of Hamas using Palestinians as human shields', *New Statesman*, 22 July 2014, <http://www.newstatesman.com/world-affairs/2014/07/jeremy-bowens-gaza-notebook-i-saw-no-evidence-hamas-using-palestinians-human>.

[169] Sherwood, H., 'In Gaza, Hamas fighters are among civilians. There is nowhere else for them to go', *Guardian*, 24 July 2014, <http://www.theguardian.com/world/2014/jul/24/gaza-hamas-fighters-military-bases-guerrilla-war-civilians-israel-idf>.

[170] Sengupta, K., 'Israel-Gaza Conflict: The Myth of Hamas's Human Shields', *Independent*, 21 July 2014, <http://www.independent.co.uk/news/world/middle-east/israelgaza-conflict-the-myth-of-hamass-human-shield-9619810.html>.

[171] 'Unlawful and Deadly: Rocket and Mortar Attacks by Palestinian Armed Groups during the 2014 Gaza/Israel conflict', *Amnesty International*, London, March 2015, pp. 45–6.

[172] 'Palestinian Armed Groups Killed Civilians on Both Sides in Attacks Amounting to War Crimes', *Amnesty International*, 26 March 2015, <https://www.amnesty.org/en/articles/news/2015/03/palestinian-armed-groups-killed-civilians-on-both-sides-in-2014-gaza-conflict/>.

[173] 'UNRWA strongly condemns placement of rockets in school', *UNRWA*, 17 July 2014, <http://www.unrwa.org/newsroom/press-releases/unrwa-strongly-condemns-placement-rockets-school>.

[174] 'Gaza: Hamas Must End Summary Executions as "Informers" Face Firing Squad', *Amnesty International*, 22 August 2014, <https://www.amnesty.org/en/articles/news/2014/08/hamas-must-end-summary-executions-informers-face-firing-squad/>.

[175] 'Gaza: Halt Executions', *Human Rights Watch*, 25 August 2014, <http://www.hrw.org/news/2014/08/25/gaza-halt-executions>.

[176] Bob, Y. J., 'NGO Asks ICC to Indict Hamas Leader Khaled Mashaal on War Crimes Charges', *Jerusalem Post*, 3 September 2014, <http://www.jpost.com/Arab-Israeli-Conflict/NGO-asks-ICC-to-indict-Hamas-leader-Khaled-Mashaal-on-war-crimes-charges-374302>.

With respect to Israel, several human rights NGOs have pointed to the excessive amount of civilian casualties and damage to civilian homes and objects indispensable to the survival of the civilian population. Amnesty International notes in an examination of eight cases in their November 2014 report 'a failure to take necessary precautions to avoid excessive harm to civilians and civilian property, as required by international humanitarian law. In all cases, no prior warning was given to residents to allow them to escape'.[177] Amnesty International also pointed to the use of imprecise munitions such as artillery in very densely populated areas.[178]

On 24 and 30 July, and on 3 August 2014, Israel targeted three UN schools in Gaza, which killed in total forty-five people, including seventeen children. According to Human Rights Watch, the 'three attacks that damaged Gaza schools housing displaced people caused numerous civilian casualties in violation of the laws of war'. It argued that the first two attacks 'did not appear to target a military objective or were otherwise unlawfully indiscriminate', and the third attack 'was unlawfully disproportionate if not otherwise indiscriminate'. It was thus considered a war crime by Human Rights Watch[179] and Amnesty International.[180] The UN Secretary-General established Board of Inquiry concluded that forty-four deaths and at least 229 injuries in UN schools sheltering civilians were caused by Israeli attacks.[181]

On 29 July, Israel bombed Gaza's only power plant. This has led to accusations of having committed acts that amounted to 'collective punishment'.[182] Human Rights Watch added that even if serving a military purpose, such an attack 'would be an unlawful disproportionate attack under the laws of war'.[183]

[177] 'Families under the Rubble: Israeli Attacks on Inhabited Homes', *Amnesty International*, November 2014, London, p. 5.

[178] 'Israel/Gaza Conflict: Questions and Answers', *Amnesty International*, 25 July 2014, <https://www.amnesty.org/en/articles/news/2014/07/israelgaza-conflict-questions-and-answers/>.

[179] 'Human Rights Watch Accuses Israel of War Crimes in Gaza', *Reuters*, 11 September 2014, <http://uk.reuters.com/article/2014/09/11/uk-mideast-gaza-war-idUKKBN0H60YD20140911>.

[180] 'Israel/Gaza: Attack on UN school in Gaza a Potential War Crime that Must be Investigated', *Amnesty International*, 30 July 2014, <https://www.amnesty.org/en/articles/news/2014/07/israelgaza-attack-un-school-gaza-potential-war-crime-must-be-investigated/>.

[181] Summary by the Secretary-General of the UN Headquarters Board of Inquiry into certain incidents that occurred in the Gaza Strip between 8 July 2014 and 26 August 2014, 27 April 2015, <https://drive.google.com/file/d/0ByLPNZ-eSjJdVy1oWXRhcFJGSjBlbFNrY241QWsxNVp1dUx3/view>.

[182] Sherwood, H., 'Gaza's Only Power Plant Destroyed in Israel's Most Intense Air Strike Yet', *Guardian*, 29 July 2014, <http://www.theguardian.com/world/2014/jul/29/gaza-power-plant-destroyed-israeli-airstrike-100-palestinians-dead>.

[183] 'Gaza: Widespread Impact of Power Plant Attack', *Human Rights Watch*, 10 August 2014, <http://www.hrw.org/news/2014/08/10/gaza-widespread-impact-power-plant-attack>.

Armed conflicts between Israel and Syria in 2014

KEY CASUALTY DATA FOR 2014

Civilian deaths:	8	(Source: media reports)
Civilians injured:	7	(Source: media reports)
Syrian military deaths:	17	(Source: media reports/UN)
Syrian military injured:	26	(Source: media reports/UN)
Hezbollah deaths:	3	(Source: media reports)

CLASSIFICATION OF THE CONFLICTS

In 2014, Israel and Syria were involved in at least four distinct, short-lived international armed conflicts (IACs).

SUMMARY OF APPLICABLE INTERNATIONAL LAW

Both parties to the conflicts were bound by customary and conventional international humanitarian law and human rights law, including customary international humanitarian law (IHL) rules of distinction, proportionality, and precautions in attacks.

Both Israel and Syria are party to the four 1949 Geneva Conventions and to the 1966 Covenant on Civil and Political Rights. Syria adhered to the 1977 Additional Protocol I in 1983.[184]

Neither State is party to the 1997 Anti-Personnel Mine Ban Convention or the 2008 Convention on Cluster Munitions.

Syria acceded to the 1992 Chemical Weapons Convention in September 2013 and was already party to the 1925 Geneva Gas Protocol;[185] Israel is a signatory to the 1992 Chemical Weapons Convention and party to the 1925 Geneva Gas Protocol.[186]

[184] When acceding, Syria made the following declaration whereby its accession 'in no way constitutes recognition of Israel nor the establishment of relations with Israel as regards the application of the provisions of the aforementioned Protocol'. Notification by the depositary addressed to the International Committee of the Red Cross (ICRC) on 23 November 1983.

[185] In 1968, when acceding to the Protocol Syria made the following declaration whereby its accession 'does not in any case imply the recognition of Israel or lead to the establishment of relations with the latter concerning the provisions laid down in the Protocol'. Schindler, D. and Toman, J., 1988, *The Laws of Armed Conflicts*, Martinus Nijhoff, p. 126.

[186] In 1969, when acceding to the Protocol Israel made the following declaration whereby the Protocol 'shall ipso facto cease to be binding on the State of Israel in regard to any enemy State whose armed forces

Neither State is party or signatory to the 2013 Arms Trade Treaty (ATT).[187]

HISTORY OF THE CONFLICT

In 2014, media reported as many as four strikes on military targets in Syria by aircraft bombing and missiles attributed to Israel.

In February 2014, Israel bombarded a Hezbollah position on the Lebanon–Syria border, according to a Lebanese security source and a Syrian NGO. While Israel did not immediately confirm or deny responsibility for the raids, their aim, shown as previous attacks, is to prevent advanced weaponry from being transferred to Hezbollah, a close ally of Damascus.[188] This attack amounts to an IAC.

Israel launched air strikes on March 2014 against Syrian military sites reportedly in response to a roadside bombing that wounded four of its soldiers, but both sides signalled they were not seeking further escalation.[189] This attack also rose to the level of an IAC.

In June, the Syrian Government said a series of Israeli airstrikes had targeted its troops in retaliation for a deadly cross-border attack which killed four people and wounded nine others. The government further declared these attacks constituted a 'flagrant violation' of Syrian sovereignty, adding however that it would not retaliate. According to the director of the Britain-based Syrian Observatory for Human Rights, the Israeli strikes destroyed two tanks, two artillery batteries, and the headquarters of Syria's 90th brigade.[190]

Syrian State media and opposition activists reported that Israeli warplanes bombed targets in territory held by the Syrian Government near Damascus on 7 December 2014. As for their previous one, these strikes appear to have been aimed at deterring shipments of Iranian missiles and other weaponry to the Lebanese Shiite Hezbollah movement.[191]

or the armed forces of its allies or the regular or irregular forces or the groups or individuals operating from its territory fail to respect the prohibitions which are the object of this Protocol'.

[187] Syria was one of three states to vote against the adoption of the ATT by the United Nations (UN) General Assembly on 2 April 2013, while Israel voted in favour.

[188] 'Israel Bombs Hezbollah Target on Lebanon-Syria Border', *The Telegraph*, 24 February 2014, <http://www.telegraph.co.uk/news/worldnews/middleeast/israel/10659467/Israel-bombs-Hezbollah-target-on-Lebanon-Syria-border.html>. See also 'Armed Conflicts between Israel and Syria in 2013'. In *The War Report 2013*, edited by Casey-Maslen, S., Oxford University Press, 2014, p. 35.

[189] 'Israel Bombs Syrian Military Sites in Retaliation for Roadside Bombing in Golan Heights', Reuters, 19 March 2014, at: <http://www.huffingtonpost.com/2014/03/19/israel-bombs-syrian-military-sites_n_4990330.html>.

[190] 'Syria: 4 Killed, 9 Wounded in Israeli Airstrikes', Fox News, 23 June 2014, at: <http://www.foxnews.com/world/2014/06/23/israel-bombs-targets-in-syria-in-response-to-boy-death/>.

[191] 'Israel Bombs Syria in Attacks Probably Aimed at Hezbollah', *The Washington Post*, 7 December 2014, <http://www.washingtonpost.com/world/middle_east/israel-bombs-syria-in-attacks-probably-aimed-at-hezbollah/2014/12/07/dc0040d6-7e3e-11e4-b936-f3afab0155a7_story.html>.

PARTIES TO THE CONFLICTS

The parties to the conflicts were Israel and Syria.

Israel is estimated to have 176,500 active frontline military personnel and a further 445,000 in reserve.[192] Syria has been estimated to have 178,000 active frontline military personnel and a further 570,000 in reserve,[193] although a different source suggested in September 2013 that active personnel stood at 125,000 of whom 80,000 were considered to be loyal.[194] In addition to a huge array of conventional weaponry held by both States, Israel possesses nuclear and chemical weapons[195] while Syria possesses chemical weapons, which are in the process of being destroyed.[196]

CASUALTIES

Israeli airstrikes and shelling on targets within Syria, including on Quneitra province on the 'Bravo side' of the Golan Heights, resulted in at least sixty-one casualties in 2014. There were at least twenty-eight deaths, including seventeen Syrian soldiers and three Hezbollah fighters and eight civilians. Another twenty-six military personnel and seven civilians were injured.[197] It was also reported that at least one of two Syrian pilots died after they plane was downed by Israeli fire.[198]

[192] 'Israel Military Strength', *Globalfirepower.com*, last updated on 27 March 2014, at: <http://www.globalfirepower.com/country-military-strength-detail.asp?country_id=israel>. The Israel Defence Forces' mission is 'To defend the existence, territorial integrity and sovereignty of the state of Israel. To protect the inhabitants of Israel and to combat all forms of terrorism which threaten the daily life', <http://www.idfblog.com/about-the-idf/idf-code-of-ethics/>.

[193] 'Syria Military Strength', *Globalfirepower.com*, last updated on 27 March 2014, at: <http://www.globalfirepower.com/country-military-strength-detail.asp?country_id=syria>.

[194] Kechechian, J., 'What is Syrian Arab Army military capability?', *Gulf News*, 8 September 2013, at: <http://gulfnews.com/news/region/syria/what-is-syrian-arab-army-military-capability-1.1228699>.

[195] See,e.g.,Fiske,G.,'AvrahamBurgPannedforBreaking"NuclearAmbiguity"',*TimesofIsrael*,8December 2013, at: <http://www.timesofisrael.com/avraham-burg-panned-for-breaking-nuclear-ambiguity/>.

[196] In late April 2014, the Organisation for the Prohibition of Chemical Weapons (OPCW) reported that the OPCW-UN Joint Mission had removed and destroyed a total of 92.5% of chemical weapons material in country covered by the Mission. The date of 30 June 2014 had been set as the deadline for completion of the disposal of Syria's chemical weapons. OPCW, '92.5% of Syria's Chemical Weapons Material Removed or Destroyed In-Country', Press release, The Hague, 22 April 2014, at: <http://opcw.unmissions.org/AboutOPCWUNJointMission/tabid/54/ctl/Details/mid/651/ItemID/305/Default.asp>.

[197] UN Security Council, S/2014/401, 10 June 2014, para. 5; 'Israeli Air Strike Kills 18 in Syria,' 15 July 2014, <http://www.aa.com.tr/en/rss/359257--israeli-airstrike>; 'Two Hezbollah Members Killed in Airstrike,' 8 December 2014, <http://www.haaretz.com/news/diplomacy-defense/1.630620>; 'Syria: 4 Killed, 9 Wounded in Israeli Airstrikes,' 23 June 2014, <http://www.foxnews.com/world/2014/06/23/israel-bombs-targets-in-syria-in-response-to-boy-death>.

This casualty has been included in the total.

[198] 'Pilots of Plane, Shot down by Israel, Died', 24 September 2014, <http://www.i24news.tv/en/news/israel/diplomacy-defense/44965-140924-report-pilots-of-plane-shot-down-by-israel-died>.

WAR CRIMES ALLEGATIONS, INVESTIGATIONS, AND PROSECUTIONS

Neither Israel nor Syria is a State party to the 1998 Rome Statute of the International Criminal Court (ICC). Syria is a signatory State to the Statute.

No allegations of war crimes are known to have been made against either Israeli or Syrian military personnel regarding any acts concerning the IACs in 2014.

Military occupation of Azerbaijan by Armenia in 2014

KEY CASUALTY DATA FOR 2014

Armenia/Nagorno Karabakh military deaths:	22–7	(Source: Media reports)
Armenia/Nagorno Karabakh military injured:	at least 7	(Source: Media reports)
Azerbaijan military deaths:	27–37	(Source: Media reports)
Azerbaijan military injured:	at least 10	(Source: Media reports)
Armenia/Nagorno Karabakh civilian deaths:	5	(Source: Media reports)
Armenia/Nagorno Karabakh civilian injured:	7	(Source: Media reports)
Armenia/Nagorno Karabakh unknown deaths:	1	(Source: Media reports)
Azerbaijan civilian deaths:	2	(Source: Media reports)
Azerbaijan civilian injured:	7	(Source: Media reports)

CLASSIFICATION OF THE CONFLICT

Armenia and Azerbaijan were involved in an international armed conflict in 2014 by virtue of continued Armenian occupation of Azerbaijani territory.

SUMMARY OF APPLICABLE INTERNATIONAL LAW

Both parties to the conflict were bound by customary and conventional international humanitarian law and human rights law, including customary international humanitarian law (IHL) rules of distinction, proportionality, and precautions in attacks; the obligation not to recruit and use children as soldiers; and by the duty to respect and protect fundamental human rights. This includes the duty to respect the rights to life and to freedom from torture or other forms of cruel, inhuman, or degrading treatment or punishment.

The law of military occupation is set out in the 1907 Hague Regulations (Articles 42–56); the 1949 Geneva Convention IV, the 1977 Additional Protocol I, and customary international law. Both States are party to the four 1949 Geneva Conventions, but only Armenia is party to the 1977 Additional Protocol I. Both States are party to the 1966 International Covenant on Civil and Political Rights and the 1966 International Covenant on Economic, Social and Cultural Rights.

The underpinning of the law of military occupation is that it is a temporary situation, which lasts until a political agreement is reached. During this period, the Occupying Power does not enjoy sovereign rights over the territories it occupies and local law that was applicable prior to the occupation remains in force. At the same time, the Occupying Power is responsible for administering the local life of the population under its control, maintaining it as it was prior to the occupation as closely as possible, and for providing security (Article 43 of the Hague Regulations).

Azerbaijan is bound domestically by customary and conventional international human rights law. In addition, international human rights law is binding on Armenia extraterritorially in the territories it occupies.[199]

Neither State is party to the 1997 Anti-Personnel Mine Ban Convention or the 2008 Convention on Cluster Munitions. Neither State is signatory or party to the 2013 Arms Trade Treaty (ATT).[200]

HISTORY OF THE CONFLICT

The re-emergence of violence in the late 1980s between ethnic Armenians and Azeris over the long-disputed region of Nagorno-Karabakh erupted into armed conflict in February 1992 between forces from Armenia and Azerbaijan as well as Nagorno-Karabakh. The armed conflict led to occupation of more than one-seventh of the territory of Azerbaijan, more than 20,000 casualties, massive refugee flows from both sides, and expulsion of ethnic Armenians from Azerbaijan and ethnic Azeris from Armenia.[201]

A ceasefire between the parties to the conflict was signed on 12 May 1994. Since February 1992, attempts to settle the conflict have been made under the framework of the Minsk Process led by the Presidents of the Organization for Security and Co-operation in Europe (OSCE), Minsk Group's Co-Chair States, namely France, the Russian Federation, and the United States of America (USA).

[199] See, e.g., International Court of Justice, *Wall* Advisory Opinion, 2004, §106. As ruled by the European Court of Human Rights, the obligation to secure in occupied territories the rights and freedoms set out in the 1950 European Convention on Human Rights derives from its effective control over occupied territory, whether it is exercised by the occupying State directly, through its armed forces, or through a subordinate local administration. See European Court of Human Rights, *Cyprus v Turkey*, Judgment, 10 May 2001, §77.

[200] Armenia was not present during the vote on the adoption of the ATT by the United Nations (UN) General Assembly on 2 April 2013, while Azerbaijan voted in favour.

[201] See, e.g., 'Nagorno-Karabakh profile', *BBC*, 30 May 2012, at: <http://www.bbc.co.uk/news/world-europe-18270325>; 'Armenia: Timeline', *BBC*, 27 February 2013, at: <http://www.bbc.co.uk/news/world-europe-17405415>; and 'Azerbaijan Profile', *BBC*, 20 March 2012, at: <http://www.bbc.co.uk/news/world-europe-17047328>.

The Minsk Process negotiations resulted in a proposal of Basic Principles put forward in November 2007 in Madrid. The Principles aimed to serve as a basis for a comprehensive settlement between Armenia and Azerbaijan and call inter alia for the return of the territories surrounding Nagorno-Karabakh to Azerbaijani control and an interim status for Nagorno-Karabakh providing guarantees for security and self-governance as well as international security guarantees that would include a peace-keeping operation.

Despite the twenty-year-long ceasefire, which is monitored by the OSCE, and continued negotiations for a peaceful settlement of the conflict, the Nagorno-Karabakh situation remains unsolved with regular violations of the ceasefire involving armed incidents along the Line of Contact between Armenia and Azerbaijan. On 12 June 2013, the OSCE's Special Representative for Conflicts warned that simmering conflict between the two might explode; he voiced continuing concern Armenia might attempt to launch regular, scheduled fixed-wing air flights between Yerevan and Karabakh, which would almost certainly provoke an Azerbaijani reaction.[202] Several days later, the Presidents of the Minsk Group's Co-Chair States issued a joint statement in which they:

> reiterate[d] that only a negotiated settlement can lead to peace, stability, and reconciliation, opening opportunities for regional development and cooperation. The use of military force that has already created the current situation of confrontation and instability will not resolve the conflict. A renewal of hostilities would be disastrous for the population of the region, resulting in loss of life, more destruction, additional refugees, and enormous financial costs. We strongly urge the leaders of all the sides to recommit to the Helsinki principles, particularly those relating to the non-use of force or the threat of force, territorial integrity, and equal rights and self-determination of peoples. We also appeal to them to refrain from any actions or rhetoric that could raise tension in the region and lead to escalation of the conflict. The leaders should prepare their people for peace, not war.
>
> Our countries stand ready to assist the sides, but the responsibility for putting an end to the Nagorno-Karabakh conflict remains with them. We strongly believe that further delay in reaching a balanced agreement on the framework for a comprehensive peace is unacceptable, and urge the leaders of Azerbaijan and Armenia to focus with renewed energy on the issues that remain unresolved.[203]

[202] International Crisis Group (ICG), Crisis Watch: Nagorno-Karabakh (Azerbaijan), 1 July 2013, available at: <http://www.crisisgroup.org/en/publication-type/crisiswatch/crisiswatch-database.aspx>.

[203] 'Joint statement on the Nagorno-Karabakh Conflict, by the Presidents of the OSCE Minsk Group Co-Chair Countries', Enniskillen, 18 June 2013, at: <http://www.osce.org/mg/102856>. See also Corboy, D., Courtney, W., Kauzlarich, R., and Yalowitz, K., 'Choices for the South Caucasus', Op-Ed, *New York Times*, 28 August 2013, at: <http://www.nytimes.com/2013/08/29/opinion/global/choices-for-the-south-caucasus.html?_r=1&>.

In December 2013, the US Co-chair of the Minsk Group, US Ambassador James Warlick, hailed the 'constructive dialogue' engaged in by the Armenian and Azerbaijani presidents who held talks in Vienna on 19 November, as the first such meeting in almost two years. The meeting was held under the auspices of the Minsk Group.[204] Two months later, in February 2014, Ambassador Warlick reported that negotiations had made progress and that there has been a decrease in incidents in the Nagorno-Karabakh region since the November meeting by the two presidents but noted that the ceasefire there remained very fragile.[205]

In July and August 2014 there was an escalation of tension near the contested territories. Azerbaijan has been breaching the ceasefire agreement more and more frequently by using sniper attacks, both in Nagorno-Karabakh and in the bordering regions of Armenia. Additionally, the President of Azerbaijan Aliyev has threatened to take military action to regain the area of Nagorno-Karanakh.[206]

PARTIES TO THE CONFLICT

The parties to the conflict were Armenia and Azerbaijan.

Armenia was estimated by one source to have some 46,500 active frontline military personnel and a further 200,000 in reserve.[207] Azerbaijan is estimated by one source to have 67,000 active frontline military personnel and a further 300,000 in reserve.[208] A wide array of conventional weaponry is possessed by both States.

Sporadic fighting along the LoC continued in 2013. In August, for example, sporadic fighting along the nearly 1,000km-long Azerbaijan–Armenia border spread to the highly sensitive Nakhichevan exclave.[209]

[204] Radio Free Europe/Radio Liberty (RFI), 'Minsk Co-Chair Cites Mutual Armenian, Azerbaijan "Respect" On Karabakh', 19 December 2013, at: <http://www.rferl.org/content/nagorno-karabakh-armenia-azerbaijan-respect/25206175.html>.

[205] RFI, 'OSCE Mediator Sees Progress in Nagorno-Karabakh Talks', 4 February 2014, at: <http://www.rferl.org/content/azerbaijan-armenia-karabakh-progress/25253225.html>.

[206] 'President of Azerbaijan Declares "State of War" with Armenia on Twitter', *The Independent*, 7 August 2014.

[207] International Institute for Strategic Studies (IISS), 2010, *The Military Balance 2010*, Routledge, London, p. 174; IISS, 2007, *The Military Balance 2007*, Routledge, London, p. 155. The Republic of Armenia armed forces website is at: <http://www.mil.am/>.

[208] 'Azerbaijan Military Strength', *Globalfirepower.com*, last updated on 27 March 2014, at: <http://www.globalfirepower.com/country-military-strength-detail.asp?country_id=azerbaijan>.

[209] ICG, Crisis Watch: Nagorno-Karabakh (Azerbaijan), 1 September 2013. Nakhichevan is a landlocked exclave of Azerbaijan bordering Armenia, Turkey, and Iran.

CASUALTIES

In 2014 at least eighty-eight casualties (between fifty-seven and seventy-two killed and at least thirty-one injured) occurred representing a large increase compared to eighteen in 2013. No comprehensive, reliable casualty figures were available for 2014. The casualty totals for 2014 are based on War Report analysis of data from media scanning the calendar year 2014.

During increased clashes in the period from late July to early August (approximately 28 July to 8 August) there were a high number of casualties among both Azeri and Armenian/Karabakh forces, with larger claims of deaths and injury by the opposing sides. Azeri media reported forty-seven Armenian military fatalities (thirty from Nagorno-Karabakh and seventeen from Armenia) and about 100 injured.[210] In contrast, a report of an Armenian Defence Ministry estimated during the period counted only five Armenian military killed and seven injured, but stated that twenty-five Azeri military were killed and thirty injured.[211]

Despite the large discrepancies between various casualty estimates reported, it was commonly stated that the level of casualties in the time period was unprecedented. The US State Department reported that it was 'the deadliest period in the conflict since the 1994 ceasefire took effect'.[212] A leading Azeri military analyst also reportedly stated that Azerbaijan 'has not suffered such losses in a single bout of hostilities since 1994, when a ceasefire was agreed'.[213] Similarly, a media article in the Armenian Weekly online said that 'statistics available for the years since 2000 make 2014 the worst year on record since the ceasefire'.[214]

The OSCE referred to there having been 'some 60 casualties in 2014' in Nagorno-Karabakh, meaning fatalities.[215] One media report summary of casualties in Nagorno-Karabakh for 2014 includes thirty-nine 'Azerbaijanis' killed and thirty-three 'Armenians' killed as a result of armed conflict such as direct combat,

[210] 'Azerbaijani Army kills 47 Armenian Servicemen in Recent Fights', 7 August 2014, <http://www.news.az/articles/karabakh/90988>.

[211] 'Armenia: Wondering About Russia's Motives in Karabakh Peace Process', 14 August 2014, <http://www.eurasianet.org/node/69551>.

[212] 'Leaders Discuss Nagorno-Karabakh Conflict; Kerry Expresses "Strong Concern"', 5 September 2014, <http://www.rferl.org/content/nagorno-karabakh-/26567727.html>.

[213] 'Five Killed in Clashes over Nagorno Karabakh,' 3 August 2014, <http://www.aljazeera.com/news/europe/2014/08/five-killed-clashes-over-nagorny-karabakh-201483212159938.html>.

[214] Sanamyan, E., 'Loose Restraints: A Look at the Increasingly Shaky Karabagh Ceasefire', 4 February 2015, <http://armenianweekly.com/2015/02/04/karabagh>.

[215] Ministry of Foreign Affairs of Serbia, 'Statement by the OSCE Chairperson-in-Office and Co-Chair of OSCE Minsk Group on the Latest Developments in the Nagorno-Karabakh Peace Process', 7 February 2015, <http://www.mfa.gov.rs/en/press-service/statements/13870-statement-by-the-osce-chairperson-in-office-and-co-chair-of-osce-minsk-group-on-the-latest-developments-in-the-nagorno-karabakh-peace-process>.

sniper fire, and landmine incidents.[216] In an incident in August three Armenian/Nagorno-Karabakh military personnel were killed when Azeri forces shot down a Mi-24 combat helicopter.[217] One Armenian/Nagorno-Karabakh died in custody in Azerbaijan 'after crossing into Azerbaijan in disputed circumstances'.[218] That casualty has been recorded with military or civilian status as unknown.

The Azerbaijan National Agency for Mine Action (ANAMA) reported that five people were killed and seventeen injured by landmines and explosive remnants of war (ERW) in Azerbaijan in 2014.[219] The Landmine Free Artsakh website reported two civilians killed and at least seven injured by landmines and ERW in Nagorno-Karabakh in 2014, including two people incurring amputations.[220] Another media article reported four people killed in mine explosions in Nagorno-Karabakh in 2014.[221]

WAR CRIMES ALLEGATIONS, INVESTIGATIONS, AND PROSECUTIONS

Neither Armenia nor Azerbaijan is a State party to the 1998 Rome Statute of the International Criminal Court (ICC), although Armenia is a signatory State.

No allegations of war crimes are known to have been made against either Armenian or Azerbaijani military personnel regarding any acts concerning the international armed conflict in 2014.

[216] According to the report, among the thirty-nine Azerbaijanis fatalities, twenty-two were enlisted soldiers (18–19-year-olds), nine contracted non-commissioned officer (NCOs), six officers, and two civilians. Among the thirty-three Armenian/Nagorno Karabakh fatalities thirteen were enlisted (19–20-year olds), six contracted NCOs and privates, eight officers, and six civilians. See Sanamyan, E., 'Loose Restraints: A Look at the Increasingly Shaky Karabagh Ceasefire', 4 February 2015, <http://armenianweekly.com/2015/02/04/karabagh>.

[217] 'Armenian Military Helicopter Shot down by Azerbaijani Forces, Killing Three', *The Guardian*, 12 November 2014, <http://www.theguardian.com/world/2014/nov/12/azerbaijani-forces-shoot-down-armenian-military-helicopter>.

[218] Armenian Captive Dies in Azerbaijan, 8 August 2014, www.eurasianet.org/node/69451.

[219] ANAMA 'Monthly Report February 2015: Mine /UXO Victims Reported—in Table', <http://anama.gov.az/site/assets/files/1/monthly_report_fevral_2015-2.pdf>.

[220] Landmine Free Artsakh, 'Victims: 2014 Accidents—Year to Date 8 Accidents, 2 Fatalities and Two Amputations', <http://www.landminefreeartsakh.com/victims>.

[221] Sanamyan, E., 'Loose Restraints: A Look at the Increasingly Shaky Karabagh Ceasefire', 4 February 2015, <http://armenianweekly.com/2015/02/04/karabagh>.

Military occupation of Cyprus by Turkey in 2014

KEY CASUALTY DATA FOR 2014

No casualties were recorded for 2014

CLASSIFICATION OF THE CONFLICT

Cyprus and Turkey were involved in an international armed conflict in 2014 by virtue of continued Turkish occupation of territory in the north of the Republic of Cyprus.

SUMMARY OF APPLICABLE INTERNATIONAL LAW

Both parties to the conflict were bound by customary and conventional international humanitarian law and human rights law, including customary international humanitarian law (IHL) rules of distinction, proportionality, and precautions in attacks; the obligation not to recruit and use children as soldiers; and by the duty to respect and protect fundamental human rights. This includes the duty to respect the rights to life and to freedom from torture or other forms of cruel, inhuman, or degrading treatment or punishment.

The law of military occupation is set out in the 1907 Hague Regulations (Articles 42–56); the 1949 Geneva Convention IV, the 1977 Additional Protocol I, and customary international law. Both States are party to the four 1949 Geneva Conventions, but only Cyprus is party to the 1977 Additional Protocol I. Both States are party to the 1966 International Covenant on Civil and Political Rights and the 1966 International Covenant on Economic, Social and Cultural Rights.

The underpinning of the law of military occupation is that it is a temporary situation, which lasts until a political agreement is reached. During this period, the Occupying Power does not enjoy sovereign rights over the territories it occupies and local law that was applicable prior to the occupation remains in force. At the same time, the Occupying Power is responsible for administering the local life of the population under its control, maintaining it as it was prior to the occupation as closely as possible, and for providing security (Article 43 of the Hague Regulations).

Cyprus is bound domestically by customary and conventional international human rights law. In addition, international human rights law is binding on Turkey extraterritorially in the territories it occupies.[222] As ruled by the European Court of Human Rights, the obligation to secure in occupied territories the rights and freedoms set out in the 1950 European Convention on Human Rights derives from Turkey's effective control over occupied territory, whether it is exercised by the occupying State directly, through its armed forces, or through a subordinate local administration. The European Court has ruled that Turkey exercises effective control over the north by virtue of its maintaining many thousands of its troops there.[223]

Both Cyprus and Turkey are party to the 1997 Anti-Personnel Mine Ban Convention. In December 2012, Cyprus was granted a three-year extension to its mine clearance deadline under the Convention on the basis that it was not in a position to clear mines in the north of the island that was occupied.[224]

Neither State is party to the 2008 Convention on Cluster Munitions, although Cyprus is a signatory. Neither State is party to the 2013 Arms Trade Treaty (ATT), but both are signatories.[225]

HISTORY OF THE CONFLICT[226]

Cyprus has been divided since 1974 when Turkey invaded the north in response to a military coup on the island backed by the Greek Government in Athens. Cyprus was effectively partitioned with the northern third inhabited by Turkish Cypriots and the southern two-thirds by Greek Cypriots. A 'Green Line' with a buffer zone, dividing the two parts from Morphou through Nicosia to Famagusta, is patrolled by United Nations (UN) troops.

UN Security Council Resolution 353 of 20 July 1974 requested the withdrawal without delay from the Republic of Cyprus of foreign military personnel. UN General Assembly Resolution 37/253 of 16 May 1983 declared that 'part of the territory of the Republic of Cyprus is still occupied by foreign forces'.

In 1983, the Turkish-held area declared itself the Turkish Republic of Northern Cyprus. Turkey recognizes only the Turkish Cypriot authorities and is believed still to

[222] See, e.g., International Court of Justice, *Wall* Advisory Opinion, 2004, §106.

[223] See European Court of Human Rights, *Cyprus v Turkey*, Judgment, 10 May 2001, §77; and *Loizidou v Turkey*, Judgment (Merits), 18 December 1996, §§52, 54, 56.

[224] See, e.g., 'Convention on the Prohibition of the Use, Stockpiling, Production and Transfer of Anti-Personnel Mines and on Their Destruction, Twelfth Meeting of the States Parties, Final Report', at: <http://www.apminebanconvention.org/fileadmin/pdf/mbc/MSP/12MSP/12MSP-FinalReport-Dec2012.pdf>.

[225] Cyprus signed the ATT on 3 June 2013 and Turkey signed on 2 July 2013.

[226] Unless otherwise stated, this section is based on 'Timeline: Cyprus', *BBC*, 13 December 2011, at: <http://news.bbc.co.uk/2/hi/europe/country_profiles/1021835.stm>.

maintain more than 10,000 troops in the north of the island. No other government has recognized the north as a State.

As European Union (EU) entry for the Republic of Cyprus approached, a UN reunification plan was put to both communities in twin referenda in April 2004. The plan was endorsed by Turkish Cypriots, although not by their leader Rauf Denktash, but was overwhelmingly rejected by Greek Cypriots. Since both sides had to approve the proposals, the island remained divided as it joined the EU in May 2004.

In April 2008, the two sides re-opened a major crossing in the divided Cypriot capital of Nicosia.[227] In September, Greek and Turkish Cypriot leaders launched intensive negotiations aimed at ending the division of the island. In January 2010, President Demetris Christofias and Turkish Cypriot leader Mehmet Ali Talat resumed talks on reunification in a downbeat mood, and no progress was made. In April, Dervis Eroglu, who favours independence, won the Turkish north's leadership contest, beating the pro-unity incumbent. The following month, re-unification talks resumed.[228]

In early March 2012, Turkey's European Affairs Minister Egemen Bağış told a Turkish Cypriot newspaper that Turkey would consider annexing northern Cyprus, which is technically EU territory, if talks between Greek and Turkish Cypriots fail to reach a deal on re-unification of the island.[229]

On 24 February 2013, Democratic Rally (DISI) leader Nicos Anastasiades won the Republic of Cyprus presidential elections leading to hopes that this might give a boost to re-unification talks as he supported a looser federation model favoured by many Turkish Cypriots. On 7 April 2013, however, Turkish Foreign Minister Ahmet Davutoğlu criticized the Greek Cypriots for not re-starting re-unification talks. A spokesman for the Republic of Cyprus Government said that the current conditions were not good.[230]

In January 2014, the UN Security Council acknowledged 'the progress made so far in the fully fledged negotiations, but notes that this has not been sufficient and has not yet resulted in a comprehensive and durable settlement, and urges the sides to continue their discussions to reach decisive progress on the core issues'.[231]

Re-unification talks finally restarted on 11 February 2014 after an eighteen-month break. Leaders of the Greek Cypriot and Turkish Cypriot communities issued a Joint Declaration emphasizing that a re-unified Cyprus would be based on political equality for Turkish Cypriots and Greek Cypriots, a single united Cyprus citizenship, a single

[227] 'Symbolic Cyprus Crossing Reopens', *BBC*, 3 April 2008, at: <http://news.bbc.co.uk/2/hi/europe/7327866.stm>.

[228] 'Timeline: Cyprus', *BBC*.

[229] 'Turkey says it could annex northern Cyprus', *Euractiv.com*, 5 March 2012 (updated 25 June 2012), at: <http://www.euractiv.com/enlargement/turkey-annex-northern-cyprus-news-511280>.

[230] International Crisis Group (ICG), Crisis Watch Database: Cyprus, 1 May 2013, available at: <http://www.crisisgroup.org/en/publication-type/crisiswatch/crisiswatch-database.aspx>.

[231] UN Security Council Resolution 2135, 30 January 2014, Operative §1.

international legal personality, and single sovereignty. Turkey supported the talks but on 9 February its Foreign Minister had suggested a two-State solution as an alternative if Greek Cypriots were to reject a new settlement deal, saying 'talks cannot and will not last forever'.[232] On 27 February, for the first time in more than four decades, chief negotiators from both Cypriot communities held official talks in Athens and Ankara, respectively.[233] In March 2014, however, just weeks after the peace talks resumed, Cypriot President Anastasiades said initial indications regarding the course of the negotiations were 'not encouraging'.[234]

Reunification talks remained stalled for many months, but on May 2015, in the biggest push in over a decade, Nicos Anastasiades, president of Greek southern sector, met Mustafa Akinci, the new leader of Turkish-occupied north to resume peace talks, raising hopes to resolve one of the longest conflicts in Europe.[235]

PARTIES TO THE CONFLICT

The parties to the conflict were Cyprus and Turkey.

Cyprus is estimated to have some 10,000 active frontline military personnel and a further 50,000 in reserve.[236] Turkey is estimated by one source to have 410,000 active frontline military personnel and a further 185,000 in reserve.[237] A wide array of conventional weaponry is possessed by both States.

The UN Peacekeeping Force in Cyprus (UNFICYP)[238] is a UN peacekeeping force established in 1964 under UN Security Council Resolution 186 to prevent a recurrence of fighting following intercommunal violence between the Greek Cypriots and Turkish Cypriots, to contribute to the maintenance and restoration of law and order and to facilitate a return to normal conditions.

According to the UN Secretary-General, the situation along the ceasefire lines was 'mostly calm and stable, with a low level of military violations' in the period from

232 ICG, Crisis Watch Database: Cyprus, 1 March 2014. 233 Ibid.

234 'President Anastasiades: Initial Indications on Cyprus Talks Not Encouraging', *Famagusta Gazette*, 17 March 2014, at: <http://famagusta-gazette.com/president-anastasiades-initial-indications-on-cyprus-talks-not-encouraging-p22699-69.htm>.

235 'Cyprus Peace Talks Raise Hopes of an End to a Conflict That Has Haunted Europe', *The Guardian*, 14 May 2015, at: <http://www.theguardian.com/world/2015/may/14/cyprus-peace-talks-raise-hopes-end-conflict-haunted-europe>.

236 'European Defence Information: Cyprus', at: <http://www.armedforces.co.uk/Europeandefence/edcountries/countrycyprus.htm>. The Republic of Cyprus armed forces website (in Greek only) is at: <http://www.army.gov.cy/?cat=1>.

237 'Turkey Military Strength', *Globalfirepower.com*, last updated on 27 March 2014, at: <http://www.globalfirepower.com/country-military-strength-detail.asp?country_id=turkey>.

238 <http://www.unficyp.org/nqcontent.cfm?a_id=778&tt=graphic&lang=l1>.

16 December 2012 to 20 June 2013[239] and remained 'mostly calm and stable' in 21 June to 5 December 2013.[240]

In the second half of 2013, the UN Secretary-General reported that:

> the two sides continued to withhold access for demining to the four known mined areas in the buffer zone, of which three are under the control of the National Guard and one under that of the Turkish Forces. There has been no progress in terms of fulfilling the Security Council call upon the parties to extend demining operations outside the buffer zone. In cooperation with the opposing forces, UNFICYP has begun reconnaissance and technical surveys of two areas where mines may have been displaced into the buffer zone through flooding.[241]

In January 2014, the UN Security Council reiterated its call to both sides 'to allow access to deminers and to facilitate the removal of the remaining mines in Cyprus within the buffer zone' and again urged both sides 'to extend demining operations outside the buffer zone'.[242]

CASUALTIES

No casualties were recorded for 2014.

WAR CRIMES ALLEGATIONS, INVESTIGATIONS, AND PROSECUTIONS

Cyprus ratified the 1998 Rome Statute of the International Criminal Court (ICC Statute) in March 2002. Turkey is neither a party nor a signatory to the Statute.

In accordance with the ICC Statute, the Court may exercise jurisdiction over war crimes alleged to have been committed by Cypriot nationals or on its territory. No allegations of war crimes are known to have been made against either Cypriot or Turkish military personnel regarding any acts concerning the military occupation in 2014.

[239] 'Report of the Secretary-General on the UN operation in Cyprus', UN doc. S/2013/392, 5 July 2013, §35.

[240] 'Report of the Secretary-General on the UN operation in Cyprus', UN doc. S/2013/781, 30 December 2013, §26.

[241] Ibid., §7.

[242] UN Security Council Resolution 2135, 30 January 2014, Operative §10.

Military occupation of Eritrea by Ethiopia in 2014

KEY CASUALTY DATA FOR 2014

No casualties were recorded for 2014

CLASSIFICATION OF THE CONFLICT

Eritrea and Ethiopia were involved in an international armed conflict in 2014 by virtue of continued Ethiopian occupation of territory in Eritrea (Badme).

SUMMARY OF APPLICABLE INTERNATIONAL LAW

Both parties to the conflict were bound by customary and conventional international humanitarian law and human rights law, including customary international humanitarian law (IHL) rules of distinction, proportionality, and precautions in attacks; the obligation not to recruit and use children as soldiers; and by the duty to respect and protect fundamental human rights. This includes the duty to respect the rights to life and to freedom from torture or other forms of cruel, inhuman, or degrading treatment or punishment.

The law of military occupation is set out in the 1907 Hague Regulations (Articles 42–56); the 1949 Geneva Convention IV, the 1977 Additional Protocol I, and customary international law. Both States are party to the four 1949 Geneva Conventions, but only Ethiopia is party to the 1977 Additional Protocol I. Both States are party to the 1966 International Covenant on Civil and Political Rights and the 1966 International Covenant on Economic, Social and Cultural Rights.

The underpinning of the law of military occupation is that it is a temporary situation, which lasts until a political agreement is reached. During this period, the Occupying Power does not enjoy sovereign rights over the territories it occupies and local law that was applicable prior to the occupation remains in force. At the same time, the Occupying Power is responsible for administering the local life of the population under its control, maintaining it as it was prior to the occupation as closely as possible, and for providing security (Article 43 of the Hague Regulations).

Eritrea is bound domestically by customary and conventional international human rights law. In addition, international human rights law is binding on Ethiopia extraterritorially in the territory it occupies.[243]

[243] See, e.g., International Court of Justice, *Wall* Advisory Opinion, 2004, §106. As ruled by the European Court of Human Rights, the obligation to secure in occupied territories the rights and freedoms

Both Eritrea and Ethiopia are party to the 1997 Anti-Personnel Mine Ban Convention. Under Article 5 of the Convention, and in accordance with the three-year extension granted by States parties in 2011, Eritrea is required to destroy all antipersonnel mines in mined areas under its jurisdiction or control as soon as possible, but not later than 1 February 2015. Under Article 5 of the Convention, Ethiopia is required to destroy all antipersonnel mines in mined areas under its jurisdiction or control as soon as possible, but not later than 1 June 2015.

Neither State is party to the 2008 Convention on Cluster Munitions.

Neither State is party or signatory to the 2013 Arms Trade Treaty (ATT).[244] In December 2009 the United Nations (UN) Security Council adopted Resolution 1907 in which it imposed an embargo on supply of arms and military equipment to and from Eritrea.[245] The embargo was imposed in reaction to findings by the UN Monitoring Group on Somalia that Eritrea had provided political, financial, and logistical support to armed groups in Somalia.[246] In July 2013, the Security Council reaffirmed the arms embargo in Resolution 2111.[247]

HISTORY OF THE CONFLICT[248]

Formerly an Italian colony, Eritrea was occupied by the British in 1941. In 1952, the UN resolved to establish it as an autonomous entity federated with Ethiopia as a compromise between Ethiopian claims of sovereignty and Eritrean aspirations for independence. However, ten years later the Ethiopian emperor, Haile Selassie, decided to annex it completely, thus triggering a thirty-two-year armed struggle. An alliance of the Eritrean People's Liberation Front (EPLF) and a coalition of Ethiopian resistance movements defeated the forces of Haile Selassie's communist successor, Mengistu Haile Mariam.

set out in the 1950 European Convention on Human Rights derives from its effective control over occupied territory, whether it is exercised by the occupying State directly, through its armed forces, or through a subordinate local administration. See European Court of Human Rights, *Cyprus v. Turkey*, Judgment, 10 May 2001, §77.

[244] Both States voted in favour of the adoption of the ATT by the United Nations (UN) General Assembly on 2 April 2013.

[245] UN Security Council Resolution 1907, adopted on 23 December 2009 by thirteen votes to one (Libya) with one abstention (China), §§5, 6.

[246] Stockholm International Peace Research Institute, 'Arms Embargo on Eritrea', last updated on 23 October 2012, at: <http://www.sipri.org/databases/embargoes/un_arms_embargoes/rritrea>.

[247] UN Security Council Resolution 2111, adopted on 24 July 2013, Operative §5.

[248] Unless otherwise stated, this section is based on 'Eritrea profile', *BBC*, 4 May 2015, at: <http://www.bbc.com/news/world-africa-13349078>.

In 1993, in a referendum supported by Ethiopia, Eritreans voted almost unanimously for independence. Ethiopia was left landlocked. In 1998, border disputes around the town of Badme erupted into open hostilities. The conflict ended with a peace deal in June 2000, but not before leaving both sides with tens of thousands of military deaths. A security zone, patrolled by UN forces until the middle of 2008, separated the two nations.

Eritrea accuses Ethiopia of refusing to withdraw from the village of Badme, where the 1998 war began, despite an Eritrea–Ethiopia Boundary Commission[249] ruling in 2002 that it belonged to Eritrea. Eritrea has repeatedly called on the international community to enforce the Commission's ruling, while Ethiopia has insisted that further border talks are needed.[250]

Renewed clashes were reported at the Eritrean–Ethiopian border in March 2012, sparking increased international concern over a potential re-ignition of the conflict.[251] Further clashes were reported in May 2012,[252] but no details were confirmed.

In July 2013, the UN Monitoring Group reported that it had 'obtained evidence of several violations of the arms embargo on Eritrea imposed by Security Council resolution 1907'.[253]

No clashes were reported in 2014.

PARTIES TO THE CONFLICT

The parties to the conflict were Eritrea and Ethiopia.

Eritrea is estimated to have some 200,000 mobilized military personnel.[254] Ethiopia is estimated by one source to have 182,500 active frontline military personnel.[255] A wide array of conventional weaponry is possessed by both States.

[249] The Permanent Court of Arbitration served as registry for the Commission, which was established pursuant to an Agreement of 12 December 2000 between the Government of the State of Eritrea and the Government of the Federal Democratic Republic of Ethiopia, with a mandate 'to delimit and demarcate the colonial treaty border based on pertinent colonial treaties (1900, 1902, and 1908) and applicable international law'. The work of the Commission can be accessed at: <http://www.pca-cpa.org/showpage.asp?pag_id=1150>.

[250] See, e.g., Plaut, M., 'Are Ethiopia and Eritrea Heading Back to War?', *BBC*, 21 March 2012, at: <http://www.bbc.co.uk/news/world-africa-17433871>.

[251] 'Eritrea "Will Not Fight Ethiopia"', *BBC*, 16 March 2012, at: <http://www.bbc.co.uk/news/world-africa-17397091>.

[252] See, e.g., International Crisis Group, 'Eritrea: Scenarios for Future Transition', Africa Report No. 200, 28 March 2013, p. 3.

[253] 'Report of the Monitoring Group on Somalia and Eritrea pursuant to Security Council resolution 2060 (2012): Eritrea', UN doc. S/2013/440, 25 July 2013, §80.

[254] Defence Web, 'Eritrean Defence Forces', 6 May 2013, at: <http://www.defenceweb.co.za/index.php?option=com_content&view=article&id=30387:eritrea&catid=119:african-militaries&Itemid=255>.

[255] 'Ethiopia Military Strength', *Globalfirepower.com*, last updated on 27 March 2014, at: <http://www.globalfirepower.com/country-military-strength-detail.asp?country_id=ethiopia>.

CASUALTIES

No casualties were recorded for 2014.

WAR CRIMES ALLEGATIONS, INVESTIGATIONS, AND PROSECUTIONS

Neither State is party to the 1998 Rome Statute of the International Criminal Court (ICC), although Eritrea is a signatory State. The ICC may not exercise jurisdiction over war crimes alleged to have been committed by a State's nationals or on its territory unless the situation is referred to the Court by the UN Security Council.

No allegations of war crimes are known to have been made against either Eritrean or Ethiopian military personnel regarding any acts concerning the military occupation in 2014.

Military occupation of Ukraine by the Russian Federation in 2014

KEY CASUALTY DATA 2014

Total deaths:	3
Total injured:	3
Ukrainian armed forces deaths:	2
Ukrainian armed forces injured:	2
Pro-Russian armed forces deaths:	1
Pro-Russian forces injured:	1

CLASSIFICATION OF THE CONFLICT

Ukraine and the Russian Federation were involved in an international armed conflict in 2014 by virtue of the Russian occupation of territory in Ukraine (Crimea).

SUMMARY OF APPLICABLE INTERNATIONAL LAW

Both parties to the conflict were bound by customary and conventional international humanitarian law and human rights law, including customary international humanitarian law (IHL) rules of distinction, proportionality, and precautions in attacks; the obligation not to recruit and use children as soldiers; and by the duty to respect and protect fundamental human rights. This includes the duty to respect the rights to life and to freedom from torture or other forms of cruel, inhuman, or degrading treatment or punishment.

The law of military occupation is set out in the 1907 Hague Regulations (Articles 42–56); the 1949 Geneva Convention IV, the 1977 Additional Protocol I, and customary international law. Both States are party to the four 1949 Geneva Conventions and to the 1977 Additional Protocol I. Both States are party to the 1966 International Covenant on Civil and Political Rights and the 1966 International Covenant on Economic, Social and Cultural Rights.

The underpinning of the law of military occupation is that it is a temporary situation, which lasts until a political agreement is reached. During this period, the Occupying Power does not enjoy sovereign rights over the territories it occupies and local law that was applicable prior to the occupation remains in force. At the same time, the Occupying

Power is responsible for administering the local life of the population under its control, maintaining it as it was prior to the occupation as closely as possible, and for providing security (Article 43 of the Hague Regulations).

Ukraine is bound domestically by customary and conventional international human rights law. In addition, international human rights law is binding on Russia extraterritorially in the territories it occupies.[256] As ruled by the European Court of Human Rights, the obligation to secure in occupied territories the rights and freedoms set out in the 1950 European Convention on Human Rights derives from effective control over occupied territory, whether it is exercised by the occupying State directly, through its armed forces, or through a subordinate local administration.[257]

Ukraine has been a State party to the 1997 Anti-Personnel Mine Ban Convention since 27 December 2005. Ukraine and Russia are neither signatory nor parties to the 2008 Convention on Cluster Munitions, while Ukraine has been a signatory party to the 2013 Arms Trade Treaty (ATT) since 23 September 2014.

Ukraine and Russia are neither signatory nor parties to the Rome Statute of the International Criminal Court. However, on 17 April 2014, the Ukraine acting government lodged a declaration under Article 12(3) of the Rome Statute, accepting the Court's jurisdiction over the alleged crimes committed in its territory between 17 November 2013 and 22 February 2014.

HISTORY OF THE CONFLICT

Since February 2014, a series of protests were carried out in the Crimean capital Simferopol and the Federal City of Sevastopol.[258] Armed men in unmarked military uniforms took control of key government buildings in the Crimean capital Simferopol, as well as airports in Crimea on 28 February. At the same time Russian marines surrounded a Ukraine Coast Guard base in Sevastopol.[259] According to Ukraine there were up to 16,000 Russian troops in Crimea under the International Agreement regarding the Black Sea fleet.

[256] See, e.g., International Court of Justice, *Wall* Advisory Opinion, 2004, §106.

[257] See European Court of Human Rights (ECtHR), *Cyprus v Turkey*, Judgment, 10 May 2001, §77; *Loizidou v Turkey*, Judgment (Merits), 18 December 1996, §§52, 54, 56; *Catan v Moldova and Russia*, Judgment, 19 October 2012, §§106–07.

[258] Crimean Tatars, pro-Russia supporters approach Crimean parliament building, Interfax-Ukraine (in English), Kyiv, 25 February 2014 at: <http://en.interfax.com.ua/news/general/192882.html>.

[259] In Crimea, the Black Sea Fleet missile boat blocked out Ukrainian border guard ships—source. UNIAN. 28 February 2014 at: <http://www.unian.ua/politics/891027-u-krimu-raketniy-kater-chf-rf-zablokuvav-vihid-ukrajinskim-prikordonnim-korablyam-djerelo.html>.

On 1 March, citing fears for the Russian speaking population in Crimea, Russian President Vladimir Putin formally asked the Federation Council for permission to 'use the armed forces of the Russian Federation on the territory of Ukraine until the normalization of the socio-political situation in that country'.[260] Hours later, the Federation Council voted unanimously to grant permission.

According to Ukrainian officials, Ukrainian troops stationed in Crimea were urged to surrender by 3 March at 5 a.m. or face an armed confrontation via an ultimatum issued by Alexander Vitko, the commander of the Russian Black Sea Fleet.[261] Russian President Vladimir Putin stated in a press conference that the soldiers occupying military bases were not Russian soldiers, but local forces of self-defence, declaring there was no need to send forces into Ukraine for the time being, but that Russia reserved the right to use 'all means' as a last resort to threats of anarchy.[262] Russian ambassador to the UN further declared that former Ukrainian President Viktor Yanukovich had sent a letter to Vladimir Putin asking him to use military force in Ukraine to restore law and order.[263]

On 5 March, unknown gunmen took hostage the UN special envoy to Ukraine Robert Serry in Simferopol.[264] UN Deputy Secretary-General Jan Eliasson said Robert Serry had been threatened but had not been kidnapped.[265] Serry was later released and continued with his role in Crimea.

Crimea's Parliament declared that the region wanted to join Russia and would let voters decide in a 16 March referendum.[266] On 6 March, Russian sailors scuttled the decommissioned cruiser Ochakov at the entrance to Donuzlav Bay in western Crimea in an attempt to prevent Ukrainian navy ships from gaining access to the Black Sea[267] and a mission of observers from the Organization for Security and Co-operation in Europe was stopped from entering the Crimean Peninsula by unidentified men in military fatigues.[268] On 8 March, the Russian military entered the territory of Chonhar village

[260] 'Lawmakers Allow Putin to Use Military in Ukraine', ABC News, 1 March 2014 at: <http://abcnews.go.com/International>.

[261] 'Russia gives Ukrainian Forces in Crimea Ultimatum To Surrender—Interfax', Reuters, 3 March 2014 at: <http://in.reuters.com/article/2014/03/03/ukraine-crisis-ultimatum-idINDEEA220EV20140303>.

[262] 'Putin: Russia Not Yet Sending Troops into Ukraine', *BBC*, 4 March 2014 at: <http://www.bbc.com/news/world-europe-26433309>.

[263] 'Yanukovich sent letter to Putin asking for Russian military presence in Ukraine', RT.com, News, 3 March 2014, at: <http://rt.com/news/churkin-unsc-russia-ukraine-683/>.

[264] 'Ukrainian officials say United Nations envoy abducted by armed men in Crimea', Daily News, 5 March 2014, at: <http://www.nydailynews.com/news/world/ukraine-prime-minister-crimea-remain-part-country-article-1.1711216>.

[265] 'Ukraine Crisis: UN Envoy Confronted by Gunmen in Crimea—live updates', *The Guardian*, 5 March 2014, at: <http://www.theguardian.com/world/2014/mar/05/ukraine-crisis-russia-nato-talks-live>.

[266] 'Ukraine Crisis: Crimea MPs Vote to Join Russia', *BBC News*, 6 March 2014 at: <http://www.bbc.com/news/world-europe-26465962>.

[267] 'Russia Sinks Ship to Block Ukrainian Navy Ships', Naval Today, 5 March 2014, at: <http://navaltoday.com/2014/03/06/russia-sinks-ship-to-block-ukrainian-navy-ships/>.

[268] 'OSCE Observers Barred from Entering Crimea: Polish Minister', Reuters, 6 March 2014, at: <http://www.reuters.com/article/2014/03/06/ukraine-crisis-osce-mission-idUSW8N0LT00Z20140306>.

in Henichesk Region of Kherson Oblast and blocked the second entrance to Crimea.[269] A couple of days later, pro-Russian forces took control over the main military hospital in Crimea.[270] Reports also emerged that several hundred residents of Crimea, mainly Crimean Tatars, have left Crimea for security reasons according to the State Border Guard Service of Ukraine.[271]

On 11 March, the Crimean Government made clear that they did not officially invite the OSCE to observe the referendum. The OSCE chair, Switzerland's Foreign Minister Didier Burkhalter, declared the referendum illegal. He further stated that as a consequence the OSCE would not send observers.[272]The European Parliament similarly rejected the upcoming referendum on independence in Crimea, which they saw as manipulated and contrary to international and Ukrainian law.[273] G7 leaders called on Russia to 'immediately' halt actions supporting the referendum on Crimea regarding its status.[274]

On 13 March, the Russian Armed Forces announced a new set of sudden military exercises in the border regions of Rostov, Belgorod, and Kursk on 13 March, involving 'artillery batteries, assault helicopters, and at least 10,000 soldiers'.[275] Amateur footage showed columns of trucks and armoured vehicles amassing at the border town of Lopan, just thirty miles outside of Kharkiv.

On 14 March a last-ditch diplomatic effort before the referendum failed in London, where Secretary of State John Kerry met with Russian Foreign Minister Sergei Lavrov amid threats of sanctions against Russia if it annexes Crimea.[276]

According to the official results from the 16 March referendum on Crimea's secession, 97% of voters supported the proposal to join Russia.[277] These reports are contested by

[269] 'Russian Military Forces Come into Chonhar Village, Kherson Region', Ukrainian News, 8 March 2014 at: <http://un.ua/>.

[270] 'Russian forces on Move Today in Crimea, Seize Military Hospital in Simferopol and Base in Bakhchisaray', Kyiv Post, 10 March 2014, at: <http://www.kyivpost.com/content/ukraine/russian-forces-on-move-today-in-crimea-seize-military-hospital-in-simferopol-338952.html>.

[271] 'Ukrainian State Border Guard Service Personnel Keep Performing Tasks on Enforcing Border Protection of South, East and West Ukrainian Border', dpsu.gov.ua, 11 March 2014 at: <http://dpsu.gov.ua/en/about/news/news_3533.htm>.

[272] 'Crimea Referendum Illegal, No OSCE Monitoring—Swiss', Firstpost, 12 March 2014 at: <http://www.firstpost.com/world/crimea-referendum-illegal-no-osce-monitoring-swiss-1429931.html>.

[273] European Parliament, 'Ukraine: MEPs Call for Firm Action on Russia to Prevent Further Escalation', 12 March 2014 at: <http://www.europarl.europa.eu/news/en/news-room/content/20140312STO38705/html/Ukraine-MEPs-call-for-firm-action-on-Russia-to-prevent-further-escalation>.

[274] 'G7 not to Recognize Crimea Referendum', Xinhua, 12 March 2014 at: <http://news.xinhuanet.com/english/world/2014-03/12/c_126258900.htm>.

[275] 'Russian Troops Mass at Border with Ukraine', *The New York Times*, 13 March 2014 at: <http://www.nytimes.com/2014/03/14/world/europe/ukraine.html?_r=1>.

[276] 'No Progress in US-Russian Talks on Ukraine' RTE News, 14 March 2014 at: <http://www.rte.ie/news/2014/0314/602187-ukraine/>.

[277] 'Crimea Referendum: Voters "Back Russia Union"', *BBC News*, 16 March 2014 at: <http://www.bbc.com/news/world-europe-26606097>.

Ukraine and the EU. The defence ministries of Ukraine and Russia agreed on a truce in Crimea until 21 March, according to the acting Ukrainian defence minister.[278]

On 17 March, the Crimean Parliament officially declared its independence from Ukraine and requested full accession to the Russian Federation.[279] Abkhazia, Nagorno-Karabakh, Russia, and South Ossetia officially recognized the independence of Crimea.[280] The next day, President of Russia Vladimir Putin addressed the State Duma deputies, Federation Council members, heads of Russian regions, and civil society representatives in the Kremlin, calling for the creation of 'two new constituent entities within the Russian Federation: the Republic of Crimea and the city of Sevastopol'.[281]

On 21 March, after the Federation Council approved on final reading the treaty of accession of the Crimea to the Russian Federation, Vladimir Putin ratified the inclusion of two new areas into the Russian Federation: the Republic of Crimea and the City of Sevastopol. The Crimean Federal District is created with Oleg Belaventsev being appointed as its Presidential Envoy. On 24 March, Ukrainian troops leave Crimea, following emotional farewells to spouses and family members left behind.

The UN General Assembly approved a resolution on 27 March, describing the Crimean 16 March referendum as illegal. One hundred countries voted in favour of the resolution and affirming Ukraine's territorial integrity. Eleven nations voted against, with fifty-eight abstentions.[282]

On 17 April, Russian President Vladimir Putin acknowledged the presence of Russian servicemen in Crimea arguing their presence was necessary to let Crimeans make the choice on the future of the region.[283]

Casualties

Following the referendum on the status of Crimea held on 16 March 2014 and the subsequent occupation of Crimea and Sevastopol[284] on 18 March by the Russian Federation,

[278] 'Ukraine and Russia Agree Truce on Crimea', RTE News, 16 March 2014 at: <http://www.rte.ie/news/2014/0316/602602-ukraine-crimea-russia/>.

[279] 'Crimean Parliament Formally Applies to join Russia', BBC, 17 March 2014 at: <http://www.bbc.com/news/world-europe-26609667>.

[280] 'BBC News—Russia's Vladimir Putin Recognises Crimea as Nation', *BBC News*, 17 March 2014 at: <http://www.bbc.com/news/world-europe-26621726>.

[281] Address by President of the Russian Federation Vladimir Putin (English transcript) (Speech), 18 March 2014, at: <http://en.kremlin.ru/events/president/news/20603>.

[282] 'Ukraine: UN Condemns Crimea Vote as IMF and US Back Loans', BBC, 27 March 2014 at: <http://www.bbc.com/news/world-europe-26776416>.

[283] 'Putin Acknowledges Russian Military Serviceman were in Crimea', RT, 17 April 2014 at: <http://rt.com/news/crimea-defense-russian-soldiers-108/>.

[284] An agreement was signed between Crimean and Russian authorities at the Kremlin on 18 March to formally initiate the inclusion of Crimea into the Russian Federation. See, The Kremlin, 'Executive Order on executing Agreement on Admission of Republic of Crimea into the Russian Federation', 18 March

at least three fatalities and three injured persons were reported. Four casualties were from the Ukrainian military; two were shot and killed and two beaten and injured. The other two casualties were pro-Russian militia one was killed and one injured.[285]

After the annexation period, a number of enforced disappearances, as well arbitrary detentions with violence and other forms of ill-treatment were recorded through the year. Many of these acts—often targeting journalists, human rights defenders and political opponents—were attributed to the Crimean 'self-defence' units and paramilitary forces.[286] On 11 June, the 'parliament of Crimea' passed a law for the integration of the Crimean 'self-defence' into a 'people's militia' with powers to assist the police.[287] At least fifteen people had gone missing since March, according to a Human Rights Watch report. A Soviet-era dissident reported that seventeen people were missing. Ukrainian authorities reported the number of missing at twenty-one.[288] In November 2014 the UN Office of the High Commissioner for Human Rights (OHCHR) reported that there had been 'a new wave of disappearances of Crimean Tatars'.[289]

WAR CRIMES ALLEGATIONS, INVESTIGATIONS, AND PROSECUTIONS

Ukraine and Russia are neither signatory nor parties to the Rome Statute of the International Criminal Court. However, on 17 April 2014, the Ukraine acting government

2014, <http://en.kremlin.ru/events/president/news/20600>; and The Kremlin, 'Address by President of the Russian Federation', 18 March 2014, <http://en.kremlin.ru/events/president/news/20603>.

[285] Walker, S., 'Putin Confirms Crimea Annexation as Ukraine Soldier Becomes First Casualty, 18 March 2014, <http://www.theguardian.com/world/2014/mar/18/putin-confirms-annexation-crimea-ukrainian-soldier-casualty>; 'Ukraine Officer "Killed in Attack on Crimea base"', 18 March 2014, <http://www.bbc.com/news/world-europe-26637296>; 'Russian Marine Kills Ukraine Navy Officer in Crimea, Says Ministry', 7 April 2014, <http://www.reuters.com/article/2014/04/07/us-ukraine-crisis-military-idUSBREA360GB20140407>; and 'Ukraine Crisis: Pro-Russian Troops Storm Naval Base as Clinton Warns of "Aggression" From Putin', 19 March 2014, <http://www.independent.co.uk/news/world/europe/ukraine-crisis-prorussian-troops-storm-naval-base-as-clinton-warns-of-aggression-from-putin-9201317.html>.

[286] OHCHR, 'Report on the human rights situation in Ukraine 15 June 2014', <http://www.un.org.ua/images/stories/Report_15_June_2014_en.pdf>.

[287] OHCHR, 'Report on the Human Rights Situation in Ukraine 15 November 2014', <http://www.ohchr.org/Documents/Countries/UA/OHCHR_seventh_reportUkraine20.11.14.pdf>.

[288] Mirovalev, M., 'Disappearing Crimea's Anti-Russia Activists', 4 December 2014, <http://www.aljazeera.com/indepth/features/2014/12/disappearing-crimea-anti-russia-activists-201412110405525656.html>; see also Human Rights Watch 'Crimea: Enforced Disappearances', 7 October 2014, <http://www.hrw.org/news/2014/10/07/crimea-enforced-disappearances>.

[289] OHCHR, 'Report on the Human Rights Situation in Ukraine 15 November 2014', <http://www.ohchr.org/Documents/Countries/UA/OHCHR_seventh_reportUkraine20.11.14.pdf>.

lodged a declaration under Article 12(3) of the Rome Statute, accepting the Court's jurisdiction over the alleged crimes committed in its territory between 17 November 2013 and 22 February 2014. On 25 April 2014 ICC Prosecutor Fatou Bensouda has opened a preliminary investigation into allegations of crimes against humanity in Ukraine.[290] No allegations of war crimes are known to have been made against Russia regarding acts related to the events in Crimea in 2014.

[290] 'ICC Opens Preliminary Investigation into Alleged Ukraine Crimes', *Jurist*, 25 April 2014, at: <http://jurist.org/paperchase/2014/04/icc-opens-preliminary-investigation-into-alleged-ukraine-crimes.php>.

Military occupation of Georgia by the Russian Federation in 2014

KEY CASUALTY DATA FOR 2014

No casualties were recorded for 2014

CLASSIFICATION OF THE CONFLICT

Georgia and the Russian Federation were involved in an international armed conflict in 2014 by virtue of continued Russian occupation of territory in Georgia (Abkhazia and South Ossetia).

SUMMARY OF APPLICABLE INTERNATIONAL LAW

Both parties to the conflict were bound by customary and conventional international humanitarian law and human rights law, including customary international humanitarian law (IHL) rules of distinction, proportionality, and precautions in attacks; the obligation not to recruit and use children as soldiers; and by the duty to respect and protect fundamental human rights. This includes the duty to respect the rights to life and to freedom from torture or other forms of cruel, inhuman, or degrading treatment or punishment.

The law of military occupation is set out in the 1907 Hague Regulations (Articles 42–56), the 1949 Geneva Convention IV, the 1977 Additional Protocol I, and customary international law. Both States are party to the four 1949 Geneva Conventions and to the 1977 Additional Protocol I. Both States are party to the 1966 International Covenant on Civil and Political Rights and the 1966 International Covenant on Economic, Social and Cultural Rights.

The underpinning of the law of military occupation is that it is a temporary situation, which lasts until a political agreement is reached. During this period, the Occupying Power does not enjoy sovereign rights over the territories it occupies and local law that was applicable prior to the occupation remains in force. At the same time, the Occupying Power is responsible for administering the local life of the population under its control, maintaining it as it was prior to the occupation as closely as possible, and for providing security (Article 43 of the Hague Regulations).

Georgia is bound domestically by customary and conventional international human rights law. In addition, international human rights law is binding on Russia extraterritorially in the territories it occupies.[291] As ruled by the European Court of Human Rights, the obligation to secure in occupied territories the rights and freedoms set out in the 1950 European Convention on Human Rights derives from effective control over occupied territory, whether it is exercised by the occupying State directly, through its armed forces, or through a subordinate local administration.[292] Furthermore:

> Where the fact of such domination over the territory is established, it is not necessary to determine whether the Contracting State exercises detailed control over the policies and actions of the subordinate local administration. The fact that the local administration survives as a result of the Contracting State's military and other support entails that State's responsibility for its policies and actions. The controlling State has the responsibility under Article 1 to secure, within the area under its control, the entire range of substantive rights set out in the Convention and those additional Protocols which it has ratified.[293]

In December 2011, the European Court of Human Rights declared admissible a case brought by Georgia against Russia, arising out of the 2008 armed conflict between Georgia and Russia.[294] In the words of the Court:

> The applicant Government submitted that, in the course of indiscriminate and disproportionate attacks by Russian forces and/or by the separatist forces under their control, hundreds of civilians were injured, killed, detained or went missing, thousands of civilians had their property and homes destroyed and over 300,000 people were forced to leave Abkhazia and South Ossetia.

As of writing, the Court had not adjudicated on the merits of this case.[295]

Neither State is party to the 1997 Anti-Personnel Mine Ban Convention or the 2008 Convention on Cluster Munitions. Both States are party to the 1972 Biological Weapons Convention and to the 1992 Chemical Weapons Convention. Neither State is party or signatory to the 2013 Arms Trade Treaty (ATT).[296]

[291] See, e.g., International Court of Justice, *Wall* Advisory Opinion, 2004, §106.

[292] See European Court of Human Rights (ECtHR), *Cyprus v Turkey*, Judgment, 10 May 2001, §77; *Loizidou v Turkey*, Judgment (Merits), 18 December 1996, §§52, 54, 56; *Catan v Moldova and Russia*, Judgment, 19 October 2012, §§106–7.

[293] *Catan v Moldova and Russia*, Judgment, 19 October 2012, §106.

[294] ECtHR, *Georgia v Russia, No. 2*, Decision on Admissibility, 19 December 2011.

[295] On 3 July 2014, the European Court of Human Rights decided on the merits of another case concerning the arrest and detention of the Georgian immigrant population in Russia in September 2006, See ECtHR, *Goergia v Russia*, n°1, Application no. 13255/07), 3 July 2014, at: <http://hudoc.echr.coe.int/sites/eng/pages/search.aspx?i=001-145546#{%22itemid%22:[%22001-145546%22]}>.

[296] Georgia voted in favour of the adoption of the ATT by the United Nations (UN) General Assembly on 2 April 2013, while Russia abstained.

HISTORY OF THE CONFLICT[297]

In 1991–2, South Ossetian and Abkhazian armed groups fought to break away from Georgia. Both regions have close ties with Moscow. On 14 May 1994, the parties signed in Moscow the Agreement on a Ceasefire and Separation of Forces, agreeing to the deployment of a peacekeeping force from the Commonwealth of Independent States (CIS) composed mainly of Russian troops. The Georgian Parliament has demanded that Russian peacekeepers in both regions be replaced by an international force.

Over the years, sporadic clashes have continued and the achievement of a comprehensive political settlement, including a settlement on the future political status of Abkhazia and South Ossetia and the return of refugees and displaced persons, remained impossible. On 7 August 2008, hostilities broke out between Georgia and South Ossetia, which led to a major Russian military intervention.

On 8 August 2008, after heavy fighting between Georgian and South Ossetian forces, Russian troops entered South Ossetia claiming the need to protect Russian citizens and supporting the separatist movement (a considerable number of South Ossetians hold Russian nationality). The intervention involved Russian troops moving beyond South Ossetian boundaries and launching strikes near the Georgian capital. On 9 August 2008, the Georgian Parliament approved a Presidential decree declaring a 'state of war'.[298]

On 12 August 2008, a ceasefire, 'the six point plan', was negotiated by the European Union. However, it was not fully respected and did not achieve a complete withdrawal of Russian forces, which continued to occupy parts of Georgia. According to the International Crisis Group (ICG), as of mid-2011, Moscow was maintaining 7,000 to 9,000 combat, security, and border forces in those two territories and is building and refurbishing permanent military bases there, in violation of the ceasefire.[299] South Ossetia remains dependent on Russian aid, both monetary and military.

In the aftermath of the 2008 conflict, South Ossetia and Abkhazia declared independence from Georgia, which has been recognized only by Russia and a few other states. This recognition was strongly condemned by the European Union (EU), the United States of America (USA), and the Organization for Security and Co-operation in Europe (OSCE). The sixteen-year-old UN Observer Mission in Georgia (UNOMIG), entrusted with overseeing the ceasefire accord between the government and Abkhaz separatists in

[297] Unless otherwise stated this section is based on 'Georgia Profile', *BBC*, 5 November 2014, at: <http://www.bbc.co.uk/news/world-europe-17301647>.

[298] See generally the report of the Independent International Fact-Finding Mission on the Conflict in Georgia (IIFFMCG–CEIIG), mandated by the Council of the European Union, at: <http://www.ceiig.ch/Report.html>.

[299] ICG, 'Georgia-Russia: Learn to Live like Neighbours', Europe Briefing No. 658, August 2011, Overview, at: <http://www.crisisgroup.org/en/regions/europe/south-caucasus/georgia/B065-georgia-russia-learn-to-live-like-neighbours.aspx>.

the country's north-western region, terminated its mandate as of 30 June 2009, following Russia's UN Security Council veto of the extension of the Mission's presence. The mandate of the OSCE Mission to Georgia active in the region since 1992 likewise expired at the end of June 2009 as a result of failure by the OSCE's participating States to reach consensus on extending the mission's mandate.

In October 2011, then Russian President Dmitry Medvedev ratified agreements concluded the previous year with Abkhazia and South Ossetia, under which Moscow would set up military bases in the breakaway republics. The treaties allow Russia to operate military bases in Abkhazia and South Ossetia for an initial term of forty-nine years, with possible extensions for an additional fifteen years.[300]

In June 2013, relations with Russia worsened over its demarcation of the Administrative Boundary Line (ABL) separating Georgian-controlled areas from South Ossetia. Georgia claimed that Russia was 'annexing' territory by installing fences deeper into areas previously under Georgian control. Russian 'border guards' also detained Georgian citizens near the ABL. Georgia's Minister of Foreign Affairs expressed concern, delivering a protest note to Russia through Switzerland. The European Union Monitoring Mission and NATO also condemned the 'borderization' process by Russian troops. On 11 June, Russian President Vladimir Putin said Moscow was willing to restore relations with Georgia 'in full scale' and called for cooperation combating crime and terrorism, but 'cannot imagine' reversal of recognition of Abkhazia and South Ossetia.[301]

On 20 July 2013, Gennady Onishchenko, head of Russia's State consumer protection agency RosPotrebNadzor and the nation's chief sanitary doctor, warned that a US-funded bio laboratory in the outskirts of Tbilisi represented 'a powerful offensive potential' and stated that Russia 'deems it to be a direct violation of the BWC [Biological Weapons Convention]'.[302] A statement by the Russian Ministry of Foreign Affairs the previous day, released in rebuttal of the US Department of State's annual report on arms control and non-proliferation, said: 'Biological-related activities of the US Department of Defense close to the Russian borders also cause our serious concern.'[303]

On 18 December 2013, the 26th round of Geneva talks involving the Georgian Government and Abkhazia and South Ossetia authorities ended in another deadlock after a previous round of discussions had seen the different parties express cautious optimism on a possible 'non-use of force' agreement.[304]

[300] 'Medvedev Ratifies Abkhazia, S. Ossetia Military Base Deployment', *RIA Novosti*, Moscow, 6 October 2011, at: <http://en.rian.ru/military_news/20111006/167440872.html>.

[301] ICG, Crisis Watch Database: Georgia, 1 July 2013, available at: <http://www.crisisgroup.org/en/publication-type/crisiswatch/crisiswatch-database.aspx>.

[302] 'Russian Official Warns Georgia over U.S.-Funded Bio Lab', *Civil Georgia*, Tbilisi, 20 July 2013, at: <http://www.civil.ge/eng/article.php?id=26288>.

[303] Ibid. [304] ICG, Crisis Watch Database: Georgia, 2 January 2014.

In late February 2014, Georgian President Giorgi Margvelashvili said that Russia's 'completely senseless' erecting of barbed-wire fences across breakaway South Ossetia's administrative boundary line sought to 'maintain[] conflict' and keep divided communities further apart.[305]

The 28th round of Geneva talks, held on 18 June 2014, involving representatives of the Georgian Government, the Russian Government, and the Abkhazian and South Ossetian de facto authorities, ended in another deadlock after delegates from the two breakaway regions walked out from the meeting demanding the issue of refugees and internally displaced persons be removed from the discussions.[306] The 29th round of the talks, held on 8 October 2014, was again marked by the de facto authorities not wishing to discuss that same issue.[307]

On 24 November 2014, the Russian Federation and Abkhazia signed the Treaty on Alliance and Strategic Partnership.[308] The treaty aims to solidify the integration of Abkhazia into the Russian Federation through incorporating the region into Russia's military, economic, social, and legal space and sets out to create a common security and defence space and joint armed forces of Russia and Abkhazia; Moscow pledges to support Abkhazia with advanced military equipment, in addition to abolishing the Georgian–Russian border along its Abkhaz section and reinforcing the occupation line. The treaty also stipulates the harmonization of the Abkhazian legislation not only with that of Russia, but also with the standards of the Eurasian Economic Union. Additionally, Russia vows to lobby for Abkhazia's international recognition and facilitate its accession to international organizations, including into those organizations that are created at Russia's initiative.[309] The same type of treaty, but with a different name, on Alliance and Integration, was signed on 18 March 2015 by Russia and South Ossetia.[310] The treaty with

[305] 'President Condemns "Borderization"', *Civil Georgia*, Tbilisi, 26 February 2014, at: <http://civil.ge/eng/article.php?id=26981>.

[306] Geneva Talks End after Walkout by Abkhaz, South Ossetian Delegates, *Radio Free Europe*, 19 June 2014, at: <http://www.rferl.org/content/geneva-talks-end-after-walkout-by-abkhaz-south-ossetian-delegates/25427723.html>.

[307] Twenty Ninth Round of Geneva Talks, *Civil Georgia*, 10 October 2014, at: <http://www.civil.ge/eng/article.php?id=27710>.

[308] 'Moscow, Sokhumi Sign Treaty on Alliance and Strategic Partnership', *Civil Georgia*, Tbilisi, 24 November 2014, at: <http://civil.ge/eng/article.php?id=27845>.

[309] Statement of the Georgian Foreign Ministry regarding the signature of the so-called treaty between Moscow and Sokhumi occupation regime, Tbilisi 24 November 2014, at: <http://usa.mfa.gov.ge/index.php?lang_id=ENG&sec_id=131&info_id=28117>; see also 'Russia Proposed Treaty with Abkhazia on Alliance and Integration', *Civil Georgia*, Tbilisi 13 October 2014, at: <http://civil.ge/eng/article.php?id=27714>.

[310] 'Putin Signs Pact With Breakaway Georgian Region', *Radio Free Europe*, 18 March 2015, at: <http://www.rferl.org/content/georgia-russia-south-ossetia/26907700.html>.

See also 'New Date Set for Signing Russia-South Ossetia Treaty', *Radio Free Europe*, 18 March 2015, at: <http://www.rferl.org/content/russia-georgia-treaty-analysis-south-ossetia/26903447.html>.

South Ossetia, amongst other things, envisages the simplification of acquiring Russian citizenship for South Ossetian inhabitants.[311] The Government of Georgia views the signing of these treaties between Moscow and the de facto Abkhazian and South Ossetian authorities as Russia annexing Georgian territories.[312]

PARTIES TO THE CONFLICT

The parties to the conflict were Georgia and Russia.

Georgia is estimated to have 37,000 active frontline military personnel and 140,000 reservists.[313] Russia is estimated to have 766,000 active frontline military personnel and almost 2.5 million reservists.[314] Russia has one of the world's largest stocks of conventional weaponry and possesses the world's greatest nuclear arsenal.[315]

CASUALTIES

No casualties were recorded for 2014.

WAR CRIMES ALLEGATIONS, INVESTIGATIONS, AND PROSECUTIONS

Georgia is party to the 1998 Rome Statute of the International Criminal Court (ICC Statute), having adhered in September 2003. Russia has signed but not ratified the ICC

[311] Договор между Российской Федерацией и Республикой Южная Осетия о союзничестве и интеграции (Dogovor mejdu Rossiiskoi Federaciei i Respublikoi Ujnaia Osetia o Soiuznichestve i Integracii), Article 6, 18 March 2015, at: <http://www.kavkaz-uzel.ru/articles/259096/>.

[312] Ministry of Foreign Affairs of Georgia, Statement of the Ministry of Foreign Affairs regarding the signature of the so-called 'Treaty on Alliance and Integration' between Moscow and the Russian Occupation regime of Tskhinvali, 18 March 2015, at: <http://www.mfa.gov.ge/News/საგარეო-საქმეთა-სამინისტროს-განცხადება-რუსეთის-(1).aspx>; Government of Georgia, Statement by Prime Minister of Georgia on the Signing of the So-Called Agreement on Alliance and Strategic Partnership between the Russian Federation and the De Facto Authorities of Abkhazia, at: <http://government.gov.ge/index.php?lang_id=ENG&sec_id=387&info_id=45791>.

[313] 'Georgia Military Strength', *Globalfirepower.com*, last updated on 27 March 2014, at: <http://www.globalfirepower.com/country-military-strength-detail.asp?country_id=georgia>.

[314] 'Russia Military Strength', *Globalfirepower.com*, last updated on 27 March 2014, at: <http://www.globalfirepower.com/country-military-strength-detail.asp?country_id=russia>.

[315] 'As of early 2013, Russia has a stockpile of approximately 4,500 nuclear warheads, of which roughly 1,800 strategic warheads are deployed on missiles and at bomber bases. Another 700 strategic warheads are in storage, along with 2,000 nonstrategic warheads.' Kristensen, H. M. and Norris, R. S., 2013, 'Russian Nuclear Forces, 2013', *Bulletin of the Atomic Scientists*, vol. 69, no. 3, at: <http://bos.sagepub.com/content/69/3/71.full.pdf>.

Statute. In accordance with the Statute, the Court may exercise jurisdiction over war crimes alleged to have been committed by Georgian nationals or on its territory.

Georgia and Russia are still conducting national investigations into the crimes allegedly committed during the armed conflict of August 2008. The ICC Prosecutor's Office Report on Preliminary Examination Activities for 2014 observed that:[316]

> … there is a reasonable basis to believe that South Ossetian forces carried out a widespread and systematic attack against the ethnic Georgian civilian population in South Ossetia and adjacent areas in the context of the armed conflict in the period from August 2008 through October 2008 that amounted to the crime against humanity of forcible transfer of ethnic Georgians under article 7(1)(d). There is a reasonable basis to believe that these forces also committed war crimes of pillaging under 8(2)(b)(xvi) and/or article 8(2)(e)(v) and destroying civilian property belonging to ethnic Georgians under article 8(2)(a)(iv) and/or article 8(2)(e)(xii) in the same period.

The progress of the national investigations for the alleged crimes committed both by Georgia and Russia, according to the report, are marred with delays, and as documented in the 2014 report and in previous annual reports from the Office, progress appears limited and no alleged perpetrators have been prosecuted, nor has there been any decision to prosecute persons concerned as a result of these investigations.[317] Hence, the Office of the Prosecutor will analyse the updated information received on national proceedings as to decide in the near future whether to seek authorization from the Pre-Trial Chamber to open an investigation into the situation in Georgia pursuant to Article 15(3) of the Statute.[318]

[316] International Criminal Court, Office of the Prosecutor, Report on Preliminary Examination Activities 2014, 2 December 2014, §140, at: <http://www.icc-cpi.int/iccdocs/otp/OTP-Pre-Exam-2014.pdf>.

[317] Ibid. §154, Report on Preliminary Examination Activities 2014

[318] Ibid.

Military occupation of Lebanon by Israel in 2014

KEY CASUALTY DATA FOR 2014

Israeli soldiers wounded 2 (Source: news media)

CLASSIFICATION OF THE CONFLICT

Israel and Lebanon were engaged in an international armed conflict in 2014 by virtue of Israel's continued military occupation of territory in Lebanon (Shebaa Farms area).

SUMMARY OF APPLICABLE INTERNATIONAL LAW

Both parties to the conflict were bound by customary and conventional international humanitarian law and human rights law, including customary international humanitarian law (IHL) rules of distinction, proportionality, and precautions in attacks; the obligation not to recruit and use children as soldiers; and by the duty to respect and protect fundamental human rights. This includes the duty to respect the rights to life and to freedom from torture or other forms of cruel, inhuman, or degrading treatment or punishment.

The law of military occupation is set out in the 1907 Hague Regulations (Articles 42–56), the 1949 Geneva Convention IV, the 1977 Additional Protocol I, and customary international law. Both States are party to the four 1949 Geneva Conventions and to the 1977 Additional Protocol I. Israel is party to the 1966 International Covenant on Civil and Political Rights and the 1966 International Covenant on Economic, Social and Cultural Rights. Lebanon is only party to the 1966 International Covenant on Economic, Social and Cultural Rights.

The underpinning of the law of military occupation is that it is a temporary situation, which lasts until a political agreement is reached. During this period, the Occupying Power does not enjoy sovereign rights over the territories it occupies and local law that was applicable prior to the occupation remains in force. At the same time, the Occupying Power is responsible for administering the local life of the population under its control, maintaining it as it was prior to the occupation as closely as possible, and for providing security (Article 43 of the Hague Regulations).

Lebanon is bound domestically by customary and conventional international human rights law. In addition, international human rights law is binding on Israel extraterritorially in the territories it occupies.[319]

Neither State is party to the 1997 Anti-Personnel Mine Ban Convention or the 2008 Convention on Cluster Munitions. Neither State is party or signatory to the 2013 Arms Trade Treaty (ATT).[320]

HISTORY OF THE CONFLICT

Shebaa Farms is a roughly eight-square-mile area of disputed land in southern Lebanon[321] that has been occupied by Israel since the 1967 Arab–Israeli war.[322] In addition to its military strategic value,[323] the area is said to be important because of the water it provides.[324] In 2001, the Arab League declared that:

> The leaders affirm their support for Lebanon for the complete liberation of its territory from Israeli occupation up to the internationally recognized boundaries, including the Shab'a farmlands.[325]

In 2005, the United Nations (UN) Secretary-General reported to the UN Security Council as follows:

> The United Nations has made abundantly clear that no violations of the Blue Line are acceptable. The continually asserted position of the Government of Lebanon that the Blue Line is not valid in the Shab'a farms area is not compatible with Security Council resolutions. The Council

[319] See, e.g., International Court of Justice, *Wall* Advisory Opinion, 2004, §106. See also European Court of Human Rights, *Cyprus v Turkey*, Judgment, 10 May 2001, §77.

[320] Both Israel and Lebanon voted in favour of the adoption of the ATT by the United Nations (UN) General Assembly on 2 April 2013.

[321] It has also sometimes been asserted that the area falls within Syrian territory.

[322] For an academic review of the history of the area, see, e.g., Kaufman, A., 2004, 'Understanding the Shebaa Farms Dispute: Roots of the Anomaly and Prospects for Resolution', *Palestine-Israel Journal of Politics, Economics and Culture*, vol. 11, no. 1 at: <http://www.pij.org/details.php?id=9>.

[323] See, e.g., Berman, Y. (Media Line), 'Shebaa Farms—Nub of Conflict', *Ynetnews.com*, 8 October 2006, available at: <http://www.ynetnews.com/articles/0,7340,L-3289532,00.html>.

[324] 'Analysis: Shebaa Farms key to Levant Hydro-diplomacy', *IRIN*, Beirut, 10 September 2009, at: <http://www.irinnews.org/Report/86092/Analysis-Shebaa-Farms-key-to-Levant-hydro-diplomacy>.

[325] Final communiqué of the Thirteenth Arab Summit Conference, Amman, Hashemite Kingdom of Jordan, 27 and 28 March 2001, §20, in Letter dated 6 April 2001 from the Permanent Representative of Jordan to the UN Secretary-General, UN doc. A/55/892 and S/2001/342, 10 April 2001, available at: <http://web.archive.org/web/20070828174552/domino.un.org/unispal.NSF/2ee9468747556b2d85256cf60060d2a6/07cd1234c61b141585256a42004e8df2!OpenDocument>.

has recognized the Blue Line as valid for purposes of confirming Israel's withdrawal pursuant to resolution 425 (1978). The Government of Lebanon should heed the Council's repeated calls for the parties to respect the Blue Line in its entirety.[326]

PARTIES TO THE CONFLICT

The parties to the conflict were Israel and Lebanon.

Israel is estimated to have 176,500 active frontline military personnel and a further 445,000 in reserve.[327] Lebanon is estimated to have some 131,000 active frontline military personnel and a further 280,000 reservists.[328]

CASUALTIES

Hezbollah claimed responsibility for attacks in the Shebaa Farms area using explosive devices on 14 March 7 and October; the latter attack wounded two Israeli soldiers.[329]

WAR CRIMES ALLEGATIONS, INVESTIGATIONS, AND PROSECUTIONS

Neither Israel nor Lebanon is a State party or signatory to the 1998 Rome Statute of the International Criminal Court (ICC). The ICC may not exercise jurisdiction over war crimes alleged to have been committed by nationals or on territory unless the situation is referred to the Court by the UN Security Council.

No allegations of war crimes are known to have been made against either Israeli or Lebanese military personnel regarding any acts concerning the Shebaa Farms area in 2014.

[326] Report of the UN Secretary-General on the UN Interim Force in Lebanon (for 21 July 2004 to 20 January 2005), UN doc. S/2005/36, 20 January 2005, §28.

[327] 'Israel Military Strength', *Globalfirepower.com*, last updated on 27 March 2014, at: <http://www.globalfirepower.com/country-military-strength-detail.asp?country_id=israel>. The Israel Defence Forces' mission is 'To defend the existence, territorial integrity and sovereignty of the state of Israel. To protect the inhabitants of Israel and to combat all forms of terrorism which threaten the daily life', <http://www.idfblog.com/about-the-idf/idf-code-of-ethics/>.

[328] 'Lebanon Military Strength', *Globalfirepower.com*, last updated on 27 March 2014, at: <http://www.globalfirepower.com/country-military-strength-detail.asp?country_id=lebanon>.

[329] Al-Monitor, 'Hezbollah Attack on Israeli Patrol Seen as Border Warning', 12 October 2014, <http://www.al-monitor.com/pulse/originals/2014/10/hezbollah-attack-shebaa-farms-israeli-soldiers-wounded.html#>.

Military occupation of Moldova by the Russian Federation in 2014

KEY CASUALTY DATA FOR 2014

No casualties were recorded for 2014.

CLASSIFICATION OF THE CONFLICT

Moldova and the Russian Federation were involved in an international armed conflict in 2013 by virtue of continued Russian occupation of territory in Moldova (Transdniestria).

SUMMARY OF APPLICABLE INTERNATIONAL LAW

Both parties to the conflict were bound by customary and conventional international humanitarian law and human rights law, including customary international humanitarian law (IHL) rules of distinction, proportionality, and precautions in attacks; the obligation not to recruit and use children as soldiers; and by the duty to respect and protect fundamental human rights. This includes the duty to respect the rights to life and to freedom from torture or other forms of cruel, inhuman, or degrading treatment or punishment.

The law of military occupation is set out in the 1907 Hague Regulations (Articles 42–56), the 1949 Geneva Convention IV, the 1977 Additional Protocol I, and customary international law. Both States are party to the four 1949 Geneva Conventions and to the 1977 Additional Protocol I. Both States are party to the 1966 International Covenant on Civil and Political Rights and the 1966 International Covenant on Economic, Social and Cultural Rights.

The underpinning of the law of military occupation is that it is a temporary situation, which lasts until a political agreement is reached. During this period, the Occupying Power does not enjoy sovereign rights over the territories it occupies and local law that was applicable prior to the occupation remains in force. At the same time, the Occupying Power is responsible for administering the local life of the population under its control, maintaining it as it was prior to the occupation as closely as possible, and for providing security (Article 43 of the Hague Regulations).

Moldova is bound domestically by customary and conventional international human rights law. In addition, international human rights law is binding on Russia extraterritorially in the territories it occupies.[330] As ruled by the European Court of Human Rights, the obligation to secure in occupied territories the rights and freedoms set out in the 1950 European Convention on Human Rights derives from effective control over occupied territory, whether it is exercised by the occupying State directly, through its armed forces, or through a subordinate local administration.[331] Furthermore in a case decided in 2012 concerning Moldova, *Catan v Moldova and Russia*, the Court stated:

> Where the fact of such domination over the territory is established, it is not necessary to determine whether the Contracting State exercises detailed control over the policies and actions of the subordinate local administration. The fact that the local administration survives as a result of the Contracting State's military and other support entails that State's responsibility for its policies and actions. The controlling State has the responsibility under Article 1 to secure, within the area under its control, the entire range of substantive rights set out in the Convention and those additional Protocols which it has ratified.[332]

The Court found that Russia had jurisdiction under Article 1 of the European Convention on Human Rights during the period relevant for the case, 2002–4: 'The "MRT" [Moldavian Republic of Transdniestria] was established as a result of Russian military assistance. The continued Russian military and armaments presence in the region sent a strong signal, to the "MRT" leaders, the Moldovan Government and international observers, of Russia's continued military support for the separatists. In addition, the population were dependent on free or highly subsidised gas supplies, pensions and other financial aid from Russia.'[333]

Moldova is party to both the 1997 Anti-Personnel Mine Ban Convention and the 2008 Convention on Cluster Munitions. Russia is party to neither treaty.

Neither State is party to the 2013 Arms Trade Treaty (ATT), though Moldova signed on 10 September 2013.[334]

HISTORY OF THE CONFLICT

The Republic of Moldova gained independence in 1991, in the aftermath of the collapse of the Soviet Union. The region east of the Dniester, which was also known as

[330] See, e.g., International Court of Justice, *Wall* Advisory Opinion, 2004, §106.

[331] See European Court of Human Rights (ECtHR), *Cyprus v Turkey*, Judgment, 10 May 2001, §77; *Loizidou v. Turkey*, Judgment (Merits), 18 December 1996, §§52, 54, 56; *Catan v. Moldova and Russia*, Judgment, 19 October 2012, §§106–107.

[332] ECtHR, *Catan v Moldova and Russia*, Judgment, 19 October 2012, §106.

[333] Ibid., §121.

[334] Russia abstained in the vote to adopt the ATT by the United Nations (UN) General Assembly on 2 April 2013.

Transdniester or Transnistria, had enjoyed formal autonomy within Ukraine prior to 1940, but was subsequently combined with the region between the rivers Dniester and Prut, formerly known as Bessarabia, to form the Moldovan Soviet Socialist Republic.[335]

Before Moldova's declaration of independence, Transdniestria, a strip of land between the river Dniester and the border with Ukraine, unilaterally declared its own independence. The move came after alarm over growing Moldovan nationalism, a possible reunification with Romania, and a 1989 language law proclaiming Moldovan as the official language. A 'Transdniestrian Moldovan Republic' (TMR) or 'Pridnestrovskaya Moldavskaya Respublica' in Russian, was proclaimed in Tiraspol on 2 September 1990. This led to localized combat, in which several hundred people were killed and thousands more displaced.

The TMR is said to have organized paramilitary 'workers' detachments' on the basis of which a fully armed and professional 'Republican Guard' was created in 1991. On 2 September 1991, Transdniestrian authorities voted to join the Soviet Union. On 28 March 1992, a state of emergency was introduced in Moldova. Fighting continued, however, with the summer of 1992 seeing a peak in armed clashes and victims, particularly in a battle over the city of Tighina/Bendery. Human Rights Watch alleged that the Russian 14th Army, stationed on the left bank of the Dniester, directly or indirectly assisted the secessionists.[336]

After peacekeeping within the CSCE or the Commonwealth of Independent States (CIS) frameworks was ruled out, a Moldovan–Russian initiative, signed in Moscow on 21 July 1992, found more success. The agreement called for an immediate ceasefire and the establishment of a demilitarized zone, 10km to the left and right of the Dniester River. A tripartite Joint Control Commission was to be set up, consisting of representatives of Moldova, Russia, and the TMR. Russian peacekeepers were brought in, alongside Moldovan and Transdniestrian ones, to stabilize the region and have remained in place ever since. In 2007, a United States (US) proposal for their replacement with an international peacekeeping contingent was rejected by the authorities in Tiraspol.

[335] Unless otherwise stated, this section is based on 'Moldova Profile', *BBC*, 20 March 2014, at: <http://www.bbc.co.uk/news/world-europe-17601580>; 'Transdniestrian conflict: Origins and main issues', based on the Background Paper, 1994, 'The Transdniestrian Conflict in Moldova: Origins and Main Issues', Vienna, 10 June 1994, CSCE Conflict Prevention Centre; Ciobanu, C., 2004, 'NATO/EU Enlargement: Moldova and the "Frozen and Forgotten" Conflicts in Post-Soviet States', US Institute of Peace, Washington DC, 22 July 2004; International Crisis Group (ICG), 2004, 'Moldova: Regional Tensions over Transdniestria', Europe Report No. 157, Chisinau; and see also European Parliament resolution on human rights violations in Transdniestria and the need for EU support for the settlement of the frozen conflict in the Republic of Moldova, Resolution No. B6-0292/2007, 10 July 2007.

[336] Human Rights Watch, 1993, 'War or Peace? Human Rights and Russian Military Involvement in the "Near Abroad"', vol. 5, no. 22 (December 1993), available at: <http://www.hrw.org/legacy/reports/1993/russia/>.

While Transdniestria enjoys de facto autonomy, the Republic of Moldova and the international community do not recognize its independence. A September 2006 Transdniestrian referendum reasserting independence and the wish for adhesion to Russia went similarly unrecognized. It is frequently referred to as a 'frozen conflict'.

In early 2012, the Moldovan Ministry of Foreign Affairs lodged a formal protest with the Russian ambassador, demanding that Moscow agree to transform the Transdniestria peacekeeping mission into a civil one with an international mandate. This followed the shooting dead of a Moldovan man by a Russian peacekeeping soldier at a checkpoint in the separatist region on 1 January 2012. On 12 January, Moldovan, Transdniestrian, and Russian representatives met to discuss tensions at checkpoints.[337]

During 2012, hopes rose for a negotiated settlement to the situation in Transdniestria. On 27 September, the European Union (EU) lifted a travel ban on the former political leadership of the Transdniestrian region in recognition of progress in negotiations to settle the conflict.[338] In February 2013, talks on Transdniestria took place in Lviv with representatives from Russia, Ukraine, the United States, the EU, and the OSCE, as well as Moldova and Transdniestria.[339]

In June 2013, Moldova was about to conclude a landmark trade deal with the EU. But the day before the agreement was signed, Transdniestria unexpectedly adopted a law transforming the administrative line separating it from the rest of Moldova into a 'State border'.[340]

In March 2014, Moldovan President Nicolae Timofti cautioned Russia against trying to annex Transdniestria in the same way it had taken control of Ukraine's Crimea.[341] The same month, NATO's most senior military commander said that Russia had amassed a large military force on Ukraine's eastern border and warned it could be planning to target Transdniestria.[342]

[337] ICG, Crisis Watch Database: Moldova, 1 February 2012, available at: <http://www.crisisgroup.org/en/publication-type/crisiswatch/crisiswatch-database.aspx>.

[338] EU Council, 'Council Lifts Sanctions to Recognize Progress in Transnistria Negotiations', *Consilium*, 27 September 2012, at: <http://www.consilium.europa.eu/uedocs/cms_Data/docs/pressdata/EN/foraff/132616.pdf>.

[339] ICG, Crisis Watch Database: Moldova, 1 March 2013, at: <http://www.crisisgroup.org/en/publication-type/crisiswatch/crisiswatch-database.aspx>. The OSCE chairs the negotiation process for a settlement of the Transdniestrian conflict. Since 2005, this process is known as the '5+2' and includes the OSCE, Russia, and Ukraine as mediators, and the EU and the United States as observers. The Mission also participates as an observer in the Joint Control Commission, which is the supervisory body for the Joint Peacekeeping Forces, composed of the delegations of the Russian Federation, Moldova and Transdniestria, with Ukraine as an additional observer. OSCE, 'OSCE Mission to Moldova', at: <http://www.osce.org/moldova>.

[340] Coalson, R., 'Moscow Counters Moldovan, Georgian Charm Offensives', Radio Free Europe/Radio Liberty, 24 June 2013, at: <http://www.rferl.org/content/moldova-georgia-breakaway-regions-moscow-counters/25026520.html>.

[341] 'Moldova Profile: Timeline', *BBC*.

[342] Harding, L., 'Russia Ready to Annex Moldova Region, Nato Commander Claims', *Guardian*, 23 March 2014, at: <http://www.theguardian.com/world/2014/mar/23/russia-ukraine-annex-moldova-trans-dniester-nato>.

In August 2014, tensions continued over Transdniestria. On 4 August, Moscow accused Moldova and Ukraine of attempting to block Russia's access to its troops in Transdniestria. The following day, the Moldovan Government called on Russia to withdraw its troops and weapons from the region.[343]

PARTIES TO THE CONFLICT

The parties to the conflict were Moldova and Russia.

Moldova was estimated in 2011 to have between 5,000 and 6,000 active frontline military personnel.[344] Russia is estimated to have 766,000 active frontline military personnel and almost 2.5 million reservists.[345] Russia has one of the world's largest stocks of conventional weaponry and possesses the world's greatest nuclear arsenal.[346]

CASUALTIES

No casualties were recorded for 2014.

WAR CRIMES ALLEGATIONS, INVESTIGATIONS, AND PROSECUTIONS

Moldova is party to the 1998 Rome Statute of the International Criminal Court (ICC Statute), having adhered in October 2010. Russia has signed but not ratified the Statute. In accordance with the ICC Statute, the Court may exercise jurisdiction over war crimes alleged to have been committed by Moldovan nationals or on its territory, including Transdniestria.

No allegations of war crimes are known to have been made against Moldovan, Russian, or Transdniestrian military personnel regarding any acts concerning Transdniestria in 2014.

[343] ICG, Crisis Watch Database, Moldova, 1 September 2014, <http://www.crisisgroup.org/en/publication-type/crisiswatch/crisiswatch-database.aspx?CountryIDs={8DA7B2AE-B336-425A-8A7D-6679D17D511A}>.

[344] Unsourced estimate. The website of the Moldovan Ministry of Defence is at: <http://www.army.md/?lng=3&action=show&cat=135>.

[345] 'Russia Military Strength', *Globalfirepower.com*, last updated on 27 March 2014, at: <http://www.globalfirepower.com/country-military-strength-detail.asp?country_id=russia>.

[346] 'As of early 2013, Russia has a stockpile of approximately 4,500 nuclear warheads, of which roughly 1,800 strategic warheads are deployed on missiles and at bomber bases. Another 700 strategic warheads are in storage, along with 2,000 nonstrategic warheads.' Kristensen, H. M. and Norris, R. S., 2013, 'Russian Nuclear Forces, 2013', *Bulletin of the Atomic Scientists*, vol. 69, no. 3 at: <http://bos.sagepub.com/content/69/3/71.full.pdf>.

Military occupation of Palestine by Israel in 2014

KEY CASUALTY DATA FOR 2014

Occupied Palestinian Territories (oPT)		
Palestinian deaths:	2,344 (including participants in hostilities)	(Source: OCHA)
Palestinian injured:	17,350 (including participants in hostilities)	(Source: OCHA)
Israeli deaths:	87 (including military personnel)	
Israeli injured:	2,629 (including military personnel)	
Israeli child deaths:	1	(Source: OCHA)
Gaza		
Palestinian deaths:	2,286	(Source: OCHA)
Palestinian injured:	11,322	(Source: OCHA)
Israeli deaths:	71*	
Israeli injured:	2,379*	
West Bank		
Palestinian deaths:	58	(Source: OCHA)
Palestinian injured:	6,028	(Source: OCHA)
Palestinian child deaths:	13	(Source: OCHA)
Children injured:	1,190	(Source: OCHA)
Israeli deaths:	16	(Source: OCHA)
Israeli injured:	250	(Source: OCHA)

* These statistics are calculated from the OCHA total for Palestine by subtracting the casualties reported for the West Bank.

CLASSIFICATION OF THE CONFLICT

Israel and Palestine were engaged in an international armed conflict in 2014 by virtue of Israel's continued military occupation of Palestinian territory. Palestine was accorded the status of non-member observer State in the United Nations (UN) by the UN General Assembly on 29 November 2012.[347]

SUMMARY OF APPLICABLE INTERNATIONAL LAW

Both parties to the conflict were bound by customary and conventional international humanitarian law and human rights law, including customary international

[347] UN General Assembly Resolution 67/19 was adopted by 138 votes to nine, with forty-one abstentions.

humanitarian law (IHL) rules of distinction, proportionality, and precautions in attacks; the obligation not to recruit and use children as soldiers; and by the duty to respect and protect fundamental human rights. This includes the duty to respect the rights to life and to freedom from torture or other forms of cruel, inhuman, or degrading treatment or punishment.

The law of military occupation is set out in the 1907 Hague Regulations (Articles 42–56), the 1949 Geneva Convention IV, the 1977 Additional Protocol I, and customary international law. Israel is party to the four 1949 Geneva Conventions but not the 1977 Additional Protocol I. Palestine adhered to the four 1949 Geneva Conventions and to the 1977 Additional Protocol I on 2 April 2014. Israel is party to the 1966 International Covenant on Civil and Political Rights and the 1966 International Covenant on Economic, Social and Cultural Rights. Palestine adhered to the two Covenants on 2 April 2014.

The underpinning of the law of military occupation is that it is a temporary situation, which lasts until a political agreement is reached. During this period, the Occupying Power does not enjoy sovereign rights over the territories it occupies and local law that was applicable prior to the occupation remains in force. At the same time, the Occupying Power is responsible for administering the local life of the population under its control, maintaining it as it was prior to the occupation as closely as possible, and for providing security (Article 43 of the Hague Regulations).

Palestine was bound domestically by customary international human rights law in 2013. In addition, international human rights law is binding on Israel extraterritorially in the territories it occupies.[348]

Neither State is party to the 1997 Anti-Personnel Mine Ban Convention or the 2008 Convention on Cluster Munitions. Neither State is party or signatory to the 2013 Arms Trade Treaty (ATT).[349]

HISTORY OF THE CONFLICT[350]

The Palestinian population of around 10 or 11 million people is divided between historic Palestine and a diaspora, mainly in neighbouring Arab countries. Efforts to create a Palestinian State on the West Bank of the River Jordan and Gaza on the Mediterranean coast have been frustrated by the continuing conflict with Israel and disputes over the status of diaspora Palestinians.

[348] See, e.g., International Court of Justice, *Wall* Advisory Opinion, 2004, §106. See also European Court of Human Rights, *Cyprus v Turkey*, Judgment, 10 May 2001, §77.

[349] Israel voted in favour of the adoption of the ATT by the UN General Assembly on 2 April 2013.

[350] Unless otherwise stated, this section is based on 'Palestinian Territories Profile', *BBC*, 28 February 2013, at: <http://www.bbc.co.uk/news/world-middle-east-14630174>.

The war that followed Israel's declaration of independence in 1948 saw the former British mandate of Palestine partitioned between Israel, Trans-Jordan, and Egypt. Hundreds of thousands of Palestinians fled or were forced out of their native land during the war, in what they call the 'Nakba' ('Catastrophe'). The demand of these refugees and their descendants to return to their former homes remains one of the most fiercely debated aspects of the dispute with Israel.

The Palestinian national movement gradually regrouped in the West Bank and Gaza, run respectively by Jordan and Egypt, and in refugee camps in neighbouring Arab States. The Palestine Liberation Organisation (PLO) emerged as its leading umbrella group shortly before the Six-Day War of 1967, during which Israel captured the West Bank, Gaza, and East Jerusalem.

The PLO under Yasser Arafat gradually won international recognition as the representative of the Palestinian people, culminating in the Oslo Accords with Israel in 1993. The accords established a Palestinian National Authority (PNA—also referred to as the Palestinian Authority, or PA) as an interim body to run parts of Gaza and the West Bank (but not East Jerusalem) pending an agreed solution to the conflict.

The PNA functions as an agency of the PLO, which represents Palestinians at international bodies. It is led by a directly elected president, who appoints a prime minister and government which must have the support of the elected Legislative Council. Its civilian and security writ runs in urban areas (Area A) under the Oslo Accords, with civilian but not security control over rural areas (Area B).

The Israeli occupation of the West Bank, with its continuing settlement building and military checkpoints, and Palestinian attacks, have slowed progress towards a final agreement and led many on both sides to dispute the worth of the Accords. Israel retains full control over bypass roads, settlements and the Jordan Valley, and makes incursions into urban areas against armed groups.

In 2005, Israel completed withdrawal of all its troops and settlers from the Gaza Strip but it retains control of the airspace, seafront, and access—including deliveries of food and other goods—apart from the crossing with Egypt. The Islamist Hamas movement, which runs Gaza, explicitly rejects the Oslo Accords and its charter calls for Israel's 'nullification'.

The beginning of 2012 was marked by an increase in violence and tension in the Occupied Palestinian Territories and Israel. Palestinian militants fired rockets into southern Israel while Israeli military forces responded with strikes in the Gaza Strip. On 14 November 2012, Israel Defense Forces (IDF) launched Operation Pillar of Defense in response to an increase of Hamas rockets following the killing, by the IDF, of Ahmed Jabari, chief of Hamas' Gaza military wing.[351] The aims of the military

[351] Wright, R., 'Who Started the Israel-Gaza Conflict?', *The Atlantic*, 6 November 2012, at: <http://www.theatlantic.com/international/archive/2012/11/who-started-the-israel-gaza-conflict/265374/>.

operation, according to the Israeli Government were to 'halt rocket attacks against civilian targets originating from the Gaza Strip'[352] and 'to disrupt the capabilities of militant organizations'.[353] According to the Israeli Government, the operation began in response to Palestinian groups launching more than 100 rockets at Israel over a twenty-four-hour period,[354] an attack on an Israeli military patrol jeep within Israeli borders by Gaza militants, and a tunnel explosion caused by improvised explosive devices (IEDs) near Israeli soldiers on the Israeli side of the fence.[355] Palestinians blamed the Israeli Government for the escalation of violence, accusing the IDF of attacks on Gazan civilians in the days leading up to the operation, and citing the blockade of the Gaza Strip, and occupation of West Bank and East Jerusalem, as the reason for rocket attacks.[356]

During Operation Pillar of Defense, the IDF struck more than 1,500 sites in the Gaza Strip, including rocket launch-pads, weapon storages, government buildings, and apartment blocks.[357] Gaza officials claimed that 133 Palestinians had been killed in the conflict of whom seventy-nine were fighters, fifty-three civilians, and one was a policeman; they also estimated that 840 Palestinians were wounded.[358] Eight Palestinians were executed by members of the Izz ad-Din al-Qassam Brigades for alleged collaboration with Israel.[359] During the eight-day conflict, Hamas, the al-Qassam Brigades, and Islamic Jihad intensified their rocket attacks on Israeli cities, in an operation codenamed Operation Stones of Baked Clay by the al-Qassam Brigades.

On 24 June 2013, Israel conducted air strikes on the Gaza Strip in response to six rockets fired into Israel in violation of the November 2012 ceasefire; no injuries were

[352] al-Mughrabi N. (Reuters), 'Hamas Leader Defiant as Israel Eases Gaza Curbs', *Chicago Tribune*, 24 November 2012, at: <http://articles.chicagotribune.com/2012-11-24/news/sns-rt-us-palestinians-israel-hamasbre8ad0wp-20121114_1_gaza-curbs-gaza-fishermen-hamas-leader>.

[353] Lappin, Y., 'IAF Strike Kills Hamas Military Chief Jabari', *Jerusalem Post*, 14 November 2012, at: <http://www.jpost.com/Defense/Article.aspx?id=291779>.

[354] Lappin, Y. and Lazaroff, T., 'Gaza Groups Pound Israel With Over 100 Rockets', *Jerusalem Post*, 12 December 2012, at: <http://www.jpost.com/Defense/Article.aspx?id=291300>.

[355] Israel Ministry of Foreign Affairs, *Operation Pillar of Defense—Selected statements*, 20 November 2012, at: <http://www.mfa.gov.il/MFA/Government/Speeches+by+Israeli+leaders/2012/Operation_Pillar_of_Defense-Statements.htm>.

[356] AFP, 'Israel Warns Hamas of "Heavy Price" For Gaza Rockets', 11 November 2012, at: <http://www.google.com/hostednews/afp/article/ALeqM5jRUtS7PreKQztfBnueg5yNep0ROg?docId=CNG.eceda380b55ad442c0c0b524c5263e34.61>.

[357] 'Factbox: Gaza targets bombed by Israel', Gaza, Reuters, 21 November 2012, at: <http://www.reuters.com/article/2012/11/21/us-palestinians-israel-gaza-idUSBRE8AK0H920121121>.

[358] 'Israeli Strikes Kill 23 in Bloodiest Day for Gaza', *News International*, 19 November 2012, at: <http://www.thenews.com.pk/Todays-News-13-18932-Israeli-strikes-kill-23-in-bloodiest-day-for-Gaza>.

[359] Rudoren, J. and Akram, F., 'Mistaken Lull, Simple Errand, Death in Gaza', *New York Times*, 16 November 2012, at: <http://www.nytimes.com/2012/11/17/world/middleeast/in-gaza-tragic-result-for-misplaced-hopes-of-cease-fire.html?hp>.

reported.[360] In July 2013, talks between Israel and Palestine were launched by the United States which it hoped would lead to a settlement of Israel–Palestine conflict during 2014. In late April 2014, the nine-month deadline for peace talks passed with nothing concrete to show for the period of intense US diplomacy. As the deadline passed some ministers in Israel's Government called for Israel to set its own borders and annex areas of the West Bank under full Israeli control. The economy minister, Naftali Bennett, said: 'We will be gradually attempting to apply Israeli law on Israeli-controlled areas.'[361]

In late April 2014, Palestinian President Mahmoud Abbas said he was still ready to extend peace talks with Israel, despite the breakdown in the process. He said a new unity government with Hamas, planned to be created within weeks, would recognize Israel and renounce violence.[362]

The Israeli occupation of the West Bank—the maintenance and expansion of the settlement enterprise, the application of Israeli domestic laws in occupied territory, and the restrictions on Palestinian movement, development and livelihoods—and Palestinian attacks from the Gaza Strip have slowed progress towards a final status agreement. Israel retains full control over bypass roads, settlements, and the Jordan Valley, and makes incursions into urban areas against armed groups.

PARTIES TO THE CONFLICT

The parties to the conflict were Israel and Palestine.

Israel is estimated to have 176,500 active frontline military personnel and a further 445,000 in reserve.[363] Palestine does not possess regular armed forces. The Palestinian National Security Forces are the paramilitary forces of the Palestinian National Authority. A number of Palestinian armed groups operate, in particular, from the Gaza Strip.

[360] International Crisis Group (ICG), Crisis Watch Database: Israel/Palestine, 1 July 2013, available at: <http://www.crisisgroup.org/en/publication-type/crisiswatch/crisiswatch-database.aspx>.

[361] Beaumont, P., 'US Has Nothing to Show as Deadline For Israel-Palestine Peace Talks Passes', *Guardian*, 29 April 2014, at: <http://www.theguardian.com/world/2014/apr/29/israel-palestine-peace-talks-deadline-passes>.

[362] 'Palestinian Leader Abbas "Still Seeks" Israel Peace Talks', *BBC*, 26 April 2014, at: <http://www.bbc.com/news/world-middle-east-27169410>.

[363] 'Israel Military Strength', *Globalfirepower.com*, last updated on 27 March 2014, at: <http://www.globalfirepower.com/country-military-strength-detail.asp?country_id=israel>. The Israel Defence Forces' mission is 'To defend the existence, territorial integrity and sovereignty of the state of Israel. To protect the inhabitants of Israel and to combat all forms of terrorism which threaten the daily life', <http://www.idfblog.com/about-the-idf/idf-code-of-ethics/>.

Ezzeddeen al-Qassam Brigades

Hamas was formed in late 1987 in the midst of the first Palestinian Intifada. Its roots are in the Palestinian branch of the Muslim Brotherhood.[364] The group's charter calls for an Islamic Palestinian State to be established in place of Israel and rejects all agreements made between the PLO and Israel.[365] More recently, Hamas publicly expressed a willingness to accept a long-term cessation of hostilities if Israel agrees to a Palestinian State based on the 1967 borders with Jerusalem as its capital. Hamas's strength is concentrated in the Gaza Strip and areas of the West Bank.

Hamas has a military wing, the Ezzeddeen al-Qassam Brigades (EQB), which was established in the 1990s and has, since then, conducted many anti-Israeli attacks in Israel and the Palestinian territories. Attacks on civilian targets have included rocket attacks and, from 1993 to 2006, suicide bombings. Military targets included Israeli outposts and border crossings and rival Palestinian militias in the occupied territories. While the group receives some support from foreign countries and movements, it remains independent.[366]

al-Quds Brigade

Islamic Jihad was formed by militant Palestinians in the Gaza Strip during the 1970s. The group is committed to the creation of an Islamic State in all of historical Palestine and the destruction of Israel through attacks against Israeli military and civilian targets. The group's central leadership resides in Syria, but the Palestinian Islamic Jihad (PIJ) maintains small regional offices in Beirut and Tehran. PIJ receives financial assistance primarily from Iran.[367] PIJ refuses to participate in the Palestinian Authority's political process and rejects all negotiations with Israel. The group's paramilitary wing—the al-Quds Brigade—has conducted numerous attacks, including large-scale suicide bombings.[368] The group has conducted numerous rocket attacks against Israeli targets near the Gaza Strip using indigenously produced rockets. The al-Quds Brigade actively participated in the 2012 eight-day conflict against Israel.

[364] National Counterterrorism Center, *Hamas*, as of 31 December 2012, at: <http://www.nctc.gov/site/groups/hamas.html>.

[365] Hamas Charter 1988, available at The Jerusalem Fund, at: <http://www.thejerusalemfund.org/www.thejerusalemfund.org/carryover/documents/charter.html>.

[366] Ezzedeen Al-Qassam Brigades-Information Office, available at: <http://www.qassam.ps/index.html>.

[367] National Consortium for the Study of Terrorism and Responses to Terrorism, *Palestinian Islamic Jihad (PIJ)*, 31 December 2012, at: <http://www.start.umd.edu/start/data_collections/tops/terrorist_organization_profile.asp?id=82>.

[368] Council on Foreign Relations, *Palestinian Islamic Jihad*, 10 April 2008, at: <http://www.cfr.org/israel/palestinian-islamic-jihad/p15984>.

CASUALTIES

OCHA statistics a total of 2,401 people killed and 19,754 injured in occupied Palestine in 2014 including Gaza and the West Bank. These figures included casualties during Operation Protective Edge an international armed conflict that occurred in Gaza in the period 8 July 2014 through 26 August 2014.[369] The vast majority of recorded casualties during 2014 were Palestinian, with 2,344 killed and 17,350 reported as injured.[370] Among the total casualties for 2014, eighty-seven Israelis were killed and 2,629 reported as injured. OCHA noted that it was 'unable to verify neither the criteria nor the number of Palestinian and Israeli injuries resulting from the July-August hostilities in Gaza'.[371]

In Gaza there were at least 2,286 Palestinians killed and 11,322 reported as injured for 2014.[372] This total includes casualties during Operation Protective Edge. OCHA reported 2,220 Palestinian deaths and 11,231 injured in Gaza during the conflict. Another seventy-one Israeli deaths during the conflict period were reported by OCHA, with sixty-six Israeli military casualties, four civilians killed, and one fatality whose role in the conflict was not known.[373] Statistics for Gaza also included eight people killed and fifty-seven injured by explosive remnants of war in 2014.[374]

In the West Bank, including East Jerusalem, there were seventy-four fatalities and another 6,278 people were injured in 2014. This included fifty-eight Palestinian deaths (this number also included three people killed in West Jerusalem) and 6,028 injured. During 2014, sixteen Israelis were recorded as killed (including six killed in West

[369] OCHA oPT, 'Fragmented lives Humanitarian Overview 2014', 26 March 2015, pp. 3–4.

[370] The War Report total of Palestinian casualties in the oPT in 2014 has been calculated by combining the number of casualties reported in the West Bank in 'Fragmented lives Humanitarian Overview 2014', 26 March 2015, p. 5. Together with the total casualties for Gaza to 29 December 2014 in OCHA oPT, 'Protection of Civilians Reporting Period: 23–9 December 2014', <http://www.ochaopt.org/documents/ocha_opt_protection_of_civilians_weekly_report_2014_01_02_english.pdf>. OCHA annual reporting cited 2,314 Palestinians killed and 17,125 injured in the OPT in 2014. However, this number is below the combined total of Palestinian injured in Gaza during Operation Protective Edge and in the West Bank reported in the same document. See 'Fragmented lives Humanitarian Overview 2014', 26 March 2015, p. 5.

[371] OCHA oPT, 'Fragmented lives Humanitarian Overview 2014', 26 March 2015, p. 3.

[372] Data covers the period from the beginning of 2014, though 29 December. OCHA oPT, 'Protection of Civilians Reporting Period: 23–9 December 2014', <http://www.ochaopt.org/documents/ocha_opt_protection_of_civilians_weekly_report_2014_01_02_english.pdf>.

[373] OCHA oPT, 'Fragmented lives Humanitarian Overview 2014', 26 March 2015, p. 4. *The War Report* calculated seventy-four Israeli deaths during Operation Protective edge: seven civilians and sixty-seven Israeli Defence Force personnel. See Israeli Ministry of Public Security, Public Information in Emergency Crisis Situations, 'Facing New Challenges: Operation Protective Edge', p. 71, <http://mops.gov.il/Documents/Publications/InformationCenter/Innovation%20Exchange/Innovation%20Exchange%2017/Public%20Information%20in%20Emergency%20Crisis%20Situations.pdf> and IDF, 'Operation Protective Edge General Information Since the beginning of the Operation', last updated 26 January 2015, <http://www.idfblog.com/operationgaza2014/#Genralinformation>.

[374] OCHA oPT, 'Fragmented lives Humanitarian Overview 2014', 26 March 2015, p. 5.

Jerusalem and one in Tel Aviv) and another 250 as injured in the West Bank. In 2014, thirteen children were killed in the West Bank, a sharp increase compared to four in 2013, the highest number recorded in the West Bank since 2006.[375] Israeli armed forces injured a total of 1,190 Palestinian children in the West Bank, a similarly high number to the 1,185 injured children in 2013.[376]

DISPLACED

In 2014, there were at least 118,200 new internal displaced persons (IDPs) in Palestine, leading to a total of 275,000 persons being internally displaced in the country as of December 2014. However, these figures are based on secondary information and surveys that use different methodologies and only reflect ad hoc occurrences of displacement. It does not reflect the full scale of displacement as no organization or mechanism monitors the number of IDPs systematically.[377]

WAR CRIMES ALLEGATIONS, INVESTIGATIONS, AND PROSECUTIONS

While Israel is not a party to the ICC, on 31 December 2014, the State of Palestine, submitted an ad-hoc declaration under Article 12(3) to the Office of the ICC Prosecutor in The Hague, accepting the jurisdiction of the ICC with respect to events that occurred after 13 June 2014—thus including the 2014 Gaza Conflict.[378] Concurrently, on 2 January 2015, Palestine submitted an instrument of accession to the Rome Statute to the UN Secretary-General.[379] On 16 January 2015, the Prosecutor announced the opening of a preliminary examination into the situation in Palestine in order to establish whether the Rome Statute criteria for opening an investigation were met, in particular, issues of jurisdiction, admissibility and the interests of justice in making this determination.

[375] OCHA oPT, 'Fragmented lives Humanitarian Overview 2014', 26 March 2015, p. 5.

[376] Statistics for the period from the beginning of 2014 through 29 December, OCHA oPT, 'Protection of Civilians Reporting Period: 23–9 December 2014', <http://www.ochaopt.org/documents/ocha_opt_protection_of_civilians_weekly_report_2014_01_02_english.pdf>.

[377] Internal Displacement Monitoring Centre (IDMC) 'Global Overview 2015', May 2015, p. 85.

[378] The declaration signed by the Palestinian Ministry of Justice, 31 December 2014 <http://icc-cpi.int/iccdocs/PIDS/press/Palestine_A_12-3.pdf>.

[379] See the ICC press release: <http://icc-cpi.int/en_menus/icc/press and media/press releases/Pages/pr1082_2.aspx>.

In addition to any allegations of arbitrary killings or torture, the transfer of populations into or from Palestine is generally considered to be a violation of international law. According to the 2013 Report of the independent international fact-finding mission to investigate the implications of the Israeli settlements on the civil, political, economic, social, and cultural rights of the Palestinian people throughout the Occupied Palestinian Territory, including East Jerusalem:

> A situation of military occupation prevails in the Occupied Palestinian Territory. …
>
> Article 49 of the Fourth Geneva Convention … prohibits the occupying Power from transferring parts of its own civilian population into the territory that it occupies. This prohibition has attained the status of customary international law. The mission notes that the Israeli settlements in the Occupied Palestinian Territory, including East Jerusalem, violate this provision and are, thus, illegal under international law.[380] …
>
> The transfer of Israeli citizens into the Occupied Palestinian Territory, prohibited under international humanitarian law and international criminal law, is a central feature of the practices and policies of Israel.[381]

The mission considered that, with regard to the settlements, Israel is committing 'serious breaches of its obligations under the right to self-determination and certain obligations' under IHL, 'including the obligation not to transfer its population into the Occupied Palestinian Territory'.[382] It noted that the ICC Statute 'establishes the jurisdiction of the International Criminal Court over the deportation or transfer, directly or indirectly, by the occupying Power of parts of its own population into the territory it occupies, or the deportation or transfer of all or parts of the population of the occupied territory within or outside that territory. Ratification of the Statute by Palestine may lead to accountability for gross violations of human rights law and serious violations of international humanitarian law and justice for victims'.[383]

[380] See for example the [ICJ] Advisory Opinion of 9 July 2004, §120; UN Security Council Resolution 471 (1980); General Assembly Resolutions 3092 (XXVIII), 47/172 and 66/225; Commission on Human Rights Resolution 2000/8; Human Rights Council Resolutions 13/7 and 16/31; and Council of the European Union, Conclusions on the Middle East Peace Process, 3166th Foreign Affairs Council Meeting, 14 May 2012.

[381] 'Report of the independent international fact-finding mission to investigate the implications of the Israeli settlements on the civil, political, economic, social and cultural rights of the Palestinian people throughout the Occupied Palestinian Territory, including East Jerusalem', Human Rights Council, UN doc. A/HRC/22/63, 7 February 2013, §§13, 16, 38.

[382] Ibid., §104. [383] Ibid.

Military occupation of Syria by Israel in 2014

KEY CASUALTY DATA FOR 2013

Israeli military killed:	0	(Source: UN)
Israeli military injured:	4	(Source: UN)
Syrian military killed by Israeli forces:	14	(Source: UN, Reuters, AFP)
Syrian military injured by Israeli forces:	19	(Source: UN)
Syrian military killed by armed groups:	At least 6	(Source: UN)
UNDOF peacekeepers injured:	4	(Source: UN)
Israeli civilian killed:	1	(Source: UN)

CLASSIFICATION OF THE CONFLICT

Israel and Syria were engaged in an international armed conflict in 2014 by virtue of Israel's continued military occupation of Syrian territory (the Golan Heights).

SUMMARY OF APPLICABLE INTERNATIONAL LAW

Both parties to the conflict were bound by customary and conventional international humanitarian law and human rights law, including customary international humanitarian law (IHL) rules of distinction, proportionality, and precautions in attacks; the obligation not to recruit and use children as soldiers; and by the duty to respect and protect fundamental human rights. This includes the duty to respect the rights to life and to freedom from torture or other forms of cruel, inhuman, or degrading treatment or punishment.

The law of military occupation is set out in the 1907 Hague Regulations (Articles 42–56); the 1949 Geneva Convention IV, the 1977 Additional Protocol I, and customary international law. Israel is party to the four 1949 Geneva Conventions. Syria is party to the four 1949 Geneva Conventions and to the 1977 Additional Protocol I. Both Israel and Syria are party to the 1966 International Covenant on Civil and Political Rights and the 1966 International Covenant on Economic, Social and Cultural Rights.

The underpinning of the law of military occupation is that it is a temporary situation, which lasts until a political agreement is reached. During this period, the Occupying Power does not enjoy sovereign rights over the territories it occupies and local law that was applicable prior to the occupation remains in force. At the same time, the Occupying Power is responsible for administering the local life of the population under its control, maintaining it as it was prior to the occupation as closely as possible, and for providing security (Article 43 of the Hague Regulations).

Syria was bound domestically by customary and conventional international human rights law in 2014. In addition, international human rights law is binding on Israel extraterritorially in the territories it occupies.[384]

Neither State is party to the 1997 Anti-Personnel Mine Ban Convention or the 2008 Convention on Cluster Munitions. Neither State is party or signatory to the 2013 Arms Trade Treaty (ATT).[385]

HISTORY OF THE CONFLICT[386]

Syria remains in conflict with Israel, which occupies part of the Golan Heights it seized in 1967 in the closing stages of the Six-Day War. Most of the Syrian Arab inhabitants fled the area during the conflict. An armistice line was established and the region came under Israeli military control. Almost immediately Israel began to settle the Golan. Today, there are around 20,000 Israeli settlers in thirty-three settlements established by Israel in occupied territory,[387] and 20,000 Syrians, mostly Druze.

Syria tried to retake the Golan Heights during the 1973 Middle East war. Despite inflicting heavy losses on Israeli forces, the surprise assault was thwarted. Both countries signed an armistice in 1974 and a UN Disengagement Observer Force (UNDOF) has been in place on the ceasefire line since 1974. Israel unilaterally annexed the Golan Heights in 1981. The move was not recognized internationally. Lebanon claims the Shebaa Farms area.

Israeli officials have argued that the Heights, which overlook northern Israel and southern Syria, provide a vantage point for monitoring Syrian movements, and that the topography provides a natural buffer against Syria. Israel also obtains a third of its domestic water supply from the occupied area, which feeds into the Jordan River. Israeli settlements in the area use the fertile volcanic soil to cultivate vineyards and orchards and to raise cattle.

[384] See, e.g., International Court of Justice, *Wall* Advisory Opinion, 2004, §106. See also European Court of Human Rights, *Cyprus v Turkey*, Judgment, 10 May 2001, §77.

[385] Syria voted against while Israel voted in favour of the adoption of the ATT by the UN General Assembly on 2 April 2013.

[386] Unless otherwise stated, this section is based on 'Golan Heights Profile', *BBC*, 10 February 2015, at: <http://www.bbc.com/news/world-middle-east-14724842>.

[387] The UN Secretary-General also reported 'ongoing exploitation by Israel of natural resources in the occupied Syrian Golan, including gas, oil, wind and water'. Report of the Secretary-General, 'Israeli settlements in the Occupied Palestinian Territory, including East Jerusalem, and in the occupied Syrian Golan', A/HRC/25/28, 12 February 2014.

Syria wants to secure the return of the Golan Heights as part of any peace deal. During peace talks brokered by the United States in 1999–2000 Israeli Prime Minister Ehud Barak had offered to return most of the Golan to Syria. But the main sticking point during the 1999 talks is also likely to bedevil any future discussions. Syria wants a full Israeli withdrawal to the pre-1967 border. This would give Damascus control of the eastern shore of the Sea of Galilee—Israel's main source of fresh water. Israel wishes to retain control of Galilee and says the border is located a few hundred metres to the east of the shore.

PARTIES TO THE CONFLICT

The parties to the conflict were Israel and Syria.

Israel is estimated to have 176,500 active frontline military personnel and a further 445,000 in reserve.[388] Syria has been estimated to have 178,000 active frontline military personnel and a further 570,000 in reserve,[389] although a different source suggested in September 2013 that active personnel stood at 125,000 of whom 80,000 were considered to be loyal.[390] In addition to a huge array of conventional weaponry held by both States, Israel possesses nuclear and chemical weapons[391] while Syria possesses chemical weapons, which are in the process of being destroyed.[392] However, Syrian forces have also dropped locally manufactured 'barrel bombs' that released chlorine gas.[393]

[388] 'Israel Military Strength', *Globalfirepower.com*, last updated on 27 March 2014, at: <http://www.globalfirepower.com/country-military-strength-detail.asp?country_id=israel>. The Israel Defence Forces' mission is 'To defend the existence, territorial integrity and sovereignty of the state of Israel. To protect the inhabitants of Israel and to combat all forms of terrorism which threaten the daily life', <http://www.idfblog.com/about-the-idf/idf-code-of-ethics/>.

[389] 'Syria Military Strength', *Globalfirepower.com*, last updated on 27 March 2014, at: <http://www.globalfirepower.com/country-military-strength-detail.asp?country_id=syria>.

[390] Kechechian, J., 'What is Syrian Arab Army Military Capability?', *Gulf News*, 8 September 2013, at: <http://gulfnews.com/news/region/syria/what-is-syrian-arab-army-military-capability-1.1228699>.

[391] See, e.g., Fiske, G., 'Avraham Burg Panned for Breaking "Nuclear Ambiguity"', *Times of Israel*, 8 December 2013, at: <http://www.timesofisrael.com/avraham-burg-panned-for-breaking-nuclear-ambiguity/>.

[392] In late April 2014, the Organisation for the Prohibition of Chemical Weapons (OPCW) reported that the OPCW-UN Joint Mission had removed and destroyed a total of 92.5% of chemical weapons material in country covered by the Mission. The date of 30 June 2014 had been set as the deadline for completion of the disposal of Syria's chemical weapons. OPCW, '92.5% of Syria's chemical weapons material removed or destroyed in-country', Press release, The Hague, 22 April 2014, at: <http://opcw.unmissions.org/AboutOPCWUNJointMission/tabid/54/ctl/Details/mid/651/ItemID/305/Default.asp>.

[393] 'Syria: Strong Evidence Government Used Chemicals as a Weapon', Human Rights Watch, 13 May 2014, at: <http://www.hrw.org/news/2014/05/13/syria-strong-evidence-government-used-chemicals-weapon>.

CASUALTIES

In the Golan Heights the UN recorded a number of casualties, mainly in incidents connected with fighting between Syrian armed forces and Syrian opposition armed groups as well as attacks involving Israeli forces. Small-arms fire, heavy weapons, and mortar rounds apparently fired by Syrian forces and Syrian armed opposition groups repeatedly struck UNDOF observation points and vehicles, injuring several peacekeepers, and Syrian opposition armed groups looted evacuated UN observation posts.[394] On 27 August, members of the Nusra Front, a Syrian opposition armed group, besieged two UN observation posts and attacked another, and captured and temporarily detained forty-five UN peacekeepers before releasing them in September; the UN evacuated its personnel to Israeli-held territory.[395] In December, armed groups used stolen UNDOF vehicles for military purposes, including an attack in Dar'a.[396]

The UN reported that Israeli forces fired artillery rounds containing phosphorus near a UN observation post on 18 March, preventing peacekeepers from observing subsequent fighting; artillery rounds and airstrikes by Israeli forces on 18 and 19 March killed two members of the Syrian armed forces and wounded seventeen others, according to Syrian authorities, while four Israeli soldiers were wounded by an explosive device.[397] On 22 June, a missile that Syria said was fired by a Syrian opposition armed group killed a teenager and injured four others driving in a truck on an Israeli military road; subsequent attacks by Israeli ground and air forces reportedly killed ten Syrian forces.[398] Israeli airstrikes responding to a Syrian rocket that hit the Golan on 15 July reportedly killed two Syrian security guards and two women.[399]

[394] 'Report of the Secretary-General on the United Nations Disengagement Observer Force for the period from 4 December 2013 to 10 March 2014', S/2014/199, 18 March 2014, <http://www.un.org/en/ga/search/view_doc.asp?symbol=S/2014/199>; and 'Report of the Secretary-General on the United Nations Disengagement Observer Force for the period from 29 May to 3 September 2014', S/2015/655, 12 September 2014, <http://www.un.org/en/ga/search/view_doc.asp?symbol=S/2014/665>.

[395] 'Report of the Secretary-General on the United Nations Disengagement Observer Force for the period from 29 May to 3 September 2014', S/2015/655, 12 September 2014; and 'Report of the Secretary-General on the United Nations Disengagement Observer Force for the period from 4 September to 19 November 2014', S/2014/859, 3 December 2014, <http://www.un.org/en/ga/search/view_doc.asp?symbol=S/2014/859>.

[396] 'Report of the Secretary-General on the United Nations Disengagement Observer Force for the period from 20 November 2014 to 3 March 2015', S/2015/177, 13 March 2015, <http://www.un.org/ga/search/view_doc.asp?symbol=S/2015/177>.

[397] 'Report of the Secretary-General on the United Nations Disengagement Observer Force for the period from 11 March to 28 May 2014', S/2014/401, 10 June 2014, <http://www.un.org/en/ga/search/view_doc.asp?symbol=S/2014/401>.

[398] 'Report of the Secretary-General on the United Nations Disengagement Observer Force for the period from 29 May to 3 September 2014', S/2015/655, 12 September 2014, <http://www.un.org/en/ga/search/view_doc.asp?symbol=S/2014/665>; 'Israeli strikes kill ten members of Syrian army: monitoring group', Reuters, 23 July 2014, <http://www.reuters.com/article/2014/06/23/us-israel-syria-border-idUSKBN0EY13O20140623>.

[399] 'Israel Warplanes Hit Syria's Golan, Killing Four: NGO', AFP, 15 July 2014, <http://news.yahoo.com/israel-warplanes-hit-syrias-golan-killing-four-ngo-104700364.html>.

The UN reported multiple 'heavy clashes between the Syrian armed forces and armed members of the opposition' in the area throughout the year, including the use of 'barrel bombs' by Syrian forces, and repeatedly observed decapitated bodies and severed heads, apparently Syrian forces killed by members of an armed Syrian opposition group.[400]

WAR CRIMES ALLEGATIONS, INVESTIGATIONS, AND PROSECUTIONS

Neither Israel nor Syria is a State party to the 1998 Rome Statute of the International Criminal Court (ICC). Syria is a signatory State to the Statute.

No allegations of war crimes are known to have been made against either Israeli or Syrian military personnel regarding any acts concerning the Golan Heights in 2014.

[400] 'Report of the Secretary-General on the United Nations Disengagement Observer Force for the period from 4 December 2013 to 10 March 2014', S/2014/199, 18 March 2014; and 'Report of the Secretary-General on the United Nations Disengagement Observer Force for the period from 11 March to 28 May 2014', S/2014/401, 10 June 2014.

Military occupation of Western Sahara by Morocco in 2014

KEY CASUALTY DATA FOR 2014

Killed (April 2014–April 2015):	4	(Source: UN Secretary-General)
Injured (April 2013–April 2014):	6	(Source: UN Secretary-General)
Estimated injuries from protest:	At least 231	(Source: Media)

CLASSIFICATION OF THE CONFLICT

Morocco and the Frente Popular para la Liberación de Saguia el-Hamra y de Rió de Oro (Polisario Front) were engaged in an international armed conflict in 2014 by virtue of Morocco's continued military occupation of Western Sahara. Western Sahara is not universally recognized as a State and is not an Observer State within the United Nations (UN) although the Sahrawi Arab Democratic Republic has been a member of the African Union since 1984.

SUMMARY OF APPLICABLE INTERNATIONAL LAW

Both parties to the conflict were bound by customary and conventional international humanitarian law and human rights law, including customary international humanitarian law (IHL) rules of distinction, proportionality, and precautions in attacks; the obligation not to recruit and use children as soldiers; and by the duty to respect and protect fundamental human rights. This includes the duty to respect the rights to life and to freedom from torture or other forms of cruel, inhuman, or degrading treatment or punishment.

The law of military occupation is set out in the 1907 Hague Regulations (Articles 42–56), the 1949 Geneva Convention IV, the 1977 Additional Protocol I, and customary international law. Morocco is party to the four 1949 Geneva Conventions and to the 1977 Additional Protocol I. It is also party to the 1966 International Covenant on Civil and Political Rights and the 1966 International Covenant on Economic, Social and Cultural Rights. The Sahrawi Arab Democratic Republic is party to none of these instruments, but is however a State party to the 1981 African Charter on Human and People's Rights.

The underpinning of the law of military occupation is that it is a temporary situation, which lasts until a political agreement is reached. During this period, the Occupying Power does not enjoy sovereign rights over the territories it occupies and local law that was applicable prior to the occupation remains in force. At the same time, the Occupying Power is responsible for administering the local life of the population under its control, maintaining it as it was prior to the occupation as closely as possible, and for providing security (Article 43 of the Hague Regulations).

The Sahrawi Arab Democratic Republic is bound by customary international human rights law and by the provisions of the African Charter of Human and People's Rights. In addition, international human rights law is binding on Morocco extraterritorially in the territories it occupies.[401]

Neither Morocco nor the Sahrawi Arab Democratic Republic is a State party to the 1997 Anti-Personnel Mine Ban Convention or the 2008 Convention on Cluster Munitions.[402] Neither is a party or signatory to the 2013 Arms Trade Treaty (ATT).[403]

HISTORY OF THE CONFLICT[404]

The status of the Western Sahara remains unresolved. Morocco annexed the territory in 1975, and a guerrilla war with Algerian-backed pro-independence forces ended in 1991. UN efforts have so far failed to break the political deadlock. The Polisario Front was set up on 10 May 1973. In a 1979 Resolution, the United Nations General Assembly noted that the Polisario Front was the representative of the people of Western Sahara.[405]. Some 100,000 refugees still live in Polisario's camps in Algeria. In February 1976, Polisario declared the establishment of the Sahrawi Arab Democratic Republic. The current President of the Republic, Mohamed Abdelaziz, was elected Secretary-General of Polisario in August 1976.

In October 1975, the International Court of Justice (ICJ) rejected territorial claims by Morocco and Mauritania.[406] The court recognized the Saharawi's right to self-determination and Spain agreed to organize a referendum. But in November 1975,

[401] See, e.g., International Court of Justice (ICJ), *Wall* Advisory Opinion, 2004, §106. See also European Court of Human Rights, *Cyprus v Turkey*, Judgment, 10 May 2001, §77.

[402] The Polisario Front is a signatory of the Geneva Call Deed of Commitment for Adherence to a Total Ban on Anti-Personnel Mines and for Cooperation in Mine Action.

[403] Morocco voted in favour of the adoption of the ATT by the UN General Assembly on 2 April 2013.

[404] Unless otherwise stated, this section is based on 'Western Sahara Profile', *BBC*, 7 January 2014, at: <http://www.bbc.co.uk/news/world-africa-14115273>.

[405] UNGA Resolution 34/37, adopted on 21 November 1979, para. 7.

[406] ICJ, *Western Sahara*, Advisory Opinion, 16 October 1975, at: <http://www.icj-cij.org/docket/files/61/6195.pdf>.

Moroccan King Hassan II ordered a 'Green March' of more than 300,000 Moroccans into the territory. Spain backed down and negotiated a settlement with Morocco and Mauritania, known as the Madrid Agreement. Signed on 14 November 1975, the deal partitioned the region. Morocco acquired two-thirds in the north and Mauritania the remaining third. Spain agreed to end colonial rule. Under international law, the Madrid agreements are not considered valid since, by virtue of the principle of self-determination, Spain could not transfer sovereignty over Western Sahara to Morocco without consulting the people of Western Sahara.[407]

In August 1978, one month after a coup, a new Mauritanian Government signed a peace deal with Polisario and renounced all territorial claims. Morocco moved to occupy areas allocated to Mauritania. Algeria in turn allowed refugees to settle in its southern town of Tindouf, where Polisario still has its main base.

In April 1991, the UN established MINURSO, the UN Mission for a Referendum in Western Sahara. Its mandate was to implement a peace plan outlined in a 1990 Security Council resolution. In September 1991, a UN-brokered ceasefire was declared. The peace plan provided for a transition period, leading to a referendum in January 1992. Western Saharans would choose between independence and integration with Morocco. While the ceasefire held, the mission was never fully deployed and nor was the transition period ever completed. A key sticking point was an 'identification process', to decide who was eligible to vote. Identification was to be based on a census carried out by Spain in 1973. Polisario wanted to rule out Moroccans who settled in Western Sahara after the Green March.

In a new bid to break the deadlock, UN Envoy James Baker submitted a 'Framework Agreement', known as the Third Way, in June 2001. It provided for autonomy for Saharawi's under Moroccan sovereignty, a referendum after a four-year transition period, and voting rights for Moroccan settlers resident in Western Sahara for over a year. This formula was rejected by Polisario and Algeria. Then in July 2003, the UN adopted a compromise resolution proposing that Western Sahara become a semi-autonomous region of Morocco for a transition period of up to five years. A referendum would then take place on independence, semi-autonomy, or integration with Morocco.

[407] As noted by Hans Corell, the then UN legal Counsel: 'On 14 November 1975, a Declaration of Principles on Western Sahara was concluded in Madrid between Spain, Morocco and Mauritania ("the Madrid Agreement"), whereby the powers and responsibilities of Spain, as the administering Power of the Territory, were transferred to a temporary tripartite administration. The Madrid Agreement did not transfer sovereignty over the Territory, nor did it confer upon any of the signatories the status of an administering Power, a status which Spain alone could not have unilaterally transferred. The transfer of administrative authority over the Territory to Morocco and Mauritania in 1975 did not affect the international status of Western Sahara as a Non-Self-Governing Territory', see Letter dated 29 January 2002 from the Under-Secretary-General for Legal Affairs, the Legal Counsel, addressed to the President of the Security Council, para. 6, available at: <http://www.havc.se/res/SelectedMaterial/20020129legalopinionwesternsahara.pdf>.

Polisario signalled its readiness to accept, but Morocco rejected the plan, citing security concerns. Envoy James Baker resigned in June 2004 and the UN process remains deadlocked. Talks resumed between Morocco and the Polisario Front in March 2008 in New York, with Mauritania and Algeria also attending. They made no progress. In November 2010, several people were killed in violent clashes between Moroccan security forces and protesters near the capital Laayoune, shortly before UN-mediated talks on the future of the territory were due to open in New York.

On 22 April 2013, a senior official from the Polisario Front warned that failure by the UN to let peacekeepers monitor human rights in Western Sahara could push the region toward armed conflict.[408] A few days later, the UN Security Council adopted Resolution 2099 in which it extended the mandate of MINURSO until 30 April 2014.[409]

In February and June 2014, periodic violent clashes took place in Laayoune between Moroccan forces and Saharawi's, calling for freedom, self-determination, and extension of MINURSO prerogatives to include human rights monitoring in Western Sahara.

In April 2014, the mandate of the MINURSO was renewed until April 2015, but without including a human rights monitoring component.[410]

Meanwhile, the deep chasm between the parties' positions remains. In a 6 November 2014 speech celebrating the anniversary of the 1975 'Green March', King Mohammed strongly reiterated Morocco's position on the issue of Western Sahara, reaffirming that 'Morocco's sovereignty over its entire territory is effective, inalienable and non-negotiable'.[411]

The mandate of the MINURSO was once again renewed until April 2016, albeit still without a human rights component.[412] The Government of Morocco and the Office of the High Commissioner for Human Rights however agreed the OHCHR would carry out a mission to Morocco and Western Sahara from 12 to 18 April 2015, while OHCHR also agreed with the Government of Algeria, as the host country, and the Polisario Front to visit the refugee camps near Tindouf from 4 to 10 May 2015.[413]

[408] Irish, J., 'U.N. failure boosts Western Sahara conflict risk: Polisario', *Reuters*, 22 April 2013, at: <http://www.reuters.com/article/2013/04/22/us-france-westernsahara-idUSBRE93L13D20130422>.

[409] UN Security Council Resolution 2099 (2013), §1. See also Reuters, <http://uk.reuters.com/article/2014/04/29/uk-westernsahara-un-idUKKBN0DF1UW20140429>.

[410] Security Council Resolution 2152 (2014); Charbonneau, L., 'U.N. renews Western Sahara mission, but without rights monitors', *Reuters*, 29 April 2014, at: <http://uk.reuters.com/article/2014/04/29/uk-westernsahara-un-idUKKBN0DF1UW20140429>.

[411] Security Council Report, Western Sahara, April 2015 Forecast, 31 March 2015, at: <http://www.securitycouncilreport.org/monthly-forecast/2015-04/expected_council_action_in_april.php>.

[412] Security Council Resolution 2218 (2015).

[413] Report of the Secretary-General on the situation concerning Western Sahara, 10 April 2015, S/2015/246, para. 54.

PARTIES TO THE CONFLICT

The parties to the conflict are Morocco and the Polisario Front.

Morocco is estimated to have some 195,000 active frontline military personnel and a further 150,000 in reserve.[414] The Polisario Front operates as the armed forces of the Sahrawi Arab Democratic Republic. At the height of its strength in the 1980s the Polisario Front consisted of approximately 15,000 personnel.[415] Its strength today is not known.

CASUALTIES

The overall number of casualties in Western Sahara in 2014 was not monitored or reported. On renewing the mandate of the UN Mission for the Referendum in Western Sahara (MINURSO), the mandate of the UN peacekeeping mission was not expanded to include human rights monitoring.[416]

MINURSO did however monitor and report casualties of landmines and explosive remnants of war (ERW) in Western Sahara. MINURSO reported that, between April 2014 and April 2015 six incidents causing casualties occurred in occupied Western Sahara, three people were killed (two civilians and one soldier) and six injured (three civilians and three soldiers).[417] Between April 2013 and April 2014, one person was killed and eighteen people injured by landmines and ERW.[418]

A political prisoner on hunger strike, who was reported to have been injured by Moroccan authorities while in prisons during 2014, died in a military hospital in Dakhla, in occupied Western Sahara on 27 September 2014. It was claimed that he was treated with negligence prior to death and did not receive adequate medical treatment.[419]

[414] 'Morocco Military Strength', *Globalfirepower.com*, last updated on 27 March 2014, at: <http://www.globalfirepower.com/country-military-strength-detail.asp?country_id=morocco>.

[415] Study of Terrorism and Responses to Terrorism, 'Terrorist Organization Profile: Polisario Front', START, at: <http://www.start.umd.edu/tops/terrorist_organization_profile.asp?id=4205>.

[416] For example: Security Council Report, 'April 2015 Monthly Forecast: Western Sahara', <http://www.securitycouncilreport.org/monthly-forecast/2015-04/expected_council_action_in_april.php?print=true>.

[417] UN Security Council, 'Report of the Secretary-General on the situation concerning Western Sahara', S/2015/246, 10 April 2015, para. 30, <http://www.un.org/ga/search/view_doc.asp?symbol=S/2015/246>.

[418] This was a decrease from the thirty-six landmine/ERW casualties identified between April 2012 and April 2013.UN Security Council, 'Report of the Secretary-General on the situation concerning Western Sahara', S/2014/258, 10 April 2014, para. 43.

[419] Stevenson, T., 'Torture and Death: A Political Prisoner's Story in Western Sahara', 2 October 2014 (last updated: 13 February 2015), <http://www.middleeasteye.net/in-depth/features/western-sahara-607501312#sthash.aLoZWicX.sPjh41oM.dpuf>,<http://www.middleeasteye.net/in-depth/features/western-sahara-607501312>.

It was reported that Moroccan authorities often forcibly dispersed protests in Western Sahara.[420] This often resulted in numerous civilians being injured, for example: on 15 January more than forty-six Sahrawi protesters were injured in El Aiun;[421] eighty protesters were injured in El Aiun on 15 March;[422] at least ten protesters were injured at the beginning of April;[423] more than seventy protesters were injured on 30 April;[424] fifteen protesters were injured on 6 June;[425] ten protesters were injured on 15 November.[426]

WAR CRIMES ALLEGATIONS, INVESTIGATIONS, AND PROSECUTIONS

Neither Morocco nor the Sahrawi Arab Democratic Republic is a State party to the 1998 Rome Statute of the International Criminal Court. Morocco has signed the Statute.

[420] Human Rights Watch, 'Annual Report 2015: Morocco/Western Sahara', <http://www.hrw.org/world-report/2015/country-chapters/moroccowestern-sahara>.

[421] 'Dozen Saharawis Injured in Occupied El Aaiun', 16 January 2014, <http://www.spsrasd.info/en/content/dozen-saharawis-injured-occupied-el-aaiun>.

[422] 'Peaceful Demonstrations "Violently" Repressed in Occupied Territories of Western Sahara', 16 March 2014, <http://www.spsrasd.info/en/content/peaceful-demonstrations-violently-repressed-occupied-territories-western-sahara>; 'Western Sahara: Moroccan police crack down on protests in occupied cities', Algeria Press Service, 16 March 2014, <http://www.aps.dz/en/world/1587-western-sahara-moroccan-police-crack-down-on-protests-in-occupied-cities>.

[423] 'Tens of Saharawis Injured in Moroccan Forces' Intervention', 2 April 2014, <http://www.spsrasd.info/en/content/tens-saharawis-injured-moroccan-forces'-intervention>.

[424] 'More than 70 Injured in Peaceful Demonstration in Occupied El Aaiun', 1 May 2014, <http://www.spsrasd.info/en/content/more-70-injured-peaceful-demonstration-occupied-el-aaiun>.

[425] 'Peaceful Demonstration "Brutally" Repressed in Occupied City of El Aaiun', 10 June 2014, <http://www.spsrasd.info/en/content/peaceful-demonstration-'brutally'-repressed-occupied-city-el-aaiun>; and 'Repression of Peaceful Demonstration Leaves Casualties in Occupied El Aaiun', 7 June 2014, <http://www.spsrasd.info/en/content/repression-peaceful-demonstration-leaves-casualties-occupied-el-aaiun>.

[426] 'Repression in El Aaiun: At Least 10 People Seriously Injured', 16 November 2014, <http://www.spsrasd.info/en/content/repression-el-aaiun-least-10-people-seriously-injured>.

Armed conflict in Afghanistan in 2014

KEY CASUALTY DATA FOR 2014

Civilians killed:	3,699	(Source: UNAMA)
Civilians injured:	6,849	(Source: UNAMA)
Civilian women killed:	298	(Source: UNAMA)
Civilian women injured:	611	(Source: UNAMA)
Children killed:	714	(Source: UNAMA)
Children injured:	1,760	(Source: UNAMA)
Afghan military and police killed:	4,634	(Source: Agence France-Presse)
ISAF military killed:	75	(Source: iCasualties.org)
US military killed:	55	(Source: iCasualties.org)
US military injured:	450	(Source: US military)
Private contractor killed:	101	(Source: US Department of Labor)
Taliban and insurgents killed:	5,377	(Source: Afghan MoI, Afghan MoD, Media)
Taliban and insurgents injured:	2,392	(Source: Afghan MoI, Afghan MoD, Media)

CLASSIFICATION OF THE CONFLICTS

Afghanistan was involved in a non-international armed conflict (NIAC) in 2014 in which the armed forces of the Government of Afghanistan and a coalition of States operating under the umbrella of the North Atlantic Treaty Organization (NATO)-led International Security Assistance Force (ISAF)[427] are fighting against the Taliban.[428] This conflict meets the threshold for the application of the 1977 Additional Protocol

[427] ISAF contributors were the following States in 2013: Albania, Armenia, Australia, Austria, Azerbaijan, Bahrain, Belgium, Bosnia and Herzegovina, Bulgaria, Canada, Croatia, Czech Republic, Denmark, El Salvador, Estonia, Finland, France, the former Yugoslav Republic of Macedonia, Georgia, Germany, Greece, Hungary, Iceland, Ireland, Italy, Jordan, the Republic of Korea, Latvia, Lithuania, Luxembourg, Malaysia, Mongolia, Montenegro, the Netherlands, New Zealand, Norway, Poland, Portugal, Romania, Singapore, Slovakia, Slovenia, Spain, Sweden, Tonga, Turkey, Ukraine, the United Arab Emirates, the United Kingdom (UK), and the United States of America (USA). All Singaporean troops were brought home from Afghanistan in mid-2013 after a six-year deployment while Canadian military involvement in Afghanistan formally ended in March 2014. See generally: <http://www.isaf.nato.int/troop-numbers-and-contributions/index.php>.

[428] The term Quetta Shura is a composite taken from the name of town in Pakistan to where Mullah Omar relocated in 2001 and the Supreme Shura that governed Afghanistan in the early 1990s. See, e.g., Dressler, J. and Forsberg, C., 'The Quetta Shura Taliban in Southern Afghanistan', Backgrounder, Institute for the Study of War, September 2009, p. 1, at: <http://www.understandingwar.org/report/quetta-shura-taliban-southern-afghanistan>.

II. In addition, there are separate NIACs with, respectively, the Haqqani Network and Hezb-e-Islami led by Gulbudin.

The position of the United Nations Assistance Mission in Afghanistan (UNAMA) in 2014 was that:

> the armed conflict in Afghanistan is a non-international armed conflict between the Government of Afghanistan and its armed forces supported by international military forces ... and non-State armed groups ... including the Taliban, Haqqani Network, Hezb-e-Islami and others ...[429]

The War Report does not consider the Islamic Movement of Uzbekistan, Islamic Jihad Union, Lashkari Tayyiba, Jaysh Muhammed, or other armed groups to have been parties to NIACs in Afghanistan in 2014. According to the Office of the Prosecutor of the International Criminal Court (ICC):

> Today ISAF, the US forces and the Government of Afghanistan (GOA) forces combat armed groups which mainly include the Taliban, the Haqqani Network, and Hezb-e-Islami Gulbuddin (HIG).[430]

SUMMARY OF APPLICABLE INTERNATIONAL LAW

All parties to the conflicts were bound by customary international humanitarian law (IHL) and human rights law, including customary IHL rules of distinction, proportionality, and precautions in attacks; the obligations of humane treatment, as set out in Common Article 3 to the 1949 Geneva Conventions; the obligation not to recruit and use children as soldiers; and by the duty to respect and protect fundamental human rights. This includes the duty to respect the rights to life and to freedom from torture or other forms of cruel, inhuman, or degrading treatment or punishment.

Afghanistan is party to the four 1949 Geneva Conventions and the 1977 Additional Protocol II. Afghanistan is also party to the 1966 International Covenant on Civil and Political Rights and the 1966 International Covenant on Economic, Social and Cultural Rights.

Afghanistan is party to the 1997 Anti-Personnel Mine Ban Convention. Under Article 5 of the Convention, and in accordance with a ten-year extension granted in 2012, Afghanistan is required to destroy all antipersonnel mines in mined areas

[429] UNAMA, 'Afghanistan, Mid-Year Report 2014, Protection of Civilians in Armed Conflict', Kabul, July 2014, p. 60, at: <http://unama.unmissions.org/LinkClick.aspx?fileticket=m_XyrUQDKZg%3d&tabid=12254&mid=15756&language=en-US>.

[430] Office of the Prosecutor of the ICC, 'Report on Preliminary Examination Activities 2014', December 2014, §78, at: <http://www.icc-cpi.int/iccdocs/otp/OTP-Pre-Exam-2014.pdf>.

under its jurisdiction or control as soon as possible, but not later than 31 March 2023. Afghanistan is also party to the 2008 Convention on Cluster Munitions, but is neither a party nor signatory to the 2013 Arms Trade Treaty (ATT).[431]

In addition, all other States parties to the 1977 Additional Protocol II operating militarily in Afghanistan are bound by that instrument in the NIAC with the Quetta Shura Taliban.[432] Other States parties to the two 1966 Covenants operating militarily in Afghanistan are also bound extraterritorially by those instruments as they are by customary international human rights law.[433]

HISTORY OF THE CONFLICT

Afghanistan has been engulfed in almost perpetual conflict since the Soviet invasion in 1979. Ongoing non-international armed conflict has now been raging for several years.

Emerging as a force in the 1990s, the Taliban—originally a group of Islamic scholars drawn from the largest ethnic group in Afghanistan, the Pashtuns—controlled about 90% of the country until late 2001, although the Taliban were recognized as the legitimate government of 'the Islamic Emirate of Afghanistan' by only three States (Pakistan, Saudi Arabia, and the United Arab Emirates). Following the attacks by Al-Qaeda in the United States of America (USA) on 11 September 2001, which were masterminded by Osama Bin Laden from Afghanistan, the Taliban refused US demands that they hand over Bin Laden. This led to the United States initiating an aerial bombing campaign in October 2001, enabling opposition groups, namely the Northern Alliance, to drive the Taliban from power. But since the fall of the regime in 2001, Taliban and other Mujahedeen fighters have re-grouped into a number of different armed groups (see below). The Taliban are conducting a widespread insurgency, particularly in the south

[431] Afghanistan voted in favour of the adoption of the ATT by the UN General Assembly on 2 April 2013.

[432] The 1977 Additional Protocol II was ratified by Afghanistan in 2009. In addition to binding Afghanistan, the Protocol is also arguably applicable to each ISAF member State that has adhered to the Protocol and which is a party to the conflict with the Taliban. This is because 1977 Additional Protocol II applies to 'all armed conflicts' which are not covered by Art. 1 of the 1977 Additional Protocol I and which take place 'in the territory of' a State party 'between its armed forces and dissident armed forces or other organized armed groups which, under responsible command, exercise such control over a part of its territory as to enable them to carry out sustained and concerted military operations and to implement this Protocol'. This applies the provisions of the Protocol to the relevant armed conflict as a whole, not merely to the armed forces of the State on whose territory the conflict is ongoing as well as the dissident armed forces or other organized armed groups fighting against those government armed forces. The United States is not a State party to the Protocol. The provisions of the Protocol that are reflected in customary IHL are binding on all States.

[433] The United States has been reluctant to accept extraterritorial application of the Covenant on Civil and Political Rights, based on its reading of Art. 2(1) of the Covenant as requiring both domestic presence of any given person within US territory and US jurisdiction over that person.

east and east of the country, while the Afghan Government has struggled to extend its effective authority beyond the capital.[434]

UNAMA documented 10,548 civilian casualties (3,699 deaths and 6,849 injured) in 2014, marking a 25% increase in civilian deaths, a 21% increase in injuries for an overall increase of 22% in civilian casualties compared to 2013 (see Casualties section below). In fact, 2014 was the deadliest year in the conflict since UNAMA began systematically recording civilian casualties in 2009.[435] UNAMA attributed three-quarters of civilian deaths and injuries to 'anti-government elements' (UNAMA's term for armed opposition groups),[436] one in nine to 'pro-government forces',[437] and one in ten to ground engagements between the two.[438]

The conflict has seen continued use of Coalition airpower, including drone strikes, against suspected Taliban and other fighters not only in Afghanistan but also in neighbouring Pakistan. Taliban and other armed groups have made widespread use of improvised explosive devices (IEDs) that have inflicted a heavy toll on Coalition troops and among the civilian population. However, whereas in previous years, the majority of civilians were killed and injured by IEDs, in 2014, more civilians were found to have been killed and injured in ground engagement and crossfire between anti-government armed groups and pro-government forces. [439]

Despite attempts, during 2013, to initiate a peace process, instability persisted throughout the year.[440] In January 2014, a Taliban suicide squad hit a restaurant

[434] See, e.g., International Crisis Group (ICG), 'Afghanistan: The Long, Hard Road to the 2014 Transition', *Asia Report No. 236*, 8 October 2012, p. 16, at: <http://www.crisisgroup.org/en/regions/asia/south-asia/afghanistan.aspx>.

[435] UNAMA, 'Afghanistan: Annual Report on the Protection of Civilians 2014', Kabul, February 2015, p. 1, at: <http://www.unama.unmissions.org/Portals/UNAMA/human%20rights/2015/2014-Annual-Report-on-Protection-of-Civilians-Final.pdf>.

[436] 'Anti-Government Elements' encompass all individuals and armed groups involved in armed conflict with or armed opposition against the Government of Afghanistan and/or international military forces. They include those who identify as 'Taliban' as well as individuals and non-State organized armed groups taking a direct part in hostilities and assuming a variety of labels including the Haqqani Network, Hezb-e-Islami, Islamic Movement of Uzbekistan, Islamic Jihad Union, Lashkari Tayyiba, Jaysh Muhammed, and other militia and armed groups pursuing political, ideological or economic objectives including armed criminal groups directly engaged in hostile acts on behalf a party to the conflict.' Ibid., p. 2.

[437] UNAMA's term for: Afghan Government National Security Forces and other forces and groups that act in military or paramilitary counterinsurgency operations and are directly or indirectly under the control of the Government of Afghanistan. These forces include, but are not limited to, the Afghan National Army, the Afghan National Police, Afghan Border Police, Afghan Local Police, the National Directorate of Security (Afghanistan's state intelligence service), and other pro-government local defence forces. Ibid., p. 2.

[438] Ibid., p. 2. [439] Ibid., p. 2.

[440] In May 2013, Taliban leader Mullah Agha Jan Mutasim called on the United States to support a peace process and warned of renewed instability if the parties did not agree on reconciliation talks; See the Afghanistan profile in the *War Report 2013*, edited by Casey-Maslen, S., Oxford University Press, 2014.

in Kabul's diplomatic quarter. This represented the worst attack on foreign civilians since 2001, causing twenty-one foreign victims including the head of the International Monetary Fund in Afghanistan.'[441]

In February, the campaign for the presidential election started, accompanied by a dramatic rise in attacks by the Taliban. Suicide bomb attacks generally intensified throughout 2014 with some estimates reporting that the number of attacks in Kabul alone has more than doubled compared to 2013.[442] The first round of the presidential election (April 2014) ended up being inconclusive, leading to a second round between Abdullah Abdullah, former Minister of Foreign Affairs, and Ashraf Ghani, former Minister of Finance. The run-off resulted in a political impasse, requiring an international audit to address allegations regarding fraudulent practices in the voting process. In early September, after five month of political stalemate, US Secretary of State John Kerry brokered a power-sharing agreement to form a national unity government led by Ashraf Ghani as president and Abdullah Abdullah as chief executive.[443]

On 30 September 2014, newly elected Afghan President Ashraf Ghani agrees to sign the Bilateral Security Agreement (BSA) according to which some 10,000 US troops can remain in Afghanistan after the conclusion of the ISAF mission at the end of 2014. Their mission would be to 'enhance the ability of Afghanistan to deter internal and external threats against its sovereignty'. That includes 'advising, training, equipping and sustaining' Afghanistan's National Defence and Security Forces and those of the National Security Directorate, the intelligence agency of the Afghan Government. The agreement also specifies that 'unless otherwise mutually agreed, United States forces shall not conduct combat operations in Afghanistan'.[444]

December 2014 and January 2015 were marked by an unprecedented wave of Taliban attacks in Kabul, including against foreigner civilians, and raised concerns over the viability of the new government.[445] As of March 2015, Afghan National Security Forces (ANSF), which since 1 January assumes formal responsibility for all combat missions, [446] launched major operation against insurgents in southern Helmand province.

[441] 'Taliban Suicide Attackers Kill at Least 21 at Kabul Restaurant', *The Guardian*, 18 January 2014, <http://www.theguardian.com/world/2014/jan/17/taliban-suicide-attack-kabul-restaurant>.

[442] 'Increased Violence and Instability in Afghanistan', Council on Foreign Relations, March 2015, <http://www.cfr.org/global/global-conflict-tracker/p32137#!/?marker=3>.

[443] 'Afghan Presidential Rivals Finally Agree on Power-Sharing Deal', *The New York Times*, 20 September 2014, at: <http://www.nytimes.com/2014/09/21/world/asia/afghan-presidential-election.html?_r=0>.

[444] 'Explainer: Key Points in U.S.-Afghan Bilateral Security Agreement', *Radio Free Europe/Radio Liberty*, 30 September 2014, at: <http://www.rferl.org/content/explainer-bsa-afghan-us-security-agreement-bsa/26613884.html>.

[445] Crisis Watch Database, at: <http://www.crisisgroup.org/en/publication-type/crisiswatch/crisiswatch-database.aspx?CountryIDs=%7bA860153E-CDC9-46DC-8FF7-7C03740C2DCF%7d&StartDate=20140901&EndDate=20150313>.

[446] ISAF Mission in Afghanistan, 13 January 2013, at: <http://www.nato.int/cps/en/natolive/topics_69366.htm>.

PARTIES TO THE CONFLICTS

The parties to the NIACs were the Afghan Government forces and ISAF against the Quetta Shura Taliban and, in separate conflicts, against the Haqqani Network and Hezb-e-Islami, respectively.

Afghan forces

Afghanistan was estimated to have 200,000 active frontline military personnel as of March 2015.[447] According to *The Independent* newspaper, the ANP were considered by the United Kingdom's Foreign and Commonwealth Office (FCO) to be 'endemically corrupt' and riven with problems including nepotism and drug abuse.[448] A confidential FCO report obtained by the British newspaper on the performance of the police observed in October: 'Unless radical change is introduced to improve the actual and perceived integrity and legitimacy of officers … the organisation will continue to provide an ineffective and tainted service to citizens … for decades to come.'[449]

As noted above, at the end of 2014, when the ISAF mission was concluded, Afghan forces assumed full security responsibility in the country.

International Security Assistance Force

ISAF was created following the Bonn Conference in December 2001. On 11 August 2003, NATO assumed leadership of the ISAF operation. The Alliance became responsible for the command, coordination, and planning of the force, including the provision of a force commander and headquarters on the ground in Afghanistan. ISAF's mandate was initially limited to providing security in and around Kabul. In October 2003, the UN extended ISAF's mandate to cover the whole of Afghanistan,[450] paving the way for an expansion of the mission across the country.

During the year 2014, ISAF stated that it has been 'assisting the Afghan authorities in maintaining security and in developing new Afghan National Security Forces (ANSF) … As transition progresses and ANSF take on their security responsibilities, ISAF will complete its shift from a combat to a supporting role. ISAF will continue to train, advise,

[447] 'Afghanistan Military Strength', *Globalfirepower.com*, last updated on 17 February 2015, at: <http://www.globalfirepower.com/country-military-strength-detail.asp?country_id=afghanistan>.

[448] Brady, B., 'Taliban Preys on Afghanistan's Corrupt Police Force', *Independent*, 23 December 2012, at: <http://www.independent.co.uk/news/world/asia/taliban-preys-on-afghanistans-corrupt-police-force-8430111.html>.

[449] Ibid.

[450] UN Security Council Resolution 1510.

and assist the ANSF until transition completion at the end of 2014. ISAF continued to provide combat support until the end of 2014'.[451]

Thirteen years after the beginning of its deployment, ISAF's mission formally ended on 18 December 2014. A new, smaller non-combat mission 'Resolute Support' was launched on 1 January 2015 to provide further training, advice, and assistance to the Afghan security forces and institutions. Some 12,000 personnel from both NATO and partner nations are deployed in support of the mission. Currently, fourteen partner countries are contributing to Resolute Support.[452]

Taliban

The largest non-State armed group fighting against the Afghan regime, the Taliban in Afghanistan (Quetta Shura Taliban) were led by Mullah Omar, an erstwhile village clergyman who lost his right eye fighting Soviet forces in the 1980s. The Taliban are thought by some to be only about 20,000 strong, but this is belied by the losses they reportedly sustained in 2013 alone, amounting to as many as 12,000 (killed, injured, and captured). His death was announced by the Taliban in July 2015. Source: The Guardian, 'Taliban officially announce death of Mullah Omar', 30 July 2015, http://www.theguardian.com/world/2015/jul/30/taliban-officially-announces-death-of-mullah-omar.

The Taliban have launched increasingly deadly attacks in 2014. Nearly 3,200 Afghan civilians were killed in the conflict between the rebel group and the army, and more than 4,600 Afghan army and police died in Taliban attacks.[453] During the summer, Taliban fighters were reported to be gaining ground in several strategic areas near Kabul, inflicting heavy losses to the Afghan forces. They were able to conduct successful military operations beyond their traditional strongholds in the rural south and are now said to dominate territory in strategic provinces like Kapisa and Nangarhar around Kabul.[454]

At the end of December 2014, the Taliban insurgents declared the 'defeat' of the United States and its allies in the thirteen-year-old war, a day after the coalition officially marked the end of its combat mission. Taliban spokesman Zabihullah Mujahid, in a statement issued on 29 December, declared that 'ISAF rolled up its flag in an atmosphere of failure and disappointment without having achieved anything substantial or tangible'.[455]

[451] NATO, 'International Security Assistance Force (ISAF): Key Facts and Figures', 1 April 2014, at: <http://www.isaf.nato.int/images/media/PDFs/2104-04-01%20isaf%20placemat-final.pdf>.

[452] NATO, Resolute Support Mission in Afghanistan, 27 February 2015, <http://www.nato.int/cps/en/natohq/topics_113694.htm>.

[453] 'Taliban Declare "Defeat" of U.S., Allies in Afghanistan', Reuters, 29 December 2014, at: <http://www.reuters.com/article/2014/12/29/us-afghanistan-war-idUSKBN0K70UC20141229>.

[454] 'Taliban Making Military Gains in Afghanistan', *The New York Times*, 26 July 2014, <http://www.nytimes.com/2014/07/27/world/asia/taliban-making-military-gains-in-afghanistan.html?_r=0>.

[455] 'Taliban Declare "Defeat" of U.S., Allies in Afghanistan', Reuters.

Hezb-e-Islami

Hezb-e-Islami Gulbuddin (HIG) is led by Gulbuddin Hekmatyar, a rebel military commander during the 1980s conflict with the Soviets and one of the key figures in the civil war that followed the Soviet withdrawal. He was Prime Minister of Afghanistan from 1993 to 1994 and again briefly in 1996. HIG has been active in eastern Afghanistan.[456]

In January 2014, Hezb-e-Islami vowed to continue its armed resistance while foreign troops remained in Afghanistan. The group, the second largest after the Taliban, had previously denied it would take part in the 2014 presidential and provincial council elections due to the presence of foreign troops in the country. But the chief of the group's political wing, Dr Ghairat Baheer, told a media outlet they had decided to participate in the elections.[457]

In July 2014, Gulbuddin Hekmatyar released a video on the group's website, where he called on fighters loyal to him not to engage in operations that harmed civilians, civil government employees such as teachers, judges, prayer leaders, engineers, doctors, and journalists. He also added that those violating Islamic teachings and torturing civilians would be expelled from party ranks.[458] In a later statement, the Hezb-i-Islami's leader criticized the signing of the Bilateral Security Agreement (BSA) between the Afghan Government and the United States allowing thousands of American troops to stay in the country after the conclusion of ISAF's mission at the end of 2014. Gulbadin Hekmatyar declared that 'everyone should recognize the fact that a continued foreign presence means nothing but war', undermining efforts at restoring peace in the country.[459]

Haqqani Network

A former anti-Soviet group in the 1980s and led by one of the most prominent families in Afghanistan's Khost, the Haqqani Network commands far fewer fighters than the Taliban, with whom they are closely allied,[460] but has been described by US military leaders as 'the most resilient enemy network out there'.[461] The network operates along

[456] See, e.g., 'Hizb-i-Islami—Gulbuddin (HIG) (Afghanistan)' in *Jane's World Insurgency and Terrorism*, Jane's Information Group, 1 February 2012.

[457] Kakar, J. H., 'HIA Vows to Continue Armed Resistance', *Pajhwok Afghan News*, Kabul, 16 January 2014, at: <http://www.pajhwok.com/en/2014/01/16/hia-vows-continue-armed-resistance>.

[458] 'Spare Civilians, Hekmatyar Directs Followers', *Pajhwok Afghan News*, 26 July 2014, <http://www.pajhwok.com/en/2014/07/26/spare-civilians-hekmatyar-directs-followers>.

[459] 'Hekmatyar calls for intra-Afghan dialogue', *Pajhwok Afghan News*, 2 October 2014, at: <http://www.pajhwok.com/en/2014/10/02/hekmatyar-calls-intra-afghan-dialogue>.

[460] See, e.g., Roggio, B., 2013, 'Afghan Taliban Condemn the Killing of Nasiruddin Haqqani', *Long War Journal*, 12 November 2013, at: <http://www.longwarjournal.org/archives/2013/11/afghan_taliban_conde.php>.

[461] See, e.g., Dressler, J. A., 2010, 'The Haqqani Network: From Pakistan to Afghanistan', Institute for the Study of War, October 2010; and Dressler, 'The Haqqani Network: A Strategic Threat'.

the border with Pakistan, where the escalating campaign against them, including drone strikes, has been targeting their fighters. At the end of April 2014, the US Department of State claimed that the Haqqani Network and the Afghan Taliban continued to find 'safe haven' in Pakistani territory. In its annual global report on terrorism submitted to the US Congress it accused Pakistani authorities of not taking 'significant military or law enforcement action against these groups'.[462] The report further claimed that a number of aggressive and coordinated attacks in Afghanistan were planned and launched from safe havens in Pakistan.[463]

After a relatively calm period during the Afghan presidential election, in July 2014, the Haqqani network resumed its activities by launching two high-profile attacks: the explosion of a huge car bomb at a market in Urgun (Paktika Province) killing at least seventy-two persons and a day after, the firing of volleys of grenades on the Kabul airport by suicide attackers. According to local and tribal officials, the insurgents are benefiting from a larger margin of action as American units began leaving border outposts. In recent months, there has been an increase in the flow of militants into the Afghan side of the border regions and this will probably continue as the Pakistani Army remains primarily focused on the militant stronghold of North Waziristan. The remote, mostly unpoliced areas of the Paktika province, provides the Haqqani network with access to central Afghanistan and also links to a corridor directed to Kabul.[464]

On 16 October 2014, two senior leaders of the Haqqani network were said to have been captured by the Afghan intelligence services during an operation in eastern Khost Province.[465]

CASUALTIES

Based on available information there were at least 23,481 (13,765 killed and 9,716 injured) casualties of conflict in Afghanistan in 2014.[466]

[462] Reuters, 'Afghan Taliban, Haqqani Network continue to find safe haven in Pakistan, claims US report', *Express Tribune*, 1 May 2014, at: <http://tribune.com.pk/story/702681/afghan-taliban-haqqani-network-continue-to-find-safe-haven-in-pakistan-claims-us-report/>.

[463] Ibid.

[464] 'Terror Group Back on the Offensive in Afghanistan', *The New York Times*, 17 July 2014, <http://www.nytimes.com/2014/07/18/world/asia/kabul-airport-comes-under-attack-from-militants.html?ref=topics>.

[465] '2 Haqqani Militant Leaders Are Captured, Afghan Officials Say', *The New York Times*, 16 October 2014, at: <http://www.nytimes.com/2014/10/17/world/asia/haqqani-leaders-arrested-afghanistan-khost.html?_r=0>.

[466] This total does not include 101 defence contractor deaths in 2014.

The United Nations Assistance Mission in Afghanistan (UNAMA) recorded 10,548 civilian casualties of conflict in Afghanistan in 2014 (3,699 people were killed and another 6,849 injured). This marked the highest number of annual civilian casualties UNAMA started systematic recording in 2009 and an increase in annual recorded civilian casualties of 22% from 2013.[467]

The rise in civilian casualties was attributed primarily to increased ground engagements, causing 54% more civilian casualties compared to 2013. Greater use of high explosive weapons systems including mortars, rockets, and grenades in populated civilian areas during ground engagements, made them the principal cause of civilian casualties in 2014.[468]

UNAMA attributed 72% of all civilian casualties to Anti-Government Elements, 14% to Pro-Government Forces (of which 2% were caused by international military forces and 12% to Afghan national security forces). The remainder of casualties occurred in ground engagements in which the civilian casualty could not be attributed to a specific party, due to explosive remnants of war and in cross-border fire. [469]

In 2014, UNAMA documented the highest number of civilian child casualties (2,474) in the five years since recording began. Annual child casualties increased by 40% compared to 2013. Ground engagements were the main cause of child casualties resulting in 1,064 children killed and injured, almost 65% more than recorded in the previous year.[470] Child casualties increased from 2013 due to IEDs (21%) and explosive remnants of war (ERW) (14%).[471] UNAMA reported 422 civilian casualties of ERW, a 20% increase compared to 2013. The majority of casualties of ERW (327) were children.[472] In 2014, UNAMA recorded 909 civilian women casualties, a 21% increase from 2013. This was also the highest number of women casualties registered by UNAMA since 2009.[473]

In November 2014 it was reported that 4,634 Afghan national security forces, Afghan National Army, and Afghan National Police personnel been had killed in the conflict during 2014, compared to 4,350 killed for all of 2013.[474] Fatality rates for Afghan National Army and Afghan National Police were reported to be 30% higher 'in the 2014 fighting season' than in the same period of the previous year.[475] It was also estimated

[467] UNAMA, 'Afghanistan: Annual Report on the Protection of Civilians 2013', Kabul, February 2014, p. 1. In 2013, UNAMA documented 8,637 civilian casualties (2,969 deaths and 5,668 injured). In 2014 UNAMA reported 8,615 civilian casualties recorded for 2013, also reflecting an increase in the total number of civilian casualties (14%) as compared to 2012.

[468] Ibid., p. 2. [469] Ibid., p. 2. [470] Ibid., p. 7. [471] Ibid., p. 7.

[472] Ibid., pp. 7 and 19. [473] Ibid., p. 12.

[474] Reported in a statement attributed to US Lieutenant General Joseph Anderson 'Mounting Death Toll for Afghan Troops is Unsustainable in Long Term: US General', Agence France-Presse, 6 November 2014, <http://www.straitstimes.com/news/asia/south-asia/story/mounting-death-toll-afghan-troops-unsustainable-long-term-us-general-2014>. Brookings reported 4,380 Afghan National Army and Afghan National Police personnel Fatalities in 2014 'through late October'. Ian Livingston and Michael O'Hanlon, 'Brookings Afghanistan Index', 10 February 2015, p. 13.

[475] 'Afghan Army Death Rate Spikes 30 Percent', 3 October 2014, <http://bigstory.ap.org/article/f0c5b2ad711b4362834f7be41adabb03/afghan-army-death-rate-spikes-30-percent> (accessed 31 March 2015).

that some 5,000 members of the Afghan National Army, Afghan National Police, and Afghan Local Police (village self-defence units) were killed in 2014, with approximately 3,200 police killed, making up the majority of national forces casualties.[476]

The online database iCasualties reported fifty-five US military deaths, of a total of seventy-five ISAF[477] coalition fatalities for 2014.[478] The US military reported fifty-six deaths for 2014, including eighteen that were either not caused by hostilities or the classification was pending verification.[479] Two of the US military fatalities were women, neither of those deaths were caused by hostilities. The fifty-six recorded US military fatalities represented a significant decrease from the 132 US military deaths reported in 2013 and marked a massive reduction from a peak of 499 annual US military deaths recorded in 2010.[480]

Four ISAF coalition and associated troops were killed and another twenty-six injured in four attacks by Afghan security forces—so-called 'green on blue' attacks—in 2014 (compared to fourteen killed and twenty-nine injured in 2013). These totals included casualties among military contractors.[481]

In 2014, 101 employees of private contractors[482] were registered as killed in Afghanistan. This represented a continuing decrease from 165 in 2013, 221 in 2012, and 386 reported in 2011.[483] Private contractors are not counted as part of the ISAF or Operation Enduring Force coalition data.[484]

[476] Casualty figures attributed to Karl Åke Roghe, Head of the European Union Police Mission in Afghanistan (EUPOL) in 'Afghan Police Lead Insurgent Fight at High Cost', (Associated Press) *New York Times*, 28 December 2014, <http://www.nytimes.com/aponline/2014/12/28/world/asia/ap-as-afghanistan-police.html?_r=0>.

[477] On 31 December 2014, the ISAF mission ended. The NATO-led Resolute Support mission, replacing the ISAF mission, began on 1 January 2015, <http://www.rs.nato.int/mission.html>.

[478] iCasualties, <http://icasualties.org/oef/>.

[479] Statistical analysis of data from the Defence Casualties Analysis System: Conflict Casualties Operation Enduring Freedom, <http://www.dmdc.osd.mil/dcas/pages/casualties_oef.xhtml>.

[480] Statistical analysis of data from Defence Casualties Analysis System: Conflict Casualties Operation Enduring Freedom, <http://www.dmdc.osd.mil/dcas/pages/casualties_oef.xhtml>. Operation Enduring Freedom ended in December 2014. See US Department of Defense, 'Obama, Hagel Mark End of Operation Enduring Freedom', 28 December 2014, <http://www.defense.gov/news/newsarticle.aspx?adbid=550008151940931585&adbpl=tw&adbpr=66369181&cid=social_20141230_38091397&id=123887>.

[481] Roggio, B. and Lundquist, L., 'Green-on-Blue Attacks in Afghanistan: The Data', 23 August 2012, data last updated on 30 January 2015, <http://www.longwarjournal.org/archives/2012/08/green-on-blue_attack.php>.

[482] These reports do not constitute the complete or official casualty statistics of civilian contractor injuries and deaths.

[483] Figures calculated according to publicly available data from the United States Department of Labor. The 2014 data was measured as the changes in number of total contractor deaths recorded since 2001: 1,582 in 2014, 1,481 in 2013; 1,316, in 2012; 1,095 in 2011; and 709 in 2010, <http://www.dol.gov/owcp/dlhwc/dbaallnation.htm>, <http://www.dol.gov/owcp/dlhwc/dbaallnation12-31-12.htm>; <http://www.dol.gov/owcp/dlhwc/dbaallnation12-31-11.htm>; and <http://www.dol.gov/owcp/dlhwc/dbaallnation12-31-10.htm>. The numbers correspond to new claims during the period. The reports are not presented as official statistics and they do not provide information on the nationality of employees.

[484] Email from the NATO operations team, Brussels, 15 April 2014.

UNAMA did not disaggregate civilian casualties from UAV/RPA (drone) strikes in 2014 reporting of casualties from aerial operations because 'comparison of different data sets would not be accurate'. This was reportedly due to improvements in 2014 in its capacity to identify the type of 'aerial platform' used. Aerial operations by international military forces caused 162 of the civilian casualties (104 killed and fifty-eight injured) reported in 2014. The decrease in civilian casualties, by 13% compared to those from aerial operations in 2013, was indicated to have been influenced by less frequent use of air strikes by ISAF and efforts by the international forces to reduce civilian harm.[485]

The Afghan Ministry of Interior Affairs (MoIA) and Ministry of Defence (MoD) in reporting Taliban and insurgent casualties daily news updates made up the majority of those recorded for 2014.[486] Of the total 7,769 Taliban and insurgent casualties recorded, 2,901 killed and 1,191 injured were from regular MoIA update reports on operations and 2,124 killed and 1,089 injured from similar MoD reports. Another 269 killed and 107 injured Taliban and insurgents were recorded from media reporting in March and April 2014, mostly from articles citing MoIA and MoD press releases that were no longer online. Another eighty-three killed and five injured Taliban and insurgents from drone strikes were recorded from media reporting.

The total of annual Taliban and insurgent casualties is not believed to capture the extent of those killed and injured in 2014, and the actual number is likely much higher. Most Taliban casualties reported by the MoIA occurred in joint operations with the Afghan National Army (MoD). Due to many Taliban and insurgent casualty reports in the same time period from both the MoIA and MoD that included some of the same areas of operation, many reports of casualties were included in the annual totals in order to avoid duplication. In addition, casualties from ISAF forces, including aerial operations, were rarely reported.

Reporting by the MoIA and the MoD frequently did not differentiate between the group allegiances of insurgent casualties, or consistently disaggregate Taliban casualties in operations from other Afghan militant groups including the Haqqani Network and Hezb-e-Islami.

UNAMA reporting does not distinguish between different 'Anti-Government Elements' in casualty reporting the cause of civilian casualties This term is used by UNAMA to include those groups who identify as 'Taliban' as well as Haqqani Network, Hezb-e-Islami, Islamic Movement of Uzbekistan, Islamic Jihad Union, Lashkari Tayyiba, Jaysh Muhammed, and armed criminal groups. However, media reporting sometimes identified casualties as being the result of activities of a specific group. For example, in

[485] UNAMA, 'Afghanistan: Annual Report on the Protection of Civilians 2013', Kabul, February 2014, p. 93.

[486] Afghan Ministry of Interior Affairs, <http://moi.gov.af/en>; and Afghan Ministry of Defense, <http://mod.gov.af/en>.

relation to a suicide attack on US military contractors in which Afghan civilians were injured a spokesman for Hezb-e-Islami claiming responsibility also said the attacker 'was looking for an opportunity to target the convoy, and not harm civilians'.[487] An attack on a volleyball game, attributed to the Haqqani Network, in November 2014 killed over sixty civilians and injured more than fifty.[488]

In 2014, UNAMA documented fifty-one civilian casualties (thirty-four killed and seventeen injured) in seventeen attacks in which Anti-Government Elements deliberately targeted humanitarian deminers. The Taliban publicly claimed responsibility for two of the attacks.[489]

The International Federation of Journalists (IFJ), recorded nine journalists killed in Afghanistan in 2014 as a result of targeted killings, bomb attacks, and cross-fire incidents.[490] The Committee to Protect Journalists (CPJ) recorded three journalists killed with the motive confirmed and two killed with unconfirmed motive.[491]

DISPLACED

At the end of 2014 there were at least 805,400 internally displaced persons (IDPs) in Afghanistan, with 156,200 civilians newly displaced by armed conflict in 2014.[492] This represented an 8% increase from 2013, which had already increased by a quarter from 2012.[493]

WAR CRIMES ALLEGATIONS, INVESTIGATIONS, AND PROSECUTIONS

Afghanistan has been a State party to the 1998 Rome Statute of the International Criminal Court (ICC Statute) since February 2003. The ICC has jurisdiction over Rome

[487] 'Kabul Car Bombing Claimed by Hezb-I-Islami Group', *Wall Street Journal*, 10 February 2014, <http://www.wsj.com/articles/SB10001424052702304558804579374440332879648>.

[488] Ibrahimkhail, S., 'Haqqani Network Behind Paktika Bombing that Killed 61: NDS', *Tolo News*, 24 November 2014, <http://www.tolonews.com/en/afghanistan/17228-haqqani-network-behind-paktika-bombing-that-killed-61-nds>.

[489] 'Afghanistan: Annual Report on the Protection of Civilians 2013', Kabul, February 2014, p. 23. Mine Action Programme of Afghanistan (MAPA) reported sixty-one casualties among its personnel (thirty-four killed and another twenty-seven injured) in thirty-seven 'security incidents'. MAPA, 'Year of Loss and Tragedy for the Mine Action Programme of Afghanistan', <http://www.macca.org.af/macca/blog/a-year-of-loss-and-tragedy-for-the-mine-action-programme-of-afghanistan>.

[490] 'Trail of Violence: Journalists & Media Staff Killed in 2014, FJ-Belgium 2015', p. 7, <http://ifj-safety.org/assets/docs/089/245/5bef559-ba3edf5.pdf>.

[491] CPJ, '27 Journalists Killed in Afghanistan since 1992/Motive Confirmed,' <https://cpj.org/killed/asia/afghanistan>.

[492] Internal Displacement Monitoring Center (IDMC), 'Global Overview 2015', May 2015, p. 82.

[493] Figures provided to UNAMA by UNHCR's IDP Task Force, 28 January 2015. UNAMA, 'Afghanistan: Annual Report on the Protection of Civilians 2013', Kabul, February 2014, p. 9; and UNAMA, 'Afghanistan: Annual Report on the Protection of Civilians 2013', Kabul, February 2014, p. 12.

Statute crimes committed on the territory of Afghanistan or by its nationals since 1 May 2003.

The Office of the Prosecutor (OTP) received 102 communications under Article 15 of the ICC Statute between 1 June 2006 and 30 September 2012. The preliminary examination of the situation was made public in 2007:

> The Office of the Prosecutor has been examining alleged crimes within the jurisdiction of the Court, including torture; attacks on humanitarian targets and the UN; attacks on protected objects; and recruitment of child soldiers.[494]

As of March 2015, the Office found that the information available provides a reasonable basis to believe that war crimes and crimes against humanity were and continue to be committed in Afghanistan.[495]

Referring to Taliban attacks, it reported that:

> The Taliban policy of attacking particular categories of civilians forms the subject of a first potential case ... The particular categories of civilians that the Taliban leadership have identified as legitimate targets include labourers involved in public-interest construction work, interpreters, truck drivers, UN personnel, NGO employees, journalists, doctors and other health workers, teachers and students, tribal and religious elders, judicial authorities, election workers, and individuals with a high public profile such as members of parliament, governors and mullahs, district governors, provincial council members, government employees at all levels, as well as individuals who joined the Afghanistan Peace and Reintegration Program and their relatives. A second potential case against the Taliban relates to attacks on girls' education (i.e., female students, teachers and their schools). The Taliban allegedly target female students and girls' schools pursuant to their policy that girls should stop attending school past puberty.[496]

With respect to pro-government forces, the Office reported that 'there is information available that the war crimes of torture, and outrages upon personal dignity, in particular humiliating and degrading treatment, have allegedly been committed by members of pro-government forces'.[497]

The report also noted that the Office had been assessing available information relating to the alleged abuse of detainees by international forces within the temporal jurisdiction of the Court.

> In particular, the alleged torture or ill-treatment of conflict-related detainees by US armed forces in Afghanistan in the period 2003-8 forms another potential case identified by the Office. In accordance with the Presidential Directive of 7 February 2002, Taliban detainees were denied the status of prisoner of war under article 4 of the Third Geneva Convention but were

494 ICC, Report on Preliminary Examination Activities 2014, at: <http://www.icc-cpi.int/iccdocs/otp/OTP-Pre-Exam-2014.pdf>.

495 Office of the Prosecutor, 'Report on Preliminary Examination Activities 2014', §80.

496 Ibid., §§85–86.

497 Ibid., §91.

required to be treated humanely. In this context, the information available suggests that between May 2003 and June 2004, members of the US military in Afghanistan used so-called 'enhanced interrogation techniques' against conflict-related detainees in an effort to improve the level of actionable intelligence obtained from interrogations. The development and implementation of such techniques is documented *inter alia* in declassified US Government documents released to the public, including Department of Defense reports as well as the US Senate Armed Services Committee's inquiry. These reports describe interrogation techniques approved for use as including food deprivation, deprivation of clothing, environmental manipulation, sleep adjustment, use of individual fears, use of stress positions, sensory deprivation (deprivation of light and sound), and sensory overstimulation ... Certain of the enhanced interrogation techniques apparently approved by US senior commanders in Afghanistan in the period from February 2003 through June 2004, could, depending on the severity and duration of their use, amount to cruel treatment, torture or outrages upon personal dignity as defined under international jurisprudence. In addition, there is information available that interrogators allegedly committed abuses that were outside the scope of any approved techniques, such as severe beating, especially beating on the soles of the feet, suspension by the wrists, and threats to shoot or kill.[498]

In *The War Report* 2013, it was noted that the Office of the Prosecutor (OTP) had analysed information about the conscription, enlistment, and use of children to participate actively in hostilities by Afghan Government forces.[499] In their 2014 report, the OTP concluded that the Office had been unable to verify the seriousness of the information received and that these allegations remained insufficiently substantiated to provide a reasonable basis to believe that war crimes have been committed. [500]

Finally, the OTP reported that:

Having analysed the information available on civilian casualties caused by air strikes, 'night raids' and escalation-of-force incidents attributed to pro-government forces, the Office assesses that the information available does not provide a reasonable basis to believe that the war crime of intentionally directing attacks against the civilian population as such or against individual civilians not taking direct part in hostilities pursuant to article 8(2)(e)(i) has been committed. In relation to allegations over proportionality, the Office recalls that the Rome Statute does not contain a provision for the war crime of intentionally launching a disproportionate attack in the context of a non-international armed conflict.[501]

[498] Ibid., §§94–95.

[499] See Afghanistan profile, *The War Report 2013*, edited by Casey-Maslen, S., Oxford University Press, 2014, p. 101.

[500] Office of the Prosecutor, 'Report on Preliminary Examination Activities 2014', §97.

[501] Ibid. §97.

Armed conflict in the Central African Republic in 2014

KEY CASUALTY DATA FOR 2014

Killed:	2,852	(Source: ACLED)
Injured:	942	(Source: ACLED)
Civilians killed:	1,896	(Source: ACLED/ASWD/Media)
Civilians injured:	688	(Source: ACLED/ASWD/Media)
Civilian women killed:	25	(Source: ACLED)
Children killed:	20	(Source: ACLED)
Humanitarian workers killed:	19	(Source: ACLED/AWSD)
Journalist killed:	1	(Source: ACLED)
Anti-Balaka killed:	121	(Source: ACLED)
Anti-Balaka injured:	11	(Source: ACLED)
Ex-Séléka killed:	191	(Source: ACLED)
Ex-Séléka injured:	34	(Source: ACLED)
Governmental forces/MISCA/MINUSCA killed:	31	(Source: ACLED)
Governmental forces/MISCA/MINUSCA injured:	15	(Source: ACLED)
Unknown combatants killed:	267	(Source: ACLED)
Unknown combatants injured:	159	(Source: ACLED)
Unknown killed:	346	(Source: ACLED)
Unknown injured:	35	(Source: ACLED)

CLASSIFICATION OF THE CONFLICT

From March 2014 onwards, the Central African Republic (CAR) was involved in a non-international armed conflict (NIAC) in which the ex-Séléka coalition of rebel forces were fighting against the 'anti-Balaka' armed group. Clashes were also reported between the armed forces of CAR (FACA) in coalition with the MINUSCA forces and the anti-Balaka. These clashes however do not meet the threshold of intensity to be qualified as a NIAC.

The ICRC in March 2014 classified the situation in 2014 as a non-international armed conflict between the ex-Séléka and the anti-Balaka.[502]

[502] ICRC 'Central African Republic: Continuing deep concern for civilians', Operational update, 7 March 2014, at: <http://www.icrc.org/eng/resources/documents/update/2014/03-07-central-african-republic-rising-violence.htm>.

SUMMARY OF APPLICABLE INTERNATIONAL LAW

All parties to the conflicts were bound by customary international humanitarian law (IHL) and human rights law, including customary IHL rules of distinction, proportionality, and precautions in attacks; the obligations of humane treatment, as set out in Common Article 3 to the 1949 Geneva Conventions; the obligation not to recruit and use children as soldiers; and by the duty to respect and protect fundamental human rights. This includes the duty to respect the rights to life and to freedom from torture or other forms of cruel, inhuman, or degrading treatment or punishment.

CAR is party to the four 1949 Geneva Conventions and the 1977 Additional Protocol II. CAR is also party to the 1966 International Covenant on Civil and Political Rights and the 1966 International Covenant on Economic, Social and Cultural Rights.

CAR is party to the 1997 Anti-Personnel Mine Ban Convention and has signed but not yet ratified the 2008 Convention on Cluster Munitions, but is neither a party nor signatory to the 2013 Arms Trade Treaty (ATT).[503]

HISTORY OF THE CONFLICT[504]

The CAR has been unstable since its independence from France in 1960. Illegal weapons proliferate across the country, the legacy of years of unrest, which has displaced tens of thousands of people, many across the border into Chad.

Three main rebel groups have been operating in CAR over the last few decades: the Popular Army for the Restoration of Democracy (APRD), which operated in the north and northwest of the country; the Union of Democratic Forces for Unity (UFDR) in the north-east of the country; and the Democratic Front of the Central African People (Front démocratique du peuple centrafricain; FDPC).[505]

In the south-east of the country, the Central African Republic Armed Forces (FACA) together with the Ugandan People's Defence Force (UPDF) had been fighting members of the Ugandan armed group, the Lord's Resistance Army (LRA), who have been active in the CAR since February 2008.[506]

[503] CAR voted in favour of the adoption of the ATT by the UN General Assembly on 2 April 2013.

[504] Unless otherwise stated, this section is based on 'Central African Republic Profile', *BBC*, 25 February 2015, at: <http://www.bbc.com/news/world-africa-13150040>.

[505] 'Report of the Secretary-General on the situation in the Central African Republic and on the activities of the United Nations Integrated Peacebuilding Office in that country', UN doc. S/2011/739, 28 November 2011.

[506] Nyakairu, F., 'Uganda: Kony Crosses into Central African Republic', *The Monitor*, 16 March 2008, at: <http://allafrica.com/stories/200803160004.html>.

Some progress towards stabilizing the country was made between 2008 and 2012. In 2008, the UFDR and APRD signed the Libreville Comprehensive Peace Agreement (CPA) with Bozizé's Government committing, inter alia, to actively participate in the disarmament, demobilization, and reintegration (DDR) programme in the north-east of the country.[507] However, the last historic armed group, the Convention of Patriots for Justice and Peace (CPJP) has remained active, especially in the north of the country where it has been responsible for attacks against the FACA, as well as civilians.[508] On 12 June 2011, a peace agreement between the CPJP and the government was signed and no more fighting was reported.

In August 2012, the CPJP, signed a peace deal. In November, however, the new Séléka rebel alliance (see below) marched south taking town after town, capturing the capital in March 2013 and ousting President François Bozize, who fled to Cameroon. FACA army chiefs pledged allegiance to the country's self-proclaimed president, Michel Djotodia, as the former rebel leader consolidated control four days after his fighters seized the capital.[509]

Djotodia suspended the Constitution and dissolved parliament in a coup condemned internationally. On 19 July 2013, the African Union Peace and Security Council decided to authorize deployment of an 'African-led International Support Mission in the CAR' (MISCA).[510] On 26 July, President Djotodia announced the creation of a new Republican Army of Central Africa Republic (ARC), comprising the former armed forces and ex-Séléka members.[511]

In August, Djotodia was sworn in as CAR's interim president. At the same time, the United Nations (UN) Security Council warned that CAR posed a risk to regional stability. UN chief Ban Ki-moon said that CAR had suffered a 'total breakdown of law and order'.[512]

During the summer of 2013 until the end of the year, the situation in CAR continued to worsen. In September, Michel Djotodia officially 'disbanded' the Séléka.[513]

[507] Spittaels, S. and Hilgert, F., *Mapping Conflict Motives, Central African Republic*, International Peace Information Service (IPIS), 17 February 2009, p. 9, at: <http://www.ipisresearch.be/mapping_car.php>.

[508] 'Report of the Secretary-General on the situation in the Central African Republic and on the activities of the United Nations Integrated Peacebuilding Office in that country', UN doc. S/2011/739, 28 November 2011.

[509] Aboa, A., 'Central African Republic Army Chiefs Pledge Allegiance to Coup Leader', *Reuters*, Bangui, 28 March 2013, at: <http://www.reuters.com/article/2013/03/28/us-centralafrica-rebels-idUSBRE92R0F420130328>.

[510] Maasho, A., 'AU plans bigger peacekeeping force for Central African Republic', *Reuters*, Addis Ababa, 19 July 2013, at: <http://www.reuters.com/article/2013/07/19/centralafrica-au-idUSL6N0FP2NP20130719>.

[511] International Crisis Group (ICG), Crisis Watch Database: Central African Republic, 1 August 2013, available at: <http://www.crisisgroup.org/en/publication-type/crisiswatch/crisiswatch-database.aspx>.

[512] 'Central African Republic in Chaos, says UN chief Ban Ki-moon', *BBC News*, 10 August 2013, <http://www.bbc.com/news/world-africa-23644384>.

[513] 'CAR's Djotodia Dissolves Séléka Rebel Group', *France24*, at: <http://www.france24.com/en/20130913-centralafrican-republic-djotodia-dissolves-seleka-rebel-group/>, 14 September 2013.

Many 'ex-Séléka', however, continued to commit acts of violence. As explained by the UN Secretary-General, 'the ex-Séléka combatants, who are not under a unified command and control of the transitional authorities, continue to commit serious violations of human rights with total impunity'.[514]

In September 2013, the UN Human Rights Council adopted Resolution 24/34 in which it decided to appoint an Independent Expert, for a period of one year, to monitor the situation of human rights in CAR and to make recommendations concerning technical assistance and capacity-building human rights.[515] In October, the UN Security Council approved the deployment of a UN peacekeeping force to support African Union troops on the ground and French troops controlling the airport.[516]

By November 2013, 400,000 persons were internally displaced persons (IDPs), 1.1 million were food-insecure, and the Office of the UN High Commissioner for Refugees (UNHCR) had recorded 66,000 refugees.[517]

Not only did the level of violence increase, its nature also changed. Whereas the conflict of the beginning of 2013 was characterized by a fight between armed groups and governmental authorities for a change of political power, during the months that followed violence became more inter-communal and was targeted against civilians. In revenge for acts of violence committed by the ex-Séléka against Christian communities, a traditional militia group, known as the 'anti-Balaka' emerged, initiating a cycle of retaliatory violence between both armed elements. Meanwhile, State authorities largely ceased to function: 'the situation is further exacerbated by the near absence of State administration and services across the country. Most of the authorities have fled and their offices have been pillaged or occupied by ex-Séléka'.[518]

In December, with turmoil continuing and rival Muslim and Christian militia accused of killing hundreds of people, France increased its contingent of troops to 1,600 in a bid to disarm the militias.

On 5 December 2013, the UN Security Council, acting under Chapter VII of the UN Charter, determining that the situation in CAR constituted a threat to international peace and security, adopted Resolution 2127 underlying its concern at the risk that the new dynamic of violence could lead CAR 'into a countrywide religious and ethnic divide, with the potential to spiral into an uncontrollable situation, including serious crimes under international law in particular war crimes and crimes against humanity, with serious regional implications'[519] and requested the establishment of an international commission

[514] 'Report of the Secretary-General on the Central African Republic submitted pursuant to paragraph 22 of Security Council resolution 2121 (2013)', 15 November 2013, §5.

[515] UN Human Rights Council Resolution 24/34, 27 September 2013, §§13–14.

[516] UN Security Council Resolution 2121, 10 October 2013.

[517] 'Report of the Secretary-General on the Central African Republic submitted pursuant to paragraph 22 of Security Council resolution 2121 (2013)', §11.

[518] Ibid., §8.

[519] UN Security Council, Resolution 2127 (2013), 5 December 2013, S/RES/2127 (2013).

of inquiry to investigate reports of violations of international humanitarian law and international human rights law.

In January 2014, President Djotodia resigned over criticism that he had failed to stop sectarian violence. Catherine Samba-Panza took over as interim leader. In February, violence continued, with attacks on Muslims a major element.

In March, the UNSC Commission of Inquiry started its investigations into possible genocide, while the International Criminal Court Chief Prosecutor Fatou Bensouda initiated a preliminary investigation into the 'extreme brutality' and whether the situation would fall into the court's remit. [520]

On 2 April, the European Union formally launched a military mission (EUFOR-RCA), with deployment foreseen in June[521] and on 10 April, the UN Security Council authorized deployment of an 11,800-strong peacekeeping force, the UN Multidimensional Integrated Stabilization Mission in the Central African Republic (MINUSCA).[522]

Sectarian violence continued. In May, ex-Séléka rebels stormed a Catholic church compound in Bangui, killing at least thirty.[523] On 23 June, anti-Balaka forces killed eighteen members of the mostly Muslim village of Bambari. Several young ex-Séléka took revenge against this attack the same day by killing ten anti-Balaka. On 8 July, seventeen people were killed when ex-Séléka forces attacked a Catholic church in Bambari, believing that the church was supposedly sheltering anti-Balaka troops. [524]

On 12 July, Michel Djotodia was reinstated as the Head of 'ex-Séléka', and the group changed its name to 'The Popular Front for the Rebirth of Central African Republic'.[525]

After three days of talks, a ceasefire was signed on 24 July 2014 in Brazzaville, Republic of Congo. The ex-Séléka representative to the ceasefire was General Mohamed Moussa Dhaffane, and the anti-Balaka representative was Patrick Edouard Ngaissona. The talks were mediated by Congolese president Denis Sassou Nguesso. Dhaffane and the Séléka delegation had pushed for a formalization of the partition of the CAR with Muslims in the north and Christians in the south. However, this demand was dropped during the talks with Ngaissona and President Nguesso.[526]

[520] 'UN launches CAR probe to prevent genocide', *Al Jazeera*, 10 March 2014 at: <http://www.aljazeera.com/news/africa/2014/03/un-launches-car-probe-prevent-genocide-201431011522234885.html>.

[521] ICG, Crisis Watch Database: Central African Republic, 1 May 2014.

[522] UN Security Council Resolution 2149, adopted on 10 April 2014.

[523] 'Rebels Kill 30 in Church Raid in Central African Republic', *Associated Press*, 28 May 2014 at: <http://www.latimes.com/world/africa/la-fg-rebels-kill-30-central-african-republic-20140528-story.html>.

[524] '17 Killed at CAR Church Shielding Thousands of Christians', *Christian Post*, 8 July 2014 at: <http://www.christianpost.com/news/17-killed-at-car-church-shielding-thousands-of-christians-122942/>.

[525] 'Central African Republic: Ex-President Re-elected Head of Rebel Movement', *Associated Press*, 13 July 2014 at: <http://www.foxnews.com/world/2014/07/13/central-african-republic-ex-president-re-elected-head-rebel-movement/>.

[526] 'Central African Republic Factions Announce Ceasefire', *BBC*, 24 July 2014 at: <http://www.bbc.com/news/world-africa-28457599>.

On 25 July, ex-Séléka's military leader Joseph Zindeko rejected the ceasefire agreement and, instead, called for the partition of the CAR into separate Christian and Muslim states.[527] Officials in Mbrès stated that thirty-four people were killed by ex-Séléka fighters in Mbrès and neighbouring villages between 10 and 15 August.[528]

In November the split of ex-Séléka into three entities was confirmed, following the 26 October establishment of the 'Unité pour la Centrafrique' (UPC) composed of Al Khatim rebels and Ali Darass Fulani supporters. On 2 November the second faction, Nouredine Adam's Front Populaire pour la Renaissance en Centrafrique (FPRC) met in Kaga-Bandoro. The third faction mostly composed of Gula and ex-Union des Forces Démocratiques pour le Rassemblement (UFDR) fighters also gathered in Bria. All factions expressed willingness to participate in January national dialogue forum. On 11 November the International Contact Group met in Bangui and approved delay for presidential and legislative elections to August 2015.[529]

On 9 April 2015 ex-Séléka leader Djotodia and anti-Balaka leader Joachim Kokate signed a controversial ceasefire agreement in Nairobi. This agreement, however, has not been recognized by the CAR Government arguing it neither participated nor was it consulted regarding the talks.[530]

In late April, international media reported a leaked UN report on sexual abuse of children by French peacekeepers in CAR in 2014. The French authorities announced on 29 April that an investigation had been launched into the matter.[531]

On 28 April the UN Security Council renewed mandate of the MINUSCA until 30 April 2016.[532]

From 4 to 11 May 2015 the National Reconciliation Forum was held in Bangui where all the major parties, including the Séléka and anti-Balaka were present in week-long talks. There was an agreement signed between the government and armed groups to disarm and to postpone the national elections from August 2015, but the overall outcome of the forum remains unclear.[533]

527 'Central African Republic Rebel Chief Rejects Ceasefire', *BBC*, 25 July 2014 at: <http://www.bbc.com/news/world-africa-28487894>.

528 'Rebel Gunmen Kill 34 in Central African Republic: Officials', *Reuters*, 17 August 2014 at: <http://af.reuters.com/article/topNews/idAFKBN0GH08120140817>.

529 ICG 'Crisiswatch Database: CAR', 1 December 2014.

530 'CAR Rebel Factions Sign Ceasefire Agreement in Kenya', *Al Jazeera*, 9 April 2015 at: <http://www.aljazeera.com/news/2015/04/car-rebels-ceasefire-agreement-150408171923689.html>.

531 'France Launches Criminal Inquiry into Alleged Sex Abuse by Peacekeepers', *The Guardian*, 7 May 2015 at: <http://www.theguardian.com/world/2015/may/07/france-criminal-inquiry-alleged-sex-abuse-french-soldiers-un-central-african-republic>.

532 'UNSC Extends Mandates of Western Sahara, CAR missions', *Africa Leader*, 29 April 2015 at: <http://www.africaleader.com/index.php/sid/232384271>.

533 'CAR Government and Rebels Sign Peace Deal', *Al Jazeera*, 11 May 2015, at: <http://www.aljazeera.com/news/2015/05/150511051147641.html>; 'CAR Reconciliation Forum Calls for Poll Delay', *The Namibian*, 13 May 2015 at: <http://www.namibian.com.na/indexx.php?id=26601&page_type=story_detail>.

PARTIES TO THE CONFLICT

The parties to the conflict in CAR in 2014 were the ex-Séléka and anti-Balaka.

Ex-Séléka

Séléka is a coalition of armed groups (the word means 'alliance' in Sango) most of whom were signatories to the 2008 Libreville Comprehensive Peace Agreement with the Government. In September 2012, however, dissident factions of the main signatory groups largely from the north of the country, the Union of Democratic Forces for Unity, the Wa Kodro Salute Patriotic Convention, and the Convention of Patriots for Justice and Peace, banded together as Séléka.[534] The coalition numbered between 1,000 and 2,000 fighters, according to one expert at the Paris-based National Centre for Scientific Research.[535] In December 2012, the Séléka took control of several major towns in the CAR and advanced on the capital, Bangui, demanding that President François Bozizé step down after failing to implement the 9 May 2008 Libreville Comprehensive Peace Agreement. The leader of the Séléka, Michel Djotodia, proclaimed himself President of CAR on March 2013 and a few months later, officially 'disbanded' the group. Being ousted, Michel Djotodia was finally reinstated as its leader on 12 July 2014.[536]

Anti-Balaka

The anti-Balaka (meaning 'anti-machete') were formed during August 2013 and at best can be described as a combination of various militia groups with the majority of fighters being youths without any schooling, with some youths as young as ten. They are currently comprised, inter alia, of the Association of Central African Farmers (ACP), an anti-Séléka peasant movement, as well as the Front for the Return to the Constitutional Order in Central Africa (FROCCA). FROCCA is a militia made up of ex-army officers loyal to the former president as well as local vigilantes annoyed with ex-Séléka's continued violence.[537] The anti-Balaka were purportedly created by the former President Bozizé to fight banditry and include some soldiers who served under Bozizé in the Central African Armed Forces (FACA). The total number of personnel that belong to the anti-Balaka remains unknown.[538]

[534] Agence France-Presse, 'Seleka, Central Africa's motley rebel coalition', Bangui, 1 January 2013.

[535] Roland Marchal, a specialist in Central African conflicts, cited in ibid.

[536] 'Central Africa Republic's ousted leader back in charge of Seleka', *Reuters*, 12 July 2014, <http://www.reuters.com/article/2014/07/12/us-centralafrica-rebels-idUSKBN0FH0NL20140712>.

[537] Report of the Secretary-General on the Central African Republic submitted pursuant to paragraph 48 of Security Council resolution 2127 (2013), para. 5, 3 March 2014, S/2014/142.

[538] 'Anti-Balaka', Terrorism Research & Analysis Consortium at: <http://www.trackingterrorism.org/group/anti-balaka>.

CASUALTIES

In 2014, 3,794 casualties were identified in the CAR from War Report analysis of information contained in the Armed Conflict Location and Event Data Project (ACLED) database.[539] Of the total casualties identified 68% (2,584) were civilians. Many records do not report on the sex or age of the casualties and therefore the number of women (twenty-five) and child (twenty) casualties confirmed through disaggregation and analysis is low compared to overall casualty numbers. Although there were casualties recorded throughout 2014, almost half (49%) of all of the casualties identified in CAR (1,884) took place over the course of the months of January and February.

During 2014, ACLED recorded at least 354 violent incidents having led to casualties in CAR involving one or more of the parties. Clashes between ex-Séléka and anti-Balaka fighters amounted to 24% of those incidents. Most clashes occurred at the beginning of 2014, principally in January. However, upsurges of violence between those two groups continued to be recorded throughout the year, in particular in May, in July/August, and again in December. Even during clashes between armed groups, civilians accounted for at least 29% of recorded casualties. One Pakistan Army peacekeeper was killed and nineteen other peacekeepers were injured in a run of clashes between anti-Balaka and United Nations Mission for Stabilization in Central African Republic (MINUSCA) from October to December 2014.[540] Another peacekeeper died from malaria in October because 'ongoing aggressive demonstrations' held by the anti-Balaka prevented emergency medical evacuation.[541]

Most casualties throughout the year (2,584) identified through ACLED data were recorded as being attributed to violence targeting civilians, often based on religious or perceived religious affiliations. At least 1,178 civilian casualties were attributed to the anti-Balaka, while it was reported that the ex-Sélékas were responsible for similarly high numbers of civilian casualties, at least 1,117 during the year.

Prior to a ceasefire agreement signed on 23 July 2014,[542] there were at least 2,689 total conflict-related fatalities in CAR, including 1,424 civilian deaths.[543] These killings

[539] Raleigh, C. and Hegre, H., 2005. 'Introducing ACLED: An Armed Conflict Location and Event Dataset'. Paper presented to the conference on 'Disaggregating the Study of Civil War and Transnational Violence', University of California Institute of Global Conflict and Cooperation, San Diego, CA, 7–8 March.

[540] Based on War Report analysis of ACLED data.

[541] MINUSCA, 'In Funeral Ceremony MINUSCA Honors its Two Peacekeepers That Died Last Week in Bangui', Press release CP#019/2014, 13 October 2014.

[542] Releifweb, 'CAR armed groups sign ceasefire agreement', AFP.

[543] The UN Panel identified 2,424 civilian deaths from 5 December 2013 through April 2014. The International Federation of Human Rights (FIDH) also documented casualties from 5 December 2013, up to June 2014. FIDH determined that some 1,000 of these occurred in the month of December. ACLED identified 1,123 civilian deaths from 1 January to 23 July 2014. 'Letter dated 26 June 2014 from the Panel of

were mainly a result of attacks against civilians by both anti-Balaka militia and the ex-Séléka. A UN Panel of Experts on CAR found that in period to June about 60% of civilian deaths were a result of anti-Balaka attacks, with the remaining 40% as a result of ex-Séléka attacks. It also found that there was a 'significant underreporting of incidents'.[544]

Also internally displaced persons (IDPs) trying to flee an area or those having found shelter in camps or churches were regularly targeted and at least 162 casualties were identified in ACLED data.

In 2014, nine Humanitarian workers were killed and ten injured in CAR.[545] In May a French journalist was also killed in a violent exchange between anti-Balaka and ex-Séléka.[546] The Committee to Protect Journalists (CPJ) reported that this was the first recorded killing of a journalist in CAR since 1992.[547]

In 2014, at least 438,500 IDPs in CAR, with more than 172,000 new IDPs were reported. Some IDPs are thought to have returned in 2014, while others fled abroad.[548]

WAR CRIMES ALLEGATIONS, INVESTIGATIONS, AND PROSECUTIONS

CAR adhered to the 1998 Rome Statute of the International Criminal Court (ICC Statute) in October 2001. In accordance with the ICC Statute, the Court has jurisdiction over Rome Statute crimes committed on the territory of CAR or by its nationals.

On 22 May 2007, the ICC Office of the Prosecutor announced the decision to open an investigation in the CAR. The trial of Jean-Pierre Bemba Gombo, alleged President and Commander-in-chief of the Mouvement de libération du Congo (MLC), has been ongoing since 22 November 2010. He has been charged with two counts of crimes against

Experts on the Central African Republic established pursuant to Security Council resolution 2127 (2013) addressed to the President of the Security Council', S/2014/452; FIDH, 'Central African Republic: They Must All Leave or Die', June 2014; and Armed Conflict Location and Event Data Project (ACLED), '2014 Realtime Complete All Africa File', last updated 22 November 2014.

[544] 'Letter dated 26 June 2014 from the Panel of Experts on the Central African Republic established pursuant to Security Council resolution 2127 (2013) addressed to the President of the Security Council', S/2014/452, p. 2.

[545] The Aid Worker Security Database, 'Security incident data for Central African Republic', last updated 9 April 2015, <http://www.aidworkersecurity.org>.

[546] 'Centrafrique: la photojournaliste Camille Lepage victime d'une embuscade', *Le Monde*, 14 May 2014.

[547] CPJ, '1 Journalist Killed in Central African Republic since 1992/Motive Confirmed'.

[548] The figure represents the number of IDPs the government and UNHCR had registered as of December 2014. The Internal Displacement Monitoring Centre (IDMC) noted that 'IDPs living in the bush and with host families, and those occupying other's homes tend to be invisible, meaning their number could be very different than estimated'. IDMC, 'Global Overview 2015', May 2015, p. 82.

humanity and three counts of war crimes.[549] On 21 November 2014, the Pre-Trial Chamber II judges confirmed the charges of corruptly influencing witnesses against Jean-Pierre Bemba and he is set to face a second trial on those charges.[550]

On 24 September 2014, the ICC Prosecutor announced the opening of investigations into CAR violence since 2012.[551] The following is an excerpt from the Prosecutor's Press Release.

In February this year, following escalating violence in CAR, I opened a new preliminary examination to assess whether or not I could proceed with an investigation into what was a dire situation in CAR. The transitional government of CAR decided to refer the situation to my Office on 30 May 2014 requesting that I investigate alleged crimes falling within ICC jurisdiction committed in the country since 1 August 2012.

My Office has gathered and scrupulously analysed relevant information from multiple reliable sources. Based on this independent and comprehensive analysis, I have concluded that an investigation is warranted. The information available provides a reasonable basis to believe that both the Séléka and the anti-balaka groups have committed crimes against humanity and war crimes including murder, rape, forced displacement, persecution, pillaging, attacks against humanitarian missions, and the use of children under fifteen in combat. The list of atrocities is endless. I cannot ignore these alleged crimes.

The 30 May 2014 referral by the CAR authorities demonstrates a commitment to fight impunity for mass crimes and to bring justice to the victims. We look forward to their full cooperation as we conduct our investigation into these crimes.

My Office will now work to directly collect criminal evidence with a view to identifying and prosecuting those responsible for the most serious crimes. As always, our investigation will be conducted in an independent and impartial manner and will be led only by the evidence.

As the investigation moves forward, we will continue to record any new crime against civilians that might be committed in CAR. Mass crimes shock the conscience of humanity and tear at the social fabric of society. Let this be a message to would-be perpetrators in CAR and beyond: such crimes will not be tolerated and will be met with the full force of the law.[552]

In December 2014 the UN International Commission of Inquiry on the Central African Republic submitted its final report to the Security Council.

[549] ICC, 'Situation in the Central African Republic, *Prosecutor v Jean-Pierre Bemba Gombo*', at: <http://www.icc-cpi.int/EN_Menus/ICC/Situations%20and%20Cases/Situations/Situation%20ICC%200105/Pages/situation%20icc-0105.aspx>.

[550] 'Bemba Faces Second ICC Trial on Charges of Corrupting Witnesses', *IJM*, 21 November 2014 at: <http://www.ijmonitor.org/2014/11/bemba-faces-second-icc-trial-on-charges-of-corrupting-witnesses/>.

[551] 'ICC opens investigation into Central African Republic violence', *Reuters*, 24 September 2014 at: <http://www.reuters.com/article/2014/09/24/us-centralafrica-warcrimes-investigation-idUSKCN0HJ1IN20140924>.

[552] ICC, Statement of the Prosecutor of the International Criminal Court, Fatou Bensouda, on opening a second investigation in the Central African Republic available at: <http://www.icc-cpi.int/en_menus/icc/press%20and%20media/press%20releases/Pages/pr1043.aspx>.

The report claimed that crimes against humanity and war crimes had been widely committed by all parties in the ongoing conflict and in view of the severely dysfunctional domestic legal system in the CAR, the commission recommended prosecutions by combination of a Special Court with a majority of international elements and the ICC.[553]

On 24 April 2015 the Central African Republic's National Transitional adopted a law to establish a Special Criminal Court within the national justice system. The special court will investigate and prosecute those responsible for war crimes and crimes against humanity in CAR since 2003. The court, as set out in the law, will be a hybrid judicial mechanism made up of Central African and international judges within the Central African justice system for a renewable five-year period. The court will have a Central African president and an international special prosecutor. There will be a majority of national judges.[554]

[553] Ibid.

[554] 'New Special Criminal Court: A Key Step Toward Justice', *FIDH*, 24 April 2015 at: <https://www.fidh.org/International-Federation-for-Human-Rights/Africa/central-african-republic/new-special-criminal-court-a-key-step-toward-justice#nb1>.

Armed conflicts in Colombia in 2014

KEY CASUALTY DATA FOR 2014

Civilians killed:	289	(Sources: NVU, PAICMA)
Civilians injured:	at least 93	(Sources: Media, PAICMA)
Children killed:	2	(Sources: Media, PAICMA)
Children injured:	13	(Sources: Media, PAICMA)
FARC killed:	235	(Source: Media)
ELN killed:	41	(Source: Media)
Military killed:	38	(Sources: Media, PAICMA)
Military injured:	163	(Sources: Media, PAICMA)

CLASSIFICATION OF THE CONFLICTS

Colombia was involved in non-international armed conflicts (NIACs) with the Revolutionary Armed Forces of Colombia (FARC-EP) and the National Liberation Army (ELN) in 2014. Both conflicts met the threshold for applicability of the 1977 Additional Protocol II.

As the Office of the Prosecutor of the International Criminal Court has noted, other armed groups engaged in armed violence are not party to a NIAC in Colombia. Notably this includes the Urabeños, the Rastrojos, and the Aguilas Negras. The Office has concluded that:

> there is not a reasonable basis to believe the Rastrojos or the Aguilas Negras are sufficiently organised to constitute a party to a non-international armed conflict. There is a reasonable basis to believe the Urabeños group is sufficiently organized because, inter alia, its members are well-disciplined; there is a hierarchical structure; effective control is exercised over its members; it exercises control over territory; it has the capacity to recruit and acquire weapons; and it has a significant number of personnel. However, the available information about the intensity of violence between the Urabeños and any of the parties to the existing armed conflict (the Government, FARC and the ELN) indicates that such confrontations are not sufficiently intense for the Urabeños to qualify as a party to the conflict. Conversely, while the available information indicates that the level and intensity of violence between the Urabeños and Rastrojos may be sufficient to constitute a non-international armed conflict, as noted above, the Rastrojos do not appear to meet the criteria to be classified as an organized armed group.[555]

[555] Office of the Prosecutor of the International Criminal Court, 'Report on Preliminary Examination Activities 2013', November 2013, §129.

SUMMARY OF APPLICABLE INTERNATIONAL LAW

All parties to the conflicts were bound by customary international humanitarian law (IHL) and human rights law, including customary IHL rules of distinction, proportionality, and precautions in attacks; the obligations of humane treatment, as set out in Common Article 3 to the 1949 Geneva Conventions; the obligation not to recruit and use children as soldiers; and by the duty to respect and protect fundamental human rights. This includes the duty to respect the rights to life and to freedom from torture or other forms of cruel, inhuman, or degrading treatment or punishment.

Colombia is party to the four 1949 Geneva Conventions and the 1977 Additional Protocol II. Colombia is also party to the 1966 International Covenant on Civil and Political Rights and the 1966 International Covenant on Economic, Social and Cultural Rights.

Colombia is party to the 1997 Anti-Personnel Mine Ban Convention. Under Article 5 of the treaty, and in accordance with a ten-year extension granted in 2010, Colombia is required to destroy all antipersonnel mines in mined areas under its jurisdiction or control as soon as possible, but not later than 1 March 2021.

Colombia has signed but not yet ratified both the 2008 Convention on Cluster Munitions and the 2013 Arms Trade Treaty (ATT).[556]

HISTORY OF THE CONFLICT[557]

Colombia has endured armed conflict between the government and several left-wing armed groups (notably the FARC-EP and the ELN) for more half a century. It is the world's longest running civil war. An underlying reason for the conflict's continuity is income generated by coca leaf traffic.[558] The International Crisis Group gives additional factors of FARC's resilience: 'First, it retains access to money, despite declining income from drug trafficking and kidnapping. Second, it has proven capable of replenishing its ranks, thus mitigating the substantial losses from combatant deaths and defections. Third, a strong institutional structure and organizational culture that have grown over five decades and have enabled FARC to absorb shifts in the balance of power and the elimination of some of its high-ranking leaders'.[559] The United States (US) Government

[556] Colombia signed the ATT on 24 September 2013.

[557] Unless otherwise stated this section is based on 'Colombia Profile', *BBC*, 19 January 2015, at: <http://www.bbc.com/news/world-latin-america-19390026>.

[558] UCDP Conflict Encyclopaedia, 'Colombian Conflict Backgrounder', December 2011, at: <http://www.ucdp.uu.se/gpdatabase/gpcountry.php?id=35&regionSelect=5-Southern_Americas#>.

[559] ICG, Colombia Peace at last, Latin America Report N°45, 25 September 2012, at: <http://www.crisisgroup.org/~/media/Files/latin-america/colombia/045-colombia-peace-at-last.pdf>, p. 4.

has also been involved in the country through Plan Colombia, an initiative originally intended to support Colombian anti-drug efforts. In that context, Colombian forces receive training and equipment to eliminate smugglers and eradicate coca crops, with US assistance.[560]

The activities of the guerrillas led to the formation of right-wing paramilitary organizations, primarily the United Self-Defence Forces of Colombia (AUC), as a means of protecting landowners, drug lords, and local businessmen from attacks and kidnappings by guerrilla forces. There have been regular accusations of linkages between the paramilitaries and the State in waging war against the guerrillas, although this has been denied by the government. Since their origins, both the guerrillas and the paramilitaries have become increasingly involved in criminal activities (such as kidnapping, extortion, bombings, murder, and hijackings), and have given a new dimension to the problem of narco-trafficking.

Over the years, the Government of Colombia has held several peace talks and negotiations with guerrilla groups, with different degrees of success. Recent years have also seen the power of the paramilitaries diminish. Following generous and controversial amnesty legislation,[561] which offered significantly reduced jail terms, by mid-2006 about 95% of the total estimated AUC force was disbanded.[562]

In October 2012, negotiators from the Colombian Government and FARC-EP rebels met for their first direct peace talks for a decade in Oslo, Norway. FARC-EP's head negotiator, Ivan Marquez, said that they came 'with an olive branch' but peace did not mean 'arms go quiet'.[563] Colombian President Juan Manuel Santos rejected FARC calls for a ceasefire, saying military operations would continue until a final agreement was reached.[564] After the launch of the process, both parties agreed to move the talks to Havana, Cuba, in November 2012. A five-point peace plan had been agreed aimed at addressing: (1) rural reform; (2) a framework for political participation of the FARC; (3) illicit drugs; (4) end of conflict and decommission; (5) victims and post-war justice.[565]

[560] McDermott, J., 'Colombia Changes Tactics in Drugs War', *BBC*, 31 August 2000, at: <http://news.bbc.co.uk/2/hi/americas/891289.stm>.

[561] Center for Justice & Accountability, *Colombia: The Justice and Peace Law*, August 2005, available at: <http://www.cja.org/article.php?id=863>.

[562] Council on Foreign Relations, *Colombia's Right-Wing Paramilitaries and Splinter Groups*, 11 January 2008, available at: <http://www.cfr.org/colombia/colombias-right-wing-paramilitaries-splinter-groups/p15239?breadcrumb=%2Fpublication%2Fpublication_list%3Ftype%3Dbackgrounder%26page%3D9>.

[563] 'Colombia and Farc Negotiators Launch Norway Peace Talks', *BBC*, 18 October 2012, at: <http://www.bbc.co.uk/news/world-latin-america-19994289?print=true>.

[564] 'Colombia's President Santos Rejects Farc Ceasefire Call', *BBC*, 7 September 2012, at: <http://www.bbc.co.uk/news/world-latin-america-19514814>.

[565] 'Colombia's War is the World's Longest-Running Conflict and Has Claimed up to 200,000 Lives, But is an End Now in Sight?', *The Observer*, 15 March 2015.

2013 was marked by ongoing peace talks, amid tensions and intermittent violence.[566] The FARC's month-long ceasefire, announced on December 2013 ended on 15 January 2014. A day later, one person was killed and more than sixty were injured in a FARC motorcycle bomb attack in Pradera (Valle). An unusually strongly worded Secretariat communiqué on 23 January acknowledged the attack and expressed 'rejection and disapproval' for the high civilian impact. The Colombian military reacted to the attack by killing twenty-seven FARC fighters and capturing twenty-one.[567]

In March 2014, President Santos again expressed his hope that a peace treaty would be signed with the FARC within the coming year.[568]

By the end of April, a new round of peace negotiations started with hopes for decisive progress on the issue of illegal drugs. The parties reached a preliminary agreement on drug policies including the institution of a national crop substitution programme and demining initiatives.[569] On 16 May, FARC and ELN announced a joint unilateral ceasefire for 20 to 28 May. In early June, the government and the FARC presented a landmark 'Declaration of Principles' to guide discussions on transitional justice (the 5th substantial issue on the Havana agenda), conveying the key message that the parties would not mutually grant themselves impunity. The parties also recognized the victims' rights to truth, justice, reparation, and guarantees of non-repetition as non-negotiable issues. On 15 June, President Santos was elected for a second mandate.[570] By the end of August, a sub-commission of military and civilian experts started consultations in Havana on the 'End of the Conflict', which represents the last substantive issue on the peace agenda.[571]

On 17 November, President Santos announced that peace negotiations with the FARC were suspended because of information that the FARC kidnapped a Colombian general, an officer, and a lawyer.[572] At the end of the month, the FARC liberated the three kidnapped persons.

On December, the FARC's lead negotiator announced the start of a unilateral ceasefire and cessation of hostilities beginning on 20 December. This was the FARC's fifth unilateral ceasefire since the peace talks started in 2012, the main difference this time being that the ceasefire was of indefinite length and the FARC suggested it could lead to an armistice.[573]

[566] See *The War Report 2013*. [567] ICG, Crisis Watch: Colombia, 1 February 2014.

[568] Watts, J. and Brodzinsky, S., 'Colombia Closes in on a Peace Deal That Could End World's Longest Civil War', *Guardian*, 16 March 2014, at: <http://www.theguardian.com/world/2014/mar/16/colombia-brink-ending-civil-war-farc>.

[569] 'Colombia and Farc Rebels Agree On Drug Trade Plan', BBC, 17 May 2014, <http://www.bbc.com/news/world-latin-america-27451784>.

[570] ICG, Crisis Watch: Colombia, 1 July 2014.

[571] ICG, Crisis Watch: Colombia, 1 September 2014.

[572] Esta fue la declaración de Santos al suspender los diálogos, El Tiempo, 17 November 2014, <http://www.eltiempo.com/politica/proceso-de-paz/suspenden-los-dialogos-de-paz-declaracion-del-presidente-santos/14841675>.

[573] FARC-EP.co, FARC-EP declara cese unilateral al fuego y a las hostilidades por tiempo indefinido, 17 December 2014, <http://www.pazfarc-ep.org/index.php/noticias-comunicados-documentos-farc-ep/estado-mayor-central-emc/2338-farc-ep-decara-cese-unilateral-al-fuego-y-a-las-hostilidades-por-tiempo-indefinido>.

In March 2015, the ceasefire was still in force, while the 33rd cycle of government-FARC negotiations were underway.

PARTIES TO THE CONFLICTS

The parties to the NIACs in 2014 were Colombia and its Armed Forces against the FARC, and against the ELN.

Colombian Armed Forces

In March 2014, Colombia was estimated to have some 445,000 active frontline military personnel and a further 62,000 in reserve.[574] In the past however, it has been claimed that the effective combat strength of the National Army (Ejército Nacional) was considerably less than that suggested by total strength figures.[575]

According to Human Rights Watch, over the past decade, the Colombian Army 'committed an alarming number of extrajudicial killings of civilians. In many cases—commonly referred to as "false positives"—army personnel murdered civilians and reported them as combatants killed in action, apparently in response to pressure to boost body counts'.[576] In June 2013, the Human Rights Unit of the Attorney General's office declared it 'was investigating 2,278 cases of alleged extrajudicial executions committed by State agents throughout the country involving nearly 4,000 victims'. According to the office, most cases were attributed to the army and occurred between 2004 and 2008. It noted however, that there had been a dramatic reduction in cases of alleged extrajudicial killings attributed to the security forces since 2009; nevertheless, some cases were reported in 2012 and 2013.[577]

Revolutionary Armed Forces of Colombia (FARC-EP)

The oldest and largest of Colombia's left-wing rebel groups, FARC-EP, was formed in 1964 with a mission to overthrow the government and install a Marxist regime through armed struggle. FARC early on gained the support of the Soviet Union, and continued

[574] 'Colombia Military Strength', *Globalfirepower.com*, last updated on 27 March 2014, at: <http://www.globalfirepower.com/country-military-strength-detail.asp?country_id=colombia>.

[575] 'Colombia—Army (Ejercito Nacional)', *GlobalSecurity.org*, 4 March 2012, at: <http://www.globalsecurity.org/military/world/colombia/colombia_army.htm>.

[576] Human Rights Watch, *World Report 2014: Colombia*, at: <http://www.hrw.org/world-report/2014/country-chapters/colombia?page=2>.

[577] Ibid.

to have strong ties to the Colombian Communist Party until the mid-1980s. When paramilitary forces fought with the group in the 1990s, FARC began financing its campaign through involvement in and taxation of the illegal drug trade,[578] as well as kidnapping and extortion. In combination with acts of violence against civilians, this led to a loss of support among the civilian population.

In 2008, the FARC was estimated to have between 10,000 and 15,000 fighters. These were organized into fronts characterized by a relatively strong hierarchy and discipline; the FARC secretariat reportedly had a high degree of control over all fronts, with centralized income and direct communication with commanders via radio. Since the death in 2008 of its long-time ideological and military leader, Pedro Antonio Marín, alias 'Manuel Marulanda', the rebel group has begun moving towards building up its urban networks and increasing its political outreach, after the military defeats suffered during Álvaro Uribe's presidency (2002–2010).[579]

In February 2012, the group pledged to renounce kidnapping although it has not renounced violence.[580] While significantly weakened, FARC remains on US and European lists of terrorist organizations. Since November 2012, the group has been actively engaged in peace negotiations with the Colombian Government. On 11 March 2013, Colombian President Santos claimed that fewer than 8,000 FARC fighters remained.[581]

National Liberation Army (ELN)

Founded in 1964, the Ejército de Liberación Nacional (ELN) is the second-largest leftist rebel group in Colombia after the FARC. ELN ideology is based on Marxism-Leninism as well as Liberation theology, a predominantly Catholic philosophy with a strong emphasis on social awareness and justice. ELN considered itself a liberation movement,

[578] According to a US Department of Justice indictment in 2006, FARC generated more than 50% of the world's cocaine and more than 60% of the cocaine that enters the United States of America (USA). See US Department of Justice, 'United States Charges 50 Leaders of Narco-Terrorist FARC in Colombia with Supplying More Than Half of the World's Cocaine', 22 March 2002, available at: <http://searchjustice.usdoj.gov/search?q=cache:mnp5e3rWob0J>; <http://www.justice.gov/opa/pr/2006/March/06_crm_163.html+FARC&output=xml_no_dtd&ie=iso-8859-1&client=default_frontend&proxystylesheet=default_frontend&site=default_collection&access=p&oe=windows-1252>.

[579] Main websites consulted: <http://www.cedema.org/>, <http://www.resistencia-colombia.org/>, <http://anncol.info/>, <http://www.abpnoticias.com/>, <https://twitter.com/#!/FARC_COLOMBIA, anncol1.blogspot.com/>.

[580] Secretariado del Estado Mayor Central de las FARC-EP, *Comunicado Publico sobre Retenciones y Prisioneros*, Montañas de Colombia, 26 February 2012, available at: <http://www.resistencia-colombia.org/index.php?option=com_content&view=article&id=1212:secretariado-del-estado-mayor-central-de-las-farc-ep&catid=22&Itemid=37>.

[581] ICG, Crisis Watch: Colombia, 1 April 2013.

formed with the goal of ousting the ruling government.[582] The group believes foreign involvement in Colombia's oil industry violates the country's sovereignty and foreign companies are unfairly exploiting Colombia's natural resources. It was long seen as more politically motivated than the FARC, staying out of the illegal drugs trade on ideological grounds.[583]

The ELN reached the height of its power in the late 1990s, carrying out hundreds of kidnappings and hitting infrastructure such as oil pipelines. The ELN ranks have since declined from around 4,000 to an estimated 1,500, suffering defeats at the hands of the security forces and paramilitaries.[584] However, in October 2009, ELN rebels were able to spring one of their leaders from jail, indicating that they were not a completely spent force. In recent years, ELN units have become involved in the drugs trade, often forming alliances with criminal gangs. ELN remains on US and European lists of terrorist organizations.[585]

CASUALTIES

The total number of casualties in Colombia from armed conflict with the FARC and ELN decreased from previous years, as work on establishing peace progressed.

In was reported that the Minister of National Defense of Colombia stated that 235 FARC and forty-one ELN guerrillas had been killed between January and November 2014.[586]

Casualties of victim-activated explosives (including anti-personnel mines, improvised explosive devices and explosive remnants of war) in incidents that occurred in 2014 were registered with the Program of Comprehensive Action against Anti-personnel Mines (Dirección para la Acción Integral contra Minas Antipersonal, formerly the Colombian Presidential Program for Mine Action—PAICMA). The programme recorded 285 casualties caused by victim-activated explosives in 2014. The total number of annually registered casualties from victim-activated explosives continued to decrease significantly in 2014, compared to 357 in 2013 and 496 in 2012.[587] Among the total casualties registered

[582] *FARC, ELN: Colombia's Left-Wing Guerrillas*, Council on Foreign Relations, 19 August 2009, at: <http://www.cfr.org/colombia/farc-eln-colombias-left-wing-guerrillas/p9272>.

[583] Portal Voces de Colombia: Ejército de Liberacion National, at: <http://www.eln-voces.com/index.php/en/>.

[584] Ibid.

[585] *Ejército de Liberación Nacional (ELN), National Liberation Army*, Globalsecurity.org, at: <http://www.globalsecurity.org/military/world/para/eln.htm>.

[586] 'COLOMBIA: In 2014 276 Guerrillas Were Killed, According to Figures from Ministry of Defense', *Entorno Inteligente*, 16 December 2014, <http://www.entornointeligente.com/articulo/4471378/COLOMBIA-En-el-2014-murieron-276-guerrilleros-segun-cifras-de-Mindefensa-16122014>.

[587] Program of Comprehensive Action against Anti-personnel Mines, 'Víctimas de Minas Antipersonal', <http://www.accioncontraminas.gov.co/estadisticas/Paginas/victimas-minas-antipersonal.aspx>.

by the programme in 2014 eight civilians were killed, including one boy and ninety injured, including one women, twelve girls, and one boy. [588] The civilian fatality total also includes 281 civilians who were registered as direct victims of homicides in armed conflict in 2014 by the National Victim's Unit (NVU).[589] A child was killed and another three civilians were reported as being injured by the FARC in media.[590]

Additionally, the Program of Comprehensive Action against Anti-personnel Mines recorded thirty-one Colombian military personnel killed and 156 injured by victim-activated explosives in 2014.[591] Another seven Colombian military personnel were killed and another seven injured in two clashes with the FARC and ELN.[592]

DISPLACED

As of December 2014 there were total of 6,044,200 IDPs in Colombia, with 137,200 people newly displaced during 2014.[593]

WAR CRIMES ALLEGATIONS, INVESTIGATIONS, AND PROSECUTIONS

Colombia adhered to the 1998 Rome Statute of the International Criminal Court (ICC Statute) in August 2002. The ICC has jurisdiction over Rome Statute crimes committed on the territory of Colombia or by its nationals since 1 November 2002, in cases where national courts are unwilling or unable to prosecute. However, the Court only

2012 data is from PAICMA casualty data, 'Situación Nacional 1990–Febrero 2013' ('National Situation 1990–February 2013'), no date, <http;//www.accioncontraminas.gov.co>.

588 Analysis of PAICMA casualty data, 'Situación Nacional 1990–Febrero 2013' ('National Situation 1990–December 2013'), no date, <http://www.accioncontraminas.gov.co>.

589 The NVU also recorded another 912 'indirect' victims of homicides in armed conflict in 2014. NVU National Information Network, 'Victims of Armed Conflict: Type of victimization causing victims', <http://cifras.unidadvictimas.gov.co/Home/Victimizaciones#>.

590 '"FARC attack" in Southwest Colombia Kills Small Child, Injures 3', 31 July 2014, <http://colombiareports.co/farc-attack-kills-small-child-3-people-injured>.

591 Analysis of PAICMA casualty data, 'Situación Nacional 1990–Febrero 2013' ('National Situation 1990–December 2013'), no date, <http://www.accioncontraminas.gov.co>, accessed 30 January 2014.

592 Jolly, A., '14 Killed in Clash Between ELN and Colombia Military,' *Colombia Reports*, 4 March 2014, <http://colombiareports.co/14-dead-fatal-clash-eln-national-army/>; Acosta, L. J., 'Eight Colombian Police, Military Killed in Guerrilla Attacks', 19 December 2014, <http://www.reuters.com/article/2014/12/19/us-colombia-rebels-idUSKBN0JX2GW20141219>.

593 The estimate represents the number of IDPs registered by the government between 1985 and 2014. Internal Displacement Monitoring Centre (IDMC) 'Global Overview 2015', May 2015, p. 83.

has jurisdiction over war crimes since 1 November 2009, in accordance with Colombia's declaration pursuant to Article 124 of the Rome Statute.[594]

The situation in Colombia has been under preliminary examination by the ICC's Office of the Prosecutor (OTP) since June 2004.[595] As reported in its November 2012 Interim Report on the Situation in Colombia, the OTP determined that a reasonable basis existed to believe that the FARC, the ELN, and paramilitary armed groups have each committed crimes against humanity under Article 7 of the ICC Statute, in the form of murder; forcible transfer of population; imprisonment or other severe deprivation of physical liberty; torture; rape and other forms of sexual violence, since 1 November 2002.[596]

The OTP has also found a reasonable basis to believe that, since 1 November 2009, the FARC and ELN have committed war crimes under Article 8 of the Statute in the form of murder; attacks against civilians; torture and cruel treatment and outrages upon personal dignity; taking of hostages; rape and other forms of sexual violence; and conscripting, enlisting and using children to participate actively in hostilities. Because paramilitary armed groups started demobilizing in 2006, they are not considered a party to the armed conflict for the period covered by the ICC's jurisdiction over war crimes.[597]

With respect to State actors, in particular members of the Colombian army, the OTP found that they have also:

> allegedly deliberately killed thousands of civilians to bolster success rates in the context of the internal armed conflict and to obtain monetary profit from the State's funds. The available information indicates that these killings, also known as 'falsos positivos' (false positives), were carried out by members of the armed forces, at times operating jointly with paramilitaries and civilians, as a part of an attack directed against civilians in different parts of Colombia, pursuant to a policy adopted at least at the level of certain brigades within the armed forces.[598]

Accordingly, the OTP has determined that a reasonable basis exists to believe that organs of the State have committed crimes against humanity in the form of murder and enforced disappearance. The Office continues to analyse whether the policy extended to higher levels within the State.[599]

The OTP further concluded that a reasonable basis exists to believe that, since 1 November 2009, members of the State's forces have committed war crimes in the form of murder and attacking civilians; torture and cruel treatment; outrages upon personal dignity; rape and other forms of sexual violence.[600]

In the context of its on-going preliminary examination, a delegation from the OTP conducted a mission to Colombia from 1 to 13 February 2015. The purpose of the mission

[594] ICC Office of the Prosecutor, 'Report on Preliminary Examination Activities 2012', November 2012, §98.

[595] OTP, 'Report on Preliminary Examination Activities 2013', November 2013, §118.

[596] Ibid., §124. [597] Ibid., §125. [598] Ibid., §126.

[599] Ibid. [600] Ibid., §127.

was 'for the Office to continue its constructive engagement with the Government of Colombia and to assess progress on national proceedings in relation to the areas of focus identified in the interim report on the situation, published in November 2012, in particular on sexual crimes, the killings known as "false positives" and forced displacement. These are three of the five areas on which the Office is focusing its attention'.[601]

[601] ICC, The Office of the Prosecutor concludes mission to Colombia, 2 March 2015, <http://www.icc-cpi.int/en_menus/icc/press%20and%20media/press%20releases/Pages/pr1090.aspx>.

Armed conflicts in the Democratic Republic of Congo in 2014

KEY CASUALTY DATA FOR 2014

Armed conflict with ADF-Nalu		
Total casualties:	721	(Source: ACLED/CPJ/media/UN)
Civilians killed:	247	(Source: ACLED/CPJ/media/UN)
Civilians injured:	8	(Source: ACLED/CPJ/media/UN)
Civilian females killed:	3	(Source: ACLED/media)
Children killed:	6	(Source: ACLED/media)
NSAG killed:	425	(Source: ACLED/media)
DRC Armed forces deaths:	34	(Source: ACLED/media)
Armed conflict with the Mai-Mai		
Total casualties:	417	(Source: ACLED/Conflict Barometer/UN/media)
Civilians killed:	62	(Source: ACLED/Conflict Barometer/UN/media)
Civilians injured:	174	(Source: ACLED/Conflict Barometer/UN/media)
Civilian females killed:	122	(Source: ACLED/Conflict Barometer/UN/media)
Children killed:	6	(Source: ACLED/UN)
Humanitarian aid worker killed:	1	(Source: ACLED/media)
NSAG killed:	109	(Source: ACLED/Conflict Barometer/UN)
NSAG injured:	7	(Source: ACLED/Conflict Barometer/UN)
DRC armed forces killed:	28	(Source: ACLED/Conflict Barometer/UN)
DRC armed forces injured:	13	(Source: ACLED/Conflict Barometer/UN)

CLASSIFICATION OF THE CONFLICTS

The Democratic Republic of Congo (DRC) and the United Nations Organization Stabilization Mission in the Democratic Republic of the Congo (MONUSCO) were engaged in different non-international armed conflicts with several armed groups including at least the ADF-NALU and the Mai-Mai. In addition, although casualties are low (and consequently they were not included in the profile), there might be a situation of NIAC with the FDLR and the Kifuafua Raïa Mutomboki. The conflicts reached the threshold for applicability of 1977 Additional Protocol II.

SUMMARY OF APPLICABLE INTERNATIONAL LAW

All parties to the conflicts were bound by customary international humanitarian law (IHL) and human rights law, including customary IHL rules of distinction, proportionality, and precautions in attacks; the obligations of humane treatment, as set out in Common Article 3 to the 1949 Geneva Conventions; the obligation not to recruit and use children as soldiers; and by the duty to respect and protect fundamental human rights. This includes the duty to respect the rights to life and to freedom from torture or other forms of cruel, inhuman, or degrading treatment or punishment.

The DRC is party to the four 1949 Geneva Conventions and the 1977 Additional Protocol II. The DRC is also party to the 1966 International Covenant on Civil and Political Rights and the 1966 International Covenant on Economic, Social and Cultural Rights. States participating in MONUSCO are bound extraterritorially by their human rights obligations.[602]

The DRC is party to the 1997 Anti-Personnel Mine Ban Convention. Under Article 5 of the treaty and in accordance with the twenty-six-month extension request granted in 2012, the DRC is required to destroy all antipersonnel mines in mined areas under its jurisdiction or control as soon as possible, but not later than 1 January 2015. On 7 April 2014, the DRC submitted a second request to extend its Article 5 deadline, this time by six years, from January 2015. States participating in MONUSCO who are party to the Anti-Personnel Mine Ban Convention are bound by this instrument. In any event, the UN Secretary-General's Bulletin requires that UN peacekeeping forces engaged as a party in an armed conflict not use anti-personnel mines.[603]

The DRC has signed but not yet ratified both the 2008 Convention on Cluster Munitions. It is not a State party or signatory to the 2013 Arms Trade Treaty (ATT).[604] States participating in MONUSCO who are party to the Convention on Cluster Munitions or the ATT are bound by those instruments.

HISTORY OF THE CONFLICT[605]

The DRC is the site of one of the world's worst ongoing humanitarian crises. Mortality studies estimate that up to 1,200 people have died each day from conflict-related causes, mostly disease and malnutrition, but also from ongoing violence. Rebel factions have been fighting the government, fighting each other, attacking civilians, and been

602 See, e.g., International Court of Justice (ICJ), *Wall* Advisory Opinion, 2004, §106; and ICJ, *Armed Activities on the Territory of the Congo (Democratic Republic of the Congo v Uganda)*, Judgment, 19 December 2005.

603 Secretary-General's Bulletin: Observance by United Nations forces of international humanitarian law, New York, UN doc. ST/SGB/1999/13, 6 August 1999.

604 The DRC voted in favour of the adoption of the ATT by the UN General Assembly on 2 April 2013.

605 Unless otherwise stated, this section is based on 'Democratic Republic of Congo Profile', *BBC*, 23 January 2015, at: <http://www.bbc.com/news/world-africa-13283212>.

subjected to infighting. The vast country, the size of Western Europe, is rich in natural resources, a fact that has often been at the heart of conflicts.[606]

The Government in Kinshasa does not effectively control large parts of the country and tension remains high in the east, particularly in North and South Kivu provinces, with conflict ongoing in a number of areas. With the help of the UN Mission in the Democratic Republic of Congo (MONUC), the country was able to overcome major logistic and political challenges to hold its first 'free and fair' elections in forty years in 2006. Joseph Kabila won the elections, but his Government faced huge challenges in rebuilding State institutions that were accountable to the Congolese people. Renewed violence in the east and brutal government crackdowns in the west underscored the country's continued fragility.

In January 2008, the 'Acte d'Engagement' was signed in Goma between the Government, the National Congress for the Defence of the People (CNDP), the Mai-Mai, and several other armed groups. However, the agreement did not include Hutu militia still active in the area, causing serious doubt as to whether or not it would be successful.[607] Indeed, in October 2008, the situation worsened significantly in the east of the country as fighting and displacement increased in North Kivu, following an advance by the CNDP.[608] Tensions between Rwanda and the DRC also escalated over alleged Rwandan support for the CNDP.

In an attempt to bring the situation under control, the Government in January 2009 invited in troops from Rwanda to help set up a joint operation against the Rwandan rebel Hutu militias active in eastern DRC. On 23 March 2009, the CNDP signed a peace treaty with the Congolese Government, where it became a political party, and up to 300 former CNDP soldiers were integrated into the DRC armed forces, the FARDC.[609] In November 2011, despite allegations of irregularities and human rights abuses against the population, elections were held confirming another term for incumbent President Kabila.

In April 2012, conflict broke out again in the Kivu province. A new militia, the M23, appeared on the scene first demanding the implementation of the 23 March 2009 peace deal, but subsequently it took the provincial capital, Goma, and threatened to move against Kinshasa.[610] The group was formed after former members of the CNDP mutinied against the FARDC to protest against the claimed inability of the Government to implement the peace

[606] Human Rights Watch, *Democratic Republic of Congo: Renewed Crisis in North Kivu*, October 2007, pp. 3–4, at: <http://www.hrw.org/reports/2007/10/23/renewed-crisis-north-kivu>.

[607] Radio France Internationale, *Accord de paix signé à Goma, RFI*, 23 January 2008, at: <http://www.rfi.fr/actufr/articles/097/article_61837.asp>.

[608] Radio Okapi, *Goma: application de l'acte d'engagement, des pistes de solution en vue*, 7 February 2008, at: <http://radiookapi.net/sans-categorie/2008/02/07/goma-application-de-l%E2%80%99acte-d%E2%80%99engagement-des-pistes-de-solution-en-vue/>.

[609] Peace Agreement between the Government and le Congrès National pour la Défense du Peuple (CNDP), 23 March 2009, available at: <http://www.iccwomen.org/publications/Peace_Agreement_between_the_Government_and_the_CNDP.pdf>.

[610] Africa Updates, *DRC Congo: M23 Rebels Capture Goma City in Eastern DRC Congo*, 11 November 2012, at: <http://www.africaupdates.com/News/News.aspx?NewsId=5604>.

agreement.[611] The group was alleged to have been supported by both Rwanda and Uganda.[612] In late December 2012, the M23 left Goma, agreed to a ceasefire, and started negotiations with the government. In early 2013, negotiations resumed and were ongoing.[613] By April 2013, however, talks between M23 and the government had stalled.[614]

On 23 February 2013, a Peace, Security and Cooperation Framework agreement for the DRC and the region[615] was signed in Addis Ababa by the DRC, Angola, the Republic of Congo, South Africa, Tanzania, Uganda, Central African Republic, Burundi, Rwanda, South Sudan, and Zambia. States agreed to abstain from interfering in the internal affairs of their neighbours, while the DRC agreed to structural and security sector reform. The UN Secretary-General, the Chairperson of the African Union Commission, the Chairperson of the Southern African Development Community (SADC), and the Chairperson of the International Conference on the Great Lakes Region (ICGLR) also signed the agreement as witnesses.

On 12 December 2013, M23 signed a peace deal with government after the army captured the last of its strongholds in the east. The agreement, which included an amnesty for those not responsible for war crimes, crimes against humanity, and genocide, required demobilization of M23 soldiers. The following month, Martin Kobler, the UN Special Representative in DRC (SRSG), said that the UN mission would not 'tolerate' a resurgence of M23. In a statement to the Security Council, he cited 'credible reports that the military recruitment of the M23 did not cease' after the peace deal. 'There are also credible reports of emerging M23 activities in Ituri in north-eastern Congo', he said.[616]

On 4 February 2014, the DRC Parliament approved a law granting amnesty for acts of insurgency and war dating back to 2006, but excluding genocide and war crimes.[617] While the National Network of Congolese Human Rights NGOs criticized the amnesty law, UN officials welcomed parliamentary approval of the law, declaring it to be the 'next step in bringing sustainable peace' to the region.[618]

[611] 'DRC: Understanding Armed Group M23', *IRIN*, 22 June 2012, at: <http://www.irinnews.org/report/95715/DRC-Understanding-armed-group-M23>.

[612] Human Rights Watch, *DR Congo: Rwanda Should Stop Aiding War Crimes Suspect*, 4 June 2012, at: <http://www.hrw.org/news/2012/06/03/dr-congo-rwanda-should-stop-aiding-war-crimes-suspect-0>.

[613] 'Congo's M23 Rebels Say Peace Deal Possible by End-February', *Reuters*, 1 February 2013, at: <http://www.reuters.com/article/2013/02/01/congo-democratic-idUSL5N0B140F20130201>.

[614] International Crisis Group (ICG), Crisis Watch Database: DR Congo, 1 May 2013, at: <http://www.crisisgroup.org/en/publication-type/crisiswatch/crisiswatch-database.aspx>.

[615] Available at: <http://www.peaceau.org/uploads/scanned-on-24022013-125543.pdf>.

[616] 'M23 Rebels Regrouping?' *Independent*, 18 January 2014, at: <http://www.independent.co.ug/news/regional-news/8612-m23-rebels-regrouping#sthash.K99bXSj8.dpuf>.

[617] ICG, Crisis Watch Database: DR Congo, 1 March 2014.

[618] 'DR Congo Parliament Approves New Amnesty Law for Insurgency and Other Crimes, as Part of Agreement with M23 Rebel Group', *International Justice Resource Centre*, 10 February 2014, at: <http://www.ijrcenter.org/2014/02/10/dr-congo-parliament-approves-new-amnesty-law-for-insurgency-and-other-crimes-as-part-of-agreement-with-m23-rebel-group/>.

On 18 January 2014 the FARDC and MONUSCO launched an offensive in the east against ADF-NALU. On 14 January, FARDC repulsed a Mai Cheka attack on Pinga in North Kivu. Four soldiers were killed in the operation while three civilians were injured.[619] On 6 January the FARDC clashed with the Mai Mai Kata Katanga in Lubumbashi and Pweto which resulted in twenty-six killed.[620]

In March 2014, the International Criminal Court found FRPI militia leader Germain Katanga guilty of war crimes for a 2003 massacre of villagers in Ituri province.[621]

In April, the FDLR's president claimed that the group had laid down its weapons and was seeking to negotiate with Rwanda. Rwanda President Paul Kagame however refused to hold talks with a group he accuses of committing genocide. MONUSCO did not believe the group had disarmed.[622]

The FARDC and MONUSCO continued to conduct joint operations in North Kivu. In an operation on 15 March, the eastern town of Lukweti was recaptured from APCLS rebels after six years. On 1 March FARDC soldiers struck an ADF-NALU base near Beni and FARDC/MONUSCO forces were engaged in minor clashes with FDLR in Virunga national park throughout the month. In sporadic retaliations ADF-NALU carried out a grenade attack on a MONUSCO vehicle on 3 March leaving five personnel injured. On 28 March the UN extended the MONUSCO and Intervention Brigade mandate to 31 March 2015.[623]

In May FARDC operations against the Alliance of Patriots for Free and Sovereign Congo (APCLS) continued in the Masisi/Walikale region. Fighting between FDLR/allied groups and Mai Mai Cheka/NDC also displaced thousands in Lubero. On 2–17 October, attacks attributed to Allied Democratic Forces (ADF) killed over eighty and displaced thousands in North Kivu.[624]

In attacks suspected by ADF-Nalu on 7 December thirty-seven civilians were killed in Oïcha and thirteen killed on 8 December 30km north of Beni.[625] Later in the month, clashes between the faction Raïa Mutomboki Ntoto and that of Nsindo in Walikale territory (North Kivu) were reported.[626]

[619] ICG, 'Crisis Watch Database: DRC', 1 February 2014. [620] Ibid.

[621] See ICC website, at: <http://www.icc-cpi.int/en_menus/icc/situations%20and%20cases/situations/situation%20icc%200104/related%20cases/icc%200104%200107/Pages/democratic%20republic%20of%20the%20congo.aspx>.

[622] 'FDLR President Seeks Peace Talks with Rwanda', *BBC*, 10 April 2014, at: <http://www.bbc.com/news/world-africa-26966751>.

[623] ICG, 'Crisis Watch database: DRC', 1 April 2014.

[624] ICG, 'Crisis Watch database: DRC', 1 November 2014.

[625] 'Ugandan Rebels Wielding Machetes Kill 36 People in Eastern Democratic Republic of Congo', *Reuters*, 8 December 2014 at: <http://www.abc.net.au/news/2014-12-08/ugandan-rebels-kill-36-in-attack-on-village-in-drc/5950254>.

[626] 'Nord-Kivu: 9 morts dans des affrontements entre deux factions de la milice Raïa Mutomboki', RO, 17 December 2014 at: <http://radiookapi.net/actualite/2014/12/17/nord-kivu-9-morts-dans-des-affrontements-entre-deux-factions-de-la-milice-raia-mutomboki/>.

A Canadian NGO signalled that the practice of kidnapping was on the rise in North Kivu, with at least 131 cases declared to the police at the end of 2014.[627]

In late January 2015, public discontent with a proposed law that would extend President Joseph Kabila's term resulted in several days of public demonstrations and clashes with the police in Kinshasa, media report. The violence resulted in at least forty-two deaths and an undetermined number of wounded individuals; the Government of DRC has cited fourteen people killed. On 23 January, Government of DRC legislators voted to cancel the national census that would have postponed the 2016 elections and prolonged Kabila's presidency. Despite the unrest, the situation did not generate large-scale humanitarian needs requiring a concerted response effort. In response to reports of abuse, the UN Office of the High Commissioner for Human Rights issued a public appeal for the Government of DRC to conduct a thorough, independent investigation into excessive use of force by law enforcement.

On 26 March 2015 the UN Security Council extended the MONUSCO mandate by one year.[628] The same month, the FARDC continued its unilateral operations against the FDLR, with reports that they had neutralized 182 rebels.[629]

PARTIES TO THE CONFLICTS

The parties to the NIACs in 2014 were the DRC and its Armed Forces and MONUSCO against ADF-NALU, the FDLR, the Mai-Mai, and possibly the Kifuafua Raia Mutomboki.

Armed Forces of the Democratic Republic of Congo (FARDC)

The FARDC is estimated to number 152,000 active frontline military personnel and a further 1,500 in reserve.[630] There have been longstanding concerns about FARDC compliance with international law.[631] In November 2012, according to a UN report, violations

[627] 'Nord-Kivu: 131 kidnappings suivis des demandes de rançon recensés en 2014', Radio Okapi, 10 March 2015, at: <http://radiookapi.net/actualite/2015/03/10/nord-kivu-131-kidnappings-suivis-des-demandes-de-rancon-recenses-en-2014/>.

[628] 'RDC: l'ONU renouvelle pour un an le mandat de la Monusco', *RO*, 26 March 2015 at: <http://radiookapi.net/actualite/2015/03/26/rdc-lonu-renouvelle-pour-le-mandat-de-la-monusco/>.

[629] 'After UN-Kinshasa Fallout, Operations Against FDLR Begin in Eastern DRC', *AA*, 2 March 2015 at: <http://africanarguments.org/2015/03/02/after-un-kinshasa-fallout-operations-against-fdlr-begin-in-eastern-drc-by-christoph-vogel/>.

[630] 'Democratic Republic of the Congo Military Strength', *Globalfirepower.com*, last updated on 27 March 2014, at: <http://www.globalfirepower.com/country-military-strength-detail.asp?country_id=democratic-republic-of-the-congo>.

[631] See, e.g., Amnesty International (AI), '10 Facts You Should Know about the Crisis in the DRC', 20 March 2013, at: <http://responsibilitytoprotect.org/index.php/component/content/article/35-r2pcs-topics/4715-amnesty-international-10-facts-you-should-know-about-the-crisis-in-the-drc>.

of human rights law and IHL by FARDC soldiers were 'perpetrated in a systematic manner and with extreme violence, mostly as FARDC units retreated from the front lines and regrouped in and around the town of Minova, Kalehe territory, South Kivu province. In this context, at least 102 women and 33 girls were victims of rape or other acts of sexual violence perpetrated by FARDC soldiers. FARDC soldiers were also responsible for the arbitrary execution of at least two people, violations of the right to physical integrity of at least 24 civilians, cases of forced labour and the widespread looting of villages'.[632] Amnesty International reported that nine soldiers from the Congolese armed forces, including a lieutenant colonel, were convicted of crimes against humanity, notably rape, regarding acts committed on 1 January in the town of Fizi, South Kivu: they were sentenced to jail in February 2012 'in a rare example of perpetrators being promptly brought to justice'.[633] In 2009, several UN officials were reported by one commentator as acknowledging privately that the army is a major problem, largely due to corruption that results in food and pay meant for soldiers being diverted and a military structure that contains many former warlords.[634] In a 2009 report alleging FARDC abuses, Human Rights Watch urged the UN to stop supporting Government offensives against eastern rebels until the abuses ceased.[635]

MONUSCO

The UN Security Council established MONUC (UN Organization Mission in the DRC) to facilitate implementation of the 'Lusaka Accord' signed in 1999 by its Resolution 1279 of 30 November 1999.[636] Later, in a series of resolutions, the Council expanded the mandate of MONUC to the supervision of the implementation of the Ceasefire Agreement and assigned multiple related additional tasks.

Extending the mandate of MONUC for the last time until 30 June 2010, the Security Council, by Resolution 1925 of 28 May 2010 decided that from 1 July 2010 it would bear the title 'United Nations Organization Stabilization Mission in the Democratic Republic of the Congo (MONUSCO)',[637] in view of the new phase reached in the country. Emphasizing that the protection of civilians must be given priority, the Council authorized MONUSCO to use all necessary means to carry out its protection mandate,

[632] UN Joint Human Rights Office (UNJHRO), 'UNJHRO Report on Human Rights Violations by FARDC and M23 in Goma, Sake, and around Minova. 15 November–2 December 2012', May 2013, Summary, at: <http://www.ohchr.org/Documents/Countries/ZR/UNJHROMay2013_en.pdf>.

[633] AI, *Annual Report 2012: Democratic Republic of the Congo*, at: <http://www.amnesty.org/en/region/democratic-republic-congo/report-2012>.

[634] Hochschild, A., 2009, 'Rape of the Congo', *New York Review of Books*, vol. 56, no. 13 (13 August 2009).

[635] Human Rights Watch, 'You Will Be Punished', 13 December 2009, at: <http://www.hrw.org/en/node/87142/section/4>.

[636] UN Security Council Resolution 1279, 30 November 1999.

[637] For further information, visit the MONUSCO webpage.

including the effective protection of civilians, humanitarian personnel, and human rights defenders under imminent threat of physical violence, as well as the protection of United Nations personnel, facilities, installations, and equipment. The Mission would also support Government efforts to fight impunity and ensure the protection of civilians from violations of international human rights and humanitarian law, including all forms of sexual and gender-based violence.[638]

UN Security Council Resolution 2098 (2013) decided that the Mission could include an 'Intervention Brigade' 'with the responsibility of neutralizing armed groups' and with 'the objective of contributing to reducing the threat posed by armed groups to state authority and civilian security in eastern DRC and to make space for stabilization activities'.[639]

On 28 March 2014, the Security Council, by its resolution 2147, extended the mandate of MONUSCO until 31 March 2015 and decided that the renewed mandate would also include MONUSCO's Intervention Brigade—'on an exceptional basis and without creating a precedent or any prejudice'—within the authorized troop ceiling of 19,815 military personnel, 760 military observers and staff officers, 391 police personnel, and 1,050 formed police units.

At the same time, the Council noted the need for a clear exit strategy and decided that the Mission's further reconfigurations and mandates should be based on the evolving situation and progress towards several objectives set out in accordance with its three priorities—protecting civilians, stabilizing the country, and supporting implementation of the Peace, Security and Cooperation Framework for the Democratic Republic of the Congo and the region.[640]

ADF-NALU[641]

The Allied Democratic Forces-National Army for the Liberation of Uganda (Forces démocratiques alliées-Armée nationale de libération de l'Ouganda, ADF-NALU) is one of the oldest but least known armed groups in the east of the DRC and the only one in the area to be considered an Islamist terrorist organization. Although it does not represent the same destabilizing threat as the M23, it has managed to stand its ground against the FARDC since 2010. Created in the DRC in 1995 and located in the mountainous DRC–Uganda border area, this Congolese–Ugandan armed group has shown

638 UN Security Council Resolution 2053, 30 June 2012.

639 UN Security Council Resolution 2098, 28 March 2013, §9.

640 For further information, visit the MONUSCO webpage.

641 This armed group profile is taken from ICG, 'Eastern Congo: The ADF-NALU's Lost Rebellion', Africa Briefing No. 93, 19 December 2012, at: <http://www.crisisgroup.org/en/regions/africa/central-africa/dr-congo/b093-eastern-congo-the-adf-nalus-lost-rebellion.aspx>.

remarkable resilience attributable to its geostrategic position, its successful integration into the cross-border economy, and corruption in the security forces.

Formed of an alliance of several armed groups supported by external actors (Mobutu Sese Seko's Zaire and Hassan al-Turabi's Sudan), the ADF-NALU initially fought the Ugandan Government of Yoweri Museveni. However, despite its Ugandan origins, it never managed to gain a foothold in its own country and instead settled in eastern Congo, particularly in the remote mountainous border areas. There it became integrated into local communities, participated in cross-border trade, and forged relationships with various armed groups in eastern Congo as well as with both Congolese and Ugandan civilian and military authorities. Given their location in this 'grey zone', the ADF-NALU's lost fighters have been able to survive despite not winning a battle in more than fifteen years and having been defeated several times, but never neutralized.

Due to the ADF-NALU's leader, Jamil Mukulu, a Christian convert to Islam, the group has transformed from a purely Congolese–Ugandan problem into one with regional dimensions, as a component of the trend of radical Islamism in East Africa. However, little is known about such purported links between ADF-NALU and radical Islamist organizations in the region.

MAI-MAI

The Mayi-Mayi, or Mai-Mai (Congolese Swahili for 'Water Water'), is a loose association of traditional Congolese local self-defence forces, which primarily fought Rwandan Government forces and their Congolese allies. It is opposed to 'Tutsi domination', but it is otherwise seemingly without clear objective and frequently changes alliances.[642] Mai-Mai are essentially self-defence militias formed on an ad-hoc basis by local leaders who arm young men in villages, often along ethnic lines.

Some of the larger ones are better known, such as the Alliance of Patriots for a Free and Sovereign Congo (APCLS), which joined the peace process in March 2009, promising to transform into peaceful political parties.

On 2 June 2010, 500 members of the Kifuafua Mai-Mai group returned to their positions in Walikale in North Kivu, claiming that their agreed integration into the army had been delayed for too long. Most Mai-Mai groups are local forces known by the name of their leader. For instance the Mai-Mai Yakutumba group can be identified as it bears the name of the 'major-general' of the group at its helm.[643]

[642] UPCD Conflict Encyclopedia, 'DRC, General Non-State Conflict', May 2015, at: <http://www.ucdp.uu.se/gpdatabase/gpcountry.php?id=38&regionSelect=2-Southern_Africa>.

[643] 'DRC: Who's Who Among Armed Groups in the East', *IRIN*, 15 June 2010 at: <http://www.irinnews.org//report/89494/drc-who-s-who-among-armed-groups-in-the-east?wptouch_preview_theme=enabled>.

FDLR

As the ICG noted already in 2005, the continued existence in the DRC of several thousand Hutu rebels with links to the 1994 genocide in their home country, Rwanda, is a key source of instability. [644] Although too weak to imperil Rwanda's Government, and although many of its members are not themselves *génocidaires*, the FDLR gave Kigali justification for interference in the DRC for many years.

FDLR is the largest foreign armed group in the DRC, even if there are contrasting estimates of the group's current strength. The UN Group of Experts estimates FDLR to include around 1,000 combatants in North Kivu and 500 in South Kivu, while the Government of Rwanda cites a total between 4,000 to 4,200 combatants. [645] The Rwanda Demobilization and Reintegration Commission (RDRC), on the other hand, believe FDLR/FOCA to have 3,000 combatants. The Enough Project and MONUSCO offer a range of 1,500[646] to 5,000 combatants, while some FDLR/FOCA defectors and UN officials have placed the figure between 700 and 800. An exact number is difficult to pin down because they are well integrated in the communities and include a growing number of Congolese.

KIFUAFUA-RAIA MUTOMBOKI

Mai-Mai Kifuafua was founded by ethnic Tembos in the early 1990s to fight Rwandan pro-Hutu militia group Democratic Forces for the Liberation of Rwanda (FDLR) and claims to have supported the Congolese army, FARDC, in operations against FDLR for years. Raia Mutomboki, meaning 'angry citizens', was loosely formed in South Kivu around 2009 but revived and took up arms against the FDLR in 2011 when government forces left empty positions in Shabunda, South Kivu.[647]

CASUALTIES

Armed conflict with the ADF-NALU

In the first half of 2014, the ADF-NALU was significantly weakened by violent exchanges and battles with both the Armed Forces of the Democratic Republic of the Congo

[644] ICG, 'The Congo: Solving the FDLR Problem Once and for All', Africa Briefing N°25, 12 May 2005, at: <http://www.crisisgroup.org/en/regions/africa/central-africa/dr-congo/B025-the-congo-solving-the-fdlr-problem-once-and-for-all.aspx>.

[645] <http://www.un.org/ga/search/view_doc.asp?symbol=S/2014/42>.

[646] <http://www.csmonitor.com/World/Africa/2015/0115/Why-the-UN-is-planning-fresh-military-offensive-in-Congo-briefing>.

[647] 'DRC: Scores Killed as Mai-Mai target Kinyarwanda Speakers', *IRIN*, 12 June 2012 at: <http://www.irinnews.org//report/95626/drc-scores-killed-as-mai-mai-target-kinyarwanda-speakers>.

(AFDRC) and the UN Peace-keeping mission MONUSCO; UN sources claimed that the chain of command was still intact and the group retained most of its command and control structures.[648] The first half of the year thus saw a high number of casualties among the ranks of ADF-NALU fighters. Overall in 2014, 425 ADF-NALU fighters were killed, whereas at least thirty-four AFDRC soldiers were killed and eight were injured.[649]

However, during the last quarter of the year, the ADF-NALU perpetrated systematic attacks on civilians of the Beni territory, in North Kivu, which led, according to UN sources, to more than 250 civilian deaths and many more injured between the months of October to December 2014.[650]

In 2014, overall, 255 civilian casualties were recorded, including 247 killed and eight injured. However, many sources only reported deaths or attacks on civilians without including disaggregated data on outcome. One journalist was also killed and two injured.[651] This constitutes a significant increase compared to civilian casualties that were recorded in 2013. Attacks against civilians were particularly violent and cruel. For example, attacks between 8 and 15 December 2014 in two remote villages near Oicha resulted in the killing of thirty-six civilians, including children, hacked to death with machetes.[652] Most civilian casualties are not disaggregated in data by sex and age but reporting regular mentions high numbers of women and children victims of ADF-NALU violence.

ARMED CONFLICT WITH THE MAI-MAI

In 2014, conflict continued between the Armed Forces of the Democratic Republic of the Congo (AFDRC) supported by the UN Peace-keeping mission MONUSCO and

[648] UN Security Council, 'Report of the Secretary-General on the United Nations Organization Stabilization Mission in the Democratic Republic of the Congo submitted pursuant to paragraph 39 of Security Council resolution 2147 (2014)', S/2014/957, 30 December 2014, p. 5; Heidelberg Institute for International Conflict Research, 'Conflict Barometer 2014', 2015, p. 64.

[649] Analysis of 'notes' and 'fatalities' in ACLED data. Raleigh, C., Linke, A., Hegre, H., and Karlsen, J., 2010, 'Introducing ACLED-Armed Conflict Location and Event Data', *Journal of Peace Research*, vol. 47, no. 5, pp. 1–10.

[650] UN Security Council, 'Report of the Secretary-General on the United Nations Organization Stabilization Mission in the Democratic Republic of the Congo submitted pursuant to paragraph 39 of Security Council resolution 2147 (2014)', S/2014/957, 30 December 2014, p. 5; UN Security Council, 'Report of the Secretary-General on the United Nations Organization Stabilization Mission in the Democratic Republic of the Congo', S/2014/956, 30 December 2014, p. 4.

[651] Committee to Protect Journalists (CPJ), 'DRC Journalist Dies From Wounds Suffered In Rebel Attack', 18 February 2014, <https://cpj.org/2014/02/drc-journalist-dies-from-wounds-suffered-in-rebel.php>; and CPJ 'Journalist Killed, Democratic Republic of Congo—Germain Kennedy Mumbere Muliwavyo, Radio Télévision Muungano, February 16, 2014, in Oïcha, Democratic Republic of the Congo', <https://cpj.org/killed/2014/germain-kennedy-mumbere-muliwavyo.php>.

[652] UN Security Council, 'Report of the Secretary-General on the United Nations Organization Stabilization Mission in the Democratic Republic of the Congo', S/2014/956, 30 December 2014, p. 4; ABC, 'Ugandan Rebels Kill thirty-six in Attack on Village in DRC', 8 December 2014.

Mai-Mai militias.[653] Mai-Mai is a general term refers to various, mostly independent, local militias claiming to represent the population against perceived foreigners. The militias ranged from well-organized, larger groups to smaller, localized units and were usually named after their commanders.[654]

Overall, there were 417 casualties related to the Mai-Mai militias recorded in 2014, be it as a result of clashes with governmental forces or of attacks and violence against civilians.[655] There were 236 civilian casualties recorded in 2014, including at least eleven women and six children.[656] On 16 August 2014 a Red Cross worker was killed when Mai-Mai Simba and government forces clashed in Lubutu territory in Maniema.[657]

Regular attacks on villages, including looting, burning houses, physical violence, and rapes were recorded in 2014, in particular in the Regions of Katanga, South Kivu, Maniema, Orientale, and North Kivu.[658] Sexual violence, in particular raping and torturing of women, were regularly reported.[659] Indeed, between 15 and 30 July, the Mai-Mai Simba were accused of raping and torturing at least 100 women in Bapaitumba and Bapakombe areas in Bapere sector, Lubero.[660] Again on 20 June 2014 the Mai-Mai Bakata Katanga attacked Kamakolo village, in Nkumba Kubukongolo area, Pweto territory, and abducted seven women, holding them in sexual slavery for two months before they escaped in early August 2014.[661]

Kidnappings of civilians and forced enrolments into militia groups, especially of children and young men were very common throughout the year.[662] In 2014, 268 kidnapping cases were recorded in addition to the overall casualty data.[663]

Displacement

As at end of December 2014 there were at least 2,756,600 internally displaced persons (IDPs) in DR Congo with 1,003,400 recorded as newly displaced in 2014. At least 561,100 IDPs returned during the year. The total figure of IDPs includes 863,431 in North Kivu, 609,566 in South Kivu, 551,374 in Katanga, 543,734 in Orientale, and 188,480 in

[653] UN Security Council, 'Report of the Secretary-General on the United Nations Organization Stabilization Mission in the Democratic Republic of the Congo', S/2014/956, 30 December 2014; and Heidelberg Institute for International Conflict Research, 'Conflict Barometer 2014', 2015, p. 62.

[654] Heidelberg Institute for International Conflict Research, 'Conflict Barometer 2014', 2015, p. 62.

[655] Analysis of ACLED data 2014.

[656] Analysis of ACLED data 2014.

[657] Radio Okapi, 'Maniema: 2 miliciens tués dans des affrontements avec des FARDC à Amalasa', 19 August 2014.

[658] Analysis of ACLED data 2014 and media reports.

[659] Analysis of ACLED data 2014 and media reports.

[660] Radio Okapi, 'RDC: 100 femmes violées et torturées en deux semaines au Nord-Kivu', 8 August 2014.

[661] Radio Okapi, 'Katanga: 7 femmes échappent aux Maï-Maï après deux mois d'esclavage sexuel', 7 August 2014.

[662] Analysis of ACLED data 2014.

[663] Analysis of ACLED data 2014.

Maniema. The Internal Displacement Monitoring Centre (IDMC) noted that figures are approximate as access to informal settlements, host communities, and the bush is difficult and movements are dynamic.[664]

WAR CRIMES ALLEGATIONS, INVESTIGATIONS, AND PROSECUTIONS

The DRC adhered to the 1998 Rome Statute of the International Criminal Court (ICC Statute) in August 2002. The ICC has jurisdiction over Rome Statute crimes committed on the territory of the DRC or by its nationals since 1 November 2002, in cases where national courts are unwilling or unable to prosecute.

The ICC Chief Prosecutor opened in June 2004 the first investigation of the ICC, after the DRC referred the situation in the country to the Court. Since then, seven arrest warrants have been issued for war crimes and crimes against humanity. Some of the high-profile cases are summarized below.

Prosecutor v Thomas Lubanga Dyilo

The trial of Thomas Lubanga Dyilo, which opened on 26 January 2009 before Trial Chamber I of the ICC, is the first trial in the history of the Court, and the first trial in the history of international law which sees victims participate fully in the proceedings.

On 14 March 2012, the ICC issued its first verdict in *Prosecutor v Thomas Lubanga Dyilo*,[665] finding the former leader of the Union of Congolese Patriots guilty, as a co-perpetrator, of the war crimes of conscripting and enlisting children under the age of fifteen and using them to participate actively in hostilities. On 10 July 2012, Mr Lubanga was sentenced to fourteen years' imprisonment by the Court. The sentence was confirmed by the Appeals Chamber on 1 December 2014.

Prosecutor v Germain Katanga and Mathieu Ngudjolo Chui

On 25 September 2009, Trial Chamber II of the ICC upheld the admissibility of the war crimes/crimes against humanity case against former Congolese militia leader Germain Katanga and former head of the Nationalist and Integrationist Front (FNI), and a colonel

[664] IDMC 'Global Overview 2015', May 2015, p. 86.

[665] ICC, Judgment pursuant to Art. 74 of the Statute, 14 March 2012, at: <http://www.icc-cpi.int/en_menus/icc/situations and cases/situations/situation icc 0104/related cases/icc 0104 0106/court records/chambers/trial chamber i/Pages/2842.aspx>.

in the FARDC, Mathieu Ngudjolo Chui.[666] Their trial started on 24 November 2009. On 18 December 2012, the Trial Chamber acquitted Mathieu Ngudjolo Chui of crimes against humanity and war crimes committed during the attack on the village of Bogoro, in Ituri district.[667] The Prosecution decided to appeal the verdict.

On 7 March 2014, Trial Chamber II found Germain Katanga guilty, as an accessory, within the meaning of Article 25(3)(d) of the ICC Statute, of one count of crime against humanity (murder) and four counts of war crimes (murder, attacking a civilian population, destruction of property, and pillaging) committed on 24 February 2003 during the attack on the village of Bogoro, in the Ituri district of the DRC. The Chamber acquitted Germain Katanga of the other charges that he was facing. On 23 May 2014 the Trial Chamber II sentenced Katanga to twelve years' imprisonment.

On 25 June 2014 the Defence notified the Appeals Chamber that Germain Katanga had decided to discontinue his appeal and that Germain Katanga accepted the judgment of the Court and its conclusions on its role as well as his conduct. Germain Katanga also indicated that he decided not to appeal against the imposed sentence. The Prosecutor subsequently informed the Appeals Chamber that she also discontinued her appeal against the judgment and that she does not intend to appeal the sentence imposed on Germain Katanga.

Prosecutor v Bosco Ntaganda

Bosco Ntaganda was the Deputy Chief of Staff and commander of operations of the Forces Patriotiques pour la Libération du Congo (Patriotic Forces for the Liberation of Congo) (FPLC). A first warrant of arrest was issued by Pre-Trial Chamber I under seal on 22 August 2006 and unsealed on 28 April 2008. The warrant listed three counts of war crimes on the basis of individual criminal responsibility: enlistment of children under fifteen; conscription of children under fifteen; and using children under fifteen to participate actively in hostilities. A second warrant of arrest was issued by Pre-Trial Chamber II on 13 July 2012. The second warrant listed seven counts of crimes as an indirect co-perpetrator under Article 25(3)(a) of the ICC Statute: four counts of war crimes (murder, attack against the civilian population, rape and sexual slavery, and pillaging) and three counts of crimes against humanity (murder, rape and sexual slavery, and persecution).[668] Mr Ntaganda voluntarily surrendered to the ICC's custody on

[666] ICC, Decision of Trial Chamber II of 12 June 2009 on the Admissibility of the Case *The Prosecutor v Germain Katanga and Mathieu Ngudjolo Chui* (Case No. ICC-01/04-01/07 OA 8), 25 September 2009, at: <http://www.unhcr.org/refworld/country,LEGAL,ICC,,COD,,4ac9dd592,0.html>.

[667] ICC, *Prosecutor v Mathieu Ngudjolo Chui*, Judgment (Case No. ICC-01/04-02/12-3), 18 December 2012, at: <http://www.icc-cpi.int/en_menus/icc/situations and cases/situations/situation icc 0104/related cases/ICC-01-04-02-12/court-records/chambers/trial chamber ii/Pages/3.aspx>.

[668] At: <http://www.icc-cpi.int/en_menus/icc/situations%20and%20cases/situations/situation%20icc%200104/Pages/situation%20index.aspx>.

22 March 2013.[669] On 5 March 2014, the Appeals Chamber confirmed the decision rejecting the Defence's request for Mr Ntaganda's interim release.[670] The charges against Mr Ntaganda were confirmed on 9 June 2014.

Prosecutor v Sylvestre Mudacumura

On 14 May 2012, the Office of the Prosecutor announced it was seeking an arrest warrant for a leader of one of the most active militia in the Kivu provinces, Sylvestre Mudacumura, the Supreme Commander of the Forces Démocratiques pour la Libération du Rwanda (FDLR-FOCA).[671] A warrant of arrest was issued by Pre-Trial Chamber II on 13 July 2012. Mr Mudacumura is allegedly criminally responsible for committing nine counts of war crimes, from 20 January 2009 to the end of September 2010, in the context of the conflict in the Kivus in the DRC on the basis of individual criminal responsibility. The alleged war crimes under Article 25(3)(b) of the ICC Statute include attacking civilians, murder, mutilation, cruel treatment, rape, torture, destruction of property, pillaging, and outrages against personal dignity.[672]

National trials

In May 2014, a mass trial of thirty-nine FARDC soldiers ended with two convicted of rape and thirteen others acquitted of rape but convicted of lesser crimes. Lawyers for the victims called the ruling an 'insult'. The UN had reported that more than 135 women and girls were raped in Minova after the army entered the town in November 2012. The incident happened when M23 rebels took control of Goma and thousands of soldiers retreated to the town of Minova to the south. Congolese soldiers told the BBC that they were 'angry and humiliated', and that they had been ordered by their superiors to begin raping women.[673]

[669] On 18 March 2013, Bosco Ntaganda surrendered to staff at the US Embassy in Kigali, ending violent infighting between M23 rebel factions in DRC that had reportedly killed more 150. Ntaganda was transferred to ICC custody on 22 March. ICG, Crisis Watch Database: DR Congo, 1 April 2013.

[670] ICC, 'Bosco Ntaganda Case: Appeals Chamber Confirms the Decision Rejecting the Defence's Request for Interim Release', Press release, 5 March 2014, at: <http://www.icc-cpi.int/en_menus/icc/press%20and%20media/press%20releases/Pages/pr985.aspx>.

[671] UN News Centre, 'ICC prosecutor pushes for arrest of rebel leaders wanted for DR Congo crimes', 14 May 2012, at: <http://www.un.org/apps/news/story.asp?NewsID=41992#.UREuntuwVrs>.

[672] ICC, 'The Prosecutor v Sylvestre Mudacumura', at: <http://www.icc-cpi.int/en_menus/icc/situations%20and%20cases/situations/situation%20icc%200104/related%20cases/icc01040112/Pages/icc01040112.aspx>.

[673] 'DR Congo Rape Trial: Many Soldiers Cleared, Two Guilty', *BBC*, 5 May 2014, at: <http://www.bbc.com/news/world-africa-27285268>.

The trial began in November 2013 after months of international pressure. But most of the soldiers accused in the trial were low-ranking, and several victims said that their rapists were not included among the thirty-nine charged. Lawyers for the victims said the ruling would discourage rape victims from coming forward. A human rights activist told the BBC the investigations were too short, and did not allow the inquiry to gather enough evidence.[674]

674 Ibid.

Armed conflict in Egypt in 2014

KEY CASUALTY DATA FOR 2014

Civilian deaths:	24	(Source: ACLED)
Child deaths:	7	(Source: ACLED)
Armed groups deaths:	515	(Source: ACLED)
Military deaths:	124	(Source: ACLED)
Police deaths:	36	(Source: ACLED)
Unknown civilian status deaths:	6	

CLASSIFICATION OF THE CONFLICT

Egypt in 2014 has been involved in a NIAC between Egyptian armed forces and the armed group known as Ansar Bayt al-Maqdis (ABM). The conflict did not reach the threshold for the applicability of the 1977 Additional Protocol II.

SUMMARY OF APPLICABLE INTERNATIONAL LAW

All parties to the conflict were bound by customary international humanitarian law (IHL) and human rights law, including customary IHL rules of distinction, proportionality, and precautions in attacks; the obligations of humane treatment, as set out in Common Article 3 to the 1949 Geneva Conventions; the obligation not to recruit and use children as soldiers; and by the duty to respect and protect fundamental human rights. This includes the duty to respect the rights to life and to freedom from torture or other forms of cruel, inhuman, or degrading treatment or punishment.

Egypt is a State party to the four 1949 Geneva Conventions and the 1977 Additional Protocol II. Egypt has signed the Rome Statute, on 26 December 2000, but has not yet ratified it. Egypt is not a party to any of the weapon conventions.

It is a party to the core human rights conventions, and in particular to the 1966 International Covenant on Civil and Political Rights, although it has not yet ratified the respective Optional Protocols. It is also a party to the 1966 International Covenant on Economic, Social and Cultural Rights, the Convention Against Torture and the Convention on the Elimination of All Forms of Discrimination against Women.

HISTORY OF THE CONFLICT

In February 2011, President Mubarak stepped down and handed the power to the Supreme Armed Forces Council (SCAF). He went on trial in August and was later sentenced to life in prison for complicity in the killing of protesters during the 2011 uprising. The protests that ousted President Hosni Mubarak in 2011 raised the hopes of those seeking democratic reform and an end to decades of a repressive regime.[675]

Following Essam Sharraf's resignation, Kamal al-Ganzouri became the new Prime Minister and head of the National unity government in December 2011.[676] After a year and a half of the interim military government, Muslim Brotherhood candidate, Mohammed Morsi won the first democratic presidential elections in half a century in June 2012.

In November, President Morsi issued a decree stripping the judiciary of the right to challenge his decisions. The same month an Islamist-dominated constituent assembly approved a draft constitution that many feared could further restrict freedom of speech and of assembly.[677] Such draft was later publicly approved by referendum.

Protests increased until in July 2013 the military, in light of the demonstrators' demands, ousted Mr Morsi and violently suppressed the protest sit-ins held by the Brotherhood in response. The month of August 2013 saw the worst incidents of State violence on demonstrators in modern Egyptian history. An example is the Rabaa massacre: on 14 August 2013 Egyptian security forces raided two camps of protesters in Cairo, one at al-Nahda Square and a larger one at Rabaa al-Adawiya Square. According to Human Rights Watch, in Rab'a Square, Egyptian security forces carried out one of the world's largest killings of demonstrators in a single day in recent history.[678] These events have been seen in light of further radicalization and deterioration of the situation in Sinai.

By the end of 2013 the government declared the Muslim Brotherhood a terrorist group, after a bomb explosion at a government building in Mansoura.[679] The Muslim Brotherhood, however, denied any involvement in the bombing, while Ansar Bait Al-Maqdis claimed responsibility for the blast, which killed sixteen people.[680] The government started drafting a new constitution and curbed media freedom.[681] On 14 and

[675] 'Egypt Country Profile—Overview', *BBC News*, 17 February 2015, at: <http://www.bbc.com/news/world-africa-13313370>.

[676] 'Egyptian Prime Minister Given Added Powers, Swears in Cabinet', *CNN*, 7 December 2011, at: <http://edition.cnn.com/2011/12/07/world/africa/egypt-prime-minister/index.html>.

[677] 'Egypt Islamists Hurriedly Approve New Constitution', *Yahoo News*, 30 November 2012, at: <http://news.yahoo.com/egypt-islamists-hurriedly-approve-constitution-043918749.html>.

[678] 'Egypt: Rab'a Killings Likely Crimes against Humanity', *Human Rights Watch*, 12 August 2014, at: <http://www.hrw.org/news/2014/08/12/egypt-rab-killings-likely-crimes-against-humanity>.

[679] 'Egypt Profile—Timeline', *BBC News*, 23 April 2015, at: <http://www.bbc.com/news/world-africa-13315719>.

[680] 'Egypt's Confused Ban on Muslim Brotherhood', *The Commentator*, 26 December 2013, at: <http://www.thecommentator.com/article/4507/egypt_s_confused_ban_on_muslim_brotherhood>.

[681] 'Egypt Country Profile—Overview', *BBC News*, 17 February 2015, at: <http://www.bbc.com/news/world-africa-13313370>.

15 January 2014, a referendum took place, where more than 90% of voters opted to ratify Egypt's third constitution.[682] However, the turnout was 38.6% of registered voters, less than the 50% predicted.[683] Egypt's new constitution strengthened the country's three key institutions—the military, the police, and the judiciary—and gave more rights to women and disabled people.[684]

Clashes between supporters of the ousted President Morsi and security forces increased ahead of, during, and after the referendum, with at least forty-nine people killed in the worst incident on 25 January.[685] While several bomb attacks took place in Cairo, multiple attacks continued in the Sinai Peninsula, which included the use of surface-to-air missile by the militants on 27 January, in order to bring down a military helicopter.[686] This attack, claimed by the Ansar Beit al-Maqdis group, represented a significant intensification of the violence in the area.

Arrests of Muslim Brotherhood supporters continued throughout the month, including 444 arrested on charges of rioting and weapons possession.[687] In March 2014, government officials declared that security forces had detained at least 16,000 people since July 2013. WikiThawra, an initiative run by the Egyptian Center for Economic and Social Rights, said that over 41,000 people had faced arrest or criminal charges since Morsi was ousted.[688]

Violence continued in February in the Sinai Peninsula as the jihadi group Ansar Beit al-Maqdis continued to carry out attacks.

On 24 March a court sentenced 529 Muslim Brotherhood members to death for murder and other offences, thus sparking domestic and international condemnation.[689]

At the end of March, Defence Minister Abdul Fattah al-Sisi resigned in order to run for the presidential election in May. Several other candidates withdrew from the

682 'Widespread Boycotts as Egyptian Voters Back New Constitution', *The Guardian*, 16 January 2014, at: <http://www.theguardian.com/world/2014/jan/16/egyptian-voters-back-new-constitution>.

683 'Egypt Constitution Approved by 98.1 Percent', *Al Jazeera*, 24 January 2014, at: <http://www.aljazeera.com/news/middleeast/2014/01/egypt-constitution-approved-981-percent-201411816326470532.html>.

684 'Widespread Boycotts as Egyptian Voters Back New Constitution', *The Guardian*, 16 January 2014, at: <http://www.theguardian.com/world/2014/jan/16/egyptian-voters-back-new-constitution>.

685 'At Least 49 Dead in Egypt as Throngs Commemorate Revolution', *CNN*, 26 January 2014, at: <http://edition.cnn.com/2014/01/25/world/meast/egypt-blast/>.

686 'Surface-to-Air Missile Attack in Sinai Spells Trouble for Israeli Airliners', *The Times*, 27 January 2014, at: <http://world.time.com/2014/01/27/missile-attack-in-sinai-spell-trouble-for-israeli-airliners/>.

687 '444 Muslim Brotherhood Arrested During 2-Day Constitution Poll', *Ahramonline*, 16 January 2014, at: <http://english.ahram.org.eg/NewsContent/1/64/91691/Egypt/Politics-/-Muslim-Brotherhood-arrested-during-day-constituti.aspx>.

688 'Egypt: New Leader Faces Rights Crisis', *Human Rights Watch*, 10 June 2014, at: <http://www.hrw.org/news/2014/06/09/egypt-new-leader-faces-rights-crisis>.

689 'Egyptian Court Sentences 529 Brotherhood Members to Death', *Reuters*, 24 March 2014, at: <http://www.reuters.com/article/2014/03/24/us-egypt-brotherhood-courts-idUSBREA2N0BT20140324>.

presidential race, and one of the former candidates, the human rights lawyer Khaled Ali called the elections a 'farce'.[690]

At the beginning of April, the EU foreign policy chief, Ashton, visited Cairo and formally announced an EU election monitoring mission.[691]

On 15 April a court in Alexandria banned Muslim Brotherhood members from running in any elections in Egypt.[692] A different court at the end of April sentenced 683 defendants to death, including Mohamed Badie, leader of the outlawed Muslim Brotherhood.[693]

At the end of May presidential elections were held and the former army chief Abdul Fattah al-Sisi was declared the winner with more than 90% of the votes.[694]

In June, the Court confirmed the death sentences against Mohamed Badie and at least 182 of his supporters.[695] The next day two protesters got killed in clashes with government forces in Cairo, while demonstrating against the sentence. Several deadly incidents took place in July along the border with Israel as well as in Cairo, where a bomb exploded outside the presidential palace. The repression against the Muslim Brotherhood continued and extended to other groups such as the Alliance for Support of Legitimacy (ASL).

In August the Grand Mufti Shawqi Allam rejected the death sentence for Mohamed Badie and later commuted his sentence to life imprisonment.[696]

Violence continued in Sinai Province as the army reportedly killed eleven militants and the jihadi group Ansar Beit al-Maqdis executed four people over alleged links to the Israeli security army.[697]

During September 2014, attacks by Ansar Beit al-Maqdis (ABM) continued in Sinai including eleven soldiers killed on 2 September, six police members killed on 16 September,

[690] 'Egypt's Election Lacks Candidates', *Al Jazeera*, 27 March 2014, at: <http://www.aljazeera.com/indepth/features/2014/03/egypt-election-lacks-candidates-20143278132166580.html>.

[691] 'US, EU Reset Egypt Policies', *AlMonitor*, 26 April 2014, at: <http://www.al-monitor.com/pulse/originals/2014/04/fahmy-visit-us-egypt-foreign-minister.html#>.

[692] 'Egypt Court Bans Muslim Brotherhood Members From Polls', *The National*, 15 April 2014, at: <http://www.thenational.ae/world/egypt/egypt-court-bans-muslim-brotherhood-members-from-polls>.

[693] 'Egypt Court Confirms Brotherhood Chief's Death Sentence', *Al Jazeera*, 11 April 2014, at: <http://www.aljazeera.com/news/2015/04/egypt-confirms-death-sentence-brotherhood-leaders-150411125719555.html>.

[694] 'Egypt: Abdul Fattah al-Sisi Profile', *BBC News*, 16 May 2014, at: <http://www.bbc.com/news/world-middle-east-19256730>. See also: 'Abdel Fatah al-Sisi Sweeps to Victory in Egyptian Presidential Election', *The Guardian*, 29 May 2014, at: <http://www.theguardian.com/world/2014/may/29/abdel-fatah-al-sisi-sweeps-victory-egyptian-election>.

[695] 'Egypt Sentences Muslim Brotherhood Leader and 182 Followers to Death', *The Guardian*, 21 June 2014, at: <http://www.theguardian.com/world/2014/jun/21/egypt-sentences-muslim-brotherhood-death>.

[696] 'Badie Death Sentence Reduced to Life in Egypt', *Al Jazeera*, 30 August 2014, at: <http://www.aljazeera.com/news/middleeast/2014/08/death-sentence-badie-reduced-life-20148305040329928.html>.

[697] ICG Crisis Watch: Egypt Profile, 1 September 2014, at: <http://www.crisisgroup.org/en/publication-type/crisiswatch/crisiswatch-database.aspx?CountryIDs={B915F536-D27C-4FAC-A808-06B2551C8ADB}#results>.

and four ABM militants reportedly killed on 23 September. ABM continued the beheadings of local Sinai residents accused of cooperating with Israeli intelligence.[698]

At the beginning of October violence continued between students and police forces in university campuses across the country, which resulted in deaths and widespread arrests.[699] Many people reportedly got killed in clashes between the army and militants in Sinai, including thirty-one soldiers on 24 October. As a result the government declared a three-month state of emergency in north and central Sinai; moreover, it closed the border with Gaza and evacuated 1,100 residents along the border to create a buffer zone.[700]

At the end of the month, the Prime Minister enacted a decree dissolving the MB-led National Alliance to Support Legitimacy (NASL).

On 10 November, Ansar Beit al-Maqdis pledged allegiance to the Islamic State armed group, which controls parts of Syria and Iraq, thus also changing its name to Province of Sinai (Welayet Sina).[701]

After President Sisi passed a law in late October expanding the jurisdiction of military courts to try civilians,[702] on 16 November a civilian criminal court referred five Al Azhar University students to a military court.[703]

At the end of November, a court designated IS and affiliated groups as terrorist organizations.[704]

According to field information gathered by Al-Monitor over the month of November, Ansar Bayt al-Maqdis had planted twenty-one bombs almost daily along several routes taken by the army and security officials in north Sinai.[705]

698 'Several Beheadings in Sinai by Terror Group', *Cherson and Molschky*, 10 September 2014, at: <http://chersonandmolschky.com/2014/09/10/beheadings-sinai-terror-group-2/>. See also: 'Egyptian Militants Swear Allegiance to Islamic State', *The Telegraph*, 10 November 2014, at: <http://www.telegraph.co.uk/news/worldnews/islamic-state/11220157/Egyptian-militants-swear-allegiance-to-Islamic-State.html>.

699 'Egypt: Security Forces Use Excessive Force to Crush Student Protests', *Amnesty International*, 17 October 2014, at: <https://www.amnesty.org/en/articles/news/2014/10/egypt-security-forces-use-excessive-force-crush-student-protests/>.

700 'Egypt Imposes State of Emergency in Sinai After Attacks', *BBC News*, 25 October 2014, at: <http://www.bbc.com/news/world-middle-east-29766945>.

701 'Egyptian Militant Group Pledges Loyalty to Islamic State in Audio Clip', *Reuters*, 10 November 2014, at: <http://www.reuters.com/article/2014/11/10/us-egypt-ansar-islamicstate-idUSKCN0IU0DD20141110?feedType=RSS&feedName=worldNews>. See also: 'Ansar Bayt al-Maqdis Joins Islamic State', *AlMonitor*, 13 November 2014, at: <http://www.al-monitor.com/pulse/security/2014/11/egypt-ansar-maqdis-sinai.html#>.

702 'Egypt: Unprecedented Expansion of Military Courts', *Human Rights Watch*, 17 November 2014, at: <http://www.hrw.org/news/2014/11/17/egypt-unprecedented-expansion-military-courts>.

703 'Egypt to Try Five Students in Military Court on Riot Charges', *Reuters*, 16 November 2014, at: <http://uk.reuters.com/article/2014/11/16/uk-egypt-military-trial-idUKKCN0J00UB20141116>.

704 'Egypt Outlaws ISIL and Affiliated Groups', *AlJazeera*, 1 December 2014, at: <http://www.aljazeera.com/news/middleeast/2014/12/egypt-outlaws-isil-affiliated-groups-20141215544430594.html>.

705 'After Joining IS, Ansar Bayt Al-Maqdis Expands in Egypt', *Al Monitor*, 1 December 2014, at: <http://www.al-monitor.com/pulse/originals/2014/12/egypt-ansar-maqdis-sinai-spread.html#ixzz3aCAoo0Bt>.

In December courts continued to issue death sentences against Muslim Brotherhood supporters,[706] while military prosecutors referred at least 820 people to military trials in Ismailia, Beheira, and Minya, signifying a marked shift toward the use of a military justice system.[707]

At the beginning of 2015, a new Sinai-based militant group emerged from the split of Ansar Beit al-Maqdis, due to a disagreement over ABM's pledge of allegiance to the Islamic State.[708]

PARTIES TO THE CONFLICT

The parties to the conflict in 2014 are Egypt and its armed forces against the Sinai Province group.

Various groups are also operating in that area, which, however, do not yet meet the organization criteria in order to be considered as being parties to the conflict.

Egypt armed forces

Egyptian armed forces are estimated to include 468,500 active frontline personnel as well as 800,000 as reserve personnel.[709]

Sinai Province

Sinai Province was previously called Ansar Beit al-Maqdis (Champions of Jerusalem), but announced a name change in November 2014 when it pledged allegiance to IS.[710] Ansar Beit al-Maqdis was an Al-Qaeda-inspired group that started its operations immediately after the January 2011 uprising that led to the fall of Egypt's long-running ruler

[706] 'Egypt Sentences 188 Muslim Brotherhood Supporters to Death', *BBC News*, 2 December 2014, at: <http://www.bbc.com/news/world-middle-east-30302258>.

[707] 'HRW: Over 800 Civilians Sent to Military Court Since October', *Mada Masr*, 19 December 2014, at: <http://www.madamasr.com/news/hrw-over-800-civilians-sent-military-court-october>. See also: 'Egypt: Surge of Military Trials', *Human Rights Watch*, 18 December 2014, at: <http://www.hrw.org/news/2014/12/18/egypt-surge-military-trials>.

[708] ICG: Egypt Profile, 5 January 2015, at: <http://www.crisisgroup.org/en/publication-type/crisiswatch/crisiswatch-database.aspx?CountryIDs={B915F536-D27C-4FAC-A808-06B2551C8ADB}#results>.

[709] 'Egypt: Manpower', *GFP*, 1 April 2015, at: <http://www.globalfirepower.com/country-military-strength-detail.asp?country_id=egypt>.

[710] 'Ansar Bayt al-Maqdis joins Islamic State', *AlMonitor*, 13 November 2014, at: <http://www.al-monitor.com/pulse/security/2014/11/egypt-ansar-maqdis-sinai.html#>.

Hosni Mubarak. The group was initially known for launching attacks on Israeli targets and interests.[711]

The exact number of fighters is difficult to assess, as estimates are different and contradictory. According to one of these, Ansar Bayt al-Maqdis militants reportedly did not exceed fifty people inside Sinai, but the group had succeeded in opening fronts inside other Egyptian districts, especially after pledging allegiance to IS. Indeed several people who supported the idea of a jihadist caliphate joined the group, in addition to defecting members from the Muslim Brotherhood.[712]

According to a different estimate, ABM's total number of fighters (with 'high strategic and technological capacity') was as high as 1,000.[713]

CASUALTIES

In 2014, at least 712 fatalities were identified in Egypt as related to conflict with Ansar Beit al-Maqdis/Wilayat Sinai and clashes in the Sinai Peninsula, through analyses of data recorded by the Armed Conflict Location and Event Data Project (ACLED). The majority of fatalities were militants, followed by military personnel and police.

Of the total number of militants recorded as killed in 2014, at least 242 were specifically recorded as having been linked to Ansar Beit al-Maqdis or 'State of Sinai' while reporting on the other conflict events with fatalities which occurred in Sinai and referred to more generally to 'militants' and 'extremists'. The months when the most fatalities were recorded (with over 100 casualties per month) were July, September, and October.[714] It was otherwise noted that 'the way the group has documented attacks on the army and police confirms its high level of preparedness and its capabilities'.[715] There were also thirty-one civilian deaths related to the conflict in Sinai Peninsula, including seven children. Most civilian casualties were not directly targeted and occurred as a result of the use of mortars, rockets, and roadside bombs.

711 'Egypt Attack: Profile of Sinai Province Militant Group', *BBC News*, 30 January 2015, at: <http://www.bbc.com/news/world-middle-east-25882504>.

712 'After Joining IS, Ansar Bayt al-Maqdis Expands in Egypt', *Al Monitor*, 1 December 2014, at: <http://www.al-monitor.com/pulse/originals/2014/12/egypt-ansar-maqdis-sinai-spread.html#ixzz3aCAoo0Bt>.

713 'Terror in the Sinai', *The Henry Jackson Society*, 2014, at: <http://henryjacksonsociety.org/wp-content/uploads/2014/05/HJS-Terror-in-the-Sinai-Report-Colour-Web.pdf>.

714 War Report analysis of ACLED data for calendar year 2014. Raleigh, C., Linke, A., Hegre, H., and Karlsen, J., 2010, 'Introducing ACLED-Armed Conflict Location and Event Data', *Journal of Peace Research*, vol. 47, no. 5, pp. 1–10.

715 Thabit al-Maamour, 'The Rise of "Wilayat Sinai": A Significant Challenge for the Sisi Regime', *Al Monitor*, 4 February 2015, <http://english.al-akhbar.com/node/23607>.

Ansar Beit-al Maqdis role in activities causing violence-related casualties increased through 2014. They were first recorded in the ACLED data in the Sinai Peninsula in November 2013. The group's tactics have often involved targeting military and security units where large scale operations militant threats frequently took place. ACLED reported that these events 'have incurred high fatality rates with military forces of Egypt being involved in the majority of conflict events and fatalities in North Sinai in 2014'.[716]

WAR CRIMES ALLEGATIONS, INVESTIGATIONS, AND PROSECUTIONS

On 1 May, International Criminal Court (ICC) prosecutors dismissed a communication filed by lawyers representing Morsi and his defunct Freedom and Justice Party seeking ICC jurisdiction in Egypt. The ICC dismissed the declaration on the grounds that the statement purporting to grant the ICC jurisdiction was not filed by the recognized Government of Egypt itself.

[716] ACLED, 'Conflict Trends (No. 30) Real-Time Analysis of African Political Violence,' September 2014, Egypt, p. 4.

Armed conflict in India in 2014

KEY CASUALTY DATA FOR 2014

Civilians killed:	128	(Source: SATP)
Police/military/militia killed:	87	(Source: SATP)
Naxalites killed:	99	(Source: SATP)

CLASSIFICATION OF THE CONFLICT

India was involved in a non-international armed conflict (NIAC) with the Naxalites (Maoists) in 2014.

SUMMARY OF APPLICABLE INTERNATIONAL LAW

Both parties to the conflict were bound by customary international humanitarian law (IHL) and human rights law, including customary IHL rules of distinction, proportionality, and precautions in attacks; the obligations of humane treatment, as set out in Common Article 3 to the 1949 Geneva Conventions; the obligation not to recruit and use children as soldiers; and by the duty to respect and protect fundamental human rights. This includes the duty to respect the rights to life and to freedom from torture or other forms of cruel, inhuman, or degrading treatment or punishment.

India is party to the four 1949 Geneva Conventions but not the 1977 Additional Protocol II. India is also party to the 1966 International Covenant on Civil and Political Rights and the 1966 International Covenant on Economic, Social and Cultural Rights.

India is not party to the 1997 Anti-Personnel Mine Ban Convention or the 2008 Convention on Cluster Munitions. India is neither a party nor a signatory to the 2013 Arms Trade Treaty (ATT).[717]

HISTORY OF THE CONFLICT[718]

India's Maoist insurgency began in the forests of the State of West Bengal in the late 1960s. Several decades later it has become, in the words of Prime Minister Manmohan

[717] India abstained from the vote on the adoption of the ATT by the UN General Assembly on 2 April 2013.

[718] Unless otherwise stated, this section is based on 'Profile: India's Maoist rebels', *BBC*, 4 March 2011, at: <http://www.bbc.com/news/world-south-asia-12640645>.

Singh, India's 'greatest internal security challenge'. The Maoists and affiliated groups are active in more than a third of India's 600-odd districts, according to the authorities. More than 6,000 people have died in the rebels' fight for communist rule in these States.

The Maoists' military leader is Koteshwar Rao, otherwise known as Kishenji. He reportedly suffered temporary paralysis in June 2010 when a police bullet hit him in the knee. In January 2011, Kishenji issued a statement saying he expected India to succumb to a Maoist revolution by 2025. Estimates in 2011 suggested he commanded at least 20,000 armed fighters. They are said to get most of their weapons by raiding police bases. Other estimates reported in 2013 suggested Maoist rebels could number up to 40,000 of which thousands 'may be armed with weapons ranging from AK-47s to light machine-guns raided from police stations or bought from dealers in Nepal. The cadre mostly comprises farmers, landless labourers, tribals and the extremely poor, including women and children'.[719]

Analysts say the longevity of the Maoist rebellion is partly due to the local support they receive. The rebels say they are fighting for the rights of indigenous tribes people and the rural poor who they say have been neglected by governments for decades. Maoists claim to represent local concerns over land ownership and equitable distribution of resources. Ultimately they seek to establish a 'communist society' by overthrowing India's 'semi-colonial, semi-feudal' form of rule through armed struggle.

The government has launched several major offensives against the rebels. In 2009, rebels gained virtual control of Lalgarh district in West Bengal barely 250 kilometres from the State capital, Calcutta. For many months, rebels, supported by local villagers, held hundreds of paramilitary forces at bay. The Maoists declared it to be India's first 'liberated zone' but Indian security forces finally overwhelmed the rebels. In April 2010, rebels ambushed paramilitary troops in the dense jungles of central Chhattisgarh State, killing at least seventy-six soldiers, in what is said to be the worst-ever Maoist attack on Indian security forces.

In 2010, the Maoists faced India's biggest ever anti-Maoist offensive. Nearly 50,000 federal paramilitary troops and tens of thousands of policemen took part in the operation across several States. While the rebels were pushed back deep into their jungle strongholds, they have continued to carry out hit-and-run attacks and numerous high-profile kidnappings. India's Government in turn pledged to crack down harder unless rebels renounced violence and entered peace talks. The Andhra Pradesh Government initiated peace talks in 2004 but the ceasefire did not hold for long. The Maoists made an offer in 2010 but the central government rejected it.[720]

[719] *Reuters*, 'Who are India's Maoists and why they are in the news', *India Insight*, 29 May 2013, at: <http://blogs.reuters.com/india/2013/05/29/who-are-indias-maoists-and-why-they-are-in-the-news/>.

[720] Ibid.

Clashes and attacks between the Maoist and government troops took place throughout 2013.[721] In November, the government deployed more than 100,000 security personnel to secure the elections in the restive Chhattisgarh region; polls saw a 75% turnout despite a Maoist boycott.[722] Several members of the security forces were killed in reported Maoist attacks in Bijapur, Munger, and Sukma districts. On 20 December, the Revolutionary Communist Party, a breakaway section of the Communist Party of India (Maoist), declared its abandonment of the Maoist armed struggle.[723]

The new government at the national level has introduced a number of new initiatives and training programmes for officials working in the naxal affected areas. This has added to the impetus provided by the last administration. Up to 144 naxalites surrendered to State authorities between May and August 2014, compared to forty-four in the same period last year. However, sporadic instances of violence occur in areas of naxal stronghold, especially in the State of Chhattisgarh.[724]

However, during 2014, clashes and violence continued. On 28 February 2014, five policemen were killed in a naxal ambush while they were deployed to provide protection to workers engaged in constructing a road in the Dantewada district of Chhattisgarh.[725]

On 11 March 2014, fifteen security personnel belonging to the Central Police Reserve Force and the State Police were killed along with one civilian, in a naxal attack, as they were engaged in a road opening exercise in the Sukma district in Chhattisgarh.[726]

On 11 May 2014, seven Police Commandos were killed in a Maoist landmine blast in the forest of Ghadchiroli district of Maharashtra.[727]

Finally, on 1 December 2014, fourteen Central Police Reserve Force personnel were killed again in the Sukma District of Chhattisgarh, the State is said to be the most affected in India from the Maoist insurgency.[728]

[721] See India profile, *The War Report 2013*, edited by Casey-Maslen, S., Oxford University Press, 2014, at p. 142.

[722] ICG, Crisis Watch Database: India (non-Kashmir), 1 December 2013.

[723] ICG, Crisis Watch Database: India (non-Kashmir), 1 January 2014.

[724] SATP, South Asia Terrorism Portal, Timeline Naxal Insurgency, at: <http://www.satp.org/satporgtp/countries/india/timeline/2014.htm>.

[725] 'Five Policemen Killed in Dantewada Naxal Ambush', *The Hindu*, 1 March 2014, at: <http://www.thehindu.com/news/national/other-states/five-policemen-killed-in-dantewada-naxal-ambush/article5736010.ece>.

[726] '16 Killed in Naxal Attack on Security Personnel in Chhattisgarh', *India Today*, 11 March 2014, at: <http://indiatoday.intoday.in/story/naxals-attack-security-forces-in-chhattisgarh/1/347813.html>.

[727] Ahmed, S., 'Gadchiroli: Landmine Blast Triggered by Naxals Kill Seven Policemen', 11 May 2014 at: <http://ibnlive.in.com/news/gadchiroli-landmine-blast-triggered-by-naxals-kill-seven-policemen/471073-3-237.html>.

[728] 'Maoist Attack Kills 14 CRPF Personnel in Chhattisgarh', 2 December 2014, at: <http://www.hindustantimes.com/india-news/13-crpf-men-killed-in-maoist-attack-in-chhattisgarh/article1-1292151.aspx>.

PARTIES TO THE CONFLICT

The parties to the NIACs in 2014 were India and its armed forces against Naxalite Maoist armed groups.

Indian armed forces

India is estimated to have 1.325 million active frontline military personnel and a further 2.14 million in reserve.[729]

Maoists[730]

Maoists are also known as 'Naxalites' because of the violent left-wing uprising in 1967, which began in the West Bengal village of Naxalbari. Although this was eventually quashed by police, over the years India's Maoists have regrouped and asserted control over vast swathes of land in central and eastern India, establishing a so-called 'red corridor'. This spans the States of Jharkand, West Bengal, Orissa, Bihar, Chhattisgarh, and Andhra Pradesh and also reaches into Uttar Pradesh and Karnataka. In 2004, several Maoist groups merged to form the Communist Party of India (Maoist), which is now the largest left-wing extremist organization in the country. Their aim is to overthrow the State and usher in a classless society. The Maoists are banned in India.[731]

CASUALTIES

The South Asia Terrorism Portal (SATP) reported a steep decline in fatalities from violence related to left-wing extremists, including the Communist Party of India-Maoist, from 1,180 in 2010 to 314 in 2014.[732] By State, the most casualties in 2014 occurred in Chhattisgarh (113) and Jharkhand (ninety-seven). Though

[729] 'Indian Military Strength', *Globalfirepower.com*, last updated on 27 March 2014, at: <http://www.globalfirepower.com/country-military-strength-detail.asp?country_id=india>. The Indian army's website contains the motto 'To be born free is an accident. To live free is a privilege. To die free is a responsibility', <http://indianarmy.nic.in/Index.aspx?flag=FNzcf7eEG9ARr6J9FBR0GA==>.

[730] Unless otherwise stated, this section is based on 'Profile: India's Maoist rebels', *BBC*, 4 March 2011.

[731] *Reuters*, 'Who are India's Maoists and Why They Are in the News', *India Insight*, 29 May 2013.

[732] SATP recorded the following total fatalities among civilians, security force personnel and CPI-Maoists related to Naxal/left wing extremist violence: 1,180 in 2010, 602 in 2011, 367 in 2012, 421 in 2013, 314 in 2014. See, 'Fatalities in Left-wing Extremism: 2005-2015', <http://www.satp.org/satporgtp/countries/india/maoist/data_sheets/fatalitiesnaxal05-11.htm>; and 'Fatalities in Left-wing Extremism: 2014', SATP, <http://www.satp.org/satporgtp/countries/india/maoist/data_sheets/fatalitiesnaxal14.htm>.

there were overall declining casualties in all States, SATP data also showed that in Chhattisgarh State the number of deaths of security force personnel increased to fifty-five in 2014 from forty-five in 2013. The majority of these casualties in Chhattisgarh however occurred in two attacks on vehicles carrying security personnel. One such attack, in March, caused fifteen security personnel fatalities and another, in December, resulted in fourteen deaths of security personnel.[733] The December attack in Chhattisgarh resulted in a rise in casualties towards the end of 2014 that was also reported in Indian media.

Ministry of Home Affairs data showed that 372 fatalities occurred in 2014: among the 222 civilians it recorded as killed ninety-one were police informants, another eighty-seven were among security personnel, and sixty-two Naxal militants were also killed.[734] According to other data reported as received from the Naxal Management Division, which was released through a freedom of information process, Naxal violence and related fatalities were reported to have dropped to lows of 1,091 and 309 respectively. This was noted as being the lowest for over a decade on both counts. The data reportedly also demonstrated that the number of recorded deaths had declined consistently between 2011 and 2013.[735]

However, due to the high number of incidents of Naxal-related violence it was stated by Baijayant 'Jay' Panda MP during debate in the lower house of India's Parliament, the Lok Sabha (Assembly of the People), that despite the ongoing decline in casualties a serious concern remained:

> If you look at left wing extremism, in 2014 alone, last year, we had 1090 incidents and 309 deaths caused by those, who call themselves Maoists. This is a very large number. It does show an improvement over the year before that. Compared to the previous year, that is, 2013, where the incidents were 1136 and deaths were 397, these have come down to 1090 incidents and 309 deaths. This, of course, is commendable that the trend is improving. But these figures are

[733] 'Maoists Kill 15 in Chhattisgarh,' *The Hindu*, 13 March 2015, <http://www.thehindu.com/news/national/maoists-kill-15-in-chhattisgarh/article5773315.ece>; and Srivastava, R. K., 'Deadly Naxal Attack in Chhattisgarh; 14 CRPF Troopers Dead, 12 Injured', *Z News*, <http://zeenews.india.com/news/chhattisgarh/deadly-naxal-attack-in-chhattisgarh-14-crpf-troopers-dead-12-injured_1507701.html>.

[734] Government of India Ministry of Home Affairs, 'Statistics of LWE violence (2010 to 2015)' in Left Wing Extremism (LWE) Division, last updated 15 April 2015, <http://mha.nic.in/naxal_new>.

[735] 'Civilians Biggest Casualty of Naxal Violence', *The Hindu*, 19 April 2015, <http://www.thehindu.com/news/national/civilians-biggest-casualty-of-naxal-violence/article7117827.ece>. Some media reports reported reversed fatality these figures for 2013 and 2014 and stated that the 'home ministry said that 309 people lost their lives in 1,090 incidents of Naxal violence in 2013 in comparison to 397 deaths in 1136 incidents in 2014'. See for example, 'J&K civilian casualties DOUBLED in 2014, home ministry reveals', 24 March 2015, <http://www.dailymail.co.uk/indiahome/indianews/article-3010142/J-K-civilian-casualties-DOUBLED-2014-home-ministry-reveals.html>; and '86.6 percent more civilian casualties in J&K in 2014: MHA', last updated 24 March 2015, <http://zeenews.india.com/news/jammu-and-kashmir/86-6-percent-more-civilian-casualties-in-jk-in-2014-mha_1567037.html>.

something to be worried about. If more than 1000 incidents continue to happen throughout the year in our country, this is something that we must all take very seriously.[736]

DISPLACED PERSONS

In 2014, there were at least 345,000 new internal displaced persons (IDPs) in India, leading to a total of 853,900 persons being internally displaced in the country as of December 2014.[737]

WAR CRIMES ALLEGATIONS, INVESTIGATIONS, AND PROSECUTIONS

India is neither a State party nor a signatory to the 1998 Rome Statute of the International Criminal Court (ICC). No allegations of war crimes are known to have been made against either Indian military personnel regarding any acts concerning the NIAC in 2014.

[736] Lok Sabha Debates, (Part I—Proceedings with Questions and Answers), 27 April 2015 (Uncorrected/Not for Publication), p. 226.

[737] Internal Displacement Monitoring Centre (IDMC) 'Global Overview 2015', May 2015, p. 84. The figure is compiled from various sources, including media and NGO reports over the last five years, and only covers regions where data is available. There are no government or international agencies that monitor displacement comprehensively.

Armed conflict in Iraq in 2014

KEY CASUALTY DATA FOR 2014

Civilians killed:	12,282	(Source: UNAMI)
Civilians injured:	23,126	(Source: UNAMI)
Military killed:	3,689	(Source: UNAMI)
Military injured:	4,281	(Source: UNAMI)
Police killed:	1,508	(Source: UNAMI)
Police injured:	2,098	(Source: UNAMI)
NSAG killed:	1,794 (1 January to 30 September)	(Source: Agence France-Presse)
NSAG injured:	278 (1 January to 30 September)	(Source: Agence France-Presse)

CLASSIFICATION OF THE CONFLICT

Iraq has been mired in violence for more than a decade. The conditions for the applicability of IHL (protracted violence and sufficient level of organizations of the armed groups) were not fulfilled. In January 2014 however a non-international armed conflict between Iraqi armed forces, supported by an international coalition, and the Islamic State erupted. Upon the invitation of the Iraqi Government the US-led coalition began air strikes against IS targets in Iraq in August 2014.

SUMMARY OF APPLICABLE INTERNATIONAL LAW

All parties to the conflicts are bound by inter alia Common Article 3 to the 1949 Geneva Conventions; the customary international humanitarian law (IHL) rules of distinction, proportionality, and precautions in attack; the obligation not to recruit and use children as soldiers; and by the duty to respect, at a minimum, fundamental human rights. This includes the duty to respect the rights to life and to dignity.

Iraq is party to the four 1949 Geneva Conventions, the 1977 Additional Protocol I but not to the 1977 Additional Protocol II. Iraq is party to the 1997 Anti-Personnel Mine Ban Convention, 1993 Chemical Weapons Convention, and the 2008 Convention on Cluster Munitions. Iraq is also party to several human rights treaties, including: the 1966 International Covenant on Civil and Political Rights, the 1966 International Covenant on Economic, Social and Cultural Rights, as well as the 1984 Convention against Torture.

HISTORY OF THE CONFLICT

Deep political tensions have been mounting in Iraq since 2011 owing to alienation of the country's Sunni minority from the Shia-dominated government in Baghdad. These tensions were vented in anti-government protests that erupted across the country in late 2011. Following violent crackdowns on anti-government protest in the Anbar province at the end of 2013, IS took advantage of the growing insecurity and greatly expanded their operations in Iraq. IS quickly managed to take control over some of the major checkpoints on the borders with Syria and Jordan, giving it the opportunity to connect the main areas under its control in eastern Syria and western Iraq.

In June 2014, Islamic State militants declared that they had established a caliphate in the territory they control stretching from Aleppo in North-West Syria to the eastern Iraqi province of Diyala. On 29 June 2014, IS released a video, entitled 'End of Sykes Picot', a reference to the agreement between France and Britain on dividing up Iraq and Syria after the First World War. In the video an IS spokesperson explains the new caliphate in Iraq and Syria and warns '[t]his is not the first border we will break, we will break other borders'.[738] Abu Bakr al-Baghdadi is declared as the leader of the new caliphate.

The rapid advance across northern Iraq (and Syria) by militant fighters from IS threw the region into chaos and led the Iraqi Government to formally invite a US-led coalition to conduct airstrikes against IS in Iraq.[739] Coalition air strikes against IS key positions began on 8 August 2014. So far the coalition has conducted at least 1,250 air strikes against IS targets in Iraq.[740] Currently it appears that IS militants in Iraq have been forced on to the back foot by the coalition action, although they remain capable of launching offensives.

IS fighters targeted a number of Iraqi dams and gained control over a number of oil fields during their advance, capturing the dam facility at Falluja in April 2014. They went on to take Mosul dam in August, before US air strikes helped force them out later that month. IS fighters also attacked the country's second largest dam at Haditha, but the area was secured by Iraqi forces in September 2014.

In early August 2014, IS began a brutal ethnic-cleansing campaign against Iraq's Yezidi minority in an area around Sinjar, in north-western Iraq. Thousands of Yezidi were killed and thousands of women and girls were raped or abducted and forced into

[738] 'Isis Announces Islamic Caliphate in Area Straddling Iraq and Syria', *The Guardian*, 30 June 2014, at: <http://www.theguardian.com/world/2014/jun/30/isis-announces-islamic-caliphate-iraq-syria>.

[739] 'Iraq Formally Asks US to Launch Air Strikes Against Rebels', *BBC News*, 18 June 2014, at: <http://www.bbc.com/news/world-middle-east-27905849>.

[740] 'Battle for Iraq and Syria in Maps', *BBC News*, 24 February 2015, at: <http://www.bbc.com/news/world-middle-east-27838034>.

sexual slavery.[741] To escape the violence many Yezidi fled up mount Sinijar. By mid-August 150,000 people were stranded up the mountain with very little access to shelter, water, food, and medical supplies. [742]

On 8 August, following an emergency session at the UN Security Council, and at the request of the Iraqi Government the United States, United Kingdom, France, and Australia began airdrops of humanitarian aid to those trapped on the mountain. In mid-August the Kurdish People's Protection Units (YPG) with the assistance of US air-strikes secured a route down the mountain thereby providing the opportunity for tens of thousands of civilians trapped on the mountain to escape.[743] Nevertheless thousands of civilians remained stranded on the mountain too fearful or frail to make the journey down. An operation conducted by approximately 8,000 Kurdish Peshmerga, with US air support, broke the IS siege of mount Sinjar in December 2014.[744]

As of March 2015 around 4,000 Yezidi women and children remain in the captivity of IS as *malak yamiin* (spoils of war), and continue to endure repeated rape, forced marriage, and sexual slavery. Some are sold in open markets while others are given as 'gifts' to fighters in Iraq and Syria. Nearly 500,000 Yezidi remain displaced living in refugee camps and abandoned buildings.[745]

In mid-February 2015, the US-led coalition began to conduct a number of air strikes against the IS targets near the militant-controlled city of Mosul, which was taken by IS in June 2014. It has been widely reported that an operation to retake Mosul will likely begin in April or May 2015 and will involve between 20,000 and 25,000 Iraqi troops. According to one official from the US Central Command five Iraqi Army brigades will soon go through training run by the US-led coalition to prepare for the mission. [746]

According to the UN Refugee Agency, the latest conflict has forced more than 2 million people to be newly or repeatedly displaced as they try to escape the conflict across

[741] *Amnesty International*, 'Escape from Hell: Torture and Sexual Slavery in Islamic State captivity in Iraq Hell', December 2014, at: <https://www.es.amnesty.org/uploads/media/Escape_from_hell_-_Torture_and_sexual_slavery_in_Islamic_State_captivity_in_Iraq_-_English.pdf>.

[742] 'Mount Sinjar: Iraq's Mountain of Death', *The Telegraph*, 19 August 2014, at: <http://www.telegraph.co.uk/news/worldnews/middleeast/iraq/11024987/Mount-Sinjar-Iraqs-mountain-of-death.html>.

[743] OHCHR, Report on the Protection of Civilians in Armed Conflict in Iraq, 6 July–10 September 2014, at: <http://www.ohchr.org/Documents/Countries/IQ/UNAMI_OHCHR_POC_Report_FINAL_6July_10September2014.pdf>.

[744] 'Mount Sinjar: Islamic State Siege Broken, say Kurds', *BBC News*, 19 December 2014, at: <http://www.bbc.com/news/world-middle-east-30539170>.

[745] 'Vian Dakhil: Iraq's Only Female Yazidi MP on the Battle to Save Her People', *The Observer*, 8 February 2015, at: <http://www.huffingtonpost.com/2015/02/08/vian-dakhil-iraqs-only-fe_n_6641480.html>.

[746] 'Up to 25,000 Iraqi Troops Preparing for Attack on Islamic State in Mosul, *The Guardian*, 20 February 2015, at: <http://www.theguardian.com/world/2015/feb/20/up-to-25000-iraqi-troops-preparing-for-attack-on-islamic-state-in-mosul>.

central Iraq and the Kurdistan Region of Iraq.[747] Those fleeing the conflict are now mainly internally displaced though some have sought refuge in other States.

PARTIES TO THE CONFLICTS

There are numerous armed actors taking part in the conflict in Iraq. The following are a selection of some of the main actors.

Iraqi Army

The Iraqi Army is understood to currently have 48,000 soldiers. Repeated jihadist attacks in 2014 left the army demoralized and led thousands of soldiers to desert, particularly after the successful operation by IS to take the city of Mosul in June 2014. The Army's sectarian make-up has also been an issue as Iraq's Sunnis feel alienated by the Shia-dominated force.[748]

Popular Mobilisation (Hashid Shaabi)

The Popular Mobilisation comprises dozens of Shia militia groups, and has been taking a lead role in Iraqi operations against IS. It was formed by the Shia-led government in June 2014 after the army collapsed in the face of an advance by IS across northern Iraq. The Popular Mobilisation is headed by Jamal Jaafar Mohammed, also known as Abu Mahdi al-Mohandis, a former Badr Organisation commander who is close to Iranian General Qassem Soleimani. Iran provides funding, weapons, and military advisers to militia in the Popular Mobilisation, and reportedly controls several of the militia groups directly.[749]

Thousands volunteered to fight in the Popular Mobilisation after Iraq's most senior Shia cleric, Grand Ayatollah Ali Sistani, called on people to take up arms and defend their country and its holy sites.

Popular Mobilisation militiamen have been accused of committing atrocities and acting with impunity. Activists say Sunni Arab civilians have been forced from their homes, kidnapped, and in some cases executed.

747 2015 UNHCR country operations profile—Iraq, at: <http://www.unhcr.org/pages/49e486426.html>.

748 'In 45 Seconds: How Strong is Iraq's Army?', *BBC News*, 2 March 2015, at: <http://www.bbc.com/news/world-middle-east-27820800>.

749 'Iraqi Forces Seek to Encircle IS Fighters in Tikrit', *BBC News*, 4 March 2015, at: <http://www.bbc.com/news/world-middle-east-31727470>.

Islamic State (IS)

Under its former name, Islamic State in Iraq and the Levant (ISIL), IS was formed in early 2013 growing out of Al-Qaeda in Iraq. In April 2013, the leader of the Al-Qaeda affiliated Islamic State of Iraq, Abu Bakr al-Baghdadi, announced that his group was merging with Jabhat Al-Nusra to form the Islamic State of Iraq and Al-Sham, also known as the Islamic State of Iraq and the Levant. However, this unilateral declaration was rejected by both the leader of Jabhat Al-Nusra, Abu Mohammed al-Jawlani, and the leader of Al-Qaeda, Ayman al-Zaqahiri. In May 2013 the group split from Al-Nusra and began acting under the name Islamic State of Iraq and Al-Sham, under the leadership of Abu Bakr al-Baghdadi.[750] Despite IS's separation from Al-Qaeda, it expanded its operations in Syria and experienced military success in both Syria and Iraq, capturing several major cities, including Raqqa, Fallujah, and Mosul. The funds seized through these invasions and seizure of oil fields in Iraq and eastern Syria combined with income from foreign donors and criminal activities, such as smuggling and the extortion of local businesses, have enabled IS to gather cash and assets worth up to $2 billion.[751]

Currently the group's precise size is unclear. Its numbers have significantly risen over the last five years. Estimates of the number of fighters vary from around 12,000[752] to 30,000. Some estimates state that about 80% of Western fighters in Syria have joined the group. IS claims to have fighters from the United Kingdom, France, Germany, and other European countries, as well as the United States, the Arab world, and the Caucasus. Despite the recruitment of thousands of Syrians the IS leadership structure is largely dominated by foreign fighters.[753]

On 29 June 2014, the group again changed its name to the Islamic State (IS), declaring a Caliphate and naming its leader Abu Bakr al-Baghdadi as Caliph; it called upon all Muslims to declare allegiance to the new Caliphate. IS gave Christians living in Mosul the choice to convert to Islam or leave the Caliphate, thousands were forced to flee before the two-day deadline expired.

There are numerous substantiated reports of serious, systematic, and widespread violations of IHL and gross human rights abuses perpetuated by IS in Iraq, including ethnic cleansing, the direct targeting of civilians and civilian infrastructure, executions and targeted killings of civilians, abductions, torture, rape, sexual slavery, and other forms

[750] 'Profile: Abu Bakr al-Baghdadi', *BBC News*, 2 August 2014, at: <http://www.bbc.com/news/world-middle-east-28749734>, at: <http://www.bbc.com/news/world-middle-east-28749734>.

[751] 'How an Arrest in Iraq Revealed Isis's $2bn Jihadist Network', *The Guardian*, 15 June 2014, at: <http://www.theguardian.com/world/2014/jun/15/iraq-isis-arrest-jihadists-wealth-power>.

[752] The Soufan Group, Foreign Fighters in Syria, June 2014, at: <http://soufangroup.com/foreign-fighters-in-syria/>.

[753] Independent International Commission of Inquiry on Syria releases its report Rule of Terror: Living under ISIS, 14 November 2014, §13.

of sexual violence against women and children, forced recruitment of child soldiers, and destruction of places of religious or cultural significance. On 15 August 2014, the UN Security Council unanimously adopted Resolution 2170 (2014), condemning the 'gross, systematic and widespread abuse' of human rights by the Islamic State. The Resolution imposes sanctions, such as travel restrictions and asset freezing, on members of IS.[754]

Kurdish Peshmerga

Since IS took control of Mosul in June 2014, the Kurdish Peshmerga have taken a lead role in trying to retake Northern Iraq. The Kurdish Peshmerga have roots leading back to groups of loosely organized tribal border guards in the late 1800s but were formally organized as the national fighting force of the Kurdish people after the fall of the Ottoman Empire in the wake of the First World War. As the Kurdish nationalist movement grew, so too did the identity of the Peshmerga who are now seen as a key part of Kurdish culture. The ultimate objective of the Peshmerga is to secure an independent Kurdish State.[755]

The Kurdish Pashmerga are thought to number around 190,000 male and female fighters. They are mainly armed with Soviet-style weapons, either seized from Saddam's army or purchased in later years from former Communist bloc countries. The Peshmerga are considered to be well trained, organized, and battle hardened fighters, and are particularly formidable in combat in mountainous terrain.[756]

The Pashmerga have received combat training from German, Italian, British, and US armed forces, which consider the group as crucial in their fight against IS.[757] Britain has supplied the Peshmerga with forty heavy machine guns and ammunition, but has denied further requests from the Pashmerga for more weaponry.[758]

In December 2014 Kurdish Pashmerga fighters swept across the northern side of Sinjar mountain freeing hundreds of Yazidis trapped there for months by IS fighters. The Pashmerga offensive was coordinated with US air support.[759]

Islamic Army of Iraq

The Islamic Army of Iraq (IAI) is one of the major Sunni armed groups that formed after the US invasion of Iraq in 2003, the group is thought to be led by former Iraqi

754 UN Security Council Resolution 2170 (2014).

755 'Profile: Who are the Peshmerga?', *BBC News*, 12 August 2014.

756 'Mapping Iraq's Fighting Groups', *Al Jazeera*, 27 June 2014.

757 'Kurdish Peshmerga Learn Tactics to Fight IS', CNN, 25 February 2015.

758 'Kurdish Pashmerga Call for Heavy Weaponry to Take Their Fight to ISIS', *The Guardian*, 22 February 2015.

759 'Yazidis Cheer Kurds on Iraqi Mountain for Breaking Islamic State Siege', *Reuters*, 20 December 2014, at: <http://www.reuters.com/article/2014/12/20/us-mideast-crisis-iraq-sinjar-idUSKBN0JY0ML20141220>.

military officers. During 2006–2007, some IAI members were thought to have joined the US-backed Awakening Councils to fight Al-Qaeda. The group also reportedly shifted its attention more towards what it considered growing Iranian influence inside Iraq, especially as US forces began to withdraw. After a relatively inactive period, the group was seen as a supporter of the anti-government protests that erupted across Iraq in 2011.[760]

In June 2014, IAI released a video allegedly showing its troops patrolling the eastern areas of Baghdad. It also proclaimed its intention to enter the Iraqi capital. IAI is thought to be more active in areas around Anbar and Baghdad.

Sadr fighters/Sadr's Peace Brigades/Saraya Al-Salam Shia

In response to IS in Iraq, powerful Shia cleric, Muqtada al-Sadr, called on his supporters to regroup to defend the people, country, religion, and holy places. In response, thousands of fighters paraded through Baghdad, Kirkuk, Basra, and Najaf on 21 June 2014.[761]

Sadr claims he has 60,000 loyal fighters who are thought to have access to one of the largest weapons arsenals in Iraq, including long-range missiles.[762] The Sadr Peace Brigade claim to be a nationalist force not a sectarian one with the objective of defeating IS for the purpose of reunifying Iraq.

CASUALTIES

In 2014, United Nations Assistance Mission to Iraq (UNAMI) recorded a total minimum number of 35,408 civilian casualties (12,282 killed and 23,126 injured). Of the total, 2,661 people were killed and 7,749 injured in Al Anbar Governorate during 2014.[763] This was a significant increase from the 27,160 civilian casualties UNAMI recorded for 2013 (10,187 people killed and 16,973 injured).[764] The number of civilian casualties (including police) in 2014 was reported to have been higher than that in 2008, when there were 26,965 civilian casualties recorded (6,787 killed and 20,178 injured).[765] UNAMI reported that it was been prevented from effectively verifying casualties in conflict

760 'Mapping Iraq's Fighting Groups', *Al Jazeera*, 27 June 2014, at: <http://www.aljazeera.com/news/middleeast/2014/06/mapping-out-iraq-fighting-groups-201462494731548175.html>.

761 Ibid.

762 'Sunni Boycott Threatens Reconciliation Efforts in Iraq', *Al Jazeera*, 23 February 2015, at: <http://www.aljazeera.com/news/2015/02/sunni-boycott-threatens-reconciliation-efforts-iraq-150223091549767.html>.

763 UNMAMI Monthly Updates, 'Civilian Casualties: Summary', <http://www.uniraq.org/index.php?option=com_k2&view=itemlist&task=category&id=159:civilian-casualties&Itemid=633&lang=en>.

764 UN, '2014 One of Iraq's Bloodiest Years as Casualty Rates Soar', UN mission reports, 2 January 2015, <http://www.un.org/apps/news/story.asp?NewsID=49725#.VT47wCGqqko>.

765 UNAMI, Monthly Updates.

areas, including Health Directorate data for Anbar Governorate and certain cases could not fully verify some incidents.[766]

From 1 June, when the conflict with ISIS spread from Anbar to other areas of Iraq, to 31 December 2014 UNAMAI reported 22,292 civilian casualties, including police (8,481 killed and 13,811 injured civilians including police personnel).[767] UNAMI monthly reporting for 2014 recorded 7,970 military and security casualties of which 3,689 killed and 4,281 injured.[768]

While not all casualties were directly related to the conflict with Islamic State (previously known as Islamic State of Iraq and the Levant/Islamic State of Iraq and Syria, often still referred to as ISIS), UNAMI attributed the sharp increase in casualties in 2014, as compared to 2013 and other previous years, to the escalation of violence in the country stemming from the armed conflict between the Iraqi Security Forces and affiliated forces, versus the ISIS and associated armed groups.[769]

Agence France-Presse (AFP) stopped reporting monthly casualty figures after September 2014.[770] AFP subsequently reported that statistics compiled by the health interior and defence ministries of Iraq had found the death toll for 2014 to be 15,538.[771]

Iraq Body Count (IBC), recorded 17,049 civilians killed in Iraq during 2014. This was almost double the number recorded in 2013 (9,743), which in turn was roughly double the number in 2012 (4,622). Of the total fatalities in Iraq recorded by IBC for 2014 some were attributable to the actions of specific armed groups: 1,748 civilians were reported killed by Iraqi military air strikes, while 4,325 were killed by ISIS and 118 civilians were recorded as killed by US-Coalition air strikes, marking the first time since the US withdrawal in 2011 that civilian deaths were directly attributed to the US-Coalition. For the majority of casualties (10,858 civilians killed) it was not possible to discern which groups were involved. The IBC casualty figures did not include combatant deaths. However IBC

[766] UNAMI and Office of the High Commissioner of Human Rights (OHCHR), 'Report on the Protection of Civilians in Armed Conflict in Iraq: 6 July–10 September 2014', p. 1.

[767] UNAMI, 'UN Casualty Figures for December; 2014 deadliest since 2008 in Iraq', 4 January 2015, <http://www.uniraq.org/index.php?option=com_k2&view=item&id=3141:un-casualty-figures-for-december-2014-deadliest-since-2008-in-iraq&Itemid=633&lang=en>.

[768] UNAMI, Monthly Updates.

[769] UNAMI and Office of the High Commissioner of Human Rights (OHCHR), 'Report on the Protection of Civilians in Armed Conflict in Iraq: 6 July–10 September 2014', p. 1.

[770] From 1 January to 30 September 2014 the AFP reported 7,054 people killed and 10,873. The June 2014 toll likely significantly higher than reported, details on all casualties were more difficult to obtain because of the militant offensive launched on 9 June, and militants have been excluded from the toll this month due to the lack of reliable independent information. Official data was released by the Iraqi Government monthly through the media; there is no single source within the government for consolidated annual figures. The figures were compiled by Agence France-Presse (AFP) and made publicly available through a link on the agency's website: <http://www.bit.ly/AFPIraqToll>.

[771] 'Iraq: 15,000 Civilians, Security Personnel Killed in 2014', Agence France-Presse, 2 January 2015, <http://english.al-akhbar.com/node/23072>.

found that in other reporting combatant deaths rose sharply in 2014 'even by the most cautious tallies' relative to previous years.[772]

IBC also noted that there were, for the first time, substantial differences between the main data tracking sources reporting totals of military and combatant fatalities deaths for 2014. It found that AFP and official statistics calculated some 4,000–5,000 combatants' deaths, whereas the sum of media reported military and security fatalities indicated totals in the area of 30,000 deaths.[773]

The International Federation of Journalists (IFJ), recorded eight journalists killed in Iraq in 2014.[774] The Committee to Protect Journalists (CPJ) recorded three journalists killed.[775]

DISPLACED PERSONS

In 2014, there were at least 2,176,800 new internal displacements in Iraq, leading to a total of 3,276,000 persons being internally displaced in the country as of December 2014. However, given the volatile security situation, the fluidity of population movements and access restrictions, the actual number of internally displaced persons (IDPs) is difficult to track.[776]

WAR CRIMES ALLEGATIONS, INVESTIGATIONS, AND PROSECUTIONS

In May 2014, the Prosecutor of the ICC announced that she has decided to re-open the preliminary examination of the situation in Iraq, previously concluded in 2006, following submission of new information received by the Office that alleges the responsibility of officials of the United Kingdom for war crimes involving systematic detainee abuse in Iraq from 2003 until 2008. While Iraq is a not a State party to the Rome Statute, the

[772] Data for calendar year 2014 up to 30 December. Iraq Body Count, 'Iraq 2014: Civilian deaths almost doubling year on year, 01 January 2015', <https://www.iraqbodycount.org/analysis/numbers/2014/>.

[773] Ibid.

[774] 'Trail of Violence: Journalists & Media Staff Killed in 2014, FJ-Belgium 2015', p. 4, <http://ifj-safety.org/assets/docs/089/245/5bef559-ba3edf5.pdf>.

[775] CPJ, '166 Journalists Killed in Iraq since 1992/Motive Confirmed', <https://cpj.org/killed/mideast/iraq>.

[776] Internal Displacement Monitoring Centre (IDMC) 'Global Overview 2015', May 2015. The figure for Iraq in this report are based on UN estimates and data published by IOM and national and local authorities.

ICC has jurisdiction over alleged crimes committed on the territory of Iraq by nationals of States parties, such as the United Kingdom. The re-opened preliminary examination will analyse, in particular, alleged crimes attributed to the armed forces of the United Kingdom deployed in Iraq between 2003 and 2008.[777]

At the domestic level, in October 2014, a US jury convicted four guards from the Blackwater company accused of manslaughter and first degree murder, relating to the 2007 Nisour Square massacre in Baghdad, which left fourteen civilians dead and seventeen wounded.[778] One of them was sentenced to life, and the three others to thirty years' imprisonment.

[777] ICC, 'Prosecutor of the International Criminal Court, Fatou Bensouda, re-opens the preliminary examination of the situation in Iraq', 13 May 2014, at: <http://www.icc-cpi.int/en_menus/icc/structure%20of%20the%20court/office%20of%20the%20prosecutor/reports%20and%20statements/statement/Pages/otp-statement-iraq-13-05-2014.aspx>.

[778] 'Former Blackwater Guards Sentenced for Massacres of Unarmed Iraqi Civilians', *The Guardian*, 13 April 2013.

Armed conflict in Libya in 2014

KEY CASUALTY DATA FOR 2014

Unknown killed:	1,188	(Source: ACLED)
Unknown injured:	980	(Source: ACLED)
Foreign civilians killed:	117	(Source: ACLED)
Civilians injured:	at least 32	(Source: ACLED)
Libyan military killed:	175	(Source: ACLED)
Libyan military injured:	142	(Source: ACLED)
Operation Dignity killed:	38	(Source: ACLED)
Operation Dignity injured:	31	(Source: ACLED)
NSAG killed:	171	(Source: ACLED)
NSAG injured:	73	(Source: ACLED)
Mixed participants in hostilities killed:	394	(Source: ACLED)
Mixed participants in hostilities killed:	122	(Source: ACLED)

CLASSIFICATION OF THE CONFLICT

In 2014, armed violence in Libya reached the threshold of a non-international armed conflict (NIAC) between several non-State armed groups, including at least the 'Libya Dignity Alliance', the group of militia known as 'Libya Dawn' and the Ansar al-Sharia armed group.

SUMMARY OF APPLICABLE INTERNATIONAL LAW

All parties to the conflict were bound by customary international humanitarian law (IHL) and human rights law, including customary IHL rules of distinction, proportionality, and precautions in attacks; the obligations of humane treatment, as set out in Common Article 3 to the 1949 Geneva Conventions; the obligation not to recruit and use children as soldiers; and by the duty to respect and protect fundamental human rights. This includes the duty to respect the rights to life and to freedom from torture or other forms of cruel, inhuman, or degrading treatment or punishment.

Libya is a State party to the four 1949 Geneva Conventions and the 1977 Additional Protocols. Moreover, it is a State party to the 1966 International Covenant on Civil and Political Rights, the 1966 International Covenant on Economic, Social and Cultural Rights, as well as the 1987 Convention against Torture.

Libya is not a State party to the ICC Statute nor to the 2008 Convention on Cluster Munitions.

HISTORY OF THE CONFLICT [779]

The situation in Libya deteriorated in May 2014, when Ahmed Maiteeq, widely perceived as backed by Misrata-based Islamist groups, was appointed as the new Prime Minister. The legality of this appointment was soon questioned[780] and Congress chairman Ezzedine Al-Amawi finally declared the vote leading to the appointment illegal.[781]

On 16–17 May 2014, former army General Khalifa Hifter formed the 'Libya Dignity Alliance' and launched a military operation in Benghazi using helicopters, jets, and ground forces, named 'Operation Dignity' against Islamist factions in eastern Libya, allegedly to 'eradicate terrorism'.[782] During a press conference, he proclaimed that the current General National Congress (GNC) was no longer representing the Libyan people and was illegitimate,[783] further explaining his primary aim was to 'purge' Islamist militants from Libya, specifically the 'terrorist' Muslim Brotherhood.[784] On 27 May 2014, the Ansar al-Sharia group declared its commitment to fight against General Hifter.[785]

In June, clashes between Ansar al-Sharia and former General Khalifa Hiftar's forces continued in and around Benghazi. On 9 June 2014 the Libyan Supreme Court ruled that Ahmed Maiteeq's appointment had been illegal.[786] As a result, Maiteeq resigned on the same day and, despite the disagreement of parts of the GNC, interim Prime Minister al-Thinni was restored.[787]

[779] Unless otherwise stated this section is based on Crisis Watch Database on Libya, at: <http://www.crisisgroup.org/en/publication-type/crisiswatch/crisiswatch-database.aspx?CountryIDs={28685262-BE79-473E-B18E-ED22761A0F17}>.

[780] 'Maiteeq Installed as Libya's New PM But Dismissed by Speaker', *Reuters*, 4 May 2014, at: <http://www.reuters.com/article/2014/05/04/us-libya-politics-idUSBREA4304720140504>.

[781] 'Libya Congress Rejects New PM Ahmed Maiteg', *BBC News*, 4 May 2014, at: <http://www.bbc.com/news/world-africa-27276153>.

[782] 'Libya's Growing Risk of Civil War', *The Washington Institute*, 20 May 2014, at: <http://www.washingtoninstitute.org/policy-analysis/view/libyas-growing-risk-of-civil-war>.

[783] 'Khalifa Haftar: My forces Will Reach Tripoli Soon', *Asharq Al-Awsat*, 22 May 2014, at: <http://www.aawsat.net/2014/05/article55332486>.

[784] 'The New Danger in Benghazi', *The New York Times*, 27 May 2014, at: <http://www.nytimes.com/2014/05/28/opinion/the-new-danger-in-benghazi.html?hp&rref=opinion&_r=0>.

[785] 'Hifter Campaign Reveals Power of Libyan Islamist Militias', *AlMonitor*, 4 June 2014, at: <http://www.al-monitor.com/pulse/originals/2014/06/libya-khalifa-hifter-ansar-sharia-benghazi-tripoli-war.html#>.

[786] 'Libyan Supreme Court Rules PM's Election Unconstitutional', *Reuters*, 9 June 2014, at: <http://www.businessinsider.com/r-libyan-supreme-court-rules-pms-election-unconstitutional-2014-09?IR=T>.

[787] 'Supreme Court in Libya Reinstates Former Prime Minister', *Financial Times*, 9 June 2014, at: <http://www.ft.com/intl/cms/s/0/933dac82-efb7-11e3-9b4c-00144feabdc0.html#axzz3ZkT4mdnD>.

Due to the opposition of the liberal factions, the UN Support Mission in Libya (UNSMIL) cancelled the political dialogue initiative initially scheduled for the 18–19 June.[788]

Parliamentary elections were held on 25 June 2014,[789] but due to boycotts and insecurity, only 188 out of 200 seats were filled and the new members of parliament decided to convene the Council of Representatives (CoR) in Tobruk instead of Tripoli.[790]

In July, the conflict spread to Tripoli where Libya Dawn, a Misrata-led militia that includes Islamist factions, wrested control of the capital from a Zintan-led militia alliance aligned to Libya Dignity. At least ninety-four people were reported killed between 13 and 27 July 2014 in the fighting between the Zintan militia and security units affiliated with Islamist-leaning Libya Revolutionaries' Operation Room (LROR) over the control of Tripoli airport.[791] Moreover, at least seventy-five people were killed mid-to late July in Benghazi during the clashes between different government forces and militias.[792]

As a result, on 14 July 2014 the UN staff was pulled out of the country, while the United States and several other embassies have been evacuated throughout the month.[793]

On 30 July 2014, Ansar al-Sharia declared the city of Benghazi an 'Islamic emirate'.[794]

Fighting between 'Libya Dawn' and the anti-Islamist Zintan-led coalition continued in Tripoli, until August, where Libya Dawn forces took control of Tripoli International Airport.[795] In the meantime, the GNC that had been replaced in the elections in June reconvened on 25 August 2014 and chose an Islamist-backed deputy as the new prime minister, leaving the country with two rival leaders and assemblies, each backed by different armed factions.[796]

[788] 'Libya: July 2014 Monthly Forecast', Security Council Report, at: <http://www.securitycouncilreport.org/monthly-forecast/2014-07/libya_11.php?print=true>. See also 'Briefing by Tarek Mitri SRSG for Libya: Meeting of the Security Council 27 August 2014', UNSMIL, at: <http://unsmil.unmissions.org/Default.aspx?ctl=Details&tabid=3543&mid=6187&ItemID=1969772>.

[789] 'Libya's Election: Dismal Democrats', *The Economist*, 28 June 2014, at: <http://www.economist.com/news/middle-east-and-africa/21605948-few-libyans-put-much-faith-weeks-general-election-dismal-democrats>.

[790] 'World Report 2015', *Human Rights Watch*, at: <http://www.hrw.org/world-report/2015/country-chapters/libya?page=3>.

[791] 'Libya Clashes Kill 38 in Benghazi', *BBC News*, 28 July 2014, at: <http://www.bbc.com/news/world-africa-28510865>.

[792] 'Heavy Shelling, Clashes Spread in Libya's Tripoli', *Reuters*, 31 July 2014, at: <http://www.reuters.com/article/2014/07/31/us-libya-security-idUSKBN0G018D20140731?irpc=932>.

[793] 'U.S. Embassy in Libya Evacuates Personnel', *CNN*, 27 July 2014, at: <http://edition.cnn.com/2014/07/26/world/africa/libya-us-embassy-evacuation/>.

[794] 'Ansar Al-Sharia Claims Control of Benghazi, Declares "Islamic Emirate" In Libya', *International Business Times*, 31 July 2014, at: <http://www.ibtimes.com/ansar-al-sharia-claims-control-benghazi-declares-islamic-emirate-libya-1645328>.

[795] 'Dawn of Libya Forces Impose Control on Tripoli', *AlMonitor*, 25 August 2014, at: <http://www.al-monitor.com/pulse/security/2014/08/libya-tripoli-control-hifter-tribal-forces.html#ixzz3ZkZEWz9W>.

[796] 'Rival Second Libyan Assembly Chooses Own PM as Chaos Spreads', *Reuters*, 25 August 2014, at: <http://www.reuters.com/article/2014/08/25/us-libya-security-idUSKBN0GP0NZ20140825?irpc=932http://www.ft.com/intl/cms/s/0/ba5639e8-1be4-11e4-adc7-00144feabdc0.html#axzz3BLCkpgeG>.

On 1 September 2014 the Tobruk-based Parliament convened and confirmed interim Prime Minister Abdullah al-Thinni as Libya's Prime Minister, creating strong instability within State institutions as neither the House of Representatives (HoR) based in Tobruk nor the General National Congress (GNC) in Tripoli could exert control.[797]

The head of GNC-backed administration, Omar al-Hassi, called for international recognition on 15 September. However, two days later at the international conference in Madrid States decided not to recognize the Tripoli-based government.[798]

On 19 October 2014, the Tobruk-based internationally recognized Parliament, the House of Representatives (HoR), formally aligned with former General Haftar initiative.[799] HoR spokesman—Farraj Hasshem—described Haftar's 'Operation Dignity' against Islamist groups as 'Libyan Army operations'.[800]

On 6 November 2014, Libya's Supreme Court ruled that Tobruk-based House of Representatives was seated unconstitutionally.[801] The judgment created even more political chaos: while leaders of the Libya Dawn coalition celebrated the court's decision, Operation Dignity members in Tobruk said the court may have ruled under duress, since the Supreme Court building was in Tripoli and surrounded by militiamen aligned with Libya Dawn.[802]

On 24 November 2014 airstrikes operated by Operation Dignity hit the Mitiga air base in Tripoli, which had served as the capital's only civilian airport since fighting over the summer destroyed Tripoli International Airport.[803]

In December 2014, the conflict between Libya's two rival political bodies and their military allies intensified, with heavy clashes and multiple new frontlines emerging across the country. On 13 December, a coalition of fighters from the Libya Dawn

[797] 'Libya: World Report 2015', *Human Rights Watch*, at: <http://www.hrw.org/world-report/2015/country-chapters/libya?page=2>.

[798] 'Al-Thinni's New Cabinet Approved amid Preparations for Negotiation Talks', *Libya Analysis*, 24 September 2014, at: <http://www.libya-analysis.com/gnc/>.

See also: 'Ministerial Conference on Stability and Development in Libya', 17 September 2014, at: <http://www.exteriores.gob.es/Portal/es/SalaDePrensa/ElMinisterioInforma/Documents/Conclusiones%20Conf%20Libia%20ENG.pdf>.

[799] 'Libya: The War Nobody Can Win', *Al Jazeera*, 19 October 2014, at: <http://www.aljazeera.com/indepth/opinion/2014/10/libya-war-nobody-can-win-2014101973131576935.html>.

[800] 'Libya Parliament Allies with Renegade General, Struggles to Assert Authority', *Reuters*, 20 October 2014, at: <http://www.reuters.com/article/2014/10/20/us-libya-security-idUSKCN0I91B620141020?feedType=RSS&feedName=worldNews>.

[801] 'Libyan Supreme Court Rules Parliament Invalid', *The New York Times*, 6 November 2014, at: <http://www.nytimes.com/2014/11/07/world/africa/libyan-supreme-court-rules-parliament-invalid.html?ref=topics>.

[802] 'Libya Faces Chaos as Top Court Rejects Elected Assembly', *Reuters*, 6 November 2014, at: <http://www.reuters.com/article/2014/11/06/us-libya-security-parliament-idUSKBN0IQ0YF20141106>.

[803] 'Bombs Hit Sole Civilian Airport in Libyan Capital', *The New York Times*, 24 November 2014, at: <http://www.nytimes.com/2014/11/25/world/africa/bombs-hit-sole-civilian-airport-in-libyan-capital.html?ref=topics>.

coalition, along with fighters from Awlad Suleiman tribe and Ansar al-Sharia, attacked forces allied with Tobruk-based Parliament in eastern Sirt basin in an attempt to take control of Sidra and Ras Lanuf oil export terminals.[804] As a consequence, the National Oil Corporation declared force majeure over both sites.[805]

PARTIES TO THE CONFLICT

The parties to the NIAC in Libya in 2014 are the Libya Dignity Alliance, backed by the Tobruk-based government; Libya Dawn, which supports the Tripoli-based government, and Ansar al-Sharia, which has now reportedly been integrated in the ISIL.

Libya Dignity Alliance

Libya Dignity Alliance is a group led by former General Hifter, together with a part of the Tobruk-based government. The faction includes tribal groups, officers who defected from Colonel Qaddafi's forces, and militias from the western mountain city of Zintan.[806] Operation Dignity has the backing of Egypt and the United Arab Emirates.[807]

Libya Dawn

Libya Dawn, a Misrata-led militia that includes Islamist factions, is an alliance of hard-line and moderate Islamist groups and members of the ethnic Berber minority, cooperating with factions from Misrata.[808] It controls Tripoli, thus supporting the Tripoli-based government and is backed by the Government of Qatar.[809]

[804] 'Libya Dawn Offensive Against the Oil Ports Kicks Off', *Libya Analysis*, 13 December 2014, at: <http://www.libya-analysis.com/libya-dawn-offensive-against-the-oil-ports-kicks-off/>.

[805] 'Force Majeure Declared over Sidra and Ras Lanuf as Fighting Rages on', *Libya Analysis*, 16 December 2014, at: <http://www.libya-analysis.com/gnc/>.

[806] 'Bombs Hit Sole Civilian Airport in Libyan Capital', *The New York Times*, 24 November 2014, at: <http://www.nytimes.com/2014/11/25/world/africa/bombs-hit-sole-civilian-airport-in-libyan-capital.html?ref=topics>.

[807] 'Libya's Haftar Confirms Military Support for Operation Dignity from Egypt and UAE', *MEA*, 30 January 2015, at: <http://www.middleeasteye.net/news/libyas-haftar-confirms-support-operation-dignity-egypt-and-uae-1265705213>.

[808] 'Here are the Key Players Fighting the War for Libya, All Over Again', *The Washington Post*, 27 August 2014, at: <http://www.washingtonpost.com/blogs/worldviews/wp/2014/08/27/here-are-the-key-players-fighting-the-war-for-libya-all-over-again/>.

[809] 'Libyan Dawn: Map of Allies and Enemies', *Al Arabiya News*, 25 August 2014, at: <http://english.alarabiya.net/en/perspective/alarabiya-studies/2014/08/25/Libyan-Dawn-Map-of-allies-and-enemies.html>.

Ansar al-Sharia

Ansa al-Sharia is a radical Islamist armed group based in Benghazi.[810] Its leader was Mohamed al-Zahawi. After his death, probably in September 2014,[811] many members of the group, including the majority of its organization in Sirte, reportedly defected to the Islamic State of Iraq and the Levant in Libya.[812] Ansar al-Sharia initially manifested as a revolutionary brigade during the 2011 Libyan revolution and gained prominence following the death of Muammar al-Qaddafi.[813] The group has been labelled as a terrorist group by the United States.[814]

CASUALTIES

Analysis of Armed Conflict Location and Event Data Project (ACLED) [815] data in the period from May to the end of December 2014 indicated that there were at least 2,089 fatalities and 1,380 people injured from 'battles' and 'remote violence' in Libya.[816] ACLED recorded 2,383 fatalities in Libya under the event classification types 'battles' and 'remote violence' for all of 2014.[817]

ACLED noted 'the fluidity of alliance formation' between armed groups in Libya in 2014 and also observed that the 'deterioration of security in Libya throughout 2014 has been characterized by a myriad of factional armed groups with complex competing claims and two divided governments'.[818] Consequently, the meaningful disaggregation of casualties on the basis of the roles of armed actors was hampered by a lack of distinction, or due to the reporting of armed groups by their own names as well as by

[810] 'Profile: Libya's Ansar al-Sharia', *BBC News*, 13 June 2014, at: <http://www.bbc.com/news/world-africa-27732589>.

[811] 'Leader of Libyan Islamists Ansar al-Sharia dies of wounds', *Reuters*, 23 January 2015, at: <http://www.reuters.com/article/2015/01/23/us-libya-security-idUSKBN0KW1MU20150123>.

[812] 'Islamic State: Inside the Latest City to Fall under Its Sway', *The Telegraph*, 10 March 2015, at: <http://www.telegraph.co.uk/news/worldnews/africaandindianocean/libya/11460124/How-Gaddafis-home-city-in-Libya-fell-under-the-rule-of-Islamic-State-jihadists.html>.

[813] 'Ansar al-Sharia in Libya (ASL)', *TRAC*, at: <http://www.trackingterrorism.org/group/ansar-al-sharia-libya-asl>.

[814] 'Terrorist Designations of Three Ansar al-Shari'a Organizations and Leaders', US Department of State, 10 January 2014, at: <http://www.state.gov/r/pa/prs/ps/2014/01/219519.htm>.

[815] War Report Analysis of ACELD data for 2014. Raleigh, C., Linke, A., Hegre, H., and Karlsen, J., 2010, 'Introducing ACLED-Armed Conflict Location and Event Data', *Journal of Peace Research*, vol. 47, no. 5, pp. 1–10.

[816] With the exclusion of casualties from direct fighting between Touareg and Tabu ethnic militia and between Gaddadfa (Qadhadhfa) and Awlad Suleiman ethnic militia during the period.

[817] ACLED, 'A Review of Libya in 2014', 21 January 2014, <http://www.crisis.acleddata.com/a-review-of-libya-in-2014>.

[818] Ibid.

the names of broader collective fighting forces and umbrella groups that they had joined in, or were associated with. These included Operation Libya Shield, Libya Dawn, and the Benghazi Revolutionaries Shura Council. Similarly while just 120 conflict fatalities were reported as 'civilian', among the casualties of unknown civilian status many (698 fatalities and 796 injured) were noted only as 'people', without reference to their participation in hostilities.[819] The United Nations Support Mission in Libya (UNSMIL) reported that distinguishing civilian casualties was a challenge exacerbated by the fact that armed group members usually did not 'wear recognizable uniforms or carry distinctive insignia'.[820] The majority of casualties with civilian status were foreign citizens from Egypt (thirty-four), Sudan (thirty-one), and Bangladesh (five).

Fatalities found in ACLED likely underrepresent the total number of people killed. Official casualty figures released by the Ministry of Health on 30 July 2014 stated that in Tripoli 214 people had been killed and 981 injured as a result of 'recent fighting'. However, statistics were not disaggregated by sex or age or between participant in hostilities and fighters and civilians.[821] The UNSMIL noted its view that the casualty figures are an underestimate of the actual situation.[822] The UN reported that an estimated 450 people were killed in fighting in Benghazi between October and November 2014.[823] ACLED reported 107 fatalities during fighting in Benghazi in the same period and 281 between May 2014 and year's end.

The Conflict Barometer 2014 report noted clashes with casualties totalling some 894 people killed and 1,311 injured in Libya for the period May through the end of December 2014. The number of injured was similar to that found through War Report analysis of ACLED data.[824] The NGO Libya Body Count recorded 2,662 violent deaths for the period from May 2014 to the end of December 2014, based on a dataset from online media reporting. The total number of violent deaths recorded by Libya Body Count for 2014 was 2,825.[825]

Two aid workers were killed in Libya in 2014. An ambulance driver for the Libyan Red Crescent Society was killed in a targeted attack and the head of the ICRC mission in Misrata was shot by masked gunmen.[826] One journalist was killed in Benghazi in May.[827]

[819] Raleigh, C., Linke, A., Hegre, H., and Karlsen, J., 'Introducing ACLED-Armed Conflict Location and Event Data', pp. 1–10.

[820] UNSMIL/OHCHR, Overview of Violations of International Human Rights and Humanitarian Law During the Ongoing Violence in Libya, 4 September 2014, p. 5, <http://www.ohchr.org/documents/countries/ly/overviewviolationslibya_unsmil_ohchr_sept04_en.pdf>.

[821] Ibid. [822] Ibid. [823] UN Security Council, S/2015/144, 26 February 2015, para. 26.

[824] The Heidelberg Institute for International Conflict Research, 2015, 'Conflict Barometer 2014', pp. 164–5.

[825] Libya Body Count 'Violent Deaths in Libya', <http://www.libyabodycount.org/table>.

[826] The Aid Worker Security Database, 'Security incident data', <https://aidworkersecurity.org/incidents>.

[827] Committee to Protect Journalists, '8 Journalists Killed in Libya/Motive Confirmed', <https://cpj.org/killed/mideast/libya>.

Displaced

As of December 2014 there were total of 400,000 Internally Displaced Persons (IDPs) in Libya, with the majority, 340,600 people, newly displaced during 2014.[828]

WAR CRIMES AND PROSECUTIONS

On 24 March 2014, the trial of thirty-seven Gaddafi-era officials and employees accused for their alleged roles during the 2011 revolution started in Tripoli. They included Saif al-Islam Gaddafi and Abdullah Sanussi, Muammar Gaddafi's former intelligence chief.

Following the Security Council referral to the ICC of the situation in Libya since 15 February 2011 with Resolution 1970 (2011),[829] on 21 May 2014 the ICC issued a final decision rejecting Libya's request to try Gaddafi domestically for crimes against humanity.[830]

However, the Libyan Government failed to uphold its legal obligation to cooperate and surrender Saif al-Islam Gaddafi, which it had been requested to do twice. As a consequence, on 10 December 2014 the ICC issued a finding of non-compliance by Libya and referred the issue to the Security Council.[831]

In the case of Abdullah Sanussi, the ICC judges approved Libya's bid to prosecute the former intelligence chief at home for his alleged role during the 2011 uprising.[832]

[828] The Internal Displacement Monitoring Centre (IDMC) noted that this figure is based on UNHCR estimates as of December 2014. Comprehensive and precise data were difficult to obtain because international organizations left the country in July 2014 due to the deteriorating security. Figures may include people displaced a number of times, which could have led to double counting. IDMC, 'Global Overview 2015', May 2015, p. 84.

[829] Security Council Resolution 1970 (2011), 26 February 2011, at: <http://www.un.org/ga/search/view_doc.asp?symbol=S/RES/1970%20%282011%29>.

[830] 'Libya: Final ICC Ruling on Gaddafi', *Human Rights Watch*, 21 May 2014, at: <http://www.hrw.org/news/2014/05/21/libya-final-icc-ruling-gaddafi>. See also: 'The Prosecutor v Saif Al-Islam Gaddafi', *ICC Case Information Sheet*, at: <http://www.icc-cpi.int/iccdocs/PIDS/publications/GaddafiEng.pdf>.

[831] 'World Report 2015', *Human Rights Watch*, at: <http://www.hrw.org/world-report/2015/country-chapters/libya?page=3>.

[832] 'Al-Senussi case: Appeals Chamber confirms case is inadmissible before ICC', *ICC Press Release*, 27 July 2014, at: http://www.icc-cpi.int/en_menus/icc/press%20and%20media/press%20releases/Pages/pr1034.aspx.

Armed conflict in Mali in 2014

KEY CASUALTY DATA FOR 2014

Total casualties:	538	
Civilians killed:	25	(Source: ACLED)
Civilians injured:	17	(Source: ACLED /ICRC/UN)
MSDF killed:	76	(Source: ACLED/ UN)
MSDF injured:	67	(Source: ACLED)
MINUSMA Peacekeepers killed:	18	(Source: ACLED)
MINUSMA Peacekeepers injured:	69	(Source: ACLED)
French military killed:	4	(Source: ACLED)
French military injured:	11	(Source: ACLED)
MNLA/MAA killed:	38	(Source: ACLED)
MNLA/MAA injured:	14	(Source: ACLED)
MUJO killed:	30	(Source: ACLED)
AQIM killed:	16	(Source: ACLED)
Other NSAG killed:	106	(Source: ACLED)
Other NSAG injured:	10	(Source: ACLED)
Unknown killed:	37	(Source: ACLED)

CLASSIFICATION OF THE CONFLICT

Mali, supported by France and the African-led International Support Mission in Mali (AFISMA) then the United Nations Multidimensional Integrated Stabilization Mission in Mali (MINUSMA), was involved in a non-international armed conflict (NIAC) with Al-Qaeda in the Islamic Maghreb (AQIM), Ansar Dine, and the Movement for Oneness and Jihad in West Africa (MOJWA), and the MNLA in 2014. The conflict met the threshold for applicability of the 1977 Additional Protocol II.

SUMMARY OF APPLICABLE INTERNATIONAL LAW

All parties to the conflict were bound by customary international humanitarian law (IHL) and human rights law, including customary IHL rules of distinction, proportionality, and precautions in attacks; the obligations of humane treatment, as set out in Common Article 3 to the 1949 Geneva Conventions; the obligation not to recruit and use children as soldiers; and by the duty to respect and protect fundamental human rights. This includes the duty to respect the rights to life and to freedom from torture or other forms of cruel, inhuman, or degrading treatment or punishment.

Mali is party to the four 1949 Geneva Conventions and the 1977 Additional Protocol II. Mali is also party to the 1966 International Covenant on Civil and Political Rights and the 1966 International Covenant on Economic, Social and Cultural Rights. France and States participating in AFISMA and MINUSMA are bound extraterritorially by their human rights obligations.[833] France and other Sates parties to the 1950 European Convention on Human Rights participating in MINUSMA are also bound extraterritorially by this instrument.

Mali is party to the 1997 Anti-Personnel Mine Ban Convention. It is also party to the 2008 Convention on Cluster Munitions. Mali ratified the 2013 Arms Trade Treaty (ATT) in December 2013.

France and States participating in AFISMA and MINUSMA that were party to the Anti-Personnel Mine Ban Convention and the Convention on Cluster Munitions were bound by those instruments. In any event, the UN Secretary-General's Bulletin requires that UN peacekeeping forces engaged as a party in an armed conflict not use anti-personnel mines.[834]

HISTORY OF THE CONFLICT[835]

Since May 2006, Mali has been engaged in low-intensity conflict in the north of the country between the Government and a number of ethnic Touareg non-State armed groups then under the umbrella of the *23 May Democratic Alliance for Change*. In July 2008, the Government and the group agreed a ceasefire after four days of talks in the Algerian capital, Algiers. Mali, Africa's third-biggest gold producer, had struggled to end the escalating militancy by the Touareg nomads who took up arms demanding greater rights for their people. The conflict followed similar rebellions in the 1960s and 1990s by the Touareg.

On 22 March 2012, a military coup in the capital, Bamako, overthrew the elected President Amadou Toumani Toure. The coup came in the aftermath of a series of losses suffered by Malian armed forces in the face of the Touareg, who had received new weaponry from Libya. On 6 April 2012, the National Movement for the Liberation of Azawad (MNLA), a new umbrella group for Touareg rebels, proclaimed the independence of

[833] See, e.g., International Court of Justice (ICJ), *Wall* Advisory Opinion, 2004, §106; and ICJ, *Armed Activities on the Territory of the Congo (Democratic Republic of the Congo v Uganda)*, Judgment, 19 December 2005.

[834] Secretary-General's Bulletin: Observance by United Nations forces of international humanitarian law, New York, UN doc. ST/SGB/1999/13, 6 August 1999.

[835] Unless otherwise stated this section is based on 'Mali Profile', *BBC*, 21 May 2015, at: <http://www.bbc.com/news/world-africa-13881370>.

the Azawad, a territory in northern Mali.[836] Among others, the African Union, the European Union, and the United States did not recognize the putative new State.[837]

On 9 April 2012, the UN Security Council reaffirmed 'the need to uphold and respect the sovereignty, unity, and territorial integrity of Mali and reject categorically any declarations to the contrary', and demanded 'an immediate cessation of hostilities in the north of Mali by rebel groups'.[838] In May 2012, the Economic Community of West African States (ECOWAS) decided to send a force of 3,000 regional soldiers to Mali in an effort to restore stability even though the military junta opposed the idea.

In May 2012, the MNLA and Islamist militant group Ansar Dine[839] sought to merge, declaring northern Mali an Islamic State. Ansar Dine began to impose Islamic law in Timbuktu. AQIM 'endorsed' the deal. But by June, the already strained relationship between Ansar Dine and the MNLA imploded, and following fierce combat with Ansar Dine and the MOJWA the MNLA was expelled from the main northern cities of Gao, Kidal, and Timbuktu by July 2012. The town of Douentza followed in September, seeing the Islamists come ever closer to Government-held territory.[840]

In November 2012, ECOWAS, backed by the UN and African Union, agreed to launch a coordinated military expedition to recapture the north. France, the United States, and the United Kingdom announced logistical support for the mission, which was planned to comprise some 3,300 military personnel.

On 11 January 2013, the French military began operations against the Islamist armed groups in Operation Serval, deploying some 4,000 troops. The first forces from the African-led International Support Mission in Mali (AFISMA) arrived on 17 January.[841] Combat operations took place throughout the first part of 2013.[842]

In April 2013, France began to withdraw some of its troops aiming to have no more than 1,000 by year's end. On 25 April, the UN Security Council adopted Resolution 2100 in which it:

> Demand[ed] that all rebel armed groups in Mali put aside their arms and cease hostilities immediately and urge[d] all such parties in Mali who have cut off all ties with terrorist organizations such as AQIM, MUJAO, Ansar Eddine and associated terrorist groups and who recognize, without conditions, the

836 The MNLA has its own website: <http://www.mnlamov.net/english.html>.

837 'Briefing: War and Peace—Mali Repeats the Cycle', *IRIN*, 29 March 2012, at: <http://www.irinnews.org/Report/95186/Briefing-War-and-peace-Mali-repeats-the-cycle>.

838 UN Security Council Press Statement on Mali, 10 April 2012, at: <http://www.un.org/News/Press/docs/2012/sc10603.doc.htm>.

839 Ansar Dine was founded by Touareg rebel Iyad Ag Ghaly.

840 RFI, 'Rupture entre le MNLA et Ansar Dine au nord du Mali', 20 March 2012, at: <http://www.rfi.fr/afrique/20120320-nord-mali-rupture-mnla-ancar-dine-touaregs-Iyad Ag Ghali>.

841 International Institute for Strategic Studies, *Military Balance 2014*, Chapter 9: Sub-Saharan Africa.

842 See the Mali Profile, *The War Report 2013*, edited by Casey-Maslen, S., Oxford University Press, 2014, p. 147.

unity and territorial integrity of the Malian State, and the transitional authorities of Mali to engage expeditiously in an inclusive negotiation process, facilitated by the Secretary-General.[843]

The Resolution further established MINUSMA, determining that authority would be transferred from AFISMA to MINUSMA on 1 July 2013.[844] The mandate of MINUSMA was to include protection, 'without prejudice to the responsibility of the transitional authorities of Mali, civilians under imminent threat of physical violence, within its capacities and areas of deployment' and to 'monitor, help investigate and report' to the Security Council on any abuses or violations of human rights or violations of IHL committed in Mali 'and to contribute to efforts to prevent such violations and abuses'.[845]

In May, an international conference pledged US$4 billion to help rebuild Mali. In June, the Government signed a peace deal with Touareg rebels to pave the way for national elections. Rebels agreed to hand over the northern town of Kidal they had captured after French troops had forced out Islamists in January. In July–August 2013, Ibrahim Boubacar Keita won presidential elections. In September, the Malian army clashed with Touareg rebels in the first fighting since the June peace accord.

In October, security in the north deteriorated. Demonstrators gathered in Gao on 10 October to protest against insecurity and weak State presence. On 23 October, the first-ever suicide attack on MINUSMA peacekeepers near Tessalit killed seven. The next day, France, MINUSMA, and the Malian army launched Operation Hydre, a joint military operation 'to avoid revival of terrorist movements' in the north.[846]

In mid-December, legislative elections were held without major incident but with a low turnout (37%); the Malian President and his allies retained a comfortable majority in Parliament. Violence and insecurity in the north, however, continued.[847]

In April 2014, President Keita appointed former rival Moussa Mara as Prime Minister in a bid to curb instability in the north of the country.[848] In May 2014, a fragile truce between the MNLA and the Malian Armed Forces broke down in the north of the country. The separatists seized control of the city of Kidal and the towns of Menaka, Agelhok, Anefis, and Tessalit.[849]

In September 2014, the Government of Mali and the separatists began a new round of talks in Algeria to try and end the conflict in the region of Northern Mali or as referred to by the separatists as 'Azawad'.[850]

[843] UN Security Council Resolution 2100, 25 April 2013, §4. [844] Ibid., §7.

[845] Ibid., §16(c)(i) and (d)(i). [846] ICG, Crisis Watch Database: Mali, 1 November 2013.

[847] ICG, Crisis Watch Database: Mali, 2 January 2014.

[848] 'New PM appointed in Mali as Entire Government Quits', *BBC*, 6 April 2014 at: <http://www.bbc.com/news/world-africa-26909113>.

[849] 'Mali: Tuareg Rebels "Defeat Government Army in Kidal"', *BBC*, 22 May 2014 at: <http://www.bbc.com/news/world-africa-27511448>.

[850] 'New Round of Mali Peace Talks Opens in Algiers', *AFP*, 1 September 2014 at: <http://reliefweb.int/report/mali/new-round-mali-peace-talks-opens-algiers>.

On 3 October, nine UN Peacekeepers were killed in an ambush in the north-east of the country. This was the deadliest attack so far on its mission in Mali.[851]

April 2015 saw an upsurge in the level of violence as the Coordination of Azawad Movements northern rebels clashed with UN Peacekeepers in Timbuktu and seized the town of Lere and attempted to recapture the town of Menaka from the pro-government forces.[852]

On 21 May 2015, it was reported that French Special Forces killed leading Al-Qaeda commanders Amada Ag Hama and Ibrahim Ag Inawalen in northern raid. Both the individuals were suspected of kidnapping and killing French citizens.[853]

PARTIES TO THE CONFLICTS

The parties to the NIACs in 2014 were Mali and its armed forces and France, AFISMA, and MINUSMA against AQIM, Ansar Dine, MOJWA, and the MNLA.

Malian armed forces

The size of Malian armed forces is estimated to be around 11,800 personnel in 2013.[854]

AFISMA

The African-led International Support Mission in Mali (AFISMA), which was initially under the auspices of the Economic Community of West African States (ECOWAS), reverted to an African Union (AU) mandate. The transition from ECOWAS to the African Union followed a review of the mission's concept of operation by the ECOWAS Committee of Chiefs of Defence Staff. The UN Security Council in Resolution 2085 authorized deployment of AFISMA for an initial period of one year, with the mandate to 'take all necessary measures, in compliance with applicable international humanitarian law and human rights law and in full respect of the sovereignty, territorial integrity and unity of Mali' to carry out a number of tasks, including:

[851] 'Nine UN peacekeepers Killed in Mali Ambush', *AJN*, 3 October 2014 at: <http://www.aljazeera.com/news/africa/2014/10/nine-un-peacekeepers-killed-mali-ambush-201410312210524407.html>.

[852] 'UN Base in Mali Hit by Deadly Suicide Bombing', *BBC*, 15 April 2015 at: <http://www.bbc.com/news/world-africa-32327252>.

[853] 'French Special Forces "Kill al-Qaeda leader in Mali"', *AJN*, 21 May 2015 at: <http://www.aljazeera.com/news/2015/05/french-special-forces-kill-al-qaeda-leader-mali-150520203048981.html>.

[854] Armed forces personnel, total, World Bank at: <http://data.worldbank.org/indicator/MS.MIL.TOTL.P1>.

To support the Malian authorities in recovering the areas in the north of its territory under the control of terrorist, extremist and armed groups and in reducing the threat posed by terrorist organizations, including AQIM, MUJWA and associated extremist groups, while taking appropriate measures to reduce the impact of military action upon the civilian population.[855]

On 1 July 2013, in accordance with UN Security Council Resolution 2100, AFISMA transferred its authority to MINUSMA in an official ceremony in Bamako, the Malian capital.

MINUSMA

In April, the UN Security Council approved the 12,600-strong MINUSMA to take over from the African-led force, authorizing them 'to use all necessary means'[856] to carry out security-related stabilization tasks, protect civilians, UN staff, and cultural artefacts, and create the conditions for provision of humanitarian aid. MINUSMA is the world's third largest UN peacekeeping force.

By unanimously adopting resolution 2164 of 25 June 2014, the Council further decided that the Mission should focus on duties, such as ensuring security, stabilization and protection of civilians; supporting national political dialogue and reconciliation; and assisting the reestablishment of State authority, the rebuilding of the security sector, and the promotion and protection of human rights in that country.[857]

Al-Qaeda in the Islamic Maghreb (AQIM)

AQIM is a Salafi-jihadist militant group operating in North Africa's Sahara and Sahel. The group was created during Algeria's earlier internal armed conflict, and has since become an Al-Qaeda affiliate. In recent months, AQIM's expanded its foothold in northern Mali.[858] AQIM has been designated as a terrorist organization by both the United States and the European Union. AQIM's main objectives include the eradication of Western influence from North Africa by overthrowing 'unbeliever' governments, and installing regimes based on Shari'a law. AQIM's tactics include the use of guerrilla-style raids, assassinations, and suicide bombings of military, government, and civilian targets.[859]

[855] UN Security Council Resolution 2085, 20 December 2012, §9.

[856] UN Security Council Resolution 2100, 25 April 2013, §17.

[857] 'Supporting Political Process and Helping Stabilize Mali', MINUSMA UN at: <http://www.un.org/en/peacekeeping/missions/minusma/>.

[858] 'Al-Qaeda in the Islamic Maghreb', *GlobalSecurity.org*, June 2011, at: <http://www.globalsecurity.org/military/world/para/gspc.htm>.

[859] Council on Foreign Relations, Al-Qaeda in the Islamic Maghreb (AQIM), January 2013, at: <http://www.cfr.org/north-africa/al-qaeda-islamic-maghreb-aqim/p12717>.

Ansar Dine

Ansar Dine (which means 'defenders of the religion' in Arabic) was created in December 2011. The group was led by Iyad Ag Ghaly, a leader of Touareg rebellions in the 1990s. Unlike the MNLA, Ansar Dine's goal is to impose Islamic law over the whole country without necessarily challenging the territorial integrity of Mali.[860] Ansar Dine's members were allegedly responsible for the destruction of UNESCO world heritage sites in Timbuktu, while imposition of Shari'a in their controlled areas led thousands to flee.[861] In November 2012, in light of the planned ECOWAS intervention, the group issued a statement whereby it rejected all forms of extremism and terrorism and committed itself in the fight against transnational organized crime.[862] This declaration seemed to mark the will for Ansar Dine to publicly distance itself from AQIM. However, a few months later, the two rebel groups were reported to be operating in close collaboration.[863]

Mouvement pour le Tawhîd et du Jihad en Afrique de l'Ouest (MOJWA)

The Mouvement pour le Tawhîd et du Jihad en Afrique de l'Ouest (Movement for Oneness and Jihad in West Africa, MOJWA) is an active terrorist group that emerged from AQIM in mid-2011. In a video announcing its creation on 12 December 2011, the rebel group openly declared its intent to spread *jihad* and impose Shari'a in West Africa, namely in Algeria and northern Mali. The MOJWA was among the rebel groups that took control of northern Mali after the military coup on 21 March 2012. On 1 September, the group seized the town of Douentza from a local self-defence militia. The capture of the town, situated in the Mopti region of Mali, was the southernmost point of the occupied territory, a fact that caused great concern in Bamako.[864] On 5 December 2012, the group was listed as a terrorist organization associated with Al-Qaeda by the UN Security Council.[865]

[860] Amnesty International UK, 'Media Briefing—Mali Unrest 2012–2013', January 2013, p. 5, at: <http://www.amnesty.org.uk/uploads/documents/doc_22968.pdf>.

[861] 'Strange Bedfellows: The MNLA's On-Again, Off-Again Marriage with Ansar Dine', *France24*, 7 June 2012, at: <http://www.france24.com/en/20120605-mali-strange-bedfellows-mnla-ansar-dine-al-qaeda-aqim-islamists-tuareg>.

[862] 'Mali: les islamistes d'Ansar Dine assurent refuser le "terrorisme"', *Le Monde*, 6 November 2012, at: <http://www.lemonde.fr/afrique/article/2012/11/06/les-islamistes-d-ansar-dine-rejettent-le-terrorisme_1786631_3212.html>.

[863] RFI, 'Au nord du Mali, Ansar Dine et Aqmi œuvrent main dans la main', 3 January 2013, at: <http://www.rfi.fr/ameriques/20130103-nord-mali-ansar-dine-aqmi-tombouctou-azawad>.

[864] GlobalSecurity.org, *Islamic Militant Group in Northern Mali Expanding Southward*, 4 September 2012.

[865] UN, 'Security Council Al-Qaida Sanctions Committee Adds One Entity to Its Sanctions List', Press release, UN doc. SC/18407, 5 December 2012, at: <http://www.un.org/News/Press/docs//2012/sc10847.doc.htm>.

National Movement for the Liberation of Azawd (MNLA)

The Movement National de Libération de l'Azawad (MNLA) is a separatist political and military organization formed mainly by Touareg and to a much smaller part by Saharian and other people living on the territory situated in Northern Mali. It was founded on 16 October 2011[866], when the National Movement of Azawad (MNA) merged with the National Alliance of Touareg in Mali (ATNM) to form the MNLA. Based in Northern Mali, the MNLA had its strongest presence in Kidal, but was also active and present in the regions of Toumbouctou, Gao, and partially Mopti. In the past and the present, some northern Malians have felt that the government has marginalized them, yet some southerners resent what they see as governments' lavish spending on demographically small regions and peoples. On 16 January 2012 the MNLA started its armed campaign with the attack on the city of Ménaka, in the Gao region.[867] Since 2013, the MNLA has reconsidered its political claim from the independence of Azawad region towards a more autonomous administration of the Azawad but still within the Malian territory. The MNLA took Ménaka over in May 2014 and lost it on 27 April 2015 against the GATIA.[868] The following day rebels attacked UN soldiers according to MINUSMA, before stating they had mistaken them for Malian military.[869] Severe fights have been ongoing since then.[870]

CASUALTIES

There was a total of 538 conflict-related casualties (350 killed and 188 injured) identified in Mali in 2014 as a result of armed conflict involving a range of actors including the Mali armed forces (Malian Defence Security Forces, MDSF), the French armed forces, the United Nations Multidimensional Integrated Stabilization Mission in Mali (MINUSMA), the National Movement for the Liberation of Azawad (MNLA) and allied groups Unity of Azawad (HCUA) and the Arab Movement of Azawad (MAA), and the Movement for Oneness and Jihad in West Africa (MUJWA) and Al-Qaeda in the Islamic Maghreb (AQIM).[871]

866 <http://reliefweb.int/report/mali/mali-humanitarian-overview-30-september-2014>.

867 <http://www.thecuttingedgenews.com/index.php?article=71898&pageid=20&pagename=Security>.

868 Gatia stands for 'Groupe autodéfense touareg Imghad et alliés', a group close to the Malian government. It was formed in August 2014, <http://www.jamestown.org/single/?tx_ttnews[tt_news]=43745&tx_ttnews[backPid]=7&cHash=00ec4c5f2c348fb01254a5fb38037614#.VVG89fDLIm0>.

869 <http://maliactu.net/urgent-mali-les-rebelles-ouvrent-le-feu-sur-les-casques-bleus-a-tombouctou/>.

870 <http://maliactu.net/mali-neuf-militaires-tues-a-quatre-jours-de-la-signature-prevue-dun-accord-de-paix/>.

871 Primarily based on war report analysis of the Armed Conflict Location and Event Data Project (ACLED) data for 2014 (with additional sources cross-referenced). Raleigh, C., Linke, A., Hegre, H., and Karlsen, J., 'Introducing ACLED-Armed Conflict Location and Event Data', pp. 1–10..

In mid May 2014, in just two incidents there were almost 100 fatalities (ninety-eight) reported and over sixty injured in clashes between Malian forces and the MNLA (with the HCUA).[872]

Among MINUSMA Peacekeepers eighteen were killed and sixty-nine injured. Peacekeeper casualties were recorded from Burkina Faso (three killed, thirteen injured), Chad (ten killed, thirty-eight injured), Guinea (one injured), and Senegal (one killed, eight injured), while in several cases the peacekeepers' nationality was not reported (four killed, nine injured). The majority of peacekeeper casualties were caused by landmines and improvised explosive devices (IEDs). There were four deaths among French military personnel, including at least one foreign national legionnaire; another eleven French military were injured.[873]

The UN Reported that IEDs and anti-vehicle mines placed along routes used by international troops severely hindered MINUSMA operations.[874] At least eleven peacekeepers were killed and forty-eight injured by landmines and IEDs according to ACLED data for 2014. In addition, four MDSF were killed and twelve injured, eight civilians killed and seven injured and two MNLA members injured by these devices.[875]

On 8 February 2014 the MUJWA kidnapped a team of five ICRC aid workers.[876] These were later freed by French military forces on 17 April in an operation that resulted in twelve MUJWA fighters being killed.[877] During 2014 three Malian aid workers were killed and two injured.[878]

Displaced

There were at least 61,600 internally displaced persons in Mali as of December 2014. During the year at least 19,200 people were newly displaced, while there were some 178,400 returnees.[879]

872 Analysis of ACLED data for 2014.

873 Analysis of ACLED data for 2014.

874 UN Security Council, Report of the Secretary-General on the situation in Mali 23 December 2014, S/2014/943, para. 17.

875 Analysis of ACLED data for 2014.

876 Afrik.com, 'Mali: retour du MUJAO qui enlève cinq membres du CICR à Kidal', 11 February 2014.

877 ICRC, 'News Release: Mali: ICRC Team Released', 17 April 2014; and 'French Troops Free Five Aid Workers Kidnapped in Mali', 17 April 2014.

878 Analysis of ACLED data for 2014; and the Aid Worker Security Database, 'Security incident data', last updated 9 April 2015, <https://aidworkersecurity.org/incidents/search?start=2014&end=2014&detail=1&country=SY>.

879 The Internal Displacement Monitoring Centre (IDMC) also noted 'The government figure is based on assessments made in close collaboration with IOM using the displacement tracking matrix. The figure is approved by the population movements commission, which has been led by the government since November 2014', IDMC, 'Global Overview 2015', May 2015, p. 85.

WAR CRIMES ALLEGATIONS, INVESTIGATIONS, AND PROSECUTIONS

Mali adhered to the 1998 Rome Statute of the International Criminal Court (ICC Statute) in 2000. The ICC has jurisdiction over ICC Statute crimes committed on the territory of Mali or by its nationals since 1 November 2002, in cases where national courts are unwilling or unable to prosecute.

On 16 January 2013, the ICC Prosecutor formally opened an investigation into alleged crimes committed on the territory of Mali since January 2012. This decision was the result of the preliminary examination of the situation in Mali that the Office of the Prosecutor (OTP) had been conducting since July 2012, following the referral of the 'situation in Mali since January 2012' by the Malian Government.[880] In its preliminary examination, the Office had determined that a reasonable basis existed to believe that war crimes within the jurisdiction of the Court had been committed in Mali since January 2012, namely:

(1) murder;
(2) mutilation, cruel treatment, and torture;
(3) the passing of sentences and the carrying out of executions without due process;
(4) intentionally directing attacks against protected objects;
(5) pillaging; and
(6) rape.

The OTP's assessment was preliminary in nature for the purpose of satisfying the threshold determination under Article 53(1) and is therefore not binding for the purpose of the investigation or any future selection of charges.[881] The situation in Mali is assigned to Pre-Trial Chamber II of the ICC.

[880] OTP, 'Report on Preliminary Examination Activities 2013', November 2013, §230, at: <http://www.icc-cpi.int/en_menus/icc/press%20and%20media/press%20releases/Documents/OTP%20Preliminary%20Examinations/OTP%20-%20Report%20%20Preliminary%20Examination%20Activities%202013.PDF>.

[881] OTP, 'Report on Preliminary Examination Activities 2013', November 2013, §231.

Armed conflict in Nigeria in 2014

KEY CASUALTY DATA FOR 2014

Total killed:	27,752	(All sources: ACLED)
Total injured:	527*	
Civilians killed:	3,900	
Civilians injured:	527*	
Military-security killed:	322	
Boko Haram killed:	2,934	
Unknown status killed:	537	
Vigilante/militia deaths:	59	

* The ACLED casualty tracking system records fatalities and therefore persons injured are included incidentally

CLASSIFICATION OF THE CONFLICT

Nigeria and its armed forces were involved in a non-international armed conflict (NIAC) with Boko Haram, which began in the middle of May 2013. As during 2014 Boko Haram seized control of various States in the northern part of Nigeria constituting a territory of about 20,000 squares metres, over which it declared the creation of an Islamic caliphate, the conflict reached the threshold for the applicability of the 1977 Additional Protocol II.

SUMMARY OF APPLICABLE INTERNATIONAL LAW

Both parties to the conflict were bound by customary international humanitarian law (IHL) and human rights law, including customary IHL rules of distinction, proportionality, and precautions in attacks; the obligations of humane treatment, as set out in Common Article 3 to the 1949 Geneva Conventions; the obligation not to recruit and use children as soldiers; and by the duty to respect and protect fundamental human rights. This includes the duty to respect the rights to life and to freedom from torture or other forms of cruel, inhuman, or degrading treatment or punishment.

Nigeria is a State party to the four 1949 Geneva Conventions and the 1977 Additional Protocol II. Nigeria is party to both the 1966 International Covenant on Civil and Political Rights and the 1966 International Covenant on Economic, Social and Cultural Rights.

Nigeria is a State party to the 1997 Anti-Personnel Mine Ban Convention. In accordance with Article 5 of the Convention, Nigeria was required to destroy all antipersonnel mines in mined areas under its jurisdiction or control as soon as possible, but not later than 1 March 2012. It announced full compliance with its clearance obligations in 2011.

Nigeria has signed but not ratified the 2008 Convention on Cluster Munitions. Nigeria signed and ratified the 2013 Arms Trade Treaty (ATT) on 12 August 2013.

HISTORY OF THE CONFLICT[882]

After lurching from one military coup to another, Nigeria now has an elected leadership. But the government faces the growing challenge of preventing Africa's most populous country from breaking apart along ethnic and religious lines. Political liberalization ushered in by the return to civilian rule in 1999 has allowed militants from religious and ethnic groups to pursue their demands through violence.

In July 2009, hundreds were killed in Borno State in north-eastern Nigeria after the Boko Haram Islamist movement launched a campaign of violence in a bid to have Shari'a law imposed on the entire country. Security forces stormed Boko Haram's stronghold and killed the movement's leader despite capturing him alive.[883]

Violence continued, however, and in July 2011 the Nigerian Government said it wanted to start negotiating with Boko Haram. The following month, a suicide bomb attack on UN headquarters in Abuja, claimed by Boko Haram killed twenty-three people. In November, at least sixty-three people were killed in bomb and gun attacks in the north-eastern town of Damaturu, for which Boko Haram again claimed responsibility. In December, nearly seventy people were killed in days of fighting between security forces and Boko Haram militants in the north-eastern States of Borno and Yobe and Christmas Day bomb attacks killed about forty people.

In April 2012, Chadian President Idriss Deby called on States neighbouring northern Nigeria to set up a joint military force to tackle Boko Haram as they continued their attacks, warning of the danger of the Islamist group destabilizing the whole Lake Chad basin area.

Violence continued throughout 2012 and 2013.[884]

[882] Unless otherwise stated, this section is based on 'Nigeria Profile', *BBC*, 1 April 2015, at: <http://www.bbc.com/news/world-africa-13949550>.

[883] 'Nigeria Policemen in Court Trial for Boko Haram Killing', *BBC*, 13 July 2011, at: <http://www.bbc.com/news/world-africa-14136185>.

[884] See Armed Conflict in Nigeria, *The War Report 2013*, edited by Casey-Maslen, S., Oxford University Press, 2014, p. 173.

On 16 December 2013, the UN Office for the Coordination of Humanitarian Affairs (OCHA) said that more than 1,200 people had been killed in forty-eight 'Boko Haram-related' attacks since May 2013. Later in December, AFP reported a video obtained of Boko Haram leader Abubakar Shekau warning that the group was not confined to Nigeria; he subsequently said that group was under instruction from Allah to 'kill, decapitate, and mutilate' non-Muslims.

On 14 April 2014, Boko Haram abducted 276 girls from their school in Chibok. Boko Haram admitted capturing the girls, saying they should not have been in school and should get married instead. Boko Haram means 'Western education is forbidden' in the Hausa language. On 9 May, UN Security Council President Oh Joon of the Republic of Korea issued a press statement in which the Council 'expressed their profound outrage at and condemned in the strongest terms the abduction' of the schoolgirls, demanded the 'immediate and unconditional release of all abducted girls still in captivity', and expressed their deep concern at statements by the alleged leader of Boko Haram 'threatening to sell these girls as slaves'.[885]

More generally, according to the International Crisis Group (ICG), 'This problem [of Boko Haram's rise] is coming from bad governance, bad governance, and bad governance. More troops, more boots on the ground won't solve anything'.[886]

After releasing a video on 5 May, claiming responsibility for the abduction of the schoolgirls,[887] Abubakar Shekau said that he would set them free in exchange for the release of all Boko Haram prisoners.[888] As a result, on 14 May, White House Press Secretary announced that the United States had started using drones and aircraft flights in Nigeria to help search for the 276 schoolgirls kidnapped by Boko Haram.[889]

On 22 May 2014, the Security Council's Al-Qaeda Sanctions Committee approved the addition of Boko Haram to its list of individuals and entities subject to the targeted financial sanctions and the arms embargo set out in paragraph 1 of Security Council resolution 2083 (2012), adopted under Chapter VII of the Charter of the United Nations.[890]

[885] UN Security Council Press Statement on Attacks in Nigeria, UN doc. SC/11387, 9 May 2014.

[886] Rinaldo Depagne, ICG West Africa Project Director, in *Time* magazine, 8 May 2014.

[887] 'Boko Haram Release Disturbing Video Threatening Schoolgirls', *The Telegraph*, 12 May 2014, at: <http://www.telegraph.co.uk/news/worldnews/africaandindianocean/nigeria/10809951/Boko-Haram-release-disturbing-video-threatening-schoolgirls.html>.

[888] 'Boko Haram Video: We'll Exchange Nigerian Girls for Prisoners', *NBC News*, 12 May 2014, at: <http://www.nbcnews.com/storyline/missing-nigeria-schoolgirls/boko-haram-video-well-exchange-nigerian-girls-prisoners-n102841>.

[889] 'U.S. Deploys Drones in Search for Kidnapped Nigerian Girls', *The Times*, 14 May 2014, at: <http://time.com/99520/us-deploys-drones-in-search-for-kidnapped-nigerian-girls/>.

[890] 'Security Council Al-Qaida Sanctions Committee Adds Boko Haram to Its Sanctions List', *UNSC Press Release*, 22 May 2014, at: <http://www.un.org/press/en/2014/sc11410.doc.htm>.

Following the Parliament approval of the extension of the state of emergency for six more months in Adamawa, Borno, and Yobe States,[891] President Jonathan on 29 May offered an amnesty to Boko Haram members.[892]

In July, the European Parliament passed a resolution condemning Boko Haram abuses and urging the Nigerian Government to ensure that efforts to tackle the insurgent violence are carried out in accordance with its obligations under international law.[893]

From July onwards Boko Haram captured and occupied more than twenty towns across Adamawa, Borno, and Yobe States.[894] On 6 August, Boko Haram captured the town of Gwoza and killed at least 600 civilians, although several sources suggested the figure was higher.[895]

In response, on the 23 July 2014, Nigeria, Niger, Chad, and Cameroon announced the formation of a joint force to tackle the growing regional threat posed by Boko Haram.[896]

In August 2014, Boko Haram leader, Abubakar Shekau, announced the creation of an Islamic caliphate in Gwoza and Adamawa[897] and later seized control of several towns in the north-east of the country. It has been estimated that Boko Haram controls about 20,000 square miles of territory.[898]

On 25 September the military reported to have killed a commander who had featured in Boko Haram's videos, claiming he was the group leader Shekau.[899] However, a week later a new video was released, purportedly of leader Shekau claiming he was still alive.

On 17 October the government announced a ceasefire had been agreed with Boko Haram.[900] However, two incidents in Nigeria's north—the reported kidnapping of more

[891] 'Nigerian Senate Approves Extension of Emergency Rule in Adamawa, Borno, Yobe', *The Times Premium*, 20 May 2014, at: <http://www.premiumtimesng.com/news/161165-nigerian-senate-approves-extension-emergency-rule-adamawa-borno-yobe.html>.

[892] 'Jonathan Offers Amnesty to Boko Haram Members', *The Nation*, 29 May 2014, at: <http://thenationonlineng.net/new/jonathan-offers-amnesty-to-boko-haram-members/>.

[893] 'Nigeria: World Report 2015', *Human Rights Watch*, at: <https://www.hrw.org/world-report/2015/country-chapters/nigeria>.

[894] 'Nigeria Profile: Amnesty International Report 2014/15', *Amnesty International*, at: <https://www.amnesty.org/en/documents/pol10/0001/2015/en/>.

[895] 'Nigeria Profile: Amnesty International Report 2014/15', *Amnesty International*, at: <https://www.amnesty.org/en/documents/pol10/0001/2015/en/>.

[896] 'West African States Pledge Regional Anti-Boko Haram Force', *Reuters*, 23 July 2014, at: <http://www.reuters.com/article/2014/07/23/us-nigeria-violence-military-idUSKBN0FS2IZ20140723>.

[897] 'Nigerian Town Seized by Boko Haram "Part Of Islamic Caliphate", Leader Says', *The Telegraph*, 24 August 2014, at: <http://www.telegraph.co.uk/news/worldnews/africaandindianocean/nigeria/11054219/Nigerian-town-seized-by-Boko-Haram-part-of-Islamic-caliphate-leader-says.html>.

[898] 'Boko Haram is Now a Mini-Islamic State, With its Own Territory', *The Telegraph*, 10 January 2015, at: <http://www.telegraph.co.uk/news/worldnews/africaandindianocean/nigeria/11337722/Boko-Haram-is-now-a-mini-Islamic-State-with-its-own-territory.html>.

[899] 'Boko Haram Fighters "Surrender" as Alleged Chief Killed', *BBC News*, 25 September 2014, at: <http://www.bbc.com/news/world-africa-29352927>.

[900] 'Nigeria Announces Cease-Fire with Boko Haram', *Al Jazeera*, 17 October 2014, at: <http://america.aljazeera.com/articles/2014/10/17/boko-haram-ceasefire.html>.

than twenty-five girls and a bomb blast killing at least five—have cast further doubt on government reports that a ceasefire deal with Boko Haram had indeed been reached.[901]

As fighting with Boko Haram continued in the north of Nigeria, President Jonathan requested another six-months' extension of the state of emergency in in Adamawa, Borno, and Yobe States to the Parliament, which however denied it.[902]

On 10 December 2014 the People's Democratic Party validated President Jonathan's candidacy for 2015 elections.[903]

PARTIES TO THE CONFLICT

The parties to the NIAC in 2014 were Nigeria and its armed forces and Boko Haram.

Nigerian armed forces

The Nigerian armed forces have been estimated to be 130,000 strong, with 32,000 reservists.[904]

Boko Haram

The Muslim cleric, Mohammed Yusuf, formed Boko Haram in Maiduguri in 2002. The group's official name is Jama'atu Ahlis Sunna Lidda'awati wal-Jihad, which in Arabic means 'People Committed to the Propagation of the Prophet's Teachings and Jihad'. But residents of Maiduguri, where it was formed in 2002, dubbed it Boko Haram. Loosely translated from the local Hausa language, this means 'Western education is forbidden'.[905]

Yusuf set up a religious complex, which included a mosque and an Islamic school. The school became a recruiting ground for jihadis. In 2009, Boko Haram carried out a spate of attacks on police stations and other government buildings in Maiduguri. This led to shoot-outs on Maiduguri's streets. Hundreds of Boko Haram supporters were killed

901 'Kidnapping, Bomb Blast in Nigeria Raise Doubts About Boko Haram Truce' *Al Jazeera*, 23 October 2014, at: <http://america.aljazeera.com/articles/2014/10/23/kidnappings-raisedoubt.html>.

902 'Senate Fails to Discuss Extension of State of Emergency', *News24 Nigeria*, 26 November 2014, at: <http://www.news24.com.ng/National/News/Senate-fails-to-discuss-presidents-request-for-extension-of-state-of-emergency-In-North-East-20141126>.

903 'ANALYSIS: Breaking with Tradition, Jonathan Attends PDP Convention a Lone Candidate', *The Times*, 10 December 2014, at: <http://www.premiumtimesng.com/news/top-news/172881-analysis-breaking-tradition-jonathan-attends-pdp-convention-lone-candidate.html>.

904 'Nigeria Military Strength', *Globalfirepower.com*, last updated on 27 March 2014, at: <http://www.globalfirepower.com/country-military-strength-detail.asp?country_id=nigeria>.

905 'Nigeria Policemen in Court Trial For Boko Haram Killing', *BBC*, 13 July 2011.

and thousands of residents fled the city. Nigeria's security forces eventually seized the group's headquarters, capturing its fighters and killing Mr Yusuf. His body was shown on State television and the security forces declared Boko Haram finished.[906]

But its fighters regrouped under a new leader, Abubakar Shekau, and increased attacks. In 2010, the United States designated it a terrorist organization, amid fears it had developed links with other militant groups, such as Al-Qaeda in the Islamic Maghreb. The deployment of troops in 2013 drove many of the fighters out of Maiduguri, their main urban base, and they retreated to the vast Sambisa forest, along the border with Cameroon. Boko Haram promotes a version of Islam which makes it 'haram', or forbidden, for Muslims to take part in any political or social activity associated with Western society. This includes voting in elections, wearing shirts and trousers, or receiving a secular education.[907]

The exact size of the Boko Haram force is not known. However, it is believed to have a fighting force of thousands of men—CIA officials had estimated around 9,000—and cells that specialize in bombings.[908]

CASUALTIES

By all accounts, the number of casualties in the conflict between Nigeria and Boko Haram leaped in 2014. Casualty tracking systems covering the conflict reported a range of total fatalities for the year from around 7,500 to some 10,000. The differences were largely comparative to the criteria applied by data collectors for including cumulative casualty estimates from attacks and violent events.

The Armed Conflict Location and Event Data Project (ACLED) reported that events related to the activities of Boko Haram, primarily in the Northeast of Nigeria, accounted for over 7,500 of the reported fatalities recorded by over the course of the year.[909] ACLED also reported that Nigeria witnessed an increase in reported fatalities by almost 150% in 2014 over 2013, 'representing a very dramatic intensification of violence in the past twelve months'.[910] ACLED's system of calculating fatalities tend to include estimates

[906] Chothia, F., 'Who are Nigeria's Boko Haram Islamists?', 7 May 2014, at: <http://www.bbc.com/news/world-africa-13809501>.

[907] Ibid.

[908] 'Who are Nigeria's Boko Haram Islamists?', *BBC News*, 4 May 2015, at: <http://www.bbc.com/news/world-africa-13809501>.

[909] ACLED, 'Conflict Trends (No. 33) Real-Time Analysis of African Political Violence (Nigeria),' January 2015, p. 8.

[910] 'Fighting associated with Boko Haram killed 6,347 civilians in 2014, said (ACLED).' Anderson, M., 'Nigeria Suffers Highest Number of Civilian Deaths in African War Zones', 23 January 2015, <http://www.theguardian.com/global-development/2015/jan/23/boko-haram-nigeria-civilian-death-toll-highest-acled-african-war-zones>.

from the lower range reported in the original sources.[911] Analysis of ACELD data on Nigeria for 2014 indicated 7,752 fatalities related to the Boko Haram conflict, at least half of all fatalities (3,900) were civilians. The 322 military and security fatalities identified in analysis of the ACLED data were mainly soldiers and military personnel, though some included police, security guards, and prison guards.[912]

The frequency and intensity of Boko Haram violence against civilians was a key feature of 2014 highlighted by ACLED, with several massacres during attacks on villages. The magnitude of anti-civilian violence by Boko Haram was believed to be associated with the increase in vigilante militias in the north-east as locals formed security units where military and police force presence was lacking, 'which may in part explain the severity and intensity of subsequent attacks on civilians'.[913]

The Nigeria Social Violence Project[914] reported a total of 7,974 fatalities due to the activities of Boko Haram and related conflict, of which 5,551 fatalities were caused directly by Boko Haram and 2,423[915] were included as 'State/Boko Haram fatalities' attributed to conflict between Boko Haram and Nigeria.[916]

Council on Foreign Relations Nigeria Security Tracker recorded a total of 10,849 fatalities related to Boko Haram in 2014, with 4,611 attributed directly to Boko Haram[917] and 6,238 recorded as 'State/Boko Haram fatalities'. Nigeria Security Tracker uses upper range reporting and estimates of fatalities.[918]

[911] According to the ACLED methodology, if source reports differ or a vague estimate is provided, the lowest number of fatalities is reported. If reports mention the terms 'several', 'many', or plural 'civilians' and 'unknown' and no other reference, '10' is recorded as the total. If a report mentions dozens, this is recorded as '12'. If a report mentions hundreds, this is recorded as '100'. If a source includes 'massacres,' 100 fatalities are recorded as a default. Raleigh, C. and Dowd, C., 2015, *Armed Conflict Location and Event Data Project (ACLED) Codebook*, pp. 20–1.

[912] War report Analysis of ACELD data for 2014. Raleigh, C., Linke, A., Hegre, H., and Karlsen, J., 'Introducing ACLED-Armed Conflict Location and Event Data', pp. 1–10.

[913] ACLED, 'Conflict Trends (No. 33) Real-Time Analysis of African Political Violence (Nigeria)', January 2015, p. 8.

[914] The Nigeria Social Violence Project of the African Studies Program at Johns Hopkins School of Advanced International Studies (SAIS), <http://www.connectsaisafrica.org/research/african-studies-publications/social-violence-nigeria>.

[915] In the system of classification 'Boko Haram fatalities are those attributed to the militant group known as Boko Haram' and 'State/Boko Haram fatalities are fatalities of or by security forces in connection with Boko Haram events'.

[916] Nigeria Social Violence Project, 'Social Violence Data Table,' <http://www.connectsaisafrica.org/wp-content/uploads/2014/10/Table3.htm>.

[917] Council on Foreign Relations, 'Nigeria Security Tracker (NST)', <http://www.cfr.org/nigeria/nigeria-security-tracker/p29483>.

[918] A member of the programme gave an interview saying, 'When we add a violent occurrence to the tracker we always take the highest reported number. We do this as we have been told by multiple non-profits on the ground that the figures range from three to five times what is actually reported.' In Ogunlesi, T., 'Have over 13,000 people been killed in Nigeria's insurgency? The claim is broadly correct', 14 October 2014, <http://africa-check.org/reports/have-13000-people-been-killed-in-nigerias-insurgency-the-claim-is-broadly-correct/>.

The Nigeria Watch monitoring project found that the intensifying Boko Haram crisis in 2014 resulted in increasing fatality numbers calculated for in each trimester of the year: 2,361 in the period January to April 2014, 3,545 in May to August 2014, and 3,978 in September to December, amounting to a total of 9,884 fatalities.[919] An analysis of fatalities from incidents related to Boko Haram in the Nigeria Watch database indicated some 10,919 associated deaths in 2014, including military and vigilante clashes with Boko Haram, attacks on local residents by Boko Haram and various other Boko Haram attacks including suicide bombings.[920]

DISPLACED PERSONS

In 2014, there were at least 975,300 new internal displaced persons (IDPs) in Nigeria, leading to a total of 1,075,300 persons being internally displaced in the country as of December 2014.[921]

WAR CRIMES ALLEGATIONS, INVESTIGATIONS, AND PROSECUTIONS

Nigeria ratified the 1998 Rome Statute of the International Criminal Court (ICC Statute) on 27 September 2001. The ICC therefore has jurisdiction over Rome Statute crimes committed on the territory of Nigeria or by its nationals from 1 July 2002 onwards.

Up to and including 1 June 2013, the Office of the Prosecutor (OTP) received sixty-five communications under Article 15 of the ICC Statute in relation to the situation in Nigeria, of which twenty-six were deemed to be manifestly outside the jurisdiction of the Court; five were found to warrant further analysis; and twenty-eight were included in the OTP's preliminary examination. The preliminary examination of the situation in Nigeria was made public on 18 November 2010.[922]

[919] Nigeria Watch Project, University of Ibadan, 'Fatality Trends Newsletter No 4, Sept-Dec, 2014', p. 6, <http://www.nigeriawatch.org/media/html/NW4.pdf>.

[920] Nigeria Watch Project, 'The Database', <http://www.nigeriawatch.org/index.php?urlaction=evtListe&cherche=1>.

[921] Internal Displacement Monitoring Centre (IDMC) 'Global Overview 2015', May 2015, p. 85. The figure represents a compilation of assessments conducted using the displacement tracking matrix, reports from the National Emergency Management Agency and the National Commission for Refugees. It includes information on IDPs in fourteen out of Nigeria's thirty-six States, but does not include people displaced before 2012.

[922] OTP, 'Preliminary Examinations: Ongoing: Federal Republic of Nigeria', at: <http://www.icc-cpi.int/en_menus/icc/structure%20of%20the%20court/office%20of%20the%20prosecutor/comm%20and%20ref/pe-ongoing/nigeria/Pages/nigeria.aspx>.

The OTP has determined there is a reasonable basis to believe that crimes against humanity have been committed in Nigeria, namely acts of murder and persecution attributed to Boko Haram. Therefore, the Prosecutor has decided that the preliminary examination of the situation in Nigeria should advance to the admissibility phase 3 with a view to assessing whether national authorities are conducting genuine proceedings in relation to those who appear to bear the greatest responsibility for such crimes, and the gravity of such crimes.[923]

At national level, the government failed to investigate deaths in custody and denied the National Human Rights Commission access to military detention facilities.[924] According to Amnesty International, the criminal justice system in 2014 remained under-resourced, blighted by corruption and generally distrusted.[925]

[923] Ibid.

[924] 'Nigeria Profile: Amnesty International Report 2014/15', *Amnesty International*, at: <https://www.amnesty.org/en/documents/pol10/0001/2015/en/>.

[925] Ibid.

Armed conflicts in Pakistan in 2014

KEY CASUALTY DATA FOR 2014

Civilians killed:	at least 161–257	(Source: news media/TBIJ)
Pakistani military killed:	200 (estimate)	(Source: news media)
Pakistani military injured:	800 (estimate)	(Source: news media)
NSAG killed:	2,000 (estimate)	(Source: news media)

CLASSIFICATION OF THE CONFLICT

Pakistan was involved in 2014 in a non-international armed conflict (NIAC) with the Tehrik-i-Taliban Pakistan (TTP/Pakistani Taliban). There might be another non-international armed conflict with TTP splinter groups such as Haqqani network, Lashkar-e-Jhangvi, Jundallah, Al-Qaeda, the East Turkestan Islamic Movement (ETIM), and the Islamic Movement of Uzbekistan (IMU), but data available does not allow a certain qualification for 2014.

SUMMARY OF APPLICABLE INTERNATIONAL LAW

All parties to the conflict were bound by customary international humanitarian law (IHL) and human rights law, including customary IHL rules of distinction, proportionality, and precautions in attacks; the obligations of humane treatment, as set out in Common Article 3 to the 1949 Geneva Conventions; the obligation not to recruit and use children as soldiers; and by the duty to respect and protect fundamental human rights. This includes the duty to respect the rights to life and to freedom from torture or other forms of cruel, inhuman, or degrading treatment or punishment.

Pakistan is party to the four 1949 Geneva Conventions, but not the 1977 Additional Protocol II. Pakistan is also party to the 1966 International Covenant on Civil and Political Rights and the 1966 International Covenant on Economic, Social and Cultural Rights.

Pakistan is not party to the 1997 Anti-Personnel Mine Ban Convention or the 2008 Convention on Cluster Munitions. Pakistan is neither a party nor a signatory to the 2013 Arms Trade Treaty (ATT).

HISTORY OF THE CONFLICT

The roots of the TTP as an organization began in 2002 when the Pakistani military conducted incursions into the tribal areas to originally combat foreign (Afghan, Arab, and Central Asian) militants fleeing from the war in Afghanistan into the neighbouring tribal areas of Pakistan.[926]

Many of the TTP's leaders are veterans of the fighting in Afghanistan and have supported the fight against the NATO-led International Security Assistance Force by providing soldiers, training, and logistics. In 2004 various tribal groups, that would later form the TTP, effectively established their authority in the Federally Administered Tribal Areas (FATA) by concurrently engaging in military attacks and negotiating with Islamabad. In December 2007 the existence of the TTP Pakistan was officially announced under the leadership of Baitullah Mehsud.[927]

The TTP differs in structure to the Afghan Taliban in that it lacks a central command and is a much looser coalition of various militant groups, united by hostility towards the central government in Islamabad.[928] In its original form, the TTP had Baitullah Mehsud as its amir. He was followed in the leadership hierarchy by Hafiz Gul Bahadur as naib amir, or deputy. Faqir Mohammed was the third most influential leader. The group contained members from all of FATA's seven tribal agencies as well as several districts of the North-West Frontier Province (NWFP), including Swat, Bannu, Tank, Lakki Marwat, Dera Ismail Khan, Kohistan, Buner, and Malakand.[929]

The Pakistani Government implicated the network in the December 2007 assassination of Benazir Bhutto although the group denies the charge. The US Central Intelligence Agency also confirmed its belief of TTP's involvement in January 2008.

In telephone interviews with news media, Mehsud claimed responsibility for the 30 March 2009 attack on the police training academy in Lahore. He told the BBC that the attack was in retaliation for continued missile strikes from American drones for which the Pakistani Government shared responsibility. In the same interview Mehsud claimed two other attacks: a 25 March 2009 attack on an Islamabad police station and a 30 March 2009 suicide attack on a military convoy near Bannu.[930]

In August 2009, a missile strike from a US drone killed Baitullah Mehsud. The TTP soon held a shura to appoint his successor. After a period of internal crisis on the issue of

[926] Zaffar, A., 'Pakistan's Undeclared War', *BBC*, 10 September 2004 at: <http://news.bbc.co.uk/2/hi/south_asia/3645114.stm>.

[927] Hassan, A., 2008, 'A Profile of Tehrik-I-Taliban Pakistan', January 2008, *CTC Sentinel*, West Point, NY: Combating Terrorism Center.

[928] Siddiqa, A., 2011, 'Pakistan's Counterterrorism Strategy: Separating Friends from Enemies', *The Washington Quarterly*, vol. 34, no. 1: pp. 149–162.

[929] *supra* note 2

[930] 'Lahore "was Pakistan Taleban op"', *BBC News*, 31 March 2009 at: <http://news.bbc.co.uk/2/hi/south_asia/7973540.stm>.

leadership Hakimullah Mehsud emerged as the new leader of the TTP in August 2009.[931] Under the leadership of Hakimullah, the TTP intensified its suicide campaign against the Pakistani State and against civilian (particularly Shia, Ahmedi, and Sufi) targets.[932]

On 10 October 2009, ten terrorists dressed in army uniforms attacked the General Headquarters of the Pakistan Army in Rawalpindi, resulting in the death of six army personnel. On 4 December 2009 at least thirty-six people were killed and eighty-three injured when six suicide bombers opened fire and hurled grenades at worshippers gathered inside the Parade Lane Mosque off Peshawar Road in Rawalpindi. All six suicide bombers were believed to have blown themselves up during the attack. The dead included a brigadier, a colonel, two lieutenant colonels, two majors, three soldiers, and seventeen children. The TTP had claimed the attack on the mosque.

The Pakistani Taliban, as well as the Afghan Taliban, claimed responsibility for the 30 December 2009 attack on Camp Chapman, a base of operations for the CIA, inside Khost Province, Afghanistan. The TTP released a video of Hakimullah Mehsud sitting next to the suicide bomber, Humam Khalil Abu Mulal al-Balawi, a Jordanian national who had been working with the CIA. In the video, al-Balawi states that the attack is in retaliation for the killing of Baitullah Mehsud. Many analysts doubted that the TTP acted alone.[933]

The militant group claimed responsibility for three separate coordinated attacks in Lahore. Ten militants targeted buildings used by the Federal Investigation Agency (FIA), the Manawan Police Training School, and the Elite Police Academy.[934]

In a May 2010 interview, US General David Petraeus described the TTP's relationship with other militant groups as difficult to decipher: 'There is clearly a symbiotic relationship between all of these different organizations: al-Qaeda, the Pakistani Taliban, the Afghan Taliban, TNSM [Tehreek-e-Nafaz-e-Shariat-e-Mohammadi]. And it's very difficult to parse and to try to distinguish between them. They support each other, they coordinate with each other, sometimes they compete with each other, [and] sometimes they even fight each other. But at the end of the day, there is quite a relationship between them.'[935]

In December 2010, the TTP claimed responsibility for a double suicide bombing upon administrative buildings in the Mohmand district's Ghalalnai village. The blast

[931] 'Hakeemullah Announced New Leader—Doubts Linger'. *Dawn News*, 23 August 2009 at: <http://www.dawn.com/news/485952/hakeemullah-mehsud-new-chief-says-faqir>.

[932] Fair, C., 2011, 'The Militant Challenge in Pakistan', *Asia Policy*, vol. 11, no. 1: pp. 105–37.

[933] 'Pakistan Taliban say they carried out CIA attack', *Associated Press*, 1 January 2010 at: <http://usatoday30.usatoday.com/news/world/2010-01-01-pakistan-cia-attack_N.htm>.

[934] Hussain, Z. and Mehsud, R., 'Wave of Deadly Attacks in Pakistan', *Wall Street Journal*, 15 October 2009.

[935] Bajoria, J. and Greg, B., 'Shared Goals for Pakistan's Militants', *Council on Foreign* Relations, 6 May 2010.

killed forty to fifty people. The purported head of the TTP in Mohmand, Omar Khalid, claimed responsibility in a telephone call with the AFP.[936]

On 10 February 2011 the TTP claimed responsibility for a suicide bombing at an army compound in Mardan that killed at least thirty-one people. Azam Tariq told the AFP that the attack was in response to repeated US drone attacks and military incursions in the tribal areas. He also threatened further attacks against 'those who protect the Americans'.[937]

On 13 May 2011 the TTP claimed responsibility for dual suicide bomb attacks on a Frontier Constabulary (FC) headquarters in Shabqadar, a town about 30 kilometres north of Peshawar, in Charsadda District. The attack killed more than eighty and injured at least 115 people. Most of the casualties were FC cadets. TTP spokesman Ehsanullah Ehsan claimed that the attack was retribution for the killing of Osama bin Laden.[938]

TTP militants abducted fifteen Pakistani paramilitary soldiers on 23 December 2011 from a fort in Mullazai. TTP spokesperson Ehsanullah Ehsan announced on 5 January 2012 that the militant group had executed the fifteen paramilitary soldiers. The bodies were recovered close to a ravine and were mutilated according to locals. On 22 January 2012 the TTP released a video showing the execution of the fifteen soldiers.[939]

On 9 July 2012 militants linked to the TTP attacked an army camp near Gujrat city that killed seven soldiers and a policeman. A pamphlet found at the scene indicated that attacks against government installations would continue as long as Pakistan allowed NATO to use its territory to transport supplies into Afghanistan.[940]

The TTP claimed responsibility for the 9 October 2012 school-bus shooting of Malala Yousafzai, a young activist blogger, and two other schoolgirls. Supporting the attack, TTP spokesman Ehsanullah Ehsan stated 'whom so ever leads a campaign against Islam and Shariah is ordered to be killed by Shariah'. He added that it is 'not just allowed... but obligatory in Islam' to kill such a person involved 'in leading a campaign against Shariah'.[941]

[936] 'Suicide Bombers Kill 40 in Mohmand Agency', *Dawn.com*, 5 December 2010 at: <http://www.topix.com/forum/religion/islam/THHISMAIQU51MQT0V>.

[937] 'Pakistan Attack: "Schoolboy" Suicide Bomber Hits Mardan', *BBC*, 10 February 2011 at: <http://www.bbc.com/news/world-south-asia-12413469>.

[938] 'Twin Blasts Kill More Than 80 in Charsadda', *Dawn*, 13 May 2011 at: <http://www.dawn.com/news/628325/twin-blasts-kill-at-least-three-in-charsadda-dawnnews>.

[939] 'Taliban Video Highlights Revenge on Pakistan Military', *Reuters*, 21 January 2012 at: <http://www.reuters.com/article/2012/01/21/us-pakistan-military-video-idUSTRE80K0NT20120121>.

[940] 'Army Camp Attack: Pamphlet Vows More Attacks if NATO Supplies Continue', *The Express Tribune*, 11 July 2012 at: <http://tribune.com.pk/story/406573/army-camp-attack-pamphlet-vows-more-attacks-if-nato-supplies-continue/>.

[941] 'Taliban use Islamic Shariah to Defend Masala Attack', *Dawn*, 10 October 2012 at: <http://www.dawn.com/news/755657/taliban-use-islamic-shariah-to-defend-malala-attack>.

On 1 November 2013, a senior Taliban source confirmed that a US drone strike in Pakistan killed Mehsud in the village of Dande Darpa Khel in North Waziristan.[942] Following the death of Hakimullah Mehsud, Mullah Fazlullah, a former commander of the TTP in Swat valley took to the leadership of the group that has seen infighting among the various factions. On 21 March 2015 it was reported widely in Pakistani media that Fazlullah had died in a drone strike in Afghanistan. The TTP have however denied these reports and no confirmation has been received so far.[943]

In 2014 a joint military offensive, Operation Zarb-e-Azb was launched by the Pakistan Armed Forces against various militant groups, including the Tehrik-i-Taliban Pakistan (TTP), Lashkar-e-Jhangvi, Jundallah, Al-Qaeda, the East Turkestan Islamic Movement (ETIM), the Islamic Movement of Uzbekistan (IMU), and the Haqqani network. The operation was launched by the Pakistan Armed Forces on 15 June 2014 in North Waziristan (part of the Federally Administered Tribal Areas along the Afghan border) as a renewed effort against militancy in the wake of the 8 June attack on Jinnah International Airport in Karachi, for which the TTP and the IMU claimed responsibility. Part of the ongoing war in North-West Pakistan, up to 30,000 Pakistani soldiers are involved in Zarb-e-Azb, described as a 'comprehensive operation' to flush out all foreign and local militants hiding in North Waziristan. The operation has received widespread support from the Pakistani political, defence, and civilian sectors.[944]

The operation has seen both ground operations as well as protracted air strikes being conducted by the Pakistani military throughout the North-West Pakistan region. On 21 June, a total of thirty militants were killed in early-morning airstrikes in uninhabited areas of Khyber and North Waziristan Agencies. Jet aircraft destroyed two hideouts near the Pakistan–Afghanistan border in Khyber Agency, killing ten militants. These surgical strikes were in line with the security forces' strategy to take on the militants across the FATA.[945]

On 30 June, early-morning ground operations began in and around Miramshah. Search operations were conducted by infantry and the Special Services Group, killing fifteen militants. Pakistani troops discovered underground tunnels and IED-preparation factories in the cleared areas, with three soldiers reportedly injured in an exchange of fire. Since the beginning of the operation 376 militants were killed and nineteen surrendered,

[942] 'Drone Strike in Pakistan Kills Head of Pakistan Taliban', *Fox News*, 1 November 2013 at: <http://www.foxnews.com/world/2013/11/01/drone-strike-in-pakistan-kills-head-pakistan-taliban-security-sources-say/>.

[943] 'No Confirmation on Mullah Fazlullah's Death: Nisar', *Tribune*, 24 March 2015 at: <http://tribune.com.pk/story/858271/no-confirmation-on-mullah-fazlullahs-death-chaudhry-nisar/>.

[944] 'Pakistan Launches Offensive Against Militants Near Afghan Border', *Associated Press*, 15 June 2014 at: <http://www.huffingtonpost.com/2014/06/15/pakistan-army-says-launch_n_5496487.html>.

[945] '30 More Terrorists Killed in NWA, Khyber Agency Strikes', *Daily Times*, 22 June 2014 at: <http://www.dailytimes.com.pk/national/22-Jun-2014/30-more-terrorists-killed-in-nwa-khyber-agency-strikes>.

with sixty-one hideouts destroyed in the operation's first phase. Seventeen soldiers were reportedly killed.[946]

In June 2014 a US drone attack reportedly killed ten members of the Haqqani network including a high-level commander, Haji Gul, in the country's tribal area of North Waziristan.[947]

On 3 September, according to ISPR, 910 militants had been killed so far in the operation. Eighty-two soldiers had also been killed (forty-two were killed in North Waziristan Agency) while 269 others have been injured, added the ISPR statement. The Pakistan Armed Forces had cleared Miramshah, Mirali, Datta Khel, Degan, Boya areas of North Waziristan which were considered strongholds of terrorists.[948]

On 27 October, Pakistani officials claimed to have found evidence of 'new sanctuaries' set up by the TTP and its affiliates in the Afghan territory near the border with North Waziristan Agency. In two separate incidents of aerial strikes, thirty-three militants were killed and nine militant hideouts were destroyed, according to ISPR. 'In early morning aerial strikes ahead of Dattakhel, 18 militants were killed. Later, in Gharlamai area another 15 militants were killed by gunship helicopters', the ISPR statement added.[949]

On 2 November 2014, a suicide bomber attempting to enter the parade arena at the India–Pakistan Wagah border, after a flag lowering ceremony, detonated explosives, killing at least sixty people, including two Pakistani Rangers, and injuring more than 110 others. Victims include ten women and seven children. Jundullah claimed responsibility for the attack, positing it as retaliation for Operation Zarb-e-Azb.[950]

The TTP claimed responsibility for the 2014 Peshawar school attack which claimed 141 lives, including 132 school children between eight and eighteen years of age, with the remaining nine fatalities being staff members of the school.[951] Following the TTP's Peshawar school massacre which in its statement was revenge for operation Zarb-e-Azb, Afghan taliban leaders condemned the TTP's actions on the school, saying it was 'Un-Islamic'.[952]

[946] 'ISPR Press Releases of 30 June', ISPR at: <https://www.ispr.gov.pk/front/main.asp?o=t-zarb-e-azb-archive>.

[947] 'Controversial US Drone Attack in Pakistan, 16 Killed', *Pakistan News.Net*, 12 June 2014 at: <http://www.jordannews.net/index.php/sid/222852683>.

[948] '910 Militants Killed Since Start of Operation Zarb-e-Azb: ISPR', *The Express Tribune*, 3 September 2014 at: <http://tribune.com.pk/story/757315/910-militants-killed-to-date-since-start-of-operation-zarb-e-azb-ispr/>.

[949] 'Two Uzbeks among 33 Militants Killed In NWA Air Strikes', *The News*, 28 October 2014 at: <http://www.thenews.com.pk/Todays-News-13-33744-Two-Uzbeks-among-33-militants-killed-in-NWA-air-strikes>.

[950] 'TTP Splinter Group Claim Wagah Attack, 60 Dead', *Dawn*, 3 November 2014 at: <http://www.dawn.com/news/1142006/ttp-splinter-groups-claim-wagah-attack-60-dead>.

[951] 'Children Targeted in Pakistan's Deadliest Militant Attack in Years; 132 Students are Killed', *Euronews*, 16 December 2014 at: <http://www.euronews.com/2014/12/16/children-targeted-in-pakistan-s-deadliest-militant-attack-in-years-132-students/>.

[952] Sridharan, V., 'International Business Times—Afghanistan: Afghan Taliban condemned "un-Islamic" Pakistan school carnage', IBT, 17 December 2014.

Reports suggest that an estimated 3,400 militants and 190 Pakistani soldiers to date have been killed in the operation.[953] Alongside this, an estimated seventy-five militants have also been reported killed by US drone strikes in the same region.[954]

As a result of the operation, 929,859 displaced civilians (from 80,302 families) were registered by Pakistani authorities as of 14 July. Financial support, relief goods, and food packages were being distributed and fifty-nine donation points were established across Pakistan by the army.[955]

PARTIES TO THE CONFLICT

The parties to the NIAC in 2014 were Pakistan and its armed forces against the TTP. As said in the introduction, there might be another NIAC with several TTP splinter groups. Available data does not allow the War Report to entirely confirm this qualification. Profiles of the armed groups involved are provided in this section for sake of more complete information on the situation of armed violence in Pakistan.

PAKISTANI ARMED FORCES

Pakistan is estimated to have 617,000 active frontline military personnel and a further 515,000 in reserve.[956]

Tehrik-i-Taliban Pakistan (TTP/Pakistani Taliban)

The TTP is an umbrella organization of various Islamist militant groups based in the north western Federally Administered Tribal Areas along the Afghan border in Pakistan. Most, but not all, Pakistani Taliban groups coalesce under the TTP.[957]

[953] 'Army Chief Raheel Sharif Vows to Hunt Down Every Terrorist', *Pakistan Tribe*, 24 December 2014 at: <http://www.pakistantribe.com/story/30391/latest-airstrikes-killed-76-militants-in-north-waziristan/>.

[954] 'Drone Strike in North Waziristan Kills 20', *The Express Tribune*, 16 July 2014 at: <http://tribune.com.pk/story/736367/drone-strike-in-north-waziristan-kills-15/>.

[955] 'US, UAE provide $51m for N Waziristan IDPs', *The Express Tribune*, 6 July 2014 at: <http://tribune.com.pk/story/731993/us-uae-provide-51m-for-n-waziristan-idps/>.

[956] 'Pakistan Military Strength', *Globalfirepower.com*, last updated on 27 March 2014, at: <http://www.globalfirepower.com/country-military-strength-detail.asp?country_id=pakistan>. The Pakistani armed force's website contains the motto 'Men at their best'. At: <http://www.pakistanidefence.com/>.

[957] Yusufzai, R., 'A Who's Who of the Insurgency in Pakistan's North-West Frontier Province: Part One—North and South Waziristan', 22 September 2008, *Terrorism Monitor* 6 (18).

In December 2007 about thirteen groups united under the leadership of Baitullah Mehsud to form the Tehrik-i-Taliban Pakistan. Among the Tehrik-i-Taliban Pakistan's stated objectives are resistance against the Pakistani State, enforcement of their interpretation of Shari'a, and a plan to unite against NATO-led forces in Afghanistan.[958]

The TTP is not directly affiliated with the Afghan Taliban movement led by Mullah Omar, with both groups differing greatly in their histories, strategic goals, and interests although they are both predominantly Pashtun.[959] The Afghan Taliban, with the alleged support of Pakistani Taliban, operate against international coalition and Afghan security forces in Afghanistan but are strictly opposed to targeting the Pakistani State.[960] The TTP in contrast has almost exclusively targeted elements of the Pakistani State although it took credit for the 2009 Camp Chapman attack and the 2010 Times Square car bombing attempt.[961]

HAQQANI NETWORK

The Haqqani network is an insurgent group which has been fighting against US-led NATO forces and the Government of Afghanistan. Maulvi Jalaluddin Haqqani and his son Sirajuddin Haqqani lead the group. The group operates on both sides of the Afghanistan–Pakistan border, and US officials believe it is based in Pakistan's Waziristan tribal frontier. The Haqqani network is allied with the Taliban.[962]

LASHKAR-E-JHANGVI

Lashkar-e-Jhangvi (LeJ), is a Sunni-Deobandi terrorist outfit formed in 1996 by a breakaway group of radical sectarian extremists of the Sipah-e-Sahaba Pakistan (SSP), a Sunni extremist outfit, which accused the parent organization of deviating from the ideals of its slain co-founder, Maulana Haq Nawaz Jhangvi. It is from Maulana Jhangvi that the LeJ derives its name. It was formed under the leadership of Akram Lahori and Riaz Basra. The LeJ aims to transform Pakistan into a Sunni State, primarily through violent means.

[958] *supra* notes 2, 10 [959] *supra* note 10 [960] *supra* note 2 [961] *supra* note 10

[962] '"No sanctuaries in Pakistan": Haqqani Network Shifts Base to Afghanistan', *Express Tribune*, 18 September 2011 at: <http://tribune.com.pk/story/254368/no-haqqani-network-sanctuaries-in-pakistan-sirajuddin/>.

JUNDALLAH

Jundallah is an Islamist terrorist militant group associated with the Tehrik-i-Taliban Pakistan (TTP). The group was commanded by terrorist Hakimullah Mehsud, the Emir of TTP, until his death on 1 November 2013. On 17 November 2014, a group spokesman told Reuters that it had vowed allegiance to the Islamic State of Iraq and the Levant, after a meeting with a three-man delegation from the group.[963]

EAST TURKESTAN ISLAMIC MOVEMENT

The East Turkestan Islamic Movement (ETIM) (also known as the Turkistan Islamic Party (TIP), Turkistan Islamic Movement (TIM), and other names) is an Islamic terrorist and separatist organization founded by Uyghur militants in western China. Its stated goals are the independence of East Turkestan from China. According to the Chinese Government, it is a violent separatist movement and is often responsible for terrorist attacks in Xinjiang. According to Chinese reports, published in 2002, between 1990 to 2001 ETIM had reportedly committed over 200 acts of terrorism, resulting in at least 162 deaths and over 440 injuries. Since 2001–2 the group has been active in Afghanistan and is currently based in North Waziristan, Pakistan.[964]

ISLAMIC MOVEMENT OF UZBEKISTAN

The Islamic Movement of Uzbekistan (IMU) is a militant Islamist group formed in 1998 by the Islamic ideologue Tahir Yuldashev, and former Soviet paratrooper Juma Namangani—both ethnic Uzbeks from the Fergana Valley. Its original objective was to overthrow President Islam Karimov of Uzbekistan, and to create an Islamic State under Shari'a; however, in subsequent years, it reinvented itself as an ally of Al-Qaeda and the Taliban.[965]

The IMU have been active in Afghanistan since 2001–2 during the American-led invasion of Afghanistan. Namangani was killed, while Yuldeshev and many of the

[963] 'Pakistan Taliban Splinter Group Vows Allegiance to Islamic State', *Reuters*, 18 November 2014 at: <http://www.reuters.com/article/2014/11/18/us-pakistan-militants-is-idUSKCN0J20YQ20141118>.

[964] '"East Turkistan" Terrorist Forces Cannot Get Away With Impunity', PRC State Council, 21 January 2002.

[965] 'Pakistan's 'Fanatical' Uzbek Militants', *BBC*, 7 October 2014 at: <http://article.wn.com/view/2014/06/12/Pakistans_fanatical_Uzbek_militants/>.

IMU's remaining fighters escaped with remnants of the Taliban to Waziristan, in the Federally Administered Tribal Areas of Pakistan. Since then, the IMU has focused on fighting Pakistani forces in the Tribal Areas, and NATO and Afghan forces in northern Afghanistan.[966]

CASUALTIES

Operation Zarb-e-Azb was launched in the Federally Administered Tribal Areas (FATA) on 15 June 2014 in response to an attack on an Airport in Karachi on 8–9 June 2014.

The Pakistan military Inter Services Public Relations said the security forces in Operation Zarb-e-Azb had killed 2,000 terrorists in North Waziristan Agency, while 200 soldiers were killed and 800 were injured.[967] From 15 June 2014, according to partial data compiled by the South Asia Terrorism Portal (SATP) during Operation Zarb-e-Azb had killed more than 1,516 militants and 204 soldiers had been killed during 2014.[968] IHS Jane's reported that by early December 2014 'military officials were claiming that its forces had killed more than 1,818 militants during the course of the operation, with a corresponding loss of at least 184 soldiers'.[969] Many sources reported that it was not possible to challenge or independently verify casualty figures provided by the military. Travel to North Waziristan was barred to journalists since the launch of Operation Zarb-e-Azb unless journalists were embedded with the military. The severe military restrictions on media access to the conflict zone made prevented assessment of civilian casualty figures.

Overall, in 2014 in Pakistan there were 4,070 fatalities from terrorism related activities including killings of 2,851 terrorists, 327 security personnel, and 892 civilians. Of these 2,863 casualties occurred in FATA, including 2,510 militants, 194 security, forces and 159 civilians killed.[970]

[966] 'Country Reports on Terrorism 2011', United States Department of State, 31 July 2012.

[967] Director General of Inter Services Public Relations Major General Asim Saleem Bajwa quoted in 'Writ of state will be ensured at all costs in NW: DG ISPR', 16 January 2015, <http://nation.com.pk/national/16-Jan-2015/writ-of-state-will-be-ensured-at-all-costs-in-nw-dg-ispr>.

[968] SATP highlights uncertainty regarding the data as no independent verification of fatalities of identities of those killed is available, as media access to the areas of conflict is severely limited. SATP, 'FATA Assessment—2015', <http://www.satp.org/satporgtp/countries/pakistan/Waziristan/index.html>.

[969] IHS Jane's Terrorism & Insurgency Monitor, 'Uncertain victory—Pakistan's North Waziristan Offensive', 28 December 2014, <http://www.janes.com/article/47302/uncertain-victory-pakistan-s-north-waziristan-offensive>.

[970] Shabbir Sarwar, 'Review: 2,841 terrorists, 327 security officials, 882 civilians killed in 2014', 1 January 2015, <http://www.dailytimes.com.pk/national/01-Jan-2015/review-2-841-terrorists-327-security-officials- 882-civilians-killed-in-2014>; based on data available in SATP, 'Detail Of Terrorism Update, Pakistan', <http://www.satp.org/satporgtp/detailed_news.asp?date1=1/1/2015&id=16#top>.

The TBIJ collected data on Pakistan air strikes including civilian casualties from the beginning of 2014 until the start of Operation Zarb-e-Azb. It found reports of 291 to 540 people killed, including between sixteen and 112 civilians.[971]

Civilian casualties were reported during airstrikes early in Operation Zarb-e-Azb. In July, after air strikes in Shawal Valley, residents reported that thirty-seven civilians had been killed, including twenty women and ten children.[972] The Pakistani military information service reported however that '35 fleeing terrorists were killed through aerial strikes in Shawal Valley'. An anonymous military source in a media interview indicated that civilians may be caught up in strikes, reflecting: 'If a terrorist is living with his family and does not abandon them even during the time of operation and we have solid ground intelligence about the terrorist and we target his hideout, what would you call it, collateral damage or what?' and 'If a terrorist is using his family as human shields what do you expect the military to do?'[973] In August Pakistan military officials declared that hundreds of militants had been killed in Operation Zarb-e-Azb 'with no *civilian casualties*'.[974] This may indicate that a distinction was made between locals as civilians, hundreds of thousands of whom were evacuated to make room for the operation, and families of militants as civilians who remained.

TTP commander Jihad Yar Wazir was reported to have said that an attack on a military school in December 2014, resulting in 145 deaths including 132 children, was carried out in retribution for civilian deaths in the bombings of FATA: 'The parents of the army school are army soldiers and they are behind the massive killing of our kids and indiscriminate bombing in North and South Waziristan'.[975] The TTP said many of their family members had been killed in Operation Zarb-e-Azb, and said the attack on the school was in revenge for those deaths.[976]

It was not specified if the casualty total for casualties for Operation Zarb-e-Azb includes US drone strike fatalities as well as casualties from Pakistani air strikes and ground engagements. A five-and-a-half month pause in drone strikes at the beginning of 2014 was the longest pause in the history of the drone campaign since 2006. From the

[971] 'Pakistan military air strikes kill hundreds, including civilians, over past six months', 23 June 2014, <http://thebureauinvestigates.com/2014/06/23/pakistan-military-air-strikes-kill-hundreds-including-civilians-over-past-six-months/>.

[972] 'Operation Zarb-e-Azb: 910 militants killed so far, 03 September 2014', <http://dunyanews.tv/index.php/en/Pakistan/235187-Operation-ZarbeAzb-910-militants-killed-so-far>.

[973] 'Civilian Casualties Fuel Outrage Over Zarb-E-Azb', 22 July 2014, <http://newsweekpakistan.com/civilian-casualties-fuel-outrage-over-zarb-e-azb/>.

[974] Iqbal, K., 'Beyond Zarb-e-Azb', *The Nation*, 10 August 2014,<http://nation.com.pk/columns/10-Aug-2014/beyond-zarb-e-azb>.

[975] Yousafzai, S., 'Taliban: We Slaughtered 100+ Kids Because Their Parents Helped America', 16 December 2014, <http://www.thedailybeast.com/articles/2014/12/16/pakistani-taliban-massacre-more-than-80-schoolchildren.html?via=twitter_page>.

[976] 'Children Massacred in Pakistan School Attack', 17 December 2014, <http://www.aljazeera.com/news/asia/2014/12/fighters-attack-army-run-school-pakistan-20141216742794184.html>.

onset of Operation Zarb-e-Azb the United States launched over twenty drone strikes in 2014. Drone Wars Pakistan reported twenty-two drone strikes with an estimated average of 151 deaths.[977] The Bureau of Investigative Journalism (TBIJ) recorded twenty-five drone strikes, 115–86 killed including 0–2 civilians and 53–76 children reported injured.[978] The Conflict Monitoring Center also recorded twenty-five drone strikes for the year.[979] Pakistan Body Count recorded twenty-four drone strikes with people 186 killed and another forty-seven injured in 2014.[980]

The International Federation of Journalists (IFJ), found that Pakistan had the most journalists killed in 2014 (fourteen). Almost all were directly targeted in shooting assassinations.[981]

DISPLACED PERSONS

In 2014, there were up to 907,000 new internal displacements in Pakistan, leading to a total of up to 1,900,000 persons remaining internally displaced in the country as of December 2014.[982]

WAR CRIMES ALLEGATIONS, INVESTIGATIONS, AND PROSECUTIONS

Pakistan is neither a State party nor a signatory to the 1998 Rome Statute of the International Criminal Court (ICC). No allegations of war crimes are known to have been made against Pakistani military personnel regarding any acts concerning the NIAC in 2014.

977 'Drone Wars Pakistan', <http://securitydata.newamerica.net/drones/pakistan/key-findings.html>; and 'Drone Wars Pakistan: Analysis', <http://securitydata.newamerica.net/drones/pakistan/analysis.html>.

978 TBIJ, 'Obama 2014 Pakistan Drone Strikes', <http://www.thebureauinvestigates.com/2014/06/11/obama-2014-pakistan-drone-strikes>.

979 Conflict Monitoring Center (CMC), the statistical division of Pak Institute for Conflict and Security Studies (PICSS), 'Drone Strikes Table 2014', 27 December 2014, <http://www.cmcpk.net/2014/12/drone-strikes-table-2014>.

980 Pakistan Body Count, 'Drone Attack: Year', <http://pakistanbodycount.org/drone_attack>.

981 'Trail of Violence: Journalists & Media Staff Killed in 2014, FJ-Belgium 2015', p. 24, <http://ifj-safety.org/assets/docs/089/245/5bef559-ba3edf5.pdf>.

982 Internal Displacement Monitoring Center (IDMC), 'Global Overview 2015', May 2015, p. 85. The figure for north-west Pakistan is based on registered IDP families as reported by UNHCR. IDMC uses an average family size of 5.2 to calculate the total. Numbers for Balochistan are based on media sources and are only rough estimates.

Armed conflict in Somalia in 2014

KEY CASUALTY DATA FOR 2014		
Civilians killed:	365	(all Sources: ACLED)
Women killed:	13	
Children killed:	22	
Somali/Puntland Military forces and police (including allies and militia) deaths:	418	
AMISOM/Ethiopia/Kenya military forces deaths:	98	
al-Shabaab killed:	1,368	
al-Shabaab injured:	74	
Unknown actor role killed:	708	

CLASSIFICATION OF THE CONFLICT

The Federal Republic of Somalia, supported by Ethiopian, Kenyan, and Ugandan armed forces, was involved in a non-international character armed conflict (NIAC) with al-Shabaab. The United States has also sent armed drones into Somalia to target al-Shabaab members and is therefore also a party to the conflict.

In 2014, the conflict again met the threshold for applicability of the 1977 Additional Protocol II, but it did not apply directly as Somalia is not party to this instrument.

SUMMARY OF APPLICABLE INTERNATIONAL LAW

All parties to the conflict were bound by customary international humanitarian law (IHL) and human rights law, including customary IHL rules of distinction, proportionality, and precautions in attacks; the obligations of humane treatment, as set out in Common Article 3 to the 1949 Geneva Conventions; the obligation not to recruit and use children as soldiers; and by the duty to respect and protect fundamental human rights. This includes the duty to respect the rights to life and to freedom from torture or other forms of cruel, inhuman, or degrading treatment or punishment.

Somalia is a State party to the four 1949 Geneva Conventions but not to the 1977 Additional Protocol II in January 2013. Somalia is party to both the 1966 International Covenant on Civil and Political Rights and the 1966 International Covenant on Economic, Social and Cultural Rights. Other States participating in military action against *al-Shabaab*, including those serving in the African Union Mission in Somalia (AMISOM), are bound extraterritorially by their human rights obligations.[983]

Somalia is a State party to the 1997 Anti-Personnel Mine Ban Convention, having become a State party on 1 October 2012. In accordance with Article 5 of the Convention, Somalia is required to destroy all antipersonnel mines in mined areas under its jurisdiction or control as soon as possible, but not later than 1 October 2022.

Somalia is signatory but not party to the 2008 Convention on Cluster Munitions.

Somalia is not a party or signatory to the 2013 Arms Trade Treaty (ATT).[984]

In March 2013, the UN Security Council partially lifted an arms embargo for one year, originally imposed in 1992, to boost the Somali Government's capacity to protect areas recovered from al-Shabaab and defend against fresh attempts by armed groups to destabilize the country. It was decided that the ban would not apply to arms or equipment sold or supplied solely for the development of the Government's security forces, but it kept restrictions in place on heavy weapons, such as surface-to-air missiles.[985]

On 5 March 2014, the Council unanimously agreed to extend the partial weapons ban on Somalia for eight months amid reports that al-Shabaab and other armed groups were able to divert arms and ammunition intended for Government forces. The resolution, which extended the ban through 25 October, cited reports by the Somalia and Eritrea Monitoring Group (SEMG) that arms had been diverted and expressed 'serious concern' that the requirements for a suspension of the embargo 'have not been fully met'.[986]

Kenya and Uganda are party to the Anti-Personnel Mine Ban Convention and signatories to the Convention on Cluster Munitions so may not use these weapons during military operations in Somalia. Ethiopia is also party to the Anti-Personnel Mine Ban Convention but not to the Convention on Cluster Munitions. The United States is party to neither instrument.

HISTORY OF THE CONFLICT[987]

Somalia has been without an effective central government since President Siad Barre was overthrown in 1991. In 2004, after protracted talks in Kenya, the main warlords and

[983] See, for example, International Court of Justice, *Wall* Advisory Opinion, 2004, §106; and ICJ, *Armed Activities on the Territory of the Congo (Democratic Republic of the Congo v Uganda)*, Judgment, 19 December 2005.

[984] Somalia voted in favour of the adoption of the ATT by the United Nations (UN) General Assembly on 2 April 2013.

[985] UN Security Council Resolution 2093, 6 March 2013.

[986] UN Security Council Resolution 2142, 5 March 2014.

[987] Unless otherwise stated, this section is based on 'Somalia Profile', *BBC*, 5 May 2015, at: <http://www.bbc.com/news/world-africa-14094503>.

politicians signed a deal to set up a new Parliament, which later appointed a president. The fledgling administration, the fourteenth attempt to establish a government since 1991, faced a formidable task in bringing reconciliation to a country divided into clan fiefdoms. Its authority was further compromised in 2006 by the rise of Islamists who gained control of much of the south, including the capital, after their militias kicked out the warlords who had ruled the roost for fifteen years.

With the backing of Ethiopian troops, forces loyal to the interim administration seized control from the Islamists at the end of 2006. Islamist insurgents—including al-Shabaab, which later declared allegiance to Al-Qaeda and in 2012 announced that it was merging with it—fought back against the government and Ethiopian forces, regaining control of most of southern Somalia by late 2008.

In May 2012, African Union and Somali Government forces captured Afgoye town south of Mogadishu, thereby cutting al-Shabaab territory in half. In August, Somalia's first formal Parliament in more than twenty years was sworn in at Mogadishu airport, in a heavily secured area of the city. This marked the end of the eight-year 'transitional period'. The same month, pro-government forces captured the port of Merca, 70 kilometres south of Mogadishu, from al-Shabaab. In October, Kismayo, the country's second-largest port, and the last major city held by al-Shabaab fell to African Union and Government forces, as did the town of Wanla Weyn 90 kilometres north-west of Mogadishu.[988]

In January 2013, the United States recognized Somalia's Government for the first time since 1991. In April, after the UN Security Council voted in favour of the partial lifting of the embargo on selling arms to Somalia for a year, US President Barack Obama cleared the way for the United States to provide military assistance to Somalia. In June 2013, veteran al-Shabaab leader Sheikh Hassan Dahir Aweys was arrested by Somali Government troops after he was ousted by the more extreme al-Shabaab figure Ahmed Abdi Godane. In September 2013, international donors promised US$2.4 billion in reconstruction aid in a three-year 'New Deal' to strengthen the Somali economy and security. The same month al-Shabaab militants seized a shopping mall and killed sixty people in the Kenyan capital Nairobi, saying they were retaliating for Kenya's military involvement in Somalia. On 12 November 2013, the UN Security Council adopted Resolution 2124 approving an additional 4,400 AMISOM troops to boost the fight against al-Shabaab; Ethiopia said it was willing to contribute.

In January 2014, new Somali Prime Minister Abdiweli Sheikh Ahmed named his cabinet, which was approved by the Somali Parliament; both President Hassan Sheikh Mohamud and Prime Minister Ahmed vowed to launch a fresh offensive against

[988] Ibid.

al-Shabaab. The 4,395 Ethiopian troops were formally merged into AMISOM on 22 January. A US drone strike on 26 January reportedly killed three al-Shabaab fighters, including senior intelligence commander Sahal Carabey.[989]

The Kenyan Government announced that Sierra Leonean troops would replace departing Kenyan AMISOM forces in Kismayo.[990] On 21 February, al-Shabaab militants attacked Villa Somalia, the official residential palace and workplace of the President of Somalia. A car loaded with heavy explosives rammed into the concrete barrier surrounding the perimeter of the Palace.[991] Nine armed men with suicide vests penetrated the palace and a lengthy firefight ensued. The assault ended when the Presidential Guard forces were reinforced by Somali Government troops and AMISOM forces. President Hassan Sheikh Mohamud was unharmed but the deputy intelligence chief, Mohamed Nur Shirbow and a close aid to the Prime Minister, Mohamed Abdulle, were among the dead.[992]

In April, al-Shabaab attacks intensified in response to the continued AMISOM and Somali Federal Government forces' offensive that had captured ten major towns, while the UN Special Representative of the Secretary-General Nicholas Kay denied reports that the UN would withdraw from Somalia if it suffered significant attacks.[993]

In September al-Shabaab leader Ahmed Ali Godane, was reportedly killed in an operation that consisted of both drones, as well manned airstrikes conducted by the United States.[994] On 29 December, the al-Shabaab Intelligence Chief Abdishakur Tahlil was also killed in a similar US airstrike.[995]

By 8 January 2015, al-Shabbab had lost control over 80% of the territory they previously held, as result of the operations conducted by the Somali Government Forces, supported by AMISOM troops and US airstrikes.[996]

On 2 April, gunmen stormed the Garissa University College in Garissa, Kenya, killing 147 and injuring at least seventy-nine people. Al-Shabaab later took responsibility

[989] ICG, Crisis Watch: Somalia, 1 February 2014.

[990] ICG, Crisis Watch: Somalia, 1 March 2014.

[991] 'Somali Presidential Palace: "Car Bomb" Attack in Mogadishu', *BBC*, 21 February 2014, at: <http://www.bbc.com/news/world-africa-26288846>.

[992] 'Militants Attack Presidential Palace in Somalia', *The New York Times*, 21 February 2014, at: <http://www.nytimes.com/2014/02/22/world/africa/somalia.html?_r=1>.

[993] ICG, Crisis Watch: Somalia, 1 May 2014.

[994] 'U.S. Forces Strike Islamic Extremists in Somalia', *Associated Press*, 2 September 2014, at: <http://www.macleans.ca/news/world/u-s-forces-strike-islamic-extremists-in-somalia/>; 'Pentagon Confirms Death of Somalia Terror Leader', 5 September 2014, *Associated Press*, at: <http://www.garoweonline.com/page/show/post/292/pentagon-confirms-death-of-somalia-terror-leader>.

[995] 'US strike in Somalia "killed al-Shabab intelligence chief"', *BBC*, 30 December 2014, at: <http://www.bbc.com/news/world-africa-30635240?print=true>.

[996] 'AU Envoys Declares That Al-Shabab Lost 80% of the Areas Under Their Control', *Goobjoog*, 8 January 2015, at: <http://goobjoog.com/english/?p=8370>.

for the attack claiming that the attack was in response to Kenya's troop deployment with the AMISOM fighting against al-Shabaab in Somalia.[997]

PARTIES TO THE CONFLICT

The parties to the NIAC in 2013 were Somalia and its armed forces, supported by Ethiopian armed forces, the Kenyan armed forces, the UPDF, against al-Shabaab.

Somalia armed forces

The Somalia armed forces have been estimated to be 12,000 strong with 24,000 reservists.[998]

Ethiopian armed forces

The Ethiopian armed forces have been estimated to be 182,500 strong.[999] Ethiopian troops entered the country in December 2006 to help Somalia's interim government oust the Union of Islamic Courts, which had taken control of much of southern Somalia. Ethiopian troop presence was violently opposed by Somali non-State armed groups.[1000] In late 2008, Ethiopia announced it would withdraw all its forces by the end of the year. Theoretically, Ethiopia's presence in Somalia ended in early 2009, when it pulled its troops under an agreement between the transitional Somali Government and moderate Islamists.[1001] In March 2012, however, Ethiopian troops openly entered Somalia and fighting ensued, with deaths reported on both sides.[1002] On 22 January 2014, 4,395 troops from the Ethiopian National Defence Forces (ENDF) are integrated into AMISOM following the adoption of Security Council resolution 2124 (2013) of 12 November 2013 which allows AMISOM to expand from 17,731 to 22,126 troops.[1003]

[997] 'Al Shabab Massacres 147 Kenyan Students', *Agence France-Presse*, 2 April 2015, at: <http://mg.co.za/article/2015-04-02-al-shabab-take-university-students-hostage-kill-15>.

[998] 'Somalia Military Strength', *Globalfirepower.com*, last updated on 27 March 2014, at: <http://www.globalfirepower.com/country-military-strength-detail.asp?country_id=somalia>.

[999] Ibid.

[1000] 'Ethiopia in Somalia: One Year On', *BBC*, 28 December 2007, at: <http://news.bbc.co.uk/2/hi/africa/7155868.stm>.

[1001] ICG, 'Somalia Conflict History', September 2008, at: <http://www.crisisgroup.org/en/publication-type/key-issues/research-resources/conflict-histories/somalia.aspx>.

[1002] *Associated Press*, 'In March 2012, Ethiopian troops had entered Somalia', 22 March 2012, at: <http://www.boston.com/news/world/africa/articles/2012/03/22/somali_ethiopian_troops_seize_town_fighters_flee/>.

[1003] 'Security Council Extends Mandate of African Union Mission in Somalia, Requests Increase in Troop Strength', at: <http://www.un.org/News/Press/docs/2013/sc11172.doc.htm>.

Kenyan armed forces

The Kenyan armed forces have been estimated to be 24,120 strong with 5,000 reservists.[1004] In October 2011, hundreds of Kenyan troops entered Somalia, escalating their efforts to fight the al-Shabaab, which it accused of kidnappings and raiding Kenyan coastal resorts and refugee camps. The group soon threatened reprisals against Kenya and witnesses reported seeing al-Shabaab fighters move toward the areas invaded.[1005] By 2012, heavy fighting was being reported between Somali and Kenyan forces and al-Shabaab in the south of Somalia. Kenyan troops were said to have killed dozens of militants.[1006] By February 2012, they had captured the Baidoa base from the militants, followed by El Bur base by the end of March 2012.[1007] The operation was making significant advances as of April 2012, with the al-Shabaab leadership was said to have become fractured following its losses.[1008]

Uganda People's Defence Force

The UPDF has been estimated to be 45,000 strong with 2,000 reservists.[1009]

AMISOM

The African Union Mission in Somalia (AMISOM) is an active, regional peacekeeping mission operated by the African Union with UN approval. It was created by the African Union's Peace and Security Council on 19 January 2007 with an initial six-month mandate paving the way for some 8,000 troops to enter the country, but leaving the origin of those forces unclear.[1010] In accordance with the decision of the African Union Peace and Security Council on 19 January 2007, AMISOM's mandate is: to provide support to the Transitional Federal Institutions of Somalia (TFIs) in their efforts towards stabilization of the situation in the country and the furtherance of dialogue and reconciliation; to

[1004] 'Kenya Military Strength', *Globalfirepower.com*, last updated on 27 March 2014, at: <http://www.globalfirepower.com/country-military-strength-detail.asp?country_id=kenya>.

[1005] Human Rights Watch, 'Kenya: Human Rights Concerns of Operation "Linda Nchi" ', 18 November 2011, at: <http://www.hrw.org/news/2011/11/18/kenya-human-rights-concerns-operation-linda-nchi>.

[1006] Somalia Report, 'Heavy Fighting in Southern Somalia', 1 May 2012, at: <http://www.somaliareport.com/index.php/post/2456/Heavy_Fighting_in_Southern_Somalia>.

[1007] 'Al-Shabab Forces Lose Somali Base of El Bur', *BBC*, 26 March 2012, at: <http://www.bbc.co.uk/news/world-africa-17516440>.

[1008] Jamestown Foundation, 2012, 'Somalia's Neighbors Making Progress against al-Shabaab Despite Threats of Retaliation', *Terrorism Monitor*, vol. 10, no. 7 (6 April 2012), at: <http://www.unhcr.org/refworld/country,,,,SOM,,4f854f9a2,0.html>.

[1009] 'Uganda Military Strength', *Globalfirepower.com*, last updated on 27 March 2014, at: <http://www.globalfirepower.com/country-military-strength-detail.asp?country_id=uganda>.

[1010] AMISOM, 'AMISOM Background', March 2007, <http://amisom-au.org/about/amisom-background/>.

facilitate the provision of humanitarian assistance, and to create conducive conditions for long-term stabilization, reconstruction, and development in Somalia.[1011]

al-Shabaab

al-Shabaab (literally, 'the youth') is a radical Islamist group of young fighters that grew rapidly in influence in Somalia, especially around Mogadishu. Placed on the United States' list of 'foreign terrorist organisations', al-Shabaab began as the militia wing of the Union of Islamic Courts (UIC). The armed group is fighting an insurgency against the Federal Government of Somalia. al-Shabaab has targeted AMISOM peacekeepers for their support of the TFG.

In 2009–10, the group controlled most of central and southern Somalia south of the autonomous region of Puntland. Since the February 2011 military offensives by AMISOM, Somali Government troops, and Somali Sufi militia forces, al-Shabaab has suffered a series of significant territorial and strategic setbacks.[1012] In February 2012, the armed group released a joint video with Al-Qaeda, announcing that the two groups had merged causing internal divisions within al-Shabaab's leadership to materialize.[1013] In April 2012, after being pushed out of central Somalia, militants moved north into Puntland in a move which the region's President claimed was driven by their desire to strengthen ties with Al-Qaeda in the Arabian Peninsula (in Yemen).[1014] The group has also repeatedly threatened the United States and the West and has demonstrated the capacity to strike beyond Somalia's borders, including in Nairobi in September 2013 and 2015.

CASUALTIES

The Armed Conflict Location and Event Data Project (ACLED) records conflict events and fatalities for Somalia. ACLED data associated with al-Shabaab—disaggregated coordinating to casualties by the War Report—found 2,957 fatalities, of 4,447 total fatalities in Somalia recorded in the ACLED dataset. [1015] Of the total 2,958 fatalities disaggregated

[1011] AMISOM, 'Status of Mission Agreement (SOMA)', 6 March 2007, at: <http://amisom-au.org/status-of-mission-agreement-soma/>.

[1012] Council on Foreign Relations, *Backgrounder Al-Shabaab*, 5 February 2013, at: <http://www.cfr.org/somalia/al-shabaab/p18650?breadcrumb=%2Fpublication%2Fpublication_list%3Ftype%3Dbackgrounder%26page%3D4>; see also CTC Sentinel, 2013, *Al-Shabab's Tactical and Media Strategies in the Wake of its Battlefield Setbacks*, vol. 6, no. 3 (March 2013), pp. 12–16.

[1013] 'Somalia's al-Shabab join al-Qaeda', *BBC*, 10 February 2012, at: <http://www.bbc.co.uk/news/world-africa-16979440>.

[1014] 'Somalia's al-Shabab Islamists Move North into Puntland', *BBC*, 11 April 2012, at: <http://www.bbc.co.uk/news/world-africa-17674996>.

[1015] Analysis of 'notes' and 'fatalities' in ACLED data. Raleigh, C., Linke, A., Hegre, H., and Karlsen, J., 'Introducing ACLED-Armed Conflict Location and Event Data', pp. 1–10.

by actor from those noted in ACLED data, the majority, 1,368, were al-Shabaab fighters. Most al-Shabaab deaths occurred in clashes with Somali National Government, police and pro-government forces, including African Union Mission in Somalia (AMISOM) and due to both ground engagement and airstrikes. Airstrikes caused at least 288 al-Shabaab deaths, including eleven in US drone strikes as found in ACLED data.[1016] The Bureau of Investigative Journalism (TBIJ) recorded a range of 2–10 casualties of US drones in three drone strikes in Somalia in 2014.[1017]

Of the 365 civilian fatalities identified from ACLED data in 2014, most died in clashes between armed groups though many were directly targeted. al-Shabaab killed twenty-five civilians in its targeting of the trade in *khat*, and several others were killed over refusal to pay taxes or 'charity' to al-Shabaab. Another twenty-seven civilians were targeted or executed by al-Shabaab on the suspicion of spying for Somali or AMISOM forces. Of the civilian casualties twenty-two were identified as children (including six killed in air strikes) and thirteen as women.

At least three members of Parliament died in targeted killing as did many other local officials. Among the 418 Somali and associated forced killed, thirty-three were police, twenty-three were military forces of Puntland, and eighty-four were soldiers of the forces of Jubaland State. Another twenty-five were other militia forces. There were 708 fatalities for which the role was not reported. Most often these included both al-Shabaab and pro-government forces where the numbers could not be distinguished in reporting.[1018]

ACLED noted there had been higher than average reported rates of civilian targeting in 2014 by al-Shabaab than previous years. A likely explanation for this change was that al-Shabaab was no longer able to allocate targeting of civilians to be carried out by unidentified armed groups and therefore themselves made use of this tactic. When al-Shabaab was dominant, their rate of civilian targeting was low. However, that low rate of violence against civilians attributed to al-Shabaab in past years was coupled with a high recorded rate of such violence by unidentified armed groups in the same places that al-Shabaab operated, indicating that unidentified armed groups 'may have been engaged in civilian targeting on behalf of Al Shabaab'.[1019]

[1016] War Report analysis of ACLED data for 2014.

[1017] TBIJ, 'Somalia: Reported US Covert Actions 2001-2015', <http://www.thebureauinvestigates.com/2012/02/22/get-the-data-somalias-hidden-war>.

[1018] Due to the nature of attacks resulting in multiple casualties, particularly the use of improvised explosive devices (IEDs) in suicide attacks (person borne IEDs) and car bombs (vehicle borne IEDs), it is not always possible to separate data on military and civilian casualties from aggregate casualty totals in media reporting. The aggregated media reporting of casualty numbers also resulted in a lack of usable data regarding women and children among casualties.

[1019] ACLED, 'The Strategic Use of Unidentified Armed Groups in Conflict Zones', <http://www.crisis.acleddata.com/the-strategic-use-of-unidentified-armed-groups-in-conflict-zones/>.

UN OCHA reported that in the period from January 2014 to 24 November 2014 more than 5,000 people with weapon-related injuries had been treated in nine hospitals in Mogadishu, Kismayo, Doolow, Mudug, and Baidoa.[1020] According to the World Health Organization (WHO) statistics, at least 5,912 civilians with conflict and weapon-related injuries were treated at four hospitals supported by WHO in Mogadishu and in Kismayo[1021] during 2013. WHO recorded some 6,680 casualties from weapon-related injuries at the four hospitals in Mogadishu in 2012.[1022]

The Committee to Protect Journalists (CPJ) documented four journalists killed in direct relation to their work in Somalia in 2014, as in 2013, this constituted a decrease from 2012, which was the noted as the 'deadliest year' on record with twelve journalists killed.[1023] In the cases of two of the four journalists killed in 2014, it was reported that they were killed in attacks by al-Shabaab.[1024]

War Report analysis of ACLED data for Kenya for 2014, found at least another 289 people were killed and ninety injured in events related to terrorist activities by al-Shabaab in Kenya in that year. The majority of those killed, 216, were civilians. Other reported fatalities included thirty al-Shabaab militants, fourteen Kenyan police, two Kenyan defence forces personnel, and twenty-seven people with their roles not defined. These casualties were not included in the War Report total for the al-Shabaab conflict with Somalia.

DISPLACED

In 2014, there were at least 89,000 new internally displaced persons (IDPs) in Somalia, leading to a total of 1,106,800 persons being internally displaced in the country as of December 2014.[1025]

1020 UN OCHA, 'Humanitarian Bulletin Somalia October 2014', 24 November 2014, p. 3.

1021 1,500 people were treated at the main hospital in Kismayo in 2013 through September. However, those injured in Kismayo likely include casualties of political violence and inter-clan rivalries not involving Al Shabaab. OCHA, Humanitarian Bulletin Somalia December 2013, 17 January 2014. p. 3, <http://somalia.humanitarianresponse.info/system/files/documents/files/OCHA%20Somalia%20Humanitarian%20Bulletin%20December%202013.pdf>.

1022 WHO, 'Somalia Emergency Weekly Health Update,' 30 December 2012, <http://www.who.int/hac/crises/som/sitreps/somalia_eha_30december2012.pdf>.

1023 CPJ, 'Attacks on the Press: Somalia', <https://cpj.org/killed/africa/somalia/>.

1024 CPJ, 'Mohamed Isaq', <https://cpj.org/killed/2014/mohamed-isaq.php>; Abdulkadir Ahmed, <https://cpj.org/killed/2014/abdulkadir-ahmed.php>; Yusuf Ahmed Abukar, <https://cpj.org/killed/2014/yusuf-ahmed-abukar.php>.

1025 Internal Displacement Monitoring Centre (IDMC) 'Global Overview 2015', May 2015, p. 86. Estimates are based on figures from UNHCR's protection and return monitoring network, which it operates with its partners, and triangulated and endorsed by the Somalia humanitarian country team.

WAR CRIMES ALLEGATIONS, INVESTIGATIONS, AND PROSECUTIONS

Somalia is not a party to the 1998 Rome Statute of the International Criminal Court.

On 27 September 2013, the UN Human Rights Council adopted Resolution 24/30 in which it expressed concern at 'reports of violations of human rights in Somalia, and underscores the need to end impunity, uphold human rights and hold accountable those who commit any such related crimes'.[1026] It also expressed concern at 'the abuses and violations perpetrated against women, including sexual violence', and emphasized 'the need for accountability for all such abuses and violations'.[1027] It further condemned violations and abuses against children, including recruitment and use of child soldiers, killing and maiming, rape and other sexual violence, abductions, attacks on schools and/or hospitals'.[1028] The Council strongly condemned 'the grave and systematic human rights abuses perpetrated against the civilian population, including women, children, journalists and human rights defenders, by Al-Shabaab and its affiliates', and called for their 'immediate cessation'.[1029]

[1026] Human Rights Council Resolution 24/30, §1.
[1027] Ibid., §2. [1028] Ibid., §3. [1029] Ibid., §5.

Armed conflict in South Sudan in 2014

KEY CASUALTY DATA FOR 2014

Civilians killed:	611	(Sources: ACLED, HRW, UN, AI)
Civilians injured:	(at least) 80	(Sources: ACLED, HRW, UN, AI)
Women killed:	(at least) 41	(Sources: ACLED, HRW, UN, AI)
Women injured (sexual violence):	(at least) 29	(Sources: ACLED, UN, AI)
Children killed:	(at least) 5	(Sources: ACLED, UN, AI)
Children injured (rape of girls):	(at least) 9	(Source: ACLED)
SPLA—In Opposition killed:	842	(Source: ACLED)
SPLA—In Opposition injured:	(at least) 2	(Source: ACLED)
Governmental forces (including police) killed:	1,049	(Source: ACLED)
Governmental forces (including police) injured:	(at least) 82	(Source: ACLED)
Uganda military killed (affiliated to Government):	3	(Sources: ACLED)
Sudan's JEM fighters killed (affiliated to Government):	8	(Sources: ACLED)
Unknown armed forces killed:	36	Sources: ACLED)
Unknown killed:	9	(Sources: ACLED)
Unknown injured:	18	(Sources: ACLED)

CLASSIFICATION OF THE CONFLICT

In 2014, South Sudan and its armed forces (the former Sudan People's Liberation Army, SPLA), supported by the Uganda People's Defence Force (UPDF), was involved in a non-international armed conflict (NIAC) with dissident South Sudan armed forces (sometimes called the SPLM/A-in-Opposition). The conflict, which began in mid-December 2013, subsequently met the threshold for applicability of 1977 Additional Protocol II.

SUMMARY OF APPLICABLE INTERNATIONAL LAW

All parties to the conflict were bound by customary international humanitarian law (IHL) and human rights law, including customary IHL rules of distinction, proportionality, and precautions in attacks; the obligations of humane treatment, as set out in Common Article 3 to the 1949 Geneva Conventions; the obligation not to recruit and use children as soldiers; and by the duty to respect and protect fundamental human rights. This includes the duty to respect the rights to life and to freedom from torture or other forms of cruel, inhuman, or degrading treatment or punishment.

South Sudan became a State party to the four 1949 Geneva Conventions and the 1977 Additional Protocol II in January 2013. South Sudan is not party to either the 1966 International Covenant on Civil and Political Rights or the 1966 International Covenant on Economic, Social and Cultural Rights. Uganda is bound extraterritorially by its human rights obligations.[1030]

South Sudan is a State party to the 1997 Anti-Personnel Mine Ban Convention, having succeeded to it in November 2011. In accordance with Article 5 of the Convention, South Sudan is required to destroy all antipersonnel mines in mined areas under its jurisdiction or control as soon as possible, but not later than 9 July 2021. It is not party to the 2008 Convention on Cluster Munitions. South Sudan is not a party or signatory to the 2013 Arms Trade Treaty (ATT).[1031]

Uganda is also party to the Anti-Personnel Mine Ban Convention and is a signatory to the Convention on Cluster Munitions so may not use these weapons during military operations in South Sudan.

HISTORY OF THE CONFLICT

South Sudan gained independence from Sudan in July 2011 as the outcome of a 2005 peace deal (the Comprehensive Peace Agreement) that ended Africa's longest-running civil war. An overwhelming majority of South Sudanese voted in a January 2011 referendum to secede and become Africa's first new State since Eritrea split from Ethiopia in 1993.[1032] In adopting Resolution 1996 on 8 July 2011, the UN Security Council determined that the situation faced by South Sudan continued to constitute a threat to international peace and security in the region. The Security Council established the UN Mission in the Republic of South Sudan (UNMISS) for an initial period of one year, starting on 9 July 2011.

In December 2013, South Sudan was plunged into crisis amid a power struggle between the President, Salva Kiir, and his Vice-President, Riek Machar, whom he had sacked. On 17 December, President Kiir accused Machar of having attempted a coup. Fighting between government troops and rebel factions erupted, and within weeks the conflict had killed thousands and prompted more than 800,000 to flee their homes. Oil production, on which South Sudan depends, fell drastically.[1033]

[1030] See, e.g., International Court of Justice (ICJ), *Wall* Advisory Opinion, 2004, §106, and ICJ, *Armed Activities on the Territory of the Congo (Democratic Republic of the Congo v Uganda)*, Judgment, 19 December 2005.

[1031] South Sudan voted in favour of the adoption of the ATT by the United Nations (UN) General Assembly on 2 April 2013.

[1032] 'South Sudan Profile', *BBC*, 23 April 2014, at: <http://www.bbc.com/news/world-africa-14069082>.

[1033] Ibid.

Clashes began in Juba, but spread rapidly to Unity and Jonglei States. Violence was particularly heavy in Bor, Jonglei, where the African Union said on 23 December that war crimes had been committed. Machar claimed Ugandan jets backing Kiir's forces bombed Bor on 21 December. Bor has changed hands several times subsequently.[1034]

Rebecca Garang, widow of the former South Sudan President John Garang, met with Kiir on 21 December but no breakthrough was achieved. On 22 December, rebel troops took Bentiu, capital of oil-rich Unity State.[1035] On 24 December, the UN Security Council increased the UNMISS peacekeeping force to 12,500, called for an 'immediate cessation of hostilities' and the 'opening of a dialogue'.[1036] Two UNMISS peacekeepers were killed in an attack on a UN base (see below casualties section). On 27 December, the Government pledged to observe an immediate ceasefire. Machar agreed to talks mediated by the regional peace and security body, the Intergovernmental Authority on Development (IGAD); talks began on 2 January 2014 in Ethiopia.[1037]

On 23 January, a ceasefire was agreed between the Government and the armed opposition following the IGAD mediation but it was quickly violated. On 28 January, the Government announced treason charges against seven opposition politicians, including Mr Machar, over the alleged December 2013 coup attempt. Ongoing clashes in Unity State forced thousands to flee in late January. Fighting continued throughout the IGAD mediation as Government forces backed by the Ugandan army retook major towns seized by armed opposition. The UN estimated that 770,000 had been displaced in fighting since December, with nearly 70,000 seeking refuge inside UN bases.[1038]

In February, violence escalated ahead of the rainy season despite the January ceasefire with reports of atrocities by both sides. The Government was increasingly fiscally unstable, even threatening non-payment of salaries to soldiers.[1039] In late March, there were fierce clashes over Malakal while a second round of talks between the Government and the opposition ended without a breakthrough. On 6 March, security officials in Lakes State intercepted eleven UN trucks transporting UNMISS firearms and uniforms; the Government accused UNMISS of plotting to arm the opposition. On 10 March, South Sudan Vice-President James Wani Igga led protests against UNMISS in Juba, calling for the resignation of the Special Representative of the UN Secretary-General and UNMISS head, Hilde Johnson. On 29 March, the UN Office for the Coordination of Humanitarian Affairs reported that more than one million people had been displaced by the conflict.[1040]

[1034] International Crisis Group (ICG), Crisis Watch Database: South Sudan, 2 January 2014, available at: <http://www.crisisgroup.org/en/publication-type/crisiswatch/crisiswatch-database.aspx>.

[1035] Ibid. [1036] UN Security Council Resolution 2132, adopted on 24 December 2013, §§4, 1.

[1037] ICG, Crisis Watch Database: South Sudan, 2 January 2014.

[1038] ICG, Crisis Watch Database: South Sudan, 1 February 2014.

[1039] ICG, Crisis Watch Database: South Sudan, 1 March 2014.

[1040] ICG, Crisis Watch Database: South Sudan, 1 April 2014.

At the beginning of May 2014, United States Secretary of State John Kerry announced that the President had agreed to hold direct talks to end the conflict with Mr Machar. Secretary Kerry warned that if the fighting continued to target civilians along ethnic lines it 'could really present a very serious challenge to the international community with respect to the question of genocide'.[1041] On 10 May, President Kiir and Mr Machar agreed a peace deal during the talks in the Ethiopia capital, Addis Ababa. The deal called for a ceasefire and the formation of a transitional government ahead of the drafting of a new constitution and the holding of new elections.[1042]

But the following day, the army and the rebels accused each other of breaching the ceasefire, only hours after it was meant to come into effect. The army said rebels attacked Government positions in the early hours of Sunday 11 May in the town of Bentiu in oil-rich Unity State. The rebels said their positions were targeted by ground attack and artillery in Unity and Upper Nile States.[1043]

On 10 June, President Kiir and rebel leader Machar agreed to end the ongoing conflict and fully engage in the Inter-Governmental Authority on Development (IGAD)-led peace process, by forming a transitional government of national unity within sixty days.[1044] The opposition refused to take part in the latest round of peace talks, saying their demands to make the negotiations more inclusive have been ignored by the mediators[1045] and later boycotted them completely as a protest against the unfair selection processes of other stakeholders to take part in the IGAD-mediated negotiations.[1046]

In June defections continued on both sides: as 3,000 soldiers deserted in the Upper Nile and Jonglei due to the non-payment of salaries,[1047] the SPLA-IO are also divided, as several ground commanders were critical of Machar's participation in the peace talks.[1048]

Because of the ongoing conflict and crisis situation in the country, the poor prevailing sanitary conditions and the beginning of the rainy season, as of 29 June 2014, a total of 2,431 cholera cases including fifty-nine deaths had been reported. [1049]

[1041] 'South Sudan Crisis: US Push for Kiir and Machar Direct Talks', *BBC*, 2 May 2014, at: <http://www.bbc.com/news/world-africa-27258765>.

[1042] 'South Sudan Rivals Kiir And Machar Agree Peace Deal', *BBC*, 10 May 2014, at: <http://www.bbc.com/news/world-africa-27353799>.

[1043] 'South Sudan Ceasefire Violated, Rebels and Government Say', *BBC*, 11 May 2014, at: <http://www.bbc.com/news/world-africa-27362508>.

[1044] 'South Sudan's Rival Leaders Agree on 60 Day Ultimatum', *Sudan Tribune*, 10 June 2014, at: <http://www.sudantribune.com/spip.php?article51294>.

[1045] 'South Sudan: Peace Process Stalls', *AllAfrica*, 20 June 2014, at: <http://allafrica.com/stories/201406210137.html>.

[1046] 'South Sudan: Rebels Boycott Peace Talks Over 'Unfair' Inclusivity', *AllAfrica*, 22 June 2014, at: <http://allafrica.com/stories/201406231658.html>.

[1047] 'S. Sudan Army Admits Soldiers Deserted Base in Jonglei State', *Sudan Tribune*, 12 June 2014, at: <http://www.sudantribune.com/spip.php?article51322>.

[1048] ICG, Crisis Watch Database: South Sudan, 1 July 2014.

[1049] 'Cholera in South Sudan', WHO Situation Report n.44, 29 June 2014, at: <http://www.who.int/hac/crises/ssd/sitreps/south_sudan_cholera_update_29june2014.pdf>.

During July 2014 heavy fights resumed as government forces attacked three towns in the Unity State, including a WFP food distribution site.[1050] Moreover, mid-month, the SPLA-IO launched an attack to gain control of Nasir, which was condemned by IGAD, UN, African Union and the United States. Indeed, according to the UN, the attack on the town was the 'most serious resumption of hostilities' since May, which, however, did not last long as on 25 July government forces retook control of the town.[1051]

On 16 July, SPLM-IO announced a proposal for the creation twenty-one new States, instead of the existing ten, based on the 1956 boundaries.[1052]

Later in the month, the UN Security Council declared that South Sudan was facing a 'catastrophic food insecurity', which constituted the worst food crisis in the world.[1053]

As the government and the opposition faction of the former vice president Machar failed to meet the 10 August deadline to conclude a peace agreement, IGAD extended the ongoing peace talks until the 28 August.[1054]

On the 25 August, IGAD announced a new ceasefire deal and a protocol for the formation of a transitional unity government, including provisions on transitional justice, finance management, and humanitarian concerns. In addition, it threatened sanctions if the government was not formed within forty-five days.[1055] Three days later, however, the SPLM-IO refused to sign the deal, as they claimed it was favouring the government side in the political settlement.[1056]

In September, new fighting erupted around the oil facilities in Upper Nile's Renk County.

During the month the SPLM-IO increased its organization as it announced the opening of an office in Kampala;[1057] moreover, a delegation visited Beijing for bilateral talks with the Chinese Government, which on 21 September halted the arms sale to the

[1050] 'South Sudan Army Attacks Food Distribution', *Radio Tamazuj*, 16 July 2014, at: <https://radiotamazuj.org/en/article/south-sudan-army-attack-food-distribution>.

[1051] 'South Sudan Rebels Break Ceasefire—Unmiss', *BBC News*, 21 July 2014, at: <http://www.bbc.com/news/world-africa-28400777>.

[1052] 'SPLM-in Opposition Proposes 21 New States, Ramciel to be the National Capital', *SSNA*, 16 July 2014, at: <http://www.southsudannewsagency.com/news/top-stories/splm-in-opposition-proposes-twenty-one-new-states>.

[1053] 'South Sudan's Food Crisis "Worst in the World"—UN', *BBC News*, 26 July 2014, at: <http://www.bbc.com/news/world-africa-28502260>.

[1054] 'IGAD extends South Sudan Peace Talks as Regional Leaders Postpone Meeting', *Sudan Tribune*, 16 August 2014, at: <http://www.sudantribune.com/spip.php?iframe&page=imprimable&id_article=52060>.

[1055] 'South Sudan Rivals Sign New Ceasefire Deal', *Al Jazeera*, 25 August 2014, at: <http://www.aljazeera.com/news/africa/2014/08/south-sudan-ceasefire-deal-2014825135823800543.html>.

[1056] 'South Sudan Crisis: Riek Machar Rebels Reject Deal', *BBC News*, 28 August 2014, at: <http://www.bbc.com/news/world-africa-28966971>.

[1057] 'Gatdet: Why Machar Opened Office in Kampala', *The Insider*, 23 September 2014, at: <http://www.theinsider.ug/gatdet-why-machar-opened-office-in-kampala/>.

government. In the meantime, peace talks resumed in order to address the details of a transitional government of national unity and the drafting of a permanent constitution, among other issues.[1058]

Fighting continued in October as SPLA-IO launched major attacks on Bentiu, prompting the government to threaten its withdrawal from the peace talks.[1059] UN Secretary-General Ban Ki Moon also condemned the renewed violence, urging all parties to participate in the negotiations so as to reach an agreement on transitional arrangements.[1060]

On 8 October, the National Assembly passed a very controversial National Security Services bill, which allows for arrests without warrants, shields officers from accountability, and provides wide powers of surveillance and authority.[1061]

The United Nations said the recruitment of children in South Sudan's civil war was 'rampant' and it estimated that there were 11,000 children serving in both the rebel, and government armies.[1062]

SPLA-IO rebels accused the government of violating the latest ceasefire deal reached in November, just hours after both sides had pledged to end the fighting.[1063] Given the continuation of hostilities, peace talks got postponed indefinitely and the Security Council extended the mandate of the United Nations Mission in South Sudan (UNMISS) until 30 May 2015, authorizing it to use 'all necessary means' to carry out its civilian protection mandate.[1064]

In early December, SPLM-IO passed a resolution agreeing to share power with Juba Government on conditions that the would-be prime minister will have full executive powers.[1065] Moreover, the rebel leadership meeting also agreed on introducing a federal system of governance based on twenty-one States.

[1058] 'Scores Killed in South Sudan Fighting as Peace Talks Resume', *Voice of America*, 22 September 2014, at: <http://www.voanews.com/content/south-sudan-death-toll-upper-nile-fighting-peace-talks-resume/2458954.html>.

[1059] 'Rebel Advance Imperils Peace Effort in South Sudan', *The Wall Street Journal*, 30 October 2014, at: <http://www.wsj.com/articles/rebel-advance-imperils-peace-effort-in-south-sudan-1414661855>.

[1060] 'South Sudan: Ban Condemns Renewed Violence Between Opposing Factions', *UN News Centre*, 30 October 2014, at: <http://www.un.org/apps/news/story.asp?NewsID=49211#.VVNhgRfva1s>.

[1061] 'South Sudan: Abusive Security Bill', *Human Rights Watch*, 15 October 2014, at: <http://www.hrw.org/news/2014/10/15/south-sudan-abusive-security-bill>.

[1062] 'Child Soldiers Still Being Recruited in South Sudan', *BBC News*, 27 October 2014, at: <http://www.bbc.com/news/world-africa-29762263>.

[1063] 'Rebels Accuse South Sudan of Breaking Truce', *Al Jazeera*, 9 November 2014, at: <http://www.aljazeera.com/news/africa/2014/11/rebels-accuse-south-sudan-breaking-truce-20141191436121865.html>.

[1064] 'Security Council Keeps in Place Peace Mission in South Sudan until 30 May 2015 as It Calls for Immediate Implementation of Cessation of Hostilities Accord', Security Council Meeting Coverage, 25 November 2014, at: <http://www.un.org/press/en/2014/sc11670.doc.htm>.

[1065] 'South Sudan Rebels Agree to Accept Non-Executive President', *Sudan Tribune*, 12 December 2014, at: <http://www.sudantribune.com/spip.php?article53317>.

On the 1 January 2015, the government declared that it would have gone ahead with preparations and plans to hold general elections in May 2015, ignoring the calls from opposition political parties to delay the vote.[1066]

Later in the month, the leaders of South Sudan's warring factions signed a symbolic deal in the Tanzanian city of Arusha in a bid to unblock efforts to end a year-long civil war,[1067] and President Kiir, former Vice-President and SPLM-IO leader Machar met in Addis Ababa to discuss the terms of a possible agreement.

At the beginning of February 2015, IGAD-led negotiations ended without a peace deal. President Kiir and Machar recommitted to a ceasefire and signed a document outlining the respective areas of agreement and disagreement regarding the proposed transitional government. However, two days later fighting erupted again in two States.[1068]

In March a rebel group freed 250 child soldiers it was using, including a girl as young as nine, and announced the imminent release of another 400 child soldiers. According to UNICEF, the rebel group hold a total of 3,000 child soldiers and thousands were still being forced to fight in the country's civil war.[1069]

PARTIES TO THE CONFLICT

The parties to the NIAC in 2014 were South Sudan and its armed forces, supported by the UPDF, against dissident South Sudan armed forces.

South Sudan armed forces

The South Sudan armed forces have been estimated to be 213,000 strong,[1070] though since the split in the SPLA the size of the effective fighting force is not known. It has been alleged that Government forces are actively recruiting child soldiers as young as thirteen.[1071]

1066 'South Sudan Says Will Hold Elections in May 2015', *Sudan Tribune*, 2 January 2015, at: <http://www.sudantribune.com/spip.php?article53517>.

1067 'South Sudan's Leaders Embark on New Peace Drive', *DW*, 22 January 2015, at: <http://www.dw.de/south-sudans-leaders-embark-on-new-peace-drive/a-18208950>.

1068 'Fighting Erupts in Two South Sudan States Days After Latest Truce', *Reuters*, 10 February 2015, at: <http://www.reuters.com/article/2015/02/10/us-southsudan-unrest-idUSKBN0LE2FQ20150210>.

1069 'South Sudan Rebel Group Frees 250 of its Child Soldiers', *Al Jazeera*, 22 March 2015, at: <http://www.aljazeera.com/news/africa/2015/03/south-sudan-rebel-group-frees-250-child-soldiers-150322173345103.html>.

1070 'South Sudan Military Strength', *Globalfirepower.com*, last updated on 27 March 2014, at: <http://www.globalfirepower.com/country-military-strength-detail.asp?country_id=south-sudan>.

1071 'South Sudan: Governement Forces Recruiting Child Soldiers', *Human Rights Watch*, 16 February 2015, at: <http://www.hrw.org/news/2015/02/16/south-sudan-government-forces-recruiting-child-soldiers>.

Dissident South Sudan armed forces

The size of the dissident South Sudan armed forces (SPLM/A-in-Opposition) is not known. A large number of soldiers have defected from the SPLA and other organized forces; estimates suggest the number to be around 35,000 fighters. Moreover, an unknown number of police forces have also joined the opposition, and if the proportion of defections was roughly similar to the SPLA, they may amount to around 10,000.[1072]

Uganda People's Defence Force

The UPDF has been estimated to be 45,000 strong with 2,000 reservists.[1073] In January 2014, Ugandan President Yoweri Museveni acknowledged that UPDF troops were fighting alongside South Sudanese Government forces against the rebels. UPDF spokesman Lieutenant-Colonel Paddy Ankunda said that Uganda had about two battalions, or 1,600 soldiers, in South Sudan.[1074]

CASUALTIES

The conflict that had started escalating in December 2013 between the South Sudan Government and the South Sudan's People Liberation Army—In Opposition (SPLA-IO) led to more than twice as many casualties in 2014 than in 2013. Indeed, while 1,011 casualties had been recorded in 2013 (703 for only the month of December), at least 2,740 had been identified by the end of December 2014. The intensity of the conflict in December 2013 was very high, and there was a continuity of conflict casualties which lasted throughout 2014.

Violence against civilians was widespread on both sides. In the period between mid-December and mid-April, armed forces on both sides targeted and killed hundreds of civilians, often because of their ethnicity, and pillaged and destroyed civilian property.[1075] Overall, at least 691 civilian casualties were recorded, including at least 611 deaths and eighty injured. Records of attacks on civilians showed serious breaches

[1072] 'The SPLM-In-Opposition', *HSBA*, 1 April 2014, at: <http://www.smallarmssurveysudan.org/fileadmin/docs/facts-figures/south-sudan/HSBA-SPLM-IO-May-2014.pdf>.

[1073] 'Uganda Military Strength', *Globalfirepower.com*, last updated on 27 March 2014, at: <http://www.globalfirepower.com/country-military-strength-detail.asp?country_id=uganda>.

[1074] 'Yoweri Museveni: Uganda troops fighting South Sudan rebels', *BBC*, 16 January 2014, at: <http://www.bbc.com/news/world-africa-25759650>.

[1075] Human Rights Watch (HRW), 'World Report 2015—South Sudan', <http://www.hrw.org/world-report/2015/country-chapters/south-sudan?page=1>; HRW, 'South Sudan's New War—Abuses by Government and Opposition Forces', 7 August 2014.

of IHL with both parties attacking displaced civilians sheltered in churches, mosques, hospitals[1076] and, on 17 April, a United Nations Mission in South Sudan (UNMISS) base in Bor, Jongei State, killing at least fifty-three civilians[1077] and two NGO Aid workers.[1078] A UNMISS Human Rights Division Special Report documenting the events of 29 October 2014 when SPLA-IO forces attacked the town of Bentiu, Unity State recorded at least twenty-four civilians killed including two women and three children, and twenty-eight injured, including twenty women forced to carry the bodies of wounded fighters and repeatedly sexually assaulted.[1079] Sexual violence was widely reported while no exact numbers were provided. According to UNMISS, 'all parties to the conflict have committed acts of rape and other forms of sexual violence against women of different ethnic groups. Credible information suggests that sexual violence took place in connection with the occurrence of human rights and humanitarian law violations before, during, and after heavy fighting, shelling, looting, and house searches'.[1080]

Violence clashes were reported throughout the year between SPLA-IO and Governmental Forces, often supported by foreign armed forces such as Ugandan soldiers and Sudan's JEM fighters. Overall, there were 2,022 casualties (1,938 killed and eighty-four injured) among parties to the conflict in 2014 identified from War Report analysis of information contained in the Armed Conflict Location and Event Data Project (ACLED) database.[1081] This included at least 1,142 Governmental forces and affiliates (1,060 killed and eighty-two injured) and 844 rebels (842 killed and at least two injured). The intensity of clashes was often very high with the use of shells and heavy ammunition on both sides, often causing collateral damage among civilians.

No casualties linked with David Yau Yau's South Sudan Democratic Movement/Army (SSDM/A) were recorded in South Sudan in 2014. Indeed, on 9 May 2014, the South Sudan Government signed a peace deal with David Yau Yau's SSDM/A Cobra faction ending a rebellion that started back in 2010. David Yau Yau was later appointed Chief Administrator or the newly created Greater Pibor Administrative Area (GPAA) counties in South Sudan's Jonglei State.

1076 Amnesty International (AI), 'Nowhere Safe—Civilians under attack in South Sudan', May 2014; HRW, 'South Sudan's New War—Abuses by Government and Opposition Forces', 7 August 2014.

1077 HRW, 'World Report 2015—South Sudan', <http://www.hrw.org/world-report/2015/country-chapters/south-sudan?page=1>.

1078 The Aid Worker Security Database, 'Security Incident Data', last updated 9 April 2015, <https://aidworkersecurity.org/incidents/search?detail=1&country=SS>.

1079 United Nations Mission in the Republic of South Sudan (UNMISS), 'Special Report: Attack on Bentiu, Unity State, 29 October 2014', 19 December 2014.

1080 UNMISS, 'Conflict in South Sudan: A Human Rights Report', 8 May 2014.

1081 Raleigh, C. and Hegre, H., 2005. 'Introducing ACLED: An Armed Conflict Location and Event Dataset'. Paper presented to the conference on 'Disaggregating the Study of Civil War and Transnational Violence', University of California Institute of Global Conflict and Cooperation, San Diego, CA, 7–8 March.

DISPLACED

As of December 2014 there were total of 1,304,200 IDPs due to conflict in South Sudan, 87% (1,304,200) of those were people newly displaced during 2014. The figure for new IDPs in 2014 brings the total figure to 1,498,200 since 15 December 2013, beginning of violent conflict in the country. There is little information on whether people displaced before 2013 have found durable solutions, were displaced again or are still displaced.[1082]

WAR CRIMES ALLEGATIONS, INVESTIGATIONS, AND PROSECUTIONS

South Sudan is neither a party nor a signatory to the 1998 Rome Statute of the International Criminal Court (ICC). The ICC may not exercise jurisdiction over war crimes alleged to have been committed by a State's nationals or on its territory unless the situation is referred to the Court by the UN Security Council.

On 30 December 2013, the African Union Peace and Security Council took an unprecedented step. For the first time in the history of the regional organization (as well as its predecessor, the Organization of African Unity), the Peace and Security Council established a commission of inquiry to investigate human rights violations and other abuses committed during the armed conflict in South Sudan.[1083] In January 2014, the African Union affirmed its commitment to begin investigation of rights violations.[1084] On 12 March 2014, the members of the African Union Commission of Inquiry on South Sudan[1085] were sworn in at the AU headquarters in Addis Ababa, Ethiopia.[1086]

In January 2014, Ivan Šimonovic, UN Assistant Secretary-General for Human Rights, said that the UN had evidence of use of child soldiers and mass war crimes committed by both sides in South Sudan. He warned that South Sudan was facing a 'horrifying human rights disaster' that had already killed thousands of civilians. Mass killings, extrajudicial killings, arbitrary detentions, and sexual violence were some of the other

[1082] Internal Displacement Monitoring Centre (IDMC) 'Global Overview 2015', May 2015, p. 86.

[1083] Dieng, A., 'Accountability in South Sudan—the African Union steps up', *Africa Renewal*, at: <http://www.un.org/africarenewal/web-features/accountability-south-sudan-%E2%80%93-african-union-steps>.

[1084] Clottey, P., 'AU to Investigate South Sudan Human Rights Violations', *Voice of America*, 21 January 2014, at: <http://www.voanews.com/content/african-union-investigate-south-sudan-human-rights-violations/1834793.html>.

[1085] <http;//au.int/en/sites/default/files/Announcement-COMMISSION%20OF%20INQUIRY%20ON%20SOUTH%20SUDAN%20-16th%20April%202014_0.pdf>.

[1086] AU, 'South Sudan Commission of Inquiry sworn-in', Press release No. 047/2014, 12 March 2014, at: <http://www.au.int/en/content/south-sudan-commission-inquiry-sworn>.

violations seen in the country, according to Assistant Secretary-General Šimonovic.[1087] In March 2014, the UN Secretary-General reported to the UN Security Council that:

> The ethnic dimension of the killings and abuses is most alarming. The affected populations and their community leaders and key stakeholders must make every effort to start the healing and reconciliation processes in order to save South Sudan from sinking into a deeper abyss. In order for reconciliation to take root and succeed, accountability too is essential. Justice will be required to right the wrongs suffered by so many.[1088]

The Secretary-General further stated that:

> Serious crimes of conflict-related sexual violence have . . . been reported in the four states directly affected by the conflict, with credible allegations that such violence has been perpetrated by SPLA, national police and anti-government forces.[1089]

South Sudan's Government has not moved to prosecute war crimes and potential crimes against humanity by its forces. Reports by investigation committees established by South Sudan's army and separately by the police service have not been made public. An investigation committee established by Kiir in January 2014 has yet to provide any report or update of its work and refused to cooperate with the AU inquiry. Authorities have also yet to pursue cases regarding a massacre in April 2014 of more than fifty people, mostly Nuer, seeking sanctuary inside the UN compound in the town of Bor.[1090]

[1087] 'UN: War Crimes Happening in South Sudan', *Al jazeera*, 18 January 2014, at: <http://www.aljazeera.com/video/africa/2014/01/un-war-crimes-happening-south-sudan-20141180817787607.html>.

[1088] 'Report of the Secretary-General on South Sudan', UN doc. S/2014/258, 6 March 2014, §78.

[1089] Ibid., §54.

[1090] 'South Sudan: One Year Later, Injustice Prevails', *Human Rights Watch*, 11 December 2014, at: <http://www.hrw.org/news/2014/12/10/south-sudan-one-year-later-injustice-prevails>.

Armed conflicts in Sudan in 2014

KEY CASUALTY DATA FOR 2014

Civilians killed:	258	(Sources: ACLED, Conflict Barometer, media)
Civilians injured:	305	(Sources: ACLED, Conflict Barometer, media)
Women injured:	221	(Sources: HRW)
Governmental forces and militias killed:	477	(Sources: ACLED, Conflict Barometer)
SRF/SLA/JEM/SPLM killed:	181	(Sources: ACLED, Conflict Barometer)
SRF/SLA/JEM/SPLM injured:	9	(Sources: ACLED, Conflict Barometer)
UNAMID killed:	11	(Source: UN Peacekeeping)
UNAMID injured:	(at least) 3	(Source UN OCHA)
Unknown killed:	21	(Sources: ACLED)
Unknown injured:	3	(Sources: ACLED)

CLASSIFICATION OF THE CONFLICTS

Sudan and its armed forces were involved in separate non-international armed conflicts (NIACs) with, at least, the Justice and Equality Movement (JEM) in Darfur, and with JEM and the Sudan People's Liberation Movement/Army-North (SPLM-North) in North and South Kordofan and Blue Nile States. Both conflicts met the threshold for applicability of the 1977 Additional Protocol II.

SUMMARY OF APPLICABLE INTERNATIONAL LAW

All parties to the conflict were bound by customary international humanitarian law (IHL) and human rights law, including customary IHL rules of distinction, proportionality, and precautions in attacks; the obligations of humane treatment, as set out in Common Article 3 to the 1949 Geneva Conventions; the obligation not to recruit and use children as soldiers; and by the duty to respect and protect fundamental human rights. This includes the duty to respect the rights to life and to freedom from torture or other forms of cruel, inhuman, or degrading treatment or punishment.

Sudan is a State party to the four 1949 Geneva Conventions and the 1977 Additional Protocol II. Sudan is party to both the 1966 International Covenant on Civil and Political Rights and the 1966 International Covenant on Economic, Social and Cultural Rights.

Sudan is a State party to the 1997 Anti-Personnel Mine Ban Convention. In accordance with Article 5 of the Convention (and the five-year extension granted by States parties in 2013), Sudan is required to destroy all antipersonnel mines in mined areas under its jurisdiction or control as soon as possible, but not later than 1 April 2019.

Sudan is not party or signatory to the 2008 Convention on Cluster Munitions or to the 2013 Arms Trade Treaty (ATT).[1091]

HISTORY OF THE CONFLICT[1092]

Sudan, once the largest and one of the most geographically diverse States in Africa, split into two countries in July 2011 after the south voted for independence following decades of conflict and violence. Continuing conflict in the western region of Darfur has driven many hundreds of thousands of people from their homes and may have already killed several hundred thousand people.

The conflict in Darfur

Fighting broke out in early 2003 when non-State armed groups seeking greater autonomy began an insurrection.[1093] Pro-government Arab militias were accused of carrying out a campaign of ethnic cleansing against non-Arab groups in the region. An African Union peacekeeping force was deployed in the Darfur region, and in 2007 the United Nations (UN) Security Council authorized a 'hybrid' UN/African Union force, UNAMID.[1094]

In April 2008, the UN Under-Secretary-General for Humanitarian Affairs, John Holmes, told the UN Security Council that the situation inside Darfur had worsened, despite the efforts of the international community. Mr Holmes said as many as 300,000 people were estimated to have died in Darfur since early 2003.[1095] This figure included deaths from disease, malnutrition, and reduced life expectancy, as well as from direct combat. In addition to the death toll, more than 2.7 million people had been displaced by the fighting, the vast majority still living within the arid region in the west of the country. Around 260,000 refugees had fled to neighbouring Chad.[1096]

[1091] Sudan abstained from the vote on the adoption of the ATT in the United Nations (UN) General Assembly on 2 April 2013.

[1092] Unless otherwise stated, this section is based on 'Sudan Profile', *BBC*, 30 April 2015, at: <http://www.bbc.com/news/world-africa-14094995>.

[1093] Darfur Australia Network, 'The Situation in Darfur', December 2010, at: <http://www.darfuraustralia.org/darfur/background>.

[1094] UNAMID was established on 31 July 2007 by UN Security Council Resolution 1769.

[1095] UNMIS, 'Media Monitoring Report', 23 April 2008, at: <http://unmis.unmissions.org/Portals/UNMIS/2008Docs/patch1/mmr-apr23.pdf>.

[1096] Ibid.

A Commission of Inquiry set up by the UN Security Council in 2004 considered allegations that war crimes and crimes against humanity had been committed during the conflict.[1097] Subsequently, arrest warrants were issued by the International Criminal Court (ICC) for a number of Sudanese Government officials and the head of the so-called *Janjaweed*.[1098] The Government refused to extradite the accused to The Hague for trial. Bahr Idriss Abu Garda, a Darfur non-State armed group member, appeared before the ICC on 18 May 2009.[1099] On 8 February 2010, Pre-Trial Chamber I refused to confirm the charges against Mr Abu Garda.

The conflict in Darfur has also strained relations between Sudan and Chad, to the west. Both countries have accused each other of cross-border incursions.[1100] In early May 2008, one of the armed groups in Darfur launched an assault on the Sudanese capital, Khartoum. The attack by the Justice and Equality Movement (JEM) was repelled, with the Government calling for JEM to be listed as a terrorist group and blaming also Chad for its alleged support for the group. Chad denied the charges and closed its border, claiming Sudan was planning an attack.[1101]

In 2010, JEM announced it was boycotting peace talks with the government, accusing it of launching new raids. There were reports of peace talks again in 2011 and in 2012;[1102] a JEM splinter group announced its interest in signing the Doha Document for Peace.[1103] A surge in government-led attacks was reported in late 2010 to early 2011 and the region remained isolated from aid workers and from UNAMID. Despite waning international attention, attacks against civilians continued in Darfur.

Fighting continued in 2013. The Sudanese Government signed a peace deal with JEM splinter faction led by Mohammed Bashar on 6 April; subsequently that month fighting erupted between JEM and Bashar's splinter faction, reportedly killing JEM-Bashar commander Saleh Mohammed Jerbo, who had been indicted by ICC

[1097] 'Report of the International Commission of Inquiry on Darfur to the United Nations Secretary-General', 25 January 2005, at: <http://www.icc-cpi.int/NR/rdonlyres/F87E244D-B27C-4A0A-BE1B-D27CECB5649E/278008/Report_to_UN_on_Darfur.pdf>.

[1098] ICC, 'Situation in Darfur, Sudan', as of 11 April 2013, at: <http://www.icc-cpi.int/EN_Menus/ICC/Situations and Cases/Situations/Situation ICC 0205/Pages/situation icc-0205.aspx>.

[1099] ICC, *Prosecutor v Bahar Idriss Abu Garda*, 18 May 2009, at: <http://www.icc-cpi.int/en_menus/icc/situations and cases/situations/situation icc 0205/related cases/icc02050209/Pages/icc02050209.aspx>.

[1100] Prunier, G., 'Chad: Caught in the Darfur Crossfire', *Le Monde Diplomatique*, March 2008, at: <http://mondediplo.com/2008/03/05chad>.

[1101] 'Assault Heralds Change in Sudan', *BBC*, 12 May 2008, at: <http://news.bbc.co.uk/2/hi/africa/7396404.stm>.

[1102] Human Rights Watch, *World Report 2012: Sudan*, January 2012, at: <http://www.hrw.org/world-report-2012/world-report-2012-sudan>.

[1103] The Doha Document for Peace in Darfur (DDPD) was finalized at the All Darfur Stakeholders Conference in May 2011, in Doha, Qatar. On 14 July, the Government of Sudan and the Liberation and Justice Movement signed a protocol committing themselves to the DDPD, which is seen as the framework for the comprehensive peace process in Darfur. See, e.g., UNAMID, *Doha Document for Peace in Darfur*, at: <http://unamid.unmissions.org/Default.aspx?tabid=11060&language=en-US>.

for war crimes.[1104] UN humanitarian chief Valerie Amos said on 22 May that some 300,000 people had fled their homes in Darfur since the beginning of the year due to an upsurge in fighting.[1105] On 17 November, JEM military leader Fidel Mohammed Rahoma was reported killed in an offensive against army facilities in Abu Zabad.[1106]

In March 2014, renewed violence occurred in Darfur; the UN estimated that some 100,000 civilians had been displaced since the beginning of the year. Following a meeting on 7 March with the head of the AU Commission, Darfur rebel groups claimed to have secured AU support for national dialogue to resolve the different armed conflicts.[1107]

Waves of attacks in Darfur by government forces however continued. Amongst reports of UNAMID actions being impeded by Khartoum, the UN Security Council on 3 April demanded for a better peacekeeping with more preventive and pre-emptive posture.[1108] On 3 July the UN started investigations into allegations of UNAMID mismanagement, misreporting of facts, failure to protect civilians in Darfur.[1109]

On 4 December, after a period of delays by the Sudanese Government, government-rebel talks were suspended indefinitely, raising fears of renewed military offensives.[1110] The Government also increased pressure on UNAMID, expelling two UN officials.[1111] The ICC on 12 December suspends a five-year long investigation into Darfur atrocities citing limited resources and UN Security Council deadlock.[1112]

On 4 January the Sudanese Parliament approves eighteen amendments to the 2005 interim Constitution, assimilating the Doha Document for Peace in Darfur (DDPD). This is viewed as reinforcing the Government's demand that DDPD serve as framework for talks with Darfur rebels.[1113]

Incumbent President Bashir won presidential election, reports claiming 95.05% of votes amid widespread voter apathy and low turnout.[1114] Arab League, AU, and IGAD

[1104] ICG, 'Crisis Watch database: Sudan', 1 May 2013 available at: <http://www.crisisgroup.org/en/publication-type/crisiswatch/crisiswatch-database.aspx>.

[1105] ICG, 'Crisis Watch database: Sudan', 1 June 2013.

[1106] ICG, 'Crisis Watch database: Sudan', 1 December 2013.

[1107] ICG, 'Crisis Watch database: Sudan', 1 April 2014.

[1108] ICG, 'Crisis Watch database: Sudan', 1 May 2014.

[1109] 'UN launches inquiry into Darfur peacekeepers', *Yahoo News*, 2 July 2014, at: <http://news.yahoo.com/un-launches-inquiry-darfur-peacekeepers-214335741.html>.

[1110] 'Sudan: AUHIP Suspends Darfur Peace Talks Indefinitely', *allAfrica*, 4 December 2014, at: <http://allafrica.com/stories/201412050167.html>.

[1111] 'Sudan expels two UN officials', *Al jazeera*, 25 December 2014, at: <http://www.aljazeera.com/news/africa/2014/12/sudan-expels-two-un-officials-2014122519274227l467.html>.

[1112] 'ICC Prosecutor Shelves Darfur War Crimes Inquiries', *BBC*, 12 December 2014, at: <http://www.bbc.com/news/world-africa-30458347>.

[1113] ICG, 'Crisis Watch database: Sudan', 2 February 2015.

[1114] 'Sudan's Bashir Wins Presidential Election in Vote Boycotted by Opposition', *WSJ*, 27 April 2015, at: <http://www.wsj.com/articles/sudans-al-bashir-wins-presidential-election-1430134646>.

observer missions all endorsed polls[1115], while the EU said on 9 April that it would not support elections.[1116] On 20 April, the United States, United Kingdom, and Norway denounced elections as not credible.[1117]

Southern Kordofan and Blue Nile States

In May–June 2011, tensions rose in Sudan between the ruling National Congress Party (NCP) and remaining forces of the former southern rebel Sudan People's Liberation Movement/Army (SPLM/A) still present in Sudan, over political and security arrangements in Southern Kordofan, Sudan's only oil-producing State, and Blue Nile State.[1118] In September 2011, fighting spread to Blue Nile and a few days later Sudanese authorities issued a ban on the Sudan People's Liberation Movement—North (SPLM-North), the successor to the SPLM after South Sudan's independence in July 2011, and arrested many of its members.[1119] According to Human Rights Watch, Sudanese forces carried out indiscriminate aerial bombardment and shelling of populated areas, killing and injuring civilians, and causing serious damage to civilian property, including homes, schools, clinics, crops, and livestock.[1120]

By the end of December 2012, Sudanese armed forces maintained control over the capital Kadugli and other main towns and areas near Dilling, Talodi, Dellami, Rashad, Abbasiya, and Abu Jibeiha. The SPLA-North controlled large areas of the countryside around Kadugli, particularly in El Buram, Um Durein, and Heiban localities, and mountainous areas north-west of Kadugli.[1121]

Fighting continued throughout 2013 and in November, the government announced its readiness to resume talks, initiated in April, with the SPLM-N.[1122]

[1115] 'Arab League, IGAD to Monitor Sudan Elections', 4 April 2015, *Sudan Tribune*, at: <http://www.sudantribune.com/spip.php?article54527>.

[1116] 'EU Says It Won't Support Sudan Election After Reform Talks Stall', *Bloomberg*, 9 April 2015, at: <http://www.bloomberg.com/news/articles/2015-04-09/eu-says-it-won-t-support-sudan-election-after-reform-talks-stall>.

[1117] 'US, UK, Norway Slam Sudan Polls as Not Credible', *AFP*, 21 April 2015, at: <http://english.alarabiya.net/en/News/middle-east/2015/04/21/U-S-UK-Norway-slam-Sudan-polls-as-not-credible-.html>.

[1118] For further details on the reasons of the tensions see Office of the UN High Commissioner on Human Rights, *Preliminary report on violations of international human rights and humanitarian law in Southern Kordofan from 5 to 30 June 2011*, August 2011, pp. 2–3.

[1119] Human Rights Watch, *Under Siege*, December 2012, pp. 18–21, at: <http://www.hrw.org/reports/2012/12/11/under-siege>.

[1120] Ibid., pp. 3–5. [1121] Ibid., pp. 20–1.

[1122] See Sudan profile, The War Report 2013, edited by Casey-Maslen, S., Oxford University Press, 2014, p. 198.

In March 2014, some 5–6,000 Arab militiamen from South Darfur returned from deployment against the SPLM/A-North in South Kordofan. The militia were accused of abuses against civilians in neighbouring North Kordofan prompting demonstrations in the North Kordofan capital, al-Obeid. Ongoing fighting in South Kordofan continued through April. On 7 April, the SAF bombed JEM positions in the region and in South Sudan's Unity State.[1123]

As government forces continued their operations, 110 SPML-N fighters were reported killed on 9 June around the Al-Atmur area, while Doctors without Borders accused the Sudanese Air Force of bombing hospital in Farandalla, South Kordofan.[1124]

In November, government and SPLM-N endorsed AUHIP draft framework agreement on conflicts in South Kordofan and Blue Nile, including roadmaps for participation of rebels in national dialogue, general elections, and transitional period. Talks were however adjourned on 17 November to give parties time to study draft agreement. Fighting nevertheless resumed in Blue Nile.[1125]

As in Darfur, parallel talks between the government and SPLM-N rebels focused on Blue Nile and South Kordofan halted on 9 December amid increasing violence in South Kordofan. As fighting in South Kordofan continued, SPLM-N in early March 2015 claimed attack on Kalogi, north of State capital Kadugli. SPLM-N chief Yasir Arman said attack was defensive and denied earlier SPLM-N claims that attacks were aimed at disrupting April 2015 elections.[1126]

PARTIES TO THE CONFLICT

The parties to the NIAC in 2014 were Sudan and its armed forces against JEM and against SPLM/A-North.

Sudan armed forces

The Sudan armed forces have been estimated to be 109,500 strong with 102,500 reservists.[1127]

[1123] ICG, 'Crisis Watch database: Sudan', 1 April and 1 May 2014.

[1124] ICG, 'Crisis Watch database: Sudan', 1 July 2014.

[1125] 'Mbeki Adjourns Talks on Sudan's Two Areas for More Consultations', *Sudan Tribune*, 17 November 2014, at: <http://www.sudantribune.com/spip.php?article53074>.

[1126] 'Sudan Call forces not involved in S. Kordofan attacks: SPLM-N', *Sudan Tribune*, 14 March 2015, at: <http://www.sudantribune.com/spip.php?article54284>.

[1127] 'Sudan Military Strength', *Globalfirepower.com*, last updated on 27 March 2014, at: <http://www.globalfirepower.com/country-military-strength-detail.asp?country_id=sudan>.

Justice and Equality Movement (JEM)

JEM is a rebel group involved in the Darfur conflict of Sudan, led by Khalil Ibrahim. Along with other rebel groups, such as the Sudan Liberation Movement (SLM), they are fighting against the Sudanese Government, including the government's proxy militia, the Janjaweed. The JEM is also a member of the Eastern Front, a rebel coalition formerly active in the east of Sudan along the Eritrean border. JEM embraces an Islamist ideology.[1128]

After years of refusing to attend peace talks with Khartoum, JEM finally signed a goodwill agreement at talks brokered by Qatar at the beginning of 2009. However, it soon fell apart after Sudanese President Omar al-Bashir expelled international development and aid groups from Darfur when the ICC in The Hague issued a warrant for his arrest in connection with international crimes allegedly committed in Darfur.[1129] JEM withdrew its support for the accord until, it said, Khartoum reinstated the aid groups. JEM signed a truce with Sudan's Government in February 2010 and until December 2012 the group has been in and out of negotiations to sign the Doha Document for Peace.[1130] JEM has also provided support to rebels in South Kordofan with its involvement said to have proven decisive in key battles.[1131]

Sudan People's Liberation Army/Movement (SPLA/M-North)

The SPLA was formed in 1983, and has since fought against the Governments of Nimeiri, Sadiq al-Mahdi, and President Omar Bashir. It is largely but not exclusively Christian and its declared aims are the establishment of a secular, democratic Sudan. Although many southerners preferred independence, it talked primarily of unity within a federal system.[1132] The SPLA/M, as the politico-military movement came to be identified, defined itself as a national movement rather than a strictly southern independence movement. Its platform promoted the concept of the 'New Sudan', a secular State that provides social, economic, and political justice for all communities.[1133]

[1128] 'Who are Sudan's Darfur rebels?', *BBC*, 23 February 2010, at: <http://news.bbc.co.uk/2/hi/africa/7039360.stm>.

[1129] Institute for the Study of Violent Groups, 'Justice and Equality Movement', December 2011, at: <http://vkb.isvg.org/Wiki/Justice_and_Equality_Movement>.

[1130] Small Arms Survey, 'Justice and Equality Movement', October 2012, at: <http://www.smallarmssurveysudan.org/fileadmin/docs/facts-figures/sudan/darfur/armed-groups/opposition/HSBA-Armed-Groups-JEM.pdf>.

[1131] Small Arms Survey, Human Security Baseline Assessment (HSBA) for Sudan and South Sudan Working Paper, *New war, old enemies: Conflict dynamics in South Kordofan*, March 2013, p. 29, at: <http://www.smallarmssurveysudan.org/project/project-summary.html>.

[1132] 'Sudan People's Liberation Army (SPLA)/Sudan People's Liberation Movement (SPLM)', Global Security.org, December 2004, at: <http://www.globalsecurity.org/military/world/para/spla.htm>.

[1133] 'Sudan People's Liberation Army (SPLA)', *Sudan Tribune*, December 2012, at: <http://www.sudantribune.com/spip.php?mot183>.

In 2005, the SPLA/M signed the Comprehensive Peace Agreement (CPA) with the Government of Sudan, ending the civil war between North and South Sudan and guaranteed the armed group prominent position in the Sudanese Government as well as the organization of a referendum for independence of South Sudan.[1134] In 2011, SPLA/M leaders announced that the group would split along a north–south divide if the results of the referendum returned a vote in favour of independence from Sudan. Since the declaration of independence of South Sudan on 9 July 2011, the northern splinter of the group has intensified its fight with the Government in Khartoum. In 2012, SPLM-North joined forces with three Darfur rebel groups: JEM, two Sudan Liberation Armies, forming a new group, the Sudan Revolutionary Front (SRF). Their declared purpose is to topple Sudanese President Al-Bashir and they have already conducted joint operations in South Kordofan.[1135]

CASUALTIES

There was a lack of detailed, disaggregated data available on the casualties caused by ongoing internal armed conflicts in Sudan for 2014. Most especially, available data fails to distinguish to which non-State armed group casualties were related, referring simply to non-State armed actors or to the Sudan Revolutionary Front, an alliance of the major armed groups working in opposition of the State, including the Sudan People's Liberation Movement in the North (SPLM-North), Justice and Equality Movement (JEM), and the Sudan Liberation Army (SLA).

Due to inconsistencies between annual reports and sources it is difficult to establish trends. Many fatalities go unreported or no disagreed numbers were provided in 2014. During the year, there were at least 1,268 casualties from armed conflict in Sudan, 948 deaths and 320 injured. However, these numbers are likely not to represent the full extent of conflict-related casualties in the country as many incidents are reported without providing exact numbers of casualties. There were 4,282 'violent deaths' in Darfur alone in 2013, according to the US Department of State. And another 975 people were killed as a result of armed conflict in South Kordofan and Blue Nile States.[1136] War Report analysis of information contained in the Armed Conflict Location and Event Data Project (ACLED) database, which was used to distinguish conflict

[1134] US Institute of Peace, 'Peace Agreements: Sudan', March 2005, at: <http://www.usip.org/publications/peace-agreements-sudan>.

[1135] 'Sudan's Darfur Region Dabbles With Peace', *BBC*, 2 March 2012, at: <http://www.bbc.co.uk/news/world-africa-17225356>.

[1136] US Department of State, 'Country Reports on Human Rights Practices 2013: Sudan', 27 February 2014.

casualties in Sudan for 2014, identified in total 3,892 fatalities in all of Sudan, from all causes.[1137]

Civilian casualties (563) amounted to more than 40% of all casualties. Both parties engaged in attacks targeting civilians, bombing areas known to be home to high numbers of civilians, looting, and destroying villages.[1138] Airstrikes targeted at civilians were conducted frequently throughout the year. For instance on 18 November, using Antonov aircraft, the Sudan Armed Forces (SAF) destroyed schools, wells, farmland, and killed cattle in several villages in North Darfur.[1139] Again on 16 June, SAF bombed and partially destroyed a hospital run by an International NGO, thus killing at least one aid worker.[1140]

Sexual violence against women was also regularly reported. For example, it was widely reported that from 30 October to 1 November 2014, SAF troops gang-raped more than 200 women and girls in the village of Tabit, North Darfur. Human Rights Watch reported at least 221 casualties and reported that it was 'able to cross-reference and verify many individual cases and allegations'.[1141] The UN-African Union Hybrid Mission in Darfur (UNAMID) expressed 'deep concern' about the allegations of mass rapes, but also 'announced it had initiated an investigation in Tabit but said that its team had found no evidence confirming the claims and received no information regarding the purported acts'.[1142]

Violent clashes between SAF and SRF-affiliated groups led to at least 477 deaths among SAF and militias, and 181 deaths and nine injured among SRF troops. However, many casualties have gone unrecorded because reports did not provide numbers or disaggregated data.[1143] The UN recorded eleven deaths of UNAMID soldiers,[1144] including

[1137] Raleigh, C. and Hegre, H., 2005, 'Introducing ACLED: An Armed Conflict Location and Event Dataset'. Paper presented to the conference on 'Disaggregating the Study of Civil War and Transnational Violence', University of California Institute of Global Conflict and Cooperation, San Diego, CA, 7–8 March.

[1138] War Report analysis of information contained in the Armed Conflict Location and Event Data (ACLED) database; Heidelberg Institute for International Conflict Research, 'Conflict Barometer 2014', 2015, pp. 80–3; Radio Dabanga, 'People Killed, Beaten, Robbed in Darfur', 29 December 2014; Radio Dabanga, 'Renewed bombing in Tawila, RSF militia arrive in Kabkabiya, North Darfur', 30 December 2014.

[1139] Heidelberg Institute for International Conflict Research, 'Conflict Barometer 2014', 2015, p. 81.

[1140] The Aid Worker Security Database, 'Security Incident Data', last updated 9 April 2015, <https://aidworkersecurity.org/incidents/search?detail=1&country=SD>.

[1141] Human Rights Watch, 'Sudan: Mass Rape by Army in Darfur', <http://www.hrw.org/news/2015/02/11/sudan-mass-rape-army-darfur>.

[1142] UN News Centre, 'UN Mission Continues Investigation into Alleged Mass Rape in North Darfur town', 14 November 2014, <http://www.un.org/apps/news/story.asp?NewsID=49339#.VViu5Pmqqko>.

[1143] War Report analysis of information contained in the Armed Conflict Location and Event Data (ACLED) database; Heidelberg Institute for International Conflict Research, 'Conflict Barometer 2014', 2015, pp. 80–83.

[1144] United Nations Peacekeeping, 'Fatalities Fatalities by Year, Mission and Incident Type up to 30 April 2015', <http://www.un.org/en/peacekeeping/fatalities/documents/stats_5a.pdf>.

three UNAMID soldiers injured in an ambush on 19 December at Nullah Crossing in South Darfur.[1145]

The vast majority of casualties (941 out of 1,268) were recorded in Darfur, while the rest took place in Kardofan and Blue Nile regions where the SPLM-North (part of the SRF) and SAF engaged in violent combat, including bombing and shelling civilian-populated areas.[1146]

DISPLACED

As of December 2014 there were total of 3,100,000 Internally Displaced Persons (IDPs) due to conflict in Sudan, with at least 557,500 people newly displaced during 2014.[1147]

WAR CRIMES ALLEGATIONS, INVESTIGATIONS, AND PROSECUTIONS

Sudan is not a party to the 1998 Rome Statute of the International Criminal Court (ICC Statute). The situation in Darfur since 1 July 2002 was referred to the Court's Prosecutor by the UN Security Council Resolution 1593 on 31 March 2005, in accordance with the ICC Statute.[1148]

There are five cases in the situation in Darfur, Sudan: *Prosecutor v Ahmad Muhammad Harun ('Ahmad Harun') and Ali Muhammad Ali Abd-Al-Rahman ('Ali Kushayb'); Prosecutor v Omar Hassan Ahmad Al Bashir; Prosecutor v Bahar Idriss Abu Garda; Prosecutor v Abdallah Banda Abakaer Nourain*; and *Prosecutor v Abdel Raheem Muhammad Hussein.*

Warrants of arrest have been issued by Pre-Trial Chamber I for President Al Bashir, Mr Harun, Mr Kushayb, and Mr Hussein. The four suspects continue to remain at large.

A summons to appear was issued for Mr Abu Garda, who appeared voluntarily before the Chamber on 18 May 2009. After the hearing of confirmation of charges, on February

[1145] OCHA, 'Weekly Humanitarian Bulletin—Sudan, Issue 51', 15–21 December 2014.

[1146] War Report analysis of information contained in the Armed Conflict Location and Event Data (ACLED) database; Heidelberg Institute for International Conflict Research, 'Conflict Barometer 2014', 2015, pp. 80–83.

[1147] Internal Displacement Monitoring Centre (IDMC) 'Global Overview 2015', May 2015, p.86. OCHA reported 3,100,000 as of 5 January 2015, including protracted and new displacement in Darfur, South Kordofan, and Blue Nile. Only limited data on urban displacement as well as on durable solutions was available.

[1148] Art. 13(b), ICC Statute.

2010, Pre-Trial Chamber I declined to confirm the charges. Mr Abu Garda is not in the custody of the ICC.[1149]

Two other summonses to appear were issued for Mr Banda and Mr Jerbo (both members of JEM) who appeared voluntarily on 17 June 2010; the confirmation of charges hearing took place on 8 December 2010. On 7 March 2011, Pre-Trial Chamber I unanimously decided to confirm the charges of war crimes brought by the ICC's Prosecutor against Mr Banda and Mr Jerbo, and committed them to trial. On 4 October 2013, Trial Chamber IV terminated the proceedings against Saleh Jerbo after 'receiving evidence pointing towards [his] death' on 19 April 2013. On 16 April 2014, Trial Chamber IV vacated the date of the opening of the trial in the case of *Prosecutor v Abakaer Nourain*, initially scheduled for 5 May 2014, in view of logistical difficulties encountered. The Chamber would 'decide in due course on the further steps to take'.[1150] Mr Nourain was charged with three war crimes under the ICC Statute: violence to life; intentionally directing attacks against personnel, installations, material, units, or vehicles involved in a peacekeeping mission; and pillaging.[1151]

On 12 December 2014, the ICC Prosecutor suspended investigations into Darfur atrocities citing limited resources and UN Security Council deadlock.[1152]

[1149] ICC, 'Situation in Darfur, Sudan', at: <http://www.icc-cpi.int/en_menus/icc/situations%20and%20cases/Pages/situations%20and%20cases.aspx>.

[1150] Ibid.

[1151] ICC, *Prosecutor v Abdallah Banda Abakaer Nourain and Saleh Mohammed Jerbo Jamus*, Case No. ICC-02/05-03/09, at: <http://www.icc-cpi.int/en_menus/icc/situations%20and%20cases/situations/situation%20icc%200205/related%20cases/icc02050309/Pages/icc02050309.aspx>.

[1152] 'ICC chief prosecutor shelves Darfur war crimes probe', *The Guardian*, 14 December 2014, at: <http://www.theguardian.com/world/2014/dec/14/icc-darfur-war-crimes-fatou-bensouda-sudan>.

Armed conflicts in Syria in 2014

KEY CASUALTY DATA FOR 2014

Total killed range:	31,253–76,021	(Source: VDC [low]; SOHR [high])
Civilians killed:	17,790–18,085	(Source: VDC [low]; SOHR [high])
Civilian women killed:	1,987–2,024	(Source: SOHR [low]; VDC [high])
Children killed:	3,501–3,698	(Source: SOHR [low]; VDC [high])
Male children killed:	2,457	(Source: VDC)
Female children killed:	1,241	(Source: VDC)
'Regime' combatant deaths (including self-defence committees, and pro-government foreign fighters):	3,795–24,794	(Source: VDC [low]; SOHR [high])
Hezbollah killed:	148–366	(Source: VDC [low]; SOHR [high])
Syrian and foreign opposition killed (including ISIS):	9,359–32,726	(Source: VDC [low]; SOHR [high])

CLASSIFICATION OF THE CONFLICTS

There are several non-international armed conflicts taking place in Syria: the Syrian armed forces are involved in a non-international armed conflict with, at least, the Free Syrian Army, al-Nusra, and Islamic State (IS), as well as other rebel groups. IS is also involved in a non-international armed conflict (NIAC) with Kurdish militias, and other rebel groups. In addition, the FSA is involved in a separate NIAC with Hezbollah, which began in May 2013.

SUMMARY OF APPLICABLE INTERNATIONAL LAW

All parties to the conflict are bound by customary international humanitarian law (IHL) and human rights law, including customary IHL rules of distinction, proportionality, and precautions in attacks; the obligations of humane treatment, as set out in Common Article 3 to the 1949 Geneva Conventions; the obligation not to recruit and use children as soldiers; and by the duty to respect and protect fundamental human rights. This includes the duty to respect the rights to life and to freedom from torture or other forms of cruel, inhuman, or degrading treatment or punishment.[1153]

[1153] In addition, the Hazzm Movement & other Free Syrian Army affiliated factions (Hazzm-FSA) signed the Geneva Call *Deed of Commitment for Adherence to a Total Ban on Anti-Personnel Mines and for Cooperation in Mine Action* and *the Deed of Commitment for the Prohibition of Sexual Violence in Situations of Armed Conflict and towards the Elimination of Gender Discrimination.* The Syrian Kurdish

Syria is party to the four 1949 Geneva Conventions but not to the 1977 Additional Protocol II. Syria is party to both the 1966 International Covenant on Civil and Political Rights and the 1966 International Covenant on Economic, Social and Cultural Rights.

Following allegations of use of chemical forces by Government forces, Syria acceded to the 1992 Chemical Weapons Convention in September 2013. Syria is neither party nor signatory to the 2013 Arms Trade Treaty (ATT).[1154]

Syria is not party to the 1997 Anti-Personnel Mine Ban Convention or the 2008 Convention on Cluster Munitions. Syria has been accused of using both anti-personnel mines and cluster munitions during the conflict. For example, it has been alleged that Government forces used anti-personnel mines during the May–June 2013 battle for Qusair, a town on the border with Lebanon.[1155] Landmine use by non-State armed opposition forces has also been recorded in the armed conflict, particularly IEDs. The Landmine monitor thus noted that booby-traps laid by Syrian insurgents (from the Nusra Front and from the Islamic State) were found in Lebanon in August 2014.[1156] With regard to cluster munitions, according to Human Rights Watch, Syrian forces used at least 249 cluster munitions in ten of Syria's fourteen governorates between July 2012 and July 2014 and credible evidence had emerged that Islamic State forces used ground-fired cluster munitions in at least one location in northern Syria.[1157]

HISTORY OF THE CONFLICT[1158]

Anti-government protests erupted in Syria in March 2011, with demonstrators calling for reforms and for the overthrowing of President Assad's regime. Government forces responded violently and, in joint operations with security forces and allied militia known as *Shabbiha*, engaged in excessive use of force, kidnappings, torture and other forms or ill-treatment. The UN Independent International Commission of Inquiry, established by the Human Rights Council, in its first report in November 2011, called the abuses

armed groups Democratic Self-Administration in Rojava/People's Protection Units/Women's Protection Units (YPG-YPJ) also signed the two Deeds of Commitment on landmines and sexual violence, as well as the one on *the Protection of Children from the Effects of Armed Conflict.*

1154 Syria was one of three states to vote against the adoption of the ATT by the United Nations (UN) General Assembly on 2 April 2013.

1155 Email from Human Rights Watch employee, 5 June 2013, in Landmine Monitor, 'Syria: Mine Ban Policy', at: <http://www.the-monitor.org/index.php/cp/display/region_profiles/theme/3074#_ftn13>.

1156 Landmine and Cluster Munitions Monitor, Syria, 30 November 2014, <http://www.the-monitor.org/index.php/cp/display/region_profiles/theme/3905>.

1157 Cluster Munitions Coalition: <http://www.stopclustermunitions.org/en-gb/cluster-bombs/use-of-cluster-bombs/cluster-munition-use-in-syria.aspx>.

1158 Unless otherwise stated this section is based on 'Syria Profile', *BBC*, 11 February 2015, at: <http://www.bbc.com/news/world-middle-east-14703856>.

carried out by Syrian authorities 'crimes against humanity'.[1159] The opposition became progressively organized when the main armed opposition group, the Free Syrian Army (composed largely of defectors from the Syrian army), and the Syrian National Council announced, in December 2011, that they would coordinate their efforts.[1160]

In November 2011, despite initially agreeing to a League of Arab States workplan aiming at ending the violence, the Syrian Government failed to cooperate and was suspended from the League, as well as being made the subject of sanctions against the United States and the European Union had already instituted sanctions against the regime.[1161] Following a year of violent clashes and the failure to adopt a Security Council Resolution on the Syrian situation,[1162] the UN Secretary-General and the Arab League appointed Kofi Annan as Joint Special Envoy with the mandate to bring a negotiated peace and the halting of hostilities.[1163]

On 27 March 2012, it was announced that the Syrian Government had agreed to a six-point plan put forth by the Special Envoy.[1164] The fragile ceasefire entered into effect on 12 April 2012 and UN observers began their monitoring work on 16 April 2012, despite reports of ongoing shellfire from Government forces in Homs and other areas.[1165]

Over a hundred civilians, including women and children, were killed in the Houla massacre on 25 May 2012, in an attack strongly condemned by the Human Rights Council and by the Security Council.[1166] Reports continued to surface of forces linked to the Syrian Government being responsible for abuses including indiscriminate attacks, extrajudicial executions, enforced disappearances, torture, and sexual violence.[1167] In June 2012, the UN announced it was suspending its mission in Syria, due to its monitors' inability to conduct patrols, and following reports of them being shot at.[1168]

[1159] 'Report of the independent international commission of inquiry on the Syrian Arab Republic', UN doc. A/HRC/S-17/2/Add.1, 23 November 2011, §1.

[1160] Combating Terrorism Center at West Point (CTC), *An Overview of Syria's Armed Revolution*, vol. 5, no. 4 (April 2012).

[1161] Council on Foreign Relations, *Syria's Crisis and the Global Response*, 3 April 2013, at: <http://www.cfr.org/syria/syrias-crisis-global-response/p28402>.

[1162] UN, 'Security Council fails to adopt draft resolution condemning Syria's crackdown on anti-government protesters, owing to veto by Russian federation, China', Press release, 4 October 2011, at: <https://www.un.org/News/Press/docs/2011/sc10403.doc.htm>.

[1163] UN, 'Secretary-General, Kofi Annan appointed joint special envoy of United Nations, League of Arab States on Syrian crisis', Press release SG/SM/14124, 23 February 2012, at: <http://www.un.org/News/Press/docs/2012/sgsm14124.doc.htm>.

[1164] 'Syrian government accepts UN-Arab League envoy's six-point plan to end crisis', UN News Centre, 27 March 2012, at: <http://www.un.org/apps/news/story.asp?NewsID=41646#.UWqmTqJA3To>.

[1165] International Crisis Group (ICG), Crisis Watch Database: Syria, 14 April 2013, at: <http://www.crisisgroup.org/en/publication-type/crisiswatch/crisiswatch-database.aspx>.

[1166] Global Research, 'SYRIA: The Houla Massacre and the Subversion of the Peace Plan', 7 June 2012, at: <http://www.globalresearch.ca/syria-the-houla-massacre-and-the-subversion-of-the-peace-plan/31300>.

[1167] Human Rights Watch, *Torture Archipelago Arbitrary Arrests, Torture, and Enforced Disappearances in Syria's Underground Prisons since March 2011*, 3 July 2012, at: <http://www.hrw.org/reports/2012/07/03/torture-archipelago-0>.

[1168] 'UN suspends monitoring activities in Syria amid escalating violence', UN News Centre, 16 June 2012, at: <http;//www.un.org/apps/news/story.asp?NewsID=42251#.UWqnPqJA3To>.

Fighting continued throughout 2012 and 2013, taking the lives of several hundreds of civilians.[1169] In late October 2012, Lakhdar Brahimi[1170] arranged for a ceasefire during Eid al-Adha in late October, but it quickly collapsed as both rebels and the Syrian Army resumed large-scale operations.[1171]

In August 2013, the Independent International Commission of Inquiry reported to the Human Rights Council that:

> The Syrian Arab Republic is a battlefield. Its cities and towns suffer relentless shelling and sieges. Massacres are perpetrated with impunity. An untold number of Syrians have disappeared.
>
> Government and pro-government forces have continued to conduct widespread attacks on the civilian population, committing murder, torture, rape and enforced disappearance as crimes against humanity. They have laid siege to neighbourhoods and subjected them to indiscriminate shelling. Government forces have committed gross violations of human rights and the war crimes of torture, hostage-taking, murder, execution without due process, rape, attacking protected objects and pillage.
>
> Anti-government armed groups have committed war crimes, including murder, execution without due process, torture, hostage-taking and attacking protected objects. They have besieged and indiscriminately shelled civilian neighbourhoods.

In September, UN weapons inspectors concluded that chemical weapons had been used in an attack on the Ghouta area of Damascus in August that killed about 300 people, but, consonant with their mandate, did not explicitly allocate responsibility for the attack. In October, President Assad allowed international inspectors to begin destroying Syria's chemical weapons on the basis of a US–Russian agreement.

In December, the United States and the United Kingdom suspended 'non-lethal' support for rebels in northern Syria after reports that Islamist rebels had seized bases belonging to the Western-backed Free Syrian Army. In January–February 2014, UN-brokered peace talks in Geneva failed, largely because Syrian authorities refused to discuss a transitional government.

In February 2014, the Commission of Inquiry reported that:

> More than 250,000 people are besieged in the Syrian Arab Republic and subjected to relentless shelling and bombardment. They are denied humanitarian aid, food and such basic necessities as medical care, and must choose between surrender and starvation. Siege warfare is employed in a context of egregious human rights and international humanitarian law violations. The warring parties do not fear being held accountable for their acts.

[1169] 'Hama Massacre: More Than 200 Killed In Tramseh, Mostly Civilians, Opposition Says', *Reuters*, 13 July 2012, at: <http://www.huffingtonpost.com/2012/07/13/hama-massacre-tramseh_n_1670255.html>.

[1170] On 17 August 2012, Brahimi was appointed by the UN Secretary-General as the new peace envoy to Syria, following Kofi Annan's resignation.

[1171] 'Syria Profile', *BBC*, 25 March 2013.

In March 2014, the Syrian Army and Hezbollah forces recaptured Yabroud, the last rebel stronghold near the Lebanese border. Indeed, by the spring of 2014, the tide of the armed conflicts in Syria seemed have shifted decisively in favour of the government with a number of key towns being recaptured from the rebels. In May 2014, the government retook Homs, Syria's third city, once dubbed the 'capital of the revolution'. An evacuation of civilians and the departure of fighters marked the end of three years of resistance in Homs. The same month, senior Iranian officials argued that Iran and President Bashar al-Assad had won the war in Syria, and 'the US-orchestrated campaign in support of the opposition's attempt to topple the Syrian regime' had failed.[1172]

The OPCW-UN Joint Mission on the elimination of Syrian chemical weapons announced in June 2014 that the removal of Syria's chemical weapons material had been completed and Syria has destroyed all declared production, mixing and filling equipment and munitions. As the mission completed its mandate, its operations drew to a close on 30 September 2014.[1173]

Islamic State militants declared they had established a 'caliphate' in the territory they control stretching from Aleppo in north-western Syria to the eastern Iraqi province of Diyala. On 29 June 2014, IS released a video, entitled 'End of Sykes Picot', a reference to the agreement between France and Britain on dividing up Iraq and Syria after the First World War. In the video an IS spokesperson explains the new caliphate in Iraq and Syria and warns '[t]his is not the first border we will break, we will break other borders'.[1174] Abu Bakr al-Baghdadi is declared as the leader of the new caliphate.

Up until July 2014, the Sunni insurgents sweeping Iraq and Syria had been variously referred to as ISIS (The Islamic State of Iraq and Syria, or the Islamic State of Iraq and al-Sham), ISIL (The Islamic State of Iraq and the Levant), or the colloquial local term 'Da'ash'. In July they declared themselves to be called the Islamic State or IS, dropping the mention of Iraq and the Levant.

In August 2014, the Independent International Commission of Inquiry presented its eighth report to the Human Rights Council. The report found that Syrian Government forces:

continued to perpetrate massacres and conduct widespread attacks on civilians, systematically committing murder, torture, rape and enforced disappearance amounting to crimes against humanity; have committed gross violations of human rights and the war crimes of murder,

[1172] Tisdall, S., 'Iran and Assad have won in Syria, say top Tehran foreign policy figures', *Guardian*, 12 May 2014, at: <http://www.theguardian.com/world/2014/may/11/syria-crisis-iran-assad-won-war-tehran>.

[1173] OPCW-UN Joint Mission Press Release, OPCW-UN Joint Mission Draws to a Close, 1 October 2014, at: <http://www.opcw.org/news/article/opcw-un-joint-mission-draws-to-a-close/>.

[1174] 'Isis announces Islamic caliphate in area straddling Iraq and Syria', *The Guardian*, 30 June 2014, at <http://www.theguardian.com/world/2014/jun/30/isis-announces-islamic-caliphate-iraq-syria>.

hostage-taking, torture, rape and sexual violence, recruiting and using children in hostilities and targeting civilians; have disregarded the special protection accorded to hospitals and medical and humanitarian personnel; have used indiscriminate and disproportionate aerial bombardment and shelling that led to mass civilian casualties and spreading terror; and have used chlorine gas, an illegal weapon. The Commission also reported that non-state armed groups (particularly IS) committed massacres and war crimes, including murder, execution without due process, torture, hostage-taking, violations of international humanitarian law tantamount to enforced disappearance, rape and sexual violence, recruiting and using children in hostilities and attacking protected objects. Specifically the Committee concluded that IS committed torture, murder, acts tantamount to enforced disappearance, and forcible displacement as part of an attack on the civilian population in Aleppo and Ar Raqqah governorates, amounting to crimes against humanity.[1175]

After weeks of fierce fighting, Tabqa airbase, near the northern city of Raqqa, was captured by IS militants in late August 2014, thereby extending their control to the entire Raqqa province. IS militants claimed on Twitter that they executed 250 Assad solders who had been guarding the airport.[1176] Photographs and videos were posted online by IS showing men being marched through the desert at gunpoint and a long line of bodies of young men lying face down in the desert.

In a televised address on 10 September 2014 US President Obama announced that he would be extending US bombing of IS targets from Iraq into Syria.[1177] On 23 September, a coalition of States (including the United States, Bahrain, Jordan, Saudi Arabia, the United Arab Emirates, and Qatar) began airstrikes against IS targets in Syria. At the time the US State department confirmed its ambassador to the UN, Samantha Power, had given her Syrian counterpart an advance indication of likely military attacks against IS in the country but strongly denied any military coordination.[1178] Power stated: [w]e warned Syria not to engage US aircraft' and in a statement the US State department affirmed:

[w]e did not request the regime's permission. We did not coordinate our actions with the Syrian government. We did not provide advance notification to the Syrians at a military level, or give any indication of our timing on specific targets.[1179]

[1175] 8th Report of Commission of Inquiry on Syria, UN doc. A/HRC/27/60, 13 August 2014.

[1176] 'Syria conflict: IS "kills dozens of Assad soldiers"', *BBC News*, 28 August 2014, at <http://www.bbc.com/news/world-middle-east-28965959>.

[1177] 'Barack Obama authorises air strikes against Isis militants in Syria', The Guardian, 11 September 2014, at <http://www.theguardian.com/world/2014/sep/10/obama-speech-authorise-air-strikes-against-isis-syria>.

[1178] For further information on this conflict, see Chapter 4 in this volume, Antonio Coco and Jean-Baptiste Maillart, 'The Conflict with Islamic State: A Critical Review of International Legal Issues'.

[1179] 'Obama administration: "No coordination" with Assad on bombing campaign', *Washington Times*, 23 September 2014, at <http://www.washingtontimes.com/news/2014/sep/23/white-house-no-coordination-assad-bombing/>.

To date, the United States, with Bahrain, Jordan, Qatar, Saudi Arabia, and the United Arab Emirates, have carried out more than a 1,000 attacks on IS in Syria since 23 September 2014. Targets have included include Raqqa, the IS's de facto capital, Deir al-Zour, Aleppo, and Kobane, a border town where IS were battling Kurdish fighters, forcing thousands to flee into neighbouring Turkey.[1180] In January 2015, Syrian Kurds eventually regained control over Kobane, ending a four-month battle for the northern Syrian town.[1181]

PARTIES TO THE CONFLICTS

The parties to the conflicts in 2014 were Syria, allied militia, and Hezbollah, the Free Syrian Army, al Nusra, IS, and the Kurdish Syrian armed groups YPG-YPJ. However, a 2013 study by IHS Jane's analyst Charles Lister estimated that as many as 1,000 rebel groups were fighting in Syria, possessing between them as many as 100,000 fighters.[1182] According to Lister:

> The insurgency is now dominated by groups which have at least an Islamist viewpoint on the conflict. The idea that it is mostly secular groups leading the opposition is just not borne out.

Syrian armed forces

The current strength of the Syrian army is unknown. It is reported that the armed forces numbered around 300,000 personnel before the conflict and have shrunk by 30–50% through desertions, defections, and deaths.[1183] In March 2013, the International Institute of Strategic Studies had reported that from a notional strength of 220,000, the army had withered to a core of about 50,000 the regime could rely on, while the Institute for the Study of War in Washington estimated the loyal core at 65,000.[1184]

[1180] 'Battle for Iraq and Syria in maps', *BBC News*, 20 February 2015, at <http://www.bbc.com/news/world-middle-east-27838034>.

[1181] 'Syrian Kurds 'drive Islamic State out of Kobane', *BBC News*, 26 January 2015, at: <http://www.bbc.com/news/world-middle-east-30991612>.

[1182] Cited in Farmer, B., 'Syria: nearly half rebel fighters are jihadists or hardline Islamists, says IHS Jane's report', *Daily Telegraph*, 15 September 2013, at: <http://www.telegraph.co.uk/news/worldnews/middleeast/syria/10311007/Syria-nearly-half-rebel-fighters-are-jihadists-or-hardline-Islamists-says-IHS-Janes-report.html>.

[1183] 'Assad's army stretched but still seen strong in Syria's war', *Reuters*, 18 September 2014, at: <http://www.reuters.com/article/2014/09/18/us-syria-crisis-military-idUSKBN0HD0M420140918>.

[1184] Borger, J., 'Iran and Hezbollah "have built 50,000-strong force to help Syrian regime"', *Guardian*, 14 March 2013, at: <http://www.guardian.co.uk/world/2013/mar/14/iran-hezbollah-force-syrian-regime>.

The Syrian army is supported by the Iranian-backed Lebanese group Hezbollah and it is estimated there are up to 5,000 Hezbollah solders in Syria.[1185] Russia has reportedly been supplying Assad's armed forces with military equipment and conventional weapons since the outbreak of the conflict, including armoured vehicles, tanks, surveillance equipment, drones, radars, electronic warfare systems, spare parts for helicopters, and various weapons including guided bombs.[1186]

Free Syrian Army

The Free Syrian Army's (FSA) formation was announced on 29 July 2011 in a video released on the internet by a uniformed group of deserters from the Syrian military who called upon members of the Syrian army to defect and join them.[1187] Although most of the FSA's members are Sunni Arabs (Syria's largest community), the organization also includes battalions made up of Kurds, Turkmen, Palestinians, and Druze. In December 2011, the Syrian opposition became more unified, with the Free Syrian Army agreeing to coordinate its efforts with the non-violence-advocating Syrian National Council.[1188]

The FSA operates throughout Syria, both in urban areas and in the countryside. Forces are active in the north-west (Idlib, Aleppo), the central region (Homs, Hama, and Rastan), the coast around Latakia, the south (Daraa and Houran), the east (Dayr al-Zawr, Abu Kamal), and the Damascus area.[1189] The FSA remains highly fractured both politically and militarily, however, in November 2012, several Syrian resistance factions came together to form an umbrella organization known as the National Coalition of Syrian Revolutionary and Opposition Forces.[1190] This new resistance group was soon recognized by several countries such as the United Kingdom, France, Turkey, and a number of Gulf Arab States.[1191] In December 2012, the FSA went through a major restructuring process bringing Brigadier-General Selim Idris to replace the army's former senior officer, Colonel Riad al-Assad.[1192]

[1185] 'Lebanon's once-mighty Hezbollah is facing attacks in Syria—and also at home', *Washington Post*, 28 October 2014, at: <http://www.washingtonpost.com/world/middle_east/lebanons-once-mighty-hezbollah-is-facing-attacks-in-syria--and-also-at-home/2014/10/27/81cd75a4-9d26-4f9b-b843-9fa0814b2471_story.html>.

[1186] 'Exclusive: Russia steps up military lifeline to Syria's Assad', *Reuters*, 17 January 2014, at: <http://www.reuters.com/article/2014/01/17/us-syria-russia-arms-idUSBREA0G0MN20140117>.

[1187] 'Free Syrian Army Founded by Seven Officers to Fight the Syrian Army', *Syria Comment*, 29 July 2011, at: <http://www.joshualandis.com/blog/free-syrian-army-established-to-fight-the-syrian-army/>.

[1188] Institute for the Study of War, 'Syria's Armed Opposition', Middle East Security Report No. 3, March 2012, p. 9, at: <http://www.understandingwar.org/sites/default/files/Syrias_Armed_Opposition.pdf>.

[1189] CTC, 'An Overview of Syria's Armed Revolution', *CTC Sentinel*, vol. 5, no. 4 (April 2012), at: <http://www.ctc.usma.edu/wp-content/uploads/2012/04/CTCSentinel-Vol5Iss41.pdf>.

[1190] Council on Foreign Relations, *Syria's Crisis and the Global Response*, 3 April 2013, at: <http://www.cfr.org/syria/syrias-crisis-global-response/p28402>.

[1191] Ibid. [1192] Ibid.

The Supreme Military Council (SMC) has thirty members, six representing each of five 'fronts' in Syria: Northern (Aleppo and Idlib), Eastern (Raqqa, Deir al-Zour and Hassaka), Western (Hama, Latakia and Tartus), Central (Homs and Rastan) and Southern (Damascus, Deraa and Suwaida).[1193] Each front has a civilian-military council and a commander. The opposition National Coalition describes General Idris as the commander of the FSA, however, observers have said the FSA is simply a loose network of brigades rather than a unified fighting force. Brigades supposedly report through the chain of command to Gen Idris, but he is yet to assert operational control and serves more as a spokesman and conduit for foreign funding and arms shipments.

Jabhat al-Nusra[1194]

Jabhat al-Nusra (al-Nusra) is a Sunni jihadist militant organization whose goal is to overthrow the Assad regime and replace it with a Sunni Islamic Government. Al-Nusra continues to thrive as one of the most prominent opposition groups in Syria. It employs both terrorist attacks and more traditional warfare against the government and Hezbollah while continuing to fight other rebel groups in some areas. Al-Nusra is Al-Qaeda's only official affiliate in Syria.[1195] The United States has blacklisted the group as a terrorist organization in response to the bombing campaigns and its status as an Islamist organization with links to Al-Qaeda.

In April 2013, Al-Nusra's leader, Abu Mohammed al-Jawlani, denied the announcement by the Al-Qaeda affiliated Islamic State of Iraq, that the two groups had merged to form the Islamic State of Iraq and Al-Sham. Instead, al-Jawlani pledged its allegiance to Al-Qaeda leader Ayman al-Zawahiri.[1196] Following this declaration, a number of Al-Nusra fighters defected to ISIS, causing further tension between the groups. By March 2014, over 3,000 fighters had been killed in battles between IS and Al-Nusra.[1197]

In contrast to IS the majority of both the leadership and members of the group are reportedly made up of local Syrians, not foreigners. Al-Nusra maintains complex

[1193] The National, Syria's southern rebels draw up new game plan, at: <http://www.thenational.ae/world/middle-east/syrias-southern-rebels-draw-up-new-game-plan#full>, 25 November 2014.

[1194] 'Profile: Syria's al-Nusra Front', *BBC*, 10 April 2013, at: <http://www.bbc.co.uk/news/world-middle-east-18048033>; Mahmood, M. and Black, I., 'Free Syrian Army rebels defect to Islamist group Jabhat al-Nusra', *Guardian*, 8 May 2013, at: <http://www.guardian.co.uk/world/2013/may/08/free-syrian-army-rebels-defect-islamist-group>.

[1195] Stanford University, Mapping Militant Organizations, November 2014, at: <http://web.stanford.edu/group/mappingmilitants/cgi-bin/groups/view/493>.

[1196] Naharnet, Al-Nusra Commits to Al-Qaida, Deny Iraq Branch Merger, 10 April 2013, at: <http://www.naharnet.com/stories/en/78961>.

[1197] Stanford University, Mapping Militant Organizations, at: <http://web.stanford.edu/group/mappingmilitants/cgi-bin/groups/view/493, November 2014>.

relationships with the FSA and the Islamic Front, sometimes cooperating with them and sometimes targeting them as enemies. In November 2014, Al-Nusra attacked and defeated the Syrian Revolutionary Front (SRF) and Harakat Hazm, both moderate rebel groups linked to the FSA and the United States.[1198]

Islamic State (IS)

Under its former name, Islamic State in Iraq and the Levant (ISIL), IS was formed in early 2013 growing out of Al-Qaeda in Iraq. In April 2013, the leader of the Al-Qaeda affiliated Islamic State of Iraq, Abu Bakr al-Baghdadi, announced that his group was merging with Jabhat Al-Nusra to form the Islamic State of Iraq and Al-Sham, also known as the Islamic State of Iraq and the Levant. However, this unilateral declaration was rejected by both the leader of Jabhat Al-Nusra, Abu Mohammed al-Jawlani, and the leader of Al-Qaeda, Ayman al-Zaqahiri. In May 2013 the group split from Al-Nusra and began acting under the name Islamic State of Iraq and Al-Sham, under the leadership of Abu Bakr al-Baghdadi.[1199] Despite IS's separation from Al-Qaeda, it expanded its operations in Syria and experienced military success in both Syria and Iraq, capturing several major cities, including Raqqa, Fallujah, and Mosul. The funds seized through these invasions and seizure of oil fields in Iraq and eastern Syria combined with income from foreign donors and criminal activities, such as smuggling and the extortion of local businesses, have enabled IS to gather cash and assets worth up to $2 billion.[1200]

Currently IS's precise size is unclear. Its numbers have significantly risen over the last five years. Estimates of the number of fighters vary from around 12,000[1201] to 30,000. Some estimates state that about 80% of Western fighters in Syria have joined the group. IS claims to have fighters from the United Kingdom, France, Germany, and other European countries, as well as the United States, the Arab world, and the Caucasus. Despite the recruitment of thousands of Syrians the IS leadership structure is largely dominated by foreign fighters.[1202]

[1198] 'US plan for proxy army to fight Isis in Syria suffers attack', *Guardian*, 2 November 2014, at: <http://www.theguardian.com/world/2014/nov/02/syria-us-proxy-army-assad>.

[1199] 'Profile: Abu Bakr al-Baghdadi', *BBC News*, 2 August 2014, at: <http://www.bbc.com/news/world-middle-east-28749734>.

[1200] 'How an arrest in Iraq revealed Isis's $2bn jihadist network', *The Guardian*, 15 June 2014, at: <http://www.theguardian.com/world/2014/jun/15/iraq-isis-arrest-jihadists-wealth-power>.

[1201] The Soufan Group, Foreign Fighters in Syria, June 2014, at: <http://soufangroup.com/foreign-fighters-in-syria/>.

[1202] Independent International Commission of Inquiry on Syria releases its report Rule of Terror: Living under ISIS, 14 November 2014, §13.

IS has extensively used explosive weapons, such as suicide or remote controlled car bombs, to cause mass civilian casualties, executed and tortured captured fighters during military operations, carried out kidnappings and public beheadings of civilians and journalists, and forcibly recruiting fighters, including children.

In November 2014, the UN Independent International Commission of Inquiry on Syria released its report 'Rule of Terror: Living under ISIS in Syria' which concludes that IS has committed war crimes and crimes against humanity. The report affirms that IS has perpetrated murder, enslavement, rape, sexual slavery, forced pregnancy, mutilation, violence, forcible displacement, enforced disappearance, the use and recruitment of children, torture and outrages upon personal dignity and that these acts have been committed as part of a widespread and systematic attack against the civilian population in Aleppo, Ar-Raqqah, Al-Hasakah, and Dayr Az-Zawr governorates.[1203]

YPG-YPJ

YPG-YPJ is 'the dominant military force' in Kurdish-populated Syria and has mainly been fighting Islamist armed groups active in Syria, notably the Islamic State and the Al-Nusra Front, since government forces largely withdrew from the areas in 2012. The Democratic Self-Administration in Rojava was formed in January 2014 and is the de facto governing authority in the Kurdish areas.[1204] YPG declared it had 50,000 fighters as of mid-2014, though independent estimates place the number at around 30,000.[1205]

Hezbollah

Hezbollah—the Party of God—is a Shi'a Islamist political, military, and social organization that wields considerable power in Lebanon. It emerged with the help of Iran during the Israeli occupation of Lebanon in the early 1980s, though its ideological roots stretch back to the Shia Islamic revival in Lebanon in the 1960s and 1970s. After Israel withdrew in 2000, Hezbollah resisted pressure to disarm and continued to strengthen its military wing, the Islamic Resistance. In some ways, its capabilities now exceed those of the Lebanese army, its considerable firepower used against Israel in the 2006 war. Starting in April 2013 (and possibly earlier), Hezbollah sent fighters across the border to support President al-Assad, a close ally of Shia-led Iran, in his struggle against the

1203 Independent International Commission of Inquiry on Syria, Rule of Terror: Living under ISIS, 14 November 2014.

1204 Geneva Call, Syria profile, at: <http://www.genevacall.org/country-page/syria/>.

1205 Kurdish People's Protection Unit YPG, Global Security.org, at: <http://www.globalsecurity.org/military/world/para/ypg.htm>.

rebels.[1206] By October 2014, there were thought to be between 4,500 and 5,000 Hezbollah fighters in Syria.[1207]

Khorasan Group

The Khorasan are reportedly made up of veteran fighters from the Afghanistan and Pakistan region who are directed by Al-Qaeda's central leadership. In 2012, the Khorasan Group began to arrive in Al-Nusra strongholds in Syria, allegedly using these relatively safe havens in Syria as a base to attack the West.[1208] In September 2014, the US Government announced that, in addition to the airstrikes it began launching against IS, it will also be targeting the Khorasan cell 'to address terrorist threats that they pose to the United States and our partners and allies'.[1209] Questions have, though, been raised as to the precise nature of the threat posed by the group.[1210]

CASUALTIES

Annual totals recorded by various datasets on conflict casualties in Syria continued to vary significantly. The Syrian Observatory for Human Rights (SOHR) reported 76,021 conflict fatalities for 2014, far greater than other sources and marking a slight increase from the 75,031 casualties that it had reported for 2013,[1211] while the Center for Documentation of Violations in Syria (VDC) recorded 31,253 conflict-related deaths in total for calendar year 2014, a significant decrease from the 43,931 deaths in Syria for 2013.[1212]

[1206] Black, I. and Roberts, D., 'Hezbollah is helping Assad fight Syria uprising, says Hassan Nasrallah', *Guardian*, 30 April 2013, at: <http://www.theguardian.com/world/2013/apr/30/hezbollah-syria-uprising-nasrallah>; see also 'Lebanon's Hezbollah movement', *BBC*, 4 December 2013, at: <http://www.bbc.com/news/world-middle-east-10814698>.

[1207] 'After losing 1,000 men in Syria, Hezbollah builds "security zone"', *Times of Israel*, 31 October 2014, at: <http://www.timesofisrael.com/after-losing-1000-men-in-syria-hezbollah-builds-security-zone/>.

[1208] 'Syria conflict: Khorasan group targeted by US air strikes', *BBC News*, 6 November 2014, at: <http://www.bbc.com/news/world-us-canada-29940096>.

[1209] Letter to the UN Security Council from US ambassador to the UN Samantha Power dated 23 September 2014. Available at <http://www.businessinsider.com/the-syria-strikes-and-international-law-2014-9>.

[1210] 'US officials unclear on threat posed by obscure Al-Qaida cell in Syria', *The Guardian*, 24 September 2014, at: <http://www.theguardian.com/world/2014/sep/25/us-officials-terror-group-khorasan-syria>.

[1211] SOHR, '76021 people killed in Syria in 2014, 1 January 2015, <http://syriahr.com/en/2015/01/76021-people-killed-in-20014>; and SOHR, 'More than 73 thousand died last year', (in Arabic) 1 January 2014, <http://www.syriahr.com/index.php?option=com_news&nid=13313&Itemid=2&task=displaynews#.U08n-le6RLw>. In 2013 and 2014 the SOHR dataset included no details on individual casualties and its dataset and verification methodology are not publicly available.

[1212] As reported at 8 April 2014, by combining both 'martyrs' and 'regime' data totals for calendar year 2013, VDC, <http://www.vdc-sy.info/index.php/en>.

Although the VDC recorded fewer casualties, it continued to make the raw data publicly available, including information on each casualty recorded. On that basis, the VDC data has been used for annual comparisons by the War Report. The most marked difference between the VDC and the SOHR data has been in the much lower number of 'regime' and pro-government casualties recoded by the VDC, but the discrepancy is not possible to verify.[1213]

The VDC data included 2,024 civilian women and 3,698 children (2,457 boys and 1,241) girls.[1214] The deaths of 3,795 Syrian 'regime' forces were also recorded by VDC as well as 148 Hezbollah deaths.[1215] VDC recorded 9,359 fatalities among anti-government rebels and militants, both national and foreign fighters, including 257 Islamic State (IS, previously known as Islamic State of Iraq and the Levant/Islamic State of Iraq and Syria, often still referred to as ISIS).

The SOHR reported aggregated fatality totals according to different definitions than VDC data: 17,790 civilian deaths, including 3,501 children and 1,987 adult women. Opposition forces included: 15,488 fighters from opposition combat battalions and national Islamic groups, 259 deserting soldiers and officers, and 16,979 ISIS and other Islamic group member non-Syrian nationals. Pro-government forces included: 12,861 regular forces of the Syrian military, 9,766 Shabiha militia, national defence forces and informants; 2,167 Shiites of non-Syrian nationality; 366 Hezbollah. There were an additional 345 'nameless victims' including unidentified persons recorded on video.[1216]

After a pause from January to August 2014, the UN OHCHR released its third outsourced analysis of multiple source data reporting fatalities in the Syria conflict since 2011. In early 2014 it had been reported that the number of reliable data sources was significantly reduced, thus preventing useful statistical analysis.[1217] The third analysis did not include SOHR data beyond April 2013.[1218] The report released in August 2014

[1213] See for example, 'Every Casualty, 'Syrian Casualties: Who's counting?', 3 June 2014, <www.everycasualty.org/newsandviews/recording_casualties_of_syrian_conflict>; Balcells, L., Beehner, L., and Schulhofer-Wohl, J., 'How should we count the war dead in Syria?', *The Washington Post*, 1 May 2014, <http://www.washingtonpost.com/blogs/monkey-cage/wp/2014/05/01/how-should-we-count-the-war-dead-in-syria/>; and Crompton, P., 'Counting death: The Syrian Observatory for Human Rights', *Al Arabiya News*, 25 April 2014, <http://english.alarabiya.net/en/perspective/features/2014/04/25/Counting-death-The-Syrian-Observatory-for-Human-Rights.html>.

[1214] The total of civilian women and child fatalities reported by the VDC included 106 women, 97 girls, and 148 boys recorded in the dataset of 'Regime' fatalities'.

[1215] Deaths recorded as 'Regime' fatalities include police and civilians. Fatalities among Hezbollah forces have been disaggregated separately.

[1216] SOHR, '76021 people killed in Syria in 2014,' 1 January 2015, <http://syriahr.com/en/2015/01/76021-people-killed-in-20014>.

[1217] 'UN abandons death count in Syria, citing inability to verify toll', 7 January 2014, <http://america.aljazeera.com/articles/2014/1/7/un-abandons-deathcountinsyria.html>.

[1218] Just three of the original sources continued to share fatality data with the OCHA analysis project in 2014.

found a total of 191,369 deaths in Syria between March 2011 and April 2014. It states that these 'can be understood as a minimum bound of the number of killings'. Of the cumulative total, 85% of people killed were male, 9% were female, while 6% of records used omitted the sex of the person.[1219] The OHCHR-commissioned reports did not disaggregate fatalities by year, nor do they include civilian or military status of the casualties.

As in past years, no tenable figures for people injured annually by the conflict in Syria were available for 2014. However, in December 2014 a representative of the WHO was quoted as stating that one million people had been injured in the conflict in Syria.[1220] A year earlier, in December 2013 the head of the ICRC in Syria estimated that at least 500,000 people had been wounded during the conflict since its beginning.[1221] These estimates do make annual comparison possible.

Israeli airstrikes and shelling on targets within Syria in 2014, including in Quneitra province on the 'Bravo side' of the Golan heights, killed at least twenty-six people in including seventeen Syrian soldiers and three Hezbollah fighters and eighteen civilians, another twenty-six people were injured.[1222] It was also reported that one of two Syrian pilots died after they plane was downed by Israeli fire.[1223]

The Committee to Protect Journalists (CPJ) reported nineteen journalists killed in Syria in 2014.[1224] Twelve journalists killed in Syria in 2014 were reported by the International Federation of Journalists (IFJ).[1225] Fourteen aid workers were reported as killed in Syria in 2014.[1226]

[1219] Price, M., Gohdes, A., and Ball, P., 'Updated Statistical Analysis of Documentation of Killings in the Syrian Arab Republic,' Commissioned by the Office of the UN High Commissioner for Human Rights, August 2014, <http://www.ohchr.org/documents/countries/sy/hrdagupdatedreportaug2014.pdf>.

[1220] Holmes, O., 'One million people wounded, diseases spreading in Syria: WHO,' 19 December 2015, *Reuters*, <http://www.reuters.com/article/2014/12/19/us-mideast-crisis-health-idUSKBN0JX0V720141219>.

[1221] 'Syria: Escalation in hostilities and severe winter weather exacerbate suffering', 22 December 2013 (Operational Update), <http://www.icrc.org/eng/resources/documents/update/2013/12-22-syria-escalation-winter-exacerbate-suffering.htm>.

[1222] UN Security Council, S/2014/401, 10 June 2014, para 5; 'Israeli air strike kills 18 in Syria,' 15 July 2014, <http://www.aa.com.tr/en/rss/359257--israeli-airstrike>; 'Two Hezbollah members killed in airstrike', 8 December 2014, <http://www.haaretz.com/news/diplomacy-defense/1.630620>; 'Syria: 4 killed, 9 wounded in Israeli airstrikes', 23 June 2014, <http://www.foxnews.com/world/2014/06/23/israel-bombs-targets-in-syria-in-response-to-boy-death>.

[1223] 'Pilots of plane, shot down by Israel, died', 24 September 2014, <http://www.i24news.tv/en/news/israel/diplomacy-defense/44965-140924-report-pilots-of-plane-shot-down-by-israel-died>.

[1224] CPJ, '81 Journalists Killed in Syria since 1992/Motive Confirmed', <https://cpj.org/killed/mideast/syria>.

[1225] IFJ, 'Trail of Violence: Journalists & Media Staff Killed in 2014', 2015, p. 9.

[1226] The Aid Worker Security Database, 'Security incident data', last updated 9 April 2015, <https://aidworkersecurity.org/incidents/search?start=2014&end=2014&detail=1&country=SY>.

The VDC recorded 181 persons who went missing during 2014 this was a massive decrease compared to 1,003 persons who went missing in Syria in 2013 and 1,191 in 2012.[1227] In 2014 another 3,609 people were detained according to VDC data.[1228]

DISPLACED

There were at least 7,600,000 internally displaced people in Syria as of December 2014. At least 1,100,000 people were newly displaced during the year in 2014. These figures reported by the Internal Displacement Monitoring Centre (IDMC) are based on OCHA information gathered from the Syrian authorities, other UN agencies and NGOs in opposition areas. Sources use different methodologies to estimate the number of IDPs.[1229]

WAR CRIMES ALLEGATIONS, INVESTIGATIONS, AND PROSECUTIONS

Syria is a signatory but not a State party to the 1998 Rome Statute of the International Criminal Court (ICC).

In May 2014 Russia and China vetoed a draft UN resolution calling for the situation in Syria to be referred to the ICC, ignoring support for the measure by sixty-five other countries and all of the other thirteen members of the Security Council.[1230]

In its eighth report the Commission of Inquiry on Syria confirmed that war crimes and crimes against humanity continue to be perpetrated by both government forces and armed groups in Syria. [1231] The report finds in the period between 20 January and 15 July 2014:

> Government forces have committed gross violations of human rights and the war crimes of murder, hostage-taking, torture, rape and sexual violence, recruiting and using children in hostilities and targeting civilians. Government forces disregarded the special protection accorded to hospitals and medical and humanitarian personnel. Indiscriminate and disproportionate

[1227] VDC, 'Missing', <http://www.vdc-sy.info/index.php/en/missing>.

[1228] VDC, 'Detainees', <http://www.vdc-sy.info/index.php/en/detainees>.

[1229] IDMC, 'Global Overview 2015', May 2015, p. 87.

[1230] 'Russia and China veto UN move to refer Syria to international criminal court', *The Guardian*, 22 May 2014, at: <http://www.theguardian.com/world/2014/may/22/russia-china-veto-un-draft-resolution-refer-syria-international-criminal-court>.

[1231] Report of Commission of Inquiry on Syria, 13 August 2014, UN Doc. A/HRC/27/60.

aerial bombardment and shelling led to mass civilian casualties and spread terror. Government forces used chlorine gas which is an illegal weapon.

With regard to armed group the report finds IS and Jabhat al-Nusra have committed massacres and war crimes, including murder, execution without due process, torture, hostage-taking, violations of international humanitarian law tantamount to enforced disappearance, rape and sexual violence, recruiting and using children in hostilities and attacking protected objects. Medical and religious personnel and journalists were targeted. Armed groups besieged and indiscriminately shelled civilian neighbourhoods, in some instances spreading terror among civilians through the use of car bombings in civilian areas. Members of the Islamic State of Iraq and Al-Sham (ISIS) committed torture, murder, acts tantamount to enforced disappearance, and forcible displacement as part of an attack on the civilian population in Aleppo and Ar Raqqah governorates, amounting to crimes against humanity.

Armed conflict in Thailand in 2014

KEY CASUALTY DATA FOR 2014 (UNTIL SEPT)

Total killed:	251	(All sources: Deep South Incident Database)
Total Injured:	545	
Civilians killed:	171	
Civilians injured:	317	
Children killed:	9	
Children injured:	26	
Military killed:	39	
Military injured:	131	
Police killed:	25	
Police injured:	62	
Paramilitary killed:	10	
Paramilitary injured:	34	
NSAG killed:	5	

CLASSIFICATION OF THE CONFLICT

Thailand and its armed forces continued to be involved in a non-international armed conflict (NIAC) with, at least, the Pattani Independence Fighters (Pejuang Kemerdekaan Pattani) and arguably also other organized armed groups operating within the National Revolutionary Front (Barisan Revolusi Nasional) until September 2014, when the level of violence fell below the required threshold.

SUMMARY OF APPLICABLE INTERNATIONAL LAW

All parties to the conflict were bound by customary international humanitarian law (IHL) and human rights law, including customary IHL rules of distinction, proportionality, and precautions in attacks; the obligations of humane treatment, as set out in Common Article 3 to the 1949 Geneva Conventions; the obligation not to recruit and use children as soldiers; and by the duty to respect and protect fundamental human rights. This includes the duty to respect the rights to life and to freedom from torture or other forms of cruel, inhuman, or degrading treatment or punishment.

Thailand is a State party to the four 1949 Geneva Conventions but not the 1977 Additional Protocol II. Thailand is party to both the 1966 International Covenant on

Civil and Political Rights and the 1966 International Covenant on Economic, Social and Cultural Rights.

Thailand is a State party to the 1997 Anti-Personnel Mine Ban Convention. Under Article 5 of the Convention, and in accordance with the nine-and-a-half year extension granted by States parties in 2008, Thailand is required to destroy all anti-personnel mines in mined areas under its jurisdiction or control as soon as possible, but not later than 1 November 2018.

Thailand is not a party or signatory to the 2008 Convention on Cluster Munitions or the 2013 Arms Trade Treaty (ATT).[1232]

HISTORY OF THE CONFLICT[1233]

Political turmoil and a decades-old conflict between the security forces and armed groups in the south of Thailand have increased since 2004. The violence is believed to have claimed more than 5,000 deaths in areas where the ethnic Malay population are predominantly Muslim (80%) in contrast with the rest of Thailand, which is essentially Buddhist. Negotiations between government officials and representatives of armed non-State actors, who have been seeking independence for the provinces of Narathiwat, Pattani, Yala, and five districts of Songkhla province: Chana, Na Thawi, Saba Yoi, Thepa, and Sadao, appear to have stalled.[1234]

Successive governments, beginning with the one of Thaksin Shinawatra (2001–6), have proved unable to control the insurgency in the south. Imposition of martial law since January 2004, as well as an emergency decree enacted in July 2005, has granted more powers to Thai security forces in the region. According to human rights groups, this law enables the Government to ban any type of political gathering, censor the media, and detain people without charge.[1235]

In April 2009, armed groups were blamed for nine deaths on 27 April, the day before the fifth anniversary of the Krue Sae mosque incident in which NSAG members launched attacks on police checkpoints, culminating in a siege of Krue Sae mosque in

[1232] Thailand voted in favour of the adoption of the ATT by the United Nations (UN) General Assembly on 2 April 2013.

[1233] Unless otherwise stated this section is based on 'Thailand profile', *BBC*, 31 March 2015, at: <http://www.bbc.com/news/world-asia-15581957>.

[1234] Zawacki, B., 2012, 'Politically Inconvenient, Legally Correct: A Non-international Armed Conflict in Southern Thailand', *Journal of Conflict and Security Law*, 18 September 2012, pp. 1–29, available at: <http://jcsl.oxfordjournals.org/content/early/2012/09/18/jcsl.krs025.full.pdf+html> (subscription needed).

[1235] International Crisis Group (ICG), *Thailand: The Evolving Conflict in the South*, Asia Report No. 241, 11 December 2012, pp. 2–3, at: <http://www.crisisgroup.org/~/media/Files/asia/south-east-asia/thailand/241-thailand-the-evolving-conflict-in-the-south.pdf>.

Pattani. Security forces were reported to have killed thirty-two people who were holed up in the mosque, sparking widespread condemnation.

Overall, however, in 2007–14, the frequency of violence had been steadily decreasing. Since early 2012, however, the pattern of violence in the south of the country has become more complex and intense. This includes attacks such as the March 2012 blast which is said to have resulted in several hundred casualties.[1236] As a result, one source reported 1,647 casualties in the first ten months of 2012, surpassing the 2011 total of 1,464.[1237]

Attacks continued in 2013, despite attempts at initiating political dialogue. In February, the Government and Muslim separatists in the south signed the first-ever peace talks deal. A BRN representative led the talks, while the Thai Government team was headed by the Secretary-General of the National Security Council, Lieutenant-General Paradon Pattanatabut, who had been tasked by Prime Minister Yingluck Shinawatra to negotiate a peace deal with insurgents. However, the exiled leader of the Pattani United Liberation Organisation, Kasturi Mahkota, said attacks by his group would continue if they were not invited to the talks. Lieutenant-General Pattanatabut said that Thailand would not agree to independence or any violation of Thailand's Constitution, but would discuss degrees of autonomy and an amnesty with the insurgents.[1238] In April, insurgents stepped up attacks in the southernmost provinces following the first meeting in the dialogue process between Bangkok and insurgent representatives on 28 March.[1239]

On 10 June, the Thai Cabinet approved the extension of the emergency decree in the southernmost provinces for another ninety days, and extension of the Internal Security Act in several districts of Songkhla province and Mae Lan district of Pattani for another year. A third round of dialogue between National Security Council and militants led by the BRN took place on 13 June in Malaysia: the two sides pledged to reduce violence during Ramadan.[1240] Instead violence surged over Ramadan and following further insurgent attacks subsequently, in October peace talks were postponed indefinitely.[1241]

According to one analyst, suspension of car-bomb operations and a drop in the deployment of motorcycle bombs by insurgents during 2013 'reflected an interest in avoiding

[1236] On 31 March 2012, a car bomb exploded in Yala, a busy commercial area and was followed by a second and a third explosion a few hours later in other crowded commercial districts in the south of the country. Deep South Watch database, 10 April 2013, at: <http://www.deepsouthwatch.org/node/3803>.

[1237] ICG, *Thailand: The Evolving Conflict in the South*, p. 4.

[1238] 'Into the south: What will it take to end fighting between the government and insurgents in Thailand's deep south?', *Al jazeera*, last modified on 28 June 2013, at: <http://www.aljazeera.com/programmes/101east/2013/06/2013626115439264456.html>.

[1239] ICG, Crisis Watch database: Thailand, 1 May 2013, at: <http://www.crisisgroup.org/en/publication-type/crisiswatch/crisiswatch-database.aspx>.

[1240] ICG, Crisis Watch database: Thailand, 1 July 2013.

[1241] Davis, A., 'Thai insurgency enters new phase', *Asia Times*, 23 October 2013, at: <http://www.atimes.com/atimes/Southeast_Asia/SEA-01-231013.html>.

civilian casualties in attacks which generally take place in urban environments and are, by their nature, indiscriminate even when directed against security force or civil administration targets. The large IEDs used in car-bombs are now being turned to what BRN appears to see as more politically useful attacks on military vehicles'.[1242]

The second major tactical shift during the 2013 involved a move away from large assaults on security forces camps by guerrillas concentrating in platoon strength (thirty to forty fighters) or more to small-scale ambushes of mobile patrols:

> Requiring less time for planning and preparation than large operations, such attacks are also more secure in that they require concentrating fewer fighters against targets which are mobile and thus more vulnerable than static defensive positions. The record also suggests smaller operations are more effective in inflicting casualties and seizing weapons.
>
> September [2013] alone provided grim evidence of this with a five-man police patrol wiped out in Thung Yang Daeng district, Pattani, on the 11th, with nine firearms seized; three Rangers killed and one wounded in Yarang district of the same province on the 12th, with three rifles and one pistol looted; and an ambush of a four-vehicle EOD (explosive ordnance disposal) convoy in Yi-ngor district, Narathiwat, on the 27th in which three policemen were severely wounded. Involving an estimated 20 fighters and two IEDs—one intended to target reinforcements (but which was disarmed)—the Yi-ngor ambush was a fairly complex operation.[1243]

In early 2014, insurgent attacks continued in the southernmost provinces, with both civilian and security force casualties, including quadruple bombing in Yala town on the 6 April which killed one person and injured at least twenty-eight.[1244]

Political turmoil intensified as the People's Democratic Reform Committee (PDRC) began series of protests in January aiming at 'shut down Bangkok' and force the cancellation of the general election on 2 February.

Although a wave of political violence in Bangkok and several provinces had risen, on 2 February the general election took place with relatively small incidents. However, anti-government protesters succeeded in stopping or disrupting the polling in over 10% of the polling stations; moreover, the voting got partially or completely cancelled in eighteen provinces. This prevented the formation of a government.

After the 21 March the Constitutional Court ruled that the general election held on 2 February was invalid because it was not held in all constituencies on same day,[1245] on the 30 April, the Election Commission announced that the day for the new elections would be 20 July.[1246]

[1242] Ibid. [1243] Ibid. [1244] ICG, Crisis Watch database: Thailand, 1 April 2014.

[1245] 'No end in sight', *The Economist*, 26 April 2014, at: <http://www.economist.com/news/asia/21601309-countrys-political-nightmare-continues-no-end-sight>.

[1246] 'Thai PM, Election Commission agree new vote in July, opposition defiant', *Reuters*, 30 April 2014, at: <http://www.reuters.com/article/2014/04/30/us-thailand-protest-idUSBREA3T09020140430>.

At the beginning of May, the Constitutional Court removed the caretaker Prime Minister Yingluck Shinawatra and nine cabinet ministers for abuse of power. The governing Pheu Thai Party called the Court ruling a 'judicial coup'.[1247]

On 22 May, the military staged a coup after months of political unrest, violence, and large-scale demonstrations: they suspended the constitution; dismissed the caretaker government and arrested hundreds of politicians, including the former Prime Minister Yingluck, democracy activists and journalists.[1248] At the end of the month, the junta chief, Prayuth, said that at least fifteen months of 'reform' were needed in order to attain 'reconciliation', before new general elections could be held.[1249] Violence in the south continued with several insurgent attacks through the month.

The coup was condemned by Australia, Canada, the United Kingdom, the United States, and the EU, which also called for punitive measures.[1250] In reaction to the coup, Jarupong Ruangsuwan, chairman of the Puea Thai Party that led the government ousted by the military, said in June that the military council had no legitimacy and he cast doubt on its promise to transfer power back to civilian authorities at some point.[1251] In the meantime, security forces continued the suppression of Red Shirt and anti-coup supporters outside Bangkok as well as inside the capital, where various arrests have been carried out, including on charges of reading George Orwell's *1984* in public.[1252]

In July, the junta National Council for Peace and Order (NCPO) tightened its grip on the power. First, it established five panels to monitor local and international media for criticism on the junta, and it further authorized legal action against journalists and outlets for 'inappropriate content'.[1253] Moreover, on 22 July the NCPO

[1247] 'Thailand court ousts PM Yingluck Shinawatra', *BBC News*, 7 May 2014, at: <http://www.bbc.com/news/world-asia-27292633>.

[1248] 'Thailand's Military Stages Coup, Thwarting Populist Movement', *The New York Times*, 22 May 2014, at: <http://www.nytimes.com/2014/05/23/world/asia/thailand-military-coup.html?_r=0>.

[1249] 'Thai junta chief declares 15 months of "reforms" before general elections', *The Guardian*, 31 May 2014, at: <http://www.theguardian.com/world/2014/may/31/thai-junta-chief-declares-15-months-of-reforms-before-general-elections>.

[1250] 'Thailand's military criticised as coup takes hold', *BBC News*, 23 May 2014, at: <http://www.bbc.com/news/world-asia-27533530>. See also: 'Thai coup draws international condemnation', *Al Jazeera*, 23 May 2014, at: <http://www.aljazeera.com/news/asia-pacific/2014/05/thai-coup-draws-international-condemnation-201452223444716458.html>.

[1251] 'Opponents of Thai military regime launch campaign for democracy', *Reuters*, 24 June 2014, at: <http://in.reuters.com/article/2014/06/24/thailand-politics-idINKBN0EZ08Y20140624>.

[1252] 'Protesting Thai reader of Orwell's 1984 dragged off by police in Bangkok', *South Asia Morning Post*. 23 June 2014, at: <http://www.scmp.com/news/asia/article/1538616/protesting-thai- reader-orwells-1984-dragged-police-bangkok>.

[1253] 'Thai junta sets up panels to crack down on critical news reports', *Reuters*, 26 June 2014, at: <http://www.reuters.com/article/2014/06/26/us-thailand-politics-idUSKBN0F10VM20140626>.

adopted an interim constitution granting amnesty to coup makers.[1254] Section 44 of the interim constitution also granted the NCPO authority over the interim government.[1255]

In August 2014, 200 members were appointed to the National Legislative Assembly (NLA), more than half of whom were active or retired senior military officials.[1256] Consequently, on 21 August the NLA unanimously elected General Prayuth as Prime Minister.[1257] Arrests continued to take place, mainly on grounds of lèse-majesté. According to Human Rights Watch, the arrest of two activists involved in a play considered by Thai military authorities to be 'insulting to the monarchy' shows the decline in freedom of expression in Thailand since the coup in May.[1258]

In September, the National Council of Peace and Order (NCPO) led by PM General Prayuth continued to consolidate political control. Reacting to the more and more stringent limitations to freedom of expression, sixty university professors from sixteen universities, on 22 September, submitted a petition to the government calling for greater respect for academic freedoms.[1259]

Violence and deadly attacks continued to take place in the South, where a member of Tha Nam Tambon Administration Organisation got killed in the beginning of the month.

After September 2014, the southern insurgency continued, in the form of small protests. Consequently, the level of violence arguably fell under the threshold required in order to classify the conflict as a NIAC.

PARTIES TO THE CONFLICT

The parties to the NIAC in September 2013 were Thailand and its police and armed forces against the BRN, particularly the Pattani Independence Fighters (Pejuang Kemerdekaan Pattani).

[1254] 'Thai King Approves Interim Constitution', *The Wall Street Journal*, 22 July 2014, at: <http://www.wsj.com/articles/thai-king-approves-interim-constitution-1406039552>.

[1255] 'Thailand: Interim Constitution Provides Sweeping Powers', *Human Rights Watch*, 25 July 2014, at: <http://www.hrw.org/news/2014/07/24/thailand-interim-constitution-provides-sweeping-powers>.

[1256] 'Thailand king endorses coup leader Prayuth as PM', *BBC News*, 25 August 2014, at: <http://www.bbc.com/news/world-asia-28923989>.

[1257] 'Thailand coup General Prayuth Chan-ocha named PM', *BBC News*, 21 August 2014, at: <http://www.bbc.com/news/world-asia-28876154>.

[1258] 'Thailand: Theater Activists Jailed for Insulting Monarchy', *Human Rights Watch*, 20 August 2014, at: <http://www.hrw.org/news/2014/08/20/thailand-theater-activists-jailed-insulting-monarchy>.

[1259] '60 scholars call on NCPO for 'freedom', *Bangkok Post*, 22 September 2014, at: <http://www.bangkokpost.com/news/politics/433500/60-scholars-call-on-ncpo-for-freedom>.

Thai Armed and Police Forces

The Thai Armed Forces have been estimated to be 306,000 strong, with 245,000 reservists.[1260] Both the army and the police have been engaged in counterinsurgency in the south of the country. It is claimed that the armed forces have struggled to adapt to fighting in a part of the country where many of the soldiers do not understand the Malay dialect spoken by the majority of the people.[1261] In addition, one Bangkok-based security company, PSA Asia, has asserted that the Thai State's efforts to reduce violence have been hampered by historical rivalry between the police and the military. This is 'an additional impediment to forming a strategic response to growing Islamic insurgent violence in south Thailand', PSA said in an advisory sent to its clients in early 2013.[1262]

BRN

The National Revolutionary Front (Barisan Revolusi Nasional, BRN) is an armed group based in northern Malaysia and operating in southern Thailand. The BRN was founded in 1963 as a response to compulsory registration by the central Thai Government of traditional Muslim boarding schools following imposition of a secular curriculum. In the beginning, the BRN's focus was more religious than military, but it also claimed independence and maintained close relationships with the communist groups in the south.[1263] The BRN fractured during the 1980s, splitting into three factions: BRN-Ulama, which renounced violence to focus on religious activities; BRN-Congress, which focused almost exclusively on military operations; and BRN-Coordinate, which engaged in both political activities and urban sabotage.[1264]

According to Amnesty International, in 2011 the BRN-Coordinate has been 'likely the strongest and best organized of the many groups fighting since 2004'.[1265] Human Rights Watch stated in 2013 that:

> The Pejuang Kemerdekaan Patani insurgents in the loose network of BRN Coordinate… are guided by a combination of extremist ethnic Malay nationalism and Islamist ideologies. They

[1260] 'Philippines Military Strength', *Globalfirepower.com*, last updated on 27 March 2014, at: <http://www.globalfirepower.com/country-military-strength-detail.asp?country_id=philippines>.

[1261] Hookway, J., 'Muslim Insurgents Widen Thailand Attacks', *Wall Street Journal*, Updated 28 February 2013, at: <http://online.wsj.com/article/SB10001424127887324906004578289220025564486.html>.

[1262] Cited in ibid.

[1263] Zawacki, B., 2012, 'Politically Inconvenient, Legally Correct: A Non-international Armed Conflict in Southern Thailand', *Journal of Conflict and Security Law*, 18 September 2012, p. 4.

[1264] Ibid., p. 6.

[1265] Amnesty International, 'They Took Nothing But His Life', Unlawful Killings in Thailand's Southern Insurgency, Doc. ASA 39/002/2011, 27 September 2011, p. 7, at: <http://www.amnesty.org/en/library/asset/ASA39/002/2011/en/bb43fb2e-dd43-49d5-b05c-824ae3d27049/asa390022011en.pdf>.

assert that Thailand's southern border provinces should be liberated from ethnic Thai Buddhists to create what they call Patani Darulsalam (Islamic Land of Patani). The insurgents use a campaign of violence and terror to oppose what they contend is an ethnic Thai Buddhist occupation. In this context, they do not tolerate the presence of the non-ethnic Malay Muslim population, and aim to drive out all Thai Buddhists, keep Malay Muslims under control, and discredit the Thai authorities.[1266]

The Pattani Independence Fighters (Pejuang Kemerdekaan Pattani) are village-level militants believed to be responsible for many of the recent attacks. Although doubts remain as to the level of their organization, they were believed to be a party to the NIAC with Thailand and its security forces in 2014.

CASUALTIES

There were at least 796 casualties in the armed conflict between Thailand and Pattani militants in the south of Thailand from 1 January 2014 to 31 August, according to Deep South Incident Database (DSID) monthly summary reporting. Of the total 251 people were killed and 545 injured. The majority of casualties, 488, were civilians. Civilian casualties included thirty-five children under the age of fifteen years, nine were killed and twenty-six injured, two Buddhist priests and one Muslim cleric were killed. Nine teachers and one student and seven foreigners were also among civilian casualties. Forty-six of the civilian casualties worked in various levels of government administration. From January through August DSID recorded 301 casualties, seventy-four killed, and 227 injured, among Thai security forces including police, military soldiers, and paramilitary (Rangers and Village Defense Volunteers). Five militant deaths were reported. In addition, for two casualties the civilian status was not reported.[1267]

The number of monthly casualties decreased from September on and the overall total casualty figures for calendar year 2014 were reported to be the lowest since 2004. In total there were at least 995 casualties, 330 people were killed, and another 665 injured, according to DSID annual summary reporting.[1268] Of the total deaths recorded by the DSID in 2014, seventy-nine security forces were killed and 268 police injured. Among

[1266] Human Rights Watch (HRW), 'Thailand: Insurgents Should Cease Attacks on Civilians', 14 February 2013, at: <http://www.hrw.org/news/2013/02/14/thailand-insurgents-should-cease-attacks-civilians>.

[1267] War Report analysis of statistics from monthly casualty reports. Deep South Watch, 'Deep South Incident Database', <http://www.deepsouthwatch.org/dsid>.

[1268] Deep South Incident Database (DSID), 'Statistics for the unrest in the southern provinces of the year 2557: the year with the fewest incidents in 11 years', as of 25 December 2014, 27 December 2014, <http://www.deepsouthwatch.org/node/6596&usg>.

civilian casualties 240 people were killed and 393 injured. There were ten insurgent fatalities.

Statistics released by the Royal Thai Police Southern Operations Centre for calendar year 2014 were similar to Deep South Watch data. The Centre noted that the situation had improved, with violent incidents declining in 2014 compared to 2013. Fatalities among security forces reported totalled sixty-eight representing a significant decrease of almost half from 129 in 2013. Eight insurgent fatalities were reported, marking a significant decrease from fifty-one in 2013. The Southern Operations Centre recorded 136 civilian fatalities.[1269]

DISPLACED

Overall in Thailand, there remained up to 35,000 Internally Displaced Persons (IDPs) as of the end of December 2014.[1270]

WAR CRIMES ALLEGATIONS, INVESTIGATIONS, AND PROSECUTIONS

Thailand has signed but not ratified the 1998 Rome Statute of the International Criminal Court.

In February 2013, Human Rights Watch declared that in February alone, insurgents:

> committed several deliberate attacks on civilians that amount to war crimes. On February 10, insurgents fired assault rifles at ethnic Thai Buddhist villagers in Pattani province's Nong Jik district, wounding four, including a 4-year-old girl. On February 5, insurgents in Krong Penang district of Yala province stormed the hut of four Thai Buddhist fruit traders, tied them up, and fatally shot them point-blank in the head and body with assault rifles and pistols. On February 1, insurgents attacked a group of Thai Buddhist rice farmers in Pattani province's Yaring district, killing two and seriously wounding 10 others.[1271]

[1269] 'Southern violence claims almost 4,000 people in 11 years, 5 January 2015', <http://englishnews.thaipbs.or.th/southern-violence-claims-almost-4000-people-11-years>; Thai Government Public Relations Office, 'Eleven Years of Efforts to Restore Peace in the Deep South', 7 January 2015, <http://thailand.prd.go.th/ewt_news.php?nid=111&filename=index>; and Davis, A., 'South Thai insurgency sees higher casualties in 2013, govt report says', *IHIS Jane's Defence Weekly*, 2 January 2014.

[1270] Internal Displacement Monitoring Center (IDMC), 'Global Overview 2015', May 2015, p. 87. The figure relies on 2007 data, the last credible information available. There are no UN or government figures.

[1271] HRW, 'Thailand: Insurgents Should Cease Attacks on Civilians', 14 February 2013.

Human Rights Watch expressed heightened concern about new abuses. After a failed attack on a Thai military camp in Narathiwat province on 13 February that left dead insurgent commander Maroso Chantrawadee and fifteen other militants, the insurgents issued a written warning against Thai Buddhist teachers and other civilians to avenge their losses. The leaflets, found in Narathiwat's Bacho district on 14 February said:

> We will retaliate in every way for our losses... From now on, we will attack and kill Buddhist Thai teachers and Buddhist Thai people. We will attack Buddhist Thai community... One Muslim life must be repaid with 10 Buddhist Thai lives.[1272]

In 2014, no investigation was initiated concerning the various attacks carried out by both parties to the conflict.

[1272] Ibid.

Armed conflicts in Ukraine in 2014

KEY CASUALTY DATA FOR 2014

Total Casualties:	14,428 Mid-April to 30 November 2014	(Source: UN OHCHR)
Total killed:	4,364 Mid-April to 30 November 2014	(Source: UN OHCHR)
Total injured:	10,064 Mid-April to 30 November 2014	(Source: UN OHCHR)
Ukrainian armed forces casualties:	4,975 Mid-April to 31 October 2014	(Source: UN OHCHR)
Ukrainian armed forces killed:	1,167 Mid-April to 31 October 2014	(Source: UN OHCHR)
Ukrainian armed forces injured:	3,808 Mid-April to 31 October 2014	(Source: UN OHCHR)
Other casualties (including civilians and members of armed groups):	8,119	
Other killed:	2,875 Mid-April to 31 October 2014	(Source: UN OHCHR)
Other injured:	5,542 Mid-April to 31 October 2014	(Source: UN OHCHR)
Donetsk killed:	1,719 Mid-April to 31 October 2014	(Source: UN OHCHR)
Donetsk injured:	2,797 Mid-April to 31 October 2014	(Source: UN OHCHR)
Luhansk killed:	858 Mid-April to 31 October 2014	(Source: UN OHCHR)
Luhansk injured:	2,745 Mid-April to 31 October 2014	(Source: UN OHCHR)
Foreign civilians killed:	298 (MH-17 flight)	(Source: UN OHCHR)
Children killed:	36 Mid-April to 31 October 2014	(Source: UN OHCHR)
Children injured:	102 Mid-April to 31 October 2014	(Source: UN OHCHR)
Russian military killed:	136–150	(Source: Media)

CLASSIFICATION OF THE CONFLICT

Ukraine was involved in two non-international armed conflicts (NIAC) in 2014 in which the armed forces of the Government of Ukraine were fighting against pro-Russian separatist armed groups which proclaimed themselves 'the Donetsk People's Republic' and the 'Luhansk People's Republic', in the east of the country. These conflicts meet the threshold for the application of the 1977 Additional Protocol II.

The ICRC has qualified the conflicts as NIACs on 23 July 2014.[1273]

[1273] The ICRC stated that: 'Fighting in eastern Ukraine continues to take its toll on civilians, and we urge all sides to comply with international humanitarian law, otherwise known as the law of armed conflict...These rules and principles apply to all parties to the non-international armed conflict in Ukraine, and impose restrictions on the means and methods of warfare that they may use', 'Ukraine: ICRC calls on all sides to respect international humanitarian law', 23 July 2014, at: <https://www.icrc.org/eng/resources/documents/news-release/2014/07-23-ukraine-kiev-call-respect-ihl-repatriate-bodies-malaysian-airlines.htm>.

There have been allegations on the presence of Russian armed groups in Ukraine, as well as their participation in combat operations. [1274] Questions on the level of control exercised by Russia on the armed groups were also raised.[1275] *The War Report* is not in the position to verify the veracity of these allegations and facts on the ground nor does it have enough information to attest of a level of control sufficient to meet the ICTY case law conditions[1276] to conclude that the conflict in Ukraine has been internationalized.[1277]

SUMMARY OF APPLICABLE INTERNATIONAL LAW

All parties to the conflict were bound by customary international humanitarian law (IHL) and human rights law, including customary IHL rules of distinction, proportionality, and precautions in attacks; the obligations of humane treatment, as set out in Common Article 3 to the 1949 Geneva Conventions; the obligation not to recruit and use children as soldiers; and by the duty to respect and protect fundamental human rights. This includes the duty to respect the rights to life and to freedom from torture or other forms of cruel, inhuman, or degrading treatment or punishment.

Ukraine is a State party to the four 1949 Geneva Conventions and the 1977 Additional Protocols to the 1966 International Covenant on Civil and Political Rights, as well as the 1950 European Convention on Human Rights and the 1987 Convention Against Torture. Ukraine has become a signatory party only in 2009 to the 1976 International Covenant on Economic, Social and Cultural Rights and has not yet ratified it.

[1274] See 'Ukraine Reports Russian Invasion on a New Front', *The New York Times*, 17 August 2014, at: <http://www.nytimes.com/2014/08/28/world/europe/ukraine-russia-novoazovsk-crimea.html?_r=2>; Swain, A., 'Further claims of Russian troop deployments follow capture of soldiers in Donetsk', the Conversation, 27 August 2014, at: <https://theconversation.com/further-claims-of-russian-troop-deployments-follow-capture-of-soldiers-in-donetsk-30945>; 'Russian military sources say soldiers crossed Ukraine border "by accident"', *The Times of India*, 26 August 2014, at: <http://timesofindia.indiatimes.com/World/Europe/Russian-military-sources-say-soldiers-crossed-Ukraine-border-by-accident/articleshow/40912541.cms>.

[1275] See 'Ukraine Leader Says "Huge Loads of Arms" Pour in From Russia', *The New York Times*, 28 August 2014, at: <http://www.nytimes.com/2014/08/29/world/europe/ukraine-conflict.html>.

[1276] The ICTY Appeals Judgment in *Tadic* stated that: '[C]ontrol by a State over subordinate armed forces or militias or paramilitary units may be of an overall character (and must comprise more than the mere provision of financial assistance or military equipment or training).... The control required by international law may be deemed to exist when a State (or, in the context of an armed conflict, the Party to the conflict) has a role in organising, coordinating or planning the military actions of the military group, in addition to financing, training and equipping or providing operational support to that group. Acts performed by the group or members thereof may be regarded as acts of de facto State organs regardless of any specific instruction by the controlling State concerning the commission of each of those acts', ICTY, *Prosecutor v Tadic*, Appeals Chamber, 15 July 1999, IT-94-I-A, para. 137.

[1277] See also the discussion by Noëlle Quenivet on the blog IntLawGrrls, 'Trying to Classify the Conflict in Eastern Ukraine', at: <http://ilg2.org/2014/08/28/trying-to-classify-the-conflict-in-eastern-ukraine/>.

Ukraine is a State party to the 1997 Anti-Personnel Mine Ban Convention since 27 December 2005. In accordance with the obligation under Article 5 of the Convention, on 29 December 2014 Ukraine indicated that all information related to the destruction of anti-personnel mines would be forthcoming later in 2015.[1278] A total of 5,584,371 anti-personnel mines remain to be destroyed.[1279] Ukraine is a party to the 1983 Convention on Certain Conventional Weapons and its Protocols.

Ukraine is neither a signatory nor a party to the 2008 Convention on Cluster Munitions, while it is a signatory party to the 2013 Arms Trade Treaty (ATT) since 23 September 2014.

Ukraine is neither a signatory nor a party to the Rome Statute of the International Criminal Court. However, on 17 April 2014, the Ukraine acting government lodged a declaration under Article 12(3) of the Rome Statute, accepting the Court's jurisdiction over the alleged crimes committed in its territory between 17 November 2013 and 22 February 2014.

Means and methods of warfare

Both sides in the conflict have reportedly made use of potentially indiscriminate weapons in populated areas. Such weapons included Grad rockets, cluster munitions, incendiary weapons, and explosive weapons with wide area effects.[1280]

Cluster munitions are munitions that are launched, dropped, or fired from the ground, the air, or the sea and that disperse or release sub-munitions or bomblets.[1281] These sub-munitions are typically small, unguided explosive devices that are designed to explode prior to, on, or after impact over a wide area normally the size of a football field. Depending on the model, the number of sub-munitions dispersed or released by a parent container can vary from several dozen to more than 600.

The use of ground-launched Smerch and Uragan cluster munition rockets with explosive sub-munitions was recorded in several parts of eastern Ukraine after June. While evidence suggests all parties may have used cluster munitions, there is particularly strong evidence that Ukrainian Government forces were responsible for several cluster munition attacks on central Donetsk in early October.[1282] In this respect, on 2 October 2014 an employee of the International Committee of the Red Cross (ICRC) was killed in

[1278] Ukraine Profile, Convention on the Prohibition of the Use, Stockpiling, Production and Transfer of Anti-Personnel Mines and on Their Destruction, at: <http://www.apminebanconvention.org/states-parties-to-the-convention/ukraine/>.

[1279] Ibid.

[1280] Human Rights Watch, World Report 2015, Section on Ukraine, at: <http://www.hrw.org/world-report/2015/country-chapters/ukraine>.

[1281] 'Cluster Munitions', *Weapons Law Encyclopaedia*, at: <http://www.weaponslaw.org/weapons/cluster-munitions>.

[1282] 'Ukraine: Widespread Use of Cluster Munitions. Government Responsible for Cluster Attacks on Donetsk', *Human Rights Watch*, news report, 20 October 2014 at: <http://www.hrw.org/news/2014/10/20/ukraine-widespread-use-cluster-munitions>.

an attack on Donetsk that included use of cluster munition rockets and which has been attributed to Ukrainian Government forces.[1283]

Grads are unguided rockets that cannot be targeted accurately and that should not be used in populated areas because of the likelihood of killing or wounding civilians.[1284] Both government and rebel forces, however, have made use of these weapons. As an example, Grad rockets launched by Ukrainian forces between 12 July and 21 July 2014 in the area of Donetsk have killed sixteen civilians and wounded many more.[1285] On the other hand, separatist rebel forces are believed to be responsible for two attacks in January 2015 which together killed at least forty-one civilians and wounded more than 100.[1286]

Incendiary weapons are any weapon or munition which is primarily designed to set fire to objects or to cause burn injury to persons through the action of flame, heat, or a combination thereof, produced by a chemical reaction of a substance delivered on the target.[1287] Evidence of use of incendiary weapons in Ukraine has been found in Donetsk in August and October 2014 by Human Rights Watch researchers.[1288]

HISTORY OF THE CONFLICT[1289]

Tensions in Ukraine began in 2013, after Russia halted imports from one of Ukraine's main confectionary makers, claiming that its products fell below safety standards, which, however, was seen as an act of retaliation for Ukraine's efforts to integrate further

[1283] Ibid.

[1284] On the use of Grads rockets in highly populated area, see Maya Brehm, 'Use of Grad Rockets in Populated Areas: What Lessons from Gotovina?', EJIL Talk, 30 July 2014, at: <http://www.ejiltalk.org/author/mbrehm/>.

[1285] 'Ukraine: Unguided Rockets Killing Civilians. Stop Use of Grads in Populated Area', *Human Rights Watch*, news report, 24 July 2014, at: <http://www.hrw.org/news/2014/07/24/ukraine-unguided-rockets-killing-civilians>.

[1286] 'Ukraine: Rising Civilian Death Toll. Unlawful Unguided Rocket Attacks on Populated Areas', *Human Rights Watch*, news report, 3 February 2015, at: <http://www.hrw.org/news/2015/02/03/ukraine-rising-civilian-death-toll>.

[1287] Art. 1(1), Protocol on Prohibitions or Restrictions on the Use of Incendiary Weapons (Protocol II) to the Convention on Conventional Weapons.

[1288] *Human Rights Watch and International Human Rights Clinic*, Incendiary Weapons: Recent Use and Growing Opposition Memorandum submitted to Convention on Conventional Weapons Delegates, November 2014, at: <http://www.hrw.org/sites/default/files/related_material/Incendiary%20Weapons_Recent%20Use%20and%20Growing%20Opposition_Nov2014_final.pdf>.

[1289] Unless otherwise stated this section is based on Crisis Watch Database on Ukraine, at: <http://www.crisisgroup.org/en/publication-type/crisiswatch/crisiswatch-database.aspx?CountryIDs=%7b8864A71C-2EC4-456D-A9BC-5E7190244489%7d>; and on 'Ukraine Profile', *BBC*, 18 February 2015, at: <http://www.bbc.com/news/world-europe-27308526>.

with the EU.[1290] On 21 November 2013, after the government's sudden decision to abandon the plans to sign an association agreement with the EU, tens of thousands of people took to the streets of central Kiev and other cities to protest against such decision, accusing the government of bowing to Russian pressure, as well as of being corrupt and unaccountable.[1291]

Consequently, on 18 December 2013, Russia announced the implementation of a $15 million aid package to help faltering Ukraine's economy, which included the lowering of Russian gas prices.[1292] Despite the new anti-protest laws passed by the government on 16 January 2015, which also amended the Criminal Code so as to restrict freedom of speech,[1293] violence escalated and in February 2014 members of security forces killed at least seventy-seven protesters in Kiev.[1294] Few days later, on 28 January 2014 the government resigned in an attempt to resolve the crisis while the Parliament first overturned the 16 January anti-protest law and, then, passed an amnesty law for the protesters.[1295]

Following further clashes with anti-government protesters, on the 21 February 2014, President Yanukovych and the opposition group agreed to form a new government and hold a new election under an EU-mediated deal. However, on 22 February, President Yanukovych fled the capital to Russia. As a result, the next day the Parliament elected the opposition leader Olexander Turchynov as interim president and issued an arrest warrant for Yanukovych.[1296]

[1290] 'Russia hits at Ukraine with chocolate war', *EurActiv*, 14 August 2013, at: <http://www.euractiv.com/europes-east/russia-hits-ukraine-chocolate-wa-news-529804>. See also 'Russia puts economic squeeze on Ukraine', *The Financial Times*, 20 March 2014, at: <http://www.ft.com/intl/cms/s/0/7ecbb1c4-b027-11e3-b0d0-00144feab7de.html#axzz3ZkT4mdnD>.

[1291] 'Ukraine protests after Yanukovych EU deal rejection', *BBC News*, 30 November 2013, at: <http://www.bbc.com/news/world-europe-25162563>. See also: 'Why is Ukraine in turmoil?', *BBC News*, 22 February 2014, at: <http://www.bbc.com/news/world-europe-25182823>.

[1292] 'Ukraine crisis: Parliament abolishes anti-protest law', *BBC News*, 28 January 2014, at: <http://www.bbc.com/news/world-europe-25923199>.

[1293] 'Ukraine's president signs anti-protest bill into law', *BBC News*, 17 January 2014, at: <http://www.bbc.com/news/world-europe-25771595>.

[1294] 'Ukraine crisis: deal signed in effort to end Kiev standoff', *The Guardian*, 22 February 2014, at: <http://www.theguardian.com/world/2014/feb/21/ukraine-crisis-president-claims-deal-with-opposition-after-77-killed-in-kiev>.

[1295] 'Ukraine president makes concession to protesters by scrapping anti-protest law', *The Guardian*, 27 January 2014, at: <http://www.theguardian.com/world/2014/jan/27/ukraine-president-scraps-anti-protest-laws>. See also: 'Ukraine crisis: Parliament abolishes anti-protest law', *BBC News*, 28 January 2014, at: <http://www.bbc.com/news/world-europe-25923199>.

[1296] 'Ukraine arrest warrant for fugitive Viktor Yanukovych', *BBC News*, 24 February 2014, at: <http://www.bbc.com/news/world-europe-26320004>.

Eastern Ukraine

After the annexation of Crimea by Russia on 21 March 2014,[1297] pro-Russian separatists seized control of over a dozen towns and cities in Eastern Ukraine leading to deadly clashes with Ukrainian armed forces. During the month of April, pro-Russian separatists occupied governmental buildings in Donetsk, Luhansk, and Kharkiv, demanding a referendum for greater autonomy and the right to join Russia. In response, the interim Prime Minister Yatsenyuk offered to devolve more powers to the eastern regions.[1298]

On 17 April 2014, the United States, Russia, the EU, and Ukraine gathered in Geneva in order to reach an agreement on the necessary steps to be taken to de-escalate the ongoing crisis, which, however, quickly broke down after the separatists occupying governmental buildings refused to leave.[1299]

Pro-Russian separatists seized the regional government headquarters in Luhansk on 29 April, and the next day, the acting President Turchynov announced that the government was no longer in control of Donetsk and Luhansk.[1300]

Although a build-up of Russian troops on the shared border in April sparked international concerns that another annexation could take place, the Russian Defence Minister Shoigu said Russia had no plans to invade Ukraine or to intervene in Eastern Ukraine.[1301]

On 11 May 2014, pro-Russian separatists in Donetsk and Luhansk declared their independence as 'People's Republics' after the referendums were held.[1302] Although the separatists announced that 90% of the people had voted in favour of the 'People's Republics', those were not recognized by Kiev or the West countries.

Presidential elections were held in Ukraine on 25 May 2014, which resulted in the election of the pro-western Petro Poroshenko as the president, who got more than 55% of the votes, although pro-Russian separatists prevented polling stations to be open in the Donetsk and Luhansk regions.[1303]

[1297] See in this volume, the Military Occupation by Russia of Crimea.

[1298] 'Ukraine leader Yatsenyuk offers powers to troubled east', *BBC News*, 11 April 2014, at: <http://www.bbc.com/news/world-europe-26984799>.

[1299] 'Ukraine crisis: Geneva talks produce agreement on defusing conflict', *The Guardian*, 17 April 2014, at: <http://www.theguardian.com/world/2014/apr/17/ukraine-crisis-agreement-us-russia-eu>.

[1300] 'Ukraine's government has lost control of east, says acting president', *The Guardian*, 30 April 2014, at: <http://www.theguardian.com/world/2014/apr/30/ukraine-government-lost-control- east-acting-president>.

[1301] 'Russian defense minister reassures US colleague on Ukraine', *Russian News Agency*, 29 April 2014, at: <http://tass.ru/en/world/729883>.

[1302] 'As Ukrainian separatists claim victory in self-rule vote, fears of all-out civil war mount', *The Washington Post*, 12 May 2014, at: <http://www.washingtonpost.com/world/europe/separatists-claim-victory-in-eastern-ukraine-kremlin-calls-for-talks-with-kiev-government/2014/05/12/135ceba9-824c-486d-98e1-e1aa49627fa3_story.html>.

[1303] 'Pro-European Businessman Claims Victory in Ukraine Presidential Vote', *The New York Times*, 25 May 2014, at: <http://www.nytimes.com/2014/05/26/world/europe/ukraine-elections.html?_r=0>.

On 20 June 2014, President Poroshenko announced a fifteen-point peace plan and declared a week-long ceasefire. The President demanded the rebels' disarmament and offered a safety corridor to Russia and freedom from prosecution in absence of 'serious crimes' for disarmed rebels; he called for a buffer zone along the border, proposed to hold early elections, decentralization and full Russian language rights.[1304] The ceasefire broke when a military helicopter was shot down over Eastern Ukraine later in the month.

On 27 June, the government signed the Association Agreement with the EU, which was later ratified on 16 September 2014.

On 17 July 2014, Malaysia Airlines flight MH17 from Amsterdam is shot down near the village of Grabove, over the Donetsk region, reportedly by Russian-made SA-11 surface-to-air missile, killing all 298 passengers on board.[1305] While pro-Russian rebels denied any involvement in the accident, pressure increased on Russia as the EU and the United States announced further sanctions, including economic ones in late July.[1306]

Violence escalated between government forces and pro-Russian rebels as the Ukrainian army attempted to encircle Donetsk and Luhansk. Reportedly, Russia stepped up to support the rebels by deploying Russian troops inside Ukraine. According to NATO, there were over 1,000 Russian troops in Ukraine and 20,000 near the border.[1307]

On August 2014, Russia sent a humanitarian aid convoy into Ukraine without the Ukrainian Government's permission while Russian President Vladimir Putin publicly congratulated the rebel forces on the latest offensives.[1308] According to NATO Secretary General Rasmussen, Russian troops were directly attacking Ukrainian forces with 'artillery support' both across the border and from within Ukraine.[1309]

[1304] 'Ukraine crisis: Details of Poroshenko's peace plan emerge', *BBC News*, 20 June 2014, at: <http://www.bbc.com/news/world-europe-27937596>.

[1305] 'Malaysia Airlines plane MH17 'shot down' in Ukraine—as it happened', *The Guardian*, 17 July 2014, at: <http://www.theguardian.com/world/2014/jul/17/malaysia-airlines-plane-crashes-ukraine-live>. See also 'Downing of MH17 jet in Ukraine "may be war crime"—UN', *BBC News*, 28 July 2014 at: <http://www.bbc.com/news/world-europe-28520813>; on some of the legal aspects of the attack, see Gibney, M., 2015, 'The Downing of MH17: Russian Responsibility', *Human Rights Law Review*, vol. 15, pp. 169–178.

[1306] 'EU and US announce new sanctions on Russia over Ukraine', *Reuters*, 29 July 2014, at <http://www.reuters.com/article/2014/07/29/us-ukraine-crisis-east-idUSKBN0FY0OX20140729>.

[1307] 'Russia has "well over 1,000 troops" in Ukraine, Nato warns', *Financial Times*, 29 August 2014, at: <http://www.ft.com/intl/cms/s/0/8275bec4-2ea2-11e4-afe4-00144feabdc0.html#slide0>. See also: 'More than 1,000 Russian troops operating in Ukraine: NATO', *Reuters*, 28 August 2014, at: <http://www.reuters.com/article/2014/08/28/us-ukraine-crisis-nato-idUSKBN0GS1D220140828>.

[1308] 'Praising Rebels, Putin Toughens Tone on Ukraine', *The New York Times*, 29 August 2014, at: <http://www.nytimes.com/2014/08/30/world/europe/ukraine-conflict.html?_r=0>. See also: 'Putin Directly Addressed Rebels In Ukraine For The First Time, And He Used A Frightening Word To Describe Them', *Business Insider*, 29 August 2014, at: <http://www.businessinsider.com/putin-addresses-pro-russia-rebels-in-ukraine-2014-8#ixzz3ZqcfrE4N>.

[1309] 'NATO: Russian Forces Provide Artillery Support To Rebels In Ukraine', *The Huffington Post*, 22 August 2014, at: <http://www.huffingtonpost.com/2014/08/22/russia-artillery-ukraine_n_5700598.html>.

After having agreed a ceasefire with the rebels, on 16 September 2014 the Ukrainian Parliament passed a law allowing a certain degree of self-government to the breakaway regions, which raised the concern that it could amount to a de facto recognition of independence.[1310]

On 26 October 2014 parliamentary elections were held and a new pro-EU Parliament was elected, although the polls were once more boycotted by the rebels in the East.[1311]

NATO Commander declared that Russian military equipment had been seen entering Ukrainian territory in early November and NATO Chief Stoltenberg urged Russia to pull back its forces.[1312]

Meanwhile, on 2 November 2014 separatists in Eastern Ukraine held their own elections for the head of State of the self-proclaimed People's Republics in Donetsk and Luhansk, which resulted in the victory of two pro-Russian leaders. While Kiev and Western States said the polls were illegitimate, Russia declared it respected the election's outcome.[1313]

On 26 December 2014, Russian President Putin implemented a new Russian military doctrine stating that the country faced threats from foreign nations installing hostile governments in neighbouring countries.[1314]

At the beginning of 2015, fighting between the army and the rebels intensified in and around Donetsk, as well as in Luhansk region resulting in heavy civilian and military casualties and further undermining the peace talks.[1315] In January, the separatist leader Alexander Zakharchenko announced a plan to take control of the entire Donetsk province.[1316] Accordingly, Kiev accused Russia of sending troops into

[1310] 'Kiev Offers "Special Status" for Breakaway Regions', *The New York Times*, 15 September 2014, at: <http://www.nytimes.com/2014/09/16/world/europe/ukraine-conflict.html>.

[1311] 'Exit polls in Ukraine's parliamentary elections show win for pro-Western blocs', *The Washington Post*, 26 October 2014, at: <http://www.washingtonpost.com/world/europe/exit-polls-in-ukraines-parliamentary-elections-show-win-for-pro-western-blocs/2014/10/26/e5ac0484-5d1a-11e4-827b-2d813561bdfd_story.html>.

[1312] 'NATO: Russia sending forces into Ukraine', *Al Jazeera*, 12 November 2014, at: <http://www.aljazeera.com/news/europe/2014/11/nato-russian-troops-ukraine-now-2014111214105962679.html>.

[1313] 'Pro-Russia separatists hold leadership elections in two Ukraine enclaves', *The Guardian*, 2 November 2014, at: <http://www.theguardian.com/world/2014/nov/02/russia-elections-ukraine-donetsk-lugansk>.

[1314] 'New Russian military doctrine says NATO top threat', *The Daily Mail*, 26 December 2014, at: <http://www.dailymail.co.uk/wires/ap/article-2887762/New-Russian-military-doctrine-says-NATO-threat.html#ixzz3ZqfN7FkX>.

[1315] 'Ukraine conflict: Battles rage in Donetsk and Luhansk', *BBC News*, 19 January 2014, at: <http://www.bbc.com/news/world-europe-30878406>.

[1316] 'Zakharchenko threatens full-scale war, says militants plan to take over all Donetsk region', *Unian News*, 23 January 2015, at: <http://www.unian.info/war/1035430-zaharchenko-threatens-full-scale-war-says-militants-plan-to-take-over-all-donetsk-region.html>.

Ukraine as well as of providing weapons and military training for separatists in Russia.[1317]

On 12 February 2015 after peace talks took place in Minsk, Russia, Ukraine, Germany, and France announced that an agreement had been reached to end the fighting and that a ceasefire would begin on 15 February. The deal also included weapons withdrawals and prisoner exchanges.[1318] The pro-Russian rebels in eastern Ukraine also signed the agreement, which included a buffer zone for heavy weapons, with a minimum of 50 kilometres between rival forces' artillery (140 kilometres for rockets).

However, despite the ceasefire, heavy fighting continued around Debaltseve.[1319]

PARTIES TO THE CONFLICTS

The parties to the NIACs were the Ukrainian armed forces against pro-Russian separatist armed groups.

Ukraine armed forces

According to the bill 'On the strength of the Armed Forces of Ukraine in 2013' signed by ex-president Yanukovych, as of 31 December the army of Ukraine had 125,482 personnel. However, on 11 March 2014 Admiral Ihor Tenuikh made a public statement declaring that de facto only 6,000 soldiers were in 'combat readiness'.[1320]

In July 2014, Ukrainian security forces estimated the government forces around 50,000 nationwide.[1321]

At present, the armament of the Ukrainian Army is 90–95% worn out or outdated. New equipment and armament is present in exceedingly small quantities and, coincidentally, it is supplied by manufacturers located predominantly in the East of Ukraine.[1322]

[1317] 'Kiev accuses Russia of sending more tanks to east Ukraine', *Reuters*, 20 February 2015, at: <http://www.reuters.com/article/2015/02/20/us-ukraine-crisis-idUSKBN0LO13420150220>.

[1318] 'Ukraine ceasefire agreed at Belarus talks', *The Guardian*, 12 February 2015, at: <http://www.theguardian.com/world/2015/feb/12/ukraine-crisis-reports-emerge-of-agreement-in-minsk-talks>.

[1319] 'Ukraine crisis: Battle rages for Debaltseve despite truce', *BBC News*, 17 February 2015, at: <http://www.bbc.com/news/world-europe-31495099>.

[1320] 'In the Army Now: Answering Many Why's', *The Ukranian Week*, 8 July 2014, at: <http://ukrainianweek.com/Politics/115444>.

[1321] Ukraine Profile, *Crisis Watch Database*, 1 August 2014, at: <http://www.crisisgroup.org/en/publication-type/crisiswatch/crisiswatch-database.aspx?CountryIDs={8864A71C-2EC4-456D-A9BC-5E7190244489}#results>.

[1322] 'In the Army Now: Answering Many Why's', *The Ukrainian Week*, 8 July 2014, at: <http://ukrainianweek.com/Politics/115444>.

'The Donetsk People's Republic' and the 'Luhansk People's Republic'

In July 2014, Ukrainian security sources estimated the rebels' strength to be in a range between 6,000 and 20,000 fighters.[1323]

Amid the escalating hostilities, the insurgents announced a call-up of new volunteer recruits in Donetsk, following a pledge by Alexander Zakharchenko, Prime Minister of the self-declared Donetsk People's Republic (DPR), to strengthen his forces to 100,000 men.[1324] In August 2014, Zakharchenko linked the rebels in Donetsk with those in Luhansk, stating that they were in possession of '150 combat vehicles, of which about 30 are actual tanks and the rest are infantry fighting vehicles and armoured personnel carriers, and 1,200 personnel who underwent four months of military training on the territory of the Russian Federation'.[1325]

CASUALTIES

A total of 14,428 casualties were reported in the conflict area of eastern Ukraine by the UN Office of the High Commissioner for Human Rights (OHCHR) from the beginning of the armed conflict period in mid-April to 30 November 2014,[1326] including 4,364 people killed and 10,064 injured.[1327] The total casualty count produced by the UN OHCHR was reported to be 'a conservative estimate by the [UN Human Rights Monitoring Mission in Ukraine] HRMMU and the World Health Organization (WHO) based on the available official data'.[1328]

[1323] Ukraine Profile, *Crisis Watch Database*, 1 August 2014, at: <http://www.crisisgroup.org/en/publication-type/crisiswatch/crisiswatch-database.aspx?CountryIDs={8864A71C-2EC4-456D-A9BC-5E7190244489}#results>; See also CNN, Who are Ukraine's pro-Russian rebels, 23 July 2014, at: <http://edition.cnn.com/2014/07/22/world/europe/ukraine-rebels-explainer/>.

[1324] 'Ukraine troops, pro-Russia rebels intensify clashes', *CBS News*, 10 February 2015, at: <http://www.cbsnews.com/news/ukraine-troops-pro-russia-rebels-intensify-clashes/>.

[1325] 'Ukraine Crisis: Rebel Fighters "Trained in Russia"', *BBC News*, 16 August 2014, at: <http://www.bbc.com/news/world-europe-28817347>.

[1326] No end of year reporting was available and subsequent OHCHR reporting crosses over the annual period. It included casualties which occurred between 1 December 2014 and 15 February 2015, with at least 1,012 people were killed and at least 3,793 were wounded in the conflict area of eastern Ukraine in that period. A massive escalation of hostilities (13 January–15 February) resulted in at least 842 of those deaths. OHCHR, 'Report on the human rights situation in Ukraine 1 December 2014 to 15 February 2015', <http://reliefweb.int/sites/reliefweb.int/files/resources/9thOHCHRreportUkraine.pdf>.

[1327] OHCHR, 'Report on the human rights situation in Ukraine 15 December 2014', p. 8. <http://www.ohchr.org/Documents/Countries/UA/OHCHR_eighth_report_on_Ukraine.pdf>.

[1328] 'Office of the United Nations High Commissioner for Human Rights Report on the human rights situation in Ukraine 15 November 2014', <http://www.ohchr.org/Documents/Countries/UA/OHCHR_seventh_reportUkraine20.11.14.pdf>.

The actual numbers of casualties are likely to be higher as both military and civilian casualties remained under reported. Over 1,000 bodies delivered to morgues in the conflict zone remain unidentified, and many sites had not been searched to recover all remains due to continued fighting and insecurity.[1329] Many people killed (especially members of armed groups) were buried without being taken to morgues. Hundreds of people were considered missing with numerous bodies pending recovery and identification, according to OHCHR reporting.[1330]

In UN OHCHR data medical establishments and local administrations reported civilians and members of armed groups without noting their participation in hostilities. In the period for which details were available, from mid-April to 31 October 2014, at least 2,875 people (including civilians and members of armed groups) were killed and 5,542 others were injured in Eastern Ukraine. This included at least 1,719 people killed and 2,797 injured in the Donetsk region (approximately 15% of casualties in the Donetsk region were reported to be women); at least 858 killed and 2,745 injured in the Luhansk region; and the 298 passengers of flight MH17 which were also included in this total.[1331]

The OHCHR casualty total for Ukrainian Armed Forces was taken from statistics reported by the National Security and Defence Council, the Prosecutor-General, the Chief Military Prosecutor, and the Ministry of Foreign Affairs. It was not reported however if this total included personnel from militia merged into the regular forces, such as the Azov Battalion and Donbas Battalion, or the Right Sector Volunteer Corps. Whereas, Ukrainian media reports clearly include Right Sector Volunteer Corps casualties among their tally of total military casualties.[1332] The Kyiv post reported in September 2014 that 'The Right Sector's Ukrainian volunteer corps is recognized as an unofficial military unit, but it is not subordinated to any government agencies'.[1333]

1329 OHCHR, 'Report on the human rights situation in Ukraine 15 December 2014', p. 8. <http://www.ohchr.org/Documents/Countries/UA/OHCHR_eighth_report_on_Ukraine.pdf>. No end of year reporting was available and subsequent OHCHRs cross over the annual period.

1330 OHCHR, 'Report on the human rights situation in Ukraine 1 December 2014 to 15 February 2015,' <http://reliefweb.int/sites/reliefweb.int/files/resources/9thOHCHRreportUkraine.pdf>.

1331 OHCHR, 'Report on the human rights situation in Ukraine 15 November 2014, <http://www.ohchr.org/Documents/Countries/UA/OHCHR_seventh_reportUkraine20.11.14.pdf>.

1332 See, for example, 'Right Sector' (or 'Praviy Sector') forces counted in the following casualty tallies: 'At least 955 Ukrainian soldiers killed in Russia's war against Ukraine,' 25 September 2014, <https://www.kyivpost.com/content/ukraine/at-least-955-ukrainian-soldiers-killed-in-russias-war-against-ukraine-365976.html>; and at least 1,184 soldiers killed in Russia's war against Ukraine, 27 November 2014, <http://www.kyivpost.com/content/ukraine/at-least-1184-soldiers-killed-in-russias-war-against-ukraine-373390.html>.

1333 'Tough but kind: Right Sector waging war,' 12 September 2014, <http://www.kyivpost.com/content/ukraine/tough-but-kind-right-sector-waging-war-364440.html>.

The number of Russian (citizen) military casualties was speculated, with no concrete or reliable cumulative statistics available.[1334] Estimates vary widely. In September 2014 one source claimed 3,500–4,000 Russian soldiers had been killed.[1335] In March 2015, the US Assistant Secretary of State for European and Eurasian Affairs claimed that 400–500 Russian military personnel had been killed in eastern Ukraine.[1336] In reply to parliamentary inquiries regarding the reported combat deaths of Russian soldiers abroad, Russian military authorities the Military Prosecutors office was reported to have responded: 'The circumstances of death of each of the servicemen indicated in the appeal outside their permanent base is being verified at the present time under the procedure established by the Code of Criminal Procedures. With that aim, highly-qualified specialists have conducted autopsies.'[1337]

At least 136 Russian military personnel killed during the Ukraine armed conflict were listed on the Ukrainian Wikipedia website, with details including name rank, regiment, and region of origin in Russia.[1338] A Russian report released in May 2015 asserted that at least 150 Russian military personnel were killed during a Ukrainian offensive in August 2014.[1339] It is not known how many Russian citizens are included among the casualty totals reported by OHCHR and therefore these casualties have not been added to the cumulative total.

On 2 October an ICRC staff member was killed in Donetsk.[1340] Human Rights Watch (HRW) found that the death of the ICRC delegate occurred in an attack on Donetsk that included the use of cluster munition rockets.[1341] The Committee to Protect Journalists (CPJ) recorded four Ukrainian journalists killed in 2014.[1342]

[1334] 'Russia Denies Ukraine War Role as Soldiers Return in Coffins,' 12 September 2014, <http://www.huffingtonpost.com/2014/09/12/russia-ukraine-soldiers-coffins_n_5809116.html>.

[1335] '3,500 Russian Soldiers Died in Putin's War in Ukraine, Rights Activists Say,' 15 September 2014, <http://www.interpretermag.com/3500-russian-soldiers-died-in-putins-war-in-ukraine-rights-activists-say>.

[1336] 'Nuland says 400-500 Russian soldiers killed in eastern Ukraine,' 10 March 2015, <http://www.kyivpost.com/content/ukraine/us-claims-400-500-russian-soldiers-killed-in-eastern-ukraine-383079.html>.

[1337] 'Russian Legislators Receive Responses from Military Officials on Soldiers Reportedly Killed in Combat in Ukraine,' 11 November 2014, <http://www.interpretermag.com/russia-update-legislators-receive-responses-from-military-officials-on-soldiers-reportedly-killed-in-combat-in-ukraine>.

[1338] 'Russian soldiers who died as a result of the Russian invasion of Ukraine (2014),' <http://uk.wikipedia.org/wiki/Російські_військовослужбовці,_що_загинули_внаслідок_російського_вторгнення_в_Україну_(2014)>.

[1339] 'Nemtsov Report Says More Than 200 Russian Soldiers Killed In Ukraine War', 15 May 2015: <http://www.rferl.org/content/russia-nemtsov-report-ukraine-war/27011532.html>; see *Putin. War*, May 2015, <http://www.putin-itogi.ru/putin-voina/>.

[1340] 'Ukraine: ICRC Delegate Killed in Donetsk,' 2 October 2014, <https://www.icrc.org/en/document/ukraine-icrc-delegate-killed-donetsk#.VHvg6cmfZdl>.

[1341] 'Ukraine: Widespread Use of Cluster Munitions,' 20 October 2014, <http://www.hrw.org/news/2014/10/20/ukraine-widespread-use-cluster-munitions>.

[1342] CPJ, '11 Journalists Killed in Ukraine/Motive Confirmed,' <https://cpj.org/killed/europe/ukraine>.

Two aid workers were killed in Ukraine in 2014, at least one during aerial bombardment.[1343]

DISPLACED

There was a total of at least 646,500 internal displaced persons (IDPs) in Ukraine as of December 2014, all were newly displaced during 2014, which marked the first year that displacement was recorded in Ukraine by the Internal Displacement Monitoring Centre (IDMC). There were 50,000 returned IDPs during 2014. The IDMC reported figures were based on official IDP registration statistics from Ukraine's State Emergency Service. The totals also include some unregistered IDPs who had approached authorities and NGOs for assistance and an estimated 17,000 IDPs within Crimea reported by UNHCR.[1344]

WAR CRIMES ALLEGATIONS, INVESTIGATIONS, AND PROSECUTIONS

On 17 April 2014, the Government of Ukraine lodged a declaration under Article 12(3) of the Rome Statute accepting the jurisdiction of the International criminal Court (ICC) over alleged crimes committed on its territory from 21 November 2013 to 22 February 2014.[1345]

On 25 April 2014 ICC Prosecutor Fatou Bensouda opened a preliminary investigation into allegations of crimes against humanity in the country.[1346]

At the domestic level, Kiev authorities opened a criminal investigation in September 2014, into alleged crimes by the pro-Kiev Aydar battalion, which have reportedly included arbitrary detention, enforced disappearances, and torture.[1347]

On May 2015, the Office of the United Nations High Commissioner for Human Rights issued its report on the human rights situation in Ukraine, alleging the scale of the human rights abuses in the country might amount to war crimes. [1348]

[1343] The Aid Worker Security Database, 'Security incident data ', <https://aidworkersecurity.org/incidents>.

[1344] IDMC, 'Global Overview 2015', May 2015, p. 87.

[1345] See ICC, Ukraine, at: <http://www.icccpi.int/en_menus/icc/structure%20of%20the%20court/office%20of%20the%20prosecutor/comm%20and%20ref/pe-ongoing/ukraine/Pages/ukraine.aspx>.

[1346] 'ICC Opens Preliminary Investigation into Alleged Ukraine Crimes', *Jurist*, 25 April 2014, at: <http://jurist.org/paperchase/2014/04/icc-opens-preliminary-investigation-into-alleged-ukraine-crimes.php>.

[1347] Human Rights Watch, *World Report 2015*, Section on Ukraine, at: <http://www.hrw.org/world-report/2015/country-chapters/ukraine>.

[1348] Available at: <http://www.ohchr.org/Documents/Countries/UA/10thOHCHRreportUkraine.pdf>.

Armed conflict in Yemen in 2014

KEY CASUALTY DATA FOR 2014

Total killed:	over 7,000 (estimate)	(All sources: Abaad Studies and Research Centre)
Civilians killed:	1,200 (estimate)	
Houthi killed:	5,000 (estimate)	
AQAP killed:	400–500 (estimate)	
Yemen military killed:	1,000 (estimate)	

CLASSIFICATION OF THE CONFLICT

Yemen and its armed forces continued to be involved in a non-international armed conflict (NIAC) with Houthi rebels in the North and with Al-Qaeda in the Arabian Peninsula (AQAP) in the South of Yemen in 2014. The conflict met the threshold for applicability of the 1977 Additional Protocol II. There was also a non-international armed conflict between the Houthi and AQAP.

SUMMARY OF APPLICABLE INTERNATIONAL LAW

Both parties to the conflict were bound by customary international humanitarian law (IHL) and human rights law, including customary IHL rules of distinction, proportionality, and precautions in attacks; the obligations of humane treatment, as set out in Common Article 3 to the 1949 Geneva Conventions; the obligation not to recruit and use children as soldiers; and by the duty to respect and protect fundamental human rights. This includes the duty to respect the rights to life and to freedom from torture or other forms of cruel, inhuman, or degrading treatment or punishment.

Yemen is a State party to the four 1949 Geneva Conventions and the 1977 Additional Protocol II. Yemen is party to both the 1966 International Covenant on Civil and Political Rights and the 1966 International Covenant on Economic, Social and Cultural Rights. Yemen is a signatory party to the Rome Statute of the International Criminal Court since 2000, but has not yet ratified it.

Yemen is a State party to the 1997 Anti-Personnel Mine Ban Convention. Under Article 5 of the Convention and in accordance with the five-year extension granted in 2008, Yemen is required to destroy all antipersonnel mines in mined areas under its jurisdiction or control as soon as possible, but not later than 1 March 2015. In

December 2013, Yemen submitted a request for a second five-year extension until 1 March 2020.

Yemen is neither signatory nor party to the 2008 Convention on Cluster Munitions or the 2013 Arms Trade Treaty (ATT).[1349]

HISTORY OF THE CONFLICT[1350]

Conflict between Yemeni forces and Houthi rebels began in 2004. Husain al-Houthi founded the Believing Youth movement in the 1990s, aimed at reviving Zaidi Islam, a branch of Shi'ism found mainly in Yemen, to counter growing fundamentalist Sunni trends in the northern Yemeni governorates where Zaidis dominate. The conflict began as isolated clashes between the Believing Youth movement (Houthis) and the army in Sa'da.[1351]

Since the clashes of 2004, there have been periods of sustained fighting, mostly in the countryside, but escalating in June 2008 to the outskirts of Sanaa. In August 2009, the government launched a major offensive against the Houthis in the Sa'da and Amran provinces, backed by air strikes and artillery fire and resulting in some of the fiercest fighting. Dozens were reportedly killed on both sides, including Houthi leaders and civilians.[1352] An estimated 200,000 persons were reportedly displaced from their homes in the northern governorates in 2009–10.[1353]

Furthermore, the conflict acquired a regional dimension, with the Yemeni authorities accusing Iran of backing the Houthis, while the Houthis accused Saudi Arabia of supporting the Yemeni Government. In October 2009, clashes broke out between the Houthis and Saudi security forces along the border of the two countries. On 4 November 2009, Houthis reportedly fought their way across the border into Saudi Arabia and took 'full control' of a mountainous section of the border region of Jabal al-Dukhan.[1354]

[1349] Yemen voted in favour of the adoption of the ATT by the United Nations (UN) General Assembly on 2 April 2013.

[1350] Unless otherwise stated this section is based on 'Yemen Profile', *BBC*, 28 March 2015, at: <http://www.bbc.com/news/world-middle-east-14704852>.

[1351] Human Rights Watch, *Disappearances and Arbitrary Arrests in the Armed Conflict with Houthi Rebels in Yemen*, 24 October 2008, pp. 10–12, at: <www.hrw.org/en/reports/2008/10/24/disappearances-and-arbitrary-arrests-armed-conflict-Houthi-rebels-yemen-0>.

[1352] *A Critical War in a Fragile Country: Yemen's Battle with the Shiite al Houthi Rebels*, Critical Threats, 31 August 2009, at: <http://www.criticalthreats.org/yemen/critical-war-fragile-country-yemens-battle-shiite-al-houthi-rebels>.

[1353] Office of the UN High Commissioner for Refugees (UNHCR), 'More than 200,000 displaced by the conflict in Yemen', Press release, 12 January 2010, at: <http://www.unhcr.se/en/media/press-releases/artikel/8e6a57b4a95019884040a369d1ead582/more-than-200000-displaced-by-the-c.html>.

[1354] Ploughshares, *Yemen (2004–first combat deaths)*, March 2012, at: <http://ploughshares.ca/pl_armedconflict/yemen-2004-first-combat-deaths/>.

A ceasefire seemed to have been reached between the Yemeni Government and the Houthis in February 2010, though episodes of violence continued to occur sporadically.[1355] An estimated 200,000 persons were displaced from their homes in the northern governorates in 2009–10.[1356] In 2011–12, the Houthis continued fighting against tribal militia, gaining control of various towns and villages near the northern Syrian border.[1357]

Violence continued in 2013, with increasing fighting between Houthis and Salafi fighters in the north as well as against Government forces. On 8 June 2013, ten people were killed and dozens wounded when the security services fired on Houthis demonstrating outside the National Security Bureau in Sana'a to demand the release of political prisoners and the disbanding of intelligence agency. The incident significantly escalated tensions between Houthis and the Government of President Abdrabuh Mansour Hadi.[1358]

In subsequent months, fighting increased in intensity between Houthis and various opposing groups in Amran, Sa'da, and Ibb, which killed dozens. A series of truces were agreed in mid to late 2013 and early 2014 but none held for long.[1359] On 24 April 2014, the UN Secretary-General's Special Adviser to Yemen, Jamal Benomar, said President Hadi and the Houthis had agreed to discuss Houthi disarmament.[1360]

In the beginning of May, following two attacks which killed around fifty people, President Hadi stated that Yemen was engaged in an 'open war' with Al-Qaeda, and that military operations will expand so as to include the areas of Baida and Marib.[1361]

Between June and August various ceasefires were agreed between the government and Houthis rebels, but they all collapsed as the Houthis took control of Amran first, on 8 July 2014, and then reached the capital, Sana'a, on 21 September.[1362] Since then, the Houthis have been patrolling the streets, operating checkpoints, controlling access to some government buildings and establishing themselves as the country's power-brokers.[1363] An example is the case of Amran, where they occupied

1355 CNN, 'Yemeni Cease-Fire Breached', 13 February 2010, at: <http://edition.cnn.com/2010/WORLD/meast/02/13/yemen.violence/index.html?_s=PM:WORLD>.

1356 UNHCR, 'More than 200,000 displaced by the conflict in Yemen', Press release, 12 January 2010.

1357 Ploughshares, *Yemen (2004–first combat deaths)*, March 2012.

1358 International Crisis Group (ICG), Crisis Watch: Yemen, 1 July 2013, at: <http://www.crisisgroup.org/en/publication-type/crisiswatch/crisiswatch-database.aspx>.

1359 'Conflict in Yemen's North Threatens Political Transition', *IRIN*, 24 February 2014, at: <http://www.irinnews.org/report/99697/conflict-in-yemen-s-north-threatens-political-transition>.

1360 ICG, Crisis Watch: Yemen, 1 May 2014.

1361 ICG, Crisis Watch: Yemen, 1 June 2014.

1362 Yemen Profile, *BBC*, 19 January 2015, at: <http://www.bbc.com/news/world-middle-east-14704852>.

1363 'Yemen is Being Reshaped by Rebellion and Intrigue', *The Guardian*, 9 October 2014, at: <http://www.theguardian.com/commentisfree/2014/oct/09/yemen-rebellion-intrigue-syria-iraq>.

government infrastructure and set up courts and prisons, taking over government functions and powers.[1364]

Despite the fact that on 21 September a ceasefire had been agreed upon, Huthi forces took control of large parts of Red Sea Coast including strategic port of Hodeidah and then moved South of Sana'a where they clashed with armed fighters affiliated with Al-Qaeda in late 2014.[1365]

On 7 January 2015, AQAP claimed responsibility for the terrorist attack to the satirical magazine *Charlie Hebdo* in Paris. On 22 January 2015, President Abdrabuh Mansour Hadi and his Government resigned and were put under house arrest.[1366] On 21 February, President Hadi fled from Sana'a and escaped first to Aden and then to Riyadh in March, after calling on the UN Security Council to authorize an intervention in Yemen under Chapter VII of the UN Charter.

On 15 February 2015 the UNSC, however, only called on Huthis to relinquish control of State institutions and to release the president and the ministers from their house arrest.

On 27 March 2015, a coalition of ten countries led by Saudi Arabia and backed by the US, launched 'Operation Decisive Storm', a countrywide air campaign against the Huthis with the aim at restoring President Hadi's Government.[1367] The campaign has been seen as reflecting the growing fears of Sunni Arab States at Iran's growing influence in Yemen, Iraq, Syria, and Lebanon.[1368]

PARTIES TO THE CONFLICT

The parties to the NIAC in 2014 were Yemen and its armed forces against the Houthi rebels and AQAP. The United States are also a party in this conflict, conducting air strikes operations mainly against Al-Qaeda, with the consent of the Yemeni Government.

At this stage it is not possible to consider Iran as a party to the NIAC. Although Iran is providing extensive material, financial, training and logistical assistance to the

[1364] Letter dated 20 February 2015 from the Panel of Experts on Yemen established pursuant to Security Council resolution 2140 (2014) addressed to the President of the Security Council, S/2015/125, 20 February 2015, at: <http://www.un.org/en/ga/search/view_doc.asp?symbol=S/2015/125>.

[1365] Amnesty International Report 2014/2015, 'The State of the World's Human Rights', at <https://www.amnesty.org/en/documents/pol10/0001/2015/en/>.

[1366] 'Yemen President Quits Amid Worsening Crisis', *Al Jazeera*, 22 January 2015, at: <http://www.aljazeera.com/news/middleeast/2015/01/yemen-president-resigns-amid-political-crisis-2015122135030512445.html>.

[1367] ICG, Crisis Watch: Yemen, 1 April 2015.

[1368] 'Air strike on Yemeni refugee camp by Saudi-led coalition kills at least 40', *The Guardian*, 30 March 2015, at: <http://www.theguardian.com/world/2015/mar/30/air-strike-refugee-camp-houthi-controlled-northern-yemen-kills-at-least-21>.

Houti rebels,[1369] to the point that US Secretary of State, John Kerry, accused Iran of 'contributing' to the Houthis' takeover in Yemen,[1370] such contribution cannot yet be regarded as 'overall control', as required by the Tadic jurisprudence of the ICTY.

Yemeni armed forces

The Yemeni armed forces are estimated to be 66,700 strong, with 71,200 reservists.[1371] In April 2013, UN Secretary-General Ban Ki-moon welcomed President Hadi's efforts to restructure the nation's security sector, in particular the armed forces 'with a view to integrating them under unified, national and professional leadership and command based on the rule of law'.[1372]

Houthi rebels

Al-Houthi is a Zaidi Shia insurgent group operating in Yemen. The group takes its name from Hussein Badreddin al-Houthi, their former commander, who was reported killed by Yemeni army forces in September 2004. The Houthi rebels have asserted that their actions are to defend Houthis against government discrimination, though the Yemeni Government has in turn accused it of wishing to destabilize the government and of 'stirring anti-American sentiment'. The group responded to the 'Arab Spring' movement by aligning with 'revolutionary youth' calling for the downfall of the regime and justice for its victims.[1373]

Al-Qaeda in the Arab Peninsula (AQAP)

Al-Qaeda in Yemen (AQY), AQAP's predecessor, came into existence after the escape of twenty-three Al-Qaeda members from a prison in Sanaa, in February 2006. AQAP emerged in January 2009 through a union of the Saudi and Yemeni branches of Al-Qaeda.[1374]

[1369] 'Does Iran Really Control Yemen?', *Al-Monitor*, 12 February 2015, at: <http://www.al-monitor.com/pulse/originals/2015/02/iran-yemen-houthis-axis-of-resistance.html>.

[1370] 'GCC moves to legitimize Aden as Yemen's capital', *Al-Monitor*, 1 March 2015, at: <http://www.al-monitor.com/pulse/politics/2015/02/yemen-aden-gcc-houthis-gulf-support.html#ixzz3ULTWzHaG>.

[1371] 'Yemen Military Strength', *Globalfirepower.com*, last updated on 27 March 2014, at: <http://www.globalfirepower.com/country-military-strength-detail.asp?country_id=yemen>.

[1372] UN, 'Yemen: Ban, Security Council Welcome Efforts to Reform Armed Forces', Press release, New York, 12 April 2013, at: <http://www.un.org/apps/news/story.asp?NewsID=44638#.UZCwtxZBvX4>.

[1373] 'Yemen's Houthi Movement in the Wake of the Arab Spring', *CTC Sentinel*, vol. 5, no. 8 (August 2012), p. 1, at: <http://www.ctc.usma.edu/posts/yemens-Houthi-movement-in-the-wake-of-the-arab-spring>.

[1374] National Counterterrorism Centre, 'Al Qa'ida in the Arabian Peninsula (AQAP)', at: <http://www.nctc.gov/site/groups/aqap.html>.

The group has been designated as a terrorist organization by the United Nations, Australia, Canada, Russia, Syria, Iran, Yemen, Saudi Arabia, the UAE, the European Union, and the United States. It is believed to have orchestrated numerous high-profile terrorist attacks, last but not least the one at the headquarters of *Charlie Hebdo* satirical magazine in Paris on 7 January 2015.

CASUALTIES

No detailed reporting on casualties in Yemen in 2014 was available and media reporting often presented overlapping and inconsonant casualty estimates that were not suitable for comparison or disaggregation. The Abaad Studies and Research Centre, a Yemeni NGO, reported that over 7,000 people were killed in 2014 due to armed clashes in Yemen during 2014. According to the findings of the Abaad Studies and Research Centre, 600 Yemeni military were killed in engagements with Houthi militia and another 400 were killed mostly by Al-Qaeda militants and other armed groups. The study estimated that more than 1,200 civilians were killed in armed clashes. It also found that there were over 5,000 fatalities among Houthis.[1375] The study said fatalities of Al-Qaeda in Yemen were estimated at between 400 and 500. Sources for the data used Abaad Studies and Research Centre in the study were not reported. The Abaad Studies and Research Centre, noted that the 2014 figures represented 'a threefold increase from of 2011, when a popular uprising broke out against the country's former president Ali Abdullah Saleh'.[1376]

At least 360 fatalities were reported in the media in the two-week period from 15 September to 30 September, after Houthi fighters entered the capital of Sanaa and took control of certain districts of the city. The majority of these casualties were believed to be combatants but no precise, disaggregated data was available. A ceasefire signed on 21 September seemed to have little immediate impact in terms of decreased casualties. Distinguishing casualties related to the Houthi conflict from casualties associated with the AQAP became increasingly difficult during 2014 as Houthi fighters moved closer to territory where AQAP were based. The September clashes in Sana'a included conflicts between Houthi fighters and AQAP fighters as well between Houthi and Yemeni military.

[1375] It was reported by the Abaad Studies and Research Centre that some 2,000 Houthis were killed in Marib, approximately 2,000 were killed in Sanaá and other cities, i.e., Hodeida and Ibb and about another 1,000 Houthis were killed in Radaá of Al-Baida. Abaad Studies and Research Centre, 'Abaad Report: 7,000 Yemenis killed in 2014, Houthis control 70% of the state army capabilities', 4 January 15, <http://www.abaadstudies.org/?p=1837&lang=en>.

[1376] Abaad Studies and Research Centre, 'Abaad Report: 7,000 Yemenis killed in 2014, Houthis control 70% of the state army capabilities', 4 January 15, <http://www.abaadstudies.org/?p=1837&lang=en>, '7,700 Yemenis killed in 2014: Study', Monday 5 January 2015 07:58 GMT, last update Friday 13 February 2015, <http://www.middleeasteye.net/news/7700-yemenis-killed-2014-study-1930042254>.

On 23 December 2014, a Red Crescent national aid worker was shot by militants while riding a motorcycle, who were likely aiming at the soldier who was also on the motorcycle.[1377]

The Bureau of Investigative Journalism (TBIJ) recorded 82–118 people killed (four to nine civilians, including one child) and seven to fourteen injured in thirteen to fifteen confirmed US drone strikes in Yemen 2014. With another forty-five to seventy-four people killed (three to twenty-two civilians, including up to three children) and eleven to seventeen injured in eighteen 'possible drone strikes' and twenty-one to twenty-two killed (nine civilians, including two children) in 'additional US attacks'.[1378]

An American journalist, who was held hostage by AQAP, was killed during a failed rescue attempt by US Special Forces in December 2014.[1379]

In 2014, there were at least 100,000 new internal displaced persons (IDPs) in Yemen, leading to a total of 334,100 persons being internally displaced in the country as of December 2014.[1380]

WAR CRIMES ALLEGATIONS, INVESTIGATIONS, AND PROSECUTIONS

Yemen has signed but not ratified the 1998 Rome Statute of the International Criminal Court.

In November 2013, Human Rights Watch called on representatives to Yemen's ongoing National Dialogue Conference[1381] to endorse a proposal to strike down Yemen's immunity law adopted by Yemen's Parliament on 21 January 2012.[1382] The Law No. 1 of 2012 Concerning the Granting of Immunity from Legal and Judicial Prosecution provided, inter alia, as follows:

> Article 1: Brother Ali Abdullah Saleh, President of the Republic, shall hereby be granted complete immunity from legal and judicial prosecution.

[1377] The Aid Worker Security Database 'Security incident data', last updated 9 April 2015, <https://aidworkersecurity.org/incidents/search?start=2014&end=2014&detail=1&country=YE>.

[1378] TBIJ, 'Yemen: Reported US covert actions 2014', <http://www.thebureauinvestigates.com/2014/01/06/yemen-reported-us-covert-actions-2014/>.

[1379] Committee to Protect Journalists (CPJ) 'Luke Somers, Freelance, December 6, 2014, in Shabwa province, Yemen', <https://cpj.org/killed/2014/luke-somers.php>.

[1380] Internal Displacement Monitoring Centre (IDMC) 'Global Overview 2015', May 2015, p. 87. The figure represents the number of IDPs the government and UNHCR had registered as of December 2014.

[1381] A UN-facilitated 'Implementing Mechanism' required the transitional government of President Hadi to convene a National Dialogue Conference to produce recommendations regarding the content of a new constitution, legal reforms, and government policies for the future Yemen. President Hadi issued a decree stating that government authorities must carry out all of the Conference's recommendations.

[1382] Human Rights Watch, 'Yemen: Strike Down Immunity Law', 20 November 2013, at: <http://www.hrw.org/news/2013/11/19/yemen-strike-down-immunity-law>.

Article 2: Immunity from criminal prosecution shall apply to the officials who have worked under the President – in state civil, military, and security agencies – in connection with politically motivated acts carried out during the course of their official duties; immunity shall not apply to acts of terrorism.[1383]

According to Amnesty International Report 2014/2015, those responsible for the killings have not been identified and no report of any prosecutions of alleged perpetrators was received.[1384]

1383 Cited in ibid.

1384 Amnesty International Report 2014/2015, 'The State of the World's Human Rights', at <https://www.amnesty.org/en/documents/pol10/0001/2015/en/>.

Part III

Thematic Chapters

A

Means and Methods of Warfare

1 The CIA Torture Report: was there a method in the madness?

Hilary Stauffer[1]

Introduction

> 'We tortured some folks.'[2]

These four words, delivered in US President Barack Obama's characteristically casual syntax, marked an official acknowledgement of what lawyers[3] for detainees held in Guantánamo Bay had long known: various agencies of the United States government tortured suspected 'terrorists' over a multi-year period in the wake of the 9/11 attacks.

The admission came in August 2014, when the furore over the proposed release of the US Senate Select Committee on Intelligence (SSCI) Report on the Central Intelligence Agency's (CIA) detention and interrogation programme[4] was reaching a fever pitch. The final document, compiled over five years[5] and at a cost of more than $40 million[6] was the subject of prolonged wrangling between the Senate and the intelligence

[1] Hilary Stauffer is a Visiting Fellow at the London School of Economics and Political Science.

[2] Gerstein, J., 'Obama: "We tortured some folks"', *Politico*, 1 August 2014, <http://www.politico.com/story/2014/08/john-brennan-torture-cia-109654.html>.

[3] Open Society Justice Initiative, 'Globalizing Torture: CIA Secret Detention and Extraordinary Rendition', 2013, <http://www.opensocietyfoundations.org/sites/default/files/globalizing-torture-20120205.pdf>, p. 34.

[4] Senate Select Committee on Intelligence: Committee Study of the Central Intelligence Agency's Detention and Interrogation Program, Declassified Executive Summary published 3 December 2014, <http://fas.org/irp/congress/2014_rpt/ssci-rdi.pdf>.

[5] Volz, D., 'Senate Releases Historic CIA Torture Report Condemning Bush-Era Detainee Treatment', *National Journal*, 9 December 2014, <http://www.nationaljournal.com/congress/senate-releases-historic-cia-torture-report-condemning-bush-era-detainee-treatment-20141209>.

[6] Volz, D., 'The Senate Torture Report Cost at Least $40 Million. But Whose Fault is That?', *National Journal*, 10 December 2014, <http://www.nationaljournal.com/defense/the-senate-torture-report-cost-at-least-40-million-but-whose-fault-is-that-20141210>.

community, with persistent allegations that the White House itself was pressuring the SSCI to be more generous in its self-censorship of key programme details.[7] Perhaps in an attempt to address the growing chorus of criticism head on (and possibly to dilute some of the more potent conspiracy theories), President Obama cut to the chase in August 2014, stating in the middle of a broader press conference about Republican Party intransigence that the United States had—in the panicked era following 9/11—'[done] some things that were wrong'.[8] In the end, the 500-page 'Executive Summary' of the reportedly 6,700 page[9] Report was released to the public in December 2014,[10] with significant redactions.[11]

Directly following the Executive Summary's publication, innumerable articles were published detailing some of the sickening techniques that US personnel once thought appropriate for interrogating suspected 9/11 plotters and their alleged cohorts. The media (and wider public's) fascination is not difficult to understand. Humans find it hard to look away from chaos, and in the multimedia analysis of the SSCI Report, chaos had been laid out in a dispassionate, systematic fashion. By one count,[12] the Report contained 310 mentions of interrogations where detainees were placed in stress positions;[13] 252 mentions of water as an interrogation method (either waterboarding or a combination of water and cold temperatures to induce confessions); and 75 mentions of slapping, hitting, or slamming detainees into objects.[14] Other approved interrogation techniques included: 'wall standing' (forcing the detainee to remain standing with his arms outstretched in front of him so that his fingers touch a wall

[7] Hudson, J., 'White House Putting up Fierce Fight to Conceal Torture Report', *Foreign Policy*, 19 November 2014, <http://foreignpolicy.com/2014/11/19/white-house-putting-up-fierce-fight-to-conceal-torture-report/>.

[8] Gerstein, 'Obama: "We tortured some folks"'.

[9] SSCI Report, Forward, p. 1

[10] Miller, G., Goldman, A., and Tate, J., 'Senate report on CIA program details brutality, dishonesty', *Washington Post*, 9 December 2014, <http://www.washingtonpost.com/world/national-security/senate-report-on-cia-program-details-brutality-dishonesty/2014/12/09/1075c726-7f0e-11e4-9f38-95a187e4c1f7_story.html?hpid=z1>.

[11] Note: the full Report of the Senate Select Committee on Intelligence remains classified, and currently, there are no indications it will be declassified at any point. Thus, in this chapter, when references are made either in the text or the footnotes to the 'Report' or the 'SSCI Report', it is exclusively referring to the Executive Summary unless otherwise indicated.

[12] Keating, D., Berkowitz, B., and Gamio, L., 'The brutal methods outlined in the senate report', *Washington Post*, 10 December 2014, <http://www.washingtonpost.com/wp-srv/special/national/cia-interrogation-report/word-count/>.

[13] Defined by the Open Society Justice Initiative as 'forcing the detainee to remain in body positions designed to induce physical discomfort'. 'Globalizing Torture', p. 16.

[14] Through techniques such as 'walling' (quickly pulling the detainee forward and then thrusting him against a flexible false wall), 'insult slaps' (slapping the detainee on the face with fingers spread), 'facial hold' (holding a detainee's head temporarily immobile during interrogation with palms on either side of the face), and 'attention grasp' (grasping the detainee with both hands, one hand on each side of the collar opening, and quickly drawing him toward the interrogator). All information in this note from Open Society Justice Initiative, 'Globalizing Torture', pp. 16–18.

four to five feet away and support his entire body weight);[15] 'cramped confinement' in a box; forced nudity; sleep deprivation while being vertically shackled; and dietary manipulation.[16]

As distressing as all these techniques are to read about, perhaps the most disturbing procedure employed by CIA interrogators was 'rectal rehydration', a rather clinical terminology for the unspeakable practice of force-feeding a detainee rectally, which in one case involved pureeing the contents of a prisoner's lunch tray and rectally 'infusing' him with the contents.[17] The Report notes that detainees often endured 'rectal rehydration' without 'evidence of medical necessity',[18] which is a detached way of saying that interrogators horribly abused the men under their control for reasons completely unrelated to effective intelligence gathering. The Report's authors remark almost as an afterthought that CIA officers 'also threatened at least three detainees with harm to their families, including threats to harm the children of a detainee, threats to sexually abuse the mother of a detainee, and a threat to 'cut [a detainee's] mother's throat'.[19]

Such salacious details have prompted widespread interest in the report, even if they leave most readers with a visceral feeling of deep revulsion at the actions their government purported to carry out in the name of national security. However, there is a corollary attraction as well, and it is the rare opportunity to see one's government categorically undercut in a very public fashion. For it was less than a decade ago, in 2006, when President George W. Bush assured Americans that '[t]he United States does not torture. It's against our laws, and it's against our values. I have not authorized it, and I will not authorize it'.[20] The publication of the Senate Report seems to directly contradict this assertion, leading many to wonder just how the Bush Administration would define 'torture', if non-medically-necessary 'rectal rehydration' doesn't qualify.

This question, and related queries regarding methodologies and motivation, will be explored in the following chapter. It is worth acknowledging that the CIA and its political supporters vehemently disagreed with some of the Report's findings and conclusions,[21]

[15] 'Globalizing Torture', pp. 16–18.

[16] 'Globalizing Torture', pp. 16–18, recounting techniques outlined in the Central Intelligence Agency's 'Memo to DOJ Command Center—Background Paper on CIA's Combined Use of Interrogation Techniques', 30 December 2004, p. 4, <http://www.aclu.org/torturefoia/released/082409/olcremand/2004olc97.pdf> (describing coercive interrogation methods applied on detainees at black sites);

[17] SSCI Report, p. 115. [18] SSCI Report, p. 100.

[19] SSCI Report, Finding and Conclusions, p. 4.

[20] Ferguson, A. and Usero, A., 'Reminder: George W. Bush Said the U.S. Didn't Use Torture', *Huffington Post*, 9 December 2014, <http://www.huffingtonpost.com/2014/12/09/george-w-bush-denies-torture_n_6295888.html>.

[21] 'Statement from Director Brennan on the SSCI Study on the Former Detention and Interrogation Program', 9 December 2014, <https://www.cia.gov/news-information/press-releases-statements/2014-press-releases-statements/statement-from-director-brennan-on-ssci-study-on-detention-interrogation-program.html>, and Memorandum from CIA Director John Brennan to Senator Dianne Feinstein and Senator Saxby Chambliss regarding 'CIA Comments on the Senate Select Committee on Intelligence Report on the

and there are allegations of partisan bias in the timing of the release.[22] Nevertheless, it must also be conceded that the CIA is not a disinterested observer, and that as an agency whose default setting is 'Top Secret', any scrutiny of its activities is unwelcome. Moreover, this particular investigation into CIA activities was initially launched after it was discovered that in 2007, the Agency had destroyed videotaped evidence of some detainees being waterboarded.[23] The CIA's credibility was even further undercut by unseemly accusations—later confirmed by the organization's own Inspector General—that some Agency employees unlawfully spied on the Senate staffers who were preparing the report.[24] For these reasons, the dissenting reactions to the report will not be scrutinized herein.[25]

Also left unexamined in this chapter are allegations about abuse and mistreatment of detainees carried out by branches of the US government other than the CIA. In 2008, the Senate Armed Services Committee undertook a separate investigation[26] of harsh interrogation techniques utilized by the Department of Defense against prisoners held in Iraq, Afghanistan, and Guantánamo Bay, finding that questionable methods such as 'sensory deprivation, sleep disruption, stress positions, waterboarding, and slapping' were all authorized.[27] Additionally, certain detainees were 'stripped naked, subjected to loud music, and made to wear a leash and perform dog tricks',[28] practices that the report concludes with almost comical understatement are 'at odds with the commitment to humane treatment of detainees in U.S. custody'.[29]

While these abuses are no less worthy of examination than the allegations of cruel, inhuman, and degrading treatment meted out by the CIA towards its detainees, it is the peculiar space occupied by the CIA within the US government and its counter-terrorism infrastructure which is the focus of this chapter. Why was the CIA such an

Rendition, Detention, and Interrogation Program', 27 June 2003, <https://www.cia.gov/library/reports/CIAs_June2013_Response_to_the_SSCI_Study_on_the_Former_Detention_and_Interrogation_Program.pdf>.

[22] Bennett, B., 'Dianne Feinstein leaving intelligence job amid clash on tactics report', *Los Angeles Times*, 7 December 2014, <http://www.latimes.com/nation/politics/la-na-feinstein-intel-20141207-story.html#page=1>; Goldman, A., '5 Questions about the CIA detention and interrogation report you wish you didn't have to ask', *Washington Post*, 8 December 2014, <http://www.washingtonpost.com/blogs/worldviews/wp/2014/12/08/5-questions-about-the-cia-detention-and-interrogation-report-you-wish-you-didnt-have-to-ask/>.

[23] Goldman, A., '5 Questions'.

[24] Office of the Inspector General of the Central Intelligence Agency: Summary of Report, 31 July 2014, available at <http://goo.gl/MIW6r6>; Miller, G., 'CIA director John Brennan apologizes for search of Senate committee's computers', *Washington Post*, 31 July 2014, <http://wpo.st/TPZE0>.

[25] Some examples of dissenting viewpoints can be found in the Statement from Director Brennan (9 December 2014), and in the following article: Landler, M. and Baker, P., 'A clash over report about U.S. torture; Republican critics say release of documents risks a backlash overseas', *International New York Times*, 10 December 2014, p. 6.

[26] Senate Armed Services Committee Inquiry into the Treatment of Detainees in US Custody, Executive Summary (2008), <http://media.washingtonpost.com/wp-srv/nation/pdf/12112008_detaineeabuse.pdf> (hereinafter SASC Inquiry).

[27] SASC Inquiry, p. xiv. [28] SASC Inquiry, p. xxi. [29] SASC Inquiry, p. xxvi.

attractive partner in this particular misadventure? Thus, this chapter will focus on the findings highlighted in the SSCI Report and the convoluted reasoning employed to justify the CIA's actions. Above all, it will seek to answer the question: was there a method to the madness? And more importantly, can we be sure it will never happen again?

A. **Origins and functions of the Central Intelligence Agency**

The CIA was created by the National Security Act (1947) to 'collect intelligence through human sources and to analyse and disseminate intelligence from all sources'.[30] It was also permitted to 'perform such other functions and duties related to intelligence affecting the national security as the President or the National Security Council may direct',[31] open-ended language which has, over time, been used to justify a multitude of covert activities and paramilitary operations.[32] However, from the time of its establishment until 2004 (when the intelligence-related activities of the US government underwent significant reform), the Agency was expressly prohibited from having any 'police, subpoena, [or] law enforcement powers'.[33] Therefore, it is not clear why—a mere 'six days after 9/11'[34]—President Bush directed the CIA to 'carry out a program to detain terrorist suspects around the world'.[35]

Detention of alleged wrongdoers is an intrinsic law enforcement capability. By its own admission, the CIA was particularly unprepared and 'lacked the core competencies

[30] Best, R. A. and Feickert, A., 'Special Operations Forces (SOF) and CIA Paramilitary Operations: Issues for Congress', *Congressional Research Service*, 3 August 2009, p. 1 <http://fas.org/sgp/crs/natsec/RS22017.pdf>.

[31] Best, R. A. and Feickert, A., 'Special Operations Forces', p. 1.

[32] Best, R. A. and Feickert, A., 'Special Operations Forces', pp. 1–2.

[33] National Security Act of 1947, Pub. L. No. 80-253, 61 Stat. 495, §102(d)(3), original version at: <http://global.oup.com/us/companion.websites/9780195385168/resources/chapter10/nsa/nsa.pdf>. The National Security Act has been amended several times over the past six decades, and underwent drastic changes enacted after the 9/11 attacks, specifically via the National Security Intelligence Reform Act of 2004; see Pub. L. No, 108-458,118 Stat. 3643 (reclassified in May 2013 as 50 U.S.C. §3001). Even after the reform, the relevant portions of the amended Act read as follows: '... (a) CENTRAL INTELLIGENCE AGENCY.—There is a Central Intelligence Agency. (b) FUNCTION.—The function of the Central Intelligence Agency is to assist the Director of the Central Intelligence Agency in carrying out the responsibilities specified in [the next section] ... (d) RESPONSIBILITIES.—The Director of the Central Intelligence Agency shall—(1) collect intelligence through human sources and by other appropriate means, *except that the Director of the Central Intelligence Agency shall have no police, subpoena, or law enforcement powers or internal security functions*' (emphasis added), 50 USC §3036 (d)(1), current as of April 2015.

[34] Statement from Director Brennan (9 December 2014).

[35] Statement from Director Brennan (9 December 2014).

required to carry out an unprecedented, worldwide program of detaining and interrogating suspected al-Qa'ida and affiliated terrorists',[36] something that the President or members of his National Security Council[37] could have been expected to know. Consequently, not only was the President directing the Agency to carry out a task it was statutorily prohibited from engaging in, he was ordering it to embark upon a multifaceted operation of sweeping scope that it was institutionally ill-suited to undertake. Why?

CONSPIRACY THEORIES AND THE COUNTER-NARRATIVE

It is tempting to assert that the Presidential administration of George W. Bush was metaphorically drunk on power and hubris and used the occasion of the 9/11 attacks to indulge in some of their deeply held fantasies of world domination, at the expense of 350 years of post-Westphalian international legal structures. Certainly, this is a charge repeatedly levelled by liberal-leaning critics in the United States and elsewhere,[38] and it is disconcerting to note that there seemed to be multiple persons working in Washington, DC, during the George W. Bush presidency that appeared to be more than willing to completely disregard long-standing domestic policies and international laws in pursuit of American power. According to this narrative, President Bush and his cronies in the CIA were looking for any excuse to meddle in the Muslim world, and 9/11 was just a pretext.

However, this analysis is overly simplistic. It neglects to acknowledge that the CIA's illegitimate overreach was not an organic, inevitable occurrence, but rather a reaction to the first military assault on American territory in six decades. Fifteen years after the 9/11 hijackings, it is easy to forget the pervasive fear that gripped the world at large in those early weeks and months after the Twin Towers fell and a plane crashed into the Pentagon. Western values—reflected in their American manifestations—were under attack.

That being said, the Bush Administration certainly capitalized on the all-encompassing alarm that was prevalent at the time to institute its own agenda and engage in some scary overreach. Those overseeing the response to the 9/11 attacks also specifically chose a partner—the CIA—that was comfortable operating in secrecy and willing to work in the grey areas on the margins of international law. In this regard, there most certainly

[36] Statement from Director Brennan (9 December 2014).

[37] Archived website detailing the composition and activities of President George W. Bush's National Security Council, at <http://georgewbush-whitehouse.archives.gov/nsc/>.

[38] Villegas, P., 'Cowardly Congress, Power-hungry President', *Orlando Sentinel*, 24 January 2003, <http://articles.orlandosentinel.com/2003-01-24/news/0301240149_1_cowardly-congress-war-powers-act-liberties>; Cole, J., 'The Trial of Richard Bruce Cheney', *Truth Out*, 11 December 2004, <http://www.truthdig.com/report/item/the_trial_of_richard_bruce_cheney_20141211>.

were methods to the madness—methodologies that must be examined and explored in order to prevent similar lapses from reoccurring in the future.

Method number 1: the ostrich approach to oversight

One of the most striking observations in reading the Executive Summary to the SSCI Report is the near-universal unwillingness of anyone in any position of potential oversight to use their investigative abilities during a period when it was clear that something was very much amiss over at the CIA's headquarters. Although the Report takes pains to describe the deceptive practices[39] and misrepresentations[40] Agency staffers engaged in to avoid external scrutiny of the detention and interrogation programme (more on these later), what comes through in parallel is an impression of executive and legislative branches adopting a policy of 'don't ask, don't tell' to the CIA's activities.

As late as 2006, by which point the programme had already been underway for five years, no one at the CIA had briefed the President on the specific interrogation techniques being employed at various CIA dark sites;[41] moreover, the President and Vice-President were completely ignorant as to the location of all but one of the Agency's detention facilities.[42] Such obfuscation on the part of the CIA seems reprehensible, but evidence abounds that the White House's ignorance was deliberate. In fact, the Report states that the White House explicitly requested that the 'secretaries of State and Defense (two principals on the National Security Council) not be briefed as to programme specifics' until a full two years after it began[43]—amid concerns they would not approve. Moreover, in emails reviewed by the Senate Select Committee, Vice President Dick Cheney 'expressed reservations about any public release of information regarding the CIA programme'.[44] Thus, not only did the White House specifically not want to know any troublesome details, they didn't want anyone else to know about them either.

But knowledge of the abuse wasn't limited only to the CIA and the White House. On at least one occasion in 2004, agents of the Federal Bureau of Investigation responded to an internal email inquiry for information from the then-Assistant Director for Intelligence about suspected maltreatment of detainees that they may have witnessed at Guantánamo Bay.[45] One response, later made public though a Freedom of Information Act request, described 'detainees chained to the floor and left without water or food for 24 hours or more, who had urinated or defecated on themselves ... [o]ne detainee was

[39] See, for example, SSCI Report, Finding and Conclusions, pp. 4–7.
[40] SSCI Report, Finding and Conclusions, pp. 4–7.
[41] SSCI Report, Finding and Conclusions, pp. 6–7.
[42] SSCI Report, Finding and Conclusions, pp. 6–7.
[43] SSCI Report, Finding and Conclusions, pp. 6–7.
[44] SSCI Report, p. 151, footnote 910.
[45] The Torture Database, 'FBI Email re: Response to Steve McCraw's Email on Detainee Abuse and Maltreatment at Guantanamo Bay (dated 2 August 2004)', 2 January 2007, <http://goo.gl/6bP2I9>.

described as almost unconscious on the floor, with a pile of hair next to him. He had apparently been literally pulling his own hair out throughout the night'.[46] It is unclear why such a distressing report didn't filter its way up the chain of command to result in some kind of public accountability for the alleged perpetrators, but by John Brennan's own admission, the use of 'such techniques' continued until December 2007,[47] so if FBI leadership knew anything, they were keeping it to themselves.

This exercise in wilful blindness went beyond the Executive Branch of the US government.[48] While Congress was almost certainly misled about the scope and effectiveness of the programme by CIA administrators,[49] there were some within Congressional leadership that had an idea of what was happening as early as 2002.[50] The Report details some ineffectual efforts on behalf of certain members of Congress to shed some light on the programme,[51] although these seem in the narrative telling to be easily stymied through mere intransigence and refusal to cooperate by the Agency,[52] without any repercussions of any kind. In an institution as partisan and porous as the US Congress, it is extremely unlikely that over the course of several years, no details would have leaked out about the detention and interrogation programme, unless there was a concerted effort on the part of legislators not to become better informed (and, therefore, not to have additional accountability).

The hypocrisy of such an approach is astonishing. These same powerbrokers would literally be up in arms if such 'interrogation techniques' were used against American POWs. Yet when the United States decides to unilaterally lower standards and single-handedly redefine 'torture', it is considered 'patriotic'. A sympathetic evaluation of such policies might label them careless, but a more accurate adjective would be 'reckless'; in any event, they represent the dark side of American Exceptionalism[53]—a recurrent theme in all discussions about this particularly ugly chapter in American history.

Method number 2: disingenuous definitions

The revelation that American policymakers passively abdicated responsibility for their oversight role of the CIA is distressing. But there were more aggressive practices

[46] Hearn, M., 'Required Reading: Prequels to the Torture Report', *ACLU Blog*, 8 December 2014 ACLU, <https://www.aclu.org/blog/human-rights-national-security/required-reading-prequels-torture-report> quoting 'FBI Email'.

[47] Statement from Director Brennan (9 December 2014).

[48] The Office of the Vice President, the Department of Justice, the Federal Bureau of Investigation and the Central Intelligence Agency are all under the purview of the federal Executive Branch; see <http://www.usa.gov/Agencies/Federal/Executive.shtml#Executive_Departments> (last accessed 26 April 2015).

[49] SSCI Report, Finding and Conclusions, pp. 2–3.

[50] SSCI Report, Finding and Conclusions, p. 5.

[51] SSCI Report, Finding and Conclusions, pp. 5–6; and SSCI Report, pp. 437–41.

[52] SSCI Report, p. 450.

[53] American Exceptionalism is the conviction that the United States holds a unique place and role in human history, due to its democratic ideals, military superiority, and economic strength.

employed during the United States' flirtation with officially sanctioned torture, methodologies that went far beyond 'don't ask, don't tell'. Although CIA Director John Brennan did belatedly acknowledge that '[c]ertain detainees were subjected to enhanced interrogation techniques', he hastened to reassure his fellow Americans that such techniques had been 'determined to be lawful [at the time]'.[54] Such dispassionate language obscures the uncompromising manner in which lawyers from the George W. Bush-era Department of Justice (DOJ) sought to reinterpret domestic and international law to their whims. In fact, the DOJ went to great lengths to completely redefine commonly understood terms in order to carve out plausible deniability for the actions of CIA agents and others involved in the detention and interrogation programme.

Before undertaking an in-depth analysis of what were colloquially called 'the Torture Memos', it's worth examining what the existing legal edicts on this prohibited practice were prior to the start of the CIA's detention and interrogation programme in September 2001. The United Nations Convention against Torture and Other Cruel, Inhuman or Degrading Treatment or Punishment (UNCAT),[55] was opened for signature in 1984.[56] Article 1 of the treaty states that:

> 1. the term 'torture' means any act by which severe pain or suffering, whether physical or mental, is intentionally inflicted on a person for such purposes as obtaining from him or a third person information or a confession, punishing him for an act he or a third person has committed or is suspected of having committed, or intimidating or coercing him or a third person, or for any reason based on discrimination of any kind, when such pain or suffering is inflicted by or at the instigation of or with the consent or acquiescence of a public official or other person acting in an official capacity.[57]

This provision expands upon an earlier iteration of the same idea that appears in the International Covenant on Civil and Political Rights (1966).[58] Article 7 of the ICCPR succinctly states that '[n]o one shall be subjected to torture or to cruel, inhuman or degrading treatment or punishment'. And the concept appears even earlier still, in Common Article 3 of the four Geneva Conventions of 1949, which prohibits 'murder, mutilation, cruel treatment, and torture, as well as ... outrages upon personal dignity'.[59]

[54] Statement from Director Brennan (9 December 2014).

[55] Convention against Torture and Other Cruel, Inhuman or Degrading Treatment or Punishment, 10 December 1984, 1465 U.N.T.S. 85 (hereinafter UNCAT).

[56] <http://www.ohchr.org/EN/ProfessionalInterest/Pages/CAT.aspx>.

[57] UNCAT, Art. 1.

[58] International Covenant on Civil and Political Rights, 16 December 1966, 999 U.N.T.S. 171 (hereinafter ICCPR).

[59] Pejic, J., 2011, 'The Protective Scope of Common Article 3: More Than Meets the Eye', *International Review of the Red Cross*, vol. 93, no. 881, p. 206, <http://www.icrc.org/eng/assets/files/review/2011/irrc-881-pejic.pdf>.

The United States has been party to the Geneva Conventions since 1955;[60] it has been party to the ICCPR since 1992;[61] and it has been party to UNCAT since 1994.[62] Thus, the long-standing prohibitions on torture were not unknown to Department of Justice lawyers, or their counterparts in the Department of State and Department of Defense. So, in order to tackle the threat posed by Al-Qaeda operatives and their Taliban cohorts, the Bush Administration need to engage in what can charitably be termed 'creative' legal interpretations.

Beginning in 2002, the DOJ drafted a series of classified memos, providing legal authorization for the torture programme. Over the ensuing decade, the contents of these memos were released into the public domain, either through leaks, Freedom of Information Act requests, or eventual declassification. They have been extensively analysed[63] elsewhere, and their legal conclusions roundly criticized.[64] Nevertheless, they bear a closer re-examination for the purposes of deconstructing the methodology of the CIA during the impetuous early years of the 'War on Terror'.

The Geneva Conventions were easily dispatched with: on 7 February 2002, President Bush signed a memo determining that the Geneva Convention did not apply to Al-Qaeda or Taliban detainees,[65] although the 'United States Armed Forces' were ordered to 'continue treating detainees humanely' (the CIA was not explicitly mentioned in this order). Another notorious memo[66] sought to assure the then-Attorney General, Alberto Gonzales, that 'enhanced interrogation techniques' (EITs) were compliant with the United States' domestic and international legal obligations, specifically UNCAT, and 18 USCS §2340-2340A,[67] the law which helped implement the Convention by criminalizing torture within the United States. In an ominous display of analytical wizardry, the memo's authors concluded that the EITs being employed by the CIA and others did not undermine the letter of the law because they weren't 'extreme'

[60] International Committee of the Red Cross, 'Treaties and States Parties to Such Treaties: The United States', <https://goo.gl/JPJ7te> (last accessed 1 May 2015).

[61] Office of the High Commissioner for Human Rights, Status of Ratification: Interactive Dashboard (United States of America), <http://indicators.ohchr.org/> (last accessed 1 May 2015).

[62] Office of the High Commissioner for Human Rights, Status of Ratification: Interactive Dashboard (United States of America), <http://indicators.ohchr.org/> (last accessed 1 May 2015).

[63] Cohen, A., 'The Torture Memos, 10 Years Later', *The Atlantic*, 6 February 2012, <http://www.theatlantic.com/national/archive/2012/02/the-torture-memos-10-years-later/252439/?single_page=true>.

[64] Hearn, M., 'Required Reading'.

[65] Memorandum from President George W. Bush Re: Human Standards of Treatment for Al-Qaeda and Taliban Detainee, 7 February 2002, <http://lawofwar.org/Bush_memo_Genevas.htm>.

[66] Memorandum from Jay S. Bybee, Assistant Attorney Gen., Office of Legal Counsel, to Alberto R. Gonzales, Counsel to the President, Re: Standards of Conduct for Interrogation Under 18 USC 2340-2340A, 1 August 2002, <http://www.justice.gov/sites/default/files/olc/legacy/2010/08/05/memo-gonzales-aug2002.pdf>. Note: the ICCPR was not explicitly addressed in these memos, most likely because the more in-depth provisions of CAT would supersede Art 7's brief mention.

[67] 18 USCS §2340-2340A.

enough.[68] The authors determined that in order to be considered torture, 'physical pain', must be of an intensity 'akin to ... that which accompanies death or organ failure',[69] and mental pain must be accompanied by 'lasting psychological harm'.[70] The memo also helpfully noted that questioning the use of EITs in the context of counter-terrorism could possibly be considered an unlawful challenge to the President's powers as Commander-in-Chief.[71]

Yet another equally infamous memo,[72] again analysing 18 USCS §2340-2340A, determined that each of the approved 'enhanced interrogation techniques', when used individually, did not rise to the level of 'severe' pain envisaged by the law. The ten techniques that the CIA sought—and received—authorization to use included: '(1) attention grasp, (2) walling, (3) facial hold, (4) facial slap (insult slap), (5) cramped confinement, (6) wall standing, (7) stress positions, (8) sleep deprivation, (9) insects placed in a confinement box, and (10) the waterboard'.[73] The memo's authors concluded that even if any physical pain or mental anguish resulting from EITs did rise to the requisite severity, such techniques would *still* not violate the Statute if the interrogator did not have a 'specific intent' to inflict pain and suffering.[74]

Savvy CIA attorneys eventually realized that the United States' obligations under CAT also extended to 'cruel, inhuman and degrading treatment',[75] and sought separate legal assurances from the DOJ that the CIA's 'enhanced interrogation techniques' were kosher in this regard. An additional memo was authored dealing with this specific question; displaying similar innovative deductions as its sister documents, its drafters determined that EITs could only be considered 'cruel, inhuman and degrading' if they 'shock the conscience',[76]

68 Bybee Memo on 'Standards of Conduct for Interrogation', pp. 6, 13.

69 Bybee Memo on 'Standards of Conduct for Interrogation', pp. 6, 13.

70 Bybee Memo on 'Standards of Conduct for Interrogation', p. 46.

71 Bybee Memo on 'Standards of Conduct for Interrogation', p. 35. The Memo's authors come to this conclusion despite the fact that Art. 2(2) of UNCAT expressly forbids this kind of loose reading, stating '[n]o exceptional circumstances whatsoever, whether a state of war or a threat of war, internal political instability or any other public emergency, may be invoked as a justification of torture'.

72 Memorandum from Jay S. Bybee, Assistant Attorney General, to John Rizzo, Acting General Counsel of the Central Intelligence Agency, on Interrogation of Al-Qaeda Operative, 1 August 2002, <https://www.thetorturedatabase.org/files/foia_subsite/pdfs/DOJOLC000780.pdf>.

73 Bybee Memo on 'Interrogation of al Qaeda Operative' p. 2.

74 Bybee Memo on 'Interrogation of al Qaeda Operative' p. 16.

75 UNCAT, Art. 16, stating: '[e]ach State Party shall undertake to prevent in any territory under its jurisdiction other acts of cruel, inhuman or degrading treatment or punishment which do not amount to torture as defined in Article I, when such acts are committed by or at the instigation of or with the consent or acquiescence of a public official or other person acting in an official capacity'.

76 See Memorandum from Steven G. Bradbury, Principal Deputy Assistant Attorney General, Office of Legal Counsel, US Department of Justice, to John A. Rizzo, Senior Deputy General Counsel, Central Intelligence Agency, Re: Application of 18 USC §§2340-2340A to Certain Techniques that May Be Used in the Interrogation of a High Value Al-Qaeda Detainee, 10 May 2005, p. 25 <https://www.thetorturedatabase.org/files/foia_subsite/pdfs/DOJOLC000864.pdf>.

which—after some circular reasoning—the authors determine is not the case.[77] However, in the interest of thorough analysis, the drafters separately conclude that even if EITs did 'shock the conscience', there still wouldn't be a violation of the United States' obligations under UNCAT because the techniques in question were being employed against non-US citizens on territory not under US jurisdiction.[78] This extremely narrow interpretation of the United States' international legal obligations is a very questionable reading of the letter of the law, and indisputably a violation of the spirit of it.

These nuanced 'definitions', such as they are, are disingenuous. They methodically undermine the protections envisaged by the drafters of UNCAT and related treaties, and exploit a very particular lacuna of international law: the lack of an ultimate enforcement authority. The United States is certainly not the only State to creatively construe its international obligations,[79] but it is one of a handful of States whose actions have the ability to actively influence developments and interpretations in international law on a comprehensive scale.[80] When it chooses to self-interestedly use this influence to diminish human rights protections, the impacts are evident far and wide. The United Kingdom, France, and Australia have almost certainly followed the US example of 'selective ignorance' of human rights obligations as inspiration for their own recent adoption of harsh new counterterrorism laws.[81]

Not only did the Bush Administration's lax interpretation of human rights law put several decades' worth of hard-won international legal protections at severe risk of being unfit for purpose—it did so for relatively little gain. The SSCI Report is scathing in its conclusions as to the merits of the CIA's detention and interrogation programme, finding that the 'use of its enhanced interrogation techniques was not an effective means of acquiring intelligence or gaining cooperation from detainees'.[82] Even more troubling, perhaps, is the fact that long before the CIA embarked on its post-9/11 misadventures, it

[77] Bradbury Memo on 'Interrogation of High Value Detainees', p. 38.

[78] Bradbury Memo on 'Interrogation of High Value Detainees', p. 39.

[79] As an example, see the discussion in this post: Spiegel, J., 'The Global Reach of the US Position on Torture', *Just Security*, 24 November 2014, <http://justsecurity.org/17749/global-reach-u-s-position-torture-convention/>.

[80] 'The United States has been at the heart of nearly all major developments in international law and the law of armed conflict over the past century and more'. Blank, L., 2012, 'Presidential Powers and Foreign Affairs', *Case Western Reserve Journal of International Law*, vol. 45, p. 107.

[81] The United Kingdom, France, and Australia are all considering (or have already implemented) stringent new law enforcement powers to proactively tackle the perceived threat from radical Islam. These laws single out primarily Muslim and ethnic minority citizens for heightened scrutiny and restrictions on freedom of speech and freedom of movement, and are almost certain to be challenged in the courts; however in the meantime, the civil liberties of certain sections of the population are being routinely undercut. A summary of the kinds of measures envisioned can be found in J.M. Berger, 'Europe Cracks Down', *Foreign Policy*, 16 January 2015, <http://foreignpolicy.com/2015/01/16/europe-cracks-down-terrorism-civil-liberties-after-paris/>.

[82] SSCI Report, Finding and Conclusions, p. 2,

had already determined from previous experience with coercive interrogations that such techniques 'do not produce intelligence', 'will probably result in false answers', and 'had historically proven to be ineffective'.[83] That it decided to engage in them anyway speaks volumes about the collective madness that gripped the country after the 9/11 attacks.

Short-sighted policies with far-reaching impacts are a dangerous combination. For centuries the United States has spent incalculable blood, treasure, and diplomatic capital to attain and maintain its status as superpower, all of which was undermined by the CIA detention and interrogation programme—the Senate concluded that 'the program caused immeasurable damage to the United States' public standing, [and] to the United States' longstanding global leadership on human rights in general'.[84] Life at the top of the food chain demands responsible leadership, for the overall health of the modern system of international relations, if nothing else. Since the beginning of the twenty-first century the US has seemed comfortable ignoring its obligations when it doesn't suit its short-term goals; however, of late it has seemed more willing to re-engage with the multilateral system in a conscientious way.

B. A renaissance in responsible leadership

One of the first acts of Barack Obama's presidency was a renunciation of 'enhanced interrogation techniques'. Under Executive Order 13491, the President ordered that:

> individuals detained in any armed conflict ... shall in all circumstances be treated humanely and shall not be subjected to violence to life and person (including murder of all kinds, mutilation, cruel treatment, and torture), nor to outrages upon personal dignity (including humiliating and degrading treatment), whenever such individuals are in the custody or under the effective control of an officer, employee, or other agent of the United States Government or detained within a facility owned, operated, or controlled by a department or agent of the United States.[85]

All previous 'executive directives, orders, and regulations inconsistent with this order, including but not limited to those issued to or by the Central Intelligence Agency (CIA) from September 11, 2001, to January 20, 2009, concerning detention or the interrogation of detained individuals'[86] were revoked to the extent of their inconsistency with the newly issued Executive Order. The CIA was explicitly ordered to 'close any detention facilities under its operational control "as expeditiously as possible," and not to open any

[83] SSCI Report, Finding and Conclusions, p. 3.
[84] SSCI Report, Finding and Conclusions, p. 16.
[85] Executive Order No. 13491, 74 Fed. Reg. 4893, 27 January 2009 (hereinafter E.O. 13491), <http://edocket.access.gpo.gov/2009/pdf/E9-1885.pdf>.
[86] EO 13491.

such future facilities … [officials were prohibited] from subjecting any detainee under effective U.S. control to any interrogation technique not listed in the current Army Field Manual on interrogation … the U.S. Supreme Court's holding in *Hamdan v Rumsfeld* that Common Article 3 of the Geneva Conventions provided the minimum standards for treatment of detainees in U.S. custody [was reaffirmed] … [and] all Bush-era Office of Legal Counsel's interpretations of Common Article 3 or the rest of the Geneva Conventions, the Convention Against Torture, and the federal criminal prohibitions on war crimes and torture [were disavowed]'.[87]

It was a bold break with the past, indirectly acknowledging that things 'contrary to American values' had been going on for far too long, with the implied—or in some cases, explicit—consent of the highest levels of government. Human rights organizations and civil liberty advocates enthusiastically welcomed the move; however, many cautioned that because its authority was based in an Executive Order (and therefore not based in legislation or binding on future presidents), it would be important to remain vigilant for any indications that torture and cruel, inhuman, and degrading treatment were once again becoming an accepted practice.[88]

Their optimism may have been rewarded in November 2014, when the United States presented its most recent report to the Committee against Torture, the treaty body of experts tasked with monitoring compliance with the Convention against Torture. Rather unexpectedly, the US delegation stated unequivocally its belief that 'torture, and cruel, inhuman and degrading treatment and punishment are forbidden in all places, at all times, with no exceptions'.[89] Even more surprisingly, and in a distinct break with past US policy, the delegation noted its understanding that 'obligations [under UNCAT] apply to a State Party in "any territory under its jurisdiction," [and that] such obligations, including the obligations in Articles 2 and 16 to prevent torture and cruel, inhuman or degrading treatment or punishment, extend to certain areas beyond the sovereign territory of the State Party'.[90] The delegation stated that the US had determined this extension applied to 'all places that the State Party controls as a governmental authority [including] the U.S. Naval Station at Guantánamo Bay, Cuba [and] U.S. registered ships and aircraft'.[91] During

[87] EO 13491; summary of content taken from Roehm, S., 'Five Years After Executive Order Ending "Enhanced Interrogations", a Return to Torture is Still Possible', *The Constitution Project*, 22 January 2014, <http://www.constitutionproject.org/documents/five-years-after-executive-order-ending-enhanced-interrogations-a-return-to-torture-is-still-possible/>.

[88] Roehm, S., 'Return to Torture is Still Possible'.

[89] Opening Statement of US Assistant Secretary of State Tom Malinowski before the Committee against Torture, 12 November 2014, <https://geneva.usmission.gov/2014/11/12/malinowski-torture-and-degrading-treatment-and-punishment-are-forbidden-in-all-places-at-all-times-with-no-exceptions/>.

[90] Opening Statement of Acting US Legal Adviser Mary E. McLeod before the Committee against Torture, 12 November 2014, <https://geneva.usmission.gov/2014/11/12/acting-legal-adviser-mcleod-u-s-affirms-torture-is-prohibited-at-all-times-in-all-places/>.

[91] Opening Statement of Acting US Legal Adviser Mary E. McLeod.

a question and answer session with the Committee, a delegation member affirmed that these protections applied to Bagram Airbase in Afghanistan as well.[92]

To characterize this as an astonishing turn of events is an understatement. The United States' last appearance before the Committee, in 2006, had been a notably combative experience. Details of the CIA's detention and interrogation programme had begun to become more widely known, through occasional media stories and persistent reports from lawyers representing detainees at Guantánamo Bay,[93] and the United States was on the defensive to explain how its counterterrorism policies were in accordance with its human rights obligations.[94] During its 2006 testimony, the US delegation suggested that certain allegations in the press about various US military and intelligence activities were 'occasionally absurd',[95] and the Committee members were somewhat patronizingly encouraged to be 'circumspect ... [and to] keep a sense of proportion and perspective'.[96] In some fraught exchanges, the Committee was chastised for asking questions 'outside the scope of the Convention',[97] and rather than respond to any line of questioning they found bothersome, the US delegation would instead refer Committee members to previously submitted written reports. Thus, the United States' 2014 appearance before the Committee—while not entirely without tension—was notable for both its more amicable overall ambiance and for the delegation's acknowledgement in its opening statement that '[a] little more than ten years ago, our government was employing interrogation methods that ... any fair minded person would believe were torture'.[98]

In parallel, the United States' presentation before the Committee against Torture was noteworthy as an overall snapshot of how the United States interprets international law in 2014, specifically with regards to the question of extraterritorial application of human rights treaties and the interplay between international human rights law, and international humanitarian law. Like many other states (but perhaps more aggressively than most), the US has long sought to limit the scope of application for human rights treaties to actions which take place within its own sovereign borders. In its 2006 appearance before the Committee, the United States reasserted its view that certain articles of the Convention did not apply to individuals outside the territory of the United States,[99] and

[92] Zarocostas, J., 'U.S. tells UN torture treaty applies to everyone, everywhere', *McClatchy DC*, 13 November 2014, <http://www.mcclatchydc.com/news/nation-world/world/article24776236.html>.

[93] See, for example, Center for Constitutional Rights, 'Report on Torture and Cruel, Inhuman and Degrading Treatment of Prisoners', July 2006, <http://ccrjustice.org/files/Report_ReportOnTorture.pdf>.

[94] Amman, D. A., 'The Committee Against Torture Urges an End to Guantanamo Detention', *ASIL Insights*, 8 June 2006, <http://www.asil.org/insights/volume/10/issue/14/committee-against-torture-urges-end-guant%C3%A1namo-detention>; Committee Against Torture, 'Summary Record of the 703d Meeting, Consideration of Reports Submitted by State Parties under Article 19 of the Convention, Second periodic report of the United States of America', CAT/C/SR.703, 12 May 2006, <http://goo.gl/wop5iY>.

[95] Summary Record of the 703d Meeting.

[96] Summary Record of the 703d Meeting.

[97] Summary Record of the 703d Meeting.

[98] Malinowski Opening Statement.

[99] See generally Amman, 'The Committee against Torture Urges an End to Guantanamo Detention', and Summary Record of the 703d Meeting.

also expressly rejected attempts to enlarge the characterization of 'territory under its jurisdiction'[100] to include Guantánamo Bay, contending that the concept that having 'de facto control' of territory was not legally equivalent to the notion of 'territory under its jurisdiction'.[101]

Thus, the United States' newfound willingness to extend the protections of the Convention against Torture to 'certain areas beyond the sovereign territory of the United States', including all places it acts 'as a governmental authority'[102] is certainly significant. While the language still does not go as far as the Committee experts would like, and is in some ways just a reiteration of Executive Order 13491, the very public method the United States chose to align itself with more mainstream interpretations of human rights obligations was a welcome (if calculated) public repudiation of the past.

Concluding remarks: a new frontier?

It is impossible to say what ramifications the Obama Administration's rapprochement with international law will have in the long term, if any. The United States will have a Presidential Election in November 2016, and it's anybody's guess whom the candidates will be, and what their foreign policy preferences will entail. It is certainly heartening for those who embrace expansive readings of human rights law to observe the United States use its 'superpower prerogative'[103] to support the notion of a capacious international legal infrastructure. Nevertheless, such optimism must be tempered by instinctive scepticism that the United States will ever act in anything other than its own self-interest. In the exact same time frame that White House lawyers and policymakers have been positively re-evaluating the United States' interpretation of international human rights law, the Administration has sought to rewrite the rules of engagement under international humanitarian law to support its secretive armed drone campaigns in Pakistan and Yemen.[104] Moreover, lingering questions remain as to whether any concrete measures of accountability will come from release of the Report—any names named, any arrests and

[100] Amman, 'The Committee against Torture Urges an End to Guantanamo Detention', and Summary Record of the 703d Meeting.

[101] Amman, 'The Committee against Torture Urges an End to Guantanamo Detention', and Summary Record of the 703d Meeting.

[102] McLeod Opening Statement.

[103] As the lone, reliably present superpower since the end of the Cold War, over the last twenty-five years, the US had tried to use military, diplomatic, and economic influence to widely promote its vision for the world, with varying degrees of success.

[104] See generally Report by Christof Heyns, the UN Special Rapporteur on extrajudicial, summary or arbitrary executions to the UN Human Rights Council, April 2013, UN doc. A/HRC/23/47, §39 <http://www.ohchr.org/Documents/HRBodies/HRCouncil/RegularSession/Session23/A-HRC-23-47_en.pdf>.

prosecutions made, any reparations paid to those who were at the brutal receiving end of the euphemistically termed 'enhanced interrogation techniques'.

However, at the very least, the publication of the SSCI report provides an important bookend to a particularly painful chapter of American history, and the questions and introspection it has prompted may help ensure that such frenzied methods are never again undertaken in the name of national security. This can only be a good thing. Vigilance will always be warranted, but transparency is always welcome.

2 Gender perspectives in armed conflicts in 2014

Megan Burke and Loren Persi Vicentic[1]

Introduction

A spectrum of serious situations of harm against women and girls in armed conflict exists in combination with sexual violence or apart from it. Anticipating the progress review of the fifteen years of implementation of UN Security Council Resolution 1325, to the end of 2014, it is therefore timely to look into some less examined issues of gender in situations of armed conflict as they occurred in that year.

This chapter highlights gender-based crimes against women and girls during situations of armed conflict in 2014, focusing on some that received less attention by the international community than the very heinous crimes of rape and sexual violence and looks at the international legal frameworks that can address them. It then looks into the numerous ways in which women participated in armed conflict—as parties to armed conflict, as peace negotiators, and as civil society activists—showing how armed conflict impacts women in their many different roles and considering the importance of their involvement and how it may impact outcomes, including issues of protection and justice.

Crimes, or elements of gender-related abuses of women and girls that may not explicitly include a sexual-violence component, or may be treated as a crime distinct from violations involving sexual violence, are many. They include trafficking, sale and slavery, forced marriage, denial of access to education, recruitment and use of child soldiers, inappropriate detention of civilians and combatants, torture and assassination—particularly of women human rights defenders—failure to observe fair trial guarantees or denial of access to justice, and outrages against personal dignity.

[1] Megan Burke and Loren Persi Vicentic are independent specialists on the casualties of, and assistance to, victims of armed conflict. Megan Burke is Director of the International Campaign to Ban Landmines and the Cluster Munition Coalition. She holds a Master's degree in International Relations from Yale University. Loren Persi Vicentic is the Victim Assistance Coordinator for the Landmine and Cluster Munition Monitor. He has worked on victim assistance issues since 2004. This chapter has been written in their independent capacity.

In all circumstances, parties to a non-international armed conflict must treat humanely persons taking no active part in hostilities including those persons who have been injured, captured, or otherwise have ceased to take part in hostilities (persons *hors de combat*), without adverse distinction, including *inter alia*, on the basis of sex.[2]

Acts against civilians and persons *hors de combat* prohibited in non-international armed conflicts 'at any time and in any place whatsoever'[3] include many that are sometimes specifically targeted towards women and girls based on their gender, such as: violence to the life, health and physical or mental well-being of persons, in particular murder as well as cruel treatment such as torture, taking of hostages, and outrages upon personal dignity, in particular humiliating and degrading treatment, rape, enforced prostitution, and any form or indecent assault and slavery. Geneva Convention IV, on the protection of civilians in armed conflict, holds in Article 27 that women 'shall be especially protected against any attack on their honour'.[4] Antecedently, Article 27 also states that all protected persons are entitled, in all circumstances, to respect for their persons and their honour.[5]

Specifically with respect to education, IHL holds the parties to conflict responsible to ensure children's access to appropriate education, noting that: 'Children ... shall receive an education, including religious and moral education, in keeping with the wishes of their parents ...'.[6]

Additional Protocols I and II to the Geneva Conventions prohibit the recruitment of children under fifteen.[7] The Rome Statute of the ICC recognizes the conscription, enlistment or use in active hostilities of child soldiers under the age of fifteen years among serious violations of the laws and customs applicable in armed conflicts.[8]

[2] Geneva Conventions (GC) Common Art. 3; and AP II, Art. 4(1).

[3] Additional Protocol II, Art. 4(1).

[4] Noting 'in particular against rape, enforced prostitution, or any form of indecent assault'.

[5] Durham, H. and K. O'Byrne, 'The Dialogue of Difference: Gender Perspectives on International Humanitarian Law', *International Review of the Red Cross*, vol. 92, no. 877 (March 2010), pp. 31–52, at p. 34.

[6] Art. 4(3)(a), Protocol additional to the Geneva Conventions of 12 August 1949, and relating to the Protection of Victims of Non-International Armed Conflicts (Additional Protocol II), 8 June 1977, in Sobhi Tawil, 'International Humanitarian Law and Basic Education', *International Review of the Red Cross*, vol. 82, no. 839 (September 2000), pp. 581–600, <https://www.icrc.org/eng/resources/documents/misc/57jqq4.htm>. Art. 24 of the Fourth Geneva Convention, also holds that 'The Parties to the conflict shall take the necessary measures to ensure that children under fifteen, who are orphaned or are separated from their families as a result of the war, are not left to their own resources, and that their maintenance, the exercise of their religion and their education are facilitated in all circumstances. Their education shall, as far as possible, be entrusted to persons of a similar cultural tradition.'

[7] ICRC, 'Customary IHL database: Rule 136. Recruitment of Child Soldiers', <https://www.icrc.org/customary-ihl/eng/docs/v1_cha_chapter39_rule136#refFn_61_1>; and Child Soldiers International, 'International Standards', <http://www.child-soldiers.org/international_standards.php>.

[8] Rome Statute, Art. 8(2)(b)(xxvi) and Art. 8(2)(d)(vii).

The Geneva Conventions do not refer to forced marriage specifically, nor is forced marriage explicitly listed among gender-based crimes under the International Criminal Court (ICC)'s Rome Statute. However, it can be argued that forced marriage is banned under the Common Article 3 3(1)(c) prohibition on 'outrages upon personal dignity, in particular humiliating and degrading treatment', which are prohibited at any time and in any place whatsoever[9] and Article 75 of Additional Protocol I to the Geneva Conventions, and Article 4 of Additional Protocol II, which include similar wording and can be applied to forced marriage in non-international armed conflict, that being the context in which such cases predominantly occur.[10]

According to the judgment in the International Criminal Tribunal for the former Yugoslavia (ICTY) case *the Prosecutor v Zlatko Alexovski* (which did not involve a sexual element to the crime), an outrage against personal dignitary is 'an act which is animated by contempt for the human dignity of another person'.[11] With regard to the crime of outrages upon personal dignity that may be applicable to the treatment of women and girls in armed conflict, it is useful to note that according to the *Alexovski* Trial Chamber outrages upon personal dignity as violations of the laws or customs of war, require that the humiliation of the victim be of an intensity such that any reasonable person would be outraged (*actus reus*). It requires (*mens rea*) that the perpetrator acted wilfully, but does not necessitate that the perpetrator has the specific intent to humiliate or degrade the victim, though they must be able to perceive that such humiliation is a foreseeable and reasonable consequence of their actions.[12]

Concerning the crime of slavery in situations of non-international armed conflict, including the sale and trade of women and girls for marriage or otherwise, the prohibition of 'slavery and the slave trade in all their forms' is recognized in Additional Protocol II as a fundamental guarantee for civilians and all persons *hors de combat*.[13]

Notably, forced marriage has been successfully prosecuted as a war crime in one instance. The Appeals Chamber of the Special Court for Sierra Leone (2008) prosecuted and made a conviction on forced marriage as a crime against humanity in the category of 'other inhumane acts'.[14] Thus far, the Special Court for Sierra Leone is the only international tribunal

[9] Nowak, M., 2014, 'Torture and Other Cruel, Inhuman, or Degrading Treatment or punishment'. In *The Oxford Handbook of International Law in Armed Conflict*, edited by Clapham, A., and Gaeta, P.: Oxford University Press, p 399.

[10] Nguyen, F., 2014, 'Untangling Sex, Marriage, and Other Criminalities in Forced Marriage', *Goettingen Journal of International Law*, vol. 6, no. 1 (October): 13, p. 26.

[11] Askin, K., 2011, 'Crimes against Women under International Criminal Law'. In *Research Handbook of International Criminal Law*, edited by Brown, B. S.: Edward Elgar Publishers, p. 99.

[12] *The Prosecutor v Zlatko Aleksovski*–Case No. IT-95-14/1-T, Trial Chamber I bis (Judges Rodrigues [Presiding], Vohrah and Nieto-Navia), 'Judgement' 25 June 1999, <http://www.icty.org/x/file/Legal%20Library/jud_supplement/supp6-e/trial.htm>.

[13] Additional Protocol II, Art. 4(2)(f), <https://www.icrc.org/customary-ihl/eng/docs/v1_rul_rule94#refFn_88_3>.

[14] Forced marriage also violates the right to freely consent to marriage found in the Universal

to have made a conviction on the grounds of forced marriage.[15] In the findings of the Court, while forced marriage may include many facets of sexual slavery, it can be differentiated due to the elements of conjectural association and implied exclusivity that constitute marriage.[16]

Considering assassination attempts on women peacemakers and activists, Additional Protocols I and II, hold that making a person the object of attack in the knowledge that she (or he) is *hors de combat* are grave breaches.[17] The Rome Statute of the International Criminal Court accordingly holds that '[v]iolence to life and person, in particular murder of all kinds ... intentionally directing attacks against the civilian population or against civilians not taking direct part in hostilities ...' are also war crimes.[18]

While all provisions of the Geneva Conventions with regard to armed forces and persons participating directly in hostilities apply without adverse distinction equally to women and men, Article 12 of Geneva Convention I, relating to the wounded and sick finds that '[w]omen shall be treated with all consideration due to their sex'. It has been argued that outdated notions of women's roles in armed conflict and combat that were held when the Geneva Conventions were drafted—particularly those incorporated in Geneva Convention I—continue to influence their application, undermining the protection, place, and the roles, of women in armed conflict.[19] This much criticized sexist approach of international humanitarian law (IHL) is underscored in the message of the still available ICRC commentary from the time on Geneva Convention I (1952), which determines that the 'special consideration with which women must be treated' is '[n]o doubt that consideration which is accorded in every civilized country to beings who are weaker than oneself and whose honour and modesty call for respect'.[20]

Declaration of Human Rights: 'Marriage shall be entered into only with the free and full consent of the intending spouses', Art. 23 of the International Covenant on Civil and Political Rights and Art. 10 of the International Covenant on Economic, Social, and Cultural Rights.

[15] See Frances Nguyen, 2014, 'Untangling Sex, Marriage, and Other Criminalities in Forced Marriage', *Goettingen Journal of International Law*, vol. 6, n. 1: pp. 13–45. The court found that forced marriage 'involves a perpetrator compelling a person by force or threat of force, through words, or conduct of the perpetrator, or anyone associated with him, into a forced conjugal association resulting in great suffering or serious physical or mental injury on the part of the victim. Special Court for Sierra Leone, Case No. SCSL-2004-16-A, *The Prosecutor of the Special Court v Alex Tamba Brima Brima Bazzy Kamara Santigie Borbor Kanu*, p. 25.

[16] Ambos, K., 2014, *Treatise on International Criminal Law: The Crimes and Sentencing, Volume II*: Oxford University Press, p. 100.

[17] Additional Protocol I, Art. 85(3)(a)–(e), and Additional Protocol II, Art. 13(2).

[18] Rome Statute Art. 8(2)(c)(i); (iii); Art. 8(2)(e)(I); (xi).

[19] See discussion on this topic in Durham, H. and O'Byrne, K., 2010, 'The Dialogue of Difference: Gender Perspectives on International Humanitarian Law', *International Review of the Red Cross*, vol. 92, no. 877 (March): 31–52, p. 33.

[20] ICRC, 'Convention (I) for the Amelioration of the Condition of the Wounded and Sick in Armed Forces in the Field. Geneva, 12 August 1949: Commentary–Art. 12. Chapter II: Wounded and sick', <https://www.icrc.org/applic/ihl/ihl.nsf/Comment.xsp?viewComments=LookUpCOMART&articleUNID=B97B83DC12AC4998C12563CD00519F56>.

Various aspects of IHL that can be applied in respect to gender-based crimes, though fragmented and inconsistent, have over time been complemented to a growing, but still limited, extent by UN resolutions, and by aspects of international human rights law, as will be explored further in relation to events in 2014.

United Nations Security Council (UNSC) resolution 1325 (2000) 'stresses the importance of women's equal and full participation as active agents in the prevention and resolution of conflicts, peace-building and peacekeeping'. Together with another six subsequent UNSC resolutions, two regarding participation and the rest focused on sexualized violence, the binding UNSC resolutions constitute a strengthened, if uneven, framework for implementing and monitoring the UN's Women, Peace and Security agenda with an array of objectives and indicators. In addition, by the close of 2014, forty-eight countries had created a National Action Plan for implementing UNSC resolution 1325.[21]

The participation of women from affected locations was an original goal of civil society groups: 'In aiming for a security council resolution [women peace activists] sought to bridge the chasm between their grassroots communities in war-torn countries and the New York skyline.'[22] By 2013, another UNSC resolution stated candidly that '[p]ersisting barriers to full implementation of UNSC resolution 1325 (2000) will only be dismantled through dedicated commitment to women's empowerment, participation, and human rights, and through concerted leadership, consistent information and action, and support, to build women's engagement in all levels of decision-making'.[23]

The development of a stronger nexus between UNSC resolutions and human rights was enhanced throughout 2014 due to the adoption in late 2013 of General Recommendation number 30 (CEDAW GR30) by the Committee on the Elimination of Discrimination against Women (CEDAW). It resulted in increased potential for synergistic implementation of those resolutions and human rights obligations.[24] CEDAW GR30 notes that international humanitarian law 'contains relevant obligations that bind non-State actors, as parties to an armed conflict (for example, insurgents and rebel groups)' in Common Article 3 and relating to the protection of victims of non-international armed conflicts in Additional Protocol II. Though not included in IHL provisions, disarmament, demobilization, and reintegration, which may be regarded as a *jus post bellum* measure, are part of the broader security sector reform framework highlighted in CEDAW GR30 as

[21] WILPF, PeaceWomen, 'Member States', <http://www.peacewomen.org/member-states>.

[22] Anderlini, S. N., 2007, *Women Building Peace: What They Do, Why It Matters*, Boulder, Colorado: Lynne Rienner, p. 72.

[23] Resolution 2122 (2013), 18 October 2013, S/RES/2122 (2013).

[24] A. Swaine, 'Substantive New Normative Provisions on Women and Armed Conflict Concurrently Adopted by the United Nations Security Council and the CEDAW Committee', American Society of International Law, ASIL Insights, vol. 18, Issue 5, 18 February 2014, <http://www.asil.org/insights/volume/18/issue/5/substantive-new-normative-provisions-women-and-armed-conflict>.

being among the first security initiatives to be established in post-conflict and transition periods.[25]

CEDAW GR30 of November 2013 raises possibilities for survivor-centred approaches to addressing non-sexual gender-based violations against women and girls in conflict with the participation of, and consultation with victims which is in greater conformity with contemporary approaches.[26] Thus CEDAW GR30 finds that:

> Women are not passive bystanders or only victims or targets. They have historically had and continue to have a role as combatants, as part of organized civil society, as human rights defenders, as members of resistance movements and as active agents in both formal and informal peacebuilding and recovery processes. States parties must address all aspects of their obligations under the Convention to eliminate discrimination against women.[27]

Pragmatic efforts to understand and address gender-based crimes require improved understanding of definitions. International agencies sometimes use the terms 'sexual violence', 'gender-based violence', and 'violence against women' interchangeably.[28] The term 'gender-based violence' refers to violence that targets individuals or groups on the basis of their gender. In its General Recommendation 19, CEDAW defines gender-based violence as 'violence that is directed against a woman because she is a woman or that affects women disproportionately'. Violence against women is defined by the UN Declaration on the Elimination of Violence against Women, adopted by the General Assembly on 20 December 1993, as 'any act of gender-based violence that results in, or is likely to result in, physical, sexual or psychological harm or suffering to women, including threats of such acts, coercion or arbitrary deprivation of liberty, whether occurring in public or in private life'. It is a form of gender-based violence and includes sexual violence.[29]

The Office of the Prosecutor of the ICC has taken a useful practical step by clarifying that 'gender-based crimes are not always manifested as a form of sexual violence' but 'may include non-sexual attacks on women and girls, and men and boys, because of their gender'.[30] However, this chapter, in discussing gender-based crimes also includes crimes whereby the victims were targeted because they were female, though not necessarily

[25] CEDAW GR30 (8) 66.

[26] UN Committee on the Elimination of Discrimination Against Women (CEDAW), General Recommendation No. 30 on women in conflict prevention, conflict and post-conflict situations, 1 November 2013, 0, p. 11.

[27] CEDAW/C/GC/30, p. 3

[28] See UN Women, 'Defining Violence against Women and Girls', <http://www.endvawnow.org/en/articles/295-defining-violence-against-women-and-girls.html>.

[29] IRIN, 'Gender-based Violence', <http://www.irinnews.org/indepthmain.aspx?InDepthId=20&ReportId=62847>.

[30] ICC, 'Policy Paper on Sexual and Gender-Based Crimes', June 2014, p. 3, <http://www.icc-cpi.int/iccdocs/otp/OTP-Policy-Paper-on-Sexual-and-Gender-Based-Cri mes-June-2014.pdf>.

being specifically the victims of 'attacks' per se. In this chapter we therefore have used the term gender based-crimes more broadly defined as prohibited acts where the victim is targeted due to gender, in these cases against women and/or girls.

A. Gender-based crimes other than sexual violence

The long neglected agenda of sexual violence in conflict has received increasing attention in recent years, and has been put at the forefront of several UNSC resolutions, raised in IHL discussion, and popularized through a massive public campaign.[31] However, it is also important to look at the situation of women more broadly, the abuses that they face during armed conflict and during transitions to often unstable post-conflict situations which differ little or may be in some cases worse than those governed by IHL. Gender-based crimes, including those that are not necessarily explicitly or exclusively sexual in nature, may be exacerbated by armed conflict but are often rooted in many other legal, social, and economic factors relating to discrimination and inequality.

The prominence given to acts of rape and sexual violence against women has raised awareness of the occurrence of these crimes, while other harms that may be more prevalent have received less attention and are rarely featured in efforts to enumerate gender-based crimes, either as data or as evidence. In exploring this predicament, Ni Aoláin has noted that the lack of quantitative analysis is influenced by their more complex, multi-factor derivations of gender-based crimes, but also, the greater attention on the sexualization of victimization. This focus on 'protection from sexual harm becomes paramount, excluding attention to the myriad of other harms women experience on a routine basis'.[32]

The strengthening of the international legal framework around protection of women in armed conflicts can also be as seen in the example of the Arms Trade Treaty (ATT), which entered into force in December 2014. A gender-specific provision in an Article of the ATT, relating to export assessments for the determination of the legitimacy of arms transfers. Article 7.4 stipulates that a State Party, in making its assessment, shall take into account the risk of the arms in question 'being used to commit or facilitate serious acts of gender-based violence'. Provisions of that same Article also determine that States

[31] The Global Summit to End Sexual Violence in Conflict in London on 10–13 June 2014 was the largest ever gathering on the subject.

[32] Fionnuala Ni Aoláin, 2015, 'The Gender Politics of Fact-Finding in the Context of the Women, Peace and Security Agenda'. In *The Future of Human Rights Fact-Finding*, edited by Alston, P. and Knuckey, S., Oxford University Press.

must 'assess the potential' that the arms could be used to commit or facilitate a 'serious violation' of international humanitarian law or international human rights law.

Recent analysis of what may constitute serious violations with regards to the ATT, finds that many violations have been recognized through various fora. Among them, there are many that strongly relate to gender-based crimes and they do not need to have been 'widespread' or 'systematic' to be considered 'serious violations'.[33] Accordingly there is agreement that in addition to rape and other sexual violations, a wider range of crimes such as enforced disappearance, deliberate targeting of civilians and civilian objects in situations of armed conflict, torture and other cruel, inhuman, or degrading treatment are considered 'serious violations'. There is also largely agreement that gender-based violence, recruitment of children into armed forces or groups, attacks on schools and education facilities, failure by States to provide conditions of detention that meet international norms may also be considered 'serious violations' (among others).[34]

As part of the growing recognition that more needed to be done to address gender-based crimes in armed conflict, the International Criminal Court (ICC) took steps to strengthen its work in this area in 2014. Following a series of trials which failed to attain a conviction of any of the defendants charged with sexual or gender-based crimes, and associated criticism of the Court's approach, in June 2014, the ICC Prosecutor published a Policy Paper on Sexual and Gender-Based Crimes.[35] Paying 'particular attention' to sexual or gender-based crimes already included of its six strategic goals in the ICC Office of the Prosecutor (OTP) Strategic Plan 2012–15, the OTP stated that the 'policy will contribute to ensuring not only the effective investigation and prosecution of sexual and gender-based crimes, but also to enhancing access to justice for victims of these crimes'.[36]

In 2014, amidst efforts to strengthen the international legal framework, commitments to ensure the protection of women in conflict as well as their participation in conflict prevention, resolution, and peace building were 'being tested' on the ground in circumstances of conflict where mass violence, humanitarian catastrophes, and human suffering are overwhelming, as highlighted by the UN Secretary-General.[37]

[33] Karimova, T., *What amounts to 'a serious violation of international human rights law?: An analysis of practice and expert opinion for the purpose of the 2013 Arms Trade Treaty*, Geneva Academy of International Humanitarian Law and Human Rights, (Academy Briefing No. 6), August 2014, pp. 5–6.

[34] Ibid.

[35] 'The Office of The Prosecutor of the ICC, Policy Paper on Sexual and Gender Based Crimes: ICC Outlines Policies to Improve Prosecutorial Outcomes, (Recent Policy Paper)', 10 December 2014, 128 *Harvard Law Review*, 793.

[36] 'The Prosecutor of the International Criminal Court, Fatou Bensouda, publishes comprehensive Policy Paper on Sexual and Gender-Based Crimes', Press Release, 5 June 2014, <http://www.icc-cpi.int/en_menus/icc/press and media/press releases/Pages/pr1011.aspx>.

[37] UNSC (S/2014/693) 27 September 2014, §3.

B. Gender-based crimes in 2014: gender-based threats to education, forced marriage, child marriage, slavery, and the recruitment of girls

Gender-based crimes in conflict rarely or never occur without a connection to sexual violence. Examining these abuses separately can provide insight into the interconnectedness of prohibited acts and the underlying influences. The prevalence of non-sexual gender-based violence in conflict may also serve as a measure of, and early warning for, an increase in the conflict and the intensity of violations and inhumane acts. Not only can this be an indicator of broader escalating violence, the crimes themselves can create a knock-on effect, bringing more women and girls into situations which lead to further violence against them. For example, gender-based attacks on education prevent access to education. Following, a lack of education has been demonstrated to make girls more vulnerable to child/forced marriage and recruitment into armed forces.[38] In another example, child recruitment can lead to forced marriage.

Targeted attacks on girls attending school were an extensive problem in 2014.[39] For example, a UN Office of the High Commissioner for Human Rights (OHCHR) report revealed that attacks on schoolgirls were 'occurring with increased regularity' from 2009 through 2014. The attacks were intentionally carried out by groups who held beliefs that women and girls should not receive an education.[40]

As a human right, the right to education is enshrined in the Convention on the Rights of the Child (CRC),[41] while Article 10 of CEDAW addresses the right to education for women on an equal basis with men. In CEDAW GR30, the Committee reiterated that in conflict-affected areas, girls' access to education is threatened by the effects of conflict as well as specifically targeted attacks and threats against girls and their teachers

[38] 'Rape, acid attacks, kidnap: girls face rising violence in fight for education-U.N.' *Reuters* 9 February, 2015, <http://www.reuters.com/article/2015/02/09/us-un-rights-girls-idUSKBN0LD1P820150209>.

[39] This issue was given wide reaching international attention due to the awarding on the Nobel Beac prize to Malala Yousafzai, from Pakistan as the 2014 co-laureate for her struggle for girls' right to education: 'After having suffered an attack on her life by Taliban gunmen in 2012, she has continued her struggle and become a leading advocate of girls' rights.' The Nobel Peace Prize 2014, 'Malala Yousafzai-Facts', <http://www.nobelprize.org/nobel_prizes/peace/laureates/2014/yousafzai-facts.html>; and UNESCO, 'Malala: Symbolizing the right of girls to education', <http://www.unesco.org/new/en/unesco/resources/malala-symbolizing-the-right-of-girls-to-education>.

[40] 'Many girls in Africa and the Middle East are under pressure to leave school', *Christian Science Monitor*, 28 February 2015, <http://www.csmonitor.com/USA/Foreign-Policy/2015/0228/Many-girls-in-Africa-and-the-Middle-East-are-under-pressure-to-leave-school>.

[41] Art. 28 of the CRC refers to the right of all children to a free primary education, it adds that children should be 'encouraged to reach the highest level of education they are capable of'.

by non-State actors. In July 2014, CEDAW commenced the elaboration of a new General Recommendation on girls' and women's right to education.[42] In that process CEDAW reported among the examples of recent cases of attacks against girls accessing education, the abduction in April 2014 of nearly 300 schoolgirls in Chibok in northeast Nigeria by the Boko Haram movement.[43]

In a statement regarding the Chibok girls' abduction, the OTP noted the responsibility of Nigeria as a State Party to the Rome Statute of the ICC: 'Under the Rome Statute, the Nigerian authorities have primary responsibility to investigate and prosecute the alleged crimes. Such cases may become admissible before the ICC if there are no relevant investigations or prosecutions in Nigeria, or if the national authorities are unwilling or unable to carry out genuine investigations or prosecutions.'[44]

The UN General Assembly resolution on child, early, and forced marriage, adopted in November 2014, was said to have marked 'the first time that UN member states have agreed upon substantive recommendations for the steps that countries, international organisations and others must take to address the problem.'[45] The resolution also noted that the risk of forced marriage is 'exacerbated in conflict and humanitarian crisis situations.'[46]

The prohibition of hostage-taking is recognized as a fundamental guarantee for civilians.[47] Boko Haram leader, Abubakar Shekau, indicated in June 2014 that the girls kidnapped from the village of Chibok would be released if Boko Haram fighters held by the government were freed in exchange.[48] It was further reported that the group had developed a list of eighteen of its members to be swapped in a hostage exchange with the abducted Chibok girls.[49] This raises questions also about whether the capture of school

[42] CEDAW, 'Right to Education Project', <http://www.right-to-education.org/keywords/cedaw>.

[43] Noted in a background paper to contribute to the development of its general recommendation on access to education, and is also to be published in advance of the 2015 High-level Review of UNSC Resolution 1325. UN rights report points to 'increasing regularity' of attacks on girls seeking education, 9 February 2015, <http://www.un.org/apps/news/story.asp?NewsID=50032#.VPRLGS5i-24>.

[44] ICC OTP, 'Statement of the Prosecutor of the International Criminal Court, Fatou Bensouda, on the abduction of schoolgirls in Nigeria', 8 May 2014, <http://www.icc-cpi.int/en_menus/icc/structure%20of%20the%20court/office%20of%20the%20prosecutor/reports%20and%20statements/statement/Pages/otp-statement-08-05-2014.aspx>.

[45] Girls Not Brides, 'Statement on UN General Assembly resolution on child, early and forced marriage', 21 November 2014, <http://www.girlsnotbrides.org/girls-brides-statement-un-general-assembly-resolution-child-early-forced-marriage>.

[46] UNGA, 'Child, early and forced marriage', 18 December 2014 A/RES/69/156.

[47] The prohibition of hostage taking on civilians and persons *hors de combat* in Additional Protocols I and II, also under the Rome Statute of the International Criminal Court, the 'taking of hostages' constitutes a war crime in both international and non-international armed conflicts. See ICRC, Customary IHL, Rule 96. Hostage-Taking, <https://www.icrc.org/customary-ihl/eng/docs/v1_rul_rule96>.

[48] Ploch Blanchard, L., 'Nigeria's Boko Haram: Frequently Asked Questions', Congressional Research Service, 10 June 2014.

[49] 'Boko Haram seeks swap of 30 Chibok girls for 18 key members', 11 September 2014, <http://www.nigerianeye.com/2014/09/boko-haram-seeks-swap-of-30-chibok.html>.

girls was a directed gender-based crime, with the consideration that the value of the girls as hostages might be higher than other potential targets. It has been noted in the press that many of the killings and kidnappings of Boko Haram had failed to gain wide-reaching international attention, and argued that therefore 'had these schoolgirls been schoolboys, we probably wouldn't be talking about it in the first place'.[50]

The Boko Haram captors of the Chibok schoolgirls declared in a video recording in November 2014 that they had converted and 'married off' the remaining 219 schoolgirls.[51] Human Rights Watch reported that in total Boko Haram was holding more than 500 women and young girls and that forced marriage was commonplace in the group's camps. Reports of forced marriages were given by some of the girls who managed to escape.[52] As in many other countries,[53] child and forced marriage in Nigeria is not limited to the affects of conflict, and occurred more frequently outside conflict. Although underage marriage was prohibited by national legislation in 2003[54]—that is not enforced in all of its states—39% of girls were married before the age of fifteen.[55]"

Forced marriage and slavery were reported in areas of Iraq controlled by the Islamic State (previously known as Islamic State of Iraq and the Levant/Islamic State of Iraq and Syria, often still referred to as ISIS) in 2014, particularly in relation to the capture and abuse of women from the Yazidi minority group. In Iraq, which is not party to the ICC Rome Statute, Amnesty international[56] and Human Rights Watch[57] reported on these

[50] Freeman, C., 'Don't forget that Boko Haram targets boys as well as girls', *The Telegraph*, 11 May 2014, <http://blogs.telegraph.co.uk/news/colinfreeman/100270947/dont-forget-that-boko-haram-targets-boys-as-well-as-girls>.

[51] 'Missing Nigerian schoolgirls "married off"', 1 November 2014, *A Jazeera*, <http://www.aljazeera.com/news/africa/2014/10/boko-haram-says-schoolgirls-married-20141031222536853563.html>.

[52] Human Rights Watch, 'Those Terrible Weeks in their Camp. Boko Haram Violence against Women and Girls in Northeast Nigeria', 2014, p. 31.

[53] World Vision reported that the countries with the highest percentages of child marriage (from 75% to 49% of girls under eighteen years; and 36% to 24% under fifteen years) were Niger, Chad, Bangladesh, Guinea, Central African Republic, Mali, Mozambique, Nepal, Malawi, Ethiopia. World Vision, 'Ten worst places for child marriage', 8 May 2014 <http://www.worldvision.org/news-stories-videos/ten-worst-places-child-marriage>.

[54] Nigeria is not however among the States parties and signatories to the Convention on Consent to Marriage, Minimum Age for Marriage and Registration of Marriages (1962), which reaffirms the consensual nature of marriage, and requires the parties to establish a minimum age by law and to ensure registration of marriages, <https://treaties.un.org/Pages/ViewDetails.aspx?mtdsg_no=XVI-3&chapter=16&lang=en>.

[55] 'Nigeria: Child brides facing death sentences a decade after child marriage prohibited', *The Guardian*, 11 March 2015, <http://www.theguardian.com/global-development-professionals-network/2015/mar/11/the-tragedy-of-nigerias-child-brides>. It has been argued that forced marriage should also be prosecuted as a crime against humanity if it occurs during a widespread or systematic attack against a civilian population even outside of conflict. Nguyen, F., 2014, 'Untangling Sex, Marriage, and Other Criminalities in Forced Marriage', *Goettingen Journal of International Law*, vol. 6, no. 1: 13–45, p. 25.

[56] 'Escape from Hell: Torture and Sexual Slavery in Islamic State Captivity in Iraq', *Amnesty International*, 23 December 2014.

[57] Human Rights Watch, 'Iraq: Forced Marriage, Conversion for Yezidis', 12 October 2014, <http://www.hrw.org/news/2014/10/11/iraq-forced-marriage-conversion-yezidis>.

crimes based on interviews with women and girls who had been captured and escaped. Sexual violence, rape, slavery, sexual slavery, and forced marriage were all reported from the accounts of these interviews.

Trafficking, sale, and slavery of women is practised by some armed groups and are also crimes committed by families and individuals affected by armed conflict. Trafficking in women and children in local markets were reported among the possible sources of revenue of ISIS.[58] Iraq's Human Rights Ministry reported that hundreds of Yazidi women were being held in schools in Mosul. A member of the Iraqi Parliament, the only Yazidi in the Parliament[59] told the Parliament that the 'women have been sold in a slavery market'.[60]

In Afghanistan, it was reported that although there are no official figures, many families of imprisoned Taliban are likely to have faced dire economic predicaments leading to them selling girl children. In one example, a suspected Taliban militant arrested for involvement laying roadside bombs sold twin eight-month-old daughters arranged through the local Jirga—an assembly of elders who make decisions based on traditional laws and customs—which also said that the girls could be bought back by the family.[61]

In 2014, the OHCHR observed that in conflict situations the risk of child, early, and forced marriage is also exacerbated, 'where the increased risks of poverty from financial instability and sexual violence leave girls even more vulnerable to this practice'.[62] It gave the example of reports from the independent international commission of inquiry on the Syrian Arab Republic[63] noting an increase in child, early and forced marriage because families believed that, in conflict, their daughters would be safer if they were already married.[64]

The Optional Protocol to the Convention on the Rights of the Child on the involvement of children in armed conflict highlights this connection, '(r)ecognizing the special needs of those children who are particularly vulnerable to recruitment or use in hostilities contrary to the present Protocol owing to their economic or social status or gender'.[65] The Optional Protocol prohibits the recruitment or use in hostilities of under

[58] 'The Islamic State in Iraq and the Levant and the Al-Nusrah Front for the People of the Levant: Report and Recommendations Submitted Pursuant to Resolution 2170' (S/2014/815), 14 November 2014, §55.

[59] Iraqi Parliament Guide, 'Vian Dakheel Saeed Khadher', <http://www.iraqiparliament.info/en/node/761>.

[60] 'Iraq Conflict: Hundreds of Yazidi Women Reportedly Captured by ISIS', 8 August 2014, <http://www.cbc.ca/news/world/iraq-conflict-hundreds-of-yazidi-women-reportedly-captured-by-isis-1.2731561>.

[61] Noor ul-Ayn, S., 'The Price of a Girl', *Afghanistan Today*, 3 June 2014, <http://www.afghanistan-today.org/article/?id=710>.

[62] A/HRC/26/22 §20.

[63] A/HRC/23/58, §35, and A/HRC/24/46, §36.

[64] OHCHR, 'Preventing and Eliminating Child, Early and Forced Marriage', 2 April 2014, A/HRC/26/22, §19.

[65] Optional Protocol to the Convention on the Rights of the Child on the involvement of children in armed conflict (2000), <http://www.ohchr.org/EN/ProfessionalInterest/Pages/OPACCRC.aspx>.

eighteen-year-olds by non-State armed groups and its Article 1 requires States Parties to 'take all feasible measures to ensure that members of their armed forces who have not attained the age of 18 years do not take a direct part in hostilities'.[66]

The issue of early, forced marriage for minors is interlinked to the issue of child soldiers. In defining 'a child associated with an armed force or armed group',[67] UNICEF refers to any person under eighteen years of age who is part of any kind of regular or irregular armed force or armed group in any capacity,[68] including girls recruited for forced marriage.[69] Reports from Syria of girls who are minors recruited as brides and enticements for fighters from militant groups, were widespread in 2014.[70] Girls were also recruited for combat and gender-specific patrolling to enforce the will of armed groups in their areas of control.[71]

The recruitment of girls in armed conflict by the Kurdish Popular Protection Units (Yekîneyên Parastina Gel-YPG), was highlighted in 2014, particularly in the battle for and around the town of Kobani and in the 'Democratic Self-Administration in Rojava' in Syria more generally.[72] Accusations also emerged in the media that female-led groups were recruiting girls at schools.[73] In July 2014, the YPG signed two 'Deed of Commitment'

[66] Art. 38 of the Convention on the Rights of the Child requires State parties to prevent anyone under the age of fifteen from taking direct part in hostilities and to refrain from recruiting anyone under the age of fifteen years. OPAC was drafted in order to raise the minimum ages set out in the Convention. Child Soldiers International, 'International Standards', <http://www.child-soldiers.org/international_standards.php>.

[67] Forced marriage may be understood to be covered in the definition, though not specifically referred to, of the Paris Principles and Guidelines on Children Associated with Armed Forces of Armed Groups (2007), Art. 2.1: 'A child associated with an armed force or armed group' refers to any person below 18 years of age who is or who has been recruited or used by an armed force or armed group in any capacity, including but not limited to children, boys, and girls used as fighters, cooks, porters, messengers, spies or for sexual purposes. It does not only refer to a child who is taking or has taken a direct part in hostilities.'

[68] Including, but not limited to, combatants, cooks, porters, messengers, and anyone accompanying such groups, other than family members. UNICEF discourages the term 'child soldier' as not accurately reflecting the range of roles in which boys and girls are recruited and used for military purposes.

[69] UNICEF, 'Child Protection from Violence', updated 22 March 2011, exploitation and abuse, <http://www.unicef.org/protection/57929_58007.html>.

[70] 'Al-Qaeda recruiting women for "jihad" in Syria: reports', 12 February 2014, <http://al-shorfa.com/en_GB/articles/meii/features/2013/12/02/feature-01>.

[71] Pandith, F. and Havlicek, S., 'The female face of terror: If we don't act now, it may not be long before we see women committing acts of terror in Western cities', *The Telegraph*, 28 January 2015, <http://www.telegraph.co.uk/news/uknews/terrorism-in-the-uk/11374026/The-female-face-of-terror.html>; al-Bahri, A., 'In Raqqa, an All-Female ISIS Brigade Cracks Down on Local Women', 15 July 2014, *Syria Deeply*, <http://www.syriadeeply.org/articles/2014/07/5799/raqqa-all-female-isis-brigade-cracks-local-women>; Sanghani, R., 'Hipster jihadis, cheesecake and miscarriages: Life inside ISIL for Western women', *The Telegraph*, 28 January 2015, <http://www.telegraph.co.uk/women/womens-politics/11374818/Isil-for-women-Hipster-jihadis-cheesecake-and-miscarriages.html>; Spencer, R., 'Target practice: Teenage British twins train in Syria', *The Telegraph*, 3 February 2015, <http://www.telegraph.co.uk/news/worldnews/middleeast/syria/11387424/Target-practice-Teenage-British-twins-train-in-Syria.html>.

[72] Human Rights Watch, 'Under Kurdish Rule: Abuses in PYD-run Enclaves of Syria', 19 June 2014.

[73] Al-Ali, J., 'Underage Kurdish girl forced into Syria war', *Ara News*, 18 May 2014, <http://aranews.net/2014/05/underage-kurdish-girl-forced-into-syria-war>.

pledges with the Swiss NGO Geneva Call, one on preventing sexual violence and gender discrimination and the other on protecting children in armed conflict.[74] Following its pledge, the YPG and its female branch, the Women's Protection Units (Yekîneyên Parastina Jinê—YPJ), demobilized 149 children.[75]

According to information received by the OHCHR, YPG continued to recruit child soldiers through 2014.[76] Some twenty teenage members of the YPJ, wearing military uniforms, armed and all under eighteen years, were reportedly observed in December. A Geneva Call representative reported that children were drawn to the YPG for a variety of reasons, including 'a lack of social and economic opportunities, insecurity and family involvement in the YPG'.[77] With the escalation of the conflict against ISIS 'dozens more children attempted to join YPG-YPJ armed forces to defend their cities and villages' and Geneva Call noted that the YPG needed to make 'a continuous effort to keep children away from hostilities'.[78]

C. Participation of women in armed conflicts and peacebuilding

The participation of women in situations of armed conflict is not new: women have long held roles as combatants and non-combatants alike, fighting wars and participating in efforts to end wars and build peace. As combatants in ongoing conflicts, women must be an essential part of any discussion of demobilization efforts as conflicts come to an end. What follows is a consideration of women's participation in armed conflict and peacebuilding in 2014.

Women participated in peace negotiations in several different countries, though participation as members of formal negotiating teams still remained the exception rather than the norm. Even while progress in advancing women's participation was slow, in

[74] The YPG signed Geneva Call's Deed of Commitment prohibiting sexual violence and gender discrimination on 5 June 2014. The YPG, the Women's Protection Units (YPJ) and the Democratic Self-Administration in Rojava signed Geneva Call's Deed of Commitment protecting children in armed conflict on 5 July 2014.

[75] Geneva Call, 'Syria: Kurdish armed forces demobilize 149 child soldiers', 7 July 2014, <http://www.genevacall.org/syria-kurdish-armed-forces-demobilize-149-child-soldiers>.

[76] 'Implementation of Security Council resolutions 2139 (2014), 2165 (2014) and 2191 (2014)' (S/2015/48), 22 January 2015, §19.

[77] 'Kurdish child soldiers battle ISIL in Syria', *Al Jazeera*, 13 December 2014, <http://www.aljazeera.com/news/middleeast/2014/12/underage-kurds-battle-isil-syria-2014127937141841 88.html>.

[78] Geneva Call, 'Syria: monitoring the prohibition of child soldiers by Kurdish armed forces', 7 October 2014, <http://www.genevacall.org/syria-monitoring-prohibition-child-soldiers-kurdish-armed-forces>.

several cases women contributed their perspectives to ongoing peace processes by developing recommendations and practical policy suggestions through civil society input—often enhancing survivor-led approaches to building sustainable peace.

The role of women as visible peace and human rights activists was yet another way that women acted in relation to conflict and violence in their countries. In several cases, women in these roles were targeted, thus highlighting the need to plan for the protection of women who speak out for humanitarian law, human rights, peace, and justice.

Women were involved as combatants, with considerable attention in the media, as part of the Syrian Kurdish Women Protection Units (YPJ), armed groups that fought alongside the People's Protection Units.[79] These units were active in 2014 on the frontlines of the battle for Kobani.[80] These female combatants will face many of the same challenges faced by female combatants in other conflicts, when considering laying down arms and reintegrating into society. These challenges must be anticipated and addressed in any sustainable peace agreement. Challenges for women in disarmament, demobilization, and reintegration of women and girls in non-State armed groups have been differentiated as including: a narrow definitions of 'fighters' preventing access to programmes, lack of physical security and the ability to care for children in demobilization camps, and not prioritizing and addressing needs more specifically identified by women, which may include equitable economic, political, and justice systems and a psychosocial support.[81]

In Ukraine, women had a prominent or visible role in the Maidan protests which began in November 2013 and turned violent, sparking the Ukrainian revolution. Women spoke out, actively resisted the forces of the authorities, and provided medical and legal assistance to protestors. In the space created by the protests, women were seen as adopting new gender roles, challenging traditional views on the role of women and gaining new political space in Ukraine.[82] In fact, the initial exclusion of women from

[79] Dirik, D., 'Western fascination with 'badass' Kurdish women', Opinion, 29 October 2014, <http://www.aljazeera.com/indepth/opinion/2014/10/western-fascination-with-badas-2014102112410527736.html>; Mona Mahmood, '"We are so proud"—the women who died defending Kobani against Isis', *The Guardian*, 30 January 2015, <http://www.theguardian.com/world/2015/jan/30/kurdish-women-died-kobani-isis-syria>.

[80] Gormlie, F., 'It Was Syrian Kurd Leftists Who Kicked Islamic State Out of Kobani', 28 February 2015, <http://sandiegofreepress.org/2015/02/it-was-syrian-kurd-leftists-who-kicked-islamic-state-out-of-kobani>.

[81] Mazurana, D., 'Women in Armed Opposition Groups Speak on War, Protection and Obligations under International Humanitarian and Human Rights Law': Report of a workshop organized in Geneva by Geneva Call and the Program for the Study of International Organization(s), 26–9 August 2004.

[82] 'Voices from Ukraine: Civil Society as a Driver for Peace', WILPF, September 2014, p. 3; Trach, N., 'EuroMaidan women warriors eager to fight injustice, sex discrimination', 13 February 2014, <http://www.kyivpost.com/guide/people/euromaidan-women-warriors-eager-to-fight-injustice-sex-discrimination-336806.html>; and Phillips, S. D., 'The Women's Squad in Ukraine's protests: Feminism,

the protests led to debates about women's roles in social change and political activism.[83] Subsequently the participation of women was highly publicized by all sides, though few examples of structural changes behind this participation were revealed.

Women continued to participate in the ongoing conflict in Ukraine in a range of roles, including as combatants. However, this participation in the conflict has been regarded by women peace activists to be largely symbolic, overturning the advances in women's influence and status that were seen during the protests. While there are women in combat roles, most are in specialized roles, such as logistical support, medics, and spokespeople.[84] It has been observed that this engagement has actually reinforced traditional roles for women as support for male combatants while deprioritizing women's equal participation in deciding on the political future of the country.[85] Women are combatants on both sides of the conflict—as members of rebel forces, of the Ukrainian army and of the volunteer battalions that fight alongside the Ukrainian army.[86]

As highlighted in CEDAW GR30, in disarmament, demobilization, and reintegration, women face particular challenges as female ex-combatants (and women and girls associated with armed groups as messengers, cooks, medics, caregivers, forced labourers, and wives). Disarmament, demobilization, and reintegration programmes often exclude women and girls or fail to respond to their specific needs and to consult them.

> Many female combatants suffer gender-based violence, in particular sexual violence, resulting in children born of rape, high levels of sexually transmitted diseases, rejection or stigmatization by families and other trauma. Disarmament, demobilization and reintegration programmes often fail to address their experiences and the psychological trauma that they have undergone. Consequently, they are unable to reintegrate into family and community life successfully.[87]

nationalism, and militarism on the Maidan', 20 August 2014, <https://euromaidanberlin.wordpress.com/2014/08/20/the-womens-squad-in-ukraines-protests-feminism-nationalism-and-militarism-on-the-maidan>; Ghosh, P., 'Ukraine Girls Really Knock Me Out: Women Playing Crucial Roles In Euro-Maidan Protests', 28 February 2014, <http://www.ibtimes.com/ukraine-girls-really-knock-me-out-women-playing-crucial-roles-euro-maidan-protests-1558508>.

[83] Phillips, S., 'The Women's Squad in Ukraine's protests: Feminism, nationalism, and militarism on the Maidan', 20 August 2014, <https://euromaidanberlin.wordpress.com/2014/08/20/the-womens-squad-in-ukraines-protests-feminism-nationalism-and-militarism-on-the-maidan>.

[84] Trisko Darden, J. and Szekely, O., 'Warfare isn't just a man's game anymore,' *Washington Post*, 9 February 2015, <http://www.washingtonpost.com/blogs/monkey-cage/wp/2015/02/09/warfare-isnt-just-a-mans-game-anymore/>; Savchuk, E., 'The women fighting on the frontline in Ukraine' *The Guardian*, 5 March 2015, <http://www.theguardian.com/world/2015/mar/05/ukraine-women-fighting-frontline>.

[85] 'Voices from Ukraine: Civil Society as a Driver for Peace', WILPF, September 2014, pp. 7–8.

[86] Lyman, R., 'Ukraine Rebels Upbeat after an Infusion of Aid,' *New York Times*, 2 February 2015, <http://www.nytimes.com/2015/02/03/world/europe/on-front-lines-in-ukraine-rebels-are-upbeat-and-eager-to-advance.html?_r=1>; and Savchuk, E., 'The women fighting on the frontline in Ukraine', *The Guardian*, 5 March 2015, <http://www.theguardian.com/world/2015/mar/05/ukraine-women-fighting-frontline>.

[87] CEDAW/C/GC/30, Security sector reform and disarmament, demobilization and reintegration (Arts 1–3, 5(a) and 7).

In Colombia, women combatants of the Revolutionary Armed Forces of Colombia (Fuerzas Armadas Revolucionarias de Colombia—FARC) have expressed concern that their reintegration process will face challenges that are unique as compared to the experiences of their male counterparts. As noted by one commentator, '[f[emale ex-combatants also face huge obstacles in reintegrating into a society whose gender roles they transgressed when they left their families and picked up weapons'.[88] This has been a factor in the gender perspectives expressed in ongoing peace negotiations.

When talking about victimization of women in armed conflict, a comprehensive approach to the protection of women must also consider the different ways that they relate to the conflict, including the situations of female combatants. In fact, within the Colombian context and likely in many other countries, the gendered victimization of women cuts across women as combatants and as non-combatants: 'When women have served as combatants and in related support roles—at least one-third of FARC are estimated to be women—many have suffered gender violence within the ranks, including forced abortions and serving as sexual slaves for their commanders.'[89]

Research on inclusive conflict resolution and peacebuilding has shown that when women participate, peace agreements are more likely to address the needs of women.[90] This includes both the protection of the rights of female civilians within armed conflict as well as the needs of female combatants in a peace process. In addition, as recognized by UNSC Resolution 1325 and further demonstrated by experience since its introduction, peace agreements are seen to be more 'durable' or lasting when the processes to reach them are inclusive of civil society, including women.[91] Women can and do make a measurably positive impact on peace processes and their exclusion correlates to a higher failure rate for peace agreements.[92] Logically this not only prolongs conflict, but also leads to more, unaddressed, gender-based crimes.

[88] Bouvier, V., 'How two women could shake up Colombia's unprecedented peace talks with the FARC', 27 November 2013, *Foreign Policy*, <http://foreignpolicy.com/2013/11/27/tables-turned>.

[89] Ibid.

[90] Not asserting simply that only women can perceive the needs of women, or that they will universally represent the same needs, but that more balanced participation tends to improve outcomes. For more detail on gender and influence on peace negations see: Sanam Naraghi Anderlini, *Women Building Peace: What they do, why it matters*', Lynne Reiner, 2007; and de Alwis, M., Mertus, J., and Sajjad, T., 'Women and Peace Processes'. In *Women and Wars*, edited by Carol Cohn, Cambridge, Malden: Polity Press 2013, pp. 169–193.

[91] UNSC 1325 states in the preamble, 'Recognizing that an understanding of the impact of armed conflict on women and girls, effective institutional arrangements to guarantee their protection and full participation in the peace process can significantly contribute to the maintenance and promotion of international peace and security ...'

[92] Nilsson, D., 2012, 'Anchoring the Peace: Civil Society Actors in Peace Accords and Durable Peace', *International Interactions: Empirical and Theoretical Research in International Relations*, vol. 38, no. 2: pp. 243–266.

In 2014, there were some notable examples of progress in the participation of women in peace processes and the consideration of the rights and needs of women in peace agreements. As well there were cases where the platforms and policy suggestions of women and their representative organizations were included in peace processes, even if women were not official members of peace negotiations, laying the ground work for such consideration in future peace agreements. The UN Secretary General's 2014 report on women, peace, and security, a review of the text of recent peace agreements found an increased number of references to women, peace, and security, largely linked to the increased inclusion of provisions on conflict-related sexual violence. Of the thirteen peace agreements signed in 2013, seven (54%) included such references, as compared with three of ten in 2012 (30%).[93]

The Government of the Philippines and the Moro Islamic Liberation Front (MILF) signed the Comprehensive Agreement on the Bangsamoro in March 2014, the result of some seventeen years of negotiation.[94] The peace process was said to have been 'one of the most gender-sensitive in the world'.[95] The responsiveness of the agreement to issues of gender was influenced by decisions to include the issues in official planning and negotiation of the peace agreement.

An important step in the process of bringing gender perspectives to the negotiating table was the much earlier inclusion—within the Philippines' 2009 'Magna Carta of Women'—of provisions on the protection of women from gender-based violence and from forced displacement from their lands and territories, relating to armed conflict. The Magna Carta of Women also called for the increase in women's membership in peace processes and the 'inclusion of women's welfare and concerns in the peace agenda ...'[96] When the Philippines became the first country in Asia to develop a national action plan on the implementation of UNSC resolution 1325 in 2010, it referred in its plan to the Magna Carta of Women and the historical contributions of women to conflict resolution.[97]

Significantly, the negotiations were concluded by parties that included women and the Government's lead negotiator was a woman, Professor Miriam Coronel-Ferrer, as was the president's adviser on the peace process. The MILF also included women on its

[93] UNSC (S/2014/693) 27 September 2014, Box 9.

[94] Government of the Philippines 'Document: The Comprehensive Agreement on the Bangsamoro', 27 March 2014, <http://www.gov.ph/2014/03/27/document-cab>.

[95] Arguillas, C., 'The women in the Bangsamoro peace process: history, herstory', Minda news, 28 January 2014, <http://www.mindanews.com/peace-process/2014/01/28/special-report-the-women-in-the-bangsamoro-peace-process-history-herstory>.

[96] Republic Act 9710, Magna Carta of Women, Chapter IV, Section 29, April 2010, <http://pcw.gov.ph/sites/default/files/documents/laws/republic_act_9710.pdf>.

[97] Miller, B., Pournik, M., and Swaine, A., 'Women in Peace and Security through United Nations Security Resolution 1325: Literature Review, Content Analysis of National Action Plans, and Implementation', May 2014, p. 121, <http://www.gwu.edu/~igis/assets/docs/working_papers/igis_wp13_ggp_wp09.pdf>.

negotiating team. As a result of a participatory gender-sensitive approach, the agreement itself is described as having 'gender responsive language' that is significant from a gender justice perspective.[98] This result also follows a struggle by the women's movement in the Philippines that laid the groundwork for women's participation in the peace process and increased awareness of protection issues for women in situations of armed conflict.

It has been argued that peace sought through the Comprehensive Agreement on the Bangsamoro faced serious challenges beyond 2014, in part because of a failing in the system to take a gender perspective during policing activities. The fallout from this threatened the ongoing peace process.[99] Similarly, CEDAW notes that it has repeatedly expressed concern that the voices of women peacemakers in leadership roles during conflict are 'silenced and marginalized in post-conflict and transition periods and recovery processes'.[100]

Parties to the Colombian peace talks in Havana agreed in June 2014, to create a subcommittee on gender with a mandate to 'integrate a gendered perspective into any agreements that result'. The gender subcommittee (an advisory group) will review the prior agreements reached and the final agreement to ensure that they have an adequate gender focus.[101] By September, for the first time, negotiations included consultations with gender experts as well as representatives from women's organizations.[102] This subcommittee aims to ensure that the final agreements address reparations for female victims and the reintegration of the many FARC ex-combatants who are women.

The creation of the gender subcommittee is the result of years of efforts by women's organizations in Colombia and globally who have successfully argued that the armed conflict impacts women, men, girls, and boys differently and thus, in order to address

[98] CO Arguillas, 'The women in the Bangsamoro peace process: history, herstory', Minda news, 28 January 2014, <http://www.mindanews.com/peace-process/2014/01/28/special-report-the-women-in-the-bangsamoro-peace-process-history-herstory>.

[99] Nario-Galace, J., 'Women Count for Peace', 9 March 2015, <http://opinion.inquirer.net/83176/women-count-for-peace>. In January 2015 forty-three members of the elite Special Action Force (SAF) unit of the Philippine National Police, were killed in fighting with members of both the Moro Islamic Liberation Front (MILF), which had signed the peace agreement and the Bangsamoro Islamic Freedom Fighters (BIFF), which had not committed to a peace agreement. A board of inquiry was to conduct an investigation into the events, including 'the apparent lack of coordination with MILF forces in the area'. Samson-Espiritu, A. Tim Hum, T., '43 Philippine police killed by Muslim rebels while hunting bomb makers', *CNN*, 27 January 2015 <http://edition.cnn.com/2015/01/26/world/philippines-maguindanao-milf-battle/>.

[100] CEDAW/C/GC/30, p. 11.

[101] 'Breaking News from Havana: Joint Declaration of Principles on Victims', Colombia Calls, 7 June 2014, <https://vbouvier.wordpress.com/2014/06/07/breaking-news-from-havana-joint-declaration-of-principles-on-victims>; and 'Gender Experts Arrive in Havana,' 16 December 2014, <https://vbouvier.wordpress.com/2014/12/16/gender-experts-arrive-in-havana>.

[102] Inclusive Security, 'Progress for Women in Colombia Negotiations,' 29 January 2015, <http://www.inclusivesecurity.org/5-amazing-stories-didnt-hear-2014/>.

these differing impacts, women should be involved in designing solutions. A first step towards more inclusive negotiations was taken in November 2013, when the Government of Colombia announced the appointment of two women to its five-person team for peace talks, one of whom was specifically tasked with ensuring the consideration of gender issues. Already, twelve of the thirty advisers registered by the FARC as part of the negotiations were women.[103]

The Colombian case provides an example of how the awareness raised around victimization of women in armed conflict, particularly through gender-based sexual violence, has created opportunities to advance a more comprehensive agenda on the protection of women and their participation in creating sustainable peace. The agreement to create the gender subcommittee was included in the 'Declaration of Principles for the Discussion of Point 5 on the Agenda: Victims' announced on 7 June 2014. This agenda item relates to the satisfaction of the rights of the victims of armed conflict, including their recognition, reparations, and participation. However, the mandate of the gender subcommittee is not limited to discussions and agreements on Point 5 of the agenda but rather all agreements made through the peace negotiations, including a retroactive review of agreements made in relation to other points of the peace agreement.[104]

The need for such participation was not always immediately planned or realized, but rather introduced while negotiations were in progress. As in Ukraine, where in the midst of peace talks in Belarus, the OSCE called for enhanced participation by women in peace negotiations and other forms of conflict resolution as a means to 'achieve security and stability'.[105]

Despite these positive examples, the UN Secretary-General's 2014 report on women, peace, and security finds that: 'Although many examples of good practice in terms of the engagement of women in conflict prevention and resolution, community security and peacebuilding have been highlighted in past reports, this area of work remains seriously underfunded. I encourage all actors, in line with resolution 2122 (2013), to increase investment in building the capacity of women's organizations and local civil society networks working in conflict and post-conflict settings and on non-violent means of resolving tensions and addressing the root causes'.[106] Indeed, as was seen to be the case in reviewing progress on the implementation of resolution 1325 after its first ten years,[107] in 2014, women's absence at peace tables remained the norm.

[103] UN S-G Sept 2014 report, §22.

[104] 'Declaración de Principios para la Discusión del Punto 5 de la Agenda: "Víctimas"', Delegación de Paz FARC-EP, <http://anncol.eu/index.php/127-farc-ep/7054-declaraqcion-de-principios-para-la-discusion-del-punto-5-de-la-agenda-victimas-ictimas>.

[105] OSCE, 5 February 2015, <http://www.osce.org/secretariat/139201>.

[106] UN S-G Report Sept 2014.

[107] '... of 31 major peace processes between 1992 and 2011, only 4 per cent of signatories, 2.4 per cent of chief mediators, 3.7 per cent of witnesses and 9 per cent of negotiators are women.' UN Women, Women's Participation in Peace Negotiations: Connections between Presence and Influence, 2012, p. 3.

In this regard CEDAW GR30 found that:

The full participation and involvement of women in formal peacemaking and post-conflict reconstruction and socioeconomic development are often not realized on account of deeply entrenched stereotypes, reflected in the traditionally male leadership of State and non-State groups, which exclude women from all aspects of decision-making, in addition to gender-based violence and other forms of discrimination against women.[108]

Unlike the advances in the participation of women in peace negotiations in Colombia and the Philippines that occurred in 2014, Syrian women were excluded as official participants in the Syrian peace talks, 'Geneva II' that were held in January. This happened despite the organization and mobilization of Syrian women and their development of concrete proposals for peace in Syria.

Recent studies found that women in Syria have had multiple and significant roles in the conflict, as victims of atrocious human rights violations, as peace activists and as humanitarian workers, providing women with first-hand knowledge of the challenges facing Syria in building peace and guaranteeing justice to the victims of the conflict there. Human Rights Watch found that 'Women have not been spared any aspect of the brutality of the Syrian conflict, but they are not merely passive victims'.[109]

Throughout 2014, a female-led young peace activists' network continued 'responding to local needs and addressing the building blocks of a peaceful society, including citizenship, education and youth issues'.[110] In these different roles, women have demonstrated the ability to develop appropriate responses to women's needs inside Syria and in refugee communities and to express their views on the best ways to achieve peace. The Women's International League for Peace and Freedom (WILPF) found that 'These [women's] groups are active on the ground in Syria and in refugee camps working hard to re-stitch the fabric of society and build foundations for their country's future'.[111]

Despite not having a seat at the table during peace negotiations, throughout 2014, women organized and developed their own demands for the peace talks as well as concrete policy suggestions to create stability in Syria and to defeat extremists.[112] UN Women convened more than fifty Syrian women activists just before the start of the 'Geneva II' talks to 'to support their collective voice and peace initiatives in the political

[108] CEDAW GR30, §37.

[109] 'Syria War's Toll on Women: Activists, Others Detained and Abused by All Sides in the Conflict', Human Rights Watch, 2 July 2014, <http://www.hrw.org/news/2014/07/02/syria-war-s-toll-women>.

[110] 'The worst scenario since World War II' Syrian peace activist paints picture of hope and despair as ISIS gains foothold', International Civil Society Action Network (ICAN), September 2014.

[111] 'Ensuring the Effective Participation and Rights of Women in the Syrian Peace and Mediation Process: A Five-Step Approach', 28 December 2013, Working Paper prepared by DemocraShe, Human Rights Watch, ICAN, Kvinna til Kvinna, Oxfam, and WILPF.

[112] Williams, K., 'Syrian Women Know How to Defeat ISIS', Inclusive Security, 16 October 2014, <http://www.inclusivesecurity.org/syrian-women-know-defeat-isis>.

process'.[113] This organization of women, with the support that the international community can give, should prepare women for the next round of talks, where the inclusion of their practical perspectives—either delivered via a seat at the negotiating table or through some other means—cannot be ignored.

The Afghan People's Dialogue for Peace's three-year 'roadmaps for peace' programme reported in 2014 that 'Afghan men, women and youth almost universally expressed the view that the inclusion of women in peacebuilding initiatives was paramount to achieving durable peace in Afghanistan. Participants further saw the need for an end to years of harmful practices against women and girls, and for women to have a more prominent role in local government positions'.[114]

Overall, participants stressed the need for 'promoting human rights and women's rights', and to attain peace measures including through strengthening security institutions, promoting responsive State institutions, ending corruption, disarming illegal armed groups, and providing employment opportunities.[115] In the second phase of the Afghan People's Dialogue on Peace, facilitated by the United Nations Assistance Mission in Afghanistan (UNAMA) in 2013, women represented almost a third (32%) of those consulted on the local road maps for peace that were developed in 2014.[116]

Only nine out of seventy appointed members of the High Peace Council in Afghanistan, around 13%, were women in 2014. Their roles were reported to be mostly symbolic.[117] A 'backlash' against women's rights in Afghanistan has been attributed to elite and urban women groups dominating national women's rights discussions. In contrast, the involvement of women in Provincial Peace Committees (PPCs)[118] was aimed at substantive engagement at the community level.[119] In 2014 there were 750 men and eighty-six

[113] 'Conference of Syrian women, convened by UN Women and the Netherlands, ends with strong recommendations for upcoming peace talks,' UN Women, 13 January 2014, <http://www.unwomen.org/en/news/stories/2014/1/press-release-on-syrian-women-meeting#sthash.MOR554Sm.dpuf>.

[114] 'Afghan People's Dialogue on Peace 'Building the Foundations for an Inclusive Peace Process', June 2014, p. 27.

[115] UNAMA, 'UNAMA welcomes Afghan civil society report presenting people's road map for peace', 10 June 2014, <http://reliefweb.int/report/afghanistan/unama-welcomes-afghan-civil-society-report-presenting-people-s-road-map-peace>; and Afghan Independent Human Rights Commission, 'Afghan Civil Society Present Road Maps for Peace to Presidential Candidates', 10 June 2014, <http://www.aihrc.org.af/home/press-release/2955>.

[116] UNSC (S/2014/693) 27 September 2014, §22.

[117] Oxfam, 'Behind Closed Doors: The risk of denying women a voice in determining Afghanistan's future', Oxfam Briefing Paper, 24 November 2014, p. 17; and Jessica Donati, 'Afghan women excluded from peace talks with Taliban: aid agency', 23 November 2014, <http://www.reuters.com/article/2014/11/24/us-afghanistan-women-idUSKCN0J806220141124>.

[118] Provincial Peace Committees (PPC) reach out to insurgents and encourage their reintegration through disarmament activities, the provision of transitional financial assistance, and livelihood skills building. UNDP-Afghanistan, 'Afghanistan Peace and Reintegration Programme (APRP)', <http://www.af.undp.org/content/afghanistan/en/home/operations/projects/crisis_prevention_and_recovery/aprp.html>.

[119] Women Peace & Security Research Institute, 'What is Women Peace & Security', <http://www.riwps-afghanistan.org>.

women (less than 15% of the total) members of the PPCs in all thirty-four provinces of Afghanistan. In 2012, the total number of women participating was seventy; the increase was attributed to advocacy of women organizations across the country. Women PPCs members expressed concerns that, while they are working to build peace, they face negative media coverage that needed to be counterbalanced by having their achievements widely publicized.[120]

A 2014 report on Afghanistan by the NGO Oxfam found that only one woman from the government was present, and only on just two occasions, during the twenty-three rounds of peace talks between the Afghan Government and the Taliban held since 2005. Similarly, minimal representation of women was recorded in negotiations with other related insurgent groups. Also alarming were the findings that no women had participated when there were international negotiators and the conclusion that 'Afghan women are excluded from efforts to negotiate peace with the Taliban and hard-won rights could be bargained away unless more is done to include them in the process'.[121]

D. Targeting of women's participation in peace, gender rights, and conflict resolution

While the demand for greater participation of women in addressing conflict and its consequences grew, in 2014, attacks on women's rights activists underscored the realities of the harm women experienced as well as the threat that is perceived by some groups or individuals when women are actively working towards gender equality. CEDAW GR30 calls attention to the multi-dimensional impact of gender-based violence and attacks on women rights defenders by State or non-State actors, in that they 'undermine women's equal and meaningful participation in political and public life'.[122]

Leading rights defender Leyla Yunus, a partner in Azerbaijan of the Dutch NGO Women Peacemakers Program (WPP), was arrested, detained, and subjected to inhumane treatment in prison in 2014.[123] Yunus had long worked with Armenian activists in advocating for the reconciliation of the two countries. The prosecutor general's office reportedly accused her, among other things, of carrying out propaganda activities aimed

[120] Women Peace & Security Research Institute, 'Forum Report: 3rd Women Peace and Security Forum, 2014', pp. 3 and 6.

[121] Oxfam, 'Behind Closed Doors: The risk of denying women a voice in determining Afghanistan's future', *Oxfam Briefing Paper*, 24 November 2014.

[122] CEDAW GR30, §37.

[123] Women Peacemakers Program, 'WPP New Year's Letter', 13 January 2015, <https://www.womenpeacemakersprogram.org/news/wpp-new-years-letter-2/>.

at getting Azerbaijan to recognize Armenian occupation of Nagorno Karabakh. The WPP also observed that the assassinations and attacks on women activists, particularly in countries of the Middle East and North Africa were indicative of the many challenges women peace activists face all over the world.[124]

A pattern of attacks on educated, professional women in Iraq by ISIS was reported by United Nations monitors, 'some after perfunctory trials'. Sameera Salih Ali al-Nuaimy an Iraqi lawyer promoting women's rights was killed by ISIS fighters.[125] An Afghan women's rights activist and parliamentarian in Shukria Barakzai, survived a blast in an attack on the armoured car transporting her in which seventeen bystanders were killed.[126] The attack was one of many on Afghan women activists and politicians in recent years.[127]

Two female human rights activists and leaders in Libya, Salwa Bugaighis and Fareha al Barqawi, were assassinated by militias in 2014 for demanding and advocating for peaceful political transition.[128] Salwa Bugaighis who was assassinated in June 2014, was a rights lawyer, deputy chair of the National Dialogue Preparatory Committee, a founding member of Libyan Women's Platform for Peace, and a member of the National Committee for Advancement of Law.[129] As Vice-President of Preparatory Commission for National Dialogue launched in January 2014 her activities were an example of mobilization of women's groups in driving preparations for national dialogue on practical solutions in transition to post-conflict political power relations.[130]

The legacy of Bugaighis' stand continued after her murder through the work of the Libyan Women's Platform for Peace, and the Cairo-based NGO Karama through its campaign 'Justice for Salwa'.[131] The Libyan Women's Platform for Peace called for use

[124] 'Azerbaijan accuses rights activist Leyla Yunus of spying for Armenia', *Agence France-Presse*, 1 August 2014, <http://www.hurriyetdailynews.com/azerbaijan-accuses-rights-activist-leyla-yunus-of-spying-for-armenia.aspx?pageID=238&nID=69849>.

[125] Cumming-Bruce, N., 'Women's Rights Activist Executed by ISIS in Iraq', 25 September 2014, <http://www.nytimes.com/2014/09/26/world/middleeast/womens-rights-activist-executed-by-islamic-state-in-iraq.html?smid=fb-nytimes&smtyp=cur&bicmp=AD&bicmlukp=WT.mc_id&bicmst=1409232722000&bicmet=1419773522000&_r=2>.

[126] P. Hassouri, 'Women's Rights Activists Between State Violence and Intervention', 25 November 2014, <http://www.merip.org/womens-rights-activists-between-state-violence-intervention>.

[127] See, Afghanistan Rights Monitor, 'Forgotten Heroes: Afghan Women Leaders Killed in Impunity Ignored in Justice', December 2012.

[128] Libyan Woman Platform for Peace, 'Libyan Women's Platform for Peace on human rights day calls for inclusive peace talks & no impunity for war lords', 10 December 2014, <https://libyanwomensplatformforpeace.wordpress.com/2014/12/10/libyan-womens-platform-for-peace-on-human-rights-day-calls-for-inclusive-peace-talks-no-impunity-for-war-lords>.

[129] 'About the National Dialogue Preparatory Commission', <http://ndpc.ly/commission-en>.

[130] Amnesty International, 'Libya must ensure proper investigation after prominent lawyer shot dead' 26 June 2014, <https://www.amnesty.org/en/articles/news/2014/06/libya-must-ensure-proper-investigation-after-lawyer-salwa-bugaighis-shot-dead>.

[131] Karaama describes Bugaighis in the light of her actions: 'As a cofounder of the Libyan Women's Platform for Peace, she engaged with women and youth leaders in leading civil society initiatives to

of Universal Periodic Review to demand implementation of UNSC Resolution 1325 and protection for human rights defenders. It also called on the State to 'enact concrete and immediate measures to fulfill the legal obligations under CEDAW General Recommendation 30 related to arms control to prevent its use for violence against women, temporary special measures for women's participation in peace and post-conflict processes, gender-responsive SSR [Security Sector Reform] and DDRR [Disarmament, Demobilisation and Reintegration and Reintegration], and prosecution of sexual violence in the conflict ….'[132]

Concluding remarks

In 2014, gender-based crimes occurring during armed conflict that were not implicitly sexual hung at the intersection of some scattered segments of IHL and a number of security council resolutions and human rights provisions—many of which squarely targeted sexual gender-based crimes. While the prosecution of non-sexual gender-based crimes was not entirely without precedent, the inability of international law to address or remedy many of these crimes that were prevalent in 2014 was apparent. However, the good intent of resolutions and recommendations prevail in the meaningful participation of women in peace processes through women's participation at national and local levels, as official members of peace negotiations and as vocal activists whose lives may be put at risk in their endeavours to ensure principles of humanitarian and human rights law or sustainable peace.

While women's participation as part of official negotiating teams remained deplorably inadequate during 2014, there were several important advances that contributed to the inclusion of more diverse gender perspectives in those instances where participation advanced. This inclusion of women in resolving conflicts by which they are directly affected, both as civilians and combatants, may be among the only, and the most effective means for both preventing and finding some recourse for addressing non-sexual crimes. Participation may open paths for victims to get some recognition and justice even when, at least currently, these crimes are unlikely to be addressed by legal systems.

confront militarization, violent extremism, and terrorism and to ensure an inclusive and just transition to democracy. As the recently appointed deputy head of the National Dialogue Preparatory Council, she pushed for open dialogue, peaceful resolution, and sustained hope in the face of ongoing obstacles.' 'Salma's Story', undated but after 24 June 2014, <http://www.el-karama.org/justice-for-salwa/about-salwa-3/salwas-story>.

[132] UN Security Council Resolution 1325 'Libyan Women's Platform for Peace on human rights day calls for inclusive peace talks & no impunity for war lords', 10 December 2014, <https://libyanwomensplatformforpeace.wordpress.com/2014/12>.

Concurrent with this enhanced engagement and participation of women, greater effort must be made by the international community to define, monitor, report, and address these as crimes both distinct from, and interconnected with, sexual violence in conflict. Actions by the international community must support and take into account the outcomes of participation by women in local contexts and national arenas.

3 The 2014 Gaza War: reflections on *jus ad bellum, jus in bello,* and accountability

Sharon Weill and Valentina Azarova[1]

Introduction

The fifty-one days of hostilities in the Gaza Strip in the summer of 2014 was the twelfth round of major fighting there since 1948 and the third one since Israel 'disengagement' from Gaza in 2005.[2] The 2014 hostilities led to an unprecedented number of civilian casualties and left 108,000 Palestinian homeless. [3] The United Nations warned that the Gaza Strip would be uninhabitable by 2020: it will become increasingly hard for residents of Gaza to access water, electricity, health, or education.[4] According to Israel's foreign ministry, the goals of the 2014 military operation were limited 'to stop the escalating barrage of rocket and mortar attacks … and to destroy Hamas's network of secret cross-border tunnels into Israel'; it also reaffirmed that 'Israel had the clear right to use force in self defence in such circumstances'.[5] However, a closer look at the events is required.

[1] Dr Sharon Weill is a lecturer and researcher at Sciences-Po Paris and CERAH, Geneva. Visiting Scholar at the Center for the Study of Law and Society, the University of California, Berkeley (2015–16). Dr Valentina Azarova is a lecturer at Al Quds University, Ramallah (Palestine). The authors wish to thank Georg Koeppinghoff and Bill Van Esveld.

[2] Filiu, J. P., 2014. 'The Twelve Wars on Gaza', *Journal of Palestinian Studies*, vol. 44, no. 1 (Autumn 2014): 52.

[3] At least 1,550 Palestinian civilian deaths, including 538 children (out of a total death toll of over 2,100 Palestinians), and six civilian deaths in Israel, including one child (out of a total death toll of seventy-four Israelis). Human Rights Watch, Israel/Palestine, World Report 2015, <https://www.hrw.org/world-report/2015/country-chapters/israel-and-palestine> (accessed 25 April 2015).

[4] United Nations, 'Gaza in 2020: A Livable Place?' (August 2012) <http://issuu.com/unrwa/docs/gaza_in_2020/1?e=0> (accessed 2 May 2015).

[5] Israel Ministry of Foreign Affairs, 'The Background to the 2014 Gaza Conflict', p. 21 <http://mfa.gov.il/ProtectiveEdge/Documents/HamasBackground.pdf>; and 'The Operation in Gaza, 7 July–26 August 2014, Factual and Legal Aspects', <http://mfa.gov.il/ProtectiveEdge/Pages/default.aspx>. See also Israel's foreign minister requesting that 'the international community should continue to demonstrate understanding for Israel to exercise its legitimate right to self-defense'. Israel Ministry of Foreign Affairs, 'FM

Two preceding events are relevant to the context in which the 2014 Gaza hostilities occurred. First, on 2 June 2014, the Palestinian political factions Fatah and Hamas formed a unity government, intended to end 'a long political and territorial division in Palestinian affairs'.[6] Analysts saw in this historical unity agreement an important step towards the renewal of Israeli–Palestinian peace negotiations, as it pledged to comply with the principles of 'nonviolence, adherence to past agreements and recognition of Israel', which Hamas had not previously accepted.[7] Israel, however, strongly opposed the move and sought to isolate the Palestinian Government internationally.[8]

The violent escalation started ten days later, when Palestinian gunmen abducted three Israeli teenagers in the West Bank. Israel claimed that Hamas was responsible for the abductions, while Hamas disavowed any involvement.[9] As riposte, Israel began a large-scale military operation across the West Bank, consisting of mass arrests of hundreds of Hamas members. Within two weeks, Israeli forces killed six Palestinians, and raided universities, newspaper offices, and over 1,000 homes.[10] At the end of June, Hamas had retaliated by launching a significant number of rockets and mortars into Israel, for the first time since the 2012 ceasefire.[11] Analysts argue that the objectives of Israel's military campaigns in summer 2014 were not only military but were connected to the

Liberman dispatches letter to foreign ministers', 9 July 2014, <http://mfa.gov.il/MFA/PressRoom/2014/Pages/FM-Liberman-dispatches-letter-to-foreign-ministers-9-July-2014.aspx> (accessed 2 May 2015).

[6] See Beaumont, P., 'Palestinian unity government of Fatah and Hamas sworn in', *The Guardian*, 2 June 2014; <http://www.theguardian.com/world/2014/jun/02/palestinian-unity-government-sworn-in-fatah-hamas> (accessed 2 May 2015).

[7] Thrall, N., 'How the West Chose War in Gaza, Gaza and Israel: The Road to War, Paved by the West', *New York Times*, 17 July 2014, <http://www.nytimes.com/2014/07/18/opinion/gaza-and-israel-the-road-to-war-paved-by-the-west.html?_r=1>.

[8] 'An Israeli government that really wanted to advance the two-state solution would have been pleased and seen the reconciliation agreement not as a threat, but as an opportunity', in Ravid, B., 'Palestinian reconciliation is an opportunity for Israel', *Haaretz*, 24 April 2014.

[9] *The Guardian* reported that 'Although Israel has insisted Hamas was responsible, it has yet to provide any hard evidence linking the kidnapping to the group', <http://www.theguardian.com/world/2014/jun/16/israel-considering-expelling-hamas-leaders-west-bank-gaza>. Hamas leader Khaled Mashal maintained that he was 'not aware of this action taken' <http://edition.cnn.com/2014/08/22/world/meast/mideast-crisis/index.html?hpt=hp_t2>.

[10] See Human Rights Watch, Israel: Serious Violations in West Bank Operations, Death, Destruction, and Massive Arrests, 3 July 2014, <http://www.hrw.org/news/2014/07/03/israel-serious-violations-west-bank-operations> (accessed 2 May 2015).

[11] Issacharoff, A., 'Hamas fires rockets for first time since 2012, Israeli officials say', Times of Israel, 30 June 2014; 'On 7 July, Hamas claimed responsibility for firing rockets for the first time in 20 months, after a series of Israeli air strikes in which several members of its armed wing were killed', in 'Gaza-Israel conflict: Is the fighting over?', 6 August 2014, <http://www.bbc.com/news/world-middle-east-28252155>. According to the Israeli Security Agency website, sixty-three rockets and eleven mortar shells launched toward Israel from Gaza by different armed groups in 2013. In 2014, there were fifty-four rockets and ten mortar shells launched from January to 31 May, and another sixty-two rockets and three mortar shells launched in June. 'Terror Data and Trends', *2013 Annual Summary* and 2014 monthly summaries, available at <http://www.shabak.gov.il/English/EnTerrorData/Reports/Pages/default.aspx> (accessed 2 May 2015).

political aim of isolating Hamas and countering the prospect of a united Palestinian Government.[12]

This chapter assesses key issues related *to jus ad bellum, jus in bello*, and accountability that are raised by the hostilities. It commences by examining the possibility of invoking the right to self-defence, as the legal justification for the use of force in the Gaza conflict context (A). The chapter then surveys specific violations of the principles on the conduct of hostilities under international humanitarian law (IHL) committed during the 2014 hostilities by the Israeli military and Palestinian armed groups (B). The final part discusses the effects of recent developments related to individual accountability for IHL violations in the Israel–Palestine setting with particular attention to the prospects of Palestine's accession to the International Criminal Court (ICC) (C).

A. **The right to self-defence under *jus ad bellum* and the Gaza 2014 conflict**

While Israel repeatedly justified its military operation in Gaza as a self-defence response to Palestinian attacks,[13] this justification has received little attention from the international legal community. The invocation of self-defence under the *jus ad bellum* regime is both a legal argument, and a powerful political narrative that seeks to frame the military operation as a just use of armed force. On the legal dimension, Israel's invocation of self-defence implicitly relies on particular interpretations of controversial legal issues, including the status of Gaza under international law, the threshold gravity of an 'armed

[12] 'As Hamas fires rockets at Israeli cities and Israel follows up its extensive airstrikes with a ground operation in the Gaza Strip, the most immediate cause of this latest war has been ignored: … Palestinian "national consensus" government that was formed in early June', Thrall, N., 'How the West Chose War in Gaza'. Filiu, a distinguished historian from Sciences–Po, Paris who concludes that: '[T]he Netanyahu government was bent on sabotaging the April 2014 reconciliation agreement. The seven-year Feud between the PA-run West Bank and Hamas-ruled Gaza was a major strategic asset the Israeli Prime minister sought to protect at all cost: Although Gaza had not been in its sights to start with, the anti Hamas campaign Israel unleashed in the West Bank in June 2014 soon led to an escalation'. In Filiu, 'The Twelve War', p 57. See also Riyad Mansour, the Permanent Observer of Palestine to the United Nations in a press conference: 'They want to do everything possible in order to discredit the national consensus government. They want to break our political system into two pieces. They want to break our homeland into two pieces and then they want to break our political system into two pieces [but] The Palestinian people are one. The government is one, the President is President Abbas', <http://www.unmultimedia.org/tv/unifeed/2014/07/un-israel-palestine/>.

[13] A representative example was Israel's statement to the UN Security Council: 'This week, Israel launched an operation of self-defense, "Protective Edge" to counter these attacks, to defend our citizens, and secure for them a life without constant threat.' For transcript, see <http://embassies.gov.il/un/statements/Pages/Prosor's-Security-Council-Siren-Speech3.aspx>. See also, above at note 5. <http://mfa.gov.il/MFA/InternatlOrgs/Speeches/Pages/Amb-Prosor-addressses-the-UN-Security-Council-10-Jul-2014.aspx>.

attack,' and the role of non-State armed groups (NSAGs). The following discussion focuses on several necessary preconditions to invoke self-defence under international law, and seeks to apply them to the case of the 2014 Gaza hostilities.

ARTICLE 51 AS AN EXCEPTION TO AN OTHERWISE ILLEGAL ACT UNDER ARTICLE 2(4): THE REQUIREMENT OF AN INTER-STATE CONTEXT

It is generally accepted that the right to self-defence has its sources both in the UN Charter and customary international law. Article 51 of the UN Charter sets out that 'Nothing in the present Charter shall impair the inherent right of individual or collective self-defence if an armed attack occurs against a Member of the United Nations, until the Security Council has taken measures necessary to maintain international peace and security'. Customary international law complements this treaty provision and provides further conditions for the exercise of self-defence: imminence, necessity, and proportionality.[14]

While the definition and scope of application of the right of self-defence are not universally accepted in all respects, some basic aspects of the right, pertinent to the Israeli–Palestinian context, are nevertheless beyond controversy. First, it is generally accepted that the right of self-defence is an exception to the prohibition of the use of force set out in Article 2(4) of the UN Charter and under international customary law.[15] Thus, Article 51 of the UN Charter allows states to use force, which would have been otherwise illegal. Second, the scope of application of Article 2(4) is limited to inter-State relations.[16] These two assumptions have a direct impact on the scope of application of the right of self-defence: Article 51 can be invoked (and the use of defensive force would be authorized) only where a foreign State is involved. Any other interpretation

[14] See, e.g., *Oil Platforms (Iran v US)*, ICJ Rep. 2003, 161, para. 51; *Legality of the Threat or Use of Nuclear Weapons*, Advisory Opinion of 8 July 1996, ICJ Rep. 226, para. 41.

[15] Art. 2(4) of the UN Charter states: 'All Members shall refrain in their international relations from the threat or use of force against the territorial integrity or political independence of any state, or in any other manner inconsistent with the Purposes of the United Nations'. This norm has been identified as a *jus cogens* norm (Brownlie, I., 2003, *Principles of Public international Law*, 6th edn, Oxford: OUP, p. 489). Among the Charter exceptions, is the authority of the UN Security Council under Chapter VII to authorize the use of force in order to maintain or restore international peace and security. For further possible exceptions, see Randelzhofer, A. and Dorr, O., 2012, 'Art. 2(4)'. In 'The Charter of the United Nations: A Commentary', edited by Simma, B. et al., 3rd edn, Oxford: OUP, Vol. I, p. 200.

[16] Weller, M., 2015, 'Introduction'. In *The Oxford Handbook of the Use of Force in International Law*, edited by Weller, M., Oxford: OUP, p. 19, noting that situation of non-international armed conflicts are not governed by the Charter but by domestic law, IHL, and International Human Rights Law.

will lead to an illogical result whereby the exception has a greater scope than the rule it is referring to.

In November 2012 Palestine was recognized as a non-Member State by United Nations General Assembly Resolution 67/19.[17] In April 2014, the State of Palestine acceded to a list of international treaties, including the 1949 Geneva and 1907 Hague Conventions—an act reserved only to States.[18] A few days later a unity agreement was signed between Fatah and Hamas, placing the Hamas Government in Gaza as a *de jure* part of the Palestinian national government.[19] All international actors affirm that Gaza is an integral part of Palestine.[20]

If Israel were to invoke Article 51 as the legal basis for its use of force in Gaza—which is applicable only between States, as being an exception to customary law and Article 2(4), as explained above—the use of this justification apparently implies that Israel recognizes Palestine as a State. A related question for the attribution of responsibility is whether or not Hamas' armed wing was acting during the 2014 hostilities on behalf of the Palestinian State, in light of the April 2014 Fatah–Hamas Unity Agreement, [21] or whether it was still operating as a non-State armed group; and whether other Palestinian armed groups that participated in the hostilities were or were not under Hamas' control.

NON-STATE ARMED GROUPS AS AUTHORS OF AN ARTICLE 51 ARMED ATTACK: A DISTINCT ISSUE

The fact that the applicability of Article 51 is limited to inter-State contexts does not mean, however, that only States may be the authors of an 'armed attack'. The UN Security Council and most academic writers have recognized, in the aftermath of

[17] The resolution was adopted by a vote of 138 to 9, with 41 abstentions.

[18] Thus the Dutch and the Swiss Governments, the depository States of these conventions, de facto recognised the status of Palestine as a State. Sweden officially recognises State of Palestine and the Parliaments of Spain, France, and the United Kingdom voted to encourage their governments to bilaterally recognize Palestine as a State.

[19] 'Text of Fatah-Hamas agreement', Jerusalem Post, 25 April 2014 <http://www.jpost.com/Arab-Israeli-Conflict/Text-of-Fatah-Hamas-agreement-376350>. A number of newly appointed ministers, such as the Justice Minister Saleem al-Saqqa, are based in Gaza.

[20] See, e.g., the EU in August 2014: 'The Gaza Strip constitutes an integral part of the territory occupied in 1967 … The situation in the Gaza Strip cannot and must not be seen separately from the broader challenges and developments on the ground that continue to make the prospect of the two-state solution increasingly difficult to attain'. <http://www.consilium.europa.eu/uedocs/cms_data/docs/pressdata/EN/foraff/144313.pdf>.

[21] On 9 July, a day after the defensive war was officially proclaimed, Palestinian President Mahmoud Abbas was reported to say that 'This is not a war against one faction or another, or against Hamas, but against the entire Palestinian people', *Haaretz* 9 July 2014 <http://www.haaretz.com/news/diplomacy-defense/.premium-1.604130>.

9/11, that acts of non-State armed groups (NSAGs), even if not attributable to a State, may constitute an *armed attack*.[22] Hence, the Article 51 exception could be applicable to armed attack by a NSAG if it was carried out in an inter-State context. Trapp thus proposes that a State could invoke Article 51 of the UN Charter in cases in which a NSAG is operating from a foreign territory, and the foreign State is unwilling or unable to repress the armed attack that originates from its sovereign territory[23]. However, if a NSAG launches an armed attack from within the State which seeks to defend itself, then Article 51 could not be invoked by that State, because the attack would fail to meet the inter-State requirement of Article 2(4). In the latter case, the use of force shall be governed by other legal frameworks such as domestic law, international human right law, and IHL (if the violence amounts to a non-international armed conflict).

A higher gravity threshold for an armed attack authored by NSAGs?

The requirement of an 'armed attack' is largely considered as a *sine qua non* for the lawful exercise of self-defence under Article 51.[24] Not any use of force will amount to an armed attack; still, there is lack of clarity over its precise definition.[25] The ICJ in

[22] As rightly stated by Judge Higgins: 'Nothing in the text of Art. 51 ... stipulates that self-defence is available only when an armed attack is made by a State'. *Legal Consequences of the Construction of a Wall in the Occupied Palestinian Territory*, Advisory Opinion of 9 July 2004, ICJ Rep. 2004, 136, Separate Opinion of Judge Higgins, para. 33. A more restricted position will required that the acts of NSAG would be attributable to a State, see *Case concerning Military and Paramilitary Activities in und against Nicaragua (Nicaragua v United States of America)*, Merits, Judgment of 27 June 1986, ICJ. Reports 1986, para. 195. But the post 9/11 practice seems not to follow this restricting view; see United Nations Security Council Resolution 1373 'Threats to international peace and security caused by terrorist acts', S/RES/1373 (2001); United Nations Security Council Resolution 1368 'Threats to international peace and security caused by terrorist acts', S/RES/1368 (2001); Greenwood, C., 2002, 'International Law and the "War on Terrorism"', *International Affairs*, vol. 78, no. 2 (April): 301, 307; Moir, L., 2015, 'Action Against Host States of Terrorist Groups'. In *The Oxford Handbook of The Use of Force in International Law*, edited by Weller, M., Oxford: Oxford University Press, p. 731; Dinstein, Y., 2001, In *War, Aggression and Self-Defence*, Cambridge: Cambridge University Press, p. 216; Lowe, V., 2007, In *International Law*, Oxford: Oxford University Press, p. 2278; Gill, T. D., 2015, 'When Does Self Defence End?'. In *The Oxford Handbook of the Use of Force in International Law*, edited by Weller, M., Oxford: Oxford University Press, p. 740; Franck, T., 2001, 'Terrorism and the right to self defence', *American Journal of international law*: 839, 840. Kretzmer, D., 2013), 'The Inherent Right to Self-Defence and Proportionality in Jus Ad Bellum', European Journal of Intl Law: vol. 24, no. 1, 235, p. 246.

[23] Trapp, K. N., 2015, 'Can Non State Actors Mount An Armed Attack?'. In *The Oxford Handbook of The Use of Force in International Law*, edited by Weller, M., Oxford: Oxford University Press, 679, pp. 694–5.

[24] Claus, K., 2015, 'The International Court of Justice and the 'Principle of Non-Use of Force'. In *The Oxford Handbook of The Use of Force in International Law*, edited by Weller, M., Oxford: Oxford University Press, p. 579; *Nicaragua*, ICJ, para. 195. *Oil Platform*, ICJ, para. 51. The controversies focus rather on the temporal element of the armed attack (whether the attack has occurred, is imminent, or anticipatory).

[25] While debate persists over the scope of the acts that could constitute *an armed attack*, it is agreed that the Art. 51 requirement of an illegal 'armed attack' sets a higher threshold than any violation of Art. 2(4) of

the *Nicaragua* case ruled that 'a mere frontier' incident would not reach the threshold of armed attack.[26] The Eritrea–Ethiopia Claims Commission excluded also 'localized border encounters between small infantry units, even those involving the loss of life'.[27]

An additional unsettled question is whether the gravity threshold of an Article 51 'armed attack' depends on whether it is authored by a State or a non-State actor. For example, some scholars hold the view that the 9/11 attacks committed by Al-Qaeda did not amount to an Article. 51 'armed attack', even though there would have been no doubt in the matter, had the same acts been committed by a State. Similarly under *jus in bello*, a mere 'one bullet incident' may be enough to apply the law of IAC, but a higher threshold of violence is required for the qualification of a NIAC (e.g., requirement of intensity, duration, organization of the party). Arguably this higher threshold should also be applied by way of analogy to the definition of an Article 51 'armed attack'; thus, for instance, the Chatham House Principles on Self-Defence state that for an imminent attack by an NSAG to qualify as an *armed attack* that justifies the use of force in self-defence, it must be part of a larger scale military operation.[28]

Armed attacks emanating from Gaza

Acts would constitute an *armed attack*, if they have reached a certain level of gravity, which is arguably higher when authored by a NSAG. The gravity question could be considered through the lens of the contested 'accumulation of events doctrine', which assumes that distinct events that do not amount to an attack in themselves could amount to one in a cumulative manner.[29] Nonetheless, given that none of the rocket attacks emanating from

the UN Charter, which prohibits the threat or *use of force*. In the *Nicaragua* case, the ICJ found that there is a need 'to distinguish the most grave forms of the use of force (those constituting an armed attack) from other less grave forms'. *Nicaragua*, ICJ, para. 191.

[26] ICJ 1986, para. 195

[27] The Eritrea–Ethiopia Claims Commission also held that 'localized border encounters between small infantry units, even those involving the loss of life, [did] not constitute an armed attack for purposes of the Charter' (para. 11).

[28] Wilmshurst, E., 2006, 'The Chatham House Principles of International Law on the Use of Force in Self-Defence', International and Comparative Law Quarterly, vol. 55, no. 4 (October 2006): p. 963. These principles were established following an expert meeting of UK international law academics and practitioners including Daniel Bethlehem, Christopher Greenwood, Vaughan Lowe, Philippe Sands, Malcolm Shaw, Colin Warbrick, Elizabeth Wilmshurst, Gerry Simpson, and Sir Michael Wood.

[29] The ICJ has implicitly referred to the doctrine in the *Oil platforms*-case, when it held that '*even taken cumulatively* ... these incidents do not seem to the Court to constitute an armed attack. (ICJ Reports 2003: para. 64). Israel has relied on the Accumulation of events Doctrine in the past. In the 2008 Gaza war Israel relied on Art. 51 of the Charter in response to 'many weeks, months, and years in which its citizens were subject to deliberate terrorist attacks'. Statement by Ambassador Gabriela Shalev, Permanent Representative Security Council, 31 December 2008, available at: <http://israel-un.mfa.gov.il/statements-at-the-united-nations/security-council/30-sitme311208>. Yet, the legal status of the doctrine still remains

Gaza from the end of the previous round of hostilities in 2012 to the hostilities that began in 2014 caused any deaths nor serious damage, it should be asked whether attacks launched by Palestinian groups in Gaza before July 2014, were sufficiently grave in terms of harm caused to Israel to amount to armed attacks for the purpose of triggering Article 51. It should be noted that in total, all Palestinian armed groups combined launched relatively few rockets and mortar shells at Israel after the November 2012 ceasefire, until June 2014. According to news reports, Hamas' armed wing itself did not conduct any such attacks from November 2012 until 30 June 2014.[30]

As noted, the threshold for an armed attack (whether determined by individual or cumulative events) is higher when the authors of attacks are NSAGs than for States. It is therefore relevant to an assessment of Israel's ability to invoke self-defence to consider whether Hamas' armed wing, the Qassam Brigades, was acting on behalf of the Palestinian State when it carried out rocket and mortar attacks before Israel began 'Operation Protective Edge'. Further, it should be asked whether other armed groups that carried out such attacks (e.g., Al-Quds Brigades, National Resistance Brigades, Abu Ali Mustafa Brigades, Al-Mujahideen Brigades) did so under Hamas' orders or were under its control.[31]

THE CASE OF AN OCCUPATION

The requirement of an extraterritorial armed attack

In its Advisory Opinion on the Wall, the ICJ rejected Israel's claim of self-defence under Article 51 because of Israel's control over the Palestinian territories. The opinion distinguished the US claim of self-defence after the NASG attacks of 9/11, and the UNSC's endorsement of that claim, from the situation in an occupied territory, by recalling that a State may not invoke self-defence against attacks originating from territory that it controls:

> Israel exercises control in the Occupied Palestinian Territory and … as Israel itself states, the threat which it regards as justifying the construction of the wall originates within, and not

unclear, in particular due to its 'cold reception' by the UN Security Council, and the impact it might cause to the immediacy principle.

[30] According to data reported by the Shabak/Israel Security Agency, in total, Palestinian armed groups in Gaza launched fewer than 140 rockets and mortar shells (combined) at Israel from the 2012 ceasefire until June 2014. See n. 11.

[31] In several reported cases, Hamas allegedly arrested and tortured members of other armed groups for launching rockets without authorization; see e.g., <http://www.jpost.com/Middle-East/Hamas-crackdown-on-Jihad-ups-tensions>; <http://www.crisisgroup.org/~/media/Files/Middle%20East%20North%20Africa/Israel%20Palestine/149-the-next-round-in-gaza.pdf> (footnote 20).

outside, that territory. The situation is thus different from that contemplated by Security Council resolutions 1368 (2001) and 1373 (2001), and therefore Israel could not in any event invoke those resolutions in support of its claim to be exercising a right of self-defence.[32]

Trapp considers that the ICJ opinion should be understood as reaffirming the precondition for the applicability of Article 51 discussed above: 'As the Court considered the West Bank to be occupied territory, Israel's construction of the wall could not engage Article 2(4) prohibitions, which applied only between sovereign states. As Art. 2(4) is inapplicable, Article 51 is equally inapplicable'.[33] The Chatham House Principles on Self-Defence also endorsed this extraterritorial requirement, and state that 'force in self-defence may be used only when … the attack is directed from outside territory controlled by the state'.[34]

Thus, a State may invoke self-defence under Article 51 only in cases where at least two States are involved, and in addition, where the 'armed attack' does not originate from a State or territory under the control of the victim State.

Another important argument supports the position whereby in cases of occupation the use of force exercised by the occupying power shall not be governed by the *jus ad bellum* framework but by *jus in bello*. The *jus in bello* framework addresses the occupying power's security concerns while taking into account the occupier's particular relations of control over a foreign civilian population; its detailed, prescriptive rules are established to protect security/military interests as well as to guarantee the welfare of protected people and their daily civilian needs. It allows the occupying State to use force in cases of necessity, but only within the scope of its provisions designed for this context. The *jus in bello* rules on military occupation achieve a delicate balance between these two interests. The *jus ad bellum* framework, by contrast, is designed to apply between equal sovereign States. Introducing *jus ad bellum* rules to allow the occupying power to use (more) force in an occupied territory would not be appropriate, as these rules do not reflect, nor take into consideration, the complex relations of control and subsequent guarantees of protection provided by *jus in bello* specialized rules.[35]

[32] *Wall*, Advisory Opinion, para. 139 (yet, *in contrario*, see the separate opinion of Judge Higgins and the declaration of Judge Buergenthal).

[33] Trapp, K. N., 'Can Non State Actors', p. 688.

[34] The Chatham House Principles note that the *Wall* Advisory Opinion 'may be read as reflecting the obvious point that unless an attack is directed from outside territory under the control of the defending state the question of self-defence in the sense of Article 51 does not normally arise'. See Principle 2 and its commentary in Wilmshurst, E., 'The Chatham House Principles'.

[35] On the distinction between *jus ad bellum* and *jus in Bello*, and the question of self defence see Okimoto, K., 2015, 'The Relationship Between Jus ad Bellum and Jus in Bello'. In *The Oxford Handbook of The Use of Force in International Law*, edited by Weller, M., Oxford: Oxford University Press, p. 1187. On the law of military occupation see Weill, S., 2014, *The Role of National Courts in Applying International Humanitarian Law*, Oxford: Oxford University Press, p. 20.

Gaza's control by Israel and the possibility to invoke Article 51

Israel cannot invoke Article 51 if it is deemed to be the occupying power in the Gaza Strip, which is determined by the extent of Israel's control over Gaza according to Article 42 of the Hague regulations.[36]

In 2005 Israel withdrew its armed forces (and civilian settlers) from Gaza and proceeded to claim that the territory is no longer subject to its belligerent occupation. Some observers have disagreed as to the extent of Israel's responsibilities in Gaza and its status as the occupier there after its unilateral 2005 'disengagement'. However, there is wide agreement and practice to suggest that both the West Bank and Gaza are occupied.[37] Israel has maintained control over Gaza's land borders, sea and air spaces, as well as its population registry, the movement of people and goods to and from the territory, and the collection of custom duties.[38] Israeli officials fixed the average daily food intake for the population of Gaza at 2,279 calories per person, and allowed supply trucks to enter the Gaza Strip on that basis.[39]

On November 2014, the ICC Office of the Prosecutor affirmed that the Gaza Strip remains 'occupied territory'.[40] Academic debate concerning the current status of the Gaza Strip has also arrived at an overwhelming consensus that the Gaza Strip remains occupied territory.[41] The points of debate have largely concerned

[36] Art. 42 of the 1907 Hague Regulations limits the applicability of occupation law to territory 'where such authority has been established and can be exercised'. Art. 6(3) of the 1949 Fourth Geneva Convention determines the extent of the responsibilities of the occupier vis-à-vis the protected population based on a factual test of the extent of its control over daily life and ability to exercise governmental authority.

[37] Curiously, this question was far less controversial in the case of the Oslo-defined 'Areas A' (and B) in the West Bank, over which Israel allocated limited jurisdiction to the Palestinian Authority; both cases have dimensions of remote control and shared responsibilities with local governments.

[38] As noted by Filiu: 'Israel's disengagement from the Gaza Strip has only changed the form of the occupation without altering its fundamentally oppressive nature. The Israeli army now implemented an innovative version of remote control occupation, saving on the military, human, and financial costs of direct control, while maintaining authority over who and what could come in and out of Gaza and when (with the close cooperation of Egypt at the southern crossing point of Rafah).' Filiu, J-P., 'The Twelve Wars on Gaza', 56; See also Gisha, 2011, 'Scale of Control: Israel's Continued Responsibility in the Gaza Strip', Tel Aviv, <http://gisha.org/publication/1660>.

[39] Bashi, S., 2013, 'Controlling Perimeters, Controlling Lives: Israel and Gaza', *Law and Ethics of Human Rights*, vol. 7, no. 2: pp. 243–82. As noted by Jean-Pierre Filiu, 'The fact that Israel could feel empowered to decide how much a Palestinian could eat on a daily basis shows how perverse and degrading the post-2005 occupation of the Gaza Strip has become'; Filiu, J-P., 'The Twelve Wars on Gaza', p. 57.

[40] See ICC decision not to open an investigation of the situation under examination on the basis of a referral by the Union of the Comoros, whose registered vessels were attacked by Israeli forces when they tried to run Israel's naval blockade of Gaza in May 2010. ICC Prosecutor Office, 'Situation on Registered Vessels of Comoros, Greece and Cambodia, Article 53(1) Report', 6 November 2014, paras. 27, 28. <http://www.icc-cpi.int/iccdocs/otp/OTP-COM-Article_53(1)-Report-06Nov2014Eng.pdf>.

[41] Dinstein advances three arguments that affirm Israel's continued position as an occupier of the Gaza Strip: the integrality of the territory of the West Bank and the Gaza Strip; the continued control by Israel over core ingredients of the administration of life in the Gaza Strip; and Israel's insistence on its ability to 'retake militarily' any part of the Gaza Strip, substantiating its continued ability 'to make its authority

the extent of Israel's control over daily life in the Gaza Strip and its consequent responsibilities.[42]

Thus, the legitimacy of invoking Article 51 could be dismissed due to the extraterritoriality requirement, discussed above, which is not fulfilled because of Israel's control over Gaza. As the Occupying Power, Israel's exercise of force in Gaza is framed by the law of belligerent occupation, including both human rights and IHL standards.

The illegal use of force to maintain an occupation and its impact on the possibility to invoke Article 51

Additional considerations support the argument that Article 51 shall not be invoked by an occupying power. First, insofar as military occupations are maintained through the use of force, prohibited by Article 2(4), the continuation of the occupation may constitute a violation of *jus contra bellum*. This issue may be particularly relevant to cases of prolonged occupation, where the continuation of the occupation cannot be justified even if the occupying power's initial resort to the use of force might have been. Consequently, the occupying State may bear responsibly for illegal use of force. In this situation, where the occupying State was responsible for creating an illegal situation, it could not resort to Article 51 to justify additional use of force in order to maintain that situation.

Israel uses force on a daily basis in order to maintain and reinforce its control over the West Bank and Gaza and to support policies that have been widely criticized for resulting in the flagrant denial of the Palestinian people's right of self-determination. Israel's use of force may therefore attract State responsibility for violations of *jus contra bellum*, which would exclude additional recourse to force under Article 51.

The 'armed attack' as constituting an illegal use of force

The right to self-defence may be invoked only against an *illegal* armed attack. A hypothetical situation in which two sides legally use force against each other is logically unfeasible.

felt', as it has done on a regular basis till this day. Dinstein, Y., 2009, *The International Law of Belligerent Occupation*, Cambridge; Cambridge University Press, paras 661–78; Darcy and Reynolds underline that 'In light of prior lack of good faith in the application of IHL to the Palestinian territories, the "disengagement" bears the hallmark of an attempt by Israel to abrogate its legal responsibilities'. Israeli authorities should be 'precluded from unilaterally deciding the extent of their own legal obligations' by situating the Gaza Strip in a position of 'legal limbo' which only stands to confirm Israel's existing 'culture of evasion and manipulation'. Reynolds, J. and Darcy, S., 2010, 'An Enduring Occupation: The Status of the Gaza Strip from the Perspective of International Humanitarian Law', *Journal of Conflict and Security Law*, vol. 15, no. 2: p. 211 .

[42] Benvenisti underscores that 'the determination whether such control exists or not at the relevant times and in the relevant place will be based on a case by case analysis'. Benvenisti, E., 2009, 'The Law

Under international law, the use of force in order to resist an unlawful territorial regime that arose from a situation of belligerent occupation does not necessarily constitute a violation of *jus contra bellum*. For instance, UN General Assembly on the 'Importance of the universal realization of the right of peoples to self-determination', adopted in 1982:

> Reaffirms the legitimacy of the struggle of peoples for independence, territorial integrity, national unity and liberation from colonial and foreign domination and foreign occupation by all available means, including armed struggle;
>
> Reaffirms the inalienable right of the Namibian people, the Palestinian people and all peoples under foreign and colonial domination to self-determination.[43]

Prolonged occupation is likely to result in the political subjugation of the local population and in the denial of their right to self-determination. Kolb and Vité argue that an occupier who adopts measures that irreversibly limit or prejudice the political and social order in the occupied territory violates the *jus cogens* principle of self-determination.[44] In cases where a people is struggling in pursuit of its internationally recognized right to self-determination, the people's right to lawfully seek and receive political, financial, military or other assistance from States in support of their struggle has in some cases been granted by the General Assembly.[45] Such cases include resistance struggles against prolonged occupations, which often consist of territorial acquisition or regime change with dimensions of economic exploitation and political subjugation.[46] Under a restricted definition of a colonial regime—limited to territories classified as mandates

on the Unilateral Termination of Occupation'. In *Veröffentlichungen des Walther-Schücking-Instituts für Internationales Recht an der Universität Kiel*, edited by Zimmermann, E., and Giegerich, T., available at <http://papers.ssrn.com/sol3/papers.cfm?abstract_id=1254523>.

[43] General Assembly Resolution 37/43 of 3 December 1982, para. 2. See also General Assembly Resolution 3070 (XXVIII) of 30 November 1973, adopted by consensus, reaffirmed the legitimacy of 'all available means, including armed struggle' and called for 'moral, material and any other assistance to all struggling' for self-determination; General Assembly Resolution 3246 (XXIX) of 29 November 1974, which approved the right of peoples to use 'all available means' to fulfil their right for self-determination.

[44] Kolb, R. and Vité, S., 2009, *Le Droit de l'Occupation Militaire: Perspectives historiques et enjeux juridiques actuels*, Bruxelles: Bruylant, pp. 213–214, 250–260.

[45] General Assembly Resolutions 2625 (XXV) of 24 October 1970, Declaration on Principles of International Law Concerning Friendly Relations, stated that in their actions against, and resistance to forcible efforts to deprive them of their right of self-determination, 'peoples are entitled to seek and to receive support in accordance with the purposes and principles of the Charter'. See also, General Assembly Resolution 3314 (XXIX), Definition of Aggression, 14 December 1974, Art. 7. Kunig, P., 2008, 'Prohibition of Intervention', *Max Planck Encyclopedia of Public International Law* (April) 4–5. Cassese, A., 1996, *Self-Determination of Peoples*, Oxford University Press, 1996, pp. 199 et seq. Roth, B. R., 1999, *Governmental Illegitimacy in International Law*, Oxford: Oxford University Press, Ch. 6.

[46] General Assembly. Resolution 35/227 (1981) recognizing SWAPO as the 'sole and authentic representative of the Namibian people', declared support for the 'armed struggle of the Namibian people' and called for 'increased and sustained support and material, financial, military and other assistance to 'SWAPO'.

by the League of Nations—Gray remarks that the only remaining struggle in the context of colonization is that of Palestine.[47]

Thus, it can be argued that the use of force by Hamas was not illegal under *jus ad bellum* (as distinct from the *jus in bello* violations it committed that may amount to war crimes, discussed below), because it amounts to legitimate resistance to illegal oppression.[48] In that case, Hamas' acts would not constitute an (unlawful) 'armed attack' for the purpose of triggering Israel's right to self-defence under Article 51.

It therefore appears that until the occupation ends, through a complete exercise of sovereignty by the State of Palestine, Israel's ability to invoke Article 51 should be set aside. Any use of force (whether legal or illegal under *jus ad bellum*) must comply with IHL. Nothing could, in any event, justify IHL violations, let alone commission of war crimes, whether by Israel or Hamas and other armed groups.

B. Principal violations of IHL during the 2014 Gaza hostilities

Much of the independent reporting on IHL violations during the hostilities was based on the work of Gaza-based field researchers employed with local human rights organizations or with investigators at international organizations. [49] It drew primarily on witness statements, and in relatively few cases on shrapnel and visual evidence that was then analysed by military experts. Investigators including those of the UN Commission of Inquiry were unable to conduct onsite investigations as Israel and Egypt placed unprecedented restrictions on international human rights groups and independent investigative missions. These restrictions mean that many facts remain unclear and the legality of specific attacks is not always ascertainable. Nonetheless, patterns of attacks

[47] Gray, C., 2010, 'The Use of Force and the International Legal Order'. In *International Law*, edited by Evans, M., Oxford: Oxford University Press, p. 620. Fox, G. H., 2008, *Humanitarian Occupation* Cambridge: Cambridge University Press. cf., discussing the 'Reagan doctrine', Henkin, L., 1995. *International Law: Politics and Values*, Boston: Nijhoff, p. 620.

[48] See how Palestinian President before the UNGA soon after the war further affirmed the Palestinians' 'legitimate right to defend themselves against the Israeli war machine' and 'their legitimate right to resist this colonial, racist Israeli occupation' (Khoury, J., 'Abbas at UNGA: Israel perpetrated genocide in Gaza, we won't forget or forgive', Israeli newspaper Haaretz, 26 September 2014, <http://www.haaretz.com/news/diplomacy-defense/1.617831>).

[49] Human Rights Watch, Egypt/Israel: Provide Rights Groups Access to Gaza, 20 August 2014 <http://www.hrw.org/news/2014/08/20/israelegypt-provide-rights-groups-access-gaza> (accessed 25 April 2015). Amnesty International, Israel: Human rights access to Gaza imperative amid renewed exchange of fire, 19 August 2014 <https://www.amnesty.org/en/articles/news/2014/08/israel-human-rights-access-gaza-imperative-amid-renewed-exchange-fire/> (accessed 25 April 2015).

are identifiable that raise concerns that serious violations of IHL were committed by all parties; some of which may amount to war crimes.

The ensuing discussion begins by two legal issues of concern arising from the Israeli military's conduct. First, it considers the obligation to take all feasible precautions to prevent harm to civilians, an underlying prerequisite for compliance with other targeting principles including the principle of distinction. Second, it assesses information regarding proportionality. The discussion then turns to reported conduct by Palestinian armed groups, including indiscriminate rocket and mortar fire at Israeli population centres, which indicate a systemic disregard for the principle of distinction.

PROTECTION OF CIVILIANS: BETWEEN PRECAUTIONS AND DISTINCTION

The author of the military attack must demonstrate that he has undertaken a careful verification of the target's status before deciding to attack.[50] IHL characterizes all persons as either combatants or civilians—and presumes them to be the latter, in case of doubt[51]—while placing the burden on the attacking party to verify that a targeted person holds a 'continuous combat function' before carrying out an attack.[52]

An emblematic case is that of the Israeli missile attacks that killed four Palestinian boys and wounded three others on a Gaza beach on 16 July 2014. An IDF official reportedly said the first missile had targeted an 'identified Hamas structure', which witness accounts identified as a shack, and that Israeli forces had then attacked again because they mistook the boys, aged ten to thirteen, for 'fleeing fighters'.[53] The Israeli military's admitted error in the second case raises serious concerns over the nature of precautions

[50] The burden of proof on the attacking party is heavy: '[W]hen there is a situation of doubt, a careful assessment has to be made under the conditions and restraints governing a particular situation as to whether there are sufficient indications to warrant an attack. One cannot automatically attack anyone who might appear dubious.' Practice Relating to Rule 6. Civilians' Loss of Protection from Attack, ICRC, Customary IHL Database, <https://www.icrc.org/customary-ihl/eng/docs/v2_rul_rule6> (accessed 20 April 2015).

[51] Additional Protocol I, Art. 52(3). Rule 10, Civilians Objects' Loss of Protection from Attack, ICRC, Customary IHL Database, <https://www.icrc.org/customary-ihl/eng/docs/v1_cha_chapter2_rule10#Fn_53_4> (accessed 20 April 2015). See also, *Prosecutor v. Stanislav Galic* (Trial Judgment and Opinion) IT-98-29-T, International Criminal Tribunal for the former Yugoslavia, 5 December 2003, para. 55.

[52] Melzer, N., 2009, Interpretative guidance on the notion of Direct participation in hostilities under international humanitarian law (ICRC) pp. 43 *et seq.* Henderson, I., 2009, *The Contemporary Law of Targeting: Military Objectives, Proportionality and Precautions in Attack under Additional Protocol I*, Leiden: Nijhoff.

[53] Human Rights Watch, Dispatches: Explaining Four Dead Boys on a Gaza Beach, 18 July 2014 <http://www.hrw.org/news/2014/07/17/dispatches-explaining-four-dead-boys-gaza-beach> (accessed 20 April 2015).

it had taken before deciding to attack. According to HRW, the attack was carried out with sensor-equipped missiles that permit the operator to see the target and divert the missiles mid-course.[54] Several other attacks using drone-launched missiles that directly targeted civilians were reported during the hostilities as resulting from errors in target verification.[55] The technological capability of drones to take real-time precautions before and throughout an attack (e.g., the ability to 'loiter' while identifying a target with sophisticated electro-optical equipment and to steer the missile away from the intended target) may indicate the inadequacy of any steps taken to minimize harm to civilians. The recurrence of such apparent errors, as indicated by independent investigations, raises concerns about the nature of the Israeli military's target verification process, its training and oversight of drone-operators, or both. Israeli practice suggests an emphasis on the success of military operations at the expense of respecting the obligation to safeguard civilians.

The link between the principles of distinction and of precautions may be explained by apparently lax targeting rules.[56] A report by the Israeli rights group Breaking the Silence, based on over 111 testimonies by soldiers who participated in the 2014 hostilities, observed that '[a]ccording to officers that operated in command centers, there was a broad range of discretion allowed for reaching decisions regarding the identification of targets … and attacks were authorized even in cases when there was partial information regarding the likelihood of harming innocent people'.[57] Some soldiers said that their commanders briefed them 'to fire at every person they identified in a combat zone, since the working assumption was that every person in the field was an enemy' and 'to shoot at

[54] Human Rights Watch, Gaza: Airstrike Deaths Raise Concerns on Ground Offensive, 22 July 2014<http://www.hrw.org/news/2014/07/22/gaza-airstrike-deaths-raise-concerns-ground-offensive>.

[55] See aerial attack on municipal workers jeep, killing two on 11 July 2014; Human Rights Watch, Israel/Palestine: Unlawful Israeli Airstrikes Kill Civilians, 16 July 2014 <http://www.hrw.org/news/2014/07/15/israelpalestine-unlawful-israeli-airstrikes-kill-civilians> (accessed 25 April 2015). Missile strike on three children playing on the roof of a residential building; Gallucci, M., 'Gaza: Three More Palestinian Children Killed By Israeli Airstrikes After Five-Hour Cease-Fire Ends, *International Business Times*, 17 July 2014 <http://www.ibtimes.com/gaza-three-more-palestinian-children-killed-israeli-airstrikes-after-five-hour-cease-fire-1631360> (accessed 25 April 2015). See also, Gaza Diaries 9, Al-Mezan Center for Human Rights, 18 July 2014 <http://www.mezan.org/en/post/19247/Gaza+Diaries9%3A+%27All+that+was+left+were+the+fragments+of+their+little+bodies+and+the+small+bag+of+chicken+food%27+Three+children+killed+on+the+roof+of+their+home+in+an+Israeli+bombardment> (accessed 25 April 2015). Similar attacks carried out with drone-fired missiles were also documented by independent investigations following the 2008–9 and 2012 hostilities. Chassay, C., 'Cut to pieces: the Palestinian family drinking tea in their courtyard', *The Guardian*, 23 March 2009 <http://www.theguardian.com/world/2009/mar/23/gaza-war-crimes-drones> (accessed 21 April 2015).

[56] Human Rights Watch, 'Gaza: Widespread Impact of Power Plant Attack', 10 August 2014 <http://www.hrw.org/news/2014/08/10/gaza-widespread-impact-power-plant-attack> (accessed 25 April 2015).

[57] See testimonies 100, 102, and 108; Breaking the Silence, *This is How We Fought in Gaza Soldiers' testimonies and photographs from Operation 'Protective Edge' (2014)* (May 2015) p. 20 <http://www.breakingthesilence.org.il/pdf/ProtectiveEdge.pdf> (accessed 5 May 2015).

any threat, imminent or suspected'.[58] Soldiers also testified about the use of 'unabated fire on "suspicious points"' which were 'not clearly define[d]', leaving soldiers to make such decisions in practice: 'almost every object or structure within the forces' eyeshot had the potential to be considered suspicious and thus targeted', such as 'movements identified in the window of a house hundreds of meters away from the forces, [which] led to a strike on that house, based on the suspicion that it was an enemy lookout'.[59]

The operational effects of the Israeli army's 'conservative approach towards uncertainty' in the targeting process[60] were also manifest during the ground incursion, when Israeli soldiers shot and killed civilians attempting to clearly convey their status by waving make-shift white flags while trying to evacuate the town of Khuza'a.[61] Repeated attacks injuring and killing medical personnel and apparently directed against ambulances during the 2014 hostilities[62] raise similar concerns with regards to the Israeli army's verification of targets and respect for the principle of distinction.

It appears that the Israeli military targeted areas or persons that it identified as military objects without sufficient certainty, as required by the 'all feasible precautions' standard.[63] This internationally accepted standard is intrinsically more demanding than Israel's standard of 'reasonableness',[64] which limits the obligation to consider alternative times or means of attack, after exhausting militarily feasible measures to verify the target, permitting the attack in the face of any uncertainty that remained.[65]

[58] See testimonies 2, 56, and 75; Breaking the Silence 2015, 17–18.

[59] See testimonies 32, 34, and 84; Breaking the Silence 2015, 18.

[60] Schmitt, M. and Merriam, J., 2015, 'The Tyranny of Context: Israeli Targeting Practices in Legal Perspective', *University of Pennsylvania Journal of International Law*, vol. 37: p. 42. Schmitt remarks that Israeli military advisers said they embrace the ICRC Interpretative Guidance but reject the 'continuous combat function' criterion, which IDF said 'creates a legal imbalance' between military and non-military members and therefore is of the view that all members of armed groups are 'targetable at all times'. See at pp. 36–7.

[61] HRW and PHR reported on the grave dangers civilians faced while trying to flee the town, including repeated shelling and the threat of attack and at least two incidents of direct shooting at civilian groups; Human Rights Watch, 'Gaza: Israeli Soldiers Shoot and Kill Fleeing Civilians', 4 August 2014 <http://www.hrw.org/news/2014/08/04/gaza-israeli-soldiers-shoot-and-kill-fleeing-civilians> (accessed 22 April 2015). Physicians for Human Rights, 2014, 'Gaza 2014: Findings of an Independent Medical Fact-Finding Mission', pp. 76 *et seq* <https://gazahealthattack.files.wordpress.com/2015/01/gazareport_eng.pdf> (accessed 22 April 2015). The report documents one case of en mass evacuation, and two cases of close-range shooting of civilians by Israeli snipers during the ground incursion in Khuza'a.

[62] Physicians for Human Rights, 2014, 'Gaza 2014: Findings of an Independent Medical Fact-Finding Mission, pp. 76 *et seq* <https://gazahealthattack.files.wordpress.com/2015/01/gazareport_eng.pdf> (accessed 22 April 2015).

[63] Merriam, J., 2015, 'Affirmative Target Identification: Operationalising the Principle of Distinction for US Warfighters', *Virginia Journal of International Law*, vol. 56.

[64] Sandoz, Y., Swinarski, C., and Zimmermann, B. (eds.), 1987, *Commentary on the Additional Protocols of 8 June 1977 to the Geneva Conventions of 12 August 1949*, Geneva: Nijhoff, Art. 57, para. 2230.

[65] Schmitt and Merriam, 'The Tyranny of Context', p. 43.

WARNINGS AND RISK TO CIVILIANS

The Israeli military made widespread use of warnings in the form of leaflets, phone calls, and text messages to mobile phones during the 2014 hostilities. However, according to Physicians for Human Rights, some warnings were ineffective, such as cases in which evacuation orders failed to indicate the time or destination of the evacuation or a route of escape.[66] Soldier testimonies collected by Breaking the Silence indicate that the wide-scale use of warnings to evacuate homes were often ineffective.[67] One warning technique, reportedly used on a wide scale, was 'roof-knocking'—the practice of firing accurate munitions without explosive warheads to warn residents that their homes would be imminently destroyed. This warning technique, according to the UN report on the 2008/9 Gaza conflict, is itself illegal since 'civilians cannot be expected to know whether a small explosion is a warning of an impending attack or part of an actual attack'.[68]

Overwhelming State practice concurs that all of an attacker's obligations remain applicable if civilians remain in the zone of operations, even after a warning was issued;[69] to lose protection from attack, a person must shield a military objective voluntarily, and must physically hinder enemy military operations or render the target legally immune from attack under a proportionality analysis (conducted as though the person was a civilian).[70]

The Israeli military's official position apparently accepts that civilians who do not heed warnings must factor into the proportionality and precautions analysis: according to Schmitt, the Israeli army position is that '[c]ivilians have no LOAC obligation to leave the target area and thus do not forfeit any of their legal protection when remaining there'.[71] However, some statements by military officials indicate that the military treated

[66] Janina Dill, 'Guest Post: Israel's Use of Law and Warnings in Gaza', *Opinio Juris*, 30 July 2014 <http://opiniojuris.org/2014/07/30/guest-post-israels-use-law-warnings-gaza/> (accessed 25 April 2015). 'The effectiveness will depend on three considerations: the clarity of the message, the credibility of the threat and the possibility of those receiving the warning taking action to escape the threat'; Human Rights Council, 'Report of the United Nations Fact-Finding Mission on the Gaza Conflict', UN Doc. A/HRC/12/48, 25 September 2009, paras. 513. See also Human Rights Council, Report of the detailed findings of the Commission of Inquiry on the 2014 Gaza Conflict, UN Doc A/HRC/29/CRP.4 paras. 235–239.

[67] Breaking the Silence 2015, pp. 20–1.

[68] Human Rights Council, Report of the United Nations Fact-Finding Mission on the Gaza Conflict, A/HRC/12/48, 25 September 2009, paras. 532–3.

[69] After people were killed and injured in the streets while fleeing their homes, many decided not to leave home even after receiving a warning. Physicians for Human Rights, 2014, 'Gaza 2014: Findings of an Independent Medical Fact-Finding Mission', p. 42 <https://gazahealthattack.files.wordpress.com/2015/01/gazareport_eng.pdf> (accessed 22 April 2015).

[70] Sassòli, M. and Quintin, A., 2014, 'Active and Passive Precautions in Air and Missile Warfare', *Israel Yearbook on Human Rights*, vol. 44: p. 114. See also, Queguiner, J.-F., 2006, 'Precautions under the Law Governing the Conduct of Hostilities', *International Review of the Red Cross*, vol .88, no. 864: p. 796.

[71] Ibid., p. 40.

areas where it had distributed flyers or otherwise issued warnings, often through SMS messages, as though all civilian residents had been evacuated. A statement by Major Amitai Kanarik suggests that the IDF even viewed people remaining in such areas as legitimate military targets that may be attacked without taking precautions:

> We try to create a situation whereby the area where we are fighting is sterile, so any person seen there is suspected of engaging in terrorist activity. At the same time, we make the utmost effort to remove the population, whether this means dropping flyers or shelling. Ultimately, we manage to convince even those who weren't at first persuaded, until we get to a situation where the neighborhood becomes a ghost town, so that anyone who suddenly surfaces automatically becomes a suspected terrorist.[72]

Soldier testimonies in Breaking the Silence's report affirmed 'a working assumption that Palestinian residents had abandoned the neighborhoods [that Israeli forces] entered due to the IDF's warnings, thus making anyone located in the area a legitimate target'.[73]

An attacking party must be able to demonstrate that it followed appropriate precautionary measures to attest to overall compliance with the law of armed conflict. Systematic failures to take all precautionary measures and acceptance of unreasonable risk to civilians, as arguably apparent from attacks during the 2014 hostilities, cannot be dismissed as genuine mistakes and indicate a relaxation of the principle of distinction.[74] Israel's obligations to take all feasible precautions to avert risk to civilians are arguably compounded by the more demanding rules on the use of force applicable in occupied territory, given its status as Occupying Power of the Gaza Strip.[75] It should be noted in this regard that Israel has extensive knowledge of the Gaza terrain, having occupied and operated in Gaza for decades, as well as 'impressive intelligence, surveillance and reconnaissance (ISR) assets'.[76]

[72] Major Kanarik heads the Military Doctrine Department at the headquarters of the Chief Infantry and Paratroopers' Officer. Bokobza, A., 2014, 'Collecting on the Frontline', *BaYabasha*, Ground Forces Journal, October, No. 29, p. 62 (Hebrew). B'Tselem, *Black Flag: The legal and moral implications of the policy of attacking residential buildings in the Gaza Strip, Summer 2014* (January 2015) p. 43 <http://www.btselem.org/download/201501_black_flag_eng.pdf> (accessed 25 April 2015).

[73] Breaking the Silence 2015, pp. 16–17.

[74] See, Pax, *Unacceptable Risk: Use of explosive weapons in populated areas through the lens of three cases before the ICTY* (November 2014) <http://www.paxvoorvrede.nl/media/files/pax-rapport-unacceptable-risk.pdf> (accessed 22 April 2015).

[75] Art. 43, 1907 Hague Regulations. Watkin, K., 2012, 'Use of Force During Occupation: Law Enforcement and Conduct of Hostilities', *International Review of the Red Cross*, vol. 94, No. 885: pp. 301 *et seq.*

[76] Schmitt and Merriam, 'The Tyranny of Context', p. 42. Orpaz, I., 'Direct and Distance Discoverer, Microphone and the Gravity: This is how tunnels are discovered and attacks', The Marker, 12 July 2014 <http://www.themarker.com/technation/1.2382546> (accessed 22 April 2015). Cahana, A., 'Hundreds of terrorists will come out of the tunnels on new year's', *NRG*, 25 July 2014 <http://www.nrg.co.il/online/1/ART2/600/825.html> (accessed 22 April 2015).

OF PROPORTIONALITY, INDISCRIMINATE ATTACKS, AND THE 'HANNIBAL' PROTOCOL

The principle of proportionality requires protection of civilians during attacks on military targets, while accepting that some civilian deaths are not unlawful if they are not 'excessive' in relation to the 'anticipated' military gain.[77]

Targeting houses

The scale of civilian death and destruction resulting from direct attacks on inhabited homes in the 2014 fighting was unprecedented. The UN estimated that about 18,000 housing units were destroyed or rendered uninhabitable, leaving approximately 108,000 people homeless. A further 37,650 housing units were damaged.[78]

The means and methods of attack on a building with civilian residents should endeavour to strike the specific apartment or room that is the military object, so as to accord with the precautions required to comply with proportionality.[79] Yet Schmitt reports that according to Israeli military legal advisers, 'the IDF treats the building as a single object such that no damage to it is legally considered collateral damage'.[80] Israeli military lawyers argue, Schmitt notes, that 'if an airstrike is planned on an apartment on the third floor but is expected to damage apartments used for civilian purposes on the floors beneath it, the expected damage need not be factored into any proportionality analysis'.[81]

While each case should be assessed on its merits—considering the military necessity and the availability of alternative munitions—it remains questioned why homes were repeatedly targeted; why the military could not have delayed some attacks intended to target individuals until they were not at home or their homes were not inhabited by large numbers of civilians; and why it could not have taken additional precautions by choosing weapons that were less likely to cause excessive harm to civilians and civilian property, as it has done in other attacks by launching accurate strikes on specific persons or apartments.[82]

[77] Arts 51(5)(b) and 57 (2)(a)(iii) of AP I.

[78] See, UN OCHA, 'Occupied Palestinian Territory: Gaza Emergency Situation Report (as of 4 September 2014, 08:00 hours)', 4 September 2014 <http://www.ochaopt.org/documents/ocha_opt_sitrep_04_09_2014.pdf> (accessed 25 April 2015). B'Tselem, *Black Flag*, January 2015; Amnesty International, *Families under the Rubble*, November 2014. Human Rights Watch, 'Israel/Palestine: Unlawful Israeli Airstrikes Kill Civilians', 16 July 2014 <http://www.hrw.org/news/2014/07/15/israelpalestine-unlawful-israeli-airstrikes-kill-civilians> (accessed 23 April 2015).

[79] Dinstein, Y., 2010, *The Conduct of Hostilities under the Law of International Armed Conflict*, Cambridge: Cambridge University Press, p. 142, para. 351.

[80] Schmitt and Merriam, 'The Tyranny of Context', p. 41.

[81] Ibid.

[82] See, Neuman, N., 2004, 'Applying the Rule of Proportionality: Force Protection and Cumulative Assessment in International Law and Morality', *Yearbook of International Humanitarian Law*, vol. 7, No. 79. Colonel Neuman currently head the IDF's International Law Department; cited in Schmitt and Merriam, 'The Tyranny of Context', p. 44.

Indiscriminate and disproportionate use of force in populated area

The large number of civilian casualties resulting from inherently indiscriminate attacks by 'statistical weapons' systems such as heavy artillery in populated areas suggests that these attacks were conducted indiscriminately and by the use of disproportionate force.[83] This was the case in Shujaiyeh, where the heavily populated neighbourhood was bombarded with at least 7,000 high explosive shells during a period of twenty-four hours, including a barrage of some 4,800 shells during a seven-hour period.[84] The scale and scope of the artillery fire used in Shujaiyeh indicated, a US military official was quoted as saying, that the IDF's intention was not to precisely target Palestinian military objectives, but rather 'laying down an indiscriminate barrage aimed at cratering the neighbourhood'.[85]

Another apparently indiscriminate attack commenced in Rafah on 1 August, 2014—dubbed 'Black Friday', it was one of the deadliest episodes of the hostilities. Israeli forces suspected that Palestinian fighters had captured an Israeli soldier alive (the military later assessed that he was killed during or shortly after the attack and that Palestinian fighters captured his remains).[86] Colonel Ofer Winter, commander of the IDF Givati Brigade, then announced the activation of the 'Hannibal protocol', which reportedly authorizes attacks intended to prevent enemy forces from taking Israeli soldiers captive.[87] Israeli ground and air force troops proceeded to direct heavy fire—including airstrikes and an estimated 800 artillery shells and 260 mortars, as reported in the military's own probe[88]—on populated residential neighbourhoods in Rafah, as far as two to three kilometres from the location where the soldier (or his body) was captured, with the stated intention to stop the capture.[89] The barrage of apparently indiscriminate fire

[83] Action on Armed Violence, *Under fire: Israel's Artillery Policies Scrutinised* (December 2014) <https://aoav.org.uk/wp-content/uploads/2015/03/AOAV-Under-Fire-Israels-artillery-policies-scrutinised.pdf> (accessed 25 April 2015).

[84] Perry, M., 'Why Israel's bombardment of Gaza neighborhood left US officers "stunned"', *Al-Jazeera America*, 27 August 2014 <http://america.aljazeera.com/articles/2014/8/26/israel-bombing-stunsusofficers.html> (accessed 22 April 2015). See also, HRW, 'Deadly cargo: explosive weapons in populated areas', 30 December 2014 <http://www.hrw.org/news/2014/12/30/deadly-cargo-explosive-weapons-populated-areas> (accessed 25 April 2015).

[85] Perry, M., 'Why Israel's bombardment of Gaza neighborhood left US officers 'stunned', *Al-Jazeera America*, 27 August 2014, <http://america.aljazeera.com/articles/2014/8/26/israel-bombing-stunsusofficers.html> (accessed 22 April 2015).

[86] Levush, R., 2014, 'Israel: Legal Aspects of Prisoner Exchanges', Report for the Law Library of Congress, November, p. 3. Margolit, R., 'Hadar Goldin and the Hannibal Directive', *The New Yorker Magazine*, 6 August 2014 <http://www.newyorker.com/news/news-desk/hadar-goldin-hannibal-directive> (accessed 23 April 2015).

[87] Schmitt and Merriam, 'The Tyranny of Context', pp. 45–6.

[88] Gili Cohen, 'Probe of Gaza op's "Black Friday": Soldiers faced "unreasonable" situation', *Haaretz*, 14 April 2015 <http://www.haaretz.com/news/diplomacy-defense/.premium-1.651743> (accessed 23 April 2015).

[89] 'The Rafah operation: Israeli fire on Gaza town raises war crimes claim', *The Associated Press*, 31 August 2014 <http://www.pennlive.com/nation-world/2014/08/the_rafah_operation_israeli_fi.html> (accessed 23 April 2015).

killed at least 114 Palestinians by the following day.[90] According to Breaking the Silence, Israeli soldiers testified that the opening-fire orders were 'disregarded when there was suspicion that a soldier was kidnapped' in Rafah and Shuyaijeh: 'During these episodes, there was fire on a much more massive scale directed into neighborhoods and populated areas, while disregarding the necessary safety ranges from the civilian population.'[91]

Breaking the Silence notes that the Israeli soldier testimonies it collected show 'a shift in the open-fire policy throughout the operation, with regard to the different targets that were authorized and the scope of injuries to innocent people that were permitted', and remarks that the policy was determined by top military echelons and changed for reasons including 'the desire to prevent Hamas from attaining a "display of victory" ahead of the ceasefire'.[92]

VIOLATIONS BY HAMAS AND PALESTINIAN ARMED GROUPS

Palestinian armed groups have reportedly engaged in serious and widespread violations of the laws of armed conflict, which were arguably more extensive in both scope and scale than previous rounds of hostilities. According to Israeli military figures, Gaza based-groups launched 4,564 projectiles from Gaza during the 2014 hostilities; of those that struck in Israel, 224 hit built-up areas.[93] Palestinian armed groups' arsenals include rockets as well as mortars; the latter target locations at shorter range and are not interceptable by Israel's anti-missile defence system, known as the Iron Dome, reported to be 95% effective against rockets.

Palestinian armed groups used these projectiles in a manner that is inherently indiscriminate: even if some were ostensibly directed at military objectives, they cannot be accurately guided or controlled when launched at Israeli population centres. Projectiles that landed in populated areas during the 2014 hostilities caused the deaths of six civilians on the Israeli side and scores of injuries, most deadly attacks reportedly resulted

[90] Lt. Col. Gino was recorded yelling at his soldiers, desperately trying to get them to stop the barrage of fire to ensure they do not kill each other; Zitun, Y., 'Hannibal Directive: Exclusive tapes reveal details of IDF's Black Friday', *Ynet*, 31 December 2014 <http://www.ynetnews.com/articles/0,7340,L-4609436,00.html> (accessed 23 April 2015). Lubell, M. and al-Mughrabi, N., 'Did Israel's "Hannibal directive" lead to a war crime in Gaza?', *Reuters*, 13 October 2014 <http://www.reuters.com/article/2014/10/13/us-mideast-gaza-warcrime-insightidUSKCN0I20FN20141013> (accessed 23 April 2015); Cohen, G., 'Israeli Army Mulling Criminal Probe Into Use of Hannibal Directive in Gaza', *Haaretz*, 15 February 2015, <http://www.haaretz.com/news/diplomacy-defense/.premium-1.643111#!> (accessed 23 April 2015).

[91] See also, testimonies 58, 60, and 103; Breaking the Silence 2015, p. 20.

[92] Ibid., pp. 22–3.

[93] According to Israeli data, 3,659 rocket and mortar impact sites were found, including those fired on IDF soldiers in Gaza. Hartman, B., '50 days of Israel's Gaza operation, Protective Edge—by the numbers', *Jerusalem Post*, 28 August 2014 <http://www.jpost.com/Operation-Protective-Edge/50-days-of-Israels-Gaza-operation-Protective-Edge-by-the-numbers-372574> (accessed 25 April 2015).

from mortar fire.[94] Some Palestinian armed groups reportedly stated their intention to attack population centres in Israel,[95] and some claimed responsibility for rocket fire at Israeli towns, which they purportedly justified as attacks 'in reprisal for Israeli abuses or aggression'.[96] In other statements, Palestinian armed groups warned Israeli civilians 'not to return to their homes [near the Gaza periphery]' and to 'remain inside shelters and protected places'.[97]

Several incidents of Palestinian fighters launching rockets and mortars from or in the vicinity of civilian areas were also reported; some of these allegations pertain to United Nations facilities, schools, graveyards, mosques, and the power plant.[98] The OHCHR and Amnesty International documented a number of cases involving rocket fire from populated areas, including reportedly at least two cases of Palestinian stray rockets that resulted in the death of at least twenty Palestinian civilians inside Gaza.[99] The IDF reported that as of 20 August 2014, 1,600 out of 3,600 rockets had been fired from civilian areas.[100] The Hamas authorities also showed disregard for individual rights by either engaging in or failing to investigate brutal summary executions of at least twenty-one Palestinians accused of collaborating with Israel during the 2014 hostilities.[101]

[94] Israel Security Agency, 'Monthly summary—August 2014', <http://www.shabak.gov.il/English/EnTerrorData/Reports/Pages/Monthlysummary-July2014.aspx>; and 'Monthly summary—July 2014', <http://www.shabak.gov.il/English/EnTerrorData/Reports/Pages/Monthly0814.aspx> (accessed 25 April 2015). Amnesty International, *Deadly and Unlawful* (March 2015). Human Rights Watch, 'Palestine/Israel: Indiscriminate Palestinian Rocket Attacks', 9 July 2014 <http://www.hrw.org/news/2014/07/09/palestineisrael-indiscriminate-palestinian-rocket-attacks> (accessed 23 April 2015). Human Rights Watch, 'Rockets from Gaza: Harm to Civilians' from Palestinian Armed Group Rockets Attacks', August 2009 <http://www.hrw.org/node/84868> (accessed 23 April 2015).

[95] Al-Quds Brigades and Qassam Brigades, Report of the United Nations High Commissioner for Human Rights on the implementation of Human Rights Council resolutions S-9/1 and S-12/1, UN Doc. A/HRC/28/80/Add.1, 26 December 2014, paras 66–7.

[96] Ibid.

[97] Ezzedeen Al-Qassam Brigades—Information Office, Military Communiqué, Press Release of Abu Obeida, Al Qassam spokesperson, 20 August 2014 <http://www.qassam.ps/statement-1509-Press_Release_of_Abu_Obeida_Al_Qassam_spokesperson.html> (accessed 25 April 2015).

[98] IDF Blog, 'New Declassified Report Exposes Hamas Human Shield Policy', 20 August 2014 <http://www.idfblog.com/blog/2014/08/20/new-declassified-report-exposes-hamas-human-shield-policy/> (accessed 25 April 2015). IDF Blog, Hamas Launches Rockets on Civilians in Gaza, 31 July 2014 <http://www.idfblog.com/blog/2014/07/31/hamas-launches-rockets-civilians-gaza/> (accessed 25 April 2015).

[99] Amnesty International, *Deadly and Unlawful* (March 2015).

[100] IDF Blog, 'New Declassified Report Exposes Hamas Human Shield Policy', 20 August 2014 <http://www.idfblog.com/blog/2014/08/20/new-declassified-report-exposes-hamas-human-shield-policy/> (accessed 25 April 2015). IDF Blog, 'Hamas Launches Rockets on Civilians in Gaza', 31 July 2014, <http://www.idfblog.com/blog/2014/07/31/hamas-launches-rockets-civilians-gaza/> (accessed 25 April 2015).

[101] Report of the United Nations High Commissioner for Human Rights on the implementation of Human Rights Council resolutions S-9/1 and S-12/1, UN Doc. A/HRC/28/80/Add.1, 26 December 2014, para. 31. '18 executed in Gaza for 'spying for Israel', Alray—Palestinian Media Agency, 22 August 2014 <http://alray.ps/en/index.php?act=post&id=5195#.U_8l38V_v90> (accessed 23 April 2015).

Storing ammunition in or firing rockets from civilian homes are acts that directly endanger civilians by turning the homes into military objectives, but do not necessarily constitute acts amounting to the use of 'human shields'.[102] The decisive test for differentiating between the failure to take passive precautions[103] and violations of the prohibition to use 'human shields', according to Sassòli and Quintin, is 'whether the simultaneous presence of civilians and legitimate targets results from the defender's efforts to obtain 'protection' for its military forces and objectives, or simply from a lack of care for the civilian population'.[104] No clear evidence has been reported that Palestinian fighters specifically directed civilians to areas where attacks were being launched, or forced them to remain in the vicinity of attacks, as required for the civilians to be considered 'human shields'.

Palestinian armed groups also reportedly operated in tunnels directly under residential neighbourhoods. Those that did so, or stored munitions in and launched attacks from the vicinity of civilian structures,[105] may have knowingly or recklessly, placed civilians on both sides in harm of injury and death. Given the stated intention of some groups to target populated areas, and the repeated failure to take precautions to protect against harm to civilians in Israel, Palestinian armed groups also appear to have engaged in attacks that are indiscriminate and fail to uphold the obligation to take all feasible precautions. Due to the gravity and widespread nature of these violations, particularly with respect to attacks on Israeli populated centres they may amount to war crimes.

C. The International Criminal Court and local investigations

On the last day of 2014, the State of Palestine, submitted an ad hoc declaration under Article 12(3) to the Office of the ICC Prosecutor in The Hague, accepting the jurisdiction of the ICC with respect to events that occurred after 13 June 2014—thus including the 2014 Gaza Conflict.[106] Concurrently, on 2 January 2015, Palestine submitted an instrument of

[102] Art. 51(7), AP I. [103] Art. 58(c), AP I.

[104] Sassòli, M. and Quintin, A., 'Active and Passive Precautions in Air and Missile Warfare', p. 34.

[105] Summary by the Secretary-General of the UN Headquarters Board of Inquiry into certain incidents that occurred in the Gaza Strip between 8 July 2014 and 26 August 2014, 27 April 2015 <https://drive.google.com/file/d/0ByLPNZ-eSjJdVyloWXRhcFJGSjBlbFNrY241QWsxNVpldUx3/view> (accessed 29 April 2015). See also, IDF Blog, Hamas Booby Traps Palestinian Houses, 27 July 2014 <http://www.idfblog.com/blog/2014/07/27/hamas-uses-palestinian-houses-as-military-compounds/> (accessed 25 April 2015).

[106] The declaration signed by the Palestinian Ministry of Justice, 31 December 2014 is available at: <http://icc-cpi.int/iccdocs/PIDS/press/Palestine_A_12-3.pdf>.

accession to the Rome Statute to the UN Secretary-General.[107] Two weeks later, the ICC Prosecutor opened a preliminary examination into the situation in Palestine—a necessary stage before starting an investigation. In determining whether to initiate an investigation, according to Article 53(1) of the Rome Statute, the Prosecutor has to consider whether: (1) there is a reasonable basis to believe that a war crime, crime against humanity, or genocide has been committed; (2) the case is admissible under the Article 17 standard of complementarity and of gravity[108] ; and (3) the investigation serves the interests of justice.

The complementarity principle—the cornerstone of the ICC—restricts the ICC's jurisdiction to cases where the relevant State is unwilling or unable genuinely to carry out investigations or prosecutions. Similarly, if the State has investigated and closed a case, it is not admissible before the ICC unless the decision resulted from the unwillingness or inability of the State genuinely to prosecute.[109]

ICC jurisprudence maintains that the Court examines the willingness and ability of a domestic system to carry out national investigations and prosecutions, only where the domestic proceedings 'encompass both the person and the conduct which is the subject of the case before the Court'.[110] Hence, for a case to be admissible, it is not necessary for national procedures to be totally non-existent. Instead, the 'same person/same conduct' test is applicable to assess the State's inaction in cases investigated by the ICC: 'where investigations exist but concern other suspects ..., or the same suspect but for conduct other than that referred to the ICC, the case is presumptively admissible'.[111] Yet, when operating 'within the parameters of an entire "situation", rather than in relation to a specific "case"',[112] without having identified specific suspects and suspected acts, how

[107] See the ICC press release: <http://icc-cpi.int/en_menus/icc/press and media/press releases/Pages/pr1082_2.aspx>.

[108] In the *Mavi Marmara Flotilla incident* (referred to the ICC in May 2013 by Comoros—the State to which the ship was registered), the ICC Prosecutor concluded on 6 November 2014 that her office would not open an investigation as 'the potential case(s) likely arising from an investigation into this incident would not be of "sufficient gravity" to justify further action by the ICC'; Situation on Registered Vessels of Comoros, Greece and Cambodia, Art. 53(1) Report, 6 November 2014, at para. 3 <http://www.icc-cpi.int/iccdocs/otp/OTP-COM-Article_53(1)-Report-06Nov2014Eng.pdf>. On July 2015 the ICC Pre-Trial Chamber requested the Prosecutor to reconsider her decision not to initiate an investigation. In its decision the Chamber set the criteria for gravity. See Pre-Trial Chamber 1, Decision on the request of the Union of the Comoros to review the Prosecutor's decision not to initiate an investigation, No. ICC-01/13, July 16, 2015, paras. 20-48.

[109] Art. 17(1)(b), Rome Statute.

[110] *Prosecutor v Lubanga*, ICC-01-04-01/06-8-US-Corr, Decision Concerning Pre-Trial Chamber I's Decision of 10 February 2006 and the Incorporation of Documents into the Record of the Case Against Mr. Thomas Lubanga Dyilo, (Lubanga Arrest Warrant Decision), 10 February 2006, para. 31; see also: Boas, G. et al., *International Criminal Procedure*, Volume III, Cambridge University Press, Cambridge, 2011, p. 72.

[111] *Katanga and Ngudjolo, Situation in the Democratic Republic of the Congo*, ICC-01/04-01/07 OA 8, AC, ICC, (Katanga Appeals Judgment) 25 September 2009, para. 78.

[112] Decision Pursuant to Art. 15 of the Rome Statute on the Authorization of an Investigation into the Situation in the Republic of Kenya, *Situation in Kenya*, ICC-01/09, PTC II, ICC, 31 March 2010 para. 44.

can complementarity be assessed at the examination stage? In the attempt to resolve this dilemma, the ICC Pre-Trial Chamber adopted a flexible reading—also known as the 'broad mirror' approach or incident-specific interpretation—that ties admissibility to a hypothetical assessment of 'one or more potential cases within the context of a situation'.[113] It specified that:

> admissibility at the situation phase should be assessed against criteria defining a 'potential' case such as (i) the ... persons involved that are likely to be the focus of an investigation for the purpose of shaping the future case(s); and (ii) the crimes within the jurisdiction of the Court allegedly committed during the incidents that are likely to be the focus of an investigation for the purpose of shaping the future case(s).[114]

The UN Security Council has the power to postpone the initiation of an investigation or its continuation for a period of twelve months, which is renewable, through a resolution adopted under Chapter VII. [115]

WAR CRIMES ALLEGATIONS AND LOCAL INVESTIGATIONS

While deciding whether to open an investigation, the ICC Prosecutor will be required to determine whether or not the Palestinian legal system is able to investigate and prosecute allegations of criminal activity committed by Palestinians. The Palestinian authority has not announced that it will conduct any investigation into the actions of Palestinian armed groups or officials during the 2014 hostilities. Given the long-running Israeli occupation, the separation between Gaza and the West Bank, and the stunted capacity and strength of its national institutions, the ability of Palestine to carry out effective investigations is questionable. As for Israel, the question before the ICC is whether it is willing to conduct independent investigations in a genuine manner and in conformity with international standards.

The 2009 report of the UN fact-finding mission into the Gaza Conflict ('The Goldstone Report') presented prima facie evidence of the commission of war crimes and crimes against humanity, and was the first international report to address the issue of Israeli and Palestinian domestic investigations of war crimes allegations. It found that Israeli military investigations did not comply with international standards, and that the Palestinian authorities had not conducted credible investigations. Two UN follow-up reports, published in 2010 and 2011, confirmed that the Israeli investigative system lacked the necessary structural independence, that its investigations were not sufficiently

[113] Ibid., para. 48. [114] Ibid., para 50.

[115] Art. 16, Rome Statute. See also, Werle, G. and Jessberger, F., 2014, *Principles of International Criminal Law*. 3rd edn, Oxford: Oxford University Press, para. 273.

transparent and prompt. It also found that it had not investigated higher-level officials and commanders.[116] Consequently, Israel mandated the Türkel Commission to examine whether Israel's investigation mechanisms were consistent with international law. The second report released by the Türkel Commission in 2013, held that the Israeli investigative system conforms to international law standards but proceeded to present a set of recommendations for the improvement of the Israeli system investigation.[117] As part of the implementation of these recommendations, a Fact-Finding Assessment Mechanism has been established.

The newly established Israeli military's investigative mechanism is designed to review 'exceptional incidents' (thus, presupposes that all infractions are to be considered exceptions), that enable the military prosecutor to reach decisions regarding whether or not to open a criminal investigation, when there is 'reasonable suspicion that the strike was not carried out in accordance with the rules and procedures applicable to IDF forces'.[118] As of March 2015, the Military Advocate General has referred at least 126 'exceptional incidents' during the Gaza fighting to the Fact Finding Assessments Mechanism, and opened nineteen (military) criminal investigations.[119] The latter include investigations into the killing of twenty-seven members of the same family, of whom nineteen were minors and two pregnant women; some looting cases; the targeting of a UNRWA school in which fifteen civilians were killed;[120] the use of persons as human shields; and firing

[116] 'Report of the Committee of independent experts in international humanitarian and human rights laws to monitor and assess any domestic, legal or other proceedings undertaken by both the Government of Israel and the Palestinian side, in the light of General Assembly resolution 64/254, including the independence, effectiveness, genuineness of these investigations and their conformity with international standards', UN Doc. A/HRC/15/50, 23 September 2010; 'Report of the Committee of Independent Experts in International Humanitarian and Human Rights Law established Pursuant to Council Resolution 13/9', UN Doc. (A/HRC/16/24), 18 March 2011.

[117] The Public Commission to Examine the Maritime Incident of 31 May 2010, known as the Turkel Commission, made up of four Israeli members and two international observers, was set up by the Israeli Government in June 2010, in the aftermath of the Flotilla incident, to examine, inter alia, 'whether the examination and investigation process for complaints and allegations raised with regard to violations of the law of armed conflict ... is consistent with the obligations of the State of Israel pursuant to the rules of international law'. Its report was published on February 2013 <http://www.turkel-committee.gov.il/files/newDoc3/The Turkel Report for website.pdf>.

[118] <http://www.law.idf.il/163-7183-en/Patzar.aspx>.

[119] In three official updates published on the *Decisions of the IDF Military Advocate General regarding Exceptional Incidents during Operation 'Protective Edge'*, the MAG released information indicating that a prominent reason for which it had closed at least 17 cases without ordering a criminal investigation is that harm was caused due to a mistake while carrying out an attack. http://www.law.idf.il/163-7183-en/Patzar.aspx and http://www.mag.idf.il/261-6958-en/Patzar.aspx

[120] In April 2015 the UN Headquarters Board of Inquiry into certain incidents that occurred in the UNRWA schools, established by the Secretary-General, released its report. The Board's mandate is limited to the establishment of the facts, and attribution of the conduct and does not include either findings of law or recommendations for compensation. It concluded that all seven cases—which resulted in forty-four civilian deaths and at least 227 injuries were caused by Israeli military attacks <http://www.bbc.com/news/world-middle-east-32479271>.

at ambulances. The only prosecution so far took place in April 2015, when the Israeli military indicted three soldiers for looting US$600 from a home in the Shuja'iyya neighbourhood, one of the largest districts of Gaza city, during the 2014 ground incursion.[121]

Thus, since summer 2014, Israel has opened multiple investigations, including dozens of preliminary inquiries that will form the basis of decisions on whether to open criminal investigations against Israeli political and military officials. As experience has shown, such processes can take years, and lead to limited instances of accountability; those that isolate individual low-ranking soldiers for their breach of military orders.[122] To discharge its burden of proof with regard to a situation of 'inaction', Israel needs to demonstrate that it is able and willing to undertake 'concrete and progressive investigative steps', and that its domestic investigations and prosecutions meet the conditions of the 'same conduct/same person' test in cases that the ICC can potentially investigate. Given the deficiency in Israel's domestic investigative practice (concentrating on exceptional cases and on the conduct of low-ranking soldiers who are suspected of having breached orders), it may not correspond to any potential ICC cases, since the ICC's *ratione materiae* jurisdiction does not extend to isolated acts of low-ranking army officials. In line with this view, the report of the UN Fact Finding Mission on the 2014 Gaza Conflict, published in June 2015 maintained:

> The commission is concerned about a number of procedural, structural and substantive shortcomings, which continue to compromise Israel's ability to adequately fulfil its duty to investigate...
>
> and it recommended to Israel to ensure that its investigations 'will not be confined to individual soldiers alone, but will also encompass members of the political and military establishment, including at the senior level, where appropriate.'[123]

Recent reports indicate that the Israeli Government decided in July 2015 to provide the ICC Prosecutor Office with information and clarifications on the ongoing work of the Israeli investigative system in the context of the ongoing preliminary examination.[124]

[121] Sobelman, B., 'Israel indicts three soldiers for alleged crimes during Gaza war', *LA Times*, 26 April 2015 <http://www.latimes.com/world/middleeast/la-fg-israel-indicts-soldiers-gaza-war-20150426-story.html> accessed July 2015.

[122] In September 2014, the leading Israeli human rights NGO B'Tselem, communicated to the MAG Corps that it has decided 'not to assist the Military Advocate General (MAG) Corps in any matter concerning such investigations ... in light of our experience with previous military actions in Gaza, which shows that investigations led by the MAG Corps do not promote accountability among persons responsible for such violations or reveal the truth' <http://www.btselem.org/download/201400904_15390_letter_to_mag_corps_regarding_protective_edge_investiations_eng.pdf>.

[123] Report of the independent commission of inquiry established pursuant to Human Rights Council resolution S-21/1, UN Doc A/HRC/29/52, 24 June 2015, paras. 618 and 681.

[124] Ravid, B., 'Exclusive: Israel Decides to Open Dialogue With ICC Over Gaza Preliminary Examination', *Haaretz*, 9 July 2015 <http://webcache.googleusercontent.com/search?q=cache:7U5F5PeR-uUJ:www.haaretz.com/news/diplomacy-defense/.premium-1.665172+&cd=1&hl=en&ct=clnk&gl=tr&client=safari>.

Israeli cooperation with the ICC is welcomed. The recent decision by the ICC Pre-Trial Chamber, requesting the ICC Prosecutor to reconsider her decision not to open an investigation into the Flotilla incident,[125] Professor Aeyal Gross of Tel Aviv University aptly remarks: 'make[s] it difficult for her [Prosecutor] not to investigate alleged war crimes by both sides in last summer's Gaza war, especially in light of the recent report by a UN commission of inquiry'. Indeed, he adds, 'the decision might accelerate her launching of an investigation into construction in the settlements as well'.[126]

The opening of an ICC investigation into the Israeli–Palestinian situation, including some cases from the summer 2014 bout of hostilities in the Gaza Strip and northern Israel, now appears to be only a matter of time.

[125] ICC Pre-Trial Chamber I requests Prosecutor to reconsider decision not to investigate situation referred by Union of Comoros, Press Release, ICC, 16 July 2015 <http://www.icc-cpi.int/en_menus/icc/press%20and%20media/press%20releases/Pages/PR1133.aspx>.

[126] Gross, A., 'ICC Decision on the Gaza Flotilla Raid Is Just the Start of Israel's Troubles', *Haaretz*, 19 July 2015 <http://www.haaretz.com/news/diplomacy-defense/.premium-1.666658>.

4 The conflict with Islamic State: a critical review of international legal issues

Antonio Coco and Jean-Baptiste Maillart[1]

Introduction

Islamic State (IS) is a radical jihadist armed group that controls vast swathes of territory in eastern Syria and across northern and western Iraq. Its exponential rise in 2014 as well as its brutality and cruel practices—including mass killings, abduction of members of ethnic and religious minorities,[2] summary executions, acts of torture, sexual enslavement, and beheadings of soldiers, journalists, and humanitarian workers—which are often filmed and released online—have sparked fear and outcry within the international community. Its existence has also raised numerous issues under international law, some of which will be addressed in the present chapter. However, before doing so, one should attempt to answer three preliminary questions in order to better understand the complexities of the issue at hand.

HOW DID IS COME TO LIFE?

The origins of IS can be traced back to 1999 when Jordanian Abu Mous'ab al Zarqawi, upon his return from Afghanistan, established Jamaat Al Tawhid Wal Djihad in Iraq, an armed group composed of ultra-violent elements which aimed primarily at countering

[1] Antonio Coco and Jean-Baptiste Maillart are PhD Candidates at the University of Geneva and Teaching Assistants at the Geneva Academy of International Humanitarian Law and Human Rights.

[2] These minorities include notably Turkmen, Christians, Yezidis, Shia Arabs, and Sabaeans. See United Nations (UN) Human Rights Council (HRC), *Report of the UN High Commissioner for Human Rights on the human rights situation in Iraq in the light of abuses committed by the so-called Islamic State in Iraq and the Levant and associated groups*, 13 March 2015, A/HRC/28/18, §16.

the US occupation.[3] In 2004, al Zarqawi pledged allegiance to Osama Bin Laden. Jamaat Al Tawhid Wal Djihad merged with Al-Qaeda and became Al-Qaeda in Iraq (AQI). Following al Zarqawi's death in June 2006 in American airstrikes, AQI merged with other Iraqi jihadist groups[4] and gave birth to Islamic State of Iraq (ISI), an umbrella organization governed by Abu Omar al Baghdadi. From then on, the organization's ranks started swelling rapidly. It first gained strong support from former members of Saddam Hussein's Baath regime and senior military officials of his long-disbanded army. All of them were looking for revenge against the American 'invasion' and the new Shia government, led by Prime Minister Nouri al-Maliki. ISI then brought to its side desperate Iraqi Sunni populations, marginalized and alienated by al-Maliki's sectarian campaign favouring the country's larger Shia population. Maliki's authoritarianism and mistreatment of the Sunni community therefore paved the way for ISI to grow. In 2010, Abu Omar al Baghdadi died and was replaced by his messenger, Abu Bakr al Baghadi, the current leader of IS. The group's activities were extended to Syria in 2012 by taking advantage of the Syrian regime's dissolution and the region's instability in the aftermath of the 'Arab Spring'. In April 2013, al Baghdadi announced the creation of Islamic State of Iraq and the Levant (ISIL) operating over vast areas in Iraq and Syria. On 29 June 2014, ISIL proclaimed itself a 'Caliphate' and was simply renamed as 'Islamic State'.[5] On 1 July, al Baghdadi called on Muslims worldwide to obey him as the Caliph and to join the new Caliphate.

IS's controlled territory is approximately 30,000 square metres[6] and includes key cities such as Falluja, Mosul, Al-Raqqa, Tikrit, as well as strategic economic sites such as dams, oil and gas fields, and transit points at the Iraqi–Syrian border. To date, IS is considered to be the richest armed group in history. Most of its income comes from the smuggling of natural resources, tax extortion, ransom payments,[7] bank robberies,[8] and allegedly, donations from charity organizations and wealthy individuals from Saudi Arabia and other Gulf States. IS has reached extremely high political and military organization, managing

[3] This group quickly ascended into notoriety due to a series of high-profile operations, such as the 2003 attack on the UN compound which led to the death of Sergio Vieira de Mello, the assassination of Laurence Foley in Amman, and the beheading of Nicholas Berg.

[4] These groups notably include *Jeish al-Fatiheen, Jund al-Sahaba, Katayeb Ansar al-Tawhid wal Sunnah*, and *Jeish al-Taiifa al-Mansoura*.

[5] IS is also often referred to as *Da'ish* or *Daesh*, which is the abbreviation of the group's name in Arabic (*al-Dawla al-Islamiya fi Iraq wa al-Sham*).

[6] IS's controlled territory is equivalent to the size of Belgium.

[7] For more related to this point, see Callimachi, R., 'Paying Ransoms, Europe Bankrolls Qaeda Terror', *New York Times*, 29 July 2014, <http://www.nytimes.com/2014/07/30/world/africa/ransoming-citizens-europe-becomes-al-qaedas-patron.html?_r=1>.

[8] For instance, some US$425 million were reportedly robbed at the Iraqi Central Bank in Mosul. McCoy, T., 'ISIS just stole $425 million, Iraqi governor says, and became the world's richest terrorist group', *Washington Post*, 12 June 2014, <http://www.washingtonpost.com/news/morning-mix/wp/2014/06/12/isis-just-stole-425-million-and-became-the-worlds-richest-terrorist-group/>.

to attract foreign fighters from over fifty States. These are estimated to be between 9,000 and 31,000, according to the late 2014 CIA finding.[9]

IS IS A STATE OR A NON-STATE ACTOR?

Although IS aspires to be a State and has put quasi-State structures in place such as its own taxation system, police (the Al-Hisbah morality police), ministries, and courts, it does not meet at least two of the four cumulative Statehood requirements provided by Article 1 of the 1933 Montevideo Convention on the Rights and Duties of States—namely 'permanent population' and 'defined territory'.[10] Therefore, the authors of the present chapter consider IS to be a non-State actor.

WHAT ARE THE MAIN DIFFERENCES BETWEEN IS AND AL-QAEDA?

Although both armed groups share common features, and can be labelled as Islamic fundamentalist, one should highlight the most important differences between the two groups. In a thorough analysis, Mohamedou points out three key differences.[11] First, IS's struggle is territorially oriented as its main aim is building a State, whereas Al-Qaeda's objective is, above all, global jihad and implementation of Sharia law worldwide. Second, IS and Al-Qaeda have different targets. Whilst IS fights all those who do not approve its extreme Sunni interpretation of Islam, i.e., non-Muslims but also Shia Muslims and

[9] Gartenstein-Ross, D., 'How Many Fighters does the Islamic State Really Have?', *War on the Rocks*, 9 February 2015, <http://warontherocks.com/2015/02/how-many-fighters-does-the-islamic-state-really-have/>.

[10] Whilst the territory controlled by IS is very large, the borders of this territory are rather vague and unstable. Furthermore, the fact that IS acquired this territory by violating international law puts its legitimacy into question. With regard to the 'permanent population' requirement, it is doubtful that the population under IS's control ties its fate to that of the group itself and that they share the same objectives. However, in view of IS's high level of organization and global network, the two remaining requirements for statehood set out in Art. 1 of the 1933 Montevideo Convention, namely 'effective government' and 'capacity to engage in relations with other States', seem to be met. For further analysis, see, e.g., Shany, Y., Cohen, A., and Mimran, T., 'Is the Islamic State Really a State?', *The Israel Democracy Institute*, 14 September 2014, <http://en.idi.org.il/analysis/Articles/isis-is-the-islamic-state-really-a-state/>.

[11] Mohamedou, M-M. O., 'ISIS and the Deceptive Rebooting of Al-Qaeda', *GCSP Policy Paper 2014/5*, August 2014, <http://www.gcsp.ch/Regional-Development/Publications/GCSP-Publications/Policy-Papers/ISIS-and-the-Deceptive-Rebooting-of-Al-Qaeda)>. See also Mohamedou, M-M. O., 'L'Etat islamique et l'ombre portée d'Al Qaeda', *Le Temps*, 25 September 2014, <http://www.gcsp.ch/Sidebar/News/Le-Temps-L-Etat-islamique-et-l-ombre-portee-d-Al-Qaida-Editorial-du-Dr-Mohammad-Mahmoud-Ould-Mohamedou>. Along the same vein, see also Byman, D. and Williams, J., 'The Foreign Policy Essay: AQ v IS and the Battle for the Soul of Jihad', *Lawfare*, 22 March 2015, <http://www.lawfareblog.com/2015/03/the-foreign-policy-essay-aq-vs-is-and-the-battle-for-the-soul-of-jihad/>.

moderate Sunnis, Al-Qaeda's enemies are those who are against the expansion of Islam, particularly the American 'far enemy' (*al 'adou al ba'eed*). Furthermore, Al-Qaeda 'consistently stressed political goals and unity among Islamist of all hues, including non-Arabs and non-Sunnis'.[12] Third, the two groups are organized differently. IS is built around a strong regional centre of gravity and functions in a pyramidal way,[13] while Al-Qaeda consists of a transnational network comprised of a series of sleeper and active cells all over the world.

A. *Jus ad bellum* considerations

The territorial control exercised by IS in Iraq and Syria has raised concern not only in the latter two States, but in the entire international community. The Caliphate's threat to expand its borders, the conditions of those individuals living under its rule, along with the considerable amount of natural resources it controls have led the US and other countries to create two differently composed international coalitions aimed at quashing IS, in Iraq and Syria respectively.[14]

Since in international law the concept of just war (*bellum justum*) has long been replaced by the concept of lawful war (*bellum legale*),[15] the moral justifications of an armed intervention against IS are to be framed in the context of the existing rules on the use of armed force (*jus ad bellum*). These rules are enshrined primarily in the United Nations (UN) Charter which, in Article 2(4), affirms that '[a]ll Members shall refrain in their international relations from the threat or use of force against the territorial integrity or political independence of any state, or in any other manner inconsistent

[12] Mohamedou, M-M. O., 'ISIS…', p. 2.

[13] However, it is worth noting here that several jihadist groups, located in other parts of the world, have pledged allegiance to IS. For instance, this is the case of *Abu Sayaaf* (Philippines), *Jund Al-Khilafa* (Algeria), *Ansar Bait Al-Maqdi* (Egypt), and *Boko Haram* (Nigeria). See Ourdan, R., Papin, D., Malécot, V., El Mokhtari, M., and Clairouin, O., 'Al-Qaida, Etat islamique: comprendre la planète djihad', *Le Monde*, 20 November 2014, <http://www.lemonde.fr/international/video/2014/11/20/djihadisme-l-etat-islamique-est-il-en-train-de-remplacer-al-qaida_4526287_3210.html>.

[14] US Department of State, webpage, *Special Presidential Envoy for the Global Coalition to Counter ISIL*, <http://www.state.gov/s/seci/index.htm>. In 2014, members of the coalition conducting military operations in Iraq include Australia, Belgium, Canada, Denmark, France, Netherlands, and the United Kingdom. Members of the coalition conducting military operations in Syria include the United States, Bahrain, Jordan, Saudi Arabia, and the United Arab Emirates. See US Department of Defense (DoD), 'Airstrikes Continue Against ISIL in Syria, Iraq', 31 December 2014, <http://www.defense.gov/news/newsArticle.aspx?id=123898>. The US operation, led by a Combined Joint Task Force, has been named 'Operation Inherent Resolve'.

[15] The terminology was used in Kunz, J., 1951, '*Bellum Justum and Bellum Legale*', *American Journal of International Law*, vol. 45: p. 528.

with the Purposes of the United Nations'.[16] The prohibition, which is deemed to have attained customary status[17] and to constitute a peremptory norm of international law,[18] knows two classical exceptions: actions undertaken in self-defence as disciplined by Article 51 of the UN Charter; military actions authorized by the UN Security Council (SC) in the framework of the UN collective security system as embodied in Chapter VII of the UN Charter. A third possible exception, relevant to the situation in Iraq and Syria, is represented by military interventions on foreign territory upon invitation or with the consent of the sovereign State. This chapter will show that the legality of such interventions is controversial when carried out in the context of an internal armed conflict.

Any actions undertaken directly by the Syrian and Iraqi armed forces on their own territories are obviously not a matter of *jus ad bellum*, which concerns the use of force in the international relations between two or more States. Such an 'international' force is instead being used by the two US-led coalitions, which started conducting airstrikes against IS-held areas on Iraqi sovereign soil in August 2014,[19] and on Syrian sovereign soil in September 2014.[20] In this analysis the legality of the foreign intervention in Iraq will be considered separately from the legality of the foreign intervention in Syria, based on a number of interrelated reasons. First, the political and factual situation in the two States in 2014 was extremely different, as Syria was amidst another civil strife, other than that opposing the government to IS. Second, considering the different ongoing relations with their respective governments, intervening States have been keen to distinguish the legal justifications of their actions in Iraq and Syria.[21] Third, some States have limited their involvement to only one of the two countries.[22] Fourth, the legality assessment over military operations in Iraq is different from the legality assessment of actions undertaken on Syrian territory. This leads to different outcomes in terms of legality.

[16] Charter of the United Nations, 24 October 1945, 1 *UN Treaty Series* XVI, Art. 2(4).

[17] Distefano, G., 2014, 'Use of Force'. In *Oxford Handbook on International Law in Armed Conflict*, edited by Clapham, A., and Gaeta, P., Oxford: Oxford University Press, pp. 545–573, 546.

[18] UN International Law Commission (ILC), 'Draft Articles on the Law of Treaties with commentaries', in *Yearbook of the International Law Commission*, 1966, vol. II, at 248, §3. In this sense, see also Abass, A., 2004, 'Consent Precluding State Responsibility: A Critical Analysis', *International and Comparative Law Quarterly*, vol. 53: 211, p. 223.

[19] US DoD, 'Statement by Pentagon Press Secretary Rear Admiral John Kirby on Airstrikes in Iraq', 8 August 2014, <http://www.defense.gov/Releases/Release.aspx?ReleaseID=16878>.

[20] US DoD, 'U.S. Begins Airstrikes Against ISIL in Syria', 22 September 2014, <http://www.defense.gov/news/newsArticle.aspx?id=123233>.

[21] Kress, C., 'The Fine Line Between Collective Self-Defense and Intervention by Invitation: Reflections on the Use of Force against 'IS' in Syria', *Just Security*, 17 February 2015, <http://justsecurity.org/20118/claus-kreb-force-isil-syria/>.

[22] France, for example, is only taking part in operations being conducted on Iraqi soil. See US DoD, 'Airstrikes Continue Against ISIL in Syria, Iraq'.

THE LEGALITY OF THE US-LED COALITION AIRSTRIKES AGAINST IS IN IRAQ

The main legal explanation provided by foreign States conducting military operations in Iraq is that they are acting upon a request for assistance coming directly from the Iraqi Government.[23] The so-called 'intervention by invitation' is frequently invoked in State practice as one of those cases in which the use of international force is lawful according to international law.[24] Such a case is not expressly spelled out in the UN Charter, but scholars have identified two possible legal avenues leading to the legality of interventions by invitation. According to a *first* strand of argument, the territorial State's consent—Iraq's consent in our case—would act as a circumstance precluding the wrongfulness of what would otherwise be a violation of its territorial integrity and sovereignty. Article 20 of the UN International Law Commission (ILC) Articles on State Responsibility (ASR), indeed, states that '[v]alid consent by a State to the commission of a given act by another State precludes the wrongfulness of that act in relation to the former State to the extent that the act remains within the limits of that consent'.[25] According to a *second* strand of argument, an intervention upon request would not actually constitute use of force against the territorial integrity or political independence of the inviting State, nor would it be in any other way inconsistent with the principles of the UN Charter. Hence, it would be perfectly compatible with the rule contained in Article 2(4) UN Charter.[26] If one were to apply this second theory to Iraq's case, it would mean that the UN Charter's prohibition on the use of force would not even apply to the international coalition's operations. Whichever legal avenue one finds most convincing, it seems undeniable that,

[23] *Letter dated 25 June 2014 from the Permanent Representative of Iraq to the UN addressed to the Secretary-General*, S/2014/440, 25 June 2014; *Letter dated 20 September 2014 from the Permanent Representative of Iraq to the UN addressed to the President of Security Council*, S/2014/691, 20 September 2014.

[24] As recognized in International Court of Justice (ICJ), *Military and Paramilitary Activities in and against Nicaragua* (Nicaragua v United States of America, Merits), Judgment, ICJ Reports 1986, pp. 14 ff., at § 246, and later implicitly confirmed in ICJ, *Armed Activities on the Territory of the Congo* (Democratic Republic of the Congo v Uganda), Judgment, ICJ Reports 2005, pp. 168 ff., inter alia at §§105–106, 113, 149. The assumption is strengthened by the definition of aggression annexed to UN General Assembly (GA), Resolution 14 December 1974, A/RES/3314 (XXIX), which in Art. 3(e) affirms that the continued presence of foreign troops on sovereign territory after withdrawal of consent constitutes an act of aggression; what means that consent can make lawful a behaviour which otherwise would constitute not only a violation of Art. 2(4), but an act of aggression. On this point, see Corten, O., 2010, *The Law against War*, Oxford: Hart Publishing, pp. 251–2.

[25] ILC, 'Articles on the Responsibility of States for Internationally Wrongful Acts' (ASR), in UN GA, Resolution 12 December 2001, A/RES/56/83, Art. 20.

[26] See Dinstein, Y., 2009, *War, Aggression and Self-Defence*, 5th edn, Cambridge: Cambridge University Press, p. 119. Bannelier, K. and Christakis, T., 2013, 'Under the UN Security Council's Watchful Eyes: Military Intervention by Invitation in the Malian Conflict', *Leiden Journal of International Law*, vol. 26: 855, p. 861; Abass, A., 'Consent Precluding State Responsibility', pp. 224–5.

if expressed in a valid manner,[27] a request for military assistance makes the subsequent use of force on the requesting State's territory compatible with the current discipline of *jus ad bellum*. Or at least this would be the general rule.

In the last thirty years, however, a considerable amount of scholars have argued that interventions by invitation are unlawful in at least one case, i.e., whenever the military intervention is aimed at helping a government to defeat the rebel side in an internal armed conflict.[28] Considering that Iraq—as it will be shown—is currently engaged in a non-international armed conflict against IS, one could argue that such a position makes an armed intervention on Iraq's side illegal under *jus ad bellum*. The theory would act as a shield for the principle of non-interference in other States' internal affairs—sanctioned by the 1970 Declaration on Friendly Relations[29]—and for the right to self-determination, which would broadly be defined here as a people's right to choose its own government (political independence *latu sensu*).[30] Once a considerable amount of people start a civil rebellion in an attempt to change its political status, intervening from the outside on the government's side would mean meddling in that State's internal affairs as much as helping the rebels. It is no coincidence that this theory was born during the 'Cold War' era, as a response to the abuse of military interventions by invitation, which were sometimes used to maintain some anti-democratic regimes' power.[31] In 1975, the *Institut de Droit International* (IDI) took the stand that '[t]hird States shall refrain from giving assistance

[27] Which means that it must not be vitiated by coercion, fraud, or corruption, clearly established, really expressed, internationally attributable to the State and given a priori. See Ben Mansour, A., 2010, 'Circumstances Precluding wrongfulness in the ILC Articles on State Responsibility'. In *The Law of International Responsibility*, edited by Crawford, J., Pellet, A., Olleson S., Oxford: OUP, pp. 439–47, at pp. 441–5.

[28] In particular, see Doswald-Beck, L., 1985, 'The Legal Validity of Military Intervention by Invitation of the Government', *British Yearbook of International Law*, vol. 56: p. 189; Christakis, T. and Bannelier K., 2004, 'Volenti non fit injuria? Les effets du consentement à l'intervention militaire', *Annuaire français de droit international*, vol. 50: p. 102; Corten, O., *The Law against War*, pp. 249–310; and Gray, C., 2008, *International Law and the Use of Force*, Oxford: OUP, pp. 67–113. See also Akande, D. and Vermeer, Z., 'The Airstrikes against Islamic State in Iraq and the Alleged Prohibition on Military Assistance to Governments in Civil Wars', *EJIL: Talk!*, 2 February 2015, <http://www.ejiltalk.org/the-airstrikes-against-islamic-state-in-iraq-and-the-alleged-prohibition-on-military-assistance-to-governments-in-civil-wars/>.

[29] UN GA, *Declaration on Principles of International Law concerning Friendly Relations and Cooperation among States in accordance with the Charter of the UN*, 24 October 1970, A/RES/2625(XXV).

[30] See Doswald-Beck, L., 'The Legal Validity of Military Intervention by Invitation of the Government', pp. 200–1; and Bannelier, K. and Christakis, T., 'Under the UN Security Council's Watchful Eyes', pp. 861–2. A different, somehow narrower, view argues instead that customary international law provides for the exercise of the right to self-determination in only three cases: *externally*, against colonial dominations or alien occupations and *internally*, against racist regimes. See Cassese, A., 2005, *International Law*, 2nd edn, Oxford: OUP, p. 62.

[31] See, for instance, the 1956 URSS' intervention in Hungary, condemned by the UN GA with Resolution 1131, 12 December 1956, A/RES/1131(XI). Other examples in Gray, C., *International Law and the Use of* Force, pp. 84–8.

to parties to a civil war which is being fought in the territory of another State'.[32] Later, in 2011, the IDI nuanced its approach, stating that '[m]ilitary assistance is prohibited when it is exercised in violation of the Charter of the United Nations, of the principles of non-intervention, of equal rights and self-determination of peoples and generally accepted standards of human rights and in particular when its object is to support an established government against its own population'.[33] The 2011 Resolution was meant to be applied only to situations of internal disturbances and riots below the threshold of a non-international armed conflict as defined in Additional Protocol II to the Geneva Conventions.[34] This notwithstanding, it gives us a useful indication as to the rationale of a possible prohibition of intervention on the government's side.

The rule, as spelled out by the IDI and by scholars, would not prohibit intervention in all non-international armed conflicts. On the contrary, it would only apply to those in which the non-governmental side exercises its right to self-determination.[35] State practice on this issue is difficult to interpret for a variety of reasons. First, intervening States have not been keen to use this legal justification for their military intervention on foreign territory when providing assistance to governments with a history of human rights violations.[36] Second, in some cases a claim of intervention by invitation in an armed conflict was coupled with a claim of action in collective self-defence, since both of these involve a request for military aid.[37] Third, in some cases the inviting State has claimed that the request for military assistance would not have been used in an armed conflict, but in law enforcement operations.[38] Fourth, sometimes the involved States have narrowed down the invitation to specific purposes, such as the protection of the invited State's nationals on the inviting State's territory, the performance of peacekeeping functions, the

[32] *Institut de Droit International* (IDI), *The Principle of Non-Intervention in Civil Wars*, Resolution 14 August 1975, Art. 2(1). A similar position was taken in a UK Foreign Policy Document n. 148, 1984. 'Is intervention ever justified?', *British Yearbook of International Law*, vol. 57: 614, p. 616.

[33] IDI, *Present Problems of the Use of Force in International Law*, Resolution 8 September 2011, Art. 3(1).

[34] Art. 2(1): 'This Resolution applies to situations of internal disturbances and tensions below the threshold of non-international armed conflict in the sense of Art. 1 of Protocol II Additional.'

[35] In this sense Van Steenberghe, R., 'The Alleged Prohibition on Intervening in Civil Wars Is Still Alive after the Airstrikes against Islamic State in Iraq: A Response to Dapo Akande and Zachary Vermeer', *EJIL: Talk!*, 12 February 2015, <http://www.ejiltalk.org/the-alleged-prohibition-on-intervening-in-civil-wars-is-still-alive-after-the-airstrikes-against-islamic-state-in-iraq-a-response-to-dapo-akande-and-zachary-vermeer/>, citing the 1975 IDI resolution's *travaux préparatoires*.

[36] For instance, France and Belgium claimed that their action was limited to the evacuation of nationals and to the re-establishment of security when, in 1978, they intervened against rebels in Mobutu's Zaire. For more on this and other examples, see Gray, C., *International Law and the Use of Force*, pp. 88–9. This is probably what also recently happened in Syria, when the United States carefully avoided any statement affirming that they were intervening on Syrian territory with Assad's government's consent. Cf. Kress, C., 'The Fine Line Between Collective Self-Defense and Intervention by Invitation'.

[37] As claimed by the United States when they decided to aid South Vietnam against a Chinese-backed invasion by North Vietnam in 1961. See Gray, C., *International Law and the Use of Force*, p. 82.

[38] The US put forward this argument when justifying their intervention in Colombia, linking it to the fight against drugs trade. See Gray, C., *International Law and the Use of Force*, p. 87.

provision of humanitarian aid, or the joint fight against terrorist groups.[39] Fifth, sometimes foreign States have been invited to intervene in an armed conflict where the rebel side has already received external aid.[40]

Commentators have argued that such an extensive use of alternative or additional justifications—even when the actual intervention's goal is different—reinforces the conviction that a rule prohibiting military intervention on the government's side in an internal armed conflict has become customary.[41] Those additional justifications invoked by the involved States would be nothing more than admissible exceptions to the prohibition.[42] Does this mean that States taking part in the 'Inherent Resolve' operation in Iraq are violating international law? Not necessarily.

First, one needs to question the intrinsic logical consistence of this prohibition. The rule's beneficiary (and the violation's potential victim) would indeed be the same inviting State, whose will is expressed by the government in power. Even admitting the breach of the rule in question, it would be interesting to explore who would be in a position to invoke such a violation. Corten notes that the rule's beneficiary would be the international community as a whole, the prohibition on the use of force being a *jus cogens* norm and engendering an *erga omnes* obligation.[43] This does not solve the issue that there have been rare occasions of States invoking the international responsibility of another State which allegedly intervened in a civil war context on the government's side. We may recall only the international community's condemnation of the Soviet Union's intervention in Hungary and of the Iraqi intervention in Kuwait.[44]

Most recent practice actually goes in the opposite direction. The International Court of Justice sanctioned the illegality of Uganda's intervention in the Democratic Republic of Congo (DRC) only after the latter's consent to the presence of Ugandan troops on the DRC's territory had been withdrawn.[45] No one protested against France's intervention

[39] France has often used the argument of protection of its nationals to justify a military intervention in internal conflicts, e.g., when intervening in Central African Republic in 1996. See Gray, C., *International Law and the Use of Force*, pp. 88–9. Cf. also Van Steenberghe, R., 'The Alleged Prohibition on Intervening in Civil Wars Is Still Alive after the Airstrikes against Islamic State in Iraq; Corten, O., *The Law against War*, at pp. 294–6; Dinstein, Y., *War, Aggression and Self-Defence*, p. 120.

[40] Doswald-Beck, L., 'The Legal Validity of Military Intervention by Invitation of the Government', p. 251; Corten, O., *The Law against War*, pp. 301–9.

[41] Doswald-Beck, L., 'The Legal Validity of Military Intervention by Invitation of the Government', pp. 251–2.

[42] Cf. for example, IDI Resolution 1975, Art. 3. Bannelier and Christakis particularly insisted on the joint fight against terrorism as one of the admissible exceptions. See Bannelier, K. and Christakis, T., 'Under the UN Security Council's Watchful Eyes', p. 867.

[43] Corten, O., *The Law against War*, p. 250. Doswald-Beck, L., 'The Legal Validity of Military Intervention by Invitation of the Government', pp. 242–3, adds that in this case the rule's primary beneficiary would not be the inviting government, but the State as a whole—as an abstract entity—since its right to choose its own political system would be violated in a manner inconsistent with the principles of the UN Charter. In this sense also Corten, ibid., pp. 288–9.

[44] See n. 31. [45] See ICJ, *Armed* Activities.

alongside the Malian governmental forces in its struggle against the rebels.[46] If the prohibition of interventions in internal conflicts did not become a rule of customary international law, then the States helping Iraq against IS would not be committing any violations of *jus ad bellum*.

Second, even if one were to accept that prohibiting military interventions in internal armed conflicts has become a rule of customary international law, it would seem reasonable to argue that such prohibition would not actually make the operations against IS unlawful. Indeed, IS is not exercising the Iraqi people's right to self-determination,[47] and therefore the armed conflict between Iraq, the international coalition, and IS is not one of those for which a foreign military intervention is prohibited. Furthermore, IS has carried out several acts of terrorism, and is listed as a terrorist organization in many countries.[48] One could also argue that IS itself is receiving a great deal of foreign assistance, in the form of foreign fighters, weapons, and other resources.[49] This would make at least one of the admitted exceptions to the purported prohibition of interventions by invitation applicable, therefore making the US-led coalition's intervention on the government's side lawful.

Hence, whilst the debate may be interesting for clarity's sake, both theoretical approaches to the legality of interventions by invitation in internal conflicts do lead to the same conclusion in practice, in that Iraq's invitation made the US-led coalition military intervention compatible with the currently applicable rules of *jus ad bellum*.

[46] Bannelier, K. and Christakis, T., 'Under the UN Security Council's Watchful Eyes', p. 858.

[47] Whilst to identify the beneficiaries of the right to self-determination has always proved difficult, and its extension to non-colonial peoples remains controversial, it seems quite clear that the exercise of the right to self-determination requires 'a free and genuine expression of the will of the peoples concerned'. See ICJ, *Western Sahara*, Advisory Opinion, ICJ Reports 1975, pp. 12 ff., §55. The way in which IS came to power and its behaviour, on the contrary, cast a serious doubt on whether the group is actually expressing the will of the Iraqi (and Syrian) people. Moreover, unlike in the IS case, self-determination is usually intended to be applicable only 'within the framework of existing sovereign states and consistently with the maintenance of the territorial integrity of those states'. See Supreme Court of Canada, *Reference re Secession of Quebec*, 20 August 1998, [1998] 2 S.C.R. 217, § 122. Finally, like other human rights, the right to self-determination is subject to limitations. Reading in conjunction with Art. 5(1) of the ICCPR and of the ICESCR—both of which enshrining the right of self-determination in Art. 1(1)—one could infer that the right to self-determination cannot be exercised at the expenses of other rights recognized in the Covenants. For further references, see McCorquodale, R., 2010, 'Group Rights'. In *International Human Rights Law*, edited by Moeckli, D., Shah, S., and Sivakumaran, S., Oxford: OUP, pp. 333–55, at pp. 336–8 and 345.

[48] The UN Committee established pursuant to Security Council resolution 1267 (1999) listed it on 18 October 2004, as 'Al-Qaida in Iraq', under the reference number 'QDe.115'. On 2 June 2014 the name 'Islamic State in Iraq and the Levant' was added <http://www.un.org/press/en/2014/sc11424.doc.htm>. The United States similarly listed it as a Foreign Terrorist Organization on 17 December 2004 <http://www.state.gov/j/ct/rls/other/des/123085.htm>.

[49] See 'Introduction', and Part II, 'State responsibility'.

THE LEGALITY OF THE US-LED COALITION AIRSTRIKES AGAINST IS IN SYRIA

As IS operates transnationally in Iraq and Syria, the US decided to intervene through military action on both territories. From a strategic point of view, this decision should be praised, the end of IS will never occur if only targeted on half of the territory it controls. However, strategic military decisions do not always comply with international law. Whilst the foreign military intervention in Iraq appears to be lawful, such is not the case for the US-led coalition airstrikes carried out in Syria.

Collective self-defence

As provided by Article 51 UN Charter, all States have an 'inherent right' of self-defence. Considered by some scholars as the 'centre of gravity in the United Nations',[50] this right is not absolute as its exercise is subjected to the fulfilment of five conditions, of which three are enshrined in the provision aforementioned ('armed attack',[51] 'until the Security Council has taken measures necessary to maintain international peace and security', and 'shall be immediately reported to the Security Council'[52]) and two are to be found in customary international law (proportionality and necessity).[53] The exercise of self-defence may be individual—when the victim State of an armed attack 'reacts alone in order to push back the aggressor'[54]—or collective—when the victim State requests the help of third States to defend itself against the armed attack. In the latter case, two additional requirements are to be met: first, 'it is the State which is the victim of an armed attack which must form and declare the view that it has been so attacked';[55] second, '[c]ollective self-defense may be exercised only at the request of the target State'.[56]

[50] Feinberg, N., 1979, *Studies in International Law with special reference to the Arab-Israel conflict*, Jerusalem: Magnes Press, p. 70.

[51] The customary nature of the 'armed attack' condition was acknowledged in ICJ, *Nicaragua*, §§193–195 and 210–211; ICJ, *Oil Platforms* (Iran v United States of America), Judgment, ICJ Reports 2003, §51.

[52] The non-customary nature of this condition was acknowledged in ICJ, *Nicaragua*, §200.

[53] ICJ, *Nicaragua*, §176: 'The Charter, having itself recognized the existence of this right, does not go on to regulate directly all aspects of its content. For example, it does not contain any specific rule whereby self-defense would warrant only measures which are proportional to the armed attack and necessary to respond to it, a rule well-established in customary international law'; ICJ, *Legality of the Threat or Use of Nuclear Weapons*, Advisory Opinion, *ICJ Reports* 1996, p. 226, §41; ICJ, *Oil Platforms*, §43; IDI, *Present Problems of the Use of Armed Force in International Law*, Resolution 27 October 2007, §2.

[54] Distefano, G., 'Use of Force', p. 552.

[55] ICJ, *Nicaragua*, §195. See further in the same paragraph: 'There is no rule of customary international law permitting another State to exercise the right of collective self-defense on the basis of its own assessment of the situation. Where collective self-defense is invoked, it is to be expected that the State for whose benefit this right is used will have declared itself to be the victim of an armed attack'.

[56] ICJ, *Nicaragua*, §199 and 232. See also IDI, §8.

States that are part of the US-led coalition justify their military strikes against IS in Syria as a lawful exercise of collective self-defence of Iraq.[57] In other words, the US and its allies would allegedly use force in Syria at the request of Iraq to defend the latter against an armed attack perpetrated by IS, a non-State armed group located in the Syrian territory. In this regard, the letter dated 23 September 2014 from the Permanent Representative of the US to the UN, Samantha Power, addressed to the Secretary-General is noteworthy:

> Iraq has made clear that it is facing a serious threat of continuing attacks from the Islamic State in Iraq and the Levant (ISIL) *coming out of safe havens in Syria*. These safe havens are used by ISIL for training, planning, financing, and carrying out attacks across Iraqi borders and against Iraq's people. For these reasons, *the Government of Iraq has asked that the United States lead international efforts to strike ISIL sites and military strongholds in Syria* in order to end the continuing attacks on Iraq, to protect Iraqi citizens, and ultimately to enable and arm Iraqi forces to perform their task of regaining control of the Iraqi borders.[58] (emphasis added)

Let's now assess whether the self-defence conditions mentioned above are met *in casu*.

On 20 September 2014, in a letter addressed to the President of the SC, the Minister for Foreign Affairs of the Republic of Iraq asserted indeed that '[the Government of Iraq] ha[s] *requested* the United States of America to lead international efforts to strike ISIL sites and military strongholds, with our express consent'.[59] Therefore, the US and their allies are intervening in Syria upon explicit request of Iraq, the target State. Moreover, besides 'armed attack', one can undoubtedly state that the other four general conditions required for the exercise of self-defence are met. The SC has been informed in this letter of Iraq's intent to resort to self-defence against IS in Syria and, so far, has not taken any Chapter VII measures necessary to 'maintain international peace and security' in the region. Regarding the proportionality requirement, it seems to be met since the coalition only strikes strategic targets such as IS bases, training camps and controlled transit points at the Iraqi–Syria border. As for the necessity requirement, such operations appear to be necessary in view of the rapid advances and exponential growth of IS in Iraq. Whether Iraq is victim of an 'armed attack' in the sense of Article 51 UN Charter

[57] It is worth noting here that regarding the airstrikes against the armed group Khorasan in Syria, the legal justification invoked by the US is distinct. Since the latter considers the former as an 'al-Qaeda element' which pose a 'threat' to the US (*Letter dated 23 September 2014 from the Permanent Representative of the United States of America to the UN addressed to the Secretary-General*, S/2014/695), the argument appears to be *individual* self-defense.

[58] Ibid. The US insists on the fact that IS plans and launches its operation from Syria. However, one could argue that the threat posed to Iraq by IS arises solely from its Iraqi branch, located in Iraq. Structurally, IS is indeed divided into two territorial branches. Furthermore, from a historical perspective, IS was born in Iraq and then extended its activities to Syria by taking advantage of the deliquescence of the Syrian regime. Nevertheless, let's note that in 2014 Ar-Raqqah (Syria) became the de facto headquarters of IS.

[59] *Letter dated 20 September 2014*...(emphasis added).

is, however, much more controversial. The fact that in the letter of 20 September Iraq does not consider the operations carried out by IS in Iraq as constitutive of an 'armed attack' but prefers to qualify them as 'a threat to the security of our people and territory' or 'terrorist attacks' shows how contentious the fulfilment of this condition is.

The customary definition of 'armed attack' is found in General Assembly Resolution 3314 (XXIX) of 14 December 1974.[60] For an attack to qualify as an 'armed attack', there are two requirements to be met. First, it must be of 'sufficient gravity' (Article 2), i.e., it must be of a certain severity and magnitude.[61] Second, and more importantly, it must be perpetrated by a State (Article 1), either directly or indirectly. In other words, an 'armed attack' must always be attributed to the State whose territory is the prospective target of an exercise of self-defence. Hence, if there is no involvement of such a State,[62] the attack does not amount to an 'armed attack' in the sense of Article 51—even if the gravity threshold is reached—and therefore the victim State cannot invoke self-defence. As rightly pointed out by Judge Higgins in her Separate Opinion in the International Court of Justice (ICJ)'s *Wall* advisory opinion, the State attribution requirement is not mentioned in Article 51.[63] Yet, it 'has been the generally accepted interpretation for more than 50 years', as noted by Judge Kooijmans in the same case.[64] Claims supporting a broad interpretation of 'armed attack' according to which States could use force against non-State actors whose conduct could not be attributed to States have been 'almost systematically'[65] rejected by the international community, in particular between the 1960s and the 1990s. For instance, the SC condemned in the strongest terms Israel's 1985 raid on the Palestinian Liberation Organisation's Headquarters in Tunisia[66] as well as the 1980s' South African incursions

[60] More precisely, Resolution 3314 provides the definition of 'aggression'. However, for the purposes of the application of Art. 51, 'armed attack' must be considered as equivalent to 'aggression'. See Distefano, G., 'Use of Force', p. 553.

[61] See also ICJ, *Nicaragua*, §191; IDI, §5. On the basis of the 'accumulation of events doctrine', a series of small-scale attacks can be weighed cumulatively and be considered as a whole as an 'armed attack'. The ICJ endorsed such an interpretation of the gravity threshold requirement. See ICJ, *Nicaragua*, §231; ICJ, *Oil Platforms*, §64; ICJ, *Armed activities*, §146.

[62] The question of what degree of State involvement is necessary to allow the victim State to use force in self-defence against the territory of the host State has led to numerous discussions, which go beyond the scope of the present chapter. For further details, see Gray, C., *International Law and the Use of Force*, pp. 132–140; Brent, M., 2009, 'Responding to Attacks by Non-State Actors: The Attribution Requirement in Self-Defense', *Australian International Law Journal*, vol. 16: p. 133; Tams, C., 'The Use of Force against Terrorists', *European Journal of International Law (EJIL)* vol. 20, no. 2: p. 359.

[63] ICJ, *Legal Consequences of the Construction of a Wall in the Occupied Palestinian Territories*, Advisory Opinion, ICJ Reports 2004, p. 136, Separate Opinion of Judge Higgins, §33: 'There is, with respect, nothing in the text of Article 51 that *thus* stipulates that self-defense is available only when an armed attack is made by a State. *That* qualification is rather a result of the Court so determining in *Military and Paramilitary Activities in and against Nicaragua* (…)'. See also in the same case the Separate Opinion of Judge Kooijmans, §35.

[64] Ibid. [65] Tams, C., 'The Use of Force against Terrorists', p. 367.

[66] E.g. UN Security Council (SC), Resolution 573 (1985), 4 October 1985, S/RES/573.

into neighbouring States.[67] The General Assembly condemned the 1986 US 'aerial and naval military attacks' on terrorist training facilities in Libya, among other targets.[68] As for the ICJ, it always required the non-State actor attack to be imputed to the territorial State.[69] However, it is worth noting that in the 2005 case *Armed Activities on the Territory of Congo*, by refusing to answer the question of the Parties 'as to whether and under what conditions contemporary international law provides for a right of self-defense against large-scale attacks by irregular forces',[70] the Court did not entirely close the door to the recognition of a right to self-defence against non-State actors absent of State imputability. Going back to the cross-borders operations carried out by IS in Iraq, whilst they are of such gravity as to amount to an armed attack,[71] it is clear that they cannot be attributed to the Syrian State, the latter being in fact involved in a non-international armed conflict against the former.[72] Therefore, it seems at first glance that these operations cannot qualify as an 'armed attack' and that, subsequently, the US-led coalition cannot rely upon the collective self-defence of Iraq argument to legally justify their airstrikes against IS targets in Syria.

However, such an 'inter-state reading of self-defense'[73] appears to be put into question since 9/11. Indeed, for the past fifteen years, there seems to be a growing acceptance of the idea that an attack perpetrated by a non-State actor which cannot be attributed to a State may be qualified as 'armed attack' in the sense of Article 51 and can justify the invocation of self-defence by the victim State. As Tams rightly states, 'the international community today is much less likely to deny, as a matter of principle, that states can invoke self-defense against terrorist attacks not imputable to another State'.[74] A quick look at the international practice shows that States have indeed recently preferred to criticize extraterritorial uses of force against non-State actors on the basis of proportionality rather than on the lack of State imputability.[75] Therefore, States are progressively

[67] e.g. UN SC, Resolution 527 (1982), 15 December 1982, S/RES/527; Resolution 546 (1984), 6 January 1984, S/RES/546; Resolution 568 (1985), 26 July 1985, S/RES/568.

[68] UN GA, Resolution 41/38, 20 November 1986, A/RES/41/38.

[69] See ICJ, *Nicaragua*, §195; ICJ, *Wall*, §139; ICJ, *Armed activities*, §146.

[70] ICJ, *Armed activities*, §147.

[71] In this regard, see the Statement by the UN SC President on 19 September 2014: 'The Security Council strongly condemns attacks by terrorist organizations, including the terrorist organization operating under the name "Islamic State in Iraq and the Levant" (ISIL) and associated armed groups, in *Iraq*, Syria, and Lebanon and emphasizes that this *large-scale offensive* poses a major threat to the region' <http://www.un.org/en/ga/search/view_doc.asp?symbol=S/PRST/2014/20>, emphasis added. This confirms that the attack is of sufficient intensity and breadth to qualify as an armed attack from a *ratione materiae* perspective.

[72] Weller, M., 2015, 'Striking ISIL: Aspects of the Law on the Use of Force', *ASIL Insights* 19(5): 'Instead of being directed by Syria, ISIL has displaced Syrian authorities in Syria (…).'

[73] Tams, C., 'The Use of Force against Terrorists', p. 383.

[74] Ibid., p. 381. See also p. 359: '… the international community during the last two decades has increasingly recognized the right of states to use unilateral force against terrorists'.

[75] For an in-depth and comprehensive review of the State practice, see Tams, C., 'The Use of Force

reconsidering their positions regarding the need for State involvement for attacks by non-State actors to trigger the right to self-defence: '[t]he vigorous and principled condemnation of the 1970s and 1980s is [being replaced] by concerns that … actions should remain proportionate'.[76] Many scholars also plead for an extension of Article 51 to non-State armed attacks. To give but some examples, the IDI declared in 2007 that '[i]n the event of an armed attack against a State by non-State actors, Article 51 of the Charter supplemented by customary international law applies as a matter of principle'.[77] Similarly, Judge Kooijmans wrote in his Separate Opinion in the ICJ case *Armed Activities on the Territory of Congo* that 'if the attacks by the irregulars would, because of their scale and effects, have had to be classified as an armed attack had they been carried out by regular armed forces, there is nothing in the language of Article 51 of the Charter that prevents the victim State from exercising its inherent right of self-defense'.[78] Therefore, there is a trend toward the recognition of a right to self-defence in cases of non-State armed attacks. Following that path, one could potentially argue that the foreign intervention in Syria is lawful, even absent of State imputability, although the definitive endorsement by customary international law of such a broad interpretation of Article 51 remains controversial.

Another complication arises from the specific terms used by the US to justify operations on Syrian soil. The US claims that self-defence applies because the 'government of the State where the threat is located is *unwilling or unable* to prevent the use of its territory for such attacks. The Syrian regime has shown that it cannot and will not confront these safe havens effectively itself'.[79] Whilst the willingness of the Syrian Government to quell IS could be argued,[80] its inability has been undoubtedly demonstrated. Besides the US, only the UN Secretary-General himself, quite surprisingly, seemed to have offered an implicit endorsement of the 'unable or unwilling test' when he noted that the US strikes took place in 'areas no longer under the effective control of the government'.[81]

against Terrorists', pp. 378–81; Ruys, T., 2010, *Armed Attacks and Article 51 of the UN Charter: Evolutions in Customary Law and Practice*, Cambridge: CUP, pp. 447–72.

[76] Tams, C., 'The Use of Force against Terrorists', p. 381. [77] IDI, §10.

[78] ICJ, *Armed activities*, 'Separate Opinion of Judge Kooijmans', §29. See also §30: 'If armed attacks are carried out by irregular bands from such territory against a neighboring State, they are still armed attacks even if they cannot be attributed to the territorial State. It would be unreasonable to deny the attacked State the right to self-defense merely because there is no attacker State, and the Charter does not so require.'

[79] *Letter dated 23 September 2014…* (emphasis added).

[80] Prior to the launch of the foreign intervention in Syria, the Syrian Government invited the US to carry out airstrikes against IS in the form of a coordinated action. See Baghdadi, G., 'Syria welcomes U.S. strikes against ISIS there, with conditions', *CBS News*, 25 August 2014, <http://www.cbsnews.com/news/syria-welcomes-u-s-strikes-against-isis-there-with-conditions/>. However, one could counter argue that Assad deliberately allowed IS to grow in importance in order to rally the international community to his side.

[81] Remarks at the Climate Summit press conference (including comments on Syria), 23 September 2014, <http://www.un.org/apps/news/infocus/sgspeeches/statments_full.asp?statID=2356#.VIrmZNFyZ9A>.

Neither the States that are part of the coalition in Syria, nor those which are not part of it but consider it lawful under international law explicitly supported this doctrine.[82] Furthermore, some other States, yet intervening in Iraq, expressed reservations about the legality of the intervention in Syria.[83] More generally, the controversy lies in the fact that although the 'unable or unwilling test' as a lawful ground for self-defence against 'independent' non-State actors is well established in the US practice[84] and receives some support in the literature,[85] it remains very controversial under international law because of the clear lack of consistent State practice.[86] The reaction of States to the airstrikes in Syria emphasizes this last point. Even Deeks, one of the most prominent defenders of the unable or unwilling doctrine, asserts that she 'found no cases in which States clearly assert that they follow the test out of a sense of legal obligation'.[87] Therefore, the authors of the present chapter argue that the 'unable or unwilling doctrine', though emerging (*de lege ferenda*), is not crystallized yet (*de lege lata*).[88] Therefore, for the time being, no one could rely upon it to make the US-led intervention in Syria lawful.

Intervention by invitation

The US never used the intervention by invitation argument in the context of Syria, the main reason being that, by doing so, they did not want to appear as implicitly approving

[82] e.g. France <http://www.reuters.com/Article/2014/09/22/us-france-fabius-airstrikes-idUSKCN0HH28920140922>, Germany <http://www.reuters.com/Article/2014/09/26/us-mideast-crisis-germany-idUSKCN0HL1BU20140926>.

[83] e.g. the Netherlands <http://www.nltimes.nl/2014/09/24/parliament-commits-troops-isis-fight/> or Australia <https://www.pm.gov.au/media/2014-09-16/interview-fran-kelly-abc-radio-national>.

[84] For instance, the 'unable or unwilling test' was also invoked by the US authorities to justify the operation in Pakistan which led to the death of Osama Bin Laden.

[85] See Deeks, A., 2012, '"Unwilling or Unable": Toward a Normative Framework for Extraterritorial Self-Defense', *Virginia Journal of International Law*, vol. 52, no. 3: p. 483; Lubell, N., 2010, *Extraterritorial Use of Force against Non-State Actors*, Oxford: OUP, p. 42; Dinstein, Y., *War, Aggression and Self-Defence*, p. 245; Stahn, C., 2003, 'Terrorist Acts as "Armed Attack": The Right to Self-Defense, Article 51 of the UN Charter, and International Terrorism', *The Fletcher Forum of World Affairs*, vol. 27, no. 2: 35, p. 47. The 'unwilling or unable' test is sometimes addressed and approved as part of the necessity requirement, see Henriksen, A., 2014, '*Jus ad bellum* and American Targeted Use of Force to Fight Terrorism Around the World', *Journal of Conflict and Security Law*, vol. 19, no. 2: 211, p. 228; UN HRC, *Report of the Special Rapporteur on Extrajudicial Summary or Arbitrary Executions, Christof Heyns*, 13 September 2013, A/68/382, § 91; Schmitt, M. N., 2011, 'Drone Attacks under the Jus ad Bellum and Jus in Bello: Clearing the "Fog of Law"', *Yearbook of International Humanitarian Law*, vol. 13: 311, p. 316.

[86] In this sense, see Heller, K. J., 'The Seemingly Inexorable March of "Unwilling or Unable" Through the Academy', *Opinio Juris*, 6 March 2015, <http://opiniojuris.org/2015/03/06/the-seemingly-inexorable-march-of-unwilling-or-unable-through-the-academy/>; and 'The Absence of Practice Supporting the 'Unwilling or Unable' Test', *Opinio Juris*, 17 February 2015, <http://opiniojuris.org/2015/02/17/unable-unwilling-test-unstoppable-scholarly-imagination/>.

[87] Deeks, A., '"Unwilling or Unable"', p. 503.

[88] See Ohlin, J. D., 'The Unwilling or Unable Doctrine Comes to Life', *Opinio Juris*, 23 September 2014, <http://opiniojuris.org/2014/09/23/unwilling-unable-doctrine-comes-life/>.

Assad's 'criminal regime'.[89] However, the controversy raised above about the legality of the US-led coalition airstrikes in Syria on the basis of collective self-defence of Iraq 'would evaporate if Syria took a path of consenting, of its own volition, to the US military action'.[90] If the Syrian regime consented to the foreign intervention on its territory, the scenario would therefore be exactly the same as in Iraq. It would be an intervention by invitation, lawful under *jus ad bellum*.[91]

Before the airstrikes began, the Syrian Government condemned, in the strongest words, any forthcoming foreign intervention to fight IS. Deputy Prime Minister Walid al Moallem was very clear saying that '[a]ny strike which is not coordinated with the government will be considered as *aggression*'.[92] However, in the first days of the US-led airstrikes, several high-level officials released statements, which appear to give tacit approval to them.[93] First, in an interview given to Reuters on 24 September 2014, the Syrian Minister for National Reconciliation stated the airstrikes were going in the 'right direction'.[94] Second, six days later, the Foreign Minister answered: '[t]his is the fact', in an interview to the Associated Press when he was 'asked whether Syria considered itself now aligned with the West because both were fighting the same enemy'.[95]

This sketch of Syrian consent was however crushed by Assad himself when he declared in the March/April 2015 issue of the magazine Foreign Affairs that the US attacks were 'illegal' since they did not ask 'permission' from the Syrian Government. In the words of Assad, 'if you want to make any kind of action in another country, you ask their permission'.[96] As Goodman rightly states, 'it looks like we may be back to square one',[97]

[89] Kress, C., 'The Fine Line Between Collective Self-Defense and Intervention by Invitation'.

[90] Goodman, R., 'Taking the Weight off of International Law: Has Syria Consented to US Airstrikes', *Just Security*, 23 December 2014, <http://justsecurity.org/18665/weight-international-law-syria-consented-airstrikes/>. In the same vein, further in the Article: 'That would take pressure off the international legal system, which has had to cope with a situation in which much of the world may support this particular exercise of US power as a matter of policy, but many, including US allies, have doubted the legality of the operations'.

[91] See Part I, Section A.

[92] Gutman, R., Youssef, N. A., and Landay, J. S., 'U.S. says airstrikes on Syria are not imminent', *McClatchy DC*, 25 August 2014, <http://www.mcclatchydc.com/2014/08/25/237643/us-says-airstrikes-on-syria-are.html> (emphasis added).

[93] For a careful analysis of these statements, see Goodman, R., 'Taking the Weight off of International Law: Has Syria Consented to US Airstrikes', *Just Security*, 23 December 2014, <http://justsecurity.org/18665/weight-international-law-syria-consented-airstrikes/>.

[94] 'Syrian minister says US-led strikes going in "right direction"', *Reuters*, 24 September 2014, <http://www.reuters.com/Article/2014/09/24/us-syria-crisis-minister-idUSKCN0HJ15P20140924>.

[95] Karam, Z., 'Syrian Foreign Minister: The US Said "We Are Not after the Syrian Army" Before Airstrikes', *Business Insider*, 30 September 2014, <http://www.businessinsider.com/syrian-foreign-minister-the-us-said-we-are-not-after-the-syrian-army-before-airstrikes-2014-9?IR=T#ixzz3MjKw64bF>.

[96] Tepperman, J., 'Syria's President Speaks', *Foreign Affairs*, 25 January 2015, <https://www.foreignaffairs.com/interviews/2015-01-25/syrias-president-speaks>.

[97] Goodman, R., 'Assad: Willing to Risk Direct Confrontation with U.S. over Moderate Rebels—and Stronger Opposition to US airstrikes', *Just Security*, 27 January 2015, <http://justsecurity.org/19419/syria-assad-risk-direct-confrontation-moderate-rebels-opposition-airstrikes/>.

the intervention by invitation cannot not be used as a valid ground to justify the foreign intervention against IS in Syria.

B. State responsibility

As explained in Part A, the activities of IS in Iraq and Syria have raised deep concern for their particular *modus operandi*. IS has established a rule of terror, characterized allegedly by serious violations of International Humanitarian Law (IHL) and International Human Rights Law (IHRL) which, if confirmed, would also entail the individual criminal responsibility of their authors as war crimes, crimes against humanity, maybe even acts of genocide against ethnic and religious groups like the Yezidis.[98] The purpose of this part however is neither to discuss the individual accountability of IS members, nor the responsibility of the group as a subject of international law.

First, Part B aims at determining whether the international responsibility of the States on whose territory the Caliphate was proclaimed, namely Syria and Iraq, could be engaged. Second, for how horrible the IS's actions have been, this armed group does not exist in a vacuum. The rise of IS has indeed arguably been facilitated by third States which, at a very minimum by virtue of their negligent behaviour in providing resources to other parties of the conflict in Syria, ultimately ended up helping IS to reinforce its position. This section will question, then, whether this provision of assistance—either willing or the result of negligence in assisting others—is such to engage those States' international responsibility. Its purpose is to understand whether third States could potentially be held responsible for having controlled, facilitated, or failed to prevent violations perpetrated by IS.

SYRIA AND IRAQ (TERRITORIAL STATES)

There is no doubt that Syria and Iraq are internationally responsible for any violation of international law—notably IHL and IHRL—committed by their organs, such as the security forces,[99] provided there is no circumstance precluding wrongfulness. However, two

[98] On Iraq, see UN HRC, *Report 13 March 2015*. On the allegations of genocide against the Yezidi minority, see §§16–20. On Syria, see UN HRC, *Report of the Independent International Commission of Inquiry on the Syrian Arab Republic*, 5 February 2015, A/HRC/28/69.

[99] Several UN organs investigated alleged violations of international humanitarian law and international human rights law committed by Iraqi and Syrian security forces and associated forces in their fight against IS. See, e.g., UN HRC, *Report 13 March 2015*, §§50–69; UN Assistance Mission for Iraq (UNAMI),

related questions about their responsibility under international law that remain controversial are discussed in the present section:

- Can Iraq and/or Syria be held internationally responsible for breaches of international law committed by IS in parts of their national territory over which they lack effective control? In more general terms, the issue at hand is the question of the territorial State's international responsibility for violations of international law committed by private persons.[100]
- Can Iraq and/or Syria be held internationally responsible for having failed to comply with their obligation to protect civilian populations under their jurisdiction?

Direct responsibility for violations of international law perpetrated by IS

As a general principle, States cannot be held internationally liable for violations of international law committed by private persons. More precisely, the wrongful conduct of a private actor is generally not attributable to the State and therefore the international responsibility of the latter cannot be engaged.[101] This principle has long been acknowledged in international judicial decisions[102] and by the ILC itself. Until 1998, it was even expressly mentioned in Article 11(1) ILC ASR, but was then deleted at the request of Special Rapporteur Crawford.[103] In the final version of the text, adopted in 2001, the principle is to be found in the Commentaries.[104]

Report on the Protection of Civilians in the Non International Armed Conflict in Iraq: 5 June—5 July 2014, 14–16; UNAMI, *Report on the Protection of Civilians in the Non International Armed Conflict in Iraq: 6 July–10 September 2014*, 18–21; UNAMI, *Report on the Protection of Civilians in the Non International Armed Conflict in Iraq: 11 September–10 December 2014*, 17–22.

[100] 'Private persons' can be defined negatively as all persons who are not 'public persons', i.e. neither State organs nor entities empowered to exercise elements of governmental authority. Ago defines 'public persons' as 'the persons or groups of persons [who] belong permanently, or even sometimes incidentally, to the machinery of the State or of separate public institutions, and act by virtue or their relationship' (Ago, R., 'Fourth Report on State Responsibility', in *Yearbook of the International Law Commission, 1972, Vol. II*, A/CN.4/SER.A/1972/Add.1, at 95).

[101] According to the 2001 ILC ASR, the international responsibility of a State is triggered if the three following cumulative conditions are met: (1) A conduct of an action or omission *attributable* to the State under international law (Chapter II); (2) A breach of an international obligation of the State (Chapter III); (3) The absence of circumstances precluding wrongfulness (Chapter V).

[102] To give some examples, the arbitrator Algot Bagge stated in the case of the *Finnish Shipowners against Great Britain in respect of the Use of Certain Finnish Vessels during the War* (1934): '[a State] has no direct responsibility under international law for the acts of private individuals' (UN, *Reports of International Arbitral Awards*, Vol. III, Sales No. 1949.V.2, 1501). Along the same vein, at the end of the nineteenth century, the US–Chile Claims Commission, established in 1892 in the *Lovett* case, had already indicated that '[a]ll the authorities on international law are a unit as regards the principle that an injury done by one of the subjects of a nation is not to be considered as done by the nation itself' (see Moore, J. B., 1900, 'History and Digest', Vol. III, at 2991).

[103] See De Frouville, O., 2010, 'Attribution of Conduct to the State: Private Individuals'. In *The Law of International Responsibility*, edited by Crawford, J., Pellet. A., and Olleson, S., pp. 257–280, at pp. 262–3.

[104] ILC, 'Draft Articles on Responsibility of States for Internationally Wrongful Acts, with commentaries', in *Yearbook of the International Law Commission, 2001, Vol. II, Part II*, A/56/10, p. 38: '... the

The rationale of this rule was well summarized by the ICJ in the *Corfu channel* case.[105] The Court stated that:

> ... it cannot be concluded from the mere fact of the control exercised by a State over its territory and waters that that State necessarily knew, or ought to have known, of any unlawful act perpetrated therein, nor yet that it necessarily knew, or should have known the authors. This fact, by itself and apart from other circumstances, neither involves *prima facie* responsibility nor shifts the burden of proof.[106]

Exceptional circumstances may arise, however, where an attribution link is found between the private person engaged in the wrongful conduct and the State. In those cases, the State's international responsibility may be engaged. The ILC recognizes five situations of this nature:

- when the private person is considered a de facto organ of the State because it acts 'on the instructions of, or under the direction or control of that State' (Article 8 ASR);
- when the conduct of the private person is carried out in absence or default of the official authorities (Article 9 ASR);
- when, following an insurrection, the private person becomes the new government of the State (Article 10(1) ASR);
- when the private person succeeds in establishing a new State (Article 10(2) ASR);
- when the conduct of the private person is acknowledged and adopted by the State as its own (Article 11 ASR).

In the case of IS, the only possible way its conduct could potentially be attributed to Syria and/or Iraq is provided in Article 10(1). If IS becomes the new government of Iraq, the State of Iraq would become retroactively responsible for all violations of international law perpetrated by IS since its creation. The same conclusion would apply to Syria: if IS removes the current Syrian Government from power and takes office, Syria would

conduct of private persons is not as such attributable to the State'. See also p. 52: '[t]he general principle, drawn from State practice and international judicial decisions, is that the conduct of a person or group of persons not acting on behalf of the State is not considered as an act of the State under international law'.

105 ICJ, *Corfu Channel* (United Kingdom v Albania), Merits, Judgment, 9 April 1949, ICJ Reports 1949, p. 4.

106 Ibid., p. 18. Writing in 1758, Vattel had expressed a similar idea: '... as it is impossible for the best regulated State, or for the most vigilant and absolute sovereign, to model at his pleasure all the actions of his subjects, and to confine them on every occasion to the most exact obedience, it would be unjust to impute to the nation or the sovereign every fault committed by the citizens. We ought not then to say in general, that we have received an injury from a nation, because we have received it from one of its members' (Kapossy, B., and Whatmore, R. (eds), 2008, *Emer de Vattel, The Law of Nations or Principles of the Law of Nature, Applied to the Conduct and Affairs of Nations and Sovereign, with Three Early Essays on the Origin and Nature of Natural Law and on Luxury*, Indianapolis: Liberty Fund, Book II, Chapter VI, §73). See also De Frouville, O., 'Attribution of Conduct to the State: Private Individuals', p. 261: '[I]t cannot be required of a State that it is in control of all the events which take place on its territory short of obliging it to become a totalitarian State'.

become retroactively responsible for IS under international law. However, this scenario seems very unlikely. IS's primary objective is not to overthrow Assad or al-Abadi but to create its own State somewhere between Mossul in Iraq and Raqqa in Syria.[107]

One could also attempt to trigger the responsibility of Syria and Iraq on the basis of Article 9. According to the ILC commentary:

> Article 9 deals with the exceptional case of conduct in the exercise of elements of the governmental authority by a person or group of persons acting in the absence of the official authorities and without any actual authority to do so.... Article 9 establishes three conditions which must be met in order for conduct to be attributable to the State: first, the conduct must effectively relate to the exercise of elements of the governmental authority, secondly, the conduct must have been carried out in the absence or default of the official authorities, and thirdly, the circumstances must have been such as to call for the exercise of those elements of authority.[108]

At first glance, these three conditions seem to be met. First, in regions under its control, IS carries out elements of governmental authority such as police, justice, and tax powers[109]. Second, neither Iraq nor Syria exercises authority in those regions. Third, the ILC considers the existence of an 'armed conflict' as to be a circumstance calling for the exercise of governmental authority.[110] However, it does not seem advisable to the authors of the present chapter to adopt such an interpretation of Article 9. Indeed, it would be absurd for a State to be responsible directly for the wrongful acts committed by those it is trying to defeat. Furthermore, this would go against the intentions of the ILC which held that '[t]he general principle in respect of the conduct of such movements, committed during the continuing struggle with the constituted authority, is that it is not attributable to the State under international law'.[111] It is only 'the conduct of an insurrectional movement which becomes the new government of a State [which] shall be considered an act of that State under international law'.[112] Moreover, ample support for this general principle is to be found in arbitral jurisprudence.[113]

Failure to comply with the obligation to protect

As demonstrated above, it is unlikely that the acts of IS will ever be attributed to Iraq and/or Syria. Therefore, these two States' international responsibility would probably never be triggered *directly* for IS's violations of international law. By contrast, their responsibility could potentially be engaged for having failed to comply with their obligation to protect.

107 See 'Introduction'. It is worth pointing out that, on the basis of Art. 10(2) ASR, if IS succeeds in its enterprise, the newly created State would be retroactively responsible for any breach of international law committed by the armed group.

108 ILC, Draft Articles... with commentaries, p. 49.

109 See 'Introduction'.

110 ILC, Draft Articles... with commentaries, p. 49.

111 Ibid., p. 50.

112 Art. 10(1) ASR.

113 For instance, one could refer to the *Sambiago* case (1904) in which it was stated that '... the very existence of a flagrant revolution presupposes that a certain set of men have gone temporarily or permanently

Under international law, States are bound by an obligation to protect, also called the obligation of due diligence. Long recognized in international jurisprudence[114] and by the ILC,[115] this obligation requires States to take all necessary measures to protect persons under their jurisdiction from harmful acts committed by private actors and to punish perpetrators of such acts.[116] Therefore, besides direct responsibility for acts of private persons, the territorial State's international responsibility may also be engaged, not for these acts directly, but 'for the action, and more often for the omission, of its organs which are guilty of not having done everything within their power to prevent the individual's injurious action or to punish it suitably in the event it has nevertheless occurred'.[117] In other words, regardless of whether the wrongful conduct of the private person is attributable to the State or not, the territorial State can be held independently 'responsible for having violated not the international obligation with which the individual's action might be in contradiction but the general or special obligation imposing on its organs a duty to provide protection'.[118] In practice, this is the most common scenario.[119] In such a situation, the act of the private person is just a pre-condition to the existence of State responsibility 'acting externally as a catalyst on the wrongfulness of the conduct of the State'.[120]

Under IHRL, the obligation to protect is part of the tripartite typology of State obligations, alongside the obligation to respect and the obligation to fulfil.[121] As stated by the UN Human Rights Committee in its General Comment 31:

> . . . the positive obligations on States Parties to ensure Covenant rights will only be fully discharged if individuals are protected by the State, not just against violations of Covenant rights by its agents, but also against acts committed by private persons or entities . . . There may be

beyond the power of the authorities; and unless it clearly appears that the government has failed to use promptly and with appropriate force its constituted authority, it cannot reasonably be said that it should be responsible for a condition of affairs created without its volition' (UNRIAA, Vol. X (Sales No. 60.V.4), 513).

[114] See, e.g., the *Tellini* case of 1923 (League of Nations, *Official Journal*, 4th Year, No. 11, November 1923, 1349).

[115] ILC, Draft Articles... with commentaries, p. 39: '... a state may be responsible for the effects of the conduct of private parties, if it failed to take necessary measures to prevent those effects'.

[116] According to Ago, '[t]his type of theory derives from Grotius' idea that the collectivity participated in a crime committed by an individual if nothing was done to prevent the crime *(patientia)* or to punish or hand over the offender *(receptus)*'. Ago, R., 'Fourth Report on State Responsibility', p. 121.

[117] Ibid., p. 123. [118] Ibid.

[119] Ibid., p. 99: '... it is generally acknowledged that the State assumes responsibility not for the action of the individual, but for the conduct, usually omissive, of some of its organs in connexion with the action of the individual'. See also Pisillo Mazzeschi, R., 1992, 'The Due Diligence Rule and the Nature of the International Responsibility of States, *German Yearbook of International Law*, vol. 35: 9 at 2pp. 5–26: '... what clearly prevails today in both legal literature and in international practice is the view that the acts of individuals *are not attributable to the State,* but they may represent only the external fact giving rise to a *different wrongful act*, consisting in the State organs' failure to prevent or punish such acts' (footnotes omitted).

[120] Ago, R., 'Fourth Report on State Responsibility', p. 97.

[121] On the three categories of human rights obligations, see generally Kälin, W. and Künzli, J., 2009, *The Law of International Human Rights Protection*, Oxford: OUP, pp. 96–113.

circumstances in which a failure to ensure Covenant rights . . . would give rise to violations by States Parties of those rights, as a result of States parties' permitting or failing to take appropriate measures or to exercise due diligence to prevent, punish, investigate or redress the harm caused by such acts by private persons or entities.[122]

At the regional human rights level, numerous cases address the issue of States' compliance with the obligation to protect.[123] The *Ilaşcu* case of 2004 is of particular interest to the current discussion. The European Court of Human Rights (ECtHR) ruled that, even where a State loses effective control over its territory, this only suspends its obligations to respect and fulfil. By contrast, its obligation to protect continues to apply and may engage its responsibility in case of failure.[124] According to the Court, if the State wants to respect this obligation, '[t]he State in question must endeavour, with all the legal and diplomatic means available to it vis-à-vis foreign States and international organisations, to continue to guarantee the enjoyment of the rights and freedoms defined in the Convention'.[125]

The ECtHR decision in the *Ilaşcu* case can be applied by analogy to Iraq and Syria. Though both States lost control over parts of their territory, it can be argued they remain bound by their obligation to protect.[126] Did they fail to comply with such an obligation? A proper answer to this question would require a thorough factual analysis, going beyond the scope of the present chapter. Nonetheless, it should be noted that, according to several UN organs, there are serious reasons to believe that Iraq and Syria failed to take all necessary measures to protect victims of IS in regions under IS' effective control. For instance, in the March 2015 Report on the Human Rights Situation in Iraq, the UN Office of the High Commissioner for Human Rights (OHCHR) recommended to the Government of Iraq to 'investigate allegations that ISF [Iraqi Security Forces]

122 Human Rights Committee (HRCee), *General Comment No. 31—Nature of the General Legal Obligation on States Parties to the Covenant*, CCPR/C/21/Rev.1/Add.13, 2004, §8.

123 See, e.g., European Court of Human Rights (ECtHR), Grand Chamber, *Osman v The United Kingdom*, Judgment, 28 October 1998; Inter-American Court of Human Rights (IACtHR), *Velasquez-Rodriguez v Honduras*, Judgment, 29 July 1988.

124 ECtHR, Grand Chamber, *Ilaşcu and others v Moldova and Russia*, Judgment, 8 July 2004, §333: '... such a factual situation reduces the scope of that jurisdiction in that the undertaking given by the State under Article 1 must be considered by the Court *only in the light of the Contracting State's positive obligations towards persons within its territory*' (emphasis added).

125 Ibid.

126 This has been acknowledged repeatedly by the UN. See, e.g., UN HRC, *Report 13 March 2015*, §72: 'Information gathered by the mission strongly suggests that international crimes may have been perpetrated and continue to be perpetrated in Iraq by ISIL. *The primary legal responsibility in addressing these international crimes lies with the State of Iraq whose duty it is to protect persons under its jurisdiction and ensure accountability*' (emphasis added). See also UNAMI, *Report ... 5 June–5 July 2014*, p. 6: 'IHRL imposes direct responsibility on the State in whose territory and under whose jurisdiction violations take place. Iraq has the obligation to ensure that action is taken so that violations are prevented and not repeated, to punish perpetrators and to ensure an adequate remedy is provided to the victims'.

and armed groups acting under its control failed to protect communities persecuted by ISIL'.[127] With regard to Syria, the Independent International Commission of Inquiry published a report on 5 February 2015 in which it declared that '[t]he human cost of the ongoing conflict in the Syrian Arab Republic is immeasurable [and that] the Syrian State has manifestly failed to protect its citizens from mass atrocities'.[128] Last but not least, if responsibility had to be apportioned between Iraq and Syria, it could be argued that Iraq seems more willing to protect its own population. First, unlike Syria, Iraq expressly requested foreign military assistance to fight IS. Second, Iraq always allowed international humanitarian operations inside its territory, whereas Syria constantly obstructed such operations.[129]

THIRD STATES

Broadening the scope of our analysis outside Iraq and Syria, it is noteworthy that there have been claims of links between other States and the various parties to the conflict in Syria, including IS. These links would include the provision of financial and military assistance, in the form of training, advice, and provision of weapons.[130] This news, alleging that some States might have willingly and directly lent assistance to IS, is not the only reason for concern. Assistance to other parties to the conflict might have also indirectly helped IS to achieve its current status.[131] Therefore, it is important to understand whether States other than Iraq and Syria (third States) could be held responsible for their direct or indirect implication in the IS's actions.

As we have already seen, there are various ways in which the responsibility of States can be engaged in view of their relationship with non-State armed groups like IS (or private actors in general). The applicability of these legal avenues depends mostly on

[127] UN HRC, *Report 13 March 2015*, §79. [128] UN HRC, *Report 5 February 2015*, §47.

[129] Ibid., §53: 'Arbitrary restrictions and obstacles to the delivery of aid continue to be imposed by all sides to the conflict, with devastating consequences for civilians in areas that are hard to reach. Humanitarian aid has been instrumentalized for military gain. The bureaucratic hurdles imposed by the Government of the Syrian Arab Republic are a calculated obstruction of aid to civilians living in areas under non-State armed group control.'

[130] See Stephens, M., 'Islamic State: Where does jihadist group get its support?', *BBC*, 1 September 2014, at <http://www.bbc.com/news/world-middle-east-29004253>, and Rogin, J., 'America's Allies Are Funding ISIS', *The Daily Beast*, 6 June 2014, at <http://www.thedailybeast.com/Articles/2014/06/14/america-s-allies-are-funding-isis.html>. See also BBC News, 'Islamic State: Where key countries stand', 4 February 2015, at <http://www.bbc.com/news/world-middle-east-29074514>.

[131] UN HRC, *Report 5 February 2015*, §120: 'Despite all the precautions allegedly taken by the States steering the process, the support given to the so-called "moderates" has ultimately consolidated the dominance of extremist groups such as ISIS and Jabhat Al-Nusra, which managed to overrun the positions of moderates and to gain loyalties among their ranks.'

the quality of the relationship between the entity providing assistance and the entity receiving it, on the level of control exercised by the State in question over members of the non-State actor, and on the type of assistance provided. With regard to third States, international responsibility could potentially arise in at least three cases: first, in a case where a third State exercised control over members of the armed group IS, so that the latter's action could be directly attributed to that State; second, in a case where the State rendered aid and/or assistance to IS, thereby becoming complicit in its violations of international law; and third, in a case where the State failed to abide by its obligation of due diligence to ensure respect for certain rules or to prevent certain violations.

Direct responsibility for violations of international law perpetrated by IS

In some cases, States are directly responsible for actions carried out by non-State actors. The question we need to ask ourselves is, then, whether any State which has provided assistance to IS can be held directly responsible for actions perpetrated by the latter.

As already seen, the ASR list cases of attribution of conducts to a State in Articles 8 to 11, and some of these Articles are applicable to acts performed by private actors. Of note, Article 8 ASR attributes responsibility to a State when private individuals are 'acting on the instructions of, or under the direction or control of, that State in carrying out the conduct'.[132] This test has been interpreted as requiring that State responsibility for non-State actors' actions can be attributed only for those violations whose perpetration was directed or enforced by the State, or performed in operations over which the State exercised 'effective control'.[133] As interpreted by the ICJ, the test is in practice really hard to satisfy. This consideration, and a careful analysis of the existing practice on the matter, led the International Criminal Tribunal for the former Yugoslavia (ICTY) Appeals Chamber to propose a new approach in its 1995 *Tadić* judgment. The Appeals Chamber claimed, in particular, that customary international law establishes a different test for attribution when non-State actors are structured in a hierarchically organized group, as it is the case for IS.[134] In those cases, indeed, State responsibility will be engaged for all actions carried out by the group, as long as the State maintains an 'overall control' over the group, 'going beyond the mere financing and equipping of such forces and involving

[132] Art. 8 ASR.

[133] ICJ, *Nicaragua*, §115; ICJ, *Application of the Convention on the Prevention and Punishment of the Crime of Genocide* (Bosnia and Herzegovina v Serbia and Montenegro), Judgment, 26 February 2007, ICJ Reports 2007, p. 43 ff., §§399-400.

[134] International Tribunal for the former Yugoslavia (ICTY), Appeals Chamber, *Tadić* (IT-94-1), Judgment, 15 July 1999, §120.

also participation in the planning and supervision of military operations'.[135] This overall control, unlike the 'effective control' test, would not require that the armed group is acting under specific instructions by the State.

An even broader test to attribute State responsibility for non-State actors' actions seems to have been proposed a few years later by the ECtHR, in the cited case *Ilaşcu*. In that case, Russia was deemed to be responsible for violations of IHRL perpetrated by the de facto authority governing Transnistria, a separatist region in Moldova. The reason for the attribution of responsibility to Russia was that the latter was exercising a 'decisive influence' over the separatist government, whose creation and survival were only possible thanks to Russian military, political, and economic support.[136] The 'decisive influence' has received little further explanation since,[137] but it is not to be excluded that the ECtHR might return to it in future cases.

Although there are several allegations that IS received external assistance from third States, none of these actually claim that that the Caliphate's actions were/are performed under the effective control, overall control, or decisive influence of any State. Therefore, none of the aforementioned tests to attribute direct State responsibility is, as things currently stand, applicable to the IS case. The hypothesis of direct attribution of IS actions to a third State will then not be explored further here, even though a change in circumstances might make it relevant again in the future.

State complicity in the violations of International Law perpetrated by IS

One should then ask whether third States could be held responsible for their involvement in the behaviour of private actors, when there is no relationship of control between them. One possibility would be to invoke the concept of 'complicity', language ordinarily used in criminal law, which has received some recognition and application also in the framework of State responsibility.[138] The idea of complicit responsibility in internationally wrongful acts committed by another State—even if under a different wording—is enshrined in Article 16 ASR, deemed to reflect customary international law.[139] According to the latter, a State is internationally responsible if it aids or assists

[135] Ibid., §§120-3 and 145. [136] ECtHR, *Ilaşcu*, §§392-3.

[137] ECtHR, Grand Chamber, *Catan and Others v Moldova and Russia*, Judgment, 19 October 2012, §111.

[138] ICJ, *Genocide*, §§419-21. See also ILC, *Draft Articles ... with commentaries*, p. 67; and Lanovoy, V., 'Responsibility for Complicity in an Internationally Wrongful Act: Revisiting a Structural Norm', paper presented at the SHARES Conference '*Foundations of Shared Responsibility in International Law*', 17–18 November 2011, Amsterdam, available at <http://ssrn.com/abstract=2170406>, pp. 4–5.

[139] See ICJ, *Genocide*, §420. Of note, Art. 41(2) ASR complements Art. 16, establishing an obligation not to render aid or assistance in maintaining a situation created by the serious breach of a *jus cogens* rule by a State. For further reference, see Jørgensen, N. H., 2010, 'The Obligation of Non-Assistance of the Responsible State', in Crawford, J., Pellet. A., Olleson, S. (eds.), pp. 687–93.

another State in the commission of an internationally wrongful act, with knowledge of the circumstances of the act itself.[140] However, as evident, Article 16 ASR only concerns cases of assistance lent to States. What then of assistance provided to armed groups like IS? It is nowadays accepted, indeed, that also non-State actors have some international obligations, especially under IHL and under IHRL.[141] If they do have international obligations, it is logical to assume that they can commit internationally wrongful acts. But is it possible to hold States responsible for having aided and/or assisted such acts?

De lege lata, the answer seems to be negative. The ASR already establish when a State is responsible via its relationship with a private actor breaching rules of international law. In that case, however, the rules applicable are those contained in Articles 8 to 11 ASR, and any relationship falling outside of those provisions would not be sufficient to hold the State responsible. And, recalling the classic 'voluntarist' approach to international law expressed by the Permanent Court of International Justice in *Lotus*, every behaviour that is not expressly prohibited in international law must be implicitly considered as allowed.[142]

De lege ferenda, one could argue that the norm on aid and assistance to violations of international law contained in Article 16 ASR is narrower than its customary international law counterpart should be.[143] If the purpose of this norm is to make violations of international law less likely by deterring acts of assistance to unlawful behaviours, it would be illogical to limit it to violations committed just by certain actors, as the system of international responsibility would then appear incomplete. And, indeed, Article 14 of the ILC Draft Articles on the Responsibility of International Organizations (DARIO) also proscribes acts of assistance to internationally wrongful acts, regardless of whether they are committed by a State or an international organization.

Of course, even if a general rule sanctioning complicity in non-State actors' violations existed, not all kinds of assistance would be enough to trigger it. We could assume that, in such a case, the same requirements contained in Article 16 ASR would still need to be satisfied. Namely, a State would only be responsible if it knew of the circumstances of the internationally wrongful act, and provided that the act performed by the non-State actor would be internationally wrongful if performed by the State itself.

[140] And if the assisting State was bound by the same rule breached by the State primarily responsible. This second requirement was not present in the original Draft Art. 25 proposed by Special Rapporteur Ago, in Ago R., 'Seventh Report on State Responsibility', A/CN.4/307 and Add. 1 and 2, in *Yearbook of the International Law Commission* (1978), vol. II (1), 60. The amendment in the current version of the ILC Articles is criticized by Lanovoy, pp. 28–32.

[141] For the seminal work on the issue, see Clapham, A., 2006, 'Human Rights Obligations of Non-State Actors', Oxford: OUP.

[142] Permanent Court of International Justice, *S. S. Lotus* (France v Turkey), 1927 PCIJ Series A, No. 10, §44.

[143] This opinion is also shared by Lanovoy, pp. 15–16.

In the case under scrutiny, there are two types of alleged aid or assistance provided to IS: (i) direct provision of assistance, in the form of delivery of weapons, funding and/or allowing the State's territory to be used by IS for oil smuggling and to provide medical treatment and training to the IS's fighters; (ii) negligence in the provision of assistance to other parties to the conflict in Syria, which ended up supporting IS activities in both Iraq and Syria.

Given the strict objectivity (i.e., the absence of a requirement of fault or intent) of the law of State responsibility,[144] even this second type of behaviour could entail the responsibility of the assisting State provided, obviously, that the assisting State had knowledge of the violations of international law which were being perpetrated by IS, and of the fact that the assistance provided to other actors would have likely ended up in the IS's hands.[145] As to the level of assistance necessary to engage a State's complicit liability, there is no indication in Article 16, nor in its commentary. This could be interpreted as meaning that any kind of behaviour, insofar as it actually facilitated the IS's violations, would be enough to engage State responsibility.

Aside from the general prohibition of aid and assistance to violations of international law, the Genocide Convention expressly includes a prohibition of complicity in acts of genocide.[146] A remarkable and relevant difference with Article 16 ASR is, however, that the Genocide Convention proscribes aid or assistance to acts of genocide regardless of whether they are perpetrated by State agents or by other entities. Forbidden acts of assistance notably include the provision of means to enable or facilitate the commission of the crime.[147] Of course, exactly as Article 16 ASR, Article III(e) implies a State's responsibility only if assistance was provided in full knowledge of the facts of the genocide,[148] including knowledge of the special intent to commit genocide by the final perpetrators.[149] A State could then, potentially, be considered as complicit in the alleged genocide of the Yezidis, if it can be proven that it somehow facilitated the genocide, in full knowledge of the IS's intent.

Similarly, some international instruments prohibit providing specific forms of assistance to certain entities. Examples relevant to our analysis could be the SC Resolution

[144] Dailler, P., Forteau, M., and Pellet, A., 2009. *Droit international public*–8ème ed., LGDJ, Paris, p. 854.

[145] The ILC commentary to Art. 16 ASR seems to implicitly affirm that a State is only responsible if it provided assistance with the intent to facilitate the perpetration of the internationally wrongful act. ILC, *Draft Articles ... with commentaries*, pp. 66, §5. This approach, however, looks to be in contradiction with the text of Article 16, and of the general objective approach to State responsibility. Special Rapporteur Ago, indeed, seemed to consider intent as implied in the deliberate provision of assistance despite the knowledge that this would have lead to an internationally wrongful act. See Ago, R., 'Fourth Report on State Responsibility', §72.

[146] Convention on the Prevention and Punishment of the crime of Genocide, 9 December 1948, Art. III(e). The ICJ considered this to be a special case of aid or assistance in an internationally wrongful act, i.e., the institute described in Art. 16 ASR. Cf. ICJ, *Genocide*, §420, and more in general §§419–432.

[147] Ibid., §419. [148] Ibid., §432. [149] Ibid., §421.

1373 (2001)[150] and the UN Convention against the Financing of Terrorism, both of which establish a duty to refrain from providing support—financial in the latter case—to entities involved in acts of terrorism.[151] Another example comes from the Arms Trade Treaty, recently entered into force, which establishes an obligation not to authorize weapons' transfer when knowing that they would be used in the commission of certain international crimes, including genocide, crimes against humanity, and certain categories of war crimes.[152] The Arms Trade Treaty also establishes an obligation to deny authorization to weapons exports whenever there is an overriding risk that they will be used to facilitate or commit—inter alia—serious violations of IHL, serious violations of IHRL, or acts of terrorism.[153] Article 11 demands that a State, before deciding whether to authorize a weapons transfer, should also assess the risk of 'diversion' of those weapons, i.e., the risk that the weapons end up in the hands of a subject other than the original recipient.[154] In the situation under scrutiny, this would mean that States could have violated one or more of these provisions when authorizing weapons transfers to other entities operating in Syria, knowing or ignoring the risk that those weapons would have ended up in the hands of IS, and used to commit one or more of the mentioned violations of international law.

In all these instances, however, the State would be responsible directly for the violation of the mentioned legal instruments, and not as an accomplice in the IS's violations. And this despite the fact that a State's behaviour in such cases is not different from the behaviour prohibited in Article 16 ASR or Article III(e) Genocide Convention.

Other provisions engaging States' responsibility for their implication in the IS violations

IS's violations could give rise to States' international responsibility in a third case, i.e., when a State did not abide by its obligation to respect and/or ensure respect for a certain body of law, or by its obligation to prevent certain violations.

Bearing in mind the IHL violations allegedly perpetrated by IS, one should question whether any States could be held responsible pursuant to Article 1 common to the 1949 Geneva Conventions, or to the similar norm included in Article 1 of Additional Protocol I. These rules, indeed, bind States Party to respect and ensure respect for the obligations contained respectively in the Conventions and in the Additional Protocol. Rule 144 identified by the International Committee of the Red Cross (ICRC) Study on customary IHL

150 UN SC, Resolution 1373 (2001), 28 September 2001, S/RES/1373, §2.

151 International Convention for the Suppression of the Financing of Terrorism, 9 December 1999, *UN Treaty Series*, vol. 2178, 197, Art. 2.

152 Arms Trade Treaty, A/CONF.217/2013/L.3, adopted by the UN GA with Resolution 2 April 2013, A/RES/67/234B, Art. 6(3) and Art. 7.

153 Ibid., Art. 7.

154 Ibid., Art. 11.

also could be relevant here, establishing a duty for States not to encourage violations of IHL, and to exert their influence to stop ongoing violations.[155]

The duty to ensure respect for IHL is nowadays considered to be not just a simple entitlement, but a fully fledged obligation owed to the international community as a whole to react against violations of IHL performed by other subjects of international law.[156] This obligation could even be considered a 'constitutional principle' of the international legal order.[157] The obligation also finds application in non-international armed conflicts with respect to common Article 3[158] and, arguably, with respect to all norms of customary international law applicable to non-international armed conflicts that logically descend from common Article 3.[159]

As far as their content, common Article 1 and its 'sister rules' impose on States a duty to undertake all reasonable and feasible steps to secure that the Conventions are respected and implemented in all circumstances in which they are applicable and by all actors—especially by parties to armed conflicts, and even by parties to those conflicts to which the State in question is not itself participating.[160] In this sense, common Article 1 also lays down an obligation (of means) to ensure compliance with IHL by non-State actors such as IS, or at least not to encourage their IHL violations.[161]

But what does this concretely mean? Finding support in the language of Rule 144 of the ICRC Customary Law Study, it could be argued that common Article 1 actually implies a duty to refrain from adopting behaviours that could encourage or facilitate or otherwise lead to a violation of the Convention.[162] Common Article 1, therefore, must

155 Henckaerts, J. M., and Doswald-Beck L. (eds), 2009, *Customary International Humanitarian Law, Volume I: Rules*, Geneva: ICRC/CUP, Rule 144.

156 Boisson De Chazournes, L. and Condorelli, L., 2000, 'Common Article 1 of the Geneva Conventions Revisited: Protecting Collective Interests', *International Review of the Red Cross (IRRC)*, vol. 82: 67 at p. 76. See also Palwankar, U., 1994, 'Measures Available to States for Fulfilling their Obligation to Ensure Respect for International Humanitarian Law', *IRRC*, vol. 76: 9. Cf. ICTY, Trial Chamber, *Kupreškić et al.* (IT-95-16), Judgment, 14 January 2000, §519; ICJ, *Nicaragua*, §220; ICJ, *Wall*, §158. *Contra*, Focarelli, C., 2010, 'Common Article 1 of the 1949 Geneva Conventions: A Soap Bubble?', *EJIL*, vol. 21: 125, claiming that the 'duty to ensure respect' should have been more correctly interpreted as referring not to other States' compliance with IHL, but the compliance with IHL of individuals under the duty-bearer's jurisdiction.

157 Boisson De Chazournes, L. and Condorelli, L., 'Common Article 1', p. 85.

158 ICJ, *Nicaragua*, §220.

159 Boisson De Chazournes, L. and Condorelli, L., 'Common Article 1', p. 69.

160 In the words of the ICRC, 'the Contracting Parties should not be content merely to apply its provisions themselves, but should do everything in their power to ensure that the humanitarian principles underlying the Conventions are applied universally'. ICRC, 1958, *Commentary on the Geneva Conventions of 12 August 1949. Volume IV*, Geneva: ICRC, p. 16. The same principle is quoted and confirmed in the ICRC, 1987, *Commentary on the Additional Protocols of 8 June 1977 to the Geneva Conventions of 12 August 1949*, Geneva: ICRC/Martinus Nijhoff Publishers, pp. 35–36. See also ICJ, *Wall*, §158.

161 ICJ, *Nicaragua*, §220. See also Brehm, M., 2008, 'The Arms Trade and States' Duty to Ensure Respect for Humanitarian and Human Rights Law', *Journal of Conflict and Security Law*, vol. 12: 359, p. 372.

162 Boivin, A., 2005, 'Complicity and beyond: International law and the transfer of small arms and light weapons', *IRRC*, vol. 87: 467, p. 479 seems suggesting this when dealing with the specific issue of arms

inform the behaviour of all High Contracting Parties with regard to any existing armed conflict, binding them to do everything in their power to prevent and avoid violations of the relevant IHL rules, by whoever perpetrated. In practice, obviously, the concrete meaning of such an obligation will depend on the circumstances, and on the State's actual ability to influence final perpetrators.[163] Nevertheless, one might assume that the obligation is breached when a State, knowingly or negligently, provided to parties to an armed conflict assistance that was used to perform IHL violations. This may well have been the case in Iraq and Syria.

Comparable considerations could be done with respect to the obligation to prevent acts of genocide, enshrined in Article I of the Genocide Convention. Article I established a direct obligation for any State Party to employ the means at its disposal to prevent acts of genocide, even when perpetrated by entities that are not under that State's authority.[164] Similar obligations are set forth in other treaties relevant to the situation in Syria and Iraq, such as the Convention against Torture[165] and the Convention against Terrorist Bombing, and the subsequent analysis could be applied to such provisions as well.[166]

As with the duty to ensure respect for IHL, the duty to prevent acts of genocide is an obligation of means, not an obligation of result. Its actual content must be determined case-by-case, depending heavily on the means at the disposal of the duty-bearer and on its capacity to effectively influence the final perpetrators. Despite this apparent looseness, the obligation resulting from Article I is quite demanding: it arises once a State learns of the risk of a genocide being committed,[167] and requires the adoption and implementation of suitable measures to prevent genocide.[168] Furthermore, it is not limited to acts of genocide being perpetrated on the territory and/or by individuals under the State's jurisdiction, but extends to cover any act of genocide wherever it is performed, insofar as a State is actually in a position to do something to prevent it.[169] States are bound to prevent acts

transfers; cf. also Brehm, M., 'The Arms Trade and States' Duty', p. 377, who considers it as an obligation of conduct. Cf. also Maslen S., Giacca G., and Bellal, A., 2012, 'Implications of International Law for a Future Arms Trade Treaty', *UNIDIR Resources, Ideas for Peace and Security*, p. 14.

163 Brehm, M., 'The Arms Trade and States' Duty', p. 374.

164 ICJ, *Genocide*, §§162 and 165–6.

165 Convention against Torture and Other Cruel, Inhuman or Degrading Treatment or Punishment, *UN Treaty Series*, vol. 1465, 85, Art. 2.

166 International Convention for the Suppression of Terrorist Bombings, adopted in GA, Resolution 52/164, 15 December 1997, A/RES/52/164, Art. 15.

167 Cassese, A., 2007, 'On the Use of Criminal Law Notions in Determining State Responsibility for Genocide', *Journal of International Criminal Justice*, vol. 5, no. 4: 875, p. 885.

168 ICJ, *Genocide*, §432.

169 Ibid., §430. Cf. also Milanović, M., 2007, 'State Responsibility for Genocide: A Follow-Up', *EJIL*, vol. 18: 669 at pp. 685–6. See also Gattini, U., 2007, 'Breach of the Obligation to Prevent and Reparation Thereof in the ICJ's Genocide Judgment', *EJIL*, vol. 18: 695, pp. 700–1.

of genocide regardless of whether the final perpetrator is a private individual, an armed group, or a State organ.[170]

Bearing in mind the alleged genocide being perpetrated by IS against the Yezidis, one should question whether third States bear any responsibility for having failed to prevent it. Potentially, Article I of the Genocide Convention may be violated by the mere fact of having allowed IS to acquire resources that were later used to perform this alleged genocide.

[170] Gaeta P., 2007, 'On What Conditions Can a State Be Held Responsible for Genocide?', *EJIL*, vol. 18: 631, p. 640.

B
Protection

5 Refugees and asylum seekers from conflict-affected States

Kristin Hausler[1]

Introduction

The United Nations High Commissioner for Refugees (UNHCR), the intergovernmental agency providing protection to displaced persons,[2] stated that the number of asylum seekers, refugees, and internally displaced peoples (commonly referred to as 'IDPs') totalled over 51 million individuals at the end of 2013, half of them being children.[3] This has been the highest number of forcibly displaced persons recorded since the Second World War. Internally displaced persons constitute the majority of forcibly displaced individuals, with over 30 million individuals, while the refugee population amounts to 16.7 million individuals, including 11.7 million under the care of the UNHCR.[4]

Wars are a major cause of forced displacement, a phenomenon which has increased dramatically in recent years as a result of the civil war in Syria, which has forced about 2.5 to 3 million individuals to become refugees or asylum seekers.[5] Other armed conflicts,

[1] Kristin Hausler is the Dorset Senior Research Fellow at the British Institute of International and Comparative Law in London. The author is grateful to Dr. Jean-Pierre Gauci for having commented on an earlier version of this chapter, as well as to Alice Law for her research assistance.

[2] According to its statute, adopted with the General Assembly Resolution 428 (v) of 14 December 1950, the UNHCR was mandated mainly to protect refugees, improve their situation, and assist them with their needs. This mandate includes asylum seekers, i.e., those who have crossed a border but whose refugee status has not yet been determined, but not IDPs. However, as a result of the General Assembly's Resolution 53/125 of December 1998, the role of the UNHCR can now extend to internally displaced persons.

[3] See 'World Refugee Day: Global forced displacement tops 50 million for first time in post-World War II era', UNHCR, News Stories, 20 June 2014, available at: <http://www.unhcr.org/53a155bc6.html>.

[4] More than half of those under the care of UNHCR (6.3 million) had, at end of 2013, been in exile for more than five years. Note that the remaining 5 million of the world's refugees were registered with the UN Relief and Works Agency for Palestine Refugees in the Near East (UNRWA), see 'World Refugee Day: Global forced displacement tops 50 million for first time in post-World War II era', UNHCR, News Stories, 20 June 2014, available at: <http://www.unhcr.org/53a155bc6.html>.

The UNHCRH Population Statistics database is available here: <http://popstats.unhcr.org/#_ga=1.98218007.901588959.1429016918>.

[5] According to an October 2014 estimate, about 9 million Syrians left their homes; while some took refuge abroad, many were displaced within Syria, see: <http://syrianrefugees.eu/>.

such as the ones in South Sudan or the Central African Republic (CAR), have also been key drivers in raising the amount of refugees and asylum seekers worldwide. In CAR, the March 2013 coup d'état led not only to a killing spree but also to the flight of more than 215,000 people across the border into Cameroon.[6]

The displacement of individuals as a result of wars comprises specific characteristics. In particular, such movement of population generally involves a large number of people and occurs rapidly, which renders adequate and timely responses very difficult. Massive waves of displacement have required the establishment of temporary housing until a final destination can be organized for those displaced, whether it means going back to their country of origin or being resettled in a third State. Refugee camps vary in size, with the largest one being in Dadaab, which is situated in Kenya about 100 kilometres from the Somali border. While its camps were first set up as a short-term solution in the early 1990s to host those fleeing the war in Somalia, it has ended up hosting people who had fled various Eastern Africa conflicts for decades.

In addition to raising many logistical issues as a result of their size and often remote location, refugee camps may also not always be the safe havens they are supposed to be. For example, the Yarmouk camp in Damascus, the largest Palestinian refugee camp in Syria, has been attacked on several occasions.[7] At the beginning of April 2015, Islamic State militants raided the camp, allegedly killing dozens of refugees. These attacks have not only led to secondary displacement but also to starvation and exposure to diseases for those not able to escape the camp, under siege for over 700 days.[8] Ongoing fighting has made it particularly arduous to provide assistance to those who had remained in the camp. As a result of the war, the Yarmouk population has been reduced from about 200,000 individuals before the conflict to about only 16,000 residents at present.[9]

Of course, the cross-border journey faced by refugees and asylum-seekers is often hazardous. The most poignant example is that of the so-called Mediterranean 'boat

[6] Nforngwa, E., 'CAR refugees "nightmare with few equivalents"', *Al-Jazeera*, 3 August 2014, available at: <http://www.aljazeera.com/news/africa/2014/07/car-refugees-nightmare-cameroon-2014722162920424272.html>.

[7] 'Syria crisis: Damascaus al-Yarmouk camp attacked', BBC News, 16 December 2012, see: <http://www.bbc.co.uk/news/world-middle-east-20747485>.

According to this article, at least eight individuals died during this particular attack. It also reports that twenty people were killed in August 2012 during a mortar attack on the camp.

[8] 'Emptied Yarmouk Camp Shows Devastation in Wake of ISIS Attack', NBC News, 6 April 2015, see: <http://www.nbcnews.com/news/world/emptied-yarmouk-camp-shows-devastation-wake-isis-attack-n336666>.

[9] Shaheen, K., 'UN warns situation in Damascus refugee camp is "beyond inhumane"', *The Guardian*, 6 April 2015, see: <http://www.theguardian.com/world/2015/apr/06/un-warns-situation-damascus-palestinian-refugee-camp-beyond-inhumane>.

Different numbers have been reported, 'Emptied Yarmouk Camp Shows Devastation in Wake of ISIS Attack', NBC News, 6 April 2015, see: <http://www.nbcnews.com/news/world/emptied-yarmouk-camp-shows-devastation-wake-isis-attack-n336666>.

This Article states that Yarmouk was the home of 500,000 Palestinians before the conflict began in 2011.

people', many of whom are seeking refuge from ongoing armed conflicts, such as those present in Syria or Libya, from countries that are still suffering from the consequences of past conflicts, such as Iraq or Eritrea.[10] In 2014, it was reported that over 218,000 migrants crossed the Mediterranean and reached European shores, mainly Italian ones.[11] However, many of those attempting to cross the Mediterranean do not survive. Between January and April 2015, the dangerous crossing is believed to have already made more than 1,500 victims at sea.[12] On 19 April, the worst capsizing on record made an estimated 800 casualties, which led EU leaders to hold a summit to discuss the allocation of more resources for search and rescue missions, as well as some pilot project for resettlement.[13] The approach of the UNHCR is more comprehensive as it seeks cooperation with European States through its Central Mediterranean Sea Initiative (CMSI), which includes measures to be taken not only within the European Union, but also in transit or first asylum countries, and in countries of origin.[14] At State level, Italy has been particularly active with its patrolling of the Mediterranean, as part of its Operation Mare Nostrum (now replaced by Operation Triton), set up after the 2013 shipwreck off the coast of Lampedusa which cost the lives of more than 350 African asylum seekers.[15]

Crossing a border is of course not the last hurdle for those fleeing a conflict to another State. Asylum seekers are likely to face many uncertainties in their transit country, from which they may have difficulties continuing their journey onto a third State or returning to their home country.[16]

From the hosting State perspective, capacity issues often arise for States on the front lines of refugee crises as they share a border with another State on which territory there is an armed conflict. For example, as a result of the war in Syria, over 3 million individuals are reported to have fled to neighbouring Turkey, Lebanon, Jordan, and Iraq.[17] Absorbing a

[10] Note that the UNHCR's 2014 High Commissioner's Dialogue, an informal policy discussion forum, was focused on 'Protection at Sea', see: <http://www.unhcr.org/5486e6b56.html>.

[11] '2015 UNHCR subregional operations profile—Northern, Western, Central and Southern Europe', UNHCR, see: <http://www.unhcr.org/pages/49e48e996.html>.

See also the website for the CMSI at: <http://www.unhcr.org/531990199.html>.

[12] Yardley, J., 'Rising Toll on Migrants Leaves Europe in Crisis; 900 May Be Dead at Sea', *New York Times*, 20 April 2015, available at: <http://www.nytimes.com/2015/04/21/world/europe/european-union-immigration-migrant-ship-capsizes.html>.

[13] 'Mediterranean migrants crisis: EU leaders gather for talks', *BBC News*, 23 April 2015, available at: <http://www.bbc.co.uk/news/world-europe-32435230>.

[14] The CMSI action plan is available at: <http://www.unhcr.org/531990199.html>.

[15] Operation Mare Nostrum was replaced by Operation Triton on 1 November 2014. While Operation Mare Nostrum was undertaken solely by Italy, Operation Triton is conducted by Frontex, the EU's border security agency, with Italy controlling it, see the press release from the European Commission, 7 October 2014, available at: <http://europa.eu/rapid/press-release_MEMO-14-566_en.htm>.

[16] See, for example, Amnesty International, 2015, *'Libya is Full of Cruelty' – Stories of Abduction, Sexual Violence and Abuse from Migrants and Refugees*, available at: <https://www.amnesty.org/en/documents/mde19/1578/2015/en>.

[17] See the 'Syrian refugees' website which cites the UNHCR at: <http://syrianrefugees.eu/>.

mass influx of refugees has been an enormous challenge for those States, putting the stability of the entire region in jeopardy. Lebanon, which counts over a million Syrian refugees for a total population of less than 4.5 million, has the highest refugee to citizen ratio in the world. As a result, it has had difficulties integrating its refugee population into its existing infrastructures, such as its education system.[18] This has in turn led its government to adopt new regulations at the beginning of 2015 in order to limit admission of Syrian nationals.[19]

Mass displacement as a result of wars may also be problematic for States that are further afield from conflict zones. For example, the number of asylum applications received in 2014 in European Union (EU) Member States has risen by 25% compared to the same period in 2013, in part as a result of the ongoing Syrian conflict and the second Libyan civil war. By October 2014, close to 150,000 Syrians had sought asylum in the European Union, with Member States continuing to pledge for additional resettlement spots, the vast majority of which being pledged by Germany.[20] In addition to a large number of Syrians, there are also a sizeable arrival into the EU of asylum seekers of Afghan or Eritrean origin, which are countries that are still recovering from past conflicts. Thus the impacts of conflicts on cross-border displacement can often be felt long after the end of hostilities.

For host nations, no matter where there are situated, integrating refugees into its own population can have dramatic budgetary repercussions. In April 2014, the EU adopted the Asylum, Migration and Integration Fund (AMIF), representing a commitment of over €3 billion for the period 2014–20, in order to complement its Member States' domestic budgets to improve their asylum systems, reception modalities, and integration policies.[21] Large movements of population as a consequence of wars also have implications for the foreign aid budgets of the world's donor nations.

This chapter seeks to frame the issues mentioned above within the legal frameworks currently applicable to those fleeing States affected by armed conflicts. It also considers how legal provisions and judicial mechanisms have been used recently to resolve some of those issues. The focus is here on refugees, i.e., individuals who have been forcibly displaced across an international border and have obtained some form of international protection (such as the refugee status), and asylum seekers, i.e., individuals who have

It is estimated that only 70,000 offers of resettlements have been made, although 3 million Syrians are in need of such opportunities.

[18] See the UN Secretary-General's Report on Children in armed conflict, A/68/878-S/2014/339 of 15 May 2014, para. 90 where it states that Lebanon has enrolled more than 102,000 Syrian children in its public school system. It is available at: <http://www.un.org/ga/search/view_doc.asp?symbol=a/68/878>.

[19] See the UNHCR, 'Syrian Refugees in Lebanon Snapshot', January-March 2015, available at: <http://data.unhcr.org/syrianrefugees/country.php?id=122>.

[20] Out of pledges to resettle about 33,000 Syrians (reported in October 2014), 85% of these spots were pledged by Germany, see: <http://syrianrefugees.eu/>.

[21] More information about AMIF is available at: <http://ec.europa.eu/dgs/home-affairs/financing/fundings/migration-asylum-borders/asylum-migration-integration-fund/index_en.htm>.

also been forcibly displaced across borders but who have not yet obtained the refugee status. It does not consider the specific issues associated with internal displacement, which is the object of another chapter;[22] however, it will point to some legal provisions which are applicable to all displaced persons, no matter if an international border has been crossed or not.

A. **International refugee law**

International refugee law aims to protect individuals seeking asylum from persecution and those who have been formally recognized as refugees with a specific set of provisions. Fleeing an armed conflict is neither a requirement nor a guarantee to be recognized as a refugee. Although refugee law overlaps with international human rights law and humanitarian law, it is here considered separately. The way international human rights law and humanitarian law protect asylum seekers and refugees is considered thereafter.

Refugee law has been enshrined in treaties, notably the United Nations Convention Relating to the Status of Refugees ('1951 Refugee Convention') and its Optional Protocol Relating to the Status of Refugees ('1967 Optional Protocol').[23] The Convention was adopted to respond to the cross-border movements of population which were the result of the Second World War. Although it was meant to address the situation of individuals having been displaced because of a war, it was not drafted in a manner that would allow all war-affected migrants to obtain the refugee status and the rights associated with it. Its scope of application was restricted in various ways. In particular, it was limited temporarily as it was only applicable in relation to events which occurred before 1 January 1951. Furthermore, contracting States could also limit the application of the Convention geographically to events which occurred in Europe only.[24]

Following a new refugee crisis in the late 1950s and early 1960s, there was a need to broaden the temporal and geographical scopes of the 1951 Refugee Convention, which led to the adoption of the 1967 Optional Protocol. While the temporal limitation was removed entirely, contracting States could retain the geographical limitation to events which occurred in Europe if they wished to do so.[25] Both of these binding instruments

[22] See Chapter 15 of this book, Marina Mattirolo, 'Protection of the Internally Displaced in Armed Conflict in 2014: A Critical Review of Law and Practice'.

[23] The 1951 Refugee Convention, which entered into force on 22 April 1954, was adopted by UNGA Resolution 429 (V) of 14 December 1950, while the 1967 Optional Protocol, which entered into force on 4 October 1967, was adopted with UNGA Resolution 2198 (XXI) of 16 December 1967.

[24] Art. 1B(1) of the 1951 Refugee Convention.

[25] Art. 1(2) and (3) of the 1967 Optional Protocol.

have been widely ratified, with 145 States being party to the 1951 Refugee Convention and 146 States being party to the 1967 Optional Protocol.[26]

SCOPE OF APPLICATION: WHO IS A REFUGEE?

The 1951 Refugee Convention first establishes the requirements that asylum seekers need to fulfil in order to be recognized as refugees by providing a definition of the term 'refugee'.

According to its Article 1(A)2, a 'refugee' is any person who:

> ... owing to well-founded fear of being persecuted for reasons of race, religion, nationality, membership of a particular social group or political opinion, is outside the country of his nationality and is unable or, owing to such fear, is unwilling to avail himself of the protection of that country; or who, not having a nationality and being outside the country of his former habitual residence as a result of such events, is unable or, owing to such fear, is unwilling to return to it.

According to this definition, there are three key requirements for someone to qualify as a refugee. The first requirement is the presence of a well-founded fear of persecution. Although the 1951 Refugee Convention does not explain what constitutes persecution, some indications as to its meaning may be inferred from a look at other articles of the Convention. For example, Article 31(1) states that no penalties should be imposed on 'refugees who, coming directly from a territory where their life or freedom was threatened', referring to the definition contained in Article 1, which includes the risk of persecution. Article 33(1) provides for the principle of non-refoulement, according to which a refugee cannot be returned to the State 'where his life or freedom would be threatened'. Therefore, a fear of persecution, as enshrined in the 1951 Refugee Convention, may include a fear of a violation of one's right to life or right to liberty. However, persecution is not necessarily limited to facing serious risks to life or liberty but may extend to risks of other human rights violations, including a violation of the principles of equality and non-discrimination.[27] Therefore, the term persecution must be understood not only by reading other Convention articles, but also through a consideration of human rights treaties,[28] the EU Qualification Directive,[29] the domestic asylum laws which have

[26] The full texts of the treaties and more information regarding their ratification is available on the website of the UNHCR at: <http://www.unhcr.org/pages/49da0e466.html>.

[27] A definition of 'persecute' given by the Merriam-Webster dictionary is 'to treat (someone) cruelly or unfairly especially because of race or religious or political beliefs', see: <http://www.merriam-webster.com/dictionary/persecute>.

[28] With regard to human rights treaties, see, for example, Arts 1 and 3 of the 1984 Convention against Torture, Art. 3 of the 1966 International Covenant on Civil and Political Rights, Art. 5 of the 1969 American Convention on Human Rights, or the Preamble, and Arts 2, 3, and 5 of the 1981 African Charter of Human and Peoples' Rights.

[29] Art. 9 of EU Directive 2011/95/EU of the European Parliament and of the Council of 13 December 2011 (recast).

implemented the 1951 Refugee Convention,[30] the relevant case law, as well as other authoritative publications.[31] What is clear is that persecution implies serious human rights violation(s), as the result of systemic mistreatment or an isolated act of torture.

In addition, the fear of persecution must be based on one (or more) of the following grounds: 'race, religion, nationality, membership of a particular social group or political opinion'. For example, in a case before the Attica Regional Asylum Office in Greece,[32] an applicant who had fled Syria was granted refugee status because, as a Christian he was considered an enemy of both parties to the conflict. Furthermore, the Syrian State was likely to consider him as a political opponent to the regime as he had lived abroad. Thus his chances of being arrested and mistreated upon return were deemed reasonable.

The formulation adopted in the 1951 Refugee Convention was based on the prohibition of discrimination, which had already been adopted in Article 2 of the Universal Declaration of Human Rights and Article 14 of the 1950 European Convention on Human Rights.[33] However, the 1951 Refugee Convention omitted some of the grounds for discrimination covered by those two instruments, such as sex or language, as it was originally drafted to protect a specific category of persons, i.e., Jews fleeing Nazi Germany.

The second requirement for someone to qualify as a refugee is being outside his or her country of nationality or outside the country of his or her former habitual residence. Therefore, the 1951 Refugee Convention does not apply to IDPs as an international border must have been crossed by the person who has been forcibly displaced.

According to the third requirement, to be considered a refugee one must be unable or unwilling, owing to a well-founded fear of being persecuted, to benefit from the protection of his or her country of nationality or former habitual residence.[34] States have an obligation to protect all individuals under their jurisdiction against human rights abuses, including those that may be considered to amount to persecution. While a State's government itself shall not carry out acts amounting to persecution, it must also ensure

[30] For example, for an analysis of US law, see Alexander Aleinikoff, T., 1991, 'The Meaning of 'Persecution in United States Asylum Law', *Int J Refugee Law*, vol. 3, no. 1: pp. 5–29.

[31] See, for example, Hathaway, J., 1991, *The Law of Refugee Status*, Butterworth, Toronto.

[32] *GT [2013] Application No. 95/000186182* (24 October 2013), Attica Regional Asylum Office (Greece), available at: <http://www.asylumlawdatabase.eu/en/case-law/greece-attica-regional-asylum-office-24-october-2013-gt-2013-application-no-95000186182#content>.

[33] The prohibition of discrimination was thereafter also enshrined in other human rights treaties such as the 1966 International Covenant on Civil and Political Rights (Art. 2), the 1969 American Convention on Human Rights (Art. 1), and the 1981 African Charter of Human and Peoples' Rights (Art. 2).

[34] The consideration of a 'well-founded' fear of persecution with regard to individuals having fled an armed conflict was considered by the Slovakian Migration Office in *A. A. S. v Ministry of the Interior of the Slovak Republic*, 10Sža/18/2013 (21 August 2013), which deemed that the fear must be real and not fictional. Its decision is available at: <http://www.asylumlawdatabase.eu/en/case-law/slovakia-migration-office-21-august-2013-aas-v-ministry-interior-slovak-republic#content>.

that non-State actors, including non-State armed groups, do not carry out such acts.[35] Any evidence of a lack of State protection from certain human rights abuses, including those committed by non-State actors, may assist in determining the likelihood of persecution and the legitimacy ('well-founded') of a fear thereof.

In addition to defining refugees, a few distinctions should also be made. For example, an 'asylum seeker' is someone who has applied for asylum but whose refugee status has not yet been granted. The qualification of 'statelessness' applies to persons who are not considered as nationals by any State but who have not generally been displaced across a border.[36] Finally, refugees are different from 'migrants', a term which refers to individuals who have chosen to move in order to improve their living conditions, such as 'economic migrants' who seek better work opportunities.

APPLYING INTERNATIONAL REFUGEE LAW TO WAR REFUGEES

Given the above requirements, the 1951 Refugee Convention is, in principle, not applicable to individuals who have crossed an international border to escape a situation of generalized violence, even if such situation amount to an armed conflict. Anyone wishing to benefit from the protection afforded by the 1951 Refugee Convention must fulfil these three requirements, including a well-founded fear of persecution. However, many of those individuals who have been forcibly displaced across borders are fleeing ongoing armed conflicts or the consequences of past hostilities, which often entail the destruction of their homes, means of subsistence, and all the infrastructure necessary for them to enjoy their rights. While there may be situations, notably in conflicts with an ethnic dimension, where individuals are fleeing because of a fear of persecution based on their 'race, religion, nationality or membership of a particular social group', as required under the 1951 Refugee Convention, this is not always the case.

In order to fill this gap left by the 1951 Refugee Convention and its Optional Protocol, additional instruments providing for refugee protection were adopted at the regional

[35] See, for example, Art. 2(1) of the Convention Against Torture, which states that 'Each State Party shall take effective legislative, administrative, judicial or other measures to prevent acts of torture in any territory under its jurisdiction'.

[36] Therefore, stateless persons are not included in the figure of 51.2 million forcibly displaced people. There are an estimated 10.5 million stateless people worldwide but this is difficult to assess with precision, see 'World Refugee Day: Global forced displacement tops 50 million for first time in post-World War II era', UNHCR, News Stories, 20 June 2014, available at: <http://www.unhcr.org/53a155bc6.html>.

Note that the 1954 Convention relating to the Status of Stateless Persons and the 1961 Convention on the Reduction of Statelessness have been adopted specifically to address the issues associated with statelessness.

level.[37] Both the 1969 Convention Governing the Specific Aspects of Refugee Problems in Africa (OAU Refugee Convention), which was adopted by the Organization of African Unity,[38] and the non-binding 1984 Cartagena Declaration on Refugees, applicable for the Central American area, expand their definitions of refugees to include persons fleeing armed conflicts or other situations of violence, in addition to the category of persons already protected under the 1951 Refugee Convention.[39] Thus, according to Article 1(2) of the 1969 OAU Convention a refugee is also someone who 'owing to external aggression, occupation, foreign domination or events seriously disturbing public order in either part or the whole of his country of origin or nationality, is compelled to leave his place of habitual residence in order to seek refuge in another place outside his country of origin or nationality'.[40] According to Article 3 of the Cartagena Declaration refugees are also those 'who have fled their country because their lives, safety, or freedom have been threatened by generalized violence, foreign aggression, internal conflicts, massive violation of human rights or other circumstances which have seriously disturbed public order'.[41] A similar understanding of the term 'refugee' was also adopted by the Asian–African Legal Consultative Organization in its 1966 Bangkok Principles on the Status and Treatment of Refugees,[42] as well as by the League of Arab States in its 1994 Arab Convention on Regulating Status of Refugees in the Arab Countries.[43] A broader understanding of the causes behind the flight of refugees was necessary in those regions given the large-scale displacement resulting from armed conflicts.

[37] In addition to the texts mentioned, the Council of Europe adopted in 1976 Recommendation 773 on the situation of de facto refugees, recognizing the inherent limitations of the 1951 Refugee Convention and thus calling its Member States to apply its definition of 'refugee' liberally.

[38] The Organization of African Unity was replaced by the African Union in 2002.

[39] The OAU Refugee Convention (1001 UNTS 45), adopted on 10 September 1969 and entered into force on 20 June 1974, counts forty-five State parties; its ratification table is available at: <http://www.achpr.org/instruments/refugee-convention/ratification/>.

The Cartagena Declaration on Refugees was adopted by the Colloquium on the International Protection of Refugees in Central America, Mexico, and Panama on 22 November 1984. Although it is not a binding instrument, it has been incorporated in several domestic laws. Furthermore, in December 2014, thirty years after the adoption of the Cartagena Declaration, the Brazil Declaration and Plan of Action was adopted by twenty-eight countries and three territories of Latin America and the Caribbean, to promote the highest standards of protection and implement innovative solutions for refugees in the region.

[40] Art. 1(1) of the OAU Refugee Convention.

[41] Art. III (3) of the Cartagena Declaration on Refugees.

[42] Art. I(2) of the Bangkok Principles states that a refugee is also 'every person, who owing to external aggression, occupation, foreign domination or events seriously disturbing public order in either part of the whole of his country of origin or nationality, is compelled to leave his place of habitual residence in order to seek refuge in another place outside his country of origin or nationality'.

[43] Its Art. I states that a refugee is also ' any person who unwillingly takes refuge in a country other than his country of origin or his habitual place of residence because of sustained aggression against, occupation and foreign domination of such country …'.

The refugee protection was also expanded within the EU Framework with the adoption of the Qualification Directive in 2004 and the recast Qualification Directive in 2011.[44] Although both Directives embrace the narrow definition of refugee,[45] as contained in the 1951 Refugee Convention, a complementary form of protection is afforded, under certain conditions, to those persons who have fled a war-caused generalized violence.[46] This 'subsidiary protection' is provided to those who do not fall under the refugee definition but who are believed to 'face a real risk of suffering serious harm' if returned to his or her country of origin or former habitual residence.[47] The Directives define 'serious harm' as either the death penalty or execution, torture or inhuman or degrading treatment or punishment, or serious and individual threat to a civilian's life or person by reason of indiscriminate violence in situations of international or internal armed conflict.[48] For example, in *MOJ & Ors (Return to Mogadishu) Somalia CG v Secretary of State for the Home Department*,[49] the Immigration and Asylum Chamber of the United Kingdom Upper Tribunal assessed the levels of conflict in Mogadishu and found that they did not amount to 'a serious and individual threat to a civilian's life or person by reason of indiscriminate violence in a situation of international or internal armed conflict' under the Qualification Directive.[50] With regard to an applicant from Afghanistan, a Hungarian court granted subsidiary protection holding that, although

[44] Council Directive 2004/83/EC (Qualification Directive), on minimum standards for the qualification and status of third country nationals or stateless persons as refugees or as persons who otherwise need international protection and the content of the protection granted, was adopted on 29 April 2004. On 13 December 2011, the EU adopted the recast Qualification Directive (2011/95/EU), applicable to all EU Member States except Denmark, Ireland, and the United Kingdom, which all remain bound by the 2004 Directive. The recast Qualification Directive was adopted to harmonize the eligibility requirements and the content of the protection among EU Member States.

[45] Art. 2(e) of the Qualification Directive and Art. 2(d) of the recast Qualification Directive.

[46] Art. 2(c) of the Qualification Directive and Art. 2(f) of the recast Qualification Directive.

[47] Art. 2(c) of the Qualification Directive and Art. 2(f) of the recast Qualification Directive. Note that the term 'humanitarian protection' has been adopted in the United Kingdom in lieu of 'subsidiary protection'.

[48] Art. 15 of the Qualification Directive and the recast Qualification Directive.

In Case C-285/12 *Diakité v Commissaire général aux réfugiés et aux apatrides* (30 January 2014), the Belgium Conseil d'État (Council of State) requested a preliminary ruling from the Court of Justice in order to ascertain whether the interpretation to be given to the concept of 'internal armed conflict' as referred to in Directive 2004/83 must be independent of the definition used in international humanitarian law and, if so, what are the requirements for a situation to be covered by it. The judgment of the CJEU is available at: <http://curia.europa.eu/juris/document/document.jsf?text=&docid=147061&pageIndex=0&doclang=en&mode=req&dir=&occ=first&part=1&cid=505934>.

[49] *MOJ & Ors (Return to Mogadishu) Somalia CG* [2014] UKUT 00442 (3 October 2014), available at: <http://www.bailii.org/uk/cases/UKUT/IAC/2014/%5B2014%5D_UKUT_442_iac.html>.

The UKUT was referring to Art. 15c of the Qualification Directive.

[50] See also the case of *M. A. N. v Ministry of the Interior of the Slovak Republic, 4Saz/2/2013* (29 May 2013), Slovakia—Kosice Regional Court, available at: <http://www.asylumlawdatabase.eu/en/case-law/slovakia-ma-n-v-ministry-interior-slovak-republic-29-may-2013-4saz22013>.

the country information was neither consistent nor coherent, the risk of serious harm was present as a consequence of indiscriminate violence in a situation of internal armed conflict, including in Kabul.[51]

Thus, under the EU system, if an individual comes from an area where there is indiscriminate violence, such as the one generated by the Syrian armed conflict, he or she must thus be granted the subsidiary protection as provided for in the Qualification Directive. However, if an individual, who comes from a conflict zone is also at personal risk of persecution, he or she may be granted the refugee status.[52] In a case before the Belgium Council for Alien Law Litigation,[53] it was decided that a Syrian national of Kurdish origin, who had sought refugee status on the grounds of his political involvement in the Syrian Kurdish Democratic Party, should not be confined to subsidiary protection as a result of the conflict in Syria but should be granted the refugee status as a result of his political activities.

Moreover, certain States have also adopted an expansive definition of the term refugee or have developed administrative or legislative measures to protect persons fleeing armed conflict specifically.

LIMITATIONS ON ELIGIBILITY FOR REFUGEE STATUS

In addition to the above-mentioned requirements that one needs to fulfil in order to be eligible to be granted refugee protection, the 1951 Refugee Convention includes a number of exclusion clauses. This is the case of those individuals who, at the time of the 1951 Convention, were already receiving protection or assistance from another organ or agency of the United Nations than the UNHCR, at the time the Convention was adopted.[54] This was mostly applicable to Koreans receiving aid from the United Nations Korean Reconstruction Agency (UNKRA) and Palestinians receiving aid

[51] *S. M. A. v Office of Immigration and Nationality (OIN), 20.K.31072/2013/9* (23 May 2013), Administrative and Labour Court of Budapest (Hungary, available at: <http://www.asylumlawdatabase.eu/en/case-law/hungary-administrative-and-labour-court-budapest-23-may-2013-sma-v-office-immigration-and#content>.

For another case regarding an Afghan applicant, where specific regional situations of conflict are discussed, see *10 C 15.12* (31 January 2013), Federal Administrative Court (Germany), available at: <http://www.asylumlawdatabase.eu/en/case-law/germany-federal-administrative-court-31-january-2013-10-c-1512#content>.

[52] There is thus a hierarchy of status as the relevant authority first checks if someone qualifies to be recognized as a refugee and, if not, considers if this person can be granted the subsidiary protection.

[53] CCE, arrêt n°103921 (30 May 2013), Belgium—Council for Alien Law Litigation, available at: <http://www.asylumlawdatabase.eu/en/case-law/belgium-council-alien-law-litigation-30-may-2013-no-103921#content>.

[54] Article 1 (D) of the 1951 Refugee Convention.

from the United Nations Relief and Works Agency for Palestine Refugees in the Near East (UNRWA), for which it continues to apply.[55] Another exclusion clause applies to persons who are given the same rights and obligations as nationals in their State of refuge.[56] Finally, the 1951 Refugee Convention does not apply to persons who are seriously believed to have committed a war crime or another serious crime.[57] The case law concerned with this particular exclusion clause is the object of Chapter 12 in this volume.[58]

In addition to the above-mentioned limitations, the refugee status is also meant to be limited to particular circumstances. It can thus be considered temporary, concluding when the situation that led to someone being recognized a refugee has ceased to exist.[59]

THE RIGHTS OF REFUGEES AND THE OBLIGATIONS OF STATES

Being granted the refugee status under the 1951 Convention means benefiting from its system of protection, which includes a number of specific rights for the refugees, as well as obligations for its State parties.

Rights of refugees

Non-refoulement principle. One of the most important rights provided under the 1951 Refugee Convention is the right not to be forcibly returned where the individual's 'life or freedom would be threatened on account of his race, religion, nationality, membership of a particular social group or political opinion'. This is known as the 'non-refoulement' principle, which is now considered part of customary international law and therefore binding on all States, whether they are a party to the Convention or not.[60] It has also been incorporated in several international human rights treaties,[61] as well as in the Fourth Geneva

[55] See UNHCR, *Handbook on Procedures for Determining Refugee Status under the 1951 Convention & the 1967 Protocol relating to the Status of Refugees*, first published in 1979 and re-issued in 2011, para 142, available at: <http://www.unhcr.org/3d58e13b4.html>.

According to para. 143, Palestinian refugees living in areas where the UNRWA does not operate are eligible for refugee status under the 1951 Refugee Convention.

[56] Art. 1(E) of the 1951 Refugee Convention.

[57] Art. 1(F) of the 1951 Refugee Convention.

[58] Ilia-Maria Siatitsa, '12. National Trials of International Crimes in 2014: Prosecuting 'Refugees' suspected of International Crimes'.

[59] Art. 1(C)(5) of the 1951 Refugee Convention.

[60] Art. 33(1) of the 1951 Refugee Convention.

[61] Art. 3 of the Convention Against Torture prohibits the forcible removal of persons to a country where there is a real risk of torture; see also Art. 7 of the International Covenant on Civil and Political Rights (Art. 7), Art. 8 of the Declaration on the Protection of All Persons from Enforced Disappearance, or Principle 5 of the Principles on the Effective Prevention and Investigation of Extra-Legal, Arbitrary and Summary Executions.

Convention of 1949.[62] The principle of non-refoulement is also prohibited in a number of regional human rights instruments, either explicitly or through interpretation.[63]

In *EM (Eritrea), R (on the app of) v Secretary of State for the Home Department*,[64] the UK Supreme Court stated that, while the asylum seeker must prove the risk of ill-treatment upon removal to a particular country, there is no requirement that the risk of ill-treatment be systematic.

Non-refoulement applies with regard to everyone seeking refuge, including asylum seekers, with the exception of those, such as terrorists, who can be reasonably believed to represent a danger for the security of the country where they are situated.[65] One does not need to have been granted the refugee status to benefit from it. When this principle is violated or threatens to be, the UNHCR intervenes with the relevant authorities, and, if necessary, will inform the public. In some circumstances, persons facing refoulement may have recourse to relevant human rights mechanisms, as non-refoulement is a principle which has also been enshrined under international human rights law, as discussed below. Importantly, the ECHR and the Convention Against Torture, which both link the prohibition of torture with the principle of non-refoulement, have a broader understanding of non-refoulement than the 1951 Refugee Convention as they extend it to everyone, including those presenting a security concern such as terrorists.[66]

Other rights. Under the 1951 Refugee Convention,[67] refugees have other specific rights including the right not to be punished for illegal entry into the territory of a contracting State (Article 31), the right not to be expelled unless strict conditions are met (Article 32), the right to public relief and assistance (Article 23), and the right to be issued identity and travel documents (Articles 27 and 28).

The 1951 Refugee Convention also contains a number of rights which were later enshrined in human rights treaties, including both civil and political rights, such as the right to freedom of religion (Article 4), the right to freedom of movement within the territory (Article 26), the right to access the courts (Article 16), and rights falling with the category of economic and social rights, such as the right to work (Articles 17–19), the right to housing (Article 21), and the right to education (Article 22). However, the 1951

[62] Art. 45(4) of the Fourth Geneva Convention relative to the Protection of Civilian Persons in Time of War, 12 August 1949.

[63] Art. 3 of the European Convention for the Protection of Human Rights and Fundamental Freedoms, Art. 22 of the American Convention on Human Rights, Art. II of the OAU Refugee Convention, and Art. 2 of the Cairo Declaration on the Protection of Refugees and Displaced Persons in the Arab World (Art. 2).

[64] *EM (Eritrea), R (on the app of) v. Secretary of State for the Home Department* [2014] UKSC 12 (19 February 2014), available at: <http://www.bailii.org/uk/cases/UKSC/2014/12.html>.

[65] Art. 33(2) of the 1951 Refugee Convention.

[66] See Art. 3 ECHR and Art. 3 CAT Convention.

[67] Note that, as already mentioned, the 1967 Protocol only extended the temporal and geographical scopes of the 1951 Refugee Convention. Thus, it contains the same rights.

Refugee Convention does not provide any explanation as to the content of these rights but, rather, provides that refugees must be treated in the same way as nationals in relation to them, or, with regard to certain aspects of these rights, at least as other foreign nationals. Therefore, it is necessary to know what rights nationals do enjoy within a particular legal system in order to understand what rights belong to refugees situated on the same territory. In particular, it is useful to consider the relevant international human rights obligations of the State in question, as discussed below.

States may grant those rights to refugees who do not fall within the 1951 Refugee Convention, in particular if they have adopted an expansive definition of the term refugee. Thus, refugees from armed conflicts, although they do not necessarily fear persecution, may benefit from a form of international protection. This is for example the case within the EU, where the Qualification Directive afford a subsidiary protection to asylum seekers originating from conflict zones, as already mentioned above.

Obligations of States

While States have no obligation to grant asylum,[68] State parties to the 1951 Convention have nevertheless a number of obligations, such as cooperating with the UNHCR in the exercise of its functions, including with its supervision of its implementation.[69] The 1951 Refugee Convention also exempts States from having to provide reciprocity, according to which, if State A grants a particular right to the citizens of State B, then State B should be granting the same right to the citizens of State A. The principle of reciprocity does not apply in relation to refugees because they do not enjoy the protection of their rights in their home country in the first place.

In addition, States must provide information to the UN Secretary-General regarding the domestic laws and regulations they may adopt to implement the Convention. The 1951 Convention does not define how States parties should determine whether an individual meets the requirements to be considered a refugee. Instead, asylum proceedings and refugee status determinations must be established at the domestic level. States are thus able to develop asylum policies in accordance with their own concerns, including economic stability or national security, for example. This has resulted in important disparities with regard to requirements, evaluation processes, as well as deadlines, which render certain jurisdictions more favourable to asylum claimants than others. For example, Syrian refugees have so far been accepted by Lebanon with few limitations while Jordan has confined most of them in camps and prohibited them to work.[70]

[68] Note however that Art. 18 of the EU Charter mentions the right to asylum (and not just the right *to seek* asylum).

[69] Art. 35 of the Refugee Convention and Art. II of the 1967 Protocol.

[70] For a summary of the treatment of refugees from Syria into neighbouring countries, see 'The fractured response of humanitarian aid in Syria', *Insight on Conflict*, 1 May 2015, available at: <http://www.insightonconflict.org/2015/05/fractured-response-humanitarian-aid-syria/>.

In any case, State parties to the 1951 Convention must grant the refugee status to asylum seekers which fit the refugee definition, which means that they are outside of their country of nationality and have a well-founded fear of being persecuted on one of the grounds mentioned in Article 1 of the Convention. This means that the decision maker must take into account both subjective and objective elements. Objective elements include facts deriving from the legal and policy frameworks of the State from which protection is sought, as well as country reports from NGOs, for example. In a case before the Swedish Migration Court of Appeal, a stateless Palestinian woman from Syria was recognized as a refugee as she was deemed not to have the option to return, following an assessment of the security situation resulting from the internal armed conflict in Syria.[71] Subjective elements entail the personal characteristics of the asylum seeker, such as gender, age, or family background. A credibility assessment is often conducted, which leads to major differences in the percentage of status granted, not only from one country to the next, but also, possibly, from one office to the next.[72]

As already mentioned, number of causes may warrant a refusal to grant asylum seekers the refugee status. These include participation in terrorist activities or commission of crimes against humanity or other particularly serious crimes. War crimes are another possible cause for exclusion. However, in general, asylum procedures are not entirely clear and objective processes.

When there is a mass movement as a result of a war, it is often not feasible to conduct individual asylum assessments in a timely manner and the reasons for fleeing are generally evident. In such circumstances, States may decide to declare groups of individuals 'prima facie' refugees. This means that they may lower the standards of proof with regard to the determination of the refugee status.[73] While States are still meant to conduct individual assessments, this determination method ensures that the asylum process is time efficient.

Despite some inevitable disparities among asylum procedures, each State should ensure that its procedure abides by the rule of law, a principle which includes equal treatment, a timely and fair process, as well as an effective remedy if their application is rejected.[74] Some States detain any individual that has crossed its borders illegally.

[71] *UM 1590-13* (26 November 2013), Sweden—Migration Court of Appeal, available at: <http://www.asylumlawdatabase.eu/en/case-law/sweden-migration-court-appeal-26-november-2013-um-1590-13#content>.

[72] See, for example, Ramji-Nogales, J., Schoenholtz, A., and Schrag, P. G., 2008, 'Refugee Roulette: Disparities in Asylum Adjudication', Stanford Law Review, vol. 60; Temple University Legal Studies Research Paper No. 2007-12, available at: <http://ssrn.com/abstract=983946>.

[73] For information on State practice with regard to 'prima facie' determination, see, for example, Albert, M., 2010, 'Prima Facie Determination of Refugee Status', Working Paper Series No. 55, Refugee Studies Centre Oxford University, January, available at: <http://www.rsc.ox.ac.uk/files/publications/working-paper-series/wp55-prima-facie-determination-refugee-status-2010.pdf>.

[74] For example, the EU provides for the right to an effective remedy in Art. 46 of Directive 2013/32/EU, which is available at: <http://eur-lex.europa.eu/legal-content/EN/TXT/?uri=CELEX:32013L0032>.

Immigration detention can be extremely problematic, in particular when there is no time limit associated with the detention, where the possibility of judicial review is missing, and where conditions of detention are inadequate. Several countries have a system of mandatory detention for all individuals arriving without a valid visa, including those seeking asylum from persecution.[75] In order to ensure that their asylum processes abide by the rule of law, States should adopt the necessary procedural safeguards. In the case of immigration detention, it means, for example, ensuring that detainees have access to judicial review and that there is a time limit to the period of detention.[76]

While the EU has tried to harmonize the requirements to benefit from international protection and the rights belonging to those who have applied for international protection,[77] it has also attempted to streamline the decision-making process with regard to the asylum procedures in place within its Member States. The Dublin system, which establishes the Member State responsible for examining asylum claims, has been heavily criticized for not being favourable to asylum seekers, such as by causing delays, encouraging the use of detention, and supporting their transfer to States with deficient asylum procedures.[78] In accordance with the Asylum Procedures Directive, which establishes minimum standards for granting refugee status within the EU, an application for asylum may be deemed inadmissible if the country of

According to its para. 5, this includes the right 'to remain in the territory until the time limit within which to exercise their right to an effective remedy has expired and, when such a right has been exercised within the time limit, pending the outcome of the remedy.'

[75] This is, for example, the case in Australia where any non-citizen who has entered the territory without a valid visa must be detained according to the Migration Act 1958 (Cth) (Migration Act), see the website of the Australian Human Rights Commission at: <https://www.humanrights.gov.au/our-work/asylum-seekers-and-refugees/projects/immigration-detention-and-human-rights>.

[76] See Fordham, M., QC, Stefanelli, J. N., and Eser, S., 2013, *Immigration Detention and the Rule of Law—Safeguarding Principles*, Bingham Centre for the Rule of Law, available at: <http://www.biicl.org/bingham-centre/news/immigrationdetention/safeguardingprinciples>.

See also UNHCR, 2012, *Detention Guidelines—guidelines on the Applicable Criteria and Standards relating to the Detention of Asylum-Seekers and Alternatives to Detention*, available at: <http://www.unhcr.org/505b10ee9.html>.

As mentioned below, IHRL also protects asylum seekers from arbitrary detention.

[77] See the recast Qualification Directive and the EU Directive 2013/33/EU laying down standards for the reception of applicants for international protection (recast).

[78] The Dublin system includes the Dublin III Regulation (No 604/2013), which replaces the Dublin Convention and Dublin II Regulation, applies to all EU Member States except Denmark, and the EURODAC Regulation, which establishes a Europe-wide fingerprinting database for unauthorized entrants to the EU. In *M.S.S. v Belgium and Greece*, App. no. 30696/09, ECtHR (21 January 2011), it was decided that Belgium, which had sent asylum seekers back to Greece under the Dublin Regulation, had violated Arts 3 and 13 of the ECHR; see also the joint cases C-411/10 and C-493/10 *N.S. v Secretary of State for the Home Department* and *M.E. and Others v Refugee Applications Commissioner and Minister for Justice, Equality and Law Reform*, Judgment of the Court of Justice of the EU (Grand Chamber) of 21 December 2011.

origin is considered safe; such country is not considered safe if it presents threats of indiscriminate violence as a result of an international or non-international armed conflict.[79] The Procedures Directive offers other procedural safeguards such as the right to have a lawyer or the right to be informed.

In 2014, the European Court of Human Rights assessed the Dublin system in *Tarakhel v Switzerland*,[80] which concerned a family from Afghanistan that originally sought asylum in Italy. After ten days in an Italian centre for asylum seekers, the family left because of the poor living conditions, and eventually applied for asylum in Switzerland. Their request was denied and they were ordered to return to Italy under the Dublin regulation. The Court ruled that returning the family to Italy constitutes a breach of Article 3 if Switzerland does not first obtain specific guarantees that the Italian authorities would take charge of the applicants in a manner adapted to the age of the children and that the family would not be separated.[81]

Once an asylum seeker has been granted the refugee status, he or she enjoys the international protection system of the 1951 Refugee Convention. The granting of the refugee status by the UNHCR may be reversed by domestic authorities. In *I.A. v The Secretary of State for the Home Department*,[82] the UK Supreme Court upheld a previous decision to not grant the refugee status to an Iranian national who had been granted that status by the UNHCR in Iraqi Kurdistan on the basis of feared persecution as a member of the Kurdistan Democratic Party of Iran (KDPI). If an individual does not meet the conditions to be granted refugee protection in the State where the asylum claim has been filed, he or she may be returned to his country of origin, unless he or she would face serious threats to his or her life or freedom if returned. In such instance, the principle of non-refoulement applies.

The 1951 Convention also sets out when refugee status terminates, such as in the case of voluntary return, the acquisition of a new nationality or a change of circumstances in the country of origin.[83]

[79] Annex II of the Council Directive 2005/85/EC of 1 December 2005 on minimum standards on procedures in member States for granting and withdrawing refugee status.

[80] *Case of Tarakhel v Switzerland*, ECtHR, App. no. 29217/12, Judgment (Merits and Just Satisfaction), Court (Grand Chamber), 4 November 2014, available at: <http://hudoc.echr.coe.int/sites/eng/pages/search.aspx?i=001-148070>.

The ECtHR referred to *M.S.S. v Belgium and Greece* (App. no. 30696/09) with regard to the particular situation of asylum seekers coming from an underprivileged and vulnerable section of the population, in need of special protection, and the special status of minors within that group.

[81] Ibid., paras 121–122.

[82] *I.A. v The Secretary of State for the Home Department* [2014] UKSC 6 (29 January 2014), available at: <https://www.supremecourt.uk/decided-cases/docs/UKSC_2012_0157_Judgment.pdf?utm_source=Weekly+Legal+Update&utm_campaign=458ab40b3b-WLU_31_01_2014&utm_medium=email&utm_term=0_7176f0fc3d-458ab40b3b-419648261>.

[83] Art. 1C of the 1951 Refugee Convention.

B. Refugees under international human rights law

As the violation of human rights (or threat thereof) can be a cause of flight, international human rights law is relevant to determine whether an individual qualifies as a refugee or not. According to the Universal Declaration of Human Rights, '[E]veryone has the right to seek and to enjoy in other countries asylum from persecution'.[84] To decide that an individual has a 'well-founded fear of persecution' amounts to assess whether one or more of his or her human rights are likely to not be respected or protected by the relevant State. Certain human rights can be derogated from by the relevant State in situations of emergency, such as one deriving from an armed conflict. However, this is not possible for several rights which are relevant here, such as the right to life or the right not to be tortured.[85] In instances of patterns of gross violations of (generally non-derogable) human rights in a conflict area, a group of people fleeing can then even be considered 'prima facie' refugees, which means that they do not need to prove a well-founded fear of persecution as it is assumed.

In addition, a consistent pattern of human rights violations in a particular State may be a reason to apply the non-refoulement principle, the cornerstone of refugee protection. Prohibiting forcible return has thus also become a part of international human rights law as it is a means of preventing human rights violations. For example, the 1984 Convention Against Torture requires its State parties not to 'expel, return ("refouler") or extradite' an individual to another State where there is a risk that the individual faces torture.[86] The 2006 Convention for the Protection of All Persons from Enforced Disappearance contains a similar provision, prohibiting the return of individuals who may be at risk of enforced disappearance.[87] It adds that such a determination must be made on the basis of all relevant considerations, including the existence of a 'consistent pattern of gross, flagrant or mass violations of human rights or of serious violations of international humanitarian law' in the State in question.[88] Furthermore, although the 1966 International Covenant on Civil and Political Rights does not explicitly prohibit 'refoulement', its monitoring body, the Human Rights Committee, has stated that it is implicit with regard to individuals at risk of violation of its Article 6, which prohibits arbitrary deprivation of life, and its Article 7, which prohibits torture and other ill-treatment.[89]

[84] Art. 14(1) of the Universal Declaration of Human Rights.

[85] For a list of non-derogable civil and political rights, see Art. 4(2) of the ICCPR. In addition, economic, social, and cultural rights are never derogable.

[86] Art. 3 of the Convention Against Torture and Other Cruel, Inhuman or Degrading Treatment or Punishment.

[87] Art. 16 of the International Convention for the Protection of All Persons from Enforced Disappearance.

[88] Ibid., Art. 16(2).

[89] Human Rights Committee, General Comment No. 31, The Nature of the General Legal Obligation Imposed on States Parties to the Covenant, CCPR/C/21/Rev.1/Add. 1326 May 2004, para. 12.

The European Court of Human Rights upheld the rights of asylum seekers not to be returned to a country where they could risk human rights abuses in *Hirsi Jamaa and Others v Italy*.[90] In this case, Italy had returned twenty-four individuals originating from Somalia and Eritrea who had been intercepted at sea by its authorities as they were attempting to reach the Italian shores, along with about 200 other individuals. The Court concluded that the return of the applicants to Libya amounted to a violation of Article 3 of the Convention and Article 4 of Protocol No 4, which prohibits the collective expulsion of aliens, which amounted to a breach of the principle of non-refoulement.[91] Returning these individuals to Libya exposed them to a risk of arbitrary repatriation.[92] The Court also deemed that Italy had failed to offer these individuals with an opportunity to lodge their complaints under Article 3 and Article 4 of Protocol No 4 with a competent authority and thus violated Article 13 of the Convention, which provides for the right to an effective remedy.[93]

Note that in order to be at risk of persecution, one does not need to be a leader or high-profile person in the country in question. In *A.A. v* Switzerland,[94] a Sudanese national, who had been the human rights officer of the anti-government Sudan Liberation Movement-Unity (SLM-Unity), had had both of his asylum claims rejected by Switzerland, which had deemed he was not a high-profile political activist. The European Court of Human Rights (ECtHR) stated that 'not only leaders and high-profile people, but also those merely suspected of supporting opposition movements are at risk of treatment ... in Sudan'. In that case, there was however an issue with the credibility of the applicant's origin. Credibility is often an issue before the courts that consider challenges to asylum claims. For example, in *A.A. and Others v Sweden*,[95] four Somali nationals, A.A. and his three children brought a case before the ECtHR after their claims for asylum had been rejected by the Swedish Migration Board and the Migration Court on the grounds of credibility concerns as to their Southern Somalia origin, on the basis of language tests. While the family complained to the ECtHR that their return to Somaliland would expose them to a real risk of being subjected to inhuman or degrading treatment because of the ongoing armed conflict in that region, the Court found that the applicants had failed to substantiate that claim. An authority may even depart from the granting of refugee status by the UNHCR if it deems there is a lack of credibility.[96]

[90] *Case of Hirsi Jamaa and Others v Italy*, ECtHR App. no. 27765/09, Judgment (Merits and Just Satisfaction), Court (Grand Chamber), 23 February 2012, available at: <http://hudoc.echr.coe.int/sites/eng/pages/search.aspx?i=001-109231>.

[91] Ibid., para. 186. [92] Ibid., para. 158. [93] Ibid., para. 207.

[94] *A.A. v Switzerland*, App. no. 58802/12, ECtHR (Second Section) (7 January 2014), available at: <http://hudoc.echr.coe.int/sites/eng/pages/search.aspx?i=001-139903>.

[95] *A.A. and Others v Sweden*, App. no. 34098/11, ECtHR 24 July 2014, available at: <http://hudoc.echr.coe.int/sites/eng/pages/search.aspx?i=001-145789>.

[96] See, for example, UNHCR and European Refugee Fund of the European Commission, *Beyond Proof—Credibility Assessment in EU Asylum Systems* (May 2013), available on the website of the

In addition to the principle of non-refoulement, international human rights law has adopted the prohibition of non-discrimination which is applicable in relation to all human rights. Accordingly, human rights belong to individuals 'without distinction of any kind, such as race, colour, sex, language, religion, political or other opinion, national or social origin, property, birth or other status'.[97] Almost all of those discrimination grounds were included in the 1951 Refugee Convention, which requires persecution to be based on such grounds. However, fear of persecution on the basis of colour, sex, or language, for example, were not included in the 1951 Refugee Convention. However, its reference to 'membership of a particular social group' may sometimes be interpreted to include those grounds. For example, being a woman in a particular country at a particular time may lead to fear of being persecuted falling under the 1951 Convention.

All individuals, no matter what their nationality, are human rights holders. Given that nationality is not a requirement to enjoy human rights, asylum seekers and refugees can also benefit from international human rights' protection. A State that has ratified an international human rights treaty must respect, protect, and fulfil the human rights enshrined therein in relation to all individuals under its jurisdiction. In addition, most human rights are (in part at least) considered part of customary international law, which means that a State does not need to have ratified a treaty to have obligations in relation to them.

Furthermore, international human rights law completes refugee law as it assists with the interpretation of the rights it contains, such as the right to education, the right to freedom of religion, or the right to a fair trial. The case law of the various human rights enforcement mechanisms has contributed to the development of standards, which may be used to interpret the provisions contained in the 1951 Refugee Convention. Moreover, international human rights law provides for a number of additional rights which may be particularly relevant for asylum seekers and refugees, such as, for example, the right not to be detained arbitrarily.[98]

Finally, human rights are relevant as their enforcement and monitoring support long-term solutions for refugees.[99] The 'durable solutions', as defined by the UNHCR, include voluntary repatriation to the country of origin, local integration into the country of asylum, and resettlement to a third country. Refugees may voluntarily decide to return and re-establish themselves in their country of origin, if conditions have changed to allow them to enjoy their human rights without fearing persecution. For example, by

CREDO Project at: <http://helsinki.hu/en/credo-%E2%80%93-improving-credibility-assessment-in-eu-asylum-procedures>.

[97] See, for example, Art. 2(1) of the International Covenant on Civil and Political Rights.

[98] Art. 9 of the International Covenant on Civil and Political Rights.

[99] See, for example, the UNHCR Executive Committee Conclusion N° 81(k), 1997.

February 2014, around 80,000 to 100,000 residents of the Dabaab camps had voluntarily repatriated to Somalia.[100] In cases where return is not possible, refugees must be assisted with their resettlement in order to be integrated and benefit from the protection of their human rights in their new country of residence, whether it is their country of asylum or a third country.

C. **Refugees under international humanitarian law**

International humanitarian law, which applies only with regard to situations of armed conflict, is thus particularly relevant to individuals fleeing conflict zones, offering them a two-tiered protection, i.e., general protection and additional protection. While international humanitarian law mentions refugees within its rules, it does not define the term but instead focuses on their situation of 'aliens' in a territory and their lack of protection from any government. In other circumstances, they benefit from the rules applicable to 'protected persons' as a result of their civilian status.

GENERAL PROTECTION

As long as asylum seekers or refugees are not directly taking part in hostilities, they benefit from their protection as 'civilians', in accordance with the principle of distinction, which means that they are protected from the effects of armed conflicts.[101] In particular, there is a general prohibition to attack civilians and civilian objects, which include refugee camps,[102] and of indiscriminate attacks, i.e., attacks which are not directed at a specific military objective.[103] In addition, when conducting an attack against a legitimate military objective, there is a duty under international humanitarian law to take all necessary precautions to spare the civilian population.[104] It is also prohibited to starve

[100] This came as a result of a November 2013 agreement between Somalia and Kenya, see Olick, F., 'Nairobi to open mission in Mogadishu', *Standard Digital*, 20 February 2014, available at: <http://www.standardmedia.co.ke/mobile/?articleID=2000105058&story_title=nairobi-to-open-mission-in-mogadishu&pageNo=2>.

[101] Arts 48, 51(2), and 52(2) of 1977 Protocol Additional to the 1949 Geneva Conventions relating to the Protection of Victims of International Armed Conflicts (AP I), Art. 13(2) of 1977 Protocol Additional to the 1949 Geneva Conventions relating to the Protection of Victims of Non-International Armed Conflicts (AP II), and Rule 1 of ICRC Customary IHL Database.

[102] For a discussion on the protection of refugee camps under IHL, see Jacques, M., 2015, *Armed Conflict and Displacement, The Protection of Refugees and Displaced Persons under International Humanitarian Law*, Cambridge: CUP, Ch. 7.

[103] Art. 51(4)(a) AP I, and Rule 12 ICRC Customary IHL Database.

[104] Art. 58(c) AP I, Art. 13(1) AP II, and Rule 22 ICRC Customary IHL Database.

the civilian population as a means of warfare and to destroy objects indispensable to its survival.[105] This also means that parties to a conflict must allow relief supplies and assistance to reach civilians in order to ensure their survival. Reprisals against civilians and their properties, which often amounts to the destruction of their homes and thus lead to population displacement, is also prohibited.[106]

The above-mentioned rules are all relevant for refugee protection as they play a role in preventing displacement. A violation of one (or several) of these rules often lead to mass displacement of civilians in situations of armed conflict. However, international humanitarian law expressly prohibits forced transfer of civilian population,[107] including the civilian population of an occupied territory both within and beyond the borders of that territory.[108] During armed conflicts, civilians may only be transferred if it is necessary to ensure their security or if there is an imperative military necessity to do so.[109] Once the hostilities have ceased in the region in question, they must then be returned to their homes. If civilians must be displaced, international humanitarian law contains rules protecting them during such transfer, in particular by requiring minimum standards with regard to shelter, hygiene, health, safety, and nutrition. In addition, family members must not be separated during such transfer.[110]

ADDITIONAL PROTECTION

In addition to the rules protecting refugees as civilians and displaced civilians, international humanitarian law provides a specific form of protection to refugees given their de facto lack of protection. When an individual seeks refuge in a State at war with its own State of origin, he or she becomes an 'enemy alien' as a national of the opposing party, which renders them particularly vulnerable. However, under international humanitarian law, a detaining power must not treat refugees as 'enemy aliens' on the basis of their nationality alone.[111] As they do not benefit from their government's protection, they cannot be automatically considered as a threat to the State they find themselves in but should rather be deemed to be opposed to their State of origin. As a result, security measures should not be applicable towards them and they

[105] Art. 54(1) AP I, Art. 14 AP II, and Rule 53 ICRC Customary IHL Database.

[106] Art. 51(6) AP I, and Rule 146 ICRC Customary IHL Database.

[107] Art. 49 of the Fourth Geneva Convention relative to the Protection of Civilian Persons in Time of War 1949 (GC IV), and Rule 129 ICRC Customary IHL Database.

[108] Art. 147 GC IV, and Art. 85(4)(a) AP I.

[109] Art. 49 (2) GC IV, and Art. 17(1) AP II.

[110] Art. 49 (3) GC IV, Art. 17(1) AP I, and Rule 131 ICRC Customary IHL Database.

[111] Art. 44 GC IV.

should be entitled to leave the territory of their asylum State. More in general, they should continue to enjoy the protections and rights which belonged to them when hostilities begun.[112]

Refugees must not be punished for having sought asylum or for having committed acts which may have made them flee their State of origin. However, their State of origin may have an opportunity to do so when it occupies their State of asylum. Therefore, in such circumstances, international humanitarian law provides that the occupying power may only arrest, prosecute, or deport refugees for offences committed after the start of the armed conflict, unless prior offences would have justified extradition in time of peace. These rules derive from their status of 'protected persons' at the start of the armed conflict.[113]

Finally, international humanitarian law has also recognized the principle of non-refoulement, albeit on limited grounds. Those who are considered 'protected persons' under international humanitarian law, such as refugees, shall thus never be transferred to a country where they may have reason to fear persecution because of their 'political opinions or religious beliefs'.[114]

Concluding remarks

As this chapter demonstrates, the legal provisions applicable to those who have fled an armed conflict across a border are fragmented and unclear. The key treaty concerned with refugees requires a well-founded fear of persecution and thus may not apply to individuals fleeing a conflict because of the general situation of violence and instability generated by it. As a result, many regional and domestic legal frameworks have adopted a subsidiary form of protection or an extended definition of 'refugee' for those not falling within the protection system of the 1951 Refugee Convention.

Despite the adoption of those additional legal provisions to cover those fleeing armed conflicts and attempts at harmonizing regional frameworks, there remains too many discrepancies from one domestic approach to asylum claims to another. In fact, as the success of asylum claims often depends not only on subjective and objective assessments, outcomes are too often unpredictable.

Of course, one of the major issues associated with individuals fleeing an armed conflict is the sheer number of those asylum seekers or refugees. This is particularly problematic for neighbouring countries which may have such capacity issues that their internal stability and security may be jeopardized when trying to absorb refugees into

[112] Art. 73 AP I. [113] Art. 73 AP I. [114] Art. 45(4) GC IV.

their own structures. It is also an issue for those countries further afield that are seen as an 'Eldorado' and may thus also end up with capacity issues.

While States should host refugees as a matter of international solidarity, cooperation, and burden-sharing, the international community should provide sufficient assistance to those States which have a massive influx of refugees as a result of wars in neighbouring regions. Burden sharing should be equitable. In 2012, the Organization of Islamic Cooperation adopted the Ashgabat Declaration on Refugees in the Muslim World, noting the challenges faced by countries hosting large number of refugees not only in terms of socio-economic impacts but also in terms of security and environmental impacts. In doing so, it noted the 'declining levels' of international assistance.[115]

Fleeing an armed conflict entails a number of risks which may be life-threatening. The continuous flow of refugees attempting to cross the Mediterranean is the most poignant example of the risks individuals are willing to take in order to escape their countries of origin, many of which are in a situation of armed conflict or a post-conflict situation. While wars are often the cause of someone's flight, they are also a continuing obstacle for anyone wishing to return safely to their country of origin. The return and resettlement of refugees are thus also linked to the resolution of the conflict they fled in the first place.

[115] 2012 OIC Ashgabat Declaration on Refugees in the Muslim World, para. 7.

6 Protection of IDPs in armed conflict in 2014: a critical review of law and practice

Marina Mattirolo[1]

Introduction

Displacement of people within their own countries owing to armed conflict is a matter of growing concern on every continent. ICRC President, Jacob Kellenberger said that: 'Internal displacement poses one of the most daunting humanitarian challenges of today. The impact not only on many millions of IDPs but also on countless host families and resident communities is hard if not impossible to measure.'[2]

In 1982, when first counted, 1.2 million IDPs were identified in eleven countries. Roughly ten years later, in 1995, the number of IDPs had grown to 20–5 million.[3] Today there is an estimate of 33.3 million people internally displaced by armed conflict, generalized violence, and human rights violation[4] with another

[1] Marina Mattirolo is a researcher at the Geneva Academy of International Humanitarian Law and Human Rights.

[2] Kellenberger, J., 2009, 'The ICRC's response to internal displacement: strengths, challenges and constraints', *International Review of the Red Cross*, vol. 91, no. 875, September, p. 475.

[3] Cohen, R. and Deng, F., 1998, *Masses in Flight: The Global Crisis of Internal Displacement*, Washington, DC: Brookings Institute Press, p. 3.

[4] Internal Displacement Monitoring Centre (IDMC), *Global Overview 2014: people internally displaced by conflict and violence*, 14 May 2014. According to IDMC, situations of armed conflict include both international and non-international armed conflict. Generalized violence refers to disturbances within the country which are characterized by a serious disruption of order resulting from acts of violence such as riots, struggles between factions or against the authorities, or inter-communal violence. Human rights violations encompass failures by any State or, where applicable, relevant non-State actors, to respect their obligations under international human rights law. The figures for conflict displacement are cumulative, taking into account both new and ongoing displacement situations and IDP returns where possible, <http://www.internal-displacement.org/assets/publications/2014/201405-global-overview-2014-en.pdf>.

22 million displaced by natural disasters.[5] Children make up at least 50% of IDPs worldwide.[6]

The definition of internally displaced persons is to be found in the Guiding Principles on Internal Displacement ('*Guiding Principles*'), adopted by the Commission on Human Rights in 1998 and representing the first universal instrument specifically addressed to persons who are internally displaced.[7] IDPs are described as persons:

> who have been forced or obliged to flee or to leave their homes or places of habitual residence, in particular as a result of or in order to avoid the effects of armed conflict, situations of generalized violence, violations of human rights or natural or humane-made disasters, and who have not crossed an internationally recognized State border.[8]

The definition encompasses people displaced by natural disasters as well as man-made disasters but this chapter will only take into account people displaced as a consequence of armed conflict, situations of generalized violence, and violations of human rights.

It is generally accepted that there are three phases of displacement: prevention of displacement or protecting people from arbitrary displacement; protection and assistance during displacement; and the achievement of durable solutions to end displacement such as return, local integration, or settlement elsewhere in the country. About the last phase of displacement, there is no absolute consensus as to when to stop considering someone an internally displaced person since, unlike for refugees, there is no cessation clause for IDPs. However, displacement is considered to end when a durable solution is achieved and those formerly displaced no longer require the specific attention given to them as IDPs.[9]

[5] Internal Displacement Monitoring Center (IDMC), *Global Estimates 2014: People Displaced by Disasters*, September 2014. The Global Estimates 2014 report, published on 17 September 2014, is based on IDMC data as of 22 August 2014. These estimates are related to disasters triggered by both weather-related and geophysical hazard events, such as floods, storms, earthquakes, volcanic eruptions, and wildfires. Displacement related to slower-onset type hazards such as drought, as well as technological hazards (such as nuclear or industrial accidents) and biological hazards (such as epidemics) is not included in these global estimates for methodological reasons. The estimates for disaster-related displacement represent the number of people newly displaced by disasters over the course of each year, <http://www.internal-displacement.org/publications/2014/global-estimates-2014-people-displaced-by-disasters/>.

[6] Office of the Special Representative of the Secretary General for Children and Armed Conflict, 2010, *The Rights and Guarantee of Internally Displaced Children in Armed Conflict*, Working Paper Number 2.

[7] UN Commission on Human Rights, *Report of the Representative of the Secretary-General, Mr Francis M. Deng, submitted pursuant to Commission resolution 1997/39. Addendum: Guiding Principles on Internal Displacement*, 11 February 1998, E/CN.4/1998/53/Add.2.

[8] *Guiding Principles*, Introduction, para. 2.

[9] See Duchatellier, M. and Phuong, C., 2014, 'The African Contribution to the Protection of Internally Displaced Persons: A Commentary on the 2009 Kampala Convention'. In *Research Handbook on International Law and Migration*, part IV, edited by Chetail, V. and Bauloz, C., Cheltenham: Edward Elgar Publishing, p. 660.

Being an IDP has been described as 'a factual state that triggers certain legal consequences' within and across international human rights law, international humanitarian law, and international criminal law.[10] The first part of this chapter will analyse what are the legal provisions of existing international law regulating the phenomenon of internal displacement and their adequacy to address the specific needs of IDPs today. The chapter will then turn into the analysis of the Guiding Principles on Internal Displacement, the first non-binding universal instrument exclusively addressed to IDPs, the impact they have had in the assistance to and protection of IDPs worldwide, and their implementation at the regional as well as domestic level.

A further section will look at the operational response put in place by the international community to face the growing needs of IDPs and examine its strengths and weaknesses. Last but not least, the chapter will briefly identify what are the current new challenges related to the protection of IDPs.

A. **The protection of IDPs under international law**

The international system set up in the aftermath of the Second World War to deal with uprooted populations fleeing persecutions did not protect displaced people inside their own countries. According to their mandate, both the UN High Commissioner for Refugees and the 1951 Convention Relating to the Status of Refugee ('Refugee Convention') only provided protection and assistance to those who:

> owing to a well-founded fear of being persecuted for reasons of race, religion, nationality, membership of a particular social group or political opinion, *is outside the country of his nationality*, and is unable to, or owing to such fear, is unwilling to avail himself of the protection of that country.[11]

The definition of refugee explicitly excluded persons that, while fleeing persecution, were not outside their country of origin. This is because, at the time of the drafting and adoption of the Refugee Convention, the vast majority of States believed that internally displaced persons had to be the exclusive responsibility of their governments. Unlike refugees who are aliens in a foreign territory, IDPs can still benefit from the protection of their country of origin and therefore are not in need of international protection.

[10] Brookings Institution, Protecting Internally Displaced Persons: a Manual for Law and Policy Makers, 13, 2008.

[11] See Art. 1(A)(2) of the Convention Relating to the Status of Refugee, 1951, emphasis added.

THE EMERGENCE OF IDPS IN THE INTERNATIONAL HUMANITARIAN AGENDA

In the 1990s the phenomenon of internally displaced persons (IDPs) emerged as one of the more 'challenging humanitarian, human rights and security issues'[12] that the international community had to face.

Unlike refugees, IDPs did not have a well-established international system to protect and assist them or help them with their recovery and reintegration. When at the end of Cold War, internal conflicts started proliferating in places such as the Balkans, Afghanistan, and Somalia, causing the number of internally displaced persons to grow dramatically, IDPs started becoming an issue of international concern. A limited group of NGOs, including the Commission of Churches on International Affairs and the Quakers,[13] began pressuring mechanisms and agencies of the United Nations system to take action against the lack of protection of people uprooted inside their own countries. Many of the displaced could not access food, medicine, or shelter and were particularly exposed to attacks, sexual violence, and other human rights abuses. In 1991, UN Secretary-General Javier Perez de Cuellar stated:

> We are clearly witnessing what is probably an irresistible shift in public attitudes towards the belief that the defence of the oppressed in the name of morality should prevail over frontiers and legal documents.[14]

A year later, the UN Human Rights Commission took up the issue of IDPs and nominated Francis Deng as Representative of the Secretary-General on Internally Displaced Persons.[15]

States experiencing displacement began recognizing that addressing the needs of IDPs was necessary in order to achieve stabilization and conflict-resolution. Western States from their part, witnessing with concern the increasing number of refugees arriving on their borders in the post-Cold War era, thought that addressing the issue of and providing assistance to IDPs in their own countries would eliminate reasons for them to flee and seek asylum in Europe and North America.[16] The assumption

[12] Cohen, R., 2014, 'Protection of Internally Displaced Persons: National and International Responsibilities'. In *Research Handbook on International Law and Migration*, part IV, edited by Chetail V. and Bauloz, C., Cheltenham: Edward Elgar Publishing, p. 589.

[13] Contat Hickel, M., 2001. 'Protection of Internally Displaced Persons Affected by Armed Conflict: Concept and Challenges', *International Review of the Red Cross*, September, vol. 83, no. 843, p. 700.

[14] UN Press Release, UN Doc. SG/SM/4560, 24 April 1991.

[15] Commission on Human Rights, *Internally displaced persons*, 5 March 1992, UN Doc. E/CN.4/RES/1992/73.

[16] Cohen, R., 'Protection of Internally Displaced Persons', p. 590.

that IDPs exclusive responsibility rested with their governments started to be questioned leaving space to the idea, backed by the newly appointed Representative of the Secretary-General, that when governments are not willing or not able to protect their displaced populations, the involvement of the international community becomes a necessity.

> The fact that they are displaced internally does not mean that the international community does not have a major responsibility to protect them.[17]

Humanitarian organizations such as the International Committee of the Red Cross (ICRC) and the UN High Commissioner for Refugees (UNHCR) had begun assisting IDPs since the 1970s, but it was during the humanitarian crises of the 1990s, when IDPs started to outnumber refugees, that it became clear that a more active engagement was necessary. That was the time where the High Commissioner for Refugees, Sadako Ogata, whose mandate excluded the protection of IDPs, asked herself:

> Should we follow the legal dictate of not exercising our mandate inside the border and thereby refrain from helping those prevented from crossing or should we stand more on realistic humanitarian grounds and extend whatever support we could?[18]

The answer was clear and not long after the High Commissioner decided to expand the 'operational coverage' of UNHCR in different internal crises to include IDPs and other affected populations.[19]

UNHCR and other humanitarian organizations soon realized that they needed a conceptual and legal foundation as a basis for their greater involvement with IDPs. That is when the role of the newly appointment Representative of the Secretary-General on Internally Displaced Persons (RSC) with the mandate to examining the human rights issues related to the protection of internally displaced persons became central.[20] Before looking at the Representative of the Secretary-General's work that helped towards the development of the Guiding Principles on Internal Displacement, the following sections include an analysis of the protection already provided to internally displaced persons by international humanitarian law and human rights law.

[17] Cohen, R., 2010, 'Reconciling R2P with IDP Protection', *Global Responsibility to Protect*, vol. 2, no. 1-2: 15–37 at p. 17.

[18] Ogata, S., 2005, *The Turbulent Decade*, New York: W. W. Norton & Co., p. 30.

[19] Ibid., p. 19.

[20] Cohen, R., 'Protection of Internally Displaced Persons', p. 592.

THE PROTECTION OF IDPS UNDER INTERNATIONAL HUMANITARIAN LAW

International humanitarian law (IHL) seeks to limit the effects of armed conflict and to protect persons who are not or no longer participating in the hostilities. IDPs are part of the civilian population and as such are entitled to the protection afforded to all civilians under IHL. Violations of IHL, such as attacks against the civilian population, ill-treating civilians, destruction of property, sexual violence, and restricted access to health care and other essential services are some of the main causes generating displacement in contemporary armed conflicts. Hence, it has been argued that 'not only IHL protects victims of internal displacement but its rules, if scrupulously applied, would make it possible to avoid the majority of displacement'.[21]

Most of the IHL provisions relating to the prevention of displacement and the protection of IDPs are contained in the four Geneva Conventions of 1949, Additional Protocol I and II of 1977, as well as in customary international humanitarian law.[22] States have the responsibility to implement these provisions in their internal legal system. As of today, the international normative framework dedicated to IDPs is of a soft law nature and most branches of international law are not accepted as being applicable to non-State armed groups, the most developed international legal norms protecting conflict-affected IDPs and binding upon all parties to an armed conflict are still to be found in IHL.[23] The following two sections will analyse IHL provisions related to the protection of conflict-induced IDPs during the three phases of displacement.

THE GENERAL PROTECTION OF IDPS AS PART OF THE CIVILIAN POPULATION UNDER IHL

When looking at the whole body of IHL, one could be fairly surprised in not finding a single mention of 'internally displaced persons' in the texts. This is because, as

[21] Lavoyer, J.-P., 1995, 'Refugees and Internally Displaced Persons: International Humanitarian Law and the Role of the ICRC', *International Review of the Red Cross*, vol. 305, 30 April, p. 162.

[22] Civilians fleeing from a non-international armed conflict (NIAC) enjoy protection very similar to that during international armed conflicts (IACs). Nonetheless provision protecting IDPs in NIACs are overall less detailed that those in IACs. Fortunately, customary IHL, composed of rules coming from a general practice accepted as law, fills the gaps left by treaty law in both IACs and NIACs and so strengthen the protection afforded to victims of armed conflict, including IDPs. See Henckaerts J.M. and Doswald-Beck, L., 2005, *Customary International Humanitarian Law*, Geneva/Cambridge, ICRC/Cambridge University Press.

[23] Ojeda, S., 2014, 'International Humanitarian Law and the Protection of Internally Displaced Persons'. In *Research Handbook on International Law and Migration*, part IV, edited by Chetail V. and Bauloz, C., Cheltenham: Edward Elgar Publishing, p. 635.

previously said, IDPs are above all part of the civilian populations whose protection is the very *raison d'être* of this branch of international law.[24]

IDPs are thus protected by all IHL rules related to the treatment of civilians. They should be treated humanely, and should not be discriminated against on the grounds of their displacement or for any other reason. IDPs are also protected from torture and other forms of ill-treatment, arbitrary deprivation of life and liberty, collective punishment, acts of terrorism, taking of hostages, slavery, and pillage.[25] Provisions regulating the conduct of hostilities also protect IDPs as part of the civilian population. These include the principle of distinction and the other central rules derived from it such as the prohibition of direct attack on civilians or civilian objects, the principle of proportionality, the obligation to take precautions in attacks and the prohibition of acts that threaten the civilian population's ability to survive.[26]

THE SPECIAL PROTECTION OF IDPS UNDER IHL

International humanitarian law specifically prohibits different forms of forced displacement,[27] namely 'forcible movement', 'forcible transfer' or 'deportation' of civilians whether within the borders of a country or across international borders.[28] Forced displacement is a serious violation of IHL and may amount to a war crime and a crime against humanity.[29]

Displacement of civilians can be considered by the authorities, exceptionally and temporarily, when justified by imperative military reasons or if the security of the population so demand.[30] ICRC Commentary to Article 17 of Additional Protocol I clearly explains how the wording 'imperative military reasons' should be interpreted:

> Military necessity as a ground for derogation from rule always requires the most meticulous assessment of the circumstances. … The situation should be scrutinized most carefully as the

[24] Contat Hickel, M., 'Protection of Internally Displaced Persons', p. 700.

[25] See Common Art. 3 to the four Geneva Conventions; Art. 75 Additional Protocol I; Art. 4 Additional Protocol II; and Chapter 5 of the ICRC Study on Customary IHL, Henckaerts, J.M. and Doswald-Beck, L., 2005, *Customary International Humanitarian Law*, Geneva/Cambridge, ICRC/Cambridge University Press.

[26] See Arts 48, 51-4, and 57-8 of Additional Protocol I; Arts 13 and 14 Additional Protocol II; Chapter I of the ICRC Study on Customary IHL, 2005.

[27] For a detailed analysis on what is 'forced' displacement as opposed to 'voluntary' displacement and the legal consequences they entail, see Ojeda, S., 'International Humanitarian Law', p. 639.

[28] See Art. 49 of Geneva Convention IV; Arts 51(7), 78(1) of Additional Protocol I; Arts 4(3)(e) and 17 of Additional Protocol II; Rules 129–130 of the ICRC Study on Customary IHL, 2005.

[29] See Art. 147 of Geneva Convention IV and Art. 85(4) of Additional Protocol I.

[30] If, for instance, a region is threatened by intense bombing, the competent authorities have the right or the duty to evacuate the region in whole or in part, transferring the inhabitants in places of refugee.

adjective 'imperative' reduces to a minimum, cases in which displacement may be ordered. Clearly, imperative military reasons cannot be justified by political motives. For example, it would be prohibited to move a population in order to exercise more effective control over a dissident ethnic group.[31]

In order to be lawful, displacement of civilians must also be 'exceptional' and 'temporary'. *Exceptional*, in the sense that the prohibition of forced displacement is the rule and that any displacement that may occur during the conflict must remain the exception; *temporary*, meaning that displaced persons should be allowed to return by the concerned party within the shortest possible period.[32] Should displacement happen, protected persons may only be evacuated to reception centres in the occupied territory in case of an IAC, or in the national territory in case of a NIAC.

During displacement, IHL rules request parties to the conflict to take all possible measures in order for the civilian population to be received under satisfactory conditions of shelter, hygiene, health, safety, and nutrition, and that members of the same family are not separated.[33] In addition, the parties to the conflict must fulfil secure adequate food supplies to the displaced persons and if they are unable to do so they should not hamper humanitarian assistance from other impartial humanitarian bodies.[34]

IHL provides special protection to children who are displaced and/or separated from their families as a result of an armed conflict. In IACs, parties to the conflict must take the necessary measures to ensure that children under fifteen, who are orphaned or are separated from their families, are not left to their own resources and that their education is facilitated in all circumstances.[35] In NIACs, children shall also receive an education, including religious and moral education.[36] As in situations of displacements children are more vulnerable to forcible recruitment into armed forces or armed groups, it has to be kept in mind that IHL, as a general rule, prohibits recruitment, forcible or voluntary, of children under fifteen years of age.[37] Also, persons over fifteen years of age shall not be subject to discriminatory practices of recruitment as a result of their displacement.

[31] Sandoz, Y., Swinarski, C., and Zimmermann, B. (eds.), 1987, *Commentary on the Protocol Additional to the Geneva Conventions of 12 August 1949, and relating to the Protection of Victims of Non-International Armed Conflict (Protocol II)*, Geneva, ICRC/Martinus Nijhoff Publishers, p. 1871, paras 4853–5.

[32] Ojeda, S., 'International Humanitarian Law', p. 640.

[33] See Art. 49 of Geneva Convention IV; Art. 17 Additional Protocol II; Rules 129, 131 of the ICRC Study on Customary IHL, 2005.

[34] See Arts 23, 50, 59, 70, and 71 of Additional protocol I; Art. 18 of Additional Protocol II; Rules 55–6 of the ICRC Study on Customary IHL, 2005.

[35] See Art. 24(1) of Geneva Convention IV. The same obligation exists for the Occupying power in the territory it occupies, Art. 50(1) of Geneva Convention IV.

[36] See Arts 4(3)(a) and 28(2) of Additional Protocol II.

[37] See Art. 77(2) Additional Protocol I; Art. 4(3)(c) Additional Protocol II; Rule 136 of the ICRC Study

As for the right to voluntary return of displaced persons, IHL provides that they shall be allowed to return to their homes or places of habitual residence as soon as the security concerns have ceased to exist in the affected area.[38] Rule 133 of the ICRC Study on Customary IHL further adds that the property rights of displaced persons must be respected. Finally, in case of separation of family members because of displacement, parties to the conflict must take all appropriate steps to facilitate their reunification.[39]

THE PROTECTION OF IDPS UNDER INTERNATIONAL HUMAN RIGHTS LAW

As citizens or residents of their state, IDPs are entitled to all human rights recognized in the said country.[40] However, the factual situation characterizing displacement—persons having to leave their homes involuntary or under coercion and being unable to return—makes IDPs particularly vulnerable and creates special needs that are qualitatively different from those of victims of other situations of violence but not forced to flee.[41] Particular needs for internally displaced persons are finding a shelter while away from their homes and protection against being coercively returned to danger zones. They also have to deal with the loss of their livelihoods and property and the subsequent difficulties in trying to regain them. Another major difficulty for IDPs in replacing their documents such as identifications cards, school leaving certificates, property deeds in order to access services. IDPs are often unable to exercise their right to vote since this can usually only be done in their place of habitual residence. Moreover, because of their situation and the consequent loss of social networks, IDPs suffer greater risk of being exposed to a variety of human rights abuses such as sexual violence or forced recruitment of children into armed forces or armed groups. They are also more vulnerable to health hazards and have restricted access to health care and other essential services.

on Customary IHL, 2005 as well as Art. 2 of the 2002 Optional Protocol to the Convention on the Rights of the Child on the Involvement of Children in Armed Conflict raises the age at eighteen years old.

[38] See Art. 49 of Geneva Convention IV; Art. 17 of Additional Protocol II and Rules 129 and 132 of the ICRC Study on Customary IHL, 2005.

[39] See Arts 26, 27, and 49 of Geneva Convention IV; Art. 74 of Additional Protocol I; Art. 4(3) of Additional Protocol II and Rule 131 of the ICRC Study on Customary IHL, 2005.

[40] In times of armed conflict, as previously mentioned, IDPs can also benefit from the protection of IHL.

[41] Kälin, W. and Künzli, J., 2009, *The Law of International Human Rights Protection*, Oxford University Press, p. 502.

KEY PROVISIONS PROTECTING IDPS UNDER INTERNATIONAL HUMAN RIGHTS LAW

Under international human rights law (IHRL), the prohibition of arbitrary displacement can be found in Article 12(1) of the International Covenant on Civil and Political Rights (ICCPR) stating everyone's right to liberty of movement and freedom to choose his or her residence. This includes the right not to leave his or her residence hence not to be displaced.[42]

During displacement, in addition to those human rights that are also vital for the non-displaced, such as the prohibition of torture and arbitrary deprivation of life, several categories of rights and guarantees are particularly relevant for IDPs. The first one is the general prohibition of discriminations based 'on race, colour, sex, language, religion, political or other opinion, national or social origin, property, birth or other status'.[43] The respect of the prohibition of discrimination is specifically important for IDPs when associated with the exercise of political rights. As a matter of fact, there are many cases of IDPs being prevented from voting and to stand for election on the basis that those are rights that may be exercised only in one's place of residence.[44]

The right to freedom of moment guarantees IDPs the right to flee from danger zones and seek refuge in another part of the country as well as the right to leave the country and seek asylum elsewhere.[45] IDPs enjoy the right not to be forcibly returned to zones where their life, safety, liberty, or health would be at immediate risk.[46] Also derived from the right to freedom of movement is the right of IDPs to move freely in and out of their camp and the prohibition, unless internment is unavoidable, of closed camps. Even when internment is lawful, it should end immediately after the conditions rendering it absolutely necessary ceased to exist.[47]

Both the Inter-American and the European Courts of Human Rights have emphasized in their jurisprudence, that the right to freedom of movement, the right to property or the right to private life and home create positive obligations for States to allow return if possible, and/or to create conditions and provide the means to enable return

[42] This interpretation was confirmed by the Human Rights Committee in General Comment No 27, Human Rights Committee, General Comment No 27 (1999), para. 7. Also the Inter-American Court of Human Rights derived the prohibition of forced displacement from the right to freedom of movement, Art. 22 of the American Convention on Human Rights. See, IACtHR, *Case of the Mapiripán Massacre v Colombia*, Series C, No. 134 (2005), para. 188.

[43] Arts 2(1) and 26 of the ICCPR, 1966.

[44] Kälin, W. and Künzli, J., *The Law of International Human Rights Protection*, p. 506.

[45] See Art. 12 of the ICCPR and Art. 14 of the Universal Declaration of Human Rights (UDHR).

[46] This is based on a similar application of the jurisprudence under Art. 3 of the European Convention on Human Rights (ECHR), Art. 7 of ICCPR, and Art. 3 of the Convention Against Torture (CAT) regarding the inhumanity of forcible return where there is a risk of torture or of deprivation of life.

[47] This is derived from an extensive interpretation of Arts 12 and 9 of ICCPR.

voluntarily in safety and dignity to their original place of residence.[48] Finally, derived from the right to freedom of movement is also the right of IDPs, once displacement has ended, to either voluntarily return to their original place of residence, to stay in the area in which they were displaced or to resettle in another part of the country.

During displacement, IDPs are often incapable of attending their most basic needs. Consequently, in order to receive food, housing, medical care, education, and other services they depend on humanitarian assistance. They have the possibility therefore to invoke their correspondent economic and social rights guaranteeing access to such items and services under human rights law.[49] It is interesting to note that in several cases, the Inter-American and the European systems have taken the position in their jurisprudence that conflict-induced IDPs in some situations can invoke forced displacement as an obstacle to the fulfilment of their right to a private and family life in addition to hampering their right to an adequate standard of living.[50] The European Court of Human Rights for instance considered 'the deliberate burning of homes by security forces' to amount, inter alia, to a violation of the right to respect to private and family life.[51] The Inter-American Court issued an analogous judgment in the case of *Ituango Massacres v Colombia*, which also dealt with the burning of homes and possessions but by paramilitary forces. The Court considered it to be a violation not only of the right to home but also of the right to private life, since: 'the individual's home and private life are intrinsically connected, because the home is the space in which private life can evolve freely'.[52]

As previously mentioned, IDPs often need to have their essential documents such as identity cards, passports, birth or marriage certificates reissued during displacement. In relation to this, it has been argued that the right to be recognized as a person before the law (Article 16 ICCPR) may be interpreted as implying that the de facto exercise of this right in the case of IDPs cannot be inhibited by requirements, such as that the document in question can only be issued at a persons' habitual place of residence, which they are unable to fulfil.[53]

48 See IACtHR, *Case of Moiwana Community v Suriname*, Series C, No. 124 (2005), paras 120–1 refers to the freedom of movement and residence and the right to property, and ECtHR, *Dogan and Others v Turkey*, App. Nos 8803–8811/02 (2004) which refers to the right to property and the right to private life and home.

49 See Arts 11, 12, and 13 of the International Covenant on Economic, Social and Cultural Rights (ICESCR) and Art. 25 of the UDHR.

50 See Art. 8 ECHR, Art. 11(2) ACHR, and Art. 11(1) ICESCR.

51 ECtHR, *Akdivar and others v Turkey* Judgment, 30 August 1996, §88. For analogous cases see also, ECtHR, *Bilgin v Turkey Judgment*, 16 November 2000, §108; *Ahmet Özkan and others v Turkey* Judgment, 6 April 2004, §405, and *Dogan and others v Turkey* Judgment, 29 June 2004, §159.

52 IACtHR, *Ituango Massacres v Colombia* Judgment, 1 July 2006, §§194 and 197, see also more recent case: *Operación Génesis v Colombia*, IACtHR, 20 November 2013, *Masacres de el Mozote v El Salvador*, 25 October 2012, *Masacre de Santo Domingo v Colombia*, 5 June 2012.

53 Kälin, W. and Künzli, J., *The Law of International Human Rights Protection*, p. 507.

B. Towards a normative framework for the protection of IDPs

In 1992, as a first task after being nominated RSC, Francis Deng, was requested by the Commission on Human Rights to conduct a comprehensive study on the issue of IDPs and, among others, to carry out:

An examination of existing international human rights, humanitarian and refugee law and standards and their applicability to the protection and relief assistance to internally displaced persons.[54]

In 1993, Deng submitted a 'comprehensive study' to the Commission on Human Rights where after raising the initial question 'whether existing international legal instrument provide sufficient protection for the internally displaced and whether what is needed is more legal prescription or simply better implementation of existing law',[55] he concluded that the urgency of the IDPs situation demanded 'for clear guidelines that could be applied to all internally displaced persons, regardless of the cause of their displacement, the country concerned, or the prevailing legal, social, political, or military situation'.[56]

Representative Deng decided to go further into studying the legal foundation for IDPs protection and developed a two-part 'Compilation and Analysis of Legal Norms' pertaining to internally displaced persons[57] respectively in 1996[58] and 1998.[59] The conclusion was that 'while existing law covers many aspects of particular relevance to internally displaced persons, there remain areas in which the law fails to provide sufficient protection for them'.[60] These areas either represent:

[54] UN Commission on Human Rights, Resolution 1992/73, para. 2.

[55] UN Commission on Human Rights, *Comprehensive Study Prepared by Mr Francis M. Deng, Representative of the Secretary-General on the Human Rights Issues Related to Internally Displaced Persons, Pursuant to Commission on Human Rights Resolution 1992/73*, annexed to UN Doc. E/CN4/1993/35, 21 January 1993, para. 55.

[56] UN Commission on Human Rights, *Comprehensive Study*, para. 75.

[57] Kälin, W., 2014, 'The Guiding Principles on Internal Displacement and the Search for a Universal Framework of Protection for Internally Displaced Persons'. In *Research Handbook on International Law and Migration*, part IV, edited by Chetail, V. and Bauloz, C., Cheltenham: Edward Elgar Publishing, p. 615.

[58] UN Commission on Human Rights, *Report of the Representative of the Secretary-General, Mr Francis M. Deng, Submitted Pursuant to Commission on Human Rights Resolution 1995/57, Compilation and Analysis of Legal Norms*, UN Doc. E/CN.4/1996/52/Add.2, 5 December 1995.

[59] UN Commission on Human Rights, *Report of the Representative of the Secretary-General, Mr Francis M. Deng, Submitted Pursuant to Commission on Human Rights Resolution 1997/39, Addendum, Compilation and Analysis of Legal Norms, Part II: Legal Aspects Relating*, UN Doc. E/CN.4/1996/52/Add.2, 5 December 1995.

[60] *Compilation and Analysis of Legal Norms 1995*, para. 410.

gaps in legal protection which occur where no explicit norms exist to address identifiable needs of the displace or where a general norm exists but a corollary, more specific right has not been articulated that would ensure implementation of the general norm in areas of particular need to internally displaced persons.[61]

The Commission on Human Rights endorsed the conclusions of the study and requested Deng to 'continue, on the basis of his compilation and analysis of legal norms, to develop an appropriate framework in this regard for the protection of internally displaced persons'.[62]

Accordingly, Deng convened a small group of legal experts[63] and, after organizing a series of consultation with UN agency and non-governmental organizations issued, in March 1998, the *Guiding Principles on Internal Displacement*.[64]

THE GUIDING PRINCIPLES ON INTERNAL DISPLACEMENT 1998

As it is stated in the Introduction, the *Guiding Principles* aim at identifying 'rights and guarantees relevant to the protection of persons from forced displacement and to their protection and assistance' in all phases of a conflict meaning 'during displacement as well as during return or resettlement and reintegration'.[65] The *Principles* do not intend to create new legal standards but they try to 'clarify relevant norms where existing treaties and conventions are unclear or may contain gaps'.[66] In doing so, they 'reflect and are consistent with international human rights law and international humanitarian law'.[67] The *Principles* should serve as guidance not only to States but also to other competent authorities, groups, and persons, and intergovernmental as well as non-governmental organizations working with internally displaced persons.[68]

[61] Ibid., para. 411.

[62] UN Commission on Human Rights, Resolution 1996/52, 19 April 1996, preamble, para. 6.

[63] The group was composed by Robert Goldman, Manfred Novak, and Walter Kälin, Jean-François Durieux from the UNHCR, Jean-Philippe Lavoyer and Toni Pfanner from the ICRC, and Daniel Helle and Maria Stavropoulou from the UN Centre for Human Rights. See Bagshaw, S., 2005, *Developing a Normative Framework for the Protection of Internally Displaced Persons*, Ardsley, Transnational Publisher, p. 128.

[64] The document was submitted to the Commission on Human Rights in March 1998, which adopted a resolution 'taking note' of the report, see Commission on Human Rights, Resolution 1998/50, UN Doc. E/CN.4/1998/177, 30 March 1998, 165, para. 1.

[65] UN Commission on Human Rights, *Report of the Representative of the Secretary-General, Mr Francis M. Deng, Submitted Pursuant to Commission on Human Rights Resolution 1997/39, Addendum, Guiding Principles on Internal Displacement,* UN Doc. E/CN.4/1998/53/Add.2, 11 February 1998, Introduction, para. 1.

[66] Kälin, W., 'The Guiding Principles on Internal Displacement', p. 621.

[67] *Guiding Principles*, Introduction, para. 3.

[68] *Guiding Principles*, Introduction, para. 3.

In the document, internally displaced persons are defined as:

Persons or groups of persons who have been forced or obliged to flee or to leave their homes or places of habitual residence, in particular as a result of or in order to avoid the effects of armed conflict, situations of generalized violence, violations of human rights or natural or humane-made disasters, and who have not crossed an internationally recognized State border.[69]

Two main criteria can be identified from this description, first, the coercive or involuntary nature of displacement, which differentiates them from persons that leave their homes for economic or similar reasons based on a voluntary decision. Second, the fact that displacement has to take place within the States' borders distinguishes them from refugees. In addition, the definition provides a list of situations that may cause displacement which is not exhaustive.[70]

The *Guiding Principles* are divided into five different sections. The first section lists some *General Principles* such as the principle of non-discrimination and highlights that 'the primary duty and responsibility to provide protection and humanitarian assistance to internally displaced persons within their jurisdiction' lies on national authorities.[71] This also entails that persons displaced inside the borders of the country of which they are nationals or permanent residents are, as such, entitled to benefit from the 'full range of human rights as well as those guarantees of international humanitarian law, which are applicable in a given situation'.[72]

Section II relates to the *Protection from Displacement* recognizing a right not to be arbitrarily displaced and providing a non-exhaustive list of forms of prohibited displacement. However, the document does acknowledge the possibility of using displacement, not arbitrarily, under exceptional circumstances, i.e., in situations of armed conflict when the security of the civilians involved or imperative military reasons so demand.[73] Principles in section III deal with *Protection during Displacement.* They restate applicable human rights law and international humanitarian law provisions formulated in general terms and they spell them out to simplify their application in contexts of internal displacement.[74] Section IV addresses the issue of *Humanitarian Assistance* reiterating

[69] *Guiding Principles*, Introduction, para. 2.

[70] Kälin, W., 'The Guiding Principles on Internal Displacement ', p. 617.

[71] *Guiding Principles*, Principle 3(1).

[72] Kälin, W., 'The Guiding Principles on Internal Displacement', p. 620.

[73] *Guiding Principles*, Principle 6 (b), (c) or (d).

[74] As Kälin interestingly points out, an example of that is Principle 6 on the right to be protected against arbitrary displacement. Neither international human rights law nor IHL explicitly mention such a right, however, IHL prohibits displacement in some specific situations and human rights law, in more general terms, guarantees not only freedom of movement but also the right to choose one's own residence. Also the right not to be displaced is present in instruments dealing with the rights of indigenous peoples. From this, the drafters of the Guiding Principles came to the conclusion that a right not to be arbitrarily displaced in already implicit in international law. See, Kälin, W., 'The Guiding Principles on Internal Displacement ', p. 619.

that the primary duty and responsibility for providing humanitarian assistance to IDPs is with national authorities and adding the right of international humanitarian organizations and other appropriate actors to offer their services in support of IDPs. The delivery of assistance by international actors needs the consent of the State concerned but cannot be denied arbitrarily.[75]

Finally, section V deals with the issue of *Return, Resettlement and Reintegration* of IDPs setting out a legal framework for finding durable solutions to end displacement. The relevant provisions stress that competent authorities:

> have the primary duty and responsibility to establish conditions, as well as provide the means, which allow internally displaced persons to return voluntarily, in safety and with dignity, to their homes or places of habitual residence, or to resettle voluntarily in another part of the country.[76]

This principle seems to acknowledge implicitly IDPs' right to choose from the three possible durable solutions which are return and sustainable integration at their former homes, sustainable local integration where they had been displaced to or sustainable integration in another part of the country.[77]

To sum up, it can be said that the *Guiding Principles* have substantially contributed in putting forward the idea that IDPs have specific needs owing to the fact that they experience a very special factual situation.

THE *GUIDING PRINCIPLES*, MORE THAN SOFT LAW?

As previously mentioned, the *Guiding Principles* are not a legally binding instrument but they have had since their adoption a significant impact as soft law. 'Soft law' can be defined as 'instruments and norms that don't give rise to binding obligations but which have certain legal effects or significance nonetheless'.[78] The legal authority of the *Guiding Principles* also stems from the fact that they reflect already binding IHL and IHRL.

Their crucial importance for the protection of IDPs was unanimously and explicitly recognized by the 2005 World Summit, which described the *Guiding Principles* as 'an important international framework for the protection of internally displaced persons'.[79]

[75] *Guiding Principles*, Principle 25. [76] *Guiding Principles*, Principle 28.

[77] Kälin, W., 'The Guiding Principles on Internal Displacement', p. 619.

[78] Bagshaw, S., *Developing a Normative Framework*, p. 99.

[79] UN General Assembly, *2005 World Summit Outcome*, UN Doc. A/RES/60/1, 24 October 2005, para. 132. During that same World Summit, States also recognized their and the UN's responsibility to protect populations from genocide, war crimes, ethnic cleansing, and crimes against humanity (paras. 138–9) and set the bases for the Human Rights Council (paras. 157–60). This position on the *Guiding Principles* was reiterated in several occasions by the General Assembly and the Human Rights Council. See UN General Assembly resolutions, UN Docs. A/RES/62/153, 6 March 2008, para. 10; A/RES/64/162, 17 March 2010,

According to some authors, the soft law nature of the *Guiding Principles* has several advantages. The more significant is the avoidance of what Kälin, calls the 'ratification gap' or the fact that 'treaties cannot be invoked against States that have not ratified them'.[80] Second, it is argued that soft law is more flexible compared to hard law and can be more easily adapted to the specific needs of each context. Also, it is said that it is easier to approach States and discuss their potential non-compliance with the *Guiding Principles* in terms of providing 'helpful guidance' or addressing 'challenges' instead of accusing them of alleged violations.[81] These are undoubtedly good points but they still fall short of addressing the issue of accountability for violations committed against IDPs and the question of redress and reparations for the victims of these violations.[82]

The question was asked if it was foreseeable to consider the *Guiding Principles* as customary international law, i.e., coming from a general practice accepted as law. In order for that to be true it would have to be proved that the *Guiding Principles* are reflected in State practice and that the international community perceives that such practice is required as a matter of law (*opinio iuris*).[83] Notwithstanding the fact that the *Principles* have been referred to by many domestic legislations and judgments and that there are at least two countries explicitly recognizing them as part of international law,[84] it seems inappropriate, today, to state that they reflect customary international law.[85] This is because State practice seems still too limited to be considered as 'general practice accepted by law' and also because, the Secretary-General's proposal to consider the *Guiding Principles* as 'the basic international norm'[86] for the protection of IDPs during the World Summit in 2005, was rejected showing that the majority of States did not want the *Guiding Principles* to become legally binding. However, their impact on the international community was significant and in 2011, the UN General Assembly noted

para. 10; A/RES/66/165, 19 December 2011, para. 12. Human Rights Council resolutions, UN Docs. A/HRC/RES/6/32, 14 December 2007, para.5; and A/HRC/RES/23/8, 20 June 2013, para. 12.

80 Kälin, W., 'The Guiding Principles on Internal Displacement', p. 628.

81 Ibid.

82 Both issues could be addressed by domestic law but this has not been the case in most of the situations we have been analysing so far. Moreover, these issues can be addressed before human rights bodies as the practice of the IACtHR and the ECtHR shows.

83 See the definition of customary law provided by the Statute of the International Court of Justice, 26 June 1945, Art. 38(1)(b).

84 The Government of Germany has stated that the Guiding Principles 'can now be considered to be customary international law'; in Iraq, the National Policy on Displacement recognizes the Guiding Principles as 'part of international law', see Kälin, W., 'The Guiding Principles on Internal Displacement', p. 629, footnote 107.

85 For a thorough discussion on the potential customary nature of the *Guiding Principles*, see Kälin, W., 'The Guiding Principles on Internal Displacement', pp. 628–630.

86 UN Secretary-General, *In Larger Freedom: Towards Development, Security and Human Rights for All*, UN Doc. A/59/205, 21 March 2005, para. 210.

that 'an increasing number of states, United Nations organizations and regional non-governmental organizations are applying them as standard'.[87]

C. Regional and national developments

Many regional and sub-regional organizations have welcomed the *Guiding Principles* calling on their member States to use them while addressing IDP-related issues at the national level.[88] The following section will provide a brief overview on how they have been and currently are treated and implemented at regional and national level.

REGIONAL INITIATIVES FOR THE PROTECTION OF IDPS

Thanks to the vigorous advocacy campaign conducted by Representative Deng in the years following the adoption of the *Guiding Principles*, a great number of regional organizations and other entities have issued public declarations and resolutions supporting them and calling for their implementation at national level. Three of these initiatives are particularly important in order to understand the current landscape related to the protection of internally displaced persons.

In Europe, the Committee of Ministers of the Council of Europe adopted in 2006 a Recommendation[89] detailing some key provisions, directly inspired by the *Guiding Principles*, which should guide the law and practice of its member States. Moreover its Committee on Migration, Refugee and Population has been stressing the importance of strengthening and ensuring the effective exercise of the rights of IDPs in Europe.[90]

[87] General Assembly, UN Doc. A/RES/66/165, para. 12. The *Guiding Principles* have also been taken into account by several UN treaty bodies when examining state reports, namely the Human Rights Committee (HRC), the Committee on the Elimination of Racial Discrimination (CERD), the Committee on the Rights of the Child (CRC), and the Committee on Economic, Social and Cultural Rights (CERCR). However, as Ojeda has pointed out, such references to the *Guiding Principles* are not systematic. For more information see: Ojeda, S., 'International Humanitarian Law', pp. 625–6.

[88] For further details, see UN Human Rights Council, *Report of the Representative of the Secretary-General on the Human Rights of Internally Displaced Persons*, Walter Kälin, UN Doc. A/HRC/13/21, 5 January 2010, 5, para. 14. See also, Organization of American States, *General Assembly Resolution on Internally Displaced Persons*, AG/RES. 2508 (XXXIX-0/09), 4 June 2009.

[89] Council of Europe, *Recommendation (2006) 6 of the Committee of Ministers to Member States on Internally Displaced Persons*, 5 April 2006.

[90] For instance, concerning the situation of conflict-induced IDPs, the Committee has adopted resolutions and recommendations on the *'Humanitarian Consequences of the War between Georgia and Russia'* or on the *'Humanitarian Situation of the Chechen Displaced Population'*. For more information, visit <http://www.coe.int/lportal/web/coe-portal>.

As the African continent is more affected by armed conflict-induced IDPs, it is not surprising that the two more important developments in terms of protection of displaced persons come from this region.[91] First of all, in 2006, the International Conference of the Great Lakes Region adopted the *Great-Lakes Protocol on the Protection and Assistance to Internally Displaced Persons* as part of its Pact on Security, Stability and Development in the Great Lakes Region.[92] Since its entry came into force in 2008, the Protocol became the first legally binding instrument exclusively addressing IDPs and, as of today, it has been ratified by eleven States.[93] The key provision of the Protocol is Article 6(3):

> Member States shall enact national legislation to domesticate the Guiding Principles fully and to provide a legal framework for their implementation within national legal systems.

This Article explicitly obliges States Parties to fully incorporate the *Guiding Principles* in their domestic law.[94]

THE 2009 KAMPALA CONVENTION

In October 2009, the African Union Special Summit of Heads of State and Governments adopted the African Convention for the Protection and Assistance of Internally Displaced Persons in Africa, the so-called 'Kampala Convention'. This instrument represents the first legally binding convention, applicable to a whole continent, exclusively addressing the phenomenon of internal displacement in a comprehensive manner. The Convention builds on the *Guiding Principles on Internal Displacement* as well as previous regional initiatives but it also reflects recent developments and the evolution of the best practices concerning the protection of IPDs.[95] Just as the *Guiding Principles*, it addresses the three phases of displacement—protection from displacement,[96] protection during

[91] Africa has more countries affected by displacement than any other continent or region and is home to more than 12 million IDPs. IDMC, *The Kampala Convention two years on: time to turn theory into practice*, Briefing Paper, 8 December 2014.

[92] International Conference in the Great Lakes Region, *Protocol on the Protection and Assistance of Internally Displaced Persons*, 30 November 2006 (entry into force, June 2008).

[93] Those States are: Angola, Burundi, Central African Republic, Democratic Republic of the Congo, Republic of Congo, Kenya, Rwanda, Sudan, Tanzania, Uganda, and Zambia.

[94] The Great Lakes Conference also adopted a *Protocol on the Property Rights of Returning Persons*, 30 November 2006, setting out the legal principles regulating the recovery of property by IDPs and the resolution of property related conflicts; and the *Protocol on the Prevention and Suppression of Sexual Violence against Women and Children* of particular relevance given the greater vulnerability of displaced women and children to sexual violence.

[95] Asplet, M. and Bradley, M., 2013, *Introductory Note to the African Union Convention for the Protection and Assistance of Internally Displaced Persons in Africa (Kampala Convention)*, 6 December 2012, American Society of International Law, International Legal Materials, vol. 52, no. 1, p. 397.

[96] Arts 4–10, Kampala Convention.

displacement[97] and the identification of durable solutions to displacement[98]—and sets out obligations to all parties potentially involved in displacement, namely States, non-State armed groups, the African Union (AU), and humanitarian actors. Establishing obligations incumbent upon non-State armed groups and humanitarian actors is quite an innovative aspect of the Convention.[99]

The text of the Kampala Convention is formulated in terms of obligations of States and other relevant actors rather than on the rights of IDPs. It reiterates the States' primary, but not exclusive, duty and responsibility to provide protection and assistance to IDPs within their territory and, where available resources are inadequate to enable them to do so the Convention states their obligation to seek the assistance of humanitarian actors.[100]

The definition provided by the Convention of internally displaced persons is identical to the one contained in the *Guiding Principles*, covering, in a holistic approach, displacement caused by armed conflict, situation of generalized violence, violations of human rights and disasters (natural or human-made).[101] One of the Convention's most progressive innovations is the strengthening of the prohibition on arbitrary displacement in international law. Article 4 of the Convention formulates a right to be protected from arbitrary displacement that covers a number of acts including discriminatory policies, violence, unjustified forced evacuations, and other grave acts not justified under international law. As it has been noted, these provisions significantly extend the notion of what constitutes arbitrary displacement and if effectively implemented could provide much greater protection to populations at risk of being displaced.[102]

The Convention also contains advanced provisions in relation to the third phase of displacement, namely the identification of durable solutions.[103] Reflecting the progressive

[97] Arts 5–9, Kampala Convention. [98] Art. 11, Kampala Convention.

[99] Art. 7 is specifically addressed to 'dissident armed forces or other organized armed groups that are distinct from the armed forces of the state' where the Convention reiterates some of the relevant obligations derived from international humanitarian law applicable in non-international armed conflict. Furthermore, it requires armed groups not affiliated with the State to protect and assist IDPs in areas under their effective control (Art. 3(2)(c)).

[100] Art. 55(1) and (6), Kampala Convention.

[101] Art. 1, Kampala Convention. The Convention also provides a definition of the phenomenon of internal displacement: 'the involuntary or forced movement, evacuation or relocation of persons or groups of persons within internationally recognized state borders', Art. 1(i), Kampala Convention.

[102] Those bound by the Convention are also obligated to ensure that individuals who commit acts of arbitrary displacement are held accountable. This obligation extends to holding non-State actors, such as armed groups, private military contractors, multinational corporations accountable for arbitrary displacement. Asplet, M. and Bradley, M., *Introductory Note to the African Union Convention*, p. 398.

[103] The Kampala Convention in relation to return, local integration, or relocation goes further, in terms of protection, than current IHL treaties. In fact, IHL in IACs just guarantees the right to return and in NIACs the right to return is not even explicitly mentioned although this gap is filled by Rule 132 of Customary IHL, providing a right to return in all situations. See, Ojeda, S., 'International Humanitarian Law', p. 648.

standards set up in the *Guiding Principles*, the Convention reaffirms the right of IDPs to 'make a free and informed choice on whether to return, integrate locally, or relocate' and stresses States' responsibility to create conditions allowing IDPs to do so.[104] The Convention, however, does not indicate when a situation of displacement is considered to have ceased and, unlike refugees, there is no cessation clause for IDPs.[105] However, it seems that there is a common agreement on the fact that in most cases, displacement does not end immediately once the causes for fleeing no longer exist.[106] The end of displacement is considered to be a process that can be rather long, and a durable solution is only achieved when IDPs no longer have any specific assistance and protection needs linked with their displacement.[107]

The Kampala Convention binds member States to provide 'effective remedies' for damage incurred as a result of displacement and just and fair compensation and other forms of reparations to IDPs,[108] showing a more progressive view in relation to the *Guiding Principles* and pushing for accountability for displacement and towards displaced persons as 'survivors' of a whole range of human rights abuses.[109]

THE CHALLENGES OF IMPLEMENTATION

The Kampala Convention undoubtedly represents an important step towards the formalizations of norms on internal displacement and, consequently, for the protection and assistance of IDPs in Africa and in the world. At present, the challenges ahead are twofold, increasing the number of ratifications of the Convention as well as ensuring its effective implementation by State parties.

As of today, the Convention, which entered into force in December 2012, has been ratified by twenty-two of the fifty-four member States of the African Union.[110] Thus, more

[104] Art. 11(1) and (2), Kampala Convention. The legal instrument goes further calling on States to create appropriate mechanisms to resolve IDPs' property disputes (Art. 11(4)).

[105] The underlying principle is that States shall take all necessary measures to avoid protracted situations of displacement. See Duchatellier, M. and Phuong, C., 'The African Contribution to the Protection of Internally Displaced Persons', p. 660.

[106] Duchatellier, M. and Phuong, C., 'The African Contribution to the Protection of Internally Displaced Persons', p. 660.

[107] Kälin, W., 'Framework on Durable Solutions for Internally Displaced Persons', in UN Human Rights Council, *Report of the Representative of the Secretary-General on the Human Rights of Internally Displaced Persons*, UN Doc. A/HRC/13/21/Add.4, 9 February 2010.

[108] Art. 12(1) and (2), Kampala Convention. Here too, the Convention goes further than IHL which does not provide a right to an individual remedy against a violation nor individual reparations. See, Ojeda, S., 'International Humanitarian Law', p. 648. Art. 12(1) and (2), Kampala Convention.

[109] Asplet, M. and Bradley, M., *Introductory Note to the African Union Convention*, p. 398.

[110] The number of signatory States amount to thirty-nine.

advocacy work needs to be done in order to increase the number of State parties. As for the second challenge, the Kampala Convention requires member States to incorporate their obligations under the Convention into domestic law by enacting or amending relevant legislation.[111] It also requires parties to the Convention to create an institutional framework for the coordination of activities related to IDPs and allocate the necessary funds for ensuring implementation.[112]

A number of African countries have already developed or are in the process of developing policies and national frameworks to address IDP-related issues.[113] In most of the cases, such policies have been issued in the aftermath of the adoption of the *Guiding Principles* and other regional initiatives such as the Great-Lakes Protocol. The next years will be crucial to appraise if the Convention is effectively implemented by member States and its effects on internal displacement in Africa. The next section will provide an overview of the development and implementation of IDP-related laws and policies at national level.

NATIONAL LAWS AND POLICIES FOR THE PROTECTION OF IDPS

To date, more than twenty countries[114] in the world have adopted domestic law and policies specifically addressing IDPs with some other countries in the process of doing so.[115] Four different models can be distinguished of how countries have enacted such laws and policies.[116]

First, a simple domestic instrument with either a reference to or adopting the *Guiding Principles*. An example of this approach is Burundi where an agreement signed with the

[111] Art. 3(2)(a), Kampala Convention.

[112] Art. 3(2)(b) and 3(2)(d), Kampala Convention. The Convention has been criticized by some for the lack of effective enforcement mechanisms. It foresees the creation of two mechanisms to monitor compliance: the Conference of State Parties and a reporting mechanism, both with no binding effects on States. For more information, see Duchatellier, M. and Phuong, C., 'The African Contribution to the Protection of Internally Displaced Persons', p. 666.

[113] Those countries are: Angola, Burundi, Central African Republic, Liberia, Sierra Leone, Sudan, Uganda, and Kenya. See Duchatellier, M. and Phuong, C., 'The African Contribution to the Protection of Internally Displaced Persons', p. 667.

[114] Colombia, Guatemala, Peru, United States, Angola, Burundi, Liberia, Sierra Leone, Uganda, India, Nepal, Sri Lanka, Tajikistan, Iraq, Turkey, Armenia, Azerbaijan, Bosnia, Georgia, Russia, and Serbia. For a compilation of laws and policies on IDPs see, Brookings-LSE project on Internal Displacement, IDP Laws and policies Index, available at: <http://www.brookings.edu/about/projects/idp/resources/idp-policies-index>.

[115] For example, Central African Republic, Somalia, and Yemen, see, Brookings-LSE project on Internal Displacement.

[116] Ferris, E., *Comparative Perspectives on Laws and Policies Addressing Internal Displacement*, Brookings-Bern Project in Internal Displacement, 27 June 2009, p. 4.

UN recognizes that 'the Government of Burundi and the International Community are bound by the United Nations Guiding Principles on Internal Displacement'.[117] Liberia went further by stating in its instrument of adoption that the *Guiding Principles* are part of its domestic law.[118]

Second, a law or policies developed to address a specific cause or stage of displacement such as in Serbia,[119] Azerbaijan,[120] Bosnia Herzegovina,[121] and Nepal.[122]

Third, a law or policy elaborated to tackle a specific right of IDPs. The Compensation Law in Turkey adopted in 2004[123] is an example of this approach as well as Angola's decree on return and reintegration of IDPs of 2002.[124]

Fourth, a comprehensive law or policy addressing all causes and phases of internal displacement. This is the case of Colombia's Law no. 387 issued in 1987 more than ten years before the adoption of the *Guiding Principles* and the subsequent 2011 Law on Victims and Restitution of Land to restore land forcibly taken from IDPs and to compensate the victims of civil conflict.[125] Uganda, as well, developed a National Policy for Internally Displaced Persons where it declared the *Guiding Principles* as one of the documents inspiring the national policy and translating many of the *Principles* into more detailed guidelines.[126] In 2007, Georgia adopted an IDP State strategy stressing that 'the government of Georgia takes into account the UN Guiding Principles on Internal Displacement'.[127]

Last but not least, Ukraine too has very recently adopted the 2014 National Policy for IDPs.[128] The *On ensuring of rights and freedoms of internally displaced persons law*, which

[117] Protocol for the Creation of a Permanent Framework for Consultation on the Protection of Displaced Persons, 7 February 2011, preamble, para. 6.

[118] Liberia, The Guiding Principles on Internally Displaced Persons Instrument of Adoption, 2004.

[119] Serbia, Protocol on Voluntary and Sustainable Return, 2006.

[120] Azerbaijan, Decree of the President of the Azerbaijan Republic regarding the approval of the 'State Program for the Improvement of living standards and generation of employment for refugees and IDPs', July 2004.

[121] Bosnia and Herzegovina, Law on Displaced Persons and Returnees in the Federation of Bosnia and Herzegovina and Refugees from Bosnia and Herzegovina, 2005.

[122] Nepal, National Policy on Internally Displaced Persons, 2007. According to the IDMC, the Government did little to implement this policy until 2010. Nepal's constitutional assembly elected in November 2013 and tasked with completing the country's draft constitution will probably clear the way for the 2007 National Policy on IDPs and its related procedural directives to be implemented. See IDMC/NRC, *Global Overview 2014*, p. 73.

[123] Turkey, Law No. 5233, The Law on the Compensation of Damages that Occurred due to Terror and the Fight Against Terrorism, July 2004.

[124] Angola, Standard Operational Procedures for the enforcement of the *Norm on the Resettlement of Displaced Populations*, Council of Ministers Decree No. 79/02, 6 December 2002.

[125] Colombia, Ley 1448 de Victimas y Restitucion de Tierras, 17 June 2011.

[126] Uganda, National Policy for Internally Displaced Persons, 2004.

[127] Georgia, State Strategy for Internally Displaced Persons—Persecutes (approved by the Government of Georgia with Decree No. 47, 2 February 2007, Chapter III, para. 1.

[128] Ukraine, National Policy for Internally Displaced Persons, *On ensuring of rights and freedoms of internally displaced persons*, 20 October 2014.

is part of the National Policy, provides IDPs with a specific set of rights and ensures protection against discrimination, forcible return, and assistance in voluntary returns. The law also simplifies access to different social and economic services, especially residence registration and unemployment benefits and it obliges the government to start developing a policy on integration of internally displaced persons.[129]

As a side note, Syria, the country most affected by internal displacement in 2014, with at least 7.6 million IDPs,[130] not only has not adopted any policy or law on the subject matter, but denies the very existence of such a phenomenon in its territory.[131] The Government of Syria, commenting on the Secretary-General's Note on the protection and assistance of IDPs in Syria, stated that his country was not suffering from a phenomenon called 'internally displaced persons' but rather had been subject to a series of terrorist attacks undertaken by armed groups. It also added that persons being assisted were referred to as 'people who left their homes as a result of the current events'.[132] The Government stressed the serious humanitarian repercussions of the sanctions imposed on the Syrian people and it detailed its efforts, such as the establishment of the High Committee for Relief, which is responsible for the immediate response to the needs of affected populations, and the Reconstruction Committee, which is mandated, inter alia, to compensate citizens for property damage and rehabilitate damaged infrastructures and public facilities.[133]

To sum up, many countries have developed IDP-related laws and policies inspired by or incorporating fully or in part the international standards set by the *Guiding Principles*. However, looking at the tragic figures on internal displacement in 2014 resulting from the growing number of internal crisis we are currently witnessing, it appears clear that more needs to be done to ensure that existing laws and policies are effectively implemented and that more States agree to endorse and incorporate the *Guiding Principles* in their domestic system.

[129] UNHCR, 'UNHCR welcomes adoption of the law by Ukrainian Parliament to protect people displaced by conflict', Press release, 20 October 2014.

[130] IDMC, Syria profile, available at: <http://www.internal-displacement.org/middle-east-and-north-africa/syria/>, as of December 2014.

[131] The issue of internal displacement has always been a sensitive matter for Syria. Before the current armed conflict, Syrian authorities only recognized as IDPs Syrians who had been displaced by Israel's invasion and occupation of the Golan in 1967. The first two years of the current conflict, the Syrian media made almost not reference to IDPs. Similarly, the Syrian's Humanitarian and Assistance Plans (HARP), developed by the Syrian Government, did not refer to IDPs but instead to 'affected populations who have moved to other areas'. See, IDMC/NRC, *Syria: Forsaken IDPs adrift inside a fragmenting state*, 21 October 2014, p. 13,

[132] Government of the Syrian Arab Republic, communications to the Special Rapporteur, 31 May and 12 June 2013.

[133] General Assembly, *Protection of and assistance to internally displaced persons: situation of internally displaced persons in the Syrian Arab Republic*, Note by the Secretary-General, 15 July 2013, UN Doc. A/67/931, paras 51–52.

D. The institutional framework for the protection of IDPs

In parallel with the development of a normative framework for the protection and assistance of IDPs, the international community started discussions on how to respond, from an operational point of view, to the specific needs of this particular group of people. As rightly pointed out by the ICRC, since displacement often continues for extended periods, 'the humanitarian challenges it brings are immense, not least for a coherent, well-coordinated and comprehensive response from the international community'.[134]

THE HUMANITARIAN REFORM AND THE *CLUSTER APPROACH*

At first, given the broad nature of IDP needs, the UN has relied on a 'collaborative approach', in which the different agencies shared the responsibility depending on their expertise. In 1991 the position of Emergency Relief Coordinator (ERC) was created and a year later the Inter-Agency Standing Committee (IASC) was established together with a task force for IDPs.[135]

The option of establishing a new agency with the specific mandate of protecting and assisting IDPs was taken into consideration. However, the lack of political will and resources at the time made this option seem unrealistic.[136] Another approach was for international agencies to expand their programme activities to meet the protection, assistance, reintegration, and developments needs of IDPs. Some organizations have had to stretch their mandates to do so. This was the case for instance of UNHCR whose mandate only included refugees' but whose involvement with IDPs continued to grow over the years.

However, in the absence of clear institutional mandates, the international community was unable to find appropriate ways to deal with the growing number of internally displaced persons. In the early 2000s it was clear that the 'collaborative approach' was not working. As eloquently declared by the US Ambassador Richard Holbrooke after visiting Angola in 2000:

A coordinated response is inadequate ... Agencies are supposed to act as 'co-heads'. In practice, however, co-heads means 'no-heads'.[137]

[134] ICRC, *Internal Displacement in Armed Conflict. Facing up to the challenges*, November 2009, p. 2.

[135] For more information, see Ferris, E., *Ten Years After Humanitarian Reform: How Have IDPs Fared?*, December 2014, Brookings-LSE, Project on Internal Displacement, p. 8.

[136] For more information see: Cohen, R., 'Protection of Internally Displaced Persons', p. 602.

[137] R. Holbrooke quoted in IASC Decide to Leave IDPS to UN Humanitarian Coordinators

The decision was made to initiate a 'humanitarian reform' programme requiring the appointment of a lead agency to coordinate the work of other agencies in its sector of expertise in each emergency. A *cluster approach* was taken with the view of ensuring a more predictable, consistent, and accountable response to each crisis.[138] Three clusters were established to specifically address the need of IDPs in conflict situations: protection, camp management, and camp coordination, and emergency shelter. UNHCR was the leading agency of these clusters in time of conflict.[139] UNICEF was the coordinating agency for water, sanitation, and nutrition, WFP was in charge of logistics, and UNDP of early recovery.[140]

After almost ten years from the adoption of the cluster approach it can be said that the international community has made significant progress in responding to the needs of IDPs. The humanitarian reform contributed to a more effective international response to IDPs crises which has alleviated suffering and saved lives.[141] Nonetheless the cluster approach has shown several flaws and weaknesses that need to be taken into account. For instance, international and especially national NGOs have a very little role to play in the cluster system although they are the one more involved in the assistance of IDPs in a long term perspective.[142] Moreover, the cluster system tends to concentrate its efforts primarily on new emergencies which results in a lack of attention and assistance to cases of protracted displacement.[143]

Shortcomings were found to be particularly critical in the *early recovery* cluster in charge of providing assistance to communities to recover from conflict and disaster by re-establishing local governance structures, judicial and law enforcement systems, basic services including schools, health care, water, and sanitation; and replacing lost documentation, creating jobs and livelihood programmes.[144] These services are generally considered as falling between the field of relief and development programmes, creating a dysfunctional gap. As a consequence, early recovery initiatives are not perceived as

[138] Cohen, R., 'Protection of Internally Displaced Persons', p. 603.

[139] In situations of natural disasters, the International Federation of Red Cross and Red Crescent Societies (IFRC) was tasked with facilitating the emergency shelter cluster while the International Organization for Migration (IOM) was to lead the cluster on camp management and camp coordination. UNHCR's engagement with IDPs follows three main principles: (1) The primary responsibility to protect and assist IDPs lies with States; (2) The rights and freedom of all IDPs must be ensured without discrimination; (3) Humanitarian organizations have a collective responsibility to ensure that their work does not undermine individual and community protection mechanisms and avoids exposing IDPs to further risk, exacerbating discrimination and negative practices. See, UNHCR, *Engaging with IDPs*, UNHCR Global Appeal 2014–15, p. 60.

[140] Cohen, R., 'Protection of Internally Displaced Persons', p. 603.

[141] Ferris, E., *Ten Years After Humanitarian Reform*, p. 12.

[142] Cohen, R., 'Protection of Internally Displaced Persons', p. 604.

[143] For more information see, Ferris, E., 2007, *Durable Solutions for IDPs in Protracted Situations: A Work in Progress*, Washington, DC, Brookings Institution, 1 June 2007, p. 25.

[144] Ferris, E., *Ten Years After Humanitarian Reform*, p. 23.

urgent and end up being overlooked notwithstanding their crucial importance for IDPs' proper recovery.[145] On this issue, Kälin has observed that:

Experience has shown that people often find themselves in the worst living situations six to twelve months after the disaster, when emergency funding has stopped. This is primarily because early recovery measures were not initiated during the emergency phase.[146]

Overall, despite a general improvement of the response mechanisms to IDPs thanks to the humanitarian reform, much more needs to be done to prevent new displacement and to find durable solutions for those who have been displaced for a long time.

E. Current challenges in protecting IDPs

The number of conflict-induced internally displaced persons has drastically increased in the past few years reaching a peak in 2014 with the worsening of the crises in countries such as in Syria, Iraq, Nigeria, and South Sudan just to name a few. The international community is thus facing new challenges in relation to internal displacement and this section will try to analyse some of them.

First of all is the difficulty of accessing IDPs in order to provide assistance and protection. This is both a logistical and a political/security problem. From a logistical view point, it can be extremely problematic to reach the displaced who for instance find themselves outside IDPs camps. As it has been said, official IDP collective sites are just the tip of the iceberg. In fact, the needs are greater outside camps especially in host communities where residents have to provide them with shelter and food. IPDs outside camps can be more difficult to reach because of lack of communication channels, configurations of the terrain or because transportation in such areas is rendered impossible by weather conditions. However, reasons for lack of access are more often a matter of political considerations and security with parties to the conflict denying access to certain areas and/or directly targeting humanitarian personnel.

In Syria, for instance, the international humanitarian response has been seriously hampered by the Syrian authorities' strict restrictions on the provision of assistance to people in need. Undoubtedly, humanitarian access in Syria is impeded by a combination of factors including security and administrative concerns, but the obstacles and restrictions imposed by the parties to the conflict through formal or informal checkpoints,

[145] The Special Rapporteur on Human Rights of IDPS made this problematic issue one of its mains priorities in December 2012,

[146] Interview with W. Kälin, 9 January 2010 in Cohen, R., 'Protection of Internally Displaced Persons', p. 607.

closure of access routes, direct attacks on humanitarian workers and vehicles, and failure to provide safe passages for civilians, are playing a greater role in hampering access to people in need.[147] As the recently published paper, *Failing Syria*, reports: 'Despite being central to the 2014 UNSC Resolutions, humanitarian access to large parts of Syria has actually diminished over the past year' adding that:

> The Government of Syria continues to hamper the work of agencies. It regularly prevents international humanitarian workers from travelling within Syria to conduct independent assessment of needs, provide impartial assistance ... Many agencies face ongoing problems with registration and with obtaining visas for their staff, severely limiting aid operations.[148]

Another issue arising from humanitarian crises that we currently witness is the phenomenon of multiple displacements. People are not only or no longer fleeing to escape generalized violence and lack of security but 'an increasing number of internally displaced persons are forced to flee again as a result of the secondary effect of conflict'. In Syria for example:

> The massive destruction of homes in certain areas, the disruption of basic services, including water, health care and sanitation, and the loss of livelihoods is depriving many Syrians of their ability to meet their most basic needs and forcing them to seek assistance and refuge in other locations.[149]

This was also the case for Nigeria, where attacks by the Islamic group Boko Haram increased dramatically from mid-2014, especially in the north-eastern part of the country. This situation caused the number of people forced within or outside the country to increase significantly. Here too, the causes of displacement vary and sometimes overlap, most people in the North flee Boko Haram attacks but government counter-insurgency and forced evictions operations and inter-communal conflicts in the Middle belt have also contributed to displacement.[150] Multiple displacements have been reported in Nigeria too, where IDPs and host communities affected by violence and lack of access to basic resources including food, water, and shelter are forced to flee again. Consequently, as the armed conflict is ongoing and the lack of resources in places of refuge worsens, IDP vulnerabilities increase at each cycle of displacement.[151]

[147] General Assembly, *Protection of and assistance to internally displaced persons: situation of internally displaced persons in the Syrian Arab Republic*, Note by the Secretary-General, 15 July 2013, UN Doc. A/67/931, paras. 42–5.

[148] *Failing Syria: Assessing the Impact of UN Security Council Resolutions in Protecting and Assisting Civilians in Syria*, Aid Agency Report, 12 March 2015, available at: <https://www.oxfam.org/en/research/failing-syria>, p. 13.

[149] General Assembly, *Protection of and assistance to internally displaced persons*, para. 17.

[150] IDMC/NRC, *Nigeria: Multiple displacement crises overshadowed by Boko Haram*, 9 December 2014, p. 1.

[151] IDMC/NRC, *Nigeria: Multiple displacement crises*, p. 8.

At last, an interesting trend has been recently identified by Elizabeth Ferris from the Brookings Institution, the risk of 'mainstreaming IDPs' also known as the decreasing visibility of IDPs on the international agenda.[152] The author refers to the danger that the progress achieved by IDPs since the adoption of the *Guiding Principles* in 1998, especially the recognition of their specific needs, risk 'being reversed as IDPs are increasingly being seen as an indistinct part of a much larger groups of people in need'.[153] According to Ferris, we face a paradoxical situation, while the number of IDPs in 2014 has reached an all-time high, they are less visible now than they were a decade ago. More and more, calls to protect IDPs have been replaced with references to 'civilians', 'vulnerable groups', and 'affected populations'. Lumping IDPs in with the larger conflict-affected populations, continues the author, risks making them invisible and makes it less likely that measures will be taken to address the specific vulnerabilities associated with displacement, namely the need of shelter, access to basic services, protection, documentation, and durable solutions.[154]

A different approach on the subject seems to be the one taken by the International Committee of the Red Cross (ICRC). The ICRC position has sometimes being considered as 'ambivalent' toward IDPs, on the one hand recognizing their special needs and on the other opposing singling out one group in order to avoid any risk of discrimination against other victims of conflict. However, ICRC's former President Kellenberger, in 2009, had a firm opinion about this. He first said that what distinguishes ICRC action from that of some other organizations is that it takes into account all the victims affected by conflict and not only IDPs.[155] Also, while he agrees that displacement adds to vulnerability, he adds that the ICRC does not believe that 'someone displaced is automatically more vulnerable than someone who is not'.[156] Moreover, he added that the organization is greatly concerned by the increasing tendency within the international community to consider the needs of IDPs as separate and distinct from those of the resident populations. 'Labelling' people and compartmentalizing humanitarian aid has introduced the danger that some groups even if in the greatest need, may be neglected.[157]

[152] Another argument put forward to support this fear is the fact that in 2010 the position of Special Representative of the Secretary-General on the Human Rights of IDPs, created in 1992 and which has served as the single most important voice on IDPs in the international community, has been replaced with the title of Special Rapporteur on the Human Rights of IDPs by the Commission on Human Rights. According to Ferris, although this change in title was part of a reform initiative of the UN Secretary-General to ensure more consistency and accountability with respect to his special representatives it nonetheless led to the perception that the position was somehow 'downgraded' within the UN system. In practice, added the author, the chance of title does affect the Special Rapporteur's access to senior officials and his ability to carry out his tasks. See Ferris, E., *Ten Years After Humanitarian Reform*, p. 40.

[153] Ferris, E., *Ten Years After Humanitarian Reform*, p. 14.

[154] Ibid., p. 14.

[155] ICRC, *Internal Displacement in Armed Conflict: Facing Up to the Challenges*, 12 November 2009, p. 20.

[156] Ibid., p. 20.

[157] Ibid., pp. 20–21.

Concluding remarks

In 2014, the number of internally displaced persons worldwide had reached an unprecedented level resulting in immense humanitarian challenges. Since the adoption of the *Guiding Principles* in 1998, developments at the international and regional level indicate the recognition of internal displacement as an issue of central concern and the will of the international community to act upon it.

Many States have adopted legislation and policies addressing internal displacement by incorporating as a whole or in part the *Guiding Principles* in their domestic regimes. At the regional level, the first legally binding instrument exclusively devoted to IDPs was adopted by the African Union in 2009, the so-called Kampala Convention, representing a crucial step forward toward the prohibition of arbitrary displacement and the recognition and protection of IDPs special needs.

Nonetheless, the present analysis shows that greater attention must be devoted first of all to prevent displacement from happening. An improved respect of international humanitarian law provisions such as for instance the basic prohibition of attacking civilians and civilian objects must be advocated as they can play an important role in reducing causes of displacement. Paramount is also the need for a greater number of States to adopt policies and legislation addressing internal displacement and specific needs of IDPs in a comprehensive manner. Even more critical is to ensure that legislation and policies are effectively implemented and respected. Moreover, when violations occur, perpetrators should be held accountable and victims should be able to achieve reparations. While the humanitarian reform has improved operational short-term response to internal displacement, it has had limited effect in either protecting people from new displacement or in finding solutions for those already displaced.[158] Thus, greater effort should also be made to end protracted displacement and find durable solutions.

[158] Ferris, E., *Ten Years After Humanitarian Reform*, p. 14.

7 The legality of detention in armed conflict

Alex Conte[1]

Introduction

The detention of persons in armed conflict calls for careful consideration of technical legal issues and practical considerations. It requires clear distinctions to be made between international versus non-international armed conflicts, as well as between combatants and civilians; and it involves a complex relationship between the application of international humanitarian law (IHL) and international human rights law. The aim of this chapter is to examine the grounds upon which persons may be detained in an armed conflict and the requirements for supervision of the lawfulness of detention in armed conflict. Consideration is not given to the various and important issues pertaining to the conditions of detention and the treatment of detainees. Nor is attention paid to the question of the detention of persons at Guantánamo Bay, which is a matter given special consideration in *The War Report 2012*.[2] For reasons of space, this chapter is restricted to the consideration of detention by States in armed conflict.

A. Applicable legal frameworks

Before examining the grounds upon which persons may be detained in armed conflict, and the question of the supervision of the lawfulness of detention, consideration must be given to the complex intersection between and complementarity of IHL and

[1] Dr Alex Conte is a Reader in International Human Rights Law at Sussex Law School, School of Law Politics and Sociology, University of Sussex, United Kingdom (contact: alex.conte@sussex.ac.uk; twitter: @alexcontelaw).

[2] Suteu, S., 2013, 'A Legal 'Black Hole'? A Decade of Detention at Guantánamo, 2002-2012'. In *The War Report: 2012*, Oxford: Oxford University Press, pp. 376–396.

international human rights law, as well as noting recent and ongoing developments relating to applicable international law and standards.

INTERNATIONAL HUMAN RIGHTS AND HUMANITARIAN LAW

It will be noted below that the International Committee of the Red Cross (ICRC) is undertaking a consultation process on how to strengthen legal protection for persons deprived of their liberty in relation to non-international armed conflicts (NIACs). The starting point in this part of the chapter is to note what is said on the ICRC's consultation page on that initiative, namely that: 'treaty law regarding deprivation of liberty of persons in relation to non-international armed conflict NIAC) is very limited'.[3] This is a troubling statement and exposes a narrow conceptualization of the ICRC initiative, as well as an omission of the position that international human rights law (a body of law that is rich in treaty law concerning the deprivation of liberty) is also applicable in times of conflict. Consideration is here given to the application of human rights in armed conflict, the principle of *lex specialis*, the extraterritorial application of human rights, and the sole application of human rights in situations not amounting to an armed conflict. This underpins later reflections in this chapter of the authorized grounds for detention in armed conflict and the review in armed conflict of the lawfulness of detention, and also identifies jurisprudence and interpretive commentary on the subject from 2014.

Application of human rights law in armed conflict

Where a situation rises to the level of an 'armed conflict' within the meaning of IHL,[4] it is now well established that the application of IHL does not preclude the application of international human rights law.[5] So long as international human rights law applies through the operation of customary international law or the territorial or extraterritorial application of human rights treaties, and subject to the principle of *lex specialis*, both IHL and human rights apply in situations of armed conflict. As early as 1970, the

[3] See International Committee of the Red Cross, 'Detention in non-international armed conflict: The ICRC's work on strengthening legal protection', <https://www.icrc.org/eng/what-we-do/other-activities/development-ihl/strengthening-legal-protection-ihl-detention.htm> (last accessed 27 March 2015).

[4] See further, in Part I of this book, 'What is an armed conflict?'.

[5] Contrast with the view of some States that human rights are part of the law of peace and international humanitarian law of the law of war (such as Israel, for example, in its position taken during the examination by the UN Human Rights Committee of its second periodic report under the International Covenant on Civil and Political Rights: see Human Rights Committee, *Concluding Observations: Second Periodic Report of Israel*, UN Doc CCPR/CO/78/ISR (2003), §11). See also Pictet, J., 1973, *Le droit humanitaire et la protection des victimes de la guerre*, Leiden, Institut Henry-Dunant, p. 13.

UN General Assembly affirmed that: 'Fundamental human rights, as accepted in international law and laid down in international instruments, continue to apply fully in situations of armed conflict'.[6] In its General Comment on the nature of obligations imposed on States parties to the International Covenant on Civil and Political Rights (ICCPR), the Human Rights Committee confirmed that:

> . . . the Covenant applies also in situations of armed conflict to which the rules of international humanitarian law are applicable. While, in respect of certain Covenant rights, more specific rules of international humanitarian law may be specially relevant for the purposes of the interpretation of Covenant rights, both spheres of law are complementary, not mutually exclusive.[7]

The Grand Chamber of the European Court of Human Rights has taken the same view concerning the application of the European Convention of Human Rights (ECHR) in times of war, ruling in its 2014 decision in *Hassan v. United Kingdom* that the ECHR applies even in the context of international armed conflicts (IACs), albeit in a modified way.[8] The Human Rights Committee has further expressed that: 'the applicability of the regime of international humanitarian law during an armed conflict does not preclude the application of the Covenant, including Article 4 which covers situations of public emergency which threaten the life of the nation'.[9] The International Court of Justice (ICJ) has confirmed this position, stressing that: 'the protection of the International Covenant on Civil and Political Rights does not cease in times of war, except by operation of Article 4 of the Covenant whereby certain provisions may be derogated from in a time of national emergency'.[10] The question of the derogability of the right to liberty under Article 9 of the ICCPR is considered later in this chapter, when looking at the grounds for the deprivation of liberty in armed conflict, as is the question of the derogability of the right to *habeas corpus*, when examining review of the lawfulness of detention.

Complementarity between IHL and human rights

The general position in situations where two bodies of law apply, reflected in the principle *lex specialis derogat lex generali*, is that the body of law that is more specialized or

[6] General Assembly resolution 2675(XXV) (1970), §1.

[7] Human Rights Committee, General Comment No. 31, 'Nature of the general legal obligation imposed on states parties to the Covenant', UN Doc. CCPR/C/21/Rev.1/Add.13 (2004), §11.

[8] *Hassan v. United Kingdom* (2014) ECHR 1162, §104.

[9] *Concluding Observations: Second Periodic Report of Israel*, §11.

[10] *Legality of the Threat or Use of Nuclear Weapons in Armed Conflict*, Advisory Opinion (1996) ICJ Reports, §24. See also *Legal Consequences of the Construction of a Wall in the Occupied Palestinian Territory*, Advisory Opinion (2004) ICJ Reports, §106; *Armed Activities on the Territory of the Congo (Democratic Republic of the Congo v. Uganda)*, Merits (2005) ICJ Reports, §§216–220.

specific to the situation should be taken to qualify the more general body of law. The rationale is that 'because special rules are designed for and targeted at the situation at hand, they are likely to regulate it better and more effectively than more general rules'.[11] That said, the exact meaning and effect of the *lex specialis* principle is contested.[12] The most radical conception of its application, concerning the relationship between IHL and international human rights law, is that of 'total displacement', under which it is argued that, in a situation of armed conflict, IHL is the *lex specialis* and displaces human rights obligations altogether.[13] Bearing in mind what has been said in the preceding section about the application of human rights law in both times of peace and times of war, however, this is not a position that finds great favour and was specifically rejected in two judicial decisions in 2014, one by the High Court in the United Kingdom and the other by the Grand Chamber of the European Court of Human Rights concerning a case brought against the United Kingdom.[14] Further reference to those decisions is made later.

The prevailing view is that of complementarity between IHL and international human rights law rather than the displacement of one set of laws in favour of the other. As indicated earlier, the Human Rights Committee has acknowledged that more specific rules of IHL may act as the *lex specialis*, but that both spheres of law are nevertheless 'complementary, not mutually exclusive'.[15] The ICJ has explained that this means that the relationship between IHL and international human rights law presents three possible situations:

> . . . some rights may be exclusively matters of international humanitarian law; others may be exclusively matters of human rights law; yet others may be matters of both these branches of international law. In order to answer the question put to it, the Court will have to take into consideration both these branches of international law, namely human rights law and, as *lex specialis*, international humanitarian law.[16]

It will be seen in the discussions below that all three situations apply to the question of the legality of detention in armed conflict: IHL acts as the more specific and therefore exclusive body of law concerning the authority to detain prisoners of war in an international armed conflict; international human rights law acts without the contradiction

[11] As observed by Justice Leggatt in *Mohammed v. Ministry of Defence* [2014 EWHC 1369, §270.

[12] See, for example, Sassòli, M., 2011, 'The Role of Human Rights and International Humanitarian Law in New Types of Armed Conflicts' and Milanović, M., 2011, 'Norm Conflicts, International Humanitarian Law, and Human Rights Law'. In *International Humanitarian Law and International Human Rights Law* edited by Ben-Naaftali O., Oxford: Oxford Scholarship Online, chs 3 and 4 respectively.

[13] This was in part argued, for example, by the Ministry of Defence of the United Kingdom in *Mohammed v. Ministry of Defence*, §271.

[14] *Mohammed v. Ministry of Defence*,§§275–281; *Hassan v. United Kingdom*, §104.

[15] Human Rights Committee, General Comment No. 31, §11.

[16] *Legal Consequences of the Construction of a Wall in the Occupied Palestinian Territory*, §106.

of IHL concerning the authority to detain persons in situations of a non-international armed conflict; and both bodies of law apply to different aspects of the obligation to review the lawfulness of detention.

In 2014, the High Court in the United Kingdom considered the question of the interaction between international humanitarian law and the UK's human rights obligations under the ECHR in the context of the UK's detention policy during the non-international phase of the armed conflict in Afghanistan. In his decision, Justice Leggatt favoured the approach of treating the *lex specialis* principle not as a matter for resolving conflicts between different bodies of law, but as a principle of interpretation.[17] He pointed to the Advisory Opinion of the ICJ in the *Legality of the Threat or Use of Nuclear Weapons in Armed Conflict* case as illustrating this approach. In that Opinion, the International Court determined that the right to life is applicable in armed conflict, but that interpretation of the meaning of the right under Article 6(1) of the ICCPR (the right not to be 'arbitrarily' deprived of life) falls to be determined, through interpretation, by IHL as the body of law regulating the conduct of hostilities.[18] In other words, so long as the killing of a person in an armed conflict complies with the norms of IHL pertaining to the conduct of hostilities, such a killing does not amount to an 'arbitrary' deprivation of life within the meaning of Article 6(1) of the ICCPR.

On the question of the interpretation of the right to liberty under Article 5 of the ECHR, Justice Leggatt determined that the exhaustive nature of the cases in which arrest or detention may be permitted under Article 5(1) meant that there was little scope for *lex specialis* to operate as a principle of interpretation. He conceded, however, that an interpretive approach, as taken by the ICJ concerning the prohibition against the arbitrary deprivation of life, might be appropriate in determining the meaning of 'arbitrary arrest or detention' under Article 9(1) of the ICCPR.[19] This is a matter turned to later in this chapter.

Extraterritorial application of human rights treaties

On the question of the extraterritorial application of human rights treaties, a very small number of States do not accept that their obligations under human rights treaties, including under the ICCPR,[20] apply to the conduct of their agents, including their armed

[17] *Mohammed v. Ministry of Defence*, §§288–292.

[18] *Legality of the Threat or Use of Nuclear Weapons in Armed Conflict*, §25.

[19] *Mohammed v. Ministry of Defence*, §§290–291.

[20] Most notably, this remains the position of the United States. See Human Rights Committee, *Concluding Observations: Fourth Periodic Report of the United States of America*, UN Doc CCPR/C/USA/CO/4 (2014), §4; and Savage, C., 2014, 'U.S., Rebuffing U.N., Maintains Stance That Rights Treaty Does Not Apply Abroad', *The New York Times*, 13 March <http://mobile.nytimes.com/2014/03/14/world/us-affirms-stance-that-rights-treaty-doesnt-apply-abroad.html?_r=3&referrer> (last accessed 24 April 2015).

forces, when acting beyond the boundaries of the State's territory. The issue here rests with the interpretation of the jurisdictional provisions of human rights treaties.[21] Under Article 2(1) of the ICCPR, each State party 'undertakes to respect and ensure to all individuals *within its territory and subject to its jurisdiction*' the rights recognized in the ICCPR (emphasis added). Article 2(1) of the Convention against Torture and Other Cruel, Inhuman or Degrading Treatment or Punishment (CAT) requires States parties to take effective measures to prevent acts of torture 'in any territory under its jurisdiction'.

The Human Rights Committee and Committee against Torture have both clarified that the obligation under Article 2 of each treaty means that the obligations under the ICCPR and CAT apply to anyone within the 'power or effective control' of the State, even in places not situated within the territory of the State.[22] The Committee against Torture has recognized that reference to 'any territory' in Article 2(1) of the CAT includes 'all areas where the State party exercises, directly or indirectly, in whole or in part, de jure or de facto effective control ... and in such places as embassies, military bases, detention facilities, or other areas over which a State exercises factual or effective control'.[23] The Human Rights Committee has similarly clarified that: 'This principle also applies to those within the power or effective control of the forces of a State Party acting outside its territory, regardless of the circumstances in which such power or effective control was obtained, such as forces constituting a national contingent or a State Party assigned to an international peace-keeping or peace-enforcement action'.[24] The ICJ has likewise affirmed the extraterritorial application of human rights treaties.[25]

As this applies to the situation of detention, it cannot be doubted that a State which detains persons in a situation of armed conflict by definition has those persons within its effective control, and thus within its jurisdiction, such that international human rights law is applicable. The European Court of Human Rights has laid to rest contrary claims, holding that the ECHR was applicable to the situation where British forces arrested and detained a suspected combatant during the international phase of the armed conflict in Iraq;[26] and, during the later non-international phase of the armed conflict in Iraq, where British forces had effective control over the operation of a detention facility in Basrah, and over persons held in that facility.[27] In its General Comment

[21] See Conte, A., 2013, 'Human Rights Beyond Borders: A New Era in Human Rights Accountability for Transnational Counter-Terrorism Operations?' *Journal of Conflict & Security Law*, pp. 3–9.

[22] Human Rights Committee, General Comment No. 31, §10; Committee against Torture, General Comment No. 2, 'Implementation of article 2 by States parties', UN Doc CAT/C/GC/2 (2008), §7.

[23] Committee against Torture, General Comment No. 2, §16.

[24] Human Rights Committee, General Comment No. 31, §10.

[25] *Legal Consequences of the Construction of a Wall in the Occupied Palestinian Territory*, §109; *Armed Activities on the Territory of the Congo*, §216.

[26] *Hassan v. United Kingdom*, §80.

[27] *Al-Jedda v. The United Kingdom* (2011) ECHR 1092, §86. See also *Al-Skeini and Others v. The United Kingdom* (2011) 53 EHRR 18, §88.

on the right to liberty, adopted in October 2014, the Human Rights Committee further affirmed that: 'Given that arrest and detention bring a person within a State's effective control, States parties must not arbitrarily or unlawfully arrest or detain individuals outside their territory'.[28]

Sole application of human rights outside armed conflict

An obvious but important point should finally be recalled, that international humanitarian law is applicable only where a situation rises to the level of an 'armed conflict' within the meaning of IHL. Outside of an armed conflict, for example in situations of banditry, unorganized and short-lived insurrections, or terrorist activities,[29] domestic law and international human rights law are the exclusive legal frameworks applicable to the determination of whether or not detention is lawful.

DEVELOPMENTS RELATING TO APPLICABLE LAW AND STANDARDS

A considerable amount of work is being undertaken at the global level to further develop and codify international law and standards relating to the detention of persons, including specifically concerning detention in armed conflict. Two documents were adopted in 2014, the Human Rights Committee's General Comment on the right to liberty and the ICRC's Opinion Paper on internment in armed conflict. 2014 also saw continued efforts concerning the rules applicable to the treatment of prisoners, the meaning and application of the right to review of detention, and the protection of persons deprived of their liberty in non-international armed conflicts. This part of the chapter provides an overview of the Human Rights Committee's General Comment, the ICRC's Opinion Paper, and the Basic Principles and Guidelines on the right to *habeas corpus* of the UN Working Group on Arbitrary Detention.

[28] Human Rights Committee, General Comment No. 35, 'Article 9 (Liberty and security of the person)', UN Doc. CCPR/C/GC/35 (2014), §63. See also Human Rights Committee, General Comment No. 31, §10; Human Rights Committee, Communication 52/1979, *Saldías de López v. Uruguay*, UN Doc. Supp. No. 40 (A/36/40) at 176 (1981), §§12.1–13; Human Rights Committee, Communication 56/1979, *Celiberti de Casariego v. Uruguay*, UN Doc. CCPR/C/OP/1 at 92 (1984), §§10.1–11; Human Rights Committee, Communications 623, 624, 626, and 627/1995, *Domukovsky et al. v. Georgia*, UN Doc. CCPR/C/62/D/623, 624, 626 & 627/1995 (1998), §18.2.

[29] As distinguished by the International Criminal Tribunal for the Former Yugoslavia in *Prosecutor v. Tadic*, Case No. IT-94-1, Judgment of 7 May 1997, §562.

Human Rights Committee General Comment on the right to liberty

In October 2014, the Human Rights Committee adopted General Comment No. 35 on the right to liberty and security of the person under Article 9 of the ICCPR, replacing its earlier General Comment No. 8 on the subject from 1982. Drawing on the Committee's jurisprudence, General Comment No. 35 considers the prohibition against arbitrary arrest and detention under Article 9(1)—relevant to the examination in the following part of this chapter of the grounds for the deprivation of liberty. It also explains the meaning and application of the right to take proceedings for release from unlawful or arbitrary detention under Article 9(4), also generally referred to as the right to *habeas corpus*—pertinent also to this chapter concerning the review of the lawfulness of detention.

Of relevance to the preceding discussion concerning the interface between IHL and international human rights law, General Comment No. 35 confirms the established position of the Human Rights Committee by stating that Article 9 applies in situations of armed conflict. It reiterates the approach of complementarity between the two bodies of law and affirms that IHL may be relevant for the purposes of the interpretation of Article 9.[30] Further relevant aspects of the General Comment are referred to later in this chapter.

ICRC Opinion Paper on internment in armed conflict

In November 2014, the ICRC issued an Opinion Paper on the rules and challenges concerning internment in armed conflict.[31] 'Internment' is defined in the Opinion Paper as 'the non-criminal detention of a person based on the serious threat that his or her activity poses to the security of the detaining authority in relation to an armed conflict'.[32] The Opinion Paper addresses the grounds of detention in an international armed conflict and in a non-international armed conflict, the latter of which is critically commented upon later in this chapter.[33]

[30] General Comment No. 35, §64.

[31] International Committee of the Red Cross, 'Internment in Armed Conflict: Basic Rules and Challenges', Opinion Paper, November 2014, <https://www.icrc.org/en/document/internment-armed-conflict-basic-rules-and-challenges> (last accessed 24 April 2015).

[32] Ibid., p. 3.

[33] See, 'Implied authority under IHL to detain in a NIAC?', in 'Deprivation of liberty in non-international armed conflicts'.

UN Working Group on Arbitrary Detention Basic Principles and Guidelines on *habeas corpus*

Under its resolution 20/16 (2012), the UN Human Rights Council requested the Working Group on Arbitrary Detention to prepare draft basic principles and guidelines on remedies and procedures on the right of anyone deprived of his or her liberty (which enshrines the principle of *habeas corpus*). The Working Group set out a first draft set of principles and guidelines ahead of its global consultation on the subject in September 2014.[34] From 2 to 5 February 2015, the Working Group met to continue its elaboration of the Basic Principles and Guidelines, resulting in the adoption of a second draft.[35] The Working Group adopted its final iteration of the document at the conclusion of its session in April 2015.[36] Although adoption of the document took place just outside the annual scope of consideration in this *War Report*, reference in this chapter is made to the final set of Basic Principles and Guidelines. Key aspects of the Working Group's Basic Principles and Guidelines are considered later in this chapter.[37]

B. **Grounds for the deprivation of liberty in armed conflict**

The grounds upon which persons may be detained in the context of an armed conflict within the meaning of IHL depends upon the status of the person concerned, primarily affected by whether the armed conflict is international or non-international in nature. As recognized in the preceding part of this chapter, international human rights law is also applicable, albeit in a potentially modified way. This part of the chapter begins with an overview of the right not to be subject to arbitrary detention under Article 9 of the

[34] Working Group on Arbitrary Detention, Global Consultation on the Right to Challenge the Lawfulness of Detention, 1–2 September 2014, Geneva, Switzerland, <http://www.ohchr.org/EN/Issues/Detention/Pages/ConsultationSept2014.aspx> (last accessed 9 April 2015).

[35] Working Group on Arbitrary Detention, 'Basic Principles and Guidelines on remedies and procedures on: The right of anyone deprived of his or her liberty by arrest or detention to bring proceedings before a court without delay, in order that the court may decide without delay on the lawfulness of his or her detention and order his or her release if the detention is not lawful', February 2015, <http://www.ohchr.org/EN/Issues/Detention/Pages/DraftBasicPrinciples.aspx#consultation> (last accessed 9 April 2015),

[36] Working Group on Arbitrary Detention, 'United Nations Basic Principles and Guidelines on remedies and procedures on the right of anyone deprived of their liberty to bring proceedings before a court', unedited version available at <http://www.ohchr.org/EN/NewsEvents/Pages/DisplayNews.aspx?NewsID=15903&LangID=E> (last accessed 30 April 2015).

[37] See, 'The right to *habeas corpus* under international human rights law', in 'Review of the lawfulness of detention'.

ICCPR. It considers the grounds for deprivation of liberty in international armed conflicts, looking at the authority to detain prisoners of war and protected persons (civilians). Consideration is then given to the grounds upon which persons may be detained in a non-international armed conflict.

DEPRIVATION OF LIBERTY UNDER INTERNATIONAL HUMAN RIGHTS LAW

The prohibition against arbitrary and unlawful detention

Article 9(1) of the ICCPR guarantees the right to liberty and security of the person. It provides that 'no one shall be subjected to arbitrary arrest or detention' and requires that any deprivation of liberty be 'on such grounds and in accordance with such procedure as are established by law'. These two phrases reflect the prohibitions against arbitrary deprivation of liberty on the one hand and unlawful deprivation of liberty on the other, although the concepts of arbitrariness and unlawfulness are interlinked. Thus, as explained by the Human Rights Committee, detention 'may be in violation of the applicable law but not arbitrary, or legally permitted but arbitrary, or both arbitrary and unlawful'.[38]

Concerning the prohibition against unlawful deprivation of liberty, Article 9(1) requires that the substantive grounds for detention must be prescribed by law. Two requirements arise from this. The first is that any detention that lacks a legal basis is both unlawful and arbitrary, and thus in violation of both aspects of the prohibition under Article 9(1) of the ICCPR.[39] The second is that the law must be defined 'with sufficient precision to avoid overly broad or arbitrary interpretation or application'.[40] If a person is detained without such legal authorization, the deprivation of liberty is unlawful and thereby in violation of Article 9(1).[41] Unlike Article 5(1) of the ECHR, the ICCPR does not list the permissible reasons for deprivation of liberty, although it

[38] General Comment No. 35, §11.

[39] General Comment No. 35, §11; Human Rights Committee, *Mika Mika v Equatorial Guinea*, Communication 414/1990, UN Doc. CCPR/C/51/414/1990 (1994), §6.5.

[40] General Comment No. 35, §22. See, for example, cases where the Human Rights Committee has considered grounds for detention to be insufficiently precise: *Concluding Observations: Combined Second and Third Periodic Report of the Philippines* (concerning vagrancy law), UN Doc. CCPR/CO/79/PHL (2003), §14; *Concluding Observations: Fourth Periodic Report of Mauritius* (concerning terrorism law), UN Doc. CCPR/CO/83/MUS (2995), §12; *Concluding Observations: Sixth Periodic Report of the Russian Federation* (concerning extremist activity), UN Doc. CCPR/C/RUS/CO/6 (2009), §24; *Concluding Observations: Initial Report of Honduras* (concerning unlawful association); UN Doc. CCPR/C/HND/CO/1 (2006), §13.

[41] General Comment No. 35, §22; Human Rights Committee, *McLawrence v Jamaica*, Communication 702/1996, UN Doc. CCPR/C/60/D/702/1996 (1997), §5.5.

expressly recognizes that individuals may be detained on criminal charges (Article 9) and it expressly prohibits imprisonment for failure to fulfil a contractual obligation (Article 11).

Any deprivation of liberty must not only be pursuant to and carried out in compliance with applicable law, the law must itself not be arbitrary, it must comply with international law and it must be implemented in a non-arbitrary manner. Deprivation of liberty will be considered arbitrary if it comes about as a result of the total or partial non-observance of international norms relating to the right to a fair trial of a grave nature.[42] The detention of a person will be arbitrary if it includes elements of inappropriateness, injustice, lack of predictability, lack of due process of law, or discrimination.[43] The concept of arbitrariness is also intended to guarantee that even reasonable conduct that is provided for by law should be undertaken in accordance with the provisions, aims, and objectives of the Universal Declaration of Human Rights and the ICCPR, such as the prohibitions against discrimination and torture or ill-treatment.[44]

Derogating from the prohibition against arbitrary and unlawful detention

Article 4(1) of the ICCPR allows a State party to derogate from (temporarily suspend the application of) certain rights in a 'time of public emergency which threatens the life of the nation and the existence of which is officially proclaimed' and 'to the extent strictly required by the exigencies of the situation, provided that such measures are not inconsistent with their other obligations under international law and do not involve discrimination'. Article 4(2) sets out a list of ICCPR rights from which no derogation may be made, even in such states of emergency. The right to liberty under Article 9 is not included in that list, which means that it is, at face value, capable of being temporarily suspended, provided that all of the procedural and substantive requirements of Article 4 are complied with, namely that such derogation: (1) is notified to the Secretary General

[42] Report of the Working Group on Arbitrary Detention, UN Doc. A/HRC/16/47 (2011), Annex, §8(c).

[43] Report of the Working Group on Arbitrary Detention, ibid., §8(e). See, for example: Human Rights Committee, *Mukong v Cameroon*, Communication 458/1991, UN Doc. CCPR/C/51/D/458/1991 (1994), §9.8; Human Rights Committee, *de Morais v Angola*, Communication 1128/2002, UN Doc. CCPR/C/83/D/1128/2002 (2005), §6.1; Human Rights Committee, *Gorji-Dinka v Cameroon*, Communication 1134/2002, UN Doc. CCPR/C/83/D/1134/2002 (2005), §5.1.

[44] Report of the Working Group on Arbitrary Detention, §8(b); Human Rights Committee, General Comment No. 16, 'The right to respect of privacy, family, home and correspondence, and protection of honour and reputation (Art 17)', (1988), §4; Human Rights Committee, *Garcia v Colombia*, Communication 687/1996, UN Doc. CCPR/C/71/D/687/1996 (2001); Siracusa Principles on the Limitation and Derogation Provisions in the International Covenant on Civil and Political Rights, UN Doc. E/CN.4/1985/4, §7.

of the United Nations; (2) takes place only in a time of public emergency threatening the life of the nation; (3) involves measures that do not exceed those strictly required by the exigencies of the situation; (4) is consistent with the State's other obligations under international law; and (5) is non-discriminatory.[45]

The Human Rights Committee has nevertheless taken the view that certain elements of Article 9 of the ICCPR cannot be made subject to lawful derogation under Article 4. In its General Comment No. 35, three points are made in this regard. First, it is reiterated that, although the existence of a state of emergency may be relevant to determining whether or not a particular arrest or detention is 'arbitrary': 'The fundamental guarantee against arbitrary detention is non-derogable, insofar as even situations covered by article 4 cannot justify a deprivation of liberty that is unreasonable or unnecessary under the circumstances'.[46] This is consistent with Rule 99 of the ICRC's catalogue of rules of customary IHL, applicable to both international and non-international armed conflicts, and which states that: 'Arbitrary deprivation of liberty is prohibited'.[47]

Second, General Comment No. 35 distinguishes between international versus non-international armed conflicts. In the context of an IAC, the Committee acknowledges that 'substantive and procedural rules of international humanitarian law remain applicable and limit the ability to derogate, thereby helping to mitigate the risk of arbitrary detention'.[48] The European Court of Human Rights has in this regard noted that it has been State practice not to derogate from the provisions of Article 5 of the ECHR or Article 9 of the ICCPR in situations of an IAC since, in effect, the Third and Fourth Geneva Conventions are treated as providing the authoritative framework authorizing the detention of persons in an IAC.[49] Outside the context of an IAC, however, the Human Rights Committee reaffirmed that 'the requirements of strict necessity and proportionality constrain any derogating measures involving security detention, which must be limited in duration and accompanied by procedures to prevent arbitrary application'.[50] This is a matter considered further below.

The third and final point to note about limits on the derogability of Article 9 concerns the right to *habeas corpus*, considered in greater detail later in this chapter.

[45] See: General Comment No. 35, §65; Human Rights Committee, General Comment No. 29, 'States of Emergency (Article 4)', UN Doc. CCPR/C/21/Rev.1/Add.11 (2001), esp. §§4–5, 8–9, and 13.

[46] General Comment No. 35, §66. See also General Comment No. 29, §§4 and 11.

[47] ICRC, *Customary IHL*, 'Rule 99. Deprivation of Liberty', <https://www.icrc.org/customary-ihl/eng/docs/v1_rul_rule99#Fn_17_7> (last accessed 24 April 2015).

[48] General Comment No. 35, §66.

[49] *Hassan v United Kingdom*, §101.

[50] General Comment No. 35, §66.

DEPRIVATION OF LIBERTY IN INTERNATIONAL ARMED CONFLICTS

Detention in an international armed conflict is regulated by the Third and Fourth Geneva Conventions and Additional Protocol I. IHL here acts as the *lex specialis* such that deprivation of liberty pursuant to and consistent with applicable provisions in the Third and Fourth Geneva Conventions and Protocol I is to be treated as compatible with Article 5(1) of the ECHR and as lawful and non-arbitrary within the meaning of Article 9(1) of the ICCPR. When considering the grounds for deprivation of liberty in armed conflict, as well as consequent rights and responsibilities, a distinction must be made between persons detained as prisoners of war and other detainees.

International humanitarian law as *lex specialis*

Applying an interpretive approach to *lex specialis*, discussed earlier, the relationship between IHL and the prohibition against arbitrary and unlawful deprivation of liberty under Article 9(1) of the ICCPR can be captured as giving rise to two general positions, each corresponding to international versus non-international armed conflicts. As to the first situation, where IHL sets out grounds for the deprivation of liberty, this will in principle amount to a lawful and non-arbitrary deprivation of liberty within the meaning of Article 9(1) of the ICCPR, so long as the relevant provisions of IHL are implemented in a non-arbitrary manner. Such is the case concerning the deprivation of liberty in international armed conflicts, in respect of which IHL sets out well-defined grounds for the detention of combatants and, in certain situations, of civilians.[51] This is accepted to be the case by the Human Rights Committee in its 2014 General Comment on the right to liberty, where it is stated that 'detention authorised and regulated by and complying with international humanitarian law in principle is not arbitrary'.[52]

This conclusion was also hinted at in the 2014 decision of the UK High Court in *Mohammed v Ministry of Defence*,[53] and is consistent with the interpretive approach adopted by the ICJ concerning the meaning of 'arbitrary' deprivation of life in the context of the conduct of hostilities under IHL.[54] It also follows the reasoning of the Grand Chamber of the European Court of Human Rights in its 2014 decision in *Hassan v United Kingdom*. The Court in that case held that Article 5 of the ECHR could be interpreted, taking into account the powers of detention under the Third and Fourth Geneva Conventions, to permit the taking of prisoners of war and the detention of civilians who pose a threat to security.[55] The Court found that the United Kingdom had not

[51] ICRC Opinion Paper, p. 3. [52] General Comment No. 35, §64.
[53] *Mohammed v Ministry of Defence*, §290.
[54] *Legality of the Threat or Use of Nuclear Weapons in Armed Conflict*, §25.
[55] *Hassan v United Kingdom*, §104.

violated Article 5 since the capture and detention of Hassan had been consistent with the relevant powers under the Geneva Conventions.[56]

The authority to detain prisoners of war

The detention of persons as prisoners of war is governed by the Third Geneva Convention Relative to the Treatment of Prisoners of War (Geneva Convention III). Article 4 of Geneva Convention III provides that persons may be held as prisoners of war (POWs) if they 'have fallen into the power of the enemy' and if they fall within one of the six categories specified in Article 4(A) including, for example members of armed forces of a party to the international armed conflict (Article 4(A)(1)), members of other armed forces who profess allegiance to a party to the conflict (Article 4(A)(3)), members of militias fulfilling certain conditions (Article 4(A)(2)), and persons who accompany the armed forces, such as civilian contractors and war correspondents (Article 4(A)(4)).

Once the trigger under Article 4 of Geneva Convention III is established, a Detaining Power is authorized under Article 21 to detain a POW subject to internment in a POW camp, or to close confinement in certain circumstances. This entitlement to hold a POW captive lasts until the cessation of active hostilities in the international armed conflict. Article 118 of Geneva Convention III requires that POWs 'shall be released and repatriated without delay after the cessation of active hostilities'. Article 75 of the First Protocol Additional to the Geneva Conventions, and Relating to the Protection of Victims of International Armed Conflicts (Protocol I) reinforces Article 118. It sets out a series of fundamental guarantees applicable to persons interned for reasons related to an IAC, which includes the right in Article 75(3) to be released as soon as the circumstances justifying detention or internment have ceased to exist. The rule in Article 118 of Geneva Convention III is a norm of customary international humanitarian law, reflected in Rule 128(A) of the ICRC's catalogue of rules of customary IHL (which uses almost identical language to Article 118).[57] Unjustifiable delay in the repatriation of POWs constitutes a grave breach of Protocol I.[58]

Additional to the requirement that prisoners of war must be released and repatriated after the cessation of hostilities, Articles 109 and 110 of Geneva Convention III impose obligations on a Detaining Power where a POW is sick or wounded. Where a POW is seriously wounded or seriously sick, she or he must be directly repatriated (in the case, for example, of a wounded POW who is unlikely to recover, according to medical

[56] Contrast this with the partly dissenting opinion of Judge Spano, joined by Judges Nicolaou, Binaku, and Kalaydjieva, esp. §19.

[57] ICRC, *Customary IHL*, 'Rule 128. Release and Return of Persons Deprived of Their Liberty', <https://www.icrc.org/customary-ihl/eng/docs/v1_rul_rule128 > (last accessed 27 April 2015).

[58] Additional Protocol I, Art. 85(4)(b).

opinion, within a year) or accommodated in a neutral country (for example, in the case of a POW whose health, according to medical opinion, is seriously threatened by continued captivity, but whose accommodation in a neutral country might remove such a threat).[59] That said, a POW may not be repatriated during hostilities if this is against her or his will.[60]

It must also be noted that combatants, namely members of the armed forces of a party to an IAC who have the right to participate in hostilities,[61] may be prosecuted for violations of IHL, in particular war crimes, or other crimes under international law such as genocide or crimes against humanity. With regard to such persons, Article 119(5) of Geneva Convention III acts as an exception to the obligation under Article 118 to release or repatriate POWs without delay after the cessation of active hostilities.[62] With respect to POWs convicted of an indictable offence or against whom criminal proceedings for an indictable offence are pending, Article 119(5) allows, but does not oblige, a Detaining Power to detain such persons until the end of the criminal proceedings or the completion of the sentence imposed following conviction.[63] Article 75(3) of Protocol I reflects this position. As mentioned, Article 75(3) reiterates the obligation to release, but it also qualifies this obligation by providing that it applies 'Except in cases of arrest or detention for penal offences'. That said, Article 115 of Geneva Convention III reflects the ability of the Detaining Power to consent to the repatriation or accommodation in a neutral country of POWs detained in connection with a judicial prosecution or conviction. The ICRC Commentary on Article 115 suggests that: 'In accordance with the spirit of the Convention, the Detaining Power should withhold consent only if it has good grounds for doing so and if its refusal would not seriously impair the state of health of the prisoners concerned'.[64]

The authority to detain protected persons in an international armed conflict

Authority for the detention of 'protected persons' (civilians) is found in the Fourth Geneva Convention Relative to the Protection of Civilian Persons in Time of War (Geneva Convention IV). The detention of a civilian, through internment or placing in

[59] Third Geneva Convention, Arts 109 and 110.
[60] Third Geneva Convention, Art. 109.
[61] This excludes members of the armed forces who are medical and religious personnel: see Art. 43(2) of Additional Protocol I.
[62] Art. 119(5) of Geneva Convention II provides that: 'Prisoners of war against whom criminal proceedings for an indictable offence are pending may be detained until the end of such proceedings, and, if necessary, until the completion of the punishment. The same shall apply to prisoners of war already convicted for an indictable offence.'
[63] International Committee of the Red Cross, 1958, *Commentary on the Geneva Conventions of 12 August 1949. Volume IV*, Geneva: International Committee of the Red Cross, p. 557.
[64] Ibid., p. 536.

assigned residence, is authorized in two contexts. The first concerns alien civilians in the territory of a party to the international armed conflict, permissible under Article 42 of Geneva Convention IV 'only if the security of the Detaining Power makes [internment or placing in assigned residence of a civilian] absolutely necessary', or if the civilian voluntarily demands this and his or her situation 'renders this steps necessary'. The International Criminal Tribunal for the former Yugoslavia has interpreted Article 42 as permitting internment only if there are 'serious and legitimate reasons' to think that the interned persons may seriously prejudice the security of the Detaining Power by means such as sabotage or espionage.[65]

The second situation in which civilians may be interned under Geneva Convention IV concerns civilians in an occupied territory, in which case Article 78 allows the Occupying Power, at the most, to subject civilians to internment or assigned residence within the frontiers of the occupied country 'if the Occupying Power considers it necessary, for imperative reasons of security, to take safety measures concerning protected persons'. It is undisputed that the direct participation of civilians in hostilities gives rise to the classification of such civilians as persons posing a serious threat to security within the meaning of Articles 42 and 78.[66] As noted by the ICRC, such persons 'are colloquially called "unprivileged belligerents" (or, incorrectly referred to as "unlawful combatants")'.[67]

Article 41 of Geneva Convention IV provides that, in considering measures of control over protected persons, a Detaining or Occupying Power 'may not have recourse to any other measure of control more severe than that of assigned residence or internment'. Reiterating Article 41, the ICRC Commentary on Articles 42 and 78 emphasizes that both internment and assigned residence are of an exceptional character and represent the most severe measures that a Detaining or Occupying Power may resort to with respect to protected persons.[68] Distinguishing between the two situations described in Articles 42 and 78 of Geneva Convention III, the Commentary further suggests that the internment of protected persons in occupied territories (under Article 78) should be even more exceptional than in the case of internment of protected persons within the territory of a party to the conflict (under Article 42).[69]

As discussed, POWs may be held captive until the cessation of hostilities, with Article 118 of Geneva Convention III requiring release and repatriation without delay after the cessation of active hostilities. The internment of civilians in an international armed conflict must similarly cease, according to Article 133(1) of Geneva Convention IV,

[65] *Prosecutor v Zejnil Delalić and Others*, Case No: IT-96-21-T, Trial Chamber, 16 November 1998, §1132.

[66] As noted in the ICRC's Opinion Paper, p. 4. [67] Ibid.

[68] *Commentary on the Geneva Conventions of 12 August 1949. Volume IV*, pp. 257, 260–1, and 368. See also the ICRC's Opinion Paper, p. 4.

[69] *Commentary on the Geneva Conventions of 12 August 1949. Volume IV*, p. 367.

'as soon as possible after the close of hostilities'. Additionally, Article 132(1) of Geneva Convention IV provides that, during hostilities or occupation, an interned civilian must be released 'as soon as the reasons which necessitated his internment no longer exist'. This is again reinforced by Article 75(3) of Protocol I, which includes—as a fundamental guarantee applicable to all persons who are in the power of a party to an IAC—the right to be released 'as soon as the circumstances justifying the arrest, detention or internment have ceased to exist'.

Whereas, due to their privileged status, combatants may only be prosecuted for violations of IHL and not for other forms of participation in hostilities, the ICRC Opinion Paper on internment reiterates that civilians who directly participate in hostilities 'can be prosecuted for having taken up arms and for all acts of violence committed during such participation, as well as for war crimes or other crimes under international law that might have been committed'.[70] For civilian internees who have been convicted and sentenced to imprisonment, or against whom criminal, non-disciplinary, proceedings are pending, Article 133(2) of Geneva Convention IV acts as an exception to the obligation under Article 133(1) to release civilian internees after the close of hostilities. Such persons may be detained until the close of pending proceedings and until completion of the sentence. This remains a wide discretionary power in the hands of the Detaining or Occupying Power.[71]

It should finally be noted that Article 147 of Geneva Convention IV establishes the 'unlawful confinement of a protected person' as a grave breach of Geneva Convention IV. Unjustifiable delay in the repatriation of civilians also constitutes a grave breach of Protocol I.[72] Grave breaches of the Geneva Conventions constitute war crimes under Article 8 of the Rome Statute of the International Criminal Court.[73]

DEPRIVATION OF LIBERTY IN NON-INTERNATIONAL ARMED CONFLICTS

The authority to detain persons in a non-international armed conflict is a matter of much controversy. While Geneva Conventions III and IV set out detailed provisions concerning the grounds and procedures for detention in an IAC, the Geneva Conventions and their Additional Protocols are silent concerning grounds or procedures for internment in the context of a NIAC. The greatest controversy surrounds the question of whether

[70] ICRC Opinion Paper, p. 5.
[71] *Commentary on the Geneva Conventions of 12 August 1949. Volume IV*, pp. 515–516.
[72] Additional Protocol I, Art. 85(4)(b).
[73] See also also Art. 2(g) of the Statute of the International Criminal Tribunal for the former Yugoslavia.

IHL implies an authority to detain in a NIAC, which is the primary subject of examination in this part of the chapter. Consideration is also given to detention in a NIAC under international human rights law, and pursuant to Security Council authorization.

Implied authority under IHL to detain in a NIAC?

Relying on Common Article 3 to the Geneva Conventions and Articles 5 and 6 of the Protocol Additional to the Geneva Conventions of 12 August 1949, and relating to the Protection of Victims of Non-International Armed Conflicts (Protocol II), it is argued by some that international humanitarian law implies a power to intern persons in a NIAC. Gill and Fleck express the following view:

> The law of non-international armed conflict is less explicit in stipulating the legal basis for operational detention than the law of international armed conflicts. However, a generic power to that effect is implicit in Common Article 3, in as much as it identifies as one category of persons taking no active part in hostilities 'those placed hors de combat by ... detention'. Articles 5 and 6 of (Protocol II) also refer to 'persons deprived of their liberty for reasons related to the armed conflict, whether they are interned or detained', which makes it clear that the deprivation of physical liberty of a person in contemplated in the law applicable to non-international armed conflicts.[74]

This is a view shared by the ICRC and forms the basis of the ICRC's assertion, in its Opinion Paper on internment in armed conflict, that Common Article 3 and Protocol II govern deprivation of liberty in NIAC.[75] Because Protocol II—which relates exclusively to non-international armed conflicts—explicitly mentions internment, the ICRC expresses the view that this confirms that internment 'is a form of deprivation of liberty inherent to NIAC', although it at the same time acknowledges that Protocol II does not refer to the grounds for internment or applicable procedural rights.[76] The Opinion Paper distinguishes between a 'traditional' NIAC, occurring in the territory of a State between government armed forces and one or more non-State armed groups, and 'NIACs with an extraterritorial element', in which 'the armed forces of one or more State, or of an international or regional organization, fight alongside the armed forces of a host State, in its territory, against one or more organized non-State armed groups'.[77] In the situation of a 'traditional' NIAC, the ICRC acknowledges that domestic law constitutes the legal framework for possible internment whereas, in the situation of a NIAC with an extraterritorial element, such as in Afghanistan for example, the ICRC contends that

[74] Gill, T. and Fleck, D., 2010, *The Handbook of the International Law of Military Operations*, Oxford: Oxford University Press, p. 471. See also Pejic, J., 2005, 'Procedural Principles and Safeguards for Internment/Administrative Detention in Armed Conflict and Other Situations of Violence' *International Review of the Red Cross*, vol. 87, no. 858, 375, at p. 377.

[75] ICRC Opinion Paper, p. 6. [76] Ibid. [77] Ibid., p. 7.

both customary and treaty IHL contain an inherent legal basis to intern.[78] This author disagrees. Common Article 3 and Protocol II do not provide a legal authority to deprive a person of liberty in NIAC, they simply guarantee a minimum level of humanitarian treatment for people who are in fact detained during a NIAC.

The opinion of the ICRC was also a position advocated by the Ministry of Defence of the United Kingdom in *Mohammed v Ministry of Defence*, a case concerning the UK's detention policy and practice during the NIAC phase of the conflict in Afghanistan. In that case, the UK High Court rejected the argument in favour of an implied power of internment in NIACs, Justice Leggatt setting out five reasons for this, with which this author agrees.[79] First, Justice Leggatt took the view that if the Geneva Conventions and their Additional Protocols had intended to provide a power to detain in a NIAC, such authority would have been expressly provided.[80] As seen in the preceding section, the authority to detain in an IAC is set out in great detail, with specific authorization and substantive grounds specified in Article 21 of Geneva Convention III (concerning prisoners of war) and Articles 42 and 78 of Geneva Convention IV (concerning civilians posing a serious threat to security). It is not genuinely conceivable that the parties negotiating the Geneva Conventions should have been so specific in the drafting of Geneva Conventions III and IV concerning international armed conflicts and then leave only a vaguely implied authorization in the context of non-international armed conflicts.

Second, Justice Leggatt considered the argument that internment in NIAC is 'contemplated' by Common Article 3 and Articles 5 and 6 of Protocol II, distinguishing between what might be contemplated in fact versus what might be contemplated in law. While these provisions may contemplate that the detention of persons in a NIAC may take place as a matter of fact, His Honour took the view that: 'It does not follow … that there is anything in these provisions which implies that internment is a measure that "can", in the sense of "may lawfully", be taken—still less that these provisions are themselves intended to provide a legal basis for detention'.[81] Common Article 3 and Articles 5 and 6 of Protocol II are provisions that apply as a consequence of detention as a matter of fact, but they in no way express or imply authority to detain as a matter of law. Such detention, as explained by Justice Leggatt, 'may be lawful under the law of the state on whose territory the armed conflict is taking place, or under some other applicable law; or it may be entirely unlawful'.[82]

[78] Ibid., pp. 7–8.

[79] The High Court's rejection of an implied authority to detain in non-international armed conflicts is also agreed with by Milanovic, M., 2014, 'High Court Rules that the UK Lacks Detention Authority in Afghanistan', *EJIL: Talk!* 3 May, <http://www.ejiltalk.org/high-court-rules-that-the-uk-lacks-ihl-detention-authority-in-afghanistan/> (last accessed 25 April 2015).

[80] *Mohammed v Ministry of Defence*, §242. [81] Ibid., §243. [82] Ibid., §243.

Third, consideration was given to the purpose of Common Article 3 and Articles 5 and 6 of Protocol II. What these provisions do is to require that any detained persons be treated humanely (Common Article 3), that they enjoy certain generally applicable rights and safeguards (such as the benefit of medical examinations under Article 5(2)(d) of Protocol II) and that they enjoy certain procedural safeguards pertaining to the prosecution and punishment of criminal offences (Article 6 of Protocol II). As noted in the ICRC Commentary: 'Like common Article 3, Protocol II has a *purely humanitarian purpose* and is aimed at securing fundamental guarantees for individuals in all circumstances' (emphasis added).[83] Justice Leggatt thus remarked: 'The need to observe such minimum standards is equally relevant to all people who are in fact detained, and does not depend on whether or not their detention in legally justified.'[84]

Fourth, it was noted that there are cogent reasons why States negotiating the Geneva Conventions and their Additional Protocols would not have wanted to establish a legal authority to detain persons in non-international armed conflicts. Given that Common Article 3 applies to 'each Party to the conflict', and that Protocol II applies to non-State armed groups that are able to implement Protocol II:

> ... providing a power to detain would have meant authorising detention by dissident and rebel armed groups. That would be anathema to most states which face a non-international armed conflict on their territory and do not wish to confer any legitimacy on rebels and insurgents or accept that such groups have any right to exercise a function which is a core aspect of state sovereignty.[85]

The High Court's final reason for rejecting the argument in favour of an implied authority to detain relied on a further comparison between international versus non-international armed conflicts. For an IAC, Geneva Conventions III and IV specify who may be detained, on what grounds, in accordance with what procedures, and for how long, whereas Common Article 3 and Articles 5 and 6 of Protocol II do not do so. In the words of Mr Justice Leggatt: 'I do not see how CA3 or AP2 could possible have been intended to provide a power to detain, nor how they could reasonably be interpreted as doing so, unless it was possible to identify the scope of the power.'[86]

Taking the latter point further, this author adds an additional, sixth, argument to reject the existence of an implied authority to detain in a NIAC. International humanitarian law prohibits arbitrary detention, Rule 99 of the ICRC's catalogue of rules of customary IHL stating, in simple terms, that: 'Arbitrary deprivation of liberty is prohibited'.[87]

[83] International Committee of the Red Cross, 1987, *Commentary on the Additional Protocols of 8 June 1977 to the Geneva Conventions of 12 August 1949*, Geneva: International Committee of the Red Cross, p. 1344.

[84] *Mohammed v Ministry of Defence*, §244.

[85] Ibid., §245.

[86] Ibid., §246.

[87] Rule 99, above n. 47.

It is explained that State practice establishes this rule as a norm of customary international law applicable in both international and non-international armed conflicts, noting also that the arbitrary deprivation of liberty is incompatible with the requirement that detainees be treated humanely, reflected in Common Article 3 as well as Additional Protocols I and II.[88] Common Article 3 and Rule 99 in this respect reinforce the general prohibition against arbitrary detention. In discussing Rule 99 in the context of the grounds for detention in NIACs, the ICRC's catalogue of rules of customary IHL points to no express or implied authority to detain. It instead recognizes that 'The prohibition of arbitrary deprivation of liberty in non-international armed conflicts is established by State practice in the form of military manuals, national legislation and official statements, as well as on the basis of international human rights law'.[89] It does not assert, nor even hint at the possibility, that Common Article 3 and Articles 5 and 6 of Protocol II imply a legal authority to detain.

A further argument is offered by this author, drawing from the 2014 General Comment of the Human Rights Committee on the right to liberty, and closely tied to Justice Leggatt's fifth reason rejecting an implied authority to detain in a NIAC. Concerning detention in armed conflict, the General Comment states that: 'Security detention *authorised and regulated by and complying with* international humanitarian law in principle is not arbitrary' (emphasis added).[90] The General Comment thereby predicates the non-arbitrary nature of detention in armed conflict as detention that satisfies three elements, namely that it is: (1) authorized by IHL; (2) regulated by IHL; and (3) thereby capable of being evaluated as to its compliance with IHL. Even if the tenuous argument of an implied authority under Common Article 3 and Protocol II was to be accepted (element (1)), proponents of that argument are unable to point to any regulation of detention in the context of a NIAC, in terms of the identification and regulation under IHL of who may be detained, on what grounds, in accordance with what procedures, and for how long (element (2)). The lack of such regulation in a NIAC not only fails element (2), it also means that it is impossible to ascertain whether any detention in a NIAC complies with IHL (element (3)). Unless detention in a NIAC is predicated on national or other law that is informed and consistent with international human rights law, it will therefore be arbitrary.

An eighth and final argument by this author also relies on General Comment No. 35 of the Human Rights Committee. As noted earlier, the General Comment makes a distinction between international versus non-international armed conflicts as this concerns any derogation from the right to liberty under Article 9. In the context of an

[88] Ibid. See also Rule 87 of the ICRC's catalogue of rules of customary international humanitarian law: ICRC, *Customary IHL*, 'Rule 87. Humane Treatment', <https://www.icrc.org/customary-ihl/eng/docs/v1_rul_rule87> (last accessed 24 April 2015).

[89] Rule 99, above n. 47.

[90] General Comment No. 35, §64.

IAC, it acknowledges that IHL includes substantive and procedural rules that help to mitigate the risk of arbitrary detention. Outside that context, however, the Committee spoke of the need for derogating measures involving security detention, which must comply with the requirements of strict necessity and proportionality and which must be limited in duration and accompanied by procedures to prevent arbitrary deprivation of liberty.[91] It is implicit in this reasoning that the Committee did not consider IHL rules pertaining to detention in a NIAC as themselves providing sufficient procedural guarantees mitigating the risk of arbitrary detention, such that any detention in a NIAC will require derogation from Article 9 of the ICCPR if it otherwise fails to comply with the normal parameters of the guarantees under Article 9.

It is therefore concluded by this author that there is no implied authority under Common Article 3 or Protocol II for the detention of persons in a non-international armed conflict. This means that there is a lacuna in international humanitarian law concerning the grounds for detention in a NIAC, the filling of which is no doubt the aim of the ICRC initiative. But this lacuna does not mean an absence of applicable law and standards. Indeed, the absence of IHL provisions means that international human rights law concerning the grounds of detention in a NIAC, and other matters such as, for example, the right to challenge the lawfulness of detention in a NIAC, apply without any contradiction arising from IHL.[92]

Detention in a NIAC under international human rights law

The foregoing discussion has led to the conclusion that detention in a NIAC must comply, in the case of States parties to the ICCPR, with the requirements of the Covenant, and that this applies without contradiction from IHL. In practical terms, this means that internment in a NIAC must either: be fully compliant with the prohibition against arbitrary and unlawful detention under Article 9(1) of the ICCPR; or be subject to a lawful derogation from Article 4 of the ICCPR.

In the first case, to be compliant with Article 9(1) of the ICCPR, detention in a NIAC must: (1) be pursuant to domestic law that is defined with sufficient precision and is compliant with international law, including international human rights law; (2) not involve elements of inappropriateness, injustice, lack of predictability, lack of due process of law or discrimination; and (3) not come about as a result of the total or partial non-observance of international norms relating to the right to a fair trial of a grave nature.[93]

[91] General Comment No. 35, §66.

[92] Doswald-Beck, L., 2011, *Human Rights in Times of Conflict and Terrorism*, Oxford: Oxford University Press, p. 277.

[93] See, 'The prohibition against arbitrary and unlawful detention', in 'Deprivation of liberty under international human rights law'.

Applied to the situation of 'security detention' not in contemplation of prosecution on a criminal charge (such as internment in a NIAC), the Human Rights Committee has concluded that that such detention presents severe risks of arbitrary detention such that it should normally be assumed that the detention is arbitrary.[94] The Committee nevertheless acknowledged that security detention may be resorted to in the absence of a derogation from Article 9, but only 'under the most exceptional circumstances'—namely where 'a present, direct and imperative threat is invoked to justify the detention of persons considered to present such a threat'—and only if the following conditions are met:

> ... the burden of proof lies on States parties to show that the individual poses such a threat and that it cannot be addressed by alternative measures, and that burden increases with the length of the detention. States parties also need to show that detention does not last longer than absolutely necessary, that the overall length of possible detention is limited and that they fully respect the guarantees provided for by article 9 in all cases. Prompt and regular review by a court or other tribunal possessing the same attributes of independence and impartiality as the judiciary is a necessary guarantee for those conditions, as is access to independent legal advice, preferably selected by the detainee, and disclosure to the detainee of, at least, the essence of the evidence on which the decision is taken.[95]

If any form of security detention in a NIAC fails to comply with these conditions, it will involve a violation of Article 9(1) of the ICCPR, unless accompanied by a derogation from Article 9(1). In the case of a derogation, such derogation must comply with the procedural and substantive requirements noted earlier,[96] and must, notwithstanding the derogation, remain consistent with the fundamental guarantee against arbitrary detention.[97] It should be noted that a derogating State has the burden of ensuring that any security detention remains necessary and proportionate, accentuated by Rule 128(C) of the ICRC's catalogue of rules of customary IHL, which provides that: 'Persons deprived of their liberty in relation to a non-international armed conflict must be released as soon as the reasons for the deprivation of their liberty cease to exist'.[98] The Human Rights Committee has otherwise not considered this situation in further depth in its General Comment No. 5, which has been characterized as a 'missed opportunity'.[99] In contrast, the Working Group on Arbitrary Detention has taken the view that internment in the context of a non-international armed conflict 'may only be

[94] General Comment No. 35, §15. [95] Ibid.

[96] See, 'Derogating from the prohibition against arbitrary and unlawful detention', in 'Deprivation of liberty under international human rights law'.

[97] General Comment No. 35, §66; Rule 99, above n. 47. [98] Rule 128, above n. 57.

[99] Fatima, S., 2014, 'UN HRC's General Comment 35 on the Right to Liberty and Security: A Missed Opportunity?', *Just Security*, 19 November, <http://justsecurity.org/17587/uns-comment-liberty-security/> (last accessed 27 April 2015).

permitted in times of public emergency which threatens the life of the nation and the existence of which is officially proclaimed'.[100]

Detention in a NIAC pursuant to Security Council authorization

The need for security internment in a NIAC to comply with human rights is not displaced by the existence of authorization for detention under a Security Council resolution. In *Al-Jedda v UK*, the United Kingdom had argued the contrary position, in a situation where the Security Council had, under its resolution 1546 (2004), authorized the multinational force operating under the United Nations Assistance Mission for Iraq to take all necessary measures to contribute to the maintenance of security and stability in Iraq 'in accordance with the letters annexed to this resolution'.[101] One of those annexed letters was from US Secretary of State Colin Powell in which he outlined the duties of the multinational force to include 'internment where this is necessary for imperative reasons of security'. Pursuant to the broad authority in resolution 1546, and the annexed letter of Colin Powell, British forces held Hilal Al-Jedda in internment at the Sha'aibah Detention Facility in Basrah from October 2004 until December 2007, which corresponds to the NIAC phase of the conflict in Iraq. Al-Jedda brought a claim before the European Court of Human Rights alleging that, since the UK had not derogated from the right to liberty under Article 5 of the ECHR, it had violated his right to liberty by making him subject to prolonged and effectively indefinite detention without trial.

Concerning the interface between Security Council resolutions and the UK's obligations under the ECHR, the UK pointed to the fact that decisions of the Security Council under Chapter VII of the United Nations Charter must be carried out by States, without discretion, by virtue of Articles 25 and 48 of the Charter. It argued that, in the event of any conflict between such decisions and a State's human rights obligations, Article 103 of the Charter requires that human rights obligations must be set aside since it holds that: 'In the event of a conflict between the obligations of the Members of the United Nations under the present Charter [here, obligations to comply with Security Council resolutions] and their obligations under any other international agreement [here, international human rights treaties], their obligations under the present Charter shall prevail'.[102]

Noting that the purposes and principles of the UN Charter include not only the maintenance of international peace and security, but also the achievement of international cooperation in promoting and encouraging respect for human rights and fundamental freedoms,[103] the European Court rejected the argument by the United Kingdom.

[100] Basic Principles and Guidelines, §49.

[101] Security Council resolution 1546 (2004), §10.

[102] *Al-Jedda v United Kingdom*, §60.

[103] See Arts 1(3), 55(c), and 56 of the Charter of the United Nations.

It concluded that the purposes and principles of the Charter, when combined with the qualified competence of the Security Council under Article 24(2) of the Charter, and the UN and Member State commitments under Articles 55(c) and 56 of the Charter, called for an interpretation of Security Council resolutions in a way that was most in harmony with the provisions of the ECHR.[104] On the facts of the case, the Court found that, although the letter from Colin Powell identified internment as one of the duties of the multinational force, where necessary for imperative security reasons, there was no explicit or implied authority from the SC to undertake internment by means of indefinite or prolonged internment without trial. The Court effectively treated Article 103 of the Charter as not being applicable since there was no irreconcilable conflict between the authority given in Security Council resolution 1546 and the human rights obligations under Article 5 of the ECHR. It held that, in the absence of a derogation, the United Kingdom had violated Article 5.[105]

It should finally be noted that, even where there is an irreconcilable conflict between human rights and the precise terms of a Security Council resolution, Article 103 of the Charter will not act to protect States' non-human rights compatible implementation of Security Council decisions. In *Al-Dulimi v Switzerland*, the European Court of Human Rights turned its mind to this situation in the context of sanctions mandated under Security Council resolution 1483 (2003). Agreeing with Switzerland, and with France and the United Kingdom who had joined as third party interveners, the Court agreed that operative paragraph 23 of Security Council resolution 1483 left Switzerland with no discretion as to the means of implementation.[106] The Court held that States nevertheless remain liable under the ECHR for all acts and omissions of their organs arising from the need to observe international legal obligations. It continued to explain that, if the organization under which such obligations arise (in this case the United Nations and its Security Council) has means of protecting human rights that are at least equivalent to the ECHR, the Court could in such cases assume that the State has complied with its obligations under the ECHR.[107] The Court concluded that no equivalent protection existed and that, accordingly, Switzerland bore full responsibility for any violation of rights under the ECHR in its implementation of resolution 1483.[108]

[104] *Al-Jedda v United Kingdom*, §102. See similar approaches concerning the interface between Security Council resolutions pertaining to the listing of terrorist entities in: Human Rights Committee, *Sayadi and Vinck v Belgium*, Communication 1472/2006, UN Doc. CCPR/C/94/D/1472/2006 (2008), Annex B, Individual opinion of Committee member Sir Nigel Rodley (concurring), un-numbered §§4–5; and *Nada v Switzerland* (2012) ECHR 2022, para. 176.

[105] *Al-Jedda v United Kingdom*, §110.

[106] *Al-Dulimi and Montana Management Inc. v Switzerland* (2013) ECHR 1173, §113.

[107] Ibid., §114.

[108] Ibid., §§118–120.

C. Review of the lawfulness of detention

Any form of detention must be subject to effective oversight. This is not only to ensure that the conditions of detention and the treatment of detainees is in compliance with international law, but also to ensure that detention is and remains neither unlawful nor arbitrary. On the latter point, Principle 4 of the UN Body of Principles for the Protection of All Persons under Any Form of Detention or Imprisonment ('the UN Body of Principles') provides that: 'Any form of detention or imprisonment and all measures affecting the human rights of a person under any form of detention or imprisonment shall be ordered by, or be subject to the effective control of, a judicial or other authority'.[109] This in part reflects paragraphs (3) and (4) of Article 9 of the ICCPR, which entail two features involving States' obligation to provide for judicial oversight. Setting aside the question of the right to be brought promptly before a court when arrested or detained for the alleged commission of an offence (as guaranteed under Article 9(3) of the ICCPR), this part of the chapter focuses on measures to review the lawfulness of detention, including through recourse to *habeas corpus* petitions (as guaranteed under Article 9(4) of the ICCPR).

THE RIGHT TO *HABEAS CORPUS* UNDER INTERNATIONAL HUMAN RIGHTS LAW

The right of anyone deprived of liberty to bring proceedings before a court, in order that the court may decide without delay on the lawfulness of the detention and obtain appropriate remedies upon a successful challenge, enshrines the principle of *habeas corpus* and is widely recognized in international and regional human rights instruments, including within Article 9(4) of the ICCPR. In the words of the UN Working Group on Arbitrary Detention: 'It is a judicial remedy designed to protect personal freedom and physical integrity against arbitrary arrest, detention, including secret detention, exile, forced disappearance or risk of torture and other cruel, inhuman or degrading treatment or punishment'.[110] The Working Group, as well as the Human Rights Committee, has confirmed that the right applies to all forms of detention, including military and security detention.[111]

[109] Body of Principles for the Protection of All Persons under Any Form of Detention or Imprisonment, adopted under General Assembly resolution 43/173 (1998), Annex.

[110] Basic Principles and Guidelines, §2.

[111] Ibid., Guideline 1 at §65(a); General Comment No. 35, §40.

As mentioned earlier, the Working Group on Arbitrary Detention has very recently adopted Basic Principles and Guidelines on the right to *habeas corpus*. Without examining in detail the content of those Basic Principles and Guidelines, it is sufficient for current purposes to note some of the key aspects of the right to *habeas corpus*, as reflected in the Working Group's final document of April 2015. First, States are obliged to provide for the right to *habeas corpus* in their national legal systems, including through the establishment of a comprehensive set of procedures to ensure that the right is accessible to all persons in all situations of deprivation of liberty.[112] Second, it is recognized that any form of detention will constitute 'effective control' by State authorities over the detained individual, thus making the person subject to the State's jurisdiction, and thereby making the right to *habeas corpus* applicable extraterritorially.[113] It explicitly recognizes, in this regard, that the right to challenge the lawfulness of detention is to be enjoyed by persons detained in armed conflict.[114]

Third, the Basic Principles and Guidelines go further than the position of the Human Rights Committee in its General Comment No. 35, in which the Committee stated that, in order to protect the non-derogable rights in Articles 6 and 7 of the ICCPR (the right to life and the prohibition of torture and ill-treatment), the right to *habeas corpus* 'must not be diminished by measures of derogation'.[115] Rather than speaking of an obligation not to diminish the right to *habeas corpus* in any derogating measure, Principle 4 of the Working Group's Basic Principles and Guidelines is more direct by stating that the right to *habeas corpus* 'must not be suspended, rendered impracticable, restricted, or abolished under any circumstances, even in times of war, armed conflict, or public emergency which threatens the life of the nation and the existence of which is officially proclaimed'.[116]

Fourth, the Basic Principles and Guidelines address the nature of the body responsible for hearing any application concerning the lawfulness of detention. They explain that such review is to be undertaken by a court established by law that bears 'the full characteristics of a competent, independent and impartial tribunal capable of exercising recognizable judicial powers',[117] including the competence to order immediate release if the detention is found to be unlawful.[118] Of final relevance for present purposes, Guideline 7

[112] Basic Principles and Guidelines, Principle 2 and Guideline 2.

[113] Ibid., Principle 3 at §21 and Principle 16 at §47. See also, 'Extraterritorial application of human rights treaties', in 'International human rights and humanitarian law'.

[114] Ibid., Principle 16 at §§47–50.

[115] General Comment No. 35, §67. See also General Comment No. 29, §§11 and 16.

[116] Basic Principles and Guidelines, Principle 4 at §22. See also the 2012 and 2014 reports of the Working Group on Arbitrary Detention: UN Doc. A/HRC/22/44 (2012), §47; and UN Doc. A/HRC/27/47 (2014), §22.

[117] Basic Principles and Guidelines, Principle 6 at §27. See also General Comment No. 35, §45.

[118] Ibid.

explains that, in order to ensure the right to bring proceedings without delay, 'no substantial waiting period shall exist before a detainee can bring a first challenge to the arbitrariness and lawfulness of detention'.[119]

PRISONERS OF WAR

As shown above, POWs may be detained through internment or close confinement from the time of capture until the cessation of active hostilities in an IAC, unless they are facing criminal proceedings or serving a criminal sentence. There may, however, be medical reasons calling for the repatriation of a POW, or transfer to a neutral State, before the cessation of active hostilities.

Because POWs may be held captive until the cessation of active hostilities, the Inter-American Commission on Human Rights has concluded that IHL is the *lex specialis* and that 'international law should not be considered to provide for any entitlement of detained combatants to be informed of the reasons for their detention, challenge the legality of their detention, or, in the absence of disciplinary or criminal proceedings, to be provided with access to legal counsel'.[120] On the face of it, this sounds reasonable. Professor Doswald-Beck nevertheless argues that the right to challenge the lawfulness of detention, through *habeas corpus*, should be respected in the case of POWs for three practical reasons, namely: (1) to determine whether a person does indeed fall within the category of a POW within the meaning of Article 4 Geneva Convention III, noting that this categorization means that the person can be detained until the cessation of active hostilities; (2) to act as a check to ensure that a seriously injured or seriously sick POW is repatriated or transferred to a neutral State; and/or (3) to act as a check to ensure that POWs are released and repatriated without delay after cessation of active hostilities.[121] This was an argument taken up by the International Commission of Jurists,[122] and accepted within the Basic Principles and Guidelines of the UN Working Group on Arbitrary Detention.[123]

[119] See also General Comment No. 35, §42.

[120] Inter-American Commission on Human Rights, *Report on Terrorism and Human Rights*, OEA/Ser.L/V/II.116, 22 October 2002, §142.

[121] Doswald-Beck, *Human Rights in Times of Conflict and Terrorism*, p. 279.

[122] International Commission of Jurists, 'Exercise of the right to challenge the lawfulness of detention by individuals detained in the context of an armed conflict, in *Panel 6: Exercise of the right by individuals detained in situations of armed conflict, state of emergency or for counterterrorism purposes*' (Working Group on Arbitrary Detention, Global Consultation on the Right to Challenge the Lawfulness of Detention, 1-2 September 2014, Geneva, Switzerland), <http://www.ohchr.org/Documents/Issues/Detention/Consultation2014/AlexConte.pdf> (last accessed 9 April 2015).

[123] Basic Principles and Guidelines, Principle 16 at §48.

PROTECTED PERSONS IN AN INTERNATIONAL ARMED CONFLICT

As mentioned, a Detaining or Occupying Power may, in considering measures of control over protected persons, have recourse to assigned residence or internment. This will either be under the authority of Article 42 of Geneva Convention IV (with respect to alien civilians in the territory of a party to the conflict) or Article 78 (with respect to civilians in an occupied territory). It has already been noted that, reiterating Article 41 of Geneva Convention IV, the ICRC Commentary on Articles 42 and 78 emphasizes that both internment and assigned residence are of an exceptional character and represent the most severe measures that a Detaining or Occupying Power may resort to with respect to protected persons.[124] It is against this background that procedures are established under Articles 43 and 78 to review the internment or assigned residence of protected persons in an IAC.

The point of such review is to ensure that a protected person is made subject to such measures only where this is required and, in the words of the ICRC Commentary, that 'no protected person should be kept in assigned residence or in an internment camp for a longer time than the security of the Detaining State demands'.[125] Concerning internment, the latter point is reflected within Geneva Convention IV and the ICRC's catalogue of rules of customary IHL. Article 132 obliges a Detaining Power to release all interned civilians 'as soon as the reasons which necessitated his internment no longer exist'. It also calls on parties to an IAC to endeavour to conclude agreements for the release, repatriation, or accommodation in a neutral country of certain classes of civilian internees, including children, wounded and sick, and those that have been detained for a long time. Rule 128(B) similarly provides that: 'Civilian internees must be released as soon as the reasons which necessitated internment no longer exist, but at the latest as soon as possible after the close of active hostilities'.

As well as recalling that Article 147 of Geneva Convention IV establishes the 'unlawful confinement of a protected person' as a grave breach of Geneva Convention IV, and that an unjustifiable delay in the repatriation of civilians also constitutes a grave breach of Protocol I,[126] consideration is here given to the procedures under Articles 43 and 78 of Geneva Convention IV and the way in which they are complemented by international human rights law concerning the right to *habeas corpus*.

[124] See, 'The authority to detain protected persons in an international armed conflict', in 'Deprivation of liberty in international armed conflicts'.

[125] *Commentary on the Geneva Conventions of 12 August 1949. Volume IV*, p. 261.

[126] See, 'The authority to detain protected persons in an international armed conflict', in 'Deprivation of Liberty in international armed conflicts'.

Alien civilians in the territory of a party to the conflict

For alien civilians in the territory of a party to an international armed conflict, who have been interned or placed in assigned residence, Article 43 of Geneva Convention IV sets out a procedure which, as described in the ICRC Commentary, is designed to ensure that parties to an IAC do not go beyond the limits of authorized resort to measures of internment or assigned residence.[127] Article 43 entitles such persons 'to have such action reconsidered as soon as possible by an appropriate court or administrative board designated by the Detaining Power for that purpose'. If the internment or assigned residence is maintained, Article 43 explains that '… the court or administrative board shall periodically, and at least twice yearly, give consideration to his or her case, with a view to the favourable amendment of the initial decision, if circumstances permit'. On the question of how Article 43 fits with international human rights law, especially the right to *habeas corpus* under Article 9(4) of the ICCPR, two issues arise: (1) the timing of the review; and (2) the nature of the reviewing body.

Reconsideration under Article 43 of an alien civilian's internment or assigned residence is to be undertaken, in the first instance, 'as soon as possible' after the act of internment or assigned residence, and thereafter on a periodic basis (at least twice each year). The expression 'as soon as possible' is not defined within Article 43, nor is an interpretation offered by the Commentary to Geneva Convention IV, although the Commentary notes that the Detaining Power 'must never forget that the Convention describes internment and placing in assigned residence as exceptionally severe measures which may be applied only if they are absolutely necessary for the security of the State'.[128] Since Geneva Convention IV is silent on this point, guidance should be taken from international human rights law. In particular, one can point to the jurisprudence of the Human Rights Committee concerning the meaning of the right in Article 9(3) of the ICCPR to be brought 'promptly' before court. Noting that this expression is also not defined, the Human Rights Committee has stated that, while the meaning of the term must be determined on a case-by-case basis, delays in bringing a person before the court must not exceed 'a few days'.[129] Bearing in mind the protected status of civilians, and the repeated reference to the exceptional nature of civilian internment or assigned residence (throughout Geneva Convention IV, its Commentary and the rules of customary IHL), the same swift approach should apply to initial reconsiderations under Article 43. This approach has been adopted within the current draft Basic Principles and Guidelines on *habeas corpus* elaborated by the UN Working Group on Arbitrary Detention.[130]

[127] *Commentary on the Geneva Conventions of 12 August 1949. Volume IV*, p. 260.

[128] *Commentary on the Geneva Conventions of 12 August 1949. Volume IV*, pp. 260–1.

[129] General Comment No. 35, §33.

[130] Basic Principles and Guidelines, Principle 16 at §47, in combination with Principles 2 and 11 and Guideline 7.

As to the nature of the reviewing body, Article 43 refers to reconsideration and periodic review undertaken by 'an appropriate court or administrative board'. The same expression is used in Article 35, concerning the review of any decision refusing to allow a civilian to leave the territory. A Detaining Power is thereby left with a choice concerning Article 43 reviews, namely whether to authorize a 'court' or an 'administrative board' to undertake such reviews. The point to be made is that this is a choice as to the nomenclature and composition of the reviewing authority, but not as to its character. According to the ICRC Commentary on Article 43: 'The existence of these alternatives provides sufficient flexibility to take into account the usage in different States'. It continues to explain, however, that even in the case of an 'administrative' decision under Article 43, such a decision 'must be made not by one official but by an administrative board offering the necessary guarantees of independence and impartiality'.[131]

This interpretation is consistent with the approach of drawing guidance from international human rights law as to the meaning of IHL, in this case drawing from the requirement in Article 14(1) of the ICCPR that the determination of a person's rights and obligations shall be made by a 'competent, independent and impartial tribunal established by law'. All determinations under Article 43 must therefore be made by a body, whether a court or administrative board, that satisfies essential requirements of competence, impartiality, and independence, and its processes must include and respect fundamental procedural safeguards.[132] This has again been reflected within the UN Working Group's draft Basic Principles and Guidelines on *habeas corpus*.[133]

Civilians in an occupied territory

With respect to civilians in an occupied territory who have been interned or placed in assigned residence, Article 78 of Geneva Convention IV provides that: 'Decisions regarding such assigned residence or internment shall be made according to a regular procedure to be prescribed by the Occupying Power in accordance with the provisions of the present Convention. This procedure shall include the right of appeal for the

[131] *Commentary on the Geneva Conventions of 12 August 1949. Volume IV*, p. 260.

[132] See for instance: Human Rights Committee, *Vuolanne v Finland*, UN Doc. CCPR/C/35/D/265/1987 (7 April 1989), §§7.2 and 9.6; European Court of Human Rights (Grand Chamber), *D.N. v Switzerland*, App. No. 27154/95 (29 March 2001), §42; Inter-American Court of Human Rights, *Chaparro Álvarez and Lapo Íñiguez v Ecuador*, Series C No. 170 (21 November 2007), §§128–130; African Commission on Human and Peoples' Rights, *Constitutional Rights Project v Nigeria*, No. 153/96, 13th Activity Report (15 November 1999) §§15–18. See also Human Rights Committee, General Comment No. 32, 'Article 14: Right to equality before courts and tribunals and to a fair trial', UN Doc CCPR/C/GC/32 (2007), §§19–24; African Commission on Human and Peoples' Rights, *Principles and Guidelines on the Right to a Fair Trial and Legal Assistance in Africa*, Principles A(4) and A(5).

[133] Basic Principles and Guidelines, Principle 16 at §47, in combination with Principle 6 and Guideline 4.

parties concerned. Appeals shall be decided with the least possible delay …'. If a decision to intern or place in assigned residence is upheld, this '…shall be subject to periodical review, if possible every six months, by a competent body set up by the said Power'. Questions of timing and the nature of the reviewing body again arise.

As to the timing of any appeal against a decision regarding assigned residence or internment, Article 78 demands that the appeal is to be decided 'with the least possible delay'. The Inter-American Commission on Human Rights, in *Coard et al v United States*, considered the application of Article 78 to the arrest and detention of seventeen claimants by US forces during the first days of a military invasion of Grenada in 1983. The petitioners were held in US custody for a total of nine to twelve days after the cessation of hostilities without access to any review of their detention. The Commission referred to the language of Article 78 as reflecting minimum safeguards against arbitrary detention.[134] Applying the approach of interpreting IHL provisions consistently with international human rights law, it found that: 'This delay, which is not attributable to a situation of active hostilities or explained by other information on the record, was incompatible with the terms of the American Declaration of the Rights and Duties of Man as understood with reference to Article 78 of the Fourth Geneva Convention'.[135] The Basic Principles and Guidelines on *habeas corpus* similarly reflect that no substantial waiting period shall apply to the hearing of a *habeas corpus* petition by an interned civilian.[136]

The right of a civilian to appeal against a decision regarding residential assignment or internment does not expressly state, within Article 78, the nature of the body that is to consider the appeal. Unlike Article 43 concerning alien civilians in the territory of a party to the conflict, it does not refer to the options of appeal by a 'court' or 'administrative body'. Article 78 is in this way more vague than Article 43 and thus even more reliant upon international human rights law for guidance as to its meaning. The ICRC Commentary explains that it is for the Occupying Power to decide on the procedure to be adopted under Article 78, but notes that it must observe the stipulations in Article 43.[137] As mentioned earlier, the Commentary speaks of the Article 43 procedure as requiring decisions by a body that offers the necessary guarantees of independence and impartiality, supplemented by Articles 9(4) and 14(1) of the ICCPR to require that the body must satisfy the essential requirements of competence, impartiality, and independence, and its processes must include and respect fundamental procedural safeguards.

Consistent with this approach is the decision of the Inter-American Commission in *Coard et al. v United States*, referred to earlier. The Commission considered that the decision to detain must 'not be left to the sole discretion of the state agent(s) responsible

[134] *Coard et al. v United States*, Report No. 109/99-Case 10.951 (1999), §54. [135] Ibid., §57.

[136] Basic Principles and Guidelines, Principle 16 at §47, in combination with Guideline 7.

[137] *Commentary on the Geneva Conventions of 12 August 1949. Volume IV*, p. 368.

for carrying it out'.[138] It expressed this requirement to be fundamental and reflecting the rationale of the right to *habeas corpus*, such that it is not capable of being overlooked in any context.[139] The Commission noted that compliance with this requirement did not have to be through recourse to the Grenadian court system but could have been accomplished through the establishment of an expeditious judicial or quasi-judicial review process, and emphasized that the appeal mechanism must have the authority to order release where warranted.[140] The approaches of the Inter-American Commission and in the ICRC Commentary are again consistent with the content of, and jurisprudence concerning, Articles 9(4) and 14(1) of the ICCPR and the UN Working Group on Arbitrary Detention's Basic Principles and Guidelines.[141]

REVIEW OF DETENTION IN A NON-INTERNATIONAL ARMED CONFLICT

It was concluded earlier that detention in a NIAC must comply, in the case of States parties to the ICCPR, with the requirements of the ICCPR, and that this applies without contradiction from IHL. It was at the same time recognized that the authority and procedures allowing for detention in a NIAC may be pursuant to a derogation from Article 9(1) of the ICCPR.[142] That said, it has also been explained that the Human Rights Committee has qualified any recourse to a derogation from Article 9 by stating that, in order to protect non-derogable rights such as the right to life and the prohibition of torture and ill-treatment, the right to *habeas corpus* must not be diminished by measures of derogation.[143] The Committee thus noted with encouragement that the United States Supreme Court, in *Boumedience v Bush*,[144] recognized the extraterritorial application of constitutional *habeas corpus* rights to aliens detained at Guantánamo Bay.[145] As also mentioned earlier, Principle 4 of the Working Group's Basic Principles and Guidelines goes further than the Human Rights Committee by stating that the right to *habeas*

[138] *Coard et al. v United States*, §§55 and 59.

[139] Ibid., §55.

[140] Ibid., §§58 and 60 respectively.

[141] Basic Principles and Guidelines, Principle 16 at §47, in combination with Principle 6 and Guideline 4.

[142] See, 'Derogating from the prohibition against arbitrary and unlawful detention', in 'Deprivation of liberty under international human rights law'.

[143] General Comment No. 35, §67; General Comment No. 29, §§11 and 16.

[144] *Boumedience v Bush* 553 US 723 (2008). Contrast this with the subsequent decision in 2010 of the US Court of Appeals, in the District of Columbia, in *Al Maqaleh v Gates* (2012, 605 F.3d 84), in which the US Court of Appeals concluded that the jurisdiction to grant *habeas* relief did not extend to aliens held in executive detention in the Bagram detention facility in Afghanistan.

[145] Human Rights Committee Concluding Observations on the Fourth Periodic Report of the United States, §3(b).

corpus under Article 9(4) of the ICCPR may not be subject to derogation, even in times of armed conflict.[146]

Thus, in any situation of detention in a NIAC, whether or not a derogation accompanies such detention, all aspects of the right to *habeas corpus* must be respected by a detaining authority.

Concluding remarks

The detention of persons in armed conflict presents a myriad of legal issues, some of which are clear and others of which give rise to controversial and hotly contested questions. Consideration has been given in this chapter to the complex intersection between international humanitarian law and international human rights law. It has been reiterated that human rights law remains applicable in armed conflict and that the complementarity of these two bodies of law presents situations in which one or both may apply to the question of the authorization for detention in armed conflict and the review of the legality of such detention. It has also been emphasized that human rights obligations are capable of applying extraterritorially, and that this is undoubtedly the case in the context of detention, since detention involves effective control by State authorities over a detained person.

It has been concluded that international humanitarian law acts as the *lex specialis* concerning the authority to detain persons in an international armed conflict, since Geneva Conventions III and IV set out detailed grounds and procedures concerning the detention of prisoners of war and civilians posing a serious threat to security. Article 9(1) of the ICCPR is to be interpreted so that it is to be assumed that, in principle, any deprivation of liberty in an IAC which is undertaken in compliance with Geneva Conventions III and IV does not amount to an arbitrary or unlawful deprivation of liberty within the meaning of Article 9(1). Concerning internment in a non-international armed conflict, a critical assessment has been undertaken of the position taken in the ICRC's Opinion Paper, namely that Common Article 3 and Protocol II imply a power to intern in a NIAC. It has been concluded that at least eight cogent arguments exist to counter the ICRC's position. Common Article 3 and Protocol II do not provide a legal authority to deprive a person of liberty in NIAC, they simply guarantee a minimum level of humanitarian treatment for people who are in fact detained during a NIAC.

[146] Basic Principles and Guidelines, Guideline 3; and the 2012 and 2014 reports of the Working Group on Arbitrary Detention.

International human rights law is instead the governing body of law, including in the context of internment regimes that might be authorized by the UN Security Council.

The final part of this chapter has considered the question of the supervision of the lawfulness of detention. In the context of detention in an international armed conflict, this involves a rich and complementary interplay between Geneva Conventions III and IV and the right to *habeas corpus*. However, in the situation of detention in a non-international armed conflict, whether or not this is accompanied by a derogation, it has been shown that all aspects of the right to *habeas corpus* under international human rights law must be respected by a detaining authority.

8 Engaging with drug lords: protecting civilians in Colombia, Mexico, and Honduras

Chiara Redaelli[1]

Introduction

In recent years, some of the most lethal episodes of violence have taken place in countries vastly affected by organized crime, such as Mexico and Honduras. Criminal groups[2] are primarily economical actors: they do not aim at constituting a parallel power system. However, they benefit from a weak State, unable to firmly control its territory, in order to create areas of impunity where they can operate undisturbed.

This chapter analyses the specific challenges of dealing with criminal organizations from an international humanitarian law (IHL) and human rights perspective.

First, I discuss how the criteria to determine the existence of a non-international armed conflict (NIAC) apply to organized crime. Broadly speaking, criminal groups are not considered party to a conflict, despite the fact that they might engage in acts of violence against the government. Nonetheless, situations such as the one in Colombia, and arguably the violence in Mexico, would suggest that criminal groups operating in these countries could be considered party to a NIAC. These organizations do not limit themselves to take advantage of the instability and weakness of the government, but directly challenge its authority, seeking to create zones of impunity where they can pursue their criminal activities. Hence, they constitute an actual and serious threat to the State.

Second, the chapter focuses on the specific challenges of dealing with organized crime. Heinous crimes against civilians demonstrate that criminal groups are unlikely

[1] Chiara Raedelli is a teaching assistant for the Master in Asian Studies and a PhD candidate in public international law at the Graduate Institute of International and Development Studies. The author would like to thank Marco Formisano for his helpful comments on successive drafts of this chapter.

[2] For the definition of 'criminal group' see next paragraph.

to respect domestic and international law. The responses adopted so far at national and international level have proved utterly unfit to face the challenges posed by criminal organizations. However, given organized crime's devastating impact on civilians, it is desirable to at least find ways to engage with these groups. The greatest difficulty lies in their economical nature and motivation: unlike opposition groups, they do not aim at overthrowing the government. Therefore, they do not seek international legitimacy and have thus fewer incentives to respect international legal obligations. The final part of the chapter thus suggests strategies to engage with criminal groups in order to improve the protection of civilians.

A. **The international framework to tackle criminal organizations**

Organized crime constitutes a serious threat to public security and global stability.[3] Concerned by its increasingly transnational dimension, the international community has started to address the issue at the international level in order to repress criminal groups and to counter their illicit activities.[4]

Specific conventions tackling drug trafficking have been adopted over the last century.[5] In particular, the Convention for the Suppression of the Illicit Trafficking in Dangerous Drugs (1936) invites States parties 'to make the necessary legislative provisions for severely punishing' acts such as 'possession, offering (for sale), distribution, purchase, sale, delivery, ... transport, importation and exportation of narcotic drugs'.[6] In the 1980s, the increasing power of and violence related to criminal organizations led to the adoption of the United Nations Convention against Illicit Traffic in Narcotic Drugs and Psychotropic Substances (1988). Despite the uncontested importance of these conventions in tackling specific drug-related activities, they do not offer a notion of criminal organizations: subjects to these treaties are all the individuals involved in the drug market. Furthermore, these conventions do

[3] Nagle, L., 2002, 'The Challenges of Fighting Global Organized Crime in Latin America', *Fordham International Law Journal*, vol. 26, no. 6: 1649, at p. 1654.

[4] Hauck, P. and Peterke, S., 2010, 'Organized Crime and Gang Violence in National and International Law', *International Review of the Red Cross*, vol. 92, no. 878 (June): 407, at p. 416.

[5] The first international treaty against drugs is the International Opium Convention (1912), adopted at the end of the Shanghai Opium Conference (1909). The Convention makes a distinction between legal and illegal drugs and its main focus is the trafficking of cocaine and opium.

[6] Convention for the Suppression of the Illicit Trafficking in Dangerous Drugs (1936 Trafficking Convention) (Geneva, 1936), Art. 2.

not establish an international cooperation framework: the criminalization of specific activities and the decision on the means to address these phenomena rest with States.[7]

It is in the light of the foregoing that the United Nations Convention on Transnational Organized Crime (UNCTOC) crucially marks a positive development in the fight against organized crime.[8] The purpose of the Convention is 'to promote cooperation to prevent and combat transnational organized crime more effectively'.[9] To this end, it binds States parties to criminalize specific acts, such as the participation in criminal groups[10] and money laundering,[11] as well as 'secondary activities' directly related to organized crime.

For the purposes of the Convention:

> 'Organized criminal group' shall mean a structured group of three or more persons, existing for a period of time and acting in concert with the aim of committing one or more serious crimes or offences established in accordance with this Convention, in order to obtain, directly or indirectly, a financial or other material benefit.
>
> 'Serious crime' shall mean conduct constituting an offence punishable by a maximum deprivation of liberty of at least four years or a more serious penalty.
>
> 'Structured group' shall mean a group that is not randomly formed for the immediate commission of an offence and that does not need to have formally defined roles for its members, continuity of its membership or a developed structure.[12]

The reasons why these definitions are of particular interest are twofold. First, the UNCTOC notion of organized criminal group requires that the groups should not be 'randomly formed'. This requirement would thus distinguish criminal organizations from less professional criminal gangs.[13] The definition specifies that the group 'does not need to have formally defined roles for its members, continuity of its membership or a developed structure'. The UNCTOC definition of organized criminal groups requires a less stringent level of organization than IHL requires for recognition of an armed group as party to a conflict.[14]

[7] Hauck, P. and Peterke, S., 'Organized Crime and Gang Violence', p. 420.

[8] United Nations Convention on Transnational Organized Crime (UNCTOC) (Palermo, 15 December 2000). The Convention is supplemented with three additional protocols which address specific activities: Protocol to Prevent, Suppress and Punish Trafficking in Persons, especially Women and Children ('Trafficking Protocol'); Protocol against the Smuggling of Migrants by Land, Sea and Air ('Migrant Smuggling Protocol'); Protocol against the Illicit Manufacturing and Trafficking in Firearms, Their Parts and Components and Ammunition ('Firearms Protocol').

[9] Hauck, P. and Peterke, S., 'Organized Crime and Gang Violence', p. 420.

[10] Art. 5 UNCTOC. [11] Art. 6 UNCTOC. [12] Art. 2 UNCTOC.

[13] Some authors distinguish between criminal organizations and gangs. The latters are defined as 'less sophisticated and are not true market players: they do not exist to provide regular goods or services professionally, but commit less well-organized and well-planned crimes without any defined clear purpose' (Hauck, P. and Peterke, S., 'Organized Crime and Gang Violence', p. 412). See e.g. Decker, S. H. and van Winkle, B., 1996, *Life in the Gang: Family, Friends, and Violence*, Cambridge: Cambridge University Press, at pp. 23–5; Franco, C., 'The MS-13 and 18th Street Gangs: Emerging Transnational Threats?', CRS Report for Congress, Congressional Research Service, Washington, DC, 30 January 2008, at p. 6.

[14] See next paragraph.

However, this does not necessarily mean that criminal groups can never be considered party to a conflict. As we shall see, several Drug Trafficking Organizations (DTOs) operating in Latin America are sufficiently organized to meet the organization requirement under IHL.[15]

Second, a criminal group commits illicit activities 'in order to obtain, directly or indirectly, a financial or other material benefit'. This would confirm the dominant view, whereby criminal organizations are mainly economical actors, while opposition groups pursue political objectives.[16] The issue will be addressed in the next section. However, the mere fact of being moved by solely economical motives does not exclude criminal groups from being party to a NIAC.[17]

B. **Criminal organizations under international humanitarian law: the organization requirement**

According to the ICTY definition, a non-international armed conflict (NIAC) is deemed to exist 'whenever there is protracted armed violence between governmental authorities and organized armed groups or between such groups within a state'.[18] 'Situations of internal disturbances and tensions, such as riots, isolated and sporadic acts of violence and other acts of similar nature',[19] as well as 'banditry, unorganized and short-lived insurrections, or terrorist activities'[20] are not considered armed conflicts.

The problem lies in determining the threshold between what is not considered a NIAC (Article 1(2) Additional Protocol II) and the notion of 'protracted armed violence' referred to in the *Tadić* decision. When does an internal conflict start? The ICTY identified a test to determine the existence of a NIAC, based on two cumulative criteria: 'the intensity of the conflict and the organization of the parties to the conflict'.[21]

As for the first requirement, the ICTY addressed the issue in the *Milošević* case, where it assessed the intensity of the violence focusing on the length or protracted nature of the conflict and seriousness and increase in armed clashes, the spread of clashes over

[15] Betti, S., 2003, 'New Prospects for Inter-State Co-operation in Criminal Matters: The Palermo Convention', *International Criminal Law Review*, vol. 3, no. 2: 151, at p. 152.

[16] Hauck, P. and Peterke, S., 'Organized Crime and Gang Violence', p. 422.

[17] This issue will be addressed further in the next section.

[18] ICTY, *Prosecutor v Tadić*, Decision on the Defence Motion for Interlocutory Appeal on Jurisdiction (Appeal Chamber) (IT-94-1), 2 October 1995, §70.

[19] Art. 1(2) Protocol Additional to the Geneva Conventions of 12 August 1949, and relating to the Protection of Victims of Non-International Armed Conflicts (Additional Protocol II), 8 June 1977.

[20] ICTY, *Prosecutor v Tadić*, Judgement (Trial Chamber) (IT-94-1), 7 May 1997, §562.

[21] Ibid.

the territory, the increase in number of governmental forces sent to Kosovo, and the weapons used by both parties.[22]

With regards the second requirement, not every situation of protracted violence raises to a NIAC: the parties 'must have a minimum degree of organization and discipline—enough to enable them to respect international humanitarian law—in order to be recognized as a party to the conflict'.[23] State authorities are presumed 'to dispose of armed forces that satisfy this criterion'.[24] With regard to armed non-State actors (ANSAs), the ICTY identified indicative factors, such as 'the existence of a command structure and disciplinary rules and mechanisms within the group; the existence of a headquarters; the fact that the group controls a certain territory; the ability of the group to gain access to weapons, other military equipment, recruits and military training; its ability to plan, coordinate and carry out military operations, including troop movements and logistics; its ability to define a unified military strategy and use military tactics; and its ability to speak with one voice and negotiate and conclude agreements such as ceasefire or peace accords'.[25]

Some authors claim the existence of a further criterion to the definition of non-international armed conflict: the motives of the ANSAs involved. According to this interpretation, only groups aiming to achieve political objectives could be party to a NIAC.[26] Criminal organizations flourish when the government is weak and their activities de facto challenge the State's control. However, these are not the main purposes of their illicit activities, but only 'collateral effects'.[27] Indeed, their principal objective is

[22] ICTY, *Prosecutor v Milošević,* Decision on Motion for Judgment of Acquittal (Trial Chamber) (IT-02-54-T), 16 June 2004, §§28–31 (hereafter *Milošević Rule 98bis Decision*). See also ICTY, *Prosecutor v Ramush Haradinaj et al.*, Judgement (Trial Chamber) (IT–04–84), 3 April 2008 (hereafter ICTY, *Prosecutor v Ramush Haradinaj et al.*), §49.

[23] ICRC, *Armed Conflicts Linked to the Disintegration of State Structures: Preparatory Document drafted by the International Committee of the Red Cross for the First Periodical Meeting on International Humanitarian Law,* Geneva, 23 January 1998.

[24] ICTY, *Prosecutor v Ramush Haradinaj et al.*, §60. See also Vité, S., 2009, 'Typology of Armed Conflicts in International Humanitarian Law: Legal Concepts and Actual Situations', *International Review of the Red Cross,* vol. 91, no. 873 (March): 69, at p. 77.

[25] ICTY, *Prosecutor v Ramush Haradinaj et al.*, §60. See also *Milošević Rule 98bis Decision*, §23, where the ICTY specified that non-State actors are deemed to be organized if they meet certain requirements, such as 'an official joint command structure, headquarters, designated zone of operations, and the ability to procure, transport and distribute arms'.

[26] See, e.g., Bruderlein, C., 2000, 'The Role of Non-state Actors in Building Human Security: The Case of Armed Groups in Intra-State Wars', *Centre for Humanitarian Dialogue,* Geneva; Petrasek, D., 2000, 'Ends and Means: Human Rights Approaches to Armed Groups', *International Council on Human Rights Policy,* Geneva, p. 5; Hauck, P. and Peterke, S., 'Organized Crime and Gang Violence', p. 433.

[27] Perret, A., 2012, 'Privatization of the War on Drugs in Mexico and Colombia. Limiting the Application of Humanitarian Law and Endangering Human Rights', *Interdisciplinary Journal of Human Rights Law,* vol. 7, no. 1: 45, at p. 62. See also Raether, J., 2012, 'Drug War: International Law and Counter-Narcotics', *University of St. Thomas Law Journal,* vol. 9, no. 3: 933, at pp. 953–954.

economical: they do not endeavour to take over the State. They would thus be prevented from being party to a NIAC.

However, this position has no legal basis under existing international humanitarian law.[28] The ICTY confirmed this approach in the *Limaj* case, where it pointed out that:

> The determination of the existence of an armed conflict is based solely on two criteria: the intensity of the conflict and organization of the parties, the purpose of the armed forces to engage in acts of violence or also achieve some further objective is, therefore, irrelevant.[29]

Furthermore, analysing the motives of the ANSAs would bring an element of confusion in the assessment of the existence of an internal conflict. Indeed, some opposition groups, such as the FARC and ELN, aim to overthrow the government, but engage also in criminal activities in order to fund their military and political operations. Conversely, criminal organizations might engage in political activities in order to facilitate their criminal ones.[30]

OPPOSITION GROUPS ENGAGING IN DRUG TRAFFICKING

Over the last fifty years, Colombia has been affected by a violent conflict between governmental forces and opposition groups, and among these groups. The main ANSAs operating in the country are the *Fuerzas Armadas Revolucionarias de Colombia—Ejército del Pueblo* (FARC) and the *Ejército de Liberación Nacional* (ELN).[31] FARC and the ELN are organized armed groups, originally led by political motivations. Both ANSAs have a high degree of institutionalization and are modelled on a hierarchical structure.[32]

FARC retains territorial control over its traditional stronghold, where it prohibits or severely restricts free movement of the local population through the so-called armed strikes.[33] Although it is not clear how often these episodes take place, it is certain that they have a dramatic impact on the local population, as access to public services, schools, and the market is prevented.[34] President Álvaro Uribe (2002–2010) started a military offensive against FARC that has been continued by President Santos and has

[28] Vité, S., 'Typology of Armed Conflicts', p. 78.

[29] ICTY, *Prosecutor v Limaj*, Judgment (Trial Chamber) (IT-03-66-T), 30 November 2005, §170.

[30] Vité, S., 'Typology of Armed Conflicts', p. 78.

[31] International Criminal Court's Office of the Prosecutor (OTP), *Report on Preliminary Examination Activities 2013* (November 2013), §§118 120.

[32] International Crisis Group (hereafter, ICG), 'Colombia: Peace at Last?', Latin America Report no. 45, 25 September 2012, p. 18.

[33] An 'armed strike' is a 'freeze in civil activities' imposed by ANSAs. See Colombia Reports, 'Authorities fail to prevent FARC "armed strike" in west Colombia', available at: <http://colombiareports.co/colombian-authorities-fail-to-prevent-farc-armed-strike/> accessed 1 May 2015; ICG, 'Colombia: Peace at Last?', p. 8.

[34] Ibid.

proved particularly effective, reducing FARC's total members from 20,000 to 7,000 combatants. Despite the fact that governmental attacks did not focus on ELN with the same intensity, the group has lost significant military power and territorial control due to the paramilitaries' expansion in the 1990s.[35]

The FARC and ELN's relations with the drug market differ substantially. ELN has been traditionally against any engagement in drug production and trafficking. This approach has always helped to build close ties with the population living in the territories under its control.[36] However, military decline and subsequent economic shortage forced ELN to break its longstanding restriction and to open to the drug market in order to fund its activities. While this decision cost ELN some local support, the group has been careful to maintain its links with the population as much as possible.[37]

In the 1980s, FARC realized that by engaging with the drug economy it could access a crucial source of funding for its activities.[38] Controlling territories with coca plantations, FARC started to protect and to tax coca growers and to set prices for buyers. Over the years, the involvement in drug trafficking has expanded and now includes all the phases of production and trafficking.[39] Not all FARC blocks are directly involved in the drug market, as this depends on the areas where they operate. Furthermore, the way in which they interact with drug traffickers largely depends on local power structure, ranging from overseeing cultivation to controlling the delivery of cocaine to international traffickers.[40]

FARC strongly denies its involvement in the drug market: the group constantly maintains that they are not drug traffickers, and that 'they simply impose a tax on all economic activities under their control, among them drug trade'.[41] Despite its denial, the ruling body of FARC is aware of the importance of the earnings coming from drug trafficking. Nevertheless, they prefer to leave drug-related activities in the hands of their subordinates in order to maintain a *plausible deniability*. As a result, drug trafficking is not centrally coordinated. If it were, FARC could gain control of the whole drug market in Colombia in a short time frame.[42] Indeed, there is ample evidence that the group is

[35] ICG, 'Left in the Cold? The ELN and Colombia's Peace Talks?', Latin America Report no. 51, 26 February 2014, p. 3.

[36] ICG, 'Left in the Cold?', p. i. [37] Ibid. [38] IGC, 'Colombia: Peace at Last?', p. 11.

[39] Ibid. FARC's leader Timochenko has strenously denied the group's involvement with drug traffickers, claiming that the only relation consists in a tax imposed to allow drug cartels to operate in territories controlled by the FARC. See ICG, 'Colombia: Peace at Last?', p. 11.

[40] Ibid., p. 12.

[41] On 17 March 2013, one of the FARC negotiators in Havana, Ricardo González, underlined that FARC is not a criminal organization: 'you aren't talking to any drug traffickers here; you're talking to an armed group'. See McDermott, J., 'The FARC: the Peace Process and the Potential Criminalisation of the Guerrillas', Insight Crime, May 2013, p. 18.

[42] McDermott, J., 'The Future of the BACRIM and Post-Conflict Colombia', Insight Crime, 2 May 2014, p. 2, available at: <http://www.insightcrime.org/investigations/future-of-the-bacrim-and-post-conflict-colombia> accessed 1 May 2015.

already one of the most powerful cartels in Colombia 'in terms of numbers, military capability, territorial control and earnings from the drug trade'.[43]

FARC has also concluded alliances with the new illegal armed groups (NIAGs), which were created after the demobilization of the paramilitary groups.[44] The Marxist group controls coca fields and production and sells coca and cocaine to Colombian BACRIMs (*bandas criminales*),[45] which sell it to the international market. This situation is ideal for FARC, allowing them to sell drugs without assuming the risks of international trafficking.[46] The alliance between FARC and BACRIM is not limited to economic relations and some authors even talk about the creation of FARCRIM.[47] For instance, in Catumbo region FARC works together with criminal groups, forming 'a common front against governmental law enforcement'.[48]

However, the FARC–BACRIM relationship is not immune from tensions. Indeed, Mexican cartels purchase cocaine from Colombia and thus seek to remove the middlemen and to negotiate directly with the guerrillas. The relationship between FARC and cartels started in 2008[49] and there is ample evidence of close ties with the Sinaloa Cartel.[50]

FARC's close ties with the drug market raise doubts with regard to its political nature, as the group is increasingly seen as a criminal organization.[51] Following the peace negotiations with the government, it is likely that some elements of the opposition group will criminalize.[52] What is still unclear is whether FARC's members will join the existing BACRIMs, or will rather create their own criminal groups, which would unavoidably increase armed confrontations and criminal violence.

In sum, both FARC and ELN engage in the illegal drug economy in order to fund their military activities. While links with the drug market have not yet transformed them into criminal groups,[53] the situation is nonetheless highly volatile and is inevitably going to evolve further at the end of the peace talks.[54]

[43] McDermott, J., 'The FARC', p. 18.

[44] See next paragraph. FARC concluded alliances also with Mexican cartels, which are increasingly involved in the Colombian drug market. See ICG, 'Improving Security Policy in Colombia', Latin America Briefing N°23, Bogotá/Brussels, 29 June 2010, p. 10.

[45] See next paragraph. [46] McDermott, J., 'The FARC', p. 22.

[47] McDermott, J., 'The Future of the BACRIM', p. 2.

[48] ICG, 'Colombia: Peace at Last?', p. 11.

[49] *The New York Times*, 'Colombian official ties FARC to Mexican drug cartels', 7 October 2008, available at: <http://www.nytimes.com/2008/10/08/world/americas/08mexico.html> accessed 1 May 2015.

[50] ICG, 'Improving Security Policy', p. 10.

[51] McDermott, J., 'Criminal Activities of the FARC and Rebel Earnings', InSight Crime, 20 May 2013, available at: <http://www.insightcrime.org/investigations/farc-criminal-activities-income> accessed 1 May 2015.

[52] McDermott, J., 'The Future of the BACRIM', p. 2.

[53] ICG, 'The Day after Tomorrow: Colombia's FARC and the End of the Conflict', Latin America Report no. 53, 11 December 2014, p. 4; ICG, 'Left in the Cold?', pp. 3, 6–7.

[54] ICG, 'Colombia: Peace at Last?', p. i.

CRIMINAL ORGANIZATIONS

Colombian *bandas criminales* (BACRIMs)

The *Autodefensas Unidas de Colombia* (AUC) was an umbrella, right-wing organization founded in 1997 to consolidate the local paramilitary groups. These self-defence groups were supported by economic elites, drug traffickers, and local communities, which lacked effective protection from the government. They claimed that their primary objective was to protect their sponsors from the guerrillas, namely FARC and ELN.[55]

In 2002, President Uribe started the demobilization of the AUC, which was concluded in 2006 and involved 31,671 paramilitaries.[56] However, the demobilization process remained partial and proved unable to bring to legality all sections of the AUC. Having pursued criminal activities for years, some members of the paramilitary groups rearmed and created successor groups, known as new illegal armed groups (NIAGs).[57]

During a meeting in 2011, the current government laid down a strategy concerning the NIAGs, whose main outcome was their definition as BACRIMs (*bandas criminales*, organized criminal organizations).[58] However, BACRIMs are more than just criminal gangs: some of the NIAGs emerged in the territories formerly controlled by the AUC and they kept the same members and practices. Furthermore, while they lack political ideology, they are rapidly evolving: groups like the *Urabeños* are increasingly involved in political violence and social control.[59] While in some areas NIAGs form alliances with opposition groups, such as FARC, in other parts of the country the army and NIAGs collaborate in order to expel the FARC.[60] Last but not least, in certain areas they benefit from tolerance and collusion of state agents.[61]

President Santos has increasingly recognized their complex nature. Colombian Ministry of Defence described them as 'nationally disjointed criminal structures, with high corrupting, intimidating and armed power that have combined the production and sale of drugs with the violent infringement of civil rights and liberties in certain rural zones and the periphery of some urban centers'.[62]

The NIAGs are thus a complex phenomenon: defining them as *bandas criminales* underestimates their role in the Colombian scenario for two reasons. First, the term

[55] ICG, 'The Day after Tomorrow', p. 5. [56] Ibid. [57] Ibid.

[58] ICG, 'Dismantling Colombia's New Illegal Armed Groups: Lessons from a Surrender', Latin America Report no. 41, 8 June 2012, p. 2.

[59] ICG, 'Cutting the Links between Crime and Local Politics: Colombia's 2011 Elections', Latin America Report no. 37, 25 July 2011, p. 10.

[60] ICG, 'Improving Security Policy in Colombia', pp. 9–10.

[61] Human Rights Watch (hereafter, HRW), *World Report 2015-Colombia*, 29 January 2015.

[62] ICG, 'Dismantling Colombia's New Illegal Armed Groups', p. 2.

BACRIM does not recognize the groups' ties with the former *autodefensas*. They are hence increasingly referred to as narco-paramilitaries, or neo-paramilitaries.[63]

Second, and most importantly, highlighting their criminal nature underestimates their link with the NIAC. Indeed, confrontations between the NIAGs on the one hand and FARC and ELN on the other are not uncommon. The narco-paramilitaries military capability and their level of organization prompted a debate on whether they should be considered parties to the internal conflict. According to Human Rights Watch, some of these organizations 'could be considered armed groups for the purposes of the laws of war'.[64]

Nevertheless, which groups might meet the organization requirement is controversial. While the AUC were 'federations of baby cartels and paramilitary groups',[65] BACRIM's organization is markedly different. Due to the constant pressure of Colombian police, these criminal groups have adopted new, unconventional forms of organization. Their criminal network is built around a series of nodes (units). If a node is taken over by the government and thus dismantled, other nodes are ready to assume the control of its activities. The absence of a traditional hierarchical structure has proved effective also at the command level. For instance, when the founder of the *Urabeños*, Daniel Rendon Herrera, alias 'Don Mario,' was captured by State forces, a new leader immediately took power and the group did not seem to suffer from the shift of leadership.[66]

In 2013, the Office of the Prosecutor (OTP) of the International Criminal Court (ICC) published a *Report on the Preliminary Examination Activities*,[67] where it analysed whether the BACRIMs are party to the NIAC: only in case of a positive answer could they be considered to commit war crimes. The OTP focused its analysis on the *Urabeños*, the *Rastrojos*, and the *Aguilas Negras* and concluded that only the first would meet the organization requirement.[68] Nonetheless, the situation is rapidly evolving and merits the highest attention. As aforementioned, at the end of the peace talks some members of the FARC will inevitably criminalize.[69] Should former members of FARC join the

63 Ibid.

64 HRW, 'Paramilitaries' Heirs: The New Face of Violence in Colombia', February 2010, p. 21.

65 McDermott, J., 'The BACRIM and Their Position in the Colombian Underworld', In Sight Crime, 2 May 2014, available at: <http://www.insightcrime.org/investigations/bacrim-and-their-position-in-colombia-underworld> accessed 1 May 2015.

66 At the moment, the Urabeños are the most powerful BACRIM in Colombia. After the demobilization of the paramilitaries, about thirty criminal organizations were formed in Colombia. In 2014, it seemed clear that the Urabeños have won the race to the leadership and now dominate the criminal market. See McDermott, J., 'The Urabeños—The Criminal Hybrid', 2 May 2014, available at: <http://www.insightcrime.org/investigations/the-urabenos-the-criminal-hybrid> accessed 1 May 2015.

67 International Criminal Court's Office of the Prosecutor (OTP), *Report on Preliminary Examination Activities 2013*.

68 OTP, *Report on Preliminary Examination Activities 2013*, §§128–9.

69 McDermott, J., 'The Future of BACRIM', p. 2.

BACRIMs, these groups would highly benefit from the expertise of the guerrillas and would pose an even more serious threat to Colombian peace and security.

Mexican drug cartels

Drug cartels have operated in Mexico for over a century.[70] These criminal organizations have highly benefited from their strategic position between countries producing drugs and the US, circumstances that allowed them 'to grow into a regional threat'.[71] In 2014 there were two main cartels operating at national levels—the *Sinaloa* cartel and *Los Zetas*.

The first was founded in the Sinaloa State, in villages with a long history of drug smuggling.[72] The *Sinaloa* leader, Joaquín 'El Chapo' Guzmán, is perhaps the most notorious of all drug traffickers, wanted both by Mexico and the US and even mentioned in the *Forbes'* list of billionaires and the *TIME* 100 'leaders and revolutionaries' lists.[73] El Chapo was arrested in 2014. Nonetheless, *Sinaloa*'s narcotics business continued with no evident change.[74]

Los Zetas are a more recent cartel, founded by Osiel Cárdenas, the leader of the Gulf Cartel, in 1999.[75] Fearing assassination 'to the point of paranoia',[76] he decided to recruit ex-soldiers and officers in order to form the armed wing of the cartel: *Los Zetas*.[77] Soon

[70] Beittel, J. S., 'Mexico's Drug Trafficking Organizations: Source and Scope of the Violence', CRS Report for Congress, Congressional Research Service, Washington, DC, 15 April 2013, p. 6.

[71] InSight Crime, 'Mexico', available at: <http://www.insightcrime.org/mexico-organized-crime-news/mexico> accessed 1 May 2015.

[72] Beittel, J. S., 'Mexico's Drug Trafficking Organizations', p. 11.

[73] Guzmán was on the *Forbes* list of the world's billionaires in 2012, at no. 1,153, and on the *Forbes* list of the world's most powerful people at no. 63. See respectively Kroll, L., 'Forbes World's Billionaires 2012', 7 March 2010, available at: <http://www.forbes.com/sites/luisakroll/2012/03/07/forbes-worlds-billionaires-2012/> and Ewalt, D. M., 'The World's Most Powerful People', 5 December 2012, available at: <http://www.forbes.com/sites/davidewalt/2012/12/05/the-worlds-most-powerful-people/> both accessed 1 May 2015. He was also included in the 2009 *Time* section 100 leaders and revolutionaries (30 April 2009), available at: <http://content.time.com/time/specials/packages/completelist/0,29569,1894410,00.html> accessed 1 May 2015.

[74] Forbes, 'One Month After Drug Lord El Chapo Guzman's Arrest, Narcotics Business Continues With No Change', 20 March 2014, available at: <http://www.forbes.com/sites/doliaestevez/2014/03/20/one-month-after-drug-lord-el-chapo-guzmans-arrest-narcotics-business-continues-with-no-change/> accessed 1 May 2015.

[75] The Gulf Cartel is based in north-eastern Mexico. After a pick of power in the 2000s, its dominance in the area started declining when *Los Zetas* took over several areas in the region. See Beittel, J. S., 'Mexico's Drug Trafficking Organizations', p. 10.

[76] Grayson, G. W., 'The Evolution of Los Zetas in Mexico and Central America: Sadism as an Instrument of Cartels' Warfare', *Strategic Studies Institute and U.S. Army War College Press*, April 2014, p. 1.

[77] The *Grupo Aeromóvil de Fuerzas Especiales* (GAFE, Special Forces Airmobile Group) is an elite special forces unit of the Mexican army. See R. Ravelo, *Osiel: Vida y Tragedia de Un Capo*, Grijalbo, Mexico City, 2009.

thereafter, other former members of the army joined the group, including former members of the Guatemalan army's elite *Kaibil* unit.[78] In 2007, following the arrest and extradition of Cárdenas, tensions started to rise between *Los Zetas* and the Gulf Cartel. In 2010, *Los Zetas* became fully independent and started operating in the north-eastern part of Mexico.[79]

At a regional level, the two major DTOs are *La Familia Michoacana* (The Michoacan's Family) and *Los Caballeros Templarios* (The Nights Templar), both operating in the Guerrero and Michoacán States.[80] *La Familia Michoacana* started operating in the 1980s as a vigilante group opposing drug trafficking in the Michoacán State, where it is based.[81] It then turned into a drug cartel and gained notoriety in 2006 for its heinous crimes. It is specialized in methamphetamines trafficking to the US, although it retains also significant parts of the marijuana, cocaine, and heroin markets.[82] *La Familia Michoacana* is described as 'a hybrid fusion of criminal drug enterprise entity and Christian evangelical beliefs'[83] as it provides religious justifications for its violence. The cartel has always made a point in projecting a 'Robin Hood' image, engaging in donations of food, and provision of heath care and education to the unprivileged members of the local communities.[84] From 2010, *La Familia Michoacana*'s role has diminished in favour of *Los Caballeros Templarios*. The latter cartel has adopted symbols similar to the one used by *La Familia Michoacana* and has emulated its commitment to social services.[85] The Knights Templar have a specific code of conduct inspired by religious beliefs and have published a booklet on its ethics.[86]

The aforementioned cartels have a hierarchical structure and rely on leaders who control their members. Hoping to weaken the cartels, President Calderon adopted the so-called 'kingpin strategy', arresting and imprisoning several heads of the DTOs. Albeit many of them retained their control of the cartels from jail, the strategy triggered instability within the groups and led to a situation of high violence.[87] In order to react to Calderon's attacks towards their leaders, the cartels have started to adopt a more

[78] ICG, 'Peña Nieto's Challenge: Criminal Cartels and Rule of Law in Mexico', Latin America Report no. 48, 19 March 2013, p. 12.

[79] Ibid. [80] Beittel, J. S., 'Mexico's Drug Trafficking Organizations', p. 10.

[81] Ibid., p. 17.

[82] Ibid. See also Finnegan, W., 'Silver or Lead', *The New Yorker*, 31 May 2010, available at: <http://www.newyorker.com/magazine/letter-from-mexico> accessed 1 May 2015.

[83] Bunker, R. J. and Sullivan, J. P., 2010, 'Cartel Evolution Revisited: Third Phase Cartel Potentials and Alternative Futures in Mexico', *Small Wars & Insurgencies*, vol. 21, no. 1 (March): 30, at p. 45.

[84] Logan, S., and Sullivan, J. P., 'Mexico's Divine Justice', *ISN Security Watch*, 17 August 2009.

[85] Beittel, J. S., 'Mexico's Drug Trafficking Organizations', p. 18. [86] Ibid.

[87] During the Calderón Government, Mexico was successful in arresting drug dealers. In particular, with the objective of removing the head of the cartels in order to weaken the DTOs. This strategy is know as 'kingpin strategy'. See Beittel, J. S., 'Mexico's Drug Trafficking Organizations', p. 3; Wotherspoon, M., 2012, 'Mexico's Drug War, International Jurisprudence, and the Role of Non-International Armed Conflict Status', *International Humanitarian Legal Studies*, vol. 3: 291, at p. 306.

horizontal structure to be more flexible and to promptly and effectively adapt to new challenges.[88]

Nevertheless, the mere fact that they have changed structure did not weaken their power.[89] Not only do they maintain the control of the drug market, but they also control substantial parts of Mexican territory. In June 2012, former President Felipe Calderón admitted that:

> Crime groups started looking to sell drugs and generate an increase of addiction and consumption in our country, particularly among our youths. This was a change with serious consequences. There came a new operative strategy of the criminals. *It changed from just control of smuggling routes and border agents to geographical expansion and control of territory and consequently fighting for territory.*[90]

The Mexican Government does not retain full control of the whole country. Hundreds of *zonas de impunidad* (zones of impunity) could be counted in Mexico in 2014. These are regions that are completely under the control of cartels, where narco-traffickers establish a quasi-State, enforcing their rule of law over members of the cartels and civilians living therein.[91] In these zones, the level of violence is alarming and has had an 'important social and economic repercussion'.[92] Businesses have closed and investments in Mexico have dropped dramatically. Due to the economic downturn, unemployment and poverty have increased and have thus provided ready recruits for the DTOs.[93]

Mexican cartels generate an annual income of US$15 to 25 billion, which is usually reinvested in weapons and recruiting.[94] Mexican and American authorities report that about 2,000 weapons are smuggled into Mexico from the United States every day.[95] As will be explained below, the cartel's weaponry arsenal includes both light and heavy weapons, such as shoulder-fired launchers.

[88] Perret, M., 'Privatization of the War on Drugs', p. 13.

[89] Wotherspoon, M., 'Mexico's Drug War'p. 306.

[90] Beittel, J. S., 'Mexico's Drug Trafficking Organizations', p. 7 (emphasis added).

[91] Manwaring, M. G., *A 'New' Dynamic in the Western Hemisphere Security Environment: The Mexican Zetas and other Private Armies*, U.S. Army War College Strategic Studies Institute, September 2009, p. 9.

[92] ICG, 'Peña Nieto's Challenge', p. 8.

[93] Beittel, J. S., 'Mexico's Drug Trafficking Organizations', p. 35.

[94] Wotherspoon, M., 'Mexico's Drug War', p. 308; Wilkason, C. and Fogel, M., 'Cartel Weapons and Their Provenance', in *The War on Mexican Cartels: Options for U.S. and Mexican Policy-Makers*, September 2012, Final Report of the Institute of Politics National Security Student Policy Group, at p. 29.

[95] Beittel, J. S., 'Mexico's Drug-Related Violence', CRS Report for Congress, Congressional Research Service, Washington, DC, 27 May 2009, p. 21; Miroff, N. and Booth, W., 'Mexico's Drug Cartel's Newest Weapon: Cold War-era Hand Grenades Made in the US, *Washington Post*, 17 July 2000, available at: <http://www.washingtonpost.com/wp-dyn/content/article/2010/07/16/AR2010071606252.html> accessed 1 May 2015.

Increasing numbers in recruits, income, and weapons have enhanced cartels' effectiveness in their fight against the government. Mexican DTOs have more frequently resorted to strategies similar to those of insurgents and terrorists, such as simultaneously attacking different cities, car bombs, and indiscriminate and planned attacks against civilians. These attacks demonstrate the ability of cartels to coordinate and carry out military operations.[96] As attacks by the governmental forces increase, the cartels tend to create alliances, notably with the *Sinaloa* and *Los Zetas*. Where alliances were formed, national forces registered an increased number of armed attacks against State facilities and personnel, such as prisons and police stations.[97]

In sum, it seems fairly clear that Mexican cartels meet the organization requirement: the existence of a defined structure and chain of command, the control over the *zonas de impunidad* and their military operational and technical capabilities confirm the existence of a high level of organization.

Maras and other criminal organizations in Honduras

Honduras is one of the least developed and most insecure countries in America, due to military rule, high rates of crime, and corruption, as well as natural disasters.[98] Located between countries that produce drugs and the United States, the major buyer, Honduras is strategic to the transport of drugs to North America. Endemic poverty and State corruption have enhanced a crime wave conducted by criminal organizations which operate mainly in drug trafficking and extortions.

The two largest and most powerful transport organizations are the *Cachiros* and *Los Valles*. They purchase drugs from the Colombian organizations and sell the product mainly to Mexican traffickers, notably to the *Sinaloa* cartel.[99] As many other trafficking organizations, they also deal in arms trafficking and money laundering.[100] The *Cachicos* and *Los Valles* are both family-run groups, hierarchically organized in a vertical command chain. Compared with the *Cachicos, Los Valles* have a relatively small number of members, which tend to maintain a low profile.[101]

Honduras is also affected by the presence of street gangs, called *maras*. The two main *maras* are the Mara Salvatrucia (MS-13) and the barrio 18 (M-18).[102] They

[96] Beittel, J. S., 'Mexico's Drug Trafficking Organizations', p. 7.

[97] Wotherspoon, M., 'Mexico's Drug War', p. 308.

[98] BBC, 'Country Profile: Honduras', available at: <http://news.bbc.co.uk/2/hi/americas/country_profiles/1225416.stm> accessed 1 May 2015.

[99] InSight Crime, 'Cachiros', available at: <http://www.insightcrime.org/honduras-organized-crime-news/cachiros-profile>; InSight Crime, 'Los Valles', available at: <http://www.insightcrime.org/honduras-organized-crime-news/lvalles> accessed 1 May 2015.

[100] InSight Crime, 'Los Valles'. [101] InSight Crime, 'Los Valles'.

[102] InSight Crime, 'MS-13', available at: <http://www.insightcrime.org/el-salvador-organized-crime-news/mara-salvatrucha-ms-13-profile>; InSight Crime, 'Barrio 18 (M-18)', available at: <http://www.insightcrime.org/honduras-organized-crime-news/barrio-18-honduras> accessed 1 May 2015.

both emerged as street gangs in Los Angeles in the 1980s. At the end of the 1990s, the United States started to deport foreigners convicted for a wide range of crimes. Several members of the two *maras* were thus sent to their home countries, where they established new cells, called *cliquas*. The MS-13 and the M-18 operate transnationally, with *cliquas* in Honduras, Guatemala, El Salvador, as well as in the United States and Canada, and close ties with the Mexican cartels, notably the *Sinaloa* and *Los Zetas*.[103]

The *maras* have a hierarchical structure. Members with more experience become the leaders of the organization and form the *direccion general* (directorate general).[104] The *maras* are locally organized in *cliquas*, which are also strongly hierarchical. *Cliquas*' members with the longest experience form the *Commission*, the leaders' committee, and have the power to enforce internal rules within the members of the *cliquas*. In particular, they can authorize the killing of a gang member in case of insubordination. Furthermore, they plan in advance extortions, homicides, and other crimes during weekly meetings. This practice contributes to maintaining the control over the subordinate members of the gang.[105]

Honduras' DTOs hold control over certain regions, where they provide alternative governance within existing national territories.[106] They also invest in political parties, human rights organizations, and the Church in order to seek allies that could help them in their fight against the government.[107]

Drug trafficking and extortion provide significant funds that are reinvested in recruitment and weapons.[108] Thanks to the control exercised over some regions, *maras* can easily recruit new members among the population. Economic advantages provided by drug trafficking and chronic unemployment have contributed to convince the local population to join the gangs.[109]

The existence of a command structure, territorial control, the ability to plan and coordinate criminal and military operation, as well as the capability to have access to weapons and to organize recruitment, all lead to conclude that the *maras*, as well as the *Cachiros* and *Los Valles*, meet the organization requirement. It is thus necessary to analyse whether the armed violence reaches the intensity required for a NIAC to exist.

[103] InSight Crime, 'MS-13'; InSight Crime, 'Barrio 18 (M-18)'.

[104] Immigration and Refugee Board of Canada, *Honduras: Information on the structure and hierarchy of main gangs; gang recruitment of children (2012-November 2014)*, 9 December 2014, available at: <http://www.refworld.org/docid/549ab6404.html> accessed 1 May 2015.

[105] Ibid. [106] Ibid. [107] Ibid.

[108] Small Arms Survey, *Violence and Firearms in Honduras*, Geneva, 2014, p. 2.

[109] BBC, 'Country Profile: Honduras'.

MEXICAN SELF-DEFENCE GROUPS

Drug cartels control substantial parts of Mexico. Especially in States like *Guerrero* and *Michoacán*, governmental forces are not able to effectively tackle the criminal groups, violence reaches the highest levels and the population is de facto in *narcos'* hands. In a more worrying development, local communities started to arm themselves in order to defend their families and properties. The first *autodefensas* (self-defence groups) were created in *Michoacán* in 2011. They then spread within the State and in 2013 they first appeared in *Guerrero* State.[110]

Mexico has a tradition of vigilantism in indigenous communities. Cartel crime and violence, together with the State inability to protect the population, led many of these communities to arm themselves for self-protection.[111] The phenomenon of the *policía comunitaria* proved to be successful: the indigenous militia guarantee security and impart justice. A *Guerrero* State law on indigenous communities, promulgated in 2011, lent legitimacy to these groups, which can lawfully carry arms and impart justice.[112] Many of the new *autodefensas* claim the same rights of the *policía comunitaria* and copy its language. However, it is paramount to distinguish the two phenomena: albeit that both originated from the same desire for self-defence against cartel violence and crime, the *autodefensas* 'do not come from local tradition and are not even rooted in indigenous communities'.[113]

Autodefensas proved to be military capable: not only have they planned and successfully organized military attacks against the cartels, but they also took control of certain areas of Guerrero and Michoacán States from DTOs' hands. Furthermore, they have access to a wide range of weapons, from guns and hunting rifles to AR-15 automatic rifles and Uzi sub-machines guns.[114] The self-defence movement is overseen by a board, whose members represent the local communities. *Autodefensas*' leaders reach decision by vote and affirm that they only move into a new territory when invited by the community.[115]

Mexican self-defence groups are a complex phenomenon. Despite their ability to successfully organize military operations, their members are moved by different

[110] ICG, 'Peña Nieto's Challenge', p. 33; ICG, 'Justice at the Barrel of a Gun: Vigilante Militias in Mexico', Latin America Briefing No. 29, 28 May 2013, p. 1; Pachico, E., 'Vigilantes Take Over Mexican Town', InSight Crime, 10 May 2011, available at: <http://www.insightcrime.org/news-analysis/vigilantes-take-over-mexico-town> accessed 1 May 2015.

[111] In 1995, indigenous communities in Guerrero created the CRAC. Its militias wear brown uniforms, don't use masks, and do not carry weapons outside their own villages. They proved able to arrest criminals and to try them according to their own rules; they even have jails, where the sentenced criminals might spend up to eighteen years. See ICG, 'Justice at the Barrel of a Gun', p. 9.

[112] Ibid. [113] Ibid., p. 2. [114] Ibid., p. 11.

[115] Althaus, D., and Dudley, S., 'Mexico's Security Dilemma: Michoacán's Militias: The Rise of Vigilantism in Mexico and Its Implications Going Forward', InSight Crime, p. 12.

motivations that tend to emerge as soon as the enemy has been defeated.[116] This is perhaps the main difference between them and the Colombian paramilitaries. Indeed, both of them were created in order to protect the local population from kidnappings and extortions perpetrated by the cartels in Mexico and by the opposition groups in Colombia. Furthermore, their relation with the government has evolved with a similar pattern. However, Colombian paramilitaries proved to be better organized and thus able to pursue a consistent policy, while the *autodefensas* seem to lack any long-term vision.[117] Consequently, Mexican self-defence groups are not sufficiently organized to be party to a conflict under IHL. Nonetheless, it should be considered that the *autodefensas* are a relatively young phenomenon in Mexico and the situation might evolve in the incoming years.

C. **Criminal organizations under international humanitarian law: the intensity requirement**

In the *Milošević* case, the ICTY assessed the intensity of the violence focusing on the escalation and the seriousness of clashes and the length of the conflict, with particular regard to the type of weaponry used.[118] In the *Ramush Haradinaj* case, the Criminal Tribunal for the Former Yugoslavia specified that:

> Trial Chambers have relied on indicative factors relevant for assessing the 'intensity' criterion, none of which are, in themselves, essential to establish that the criterion is satisfied. These indicative factors include the number, duration and intensity of individual confrontations; the type of weapons and other military equipment used; the number and calibre of munitions fired; the number of persons and type of forces partaking in the fighting; the number of casualties; the extent of material destruction; the number of civilians fleeing combat zones. The involvement of the UN Security Council may also be a reflection of the intensity of a conflict.[119]

COLOMBIA

In 2014 the intensity criterion was surely met with regard to the clashes between FARC and ELN on the one hand and the Colombian Government on the other. Notwithstanding the peace talks between the government and the FARC, clashes and

[116] Ibid., p. 16. [117] Ibid., p. 18. [118] *Milošević Rule 98bis Decision*, §§28–31.
[119] ICTY, *Prosecutor v Ramush Haradinaj et al.*, §49; *Milošević Rule 98bis Decision*, §§28–31.

violence did not stop and are still on-going.[120] The UN Office for the Coordination of Humanitarian Affairs (OCHA) reported that in 2014 an average of fifty-seven armed actions per month took place in Colombia, mainly between opposition groups and governmental forces, close to the average of sixty-one armed clashes per month which took place in 2013.[121] Furthermore, between November 2012 and September 2014, each month about 15,000 Colombians were displaced by violence.[122] Albeit mass displacement declined by 40% in 2014 compared with 2013, this positive trend does not correspond to a decrease of armed violence. The reason for the reduction in mass displacement might be due to a change in the *modus operandi* of ANSAs, which are avoiding highly visible actions, despite the fact that overall targeted violence did not drop.[123]

Determining whether the BACRIMs are party to the conflict is a more difficult task. As mentioned before, the OTP's *Report on the Preliminary Examination Activities* concluded that only the *Urabeños* are sufficiently organized, while the *Rastrojos* and the *Águilas Negras* do not meet the organization requirement under IHL.[124] With regard to the intensity of violence, available information would suggest that armed episodes between the *Urabeños* and the other two BACRIM would reach the intensity threshold. However, as the latter are not sufficiently organized, it is not possible to conclude the existence of a NIAC among these criminal organizations. On the other hand, clashes between the *Urabeños*, the opposition groups and the governmental forces are not sufficiently intense and violent.[125]

As aforementioned, the situation might evolve at the end of the peace talks. Due to the possible demobilization of the FARC, some members of the Marxist group are likely to become criminalized and could join the BACRIM or create new criminal groups. In both cases, the current situation is going to change and violence between BACRIMs will likely increase.

MEXICO

Violence has affected Mexico for several years. Since at least late 2006, armed confrontations between the government and the cartels have been intense and sustained.[126] The character of the clashes range from 'shoot and run' scenarios to more intense and

[120] ICG, 'Left in the Cold?', p. 18.
[121] Gómez, G., 'Monthly Humanitarian Bulletin—Colombia', OCHA, Issue 32, 1–31 October 2014.
[122] OCHA, 'Annual Report 2014 on Colombia', 2014, p. 2.
[123] Egeland, J., 'Monthly Humanitarian Bulletin—Colombia', Issue 34, January 2015, p. 3.
[124] OTP, *Report on Preliminary Examination Activities 2013*, §§128–9.
[125] Ibid.
[126] Perret, A., 'Privatization of the War on Drugs', p. 12.

protracted situations.[127] Often fights between cartels and State forces are brief guerrilla-style clashes, where the DTOs attack the police and military forces with light weapons.[128] However, 'urban warfare with commando-style raids' have emerged and are becoming a common practice.[129]

The weaponry arsenal of the cartels is highly sophisticated and not limited to light weapons. Mexican authorities have discovered anti-tanks rockets, unguided rocket-propelled projectiles such as rocket-propelled grenades (RPGs) of Soviet manufacturing origin, semi-automatic rifle such as AR-15, .50 calibre sniper rifles, hand-grenades, and dynamite. To respond to police and State army offensives, the cartels' array of weapons is becoming increasingly destructive. Notably, the use of shoulder-fired rocket launchers raises particular concerns due to their destructive potential, with a high explosive power and the capacity to reach up to 900m.[130]

The inadequacy of the normal Mexican police forces to enforce law and order in the country is a relevant factor to evaluate the intensity of the conflict. The necessity to deploy military forces is a clear sign that the capabilities of the cartels exceed those of the Mexican police.[131] When President Peña Nieto took office in December 2012, one of the major promises he repeatedly affirmed during the electoral campaign was the creation of the *gendarmería nacional*: 'a civilian commanded police force staffed with elite military troops'[132] to improve security in areas where ANSAs operate.[133] The first members of the gendarmerie were dispatched for the first time in September 2014, with 5,000 police agents.[134] However, clashes between governmental forces and cartels have dropped in 2014.

President Calderon deployed 45,000 Mexican military personnel to various areas of operation throughout the Mexican border and interior. 'To put this into perspective, this is more military personnel than the United States committed to Operation Enduring Freedom in Afghanistan during any given year from 2001 to 2009.'[135] Furthermore, in September 2014 President Nieto had deployed the new gendarmerie, formed by 5,000

[127] Wotherspoon, M., 'Mexico's Drug War', p. 10. [128] Ibid.

[129] Beittel, J. S., 'Mexico's Drug Trafficking Organizations', p. 10.

[130] Wotherspoon, M., 'Mexico's Drug War', p. 11; Sánchez, A. N., 2013, 'Mexico's Drug "War": Drawing a Line between Rethoric and Relity', *Yale Journal of International Law*, vol. 38: 467, p. 483; TIME, 'Mexico's Drug Lords Ramp Up Their Arsenals with RPGs', 25 October 2012, available at: <http://world.time.com/2012/10/25/mexicos-drug-lords-ramp-up-their-arsenals-with-rpgs/> accessed 1 May 2015.

[131] Raether, J., 'Drug War',p. 21.

[132] Justice in Mexico Project, *Drug Violence in Mexico: Data and Analysis Through 2013*, April 2014, p. 40.

[133] ICG, 'Justice at the Barrel of a Gun', p. 3.

[134] U-T San Diego, 'New gendarmerie in Baja California', 5 September 2014, available at: <http://www.utsandiego.com/news/2014/sep/05/gendarmerie-mexico-baja-california-organized-crime/> accessed 1 May 2015. NYT, 'Elite Mexican Police Corps Targets Persistent Violence, but Many Are Skeptical', 22 August 2014, available at: <http://www.nytimes.com/2014/08/23/world/americas/familiar-flaws-seen-in-mexicos-new-elite-police-force.html?_r=0> accessed 1 May 2015.

[135] Wotherspoon, M., 'Mexico's Drug War', p. 12.

members. On the DTO side, the number of members of the cartels is about 100,000 or more, which is close to the total number of Mexican armed forces.[136]

The violence in Mexico is highly intense. In 2014 alone, the number of persons killed in drug related violence was between 6,400 and 8,000.[137] Drafting a complete dataset on casualties and clashes is not an easy task, especially with regards to confrontations between cartels and *autodefensas*, and among cartels themselves. The situation is further complicated by the government tendency to withhold figures and data on drug-related violence.[138] It is also worth noting that about 115,000 people have been displaced by Mexico's drug-related violence.[139]

Autodefensas groups are emerging as a third party to the conflict.[140] In 2014, they have engaged in fights with the cartels as well as with State forces. The situation is extremely delicate in *Michoacán* State, where the phenomenon of vigilantes started.

The government's first reaction was to define the *autodefensas* as criminals. The situation changed in 2013, where President Nieto ignored the self-defence groups for almost the entire year. This strategy proved to be ineffective, as it downplayed the groups' success in *Michoacán*.[141] At the beginning of 2014 the *autodefensas* seized towns in the hands of *Los Caballeros Templarios*. On 13 January 2014, *autodefensas* took control of the small town of Nueva Italia (*Michoacán*), which was under the control of *Los Caballeros Templarios*. After days of clashes with the Knights Templar, about 100 armed members of the *autodefensas* entered Nueva Italia and disarmed the local police.[142] In order to stop clashes, soldiers deployed in Western *Michoacán* intervened and tried to disarm the vigilantes. However, most groups ignored the order to lay down their weapons and the fight ended with the self-defence groups disarming State forces.[143]

Following days of intense clashes, President Nieto named the former Mexico State Attorney General Alfredo Castillo as special envoy in *Michoacán*. Castillo reached an agreement with the militias whereby the *autodefensas* are required to register themselves and their weapons with the State authorities. Furthermore, the government announced a plan intended to enhance the living conditions in *Michoacán*, targeting unemployment,

[136] Beittel, J.S., 'Mexico's Drug Trafficking Organizations', p. 19.

[137] Heinle, K., Molzahn, C., and Shirk, D. A., *Drug Violence in Mexico: Data and Analysis through 2014*, Justice in Mexico Project, April 2015, p. 21.

[138] J. Raether, 'Drug War', p. 950; Tracy Wilkinson, *Mexico Government Sought to Withhold Drug War Death Statistics, L.A. Times*, 11 January 2012, available at: <http://articles.latimes.com/2012/jan/11/world/la-fg-mexico-dead-numbers-20120112> accessed 1 May 2015.

[139] Sánchez, A. N., 'Mexico's Drug "War"', p. 18.

[140] BBC, 'Mexican vigilantes clash with soldiers in Michoacán state', 15 January 2014, available at: <http://www.bbc.com/news/world-latin-america-25739937> accessed 1 May 2015.

[141] Althaus, D., and Dudley, S., 'Mexico's Security Dilemma', p. 12.

[142] BBC, 'Mexico vigilantes clash with Knights Templar cartel in Michoacán', 13 January 2014, <http://www.bbc.com/news/world-latin-america-25708297> accessed 1 May 2015.

[143] BBC, 'Mexican vigilantes clash with soldiers'.

education, and social development.[144] These decisions fostered the relationship between the government and the self-defence groups to the point that they started organizing joint operations to seize towns in the cartels' hands.[145] However, the cooperation quickly came to an end when State forces started targeting the militias' leaders. This triggered new clashes between the *autodefensas* and the government.[146]

State's ambivalent attitude towards the self-defence groups underlines State's incapacity to tackle the problem with a clear and consistent approach. The problem is now to decide what to do with these groups. So far, the government has reacted to the *autodefensas* individually: it has incorporated some members in its forces, while it has prosecuted others. 'The message is clear: behave and get security force and possibly public monies; cross the government and receive no support and possibly criminal charges.'[147] While this approach has the positive outcome to differentiate between the members of the militias, this ambiguity might create instability in the dismantling process. Another solution could be to integrate these groups into the State forces. However, President Nieto does not seem willing to assume such a political risk.[148] At the moment, the government seems more inclined to delegitimize and disarm the groups.[149] However, this approach could lead to new tensions and clashes between State forces and the self-defence groups.

In sum, the militias lead to a positive outcome, namely the weakening of *Los Caballeros Templarios*, but constitute also a threat to Mexican peace and security. In 2014, apart from some high-intensity armed episodes, the government proved able to keep these groups under control. However, the situation might change, depending on who will fill the vacuum left by the Knights Templar.[150]

HONDURAS

High rates of violence affect Honduras, mostly related to disputes between *maras*. There is a 'clear link between contested trafficking areas and murder rates' and 'some of the most violent areas in the world lie along the Honduran coast'.[151] This circumstance, together with extortion and forced recruitment, is one of the main causes of internal displacement: in recent years, at least 17,000 people were forced to flee their homes.[152] In 2014, UNHCR has registered a dramatic increase of asylum seekers from Honduras, Guatemala, and El Salvador, directed to the United States and Canada, as well as

[144] Althaus, D., and Dudley, S., 'Mexico's Security Dilemma', p. 13. [145] Ibid., p. 14.
[146] Ibid., p. 16. [147] Ibid., p. 20. [148] Ibid., p. 19. [149] Ibid. [150] Ibid., p. 20.
[151] United Nations Office on Drugs and Crime (UNODC), *Transnational Organized Crime in Central America and the Caribbean: A Threat Assessment*, September 2012, p. 11.
[152] World Bank, *World Development Report 2011: Conflict, Security, and Development*. Washington, 2011, p. 1.

Mexico, Panama, Belize, and Costa Rica.[153] Particularly worrying is the increased number of unaccompanied minors who have reached the United States and Canada in 2014, mainly fleeing criminal violence.[154] Criminal organizations constitute a serious threat for the population. In 2014, roughly 12,000 people are estimated to be active members of the *maras* in Honduras.[155] They mainly use 9mm handguns, but also revolvers and semi-automatic and automatic rifles.[156]

In order to tackle criminal groups' operation and to retake territorial control, in December 2011 the government enacted an emergency decree whereby armed forces could execute raids and military operations with the national police against criminal organizations.[157] In 2014 the government declared its intent to use the *mano dura* (iron fist) against drug traffickers and street gangs and established ad hoc military forces to this end.[158] The *Tropa de Inteligencia y Grupos de Respuesta Especial de Seguridad* (TIGRES, Intelligence Troops and Groups for Special Response on Security) is an elite police force created to tackle organized crime and to protect the security of the population. The TIGRES began operating at the beginning of 2014 and is financed through loans from the Inter-American Development Bank.[159] In the same period, the *Fuerza Nacional de Seguridad Interinstitucional* (FUSINA, National Inter-institutional Security Force), and the *Policía Militar del Orden Público* (PMOP, Military Police for Public Order), created respectively in 2014 and 2013, were deployed in areas affected by the highest rates of violence.[160] These measures raise concerns with regard to the protection of human rights. Indeed, State armed groups are not always sufficiently trained and they committed significant human rights violations during their law enforcement operations.[161]

The organization of the parties and the State response against the *maras* meet the threshold identified by the ICTY for a NIAC to exist. However, the number, intensity and duration of individual confrontations and the number of casualties directly related to clashes between the army and the criminal groups are still limited and are not enough to consider the situation in Honduras as a NIAC. Albeit the country is one of the most violent places and has the highest homicide rate in the world,[162] violence is mainly directed

[153] UNHCR, 'Children on the Run: Unaccompanied Children Leaving Central America and Mexico and the Need for International Protection', Washington, 2014, p. 4.

[154] Ibid., p. 11. [155] Small Arms Survey, p. 3. [156] Ibid., p. 2

[157] Immigration and Refugee Board of Canada, *Honduras: State response to gang- related violence and criminal activity, including the efforts of the army (2012-November 2014)* (hereafter *Honduras*), 10 December 2014, available at: <http://www.refworld.org/docid/549ab5464.html> accessed 1 May 2015.

[158] Amnesty International, *Amnesty International Report 2014/15-Honduras*, 25 February 2015, available at: <http://www.refworld.org/docid/54f07de415.html>; InSight Crime, 'Soldiers on Honduras Street Provide Preview of Security Strategy', 28 January 2014, available at: <http://www.insightcrime.org/news-briefs/new-honduras-president-sends-soldiers-to-streets-in-opening-security-move?highlight=WyJ0aWdyZXMiXQ> accessed 1 May 2015.

[159] Immigration and Refugee Board of Canada, *Honduras.* [160] Ibid.

[161] Amnesty International, *Amnesty International Report 2014/15—Honduras.* [162] Ibid.

against the population. In order to conclude for the existence of an internal armed conflict, the degree of violence refers to clashes between State forces and ANSAs or between such groups. Therefore, Honduras is not affected by a non-international armed conflict.

D. *Zonas de impunidad*: human rights obligations of criminal organizations

As discussed above, certain ANSAs in Colombia, Mexico, and Honduras are not involved in a NIAC. In situations short of armed conflict, IHL is not applicable and the legal framework is thus limited to international human rights law (IHRL) and law enforcement. The latter are bound only State forces, as they retain the monopoly of the right to enforce law. Clearly, States are also bound by IHRL, whose rules are enshrined in international and regional conventions, as well as established by customary norms.[163] Whether non-State armed groups are bearers of human rights obligations under international law is still debated.

Those objecting to the possibility of applying IHRL to ANSAs ground their position on four main reasons. First, the traditional view is that only States can breach IHRL, whereas non-State armed groups can solely commit criminal acts. Second, human rights treaties directly address only States, hence they do not bind non State actors explicitly. Third, applying IHRL to rebel groups might grant them a de facto recognition and legitimacy, equalizing them to States. Fourth, as IHRL was designed for States, opposition groups might not have the capabilities to comply with human rights obligations.[164]

However, practice of relevant UN bodies[165] shows a new trend towards the application of IHRL to non-State armed groups, at least when they exercise an effective control over part of the territory. Part of the scholarship tends to favour this evolution of the

[163] See, e.g., Universal Declaration of Human Rights (1948); Convention on the Elimination of All Forms of Racial Discriminations (1965); International Covenant on Civil and Political Rights (1966); International Covenant on Economic, Social and Cultural Rights (1966); Convention on the Elimination of All Forms of Discriminations against Women (1979); Convention against Torture and Other Cruel Inhuman or Degrading Treatment or Punishment (1984); Convention on the Rights of the Child (1989); International Convention on the Protection of the Rights of All Migrant Workers and Members of Their Families (1990); Convention on the Rights of Persons with Disabilities (2006).

[164] Clapham, A., 2006, *Human Rights Obligations of Non-State Actors*, Oxford: Oxford University Press, pp. 271–286.

[165] See, e.g., 'Report of the Commission of Inquiry to investigate all the alleged violations of international human rights law in the Libyan Arab Jamahiriya', UN Human Rights Council, UN doc. A/HCR/17/44, 1 June 2011, §72; 'Report of the Independent International Commission of Inquiry on the Syrian Arab Republic', UN doc. A/HCR/19/69, 22 February 2012, §106; UN doc. A/HCR/21/50, 16 August 2012, §10.

law.[166] The *raison d'être* of human rights law is to guarantee the protection of individuals who live under the authority of a government. In normal situations, this relationship is between individuals and the State. However, in case non-State armed groups exercise an effective control over the territory, 'elements of governmental authority have fallen into their hands'.[167] In these circumstances, the reality of the human rights equation is satisfied: individuals are at the mercy of a power over whose actions the State government is impotent.[168] Consequently, non-State armed groups can be considered as de facto governments and are thus bearers of human rights obligations.[169]

These considerations are particularly important in the light of the analysis conducted above. Indeed, nearly all ANSAs in Colombia, Mexico, and Honduras have territorial control over more or less vast zones of these States. Consequently, they bear the obligation to respect human rights of the population under their control. ANSAs' disregard for IHRL is one of the main causes of the creation of paramilitary groups, like the AUC in Colombia and the *autodefensas* in Mexico. The last part of this chapter will suggest ways to engage with criminal organizations, in particular where they have territorial control and are hence bearers of human rights obligations.

E. The responsibility of criminal organizations under international criminal law

Whenever there is a resort to violence between governmental forces and criminal organizations or between such groups within a State, which reaches the threshold of

[166] See, e.g., Clapham, A., *Human Rights Obligations*; Tomuschat, C., 2004, 'The Applicability of Human Rights Law to Insurgent Movement'. In *Krisensicherung und Humanita ̈rer Schutz—Crisis Management and Humanitarian Protection: Festschrift für Dieter Fleck*, edited by Horst Fischer, Ulrika Froissart, Wolff Heintschel von Heinegg, and Christian Raap, Berlin: Berliner Wissenschafts-Verlag; Bellal, A., and Casey-Maslen, S., 2001, 'Enhancing Compliance with International Law by Armed Non-State Actors', *Goettingen Journal of International Law*, vol. 3: 175.

[167] Tomuschat, C., 'Applicability of Human Rights Law', p. 588.

[168] Rodley, N., 1993, 'Can Armed Opposition Groups Violate Human Rights?'. In *Human Rights in the Twenty-first Century: A Global Challenge*, edited by Mahoney, K. E., Mahoney, P., Dordrecht: Martinus Nijhoff, at p. 313; Zegveld, L., 2002, *Accountability of Armed Opposition Groups in International Law*, Cambridge: Cambridge University Press, pp. 148–9; Bellal, A., and Casey-Maslen, S., 2011, *Rules of Engagement: Protecting Civilians through Dialogue with Armed Non-State Actors*, DCAF and Geneva Call, Geneva, at p. 25.

[169] Bellal, A. and Casey-Maslen, S., 'Enhancing Compliance with International Law', p. 14; Clapham, A., *Human Rights Obligations*, p. 283. Part of the scholarship affirms that ANSAs are bearers of human rights obligations also when they do not control part of State's territory. However, practice suggests that it is too early to reach such a conclusion, albeit it seems to be going in that direction. See Clapham, A., *Human Rights Obligations*, pp. 271–99.

NIAC, international humanitarian law (IHL), international human rights law (IHRL) and international criminal law (ICL) are applicable. All the parties to a conflict bear obligations under IHL. This does not prevent States from punishing criminal organizations under domestic criminal law. However, the members of these groups would also be accountable for violations of IHL.[170] The primary responsibility for sanctioning criminal groups relies in State's hands. Nonetheless, high levels of corruption among governmental authorities at nearly every level of the hierarchy might raise doubts about the effectiveness of State interventions.[171]

Article 7 of the Rome Statute[172] defines crime against humanity as 'any of the following acts when committed as part of a widespread or systematic attack directed against any civilian population, with knowledge of the attack'. It then lists acts such as murder, enslavement, imprisonment, torture, and enforced disappearances of persons.

Article 7(2) specifies that:

> Attack directed against any civilian population' means a course of conduct involving the multiple commission of acts referred to in paragraph 1 against any civilian population, pursuant to or in furtherance of a State or organizational policy to commit such attack.

In the words of the ICTY, 'it is by now a settled rule of customary international law that crimes against humanity do not require a connection to international armed conflict. Indeed ... customary international law may not require a connection between crimes against humanity and any conflict at all'.[173] Therefore, criminal groups could be held responsible under ICL albeit they are not party to a NIAC.[174] However, not any ANSA can commit crimes against humanity: it needs to have 'the capacity to orchestrate a widespread or systematic attack against a civilian population'.[175] The degree of organization required under Article 7(2) is highly controversial. Some scholars do not use the same criteria that apply to groups party to a NIAC, but use different ones, such as 'power and use of force comparable to those of state institutions'.[176] The ICC specified that:

> In the view of the Chamber, the determination of whether a given group qualifies as an organization under the Statute must be made on a case-by-case basis. In making this determination, the

[170] Hauck, P. and Peterke, S., 'Organized Crime and Gang Violence', p. 435; McConville, M., 2000, 'Global War on Drugs: Why the United States Should Support the Prosecution of Drug Traffickers in the International Criminal Court', *American Criminal Law Review*, vol. 37, no. 1: 90.

[171] La Rosa, A., and Wuerzner, C., 2008, 'Armed Groups, Sanctions and the Implementation of International Humanitarian Law', *International Review of the Red Cross*, vol. 90, no. 870: 327, at p. 335.

[172] Rome Statute of the International Criminal Court (2002).

[173] ICTY, *Prosecutor v Tadić*, Decision on the Defence Motion for Interlocutory Appeal on Jurisdiction, §141.

[174] Dugard, J., 1998, 'Bridging the Gap Between Human Rights and Humanitarian Law: The Punishment of Offenders', *International Review of the Red Cross*, vol. 38, no. 324 (September): 445.

[175] Rodenhauser, T., 2014, 'Beyond State Crimes: Non-State Entities and Crimes against Humanity', *Leiden Journal of Int'l Law*, vol. 27, no. 4: 913, at p. 914.

[176] Hauck, P. and Peterke, S., 'Organized Crime and Gang Violence', p. 434.

Chamber may take into account a number of considerations, inter alia: (i) whether the group is under a responsible command, or has an established hierarchy; (ii) whether the group possesses, in fact, the means to carry out a widespread or systematic attack against a civilian population; (iii) whether the group exercises control over part of the territory of a State; (iv) whether the group has criminal activities against the civilian population as a primary purpose; (v) whether the group articulates, explicitly or implicitly, an intention to attack a civilian population; (vi) whether the group is part of a larger group, which fulfills some or all of the aforementioned criteria. It is important to clarify that, while these considerations may assist the Chamber in its determination, they do not constitute a rigid legal definition, and do not need to be exhaustively fulfilled.[177]

This is not the place to analyse this complex provision. Nonetheless, it is clear that not many criminal organizations which operate in Mexico and Honduras meet all of the aforementioned criteria.[178] With regard to Colombia, the OTP of the ICC specified in its *Interim Report* that 'there is a reasonable basis to believe that each of the non-State actors under the analysis, the FARC, ELN and paramilitaries, have committed crimes against humanity'. Indeed, 'the required elements appear to be met for each group taken individually'.[179]

Article 8(2)(f) of the Rome Statute specifies that war crimes—i.e., serious violations of the laws and customs of IHL—can be committed during a NIAC. Clearly, only criminal organizations that are party to a conflict can be held accountable for war crimes. The 2013 OTP *Report on Preliminary Examination Activities* examines the situation in Colombia, concluding that:

There is ... a reasonable basis to believe that the FARC and ELN have committed war crimes under article 8 of the Rome Statute in the form of murder; attacks against civilians; torture and cruel treatment and outrages upon personal dignity; taking of hostages; rape and other forms of sexual violence; and conscripting, enlisting and using children to participate actively in hostilities, since 1 November 2009. Because the paramilitary armed groups started demobilizing in 2006, they are not considered a party to the armed conflict for the period covered by the ICC's jurisdiction over war crimes.[180]

As aforementioned, the ICC does not consider the BACRIMs to be party to the NIAC due to their lack of organization or because they are involved in tensions that do not meet the intensity threshold. Nonetheless, the situation might change in the near future.[181]

[177] ICC, *Situation in the Republic of Kenya*, Decision Pursuant to Article 15 of the Rome Statute on the Authorization of an Investigation into the Situation in the Republic of Kenya, ICC-01/09, 31 March 2010, §93.

[178] Hauck, P. and Peterke, S., 'Organized Crime and Gang Violence', p. 434.

[179] OTP, *Situation in Colombia—Interim Report*, November 2012, §37.

[180] OTP, *Report on Preliminary Examination Activities 2013*, §§124–125.

[181] Ibid., §§128–129.

With regard to the situation in Mexico, massacres of civilians committed by some cartels could lead to the conclusion that these criminal groups have committed crimes against humanity and war crimes.[182]

The situation in Honduras does not amount to an internal armed conflict. Nonetheless, 'since the coup in 2009, violence ... has increased significantly'.[183] The OTP has mainly investigated acts committed by the State, which could amount to crimes against humanity, notably rape and sexual violence, deportation and forcible transfer, and persecution.[184] In addition, it would be interesting to analyse the acts committed by the *maras*, which could entail the responsibility of gangs' members under Article 6 of the Rome Statute.

F. Engaging with drug lords

THE CHALLENGES OF ENGAGEMENT

The previous sections have analysed situations of NIAC and short of armed conflict, as well as ANSAs' obligations under international law. Demonstrating that drug trafficking organizations are bearers of IHL and human rights obligations risks to remain an academic exercise. Criminal groups are famous for their brutality and their disregard for legal obligations. Massacres of civilians, such as those that took place in Mexico, confirm that DTOs are unlikely to respect domestic and international law.[185]

Over the past years, both scholars and humanitarian workers have highlighted the importance of engaging with armed groups involved in NIACs.[186] This trend is not seen favourably by States, as they fear that any contacts with ANSAs would give them a privileged status. Nevertheless, States' reluctance has not prevented humanitarian organizations and NGOs such as Geneva Call to engage with ANSAs in a constructive dialogue.[187]

The first approaches in this direction were seen with scepticism by States and scholars. Nonetheless, they proved to be effective to some extent. Some ANSAs have adopted deeds of commitment, declarations, and codes of conduct, which refer to human rights

[182] Spencer, T., 2012, 'A Complementarity Conundrum: International Criminal Enforcement in the Mexican Drug War', *Vanderbilt Journal of International Law*, vol. 45: 599, at pp. 605–18.

[183] OTP, *Report on Preliminary Examination Activities 2013*, §62.

[184] Ibid., §§67–9.

[185] Carpenter, A. C., 2012, 'Civilian Protection in Mexico & Guatemala: Humanitarian Engagement with Druglords', *Homeland Security Review*, vol. 6: 109, at pp. 110–11.

[186] Sassòli, M., 2010, 'Taking Armed Groups Seriously: Ways to Improve their Compliance with International Humanitarian Law', *Journal of International Humanitarian Legal Studies*, vol. 1: 5, Clapham, A., *Human Rights Obligations* , p. 291.

[187] Carpenter, A. C., 'Civilian Protection in Mexico & Guatemala', p. 118.

standards.[188] Others have concluded written agreements with States, where non-State actors assumed the obligation to respect human rights and humanitarian law.[189] This dialogue has been taking place with ANSAs engaged in NIACs and other groups, such as the PKK (*Partiya Karkerên Kurdistani*, Kurdistan Workers' Party), some of them considered terrorist organizations by certain States and international/regional organizations. Nonetheless, 'there is as yet no inclusion of more criminal and commercially minded armed groups in these arrangements'.[190]

Given criminal groups' impact on civilians, it is at least desirable to start a constructive dialogue with them. However, engaging with criminal groups is particularly challenging due to three main reasons. First and foremost, DTOs and other criminal organizations have no political interests, thus they don't need to gain legitimacy in the eyes of the international community. They do not aim at overthrowing the government: their objective is to gain economic interests through illicit trafficking of drugs *et similia*. Therefore, convincing them to comply with IHRL and IHL—when applicable—seems an impossible task.[191]

Hauck has correctly highlighted that:

> As their violence is not driven by an ideology or legitimate political intentions, the criminal organizations not only have no interest in confronting the government and assuming its powers and responsibility, they also have no interest in imposing disciplinary rules and mechanisms to guarantee respect for IHL.[192]

Second, the deep cultural and political prejudice against criminal groups in many countries is an obstacle to formal conversations with such groups. However, clandestine ties do exist between DTOs and governments. Third, engaging with drug traffickers triggers security risks—inasmuch as they are extremely dangerous organizations[193]—and tactical risks—as they might use the engagement to bargain benefits.[194]

Increasing human rights violations committed by cartels calls for urgent action in order to improve civilians' protection. To this end, two approaches could be adopted. First, the government could conclude a truce with the DTOs. As we shall see, in El Salvador MS-13 and M-18 concluded a truce in 2012 that proved to have reduced substantially the number of casualties in the country, especially among civilians. Second, although criminal organizations do not seek international legitimacy, they do benefit

[188] Clapham, A., *Human Rights Obligations*, p. 189; La Rosa, A., and Wuerzner, C., 'Armed Groups', pp. 332–3.

[189] See, e.g., *San José Agreement on Human Rights*, concluded between El Salvador and the *Frente Farabundo Martí para la Liberación Natcional* (FMLN). See Clapham, A., *Human Rights Obligations*, p. 272.

[190] Bellal A. and Casey-Maslen, S., *Rules of Engagement*, p. 18.

[191] Hauck, P. and Peterke, S., 'Organized Crime and Gang Violence', p. 433

[192] Ibid.

[193] Carpenter, A. C., 'Civilian Protection in Mexico & Guatemala', p. 129.

[194] Ibid.

from the local kind, especially in the territories under their control. Antagonizing the local population has proved counterproductive, as the *autodefensas* phenomenon in Michoacán and Guerrero States demonstrate. Consequently, DTOs could benefit from the support of the civilians, assistance that they could get only by regaining the lost legitimacy in the population's eyes.

CONCLUDING TRUCES WITH CRIMINAL ORGANIZATIONS

At the beginning of 2012, in El Salvador, the leaders of the Mara Salvatrucha (MS-13) and the Barrio 18 (M-18) agreed a truce with the mediation of the Church.[195] Albeit at first both the *maras* and the government claimed that the authorities were not involved in the negotiations, it then appeared clear that the government played a substantial role in the process.[196] Notably, the *maras* have agreed to reduce violence in exchange for reintegration programmes for group members and transfer to low-security prisons for their leaders.[197] Thanks to the truce, El Salvador saw violence dropping by 60%.[198] However, by the end of 2013 the truce collapsed, murders raised by 57% and by June violence was back to pre-truce levels.[199]

Despite the overall failure of this attempt, it did have some positive outcomes. First, it caused a dramatic drop in homicides while the truce lasted, which is perhaps the greatest benefit of the deal. Furthermore, the truce helped to have an insight on the *maras*' structure. Maintaining the truce for more than one year, these criminal gangs proved to have a significant hierarchical control over their members. Controlling 'well-armed,

[195] Stone, H., 'El Salvador Gangs Confirm Truce', InSight Crime, 23 March 2012, available at: <http://www.insightcrime.org/news-briefs/el-salvador-gangs-confirm-truce>; TIME, 'Central America's Gang War', August 13, 2012, available at: <http://world.time.com/2012/08/13/central-americas-gang-wars-a-truce-leads-to-an-unusual-peace/> accessed 1 May 2015.

[196] Martinez, C. and Sanz, J. L., 'The New Truth about El Salvador Gang's Truce', InSight Crime, 14 September 2012, available at: <http://www.insightcrime.org/news-analysis/the-new-truth-about-the-gang-truce> accessed 1 May 2015.

[197] It is worth mentioning that the Organization of American States (OAS) supported the truce, welcoming the drop in the murder rate. See Stargardter, G., 'Organization of America States backs fragile El Salvador gang truce', InSight Crime, 25 July 2013, available at: <http://www.reuters.com/article/2013/07/26/us-elsalvador-violence-idUSBRE96P03X20130726> accessed 1 May 2015. With regard to the government's involvement in the truce, see Stone, H., 'Why El Salvador Truce is Illegal, and Why it Matters', InSight Crime, 27 March 2013, available at: <http://www.insightcrime.org/news-analysis/el-salvador-gang-truce-illegal> accessed 1 May 2015.

[198] Stone, H., 'El Salvador Sees Almost 60% Drop in Murders in April, As Gang Truce Holds', InSight Crime, 1 May 2012, available at: <http://www.insightcrime.org/news-briefs/el-salvador-sees-almost-60-drop-in-murders-in-april-as-gang-truce-holds> accessed 1 May 2015.

[199] Lohmuller, M., 'El Salvador Gang Truce "Technically" Finished: Police', Insight Crime, 4 March 2014, available at: <http://www.insightcrime.org/news-briefs/el-salvador-gang-truce-technically-finished-police> accessed 1 May 2015.

unemployed young men and women is difficult in any circumstances'. However, *maras*' leaders were capable of enforcing a common policy.[200]

Finally, the truce demonstrated that a 'soft' approach, as opposed to the *mano dura* (iron fist), can be more effective to protect civilians:

> For perhaps the first time, local and federal government bureaucrats, politicians, and functionaries are asking themselves what they need to do to establish effective prevention and rehabilitation programs. They are trying to calculate the costs, they are turning to those who have long worked with at-risk youth, and they are developing programs in conjunction with international donors.[201]

Given the positive outcomes of the truce in El Salvador, Honduras tried to reproduce it. However, the attempt did not lead to similar positive effects.[202] The main reasons for this failure are to be found in some key differences between the two countries. First, in Honduras the dominant *maras* is the M-18, while in El Salvador it is the MS-13. What might be seen as a minor difference proved crucial in order to successfully implement the truce. Indeed, the barrio 18 has a more decentralized structure that makes it more difficult to implement the truce at every level of the group.[203] Furthermore, the government benefits from more credibility in El Salvador than in Honduras. While the Salvadorian authorities have reliable institutions through which negotiations with the *maras* could take place, the same cannot be said for Honduras, whose former President Zelaya was ousted in 2009 and where recent elections have been contested.[204]

The truces have not been as successful as hoped. Nevertheless, they could be an effective instrument to reduce violence and to enhance protection of civilians. They have shown that the *maras* are not simply criminal gangs, but are able to negotiate with the authorities and to implement agreements within their members. As it has been correctly pointed out:

> The truce has changed the conventional thinking about who the gangs are and what is the best way to handle the most difficult law and order issue in the Northern Triangle countries of El Salvador, Guatemala and Honduras.[205]

[200] Dudley, S., '5 Things the El Salvador Gang Truce Has Taught Us', InSight Crime, 12 March 2013, available at: <http://www.insightcrime.org/news-analysis/5-things-el-salvador-gang-truce-taught-us> accessed 1 May 2015.

[201] Dudley, S., 'El Salvador Gangs' Truce: Positives and Negatives', InSight Crime, 11 June 2013, available at: <http://www.insightcrime.org/investigations/el-salvadors-gang-truce-positives-and-negatives> accessed 1 May 2015.

[202] Bargent, J., 'Murders in Honduras Rising Despite Gang Truce', InSight Crime, 5 August 2013, available at: <http://www.insightcrime.org/news-briefs/murders-in-honduras-rising-despite-gang-truce> accessed 1 May 2015.

[203] Dudlye, S., '5 Differences Between El Salvador, Honduras Gang Truces', InSight Crime, 12 January 2013, available at: <http://www.insightcrime.org/news-analysis/5-differences-between-el-salvador-honduras-gang-truces> accessed 1 May 2015.

[204] Dudlye, S., '5 Differences Between El Salvador, Honduras Gang Truces'.

[205] Dudlye, S., 'El Salvador's Gang Truce: Positives and Negatives', InSight Crime, 11 June 2013, available at: <http://www.insightcrime.org/investigations/el-salvadors-gang-truce-positives-and-negatives> accessed 1 May 2015.

New attempts to conclude truces would constitute important opportunities to reduce violence. However, to be successful all the parties involved should consider the specific challenges that led to the collapse of previous attempts. Notably, the government should never forget that gangs like the *maras* and Mexican cartels are international criminal organizations with bases and ties in most of the Latin American countries. Furthermore, criminal groups are not independent actors: they are incorporated in international criminal networks, as well as into the State 'through networks connected with corrupt civic actors, bureaucrats, and politicians'.[206] Indeed, corruption among authorities is not uncommon and generates close ties between criminal organizations and public officeholders.

To conclude, truces could be a useful instrument to reduce violence and to start a constructive dialogue with criminal groups. In a climate of enhanced trust and cooperation, the government would be able to focus on the main causes of criminal violence and on the possible ways to dismantle these organizations. Truces should not be considered the end of the process: they are the start.[207]

CRIMINAL ORGANIZATIONS BETWEEN TERRITORIAL CONTROL AND LOCAL LEGITIMACY

As aforementioned, criminal groups do not aim to take over the State. Their objectives are primarily economic.[208] In order to continue their illegal activities undisturbed, they need areas inaccessible to the government.[209] They don't intend to constitute a parallel power system. Nonetheless, they establish control over certain zones in order to pursue their economic interests. They thus benefit from a weakened state, unable to firmly control every part of the country.[210]

In order to exert control over the territory, criminal groups need to engage with the local population, offering services, jobs, and security. However, they also use force and exemplary punishments in order to spread fear among the population and to show what happens when someone tries to disobey them.[211] Some DTOs, such as *La Familia Michoacana* and *Los Caballeros Templarios*, have started 'to build community solidarity

[206] Muggah, R., Carpenter, A., and McDougal, T., 'The Inconvenient Truth About Gang Truces in the Americas', InSight Crime, 5 December 2013, available at: <http://www.insightcrime.org/news-analysis/the-inconvenient-truth-about-gang-truces-in-the-americas> accessed 1 May 2015.

[207] Ibid.

[208] Davis, D. E. and Pereira, A. W. (eds.), 2008, *Irregular Armed Forces and their Role in Politics and State Formation*, Cambridge: Cambridge University Press, at p. 407; Bellal, A., and Casey-Maslen, S., *Rules of Engagement*, p. 17.

[209] Bellal, A., and Casey-Maslen, S., *Rules of Engagement*, p. 17.

[210] Ibid. [211] Raether, J., 'Drug War', p. 942.

through employment opportunities, for instance by building infrastructures and by providing goods and services to the community'.[212]

Criminal organizations do not seek international legitimacy. Unlike some opposition groups, they do not feel obliged to comply with international law in order to gain legitimacy in the eyes of the international community.[213] However, they do need the local population. In order to pursue undisturbed their criminal activities, cartels need to control part of State territory. To this end, they take advantage of the geographical isolation of certain areas, as well as of the absence and weakness of the government, to establish the so-called *zonas de impunidad*. There, criminal groups can arrive to provide services to the local population, from health care to justice. In areas where the State is completely absent, these services are crucial. Meeting the needs of the local population, criminal groups gain legitimacy in their eyes, to the detriment of State authorities. As a result, civilians might prefer to back the DTOs instead of the government, as the first are able to provide protection, jobs, and services that would be otherwise unavailable.[214]

In recent years, a new trend has started whereby criminal groups do not seek to be legitimate in the eyes of the local population, but rather maintain their control over territory through fear and violence. This is particularly true in Mexico. Following the kingpin strategy, a new generation of young and crueller bosses has emerged. This led to a deterioration of the security of the civilian population living in territories controlled by the cartels.[215]

If DTOs again start to guarantee protection to the local population, they could regain their lost legitimacy. This would have positive consequences: if criminal organizations protect civilians, the latter would not create self-defence groups, like the Colombian paramilitaries and the Mexican *autodefensas*. Therefore, there would be fewer casualties among civilians and the DTOs would not need to disperse their forces fighting both vigilantes and the State.[216]

Some could see this approach as a de facto help to DTOs. Governments in particular might be sceptical. However, the situation at the moment is unacceptable. Due to high

[212] Bellal, A., and Casey-Maslen, S., *Rules of Engagement*, p. 18. For instance, *La Familia Michoacana* has donated food and medicines to the poor (J. Raether, 'Drug War', p. 943). La Tuta, head of *Los Caballeros Templarios*, distributes money to get accepted by the local community—in contrast with the State which is absent and the local authorities that are corrupted—and also in order to recruit new people among the local population; see <https://www.youtube.com/watch?v=ht1Y78sdsoQ> accessed 1 May 2015.

[213] Clapham, A., *Human Rights Obligations*, p. 288.

[214] Bellal, A., and Casey-Maslen, S., *Rules of Engagement*, p. 17; Carpenter, A. C., 'Civilian Protection in Mexico & Guatemala', p. 115.

[215] Grayson, G. W., 'The Evolution of Los Zetas in Mexico and Central America: Sadism as an Instrument of Cartel Warfare', US Army War College—Strategic Studies Institute, April 2014, p. 9; Carpenter, A. C., 'Civilian Protection in Mexico & Guatemala', p. 119.

[216] Bruderlein, C., 'The Role of Non-State Actors in Building Human Security: The Case of Armed Groups in Intra-State Wars', Centre for Humanitarian Dialogue, Geneva, May 200, p. 12.

levels of corruption and lack of resources, it is highly unlikely that governments will be able to provide effective protection to the local population. The dramatic events that are affecting civilians, especially in areas under cartels' control, are unlikely to end any day soon. Engaging with criminal groups is thus paramount to tackle the humanitarian crisis caused by these organizations.

9 Protecting the right to protest in armed conflict

Milena Costas Trascasas[1]

Introduction

In recent years the direct connection between the right to protest and armed conflict has come to the fore. The wave of protest movements that have rocked the Arab world since 2011 has put the spotlight on the right to freedom of assembly and the State's obligation under international human rights law to facilitate and protect peaceful protest. At the same time, the 'Arab Spring' has made evident the potential of mass protests, which are capable of bringing a nation to democracy (Tunis), to civil war (Syria), to collapse (Libya, Yemen), or even, ultimately, to a situation in which a pre-existing authoritarian regime is reinforced (Egypt). [2]

Social protest has increasingly become a common way of exercising the rights to freedom of peaceful assembly and of expression. The Human Rights Council has recognized that 'everyone must be able to express their grievances or aspirations in a peaceful manner, including through public protests'.[3] Individuals do not, though, have a 'right' to protest as such. Rather, protests are situations that provide them with the opportunity to simultaneously exercise a number of rights, the guarantee of which is essential and inherent to any reputable democratic system.

Allowing peaceful protests to take place is a sign of democratic health and an important indicator of the rule of law. Protests may be seen as 'a positive contribution to the development, strengthening and effectiveness of democratic systems and to democratic processes',[4] but also as a threat to national security, an incitement to violence, or a challenge to public order. In fact, because those protesting convey a message of opposition

[1] Dr. Milena Costas Trascasas is an independent researcher.

[2] See in general, Bellal, A. and Doswald-Beck, L., 2011, 'Evaluating the Use of Force During the Arab Spring', *Yearbook of International Humanitarian Law*, vol. 14, pp. 3–35.

[3] HRC, 'The promotion and protection of human rights in the context of peaceful protests', A/HRC/RES/25/38, 28 March 2014.

[4] Ibid.

or criticism to those in power, States tend to adopt repressive policies and practices in handling these situations. Recent events show that numerous countries do not perceive the political and social benefits of creating a climate where the right to protest may be exercised in freedom and without fear. This fact has led to some concerning patterns that have been addressed by human rights bodies over the past decades.

The aim of this chapter is to determine the scope of the State's obligations when protests take place in a context of armed conflict or occupation. Such situations certainly pose a number of challenges to national authorities, not only regarding the circumstances under which the holding of protests might be restricted or banned due to security or public order reasons but also in the determination of the applicable rules governing the use of force in the dispersal of non-authorized or otherwise unlawful protests, as for example, where protesters undertake violent or armed actions against security forces.[5]

A. **Legal regime applicable to protests**

There is no doubt that ongoing armed hostilities may gravely reduce the space for exercising political rights.[6] As a matter of fact, 'in situations of armed conflict, individuals who desire to assemble and associate freely, even to address emergency needs or to call for the end of violence, may meet drastic restrictions that may amount to a strict denial of their rights'.[7] As a matter of law, protests may also be banned because of the risk of clashes, because active fighting is actually taking place, or due to restrictions imposed by armed groups.[8]

In principle, even when facing a threat to national security, the State continues to bear the duty to guarantee the right to hold protests peacefully as well as that to protect without discrimination the rights of all persons under its jurisdiction. However, hostilities or a lack of control of certain parts of the territory may justify an adjustment in the scope of the State's human rights commitments. This may imply the temporary restriction or the exceptional suspension of certain rights until the situation of normality is fully re-established.

[5] For the purposes of this chapter the term 'security forces' refers to those State agents that may be involved in the policing of a protest being the members of the police and members of the armed forces carrying out law enforcement tasks. It includes also private security providers. See Commentary to Art. 1 of the 1979 Code of Conduct for Law Enforcement Officials.

[6] Dinstein, Y., 2014, *Non-international Armed Conflicts in International Law*, Cambridge University Press, p. 746.

[7] A/HRC/20/27, 21 May 2012, §22.

[8] OHCHR, 'Report on the human rights situation in Ukraine, 16 September 2014', §178 r) and §159; 'Report on the human rights situation in Ukraine, 17 August 2014', §73.

The body or rules called to protect the rights of protesters during protests is human rights law (HRL), generally applicable in situations of armed conflict or occupation.[9] International humanitarian law (IHL) contains rules that are also applicable in those situations. However, it does not specifically regulate the handling of demonstrations or other situations of law enforcement but the conduct of hostilities and the protection of the victims of armed conflicts more broadly. In fact, situations of disturbances, riots, and other situations that may imply acts of sporadic or isolated violence are generally considered as falling outside the scope of non-international armed conflict and therefore the application of IHL.[10]

Human rights treaties and national constitutions recognize in very similar terms the right of peaceful assembly. According to Article 21 ICCPR; 'The right of peaceful assembly shall be recognized. No restrictions may be placed on the exercise of this right other than those imposed in conformity with the law and which are necessary in a democratic society in the interests of national security or public safety, public order (*ordre public*), the protection of public health or morals or the protection of the rights and freedoms of others.'[11]

Protests constitute a particular type of assembly, where protesters tend to send a message of dissent, opposition, response, or reaction, usually against the policies or actions of the ruling government. Particularly when public demonstrations are spontaneous events, or gather hundreds of thousands of protesters, they may pose a great challenge for those in charge of policing these events. But regardless of their size, the way in which a protest is handled is a very sensitive issue from a political and social point of view; one which puts the focus on the security forces' intervention.

As a general rule, national laws and authorities should tend to facilitate—rather than discourage—the holding of peaceful protests. The State must refrain from interfering with the right of individuals to organize and to freely participate in these events at all levels (administrative, criminal, and while policing protests). National authorities not only have the duty to favour the holding of protests, they have also an obligation to guarantee actively the peaceful character of such events.[12] Peaceful protesters must be actively protected against any conduct aimed at temporarily hindering, impeding, or

[9] ICJ, 'Legal Consequences of the Construction of a Wall in the Occupied Palestinian Territory', Advisory Opinion, 9 July 2004, §106.

[10] Art. 1(2) APII. See Costas Trascasas, M., 2008, *Violencia Interna y protección de la persona: una laguna jurídica del Derecho Internacional*, Tirant Lo Blanch, pp. 460–92.

[11] See also Art. 20 of the 1948 Universal Declaration on Human Rights; Art. 11 of the 1950 European Convention on Human Rights and Fundamental Freedoms; Art. 15 of the 1969 American Convention on Human Rights; Art. 11 of the 1987 African Charter on Human Rights and Peoples' Rights; Art. 24 of the 2003 Arab Charter on Human Rights.

[12] The ECtHR has said that the authorities 'have a duty to take appropriate measures with regard to lawful demonstrations in order to ensure their peaceful conduct and the safety of all citizens'. *Oya Ataman v Turkey*, Judgement, 5 December 2006, §35.

obstructing the protest as well as against any sporadic or isolated act of violence that may arise. The life and physical integrity of those protesting should be particularly protected from violence from others, i.e. counter-demonstrators, non-State actors, and[13] *'agents provocateurs'*.[14]

In the course of actively protecting those taking part in the protests against any interference or disruption security forces should act without discrimination. They should not side with political parties or movements and act with impartiality regardless of the political affiliation of the protesters or the content of the message. Positive measures should be adopted and implemented in order to prevent the escalation of violence as well as excesses in the response of the security forces, particularly to avoid the resort to firearms when resorting to force.[15]

Against the backdrop of a situation of armed conflict or occupation the risk of a biased intervention of the security forces leading to cases of abuse of authority is particularly high. This might contribute to the escalation of the situation. As the Special Rapporteur on extrajudicial, summary, or arbitrary executions has warned: 'the indiscriminate use of force against a crowd as a whole can persuade the more restrained members of the group to also resort to the use of force in order to protect their fellow group members'.[16]

The situation may require specific measures to protect persons not involved in the protests (such as passers-by and observers). States are also called upon to implement specific measures to ensure that security forces are aware of the rights of particularly vulnerable groups (such as children and women) as well as of those professionals carrying out their duties during the protests such as journalists, doctors, and lawyers or human rights defenders. Regardless of the general context under which the protests take place, legally speaking, the State continues to bear the duty to protect those who peacefully participate in such events against violations of their rights.

CAN THE RIGHT TO PROTEST BE SUSPENDED?

To be able to confront effectively the threat that a situation of armed conflict or civil unrest may pose, the State can have recourse to the declaration of a 'state of emergency' as provided for in Article 4 ICCPR.[17] Emergency powers are however very often used in

[13] A/HRC/23/39, 24 April 2013, §49 and A/HRC/19/40, 19 December 2011, §14.

[14] The infiltration of 'agents provocateurs' is sometimes tolerated by security forces as a justification to terminating or forcibly dispersing the assembly. See OSCE ODIHR, 2010, *Guidelines on Freedom of Peaceful Assembly*, Warsaw, §167.

[15] Basic Principle no. 11 of the 1990 Basic Principles on the Use of Force and Firearms (BRUFF), (hereafter Basic Principles).

[16] A/HRC/17/28, 23 May 2011, §112.

[17] Art. 15 of the 1950 European Convention on Human Rights and Fundamental Freedoms; and Art. 27 of the 1969 American Convention on Human Rights. The declaration of the state of emergency is also regulated in domestic law.

practice to illegitimately limit the exercise of the right to protest, particularly in situations that fall short of armed conflict. In the aftermath of the *coup d'état* that took place in 2009 in Honduras, for example, the de facto government suspended the right to freedom of assembly along with other constitutional guarantees. Public meetings or assemblies were prohibited 'in order to prevent uprisings' during the curfew hours and unless authorized by the police or military authorities.[18] The Inter-American Commission on Human Rights considered that such restrictions were not justified, among other things, because they were ordered 'without any explanation of their reasons or their relevance to the situation that prompted the state of emergency'.[19]

In view of the abusive use of the derogation clause made by States, human rights bodies have recalled that some elements of the right of peaceful assembly can only be suspended where the strict requirements of the derogation clause are met.[20] Extraordinary measures can only be adopted in situations posing a real, grave, and imminent threat to the existence of the nation and when ordinary limitation measures are plainly inadequate to address the situation. Measures must be proportionate and adequate to address the threat.[21] For the Human Rights Committee situations of mass violent demonstrations could usually be faced through normal possibilities for limitation and without resorting to derogation.[22] A lasting or total prohibition of the right to hold assemblies would be therefore very rarely justifiable.[23] In any case, this could not affect the enjoyment of other 'core rights' such as the right to life or the prohibition of torture that must be respected under any circumstances. Furthermore, 'states parties may in no circumstances invoke Article 4 of the Covenant as justification for acting in violation of international humanitarian law or peremptory norms of international law, for instance by taking hostages, by imposing collective punishments, through arbitrary deprivations of

[18] National authorities justified the suspension 'because groups of persons who abuse the right to peaceful demonstration and freedom of association for lawful purposes are staging violent takeovers at strategic points along streets, avenues, bridges, highways and public buildings. Acts of vandalism are being committed that seriously endanger persons who have nothing to do with these events. The repeated clashes with police forces have resulted in excessive use of force by the police, which has claimed a regrettable number of victims'. IAComHR, 'Honduras: human rights and the coup d'état', OEA/Ser.L/V/II. Doc. 55, 30 December 2009, §217.

[19] Ibid., §§219–220.

[20] In order to adopt measures derogating from the provisions of the Covenant the threat must be of an exceptional and temporary nature and amount to a public emergency which threatens the life of the nation (necessity). Measures must be limited to the extent strictly required by the exigencies of the situation (proportionality). The state of emergency has to be officially proclaimed and notified. See Human Rights Committee, General Comment no. 29. 'States of emergency (Article 4)'. UN Doc. CCPR/C/21/Rev.1/Add.11, 31 August 2001.

[21] 'Siracusa Principles on the Limitation and Derogation Provisions in the International Covenant on Civil and Political Rights', E/CN.4/1985/4, Annex (1985), §§40 and 53.

[22] General Comment no. 29, §5. Nowak, M., 2005, *CCPR Commentary*, Engel Publishers, §§90–91.

[23] Doswald-Beck, L., 2011, *Human Rights in Times of Conflict and Terrorism*, Oxford University Press, p. 443.

liberty or by deviating from fundamental principles of fair trial, including the presumption of innocence'.[24]

Recent events in Ukraine show that despite situations of ongoing armed conflict the right to freedom of assembly may be guaranteed both by law and in practice, without particular restriction except in the areas controlled by the armed groups.[25] With respect to an occupied territory the occupying power is entitled to adopt measures of derogation in conformity with international law.[26] However, this is not always the case. In reference to the long-term measures aimed at curtailing the exercise of the right to peaceful assembly on security grounds in the Occupied Palestinian Territory, the Human Rights Committee has reminded Israel that they are no longer justified in light of current circumstances.[27]

ORDINARY RESTRICTIONS TO THE RIGHT TO PROTEST

Restricting the exercise of the right to protest through ordinary legislation is a common practice. In accordance with Article 21 ICCPR national legislation can limit exercise of the right to freedom of peaceful assembly in order to protect national security, public order, or the protection of the rights and freedoms of others.[28] Nevertheless, the State must 'refrain from applying unreasonable indirect restrictions upon that right. In view of the essential nature of freedom of assembly and its close relationship with democracy there must be convincing and compelling reasons to justify an interference with this right'.[29]

It is implicit in the exercise of the right to peaceful assembly that protests may cause disruption to the daily life of others and cause isolated or sporadic problems of public order.[30] Restrictions are only justified on the prevention of imminent danger of violence or avoidance of the negative consequences that these events may have on the rights of

[24] General Comment no. 29, §11. See also §§7 and 16.

[25] In the Autonomous Republic of Crimea, for example, those responsible for guaranteeing all fundamental rights to all persons, including freedoms of peaceful assembly, are the authorities in Crimea and the de facto governing authority of the Russian Federation. OHCHR, 'Report on the human rights situation in Ukraine', 16 September 2014, §178 r).

[26] Sassòli, M., 2011, 'New Types of Armed Conflicts'. In Ben-Naftali, O., *International Humanitarian Law and International Human Rights Law*, Oxford University Press, p. 66.

[27] CCPR/C/ISR/CO/4, 21 November 2014, §10. The High Court of Justice has been recently asked to declare the existence of a state of emergency void, or alternatively, order that it is to be immediately terminated. A/HRC/WG.6/3/ISR/1, 25 September 2008, §§98 and 102; CCPR/C/ISR/CO/4, 21 November 2014, §10.

[28] OSCE ODIHR, 2010, *Guidelines on Freedom of Peaceful Assembly*, Warsaw, §72. In Ukraine, for example, courts or local authorities have prohibited protests in the name of public order and safety, particularly to prevent rival protests that could potentially turn violent. OHCHR, 'Report on the human rights situation in Ukraine 1 December 2014 to 15 February 2015', §58.

[29] ECtHR, *Makhmudov v Russia*, Judgement, 26 July 2007, §64.

[30] IAComHR, 'Report on citizen security and human rights', OEA/Ser.L/V/II, Doc. 57, 31 December 2009, §198.

others.[31] As the ECtHR has noted, interference in the enjoyment of this right are justified 'for the prevention of disorder or crime and for the protection of the rights and freedoms of others where demonstrators engage in acts of violence'.[32] However, 'the threat must be associated with that particular assembly, and the state should not inflate the risk of violence as a means of simply preventing the assembly from taking place'.[33]

Protests might be prohibited or limitations on the 'time, place and manner' imposed to address a serious threat of violence and disorder. Such decisions cannot be discriminatory nor subordinated to political considerations.[34] Restrictions or prohibitions cannot be imposed only on the basis of the content of the protest's message, such as criticisms of government policy. A prohibition of a specific protest would nevertheless be permitted in extreme situations as for example when the organizers promote hatred or discrimination towards certain groups, incite violence, or promote lawless or disorderly acts.[35]

The decision on banning a protest requires considering the specific circumstances of each situation and, thus, sweeping restrictions for a protracted period of time would normally amount to a violation of the right to peaceful assembly. In this vein, the Special Rapporteur on the freedoms of peaceful assembly and association has affirmed that: 'blanket bans, are intrinsically disproportionate and discriminatory measures as they impact on all citizens wishing to exercise their rights to freedom of peaceful assembly'.[36]

UNAUTHORIZED PROTESTS

Under a number of domestic laws organizers of a protest are required to give advance notice or seek authorization from the authorities. Such a requirement may enable the authorities to facilitate the holding of the protest without disturbing the normal activities of the rest of the community and allow them to put in place 'reasonable and appropriate measures ... to ensure that a demonstration passes off smoothly'.[37] Practice shows nevertheless that such procedures are open to misuse: unduly or excessive bureaucratic

[31] The exercise of the right to protest can only be limited on a temporary basis when strictly necessary to achieve that aim, provided that the measures adopted are necessary and proportionate.

[32] ECtHR, *Giuliani and Gaggio v Italy*, Judgement, Grand Chamber, 24 March 2011, §251.

[33] OSCE ODIHR, *Handbook on Monitoring Freedom of Peaceful Assembly*, 2011, p. 22.

[34] IAComHR, 'Report on the Situation of Human Rights Defenders in the Americas', OEA/Ser.L/V/II.124 Doc. 5 rev.1, 7 March 2006, §60.

[35] Art. 20(2) ICCPR allows the prohibition of any war propaganda or advocacy of racial, national, or religious hatred that constitutes incitement to hostility, violence, or discrimination. See also Art. 4(a) of the Convention on the Elimination of Racial Discrimination; A/HRC/2/39, 24 April 2013, §59.

[36] A/HRC/23/39, 24 April 2013, §63.

[37] IACHR, 'Report on the Situation of Human Rights Defenders in the Americas', §56.

procedures may seek to provoke a chilling effect; domestic regulations may also grant national authorities a great discretion in the decision of banning.[38]

When organizers decide to ignore the prohibition and hold a protest, national authorities may be much more prone to adopt a biased approach in the policing of the protest. This is particularly true in a situation of armed conflict or occupation where the police are generally the body in charge of authorizing the holding (or not) of a protests, sometimes with great discretion.[39] Under Israeli law, for example, the authority may decide whether to grant or not a permit on the basis of the police's ability to cope with the demonstration 'in the context of the other challenges they face'.[40] In the same vein, Article 9(1)(a) of the South African Regulation of Gathering Act no. 205 (1993) provides the police with the power to notify the convener of a gathering 'that will not be able to provide adequate protection for the people participating in such a gathering or demonstration'.

Recent practice shows that many protests are genuinely spontaneous and respond to a particular event that triggers the gathering. In other cases, protesters may decide to bypass formal requisites and to gather without informing national authorities or without complying with domestic procedures or legal requirements, and this for several reasons: because they do not recognize the authority of the government or the occupied power, because they fear reprisals or criminal sanctions, or simply because they are persuaded that national authorities will not provide them with the permit to protest.

In a number of domestic laws the fact that a protest had not been authorized renders it 'unlawful' meaning that the authorities may forcibly disperse such events.[41] In this respect, the guiding principle is that States need to show a certain degree of tolerance toward peaceful assemblies, even when procedural requirements are not respected. The ECtHR case law has emphasized that the holding of an unauthorized peaceful protest does not affect the obligation of the State to allow the protest to continue as far as remains peaceful and is not obstructive.[42]

In general, as long as assemblies remain peaceful, they should not be dispersed. This should apply also to the protests that have been banned. In the absence of violent conduct by the participants, the forcible dispersal of a protest only on the basis that it was not either authorized or notified amounts to a disproportionate restriction of the freedom of peace ful assembly.[43] An inadequate, unnecessary, or excessive use of force in the dispersal of an unauthorized protest may provoke an initially peaceful protest to turn violent endangering

[38] A/HRC/23/39, 24 April 2013, §54.

[39] Costas Trascasas, M. and Casey-Maslen, S., 2014, 'Facilitating Peaceful Protests', Geneva Academy Briefing, January, p. 11 <http://www.geneva-academy.ch/docs/publications/briefing5_web_singles8.pdf>.

[40] Baumgarten-Sharon, N., 2010, 'The Right to Demonstrate in the Occupied Territories. Position Paper,' July, p. 5, at: <http://www.btselem.org/sites/default/files2/publication/20100715_right_to_demonstrate_eng.pdf>.

[41] See Basic Principle no. 13 BPUFF.

[42] ECtHR, *Oya Ataman v Turkey*, Judgement, 5 December 2006, §42.

[43] ECtHR, *Bukta and Others v Hungary*, Judgment, 17 July 2007, §36.

thereby the lives of those attending the event, including members of the security forces and other uninvolved people.

Participants that do not comply with the orders of the security forces to disperse are usually arrested on administrative or criminal grounds. Organizers or those participating in an unauthorized protest may also be sanctioned after an assembly for violating applicable laws and lack of compliance with legal requirements respectively.[44] Likewise, those having committed criminal offences may be arrested and prosecuted for those acts.

Nevertheless, excesses are frequently committed in the policing of protests. The practice of massive arbitrary detentions, the criminalization of peaceful demonstrators and the imposition of disproportionate sanctions may certainly have a chilling effect. Stop and search powers of the police are also frequently abused in relation to demonstrations and against peaceful protestors.[45] Human rights case law has referred to these practices as amounting to a violation to the rights to security and freedom from arbitrarily arrest as well as of the right to freedom of assembly.[46] Regardless of the fact that a protest had been authorized or not, peaceful protesters cannot be sanctioned only for exercising their right to protest.

B. **Use of force in protests**

Lack of restraint in the policing of mass protests was one of the factors that contribute to trigger armed hostilities in some recent cases. In Libya, arbitrary and indiscriminate use of force against peaceful protesters intensified the uprising that spread across the country in only one week.[47] Also the brutal repression of the 2011 protests across the country inflamed the Syrian conflict, quickly turning from peaceful protests with sporadic and isolated acts of violence into armed hostilities.[48] Likewise, it is admitted that failures in the policing

[44] The excessive use of criminal sanctions applied to those who legitimately exercise their right to protest could result in the criminalization of protests and, as a consequence, the intimidation of those who want to exercise this means of participating in public life in order to demand their rights. IAComHR, 'Democracia and Human Rights in Venezuela', OEA/Ser.L/V/II.Doc.54, 30 December 2009, §151.

[45] Section 44 of the UK Terrorism Act 2000 allowing the Home Secretary to authorize police to make random searches in certain circumstances was declared by the ECtHR contrary to Art. 8 of the ECHR. *Gillan and Quinton's v UK*, Judgement, 12 January 2010.

[46] IAComHR, 'Report on the Situation of Human Rights Defenders in the Americas'§§56 and 108.

[47] A/HRC/17/44, 1 June 2011, §36.

[48] The Secretary-General in 2012 reported that: 'the State's campaign of violently suppressing dissent, which from the outset employed excessive and lethal force against peaceful demonstrators' was followed by defections and the formation of anti-Government armed groups. S/2012/523, 6 July 2012, §2.

of the *Maidan* demonstrations in Ukraine triggered further protests and fuelled violence in some areas of the country.[49]

Police operations directed against civilians in the course of protests, riots, or other situations of civil unrest are not covered by IHL rules.[50] Outside the conduct of hostilities, conditions for the lawful use of force (both lethal and less-lethal) are governed by HRL rules on 'law enforcement'. Rules regulating the use of force during protests are mainly the same as those that apply to any use of force. The 1990 Basic Principles on the Use of Force and Firearms by Law Enforcement Officials (BPUFF), as subsequently interpreted by human rights case law, set the reference framework for any lawful use of force.[51]

In the course of a peaceful protest, force should generally not be used at all against peaceful protesters. When necessary and proportionate, force may be gradually increased and police may have to resort to different less-lethal means (i.e. truncheons, water cannons, rubber bullets, or tear gas).[52] The principles of necessity and proportionality apply not only to firearms but also to all other weapons.[53] This is important bearing in mind that less lethal weapons can easily be misused so as to produce lethal effects.[54]

As a general principle, the use of firearms and other lethal means should not be permitted in the policing and dispersal of peaceful protests, authorized or not.[55] While policing violent protests, lethal force is only allowed in self-defence or to protect life or against the imminent threat of serious injury.[56] Security forces must, however, act with restraint so as to minimize the damage and injury to the greatest extent possible.[57] Those provoking acts of violence must still be treated with humanity.[58] The use of potentially lethal force against those not posing a real or imminent risk to the life of others may amount to an arbitrary deprivation of life or cruel or inhumane treatment. In any event, the minimum necessary use of force should be made. Potentially lethal force may

[49] Forceful dispersal of protesters on 30 November 2013 was the first instance of the excessive use of force against peaceful *Maidan* demonstrators and triggered further protests. OHCHR, 'Report on the human rights situation in Ukraine 15 April 2014', §2.

[50] See Art. 1(2) AP II.

[51] See in particular, Basic Principles nos. 12–14 BPUFF.

[52] Basic Principle nos. 2 and no. 3 BPUFF.

[53] HRW, Turkey: End Incorrect, Unlawful Use of Teargas, 17 July 2013; <http://www.hrw.org/news/2013/07/16/turkey-end-incorrect-unlawful-use-teargas>.

[54] See Dymond-Bass, A. and Corney, N. 2014, 'The Use of "Less-Lethal Weapons" in Law Enforcement'. In *Weapons under International Human Rights Law*, edited by Casey-Maslen, S., Cambridge University Press, pp. 32–52.

[55] Basic Principles nos. 12 and 13 BPUFF. Further, in view of the consequences for persons who are present but not involved in the violent acts and the additional risks posed by a violent protest 'large crowds, confusion and disorganization' it has been questioned whether the use of firearms is admissible and practicable at all while policing such situations. ICRC, *Violence and the use of force*, 2011, p. 44.

[56] Ibid., §119 and Commentary on Art. 3 of the 1979 Code of Conduct for Law Enforcement Officials.

[57] Basic Principle no. 14 BPUFF.

[58] *Neira Alegria et al. v Peru*, Judgment of 19 January 1995, §75.

be required and legally used when other means are ineffective against an imminent threat to life or of serious injury.[59]

Where violent actions break out security forces must intervene to control the situation as well as to protect the safety of all citizens by avoiding or preventing any threat to their lives or security. The level of force must be increased progressively starting with non-violent means when circumstances allow for this. The use of deadly force is only allowed when a protester by his or her own action is posing a threat to the life of another, including the life of the member of the security forces. In situations of chaos and disorder the use of firearms and other potentially lethal means may lead to erroneous targeting and to incidental death or casualties as an unintended outcome. Its use is therefore only allowed provided that the targeting of the specific 'aggressor' is possible and where the risk of causing death or damage within the crowd is minor, and in any case proportionate to the threat posed by the violent protester.

The HRC has encouraged States to make non-lethal weapons available, while pursuing international efforts to regulate and establish protocols for the training and use of non-lethal means.[60] Police are required to take all necessary precautions to avoid unnecessary injury, in accordance with the principles that govern the use of any kind of force and common best practices. Though prohibited as a method of warfare, the use of tear gas for law enforcement purposes (i.e. in the dispersal of non-authorized protests) is an extended practice.[61] In response to a number of recommendations and critical judgments by several human rights bodies, Turkey has enacted regulations containing a number of guidelines on the use of tear gas during protests. As a general principle, police should avoid the use of tear gas unless there is actual aggression or physical resistance to their lawful acts, and stop using gas when such opposition ends.[62]

This general framework must of course be adjusted to the particular features that characterize a protest taking place in the context of an armed conflict or cases of internal violence or occupation. It cannot be underestimated that in a general ambience of political tension the probability that protesters turn violent and undertake harmful actions is very high. Protesters may also very frequently carry weapons for self-defence and be organized in their actions against the State agents. Fighters might take advantage of the situation of disturbances to infiltrate peaceful protesters and attack members of the security forces. Sometimes they can also be voluntarily uncovered by the crowd.

[59] Basic Principle no. 9 BPUFF.

[60] A/HRC/RES/25/38, 25 March 2014, §14.

[61] The use of riot control agents as a method of warfare is prohibited. Tear gas may be nevertheless used in law enforcement operations, including during a situation of armed conflict. See Art. II(9)(d) of the 1993 Convention, affirmed by ECtHR, *Ali Güneş v Turkey*, Judgment, 10 April 2012, §37 and *Abdullah Yaşa and Others v Turkey*, Judgment, 16 July 2013, §§48–51.

[62] HRW, 'Turkey: End Incorrect, Unlawful Use of Teargas', 17 July 2013; <http://www.hrw.org/news/2013/07/16/turkey-end-incorrect-unlawful-use-teargas>.

THE LAW ENFORCEMENT MODEL

In some circumstances doubts may arise as to whether HRL is the more suitable applicable legal regime for national authorities facing a situation that poses a great threat to national security. Since the purpose of human rights rules is to protect individuals from State abuse of power, they take a very 'protective' stand for protesters. HRL contains no rules that either define or distinguish civilians from combatants and other military targets as such, much less allow a civilian to be lawfully attacked during military operations. On the contrary, the right to protest must be facilitated and the use of firearms must be considered only as a last resort. Furthermore, requirements for the lawful use of potentially lethal force are quite stringent in the light of human rights case law.[63] Security forces must try *in primis* to arrest those who commit criminal acts but are not threatening the life or limb of others. Only violent protesters or those who are suspected to have committed offences or resist authority can be legally detained.[64] In addition, under HRL 'collateral damage' is rarely a lawful outcome of a law enforcement operation.

Instead, under IHL the State may adopt a 'reactive' mode in the conduct of the hostilities. In an armed conflict potentially lethal force may be used against 'military objectives' which includes not only 'enemy' combatants (in an international armed conflict) or members of the opposed armed group (in a non-international armed conflict) but also civilians who have lost protection because they are taking a direct part in hostilities.[65] These persons can be targeted, possibly regardless of whether they can be captured or arrested. The resulting civilian casualties may be assumed to be a lawful 'collateral' consequence of the hostilities provided that the operation fulfils the test of proportionality, i.e. in the light of the military advantage anticipated from the attack.[66] National authorities may also have broader discretion in the power to detain civilians on security grounds.[67]

Under HRL law the meaning of 'arbitrary killings' depends on whether the deprivation of the right to life or other injury takes place as a consequence of the conduct of hostilities or a law enforcement operation.[68] IHL leaves States a broader leeway allowing as lawful acts of war or otherwise lawful deprivations of life,[69] the targeting of combatants, fighters, and civilians taking direct part in hostilities.[70]

[63] Nevertheless in the interpretation of the principles of necessity and proportionality the ECtHR commonly takes into account the situation of violence and the circumstances that surrounded the event that provoked the resort to lethal force by part of the State agents.

[64] See HRC, *Guerrero v Colombia*, Comm. no. 45/1979, 5 February 1979, §13.3.

[65] See Art. 3 IVCG and Arts 51(3) API and 13(3) AP II.

[66] See Art. 57 API and Arts 48-51 AP I.

[67] See Arts 42 and 78 IV CG. But see the chapter in this volume on detention by Alex Conte.

[68] Human Rights Committee, General Comment no. 29 (2001).

[69] According to Art. 15(2) ECHR, no derogation from Art. 2 (right to life) is allowed except in respect of deaths resulting from lawful acts of war.

[70] The notion of direct participation in hostilities refers to conduct which, if carried out by civilians, suspends their protection against the dangers arising from military operations. Derived from Art. 3

Indeed, requirements for the use of potentially deadly force outside a situation of open hostilities are much stricter. Under Basic Principle 9 of the BPUFF, potentially lethal force may only be used in self-defence or in response to an imminent threat to life or serious injury.[71] This means that firearms cannot be used with the purpose of dispersing protests or with the sole scope of protecting property from acts of vandalism.[72] Internal political instability or any other public emergency may not be invoked to justify 'special use-of-force regimes' or any departure from these basic principles or to shelter national authorities from observing due diligence in the policing of protests.[73] Particularly, the involvement of the army or deployment of military units in support of law enforcement operations does not alter these limits or change the constraints on the use of lethal force while policing protests.

Human rights case law shows that, in practice, violations of other fundamental rights in particular the right to life during the policing of protests often occur due to the lack of adequate domestic legislation regulating the use of force in accordance with international standards.[74] Likewise, in many cases, operational rules and regulations are not sufficiently precise or do not include clear guidance on how to escalate the use of force according to the different settings.[75] Operational planning and procedures may aim to curb rather than facilitate protests and therefore allow greater discretion for members of the security forces to resort to lethal force when violence breaks out.[76] Lack of an appropriate legislative framework coupled with shortcomings in the organization and preparation of a policing operation and lack of training of law-enforcement personnel may end up with the life of demonstrators being endangered.[77] Likewise, lack of adequate equipment is a challenging and concerning issue since 'police who do not have protective gear will, understandably, resort more easily to the use of lethal force or firearms to defend themselves'.[78] In the policing of protests decisions need to be taken on the spot: this requires specific training in the policing of riots and violent protests as well as clear and specific operational protocols with instructions on the gradual escalation in the use of force.[79]

common to the Geneva Conventions and present in many other provisions, no definition is provided by any IHL instrument. Melzer, N., 2009, 'Interpretative Guidance on the Notion of Direct Participation in Hostilities', ICRC, p. 12.

[71] Art. 2(a) and (c) ECHR. [72] A/HRC/26/36, 1 April 2014, §72.

[73] Basic Principle no. 8 BPUFF. A/HRC/17/28, 23 May 2011, §95.

[74] Basic Principles nos. 1 and 11 BPUFF. IACtHR, *Nadege Dorzema and others v Dominican Republic*, 24 October 2012, §80.

[75] A/HRC/26/36, 1 April 2014, §47.

[76] IACtHR, *Caracazo Case. Reparations*, Judgment of 29 August 2002, Series C. N. 95, §127.

[77] ECtHR, *Giuliani and Gaggio v Italy*, Judgment, Grand Chamber, 24 March 2011, Joint Partially Dissenting Opinion of Judges Rozakis, Tulkens, Zupančič, Gyulumyan, Ziemele, Kalaydjieava and Karakaş, §§12 and 18.

[78] A/HRC/17/28, 23 May 2011, §104. IACHR, 'Report on Citizen Security and Human Rights', OEA/Ser.L/V/II. Doc. 57 31 December 2009, §193.

[79] See, e.g., the 'Manual de Derecho Operational' of Colombia (2009).

When the situation poses a great threat to national security there is a risk that a loose interpretation of standards on the use of force in order to justify resort to lethal force be implemented. The adoption of military tactics by the police or the engagement of the army in law enforcement may constitute the first step in that direction. Military forces may be called to assist the police in performing law enforcement tasks; this supporting role is foreseen by a number of domestic laws. However, it is a matter of fact that soldiers are usually trained to use immediate lethal force when facing a military objective and frequently are not adequately equipped to perform law enforcement tasks.[80] On top of that, armed forces do not always have clear procedures as to when they are allowed to use deadly force and on the modalities of intervention during protests.[81]

Whilst the engagement of the military in response to a protest might be exceptional in peacetime, in a war-like situation or occupation this situation can be much more common. The risk of unlawful and excessive use of lethal force against protesters might be exacerbated if soldiers do not conform to law enforcement standards nor are properly trained and equipped for crowd control.[82] As has been observed, placing combat-ready soldiers in such highly volatile environments without law enforcement training and crowd control devices is a 'recipe for disaster'.[83]

DISTINCTION BETWEEN PEACEFUL, VIOLENT, AND ARMED PROTESTS

In practice, the fact that human rights treaties specifically refer to 'peaceful' assemblies constitutes an important constraint for the correct application of human rights' standards on the use of force to protests.[84] On this basis, States have frequently advanced the

[80] A/HRC/17/28, 23 May 2011, §104. IACHR, 'Report on Citizen Security and Human Rights', OEA/Ser.L/V/II. Doc. 57 31 December 2009, §99. Likewise, armed forces are not well suited to policing peaceful protests. Units not specifically trained or equipped to intervene in law enforcement should only exceptionally be involved in the task of policing non-peaceful protests.

[81] A best practice in this regard has been followed by some countries in establishing specifically in national laws the specific cases and circumstances where soldiers may intervene in support of police. See, e.g., the Mexican Law: Ley que regula el uso de la fuerza de los cuerpos de seguridad pública del Distrito Federal (2008); <http://www.aldf.gob.mx/>.

[82] The Inter-American Court of Human Rights has recalled that 'states must restrict to the maximum extent the use of armed forces to control domestic disturbances, since they are trained to fight against enemies and not to protect and control civilians, a task that is typical of police forces'. IACtHR, *Montero-Aranguren and others (Detention Center of Catia) v Venezuela*, Judgment, 5 July 2006, §78. Ibid., §§17–18 and 40.

[83] HRW, 'Violent response: the US Army in Al-Falluja', June 2003, <http://www.hrw.org/reports/2003/iraqfalluja/iraqfalluja.pdf>.

[84] The direct consequence of the requirement of peaceful assembly is the prohibition to carry arms, weapons or any weapon-like designed instrument during a demonstration or a public assembly. This is

argument that 'violent' or even peaceful but 'non-authorized' protests are not protected.[85] This approach has led to the misunderstanding that security forces have a broader leeway during the policing of such situations to use force against persons attending unlawful events as well as in the use of deadly force against those who are engaged in violent or hostile actions. This reasoning does not conform to the spirit and object of human rights treaties.

As a general rule, peaceful protesters are fully protected by HRL. A protest must be presumed to be peaceful if its organizers have professed their peaceful intentions and the conduct of the assembly is non-violent.[86] Protesters cannot be deprived of their right to peaceful assembly as a result of sporadic violence or other punishable acts committed by others in the course of a demonstration.[87] Peaceful protests have been defined as those that are not violent, and where participants have peaceful intentions and respect the rights of other persons or groups of persons.[88] When a protester bears arms or weapons capable of causing indiscriminate damage and casualties, it can be presumed that he or she has no peaceful intentions.[89]

Under a number of national laws carrying objects that could be used as weapons in the area where the demonstration is taking place is prohibited. For example, Article 23 of the Turkish Law No. 2911 of 6 October 1983, 'on Meetings and Demonstrations Law' prohibits 'the possession of weapons or explosives, sharp objects, stones, sticks, iron or plastic bars, metal ropes or chains that can cause injuries or be used to strangle, toxic substances that can burn, corrode or injure, or any other poisonous substances or smoke, gas and other similar substances'.[90] The violation of this law renders the protest illegal, which is the precondition for dispersal.[91]

endorsed in many national constitutions and laws by explicitly requiring that this right should be exercised without recourse to 'arms' or the use of 'weapons'.

[85] In part, this argument is based on a misleading understanding of the statements of some human rights bodies. See A/HRC/22/28, 21 January 2013, §10. There is also a worrying tendency in national legislation and police practice to assimilate non-authorized (or unlawful) protests to violent protests. See 'Protocolos para el mantenimiento del orden público', Chile, 25 July 2014. <http://www.indh.cl/wp-content/uploads/2014/08/PROTOCOLO-PARA-EL-MANTENIMIENTO-DELORDEN-PUBLICO.pdf.>

[86] Unless there are compelling and demonstrable evidences that the organizers or participants intend to use, advocate, or incite imminent violence. OSCE ODIHR, 2010, *Guidelines on Freedom of Peaceful Assembly*, Warsaw, §25.

[87] A/HRC/RES/25/38, 28 March 2014.

[88] OSCE ODIHR, 2010, *Guidelines on Freedom of Peaceful Assembly*, Warsaw §72; IAComHR, 'Citizens Security and Human Rights', §194.

[89] The concept of civilian set in common Art. 3 IV GC implies that the individuals do not bear arms on behalf of a party to the conflict. ICRC Guidance, p. 28, referring to the Commentary on the IV GC.

[90] Max Plank Institute for Comparative Public and International Law, 2014, 'Comparative Study: Freedom of Peaceful Assembly in Europe', March, p. 67. In other cases, this prohibition is not absolute. For example, the Federal Act on Assemblies and the corresponding Land laws allows the participants of demonstrations to carry arms following prior authorization of the competent authorities.

[91] Arts 23–4, Turkish Law on Meetings and Demonstrations. Under French legislation, participation in an '*attroupement*' likely to disrupt public order constitutes a misdemeanour and the crowd can therefore be dispersed. Once legal warnings have been made to the demonstrators, it is an offence to continue participating in that crowd. Penal Code, Vol. IV–Offences against the Nation, the State and public peace,

Though organizers may have professed non-peaceful intentions a protest does not become violent until a confrontation between the participants and the security forces or among counter-demonstrators actually breaks out. Isolated acts of violence committed by others do not deprive peaceful individuals of their rights. The mere presence of 'combatants' or 'fighters' within the crowd does not automatically render the whole crowd to be treated as 'armed' or 'violent'. In order to qualify a protest as violent in its whole a significant percentage of the protesters should engage in violent actions or behave or demonstrate in any other way a violent attitude or intention.[92]

The fact that an individual or some individuals may be armed with weapons does not mean to automatically treat whole protest as 'violent'. Protesters may, for example, be carrying traditional arms (i.e. spears or machetes) or home-made tools with the only intention of using them in self-defence or to defend the others from possible unlawful aggressions.[93] Under such circumstances 'armed' crowd is not necessary equal to a 'violent' crowd. Conversely, a protest where protesters throw stones or 'Molotov' cocktails at the security forces could be rightly qualified as a 'violent' protest but not as an 'armed' one.[94]

Instead, when a number of protesters bear arms and proactively use them against the security forces the protest may well be qualified as an 'armed' protest. The characterization of a protest as armed may be indicative of the violent intentions of some protesters and also shows that there might be some kind of coordination and previous planning of the hostile actions. However, an 'armed crowd' is not synonymous with 'armed group' under IHL or domestic criminal law. Particularly, violent acts committed in the course of protests may only be prosecuted as acts of terrorism when they meet the legal requirements of such a qualified crime. Human rights bodies are concerned by the fact that many countries use anti-terrorism laws and related legislation against participants of demonstrations and in a discriminatory way to curtail political dissidence. In past years, the UN Special Rapporteur on the promotion and protection of human rights and fundamental freedoms while countering terrorism has urged States to refrain from applying anti-terrorism legislation in connection with protests.[95]

Title III–Offences against the authority of the State, Chap. I–Breaches of public peace, Sect. 2–Criminal involvement in a crowd, Art. 431-3.

[92] Costas Trascasas, M. and Casey-Maslen, S., 'Facilitating Peaceful Protests', p. 18.

[93] See AI: 'Peru: Five years on from Bagua violence and still no justice for victims', 5 June 2014; <https://www.amnesty.org/en/articles/news/2014/06/peru-five-years-bagua-violence-and-still-no-justice-victims/>.

[94] The ECtHR qualified as violent an unauthorized demonstration where demonstrators had thrown stones at law enforcement officers. *Abdullah Yaşa et autres v. Turquie*, Judgment, 16 July 2013, §41. During demonstrations in the Gaza Strip the army normally responds to protesters and stone-throwers with live firing. These events raise a grave suspicion of illegal and unjustified use of live ammunition when soldiers were in no danger whatsoever. See <http://www.btselem.org/press_releases/20120405_live_ammunition_on_demonstrators_in_gaza>.

[95] 'UN expert urges Chile to stop using anti-terrorism legislation and to adopt national strategy to address the Mapuche question'; <http://www.ohchr.org/EN/NewsEvents/Pages/DisplayNews.aspx?NewsID=13599&LangID=E#sthash.HkHtESsD.dpuf>.

The conflation of all these different categories is often abused by national authorities to justify arbitrary detention of otherwise peaceful protesters as well as the use of lethal force against persons not representing a real and imminent threat to the lives of others. In fact, labelling protestors as 'criminals', 'fighters', or 'terrorists' is often a political device to make dissenters or opponents appear as legitimate targets in the public eye.[96]

CAN VIOLENT ACTIVITIES BE CONSIDERED AS DIRECT PARTICIPATION IN THE HOSTILITIES?

Arguably, under the conduct of hostilities model when protesters engage in certain types of hostile acts they might lose the protective benefits pertaining to peaceable civilians.[97] In the *Tablada* case the Inter-American Commission on Human Rights said that 'specifically, when civilians ... assume the role of combatants by directly taking part in fighting, whether singly or as a member of a group, they thereby become legitimate military targets. As such, they are subject to direct individualized attack to the same extent as combatants'.[98]

Civilians can therefore sometimes lose the protection against attack afforded by IHL rules. According to the ICRC 'Interpretative Guidance on Direct Participation in Hostilities', under certain circumstances civilians could be targeted as if they were combatants, i.e., 'at all times and in all places' if they participate directly in hostilities and are members of an armed group who have a 'continuous combat function'. However, a given act only amounts to 'direct participation in hostilities' if it causes directly a certain threshold of harm and is specifically designed to support the military operations of one party to the detriment of the other party.[99]

In the light of this, it could be questioned whether the actions of protesters may be legally assimilated to 'direct participation in the hostilities' in accordance with IHL. Hypothetically, the targeting of protesters with potentially lethal force could only be justified if a single conduct fulfils these conditions, i.e., provided that the protester is a member of an armed group performing a function (not necessarily as a combatant) for a sufficient time as to provide a substantial support to one party. But the likelihood that circumstances allow for legally 'shooting-to-kill' a protester would be fairly exceptional under the rule of law, as will be explained.

[96] See A/HRC/17/28, 23 May 2011, §25. [97] See Art. 13(3) of AP II.

[98] IAComHR, *Juan Carlos Abella v Argentina (The Tablada case)*, Case no. 11.137, Report no. 55/87, 30 October 1997, §178.

[99] ICRC/N. Melzer, 'Interpretative Guidance on the Notion of Direct Participation in Hostilities', ICRC, 2009 (hereafter ICRC Guidance).

It is true that facts are often blurred complicating the decision over the most adequate model of use of force to be applied. In the context of anti-governmental protests a crowd may collectively engage in violent acts and systematically provoke violent actions against the security forces. Contemporary protests may be well organized and planned or have a protracted nature.[100] In some instances, clashes between protesters and security forces may reach a high threshold of harm and level of violence, sometimes comparable to that derived from belligerent hostilities. This may include looting, clashes, and exchange of fire with the security forces, damage to the property, the blocking of roads leading to a strategically important area and threat to the lives of others.

But despite the damage provoked, for such actions to amount to direct participation in hostilities typically they must be of a military or military-like nature. Further, they must be specifically designed to support a party to an armed conflict 'by directly causing the required threshold of harm to another party'. Moreover, it must be demonstrated that there is a connection between confrontations and hostile activities occurring during a protest with the ongoing armed hostilities.[101]

The so-called 'belligerent nexus' will be clearly lacking in most cases when those protesting seek first and foremost to express their dissatisfaction with the territorial or detaining authorities. Violent actions that may break out commonly have an isolated and sporadic character and unlike, military operations, do not use to be 'carefully planned, coordinated and executed' nor specifically designed to support one of the party in detriment to the other. Consequently, such actions of protest do not meet the requirements of direct participation in hostilities.[102] In fact, it seems that in the more likely scenario the contribution of a specific hostile action taking place in the course of a protest to a 'party' (be that the belligerent party or the organized armed group) will be in most cases rather indirect and with a limited military impact.[103]

[100] In the Occupied Palestinian Territory, peaceful demonstrations against occupation and continued illegal land acquisitions resulting from a policy of settlement expansion have been hold systematically for years. Dinstein, Y., *Non-international Armed Conflicts in International* Law, §106.

[101] ICRC Guidance, pp. 61–3 and p. 64.

[102] In the *Tablada* case, which involved an attack by a group of civilians against a military barracks in Argentina, the Inter-American Commission on Human Rights reached the conclusion that the events constituted a non-international armed conflict. The Commission said that 'what happened there was not equivalent to large scale violent demonstrations, students throwing stones at the police, all forms of domestic violence not qualifying as armed conflicts'. *Juan Carlos Abella v Argentina (La Tablada)*, Inter-American Commission on Human Rights, Case no. 11.137, Report no. 55/87, 30 October 1997.

[103] According to the ICRC Guidance, 'Civil unrest may well result in death, injury and destruction and, ultimately, may even benefit the general war effort of a party. Likewise, the use of armed force by civilian authorities to prevent looting and maintain law and order in a conflict area may cause death and injury, but generally it would not constitute part of the hostilities conducted between parties to an armed conflict'. ICRC Guidance, p. 63.

Similarly, extending the notion of 'combat function' to protesters would be problematic from a human rights perspective.[104] In fact, this category leaves open the likelihood of using lethal force against civilians 'all the time' on the basis of a diluted interpretation of the existing standards regarding the direct participation in hostilities.[105] In light of the previous criteria it is generally admitted that persons who engage in sporadic or episodic direct participation (and may only be attached during their participation) or have a general war support function or form the political wing of an organized group, cannot be considered as legitimate targets of violence under IHL.[106]

Protests are certainly political activities that might contribute to the general war effort and sometimes have an impact on the military capacity. Protesters may contribute to undermine the territorial authority and control of another party and may generally support the war effort through 'political pressure, economic insecurity, destruction and disorder violent actions'. But despite this such activities cannot be legally qualified as 'direct participation in hostilities'. Particularly, there are no legal grounds or arguments supporting the idea that protesters' actions may fall within the notion of 'combat'.[107]

By definition, the scope of IHL rules related to the conduct of hostilities cannot be extended to persons that are not directly participating in such events by undertaking hostile, organized, and armed activities aimed at directly damaging and weakening the 'enemy' or the 'counterpart' in military terms. The general rule that emerges is that the mere fact of participating in a protest, even when engaging in violent acts, cannot be regarded as individual conduct that constitutes part of the hostilities in support of one party. Thus, as a matter of law enforcement, an escalation procedure in the use of force must be followed. Persons can only be intentionally targeted with potentially lethal force at the moment they are committing an act that poses an imminent threat to the lives of others. These rules should apply 'by default': in case of doubt, the most protective position for the person should be taken.[108]

[104] According to the Guidance 'under IHL, the decisive criterion for individual membership in an organized armed group is whether a person assumes a continuous function for the group involving his or her direct participation in hostilities'. Individuals whose continuous function involves the preparation, execution, or command of acts or operations amounting to direct participation in hostilities are assuming a continuous combat function. ICRC Guidance, pp. 33 and 34.

[105] A/HRC/14/24/Add.6, 28 May 2010, §65.

[106] A/HRC/14/24/Add.6, §66.

[107] Particularly, the use of force by civilians to defend themselves against unlawful violence lacks belligerent nexus. Similarly, the use of armed forces by security forces to suppress riots and other forms of civil unrest would not constitute part of the hostilities. Therefore, the use of necessary and proportionate force in such situations cannot be regarded as direct participation in hostilities. ICRC Guidance, p. 63.

[108] At least where the State operates in its own territory or territory in which it effectively exercises authority. Experts Meeting, CUDH-UCHL 'Expert Meeting on the right to life in armed conflicts and situations of occupation' (hereafter Experts Meeting), 1–2 September 2005, p 40; <http//www.geneva-academy.ch/docs/expert-meetings/2005/3ra$ort_droit_vie.pdf> p. 40.

USE OF LETHAL FORCE AGAINST PROTESTERS

Increasingly, national laws and practices endorse policies that suggest that the use of lethal force might sometimes not be the last resort. Sometimes national laws practically provide police and armed forces with a 'licence to kill'.[109] Common expressions such as 'shoot-to-kill', 'shoot on sight', or ordering to use the 'utmost force' exemplify this approach. In many cases States distort the magnitude of the threat to be faced in order to justify the application of the looser IHL standards on targeting in situations that are essentially matters of law enforcement. In this regard the UN Special Rapporteur on extrajudicial, summary, or arbitrary executions has noted that 'shoot-to-kill' policies violate human rights law: 'under human rights law, a targeted killing in the sense of an intentional, premeditated and deliberate killing by law enforcement officials cannot be legal because, unlike in armed conflict, it is never permissible for killing to be the sole objective of an operation'.[110]

When 'combatants' or 'fighters' infiltrate the crowd and are intermingled in the protest with civilians this conclusion could be challenged.[111] They can be proactively engaged in acts of open hostility with the security forces while taking advantage of the crowd acting as 'human shields'.[112] Could this hypothetical situation temporarily activate IHL rules on targeting with regard to certain individuals? According to the rules on the conduct of hostilities this is possible in principle: a fighter could be legitimately targeted at any moment. However, the fact that he or she be intermingled with civilians, who are protected under IHL, may lead to a different conclusion in the light of the core rule of proportionality.[113] In fact, unlawful use of civilians as human shields does not generally affect the other side's obligation to ensure that attacks do not cause civilian casualties in excess of the anticipated military advantage of killing the targeted fighter.[114]

While under the conduct of hostilities model the use of lethal force against legitimate targets is the rule, under the human rights framework, it is the exception. The State's

[109] E/CN.4/2006/53, 8 March 2006, §46. In Peru, for example, a law that entered into force in January 2014 grants exemption from criminal liability to law enforcement personnel, including the military, 'who cause injury or death in the performance of their duties through the use of service weapons or any other means'. See 'Ley que modifica el inciso 11 del artículo 20 del Código Penal, referido al uso de armas u otro medio de defensa por personal de las fuerzas armadas y de la policía nacional del Perú'. Ley no. 30151, 12 January 2014; <http://www2.congreso.gob.pe>.

[110] A/HRC/14/24/Add.6, 28 May 2010, §33.

[111] While in an IAC members of the enemy armed forces and members of organized resistance movements fulfilling the requirements of Art. 4(A)(2) GC III can be targeted on sight and on the basis of their combatant status alone, in a NIAC rebel fighters cannot be targeted simply for the fact of being members of a rebel group and on the basis of their previous involvement in hostilities; instead, they should be arrested. A similar solution should be applied in cases of occupation where former members of the armed forces of the occupied country may be interned. Expert Meeting, pp. 18 and 23.

[112] See Art. 28 GC IV; Art. 52(7) AP I.

[113] See Art. 51(2), 52–6 P I; Art. 85(3) P I; Art. 13 P II.

[114] Arts 51(7) and 50(3) AP I.

duty to protect the right to life allows for very few exceptions.[115] Lethal force is the last resort and must be 'absolutely necessary'.[116] Human rights law only permits its use when it is strictly necessary in self-defence or to protect the lives of others against 'the imminent threat of death or serious injury'.[117] Thus, the only grounds allowing the police to use firearms or other potentially lethal force against protesters is to save the lives of other persons against lawless violence. Any other grounds such as protection of public buildings or property against widespread looting are not admissible. Shooting a person who is not posing any more danger to the life or limb of others such as an unarmed or defenceless person or someone who has surrendered, would amount to a violation of the right to life.[118]

Before resorting to firearms non-lethal tactics must be attempted and exhausted if feasible. Where possible, security forces must provide warnings, give suspects the opportunity to surrender and employ force in a differentiated and graduate manner. An immediate resort to lethal force may be required however in pressing circumstances when strictly unavoidable to prevent an even greater loss of life.[119] Preventive measures aimed at minimizing the consequences of the use of firearms or other potentially lethal means should be adopted. Particularly important is that national authorities ensure that medical assistance is available.[120]

Proportionality requires that use of force be proportionate to the risk that the targeted person poses to others.[121] Moderation in the use of force implies that a balance must be achieved between the aim pursued and the means employed to achieve it.

[115] For an overview of the most preeminent case law see Casey-Maslen, S., 2014, 'Crowd Management, Crowd Control, and Riot Control'. In *Weapons under International Human Rights Law*, edited by Casey-Maslen, S., Cambridge, pp. 53–79.

[116] *McCann and Others v United Kingdom*, Judgment, 27 September 1995, §149.

[117] Basic Principle no. 9 BPUFF. Ibid., 'The guiding principle in respect of the lethal use of firearms is defence of one's own life or that of others', §60.

[118] IAComHR, *Carandiru* Case 11.291, Report no. 34/00 Brazil, 13 April 2000, §67.

[119] For example, when the criminal is already in the process or visibly on the verge of using a weapon, there can be little doubt regarding the inevitability of violence if immediate recourse to lethal force is not taken. E/CN.4/2006/53, 8 March 2006, §§48–49.

[120] Basic Principle no. 5 BPUFF. The ECtHR case law has clearly established in this regard that not providing adequate medical service or impeding the access to those services to attend those after the use of lethal force will amount to a violation of the right and ultimately to a breach of the positive obligations derived from the obligation to protect the right to life. ECtHR, *Giuliani and Gaggio v Italy*, Judgement, Grand Chamber, 24 March 2011, §251; *Ergi v Turkey*, 28 July 1998, §79; See also *Finogenov & Others v Russia*, 20 December 2011, §266. The Court has said that it would be desirable at least to have the presence of first-aid services at the site of demonstrations.

[121] In reference to Israeli security forces response to stone-throwing by Palestinian youths, the Special Rapporteur has observed that: 'the plausibility of the use of firearms in self-defence or the defence of others against the imminent threat of death or serious injury is questionable in many of the cases involving Palestinians exercising their right to peaceful protest'. A/HRC/28/78, 22 January 2015, §43. The Israel Government admitted that civilians were killed during violent clashes between Palestinians and Israeli security forces in the course of which Israel Defence Forces soldiers were subject to severe acts of violence, including the throwing of stones, Molotov cocktails, and improvised explosives. Ibid., §47.

Particularly, when resorting to self-defence as a justification of the use of lethal force, a careful assessment on the threat posed by the targeted protestor and the suitability of the arms used to effectively create an imminent danger to the lives of the others must be done.[122] Protesters may in some cases carry arms or weapons for example with the aim of defending themselves against the likelihood of being the object of unlawful use of force from the security forces.

In a context of armed conflict or occupation, the chances of excessive and indiscriminate use of lethal force are multiplied, particularly due to the normal involvement of armed forces units in law enforcement tasks and the likelihood that security forces will be armed routinely.[123] While repressing the civil uprising of January 2011 Libyan security forces used fighter jets and live ammunition against protesters in the capital. Mortar and artillery shelling was also used in operations to quell demonstrations. Authorities disputed these claims, explaining that there were ammunition dumps in remote areas away from residential areas.[124] Referring to the means used by the Yemeni Government against demonstrators in 2011, the OHCHR said that 'there can be no justification for the hasty resort to excessive use of lethal force and heavy weaponry, including the deployment of tank in cities, to quell street demonstrations or to clear out sit-ins'.[125]

Lethal force must be specifically targeted to the person that is actually posing a threat to the life of the others. Shooting indiscriminately into a crowd or shooting-to-kill unarmed protesters not representing such a threat is manifestly unlawful.[126] Resorting to weapons (e.g., automatic or semi-automatic arms) that do not allow discrimination between violent and non-violent protesters should not be permitted. Likewise, it is unlawful to use heavy combat weapons to repress a peaceful protest, particularly if they take place in a populated area.[127]

Even when an operation involves the use of lethal force by the security forces, it remains that the aim of the operation is to protect lives from unlawful violence. Police action must always seek to reduce to a minimum personal injury and the loss of human life and take appropriate care to ensure that any risk of life is minimized

[122] In the *Carandiru* case, related to the repression of a riot in Brazil, the IAComHR noted that the deaths 'did not take place in situations of self-defense or to disarm the inmates since the prisoners' weapons were of the homemade variety and had been thrown down on to the patio when the police entered. No firearms were found in the possession of the rioters nor had any shots been fired against the police. Their initially violent attitude was quickly overcome by the entry en masse of the heavily armed police'. IAComHR, *Carandiru* Case 11.291, Report no. 34/00 Brazil, 13 April 2000, §63.

[123] The use of firearms in the policing of peaceful protest should be generally prohibited by domestic laws.

[124] A/HRC/21/50, 15 August 2012, §22 and 90.

[125] A/HRC/18/21, §78.

[126] A/HRC/RES/25/38, 28 March 2014, OP.11. In Syria, according to individual testimonies, State forces shot indiscriminately at unarmed protesters. Most were shot in the upper body, including in the head. Defectors from military and security forces received orders to shoot at unarmed protesters without warning. A/HRC/S-17/2/Add.1, 23 November 2011, §§41 and 43.

[127] ECtHR, *Isayeva v Russia*, 24 February 2005, §191.

and that the choice of action is not made in a negligent manner.[128] The use of tanks and helicopters, for example, to fire on non-violent demonstrators constitutes an unlawful and unnecessary use of force.[129] Massive use of indiscriminate weapons will stand in flagrant contrast with the principle of distinction and proportionality and cannot be considered compatible with the standard of care required in a law enforcement operation. In the case *Isayeva v Russia*, for example, the ECtHR considered that using bombs and other non-guided heavy combat weapons in a populated area, outside wartime, and without prior evacuation of the civilians, is impossible to reconcile with law-enforcement standards.[130]

The lack of adequate means does not justify resorting to weapons that may lead to disproportionate victims, damages, or results. In this sense, it is regrettable that too often a resort to firearms is made because police are not equipped with any alternatives as to gradually increase the level of force. In a case on Turkey, the ECtHR found that the right to life of a demonstrator was violated due to the use of a very powerful weapon because the police apparently did not have other less-lethal means. The Court said that the lack of such equipment was all the more incomprehensible and unacceptable in the light of the circumstances of the case since the state of emergency had been declared in the region and therefore, disorders should have been expected to happen.[131]

C. **Right to protest in occupied territories**

Many of the previous considerations must be extended to cases where protests take place in the context of occupation where the exercise of right to freedom of assembly, is commonly restricted.[132] According to Article 43 of the 1907 Hague Regulations the occupying power is responsible for administering the local life of the population under its control, and for providing security. This includes the adoption of any measures 'to restore, and ensure, as far as possible, public order

[128] ECtHR, *Giuliani and Gaggio v Italy*, Grand Chamber, 24 March 2011, §249. *Isayeva v Russia*, 24 February 2005, §181.

[129] HRW, 'End unlawful use of force against civilians in Gaza', 20 May 2004; <http://electronicintifada.net/content/end-unlawful-use-force-against-civilians-gaza/1672>.

[130] 'The massive use of indiscriminate weapons stands in flagrant contrast with this aim and cannot be considered compatible with the standard of care prerequisite to an operation of this kind involving the use of lethal force by State agents'. *Isayeva v Russia*, 24 February 2005, §191.

[131] ECtHR, *Güleç v Turkey*, Judgment, 27 July 1998, §§71 and 73. The police were apparently not equipped with 'less-lethal' weapons, deployed two armoured vehicles, and fired bullets at the crowd.

[132] ACLU, 'Take back the streets. Repression and criminalization of protests around the world', p. 11; <https://www.aclu.org/sites/default/files/field_document/global_protest_su§ression_report_inclo.pdf>.

and safety, while respecting, unless absolutely prevented, the laws in force in the country'.[133]

Such an obligation comprises the duty to secure respect for the applicable rules of HRL and IHL, to protect the inhabitants of the occupied territory against acts of violence, and not to tolerate such violence by any third party.[134] Where absolutely necessary to restore and maintain public order the occupying power may suspend any former law that may 'affect its own security'.[135] Protests or riots may pose a significant threat to the security of the occupying power particularly when violent clashes occur and public order may be a valid ground for limiting some rights, including the right of public assembly.[136]

The responsibility to maintain security and order may include the use of force. Again, any use of force in circumstances outside combat, whether by soldiers or police officers, must be consistent with international law enforcement standards, i.e., does not allow targeting civilians deliberately and requires minimizing harm.[137] The mere use of military force by the occupied power to control violence does not allow equating such violence to armed hostilities. As has been observed in a 'calm' situation the occupying power 'cannot simply conduct a military operation, create hostilities, and then claim that the rules of IHL now govern'.[138] Where faced with riots and ordinary criminal activity, the occupying power must respond in accordance with the law enforcement model. As recalled by Human Rights Watch in the context of the US-led military occupation of Iraq, 'the hostile environment and risk of attacks opposed to the occupation does not absolve the military from its obligations to use force in a restrained, proportionate and discriminate manner, and only when strictly necessary'.[139]

Recent practice shows that situations of occupation nearly always encompass a challenging security situation that may be addressed by the occupying power by enacting

[133] Art. 43 of the 1907 Hague Regulations. The occupying power has the obligation to abolish any legislation which contravene IHR standards and to replace it by additional legislation aimed at genuinely protecting human rights. See Sassòli, M., 2005, 'Legislation and Maintenance of Public Order and Civil Life by Occupying Powers', *The European Journal of International Law*, vol. 16, no. 4, pp. 676–7.

[134] ICJ, *Armed Activities on the Territory of the Congo (Democratic Republic of Congo (DRC) v Uganda*, Judgment, 19 December 2005, §§205–212.

[135] See, for example, §11.25 of the *UK Joint Service Manual of the Law of Armed Conflict* (2004).

[136] In 2013, for example, more than 60% of injuries occurred in the Gaza Strip resulted from clashes between Palestinian protesters and Israeli forces during demonstrations. Casey-Maslen, S. (ed.), 2014, *The War Report. Armed Conflict in 2013*, Oxford University Press, p. 77.

[137] AI, 'Iraq: Responsibilities of the Occupying Powers,' 15 April 2003, p. 8; <https://www.amnesty.org/en/documents/MDE14/089/2003/en/>.

[138] Experts Meeting p. 27; <http://www.geneva-academy.ch/docs/expert-meetings/2005/3ra§ort_droit_vie.pdf>.

[139] HRW, 2003, *Hearts and Minds: Post-war Civilian Deaths in Bagdad Caused by US Forces*; <http://www.hrw.org/reports/2003/iraq1003/iraq1003full.pdf>.

legislation aimed at curtailing the right to protest. This usually leads to empowering police with excessive powers to prohibit and forcibly break up unauthorized protests. In the Occupied Palestinian Territory excessive use of force is employed to curtail demonstrations that usually are not authorized, due to security or public order reasons or because the organizers simply interpret that asking for a permit amounts to recognizing the authority of the occupying power.[140] Protesters are usually charged with organizing and leading demonstrations without proper military authorization, inciting the demonstrators to harm the security forces or stone throwing.[141] Israeli Military Order No. 101 'Regarding Prohibition of Incitement and Hostile Propaganda Actions', applicable to the West Bank and in force since 27 August 1967, virtually prohibits all protest activity, including vigils, processions, and even personal items expressing a political viewpoint.[142] The order empowers 'any soldier' with the authority 'to use the required degree of force' to enforce this Military Order.[143] In addition, Military Order No. 1651 'Regarding Security Provisions, Consolidated Version' allows the imposition of a closed military zone, thereby declaring a certain area off limits for certain periods of time. Reportedly, this order is often used to deny the right to peacefully demonstrate, or as a pretext to use excessive force to disperse demonstrators.[144]

Also in the context of the US-led military occupation of Iraq in 2003–4, there were allegations of excessive use of force in the response of the coalition to the increasing armed resistance from individuals or small groups protesting against the occupation.[145] According to Amnesty International, the Coalition Provisional Authority reaction to disorder was far from being adequate: 'the occupying powers did not deploy forces in sufficient numbers and with the right training and equipment to restore law and order'.[146]

[140] In Palestine, for example, since 1967, few Palestinians have submitted requests to hold a demonstration as an act of protest against the occupation.

[141] Israel's Knesset Parliament has recently introduced legislation allowing stone-throwers to be sentenced to prison terms of up to twenty years. <http://www.irishtimes.com/news/world/middle-east/stone-throwers-can-be-jailed-for-20-years-under-new-israeli-law-1.2292410>.

[142] Assembly is defined as 'ten or more persons who have gathered in a place in which a speech is being made on a political subject, or which may be construed as political, or to discuss such a subject'; <http://www.btselem.org/download/19670827_order_regarding_prohibition_of_incitement_and_hostile_propaganda.pdf>.

[143] Violations of the order are punished with imprisonment for ten years or a fine of ten thousand liras, or both. The order establishes that a person who violates its provisions shall be liable to ten years' imprisonment, a fine, or both penalties together.

[144] AI, 'Trigger-happy. Israel's use of excessive force in the West Bank', February 2014; <http://www.amnestyusa.org/pdfs/mde150022014en.pdf>.

[145] HRW, 'Violent response: the US Army in Al-Falluja', June 2013, <http://www.hrw.org/reports/2003/iraqfalluja/iraqfalluja.pdf>.

[146] AI, 'Iraq: Responsibilities of the Occupying Powers,' 15 April 2003, p. 8; <https://www.amnesty.org/en/documents/MDE14/089/2003/en/>.

Concluding remarks

The right to protest continues to serve a critical democratic role even in exceptional situations such as armed conflicts or occupation. But despite this, in many countries, protests are systematically banned or otherwise heavy-handedly repressed. National security and public order are often invoked to violently disperse protests, and many domestic laws frequently afford security forces great powers and discretion in the use of force. Police may carry out massive arrests and resort to live ammunition or other unlawful means as a way of deterring protesters. Protesters are often stigmatized, accused, and prosecuted on the basis of criminal law on grounds of terrorism, treason, or even full-scale rebellion.

When protests do take place against the background of armed hostilities or a situation of occupation there are factors that complicate the assessment on the applicable legal framework. Political sensibilities, biased police interventions, resort to armed forces and an ambient of impunity leads to a blurred panorama where it is sometimes difficult to determine the applicable standards. This uncertainty is particularly critical when ambiguities refer to the protection of core rights such as the right to life, the right to liberty and security of the person, the prohibition of torture, or the right to a fair trial.

In the last few years, however, a number of standards have been identified by human rights bodies. The main is the 'protect life principle' advocated by the UN Special Rapporteur on extrajudicial, summary, or arbitrary executions, i.e., that intentional lethal force is only allowed when strictly unavoidable in self-defence or to safeguard another's life. This principle, essential in the law enforcement model, is particularly applicable to the policing of protests, regardless of the context in which they take place. States cannot pretend that deaths taking place outside the conduct of hostilities and not having any *nexus* to the armed operations be considered 'lawful acts of war' or otherwise 'lawful deprivations of the right to life'.

Sporadic or isolated incidents of violence or even clashes or confrontations with the security forces provoking a high threshold of harm may arise during protests, but do not modify the legal regime that is generally applicable to such situations: HRL. For a protest to evolve into real combat operations, calling for the application of IHL rules, violence must surpass a certain degree of intensity and the security forces must face a situation that cannot be addressed as a normal law enforcement operation: because fighters or combatants outnumber the protesters, because they act in an assembled and organized way, and because they undertake military operations or combat actions encompassing the use of armed force.

Civilians may only lose the full protection of IHL for such time as they directly participate in hostilities. Common sense and a teleological interpretation of both HRL and IHL prevents the opening of a door allowing States to include protesters as a new category of people who can be lawfully targeted and killed on sight. IHL cannot offer the legal basis for the systematic harassment and persecution of political dissenters.

10 Youth as main victims and perpetrators of violence: are the mechanisms behind joining 'criminal' gangs similar to those for joining violent extremist groups?

Sylvie Girard[1]

Often, in an attempt to find a sense of identity, . . . children create their own subculture with its own rites of passage into adulthood. The sometimes bizarre array of subcultures to which young people belong is actually a reflection of a deep spiritual impulse that is not being fulfilled by the larger culture. Richard Moss[2]

Introduction

Why discuss youth and violence in a journal dedicated to the study of war? On the one hand, research and the facts on the ground show that urban centres will increasingly become the next battle grounds, with the number of violence-related deaths in some cities far exceeding those of many ongoing civil wars.[3] According to the Geneva

[1] Sylvie Girard is a former ICRC Youth Adviser.

[2] Moss, R., 1986, *The Black Butterfly: An Invitation to Radical Aliveness*, Celestial Arts, Berkeley, California, p. 242.

[3] Muggah, R., 2012, 'Researching the Urban Dilemma: Urbanization, Poverty and Violence', International Development Research Center, Canada (IDRC) and Department for International Development, UK (DFID).

Declaration, 'only one in ten killings is the result of terrorism or armed conflict' and, since 2006, '90% of violent deaths in the world took place outside situations conventionally understood as armed conflict or terrorism'.[4] In the words of Robert Muggah, cities are experiencing 'a "new kind" of armed conflict … a variation of warfare, often in densely populated slums and shantytowns …' featuring 'pitched battles between state and non-state armed groups and among armed groups themselves'. He points out that 'to some analysts, these "other situations of violence" exhibit many of the key characteristics—intensity and organization—of conventional armed conflicts despite not being recognized as such by the international community'. He further argues that 'Military doctrine in a number of developed countries is beginning to reflect the primacy of the urban battlespace as the dominant site and model of conflict in the twenty-first century'.[5] Indeed, the peasant wars of the twentieth century have given way to the urban wars of the twenty-first century as rapid urbanization overtakes the capacity of communities, social organizations, and the State to cope with the massive influx of displaced and marginalized newcomers to the cities' peripheries. As quoted by Hagedorn,[6] journalist Silla Boccanero remarked that 'Until recently, a rebellious youth from Central America would go into the mountains and join the guerrillas. Today, he leaves the countryside for the city and joins one of the street gangs engaged in common crime without political objectives'. Today's conflicts increasingly have social and economic causes: the decay of the social fabric and the loosening of community bonds, together with the concentration of poverty in cities' peripheries. New actors of conflict are complex, varied, and often made up of private individuals, from violence entrepreneurs such as cartels and other forms of mafia organizations, to large groups of children and youth active in armed violence, to administrative remnants of failed States.[7]

Where do youth come in? While children and young people under the age of twenty-five represent close to 50% of the world population, 85% of them live in developing countries, with cities offering a demographic concentration of youth. It is precisely children, adolescents, and young adults who are at the centre of these battles, as both primary victims, perpetrators, and witnesses of violence. According to the World Health Organization,[8] of the total number of homicides that occur worldwide each year, 43%, or some 200,000, occur among youth aged ten to twenty-nine. In all countries, young males are the majority of victims and perpetrators of violence. Rapid and uncontrolled

[4] Geneva Declaration, 2011.

[5] Muggah, R., 2012. 'Urban Violence and Humanitarian Action: Engaging the Fragile City', *The Journal of Humanitarian Assistance*, January 19, p. 1.

[6] Hagedorn, J. M., 2005, 'The Global Impact of Gangs', *Journal of Contemporary Criminal Justice*, Vol. 21, No. 2, May, p. 161.

[7] Badie, B. and O. M., Mohammad-Mahmoud, 'L'insaisissable conflit du XXIème siècle'. In *Le Temps*, 6 May 2014.

[8] WHO, Youth Violence, Fact Sheet No. 356, January 2015.

urbanization is a prime driver for the proliferation of gangs. It is in Latin America, Africa, and Asia, where the most rapid and uncontrolled urbanization has taken place, that the vast majority of youth gangs live. Unsupervised youth living in the streets are at risk of being recruited by criminal groups or by nationalist or religious militias. With youth unemployment reaching epidemic proportions, in certain areas, criminal and armed groups are often young people's main employers. Only a few young people manage to 'mature out' of a gang. Most end up incarcerated or killed.

Young people are not only at the core of urban violence. They are also linked to organized armed violence and armed conflict, including civil conflict. Since the mid-1990s, research on the 'demographic youth bulge'[9] has established a link between high concentrations of unemployed youth and armed conflict. It is reported, for example, that between 1970 and 1999, 80% of civil conflicts occurred in countries where at least 60% of the population were under the age of thirty. Another finding was that 90% of countries with very young structures had autocratic or weak democratic governments at the end of the twentieth century.[10] Today, the greatest 'youth bulges' are found in sub-Saharan Africa, southern Asia, and the Middle East. In the Middle East, where 60% of the population is under twenty-five, civil strife is more likely, especially when large populations of disaffected youth look to extremist interpretations of Islam as alternatives to social mobility. Of the twenty-seven largest 'youth-bulge' societies in the world, thirteen are Muslim.[11]Given the developments of the so-called 'Arab Spring', starting in 2011, these were indeed prescient findings.

Youth, as members of gangs and main victims and perpetrators of violence, are therefore a core component of the dynamics of urban violence. They are also at the centre of movements seeking the radical transformation of societies, often as positive agents of social and political change. Yet they can also be caught up in ideological movements that are prone to extreme forms of violence. Witness the increasing numbers of adolescents from stable, relatively affluent democracies (in Europe, the United States and Canada, Australia, and New Zealand) who are joining the so-called Islamic State (IS) and other extremist organizations in Syria and Iraq to carry out violent acts in the name of an idea or for other motivations.

This chapter will not be looking at the structural or root causes of youth violence and urban violence, as those are already well documented. Neither will it look at interventions around urban renewal, crime prevention, firearm legislation, or macro-level State

[9] Proponents of the 'youth bulge' social theory are Gunnar Heinsohn, Gary Fuller, and Kack A. Goldstone.

[10] Leahy, E., Engelman, R., Gibb Vogel, C., Haddock, S., and Preston, T., 2006, 'The Shape of Things to Come: Why Age Structure Matters to a Safer, More Equitable World'. In *Population Action International*.

[11] Beehner, L., 2007, 'The Effects of 'Youth Bulge' on Civil Conflicts', *Council of Foreign Relations*, 27 April.

interventions. It will instead focus on what humanitarian and development organizations can do, as well as local and international NGOs, along with grassroots associations and civil society, to design projects with and for young people at risk of joining gangs or violent extremist organizations.

To design effective programmes, it is necessary to understand the emotional and cognitive specificities that make adolescents different from both children and adults, therefore justifying tailor-made programming, as well as grappling with the motivations behind youth joining 'criminal' gangs or extremist political groups and movements. Top-down programming designed by adults who think they 'know better', without the active involvement of young people themselves, is doomed to fail.

We will focus on at-risk youth in mainly Latin America and Europe and narrow the age range to that particular period when the adolescent is weighing the pros and cons of joining, roughly between ages ten and eighteen.

We will look at how youth is defined by different humanitarian and development organizations, what it means to be an adolescent, which different push and pull factors are at work in causing young people to join violent groups and which programmes seem to work best and why.

A. **Defining youth**

Youth or the experience of 'being young' is generally considered a time of transition between childhood and adulthood, a time of identity formation when the individual is becoming an independent and socially responsible adult. The age range when this is occurring can vary according to social and cultural constructs and across regions and countries. The African Youth Charter, for example, defines 'youth' as 'every person between the ages of 15 to 35 years'[12] while the UN defines youth as 'those persons between the ages of 15 and 24 years, without prejudice to other definitions by member States…'[13] and defines adolescents as spanning the ten to nineteen age range.[14] Some African countries apply the Commonwealth definition of youth with an age range between fifteen and twenty-nine.[15] The International Federation of Red Cross and Red Crescent Societies defines young people as 'people in the age range of 5 to 30 years'.[16]

[12] African Youth Charter, July 2006.

[13] Secretary-General's Report to the General Assembly, A/36/215, 1981.

[14] UNICEF: The State of the World's Children—Adolescence: An Age of Opportunity, New York, 2011.

[15] Commonwealth Secretariat definition of youth.

[16] International Federation of Red Cross and Red Crescent Societies, Youth Policy as adopted by the 18th General Assembly held on 23–25 November 2011 in Geneva. 'The terms "youth" and "young people" in the International Federation cover people in the age range of 5 to 30 years. This includes children (5 to 11 years old), adolescents (12 to 17 years old), and young adults (18 to 30 years old).'

As for defining 'youth at risk', one of the best definitions was provided at the International Conference on Urban Youth at Risk hosted by UN Habitat in Monterrey, Mexico in October 2004: 'Youth at risk can be defined as young people whose background places them "at risk" of future offending or victimization due to environmental, social and family conditions that hinder their personal development and successful integration into the economy and society.'[17] It recognizes the double dimension of youth as both victims and perpetrators of violence and points to the multiple factors at work creating the conditions of risk.

B. **Defining gangs**

As we will see, reasons for joining gangs are different in low and middle income countries than in more affluent societies, but gang membership generally offers disaffected, disenfranchized, and marginalized youth a means of fulfilling social and cultural needs as well as protection. In the words of Hagedorn 'gangs today are organizations of the socially excluded'.[18] A good rights-based definition of youth gangs was devised by the OAS:[19]

Youth gangs represent a spontaneous effort by children and young people to create, where it does not exist, an urban space in society that is adapted to their needs, where they can exercise the rights that their families, government and communities do not offer them. Arising out of extreme poverty, exclusion and a lack of opportunities, gangs try to gain their rights and meet their needs by organizing themselves without supervision and developing their own rules, and by securing for themselves a territory and a set of symbols that gives meaning to their membership in the group. This endeavor to exercise their citizenship is, in many cases, a violation of their own and others' rights, and frequently generates violence and crime in a vicious circle that perpetuates their original exclusion.

C. **Age and gang membership**

There seems to be a general consensus among gang researchers that the age of gang membership, although highly variable, ranges between twelve and twenty-four.[20] Ages

[17] International Conference on Urban Youth at Risk in Latin America and the Caribbean: Strong Families, Caring Communities and Inclusive Cities: the Latin America and Caribbean Experience, Monterrey, October 2004 (UN Habitat: <http://ww2.unhabitat.org/prgrammes/safercities/uyr.asp>).

[18] Hagedorn, 'The Global Impact of Gangs', p. 156.

[19] Organization of American States (OAS), 2007 Definition and classification of gangs: Executive summary, Washington DC: Department of Public Security.

[20] Higginson, A., Mazerolle, L., Benier, K., and Bedford, L., 2013, 'Predictor of Youth Gang Membership in Low-and Middle-Income Countries: A Systematic Review' in *The Campbell Collaboration*.

of 'hard core' gang members range between eighteen and twenty-five. Beyond the age of twenty-five, gang members in Latin America tend to be in prison or dead. The mean age for joining gangs seems to be fifteen, which is interesting, as that is also the age (fourteen to fifteen) in which adolescents are most susceptible to joining organizations such as IS or, in other circumstances, decide to run away from home.[21] In the United States, the average age a teenager becomes homeless is 14.7.[22]

In Latin America, the age for joining gangs can be much lower, often motivated by the fact that gang leaders need to recruit younger children who can commit targeted assassinations or other criminal acts with relative legal impunity. According to José Miguel Cruz[23] the age range of the original Salvadoran *maras*,[24] before the end of the civil war in 1992, was between seven and thirty-five years. In Honduras, children as young as seven have been killed for refusing to join a gang.[25]

With young people joining extremist groups, children as young as fourteen, both girls and boys, have been travelling to Syria on their own.[26] In the United Kingdom, an evaluation of the government's Channel programme,[27] which seeks to identify and help young people at risk of radicalization, revealed that the majority of referrals involved children and young people between the ages of thirteen and twenty-five: 26% were under sixteen and 5% were under twelve.[28]

For the purposes of this article, we will narrow our focus on the age range where children and adolescents are most at risk of joining gangs and/or violent groups, i.e., roughly between ten and eighteen, with particular emphasis on the critical ages of fourteen to sixteen.

[21] Tucker, J. S., Edelen, M. O., and Klein, D. J., 2011, 'Running Away From Home: A Longitudinal Study of Adolescent Risk Factors and Young Adult Outcomes', *Journal of Youth and Adolescence*, May.

[22] <https://www.dosomething.org/facts/11-facts-about-homeless-teens>.

[23] Cruz, J. M., 2014, 'Maras and the Politics of Violence in El Salvador'. In *Global Gangs: Street Violence across the World*, edited by J. M. Hazen and D. Rodgers, University of Minnesota Press.

[24] The term 'maras' generally refers to the notorious youth gangs (notably Mara Salvatrucha or MS-13 and Mara 18) in El Salvador, Honduras, and Guatemala with ties to organized crime and to Hispanic youth gangs in Los Angeles, USA. The terms *pandillas* (used mainly in Central America and Mexico) and *combos* or *clicas* (Colombia) tend to refer to loosely organized youth groups with little or no ties to organized crime.

[25] BBC World News, 'Honduras child killings: probe into "gang links"', 3 May 2014; El Nuevo Diario. 'En Honduras, Niños asesinados por negarse a ser pandilleros', 7 May 2014

[26] France, from where many of these teenagers originate, introduced a law on 1 January 2013, allowing French nationals as young as fourteen to travel within Europe without written authorization ('autorisation de sortie de territoire') from their parents or legal guardians.

[27] The Channel programme is one component of the UK Government's PREVENT programme, itself part of a wider anti-terrorism government strategy called CONTEST.

[28] Prevent Strategy: presented to Parliament by the Secretary of State for the Home Department by Command of her Majesty, June 2011.

D. Youth gangs in recent history

Traditionally, in Europe and the United States[29] joining a gang was seen as a transition to adulthood. In France, for example, most male youth who joined gangs in the 1950s, 1960s, and 1970s had working class backgrounds and did so as a way of delaying the passage into 'responsible' adulthood, meaning marriage and factory work. Compulsory military service also served as a clear transition between adolescence and adulthood. As a result, gang membership was short-lived and a matter of choice.[30] What changed in the 1970s, in both Europe and the United States was the transition from a manufacturing to a service-based, high-tech economy, meaning that unskilled youth could no longer rely on factory work. With no prospects for upward economic mobility, they slid into the underclass, where means of survival included drug dealing and street crime. Once drugs are involved, not only is violence exacerbated, but gang membership tends to become a way of life, a means of survival. This is the case for marginalized youth from deprived backgrounds in low and middle income countries, with the added difference that, while gang members in the United States or Europe can eventually opt out, leaving a gang in Latin America is difficult and fraught with danger, as it leaves the young person exposed to being killed by rival gangs, by the police or, more often than not, by their own gang—in retaliation. Leaving the gang is seen as the ultimate form of disloyalty and the usual punishment is death.

E. Adolescence: a potentially dangerous transition

Who are adolescents? Although it seems self-evident to say they are neither children nor adults, it is interesting to note that neuroscience has recently shown that teenage brains function differently from either. While it was generally accepted that personality traits shaped by the environment were very much fixed by age six, given the fact that brain size reaches 95% of its adult size by that age, recent research[31] has shown that, just as there is a burst of brain growth and activity as the fetus develops, until around eighteen months, there is another burst of what scientists call an 'overproduction' of grey matter around

[29] Howell, J. C., 1998, 'Youth Gangs; An Overview', *Juvenile Justice Bulletin*, August: p. 2.

[30] Mohammed, M., 2014, 'From Black Jackets to Zulus: Social Imagination, Myth, and Reality Concerning French Gangs'. In *Global Gangs: Street Violence Across the World*, edited by J. M. Hazen, D. Rodgers, University of Minnesota Press.

[31] Giedd, J., 2014, interviewed in *Frontline*, 'Inside the Teenage Brain'.

the period of pre-puberty, peaking at age eleven in boys and twelve in girls. As the grey matter thickens, new cells and new connections are made, setting the stage for greater learning potential and preparing the teen for adulthood. It is a time of opportunity but also of great risk.[32] What is interesting is that, after this phase of 'overproduction' the next stage consists of the whittling down of the connections not being used, a bit like a sculpture, whereby the final shape is achieved by taking away matter from the original building block. This means that, whatever activities the adolescent chooses to engage in, it will become hardwired in the brain, as those are the neural pathways and connections that will remain. At the same time, the parts of the brain responsible for forward planning, controlling impulses, judgment, and connecting actions to consequences do not develop fully until the early twenties. Brain scans also show that adolescents respond with greater intensity to emotionally strong images and situations than either adults or children,[33] which goes some way to explaining why, when bombarded with images of suffering children or women in Syria, Iraq, or elsewhere, some particularly sensitive adolescents decide they want to take action 'right now'.

Paradoxically, adolescence is a time of selfishness, but also of altruism and idealism. Such altruism means adolescents are naturally inclined to move towards a wider social circle, including community and society, seeking to be of service and embrace a greater cause they can believe in. Idealism means they have a propensity to see reality as either black or white, without the nuances afforded by age, making it all the more natural for them to adopt extremist views and behaviours. It is also a time of fragility in which the young person is struggling to forge his or her identity, more often than not in association and identification with peers and in opposition to parents or authority figures. For adolescents, it is paramount to 'fit in' and conform to the dominant culture of their peers, to be part of the 'in-crowd', the group, the 'gang', which often goes hand in hand with a rejection of parents and authority figures.

Richard Moss captures perfectly the underlying soul-searching of many adolescents, which today seems to propel some children and young people to find meaning by joining organizations such as IS, including by volunteering for suicide missions:

> . . . conformity without the integrative presence of an alive spiritual consciousness becomes the submersion of one's uniqueness into a selfish, relatively lifeless and soulless mediocrity. Even the negative identity that comes from rejection of the soulless social norm is better than conformity to something that has no sense of deeper integrity. Sadly, in adolescence the search for identity

[32] According to the National Institute of Mental Health, 2011, 'Rates of death by injury between ages 15 to 19 are about six times that of the rate between ages 10 and 14.' 'The Teen Brain: Still Under Construction', National Institute of Mental Health, Bethesda, Maryland, NIH Publication No. 11-4929, 2011, p. 1, introduction: <http://www.nimh.nih.gov/health/publications/the-teen-brain-still-under-construction/index.shtml>.

[33] Morris, S., 2014, 'Teenage Wasteland; Why Do So Many Efforts To Stop Young People From Joining Extremist Groups Fail?'. In *Foreign Policy*, November 4.

often results in violent rejection of the norm and/or the self. Adolescents subconsciously recognize that the passage to adulthood represents dying to structures of the past—the end of childhood. But, without a social awareness that invites a meaningful participation in society and provides a base for understanding the transformation, it is easy to lash out against the world . . . or confuse this development with suicide. Suicide then becomes a ritual of transformation and an attempt to demonstrate potency . . . In recognition of this, some cultures provide a ritual death for their adolescents to symbolize the passage from childhood to adulthood.[34]

F. **Push and pull factors**[35]

Although it would seem that the two acts—choosing to join a gang in Honduras, on the one hand, and joining a youth brigade in Syria to carry out 'jihad' on the other—stem from different dynamics, it could be argued that there are similar mechanisms at work in the decision of the young person to join. While one appears to be an act of survival, and therefore more subject to a 'push' factor, the other appears to respond, in part, to a need for meaning, a form of idealism and a need for adventure—thus subject to a 'pull' or 'attraction' factor. Although there are push and pull factors in both cases, the common denominators are: (1) adolescence; (2) a sense of exclusion; and (3) urban environments. It is therefore conceivable that some of the interventions that have yielded results in urban violence programmes could also work with youth at risk of joining extremist ideological groups.

The propensity of children and adolescents to join gangs or extremist groups can also reflect severe dysfunctions within the family and society.

Studies consistently show that it is a combination and accumulation of several risk factors that predisposes children to join gangs. According to James C. Howell 'children who experience 7 or more risk factors at ages 10 to 12 are 13 times more likely to join a gang in adolescence than children who experience only one risk factor or none . . .'.[36] This is why, as we shall later see, programmes need to start at around age ten.

[34] Moss, *The Black Butterfly*, p. 242.

[35] Most gang literature discusses 'push and pull factors'. Push factors are akin to 'risk' factors and are negative social, economic, and cultural circumstances which 'push' young people away from their families and into gangs. Typical 'push' factors are poverty, growing up in a community with low levels of social integration, absence of biological parents or violent or dysfunctional family environments, low student commitment to school and to teachers, low self-esteem, numerous negative life events etc. When 'push' factors are involved, the gang is perceived as a form of protection. 'Pull' factors are those that *attract* youth into gangs, such as increased reputation and social status associated with gang membership, desire to join like-minded peers, the promise of money, drugs, power, fun, and excitement. Push and pull factors work in synergy, reinforcing each other.

[36] Howell, 'Youth Gangs; An Overview', p. 8.

It stands to reason that the push factors involved in youth joining gangs, especially in low and middle income countries, are more numerous than the pull factors. These include social and economic marginalization, absent or dysfunctional parents or caregivers, violence in the home, including incest and drug and alcohol abuse, a lack of adult role models, especially male role models, and, at an individual level, low self-esteem, an accumulation of negative life events, and easy access to drugs. Poor school attachment is also a consistent predictor of potential gang membership. If a teenager is bullied at school or feels inadequate, if he or she doesn't see school as 'worth his while', as a way out from difficulties at home or as a viable outlet to his or her need for social connections and a sense of 'belonging', he or she may well seek these out in the streets. In the case of girls, teenage pregnancy pushes them away from school, compounding the fact that girls may already have low expectations of academic achievement, owing to the family and cultural climate. Other push factors involve the lack of job prospects and the need to make a living.

On the attraction or 'pull' side of the equation, the emotional dynamics that stand out are the need to belong to a group of like-minded peers who can offer protection, companionship, status, identity, and, last but not least, self-esteem. Other pull factors include a sense of adventure and fun, even of danger (*la vida loca* or 'the crazy life'), an exhilarating sense of power, an ability to make quick money (from petty crime, extortion, selling drugs). Youth from the *barrios* and *favelas* in Latin America often look up to gang members as role models. They may have a brother or cousin already in the gang and consider it a normal, if not glamorous way of life. The girls tend to aspire to become the girlfriend of a gang leader as a way of gaining status and respect.[37]

Push factors can also be strong when it comes to children and youth in IS-controlled territories, with outright kidnapping or paying destitute parents to let their children enrol in IS schools part of the recruitment strategy.[38] However, with youth from relatively affluent Western societies joining extremist groups such as IS, the pull factors tend to be far more numerous and powerful than in the case of Latin American or African youth, with push factors generally limited to a sense of exclusion from mainstream society and poor job prospects. Rarely do push factors involve absence of adequate parenting or severe economic deprivation. Instead, arguments used by extremely sophisticated recruiters via social media show a keen understanding of teenage psychology and appeal to a wide range of teenagers: male and female, Muslims and children or grand-children of immigrants, newly converted youth from middle class white Christian or atheist families,[39]

[37] From conversations with teachers and youth workers in Honduras, Mexico, Colombia, and Brazil.

[38] Masi Alessandria, 'ISIS Youth Recruitment: Life in ISIS-ruled Raqqa so grim, Parents Are Giving Up Their Children', *International Business Times*, 6 November 2014.

[39] According to a ninety-page report commissioned by the Centre de Prévention contre les dérives sectaires liées à l'Islam(CPDSI), 80% of families who called the centre to seek help for a son or daughter at

relatively well-to-do young people with a university education[40] or disaffected youth from the *banlieues.* Social isolation, depression, idealism, and sensitivity are risk factors. Increasingly more girls and young women, many with very good academic records, are attracted. They are being particularly targeted; by marrying IS fighters and starting a family, they contribute to fixing the men in a given territory, providing the building blocks for a future State. Single women not planning to marry an IS fighter are actively dissuaded from joining IS. Although a few of the young women and girls who join would like to take an active part in the fighting, females are so far officially barred from combat duties by the IS hierarchy. Most women and girls seem to join essentially for three reasons: to counter what they perceive as the generalized oppression of Muslims, to embrace a new vision of society as an Islamic Utopia while rejecting the Western culture they grew up in, and to fulfil what they believe to be a religious duty by joining the jihad and thus becoming worthy of entering heaven. A strong sense of sisterhood with other women who join also seems to be a very powerful pull factor. Although the IS vision for women is essentially one of domesticity, their whole-hearted endorsement of violence is just as high as that of their male counterparts.[41] While many Western observers tend to find it perplexing that Western women and girls should willingly join an organization and a belief system reputed to oppress women, Christina Baudin warns that 'despite our instincts to focus on events such as Boko Haram's kidnapping of school girls, or ISIS's sexual violence and forced marriages, the fact of the matter is that despite their perceived oppression, women have found a reinforced sense of personal identity with these groups'.[42]

risk of joining IS in Syria or Iraq declared themselves atheist and only 10% of the young people involved had an immigrant grand-parent. Most were from the middle class (67%), 16% from working class backgrounds, and 17% from the upper middle class. The study also found that 63% of their sample group of young people were between fifteen and twenty-one years old. As reported in *Le Parisien*, 17 November, 2014 'Rapport: pourquoi ces jeunes sont attirés par le Jihad?'.

[40] Research conducted by Kamaldeep Bhui, Professor of Cultural Psychiatry and Epidemiology at Queen Mary University, London, found that youth at risk of radicalization were more likely to be lonely or depressed, 'feel bored with their lives', under the age of twenty, in full time education, or coming from families earning more than US$120,000 a year. Recent immigrants were less likely to become radicalized as they were too busy struggling to make a living and had recent experiences of escaping adversity. Girls were slightly more likely to become radicalized than boys. As reported by Pizzi, M. in *Al Jazeera America*, 19 March 2014, 'Study finds unexpected risk factors for violent radicalization' and Knapton, S. in *The Telegraph* 'British jihadis are depressed, lonely and need help, says Professor Kamaldeep Bhui', 15 October 2014. However, according to the UK Citizenship Survey in 2010, 'approval of violent extremism is higher amongst young people and for people from lower income and socio-economic groups.' The highest approval rating (18%) was among the sixteen to nineteen year age group (quoted in 'Prevent Strategy: presented to Parliament by the Secretary of State for the Home Department by Command of her Majesty', June 2011).

[41] Hoyle, C., Bradford, A., and Frenett, R., 2015, 'Becoming Mulan? Female Western Migrants to ISIS', Institute for Strategic Dialogue.

[42] Baudin, C., 'The Women of Terror', *International Policy Digest*, 12 February, 2015.

A much discussed survey on support for IS by citizens from Germany, France, and the United Kingdom[43] commissioned by the official Russian news agency, Rossiya Segodnya, showed that generally favourable opinions of IS among the French sample was 16%, 7% for the UK, and 2% in Germany. In France, 27% of those aged eighteen to twenty-four had favourable opinions. Figures for that age group in the UK and Germany were 4% and 3%, respectively. The survey was administered by telephone to 1,006 people in France, 1,001 in Germany, and 1,000 in the UK, all representing the general population, based on quotas for age, gender, and geographical areas. These figures, which seem particularly high for France, can be compared to similar polls conducted in October 2014 in some Arab countries[44] by the Washington Institute for Near East Policy which showed a 5% support for IS in Saudi Arabia, 3% in Egypt, and almost none in Lebanon.

Some explanations for the high figure in France include a growing disaffection among French youth with mainstream politics and the 'establishment', the high proportion of Muslims in France, many of whom feel excluded from mainstream society, high unemployment rates, and the French Government's insistence on secular values. According to a Senate report published on 8 April 2015, of the 3,000 Europeans who have joined extremist groups in Syria and Iraq, half are from France. The figure for France represents an 84% increase with respect to January 2014.[45]

It is interesting to note that, while in France, those who join IS tend to be disaffected youth from the *banlieues* with few prospects for upward mobility, in the UK, it seems to be the ones with a higher education and good incomes who choose to leave.

Depending on gender and the young person's personal circumstances, motivations for joining seem to range from:

1. Seeking the *thrill of violence* and fighting in a war; this includes self-directed violence, as a number of young people join for the specific purpose of becoming suicide bombers;
2. A sense of boredom, disaffection with life in the West and its perceived lack of *values*, including spiritual values; seeking *adventure*;
3. Revenge for feelings of *humiliation*, wounded self-esteem; seeking *dignity* and honour (especially true in the case of French Muslims) and a sense of *identity*;

[43] ICM Research: New EU Members Survey—CATI fieldwork: 11–13 July 2014 <http://www.icmunlimited.com/data/media/pdf/New%20EU%20Members-Combined-July>.

[44] Pollock, D., 'ISIS Has Almost No Popular Support in Egypt, Saudi Arabia, or Lebanon', policy analysis in *The Washington Institute for Near East Policy*, 14 October 2014.

[45] FranceTVInfo and AFP: 'Le nombre des départs de Français pour la Syrie en forte hausse, selon un rapport parlementaire', 8 April 2015.

4. A sense of *belonging* to a group of like-minded peers, camaraderie, friendship, kinship;
5. A sense of *purpose*, of being of service, of being part of history, of something larger than themselves;
6. Fighting to redress *injustice* (many, especially the young women/girls, are profoundly affected by images of civilian suffering, especially of children, in Syria, and blame the West for its inaction);
7. The thrill of participating in the *building* of *a new society*, an ideologically pure State (the self-proclaimed Islamic Caliphate);
8. The thrill of being part of an *epic narrative* in which the forces of Islam will battle the forces of the 'infidels' in a foretold Apocalypse;
9. A sense of *religious duty* towards Islam;
10. For girls, *getting married* to a brave, heroic and noble man/fighter and helping to build a new society by being dutiful wives and good mothers.[46]

According to most reports, most of those who join have little or no knowledge of Islam.[47] If anything, religious education may in fact protect against radicalization.[48]

In this sometimes chilling list, we see many of the usual preoccupations of adolescence: boredom, adventure, romance, danger, humiliation, omnipotence, belonging/friendship, idealism, manicheist world view, generosity and altruism, the search for meaning and purpose, the need to belong to something larger than oneself by building a new, 'ideal' society.

[46] For a larger discussion of female motivations, see above under 'Push and pull factors'.

[47] Atran, S., 2011, *Talking to the Enemy: Faith, Brotherhood and the (Un) Making of Terrorists*, Harper Collins. Sageman, M., 2004, *Understanding Terror Networks*, University of Pennsylvania Press. According to Atran, 'Western volunteers for ISIS are mostly youth in transitional stages in their lives—immigrants, students, between jobs or girlfriends, having left their homes and looking for new families. For the most part they have no traditional religious education and are "born-again" to religion ... what inspires the most lethal terrorists in the world today is not so much the Qur'an or religious teachings as a thrilling cause and call to action that promises glory and esteem in the eyes of friends.' (Atran as quoted in *The Guardian*, 4 September 2014: 'Jihad's fatal attraction'). Similarly, Sageman argues that young Muslims have a limited understanding of Islam, which is precisely what makes them more vulnerable to extreme interpretations. Both Atran and Sageman argue that it is a sense of moral outrage at perceived attacks by the West on the global Muslim community (or Ummah) and bonding with like-minded friends that drives young people to kill or be killed to protect and avenge friends or the larger Muslim community.

[48] According to Matthew Wilkinson, an expert on Islam and director of the think-tank 'Curriculum for Cohesion', part of the solution to radicalization lies in better religious education, given the fact that 89% of British Muslim youth see Islam as their main identifier even if they have little or no knowledge of religion. In *BBC News*, Frank Gardner, 'Prevent Strategy: is it failing to stop radicalisation?' 6 March 2015.

PLAYING OUT THE KARPMAN TRIANGLE

According to the Karpman Drama Triangle[49] human interactions can be fixed from an early age into unconscious role-plays in which one is either a victim, a persecutor, or a rescuer, with the same person being able to switch from one role to another in relatively quick succession, depending on the psychological needs being fulfilled from playing either of the roles.

With the story of young Westerners joining IS, the whole spectrum of the triangle is being acted out. They perceive themselves and others like them (my people) as victims, decide to rescue them (by going to fight), while at the same time becoming persecutors to those whom they consider to be the original persecutors (brutal killings of those deemed 'infidels').

With youth gangs, the 'game' is more two-dimensional, with victimized children becoming bullies and persecutors because, in this case, being the persecutor is a more comfortable role than being a victim. Brutal initiation rites are meant to toughen the new recruit so that they can never be a victim again.

The whole point of the Karpman Triangle model, of course, is that to be a responsible adult who respects his own boundaries and those of others, it is necessary to move out of the triangle altogether.

CULTURAL RESISTANCE IDENTITIES: HIP-HOP AND ISLAM, 'MÊME COMBAT'?

The parallels between young people joining gangs and adolescents joining extremist political groups can be partly explained by what Hagedorn calls *resistance identities*, i.e., 'identities formed in opposition to the dominant culture and the uncertainties of an unstable modernity',[50] with globalization inviting a hardening of national, ethnic, and religious identities and the binary 'us versus them' mentality, so prominent in gang culture but also among young people attracted to extremist ideologies. The attitude of young Muslims in the West can be understood in light of Hagedorn's observation that 'Nationalist, religious and ethnic cultures have grown strong by resisting the homogenizing influence of westernization. Islamic fundamentalism today is but one example of the strength of cultural resistance identities'.[51] Youth gangs in Latin America or

[49] Karpman drama triangle is 'a psychological and social model of human interaction in transactional analysis, first described by Stephen Karpman in 1968' source: Wikipedia.

[50] Hagedorn, 'The Global Impact of Gangs', p. 158.

[51] Ibid.

Africa, however, are caught between rejection of the dominant culture or social class and the aspiration to embrace the values of consumerism, with gang members sporting the latest iPhones, designer shades, and gold jewellery as so many trophies.

Just as a Latin American youth will use street dance, rap, hip-hop and *reggaeton*,[52] along with distinctive clothing, artefacts, and tattoos as a buffer, shield, or refuge against the dominant culture, so will young Muslims in Europe use religion and dress (scarf, veil, or niqab for women) to affirm their identity against a culture perceived as exclusive and oppressive. What's more, in the West, especially in Europe, young Muslims from the *banlieues* and other segregated neighbourhoods are into hip-hop as a form of lyrical resistance music against perceived oppression—a role it has traditionally taken, given its roots in Black rebellion against White authority in the United States. In fact, some of the most successful and well-known hip-hop artists in Europe are Muslim, either the children of immigrants or converts. Britain has recently seen its first female hip-hop duo, 'Poetic Pilgrimage', a paradox only in appearance. These two young women, while trying to 'reconcile their conversion to Islam with their strong feminist sensibilities and Jamaican roots'[53] are also surfing on the appeal this kind of music has on young people in general and on young European Muslims in particular. While their brand of hip-hop seeks to 'uncover the hidden nuances and natural cultural overlaps' in order to create a 'bridge between two seemingly opposed camps',[54] such is not the case of many rap and hip-hop artists. European government officials have been increasingly worried about the effects of so-called 'Muslim hate-rap' on youth and its supposed link to violent extremism. As a result, since around 2004, Western governments have been trying to coopt rap and hip-hop culture, using it to lure young people away from extremist ideas. Since the 2005 youth riots in the *banlieues*, the French Government has heavily invested in hip-hop initiatives by local associations in the hope of fostering a youth culture conducive to integration.[55] In the UK, a government-sponsored initiative called PREVENT, created in the aftermath of the London July 2005 bombings, uses hip-hop and other art forms to attract Muslim youth and offer a 'safe space' to discuss and explore issues around religion and extremism, hoping to build communities' resilience to violent extremism. The hip-hop concerts invite more mainstream artists to 'use their music to cast a critical eye on current affairs, talk about social justice, express their faith and inspire action'.[56] Hip-hop

[52] A Spanish-language cross between hip-hop and reggae that originated in Puerto Rico in the mid-1990s.

[53] Reizel, M., 'Hip-Hop Hijabis; a musical journey of faith that follows Britain's first female Muslim hip-hop duo on tour', *Al Jazeera*, 5 March 2015.

[54] Ibid.

[55] Aidi, H., 'Don't Panik! Islam and Europe's "Hip-Hop" Wars; the debate over Islam and hip hop in Europe is heating up as governments wade in', *Al Jazeera*, 5 June 2012.

[56] Create/Participate: a selection of six case studies working creatively with Prevent strategy objectives; Creativity, Culture and Education (CCE).

is also at the heart of US embassies' strategies to reach Muslim youth and 'convey a "different narrative" to counter the foreign "violent ideology" that youth are exposed to'.[57] Although these kinds of initiatives often offer the right mix of incentives (pull factors), the problem is they can be perceived by young people and rap artists alike as attempts by established authorities to coopt youth into more mainstream culture.

A similar narrative emerged in Puerto Rico in the mid-1990s with the *reggaeton* revolution, which took youth from the *barrios* and shantytowns by storm. Its explicit sexual lyrics and no-holds-barred commentaries on drug violence, government corruption, failing schools, and high unemployment rates shocked middle-class values and drew fierce attacks from the government who saw it as a threat to social order and a corruptor of young minds. In the words of Daddy Yankee, the genre's biggest star, 'the government tried to stop us ... people from other social extractions ... looked down on young people from the barrios, underestimating and seeing us as outcasts'.[58] Early censorship of *reggaeton* only enhanced its appeal among marginalized and rebellious youth, of course. Yet in a 'if you can't beat them, join them' reversal, by 2003, an electoral year, politicians trying to appeal to younger voters did not hesitate to dance the *reggaeton* at political rallies, flanked by *regaaetton* stars. The genre has since joined mainstream pop culture and become a huge international commercial success.

G. **The use and role of violence**

In both groups, the use of radical violence is not only a byproduct of joining but is also considered a necessity by the youth involved. Often, young people consider that violence is the only effective way of repairing damaged self-esteem. In the case of gangs, initiation rituals themselves often involve violence (typically, severe beatings for boys and gang rapes for girls). Most of the violence is directed at other gangs in defence of turf, drug routes, and street-corner business.[59] Violence against rival gangs also serve to cement group cohesion.[60] Honour, especially sexual honour, as understood in machismo culture, is also cause for violence. Among young people joining extremist groups, violence ranges from self-directed violence (suicide bombings) to combat duties and targeted executions. It is interesting to note that, even those who join for

[57] Aidi, 'Don't Panik!'.

[58] Quoted by Negrón-Muntaner, F. and Rivera, R. Z., 'Reggaeton Nation' in *NACLA*.

[59] Howell, 'Youth Gangs; An Overview'.

[60] Decker, S. H., 1996, 'Collective and Normative Features of Gang Violence', *Justice Quarterly*, Vol. 13, No. 2, June.

idealist reasons, including young women attracted by the idea of contributing to a humanitarian cause, violence is not merely tolerated but celebrated. In a study of girls and young women joining jihad in Syria, the authors found that, in spite of humanitarian motivations, the divide between 'us' and 'them' was such that tweets and other social media messages expressed very strong approvals of beheadings and other acts of violence against Western hostages, to the point where some of the women tweeted they wished they had inflicted the violence themselves.[61] Research shows that the common goal of violent acts is retribution and that impulses towards resolving conflicts through violence does not stem from 'an absence of values but from a value system in which violence is acceptable'.[62] This notion is in line with the findings and operating premises of the NGO 'Cure Violence', which maintains that violence is a learned behaviour that can be 'unlearned'. It sees violence as an epidemic and a health issue that can be 'cured'.[63]

WHAT WORKS

Potential areas of intervention

Levels of intervention include the individual, the family, the school, peers, and the community. Ideally, the more levels are intervened in parallel, the higher the probability of having an impact. Moreover, studies repeatedly show that the earlier the intervention, the higher the likelihood of reducing at risk behaviour and participation in violence later.[64] These early interventions include teaching parenting skills and monitoring the welfare of infants and toddlers, especially children of adolescent mothers, and administering pre-school enrichment programmes, all of which are highly resource-intensive interventions. It is therefore difficult to reach children individually and to intervene at the family level. This leaves the school, peers, and the community as the most likely and cost-effective areas of intervention.

[61] Hoyle, Bradford, and Frenett, 'Becoming Mulan?'.

[62] Crawford, D. K. and Bodine, R. J., 2001, 'Conflict Resolution Education: Preparing Youth for the Future', *Juvenile Justice Journal*, vol. VIII, no. 1, June, p. 21.

[63] Cure Violence was founded in 2000 by Doctor Gary Slutkin, an American physician who worked with the World Health Organization (WHO) in Africa on large-scale epidemics. The methodology involves well-trained locally hired community workers, often ex-gang members, who work as 'violence interrupters', outreach behaviour change agents, and community coordinators to detect and interrupt potential violence, identify and treat those at highest risk of committing violence and mobilizing the community to change norms. Apart from the United States, Cure Violence is present in eight countries, including Honduras, Mexico, Colombia, South Africa, Iraq, and Syria.

[64] WHO, Series of briefings on violence prevention, 2009.

Age of intervention

By age nine or ten, children tend to move away from family influences and become far more susceptible to peer influence, with school also a strong influence between the ages of six and fifteen. By eighteen, the community becomes a strong influence. As already discussed in the section on risk factors, it would seem that programming from ages seven to eighteen, with particular emphasis on ages ten to sixteen, cover the spectrum of the highest risk as well as having the advantage of being able to reach most youth in schools.

Types of intervention

Literature on gangs describe progammes as falling into the category of primary prevention, secondary prevention, gang intervention and targeted suppression.[65] Primary prevention programmes target all youth living in a community where gangs are present, secondary prevention targets youth who are at risk of joining gangs, gang intervention targets youth already in gangs or associated with them, yet who aren't in the highest offending category, while targeted suppression targets older gang members who have become chronic and violent offenders. While prevention programmes are more cost-effective than either suppression or gang-intervention programmes, within the prevention category, targeting youth at risk of joining gangs (or an extremist organization) is considered by most practitioners as the top prevention priority, 'because youth in this group are most likely to confront the decision of whether or not to join a gang in the near future'.[66] Moreover, once in a gang, interventions become far more difficult, especially in Latin America, where being in a gang is a way of life and leaving it is simply not an option. We will therefore focus our attention on programmes and interventions targeting at-risk youth. Activities offered can be school-based or community-based and involve arts (theatre, street art, street dance), sports, psychosocial support, vocational training, youth community involvement, or, better still, a combination of all these. We will see that the bottom line, when it comes to programming for this category of youth, is that the activities envisaged are more attractive, from the point of view of the child or young person, than what the gang or extremist organization may appear to offer.

[65] James C. Howell: "Gang Prevention: An Overview of Research and Programs" in Juvenile Justice Bulletin, US Department of Justice, December 2010, Howell, 2010.

[66] Howell, 2010, p. 12.

PROGRAMMING EXAMPLES

ERPV (REGIONAL STRATEGY FOR VIOLENCE PREVENTION FOR CENTRAL AMERICA AND THE CARIBBEAN) 2008–2012

Description: A series of eleven projects implemented by National Red Cross Societies in eight countries of Central America and the Caribbean simultaneously, supported by the Spanish Red Cross, with technical and financial support from the Spanish Agency for International Cooperation and Development. The projects were developed in urban neighborhoods (*barrios*) with high levels of gang violence, intra-family, sexual, and gender-based violence.

Programming goals: Prevent young people at risk of social exclusion from joining gangs by promoting their rights and responsibilities and strengthening their involvement in civil society (local community structures) and including a gender-based perspective in all activities.

Methodology: Children and youth at risk, aged fourteen to twenty-one, were approached in the streets in order to design, together with them, pedagogical/recreational activities. The focus was on transformative leaderships, urban culture, popular education, critical thinking.

Impact/recommendations: In most countries, the projects had a significant impact on the beneficiaries themselves in terms of building self-esteem, life skills, leadership, and positive attitudes towards the future. Youth were involved in the design, implementation and evaluation of the projects. Relationships with other youth and with families improved. However, the goal of including young people in the decision-making processes of local community structures was achieved only in El Salvador. In practice, working in the streets and achieving the goal of reclaiming public spaces turned out to be difficult or impossible, given an acute resurgence of gang and drug-related violence in the region at the time. The experience showed that working from a 'safe space' (a community building) was beneficial to the young people involved. During the course of the programme, it also became clear that determining the age of participation in an arbitrary manner is often not possible or even desirable. Many children younger than fourteen needed and wanted to be part of the programme and were often informally included. Some of the weaknesses of the programme were its lack of sustainability and the fact that, once empowered, the beneficiaries had little or no job opportunities or avenues to express their leadership or entrepreneurial skills. This raises the important question of potential frustration when new expectations are not met with corresponding concrete solutions. Adult mentorship was an important aspect of the programmes. Children and youth became very attached to staff implementing the projects and thrived as a result. When the project ended and the staff had to leave, some youth were deeply affected. This raises the issue of ensuring that mentors are part of the community and 'there to stay'.

PAO (PROYECTO AMPLIANDO OPORTUNIDADES—EXPANDING OPPORTUNITIES PROJECT) 2002–ONGOING

Description: A community-based violence prevention project targeting some 8,000 young people between the ages of twelve and twenty-five in five different neighbourhoods of Tegucigalpa, Honduras. It is implemented by the Honduran Red Cross with technical and financial support from the Italian Red Cross, the Swiss Red Cross, and the International Committee of the Red Cross (ICRC).

Programming goals: To limit social exclusion and provide vulnerable and marginalized youth and their families with opportunities for personal development away from violence.

Methodology: A community-based integrated approach focusing on health, education (remedial education for school dropouts and illiterate adults, citizenship education, and the promotion of humanitarian principles), vocational training to facilitate youth employment and schools for parents to promote parenting skills. Overall promotion of solidarity networks at the community level with training of youth community volunteers.

Impact/recommendations: The project has had a major impact in drastically reducing the level of violence in a circumscribed location by mobilizing youth in favour of their community and providing them with useful skills. The building of solidarity networks strengthened the social fabric and hence community resilience. Young people became proud of belonging to their community and gang members with organic links to the community benefited from and participated in the project. The success of the project led members of the Red Cross consortium to replicate it, successfully, in a violence-affected neighbourhood of San Salvador. However, in spite of having involved government entities (the National Institute for Vocational Training, the Ministries of Health and Education, the National Youth Institute, universities, etc.), the project has been struggling to achieve sustainability insofar as the community and local authorities have not managed to take over full responsibility for the project.

AEH (ABRIENDO ESPACIOS HUMANITARIOS—CREATING HUMANITARIAN SPACES) ICRC, 2009–2015

Description: Intra-curricular school-based programme for secondary-school children (ages twelve to eighteen) in selected violence-affected neighbourhoods (*barrios* or *favelas*) of Rio de Janeiro (Brazil), Medellín (Colombia), Ciudad Juárez and the State of Guerrero (Mexico), and Honduras.

Programming goals: By providing children and young people with life-skills and alternatives to risk-taking behaviour, increase the resilience of youth at risk of joining gangs and provide them with the opportunity to make more informed choices about joining or not. The programme acts as a vector to enable the ICRC to carry out its humanitarian work in otherwise difficult to access violence-affected communities.

Methodology: Based on strong buy-in by the Ministry of Education, curricular intervention with modules developed for the last three years of secondary school and designed together with teachers and with the input of students. Aims to develop life skills such as critical thinking, debating, active listening, tolerance and empathy, conflict management, teamwork, planning for one's future and basic project management. Contents include the concept of human dignity, the study of dilemmas through case studies, basic humanitarian principles, and violence in the community. In the last year, students are encouraged to design and implement a small project in favour of their community, putting into practice what they've learned. Curricular intervention is combined with first aid training for teachers, safe behaviour workshops for both teachers and students, physical upgrades to the school buildings and surroundings to protect them from stray bullets, and psychosocial support to both students and teachers, including through art therapy.

Impact/recommendations: Although the project as a whole has yet to benefit from a proper external evaluation, partial evaluations and interviews with stakeholders show that the progamme has achieved behavioural change in students and raised academic achievements and school attrition rates, keeping more young people in schools. Teachers living in fear in neighborhoods with exceptionally high levels of violence have felt supported and empowered. Teacher–student relationships improved, as did relationships among students and between students and their parents. Students' self-esteem, social skills and sense of initiative improved. Discussing violence in the community was no longer taboo. The school was perceived as a safe space in which students could discuss their problems and voice their opinions. What sets this programme apart is the fact that it is school-based and sustainable. It has the buy-in of teachers and the Ministry of Education, the modules are integrated in the main curriculum and handover to the Ministry of Education is programmed from the very start.

LUTA PELA PAZ—(FIGHT FOR PEACE) 2000–ONGOING

Description: The project, based in the Complexo da Maré *favela* in Rio de Janeiro, was founded by Luke Dowdney, a former boxing champion and author of 'Children of the Drug Trade' (2003) and 'Neither War nor Peace: international comparisons of children and youth in organized armed violence' (2005). He is also the founder of COAV (Children in Organized Armed Violence), a website that documents cases of children and youth involved in armed groups in countries not at war.

Programming goals: Enable children and young people to realize their potential in communities affected by crime and violence, providing alternatives to violence, gang membership, and drug trafficking, thus contributing to overcoming division and violence in the community.

Methodology: Sports activities that are attractive to young people, mainly boxing and martial arts training and competition, combined with personal development and formal education, job training and work access, youth leadership (training to become part of the Youth Council), and youth support services (mentoring and case work). Youth Councils have a say in programming.

Impact/recommendations: Research conducted in 2013 by the Centre for Social Justice and Change, School of Law and Social Sciences, University of East London and an evaluation by independent consultant, Conor Foley, in 2014 found that, overall, participants' behaviour, self-esteem, and ways of thinking were positively impacted. 92% of young people reported having successfully acquired life-skills and 99% reported feeling more positive towards their own future. The programme also helped to break down the 'invisible' barriers created by territorial disputes between different gangs, with 79% of young people in the programme reporting they felt safe enough to visit the other communities where the programme was established. While the evaluations showed significant behaviour change in the beneficiaries, it also pointed out that 'Accepting existing social and economic conditions as a given, which must be either lived or escaped from, quite obviously ignores the third possibility of seeking to influence public policy to change things for the better'.[67] The author therefore recommended that 'Luta pela Paz ... should develop an outreach strategy with the city and state authorities in Rio de Janeiro and to increase the project's impact on public policy decision-making.'

AMANDLA EDUFOOTBALL, KHAYELITSHA TOWNSHIP, CAPE TOWN, SOUTH AFRICA, 2007–ONGOING

Description: The project was founded by Florian Zech, a German national who worked for a year in a Khayelitsha orphanage as part of his civil service. It uses football as a catalyst for social change and youth empowerment in marginalized, violence-affected urban environments. Between 2011 and 2014, it was partly funded by the ICRC, which also carried out impact research.

Programming goals: A sports-based violence-prevention programme which provides youth at risk of joining gangs or engaging in anti-social behaviour with a 'safe-hub' and alternatives to risk-taking behaviour. In 2014, Amandla catered to at least 3,000 children and young people between the ages of eight and twenty-five. Special focus is placed on males aged fourteen to seventeen, as these are the most likely to become gang members.

Methodology: 'Fair-play' football coaching and league games which take place at times when youth are most likely to engage in at-risk behaviour (after school, Fridays and Saturday evenings, holidays). The 'fair-play system' awards points for pro-social behaviour on and off the football pitch. The games are therefore opportunities to instil life-skills and promote behaviour change. At the same time, the technical quality of

[67] Foley, C., 'Maré United—An External Evaluation, April 2014.

the coaching and competitiveness of the games is such that the most difficult group (males aged fourteen to seventeen) are attracted. The sports component is supplemented with academic tutoring, life-skills programming and a leadership programme which supplies Amandla with peer mentors aged seventeen to twenty-five. Former 'gangsters' are also involved in workshops as facilitators. Amandla is very strong on evidence-based programming. It monitors and evaluates all the activities, conducting baseline surveys and using control groups. It even goes so far as using biometric data to monitor attendance of beneficiaries.

Impact/recommendations: Indicators include the improvement of behaviour in areas such as teamwork, the respectful treatment of others, and conflict-management skills. Measurable impacts have included a 49% improvement in school results and a significant drop in violence ('contact crime') within a 600 metre radius of the project. The success of Amandla EduFootball seems to stem from the concept of a 'safe hub' where youth at risk find it enjoyable and useful to spend time in (strong pull factor), the use of peer-to-peer coaching and mentorship, and the combination of sports with life-skills and academic tutoring. For youth at risk, the Amandla programme becomes a 'second family' where they are encouraged to reach their potential in a safe and nurturing environment. For those who progress to the leadership programme, incentives include travelling abroad to participate in global youth leadership events and help with securing scholarships to study.

STREET MEDIATION—NORWEGIAN RED CROSS, OSLO AND EIGHT OTHER CITIES AND DISTRICTS IN NORWAY, CENTRAL AMERICA, DENMARK, LEBANON, AND ROMANIA, 1998–ONGOING

Description: A street-based, conflict management programme aimed at youth aged thirteen to twenty-five at risk of joining gangs or engaging in anti-social behaviour, including murder. In Norway, the programme caters mostly to young people from immigrant backgrounds.

Programming goals: Based on the premise that 'violence is the tragic expression of unmet needs', the programme intervenes proactively, through workshops, and reactively, through on-the-spot and *in situ* mediation to prevent conflicts from escalating into violence. Eventually, a large pool of young people trained in conflict management and mediation can deal reactively to conflicts as they arise in the community.

Methodology: Uniformed Red Cross volunteers or employees actively recruit young people in the streets, encouraging them to join a set of workshops on conflict management and mediation. They work from Street Mediation Units strategically located across the city in either a local Red Cross Resource Center, offices of the municipality or a local NGO, such as the Islamic Cultural Center. In Norway, the programme works in partnership with the local police force and child welfare services. The workshops are inspired by concepts such as restorative justice, peace circles, non-violent communication, conflict mediation, and conferencing etc. and uses role plays, games, and reflective dialogue and discussions. There are three levels to the workshops. The 'Conflict Workshop' enables participants to understand conflict and their own triggers, encouraging self-awareness. The 'Mediation Workshop' explores tools to help two parties solve a conflict and the 'Instructor Workshop' enables interested young people to become peer instructors in conflict management. Within the programme, youth instructors and adult instructors have equal status.

Impact/recommendations: No comprehensive impact research has been carried out but there are strong indications that the peer-to-peer approach works well and is therefore well regarded by local authorities responsible for crime prevention. Challenges include following up on young street mediators once they have completed the workshop and providing them with a network they can tap into when needed.

GOVERNMENT-LED PROGRAMMES; A CASE IN POINT

PREVENT PROGRAMME—HOME OFFICE, UK, 2005–ONGOING. REVISED IN 2006 AND 2011

Description: Part of CONTEST, the government's four-pronged counter-terrorism strategy. The other three strands are PREPARE (for attacks), PROTECT (the public), and PURSUE (the attackers)

Programming goals: To stop people, especially young people, from becoming terrorists or supporting terrorism. Seeks to reinforce community cohesion and resilience to terrorist ideology.

Methodology: Distribution of tens of millions of pounds (£140 million in 2008–2009) to local councils, voluntary sector organizations, and Muslim organizations and mosques, targeting Muslim communities, young people, and women. Areas of intervention include 'safe space' debates to discuss current affairs or grievances, presentations to schools about Islamic beliefs and culture, arts, and cultural activities as well as sports and recreation. Within PREVENT, the Channel programme (started in 2007) encourages local governments, schools, health professionals, and youth workers to observe individuals' behaviour for signs of radicalization and refer them to local councils for support.

Impact/recommendations: Within the overall CONTEST strategy, which is generally viewed as effective, the PREVENT component has been challenged from its inception, with criticism ranging from its stigmatization of the Muslim community to diverting public funds away from more mainstream community projects. Pressure on teacher and youth workers to share information with the police on individuals' potential vulnerability to radicalization was seen as a form of spying.[68]

In France, recent plans to prevent and detect radicalization[69] involve, among a series of other measures, teaching young people about religion from a secular standpoint, helping them process internet content with a critical eye, and training social workers, judges dealing with minors, as well as teachers and school staff, in Islamic values, based on the finding that State officials who interact with children and young people on a daily basis often have little or no understanding of Islam, making a constructive dialogue with those tempted by radicalization difficult. Some innovative measures involve entrusting civil society and local associations, rather than the State, with leading the counter-narrative to jihadist propaganda as well as encouraging disillusioned returnees to tell their stories to young people at risk of radicalization.

[68] Dodd, V., 'Government anti-terrorism strategy "spies" on innocent; data on politics, sexual activity and religion gathered by government', *The Guardian*, 16 October 2009; Holehouse, M., 'Tony Blair's anti-jihadist programme has failed, says ex-MI5 chief', *The Telegraph*, 14 January 2015; Murray, D., 'The Prevent Strategy: a textbook example of how to alienate just about everybody', *The Telegraph*, 31 March 2010; Khan, H. on *BBC Radio 5*, 26 August 2014, 'A senior figure in the Muslim Council of Britain says PREVENT, a key government anti-terrorism strategy has "failed"'; Gardner, F., 'Prevent strategy: Is it failing to stop radicalisation?' in *BBC News*, 6 March 2015; Casciani, D., 'Analysis: The Prevent strategy and its problems', *BBC News*, 26 August, 2014; St Vincent, Sarah, 'Change the Channel: How UK's Adoption of a Mandatory Anti-Radicalization Program Could Violate Human Rights', Center for Democracy and Technology, 14 January 2015; Bartlett, J. and Birdwell, J., 'From Suspects to Citizens: Preventing Violent Extremism in a Big Society', DEMOS Report, July 2010. The report recommends abolishing the programme, arguing that 'It is widely believed that Prevent has alienated Muslim communities, increased inter-community tensions, and threatens to undo a number of good initiatives that contribute to community cohesion because of the link to counter terrorism'. Jahangir, M. and Dr Siddiqui, A., 2013, 'The Prevent Strategy: a Cradle to Grave Police State', CAGE.

[69] Graff, V., 'Lutte contre le jihadisme: ce que proposent les sénateurs', *FranceInfoTV*, 8 April 2015.

PROGRAMMES AIMED AT REINTEGRATING RETURNING WOULD-BE JIHADISTS

Although European anti-radicalization programmes focus mainly on preventing youth from joining extremist groups, governments are increasingly grappling with the issue of what to do with those who return. On 29 April 2015, Manuel Valls, head of the French Government, unveiled the country's plan for returning 'jidhadi' or would-be 'jihadis', which involved setting up a rehabilitation centre offering returnees not subject to prosecution psychosocial support, on a voluntary basis. He took the opportunity to highlight the latest figures concerning the number of French nationals identified as having been radicalized. According to government figures, since 29 April 2014, 1,900 people were reported as being radicalized, of which 25% are minors and 43% women or girls.[70] The increase in the number of French women and girls seeking to join IS in Syria is indeed noteworthy.

In terms of reintegration, Denmark seems to have gone the furthest, with its programme in Aarhus, the country's second largest city, often cited as a model.[71] The programme, a collaboration between social services, schools, and the police, has been running since 2013 and offers counselling and career advice to returnees. There are no interrogations on participants' activities in Syria or Iraq. Instead, psychologists and adult mentors listen to their stories and provide practical advice and support on a case-by-case basis.

Although it is necessary, for security reasons, to monitor the activities and whereabouts of returnees, it is crucial to provide counselling and practical support to avoid further radicalization. In the words of Richard Barrett, senior vice-president of the Soufan Group, 'The treatment of returning foreign fighters by the authorities of their home States will have an important impact on their future behaviour. Returnees who have been motivated to go to Syria by humanitarian concerns and have done no fighting, may be radicalized and alienated if treated roughly on their arrival home'.[72] Beyond being helped with the practical aspects of reintegration, young returnees who left for Syria on a humanitarian impulse can avoid frustration if their idealism is channelled towards helping their peers make more informed decisions about joining or not. As Richard Barrett rightly points out: 'Returning fighters themselves could play a significant role in helping the State or their community to understand these issues and so mitigate the threat, and this also argues for careful treatment of each returnee on a case-by-case basis. A returning fighter will have a great deal of credibility in radical circles at home, and if he argues against participation in the war ... this is likely to be more effective than anything a government can do.'[73]

[70] 'Valls annonce une structure pour les Français qui renoncent au jihad', *Le Parisien*, 29 April 2015.

[71] Bernard, M.-V., 'Danemark: à Aarhus, "on aide les anciens jihadistes, on ne les traite pas comme des terrorists"', *FranceInfoTV*, 24 October 2014 and Gidda, M., 'No place like home: what to do when jihadists return', *BBC News*, 18 November 2014.

[72] Barrett, R., 'Foreign Fighters in Syria', *The Soufan Group*, June 2014.

[73] Ibid.

THE COMMON DENOMINATORS BETWEEN PROGRAMMES THAT WORK

We will start from the basic premise that prevention and programmes geared towards social integration not only have a better chance of working than those focused on repression; they also cost less. As pointed out by Adam Baird[74] 'Lessons learned indicate that "demobilizing" youths already involved with gangs involves expensive and long-term life-cycle projects, which are beyond the scope of … funding opportunity'. At the other end of the spectrum, it is difficult to 'catch' potentially at risk youth in their infancy, i.e., through their families, as this would require structural interventions and 'social engineering' on a scale only a very strong State could hope to achieve.

There are therefore two areas where moderately funded and focused interventions have a reasonable chance of making an impact. These are school and community-level interventions.

Schools

Remaining in school is often a protective factor in and of itself. To take only one example, most of the 5,300 children and adolescents murdered in El Salvador between 2005 and 2011 were out of school and in gangs.[75] What does it take to keep adolescents in school?

In both urban violence contexts and in situations where young people are attracted to extremist ideologies, the school, as the prime scene of socialization for children and adolescents is a crucial area of intervention. When the family environment has failed a child, schools can offer a second chance.

Schools offer not only a 'captive audience' of potentially at-risk youth, including some already involved in gangs, but in very violent neighbourhoods, schools can act as springboards from which to reach the rest of the community, mainly through teachers, parents and caretakers. By working in schools, it is therefore possible to reach individual families and the community at large. In violent neighbourhoods, the role of the school as a 'safe hub' can be deliberately enhanced. However, for this to happen, the attractiveness of the school needs to be reinforced.

Schools become attractive when they offer a safe haven, when they allow young people to express themselves without being judged, when the subject matters are relevant to their everyday life, when extra-curricular activities are interesting enough to act as

[74] Baird, A., 2011, *Community-Building to Combat Crime: Project Proposal, 'South-Side Youth Success: Pathways to employment for young men at risk of joining gangs in Belize City'*, UNDP, Belize.

[75] UNICEF: <http://www.insightcrime.org/news-briefs/majority-of-minors-killed-in-el-salvador-involved-in-gangs-unicef>.

a social pull factor and when schools offer avenues for social and community involvement. As the French Government rightly identified, teachers are at the forefront of the 'battle against radicalization'.[76] They are also among the first victims of urban violence, often subject to extortion and threatened by their own students.

Schools need to become places where 'taboo' subjects such as violence in the community (or at home) and joining extremist groups can be discussed safely and openly. Programmes such as AEH in Latin America have shown that this is possible. It means teachers need to be trained in basic psychosocial support and in truly participative teaching methodologies. Often, it is the methodologies themselves rather than the subject matter that carry the seeds of transformation. More civics classes or discourses on 'morals' and 'values' are not going to do the trick. Methodologies based on critical thinking, debating, teamwork, role plays, active listening, and conflict management have the power to raise young people's self-esteem, increase their social and life skills, and enable them to put themselves in others' shoes, therefore helping them to tolerate and understand other points of view. As we have seen, in both attraction to gangs and to extremist groups, lack of self-esteem, peer pressure (not knowing one's own mind), and an 'us versus them' mentality (intolerance for different points of view) are key elements leading to gang membership or radicalization.

Beyond classroom sessions, whenever possible, schools catering to at-risk youth need to fill in those critical after school hours with extra-curricular activities that are both attractive and empowering. In particularly deprived neighbourhoods, where cultural centres or other 'glues' of the social fabric are missing, the schools, as physical structures, can replace those centres and act as bridges to the surrounding community. Schools can also become places from which young people, with the help of teachers or outside resources, can dream up, design, and carry out small projects in favour of their community, thus filling in a basic need of adolescents of being of service and part of something larger than themselves. Such activities also serve to attenuate the stigma associated with young people in violence-affected neighbourhoods.

Community-based programming for school drop-outs or to fill after-school hours

As we have seen from some of the projects described above, among the elements of success are:

- finding incentives or levers, such as sports, art, hip-hop, that attract young people and are perceived as 'cool'; adolescents, especially older ones, will join only if their peers do;

[76] Donadio, R., 'French Teachers, on the Front Lines; Charlie Hebdo Attack Puts Schools under Scrutiny', *The New York Times*, 10 February 2015.

- creating a physical space, such as a drop-in centre, a youth community centre, or a safe-hub where children and young people feel they can meet friends in a safe environment to participate in an activity they enjoy while benefiting from adult mentorship and life-skills training;
- life-skills include transformative leadership training, conflict management, planning for the future, open discussions in a safe environment, communication skills, tutoring;
- adult mentorship and peer-to peer support;
- the fact that the activities and life-skills proposed follow a progression, with established incentives, such as diplomas, becoming a peer-to-peer instructor or participating in outside sports or arts competition;
- last but not least, young people need to feel they have been consulted on the activities proposed and have an active role in designing and monitoring the project. Programmes either run by former gang members or involving them in significant ways have also proven effective, especially for young people trying to leave gangs.

Programmes that are implemented together with local community-based associations and with local authorities have the advantage of building in sustainability. Whenever possible, NGOs and INGOs should therefore deliberately involve local actors, both grassroots organizations and government entities at both the national and municipal level.

BEYOND VOCATIONAL TRAINING AND JOB PLACEMENT

While vocational training and job placement initiatives have proven particularly useful in preventing gang involvement and rehabilitating former gang members,[77] with young people at risk of radicalization, whether in Europe, Pakistan, Nigeria, or Somalia, poverty and lack of jobs are not the main drivers of extremism, which is why the kinds of responses needed seem to be both simpler and more complex. As we have seen, it is often social and political marginalization, as well as idealism and the need to fit into a larger, heroic narrative that seems to propel teenagers to join the ranks of extremist groups in Syria, Iraq, or elsewhere. As pointed out by Sharon Morris,[78] they want to 'change the world, to fight injustice, to earn respect, and … to

[77] The best-known initiative is Los Angeles-based Homeboy Industries, founded in 1988 by Father Greg Boyle, a Jesuit priest. It created several social business enterprises which provide job training to former gang members, along with remedial education, psychosocial support, anger management, tattoo removal, treatment for substance abuse, legal assistance, and job placement services. Interestingly, members of rival gangs work side by side.

[78] Morris, S., 2014, 'Teenage Wasteland; why do so many efforts to stop young people from joining extremist groups fail?' *Foreign Policy*, November 4.

challenge the status quo'. Which means that 'as long as the answers to the problem of radicalized youth are primarily focused on priorities such as finding a job or staying in school—sensible, adult concerns that ignore the emotional, black-and-white way many teen-agers see the world—assistance is likely to miss the mark or even make things worse'.[79] If traditional job creation programmes miss the point, the challenge for governments and other programming bodies is to come up with alternative narratives and worthwhile causes that are more exciting than those peddled by extremist groups. A tall order, particularly if young people feel the societies they live in have either reached a dead end or are excluding them, and if well-meaning government programming is viewed suspiciously (as in the case of PREVENT). If some of this energy and idealism is to be harnessed, then programmes need to take into account the needs, views, and ideas of the very people they are trying to help and offer avenues for meaningful engagement in social and political transformation, starting with the communities in which they live.

Concluding remarks

Young people are truly at the centre of violence and social upheavals, while also representing a strong potential for positive change and transformation. They also have needs that are different from those of younger children and adults. Recognizing this, many humanitarian organizations have increasingly been programming specifically for this segment of the population. Witness, for example, the United Nations High Commissioner for Refugees (UNHCR), which recently added a Youth Unit, separate from already existing Education and Child Protection Units, to cater for displaced and refugee youth. UNHCR youth programmes also build upon the valuable contributions youth can make to their communities as leaders and activists by helping them implement their own projects and partnering with youth groups. [80]

Although the motivations young people have for joining a gang in Latin America or joining IS in Syria stem from different dynamics, we have seen there are common denominators in both cases, including age (fifteen to eighteen), feelings of marginalization and humiliation (and its flip side, omnipotence), peer influence, a search for identity and meaning and the need to belong to a group of like-minded peers who will provide protection and/or family-like ties and help them forge a sense of identity. In both instances, urban settings, whether the *barrio*, *favela*, or the French *banlieue*, with its

[79] Ibid.

[80] From conversations with Nick Sore, Youth Officer at UNHCR Headquarters, Geneva, March 2015.

disjointed social fabric, provide the backdrop where these children grow up to become frustrated, angry, or desperate teens.

In both cases, situations of anomie[81] exacerbate the propensity for young people to seek a sense of kinship, belonging, and meaning elsewhere. In fact, gangs are often an attempt to recreate the social fabric. In Central America, for example, some gangs provide an element of social cohesion in the absence of State institutions and services and protect the community from police brutality or from incursions from other gangs. For young people joining IS, feelings of sisterhood and brotherhood around a common cause seem to be paramount.

In the case of young Westerners joining groups such as IS, especially from the more affluent countries and social classes, there is yet another dynamic at work: a profound disaffection with what they perceive as the shallow and materialistic values of Western societies, leading them to search for meaning, including spiritual, elsewhere.

This is why so many of the interventions aimed at preventing youth from joining gangs or extremist organizations focus on social cohesion and community integration. The problem is that, when these interventions are implemented from the top down, attempting to translate theory into practice, as in the case of PREVENT, they seldom work. Recreating or strengthening the social fabric is indeed crucial to create the conditions in which marginalized youth can start to feel integrated, but for programmes to work, direct beneficiaries and local communities need to be an integral part of the initiatives, particularly at the planning stage. If programming activities aimed at youth are ultimately going to help build solidarity networks within the community, they need to grow organically in response to real needs and fully take into account the ability of young people to shape such initiatives.

[81] The term was popularized by French sociologist Emile Durkheim and describes a condition in which there is a mismatch between personal and group aspirations and wider social norms and standards, resulting in a breakdown of social bonds between individuals and the community, a fragmentation of the social fabric and a crisis in values.

C
Accountability

11 Extraordinary rendition and the European Court of Human Rights

Silvia Suteu[1]

Introduction

The most visible event of 2014 with regard to counter-terrorism may well have been the US Senate Select Committee on Intelligence *Study of the Central Intelligence Agency's Detention and Interrogation Program* declassified in early December.[2] It unequivocally admitted that the Central Intelligence Agency (CIA) had engaged in so-called 'enhanced interrogation techniques' of suspected terrorists detained at secret sites which amounted to torture, that these methods were not effective in yielding intelligence, and that the CIA had misrepresented the programme. The report sent shockwaves through the world, not so much due to the novelty of the findings—most of which had previously been suspected and then documented in reports by international and non-governmental organizations[3]—but due to their source. Here was the US Senate itself pointing the finger at CIA practices which had long been criticized as amounting to serious human rights violations in a (albeit redacted) 6,700-page report which immediately triggered calls for prosecutions.[4]

[1] PhD research student at the University of Edinburgh School of Law and Associate Director for Research Engagement, Edinburgh Centre for Constitutional Law. Email: s.suteu@sms.ed.ac.uk.

[2] *Study of the Central Intelligence Agency's Detention and Interrogation Program*, United States Senate Select Committee on Intelligence, Approved 13 December 2012; Updated for Release 3 April 2014; Declassification Revisions 3 December 2014, <http://www.intelligence.senate.gov/study2014.html>.

[3] Examples of such reports abound, but one comprehensive source is The Open Society Justice Initiative's *Globalizing Torture: CIA Secret Detention and Extraordinary Rendition*, 2013, <http://www.opensociety-foundations.org/reports/globalizing-torture-cia-secret-detention-and-extraordinary-rendition>.

[4] See 'UN expert calls for prosecution of CIA, US officials for crimes committed during interrogations', *UN News Centre*, 9 December 2014, <http://www.un.org/apps/news/story.asp?NewsID=49560#.VJhX2kACB> and 'Human rights groups call for special prosecutor to investigate CIA torture', *The Guardian*, 22 December 2014, <http://www.theguardian.com/law/2014/dec/22/aclu-human-rights-watch-ask-eric-holder-prosecute-cia-torture>.

Less visible was the European Court of Human Rights (ECtHR) continuing on its path to address extraordinary rendition in Council of Europe (CoE) member States. In its judgments in *Al Nashiri v Poland*[5] and *Husayn (Abu Zubaydah) v Poland*,[6] the Court built on its jurisprudence in this area—most prominently on the *El Masri v Former Yugoslav Republic of Macedonia* (FYROM)[7] case decided in 2012—and added one more brick to the judicial edifice surrounding what was previously termed a 'black hole'[8] in international law: extraordinary measures, such as rendition and black site detention, as part of counter-terrorism efforts by States. As this chapter will show, from a certain point of view, the 2014 judgments of the ECtHR may be viewed as even more significant than the US Senate's CIA report. For while the latter adds a crucial piece to the massive evidentiary trove detailing torture at secret detention sites, the European Court's judgments actually advance the fight against impunity of those responsible for such human rights violations. The fact that responsibility was attributed to a State for the illegal detention, transfer, and treatment of terrorism suspects by a court of law[9] is a significant step forward in ensuring accountability in the murky area of counter-terrorism.

The chapter proceeds by, first, defining extraordinary rendition and the elements which distinguish it from other types of transfer of detainees under international law. Second, the chapter delves into Strasbourg case law on this matter, with special attention provided to the *El Masri* and *Al Nashiri* cases (the *Abu Zubaydah* case is referenced only insofar as it adds distinct elements from the latter). The atypical position of Strasbourg emerges from these comparisons: as a bold institutional actor asserting the need to protect human rights and the rule of law despite governments' appeals to State secrets and national security exceptions. Third, I temper this praise by outlining four areas which remain problematic in the European Court's extraordinary rendition jurisprudence: the attribution of responsibility for the transfers of detainees; the right to the truth; rendition as a case of enforced disappearance; and the reliance on diplomatic assurances when analyzing the *non-refoulement* principle. The chapter concludes by cautioning against exaggerated optimism regarding extraordinary rendition cases in Strasbourg and by looking to the future at cases still pending before the ECtHR and other international developments likely to impact its jurisprudence in this area.

[5] App. no. 28761/11, Judgment, 24 July 2014. [6] App. no. 7511/13, Judgment, 24 July 2014.

[7] App. no. 39630/09, Judgment, 13 December 2012.

[8] Lord Steyn, J., 2004, 'Guantanamo Bay: The Legal Black Hole', *International and Comparative Law Quarterly*, vol. 53 (January): p. 1.

[9] On the importance of the ECtHR's role as a court of law pronouncing on these matters, see Fabbrini, F., 2014, 'The European Court of Human Rights, Extraordinary Renditions and the Right to the Truth: Ensuring Accountability for Gross Human Rights Violations Committed in the Fight Against Terrorism', *Human Rights Law Review*, vol. 14: p. 99.

A. Defining extraordinary rendition

Before looking in depth at its case law, it is worthwhile knowing what the ECtHR understands by extraordinary rendition in the counter-terrorism context. The definition the Court relies upon in *El Masri* (§221) and subsequently in *Al Nashiri* (§454) is taken from a previous case, *Babar Ahmad and Others v the United Kingdom*, wherein it defined extraordinary rendition as:

> the extra-judicial transfer of persons from one jurisdiction or State to another, for the purposes of detention and interrogation outside the normal legal system, where there was a real risk of torture or cruel, inhuman or degrading treatment.[10]

This definition, albeit adopted by the ECtHR from a UK Intelligence and Security Committee special report on rendition submitted in the *Babar* case,[11] mirrors those employed by other European institutions in their resolutions on and inquiries into the legality of renditions in their member States. The Council of Europe Parliamentary Assembly, in a resolution from as early as 2005, had defined rendition as 'removal of persons to other countries, without judicial supervision, for purposes such as interrogation or detention'.[12] The Venice Commission had adopted a similar definition, emphasizing that rendition was 'a general term referring more to the result—obtaining of custody over a suspected person—rather than the means' and could be unlawful, particularly if it breached international human rights law.[13] In fact, the Commission stressed that '[t]he term "extraordinary rendition" appears to be used when there is little or no doubt that the obtaining of custody over a person is not in accordance with the existing legal procedures applying in the State where the person was situated at the time'.[14] Subsequent CoE documents used even stronger language and understood rendition to be aimed at illegally transferring persons 'often to be handed over to States who customarily resort to degrading treatment and torture'.[15] The European Parliament had also emphasized

[10] Partial Decision as to the Admissibility of Application nos. 24027/07, 11949/08 and 36742/08 by Babar Ahmad, Haroon Rashid Aswat, Syed Tahla Ahsan, and Mustafa Kamal Mustafa (Abu Hamza) against the United Kingdom, 6 July 2010: §113.

[11] See *Babar Ahmad and Others v the United Kingdom*, §81.

[12] Resolution 1433 (2005): Lawfulness of Detentions by the United States in Guantánamo Bay, Council of Europe Parliamentary Assembly: vii.

[13] Opinion on the International Legal Obligations of Council of Europe Member States in Respect of Secret Detention Facilities and Inter-State Transfer of Prisoners, European Commission for Democracy through Law (Venice Commission), Opinion no. 363/2005, CDL-AD(2006)009, 17 March 2006: §30.

[14] Ibid., §31.

[15] *Alleged Secret Detentions and Unlawful Inter-state Transfers of Detainees Involving Council of Europe Member States* ('the 2006 Marty report'), Council of Europe Committee on Legal Affairs and Human Rights, Doc. 10957, 12 June 2006: p. 4.

the extra-judicial nature of rendition and its breach of international human rights law, at the same time as it directly linked the practice to US involvement:

> the programme of extraordinary rendition is an extra-judicial practice which contravenes established international human rights standards and whereby an individual suspected of involvement in terrorism is illegally abducted, arrested and/or transferred into the custody of US officials and/or transported to another country for interrogation which, in the majority of cases, involves incommunicado detention and torture.[16]

The Court's definition is also consistent with scholarly views on the meaning of extraordinary rendition. While scholars and non-governmental organizations have striven to distinguish this practice from other forms of rendition[17] and transfers of prisoners,[18] it is clear the term 'rendition', with the usual qualifiers 'extraordinary' or 'irregular', has acquired 'the unambiguously negative connotation of removal of a suspected terrorist to another state, without judicial supervision, particularly for coercive interrogation and/or indefinite or extrajudicial detention'.[19] As Silvia Borelli has pointed out, the common features in all these definitions are: a 'territorial state' consenting to US agents' actions (with its own local agents involved to varying degrees); certain modalities of transfer which often include so-called 'rendition flights' operated by the CIA or the US military; and States of destination which are principally outside Europe (exceptions are Lithuania, Poland, and Romania) and where victims of rendition are placed in detention facilities operated by local authorities or, again, the United States.[20]

The European Court's adopted definition may thus be said to be comparatively restrained in the connection it draws between extraordinary rendition and the 'real risk'—rather than the intended purpose—of torture or cruel, inhuman, or degrading treatment. Its emphasis on the extra-legal nature of both the transfer and the detention and interrogation of the victim of rendition, however, retain the core of what makes this practice 'extraordinary' in the worst sense of the term.

[16] *Report on the Alleged Use of European Countries by the CIA for the Transportation and Illegal Detention of Prisoners (2006/2200(INI))* ('the Fava report'), European Parliament Temporary Committee on the alleged use of European countries by the CIA for the transportation and illegal detention of prisoners, A6-0020/2007, 30 January 2007: §36.

[17] See *Globalizing Torture*, p. 120.

[18] Satterthwaite, M. L., 2015, 'The Legal Regime Governing Transfer of Persons in the Fight Against Terrorism'. In *Counter-Terrorism Strategies in a Fragmented International Legal Order: Meeting the Challenges*, edited by van den Herik, L. and Schrijver, N., Cambridge: Cambridge University Press, pp. 589–638.

[19] Borelli, S., 2014, 'Extraordinary Rendition, Counter-terrorism, and International Law'. In *Research Handbook on International Law and Terrorism*, edited by Saul, B., Cheltenham: Edward Elgar Publishing, p. 362.

[20] Ibid., pp. 363–364.

B. Strasbourg expands its extraordinary rendition doctrine

THE *AL NASHIRI, ABU ZUBAYDAH,* AND *EL MASRI* CASES

The *Al Nashiri* case concerned the application of Abd al-Rahim Hussayn Muhammed Al Nashiri, a Saudi Arabian who claimed to have been held incommunicado and tortured by CIA agents in the Polish prison Stare Kiejkuty between December 2002 and June 2003, having previously been detained and tortured at the notorious 'Salt Pit' secret CIA-run prison in Afghanistan and at another black site in Thailand. Polish authorities then assisted US agents in flying Al Nashiri out of the country, with the US Government finally acknowledging his detention at Guantánamo Bay in September 2006. The facts up to this point are similar in Abu Zubaydah's case. Proceedings against Al Nashiri were initiated before a military commission in Guantánamo in December 2008, dropped in February 2009, and then reinstated in April 2011. He was charged for his alleged role in the attack on the *USS Cole* in 2000 and the attack on the French civilian oil tanker *MV Limburg* in the Gulf of Aden in 2002, charges which carry the death penalty.[21] The same year he filed an application with the ECtHR against Poland, Al Nashiri also began proceedings against Romania[22] as a country in which he was also allegedly rendered and tortured. That case is still pending before the Court.

The *Al Nashiri* judgment was not the first in which the ECtHR addressed extraordinary rendition. Its 2012 decision in the *El Masri* case was the first time the Court did so, and it did this with a bang. That case concerned a German national, Khaled El Masri, who had been detained incommunicado and without charge and ill-treated for several months on the territory of the Former Yugoslav Republic of Macedonia (hereinafter 'FYROM' or 'Macedonia'), after which he had been transferred—on a flight operated by, and following procedures typical of, the CIA—to a black site in Afghanistan (the 'Salt Pit' prison also used for Al Nashiri). Following torture and ill-treatment there, he had been returned to Kosovo and from there he had returned to Germany, still never having been charged. El Masri subsequently began proceedings both in Macedonia and Germany, as well as in the United States. He lodged his application in Strasbourg following the failure of either of these to reach a verdict in his case.

In *El Masri*, the ECtHR found Macedonia guilty of having violated Articles 3, 5, 8, and 13 of the European Convention on Human Rights (hereinafter 'Convention' or

[21] See *Al Nashiri*, §122.

[22] See Information Note on the Court's case law No. 155, August-September 2012, *Al Nashiri v Romania* (communicated case) 33234/12.

'ECHR'). It also found that the six-month limit on beginning proceedings before it following the exhaustion of domestic remedies had not been breached. Importantly, the Court also engaged in an extensive factual analysis, reaching a conclusion which also built on indirect evidence (notably reports by international organizations and NGOs) and which largely supported the applicant's version of events. In *Al Nashiri*, the ECtHR found Poland in breach of Articles 2, 3, 5, 6, 38, and 46 of the Convention. The most significant findings in the Court's judgments in these two cases are briefly examined in what follows.

THE SIX-MONTH RULE

The Court in *El Masri* had to first deal with a jurisdiction challenge based on the six-month rule incorporated in Article 35(1) of the Convention. The Macedonian Government had argued that the rule had been breached and that El Masri had lodged his application with domestic authorities more than four years after the events complained of, and against an unidentified perpetrator. The ECtHR clarified that the relevant question was 'whether, in the particular circumstances of the present case, a criminal complaint was an effective remedy to be used by the applicant in order to seek redress for his Convention grievances' (§138). The Court found that, given the complexity of the case and the 'policy of obstruction' he faced, it was reasonable for the applicant to pursue his domestic case only insofar as he had corroborative evidence (§142). The Court thus concluded that the six-month period began when the final decision regarding his criminal complaint became known to the applicant (§147).

The significance of the Court's findings on this procedural matter is great. ECtHR case law prior to *El Masri* paints a picture wherein the Court was less willing to take into account the special circumstances involved in extraordinary rendition when assessing procedural jurisdictional challenges. The case of *Alzery v Sweden* concerned an Egyptian national who was denied asylum in Sweden as a suspected terrorist and returned to Egypt on the basis of diplomatic assurances that he would be afforded a fair trial and not be mistreated. His expulsion was implemented by the Swedish secret service with the help of American authorities who provided a plane and, allegedly, was done with the suspect in shackles and handcuffs for the duration of the flight. Once in Egypt, he was immediately imprisoned and allegedly ill-treated and tortured. The ECtHR never got to opine on the veracity of Alzery's case as it dismissed his application on procedural grounds.[23] The Court was not swayed by either the gravity of the alleged

[23] Decision as to the Admissibility of Application no. 10786/04 by Mohammed Alzery against Sweden, 26 October 2004.

violation (torture), nor by the exceptional circumstances of the case (the applicant being imprisoned in Egypt at the time of the application being lodged) and dismissed the case for being out of time. Interestingly, however, the Court did mention that 'the Swedish Government has had to answer to other international human rights bodies, notably the UN Human Rights Committee and the Council of Europe Commissioner for Human Rights'.[24] It thus seemed to find some reassurance in the fact that the very serious violations invoked in the case still found redress, even if not before it.[25]

The *Alzery* decision was handed down in 2004, at a radically different time from *El Masri* and *Al Nashiri*. The wealth of evidence on extraordinary rendition was not yet present in the public domain and the Court found little reason to deviate from its procedural strictures in admitting the application before it. One can only speculate as to whether the Court would have reached a different conclusion were the case before it at a different time. What this case does show, however, is just how noteworthy the *El Masri* decision was, even at the jurisdictional level. The six-month rule would not feature in the *Al Nashiri* case. However, the complex nature of cases involving allegations of extraordinary rendition makes it likely that procedural arguments rooted in the late lodging of applications may yet be invoked. The ECtHR's careful weighing of the law on this matter was therefore a step in the direction of precluding procedural technicalities from automatically rendering cases inadmissible.

ARTICLE 3 ECHR VIOLATIONS

The ECtHR approached the Article 3 problem both under its substantive aspects and by inquiring into whether an effective investigation had taken place. In *El Masri*, the latter was found to have been missing, despite it constituting *ipso facto* an obligation for the State given the amount of evidence from international investigations corroborating the applicant's claims (§186). However, the Macedonian Government had conceded that its investigation had not been effective (§§174, 190). The issue was more contentious in *Al Nashiri*, wherein the Polish Government contended that it 'was in fact the only country that was conducting a proper criminal investigation into the allegations of rendition and secret detention' (§463). To the government's arguments about the extraordinary complexity and international character of the case, the applicant retorted that 'the investigation had been neither promptly begun, nor had been promptly carried out' (§472); that it 'was not sufficiently independent' (§473); that it lacked transparency,

[24] Ibid., p. 8.

[25] In fact, the UN Human Rights Committee did find Sweden guilty of breaching the *non-refoulement* principle in Alzery's case. See *Mohammed Alzery v Sweden*, CCPR/C/88/D/1416/2005, UN Human Rights Committee (HRC), 10 November 2006.

having been shrouded in secrecy (§474); and that he had been denied access to his file, thus preventing his lawyers from adequately representing his interests (§475). The Court agreed with the applicant, finding that the national investigation 'failed to meet the requirements of a "prompt", "thorough" and "effective" investigation' (§499). It also expressed concern about 'a more general problem of democratic oversight of intelligence services' as a required national safeguard against abuses of Convention rights at their hands (§498).

On the substantive front, the ECtHR unequivocally found both the treatment of applicants while in detention and their transfers as amounting to violations of Article 3 ECHR. In *El Masri*, the Court first established that the applicant's secret and incommunicado detention in a hotel amounted to inhuman and degrading treatment (§204). The Court also established that the applicant's transfer and the treatment suffered during it were contrary to Article 3 and that FYROM authorities were responsible for the acts committed by CIA agents when transferring him (more on this below).

In *Al Nashiri*, the Court relied on exhaustive evidence to conclude that 'the treatment to which the applicant was subjected by the CIA during his detention in Poland at the relevant time amounted to torture within the meaning of Article 3 of the Convention' (§516). The novelty of this attribution of responsibility for torture to the CIA will be discussed below. With regard to Poland's responsibility, the ECtHR admitted that it was unlikely that Polish authorities had witnessed or knew exactly what was occurring at the Polish black site (§517). Nevertheless, the Court concluded:

> Under Article 1 of the Convention, taken together with Article 3, Poland was required to take measures designed to ensure that individuals within its jurisdiction were not subjected to torture or inhuman or degrading treatment or punishment, including ill-treatment administered by private individuals (§517).

It thus found that 'Poland, for all practical purposes, facilitated the whole process, created the conditions for it to happen and made no attempt to prevent it from occurring' (§517). Moreover, the Court stated, authorities 'must have been aware of the serious risk of treatment contrary to Article 3 occurring on Polish territory' (§517) and were 'aware that the transfer of the applicant to and from its territory was effected by means of "extraordinary rendition"' (§518). In other words, the Court left no doubt that European countries could neither feign ignorance nor minimize their roles in order to eschew responsibility for extraordinary renditions.

VIOLATIONS OF ARTICLE 5 ECHR

Other Convention rights were also implicated in the cases under discussion. Perhaps most significantly, both *El Masri* and *Al Nashiri* dealt with the question of whether the right to liberty and security, incorporated in Article 5 ECHR, had been violated. In the former, the ECtHR had to rule on whether El Masri's incommunicado detention without any arrest warrant having been issued constituted a breach of this right. The Court acknowledged the special circumstances involved in terrorism-related cases, but nevertheless ruled that these did not amount to giving governments *carte blanche*:

> although the investigation of terrorist offences undoubtedly presents the authorities with special problems, that does not mean that the authorities have carte blanche under Article 5 to arrest suspects and detain them in police custody, free from effective control by the domestic courts and, in the final instance, by the Convention's supervisory institutions, whenever they consider that there has been a terrorist offence (§232).

As such, the Court found Macedonia to have violated Article 5 when detaining El Masri in an 'unacknowledged detention' in a Skopje hotel (§237). Significantly, it went further and explained that Article 5 prevents not just active infringements, but also requires that the State 'take appropriate steps to provide protection against an unlawful interference with those rights to everyone within its jurisdiction' (§239). As a consequence, FYROM was found responsible for a breach of Article 5 for the duration of El Masri's entire captivity, including in Afghanistan (§241).

In *Al Nashiri* we see the Court, again based on the exhaustive evidence before it, even more confidently condemning the secret detention to which the applicant had been subjected in breach of Article 5. It stated that 'secret detention of terrorist suspects was a fundamental feature of the CIA rendition programme', whose rationale was to place suspects beyond the reach of either domestic or international law (§530). Cooperation of States with this programme was what allowed the CIA-run facilities to serve this function, and the Court unequivocally condemned any such aid:

> The rendition operations had therefore largely depended on cooperation, assistance an active involvement of the countries which put at the USA's disposal their airspace, airports for the landing of aircraft transporting CIA prisoners and, last but not least, premises on which the prisoners could be securely detained and interrogated (§530).

Just as in the case of Article 3, Article 5's procedural requirements were breached by both countries' failure to conduct effective investigations (*El Masri* §242, *Al Nashiri* §531).

VIOLATIONS OF ARTICLE 6 AND OF ARTICLES 2 AND 3 IN CONJUNCTION WITH ARTICLE 1 OF PROTOCOL 6 OF THE CONVENTION

Al Nashiri's case differed from El Masri's in respect of his transfer to Guantánamo and subsequent indictment on capital charges before a US military commission. He argued before the ECtHR that his transfer by CIA agents had put him at 'a real and serious risk of being transferred to a jurisdiction where he would be subjected to a flagrantly unfair trial, in breach of Article 6 §1 of the Convention' (§552). The Court agreed and concluded that the military commission set to try him 'did not offer guarantees of impartiality of independence of the executive as required of a "tribunal" under the Court's case-law'; 'that it did not have legitimacy under US and international law…and that, consequently, it was not "established by law" for the purposes of Article 6 §1'; 'and that there was a sufficiently high probability of admission of evidence obtained under torture in trials against terrorist suspects' (§567). As such, the ECtHR stated, at the time of Al Nashiri's transfer from Poland, 'there was a real risk that his trial before the military commission would amount to a flagrant denial of justice' (§567).

Also present in *Al Nashiri* but not in *El Masri* was the alleged breach of Articles 2 and 3 in conjunction with Article 1 of Protocol 6 of the Convention, the latter of which prohibits the death penalty. Al Nashiri argued that it had been a matter of public knowledge at the time of his transfer from Poland that he would face the death penalty following an inherently unfair trial in the United States (§572). He also invoked the ECtHR's prior case law, notably *Al Saadoon and Mufdhi v the United Kingdom*[26] wherein the Court had found that the 2005 transfer of two Iraqi detainees from UK to Iraqi custody amounted to a breach of Article 3 due to the risk of capital punishment they faced in the Iraqi criminal system. Moreover, Al Nashiri argued, based on the Court's previous decision in *Ocalan v Turkey*,[27] 'that the imposition of the death penalty following an unfair trial would amount to an arbitrary deprivation of life in violation of Article 2 and also of Article 3, as it would subject a person wrongfully to the fear that he was going to be executed' (§573). The Court agreed and found that at the time of Al Nashiri's transfer, there was 'a substantial and foreseeable risk that he could be subjected to the death penalty following his trial before the military commission' and, given the confirmation of his charges, that that risk had not diminished (§578).

C. **Outstanding problematic aspects of Strasbourg's extraordinary rendition doctrine**

Despite the enthusiasm with which these recent Strasbourg decisions have been met in both the legal and scholarly communities, there remain causes for caution. It is worthwhile remembering that, desirable and weighty though a court pronouncement may

[26] App. no. 61498/08, Judgment, 2 March 2010.
[27] App. no. 46221/99, Grand Chamber Judgment, 12 May 2005.

be in these matters, it also carries its limitations. One of the most obvious ones with regard to extraordinary rendition cases, and counter-terrorism cases more generally, is the question of time. One must note that all three applicants only found redress a full twelve years after their initial capture, following arduously fought cases which required extensive resources. Moreover, as one author puts it, the ECtHR became involved in rendition cases late compared to other regional human rights bodies.[28] Such a prolonged process, however unfortunate, is likely unavoidable precisely because of the complexity of cases involving counter-terrorism suspects. The same rigour which lends the judicial process its prestige is also likely to result in years-long proceedings and delayed resolution.

While that is an inherent characteristic of the legal process, other problematic aspects of Strasbourg's doctrine in this area may not have been similarly inevitable. In what follows, I explore four issues which the Court addressed in *El Masri* and *Al Nashiri*, not necessarily coherently, and which may leave room to question whether the ECtHR has taken the most human rights-protective stance possible.

ATTRIBUTION OF STATE RESPONSIBILITY

One such issue concerns the attribution of State responsibility for the transfer, detention of, and treatment suffered therein by the applicants. The Court may be said to have taken a bold step by finding member States responsible not just for the detention of terrorist suspects on their territory and for their transfer, but also, given their collusion and knowledge of likely outcomes, for the treatment they suffered once rendered. This was in fact as far as the Court would go in *El Masri*. In that case, the Court found Macedonia directly responsible for violations of Convention rights having occurred during the applicant's extraordinary rendition:

> The respondent State must be considered directly responsible for the violation of the applicant's rights under this head since its agents actively facilitated the treatment and then failed to take any measures that might have been necessary in the circumstances of the case to prevent it from occurring (§211).

The Court further clarified that any liability it would find would have been incurred solely by Macedonia as the sending State in the instant case of extraordinary rendition:

> There is no question of adjudicating on or establishing the responsibility of the receiving country, whether under general international law, under the Convention or otherwise. In so far as any liability under the Convention is or may be incurred, it is liability incurred by the sending

[28] Borelli, S., 'Extraordinary Rendition', p. 377.

Contracting State by reason of its having taken action which has as a direct consequence the exposure of an individual to proscribed ill-treatment (§212).

A significant change in *Al Nashiri* and *Abu Zubaydah* as compared to *El Masri*, also noted by commentators such as Martin Scheinin,[29] concerns the language used to describe the CIA's responsibility in these cases. Where the Court in *El Masri* found that 'the respondent State must be regarded as responsible under the Convention for acts performed by foreign officials on its territory with the acquiescence or connivance of its authorities' (§206), it took a more assertive stance in the two 2014 cases. In *Al Nashiri*, it 'conclude[d] that the treatment to which the applicant was subjected *by* the *CIA* during his detention in Poland at the relevant time amounted to torture within the meaning of Article 3 of the Convention' (§516, emphasis added; see also *Abu Zubaydah*, §511). Noting this newfound assertiveness, Scheinin asks:

> whether the ECtHR through its formulations in paras. 516-517 created a situation where the US was an *indispensable third party*, to the effect that the finding in respect of the lawfulness of conduct by the US was a prerequisite for a conclusion in relation to Poland, even if the Court obviously did not consider the US participation in the proceedings (or consent to its jurisdiction) to be indispensable.[30]

Scheinin goes on to ask whether the ECtHR could not make creative use of Article 36 of the Convention, according to which the President of the Court may ask 'any person concerned who is not the applicant to submit written comments or take part in hearings', to invite non-European States to intervene in cases where they are implicated by the facts. In cases such as those involving extraordinary rendition, the US would likely refuse to do so, but the invitation in itself 'would strengthen the legitimacy of the ECtHR', Scheinin argues.[31]

The concern here, shared by Scheinin and others, is to ensure accountability for these wrongs from those most responsible, i.e., those having set up and led the extraordinary rendition programme. Important though the *El Masri*, *Al Nashiri*, and *Abu Zubaydah* cases were, they addressed only a minute share of the responsibility for the human rights violations suffered by the applicants. Given that the prospect of US prosecutions reaching the CIA and other officials involved is unlikely, even in the aftermath of the 2014 Senate report disclosures, perhaps Scheinin's hypothesis is not as far-fetched as it may appear initially. It would be a path which the Court might wish to entertain taking with a view to ensuring a more meaningful end to impunity.

[29] Scheinin, M., 2014, 'The ECtHR Finds the US Guilty of Torture—As an Indispensable Third Party?', EJIL: *Talk!*, 28 July, <http://www.ejiltalk.org/the-ecthr-finds-the-us-guilty-of-torture-as-an-indispensable-third-party/>.

[30] Ibid. [31] Ibid.

THE RIGHT TO TRUTH

The same concern with ending impunity, and ensuring both a public and an individual right to the truth, featured in these cases, particularly in *El Masri*. There, in answering the question of whether an effective investigation had been conducted, the Court also addressed the right to truth, particularly as it interacted with the doctrine of State secrets (§191). The Court acknowledged the complex circumstances in such cases but deemed them insufficient so as to justify impunity for serious human rights violations (§192). Because of the disputed nature of the facts, the ECtHR proceeded to establish them itself based on the abundance of evidence before it, including circumstantial, and explained that '[i]n the proceedings before the Court, there are no procedural barriers to the admissibility of evidence or pre-determined formulae for its assessment' (§151). It categorically refused to accept that the doctrine of State secrets prevented it from doing so: 'The concept of "State secrets" has often been invoked to obstruct the search for the truth' (§191). Furthermore, because the majority of the evidence was in its hands, the Court reversed the burden of proof and entrusted it to the government (§152). Finally, the Court explained that the right to the truth had both a private and a public dimension, and 'underline[d] the great importance of the present case not only for the applicant and his family, but also for other victims of similar crimes and the general public, who had the right to know what had happened' (§191).

This embrace of the right to the truth was lauded by commentators who praised *El Masri* as 'the first judicial decision which officially recognises the events, and the first verdict that effectively holds a government accountable for them'.[32] Others have pointed to the right to truth and freedom of information mechanisms more generally as useful both in litigation and in obtaining crucial evidence in counter-terrorism contexts.[33]

The ECtHR's embrace of this new paradigm was partial, however.[34] Two separate opinions attached to the judgment disputed both the place of the right to truth within the Convention and its necessity and reach. Thus, the four judges signing the first separate opinion saw the right to truth as 'more appropriately situated in the context of Article 13 of the Convention'.[35] Read in this context, they argued, the right to truth, 'far from being either innovative or superfluous',[36] could be seen as a logical development of ECtHR case law. Conversely, the two judges writing the second separate opinion saw the recourse to a right to the truth 'as something different from, or additional to, the requisites already established in such matters by the previous case-law of the Court' and as such as being unnecessary.[37] Moreover, the two wrote, the right to a serious investigation

[32] Fabbrini, F., 'The European Court of Human Rights', p. 96.

[33] Duffy, H., 2015, 'Accountability for Counter-Terrorism: Challenges and Potential in the Role of the Courts'. In *Critical Debates on Counter-Terrorism Judicial Review*, edited by Davis, F. F. and de Londras, F., Cambridge: Cambridge University Press, pp. 356–7.

[34] See also Fabbrini, F., 'The European Court of Human Rights', pp. 101–2.

[35] *El Masri*, Joint Concurring Opinion of Judges Tulkens, Spielmann, Sicilianos, and Keller, §4.

[36] Ibid., §7.

[37] *El Masri*, Joint Concurring Opinion of Judges Casadevall and Lopez Guerra.

applies irrespective of the publicity attached to the case, and they thus negated the public dimension of the right to the truth identified in the judgment: 'Therefore, as far as the right to the truth is concerned, it is the victim, and not the general public, who is entitled to this right as resulting from Article 3 of the Convention, in the light of the Court's case-law.'[38]

There is merit to all these disparate points of view. One can agree with the judgment in its adoption of a right to truth paradigm in a context—national security—which, like the original setting in which the concept of this right was developed (enforced disappearances, more on which shortly), has also suffered at the hands of opaque and obstructing official action. One can also see the potential unintended consequences resulting from developing a right to truth doctrine, whether linked to Article 3 violations or to Article 13, if its protection were to depend on the nature of the alleged violation. The split in the Court may have attenuated the 'possibly... novel standard'[39] to be applied to investigations in national security cases. However, if *Al Nashiri* and *Abu Zubaydah* were the testing ground for the embrace of a right to the truth doctrine as enunciated in *El Masri*, then it proved successful (§495 and §489, respectively). It remains to be seen how the finer points of contention above, notably which Convention right(s) the right to truth attaches to, will be decided in future case law.

EXTRAORDINARY RENDITIONS AS CASES OF ENFORCED DISAPPEARANCE

Extraordinary rendition can be seen as a case of, or also implicating, enforced disappearance, even while the ECtHR in both *El Masri* and *Al Nashiri* went further by also finding, primarily, violations of Article 3 ECHR. This does not negate that both crimes 'violate a multiplicity of human rights and that such violations are inherently cumulative, being part of a single conduct having the effect of placing the person concerned outside the protection of the law'.[40] Thus, in *El Masri* the Court found that:

> the applicant's abduction and detention amounted to 'enforced disappearance' as defined in international law... The applicant's 'enforced disappearance', although temporary, was characterised by an ongoing situation of uncertainty and unaccountability, which extended through the entire period of his captivity (§240).

[38] Ibid. [39] Fabbrini, F., 'The European Court of Human Rights', p. 102.

[40] Mussi, F., 2013, 'Extraordinary Renditions as Enforced Disappearances? The Jurisprudence of the European Court of Human Rights', *Diritti umani e diritto internazionale*, vol. 2 (May-August), pp. 365–78.

Similarly, in *Al Nashiri* the ECtHR found the rationale behind the applicant's treatment to be to facilitate impunity for torture and enforced disappearance:

> as can be seen from the CIA declassified documents, the rationale behind the programme was specifically to remove those persons from any legal protection against torture and enforced disappearance and to strip them of any safeguards afforded by both the US Constitution and international law against arbitrary detention, to mention only the right to be brought before a judge and be tried within a reasonable time or the *habeas corpus* guarantees (§530).

As was argued by many of the third party interveners in both cases, the right to truth and the protection against enforced disappearance are inherently linked.[41] This connection has long been acknowledged in scholarship on the emergence of an actionable right to the truth;[42] the context of extraordinary renditions may be said to provide yet another instantiation of an array of human rights violations accompanied by silence on the part of national authorities.

The commonalities between enforced disappearances and renditions thus also extend to the behaviour of national and international bodies when faced with investigations into their conduct. This was shown by 'the comprehensive governmental silence' amounting to a 'wall of silence', also encompassing NATO and the CIA, exhibited in the *El Masri* case.[43] The silence in *El Masri* was pierced by the intervention of the former Minister of Interior of Macedonia as witness in the case, but solely for the purposes of that case and only following increased international scrutiny, including by the Council of Europe and the European Parliament.[44] By 2014 when the *Al Nashiri* judgment was rendered, the amount of evidence corroborating the applicant's allegations was too overwhelming and credible to overlook. Nevertheless, the Court's pronouncements on rendition as enforced disappearance were sparse in both *El Masri* and *Al Nashiri* and are perhaps riper for scholars to debate than central to Strasbourg's doctrine on these matters. Indeed, its enforced disappearance doctrine may itself be in flux, with recent cases showing a less determined Court with respect to enforcing the right to truth.[45]

[41] See, inter alia, the UN High Commissioner for Human Rights making this argument in *El Masri* at §175 and, on the risk that secrecy of detention and transfer could expose suspects to torture, enforced disappearance, and extrajudicial killing, the UN Working Group on Arbitrary Detention in *Al Nashiri*, §216.

[42] Naqvi, Y., 2006, 'The Right to the Truth in International Law: Fact or Fiction?', *International Review of the Red Cross*, vol. 88 (June), pp. 248–9.

[43] Keller, H. and Heri, C., 2014, 'Enforced Disappearance and the European Court of Human Rights: A "Wall of Silence", Fact-Finding Difficulties and States as "Subversive Objectors"', *Journal of International Criminal Justice*, vol. 12: p. 742.

[44] Ibid., p. 743.

[45] See Heri, C., 2014, 'Enforced Disappearance and the European Court of Human Rights' *Ratione Temporis* Jurisdiction: A Discussion of Temporal Elements in *Janowiec and Others v. Russia*', *Journal of International Criminal Justice*, vol. 12: p. 767.

DIPLOMATIC ASSURANCES

A final point of concern to be discussed here refers to the ECtHR's reliance on diplomatic assurances in its extraordinary rendition cases. In *El Masri*, for instance, the Court bemoaned that 'the respondent State did not seek any assurances from the US authorities to avert the risk of the applicant being ill-treated' (§219). In *Al Nashiri*, the Court similarly explained that in cases of removal from a territory, irrespective of the procedure to achieve it:

> the Court may require the State concerned to "take all possible steps" to obtain the appropriate diplomatic assurances from the destination State. Those representations may be required even if an applicant has already been transferred from the territory of the respondent State but the risk still continues (§587).

The court held these principles to apply *a fortiori* in cases involving extraordinary rendition (§588). It further found that Poland should have sought assurances against Al Nashiri being subjected to the death penalty (§589).

This reliance on diplomatic assurances with regard to transfers likely to result both in torture or ill-treatment and in subjection to the death penalty places the Court in unwelcome company when it comes to accepting the value of such assurances. A former CIA Director virtually admitted their irrelevance once a person is rendered.[46] The Task Force set up by President Obama upon taking office in 2009 to review the extraordinary rendition programme admitted that mechanisms to obtain, evaluate, and monitor assurances needed to be strengthened.[47]

More significantly, however, the United Nations has long called into question the reliability of assurances in protecting against torture. In a report from as early as 2002, the UN Special Rapporteur on Torture cautioned against their use unless the receiving State could offer an 'unequivocal guarantee' that the transferred person would not be subjected to torture and that there would be monitoring of compliance.[48] Assurances from countries which systematically practise torture are meaningless when seeking to respect the principle of *non-refoulement*.[49] The ECtHR's own doctrine in this area, built around cases in which there was a risk that the death penalty would apply to persons extradited from its member States, requires careful assessment of the human rights record of the

[46] Porter Goss Congressional testimony cited in *Globalizing Torture*, p. 15.

[47] Cited in Fabbrini, F., 2011, 'Extraordinary Renditions and the State Secret Privilege: Italy and the United States Compared', *Italian Journal of Public Law*, vol. 2: fn 3.

[48] *Interim Report of the Special Rapporteur on Torture, Theo van Boven, to the General Assembly A/57/173*, 2 July 2002.

[49] See also '"Diplomatic Assurances" against Torture: Questions and Answers', Human Rights Watch, 10 November 2006, <http://www.hrw.org/news/2006/11/10/diplomatic-assurances-against-torture>.

receiving country and the possibility of post-transfer monitoring of compliance with the assurance.[50]

It is unclear how much use diplomatic assurances could have been in the muddy area of extraordinary renditions. Given the secrecy of entire operations, with suspects hauled from one corner of the world to another never having been documented, let alone charged with a crime, it seems unlikely that a request of diplomatic assurance would have gained much traction; indeed, the territorial State likely would not even have known which State to request the assurance from. The ECtHR's legalistic insistence on assurances from the 'destination State', therefore, seems misguided. Furthermore, asking for an assurance from the US Government would not have proven more effective. To seek any guarantee against torture from a government whose agents have since been proven to have secretly and systematically engaged in such treatment would have been hopeless.

Concluding remarks

The cases discussed in this chapter were undoubtedly victories for the protection of human rights and the rule of law in the counter-terrorism context. They brought welcome accountability in instances of extraordinary rendition which had hitherto escaped it. Moreover, and not to be taken lightly, there is great value in having the evidence substantiating these renditions not just in the public domain (which they already largely were), but endorsed by a judicial ruling. The great lengths to which the ECtHR went to describe in detail these transfers, detentions, and mistreatments is thus to be commended. Even more so as other cases have already been lodged with the Court, both against Romania[51] and against Lithuania,[52] the two other European countries besides Poland accused of operating 'black detention sites' on their territories. Following the 2014 release of the US Senate's report, the European Parliament reopened its investigation into CIA run detentions and transfers in EU countries;[53] this may yet lead to new evidence and possibly new cases of human rights violations.

[50] See Izumo, A., 2010, 'Diplomatic Assurances Against Torture and Ill Treatment: European Court of Human Rights Jurisprudence', *Columbia Human Rights Law Review*, vol. 42 (Fall): pp. 233–277.

[51] See n. 22.

[52] *Abu Zubaydah v Lithuania*, App. no. 46454/11, lodged on 14 July 2011. See also *Human Rights Monitoring Institute v Republic of Lithuania*, lodged 20 December 2012.

[53] 'Parliament to Resume Investigations into CIA-led Operations in EU Countries', *European Parliament News*, 11 February 2015, <http://www.europarl.europa.eu/news/en/news-room/content/20150206IPR21212/html/Parliament-to-resume-investigations-into-CIA-led-operations-in-EU-countries>.

Scholarly opinion on these developments has largely been optimistic. One author has argued it is now possible to set out a minimum legal standard to be upheld in all settings of transfers of detainees.[54] This standard, she argues, would be 'most relevant for informal transfers, since they are almost always accomplished without regard to the full set of protections due to the individual being transferred'.[55] Others have focused on the positive role played by the ECtHR as a supranational human rights body.[56] They have argued that 'supranational criminal proceedings provide both a catalyst and an alternative to pursue accountability where the offending state does not assume the responsibility'.[57] Helen Duffy even speaks of complementarity between criminal, civil, and international human rights courts and identifies a welcome momentum behind legal proceedings and investigations in this matter.[58]

True as these observations may be, experience also dictates caution. Writing about domestic counter-terrorism cases which also, in their time, were heralded as human rights victories, David Jenkins warns against the phenomenon of 'good cases going bad'.[59] What he means by this is that 'over time, governments found ways around those decisions, either by taking advantage of their doctrinal weaknesses and ironically using them as justifications for expansions of national security powers, or resisting their implementation in other ways'.[60] Initial triumphs for human rights thus transformed into pyrrhic victories and there is no reason to assume governments today are any less inclined to eschew the reach of the law in an area they have traditionally viewed as their sole domain.[61] A 'blinkered, case-focused view'[62] may thus be particularly risky in the field of counter-terrorism. Continued vigilance, and not just in the European context,[63] remains necessary if accountability and an end to impunity for extraordinary renditions are to be more fully achieved.

[54] Satterthwaite, M., 'The Legal Regime', p. 595. [55] Ibid.

[56] Fabbrini, F., 'The European Court of Human Rights', p. 97 and Duffy, H., 'Accountability for Counter-Terrorism', p. 363.

[57] Duffy, H., 'Accountability for Counter-Terrorism', p. 363. [58] Ibid.

[59] Jenkins, D., 2014, 'When Good Cases Go Bad: Unintended Consequences of Rights-friendly Judgments'. In *Critical Debates on Counter-Terrorism Judicial Review* edited by Davis, F. F. and de Londras, F., Cambridge: Cambridge University Press, p. 95.

[60] Ibid.

[61] On the United Kingdom doing precisely this see Fenwick, H., 2014, 'Post 9/11 UK Counter-terrorism Cases in the European Court of Human Rights: A "Dialogic" Approach to Rights Protection or Appeasement of National Authorities?'. In *Critical Debates on Counter-Terrorism Judicial Review*, edited by Davis, F. F. and de Londras, F., Cambridge: Cambridge University Press, pp. 302–23.

[62] Jenkins, D., 'When Good Cases Go Bad', p. 96.

[63] Indeed, extraordinary renditions appear to have continued as late as 2014. See 'Fears build as CIA's "ghost prisoners" vanish into Afghan jails', *The Guardian*, 20 December 2014, <http://www.theguardian.com/us-news/2014/dec/20/cia-ghost-prisoners-torture-afghan-jails>.

12 National trials of international crimes in 2014: prosecuting 'refugees' suspected of international crimes

Ilia Maria Siatitsa[1]

Introduction

Over the past few years, there has been an increasing focus on initiating criminal proceedings against suspects of international crimes.[2] The attention on perpetrators of international crimes inevitably influenced the use of the exclusion clause in the 1951 Convention relating to the Status of Refugees.[3] The term 'refugee', referring to an individual 'deserving' asylum protection, in the title of the chapter is used only figuratively. Article 1F(a) of the 1951 Convention excludes any asylum seeker 'with respect to whom there are serious reasons for considering that: [among others] he [or she] has committed a crime against peace, a war crime, or a crime against humanity' from refugee protection. A State can also revoke refugee protection if the authorities later receive information regarding a suspected criminal act.

Until recently, the exclusion clause was rarely invoked.[4] Over the past decade, though, many perpetrators of international crimes have sought refugee status in countries around the world.[5] Applying the exclusion clause in refugee law meant that the asylum seeker does

[1] Ilia Maria Siatitsa is a PhD candidate at the Faculty of Law of the University of Geneva. She holds a fellowship from Swiss National Science Foundation 2015–2016.

[2] For the purpose of this chapter, 'international crimes' refer to war crimes, crimes against humanity, and genocide.

[3] The 1951 Convention defines who is a refugee, their rights, and the obligations of States, Convention Relating to the Status of Refugees, 28 July 1951 (hereinafter '1951 Convention').

[4] Kosar, D., 2013, 'Inclusion before Exclusion or Vice Versa: What the Qualification Directive and the Court of Justice Do (Not) Say', *Int'l J. Refugee L.*, vol. 25: p. 87.

[5] The first big wave of refugees came from the former-Yugoslavia and Rwanda. Since then, flows of refugees come from every country with a situation of extreme violence, especially from the African continent and Middle East.

not deserve the refugee protection and the State can send the applicant back to the country where he or she fears persecution.[6] However, the emergence of international criminal law and the establishment of the *non-refoulement* principle in international human rights law introduced new parameters. It is no longer as simple as excluding and deporting. Different cases in 2014 demonstrate the complexity and the legal implications the application of the exclusion from refugee protection clause might have.

This article is divided into two sections. First the legal framework that applies in cases of suspects of international crimes found in the territory of a third State is presented (section A). Then, the different scenarios of what follows when a suspected criminal is denied refugee protection on the basis of 2014 developments are examined (section B). The host State needs to decide whether to extradite, prosecute, or deport the alleged perpetrator of international crimes. However, the State might not be able to do any of the above and so would be obligated to continue hosting the suspect.

A. **The legal framework**

IN THE INTERSECTION BETWEEN DIFFERENT BRANCHES OF INTERNATIONAL LAW

International Refugee Law

The refugee status has been created to provide protection to individuals fleeing their country of origin or residence because of a well-founded fear of being persecuted.[7] The European Union (EU) Qualification Directive has extended protection to those facing a real risk of suffering serious harm (subsidiary protection). Thus, the individuals found in the territory of one of the EU members are also eligible for protection.[8] An asylum seeker is excluded from refugee (and subsidiary) protection if she or he is suspected to have committed one of the acts enumerated in Article 1F of the 1951 Convention (or

[6] Bliss, M., 2000, 'Serious Reasons for Considering: Minimum Standards of Procedural Fairness in the Application of the Article 1F Exclusion Clauses', *Int'l J. Refugee L.*, vol. 12: p. 92.

[7] Art. 1A of 1951 Convention.

[8] Art. 2(f) of Directive 2011/95/EU of the European Parliament and of the Council of 13 December 2011 on standards for the qualification of third-country nationals or stateless persons as beneficiaries of international protection, for a uniform status for refugees or for persons eligible for subsidiary protection, and for the content of the protection granted (recast), *Official Journal of the European Union* L337/9 (hereinafter 'Qualification Directive').

Articles 12 and 17 of the Qualification Directive).[9] The same exclusion clause is repeated in the EU Directive on temporary protection.[10] Accordingly, a person suspected of having committed an international crime cannot benefit from any protection, even if there is a real risk of being persecuted or suffering a serious harm. Once excluded, international refugee law has nothing more to say about the fate of the person excluded from protection. The 1951 Convention provides rules for those protected by the refugee status; it does not cover those excluded by it.[11] In the absence of international criminal law and international human rights law, the host State could simply expel the suspect.

International Humanitarian Law and International Criminal Law

Since 1951, the interest in ensuring the prosecution of international crimes has increased and international criminal law rapidly developed. The two international criminal tribunals established by the UN Security Council (one for the former-Yugoslavia and one for Rwanda) paved the way for the creation of the International Criminal Court (ICC). In addition, many States have adopted laws allowing the prosecution of international crimes by their national courts. Today, States (members of the ICC) have an obligation to surrender suspects to the Court.[12] However, there is still no agreement that the States have a general obligation to ensure the prosecution of any other person suspected of international crimes found in their territory.[13] A State could ensure prosecution by either extraditing the suspect to a State that will prosecute them or by enabling its own judicial authorities to try them.

[9] Apart from international crimes (paragraph a), the 1951 Convention excludes those who have committed a serious non-political crime outside the country of refuge prior to his admission to that country as a refugee (paragraph b); and those who have been guilty of acts contrary to the purposes and principles of the United Nations (paragraph c). The Qualification Directive reproduces the same exclusion clauses for both refugee and subsidiary protection (Arts 12(2) and 17(1), Qualification Directive). This chapter focuses on the first of the exclusion clauses, namely exclusion due to the applicant being suspected of committing one of the enumerated crimes.

[10] The directive on temporary protection aims at addressing situations of mass influx when the individual determination of refugee status is impossible. It provides a minimum standard of protection to all the people that fled from a conflict or natural disaster and they cannot return. Art. 28 excludes suspects of international crimes from protection. The directive on temporary protection has not been used so far. Council Directive 2001/55/EC of 20 July 2001on minimum standards for giving temporary protection in the event of a mass influx of displaced persons and on measures promoting a balance of efforts between Member States in receiving such persons and bearing the consequences thereof, *Official Journal of the European Union* L212/12, 7 August 2001.

[11] Guidelines on International Protection: Application of the Exclusion Clauses: Art. 1F of the 1951 Convention relating to the Status of Refugees, UNHCR, UN Doc. HCR/GIP/03/05, 4 September 2003, para. 2 (hereinafter UNHCR Guidelines).

[12] Art. 89 of the Rome Statute of the International Criminal Court.

[13] The obligation to extradite or prosecute (*aut dedere aut judicare*), Final Report of the International Law Commission, 2014, *Yearbook of the International Law Commission*, vol. II (Part Two), paras. 53–4; Cryer, R. 2010, *An Introduction to International Criminal Law and Procedure*, Cambridge University Press, p. 52.

An established treaty-based obligation to extradite or prosecute is found in the Geneva Conventions and the first Additional Protocol; however, it is limited to grave breaches and so only covers a limited number of the war crimes committed in an international armed conflict.[14] Conversely, for most of the other international crimes that are now considered to be the core international crimes—including war crimes committed during a non-international armed conflict, crimes against humanity, and genocide—there is no established legal obligation to ensure the prosecution of suspects. Law certainly gives States the right to do so, but it has not yet imposed an obligation. Universal jurisdiction, which gives the courts of the host State the ability to prosecute, is distinct from an obligation to prosecute.[15] Thus, in relation to many suspects who are not brought before the ICC, there are few legal obligations. In any event, even if one accepts that there is an obligation to prosecute, this does not necessarily mean that the proceedings will be initiated and even less that the suspect will be punished.[16]

International human rights law and the principle of *non-refoulement*

Today, though, deportation of persons excluded from refugee protection is not as simple as it might appear. Indeed, even if the concerned persons are excluded from protection and there are no criminal proceedings, the State still might not be able to deport the suspect due to its human rights obligations. The development of the principle of *non-refoulement* in international human rights law could prevent the State from expelling the suspect. The principle of *non-refoulement* was also introduced in Article 33 of the 1951 Convention. According to this, the host State cannot expel or return ('refouler') 'a refugee...where his [or her] life or freedom would be threatened on account of his race, religion, nationality, membership of a particular social group or political opinion'. However, a person excluded from refugee protection is not covered by this article, even if he or she fears persecution or suffering of serious harm.

In international human rights law the principle of *non-refoulement* is broader. It is not limited to refugees and asylum seekers. It protects all individuals irrespective of their status,

[14] Art. 49 of First Geneva Convention; Art. 50 of Second Geneva Convention; Art. 129 of Third Geneva Convention; Art. 146 of Fourth Geneva Convention; Art. 85 of Additional Protocol I. The Genocide Convention provides an obligation to try the responsible within the state that the violations occurred or to surrender them to an international tribunal (Art. 6 of Convention on the Prevention and Punishment of the Crime of Genocide). In the recent *Hissène Habré* case, before the International Court of Justice, the question was limited to the existence of an obligation to prosecute or extradite provided by the Convention again Torture and not under customary law. *Questions relating to the Obligation to Prosecute or Extradite (Belgium v Senegal)*, Judgment, ICJ, 20 July 2012, ICJ Reports 2012, 422.

[15] See below.

[16] On the relationship between the international criminal law and Art. 1F(a) see Bauloz, C., 2014, 'L'apport du droit international penal au droit des réfugiés: etude de l'article 1F(a) de la Convention de Genève relative au statut des réfugiés'. In *Asile et extradition Théorie et pratique de l'exclusion du statut de réfugié* edited by Chetail, V. and Laly-Chevalier, C., Bruxelles: Bruylant, p. 33.

including any criminal or suspect of international crimes found in the territory of a third State.[17] In addition, contrary to refugee law (where a State can still return a refugee if he or she poses a threat to national security[18]), international human rights law does not allow such exceptions.[19] Thus, a State cannot send an individual found in its territory to a place where they may be at risk of serious human rights violations.[20] The prohibition has been mostly used in cases where there is a risk of torture, cruel, inhuman or degrading treatment or punishment, or an arbitrary deprivation of life.[21] However, it also covers cases of slavery and forced labour,[22] enforced disappearances,[23] special cases for protection of children,[24] and flagrant violations of the right to a fair trial.[25]

That said, it may be the case that the host State will not extradite or prosecute a suspected criminal due to the absence of a legal basis or simply because of a lack of evidence.

[17] Among many, CCPR, General Comment No. 31, The Nature of the General Legal Obligation Imposed on States Parties to the Covenant, 26 May 2004, UN Doc. CCPR/C/21/Rev.1/Add.13, para. 12; CCPR, General Comment No. 20, Prohibition of Torture, or other Cruel, Inhuman or Degrading Treatment or Punishment (Art. 7), 3 October 1992, UN Doc. CCPR/C/21, para. 9; ECtHR, *Chahal v UK* (App. no. 70/1995/576/662), Judgment, 15 November 1996, par. 80; IACtHR, *Ca-so Familia Pacheco Tineo v Estado Plurinacional de Bolivia*, 25 November 2013, Series C No. 272, para. 151; CAT, *Aemei v Switzerland* (Communication No. 34/1995), 29 May 1997, UN Doc. CAT/C/18/D/34/1995, para. 9.8.

[18] Art. 33(2) of 1951 Convention.

[19] The European Court of Human Rights has underlined that it applies irrespective of the reprehensible nature of the conduct of person in question. A State cannot send a migrant to a place where he or she faces irreparable harm, ECtHR, *D. v UK* (App. no. 30240/96), Judgment, 2 May 1997, para. 47; CCPR, *Maksudov and Rakhimov v Kyrgyzstan* (Communication No. 1461, 1462, 1476 1477/2006), 31 July 2008, UN Doc. CCPR/C/93/D/1461, 1462, 1476 and 1477/2006, para. 12.4. ECtHR, *Othman v UK*, App. no. 8139/09, Judgment, 17 January 2012, para. 260.

For a detailed presentation on the main points of the *non-refoulement* principle see: Information Note on the Principle of Non-Refoulement, April 2014, IOM (International Migration Law Unit).

[20] Chetail, V., 2004, 'Le droit des réfugiés à l'épreuve des droits de l'homme: bilan de la jurisprudence de la Cour européenne des droits de l'homme sur l'interdiction du renvoi des étrangers menacés de torture et de traitements inhumains ou dégradants', *Revue Belge de Droit International*, vol. 37(1), 155.

[21] Regarding torture, inhuman, and degrading treatment, see among others, Art. 7 of the International Covenant on Civil and Political Rights; Art. 2 of the Convention Against Torture and Other Cruel, Inhuman or Degrading Treatment or Punishment; and Art. 5(2) of the Inter-American Convention on Human Rights. See also, ECtHR, *Saadi v Italy* (App. no. 37201/06), Judgment, 28 February 2008, para. 134.

Regarding the right to life see among others, ECtHR, *Al-Saadoon v UK* (App. no. 61498/08), Judgment, 2 March 2010, para. 143; CCPR, *Baboeram et al. v Suriname* (Communication 146/1983), 4 April 1985, UN Doc. CCPR/C/24/D/146/1983, para. 14.3; CCPR, General Comment No. 6, The right to life (art. 6), 30 April 1982, para. 3; IACnHR, *The Haitian Centre for Human Rights et al. v US*, Report No. 51/96, Inter-AmCHR, 1997, para. 168.

[22] ECtHR, *Mohammed Lemine Ould Barar v Sweden* (App. no. 42367/98), Decision, 19 January 1999, para. 1.

[23] Art. 16(2) of the International Convention for the Protection of All Persons from Enforced Disappearance.

[24] CRC, General Comment No. 6, Treatment of unaccompanied and separated children outside their country of origin, 1 September 2005, UN Doc. CRC/GC/2005/6, para. 27.

[25] Fair trial violations must go 'beyond mere irregularities or lack of safeguards in the trial procedure' and the breach must be 'so fundamental as to amount to a nullification or destruction of the very essence, of the right'. However, cases usually concern trials that may lead to death penalty or torture: ECtHR,

Still, it may not be able to expel the suspect because of international human rights law restrictions. The question then arises with respect to the fate of these suspects. The State cannot detain someone on the basis of the exclusion clause for a long period, but, at the same time, it does not need to provide the suspect with any legal papers, for instance, papers that would allow them to work. The exclusion clause determination is an administrative procedure, not a criminal trial. Before going into the details of recent cases of asylum seekers that had been excluded from protection, it is useful to highlight the main differences between the exclusion clause and the criminal proceedings.

Exclusion clause v. criminal proceedings

The exclusion of persons suspected of international crimes under the 1951 Convention differs substantially from criminal proceedings. First, the *standard of proof* for excluding a suspected criminal from refugee protection is lower than that under criminal law.[26] Article 1F(a) requires 'serious reasons for considering' that the individual has committed or participated in the commission of such acts. The immigration authorities do not have to prove the guilt beyond reasonable doubt, as it is required in criminal law. However, the UN High Commissioner for refugees (UNHCR) emphasizes that it is still a high standard of proof. Reliable, credible, and convincing evidence should be used to determine whether an asylum seeker has committed such crimes.[27] Nevertheless, it is not clear what *evidence* can or cannot be used by immigration authorities.[28] The immigration authorities are alleged to mainly rely on the personal accounts of the applicant in combination with authoritative reports, which generally describe the activities of the organization the applicant claimed to be part of.[29]

Under criminal law, it is necessary to prove beyond reasonable doubt that the accused has committed specific acts with the required mental element. Conversely, under refugee law, even though the mental element should be taken into account, in exceptional circumstances, the mere participation in a group is sufficient to exclude a refugee from protection.[30] In addition, the *degree of involvement* of the suspect (whether the accused is a perpetrator, aider, or abettor) and any mitigating circumstances are taken into account

Soering v UK (App. no. 14038/88), Judgment, 7 July 1989, para. 113; ECtHR, *Mamatkulov and Askarov v Turkey* (App. nos. 46827/99 and 46951/99), Judgment, 4 February 2005, para. 88; IACtHR, *Hilaire, Constantine and Benjamin et al. v Trinidad and Tobago*, Judgment, 1 September 2001, para. 148.

[26] UNHCR Guidelines, paras 34–6. [27] Ibid.

[28] Bliss concludes that evidence should include 'credible confession by the asylum seeker of involvement in excludable crimes; verified and legitimate conviction of an excludable crime; indictment by an international tribunal; and other clear and convincing evidence'. Bliss, M., 'Serious Reasons for Considering', p. 120.

[29] Moore, B. and van Wijk, J., 2014, 'Asylum-Seekers Falsely Implicating Themselves in International Crimes: Should They Be Informed of the Existence of Article 1F of the Refugee Convention?', *Migration Letters*, vol. 12, no. 1: pp. 91, 92.

[30] UNHCR Guidelines, paras 18–19.

at least at the sentencing stage. These factors do not really matter in refugee law. On the contrary, there is only one consequence—namely the exclusion from refugee protection.[31] There is an increasing understanding that some form of *balancing* is necessary between the level of the persecution the asylum seeker faces if returned and the nature of the crimes suspected to have been committed (proportionality test).[32] However, case law is not consistent on the matter and it would probably not apply in the case of Article 1F(a).[33] In practice, it is very difficult to control whether or not such a balancing has been made.

Furthermore, the asylum seeker does not have the same *procedural safeguards* as in criminal proceedings.[34] A list of minimum requirements of procedural fairness has been suggested, but States in practice continue to provide substantially fewer procedural safeguards.[35] As a result, the asylum seekers that were unjustifiably denied protection on the basis of Article 1F(a) of 1951 Convention do not have any *remedies* for unnecessary harm suffered.

The exclusion from refugee protection on the basis of Article 1F(a) resembles partial conviction, with unpredictable consequences. Ideally, an exclusion clause determination is followed by criminal proceedings, which determine guilt. The suspect is either extradited to be tried or prosecuted by the host State. However, there might be other cases where the host State will not be able or willing to ensure the prosecution of a suspect of international crimes.

B. **Developments in 2014**

EXTRADITION CASES

If there is a court willing to prosecute the suspects, the host State will be able extradite the asylum seekers who are excluded from refugee protection on the basis of Article 1F(a) of the 1951 Convention. In some cases, the host State can hand over the suspect for trial to the International Criminal Court or to any other international or quasi-international judicial body. In other cases, the State of origin (or any other) might

[31] Bond, J., 2012, 'Excluding Justice: The Dangerous Intersection between Refugee Claims, Criminal Law, and "Guilty" Asylum Seekers', *Int'l J. Refugee L.*, vol. 24: 37 at pp. 37–59.

[32] UNHCR Guidelines, para. 24.

[33] Ibid; Bliss, M., 'Serious Reasons for Considering', p. 110.

[34] Bliss, M., 'Serious Reasons for Considering', p. 97.

[35] Bliss has suggested the following procedural safeguards: an individual determination of the claim for protection; the right to be informed of the nature of proceedings; the right to an oral hearing or interview; the right to have evidence on which the decision-maker intends to rely presented to him or her, and to be given an opportunity to comment on it; the right to an interpreter if required; the right to assistance; the right to written reasons for decision; and the right to appeal a first instance decision to exclude. Ibid., pp. 99–100.

issue an extradition request. The host State will extradite the alleged criminal only if there are reasonable grounds for the arrest warrant and if there are assurances that the suspect will receive a fair trial. Nevertheless, the host State cannot extradite an individual if there is reasonable belief that the person will be killed or inhumanely treated.[36]

Until recently, European States would not extradite Rwandan nationals to be tried by Rwandan courts. For instance, a 'Gacaca' court in Rwanda had already convicted Stanislas Mbanenande,[37] but a Swedish court retried him because Swedish law does not recognize Gacacas.[38] Lately, though, certain States have started accepting the extradition of Rwandan international crime suspects to Rwanda to be tried. This trend seems to have been justified on the basis that concerned States have received sufficient assurances from Rwanda that measures have been taken to improve the judicial system and the authorities will do everything possible to ensure a fair trial.[39]

Charles Bandosra, whose trial hearings began in Kigali in 2014, was the first genocide suspect to be extradited to Rwanda on 10 March 2013.[40] Bandora was a high-ranking member of the National Republican Movement for Democracy and Development (MRND) party in Bugesera, Rwanda. He is accused of having ordered the killing of hundreds of Tutsis in Ruhula church in April 1994.[41] He was arrested on 9 June 2010 at an airport in Norway under the suspicion of travelling with a fake passport. It is reported that he applied for asylum in Norway but Rwanda requested his extradition. He was extradited from Norway to Rwanda after having exhausted all legal avenues to stop his return.[42]

On 17 June 2014, the Supreme Court of the Netherlands upheld a decision confirming the legality of the extradition of the Rwandan Jean-Claude Iyamuremye. He allegedly committed crimes against humanity, genocide, and war crimes. He is accused, with others, of having organized the *Interahamwe* massacre in the Official Technical School (ETO) in Kigali, Rwanda.[43] According to the Court, there was not enough evidence to support

[36] Particularly on extradition and human rights see Matrigne, J., 2014, 'La situation de l'exclu au regard de l'extradition'. In *Asile et extradition Théorie et pratique de l'exclusion du statut de réfugié* edited by Chetail, V. and Laly-Chevalier, C., Bruxelles: Bruylant, p. 257.

[37] See below section under 'Convictions for immigration fraud'.

[38] Gacaca courts were originally used to try village or familial disputes. The trials are conducted by the people of the village with the active participation of the victims.

[39] The policy shifted after the *Uwinkindi* decision by the International Criminal Tribunal for Rwanda (ICTR) to transfer an accused to Rwanda. The European Court of Human Rights (ECtHR), relying mainly on ICTR's previous decision, concluded that the Swedish decision to extradite a Rwandan national to Rwanda for trial did not violate the European Convention. Appeals Chamber Dismisses Uwinkindi's Motion for Stay of Transfer to Rwanda, United Nations International Criminal Tribunal for Rwanda, ICTR, 19 April 2012; ECtHR, *Ahorugeze v Sweden* (App. no. 37075/09), Judgment, Fifth Section, 27 October 2011.

[40] TRIAL, Profiles—Charles Bandora (last modified in 27 October 2014).

[41] Ibid.

[42] Ibid.

[43] TRIAL, Profiles—Jean-Claude Iyamuremye (last modified 22 August 2014).

the assertion that he would suffer any flagrant violation of his right to a fair trial.[44] Iyamuremye has lived for twenty years in the Netherlands with his family. At the time of writing, he is still being held in the Netherlands awaiting the decision of the Dutch Minister of Security and Justice on his extradition.[45]

Early 2015, Norway's Supreme Court upheld the decision that Eugene Nkuranyabahizi should be extradited to Rwanda to be tried for his alleged involvement in the 1994 Rwandan genocide.[46] Nkuranyabahizi lived in Norway since 1999. His citizenship request was denied because of suspicions regarding his involvement in the genocide. The Norwegian court relied on the validity of the allegations and on assurances that he would be offered a fair trial to decide whether the extradition claim was justified.[47]

However, a recent French decision shows how fragile any extradition practices are. The Supreme Court of France decided that it was not possible to extradite any individual to Rwanda to be tried for genocide. On 26 February 2014, the *Court de Cassation* in France overturned an appeals court's judgment that allowed the extradition of Claude Muhayimana and Innocent Musabyimana to Rwanda in order to stand trial. It also upheld the decision not to extradite Laurent Serubuga.[48] They all moved to France after the Rwandan genocide. Muhayimana is accused of taking part in the massacre of Tutsis in the western town of Kibuye. Musabyimana is suspected of taking part in the killings in the north-western province of Gisenyi. Serubuga was Rwanda's deputy army chief-of-staff at the time of the genocide.[49] The French decision concluded that the crime of genocide was not defined in the Rwandan criminal code in 1994; therefore, the accused could not be retroactively tried for genocide—this aspect has never been examined before by any other court.[50] This case is significant because it questions the legality of all the trials that have taken place in Rwanda so far and also undermines all other extradition decisions.[51]

Arguably these are (ideal) extradition cases where the individual who was excluded from refugee protection was sent back to their country of origin for trial. Upon release, the accused (either after serving their sentence or after their acquittal) can start their life legally in their country of origin. Alternatively, the host State can initiate criminal proceedings against the suspect. This depends on whether the national laws allow for such prosecution.

[44] ICD—Jean-Claude Iyamuremye, International Crimes Database, Asser Institute.
[45] TRIAL, Profiles—Jean-Claude Iyamuremye (last modified 22 August 2014).
[46] Ahman, M., 'Norway's Supreme Court Upholds Extradition of Rwanda Genocide Suspect'.
[47] TRIAL, Profiles—Eugene Nkuranyabahizi (last modified 21 October 2014).
[48] Bradfield, P., 2014, 'France v the Rest of the World—Who Is Right?', Beyond The Hague Blog.
[49] Ibid. [50] Ibid.
[51] Ibid.

PROSECUTION OF SUSPECTS OF INTERNATIONAL CRIMES IN THE HOST COUNTRY

Many States have today passed legislation giving their courts universal jurisdiction to try suspects of international crimes. 'The term "universal jurisdiction" refers to jurisdiction established over a crime without reference to the place of perpetration, the nationality of the suspect or the victim or any other recognized linking point between the crime and the prosecuting state.'[52] Universal jurisdiction is mostly limited to specific crimes. The list of crimes might differ from one country to another, but the international crimes discussed in this chapter are largely covered by most universal jurisdiction laws. States often require that the suspect is found in their territory ('conditional' universal jurisdiction).[53] In 2014, Spain also opted to revise its infamous law and limit its courts' universal jurisdiction over international crimes to cases in which there are Spanish victims or the alleged perpetrator is on Spanish soil.[54] Domestic courts around the world more and more often apply universal jurisdiction to try individuals who are found within their territory and who were excluded from refugee protection as they are suspected of having committed international crimes.

Completed trials against suspects of international crimes

Procedures related to the Syrian conflict. For the first time since the beginning of the Syrian conflict, a Syrian refugee was convicted in early 2015 for war crimes committed before he fled from the conflict.[55] A Swedish court sentenced Mouhannad Droubi to five years of imprisonment for abusing a captured member of the Syrian armed forces. The convicted was a member of the Free Syrian Army at the time of the assault. He had applied and obtained asylum in Sweden in 2013. The court was able to build a case against Droubi because he had posted a video of the assault showing him beating and striking the prisoner with several objects on social media. He was charged with attacking an enemy who was defenceless.[56] Most probably, the convicted will file an appeal.

[52] In some cases, where the asylum seekers have already obtained the citizenship of the host country, they might be tried on the basis of the nationality principle. The States are entitled to pass laws to try their own nationals for crimes they committed abroad. International crimes are covered by such laws. Often though, it is required that the perpetrator had the nationality at the time of commission of crime. Cryer, R., *An Introduction to International Criminal Law and Procedure*, pp. 48 and 51.

[53] Ibid., p. 52.

[54] Spanish law had one of the broadest universal jurisdiction laws. It allowed Spanish courts to try any case of international crimes, irrespective of where the crime was committed or against whom and irrespective of where the alleged criminal was found. Kassam, A., 'Spain Moves to Curb Legal Convention Allowing Trials of Foreign Rights Abuses', *The Guardian*, 11 February 2014.

[55] It is also one of the rare cases where a fighter is only convicted for a war crime. BBC, 'Sweden Convicts Syrian Rebel', 26 February 2015.

[56] JURIST, 'Al. Sacriponte, Syria Rebel Sentenced to 5 Years for War Crimes', 26 February 2015.

Procedures related to Rwandan genocide. In 2014 and late 2013, judicial proceedings against Rwandan nationals that had fled to Europe and other western countries after the genocide in 1994 were completed. For all these trials, the investigating authorities had to travel around the world to interview witnesses and collect additional evidence. The investigation processes have been lengthy and costly.

Closing the first trial connected to the Rwandan genocide in Germany, on 18 February 2014, a German court sentenced Onesphore Rwabukombe to fourteen years in prison for aiding and abetting genocide. Rwabukombe was allegedly responsible for thousands of killings. However, the Court was not able to establish his direct responsibility in committing genocide. Rwabukombe was granted refugee status in Germany in 2002, but now it will probably be revoked.[57]

On 14 March 2014, in a landmark decision by a French court, Pascal Simbikangwa was found guilty of complicity in genocide. He is considered to be one of the key figures behind the genocide and was involved in numerous massacres, assassinations, and other attacks against opposition parties.[58] The French court sentenced him to twenty-five years of prison (instead of imprisonment for life) as one of the instigators and authors of the Rwandan genocide.[59] He is the first person to be convicted in France in connection to the genocide in Rwanda. It is one of many investigations taking place in France that has been accused of sheltering senior Hutu figures within the territory.[60]

On 19 June 2014, a Swedish appeal court upheld a decision convicting Stanislas Mbanenande to life imprisonment for crimes against humanity and genocide. It is the first time a Swedish court has convicted someone for the crime of genocide and the first time they have convicted someone for the Rwandan conflict. According to the decision, Mbanenande had been involved in killings, attempted killings, and kidnapping of civilians in Kibuye area. The court established that he committed all crimes with genocidal intent to destroy the Tutsi ethnic group. Mbanenande fled to Sweden in 2007, where he was recognized as a refugee and was later granted Swedish citizenship.[61] His citizenship will now probably be revoked.

In Canada, on 18 December 2014, the Supreme Court rejected the appeal of Désiré Munyaneza.[62] The Superior Court of Quebec had convicted Munyaneza for genocide, crimes against humanity, and war crimes committed during 1994 in Rwanda.[63] It is the

[57] TRIAL, Profiles—Onesphore Rwabukombe (last modified 24 March 2104); BBC, 'Germany Finds Rwanda Ex-Mayor Guilty', 18 February 2014.

[58] TRIAL, Profiles—Pascal Simbikangwa (last modified 16 May 2014).

[59] BBC, 'Rwanda Ex-Spy Chief Jailed in France', 14 March 2014.

[60] Lichfield, J., 'Pascal Simbikangwa Jailed in Paris: Rwandan Genocide Conviction Could Pave the Way for More French Trials', *The Independent*, 15 March 2014.

[61] ICD—*Public Prosecutor v Stanislas Mbanenande*, Asser Institute; TRIAL, Profiles—Stanislas Mbanenande (last modified 19 July 2014).

[62] TRIAL, Profiles—Desire Munyaneza (last modified 26 January 2015).

[63] Court Proceedings—War Crimes and Crimes Against Humanity, Department of Justice, Government of Canada.

first time the Crimes against Humanity and War Crimes Act (adopted in 2000) has been used to convict an individual. Munyaneza fled to Canada in 1997 and immediately filed a refugee claim. His request was rejected because they already suspected his involvement in the Rwandan genocide. Nevertheless, he was only arrested in 2005. The investigations lasted for another five years and the legal proceedings went on until 2014.[64]

Munyaneza was left for more than ten years in Canada waiting to be tried, while the second person to be indicted under the Crimes against Humanity and War Crimes Act has been acquitted. Jacques Mungwarere, also a Rwandan national, was granted refugee status in 2002. The investigation around him started in 2003. He was officially indicted for genocide and crimes against humanity in 2010.[65] On 5 July 2013, the judge concluded that Mungwarere was probably guilty, but the prosecution was not able to prove its case beyond reasonable doubt. Mungwarere might still lose his refugee status.[66] This decision demonstrates the fragile relationship between criminal and refugee determination proceedings. Despite his acquittal in a criminal trial, Mungwarere might still face deportation on the basis of the exclusion clause.

In 2013, Yvonne Basebya, a Rwandan-born Dutch citizen, was convicted for inciting genocide in Rwanda in 1994. She received the maximum sentence of six years and eight months in jail. She was cleared of other charges, including perpetrating genocide, murder, and war crimes. Basebya had arrived in the Netherlands in 1998 and hid her previous activities when seeking refugee protection.[67]

Arrests of suspects in relation to the first Liberian civil war

The first ever arrests in Europe related to crimes committed during the first Liberian civil war (1989–96) are among the major developments of 2014.[68] Charles Taylor, the former Liberian president, is now serving a fifty-year sentence in Britain for crimes committed during the civil war in Sierra Leone and not in Liberia.[69] On 17 September 2014, Martina Johnson, a former front line Commander of the National Patriotic Front of

[64] TRIAL, Profiles—Desire Munyaneza (last modified 26 January 2015).

[65] Apparently, the testimonies seemed to be contradictory and the judge had to drop the last part of the charges after discovering that it was fabricated. Court Proceedings—War Crimes and Crimes Against Humanity, Department of Justice, Government of Canada; TRIAL, Profiles—Jacques Mungwarere (last modified 4 February 2014).

[66] CBCNews, 'Ontario Judge Clears "Probably Guilty" Rwandan of War Crimes', 5 July 2013.

[67] She was also tried and convicted in absentia by a Gacaca trial. TRIAL, Profiles—Yvonne Ntacyobatabara Basebya (last modified 12 May 2014).

[68] The two back-to-back civil wars ended in 2003 and they are estimated to have cost over 250,000 lives. Macdougall, Cl., 'A Former Commander of Liberian Rebels Is Arrested in Switzerland', *The New York Times*, 16 January 2015.

[69] *Prosecutor v Charles Ghankay Taylor*, Case No SCSL-03-01-A-1389, Appeal Chamber Judgment, Special Court for Sierra Leone, 26 September 2013.

Liberia (NPFL) of Charles Taylor, was arrested and indicted in Belgium. She is accused of participating in war crimes and crimes against humanity (including mutilation and mass killing) committed in 1992.[70] Not long after, on 14 November 2014, Alieu Kosiah, a former commander of the United Liberation Movement of Liberia for Democracy (ULIMO), a rebel group that fought against Charles Taylor's NPFL, was arrested in Switzerland. He is accused of having committed international crimes, including systematic killings of civilians in north-western Liberia between 1993 and 1995.[71]

These arrests encourage discussion of the prosecution and punishment of perpetrators of international crimes during the civil wars in Liberia. Until now there have been no efforts to investigate and prosecute these crimes. The Truth & Reconciliation Commission, created to investigate, among others, gross human rights violations and violations of international humanitarian law, published a lengthy report in 2009.[72] It recommended the prosecution of perpetrators, but there has been no follow-up so far.[73] The trials in Europe have not yet taken place and no one can predict their outcome, meanwhile, the two suspects risk losing their residence permits.

After the proceedings are completed

Most of the above-mentioned persons convicted of international crimes will be sent back to their country of origin after they serve their sentence, or even if they are acquitted. By the time the Rwandan nationals serve their sentences, the 'host' States should be able to send them back to Rwanda.[74] For others, however, the situation in their country of origin will not allow them to be sent back. The host State will be obligated to keep them in its territory, unless another country is willing to receive them. Remaining in the host State's territory, without refugee protection or residence permit, will put them in an uncertain legal situation.

For instance, the Swedish court did not order Droubi's deportation due to the situation in Syria, but it is very likely that he will lose his Swedish residence permit and refugee protection.[75] Therefore, after he serves his sentence, the deportation decision will be

[70] 'Martina Johnson, Former Liberian NPFL Rebel Commander, Arrested and Indicted in Belgium for Alleged War Crimes and Crimes Against Humanity', Press Release, Civitas Maxima, 18 September 2014.

[71] Alieu Kosiah is the first ever member of ULIMO to be prosecuted. It is significant that the two cases concern former commanders of two opposing sides. Former Liberian ULIMO Rebel Commander Arrested in Switzerland for Alleged War Crimes, Press Release, Civitas Maxima, 16 January 2015.

[72] See website of Truth and Reconciliation Commission of Liberia.

[73] 'Executive Summary and Priority Recommendations: A House with Two Rooms: Final Report of the Truth & Reconciliation Commission of Liberia Diaspora Project', Volume 3, Appendices VII, 30 June 2009, pp. 23–4.

[74] See above section under 'Extradition cases'. European States have started already extraditing people to Rwanda. What will happen though if Rwanda intends to try them again, though, is not certain.

[75] Al Akhabar English, 'Sweden Sentences Former Syrian Rebel to 5 Years in Prison for War Crimes', 26 February 2015.

re-examined. Once the situation in Syria improves, he will be sent back. However, for as long as the Syrian conflict continues, Sweden cannot deport him. It is likely that after he serves his sentence he will be left waiting, in an uncertain legal status, until the situation in Syria improves.

These cases still concern suspects of international crimes convicted by a court. In the meantime, many exclusion cases do not necessarily lead to an extradition or a prosecution. Alternatively, asylum seekers suspected of international crimes might be convicted for immigration fraud, be deported, or none of the above.

CONVICTIONS FOR IMMIGRATION FRAUD

On 10 February 2014, Jorge Sosa Orantes, accused of committing crimes against humanity, genocide, and war crimes during the Guatemalan dictatorship (1982), was found guilty for immigration fraud in the United States. He was convicted for lying to the US immigration authorities. He had not mentioned in his application for US citizenship that he had been a member of a military organization and he had answered negatively to the question regarding the commission of a crime. He was sentenced to ten years in prison, which is the maximum penalty for immigration fraud, and was stripped of his US citizenship. Orantes is wanted by the Guatemalan and Spanish authorities for his participation (among others) in the Dos Erres massacre of 1982. During Efrain Rios Montt's dictatorship, Orantes was a sub-lieutenant and an instructor at the Kaibil School, which trained special commando units. Guatemala has asked for his extradition. Orantes will most probably be extradited after his prison term ends. Based on the above, Orantes will serve ten years for hiding information about his previous activities and then he will be extradited to be tried for the actual activities.

In an older case in Canada, the court decided to revoke the Canadian citizenship of Branko Rogan because he deliberately gave false information to the immigration authorities about his past. Rogan came to Canada from Bosnia–Herzegovina in 1994 after the war and became a Canadian citizen. An investigation was initiated against him after he was recognized by a Bosnian Muslim refugee also residing in Canada. The testimonies of four former prisoners and a specialist in history were allegedly used to justify the decision.[76] In addition, he has been asked to pay the costs for the citizenship revocation procedures (allegedly close to $300,000).[77]

[76] Humphreys, A., 'The Cost of Being Stripped of Citizenship', *National Post*, 10 October 2011.

[77] Court Proceedings—War Crimes and Crimes against Humanity, Department of Justice, Government of Canada.

There are two paradoxes with these convictions. First of all, the two suspected criminals are not tried for the international crimes they committed; instead, they are severely punished for immigration fraud. Orantes will stay in prison for ten years before any trial for the international crimes he is suspected of committing even begins; Rogan was made to pay an incredible administrative fine, without being tried. Immigration fraud is a serious offence. However, it does not seem reasonable to make the effort to prove the previous crimes in order to establish immigration fraud and then not punish them for these previous crimes.

In addition, these sentences seem quite severe for punishing immigration fraud during asylum determination procedures. It is not uncommon for an asylum seeker to fabricate events in order to ensure a successful application. Apart from criminals who try to hide their past, individuals might lie about their membership of a particular group because they have been incorrectly advised that this will secure refugee status.[78] Such severe sanctions for lying to the immigration authorities resemble the criminal charges for the perpetration of international crimes. There is no doubt that authorities need to take measures to ensure that asylum seekers are telling the truth; however, there should be some limits in terms of the consequences.

DEPORTATIONS

The exclusion clause is still a very good excuse for simply deporting asylum holders without them standing trial. For instance, the US authorities have been investigating and gradually deporting Bosnians because it is believed that they took part in war crimes and ethnic cleansing during the conflict in the former Yugoslavia. The about-to-be-deported-suspected-criminals have no form of protection against such decisions. There have been allegations that the immigration authorities base their deportation decisions purely on the participation of suspects in the Bosnian–Serb army or because they happened to have been close to Srebrenica when the genocide took place. The defence lawyers argued that there is often no other evidence that the deportees had committed crimes during the war.[79] There is no indication that they have been deported to face trial in Bosnia–Herzegovina or elsewhere. These allegations bring to light a reoccurring problem: the standard of proof for stripping someone from any kind of protection is much lower than convicting someone under criminal law.[80]

[78] Moore, B. and van Wijk, J., 'Asylum-Seekers Falsely Implicating Themselves', p. 92.

[79] Lichtblau, E., 'U.S. Seeks to Deport Bosnians Over War Crimes', *The New York Times*, 28 February 2015; BBC, 'US "to Deport Bosnian War Suspects"', 1 March 2015.

[80] See above section under 'Exclusion clause v. criminal proceedings'.

STUCK IN THE HOST STATE

Finally, there is a last scenario. Even though the authorities can exclude an asylum seeker if there are serious and actual reasons for considering that the applicant has committed international crimes, it is quite often the case that the authorities will not be able to prosecute, extradite, or deport a suspect for a variety of reasons. There might be no State willing to start a trial against them; the host State might not have jurisdiction to try them; or there might not be enough evidence to prosecute the suspects. Also, the host State might not be able to send them back, due to the situation at the country of origin. The United States is able to send people back to Bosnia, but the Netherlands cannot currently send Syrian nationals, suspected of having committed international crimes, back to Syria.[81] In such cases, on the one hand, the State finds itself in a very sensitive situation where it is accused of hosting suspects of international crimes. On the other hand, the excluded individuals, who have no right to refugee protection, may become undocumented immigrants, at risk of being deported at any time, and labelled as alleged perpetrators of international crimes without ever standing trial and being convicted.[82]

Concluding remarks

There is no doubt that States should ensure that perpetrators of international crimes do not benefit from refugee protection. It is crucial that several States are already taking steps to prosecute and punish their own nationals[83] or persons in their territory who are suspected of being responsible for international crimes. The red flag is not raised with regard to those asylum seekers (suspected of international crimes) who, after their exclusion from refugee protection, are extradited to stand trial or who are prosecuted by the host State. The problem is rather when there is no follow up after the exclusion determination. The consequences of excluding someone from the refugee protection can be devastating. Yet, the determination of the exclusion clause is an administrative procedure with a quasi-criminal character—it is the immigration authorities who make

[81] Bolhuis, M., 'The Syrian Exodus and Perpetrators of International Crimes, Center for International Criminal Justice', Center for International Criminal Justice, 17 December 2014.

[82] Moore, B. and van Wijk, J., 'Asylum-Seekers Falsely Implicating Themselves'.

[83] At the moment there are ongoing trials in Latin American countries (Argentina, Guatemala, Haiti, a.o.), in the Balkan countries of former-Yugoslavia (Bosnia–Herzegovina, Croatia, Kosovo, and Serbia), Bangladesh, and many African countries (DRC, Uganda). Countries that slowly recover from events of extreme violence, such as Nepal and Sri Lanka, are discussing the adoption of new laws to punish the perpetrators of past crimes (Sri Lanka after UN pressure and Nepal court). At the same time, complicated proceedings in the United States continue to unfold (Abu Ghraib case).

a decision on whether or not the applicant was involved in any of the criminal activities enumerated in Article 1F(a).[84]

There is an urgent need to properly regulate the process and a minimum level of procedural safeguards should be provided. The asylum seeker who is excluded protection should be at least given a fair opportunity to defend their case. The obligation to extradite or prosecute should be explicitly recognized. Certainly, there are insurmountable procedural and economic barriers to cross in order to institute criminal proceedings. In some cases (where neither extradition nor prosecution are available) additional obligations to gather evidence before deporting a person suspected of international crimes should be made. Review processes should be available. Finally, the status of those persons excluded protection but who cannot be sent back because of the situation in their country of origin should be clarified. Safeguards similar to refugee protection should still be provided to them. Maybe perpetrators of international crimes do not 'deserve' refugee status, but putting them in an uncertain legal situation and leaving them hanging for years is more likely to push them to further criminal activities, rather than protecting the host State's society.

84 Bliss, M., 'Serious Reasons for Considering', p. 99.

13 War crimes trials at Guantánamo Bay: key developments in 2014

Dru A. Brenner-Beck[1]

Introduction

Observing the Guantánamo military commissions can sometimes be a surreal experience. Set up in 2006 by the United States (US) Congress to try 'alien unprivileged enemy belligerents' for war crimes,[2] the commissions have been described even by the defendants as 'a very unique and strange court'.[3] Conducted in a specially designed courtroom, the proceedings are broadcast to courtroom observers sitting behind a soundproof glass partition after a forty-second delay. This delay is designed to allow security personnel time to mute any reference to classified information, which prior to 9 December 2014 included all references to the torture, detention, and interrogation of the defendants after their capture. Thus, observers watch and listen to the proceedings on closed circuit

[1] Lieutenant Colonel (Retired), US Army Judge Advocate General's Corps. Formerly served as Deputy Legal Counsel, US Army's Office of the Inspector General and Chief, Military and Civil Law, US Army Europe. She graduated from Georgetown University's School of Foreign Service, and Boston University's School of Law. After retirement, Ms Brenner-Beck served as a law clerk to the Honorable Carlos F. Lucero, US Court of Appeals for the Tenth Circuit, and as a legal consultant on international law matters. She is the President of the National Institute of Military Justice, and has observed the military commission trial of the alleged 9/11 conspirators at Guantánamo Bay Naval station six times since June 2013. The views expressed in this chapter are those of the author and not of the National Institute of Military Justice.

[2] See Pub. L. 109–366, 120 Stat. 2600, codified at 10 U.S.C. §§948a *et seq.* (2006) [hereinafter 2006 MCA] (§948b(a) uses the term 'alien unlawful enemy combatants'); Pub. L. 111–184, 123 Stat. 2190, 2574 *amending* 10 U.S.C. 948a *et seq.* [hereinafter 2009 MCA] (§948b(a) changing term to 'alien unprivileged enemy belligerents'). All current commission cases are being conducted under the 2009 MCA. Although the original post-9/11 military commissions were authorized by Presidential order, the 2006 MCA was passed after the Supreme Court held the original commissions invalid in *Hamdan v Rumsfeld*, 548 U.S. 557 (2006).

[3] See 'Unofficial/Unauthenticated Transcript of the Al Nashiri (2) Hearing Dated 02/19/2014, 9:06 AM to 10:14 AM,' in *United States v Al-Nashiri*, dated 2/19/2014.

television as they occurred forty seconds in the past, while simultaneously watching the actual proceedings in the courtroom. Adding to the cognitive dissonance caused by the unique observation conditions, legal issues in the Guantánamo military commissions are complex, involving intertwining issues of international law, international humanitarian law,[4] and domestic US constitutional, statutory, military, and common law. As a newly created court, the commissions lack the over 200 years of binding precedent present in both the US courts-martial and federal judicial systems. Thus, issues long settled in courts-martial and federal practice must be litigated anew.

Although the military commissions were proceeding slowly but steadily, as would be expected of a judicial system in which little binding precedent exists, stagnation is the word that best describes the Guantánamo military commissions in 2014. Encompassing both the appellate and trial levels of ongoing military commission cases, the expected resolution of significant jurisdictional issues by the US Court of Appeals for the DC Circuit in *United States v Al-Bahlul*[5] and anticipated progress in the pre-trial hearings in both the *USS Cole* bombing and 9/11 cases did not materialize. Instead, continuing legal uncertainty regarding the permissible jurisdiction of military commissions plus continuing interferences with the military commissions by outside entities resulted in significant delays as the commissions grappled with the legal questions raised, halting the consideration of some or all of the pending pre-trial motions in both cases until these critical issues could be resolved.

A. Charges and Procedures

From approximately 2012 until the middle of 2014, only two cases were being tried before Guantánamo military commissions—the 9/11 case, involving defendants Khalid Sheik Mohammad, Walid Bin 'Attash, Ramzi Bin Al Shibh, Ali Abdul Aziz Ali (aka Ammar Al-Baluchi), and Mustafa Al-Hawsawi; and the *USS Cole* bombing case against Abd Al-Rahim Al-Nashiri.[6] Congress, in specifying the subject-matter jurisdiction of

[4] Also called the law of war or the law of armed conflict.

[5] *Al-Bahlul v United States*, 767 F.3d 1 (D.C. Cir. 2014) (*en banc*). Normally, in US Courts of Appeal, appeals are decided by a panel of three judges. A panel decision establishes Circuit precedent on that issue, and can be overruled only by a contrary decision of the US Supreme Court or an *en banc* opinion of the entire Court of Appeals. An appellant or appellee can seek either initial consideration or reconsideration by the *en banc* court, consisting of all active judges on the Circuit Court, which is referred to as *en banc* review. The number of active judges on a Circuit Court of Appeals ranges from six to twenty-nine, with the DC Circuit authorized eleven active judges.

[6] For those readers unfamiliar with the allegations against Al-Nashiri, he is accused of planning and orchestrating Al Qaeda's boats operation, which is alleged to encompass three separate terrorist attacks conducted in or near Aden and Al-Mukallah harbours in Yemen—the attempted bombing of the *USS The*

military commissions in the Military Commissions Act of 2009 ('2009 MCA'), required all charged offences to have been 'committed in the context of and associated with hostilities',[7] which for current commission cases is the transnational non-international armed conflict (NIAC) the United States asserts exists between itself and Al Qaeda and associated forces. The requirement that offences be committed within the context of an armed conflict in order to be considered a 'war crime' is hardly controversial. In contrast, there remains substantial controversy over the existence of the claimed NIAC between the US and Al Qaeda, as well as the characterization of some of the charged offences in current commission trials as 'war crimes.'

CHARGES

For those readers not familiar with American criminal or military procedure, the 2009 MCA enumerates thirty offences which the US Congress proscribed as war crimes or other offences subject to trial by military commissions, ranging from war crimes widely recognized under the international law of war to offences such as spying,[8] terrorism, murder in violation of the law of war, material support for terrorism, and inchoate conspiracy, which are much more controversial under both domestic and international law.[9] The charges in the 9/11 and *USS Cole* bombing cases both include charges widely

Sullivans in January 2000, the completed bombing of the *USS Cole* in October 2000, and the completed bombing of the French-flagged *M/V Limburg* in October 2002. The charges and filings in both these cases, as well as other military commission cases, are available on the military commission website. See *United States v Khalid Sheik Mohammad, et. al. (2)* [hereinafter *Khalid Sheik Mohammad,* et al.], and *United States v Abd Al-Rahim Hussein Muhammed Abdu Al-Nashiri (2),* [hereinafter *Al-Nashiri*], both available at <http://www.mc.mil/CASES.aspx>.

[7] §950p(c), 2009 MCA (hostilities are defined as 'any conflict subject to the laws of war').

[8] For the charges of spying or unlawful belligerency, the US contends that although these charges are not violations of the international law of war, international law has long countenanced their trial by domestic military commission. Separate statutory authority has long existed for military commission trial of the offences of spying and aiding the enemy. See 10 U.S.C §§904, 906.

[9] See §950t, 2009 MCA (charges under the 2009 MCA include: murder of protected persons; attacking civilians; attacking civilian objects; attacking protected property; pillaging; denying quarter; taking hostages; employing poison or similar weapons; using protected persons as a shield; using protected property as a shield; torture; cruel or inhuman treatment; intentionally causing serious bodily injury; mutilating or maiming; murder in violation of the law of war; destruction of property in violation of the law of war; using treachery or perfidy; improperly using a flag of truce; improperly using a distinctive emblem; intentionally mistreating a dead body; rape; sexual assault or abuse; hijacking or hazarding a vessel or aircraft; terrorism; providing material support for terrorism; wrongfully aiding the enemy; spying; attempts; (inchoate) conspiracy; and solicitation). The 2006 MCA listed the same offences, albeit in a slightly different arrangement. See §950t, 2006 MCA. Inchoate conspiracy is an Anglo-American criminal charge that requires an agreement to commit a criminal act and the commission of an overt act in furtherance of the conspiracy. It does not require the completion of the underlying criminal offence, and may be charged separately from the underlying criminal act if it is completed.

recognized under the international law of war, such as deliberately attacking civilians, as well as other more controversial charges, such as material support for terrorism, inchoate conspiracy, and murder in violation of the law of war.[10] Material support for terrorism and inchoate conspiracy were the primary charges in earlier military commission trials, to include those of Salim Hamdan (Osama Bin Laden's driver) and Ali Al-Bahlul (Al Qaeda's propagandist), and it is the viability of those charges as violations of the law of war that is the subject of their appeals.

Complicating the issue of subject-matter jurisdiction is the fact that the majority of the conduct of the defendants currently subject to trial by the Guantánamo military commissions occurred well before the passage of the 2006 Military Commissions Act. As a result, that conduct must have been unlawful and subject to trial by military commission prior to that date in order to survive an *ex post facto* or legality challenge.[11] For the US Supreme Court, the sole statutory authority providing military commission jurisdiction over war crimes prior to the enactment of the 2006 MCA is Article 21 of the US Uniform Code of Military Justice (UCMJ),[12] which preserved the pre-existing jurisdiction of military commissions over violations of the laws and customs of war. Accordingly, even where an offence is enumerated in the 2006 MCA, the *ex post facto* consideration necessitates a finding that the statute merely codified a pre-existing violation of the laws and customs of war and did not establish a completely new offence.

[10] The charges against the 9/11 defendants include attacking civilians, attacking civilian objects, murder in violation of the law of war, destruction of property in violation of the law of war, hijacking or hazarding a vessel or aircraft, terrorism, intentionally causing serious bodily injury, and conspiracy to commit the prior seven offences; while the case against Al-Nashiri involves allegations based on Al Qaeda's attempted bombing of the *USS The Sullivans* in January 2000, its completed bombing of the *USS Cole* in October, 2000, and its bombing of the French-flagged *MV Limburg* in October of 2002 involving charges of using treachery or perfidy, murder in violation of the law of war, attempted murder in violation of the law of war, terrorism, conspiracy to commit terrorism and murder in violation of the law of war, intentionally causing serious bodily injury, attacking civilians (*MV Limburg*), attacking civilian objects (*MV Limburg*), and hijacking or hazarding a vessel or aircraft.

[11] The *Ex Post Facto* Clause prohibits Congress from passing laws, particularly criminal laws, with retroactive effect. US Const. Art. I, §9, cl. 3 ('No bill of attainder or *ex post facto* Law shall be passed'). This prohibition reflects the international principle of legality as 'ancient as the law itself.' See also Brenner-Beck, D., 2015, 'Trial and Punishment for Battlefield Misconduct', in *The War on Terror and the Laws of War: A Military Perspective*, 2nd edn, p. 216.

[12] *Hamdan v Rumsfeld*, 548 U.S. 557, 593 (2006). The UCMJ is the specialized body of law that governs criminal prosecutions of members of the US military. It also preserves the pre-existing military commission jurisdiction to try violations of the law of war. See 10 U.S.C. §821/Article 21, UCMJ ('Jurisdiction of courts-martial not exclusive. The provisions of this code conferring jurisdiction upon courts-martial shall not be construed as depriving military commissions, provost courts, or other military tribunals of concurrent jurisdiction in respect of offenders or offenses that by statute *or by the law of war may be tried by such military commissions*, provost courts, or other military tribunals'); see also *Ex parte Quirin*, 317 US 1, 28 (1942) ('By the Articles of War, and especially Article 15 [the precursor to Article 21, UCMJ], Congress has explicitly provided, so far as it may constitutionally do so, that military tribunals shall have jurisdiction to try offenders or offenses against the laws of war in appropriate cases').

In other words, the nature of the offence as a violation of the law of war became a critical determination in validating military jurisdiction over it.

PROCEDURE

The criminal procedures in the 2009 (and 2006) MCAs are based primarily on the criminal procedures in US military courts-martial, with omissions of certain statutory rights and some alterations to traditional hearsay rules to accommodate battlefield conditions.[13] A criminal case in a US court-martial or military commission is commenced by the swearing of criminal charges against a defendant (called 'preferral'). The case is then 'referred' by the military convening authority for trial by court-martial or commission. For serious courts-martial, high level military commanders normally act as the convening authority for their military units. The Guantánamo military commissions are convened by the US Secretary of Defense, or any officer or official of the US designated by him for that purpose.[14] Courts-martial and military commissions are not standing permanent courts; instead they are 'convened' or created by order of the convening authority for each case. The convening authority also makes determinations on the allocation of resources to the prosecution (called a trial counsel in military practice) and the defence, as well as deciding what charges to refer for trial, and whether the commission is authorized to impose the death penalty for charges authorizing such a penalty. The convening authority also takes 'final action' to approve, modify, or disapprove the final findings (on the charges) and/or sentence of the commission.

The MCA also created an appellate process analogous to that provided for servicemembers convicted by courts-martial. For the current Guantánamo military commissions, once the convening authority takes final action on any conviction and sentence, the case is referred for appellate review to the Court of Military Commission Review (CMCR),[15] with subsequent appeals to the US Court of Appeals for the DC Circuit,[16] and a subsequent

[13] See §948b(d), 2009 MCA. The protections of Arts 10, 31, and 32 of the UCMJ (120-day speedy trial rule, preliminary investigation/inquiry, and affirmative rights warning requirement) were specifically made inapplicable to military commissions under the 2006 and 2009 MCA. Under Art. 32, UCMJ, a preliminary investigation/inquiry is required prior to referral of charges to a general court-martial (the highest level court which tries serious felonies). There is no such requirement for military commissions under the MCA.

[14] §948h, 2009 MCA.

[15] §§950c, 950f, 2009 MCA. A panel on the CMCR shall consist of not less than three appellate military judges who shall be either appellate military judges assigned by the Secretary of Defence to be judges on the court, or a person appointed by the President with the advice and consent of the Senate to serve as an appellate judge on the CMCR. See §950f(b)(2) and (3), 2009 MCA.

[16] §950g, 2009 MCA. 'DC Circuit' stands for the District of Columbia Circuit. US federal appellate courts are divided into twelve regional circuits (1-11 and the DC Circuit) which hear appeals from the district courts within their respective geographical regions, and the Court of Appeals for the Federal Circuit

potential grant of discretionary review by the US Supreme Court through a *writ of certiorari*. The United States may seek interlocutory appeal to the CMCR only in cases where the ruling of the presiding military judge terminates the proceedings with respect to a charge or specification, excludes evidence that is substantial proof of a fact material in the proceeding, or involves disclosure of classified information.[17]

STAGNATION IN 2014

At the appellate level, the much anticipated *en banc Al-Bahlul* decision, which will be discussed extensively later in this chapter, failed to resolve the question of which 'law of war' was referred to in Article 21 of the UCMJ, the sole statutory authority providing jurisdiction for military commissions over war crime offences which pre-dated the 17 October 2006 passage of the 2006 Military Commissions Act.[18] This highly anticipated decision skirted definitive resolution of the decisive question: whether this provision referred to the 'international law of war' as determined by the October 2012 DC Circuit decision in *Hamdan v United States (Hamdan II)*,[19] or instead referred to a broader conception of the law of war to include the 'US common law of war'. As a result, uncertainty remains as to the viability of pre-2006 charges of inchoate conspiracy which arguably do not qualify as violations of the international law of war, and would therefore be valid only under the 'US common law of war' theory articulated by the United States.

In addition to the failure of *Al-Bahlul* to resolve important jurisdictional questions, an interlocutory appeal in *Al-Nashiri* of the dismissal of the *M/V Limburg* charges by the military commission limited not only the matters on which the Commission could move forward in that case, but also resulted in the cancellation of scheduled pre-trial hearings in September, October, and December 2014. The DC Circuit's November 2014 issuance of a stay of the CMCR's consideration of that interlocutory appeal has resulted in further delay as the DC Circuit considers Al-Nashiri's petition for a writ of mandamus and prohibition[20] challenging the composition of the CMCR under the 2009 MCA.

which has nationwide jurisdiction to hear specialized appeals, such as those involving patent laws and cases decided by the Court of International Trade and the Court of Federal Claims.

[17] §950d(a), 2009 MCA.

[18] 2006 MCA. Although the legality or *ex post facto* issue depends upon the date of the enactment of the 2006 MCA, current commission trials are conducted under the authority of the 2009 MCA.

[19] 696 F.3d 1238 (D.C. Cir. 2012) (hereinafter *Hamdan II*).

[20] Al-Nashiri sought both a writ of mandamus and a writ of prohibition to disqualify the two military judges on the Court of Military Commission Review and prohibit their participation on the CMCR panel reviewing the interlocutory appeal in his case. He contends that the process of appointing military appellate judges to the CMCR violates the US Constitution, and therefore, their participation on the CMCR is a violation of the law. A writ of mandamus is an *extraordinary* writ issued by an appellate court which compels a judicial body to perform a duty that the law clearly requires. A writ of prohibition, alternately,

An equally important cause of the stagnation in the two primary military commission cases, *United States v Khalid Sheik Mohammad, et al.* and *United States v Al-Nashiri*, involves various interferences with the commissions by outside entities which have created serious legal issues involving government intrusion into the defence function. In early 2014, while the 9/11 commission case was halted pending a competency determination on one of the five defendants,[21] defence attorneys became aware that Federal Bureau of Investigation (FBI) agents had approached various members of the defence teams and recruited or attempted to recruit them as confidential informants. Such intrusion into the defence function raised the issue of a real or potential conflict of interest for the attorneys leading each team, as well as the potential of compromise of confidential or privileged defence information. Because the defendants are entitled to conflict-free counsel in their trials,[22] resolution of this issue has prevented any other action by the military commissions in the 9/11 case as this issue is litigated.

Further, recent interferences affecting the progress of the commissions include the in-court surprise identification by Mr bin Al-Shibh of a former Central Intelligence Agency (CIA) black site interpreter on his defence team in February 2015, and the ill-conceived December 2014 initiative (alleged to amount to unlawful influence) by the military commission convening authority to change the regulation governing trial by military commission to require all military judges officiating over commission trials to relocate to the Guantánamo Naval Base for the duration of the trials.[23] Resolution

prevents a judicial body from exercising its power in a manner unauthorized by law. Because these writs are extraordinary, they may only be issued in rare cases where the right to relief is 'clear and indisputable' and there is 'no other adequate means' by which the petitioner may attain the relief he seeks, such as through ultimate post-trial appeal. *Cobell v Norton*, 334 F.3d 1128, 1137 (D.C. Cir. 2003).

[21] On 19 December 2013, pre-trial hearings in the 9/11 case were halted by the US Government's request for a competency determination on Mr bin Al-Shibh, one of the 9/11 defendants, based on his repeated disruptions of the commission proceedings during that week of sessions. Such a request halted all further Commission proceedings in the 9/11 case, absent severance of that defendant from the joint trial, until it could be determined that the defendant was competent to assist in his defence. While that issue and the ensuing delay was not due to any interference with the Commissions, the defendant's competence had not yet been determined by April 2014 when the FBI investigations came to light, requiring the Commissions to address their effect on the trial process before any other issue, to include the lingering competency issue. Mr Al-Shibh's defence counsel has repeatedly asserted that his client is competent.

[22] See AE 292QQ, 'Amended Order, Emergency Defense Motion to Abate Proceedings and Inquire into Existence of Conflict of Interest Burdening Counsel's Representation of Accused', 16 December 2014 (original order dated 24 July 2014), in *Khalid Sheik Mohammad, et al.*; *Smith v Lockhart*, 923 F.2d 1314, 1320 (8th Cir. 1991); *United States v Blount*, 290 F.3d 201, 210 (2d Cir. 2002) (citing *Wood v Georgia*, 450 U.S. 261, 271 (1981) and *Holloway v Arkansas*, 435 U.S. 475, 481–482 (1978)).

[23] On 9 December 2014, the Convening Authority sought a change in the Regulation for Trial by Military Commission (2011 Ed.), to require the establishment of 'military commissions as the exclusive judicial duty for the military judges…and designat[ing] the judge's place of duty as the venue where the military commission is to take place'. See Memorandum, 'Assessment of Office of Military Commissions, Dec. 9, 2014, from Mr Vance A. Ary, Convening Authority and Director, Office of Military Commissions, to Deputy Secretary of Defense'.

of collateral issues, such as certain defendants' objections to being touched by female guards because of their religious beliefs, have also required time-consuming litigation to ensure the smooth operation of the commissions.

Although the military commissions accomplished little forward progress in 2014, new charges were brought against both Ahmed Al-Darbi[24] and Abd Al-Hadi Al-Iraqi.[25] Perhaps most critical to the legitimacy and progress of the Guantánamo military commissions was the 9 December 2014 release of the US Senate Select Committee on Intelligence (SSCI) *Study on the Central Intelligence Agency's Detention and Interrogation Program*,[26] which is expected to produce some positive results in discovery and transparency as more of the proceedings will be open to the public.

After first discussing the issues raised in the *Al-Bahul* and *Al-Nashiri* appeals, this chapter will turn to the various interferences and collateral issues slowing the progress of the military commissions, as well as new charges brought in 2014. It will then examine the positive results expected to flow from the release of the SSCI Torture Report on the efficiency and transparency of the Guantánamo Commissions.

B. **Appellate issues**

AL-BAHLUL v UNITED STATES

Judicial determination of the scope of current Guantánamo military commission subject-matter jurisdiction has two important predicate questions: first, whether the charged offence is a violation of the 'law of war' referred to in Article 21, UCMJ, such that pre-October 2006 conduct can be tried before a military commission (and significantly, what body of law is referred to by the phrase 'law of war' in Article 21); and second, whether congressional power to include enumerated war crimes within the jurisdiction of military commissions is limited by the international law of war or other US constitutional restrictions. The first issue on the content of the 'law of war' under Article 21 was directly raised in the appeals of the 2008 military commission convictions of Salim Hamdan and Ali Al-Bahlul. Salim Hamdan was tried before a military commission and found guilty of material support for terrorism for his role as Osama Bin Laden's driver; he was acquitted

[24] 'Referred Charges', 5 February 2014, in *United States v Ahmed Al-Darbi* [hereinafter *Al-Darbi*), available at <http://www.mc.mil/CASES.aspx>.

[25] See 'Referred Charges', 2 June 2014, in *United States v Abd Al-Hadi al-Iraqi* [hereinafter *Al-Hadi*], available at <http://www.mc.mil/CASES.aspx>.

[26] Senate Select Committee on Intelligence, The Senate Intelligence Committee Report on Torture, Committee Study on the Central Intelligence Agency's Detention and Interrogation Program [hereinafter SSCI Executive Summary], available at <http://www.intelligence.senate.gov/study2014.html>.

of conspiracy charges. Ali Al-Bahlul was tried and convicted of material support for terrorism, conspiracy, and solicitation to commit war crimes for his direct support to Osama Bin Laden and his role as Al Qaeda's propagandist and public relations director, specifically including his creation of videos glorifying Al Qaeda's attacks on the *USS Cole* (a US Navy warship attacked in a Yemeni port) which were used to recruit new members for Al Qaeda and to incite terrorist attacks. Although the DC Circuit's opinion in Salim Hamdan's appeal, *Hamdan II*, purportedly resolved the test to be applied to resolve the first issue—that Article 21 refers solely to the 'international law of war'—its holding was weakened, as discussed below, but not overruled by the *en banc* decision in *Al-Bahlul*.

In the US legal system, the powers of the national federal government, although broad, are limited to those enumerated in the Constitution. This division of powers between federal and state governments, as well as the separation of powers between the three branches of the federal government,[27] are designed to protect the liberty of the individual, and any statute enacted in excess of the powers vested by the Constitution in the federal government or its specific prohibitions is void.[28] As in any case challenging a statute passed by the US Congress, a determination of the source of authority to legislate under the US Constitution is necessary. In the *Hamdan II* and *Al-Bahlul* appeals, identification of the source of Congress's powers to proscribe war crimes and subject them to trial by military commission, and any limits to those powers, is relevant to determine both the scope of the 'law of war' referenced by Article 21 of the UCMJ for pre-2006 conduct (what *did* Congress include in Article 21), and its power to prospectively subject the offences listed in the 2006 and 2009 MCAs to trial by military commission (what *can* Congress include). Additionally, because US law recognizes that Congress can legislate in violation of international law if it clearly indicates its intention to do so,[29] the intertwined issues of the source and limits of congressional power arising from the Constitution pose, at least for the purposes of domestic US law, the operative constraints on US military commission jurisdiction.

In *Ex parte Quirin* and *In re Yamashita*,[30] two cases evaluating the legitimacy of the Second World War law-of-war military commission trials, the Supreme Court premised congressional authority to proscribe violations of the law of war and subject them to trial by military commission on the Define and Punish Clause of the US Constitution,[31] and identified the law of war as part of the law of nations referenced in that

[27] The Executive (President), Legislative (Congress), and Judicial branches.

[28] See *Bond v United States*, 131 S.Ct. 2355, 2364-65 (2011); ibid. at 2367 (Ginsburg, J., concurring) ('In short, a law "beyond the power of Congress,' for any reason, is 'no law at all"') (citing *Nigro v United States*, 276 U.S. 332 (1928)).

[29] Raustiala, K., 2009, *Does the Constitution Follow the Flag? The Evolution of Territoriality in American Law*, OUP, pp. 99, 269 n. 20 (citing *Whitney v Roberts*, 124 US 190 (1888)).

[30] *In re Yamashita*, 327 U.S. 1, 11 (1946); *Ex parte Quirin*, 317 U.S. 1, 7 (1942).

[31] US Const. art. I, §8, cl. 10 ('The Congress shall have Power To...define and punish Piracies and Felonies committed on the high Seas, and Offences against the Law of Nations ...').

clause.[32] However, while these cases provide solid authority for the proposition that international law provides the basis for criminal sanction by military tribunals, they did not address the question of whether international law operates as a constraint on congressional power to enumerate offences subject to trial by military commission. Although Congress may have the power to criminalize conduct, its power to subject an offence to trial before a military commission is limited, at least according to *Quirin* and *Yamashita*,[33] by the content of the law of war as part of the law of nations. Relying on these two cases, both Hamdan and Al-Bahlul argued in their appeals that 'Congress's authority under the Define and Punish Clause is limited to proscribing offences that are already illegal under international law',[34] and that violations of the law of war under Article 21 of the UCMJ, similarly incorporated international law both as a source and limit on congressional power.

In *Al-Bahlul v United States*, Al-Bahlul contested his commission convictions for material support for terrorism, solicitation of others to commit war crimes, and conspiracy on the basis that these offences were not war crimes under the international law of war, and

[32] *Ex parte Quirin*, 317 U.S. 1, 28 (1942) ('From the very beginning of its history this Court has recognized and *applied the law of war as including that part of the law of nations* which prescribes, for the conduct of war, the status, rights and duties of enemy nations as well as of enemy individuals. By the Articles of War, and especially Article 15, Congress has explicitly provided, so far as it may constitutionally do so, that military tribunals shall have jurisdiction to try offenders or offenses against the law of war in appropriate cases. Congress, in addition to making rules for the government of our Armed Forces, *has thus exercised its authority to define and punish offenses against the law of nations* by sanctioning, within constitutional limitations, the jurisdiction of military commissions to try persons for offenses which, *according to the rules and precepts of the law of nations, and more particularly the law of war,* are cognizable by such tribunals') (emphasis in original); *In re Yamashita*, 327 U.S. at 7 ('In *Ex parte Quirin*, 317 U.S. 1, we had occasion to consider at length the sources and nature of the authority to create military commissions for the trial of enemy combatants for offenses against the law of war. We there pointed out that Congress, in the exercise of the power conferred upon it by Article I, §8, Cl. 10 of the Constitution to "define and punish…Offences against the Law of Nations…" of which the law of war is a part, had by the Articles of War (10 U.S.C. §§1471-1593) recognized the "military commission" appointed by military command, as it had previously existed in United States Army practice, as an appropriate tribunal for the trial and punishment of offenses against the law of war'); *Hamdan II*, 696 F.3d at 1248-49; *Hamdan v Rumsfeld*, 548 U.S. at 601 (plurality op.); see also ibid. at 641 (Kennedy, J. concurring in part) (the law of war 'derives from "rules and precepts of the law of nations"; it is the body of international law governing armed conflict') (citing *Quirin*, 317 U.S. at 28); see generally Hafetz, J., 2014, 'Policing the Line: International Law, Article III, and the Constitutional Limits of Military Jurisdiction', Wis. L. Rev. vol. 4, pp. 681, 694–697.

[33] *Quirin*, 317 U.S. at 28; *Yamashita*, 327 U.S. at 7; see also *Hamdan v Rumsfeld*, 548 U.S. at 595–618 (plurality op.) (although the plurality opinion held that Presidential authority to subject offences to trial by military commission was limited by the international law of war, Justice Stevens qualified this portion of the decision to apply 'in the absence of Congressional legislation', implying a different standard might apply to congressional legislation defining war crimes subject to trial by military commission); ibid. at 655 (Kennedy, J., concurring in part) ('In light of the conclusion that the military commissions at issue are unauthorized, Congress may choose to provide further guidance in this area. Congress, not the Courts, is the branch in the better position to undertake the "sensitive task of establishing a principle not inconsistent with the national interest or with international justice" ').

[34] See *Al-Bahlul*, 767 F.3d at 72 (Kavanaugh, J., concurring in the judgment in part and dissenting in part); *Hamdan II*, 696 F.3d at 1246.

that the military commission therefore lacked subject-matter jurisdiction. In *Hamdan II*, Salim Hamdan made the same argument to successfully contest his convictions for material support for terrorism. In both these cases, the United States asserted that the 'law of war' referenced in Article 21 extended beyond the international law of war recognized in *Quirin* and *Yamashita*,[35] 'to encompass a separate body of domestic law known as the US common law of war'.[36] This novel assertion of an American common law of war relied on an expanded consideration of historical military commissions to include commissions from the American Civil War. However, as Justice Stevens warned in *Hamdan v Rumsfeld*, nineteenth-century Civil War commissions should be 'considered with caution'[37] because they 'operated as both martial law or military government tribunals and law-of-war commissions… [and] regularly tried war crimes and ordinary crimes together,… mixing elements of crimes ordinarily triable in civilian courts (like treason) and violations of the laws of war'.[38] In *Hamdan II*, the DC Circuit rejected the US Government's US common law of war claim, and relying directly on *Quirin*, held that 'the "law of war" cross-referenced in [Article 21] is the *international* law of war'. [39] Accordingly, the court held that the international law of war, and therefore Article 21 of the UCMJ, did not proscribe material support for terrorism as a war crime.[40] As a result, the court vacated Hamdan's military commission convictions.

Closely following and applying the holding in *Hamdan II*, the DC Circuit panel considering Al-Bahlul's appeal summarily vacated his convictions after the US

[35] *In re Yamashita*, 327 U.S. 1, 11 (1946); *Ex parte Quirin*, 317 U.S. 1, 7 (1942).

[36] Hafetz, J., 'Policing the Line'. For a description of the American common law of war position, see Brief of the United States, *Hamdan II*, 696 F.3d 1238; *Hamdan II*, 696 F.3d at 485; Brief of the United States, *Al-Bahlul v United States*, 767 F.3d 1 (2014); Supplemental Brief of the United States, ibid. The actual historical underpinnings of the American common law of war theory have been extensively evaluated, resulting in diametric conclusions as to its validity. Compare Glazier, D., 2014, 'The Misuse of History: Conspiracy and the Guantánamo Military Commissions', Baylor L. Rev., vol. 66, p. 265 (evaluating the American law of war theory), and Thravalos, H. V., 2012, 'History, Hamdan, and Happenstance: "Conspiracy by Two or More to Violate the Laws of War by Destroying Life or Property in Aid of the Enemy"', Harv. Nat'l Sec. J., vol. 3, p. 223.

[37] *Hamdan*, 548 U.S. at n.27 (plurality op.).

[38] 548 U.S. at 596 n.27, 608, 609 n.37 (plurality op.) (Justice Stevens explained that commissions had historically been used in three situations: they have substituted for civilian courts at times and in places where martial law has been declared; been established to try civilians 'as part of a temporary military government over occupied enemy territory or territory regained from an enemy where civilian government cannot and does not function[;] … and convened as an "incident to the conduct of war" when there is a need "to seize and subject to disciplinary measures those enemies who in their attempt to thwart or impede our military effort have violated the law of war"'. Ibid. at pp. 595–6 (citations omitted)).

[39] *Hamdan II*, 696 F.3d at 474 (citing *Quirin*, 317 U.S. at 27–30), 478 (citing *Hamdan v Rumsfeld*, 542 U.S. at 603, 610 (plurality); ibid. at 641 (Kennedy, J., concurring); *Quirin*, 317 U.S. at 27–30).

[40] *Hamdan II*, 696 F.3d at 474, 479–86. The court also declined to answer the question of the extent of congressional authority to subject offences to trial by military commission as that issue was not necessary for resolution of the appeal. Ibid. at 479–80. Judge Kavanaugh alone stated in a concurring footnote that Congress was not limited prospectively to the limits imposed by the international law of war. See *Hamdan II*, 696 F.3d at 1246 n.6.

Government conceded that inchoate conspiracy and solicitation did not violate the international law of war.[41] Because a decision of a panel of a federal appellate court, such as the DC Circuit, establishes circuit precedent which can be overruled only by a contrary decision of the US Supreme Court or an *en banc* opinion of the entire Court of Appeals, the United States sought *en banc* reconsideration of Al-Bahlul's appeal seeking to overturn the holding the *Al-Bahlul* panel had impliedly incorporated from *Hamdan II*—that Article 21 referenced only 'the international law of war'. After extensive briefing and argument in which the United States once again asserted its 'US common law of war' theory, the *en banc* Court upheld Al-Bahlul's conspiracy convictions, but vacated his convictions for material support for terrorism and solicitation. This ruling, however, avoided deciding the key issue presented—the nature of military commission war crimes jurisdiction. Instead, the court relied on the plain error doctrine which substantially limited the scope of its review. In US appellate practice, if a party to a case fails to object to an issue at trial, that error is reviewed only for plain error on appeal.[42] Under this standard of review, only plain errors that affect substantial rights and seriously affect the fairness, integrity, or public reputation of the judicial proceedings may, at the discretion of the reviewing court, be remedied.[43] While meeting this exacting standard in challenging his convictions for material support for terrorism and solicitation, Al-Bahlul's challenge to his convictions for inchoate conspiracy failed. The procedural basis for the decision, however, significantly undermined its value in providing guidance in future cases.

Although the Court agreed that the charges of material support for terrorism and solicitation of others to commit war crimes could not traditionally be tried by law-of-war military commissions, its invocation of plain error review did not require the Court to determine what law was referenced by Article 21—the international law of war or the US common law of war. Nor did it decide whether the *Ex Post Facto* clause (U.S. Const. art. I, §9, cl. 3) applied at Guantánamo. Instead, accepting, without deciding, that the *Ex*

[41] *Al-Bahlul v United States*, 2013 WL 297726 (D.C. Cir. Jan. 25, 2013) (order vacating Al-Bahlul's convictions for conspiracy, solicitation, and material support for terrorism under rationale of *Hamdan II*).

[42] At his military commission trial Al-Bahlul sought to represent himself, and was ultimately denied the right to do so. Although appointed a military defence counsel, both Al-Bahlul and his appointed counsel (at his direction) refused to participate in the proceedings as a protest against the denial of the right of self-representation. Al-Bahlul, 767 F.3d at 7; see also Posting of David Frakt, *Guest Post: David J.R. Frakt on the Al-Bahlul Amicus Brief*, to OpinioJuris Blog, <http://opiniojuris.org/2013/07/28/guest-post-david-j-r-frakt-on-the-al-bahlul-amicus-brief/> (Jul. 28, 2013, 12:51 p.m.). Despite this boycott, Al-Bahlul did make certain statements regarding the charges at his hearing, and various judges on the DC Circuit drew different conclusions from these statements on whether Al-Bahlul had preserved issues for appeal or instead if the appeal would be reviewed only for plain error. The majority of the Court determined that Al-Bahlul, in refusing to participate, had forfeited the arguments raised on appeal, and accordingly, they would be reviewed only for plain error despite the lack of clarity for analysis of future military commissions charges that would result from such a standard of review. *Al-Bahlul*, 767 F.3d at 10–11.

[43] See *Al-Bahlul*, 767 F.3d at 9–10.

Post Facto clause did apply to Guantánamo military commissions,[44] the Court held that Al-Bahlul's conspiracy charge did not violate that restriction for two independent reasons.

First, the Court held that because the conduct for which Al-Bahlul was convicted was already criminalized under 18 U.S.C. §2332(b), the federal statute criminalizing conspiracies outside of the United States to kill US nationals, it 'was not "plain" that it violated the *Ex Post Facto* Clause to try a pre-existing federal criminal offence in a military commission'.[45] This conclusion depended heavily on the plain error review standard, and was roundly criticized by other judges on the DC Circuit as being without legal support, contrary to the *Ex Post Facto* clause and Supreme Court precedent, and prohibited by the laws of war.[46]

Second, the Court also held that it was 'not "plain" that [inchoate] conspiracy was not already triable by law-of-war military commission under [Article 21] when Bahlul's conduct occurred'.[47] To substantiate this conclusion the court first discussed the four-three split in the Supreme Court in *Hamdan v Rumsfeld* on the validity of the charge of inchoate conspiracy as a violation of the law of war, an issue left unresolved in that opinion.[48] Next, the court acknowledged the two differing views of what body of law was referenced by Article 21. In light of the split in the Supreme Court and the views of at least two judges of the DC Circuit that Article 21 might not be limited to the international law of war, and its evaluation of the historical evidence underlying the US Government's common law of war position,[49] the *en banc* court concluded that subjecting Al-Bahlul to trial by military commission for conspiracy was not plain error.[50]

[44] *Al-Bahlul*, 767 F.3d at 18. The US Constitution's *Ex Post Facto* clause prohibits Congress from passing criminal laws that apply retrospectively, thereby criminalizing conduct that was legal when originally performed. *See Ex Post Facto* Clause. This constitutional prohibition embodies the international principle of legality.

[45] Ibid. at 18 ([t]he court also held that any difference between the elements of that offense and the conspiracy charge in the 2006 MCA does not seriously affect the fairness, integrity or public reputation of judicial proceedings).

[46] Ibid. at 77–8 (Kavanaugh, J., concurring in the judgment in part and dissenting in part) (finding this suggestion to be unsupported by precedent, scholarly commentary, or legislative history); ibid. at 49–50 (Rogers, J., concurring in the judgment in part and dissenting) (condemning this argument as 'a standardless exercise in crime by analogy' which has been condemned by the Supreme Court and forbidden by the law of war).

[47] *Al-Bahlul*, 767 F.3d at 18.

[48] As was the question of what body of law was meant by the term 'law of war' in §821/Article 21, UCMJ.

[49] Critics of this analysis highlighted Justice Stevens' instruction in *Hamdan v Rumsfeld* that '"[t]he Civil War precedents must...be considered with caution" because military commissions "operated as both martial law or military government tribunals and law-of-war commissions" and thus "often charged hybrid crimes mixing elements of crimes ordinarily triable in civilian courts (like treason) and violations of the law of war." Hamdan, 548 U.S. at 596 n. 27, 609 n. 37 (plurality op.)'. *Al-Bahlul*, 767 F.3d at 43 (Rogers, J., concurring in the judgment in part and dissenting).

[50] Use of the plain error review standard was criticized by other judges on the *en banc* panel. *Al-Bahlul*, 767 F.3d at 48 (Rogers, J., concurring in part and dissenting); ibid. at 51 (Brown, J., concurring in the judgment in part and dissenting in part); ibid. at 62–3 (Kavanaugh, J., concurring in the judgment in part

In both *Hamdan II* and *Al-Bahlul*, the DC Circuit avoided the most important question related to military commission jurisdiction: the scope of congressional power to subject offences to trial by military commission. In *Hamdan II*, Hamdan's convictions for material support for terrorism involved only pre-2006 conduct. This fact limited the judicial inquiry to determining what offences were incorporated by Article 21's reference to the law of war prior to the MCA's enumeration of this offence within the scope of military commission jurisdiction. Because *Hamdan II* concluded that Article 21 incorporated the *international* law of war, and because *Quirin* and *Yamashita* established that the Define and Punish clause authorized Congress to subject violations of the international law of war to trial by military commission,[51] it was unnecessary to reach the question of whether Congress had, in Article 21, criminalized conduct based on the distinct US law of war instead of internationally recognized law of war violations. Under either conception of the "law of war" in Article 21, material support to terrorism was not a war crime. In *Al-Bahlul*, however, the viability of the offence of inchoate conspiracy did depend on which body of law the court determined was incorporated by Article 21,[52] but this issue was avoided when the court invoked the plain error doctrine.

By relying on plain error review, *Al-Bahlul* also avoided deciding the key domestic law questions raised by challenges to military commission jurisdiction, which are distinct from the legitimacy of the Guantánamo military commissions under international law. These questions include: what sources of power under the US Constitution authorize Congress to proscribe specific conduct as war crimes and subject these offences to trial by military commissions; what degree of deference is due to Congress by the courts when evaluating such an exercise of congressional authority; and finally, whether congressional discretion in this area is limited by international law, constitutional provisions, or some other source of law. The US Government's constitutional arguments in both *Hamdan II* and *Al-Bahlul* asserted that the appellants' 'focus on the Define and Punish Clause alone is misplaced [because Congress's war powers,] as supplemented by the Necessary and Proper Clause, independently authorize Congress to establish military commissions to try an enemy's war crimes, [and that these broad independent war powers are] not constrained by

and dissenting in part). Additionally while six of seven judges upheld the legitimacy of conspiracy charges based on pre-2006 conduct under plain error review, they based their conclusions on very different rationales. See Brenner-Beck, D., 2015, 'Trial and Punishment for Battlefield Misconduct', at p. 195, n.9.

[51] *Quirin*, 317 U.S. at 28 ('the jurisdiction of military commissions to try persons for offenses which, *according to the rules and precepts of the law of nations, and more particularly the law of war*, are cognizable by such tribunals').

[52] A decision that Art. 21 incorporated the US common law of war, and broadened the scope of permissible military commission jurisdiction, would have required analysis of the limits of congressional power under the Define and Punish Clause, as well as what other authority might empower Congress to legislate without regard to international law in this area.

the evolving and often difficult to discern standards of international law'.[53] The plain error review standard enabled the *en banc* court to avoid these issues as well.

Regardless, debate over these core constitutional issues feature prominently in the separate concurring and dissenting opinions in *Al-Bahlul*. While one judge concluded that Congress's powers were limited by the international law of war, at least two of the judges on the *en banc* court concluded that Congress had almost unlimited constitutional authority to prospectively subject non-international law of war offences to trial by military commission.[54] Such a broad conception, however, certainly implicates the concern articulated in *Hamdan v Rumsfeld* that the limitations on military commission jurisdiction were essential to ensuring the constitutional limits on the accumulation of power in military hands,[55] and 'raises separation-of-powers concerns of the highest order'.[56] The structural limitations imposed by the Constitution's separation of powers arguably pose additional limitations on unrestrained congressional discretion as to the limits of military commission jurisdiction even if the source of its authority extends beyond the Define and Punish Clause.[57]

[53] *Hamdan II*, 696 F.3d at 1246; Brief of the United States, *Al-Bahlul*; see also *Hamdan v Rumsfeld*, 548 U.S. at 591–2 (concluding that exigency alone 'will not justify the establishment and use of penal tribunals not contemplated by Art. I, §8, and Art. III, §1, of the Constitution unless some other part of that document authorizes a response to the felt need… [a]nd that authority, if it exists, can derive only from the powers granted jointly to the President and Congress in time of war'. The Court then listed these powers: 'The Constitution makes the President the "Commander in Chief" of the Armed Forces, Art. II, §2, cl. **1**, but vests in Congress the powers to "declare War…and make Rules concerning Captures on Land and Water", Art. I, §8, cl. 11, to "raise and support Armies", id., cl. 12, to "define and punish…Offences against the Law of Nations," id., cl. 10, and 'To make Rules for the Government and Regulation of the land and naval Forces', id., cl. 14'). Additionally the Constitution reposes in Congress the "Power…To make all Laws which shall be necessary and proper for carrying into Execution the foregoing Powers, and all other Powers vested by the Constitution in the Government of the United States, or in any Department or Officer thereof" U.S. Const. Art. I, §8, cl. 18 (Necessary and Proper Clause).

[54] Two judges, in *Al Bahlul*, see few limits to congressional authority under either the Define and Punish, Declare War, and Necessary and Proper clauses, and would accord extraordinary deference to congressional action in this area, while another judge concluded that international law did provide a limit. Compare *Al-Bahlul*, 767 F.3d at 52–61 (Brown, J., concurring in the judgment in part, dissenting in part); ibid. at 72–3 (Kavanaugh, J., concurring in the judgment in part, dissenting in part); and ibid. at 36–7 (Rogers, J., concurring in the judgment in part and dissenting); see also Hafetz, J., 'Policing the Line', at pp. 703–5. Because the composition of the D.C. Circuit has changed significantly since 2013 with the addition of four new judges appointed by President Obama, use of these opinions to predict future D.C. Circuit action in this area is unreliable.

[55] *Hamdan v Rumsfeld*, 548 U.S. at 602.

[56] *Hamdan v Rumsfeld*, 548 U.S. at 638 (Kennedy, J., concurring in part); see also *Perez v Mortg. Bunkers Assn.*, 135 S.Ct. 1199 (2015) (Thomas, J., concurring in the judgment) (in depth discussion of historical underpinning of the separation of powers).

[57] *Al-Bahlul*, 767 F.3d at 35, 42 (Rogers, J., concurring in the judgment in part and dissenting) (citing *Quirin*, 317 U.S. at 29) (arguing that military commission subject matter jurisdiction required both that the offense be a violation of the international law of war *and* recognized in US military commissions, because 'there may be, "acts regarded in other countries, or by some writers on international law, as offenses against the law of war which would not be triable by military tribunal here, either because they are

'Every extension of military jurisdiction [in the US system] is an encroachment on the jurisdiction of the civil courts, and, more important, acts as a deprivation of the right to jury trial and of other treasured constitutional protections.'[58] Article III of the US Constitution vests the judicial power of the United States in the federal courts.[59] Both Article III itself and the judicial process guarantees of the Fifth and Sixth Amendments to the US Constitution may pose structural and specific constraints on Congress's ability to subject offences to criminal trial by military commission.[60] While *Quirin* recognized a limited exception to Article III for military commission trials of law-of-war violations, that exception was premised upon a violation of the international laws of war. The Supreme Court in *Quirin*, also 'specifically rejected defendants' Article III and Fifth and Sixth Amendment jury trial objections to trial by military commission'.[61] Although various judges on the DC Circuit in *Al-Bahlul* have argued for a broader discretion for Congress untethered by international law, the *en banc* decision did not resolve the extent to which international law operates as a hard constraint on congressional authority in the context of military commission jurisdiction. That question and any structural limits posed on congressional power by Article III and the US Constitution's separation-of-powers have not yet been determined, but could be addressed in the near future.

The *en banc Al-Bahlul* court remanded four issues to the original *Al-Bahlul* appellate panel for consideration. Among these issues were whether: (1) 'Congress exceeded its Article I, §8 authority by defining crimes triable by military commission that are not offences under the international law of war; [and whether] (2) the Congress violated Article III by vesting military commissions with jurisdiction to try crimes that are not offences under the international law of war.'[62] Just as the suspension clause was

not recognized by our courts as violations of the law of war or because they are of that class of offenses *constitutionally triable only by a jury*"') (emphasis added); *accord* Glazier, D., 2014, 'The Misuse of History', at p. 22 (under *Quirin*, the American common law of war is more limited than the international law of war).

[58] *Al-Bahlul*, 767 F.3d at 35 (Rogers, J., concurring in the judgment in part and dissenting) (citing *Reid v Covert*, 354 U.S. 1, 21, 77 (1957) (plurality op.); *see* ibid. at 41 (Frankfurter, J., concurring in result)).

[59] U.S. Const. art. III, §1 ('The judicial power of the United States, shall be vested in one Supreme Court, and in such inferior courts as the Congress may from time to time ordain and establish....').

[60] Hafetz, J., 'Policing the Line', at pp. 718–9 (citing Vladeck, S. I., 2010, 'The Laws of War as a Constitutional Constraint on Military Jurisdiction', J. Nat'l Sec. L. & Pol'y, vol. 4, p. 295); *see* U.S. Const. amend. V; U.S. Const. amend. VI (relevant portions of the Fifth Amendment require presentment or indictment by a grand jury before a person may be tried for a capital or infamous crime, while the Sixth Amendment preserves the right to a jury trial, among other trial rights).

[61] See *Quirin*, 317 U.S. at 29 (describing law of war as branch of international law), 38–45; see also *Al-Bahlul*, 767 F3d at 73–5 (Brown, J., concurring in the judgment in part and dissenting in part).

[62] *Al-Bahlul*, 767 F.3d at 31 (two other issues were also remanded for panel consideration—whether Al-Bahlul's convictions violate the First Amendment to the US Constitution and whether the 2006 MCA discriminates against aliens in violation of the equal protection component of the Due Process Clause of the US Constitution). Article I, §8 refers to the portion of the US Constitution listing the powers of Congress.

recognized in *Boumediene v Bush*[63] as 'an indispensable mechanism for monitoring the separation of powers',[64] so too may be the requirement that law-of-war military commissions adjudicate only violations of the international law of war.[65] The panel considering these issues heard argument in late October 2014, and their ultimate decision may provide additional guidance on the role of international law in circumscribing congressional authority to subject non-international law-of-war crimes to trial by military commission.[66] Alternatively, the panel may determine that these issues too were not preserved for appeal, or are controlled by the *Quirin* decision.

Finally, the DC Circuit's *Hamdan II* decision precipitated the late 2013 appeals of the 2007 and 2010 convictions of David Hicks and Omar Khadr, respectively. As a result of the 2014 *Al-Bahlul en banc* decision, the Court of Military Commission Review vacated David Hick's convictions for material support for terrorism on 18 February 2015.[67] Omar Khadr's appeal, involving additional charges beyond material support to terrorism, is still pending.

UNITED STATES v AL-NASHIRI

In explaining the prerequisites for law-of-war military commission jurisdiction, the plurality opinion in *Hamdan v Rumsfeld* listed four requirements: personal jurisdiction over the

[63] 553 U.S. 723 (2008). *Boumediene* addressed the constitutional permissibility of suspending the right of habeas corpus for Guantánamo detainees under the Suspension Clause (U.S. Const. art. IX, cl. 2).

[64] *Boumediene*, 553 U.S. at 765 (Kennedy, J., concurring in judgment).

[65] Jonathan Hafetz argues that such a requirement would appropriately police the line between Art. III courts with its guarantees of judicial independence and umbrella of procedural protections and the appropriate jurisdiction of military commissions. Hafetz, J., 'Policing the Line', at p. 719. The lack of judicial independence has been a continuing criticism of the Guantánamo military commissions.

[66] On 12 June, 2015, the DC Circuit panel vacated Al-Bahlul's remaining convictions for conspiracy, concluding that the Article III exception for law of war military commissions does not extend to the trial of domestic crimes, except for spying and aiding the enemy which have been subject to military jurisdiction since the ratification of the Constitution. See *Al-Bahlul v United States*, xx F.3d xxx (2105), 2015 WL 3687457. On 27 July 2015, the US Government filed a petition seeking *en banc* review of the panel's conclusion on the Article III question by the entire DC Circuit.

In 2010 and 2012 the Department of Defense explicitly decoupled the Guantánamo military commissions' jurisdiction from the international law of war for certain offences, to include intentionally causing serious bodily injury, murder in violation of the laws of war, destruction of property in violation of the law of war, and spying (which has its own long statutory history of trial by military commission regardless of its status under the international law of war). Such an untethering of commission offence from the international law of war raises considerable questions about the legitimacy of these commissions under international law, but also could have the perverse effect of subjecting US military personnel to similarly subjective interpretations of criminal liability for military operations, as well as the domestic separation-of-powers questions discussed above. See Brenner-Beck, D., 'Trial and Punishment for Battlefield Misconduct', at p. 224.

[67] See 'Opinion,' dated 18 February 2015, in *David M. Hicks v United States*, No 13-004, (C.M.C.R. Feb. 18, 2015).

defendant; that the offence be a violation of the law of war;[68] that the offence be committed within the theatre of war; and that the offence occur during the period of war, with no jurisdiction existing for offences which occurred before or after the war.[69] These temporal and geographical requirements pose additional restrictions on the jurisdiction of military commissions, restrictions which were recognized by Congress when it drafted the 2009 MCA, the statute authorizing the current Guantánamo military commissions. Every listed offence requires, both jurisdictionally and as an element of the offence, that the offence be 'committed in the context of and associated with hostilities',[70] with hostilities defined by the statute as 'any conflict subject to the laws of war'.[71] These requirements recognize that in order to constitute a war crime, the law of armed conflict must apply at the time of the alleged misconduct—for only in an armed conflict can the laws of war be violated.[72]

The Interlocutory Appeal

Al-Nashiri, the alleged mastermind of Al Qaeda's boats operation,[73] has challenged the jurisdiction of his military commission to try him, by collateral attack in US federal courts[74] and before his military commission.[75] In these challenges Al-Nashiri contends

[68] The law of war is currently termed the law of armed conflict (LOAC). LOAC is triggered by the existence of an armed conflict. *See* Brenner-Beck, D., 'Trial and Punishment for Battlefield Misconduct', at p. 197. ('War crimes prosecutions are based on a legally simple but factually complex jurisdictional predicate: a violation of the proscriptions established by the international law of armed conflict. Accordingly, any war crime allegation must rest on a two-pronged foundation: first, that the LOAC applied at the time of the alleged misconduct; and second, that the defendant's acts or omissions violated a proscription established by that law'). While the first proposition is reflected in the 2009 MCA, the second is the subject of the debates over the composition of the 'law of war' discussed above in *Hamdan II* and *Al-Bahlul*.

[69] *Hamdan v Rumsfeld*, 548 U.S. at 597–8 (plurality op.) (citing William Winthrop, Military Law and Precedents).

[70] §950p(c), 2009 MCA. [71] §948a(9), ibid.

[72] See Brenner-Beck, D., 'Trial and Punishment for Battlefield Misconduct' at pp. 197–9 (criticism of the 2009 MCA includes the fact that the statute does not differentiate between international armed conflicts and non-international armed conflicts, nor does it recognize that some law-of-war offences are applicable or inapplicable in certain types of conflicts).

[73] See *supra* note 5.

[74] See *Al-Nashiri v MacDonald*, 2012 WL1642306 (W.D. Wash. May 10, 2012) (dismissing case on procedural grounds in which Al-Nashiri claims that the charges against him were not committed 'in the context of and associated with hostilities' because the United States was not in an armed conflict with Al Qaeda in Yemen in 2000 as required by the 2009 MCA and international law; and that absent an armed conflict, his conduct, while it may have been criminal, cannot have been a war crime subjecting him to trial by military commission), 2013 WL 6698066 (9th Cir. Dec. 20, 2013) (affirming dismissal); *Supplemental Petition for a Writ of Habeas Corpus, Al-Nashiri v Hagel, et al.*, No. Cv-08-1207 (D.D.C. filed Apr. 21, 2014) (same claim); *Al-Nashiri v Obama, et al.*, No. Cv-08-1207 (RWR), (D.D.C. Dec. 29, 2014) (order rejecting the request for an injunction and staying the habeas case as a matter of comity and judicial economy for the duration of the military commission case).

[75] AE 104F, 'Order, Defense Motion to Dismiss Because the Convening Authority Exceeded His Power in Referring this Case to a Military Commission', 15 January 2013, in *Al-Nashiri*.

that all the alleged offences were not committed during time of war or in a theatre of war. His recent challenge to the charges involving the October 2002 bombing of the *M/V Limburg*, however, focused specifically on his contention that these charges were not, as required, 'committed in the context and associated with hostilities', because the attack on a French-flagged vessel in the Gulf of Aden was not part of an armed conflict existing between the US and Al Qaeda at the time. In response the US Government argued that two alternatives exist to bring the attack on the civilian French-flagged vessel within the armed conflict it claims existed between the United States and Al Qaeda: France's status as a coalition partner with the United States in Afghanistan, and because the attack was aimed at harming or influencing the United States.[76]

Responding to Al-Nashiri's latest challenge in September 2014, the military judge[77] dismissed the charges involving the *M/V Limburg*. His decision was not based on the merits of the legal question presented,[78] but instead because the 'Prosecution failed to request an evidentiary hearing and offer any documentary or testimonial evidence into the record to factually support their assertion of jurisdiction as to the charges and specification involving the *M/V Limburg*,... [and] has thus failed to meet its burden of persuasion in this interlocutory matter'.[79] The US Government filed an interlocutory appeal with the Court of Military Commission Review (CMCR) contesting this dismissal.[80] The US Government claims that it is not required to produce evidence on this issue at the pre-trial stage of the case, but may instead wait until the full trial on the merits to do so. Although the prosecution must establish the jurisdictional matter by a preponderance of the evidence,[81] and must prove every element of the crime beyond a reasonable doubt,[82] the 2009 MCA does not clarify

[76] The challenge to these charges centered on the underlying legal issue of 'when, if at all, a terrorist group's attack upon a civilian ship of one nation (here, France) might be deemed part of an armed conflict between that group and a different nation (the US)'. Posting of Marty Lederman, 'The jurisdictional issue delaying the Al-Nashiri commission: Saudi defendant + French ship + Malaysian shipper + Iranian oil + Bulgarian casualty − trial is a US military commission?' on JustSecurity Blog, <http://justsecurity.org/15258/issue-delaying-al-nashiri/>. The referred charges include the assertion that the attack *M/V Limburg* attack was done 'in a manner calculated to influence and affect the United States government by intimidation and coercion and to retaliate against the United States government'. See 'Referred Charges', 28 September 2011, in *Al-Nashiri*.

[77] Colonel Vance Spath replaced Judge James Pohl as the presiding military judge in the *Al-Nashiri* case in July 2014.

[78] *i.e.*, the subject-matter jurisdiction question of the charges being committed in the context of and associated with hostilities between the US and Al Qaeda.

[79] AE 168G/AE 241C, 'Order, Defense Motion to Dismiss Charges VII-IX for Lack of Jurisdiction Under International Law', 11 August 2014; AE 168K/AE 241G, 'Ruling Government Motion to Reconsider AE 168G/AE 214C and Reopen Matters for an Evidentiary Hearing on Personal Jurisdiction,' 16 Sep. 2014, both in *Al-Nashiri*.

[80] *United States v Al-Nashiri*, No. 14-001 (C.M.C.R. filed Sep. 29, 2014).

[81] A preponderance of evidence has been described as just enough evidence to make it more likely than not that the fact the claimant seeks to prove is true.

[82] See Brief of the United States, 29 September 2014, in *United States v Al-Nashiri* (C.M.C.R. 2014) (No. 14-001). Prior military commission precedent includes both the requirement to prove jurisdiction at the

when such burdens must be met. To support its claim, the US relies on federal jurisprudence which does not require the production of evidence to survive a motion to dismiss a charge at the pre-trial stage. The prosecution claims it will produce evidence at the trial on the merits to both prove the existence of jurisdiction, as well as the element of each charge requiring the offence to have been 'committed in the context of and associated with hostilities'. In his ruling, however, the military judge relied on courts-martial jurisprudence to require the prosecution to produce evidence at the pre-trial phase to support its jurisdictional claim by a preponderance of the evidence.

Both military and federal jurisprudence are sources of persuasive legal authority in arguments before the commission. However, the procedures for military commissions are based upon those for trial by general courts-martial, and the MCA explicitly makes judicial construction and application of procedures for trial by general courts-martial 'instructive' in interpreting procedures for military commissions (unless inapplicable by their terms).[83] Only in the construction of the rules regarding the protection of classified information is federal judicial construction made authoritative.[84] This statutory directive accords with *Hamdan v Rumsfeld's* conclusion that deviations between practice in general courts-martial and military commissions must be justified by evident practical need in order to comply with Common Article 3 of the Geneva Conventions.[85] The 2009 MCA lacks any procedure to evaluate the evidence prior to referral for trial, such as the Article 32 pre-trial investigation in military practice or the grand jury investigation in federal practice. Because of this, the military judge's reliance on military precedent requiring the production of a preponderance of evidence to survive a pre-trial challenge to a charge more closely accords with both *Hamdan v Rumsfeld's* mandate that courts-martial procedures are the standard against which to measure those of military commissions and the MCA's affirmative instruction that judicial construction of courts-martial procedures are to be instructive in interpreting the MCA. Although resolution of this interlocutory appeal may decide the procedural issue of how and when a military commission is able to determine its own jurisdiction, it will not

pre-trial hearing stage by a preponderance of the evidence, or alternatively, allowing the judge to defer ruling on the motion to dismiss after the presentation of the evidence at the prosecution's case-in-chief. Both approaches agree that the issues are distinct. Compare AE 048, 'Ruling D-023, Defense Motion for an Article 5 Status Determination, or Alternatively, Dismissal for Lack of Personal Jurisdiction', in *United States v al-Qosi*, 3 December 2009, with AE 083, 'D-007 Ruling on Defense Motion to Dismiss—Lack of Subject Matter Jurisdiction', 24 September 2008, in *United States v Jawad*. Additionally, unlike US courts-martial jurisprudence where subject-matter and personal jurisdiction depend on the status of the accused, military commission subject-matter jurisdiction is not determined solely by that criteria.

[83] The MCA explicitly excludes only the application of Arts 10 (speedy trial rule), 31 (rights warning as to compulsory self-incrimination), and 32 (pre-trial investigation) in trials by military commissions, while making federal jurisprudence on classified information procedures authoritative in interpreting similar provisions in the MCA. See §§948b(c) and (d), 949a, 2009 MCA.

[84] §949-pl(d), 2009 MCA.

[85] See *Hamdan v Rumsfeld*, 548 U.S. at 634 (plurality op.); ibid.at 645–646 (Kennedy, J., concurring in part).

resolve the underlying legal issue of whether the *M/V Limburg* charges were 'committed in the context of and associated with hostilities' on the merits, as the motion was not decided on that basis.

Mandamus

Consideration of this interlocutory appeal by CMCR, however, was stayed in November 2014 by the DC Circuit to allow its consideration of a petition for a writ of mandamus and prohibition[86] filed by Al-Nashiri seeking to disqualify the two military judges on the CMCR and prohibit their participation on the CMCR panel reviewing the interlocutory appeal in his case. He contends that the process of appointing military appellate judges to the CMCR violates the US Constitution, and therefore, their participation on the CMCR must be prohibited. Because these writs are extraordinary, they may only be issued if the right to relief is 'clear and indisputable' and there is 'no other adequate means' by which the petitioner may attain the relief he seeks, such as through ultimate post-trial appeal.[87] Before reaching the merits of Al-Nashiri's petition, however, the DC Circuit must first determine if it has mandamus jurisdiction over the CMCR.[88] Only if the DC Circuit determines that such jurisdiction exists can it then determine if Al-Nashiri has met the stringent conditions required to grant such a writ.

Mandamus jurisdiction. Although section 950g of the 2009 MCA gives appellate jurisdiction to the DC Circuit only for final judgments rendered by the military commissions (a narrow grant), the All Writs Act gives the DC Circuit the authority to issue all writs necessary or appropriate in the aid of its jurisdiction,[89] a broad grant of authority that has been 'interpreted to authorize writs of mandamus in *advance* of a final judgment in order to "protect" the appellate court's jurisdiction'.[90] Narrow language similar to that

[86] See *In re Al-Nashiri*, No. 14-1203 (D.C. Cir. Nov. 12, 2014) (order staying consideration of appeal by the Court of Military Commission Review); *In re Al-Nashiri*, No. 14-1203 (D.C. Cir. filed Oct. 14, 2014) (petition for writ of mandamus and prohibition). A writ of mandamus is an *extraordinary* writ issued by an appellate court which compels a judicial body to perform a duty that the law clearly requires. A writ of prohibition, alternately, prevents a judicial body from exercising its power in a manner unauthorized by law. See *supra* note 19.

[87] See *Cobell v Norton*, 334 F.3d 1128, 1137, 1144-45 (D.C. Cir. 2003); Posting of Steve Vladeck, 'Argument Recap: The Critical Difference in How al-Nashiri Loses,' on Lawfare Blog, available at <http://www.lawfareblog.com/2015/02/argument-recap-the-critical-difference-in-how-al-nashiri-loses/>.

[88] See Posting of Steve Vladeck, 'The D.C. Circuit's Mandamus Jurisdiction and the Legitimacy of the Military Commissions', on Lawfare Blog, <http://www.lawfareblog.com/2014/12/the-d-c-circuits-mandamus-jurisdiction-and-the-legitimacy-of-the-military-commissions/>; *al-Nashiri Argument Preview: The CMCR's Appointment Clause Problem*, on Lawfare Blog, <http://www.lawfareblog.com/2015/02/al-nashiri-preview/> (discussing *Cobell v Norton*, 334 F.3d 1128, 1137, 1144-45 (D.C. Cir. 2003) (mandamus may be available in the context of motions to disqualify lower court judges)).

[89] 28 U.S.C. §1651.

[90] Posting of Steve Vladeck, 'The D.C. Circuit's Mandamus Jurisdiction'.

used in section 950g, has been interpreted to not bar military appellate courts from issuing such extraordinary relief prior to a final judgment under Articles 66 and 67 of the UCMJ.[91] Again, a similar interpretation here would be more in accordance with military practice as instructed by *Hamdan v Rumsfeld* and the 2009 MCA. Although the DC Circuit may decide that Al-Nashiri's interests can be protected through a post-conviction appeal, its determination of whether mandamus jurisdiction over government interlocutory appeals of military commission orders is available, akin to the authority of federal appellate courts over lower federal courts, is key to the perception of the fairness of the commission's process. Treating the commissions in the same fashion as subordinate lower federal courts would only contribute to the commission's legitimacy.[92]

Mandamus merits. In his petition seeking mandamus/prohibition, Al-Nashiri makes two claims to justify the issuance of the writ.[93] Of the two, his claim that the method of appointing military appellate judges to the CMCR violates the US Constitution's Appointments Clause is stronger. Al-Nashiri claims that because the judges on the CMCR are principal (as opposed to inferior) officers of the United States for purposes of the US Constitution's Appointments Clause[94] they must be appointed in conformity with that clause—requiring appointment by the President, by and with the advice and consent of the Senate.[95] In his petition, Al-Nashiri contends that the judges on the CMCR are different from the seemingly similar military judges on the military service Courts of Criminal Appeals (CCA), because the CMCR judges have the power to issue final decisions on the part of the Executive Branch. Because of this power Al-Nashiri claims,

[91] Ibid. [92] See Posting of Steve Vladeck, 'The D.C. Circuit's Mandamus Jurisdiction'.

[93] In his first claim, Al-Nashiri makes a convoluted argument concerning the President's constitutional power as Commander-in-Chief (under Art. II of the US Constitution) to reassign the military judges on the CMCR and the effect of this power on the judicial independence and impartiality of these judges. Similar to protections for military judges in the US courts-martial system, the 2009 MCA prohibits reassignment of CMCR judges in order to influence their decisions on the court. Because the Supreme Court has held that these protections adequately protect judicial independence in the courts-martial system Al-Nashiri is unlikely to prevail on this claim to disqualify the military CMCR judges. See Posting of Marty Lederman, 'The merits of the judge-disqualification petition in al-Nashiri', on JustSecurity Blog, <http://justsecurity.org/17411/merits-or-lack-thereof-judge-disqualification-petition-al-nashiri/> (arguing that although Al-Nashiri is probably correct that the judges on the CMCR are principal officers because their decisions are not reviewed by any intermediate executive branch officers, the requirement of the Appointments Clause *has been satisfied*: the two judges *have been* appointed by the President, by and with the advice and consent of the Senate, which is sufficient so long as the duties as CMCR judges are germane to their duties as military officers).

[94] U.S. Const. art. II, sec. 2, cl. 2 ('The President shall…nominate, and by and with the Advice and Consent of the Senate, shall appoint…all other Officers of the United States, whose Appointments are not herein otherwise provided for, and which shall be established by Law: but the Congress may by Law vest the Appointment of such inferior Officers, as they think proper, in the President alone, in the Courts of Law, or in the Heads of Departments').

[95] Posting of Marty Lederman, 'Merits of Judge Disqualification'.

the CMCR judges are 'principal' not 'inferior' officers, and must therefore be separately nominated by the President and confirmed by the Senate. In *Weiss v United States* and *Edmond v United States*,[96] the Supreme Court upheld the assignment of military judges to the military CCAs without a separate appointment because they had already been appointed as military officers in conformity with the Appointments Clause and because assignment to new duties as military judges was 'germane' to their duties as military officers. However, in *Weiss* and *Edmond* the judges on the military CCAs did not issue final decisions on behalf of the Executive Branch because their decisions are reviewed by the Court of Appeals for the Armed Forces (CAAF) whose judges are properly appointed principal officers. Because the CMCR does have the power to issue final decisions for the Executive Branch,[97] which are then directly reviewed by the DC Circuit with no intervening executive appellate court such as CAAF, they are likely to be considered as 'principal' officers requiring a separate appointment. Nevertheless, to merit the extraordinary writ he is seeking, Al-Nashiri would have to show that there are 'no other adequate means' to obtain the relief he seeks, to include through an ultimate post-trial appellate review.[98]

Regardless of how the interlocutory appeal and petition for mandamus/prohibition are resolved, pre-trial hearings in the *Al-Nashiri* military commission were substantially halted by this interlocutory appeal, causing the cancellation of the scheduled September, October, and December 2014 hearings. In the interim only limited hearings addressing the litigation of proposed hearsay admissions, challenges to the processing of summaries of classified information under 2009 MCA procedures, and the evaluation of the sufficiency and multiplicity of the remaining charges against Al-Nashiri have occurred in September and November 2014. After six days of hearings in February/March 2015, the US Government filed a separate interlocutory appeal contesting the military judge's order excluding certain evidence allegedly showing Al-Nashiri's wanton disregard for human life relating to the terrorism charge against him.[99] As a result of this second

[96] 510 U.S. 163 (1994); 520 U.S. 651 (1997).

[97] Compare Posting of Steve Vladeck, 'Argument Preview' (discussing whether military judges as 'inferior' officers can be reassigned to duties as 'principal' officers absent a separate appointment in accordance with the Appointment clause), with Posting of Marty Lederman. ('The Supreme Court has already held, in *Weiss v United States*, that where, as here, the statute in question insulates military judges from the effects of command influence over their decision-making, the Due Process Clause does not require a fixed term of office, let alone lifetime tenure, in order to guarantee sufficient protection of judicial impartiality. Therefore, the fact that the military judges on the CMCR can be reassigned for "military necessity"—something that presumably was true with respect to the military judges in the *Weiss* case, too—raises no serious constitutional problem').

[98] *See In re* Al-Nashiri, 791 F.3d 71 (D.C. Cir. 2015)(concluding that the DC Circuit has mandamus jurisdiction and that Al-Nashiri is not entitled to mandamus relief because his challenges can be considered on direct appeal after trial, but also suggesting that the President and Congress might decide to re-nominate and re-confirm the military judges to be CMCR judges to obviate the issue).

[99] See AE248T, 'Government Certificate of Notice of Appeal,' 27 March 2014; AE 248S, 'Ruling (Corrected Copy), Government Motion to Reconsider AE 248G, ¶5, and Allow the Prove the Accused's 'Wanton Disregard for Human Life' by Introducing Relevant and Probative Evidence Relating to Foreign

interlocutory appeal, the military judge cancelled all scheduled 2015 hearings in the case pending resolution of the interlocutory appeals.[100]

C. Interferences and collateral issues delaying the commissions

Although the legal motions practice at the military commissions is extensive and complex, as would be expected in any new hybrid judicial system, the greatest delays in 2014 arose from the FBI's investigations of the 9/11 defence teams which have resulted in a complete cessation of substantive progress toward trial since February 2014, a delay which is expected to continue for the foreseeable future. Additionally, in December 2014, the Commission's Convening Authority instigated a change to a Department of Defence regulation governing the military commissions at Guantánamo in an ill-advised attempt to speed up the commission process. This change mandated the permanent relocation of officiating military judges to the Guantánamo Naval Base and prohibited their acting in any other military justice matter. The defence in the 9/11, *Al-Nashiri*, and *Al-Hadi* cases challenged this change on the basis that it was an attempt to unlawfully influence and intimidate military commission judges. As a result of consideration of these motions and resulting orders by the military judges, the regulatory change was rescinded on 26 February 2015. Nevertheless, its consequences have become another ongoing source of delay. Additionally, in October 2014, Guantánamo defendants filed motions contesting the use of female guards to escort them to meetings with their attorneys, claiming a burden on their rights of free exercise of their religion as well as interference with their right to assistance of counsel, another issue that took priority over normal Commission business.

CONFLICTS OF INTEREST AND THE RIGHT TO CONFLICT-FREE COUNSEL

In December 2013, the 9/11 case was halted by the prosecution's request for a competency evaluation of Mr bin Al-Shibh. Although Mr Al-Shibh was not cooperative in the competency determination process under Rule for Military Commission (RMC)

Nationals Located On or Around the USS Cole (DDG 67) at the Time of the Attack', 25 March 2015 (order holding the Government to its charging decision, and excluding evidence of the danger to foreign national protected persons on boats in the harbour, and not on the *USS Cole* to show the alleged wanton disregard for human life), both in *Al-Nashiri*.

[100] AE 203N, 'Order Cancel Future Sessions', 16 April 2015 (Order cancelling all scheduled hearings for 2015 until resolution of Government's interlocutory appeals), in *Al Nashiri*.

706,[101] the prosecution was poised to resolve any question of his competence to assist in his defence during pre-trial hearings in April 2014 by presenting evidence to support the presumption of competence established in RMC 909.[102] A complete resolution of this issue, however, was overcome by events as defence counsel for Mr Al-Shibh, joined by counsel for the other four defendants, filed an emergency motion to address newly discovered attempts by the FBI to infiltrate the 9/11 defence teams as part of ongoing FBI investigations, the ultimate purposes of which have not yet been disclosed publicly.[103]

Shortly before the April 2014 hearings, defence counsel became aware of FBI overtures to the Defense Security Officer (DSO) on Mr Al-Shibh's defence team. As part of its investigation the FBI sought to enlist the DSO as a confidential informant and had him sign a non-disclosure agreement prohibiting him from disclosing his relationship with the FBI to anyone. It later became known that the FBI had also approached an investigator on the Al-Shibh team, and, in a separate January 2013 investigation, a linguist on the Mohammad team. Because the FBI's infiltration of the defence teams may have involved the unauthorized disclosure of privileged or confidential defence information, the Chief Prosecutor appointed a Special Review Team (SRT) counsel to act for the United States in the litigation and investigation of this matter, with the regular prosecution team walled off from this issue in order to avoid disqualification if privileged or confidential information was disclosed. At the June 2014 hearing, the SRT counsel asserted that both investigations had been closed, and argued that under existing case law no potential or actual conflict of interest could exist if there were no active investigation. In addition to contesting this legal argument, defence counsel asserted that the investigations involving Mr Al-Shibh's DSO and investigator and Mr Mohammad's linguist affected other defence teams as they shared investigator and linguist assets in their pre-trial investigation and preparation under their joint defense agreement.

On 24 July 2014, seeing no quick resolution of these conflict issues, the military judge ordered both the appointment of independent conflict counsel for Mr Al-Shibh and his severance from the joint 9/11 trial.[104] In doing so, the Commission determined that the issues involved in the conflict-of-interest motions were 'broader than the Special Review Team's assertion that "[b]ecause there is no... investigation there is no possible conflict of interest"'.[105] For the Commission, the nature of this case, a capital criminal trial involving the highest level national security information, differentiated its analysis from the normal criminal trial, where 'the criminal activities of the client and the

[101] R.M.C. 706, U.S. Dep't of Defense, Manual for Military Commissions, Rule for Military Commission 706 (2012) (hereinafter MMC).

[102] R.M.C. 909, MMC, ibid. [103] See, e.g., AE 292 series, in *Khalid Sheik Mohammad, et al.*

[104] See AE 292QQ; AE 312, 'Severance Order', 24 July 2014, in *Khalid Sheik Mohammad, et al.*

[105] See AE 292QQ at p. 22.

attorney are separate acts, and unless the attorney is actually acting in their own best interests at the expense of the client, there is no conflict'.[106] Because defence counsel have 'an independent duty to investigate the circumstances of the crimes alleged, and gather information for use in the case-in-chief and, if necessary, for mitigation',[107] a requirement that involves voluminous classified or potentially classified information, the Commission concluded that the risk of a breach of the security constraints is always present. Here, where the investigation of counsel may involve allegations of such breaches, the interests of the attorney and the client cannot easily be segregated, and the analysis of a potential conflict of interest therefore requires a more cautious evaluation.[108] The Commission also recognized that the nature of the case mandated that the scope of potential conflict-causing investigations be similarly broad, to include administrative or intelligence investigations that could also affect an attorney's personal interests.[109] In its Order, the Commission recognized the fundamental right involved: '[t]he Accused are entitled to the undivided loyalty of their counsel, and by extension, of the paralegals and other members of the Defence Team who fall under the umbrella of privilege, as a critical component of their right to assistance of counsel'.[110]

The Government contested the *sua sponte* severance order,[111] and requested reconsideration of both it and the order providing independent counsel to Mr Al-Shibh, arguing that severance was too severe a remedy for the delays caused by Mr Al-Shibh's various issues. The United States also reiterated its argument that no ongoing investigations supported the claim of a potential conflict of interest. After argument in August 2014, the military judge suspended his severance order,[112] but maintained the requirement that independent counsel be appointed to act on Mr Al-Shibh's behalf to investigate, evaluate, and advise Mr Al-Shibh on any actual or potential conflict of interest. Independent counsel was appointed in early August, and obtained the necessary clearances to meet with Mr Al-Shibh in late October. Both the October and December pre-trial hearings were cancelled to allow the SRT Counsel and the independent conflict counsel for Mr Al-Shibh to work out discovery on the content and focus of the FBI investigations, information necessary for the independent counsel to determine if an actual or potential conflict of interest existed. In the interim there were eight *ex parte* filings made by the SRT Counsel to the Commission, and two *ex parte* orders issued by the military judge.[113]

106 Ibid. at p. 28. 107 Ibid. at p. 27.

108 Ibid. at pp. 27–28. 109 Ibid. at pp. 28–30. 110 Ibid. at pp. 22–23.

111 *Sua sponte* is Latin for 'on his own accord' and refers to an action taken by a judge without a prior motion or request from the parties.

112 Called an 'abatement' in military practice. The order remains valid but its implementation is suspended. An abatement can also apply to a military judge's order to halt proceedings in a case until a condition is met.

113 Defence counsel for all defendants except Mr Al-Hawsawi have opposed the *ex parte* filings on the conflict issue and seek access to the FBI investigations in order to meet their own ethical obligations to withdraw if they determine a non-waiveable conflict exists, or if the conflict may be waived, to provide

As of the February 2015 pre-trial hearings, the independent counsel had been provided access to only one of these *ex parte* filings and none of the classified evidence underlying the FBI investigations. At that hearing the military judge indicated that he did not consider the potential conflict he had identified in his July 2014 order to have been eliminated by the information provided by the SRT counsel.

Because of this, the military judge asked the prosecution if it still opposed severance despite the likely lengthy delay necessary to resolve the conflict issue, an issue that had already delayed progress in the case for ten months.[114] The prosecution continued to oppose severance despite expected delay for the 'foreseeable future'.[115] Complicating the normal conflict resolution method is the fact that the information contained within the FBI investigations is classified,[116] which the Government contends cannot be provided to the defendants. If independent counsel and/or the Commission determines that an actual or potential conflict exists, how a knowing and voluntary waiver of a conflict can be obtained when the facts creating the conflict cannot be shared with the defendant remains an unresolved issue that will likely delay resolution of this conflict issue even further.

The April 2014 discovery of the intrusions by the FBI into the defence teams, whatever their purpose, was only one in a continuing litany of interferences with the defence function alleged by the defence, all of which have the subject of intense litigation at the commissions since 2012. These include: the October 2011 'base-line review' in which Joint Task Force, Guantánamo seized all legal and attorney–client privileged documents from the defendants' cells and subsequently inventoried and translated them; implementation of the Woods orders[117] interfering with privileged meetings and

the necessary facts to their clients to seek a knowing and voluntary waiver of that conflict (in addition to the independent advice they believe must be provided to their clients from independent counsel). Counsel for Mr Al-Hawsawi concluded that any potential conflict of interest did not affect his defense team or Mr Al-Hawsawi.

[114] Mr Al-Hawsawi had moved for severance for the case on the basis that this delay interfered with his right to a speedy trial, and the delay in justice was one of the rationales used by the military judge in his original July 2014 severance order. See AE 299, 'Mr Al-Hawsawi's Motion to Sever', 21 May 2014, in *Khalid Sheik Mohammad, et al.* Hearings in June and August, 2015 were also cancelled.

[115] In response to queries by the military judge, the US Government adamantly opposed the severance of Mr Al-Shibh and accepted that resolution of the conflict issue could take additional months to resolve, and that the delay was satisfactory to the government. See 'Transcript Unofficial/Unauthenticated Transcript of the Khalid Shaikh Mohammed et al (2) Hearing Dated 2/11/2015 from 11:16 AM to 11:46 AM' in *Khalid Sheik Mohammad, et al.*

[116] The SRT has filed numerous classified *ex parte* filings on AE 292. The contents or target of the investigations are either classified and/or protected from public disclosure.

[117] The Woods orders were two written orders issued by the Joint Task Force (JTF) Guantánamo Commander governing attorney visits and legal mail. These orders required that all documents and attorney-client notes brought into or out of attorney-client meetings, as well as all legal and non-legal mail, be reviewed by a 'privilege team' consisting of government personnel, and the contents disclosed to the Commander if a security threat or violation of the rules were discovered. Acceptance of such a

written communications between defence counsel and the defendants from October 2011 until the issuance of a final protective order by the military judge in November 2013; the discovery of microphones disguised as smoke detectors in the attorney–client meeting rooms at Camp Echo; the discovery that an original Classification Authority (OCA), likely the CIA, had been monitoring the ungated microphone feed from the courtroom and had the capability to activate the muting feature on the public audio feed of the courtroom without the military judge's knowledge, with the accompanying concern that because the microphone array in the courtroom was so sensitive it allowed the CIA to monitor attorney–client communications within the courtroom itself; the discovery that the defence computer network was on a common server with that of the prosecution without sufficient safeguards to protect defence information; and continued allegations of seizure of marked attorney-client privileged documents from defendants' cells.[118]

Although litigation of these interferences resulted in no showing of actual intrusions into privileged defence communications by the prosecution, they necessitated both litigation of the issues and the concomitant delay. Many of these fundamental issues are shared in the *Al-Nashiri* case. At the very least these interferences reinforced the defendants' distrust of the military commission process, impeded the development of any relationship of trust between the defendants and their attorneys, and forced defence attorneys to limit their communications with their clients in order to meet their ethical obligations to protect privileged and confidential information.[119] In February 2015, Mr Al-Shibh's surprise in-court identification of a former CIA black site interpreter on his defence team created yet another issue that requires resolution prior to the 9/11 military

requirement would destroy the privilege. The orders also prohibited certain 'information contraband' being shared with the detainees, such as historical perspectives on jihadist activities; discussions the defence contended were necessary for the preparation of the defence.

[118] The following series of motions, and oral argument in the January–February 2013, June 2013 and October 2013 sessions illustrate these alleged interferences. See, e.g., AE013 (protective order for national security information), AE018 (interference with privileged written communications), AE032 (appropriate relief for invasion of attorney-client privileged communications), AE133 (electronic monitoring of attorney-client communications), AE155 (security of defence computer network), AE168 (intrusion into attorney-client communications), in *Khalid Sheik Mohammad, et al.* Similar issues were raised in the *Al-Nashiri* case.

[119] See, e.g., National Association of Criminal Defense Lawyers, Ethics Advisory Committee, *Opinion 12-01*, 'Disclosure of attorney-client privileged communications to third-party (Guantánamo Bay, Cuba)', 19 February 2012; Memorandum of Dep't of Defense, Office of Chief Defense Counsel to Office of Chief Defense Counsel, 'Subject: Professional Responsibility Guidance on the JTF-CDR-GTMO Orders Governing Written Communications Management for Detainees Involved in Military Commissions of 27 December 2011 and Governing Logistics of Defense Counsel Access to Detainees Involved in Military Commissions of 27 December 2011' (directing defence attorneys in Office of Chief Defense Counsel not to submit attorney-client privileged material for review by the JTF privilege team controlled by US Government).

commission being able to resume normal pre-trial hearings.[120] But more significantly, this litany has resulted in increasing perceptions of unfairness, perceptions that linger and irreparably taint the commissions in the eyes of many.

UNLAWFUL INFLUENCE

Action taken by the Convening Authority on 9 December 2014 seeking a change to the Department of Defence regulation governing trial by military commission resulted in motions by the defence in the 9/11, *Al-Nashiri*, and *Al-Hadi* trials[121] alleging an unlawful attempt to influence the commissions' military judges. This initiative was intended to remedy the perceived slow progress and high cost of the commissions,[122] and resulted on 7 January 2015 in a change to the regulation. This change would have required the military judges presiding over Guantánamo military commissions to relocate to Guantánamo for the duration of the trials and would have prohibited them from presiding over any other military justice trials.[123] As a result of defence motions, the military judge in the 9/11 case found that a perception of unlawful influence had been created by the action of the convening authority; and as a result, he ordered the suspension of the case on 25 February 2015, to last until the regulation was rescinded.[124] On 26 February 2015, the regulation was rescinded, resulting in the judge's rescission of the suspension a day later.[125] The military judge in the *Al-Nashiri* case held an evidentiary hearing on the allegation of unlawful influence in February 2015, and as a result disqualified the Convening

[120] See 'Unofficial/Unauthenticated Transcript of the Khalid Shaikh Mohammed, et al. (2), Hearings dated 2/9/2015 from 9:07 AM to 10:57 PM,' at 8248, lines 19–23, in *Khalid Sheik Mohammad, et al.*

[121] See AE343, 'Joint Defense Motion to Dismiss for Unlawful Influence on Trial Judiciary', 30 January 2015, in *Khalid Sheik Mohammad, et al.*; AE332, 'Defense Motion to Dismiss for Unlawful Influence and Denial of Due Process for Failure to Provide an Independent Judiciary', 13 January 2015, in *Al-Nashiri*; AE 032, 'Defense Motion to Dismiss for Unlawful Influence and Denial of Due Process for Failure to Provide an Independent Judiciary', 22 January 2015, in *Al-Hadi*.

[122] The proposal submitted by the Convening Authority to the Deputy Secretary of Defense stated that the commissions had been in session for only 107 hours and forty minutes in FY 2014, costing over $78 million in FY 2014 (not including the military personnel costs for 158 military personnel). Memorandum, 'Assessment of Office of Military Commissions'. *The Guardian* newspaper also reported that Mr Ary described the cost of the lethargic commissions at $7,647 per minute, or $458,823 per hour that the Commission met in 2014. See 'Guantánamo Bay: wheels of justice turn slowly—at $7600 a minute', *The Guardian*, 9 February 2015.

[123] See Change 1 to the Dep't of Defense, Regulation for Trial by Military Commission, (2011) (changing ¶6-2).

[124] AE 343C, 'Ruling Defense Motion to Dismiss For Unlawful Influence on Trial Judiciary', 25 February 2015, in *Khalid Sheik Mohammad, et al.*

[125] AE343D, 'Government Notice of Rescinding of Change 1 of the Regulation for Trial by Military Commission', 27 February 2015; AE343E, 'Order Defense Motion to Dismiss for Unlawful Influence on Trial Judiciary', 27 February 2015, in *Khalid Sheik Mohammad, et al.*

Authority from taking any further action in the case.[126] On 11 March 2015, the defence in the 9/11 case filed a joint motion seeking the disqualification of the Convening Authority from taking any further action in that case based on unlawful influence, in effect seeking the same remedy as that granted by the military judge in the *Al-Nashiri* case.[127] On 18 March, the Convening Authority submitted his voluntary resignation,[128] seemingly resolving the immediate issue.

FEMALE GUARDS

In October 2014 at least two high value detainees, Mr Bin 'Attash (one of the defendants in the 9/11 case) and Mr Al-Hadi filed motions objecting to the use of female guards to perform duties as escorts when moving them from Camp 7, their detention facility, to Camp Echo, where meetings with their attorneys occur.[129] They raised these objections only if the female guards were required to physically touch them because their religious beliefs prohibited their being touched by a female who was not a wife or close relative. The possibility of being touched by unrelated females resulted in the defendants refusing meetings with counsel, which the defence alleged adversely impacted effective attorney–client communication. As a result of this alleged encumbrance, military judges in both cases issued interim orders prohibiting female guards from touching the accused, absent exigent circumstances, when transporting them to legal meetings until the issue could be litigated.[130] The defendants based these claims on the Religious Freedom Restoration Act

[126] 'Unofficial/Unauthenticated Transcript of the Al Nashiri (2) Motions Hearing Dated 3/2/2015 from 10:30 AM to 11:13 AM', in *Al-Nashiri*.

[127] AE343F, 'Joint Defense Motion to Disqualify the Convening Authority Due to Unlawful Influence', 11 March 2015, in *Khalid Sheik Mohammad, et al.*

[128] Posting of Wells Bennett, 'The New (Old) Interim Convening Authority for Military Commissions', on LawfareBlog, <http://www.lawfareblog.com/2015/03/the-new-old-interim-convening-authority-for-military-commissions/>.

[129] See AE 254Y(WBA), 'Emergency Defense Motion to Bar Regulation Substantially Burdening Free Exercise of Religion and Access to Counsel', 20 October 2014, in *Khalid Sheik Mohammad, et al.*; AE021, 'Emergency Defense Motion for Appropriate Relief to Cease Physical Contact with Female Guards', 16 October 2014, in *Al-Hadi*. Mr Al-Hawsawi, Mr Al-Shibh, and Mr Mohammad joined Mr Bin 'Attash's emergency motion. Counsel cannot visit the defendants at Camp 7, and currently no telephonic contact is authorized. See AE254Y (MAH Sup.), AE 254Y (RBS Sup.), and 254Y (KSM Sup.), respectively, in *Khalid Sheik Mohammad, et al.*

[130] See AE 254JJ, 'Interim Order. Emergency Defense Motion to Bar Regulation Substantially Burdening Free Exercise of Religion and Access to Counsel', 7 January 2015, in *Khalid Sheik Mohammad, et al.*; AE021B, 'Interim Order. Emergency Defense Motion for Appropriate Relief to Cease Physical Contact with Female Guards', 7 November 2014, in *Al-Hadi*. The interim orders eliminated the likelihood that the defendants would have to be forcibly extracted from their cells for transport to the commissions proceedings, at least until the issue was fully litigated. Female military guards at Guantánamo thereafter filed an equal opportunity complaint against the military judges alleging gender discrimination. See Rosenberg, C., 'Female Guards File Discrimination Complaints Against Guantánamo Judges', *Miami Herald*, 27 January 2015.

(RFRA),[131] various amendments to the US Constitution,[132] and finally as a violation of Common Article 3 of the Geneva Conventions' prohibition on outrages to personal dignity under customary international law.[133] After extensive hearings, the military judge in *Al-Hadi*, rejected his RFRA claim, relying on case law from the DC Circuit holding that the statute does not apply extra-territorially, and that the term 'persons' in the Act did not include detainees at Guantánamo. As a result the Judge did not apply strict scrutiny to evaluate the policy of using female guards to escort the defendants, but instead analysed the claim under *Turner v Safley*, under which restrictions on an inmate's constitutional rights are valid if they are reasonably related to a legitimate penological interest.[134] The Commission found the policy to be rationally related to the legitimate government interests of running a well-functioning detention facility and eliminating gender discrimination in the military.[135] Significant to the analysis, however, was testimony substantiating the difficulty of filling the units that deploy to Guantánamo to execute the detention mission with soldiers that have Top Secret/SCI clearances, a requirement that appears to rest on the high level security classification of the defendants' treatment by the CIA before their transfer to Guantánamo, and because of assertions by the United States that it can classify the defendants' memories and life experiences of such treatment. The issue is still outstanding in the 9/11 case, although the prosecution has moved for reconsideration of the interim order in that case.[136]

D. New charges

Although the military commissions accomplished little in 2014, new charges were brought against both Ahmed Al-Darbi[137] and Abd Al-Hadi al-Iraqi.[138] Mr Al-Darbi agreed to, and did plead guilty to charges involving the attack on the *M/V Limburg*,

[131] 42 U.S.C. §2000bb *et seq.*

[132] To include the protection of religious exercise under the First Amendment and against cruel and unusual punishment under the Eighth Amendment. U.S. Const. amend. I & VIII.

[133] AE 245Y.

[134] AE021DD, 'Ruling. Emergency Defense Motion for Appropriate Relief to Cease Physical Contact with Female Guards', 24 February 2015 (citing *Turner v Safley*, 482 U.S. 78 (1987)), in *Al-Hadi*. Strict scrutiny, in contrast, would have required a compelling government interest and that the policy was the least intrusive means to accomplish the compelling government interest.

[135] Ibid. at 14.

[136] AE254LLL, 'Government Motion to Reconsider AE 254JJ Interim Order Enjoining Female Guards From Physical Contact While Participating in Movements to and from Attorney-Client Meetings and Commission Hearings and Notice of Subsequent Persuasive Authority', 2 March 2015, in *Khalid Sheik Mohammad, et al.*

[137] 'Referred Charges', 5 February 2014, in *Al-Darbi*.

[138] See 'Referred Charges', 2 June 2014, in *Al-Hadi*.

and as part of his pre-trial agreement with the US Government agreed to provide assistance in the case against Mr Al-Nashiri. The case against Mr Al-Hadi includes some charges alleging inchoate conspiracy that post-date the enactment of the 2006 Military Commissions Act. His trial will thus present the domestic law issues not resolved in *Al-Bahlul v United*, discussed earlier. Thus, the US constitutional law question of what, if any, limits apply to Congress's power to prospectively proscribe conduct and subject it to trial by military commission will be squarely presented. This domestic law question is apart from the legitimacy, or lack thereof, under international law of trying inchoate conspiracy as a war crime. Nevertheless, if a court determines that Congress's power in this area is limited by the international law of war, by virtue of its interpretation of the Define and Punish Clause or by other limitations in Article III or the criminal process protections of the Fifth and Sixth Amendments, international law may indeed be relevant to a determination of this domestic law issue.[139]

E. **Torture Report**

Although the release of the US Senate Select Committee on Intelligence (SSCI) *Study on the Central Intelligence Agency's Detention and Interrogation Program* ('the *Torture Report*') was approved by the SSCI in December 2012, it took another two years to have its Executive Summary, including its unredacted findings and conclusions, declassified and released to the public. The redacted portions of the Executive Summary, the full 6,700-page report, as well as the over 6 million official government documents reviewed by the SSCI task force remain classified, although efforts are ongoing to review the appropriateness of their classification as well. The 9 December 2014 release of this report has already increased the transparency of the military commissions by allowing defence attorneys for the first time to raise allegations of torture experienced by their clients in open commission sessions and public forums.[140] This transparency is limited, however, by the fact that the declassified information from the SSCI Executive Summary is what

[139] On 12 June, 2015, the remand panel in *Al-Bahlul* did decide that Art. III of the US Constitution prohibits the Guantánamo military commissions from trying 'domestic' criminal offenses, as 'war crimes' and subjecting them to trial by military commission. See *Al Balhul*, xxx F.3d xx (2015), 2015 WL 3687457. On 27 July 2015, the United States filed a petition for rehearing *en banc* contesting that ruling; a petition that was opposed by Al-Bahlul on 13 August 2015.

[140] Press Release of Mr Walter Ruiz ('The Senate report released on Tuesday is the sanitized tip of a 6000 page iceberg revealing acts of unspeakable horror, depravity, dishonesty, and an overall shocking breach of our core values and beliefs'), 10 December 2014; Press Conference (Defense), 15 February 2015 at Guantánamo Bay; Statement of Walter Ruiz, Counsel for Mr Al-Hawsawi, before the Inter-American Commission on Human Rights, 16 March 2015.

one defence attorney calls 'only the tip of the iceberg' of the full details concerning the defendants' treatment by the US Government.[141]

Defence counsel have complained that classification of the details of the defendants' treatment by the CIA after capture has impeded both the investigation of their cases and advocacy for their clients. Prior to the declassification of the SSCI Torture Report Executive Summary, counsel were precluded from discussing the CIA's Rendition, Detention, and Interrogation (RDI) programme in open sessions of court because all aspects of this programme were classified at the Top Secret/Sensitive Compartmented Information (TS/SCI) level. Their ability to discuss or use classified information in their pre-trial investigations was also significantly affected by the laws governing national security information and by the protective order entered by the military commissions to protect such information in each case.[142] Complicating this situation, the Government has also claimed that the defendants' memories and experiences of their torture are classified, and as such could not be disclosed, either by defence attorneys or the defendants themselves.[143] Finally, the protective orders issued in the 9/11, *Al-Nashiri*, and *Al-Hadi* cases required heightened handling procedures and additional restrictions on disclosure for any classified information concerning the CIA's RDI programme involving commission defendants, to include information received from the defendants themselves.[144]

Immediately following the 9 December 2014 release of the SSCI Executive Summary, the military commission judge in the 9/11 case ordered the US Government to examine the protective order and to propose changes based on the newly declassified

[141] Statement of Walter Ruiz, Counsel for Mr Al-Hawsawi, before the Inter-American Commission on Human Rights, 16 March 2015.

[142] If requested by the prosecution the entry of a protective order to protect national security information is mandated by the 2009 MCA. See Section 949p(3), 2009 MCA. See also AE 200II 'Order, To Defense Motion to Dismiss Because Amended Protective Order #1 Violates the Convention Against Torture', 16 December 2013 ('The provisions of the protective order do not prevent attorney-client communication nor or the ability of the defense to conduct their mitigations investigations, although 'the manner in which questions are asked and information is sought must be adjusted to account prevent (*sic*) the inadvertent disclosure of classified information'), in *Khalid Sheik Mohammad, et al.* Additionally, US Government policy prohibits the disclosure of classified information by individuals holding a security clearance even if the information has been leaked and is otherwise available publicly; as a result counsel may only publicly discuss information which has been officially declassified.

[143] See 'Unofficial/Unauthenticated Transcript of the KSM *et al.* (2). Motions Hearing, dated 23 October 2013, from 10:51 a.m. to 12:23 p.m.', at 6670–1, *Khalid Sheik Mohammad, et al.*

[144] As an illustrative example of these restrictions, see, e.g., para. 2g of the protective order which specifically included the following in the definition of classified information: information surrounding the capture of the defendants; the foreign countries in which the defendants were held from their capture until their transfer to Guantánamo in 2006; information on the persons involved in the capture, transfer, detention, or interrogation of the defendants; the enhanced interrogation techniques applied to the defendants, to include the duration, frequency, sequencing, and limitations of these techniques; and descriptions of the conditions of confinement from capture to transfer to Guantánamo. These categories originally specifically included the observations and experiences of the defendants. See AE 013AA, 'Amended Protective

information.[145] On 30 January 2015, the CIA provided additional classification guidance concerning the former RDI programme and information released in the SSCI Torture Report to the Commission Chief Prosecutor.[146] As a result, in early February 2015 the prosecution moved to amend the protective orders in the three ongoing military commission cases by requesting removal of the restrictions concerning the enhanced interrogation techniques used on the defendants and their conditions of confinement from capture to their transfer to Guantánamo in September 2006.[147] On 20 February 2015, this motion was granted in the *Al-Nashiri* case, and in the *Al-Hadi* case on 11 March 2015, and finally in the 9/11 case on 6 July 2015.[148]

Order #1 To Protect Against Disclosure of National Security Information', 9 February 2013, at ¶ 7, 4; AE 013DDD, 'Second Amended Protective Order', (same restrictions), 17 December 2013, in *Khalid Sheik Mohammad, et al.*

[145] See AE 013RRR, 'Government Motion to Amend AE 013DDD Second Amended Protective Order #1 to Protect Against Disclosure of National Security Information', 30 January 2015, at 5-6, in *Khalid Sheik Mohammad, et al.*

[146] In the US Government's motion is the following unclassified representation summarizing the changes to the classified CIA's classification guidance, stating that the following information is no longer classified:

- The fact that the former RDI Program was a covert action program authorized by the President. The fact that the former RDI Program was authorized by the 17 September 2001 Memorandum of Notification (MON);
- General allegations of torture by HVDs unless such allegations reveal the identities (e.g., the names, physical descriptions, or other identifying information) of CIA personnel or contractors; the locations of detention sites (including the name of any country in which the detention site was allegedly located); or any foreign intelligence service involvement in the HVD's capture, rendition, detention, or interrogation;
- The names and descriptions of the thirteen Enhanced Interrogation Techniques (EITs) that were approved for use, and the specified parameters within which the EITs could be applied;
- EITs as applied to the 119 individuals mentioned in Appendix 2 of the SSCI Executive Summary acknowledged to have been in CIA custody;
- Information regarding the conditions of confinement as applied to the 119 individuals mentioned in Appendix 2 of the SSCI Executive Summary acknowledged to have been in CIA custody;
- Information regarding the treatment of the 119 individuals mentioned in Appendix 2 of the SSCI Executive Summary acknowledged to have been in CIA custody, including the application of standard interrogation techniques;
- Information regarding the conditions of confinement or treatment during transfer ('rendition') of the 119 individuals mentioned in Appendix 2 of the SSCI Executive Summary acknowledged to have been in CIA custody.

Ibid. at 5–6.

[147] See, e.g., AE013RRR. As a result the Government moved to remove the corresponding restrictions in the applicable protective orders.

[148] AE013S, 'Second Amended Protective Order #1', 20 February 2015, in *Al-Nashiri*; AE013K, 'Third Amended Protective Order 1-To Protect Against Disclosure of National Security Information', 11 March 2015, in *Al-Hadi*. The delay in ruling on the motion in the 9/11 case was, in all likelihood, due to the requirement of resolving related defence motions, while balancing the requirement to resolve the conflict-of-interest issue prior to the commission proceeding to other business.

These proposed amendments bring the protective orders into alignment with the SSCI Executive Summary's declassification of RDI information for two categories: the conditions of the defendants' confinement and the interrogation techniques applied to the defendants. Although the modification of the protective order and what is known of the new CIA classification guidance[149] indicate that significant information concerning the CIA's RDI programme and its approved Enhanced Interrogation Techniques is no longer considered classified, information outside that contained in the declassified SSCI Executive Summary must now be evaluated against the classification guidance and be formally declassified by the Original Classification Authority (OCA). The protective order and the classification of information about the former RDI programme remain separate, albeit linked, processes. The intent of the Government appears to be to remove impediments to both defence counsels' and defendants' ability to publicly discuss their allegations concerning the defendants' torture and conditions of confinement and enhance the transparency and fairness of the trial process.

Despite this intent, some ambiguities exist between the CIA's new classification guidance and the provisions of the proposed protective order. First, the CIA classification guidance indicates that two of the categories—'the names and descriptions of the thirteen Enhanced Interrogation Techniques (EITs) that were approved for use, and the specified parameters within which the EITs could be applied' and 'EITs as applied to the 119 individuals mentioned in Appendix 2 of the SSCI Executive Summary acknowledged to have been in CIA custody'—are no longer classified. A strict reading of these categories, however, leaves open the question of whether other torture or cruel, inhuman, or degrading treatment (CIDT) alleged to have been applied to the defendants (i.e., not falling within the thirteen approved EITs or included in the SSCI Executive Summary) remain classified. The fact that techniques falling outside the thirteen EITs are detailed in the SSCI Torture Report support the inference that other 'non-approved' techniques may have been used. Additional ambiguities also exist as to the ability of the defence attorneys to refer to specific information that falls within the remaining provisions of the protective order but which were declassified and included within the SSCI Executive Summary, such as the pseudonyms used by the SSCI to describe the locations of the black sites, and the information about capture and foreign partners identified in the declassified SSCI Executive Summary.[150] Similar ambiguities exist as to the treatment of the defendants' memories and experiences of their torture.

[149] The CIA Classification guidance is classified, although the government's motion includes an unclassified summary. See AE 013RRR, at 4–5.

[150] AE013SSS, 'Mr al Baluchi's Response to Government Motion to Amend AE013DDD Second Amended Protective Order #1 to Protect Against Disclosure of National Security Information', 23 February 2015, in *Khalid Sheik Mohammad, et al.*

The declassification of the SSCI Executive Summary and the new CIA classification guidance would seem to permit the defendants and their attorneys to discuss this information publicly and provide it to appropriate international or national bodies, such as the March 2015 presentation to the Inter-American Commission on Human Rights. Nevertheless information on the capture/persons/places involved in the RDI programme,[151] would, according to the previously articulated US position, continue to be classified and subject to the protective order and existing legal protections for national security information, even if derived from the memories of the defendants.[152]

Even given these current ambiguities, the declassification and disclosure of the information on the former RDI programme in the SSCI Executive Summary is a significant step forward for the transparency and fairness of the commissions. Although neither the CIA's new classification guidance nor the proposed changes to the protective orders ensures future declassification of the information contained within the still classified full SSCI Torture Report and its millions of underlying documents, or information on other torture/CIDT not strictly included within the thirteen approved EITs listed in the CIA's classification guidance, existing procedures in the military commissions provide a mechanism to resolve any ambiguities in current guidance. Defence counsel may confidentially submit information to their Defence Security Officers and obtain a classification determination from an Original Classification Authority (OCA). This procedure should allow the defence to clarify information that falls within the ambiguous areas discussed above without forfeiting any privilege.

Nevertheless, the release of the SSCI Executive Report, and the declassification of significant categories of information in the former RDI programme, have begun to make commission practice more open, and is a significant step forward in increasing the transparency of the Guantánamo military commissions. These changes have enabled defence counsel to publicly present details of their clients' torture for the first time, both within the commissions and in other forums.[153] Declassification of the entire SSCI Report and its

[151] The CIA has not declassified information detailing the capture of the defendants and the identities of CIA personnel or contractors, or foreign involvement in their capture, transfer, detention, rendition, or interrogation (capture/persons/places caveat). See note 142 and 144.

[152] The US Government's position is that it can classify the thoughts and memories of the defendants of their torture experiences because they constitute sensitive intelligence methods and sources. See Transcript of 23 October 2013. The release and declassification of the RDI information in the SSCI Executive Summary and the resulting new CIA classification guidance would logically also apply to the memories of the defendants, potentially resulting in a widening of their ability to communicate complaints of their torture.

[153] See Press Release of Mr Walter Ruiz ('The Senate report released on Tuesday is the sanitized tip of a 6000 page iceberg revealing acts of unspeakable horror, depravity, dishonesty, and an overall shocking breach of our core values and beliefs'), 10 December 2014, available at <https://www.documentcloud.org/documents/1380449-hawsawi-defense-lawyer-news-release-dec-10-2014.html>; Press Conference (Defense), Feb. 15, 2015 at Guantánamo Bay; Statements of Walter Ruiz, Counsel for Mr Al-Hawsawi, and James Connell III, Counsel for Mr Al-Baluchi, before the Inter-American Commission on Human Rights, Mar. 16, 2015.

underlying documentation is also being evaluated, both as a part of the discovery process and more generally.[154] Should full declassification of all the torture and CIDT experienced by the defendants occur, practice before the Guantánamo military commissions will be made infinitely less complicated and more transparent, as well as making the required investigation by defence counsel into their case less fraught with the peril of inadvertently violating security restrictions.[155]

Concluding remarks

The law of war has always evolved in response to new and emerging challenges in warfare. This inherent pragmatism is certainly central to the US decision to characterize its conflict with Al Qaeda as an armed conflict. While this interpretation of the law remains controversial, it is an established fact for US purposes, and provides the legal foundation for a range of responsive measures, including the use of military commissions. Accordingly, use of military tribunals to try these unlawful alien enemy belligerents, whatever their imperfections, may be the first step in the development of international law to apply the laws and customs of war to transnational organized armed terrorist groups. Holding members of these groups accountable for war time atrocities while 'affording [them] all the judicial guarantees which are recognized as indispensable by civilized peoples'[156] is the challenge that the Guantánamo military commissions were created to meet. Although the initial decision to use military commissions was made by the President, subjecting members of Al Qaeda and associated groups to punishment for conduct that violates the law and customs of war was the aim of the US Congress when it implemented, and improved, the Guantánamo military commissions in the 2006 and

[154] *Chief Prosecutor Mark Martins Remarks at Guantánamo Bay 13 December 2014* (referring to February 2014 CIA ongoing efforts to declassify certain information relating to the former RDI program in support of current military commission proceedings, and stating that 'Tuesday's declassification increases the likelihood that more of these processes will be open to the public and assures the accused will be able to see and consult with defense counsel about certain information not previously available to them.'); Rosenberg, C., 'Prosecutor "Torture Report" should make 9/11 trial more transparent', *Miami Herald*, 14 December 2014.

[155] Additionally, the ability to accomplish the detention mission at Guantánamo may be made less difficult by reducing the requirement for high level clearances for guards who interact with the defendants.

[156] Common Art. 3, Geneva Conventions. Geneva Convention for the Amelioration of the Condition of the Wounded and Sick in Armed Forces in the Field, 12 August 1949, T.I.A.S. 3362, Art. 3; Geneva Convention for the Amelioration of the Condition of Wounded, Sick, and Shipwrecked Members at Sea, 12 August 1949, T.I.A.S. 3363, Art. 3; Geneva Convention Relative to the Treatment of Prisoners of War, 12 August 1949, T.I.A.S. 3364, Art. 3; Geneva Convention Relative to the Treatment of Civilian Persons in Time of War, 12 August 1949, T.I.A.S. 3365, Art. 3; *Hamdan v Rumsfeld*, 558 US at 630.

2009 MCAs.[157] Judicial scrutiny, through the appellate process, however remains the key means to align this congressional goal with the international and domestic law underlying the Guantánamo military commissions.

Unfortunately, judicial decisions pronounced in 2014 failed to advance the law in any meaningful way, and in some ways actually exacerbated legal uncertainty related to these tribunals. Relying on the plain error doctrine, the *Al-Bahlul* decision not only cast doubt on the clear holding enunciated in *Hamdan II* at the end of 2012 that Article 21 of the UCMJ referenced the 'international law of war', but also failed to provide any definitive guidance for Congress or the Commissions going forward. The continued reliance by the US Government on its novel (and in my opinion and that of many others, specious) 'US common law of war' theory to expand the permissible jurisdiction of law of war military commissions has undermined their domestic and international legitimacy, created significant US constitutional separation of powers issues, and supplied precedent for other nations to similarly expand the jurisdiction of their military commissions based on idiosyncratic national histories. This claim to a US law of war 'contradicts the essential nature of the law of war, which has always been understood to be a subset of public international law',[158] a fact recognized by most military professionals and the Supreme Court in *Quirin* and *Yamashita*. Law in general, and international humanitarian and human rights law in particular, have developed substantially in the 150 years since the American Civil War. The modern law of war was in its infancy during the Civil War, with modern war crimes jurisprudence developing only since the Second World War.[159] By undermining the clear holding of *Hamdan II*, the *en banc Al-Bahlul* court muddied the waters on the scope of permissible military commission jurisdiction and further diminished the perceived legitimacy of the Guantánamo military commissions. The interlocutory appeal in *Al-Nashiri* has also delayed progress in that case, as the CMCR and the DC Circuit decide key procedural issues affecting the commissions, issues decided long ago in both federal and courts-martial practice.

The two main military commission cases, the *United States v. Khalid Sheik Mohammad, et. al.*, and *United States v. Al-Nashiri*, remained stagnant in 2014 as the commissions were required to litigate significant legal issues caused by continued interferences by outside entities. These interferences by US Government entities, separate from and uncontrolled by the commission prosecutor, have adversely affected the relationship between the defendants and their defence counsel, a relationship necessary to the provision of a fair trial under both international and US law. Clearly, the US Government has the right, and the duty, to investigate alleged violations of the laws protecting classified defence information. Nevertheless, appropriately tailoring such investigations to be

[157] See, e.g., §948b(f), 2006 MCA.
[158] Glazier, D., 'The Misuse of History', at p. 3.
[159] Glazier, D., 'The Misuse of History', at p. 3.

sensitive to their effects on the attorney-client relationship will protect national security, while ensuring orderly proceedings in the commissions and protection of the core relationship between defence counsel and the defendants. If the United States is going to use military commissions to prosecute war crimes committed by members of transnational organized armed terrorist groups such as Al Qaeda, its commitment to providing a fair trial, one that affords all the judicial guarantees which are recognized as indispensable by civilized peoples mandated by both international law and the US Congress, must take priority over continued intelligence operations against the defendants. If the US practice of using military commissions to prosecute members of belligerent terrorist groups such as Al Qaeda for their violations of the laws and customs of war is to shape the development of international law, as did US practice in the military tribunals following the Second World War, the United States must protect the attorney–client relationship upon which a fair trial depends.

The lack of a national commitment to this end can be seen by the creation of significant collateral issues that have delayed the prosecution of the military commission trials, delaying justice for the victims and families of the terrorist attacks of 9/11 and the *USS Cole* bombing. The FBI investigations and intrusions into the 9/11 defence teams alone have resulted in a delay of over sixteen months, with no resolution in sight. New collateral issues involving the use of female guards and the serious allegation of unlawful influence on the part of the Convening Authority consumed military commission resources at the end of 2014, with their resolution extending into 2015. Resolution of motions pending since arraignment in 2012 and 2013, as well as critical motions to compel discovery so essential to the ultimate preparation for trial on the merits have been pushed back by these exigent issues. Clearly, once these issues arise, they must be fully litigated to ensure that defendants before military commissions receive a fair trial. But the record to date raises a legitimate question of whether more credible and cautious management of inter-agency relationships might avert the generation of these issues in the first instance.

The stagnation caused by interferences and collateral issues was offset only by the referral of two new military commission cases (against Al-Darbi and Al-Hadi), and by the long-awaited release of the SSCI Torture Report. If the declassification of the specifics of the post-capture treatment of the Guantánamo military commission defendants continues, it can only contribute to the transparency of the process, and may ultimately reduce many of the collateral issues and interferences that have derailed the trials to date. The decision by the US to torture and maltreat the defendants made their subsequent prosecution infinitely more difficult regardless of what forum was chosen to try them. Military commissions, federal courts, or courts-martial, all viable choices, would have to deal with the complications caused by the torture of the current defendants. The Commissions, at least, are fully litigating every viable issue as they endeavour to ensure a fair trial to the defendants. Nevertheless, in 2014, rather than the rapid progress toward trial anticipated for the Guantánamo military commissions, at the end of the year the Commissions were further away from their goal of a trial on the merits than when the year began.

None of this, however, should cloud the broader question of accountability. Perhaps trial by military commission was controversial at inception; perhaps the government is trapped within its own self-inflicted morass; perhaps these tribunals will begin to gain momentum and move towards just outcomes; or perhaps they will be abandoned in favour of Article III trials. These are all important questions related to legitimacy, efficiency, and the evolution of the laws and customs of war. But ultimately, the individuals responsible for these alleged wartime atrocities and acts of terror must be held to account for their conduct.

14 Tackling impunity for sexual violence

Alice Priddy[1]

Introduction

Despite international attention to sexual violence in armed conflict being at an all-time high, sexual violence continues to be a prominent and persistent feature of all of today's armed conflicts. Deeply entrenched discrimination, combined with a lack of security, effective law enforcement, and political will has allowed often systematic and large scale sexual violence during armed conflict to perpetuate.

Sexual violence is a weapon, 'as deadly as any bullet and as destructive as any gun',[2] and it can be a highly effective: it devastates and terrorizes the victim, witnesses, and their community. In today's conflicts sexual violence is used to advance military objectives, to terrorize and gain control over the victim and their communities, to illicit information, to ensure compliance, to punish, and to assert control over territory and/or resources. Sexual violence in armed conflict also includes acts that are conducted within a family or community where perpetrators take advantage of the lack of security and breakdown of the rule of law.

Rape, forced prostitution, sexual slavery, forced impregnation, forced marriage, genital mutilation, and deliberate infection with HIV/AIDS and other sexually transmitted infections are just some of the forms of sexual violence occurring in today's armed conflicts.[3] It is a common misconception to think of sexual violence as not purely a sexual act. It is in fact an act of aggression and one that is not always committed for sexual gratification, for example electrocution of male genitalia as an interrogation technique.

[1] Alice Priddy is a researcher at the Geneva Academy of International Humanitarian Law and Human Rights.

[2] Foreword by the United Nations (UN) Special Representative of the Secretary-General on Sexual Violence in Conflict, in Team on Experts, Rule of Law/Sexual Violence in Conflict, *Annual Report 2012*, 10 April 2013.

[3] See the UN Special Representative of the Secretary-General on Sexual Violence in Conflict latest report for a full overview of type of sexual violence being committed in today's armed conflict. 'Conflict-related sexual violence, report of the Secretary-General', UN Doc. No. S/2015/203, 23 March 2015.

Force is also not a necessary component, for example there have been repeated reports of humanitarian workers offering aid in exchange for a sexual act.[4] Aside from the immediate pain, terror, and trauma, victims often face long-term physical health problems, psychological trauma, and social isolation. Victims may be left with life threatening or life changing debilitating physical injuries, and females face the added risk of unwanted pregnancy.[5] More often than not in the conflict setting survivors will not have access to treatment for the injuries that they have sustained.

Sexual violence is not limited to any type of conflict or geographical region or cultural context, nor its victims, its perpetrators, or its setting. Victims include fighters, civilians, detainees, displaced persons, and refugees. Those who are internally displaced, refugees, children, detainees, those belonging to a specific ethnic group, female heads of household, and those with disabilities are particularly vulnerable. Perpetrators include all sections of society: members of armed forces, armed non-State actors, police, civilians, peace keepers, and humanitarian personnel. Sexual violence occurs at check points, on the street, in places of detention, in homes, and in places of refuge.

Although we know tens, if not hundreds, of thousands of people are affected by conflict-related sexual violence every year, due to under-reporting exact numbers are not known. Under-reporting continues for a multitude of reasons including insecurity, social stigma, cultural taboos, fear of reprisals, fear of cultural practices (such as so-called 'honour killing') or traditional justice arrangements (such as forcing the survivor to marry the perpetrator), fear of criminal prosecution, geographical barriers, economic and geographical obstacles, apathy, insufficient or adequate domestic criminal law, corruption, and ineffective or unwilling police services. The context of the sexual violence must also be remembered. In an armed conflict the immediate concerns of the survivor or witness, are likely to be: Where is my missing partner or child? Where am I going to live now my home has been destroyed? How am I going to secure food and water for myself and family? Reporting sexual violence is likely to be at the bottom of a list of immediate priorities. Unless there is social support in place to address the immediate needs of the survivor, or witness, they are unlikely to make a formal complaint or testify in a criminal process.

Whilst the vast majority of survivors and their communities remain traumatized, marginalized, and without redress, perpetrators continue to enjoy almost guaranteed impunity. At least 50,000 women were raped during the three-year Bosnia war, yet there have been fewer than forty prosecutions at the international and national courts combined.[6]

[4] Office of the UN High Commissioner for Refugees (UNHCR) and Save the Children, 'Sexual violence and exploitation: the experience of refugee children in Guinea, Liberia, and Sierra Leone', February 2002.

[5] Sadler, A. G. et al., 2000, 'Health-Related Consequences of Physical and Sexual Violence: Women in the Military', *Obstetrics and Gynaecology*, vol. 96, no. 3, pp. 473–80.

[6] Wallström, M., 2012, 'Introduction: Making the Link Between Transitional Justice and Conflict-Related Sexual Violence', Wm. & Mary J. Women and Law, vol. 19, no. 1, p. 4.

At least 250,000 women were raped during the genocidal campaign in Rwanda yet the International Criminal Tribunal for Rwanda has prosecuted less than a dozen people for these crimes.[7] In Columbia, where sexual violence is a persistent and widespread feature of the ongoing armed conflict, the impunity rate runs at 98%.[8] The high level of impunity will come as no surprise to readers who are aware of the pitiful statistics on rape prosecutions in national courts. Within Europe, for example, only 6% of rape cases brought to court lead to a successful prosecution.[9] However, in the conflict setting the continued culture of impunity aggravates ethnic, sectarian, or other divisions within the community and undermines peace-building efforts thereby preventing long-term peace and reconciliation. It also sends the message that sexual violence is somehow socially acceptable thereby perpetuating a culture of tolerance. Considering which, it is unsurprising that in the aftermath of many conflicts levels of sexual violence have risen.[10]

We know sexual violence continues to be perpetrated on a large scale in today's armed conflicts, we also know the devastating consequences of this for the survivor, their community, and for long-term peace and security. We have the legal framework and there seems to be a political will to address the issue in some States at a national level,[11] as well as at the international level, so why does implementation of law and policy remain an elusive goal and impunity remain the norm? And are there other options for securing prosecutions? This chapter will firstly outline the sex and gender aspects of sexual violence, as well as the international legal framework prohibiting sexual violence before turning to these questions and looking at possible alternative criminal justice mechanisms that might be worth consideration.

A. **Sex, gender, and sexual violence**

The prevailing inequality between women and men in nearly all societies, whereby women are viewed and treated as subordinate and inferior to men results in women in all contexts being the target for sexual violence. However, during periods of insecurity

[7] 'Rwanda's Women Make Strides towards Equality 20 Years after the Genocide', *The Guardian*, 7 April 2014.

[8] Global Justice Centre Blog, 'Ending Impunity for Widespread and Systematic Use of Sexual Violence in Columbia's Ongoing Armed Conflict', 9 December 2013.

[9] Madeleine Rees, speaking at the Chathem House event 'Sexual Violence in armed conflict—what use is the law?' 23 January 2015. A video of Madeleine Rees's presentation can be found at <http://www.chathamhouse.org/event/sexual-violence-conflict-what-use-law>.

[10] Cohen, D. K. and Nordas, R., 2014, 'Sexual Violence in Armed Conflict: Introducing the SVAC Dataset, 1989–2009', *Journal of Peace Research*, vol. 51, 418, at p. 425.

[11] The Democratic Republic of Congo, for example, has taken unprecedented (though long overdue) steps to prosecute the perpetrators of sexual violence during conflict and pay reparations to survivors.

the plight of women is exacerbated, since '[c]onflict creates a free-fire zone, a sort of "free-for-all" in which pre-existing ideas about women as inferior, and other discriminatory and misogynist ideas, may be given free expression by frequently all-male groups of solders and other combatants'.[12]

Women and girls are often perceived as merely an extension of the opposition's male fighters, a vessel for procreation (including as a form of ethnic cleansing), an object for fighters' pleasure, a 'warriors reward', or a commodity. The thousands of Yazidi girls and women who have been abducted by IS in the past six months and used as sex slaves, sold, or given away as 'prizes' or 'gifts' to the 'best' IS fighters and supporters provides repulsive evidence of this.[13] Women are particularly vulnerable when they do not have the capacity to flee the conflict due to lack of economic means, being encumbered by cultural or religious constraints that limit their ability to move freely without the presence or even permission of a male, pregnancy, or being responsible for the care of children and elderly relatives. Women that do manage to flee the immediate violence all too often find themselves still vulnerable to sexual violence during flight and once displaced. Survival sex, where desperate individuals and families agree to 'marriages', often of young girls, in exchange for food, shelter, or 'protection' is a common occurrence in many refugee and displacement camps.[14]

For a woman or girl who has been raped the ability to freely access medical services, including emergency contraception and termination is vital. Yet in States where conflict-related sexual violence is most prevalent women and girls are still being denied access to safe and legal termination services. The risks associated with pregnancy are real for all women: maternal mortality is so grave a problem that everyday 800 women die as a result of complications in pregnancy and childbirth.[15] The risks will be even greater in States where health care services are not available and for young girls whose underdeveloped bodies struggle to cope with pregnancy—aside from the internal injuries sustained during rape.[16] I would argue that any policy that denies access to emergency contraception

'Conflict-related sexual violence, report of the Secretary-General', UN Doc. No. S/2015/203, 23 March 2015, §§23–26.

[12] Bennounce, K., 2006, 'Do We Need New International Law to Protect Women in Armed Conflict?', *Case Western Reserve Journal of International Law*, vol. 38, p. 370.

[13] Amnesty International, *Escape from Hell: Torture and Sexual Slavery in Islamic State Captivity in Iraq*, November 2014; Report of the Office of the United Nations High Commissioner for Human Rights on the human rights situation in Iraq in the light of abuses committed by the so-called Islamic State in Iraq and the Levant and associated groups*, UN Doc. No. A/HRC/28/18, 13 March 2015, §§35–43.

[14] Save the Children, 2013, *Unspoken Crimes against Children: Sexual Violence in Conflict*, Save the Children, London, March 2013, p. 11; UNHCR, 2011, 'Action against Sexual and Gender-Based Violence: An Updated Strategy', Geneva, June 2011.

[15] World Health Organization, 2013, *Global Health Observatory: Maternal Mortality*.

[16] In peacetime, girls aged fifteen and under are five times more likely to die during pregnancy and childbirth compared to those aged over twenty; this risk will be even higher during periods of insecurity. Save the Children, 2013, *Unspeakable Crimes against Children: Sexual Violence in Conflict, Save the Children*, London, March 2013, p. 16.

and termination services, thereby failing to take into account the often inevitable consequences of the rape of females, is prohibited under international law as equates to both discrimination on the grounds of gender,[17] and amounts to cruel, inhuman, or degrading treatment where this forces a female to either undergo a dangerous illegal termination or carry an unwanted pregnancy.[18] As asserted by Louise Doswald-Beck, women raped in armed conflict are also entitled to treatment under international humanitarian law as 'wounded and sick'[19] and '[e]xclusion of one medical service, abortion, from the comprehensive medical services provided to the "wounded and sick" in armed conflict, where such service is needed by only one gender, is not only a violation of their [females] right to medical care, but also a violation of the prohibition on "adverse distinction" found in common Article 3, the Additional Protocols to the Geneva Conventions, and customary international law'.[20]

The gender stereotypes and discrimination that gives rise to female directed sexual violence also leads to acts of sexual violence being committed against men and boys. Male victims of sexual violence often report feeling that their masculine identity has been destroyed and that they have somehow been 'feminized' by the attack; a statement that illustrates the prevailing noting of women being of lesser status in some societies.[21] Sexual violence is an act of dominance and power over the victim; therefore when perpetrated against males in societies where masculinity is closely associated with dominance, strength, and power, the victim is disempowered and demoralized, particularly

[17] 1966 International Covenant on Civil and Political Rights (ICCPR), Art. 26; 1966 International Covenant on Economic, Social and Cultural Rights, Art. 2(2); 1950 European Convention on Human Rights (ECHR), Art. 14; 1969 American Convention on Human Rights (ACHR), Art. 1; 1981 African Charter on Human and Peoples' Rights (ACHPR), Art. 2; 2004 Arab Charter on Human Rights (ArCHR), Art. 3; 1979 Convention on the Elimination of All Forms of Discrimination against Women (CEDAW).

[18] 1984 Convention against Torture and Other Cruel Inhuman or Degrading Treatment or Punishment (CAT); ICCPR, Art. 7; ACHR, Art. 5; the 1985 Inter-American Convention to Prevent and Punish Torture and Inhuman or Degrading Treatment; ECHR, Art. 3; ACHPR, Art. 5; Common Art. 3 to the four Geneva Conventions. The prohibition on torture is also a norm of *jus cogens*.

[19] Under IHL, the basic requirement to give the necessary medical care to the wounded and sick reflects customary law. The International Committee of the Red Cross (ICRC) Customary IHL Study, Rule 10, confirms that, in both international and non-international armed conflicts: '[T]he wounded, sick and shipwrecked must receive, to the fullest extent practicable and with the least possible delay, the medical care and attention required by their condition. No distinction may be made among them founded on any grounds other than medical ones'. As Louise Doswald-Beck asserts, '[t]here can be no doubt that persons who are raped fall into the category of "wounded and sick", due to severe mental, and often physical, trauma suffered'. L. Doswald-Beck's open letter to President Obama, 10 April 2013, on file with the author.

[20] L. Doswald-Beck's open letter to President Obama, 10 April 2013, on file with the author. For further discussion on this point see Bellal, A., 2015 (forthcoming), 'Who is Wounded and Sick?'. In *Commentary to the Geneva Conventions*, edited by Clapham, A. and Gaeta, P., Oxford University Press.

[21] Sivakumaran, S., 2007, 'Sexual Violence Against Men in Armed Conflict', *European Journal of International Law*, vol. 18, pp. 253–76.

when the violence is perpetrated in public.[22] Conversely, the perpetrator may be seen as more masculine through their dominance of the victim.[23]

Sexual violence against men and boys is still a taboo subject and is rarely reported and significantly under researched.[24] Men and boys are particularly unlikely to report being a victim of sexual violence. Inability or unwillingness to report the violence might be for a multitude of reasons including; shame, fear of social stigma, fear of criminal prosecution under-anti sodomy laws,[25] discriminatory and inadequate domestic law,[26] lack of or inaccessible services (the majority of which are only tailored to the needs of women and girls), and lack of access to justice. Fear of being labelled weak, a homosexual, or even a paedophile (where the victim was forced to perform a sexual act on a child) also has a silencing effect. This fear will be particularly acute in homophobic societies.[27] Furthermore, research indicates that males struggle to come to terms with being a 'victim' as they feel it is incompatible with being a 'man', either in terms of the attack itself (as a man should be able to protect himself) or in the aftermath (a man should be able to cope 'like a man').[28]

A vicious cycle exists where males are unwilling or unable to report the violence that they have suffered, resulting in a lack of data and therefore ignorance of the scale and characteristics of the violence persists, resulting in resources not being allocated to prevention and services for survivors, meaning males have nowhere to report the abuse they have suffered and seek rehabilitation. Impunity continues to prevail and no action is taken to address the root causes of the violence or the discriminatory norms that silence survivors.

Discriminatory and incorrect understandings about gender norms in situations of armed conflict, where men are seen as naturally aggressive, dominant, sexual

[22] Oosterhoff, P. et al., 2004, 'Sexual Torture of Men in Croatia and Other Conflict Situations: An Open Secret', *Reproductive Health Matters*, pp 71, 74–5.

[23] Lewis, D., 2009, 'Unrecognized Victims: Sexual Violence Against Men in Conflict Setting under International Law', *Wisconsin International Law Journal*, vol. 27, no. 1, pp. 1–49.

[24] My chapter in last year's *War Report* was dedicated to this subject; Priddy, A., 2014, 'Sexual Violence against Men and Boys in Armed Conflict'. In *The War Report Armed Conflict in 2013*, edited by Casey-Maslen, S., Oxford: Oxford University Press. See also Sivakumaran, S., 2007, 'Sexual Violence Against Men in Armed Conflict', *European Journal of International Law*, vol. 18, pp. 253–76.

[25] The Ugandan Penal Code, for example, criminalizes sodomy and places the burden on the prosecution to prove the victim did not consent, thereby creating string disincentives for male victims to report the crime. Ugandan Penal Code Act of 1950 (Ch. 120) (as amended) s. 145: 'Unnatural offences'.

[26] The Ugandan Penal Code, for example, defines rape as 'the unlawful carnal knowledge of a women or a girl' thereby excluding male victims. Ugandan Penal Code, of 1950 (Ch.120) (as amended) s. 123: 'Offences Against Morality'.

[27] Sivakumaran, S., 2005, 'Male/Male Rape and the "Taint" of Homosexuality', *Human Rights Quarterly*, vol. 27, pp. 1274–1306.

[28] Sivakumaran, S., 2007, 'Sexual Violence Against Men in Armed Conflict', *European Journal of International Law*, vol. 18, pp. 253–76.

demanding, and invulnerable and women as passive, weak, subordinate, and victims has led to the widely held view that men are always the perpetrators of sexual violence and never the victims.[29] This over-simplistic and incorrect gender analysis disempowers women, reinforces chauvinistic stereotypes, and fails to recognize female fighters as well as male victims of sexual violence during conflict.[30] This can be seen at the international law and policy level where the prevailing approach is to focus on females as victims of sexual violence thereby ignoring the plight of male victims and the differing roles females play in armed conflict, including as fighters.[31] Until these gender stereotypes are challenged from the societal to the international level we have no hope of preventing and tackling sexual violence or providing adequate services for survivors.

B. Sexual violence under international law

All forms of sexual violence in armed conflict are prohibited through a strong and complementary legal framework made up of international humanitarian law, international human rights law, and international criminal law.

Turning first to international humanitarian law (IHL), IHL has long prohibited sexual violence during armed conflict, albeit implicitly and conservatively.[32] Of the four Geneva Conventions of 1949, only Geneva Convention IV expressly refers to sexual violence. This reference only concerns women and is framed in archaic and discriminatory language feeding the stereotype of women as weaker than their male counterparts.

[29] Special Representative of the Secretary-General on Sexual Violence in Conflicts, *Report of the Workshop on Sexual Violence against Men and Boys in Conflict Situations*, New York, 2 December 2013

[30] Stemple, L., 2009, 'Male Rape and Human Rights', *Hastings Law Journal*, vol. 60, pp. 605–647, at p. 612.

[31] A recent study of the language used by the Independent Commission of Inquiry for Syria and the UN Human Rights Council in their reports found that women are nearly exclusively referred to as powerless victims of sexual violence. Conversely, men have multiple and important identities ascribed to them, variously mentioned as; civilians (as if women are not civilians), combatants, medical personnel, or journalists. This language feeds gender stereotypes and acts as a disincentive to ensure that women are involved in peace processes in roles that go beyond being 'victims'. As Madeline Reese points out [i]f women are seen as powerless agents then their participation in peace processes is not going to be viewed as necessary or valuable'. Women's International League for Peace and Freedom and the Graduate Institute of International and Development Studies, 'A gendered analysis: examining how women and gender in the Syrian conflict are addressed by the UN Human Rights Council', December 2014.

[32] The 1863 Lieber Code prohibited, and made punishable by death 'all wanton violence committed against persons in the invaded country… [including] all rape… of such inhabitants'. 1863 Lieber Code, General Orders No. 100, 24 April 1863, Art. 44. The code also provided that 'unarmed citizens were to be spared in person, property and honor' and that 'persons of inhabitants, especially those of women; and the sacredness of domestic relations' require protection. 1863 Lieber Code, General Orders No. 100, 24 April 1863, Arts 22 and 37.

Article 27 states: 'Women shall be especially protected against any attack on their honour, in particular against rape, enforced prostitution, or any form of indecent assault', thereby placing such violence in a protection framework rather than expressly prohibiting this conduct. Furthermore, the violence is identified as attacks on women's 'honour' rather than as violent crimes.

Despite male directed sexual violence not being expressly mentioned in any of the four Geneva Conventions, males are implicitly protected from sexual violence under Common Article 3, which prohibits 'at any time and in any place whatsoever... outrages upon personal dignity, in particular humiliating and degrading treatment'.

The 1977 Additional Protocol I (AP I), which governs IAC, abandons the language of honour but still treats women as persons in need of 'special respect' and protection. AP I only envisages female victims, and makes no express reference to males. Article 27 of 1977 Additional Protocol I states: '[w]omen shall be the object of special respect and shall be protected in particular against rape, forced prostitution and any other form of indecent assault.' Although Article 27 does not apply to men, Article 75 lists fundamental guarantees that must be enjoyed 'without any adverse distinction' based upon, inter alia, 'sex', including the prohibition of outrages upon personal dignity, in particular humiliating and degrading treatment, enforced prostitution and any form of indecent assault', under which sexual violence clearly falls.

The 1977 Additional Protocol II, which governs non-international armed conflicts (NIAC), takes a gender-neutral approach. Article 4(2) contains fundamental guarantees that prohibit 'violence to the life, health and physical or mental well-being of persons... [;] cruel treatment such as torture, mutilation': and 'outrages upon personal, in particular humiliating and degrading treatment, enforced prostitution and any form of indecent assault'.[33] All of which clearly encompass sexual violence.

Sexual violence in armed conflict is also prohibited under customary international law in both IAC and NIAC, as reflected in Rule 93 of the International Committee of the Red Cross (ICRC) 2005 study.[34] The prohibition codified in Rule 93 is gender-neutral, applying equally to male-directed sexual violence as it does to female-directed sexual violence.

Controversially, sexual violence is not explicitly included as a grave breach in the 1949 Geneva Conventions or the 1977 Additional Protocols. Instead, sexual violence falls under the umbrella of wilfully causing great suffering or serious bodily injury to body or health.[35] Spurred by the atrocities that occurred during the conflict in Bosnia and Herzegovina and pressure from human rights activists, the ICRC issued an *Aide-Mémoire*

[33] 1977 Additional Protocol II, Art. 4(2) (a) and (e).

[34] Henckaerts, J. and Doswald-Beck, L., 2005, *ICRC Customary International Humanitarian Law, Volume I: Rules*, Cambridge University Press, p. 323.

[35] 1949 Geneva Convention IV, Arts 146 and 147.

to clarify that the grave breach regime 'obviously not only covers rape, but also any other attack on women's dignity'.[36] Furthermore, in the explanation on Rule 156 of the ICRC study, on the definition of war crimes, the ICRC reiterated that although rape was not 'explicitly listed as a grave breach... [it] would be considered a grave breach on the basis that it amounts to a inhumane treatment or wilfully causing great suffering or serious injury to body or health'.[37]

It is important to ascertain whether or not an offence is recognized as a grave breach since States are obligated to exercise universal jurisdiction over such breaches.[38] Under the principle of universal jurisdiction, any State can investigate and prosecute any individual in respect of international crimes committed abroad, regardless of the nationality of the perpetrator or victim and even if the accused is not present in the State seeking to prosecute.[39] Universal jurisdiction is based on the principle that certain crimes are so heinous that every State should have the possibility and responsibility to hold account perpetrators. Unfortunately as the grave breaches regime only applies to IACs not NIACs the regime offers little help for survivors of sexual violence in today's armed conflicts which are nearly exclusively NIACs.[40] That said there is nothing to stop States that are serious about tackling impunity for sexual violence in armed conflict from extending their understanding of the grave breaches regime to apply to NIACs.

Turning to international human rights law (IHRL), sexual violence is prohibited under IHRL primarily through the prohibition of torture and other forms of cruel, inhuman, or degrading treatment or punishment, as well as the prohibition of slavery. The prohibitions of torture and slavery have been enshrined as absolute and non-derogable and are accepted to be norms of *jus cogens* status meaning that the prohibitions apply at all times,[41] including in armed conflict. Thus any form of sexual violence committed during armed conflict that constitutes torture or slavery would be a violation of IHRL. Many acts of sexual violence that are being carried out in today's armed conflicts, such as

[36] ICRC, Update on *Aide-Mèmoire* of 3 December 1992; Meron, T., 1993, 'Rape as a Crime under International Law', *American Journal of International Law*, vol. 87, p. 427.

[37] The ICRC Customary IHL Study, Rule 156 Definition of War Crime, *(ix) Committing sexual violence, in particular rape, sexual slavery, enforced prostitution and enforced pregnancy.*

[38] 1949 Geneva Convention I, Art. 49; 1949 Geneva Convention II, Art. 50; 1949 Geneva Convention III, Art. 129; 1949 Geneva Convention IV, Art. 146.

[39] Unless the legal system of the state seeking to prosecute permits trials in absentia, national law may require the presence of the accused within its territory to initiate proceedings.

[40] Although some diverging views on this do exist: see Separate Opinion on George Abi-Saab on ICTY, *Prosecutor v Tadić*, Decision on Jurisdiction (Appeals Chamber) (Vase No. IT-94-1), 15 July 1999.

[41] On the status of torture as jus cogens see IACtHR, *Caesar v Trinidad and Tobago*, Judgment, 2005, §70; Rodley, N., 2006, 'The Prohibition on Torture: Absolute Means Absolute', *Denver Journal of International Law and Policy*, vol. 34, p. 145; de Wet, E., 2004, 'The Prohibition of Torture as an International Norm of Jus Cogens and its Implications for National and Customary Law'; *European Journal of International Law*, vol. 15, no. 1, p. 97.

electrocution of genitalia and rape have been repeatedly affirmed to constitute torture,[42] and sexual slavery and forced marriage would undoubtedly constitute slavery.[43]

Although it is clear that sexual violence is prohibited under IHRL further questions arise regarding States' obligations under these prohibitions and when a State can be held accountable for such acts. On the question of what obligations these prohibitions entail, States are bound by the usual positive and negative obligations that exist under IHRL. States are clearly obligated *not* to participate in acts of slavery, torture or cruel, inhuman, or degrading treatment (negative obligations), but they also have a positive obligation to protect those within their jurisdiction from such acts, including by criminalizing these acts in national legislation and enforcing that legislation.[44] States also have a positive obligation to promptly and effectively investigate allegations of torture, or of cruel, inhuman, or degrading treatment promptly and effectively.[45] Importantly, in the context of conflict-related sexual violence, the Human Rights Committee has concluded that the duty to investigate extends to acts of a prior regime. This means that not

[42] See, among others, Committee against Torture, General Comment No. 2, UN doc. CAT/C/GC/2, 24 January 2008 §§12 and 18; ECtHR, *Aydin v Turkey*, Judgment, 25 September 1997, §86; IACtHR, *Miguel Castro-Castro Prison v Peru*, Judgment, 25 November 2006 Furthermore the Committee against Torture has found that female genital mutilation and sex trafficking constitute acts of torture or ill-treatment. Committee against Torture, General Comment No. 2, 24 January 2008, §18.

[43] Adapted from the 1929 Slavery Convention, today slavery can be understood to mean 'the status or condition of a person over whom any or all of the powers attaching to the right of ownership are exercised, including sexual access through rape and other forms of sexual violence'. Special Rapporteur on the situation of systematic rape, sexual slavery, and slavery-like practices during wartime, Final Report', UN doc. E/cn.4/sub.2/1998/13, 1998 §27. Implicit within this definition is the limitation on the ability of the victim to exercise autonomy and freedom of movement. The ability of the victim to extract her or himself from the condition of slavery should not be interpreted as nullifying a claim of slavery, rather: '[I]n all cases, a subjective, gender-conscious analysis must also be applied in interpreting an enslaved person's reasonable fear of harm or perception of coercion. This is particularly true when the victim is in a combat zone during armed conflict, whether internal or international in character, and has been identified as a member of the opposing group or faction'. Special Rapporteur on the situation of systematic rape, sexual slavery, and slavery-like practices during wartime, Final Report', UN doc. E/cn.4/sub.2/1998/13, 1998 §29.

[44] CAT, Art. 1 (applies only to acts of torture); ICCPR, Art. 2(2); ECtHR, *M. C. v Bulgaria*, Judgment, 3 December 2003, §151. IACtHR, *Velasuez-Rodriguez v Honduras*, Judgment, 29 July 1982, §172. Although CAT recognizes torture and other cruel, inhuman or degrading treatment only when committed at the instigation, or with the consent or acquiescence of, a public official, the Committee against Torture has affirmed that where state authorities 'know or have reasonable ground to believe that acts of torture or ill-treatment are being committed by non-state officials or private actors and they fail to exercise due diligence to prevent, investigate, prosecute or punish such non-State officials or private actors... the State bears responsibility... under the Convention'. General Comment No. 2. §18.

[45] CAT, Art. 2; Human Rights Committee, General Comment No. 20 §14. See, amongst others: ECtHR *Ribitsch v Austria*, Judgment, 4 December 1995, §§108-11; ECtHR, *M. C. v Bulgaria*, Judgment, 3 December 2003, §153; IACtHR, *Vargas Areco v Paraguay*, Judgment, 26 September 2006, §53; ECtHR, *Colibaba v Moldavia*, Judgment, 23 October 2007, §53; Committee against Torture, *Blanco Abad v Spain*, Views, 14 May 1998, §8.2; Committee against Torture, *Ristoc v Yugoslavia*, Views, 11 May 2001, §9.5; Human Rights Committee, *Rodridguez v Uruguay*, Views, 19 July 1994; ECtHR, *Asseno v and others v Bulgaria*, Judgment, 28 October 1998.

only do the governments of a State in which sexual violence is being perpetrated today have a duty to investigate but so do future governments.[46] Furthermore, States are obligated to ensure redress, including compensation, to survivors of slavery, torture, or cruel, inhuman, or degrading treatment.[47]

Finally, under international criminal law (ICL), rape, sexual slavery, enforced prostitution, forced pregnancy, enforced sterilization, 'or any other form of sexual violence of comparable gravity' are all included in the 1998 Rome Statue of the International Criminal Court (ICC Statute) as crimes against humanity as well as war crimes.[48] The contextual elements will determine whether the offence is a crime against humanity or a war crime. To constitute a crime against humanity the acts must be 'committed as part of a widespread or systematic attack directed against a civilian population' with the perpetrator's knowledge that the conduct was part of such an attack.[49] To constitute a war crime, the offence must have taken place in the context of, and be associated with, either an IAC or an armed conflict 'not of an international character' with the perpetrator's awareness of the 'factual circumstances that established the existence of an armed conflict'.[50]

As well as crimes within their own right, rape and other forms of sexual violence can constitute genocide when committed with intent to destroy in whole or in part a national, ethical, racial, or religious group.[51] Sexual violence as a tool for genocide may be perpetrated through preventing births of a particular group by rape (where a woman is deliberately impregnated by a man of another group, with the intent to have her give birth to a child who will consequently not belong to its mother's group),[52] forced

[46] Human Rights Committee, General Comment No. 20, §5; *Rodriguez v Uruay*, Views, 11 May 2001, §12.4.

[47] CAT, Art. 14; Committee against Torture, General Comment No 3 (2012); Committee against Torture, *Agiza v Sweden*, Views, 20 May 2005, §13.6; ICCPRA, Art. 2(3); ECtHR, *Assanidez v Georgia*, Judgment, 8 April 2008, §198; ACHR, Art. 3(1).

[48] ICC Statute, Art. 7(1)(g) (crimes against humanity); Art. 8(2)(b)(xxii) (war crimes in an IAC); Art. 8(2)(e)(vi) (war crimes in a NIAC). To bring a case to the ICC the accused must be a national of a state that has ratified the ICC Statute, or the crime must have occurred in a State that has accepted the court's jurisdiction or in a specific situation that has been referred to the ICC Prosecutor by the UN Security Council. Furthermore national courts must be unwilling or unable to prosecute and the crime must be of 'sufficient gravity'. Rome Statute, Art. 17(1)(a)–(d).

[49] Elements of Crimes, common elements in sub-paras. 3 and 4, to Art. 7(1)(g): rape; sexual slavery; enforced prostitution; enforced sterilization; and sexual violence: and sub-paras. 2 and 3 to Art. 7(1)(g), forced pregnancy.

[50] Elements of Crimes, common elements in sub-paras. 3 and 4, to Art. 8(2)(b)(xxii): rape, sexual slavery, enforced prostitution, forced pregnancy, enforced sterilization, and sexual violence (for IACs); and common elements in sub-paras. 3 and 4 to Art. 8(2)(e)(vi): sexual slavery, enforced prostitution, forced pregnancy, enforced sterilization, and sexual violence (for NIACs).

[51] 1948 Convention on the Prevention and Punishment of the Crime of Genocide; ICTR, *Prosecutor v Akayesu*, Judgment (Trial Chamber) (Case No. 96-4-T), 2 September 1998, §597; ICTR, *Prosecutor v Musema*, Judgment (Trial Chamber) (Case No. ICTR-96-13-A), 27 January 2000.

[52] ICTR, *Prosecutor v Akayesu*, Judgment (Trial Chamber), 2 September 1998, §507.

sterilization, sexual mutilation, or separation of the sexes.[53] Furthermore sexual violence has been prosecuted as an act of terrorism by both the ICTY and the Special Court for Sierra Leone (SCSL).[54] In considering the widespread and systematic use of sexual violence by the Revolutionary United Front during the conflict in Sierra Leone the SCSL found that 'the nature and manner in which the female population was a target of sexual violence portrays a calculated and concerted pattern on the part of the perpetrators to use sexual violence as a weapon of terror'.[55] The SCSL determined that the acts of sexual violence 'were not intended merely for personal satisfaction or a means of sexual gratification for the fighter' rather 'these acts were committed with the specific intent of spreading terror among the civilian population as a whole, in order to break the will of the population and ensure their submission to the AFRC/RUF control'.[56] It concluded that 'rape, sexual slavery, "forced marriages" and outrages on personal dignity, when committed against a civilian population with the specific intent to terrorise, amount to an act of terror'.[57]

Before we look at each of the specific offences of sexual violence it is important to note that under ICL, not only can identified soldiers be prosecuted for their crimes but also their commanders, under the ICL doctrine of command responsibility.[58] At its essence command responsibility imposes criminal responsibility on a commander for their 'failure to act when under a duty to do so'.[59] Thus, a commander will be criminally responsible 'if he or she knows or has reasons to know that his or her subordinates are about to commit or have committed crimes, unless the superior prevents the subordinates' crimes or punishes the perpetrators after the crimes are committed'.[60] Therefore, it is not necessary that commanders order or encourage crimes; if they have reason to know that soldiers under their command are about to commit, or have committed, an act of sexual violence and turn a blind eye they can be prosecuted for the offence.[61]

[53] Genocide Convention, Art. II(d); *Prosecutor v Akayesu*, Judgment (Trial Chamber), 2 September 1998, §508.

[54] The constitutive elements of the offence of terrorism are: (1) acts or threats of violence; (2) the accused made the civilian population or individual civilians not taking part in hostilities the object of those threats of acts of violence; (3) the acts or threats of violence were carried out with the specific intent of spreading terror among the civilian population. *Sesay, Kallon and Gbao* (Judgment) SCSL-04-15-T, 2 March 2009, §113.

[55] *Sesay, Kallon and Gbao* (Judgment) SCSL-04-15-T, 2 March 2009, §1347.

[56] Ibid., §1348.

[57] Ibid., §1348

[58] The doctrine of command responsibility is contained in, among others, Arts. 86 and 87 of 1977 Additional Protocol I; Art. 7(3) Statute of the ICTY; Art. 6(3) Statute of the Special Court for Sierra Leone; and Art. 28 of the ICC Statute.

[59] Judge Bakone Justice Moloto, 2009, 'Command Responsibility In International Criminal Tribunals', *Berkeley Journal of International Law Publicist*, vol. 3, p. 12.

[60] Ibid., p. 13.

[61] Indeed the perpetrator need not even be identified, it is sufficient that the perpetrators are identified as belonging to a unit or group controlled by the superior. *Prosecutor v Blaskic*, Judgment (Appeals Chamber) (Case No. IT-95-14-A), 29 July 2004, §217.

RAPE

A clear definition of rape did not exist in international law until 1998 when the International Criminal Tribunal for Rwanda (ICTR) defined rape as 'a physical invasion of a sexual nature, committed under circumstances which are coercive'.[62] Building upon this definition, and the jurisprudence of the other ad hoc tribunals,[63] rape is defined in the ICC Elements of Crimes as having two components. First, the perpetrator must have 'invaded the body of a person resulting in penetration however slight, of any part of the body of the victim or of the perpetrator with a sexual organ, or the anal or genital opening of the victim with any object or any part of the body'. A footnote to this element makes clear that such 'invasion' is to be regarded as gender-neutral, thereby incorporating both female and male victims. Second, the invasion must have been 'committed by force, or by threat of force or coercion, such as that caused by fear of violence, duress, detention, psychological oppression or abuse of power, against such a person on another person, or by taking advantage of a coercive environment, or the invasion was committed against a person incapable of giving genuine consent'. A footnote to this element states: 'it is understood that a person may be incapable of giving genuine consent if affected by natural, induced or age-related incapacity'.[64]

The ICTY came to consider whether consent could ever be given in coercive circumstances in the *Kunarac* case. The case concerned women and girls who were held in de facto military headquarters, detention centres, and apartments maintained as soldiers' residences where they were considered the legitimate sexual prey of their captors and were repeatedly raped, often by several men and on a daily basis. Those who sought aid or resisted 'were treated to an extra level of brutality'. The Appeals Chamber of the ICTY held that 'such detentions amount to circumstances that were so coercive as to negate *any* possibility of consent'.[65] Today it can be said that under ICL the use of force, threat of force, or coercion defeat the possibility of 'genuine consent' such that any person who engages in prohibited sexual violence in these circumstances is committing an act of rape, or another form of sexual violence.[66] Whether or not the victim of the violence put

[62] ICTR, *Prosecutor v Akayesu*, Judgment (Trial Chamber) (Case No. 96-4-T), 2 September 1998, §597.

[63] Shortly after *Akayesu* the ICTY defined rape as: 'the sexual penetration, however slight: of the vagina or anus of the victim by the penis of the perpetrator or any other object used by the perpetrator; or of the mouth of the victim by the penis of the perpetrator; by coercion or force or threat of force against a victim or third person'. *Prosecutor v Furundžija*, Judgment (Trial Chamber) (Case No. IT-95-17/1), 10 December 1998,§185.

[64] Elements 1 and 2 of the Elements of Crimes relating to Art. 7(1)(g); Art. 8(2)(b)(xxii); and Art. 8(2)(e)(vi). For discussion of sexual autonomy and the concept of consent, see, e.g., Amnesty International, *Rape and Sexual Violence: Human Rights Law and Standards in the International Criminal Court*, AI Index: IOR 53/001/2011, Amnesty International, London, March 2011, p. 13.

[65] ICTY, *Prosecutor v Kunarac, Kovać and Vuković*, Judgment (Appeals Chamber) (Case No. IT-96-23), 12 June 2002, §§131–2.

[66] Use or threat of force has been held to be 'clear evidence of non-consent': *Prosecutor v Kunarac, Kovać and Vuković*, Judgment (Appeals Chamber), 12 June 2002, §99.

up a fight or resisted is irrelevant.[67] Coercive circumstances would include, for example, a soldier entering a home at night with arms.[68]

It is accepted under ICL that rape can constitute torture given that severe pain or suffering, an element of the definition of torture,[69] can 'be said to be established once rape has been proved, since the act of rape necessarily implies such pain or suffering'.[70] Furthermore, unlike under the 1984 CAT ICL does not require the perpetrator of an act of torture to be a public official or a person acting with the acquiescence of a public official.[71]

SEXUAL SLAVERY AND ENFORCED PROSTITUTION

Sexual slavery is defined under the ICC Elements of Crimes to exist where the 'perpetrator exercised any or all of the powers attaching to the right of ownership over one or more person, such as by purchasing, selling, lending or bartering such a person or persons, or imposing on them a similar deprivation of liberty' and causing that person 'to engage in one or more acts of a sexual nature'.[72]

The ICC Elements of Crimes define enforced prostitution to be where the 'perpetrator caused one or more persons to engage in one or more acts of a sexual nature by force, or by threat of force or coercion, such as that caused by fear of violence, duress, detention, psychological oppression or abuse of power, against such person or persons or another person, or by taking advantage of a coercive environment or such person's or persons' incapacity to give genuine consent' and the perpetrator or another person obtained or expected to obtain pecuniary or other advantage in exchange for or in connection with the acts of a sexual nature.[73] It is the latter requirement that distinguishes the crime of enforced prostitution from that of slavery.

[67] *Prosecutor v Kunarac, Kovać and Vuković*, Judgment (Appeals Chamber), 12 June 2002, §128. Rule 70 of the ICC Rules of Procedure and Evidence provides that '[c]onsent cannot be inferred by reason of the silence of, or lack of resistance by, a victim to the alleged sexual violence'.

[68] See comments of the Pre-Trial Chamber of the ICC in *Decision on the Confirmation of charges, Situation in the Central African Republic in the case of Jean-Pierre Bemba Gombo, Decision Pursuant to Article 61(7)(a)and (b) of the Rome Statute on the Charges of the Prosecutor Against Jean-Pierre Bemba Gombo*, 15 June 2009, Case ICC-01/-5-01/08, §172.

[69] The ICC Statute defines torture as the 'intentional infliction of severe pain or suffering, whether physical or mental': Art. 7(2)(e).

[70] *Prosecutor v Kunarac, Kovać and Vuković*, Judgment (Appeals Chamber), 12 June 2002, §151.

[71] *Prosecutor v Kvocka and ors*, Judgment (Appeals Chamber) (Case No. IT-98-30/1-A), 28 February 2005, §284.

[72] Art. 7(1)(g); Art. 8 (2)(b)(xxii); and Art 8(2)(e)(vi). For further reading on the ICC's approach to sexual slavery see, e.g., Oosterveld, V., 2004, 'Sexual Slavery and the International Criminal Court: Advancing International Law', *Michigan Journal of International Law*, vol. 25, p. 607.

[73] Art. 7(1)(g); Art. 8(2)(b)(xxii); and Art. 8(2)(e)(vi).

In practice, the distinction between enforced prostitution and sexual slavery is blurred. Indeed, a number of survivors as well as commentators advocate that enforced prostitution is better characterized as sexual slavery and should be prosecuted as such.[74] This is the position of the former Special Rapporteur on the issue of systematic rape, sexual slavery, and slavery-like practices in armed conflict, Gay McDougall, who argues that in armed conflict 'most factual scenarios that could be described as forced prostitution would also amount to sexual slavery and could more appropriately and more easily be characterized and prosecuted as slavery'.[75] Survivors have expressed concern 'that the term "forced prostitution" obscures the terrible gravity of the crime, suggests a level of voluntarism, and stigmatizes its victims as immoral or "used goods"'.[76] However, by retaining enforced prostitution within the ICC Statute, sexual violence that does not meet the conditions required to meet the definition of sexual slavery will still fall within the jurisdiction of the ICC, thereby providing a further avenue for prosecution.

FORCED MARRIAGE

Forced marriage has been confirmed to be a crime against humanity by the SCSL.[77] The Appeals Chamber held that a separate crime of forced marriage existed in the context of Sierra Leone because a unique element was found in the 'bush marriages' that occurred in the region. The Court held that forced marriage involved a perpetrator compelling a person by force or threat of force, through words, or conduct of the perpetrator, or anyone associated with him, into a forced conjugal association. It concluded that this results in great suffering or serious physical or mental injury on the part of the victim.[78] The Court noted that the crime of forced marriage was not exclusively, or predominantly, sexual, and as such was

[74] Forced prostitution and forced servitude constitute a violation of the *jus cogens* norm prohibiting enslavement or slavery.

[75] 'Final report on systematic rape, sexual slavery and slavery-like practices during armed conflict: Gay J. McDougall, Special Rapporteur', UN doc. E/CN/.4/Sub.2/1998/13, 22 June 1998, §33.

[76] Argibay, C. M., 2003, 'Sexual Slavery and The Comfort Women of World War II', *Berkeley Journal of International Law*, vol. 21, no. 375, p. 12.

[77] Special Court for Sierra Leone (SCSL) *Prosecutor v Alex Tamba Brima*, Judgment (Appeals Chamber) (SCSL-2004-16-A), 22 February 2008. The ICTY had previously been referred to forced marriage as a possible form of sexual violence; see *Prosecutor v Kvočka and ors*, Judgment (Trial Chamber) (Case No. IT-98-30/1), 2 November 2001, §180. For discussion of this case and the crime of forced marriage in general see Jain, N., 2008, 'Forced Marriage as a Crime Against Humanity: Problems of Definition and Prosecution' *Journal of International Criminal Justice*, vol. 6, pp. 1013–32; Park, A. S. J. and Frulli, M., 'Advancing International Criminal Law: the Special Court for Sierra Leone Recognizes Forced Marriage as a "New" Crime Against Humanity', *Journal of International Criminal Justice*, vol. 6, pp. 1033–42. Note also that forced marriage is prohibited under international human rights law (IHRL); see Art. 23(3), ICCPR; and Art. 16, CEDAW.

[78] *Prosecutor v Alex Tamba Brima*, Judgment (Appeals Chamber), 22 February 2008, §183.

not fully encompassed by the crime of sexual slavery. The women who testified in the case described the marriages as having encompassed a series of abuses, including abduction, forced labour, deprivations of liberty, corporal punishment, assaults, and sexual violence. The Court concluded that forced marriage might also include one or more international crimes such as enslavement, imprisonment, rape, sexual slavery, or abduction.

Forced pregnancy

Forced pregnancy consists of two elements: forced impregnation and forced denial of access to a termination.[79] The ICC definition is, however, limited to circumstances where there is 'intent of affecting the ethnic composition of any population'.[80] This is the only crime against humanity that requires an additional element of intent. Religious objections are obviously the motivation for including this further element of intent. Indeed, the provision includes the rider that the definition 'shall not in any way be interpreted as affecting national laws regarding pregnancy'.[81] As Chinkin posits, forced pregnancy 'constitutes a very particular denial of a woman's autonomy and bodily integrity by forcing her to bear a child. Yet in this one instance the continuing insistence for control over women's reproductive capacity has subjugated gender identity, (that the crime was committed against her because she is a woman) to ethnic identity'.[82]

ENFORCED STERILIZATION

The ICC Elements of Crimes describes enforced sterilization to take place where the perpetrator 'deprived one or more persons of biological reproductive capacity' and the conduct was 'neither justified by the medical or hospital treatment of the person' nor 'carried out with their genuine consent'.[83] It is noted in the Elements of Crimes that deception is incompatible with genuine consent.

SEXUAL VIOLENCE

Sexual violence is defined in the ICC Elements of Crimes to be where 'the perpetrator committed an act of sexual nature against one or more persons or caused such person

[79] ICC Elements of Crimes: Art. 7(1)(g); Art. 8 (2)(b)(xxii); and Art. 8(2)(e)(vi).

[80] ICC Statute, Art. 7(2)(f). [81] ICC Statute, Art. 7(2)(f).

[82] Chinkin, C., 2014, 'Gender and Armed Conflict'. In *Oxford Handbook of International Law in Armed Conflict*, edited by Clapham, A. and Gaeta, P., Oxford University Press, p. 675.

[83] ICC Elements of Crimes: Art. 7(1)(g); Art. 8(2)(vi); and Art. 8(2)(b)(xxii).

or persons to engage in an act of sexual nature by force, threat of force or coercion, such as that caused by fear of violence, duress, detention, psychological oppression or abuse of power, against such person or persons or another person, or by taking advantage of a coercive environment such person's or persons' incapacity to give genuine consent'.[84]

The ICTR has broadly defined sexual violence to be 'any act of a sexual nature committed under circumstances that are coercive', explaining that 'sexual violence is not limited to a physical invasion of the human body and may include acts that do not involve penetration or physical contact. Sexual violence covers both physical and psychological attacks directed at a person's sexual characteristics'.[85] Similarly, the ICTY has held that sexual violence 'embraces all serious abuses of a sexual nature inflicted upon the integrity of a person by means of coercion, threat of force or intimidation in a way that is humiliating and degrading to the victim's dignity'.[86] In light of the sexual violence commonly being witnessed in today's conflicts, such as forced nudity and electrocution of genitalia,[87] one would hope that the any court presiding over these acts would adopt a broad interpretation of sexual violence.

C. (Lack of) Prosecutions for sexual violence at the International Court and ad hoc Tribunals

It should be borne in mind that the primary responsibility to investigate and prosecute sexual violence is with the State. Where the State is unable or unwilling to investigate—or national criminal law is inadequate and domestic remedies have been exhausted—international criminal justice, in theory, should step in. However, despite all forms of sexual violence, from rape to forced nudity, being clearly prohibited under IHL, IHRL, and ICL, the International Criminal Court and the ad hoc tribunals have secured only a miniscule number of prosecutions compared to the scale of sexual violence that has been committed during armed conflict in recent history.

The ICC has failed to prosecute a single case of sexual violence. In the first successful prosecution by the ICC, the Lubanga case, charges were limited to recruitment of children

84 ICC Elements of Crimes: Art. 7(1)(g); Art. 8(2)(b)(xxii); and Art. 8(2)(e)(vi).

85 *Prosecutor v Akayesu*, Judgment (Trial Chamber), 2 September 1998, §§598 and 688. Similarly, Triffterer asserts: 'Sexual violence is a term broader than rape. The term is used to describe any kind of violence carried out through sexual means or by targeting sexuality'. Triffterer O. (ed.), 2008, *Commentary on the Rome Statute of the International Criminal Court*, 2nd edn, Hart Publishing, UK, p. 214.

86 *Prosecutor v Stakic*, Judgment (Trial Chamber) (Case No IT-97-24), 31 July 2003, §757.

87 'Conflict-related sexual violence, report of the Secretary-General', UN Doc. No. S/2015/203, 23 March 2015.

despite ample evidence of sexual slavery and rape. In her dissenting opinion Judge Obio Benito expressed her frustration at this and highlighted that the exclusion of charges related to sexual violence restricts a judge's ability to render justice to victims.[88] In the courts only other successful prosecution, Germain Katanga was convicted on four counts of war crimes and one count of a crime against humanity for his part in killing more than 200 people in a massacre in 2003 in north-eastern DRC.[89] However, Katanga was cleared of all charges of sexual violence despite the initial ICC investigation finding that women who survived the 2003 massacre had been raped and/or kept as sex slaves.[90] Prosecutors tried to show that rape and sexual violence took place as a result of a common plan directed by Katanga, however they failed to do so largely because the evidence linking Katanga to crimes of a sexual nature was deemed insufficient. Prosecutors appear to have missed a trick here. Instead of charging sexual violence as part of a planned attack, the command responsibility mode of liability could have been invoked, according to which prosecutors would just have to show that Katanga knew about the crimes but did not take steps to prevent or punish his subordinates for committing them, rather than having to prove that the sexual violence was part of a pre-planned tactic. The Office of the Prosecutor, following much criticism of its handling of the case, has said that in future cases it plans to prosecute sexual violence under broader modes of liability, including command responsibility.[91]

A major barrier to international prosecutions is that international courts and tribunals will only have jurisdiction where authorized by the State concerned or the UN Security Council. Taking Syria as an example, accessing criminal justice is not a realistic prospect for today's survivors of sexual violence as Syria is not a State party to the ICC Statute meaning that the court has no territorial jurisdiction over the crimes being committed there. Nevertheless the ICC may still be able to prosecute the perpetrators of crimes in Syria who are nationals of a State party to the ICC Statute, through personal jurisdiction, meaning a British foreign fighter, for example, who commits a war crime in Syria may, in theory, be prosecuted by the ICC. However, at this point in time the ICC Office of the Prosecute has said it will be not be pursuing prosecutions through personal jurisdiction as the ability to conduct investigations in Syria 'appear limited'.[92] The only further avenue for the ICC to exercise jurisdiction is for the situation to be referred to it by the Security Council under Chapter VII of the UN Charter. However,

[88] *Prosecutor v Thomas Lubanga*, Decision on Sentencing (Trail Chamber) (Case No. ICC-01/04-01/06-2901) 10 July 2012, §60.

[89] *Prosecutor v Germain Katanga*, Judgment (Trial Chamber II) Case No. ICC-01/04-01/07, 8 March 2014.

[90] *Prosecutor v Katanga and Mathieu Ngudjolo Chui*, Decision (Pre-Trail Chamber I) (Case No. ICC-01/04-01/07), 30 September 2008, §§347–54.

[91] ICC Policy Paper on Sexual and Gender Based Crimes, June 2014, §78.

[92] Statement of the Prosecutor of the International Criminal Court, Fatou Bensouda, on the alleged crimes committed by ISIS, 8 April 2015.

the Security Council has already failed to make a referral and considering the continued Chinese and Russia opposition to an ICC referral it is extremely unlikely to change its position.[93] Failing a regime change, it seems that the only hope for survivors in Syria is the formation of a special tribunal dedicated to prosecuting mass crimes committed in Syria. This is something that the UN Independent Commission of Inquiry on Syria is pushing for but in reality is lacking political support and is unlikely to be achieved any time soon.[94]

Evidentiary issues are another reason why there have been so few prosecutions for sexual violence at the international court and the ad hoc tribunals. It is seen, by some, as harder to gather evidence in cases concerning sexual violence and argued that by the time the security situation has stabilized enough to allow investigations to begin; evidence is often diminished or destroyed. It is true that unlike a massacre where there are likely to be mass graves, the physical evidence of mass rape, for example, will be harder to come across. However, there will still be mass survivors and witnesses who are able to give first hand testimony of their experiences and may be able to provide medical evidence. To access this evidence the reasons why survivors and witnesses may not come forward need to be addressed; including addressing survivors immediate needs, social stigma, and fear of reprisals. Considering the difficulties associated with securing witness testimony, and the problem of witness intimidation,[95] it is encouraging that the ICC's Office of the Prosecutor has said that as part of its renewed focus on sexual violence and gender-based crimes greater efforts will be made to gather documentary evidence, such as hospital records, and forensic investigation strategies. Social media may also provide a new and vital source of evidence for future prosecutions, as many armed groups have taken to filming their crimes and widely disseminating the footage on social media.

The international nature of investigations and prosecutions has also been blamed for the low number of prosecutions. Securing and exercising an arrest warrant, collecting evidence and securing witness testimony in court is not an easy task when the perpetrator, physical evidence, witnesses, and the court are across several States or regions. However, although difficult this is not an impossible task, and prosecutions for other crimes with the same geographical hurdles have been secured. In the case of Somali maritime piracy, by way of example, despite the perpetrator being Somali, the crime being committed in international waters where evidence is easily dumped into the

[93] UN Press Release, *Russia, China block Security Council referral of Syria to International Criminal Court*, 22 May 2014.

[94] Report of the Independent International Commission of Inquiry on the Syrian Arab Republic*, UN Doc. No. A/HRC/28/69, 5 February 2015, §96

[95] It has been claimed that witness intimidation was the main reason why rape charges were not brought in cases against Kenyan deputy president William Ruto and former broadcaster Joshua Arap Sang. Institute for War and Peace, 'ICC Restates Commitment on Crimes of Sexual Violence' 10 June 2014.

ocean and the victims and witnesses being spread across the globe, a number of successful prosecutions have been made.[96]

A further hurdle to securing prosecutions for sexual violence is that all forms of sexual violence—against both males and females—is too often recorded and therefore prosecuted, as solely an act of torture or abuse rather than an act of sexual violence. In the *Tadić* case, for example, Duško Tadić was prosecuted, in part, for the role he played in the abuse of detainees, including forcing a male detainee to perform fellatio on another detainee and then bite off his testacies.[97] However, charges were limited to cruel treatment and inhumane acts (crimes against humanity), rather than rape or other forms of sexual violence of comparable gravity. This is a concern because although rape and other forms of sexual violence are also forms of torture or cruel, inhuman, or degrading treatment it is essential for our understanding of the scale, manifestations, and characteristics of sexual violence that it be correctly documented. Accurate recording is also essential for prosecution, truth and reconciliation, and historical purposes, as well as to dispel discriminatory stereotypes and assumptions.

ARE THERE BETTER ALTERNATIVES TO EXISTING CRIMINAL JUSTICE MECHANISMS?

Considering the void that exists between the international legal framework that prohibits sexual violence and its implementation—which allows almost total impunity to prevail—is now the time to harness the political will that seems to be at an all-time high,[98] and consider new criminal justice mechanisms in the hope that they will do better job of securing prosecutions?

One option would be to establish an international tribunal dedicated to only prosecuting sexual violence in armed conflict—any conflict. Such a thematic tribunal would have the benefit of specialized expertise, something that appears to be missing in existing mechanisms. A thematic tribunal may also allow the politics of country-specific tribunals to be by-passed. It is much harder for a State to object to the investigation of sexual violence in armed conflict *wherever* it may occur than it is to object to an investigation into one specific State, which may be an ally. Such a thematic tribunal would send a very clear message that sexual violence is not acceptable at any time and the

[96] See Guilfoyle, D., 2012, 'Prosecuting Somali Pirates', *Journal of International Criminal Justice*, vol. 10, no. 4, pp. 767–96.

[97] *Prosecutor v Tadić*, Opinion and Judgment (Case No. IT-96-1-T), 7 May 1997, §206.

[98] Take for instance the 2014 Global Summit to End Sexual Violence in Conflict held in London in June 2014. During the summit the International Protocol on the Documentation and Investigation of Sexual Violence in Conflict was launched.

international community is serious about accountability. It would also have a greater chance, if well resourced, of securing larger number of prosecutions of perpetrators of varying ranks than the ICC, which is notoriously slow and appears to only be concerned with high-ranking officials. This option obviously comes with all the issues that setting up an ad hoc tribunal brings including: resources, time to set it up, regional presence, balanced geographical representation as well as jurisdiction and procedural methods.

To avoid setting up an entirely new tribunal a specialized chamber that is tacked onto the ICC could be established. Thereby ensuring the expertise of a specialized tribunal but also having the benefit of an already established court and its evidentiary, procedural, and jurisdictional issues settled. Based on the limited data that is available it does appear that sexual violence is being committed on such a huge scale as to warrant special treatment by the ICC. That said singling out sexual violence offences, rather than genocide, for example, will be unpopular with purists and the same politics and jurisdiction issues that appear to hinder the ICC now would equally apply to a specialized chamber attached to it.

If establishing a new tribunal or chamber is considered too radical or complex, national courts could be turned to. Indeed, as has been noted by prominent international judges, the development of the international criminal courts and ad hoc tribunals does not replace the important role of national courts in prosecuting the perpetrators of serious international crimes.[99] There is nothing to stop a coalition of like-minded States from collectively developing a prosecution strategy and agreeing to share resources and expertise to prosecute sexual violence in their national courts. Such a coalition would have the benefit of sharing expertise on investigation and prosecution and be the most resource-efficient option. Such a coalition could exercise various modes of jurisdiction to secure convictions including universal jurisdiction over sexual violence in any conflict (IAC or NIAC),[100] active personality jurisdiction (based on the nationality of the perpetrator, under which a State may prosecute one of its nationals for offences committed abroad); and passive nationality jurisdiction (based on the nationality of the victim, under which a State party may prosecute a non-national for acts committed against a national abroad). Of course this option, like the others, will still have to overcome the hurdles of implementing arrest warrants and securing evidence in an international context. However, it certainly seems a better option than allowing the status quo to continue and would give real teeth to a number of States' commitment to tackling impunity.

[99] Judges Higgins, Kooijmans and Buergenthal in Arrest Warrant of 11 April 2000 (*Democratic Republic of Congo v Belgium*), Judgment, ICJ Reports 2002, p. 3, Joint Separate Opinion of Judges Higgins, Kooijmans and Buergenthal, pp. 78–9, para. 51.

[100] Indeed a number of States have exercised universal jurisdiction to prosecute other war crimes including Australia (High Court of Australia, *Polyukhovich v Australia and anor*, 172 CLR 501 14 August 1991); Canada (Supreme Court of Canada, *R. v Finta*, File No. 23097, 24 March 1994): and the United Kingdom (United Kingdom Court of Appeal *R v Sayoniuk*, 10 February 2000).

Concluding remarks

Whilst increased political will has led to new initiatives to tackle sexual violence in armed conflict the fact remains that sexual violence continues to be a prominent feature of armed conflict in 2015 and survivors and their communities remain traumatized, stigmatized, and without redress whilst perpetrators continue to enjoy impunity.

Tackling impunity for sexual violence in armed conflict requires sustained political will, targeted prosecution strategies, and timely collection of evidence. Gender-sensitive training of investigators, prosecutors, and the judiciary is essential. Medics working in conflict-affected States also need training on the medico-legal aspects of sexual violence, including on how to correctly document forensic evidence and refer patients to law enforcement agencies.[101] One-stop shops that provide medical and legal services for survivors have the potential to be very effective in increasing prosecutions, so long as they are accessible to all survivors and not just females and children.[102]

Securing prosecutions is an impossible task without taking into account the immediate needs arising from the conflict for the survivor, such as securing shelter or locating a missing loved one. It is only once these immediate concerns are addressed that survivors will be inclined to report the violence. Survivors also need education on the criminal justice options available to them and free legal assistance to pursue a complaint should they choose to do so. As well as a safe and supportive environment in which survivors and witnesses feel empowered and secure enough to come forward and report the crime.

Traditional criminal justice mechanisms are of course not enough to challenge impunity and prevent future acts of sexual violence. Transitional justice mechanisms such as truth commissions, which can play a particularly important role in breaking social stigma, and gender-sensitive reparations—including compensation, satisfaction, rehabilitation, and guarantees of non-reoccurrence,[103] are equally important and should go hand in hand with seeking criminal accountability.[104] Women must be fully integrated and involved in any peace agreement, and in roles that reflect their different identities rather than as solely victims. Addressing sexual violence should be a key feature in

[101] The International Protocol on the Documentation and Investigation of Sexual Violence in Conflict does provide some guidance to medical practitioners on how to collect and store forensic evidence. June 2014, p, 70.

[102] Access to Justice for Children, Report of the United Nations High Commissioner for Human Rights, UN Doc. No. A/HRC/27/21, 15 December 2013, §50.

[103] Basic Principles and Guidelines on the Right to a Remedy and Reparation for Victims of Gross Violations of International Human Rights Law and Serious Violations of International Humanitarian Law, Principle 18.

[104] Note the Guidance note of the UN Secretary-Generals on Reparations for Conflict-related Sexual Violence, June 2014.

all peace agreements and sexual violence should always be totally excluded from any amnesty.

Finally, we do not want a would-be perpetrator not to commit acts of sexual violence because they feel they should respect the law or they fear prosecution; rather we want them not to commit acts of sexual violence because they don't want to commit a morally wrong and socially unacceptable act. To achieve this more needs to be done to tackle the deeply entrenched misogynistic and discriminatory attitudes that feed sexual violence committed against men, women, boys, and girls—in both peace time and armed conflict, in this respect it must be remembered that taking sexual violence in armed conflict is part of the bigger picture to secure equality.

15 A review of the work of the International Criminal Court in 2014

Damien Scalia[1]

Introduction

This chapter presents and analyses the main substantive contributions to international criminal law made by the International Criminal Court (ICC) in 2014. During the last year, there have been many developments related to the preliminary examinations made by the Prosecutor. Moreover, the ICC issued one condemnation judgment (in the *Katanga* Case), one appeal judgment (in the *Lubanga* Case), some decisions concerning the confirmation of charges, and many decisions related to admissibility, jurisdiction, and procedural issues. While these decisions provide detail about the forms of responsibility and elements of admissibility, only a few elements of crimes were analysed. One could think this is an indication that after fifteen years of activities, the definitions of crimes are sufficiently clear and the only remaining problems concern the forms of responsibility and the relationships with State parties.

After initially presenting the developments related to the preliminary examinations (section A) and the main decisions concerning admissibility and the jurisdiction of the Court (section B), this chapter will outline some of the issues regarding the *Katanga* and *Lubanga* judgments (section C) and, in relation to them, the pronounced penalties (section D).

A. Preliminary examinations and preliminary stages

As explained by the Prosecutor, 'the preliminary examination of a situation may be initiated on the basis of: a) information sent by individuals or groups, States,

[1] Dr Damien Scalia is an Advanced Researcher FNS and UCLouvain-CRID&P.

intergovernmental or non-governmental organizations; b) a referral from a State Party or the Security Council; or (c) a declaration accepting the jurisdiction of the Court lodged pursuant to Article 12(3) by a State which is not a Party to the Statute'.[2] In 2014, the Office of the Prosecutor of the ICC conducted preliminary examinations regarding a number of situations: Honduras, Iraq, Ukraine, Afghanistan, Colombia, Georgia, Guinea, and Nigeria. Other preliminary examinations were completed regarding three situations: Central African Republic, Republic of Korea, and registered vessels of Comoros, Greece, and Cambodia.[3] While some of these preliminary examinations do not warrant comment, others are more crucial. This section will highlight a few elements in this latter category.

First, concerning Afghanistan, the *Report on Preliminary Examination Activities 2014* of the Office of the Prosecutor delivers important information: the Prosecutor examines potential crimes committed by US forces on detainees in Afghanistan. This report was the subject of many comments[4] and states that:

> The Office has been assessing available information relating to the alleged abuse of detainees by international forces within the temporal jurisdiction of the Court. In particular, the alleged torture or ill-treatment of conflict-related detainees by US armed forces in Afghanistan in the period 2003-2008 forms another potential case identified by the Office. In accordance with the Presidential Directive of 7 February 2002, Taliban detainees were denied the status of prisoner of war under article 4 of the Third Geneva Convention but were required to be treated humanely. In this context, the information available suggests that between May 2003 and June 2004, members of the US military in Afghanistan used so-called 'enhanced interrogation techniques' against conflict-related detainees in an effort to improve the level of actionable intelligence obtained from interrogations. The development and implementation of such techniques is documented *inter alia* in declassified US Government documents released to the public, including Department of Defense reports as well as the US Senate Armed Services Committee's inquiry. These reports describe interrogation techniques approved for use as including food deprivation, deprivation of clothing, environmental manipulation, sleep adjustment, use of individual fears, use of stress positions, sensory deprivation (deprivation of light and sound), and sensory overstimulation.[5]

[2] ICC, *Report on Preliminary Examination Activities 2014*, OTP, 2 December 2014, §§2.

[3] Ibid.

[4] Goodman, R., 'Int'l Criminal Court's Examination of U.S. Treatment of Detainees Takes Shape', in Justsecurity.org, 3 December 2014, consulted on 28 February 2015 in <http://justsecurity.org/17948/international-criminal-courts-examination-u-s-treatment-detainees-takes-shape/>; Vogel, R., 'ICC Prosecutor Advances Examination of U.S. Detention Policies in Afghanistan', in lawfareblog.com, consulted on 28 February 2015 in <http://www.lawfareblog.com/2014/12/icc-prosecutor-advances-examination-of-u-s-detention-policies-in-afghanistan>; Heller, K. J., 'The OTP's Afghanistan Investigation: A Response to Vogel', 4 December 2014, consulted on 28 February 2015 in <http://opiniojuris.org/2014/12/04/otps-afghanistan-investigation-response-vogel/>.

[5] ICC, *Report on Preliminary Examination Activities 2014*, OTP, 2 December 2014, §§94.

This is still crucial. The report adds also that:

> Certain of the enhanced interrogation techniques apparently approved by US senior commanders in Afghanistan in the period from February 2003 through June 2004, could, depending on the severity and duration of their use, amount to cruel treatment, torture or outrages upon personal dignity as defined under international jurisprudence. In addition, there is information available that interrogators allegedly committed abuses that were outside the scope of any approved techniques, such as severe beating, especially beating on the soles of the feet, suspension by the wrists, and threats to shoot or kill . . . While continuing to assess the seriousness and reliability of such allegations, the Office is analysing the relevance and genuineness of national proceedings by the competent national authorities for the alleged conduct described above as well as the gravity of the alleged crimes.[6]

This is the first time that the Office of the Prosecutor has conducted an examination on crimes committed by the United States. Admittedly, it is only a preliminary examination (and the Prosecutor can stop these whenever they want) but it is symbolically important—at a time when the Court is accused of being 'racist' or politically employed.

Then, the question of the stage of the preliminary examination should be raised. As explained by the Office of the Prosecutor, it 'applies a holistic approach throughout the preliminary examination process' divided into four phases.[7] According to Goodman, 'it appears that the examination of US detention operations has reached the third phase and crossed over the important threshold of a finding that there is a reasonable basis to believe US forces committed war crimes within the jurisdiction of the Court'.[8] It means that the Office of the Prosecutor 'is specifically considering whether US forces are responsible for war crimes relating to detainee treatment in Afghanistan'.[9]

[6] Ibid., §§95–96.

[7] The Office of the Prosecutor distinguishes among four phases: 'Phase 1 consists of an initial assessment of all information on alleged crimes received under article 15 ("communications"). The purpose is to analyse the seriousness of information received, filter out information on crimes that are outside the jurisdictions of the Court and identify those that appear to fall within the jurisdiction of the Court. Phase 2, which represents the formal commencement of a preliminary examination, focuses on whether the preconditions to the exercise of jurisdiction under Art. 12 are satisfied and whether there is a reasonable basis to believe that the alleged crimes committed in the situation at hand with a view to identifying potential cases falling within the jurisdiction of the Court. The Office may further gather information on relevant national proceedings if such information is available at this stage. Phase 3 focuses on the admissibility of potential cases in terms of complementary and gravity. In this place, the Office will also continue to collect information on subject-matter jurisdiction, in particular when new or ongoing crimes are alleged to have been committed within the situation. Phase 4 examines the interests of justice consideration in order to formulate the final recommendation to the Prosecutor on whether there is reasonable basis to initiate an investigation' (ICC, *Report on Preliminary Examination Activities 2014*, OTP, 2 December 2014, §15).

[8] Goodman, R., 'Int'l Criminal Court's Examination of U.S. Treatment of Detainees Takes Shape', in Justsecurity.org, 3 December 2014, consulted on 28 February 2015 in <http://justsecurity.org/17948/international-criminal-courts-examination-u-s-treatment-detainees-takes-shape/>.

[9] Heller, K. J., 'The OTP's Afghanistan Investigation: A Response to Vogel', 4 December 2014, consulted on 28 February 2015, in <http://opiniojuris.org/2014/12/04/otps-afghanistan-investigation-response-vogel/>.

Finally, it is worth noting that the Office of the Prosecutor highlights the 'interrogation techniques apparently approved by US senior commanders in Afghanistan'. It seems that the examinations of the Prosecutor targets the high level people. While no one could assume the following procedure will be made after this preliminary examination, one could hope that this announcement will set an important precedent for international criminal justice. In spite of this, one should recall the agreement signed between the Government of Afghanistan and the Government of the United States of America regarding the surrender of persons of the ICC.[10] By this agreement, the Parties agreed that the 'person of one Party present in the territory of the other shall not, absent the expressed consent of the first Party, (a) be surrender or transferred by any means to the International Criminal Court for any purpose'.[11]

Second, it is important to note that the Office of the Prosecutor closed the preliminary investigations concerning the Union of the Comoros. This preliminary investigation was related to registered vessels of Comoros, Greece, and Cambodia. At the same time as analysing this preliminary investigation, it is necessary to analyse the development related to the situation in Palestine and the recent preliminary examination started at the beginning of 2015. 'On 14 May 2013, the Office of the Prosecutor received a referral on behalf of the authorities of the Union of the Comoros ("Comoros") with respect to the 31 May 2010 Israeli interception of a humanitarian aid flotilla bound for the Gaza Strip. On the same day, the Prosecutor announced that it had opened a preliminary examination on the basis of the referral.'[12] Remember that on 3 January 2009, Israel imposed a naval blockade off the coast of the Gaza Strip, following the Hamas victory in the elections. In response, the *Free Gaza Movement* was created and a humanitarian flotilla had been chartered for the purpose of bringing aid to Gaza and to 'break the Israeli blockade, and draw international attention to the situation in Gaza and the effects of the blockade'.[13] On 31 May 2010, the Israeli Defence Forces intercepted the flotilla and ten passengers were killed. One of the vessels was registered in Comoros. It was the first referral made by a State concerning a situation occurring on a boat.[14] At the outset, the Prosecutor stated that 'the information available indicates that there is a reasonable basis to believe that war crimes were committed on board the Mavi Marmara during the interception of the flotilla on 31 May 2010 in the context of an international armed conflict, namely: (1) wilful killing pursuant to article 8(2)(a)(i);

[10] Agreement between the Government of the Transitional Islamic State of Afghanistan and the Government of the United State of America regarding the surrender of persons to the International Criminal Court, 20 September 2002, consulted on 28 February 2015, in <http://www.law.georgetown.edu/library/research/guides/upload/Afghanistan03-119.pdf>.

[11] Ibid., p. 1.

[12] ICC, *Report on Preliminary Examination Activities 2014,* OTP, 2 December 2014, §246.

[13] ICC, *Situation on Registered Vessels of Comoros, Greece and Cambodia Article 53(1) Report,* OTP, 6 November 2014, §11.

[14] Bitti, G., 'Chronique de droit international pénal', *RSC*, October–December 2013, pp. 941–70, pp. 3–4.

(2) wilfully causing serious injury to body and health pursuant to article 8(2)(a)(iii); and (3) committing outrages upon personal dignity pursuant to article 8(2)(b)(xxi) of the Statute'.[15] Nevertheless, 'having carefully assessed the relevant considerations, the Office has concluded that the potential case(s) that would likely arise from an investigation of the flotilla incident would not be of sufficient gravity to justify further action by the Court, in light of the criteria for admissibility provided in Article 17(1)(d) and the guidance outlined in article 8(1) of the Statute'.[16]

To conclude, the Prosecutor added that 'the interception of the flotilla took place in the context of the Israel-Hamas conflict, the Court does not have jurisdiction over other alleged crimes committed in this context, nor in the broader context of any conflict between Israel and Palestine'.[17]

In this regard, an important development must be underlined in connection with Palestine. In early 2014, the Prosecutor of the Court refused to open a preliminary investigation into crimes allegedly committed in Palestine. Indeed, the Prosecutor considered that, on the one hand, Palestine was not a party to the ICC Statute and, on the other hand, the Court had not received any communication accepting the jurisdiction of the Court or requesting an investigation into crimes committed after November 2012, that is to say after the Resolution (67/19) of the General Assembly of the United Nations granted Palestine the status of non-member State.[18] This deficit was filled on 1 January 2015, when the Registrar of the Court received a declaration of acceptance of jurisdiction of the ICC by the government of the Palestine from 13 June 2014. The day after (on 2 January 2015) the State of Palestine acceded to the Rome Statute and became the 123rd signatory of the ICC Statute. There are two comments of note in this regard. First, Palestine accepted the acceptance of the jurisdiction of the Court before it ratified the Statute, because membership cannot be retroactive, while the declaration of acceptance can be. Second, the date of 13 June 2014 is not insignificant: on 12 June 2014, three Israeli teenagers were kidnapped and killed and the crimes were attributed to the Hamas. Following the ratification of the Statute, on 16 January 2015, the Prosecutor opened a preliminary examination into the situation in Palestine. Nevertheless, the Prosecutor clarified that 'a preliminary examination is not an investigation but a process of examining the information available in order to reach a fully informed determination on whether there is a reasonable basis to proceed with an investigation pursuant to the criteria established by the Rome Statute. Specifically, under Article 53(1) of the

[15] ICC, *Situation on Registered Vessels of Comoros, Greece and Cambodia Article 53(1) Report*, OTP, 6 November 2014, §19.

[16] Ibid., §24. [17] Ibid., §25.

[18] Heller, K. J., 'Three Thoughts on the OTP's Rejection of Jurisdiction over the Situation in Palestine', Opinio Juris, 5 August 2014, consulted on 29 February 2015 in <http://opiniojuris.org/2014/08/05/breaking-otp-rejects-jurisdiction-situation-palestine/>.

Rome Statute, the Prosecutor must consider issues of jurisdiction, admissibility and the interests of justice in making this determination. The Office gives due consideration to all submissions and views conveyed to the Office during the course of a preliminary examination, strictly guided by the requirements of the Rome Statute in the independent and impartial exercise of its mandate'.[19]

Before analysing the decisions related to admissibility and the jurisdiction of the Court, it is important to highlight two further factual circumstances before the ICC. First, the Prosecutor decided to withdraw the charges against Uhuru Muigai Kenyatta.[20] This decision followed the Trial Chamber's rejection of the Prosecution's request for an adjournment.[21] The Prosecutor justified his decision stating that 'the evidence has not improved to such an extent that Mr Kenyatta's alleged criminal responsibility can be proven beyond reasonable doubt'.[22] He explained the decision by arguing that 'several people who may have provided important evidence regarding Mr Kenyatta's actions, have died, while others were too terrified to testify for the Prosecution; key witnesses who provided evidence in this case later withdrew or changed their accounts, in particular, witnesses who subsequently alleged that they had lied to my Office about having been personally present at crucial meetings; and the Kenyan Government's non-compliance compromised the Prosecution's ability to thoroughly investigate the charges, as recently confirmed by the Trial Chamber'.[23] Nonetheless, such a decision is surprising after five years of investigation. It might be thought that this decision is linked to the fact that M. Kenyatta is a President-in-Office. In the same vein, the Prosecutor suspended his works in the situation of Darfur,[24] in stating that 'given this Council's lack of foresight on what should happen in Darfur, I am left with no choice but to hibernate investigative activities in Darfur as I shift resources to other urgent cases, especially those in which trial is approaching. It should thus be clear to this Council that unless there is a change of attitude and approach to Darfur in the near future, there shall continue to be little or nothing to report to you for the foreseeable future'.[25] Although the purpose of this announcement could be to force the Security Council to act, both decisions demonstrate the lack of power of the ICC against political bodies.

[19] ICC, *The Prosecutor of the International Criminal Court, Fatou Bensouda, opens a preliminary examination of the situation in Palestine*, Press Release, OTP, ICC-OTP-20150116-PR1083, 16 January 2015.

[20] ICC, *The Prosecutor v Uhuru Muigai Kenyatta*, Notice of withdrawal of the charges against Uhuru Muigai Kenyatta, Bureau du Procureur, ICC-01/09-02/11, 5 December 2014.

[21] Ibid. [22] Ibid., §2.

[23] ICC, *Statement of the Prosecutor of the International Criminal Court, Fatou Bensouda, on the withdrawal of charges against Mr Uhuru Muigai Kenyatta*, Press Release, OTP, 5 December 2014.

[24] UN News Center, *Security Council inaction on Darfur 'can only embolden perpetrators'*—ICC prosecutor, 12 December 2014, consulted on 28 February 2015 in /,http://www.un.org/apps/news/story.asp?NewsID=49591#.VRF322ajzw4>.

[25] Ibid.

B. Admissibility and jurisdiction

In terms of admissibility, this chapter analyses two main decisions. The first is related to the *Simone Gbagbo* case in Côte d'Ivoire's situation. The ICC indicted her four charges as crimes against humanity. After the Court has asked the State to execute the arrest warrant issued (on 29 February 2012 but unsealed on 22 November 2012) against her, Côte d'Ivoire refused, on 30 September 2013, and challenged the warrant's admissibility, arguing that a case against the same person for the same crime was being prosecuted at national level.[26] On 11 December 2014, the Pre-Trial Chamber issued a decision about admissibility. In the decision, the Judges rejected the argument of the Côte d'Ivoire arguing that 'the documentation provided as part of, and in addition to, the Admissibility Challenge does not demonstrate that concrete, tangible and progressive investigative steps are being undertaken by the domestic authorities of Côte d'Ivoire in order to ascertain Simone Gbagbo's criminal responsibility for the same conduct as that alleged in the proceedings before the Court. Nor does this documentation indicate that Simone Gbagbo is currently being prosecuted by Côte d'Ivoire for the same conduct attributed to her in the case before the Court'.[27] At the beginning of 2015, Simone Gbagbo was condemned in Côte d'Ivoire for '*attentat contre l'autorité de l'Etat, participation à un mouvement insurrectionnel et trouble à l'ordre public*'[28]. The Côte d'Ivoire requested an appeal against the Pre-Trial Chamber's decision.

Again concerning admissibility, in 2014 the ICC issued another important decision. It related to the Libya situation. On 21 May 2014, the Appeals Chamber of the ICC confirmed a decision issued by the Trial Chamber,[29] which Libya appealed against. The Appeals Chamber specified various elements of admissibility. First, concerning the incidents tried both at national and international level, Judges of the Chamber explained that 'the real issue is the degree of overlap required as between the incidents being investigated by the Prosecutor and those being investigated by a State—with the focus being upon whether the conduct is substantially the same. Again, this will depend upon the facts of the individual case. If there is a large overlap between the incidents under investigation, it may be clear that the State is investigating substantially the same conduct; if the overlap is smaller, depending upon the precise facts, it may be that the State is still investigating substantially the same

[26] ICC, *The Prosecutor v Simone Gbagbo*, Decision on Côte d'Ivoire's challenge to the admissibility of the case against Simone Gbagbo, Pre-Trial Chamber, ICC-02/11-01/12, 11 December 2014, §3.

[27] Ibid., §78.

[28] AFP, 'Côte d'Ivoire: Simone Gbagbo condamnée à vingt ans de prison', in *Libération*, 9 March 2015, consulted on 9 March 2015 in <http://www.liberation.fr/monde/2015/03/09/cote-d-ivoire-simone-gbagbo-condamnee-a-20-ans-de-prison_1217735>.

[29] ICC, *The Prosecutor v Saif Al-Islam Gaddafi*, Decision on the admissibility of the case against Saif Al-Islam Gaddafi, ICC-01/11-01/11-344-Conf, 31 May 2013.

conduct or is investigating only a very small part of the Prosecutor's case. For example, the incidents that it is investigating may, in fact, form the crux of the Prosecutor's case and/or represent the most serious aspects of the case. Alternatively, they may be very minor when compared with the case as a whole. What is required is a judicial assessment of whether the case that the State is investigating sufficiently mirrors the one that the Prosecutor is investigating. The Appeals Chamber considers that to carry out this assessment, it is necessary to use, as a comparator, the underlying incidents under investigation both by the Prosecutor and the State, alongside the conduct of the suspect under investigation that gives rise to his or her criminal responsibility for the conduct described in those incidents'.[30] Moreover, the interest of victims should also be taken into consideration.[31] Libya did not transfer Gaddafi to the ICC. The Court requested the cooperation of the Security Council and then referred the matter on to it.[32]

In the same situation, the Judges of the Appeals Chamber answered a crucial question related to the respect of human rights as an element to be taken into account to evaluate the admissibility of a case. Indeed, since the establishment of the ICC and the writing of Article 17 of the Rome Statute, authors have discussed the status of human rights in relation to the complementarity principle:[33] should the Court analyse the respect of human rights to declare a case admissible before it? Judges declined to deal with this argument and clarified that 'the Court was not established to be an international court of human rights, sitting in judgment over domestic legal systems to ensure that they are compliant with international standards of human rights'.[34] This clarifies an important issue in reaffirming the criminal character of the ICC. This position could be criticized, but it seems to be realistic and pragmatic. As concluded by the Court, founding its reasoning especially on the *travaux préparatoires* of the Rome Statute:

1) For a case to be admissible under article 17 (2) (c) it must be shown that the proceedings were not or are not being conducted independently or impartially and that the proceedings were or are being conducted in a manner which, in the circumstances, is inconsistent with an intent to bring the person concerned to justice.

[30] ICC, *The Prosecutor v Saif Al-Islam Gaddafi et Abdullah Al-Senussi*, Judgment on the Appeal of Libya against the decision of Pre-Trial Chamber I of 31 May 2013 entitled 'Decision on the admissibility of the case against Saif Al-Islam Gaddafi', case n° ICC-01/11-01/11, 21 May 2014, §§72-73.

[31] Ibid., §74.

[32] ICC, *The Prosecutor v Saif Al-Islam Gaddafi*, Decision on the non-compliance by Libya with requests for cooperation by the Court and referring the matter to the United Nations Security Council, Pre-Trial Chamber, ICC-01/11-01/11, 10 December 2014.

[33] For example: Fry, E., 'Between Show Trials and Sham Prosecutions: The Rome Statute's Potential Effect on Domestic Due Process Protections', *Criminal Law Forum*, 2012, pp. 35–62; Bernard, B., 2014, *Juger et juger encore les crimes internationaux, Etude du principe ne bis in idem*, Bruxelles, Bruylant.

[34] ICC, *The Prosecutor v Saif Al-Islam Gaddafi and Abdullah Al-Senussi*, Judgment on the appeal of Mr Abdullah Al-Senussi against the decision of Pre-Trial Chamber I of 11 October 2013 entitled 'Decision on the admissibility of the case against Abdullah Al-Senussi', case n° ICC-01/11-01/11, 24 July 2014, §§219 et 221-230.

2) Taking into account the text, context, object and purpose of the provision, this determination is not one that involves an assessment of whether the due process rights of a suspect have been breached per se. In particular, the concept of proceedings 'being conducted in a manner which, in the circumstances, is inconsistent with an intent to bring the person concerned to justice' should generally be understood as referring to proceedings which will lead to an suspect evading justice, in the sense of not appropriately being tried genuinely to establish his or her criminal responsibility, in the equivalent of sham proceedings that are concerned with that person's protection.
3) However, there may be circumstances, depending on the facts of the individual case, whereby violations of the rights of the suspect are so egregious that the proceedings can no longer be regarded as being capable of providing any genuine form of justice to the suspect so that they should be deemed, in those circumstances, to be "inconsistent with an intent to bring that person to justice.[35]

Thus, the non-respect of human rights could be taken into consideration if the purpose is to not bring a person to justice. The ICC is not a supranational court of human rights, which assesses the respect of them by national courts and tribunals. Even if the ICC has to respect them in its procedures and trials, what is happening at the national level does not concern if it is not an obstacle of the fight for impunity. If it were otherwise, the Court would not meet its objectives and could overflow.

C. *Katanga* and *Lubanga* judgments

In 2014, the ICC issued one condemnation judgment (in the *Katanga* Case) and one appeal judgment (in the *Lubanga* Case). In both, legal contribution is more related to the forms of responsibility (1) than the definition of crimes (2), which seems to be now approximately clear.

FORMS OF RESPONSIBILITY

Concerning the forms of responsibility, the *Katanga* Judgment is important:[36] on the one hand (and particularly) because of the use of the Regulation 55 of the Regulations of the Court; and, on the other hand, because the judges clarified the definition of contribution to the commission of a crime, as stated by Article 25-3-d of the Rome Statute.

[35] Ibid., §230.
[36] ICC, *The Prosecutor v Germain Katanga*, Jugement rendu en application de l'article 74 du Statut, Chambre de première instance, ICC-01/04-01/07, 7 March 2014.

Regulation 55 enabled Judges to condemn M. Katanga by virtue of his responsibility for acts concerning that for which he was not indicted. M. Katanga was indicted, by virtue of Article 25-3-a, which targets persons who commit a 'crime, whether as an individual, jointly with another or through another person, regardless of whether that other person is criminally responsible', the 'so-called' author and co-author responsibility. With this responsibility, M. Katanga was indicted for the following crimes: wilful killing as a war crime under Article 8-2-a-i of the Statute; murder as a crime against humanity under Article 7-1-a of the Statute; directing an attack against a civilian population as such or against individual civilians not taking direct part in hostilities, as a war crime under Article 8-2-b-i of the Statute; destruction of property as a war crime under Article 8-2-b-xiii of the Statute; and pillaging as a war crime under Article 8-2-b-xvi of the Statute, in the knowledge that this crime would occur in the ordinary course of events; and, jointly committing, within the meaning of Article 25-3-a of the Statute, the war crime of using children under the age of fifteen years to participate actively in the hostilities, under Article 8-2-b-xxvi of the Statute. M. Katanga was condemned for murder as crime against humanity and for four war crimes, but this condemnation was founded under Article 25-3-d and not under Article 25-3-a of the Rome Statute.

This modification of charges is possible by the Regulation 55, which states that 'in its decision under article 74, the Chamber may change the legal characterization of facts to accord with the crimes under Articles 6, 7, or 8, or to accord with the form of participation of the accused under Articles 25 and 28, without exceeding the facts and circumstances described in the charges and any amendments to the charges'. But, what was very problematic in the *Katanga* case was the time when the Judges made the change. The Judges made the modification after the defence of Katanga had made many of its arguments against the Article 25-3-a responsibility. The modification was particularly based on these arguments. According to Judge Van den Wyngaert, who issued a strong minority opinion at the same time of the judgment,[37] many authors analysed the modification as a violation of fair trial and the right against self-incrimination.[38] Analysing Regulation 55, Judge Van den Wyngaert denounced its use in the *Katanga* case. For her, this use violated various accused's rights: the right not to be compelled to testify and the right to be informed of the charges and to have adequate time and

[37] ICC, *The Prosecutor v Germain Katanga*, Jugement rendu en application de l'article 74 du Statut, Chambre de première instance, Minority Opinion of Judge Christine Van den Wyngaert, ICC-01/04-01/07-3436-AnxI, 7 March 2014.

[38] Ambos, K., 2014, 'A Workshop, a Symposium and the Katanga Trial Judgment of 7 March 2014', *Journal of International Criminal Justice*, vol. 12, pp. 219–229; Heller, K. J., 'Another Terrible Day for the OTP', in Opinio Juris, 6 March 2014, consulted on 28 February 2015 in <http://opiniojuris.org/2014/03/08/another-terrible-day-otp/>; Jacobs, D., 2014, 'The ICC Katanga Judgment: A Commentary (part 1): Investigation, Interpretation and The Crimes'. In *Spreading the Jam*, 10 March 2014, consulted on 28 February 2015 in <http://dovjacobs.com/2014/03/10/the-icc-katanga-judgment-a-commentary-part-1-investigation-interpretation-and-the-crimes/>.

facilities for the preparation of the defence. Some academics have considered that M. Katanga should have been acquitted before the modification of the form of responsibility and that he was tried by his own accuser.[39] Judge Van den Wyngaert agreed with this analysis when she spoke about the 'Majority case' in the dissenting opinion.

There are two further clusters of comments. First, concerning the use of Regulation 55, it has to be strictly read in order to protect the right to have a fair trial. Moreover, the term 'facts and circumstances' written in the Regulation have to be better defined and clarified. Finally, protection against self-incrimination should be provided; if not, many accused will not take the risk of testifying during an ICC Trial and will only use their right to remain silent. International criminal justice will then be all the more opaque.

My second comment is related to the dissenting opinion made by Judge Van den Wyngaert (it is some 170 pages long) and, specifically, the Concurring Opinion of Judges Fatoumata Diarra and Bruno Cotte.[40] To our knowledge, this is the first time that the majority of Judges have issued an opinion declaring that they agree with themselves. Once again, this demonstrates that the dissenting opinion should be banned in (international) criminal law.[41] Dissenting opinions are not understood by the accused and they give rise to doubt about the decision made by the court. Moreover, one could question if, with a dissenting opinion, the secrecy of deliberations is respected.

Lastly, in the *Katanga* case, Judge Van den Wyngaert did not sign the judgment. Perhaps this is only an oversight. But if not, one could question the validity of the judgment (even if nothing is written in constitutive texts of the ICC) or the respect of the Code of Judicial Ethics[42] by the non-signature of the judgment, even if this Code is only a guideline 'on the essential ethical standards required of judges in the performance of their duties'.

[39] Jacobs, D., 2014, 'The ICC Katanga Judgment: A Commentary (part 2): Regulation 55 and the Modes of Liability'. In Spreading the Jam, 10 March 2014, consulted on 28 February 2015 in <http://dovjacobs.com/2014/03/11/the-icc-katanga-judgment-a-commentary-part-2-regulation-55-and-the-modes-of-liability/>.

[40] ICC, *The Prosecutor v Katanga*, Jugement rendu en application de l'article 74 du Statut, Concurring opinion of Judges Fatoumata Diarra and Bruno Cotte, ICC-01/04-01/07-2426-AnxII, 7 March 2014.

[41] Scalia, D., 'Jurisprudence in the Ad Hoc International Criminal Tribunals in 2012: Contributions and Controversy. In *The War Report 2012*, edited by Casey-Malsen, S., Oxford: OUP, p. 472.

[42] As a reminder, see the following articles of the code:

Article 3 Judicial independence

1. Judges shall uphold the independence of their office and the authority of the Court and shall conduct themselves accordingly in carrying out their judicial functions.
2. Judges shall not engage in any activity which is likely to interfere with their judicial functions or to affect confidence in their independence.

Article 4 Impartiality

1. Judges shall be impartial and ensure the appearance of impartiality in the discharge of their judicial functions.
2. Judges shall avoid any conflict of interest, or being placed in a situation which might reasonably be perceived as giving rise to a conflict of interest.

That said, the *Katanga* Judgment has also clarified the form of responsibility stated at Article 25-3-d. First, the Court started explaining that this article allows '*de retenir la responsabilité de personnes ayant contribué 'de toute autre manière' à un crime relevant de la compétence de la Cour*'.[43] So it is a residual form of responsibility allowing for the condemnation of people who have not participated under Article 25-3-c of the Rome Statute.[44] The Chamber then defines the participation as follows: '*les personnes qui ont commis le crime faisaient partie d'un groupe de personnes agissant de concert dans la poursuite d'un dessein commun; l'accusé a contribué de manière significative à la commission du crime; la contribution était intentionnelle; et la contribution de l'accusé a été faite en pleine connaissance de l'intention du groupe de personnes de commettre le crime*'.[45] The more important elements are the common purpose and the contribution of the accused. The criminal objective implies the definition of the purpose pursued (it has to be criminal, even if it is not a crime under the jurisdiction of the court[46]), its impact, the victims, and the members of the group, even if all persons are not identified.[47] Moreover, the accused is not necessarily a member of the group, but his contribution should be significant. That means that '*qu'elle aura influencé soir sur la survenance du crime soit sur la manière dont il a été commis, soit les deux*'.[48] Thus, it means that the crime does not necessarily depend on the contribution:[49] it is not necessary to establish a direct link between the behaviour of the accomplice and that of the principal author.[50] Finally, the accused has to be aware of the intent of the group when he provided his contribution.[51]

Article 5 Integrity

1. Judges shall conduct themselves with probity and integrity in accordance with their office, thereby enhancing public confidence in the judiciary.
2. Judges shall not directly or indirectly accept any gift, advantage, privilege or reward that can reasonably be perceived as being intended to influence the performance of their judicial functions.

Article 6 Confidentiality

Judges shall respect the confidentiality of consultations which relate to their judicial functions and the secrecy of deliberations.

Article 7 Diligence

1. Judges shall act diligently in the exercise of their duties and shall devote their professional activities to those duties.
2. Judges shall take reasonable steps to maintain and enhance the knowledge, skills and personal qualities necessary for judicial office.
3. Judges shall perform all judicial duties properly and expeditiously.
4. Judges shall deliver their decisions and any other rulings without undue delay.

[43] ICC, *The Prosecutor v Germain Katanga,* Jugement rendu en application de l'article 74 du Statut, Trial Chamber, ICC-01/04-01/07, 7 March 2014, §1618.

[44] Ibid. [45] Ibid., §1620. [46] Ibid., §1627.

[47] Ibid., §1626. [48] Ibid., §1633. [49] Ibid. [50] Ibid., §1635. [51] Ibid., §1642.

Concerning the form of responsibility, in another judgment (the *Lubanga* case[52]), the Appeals Chamber of the ICC clarified the intent of the co-author under Article 25-3-a. In this case, the Trial Chamber stated that 'it is necessary, as a minimum, for the prosecution to establish the common plan included a critical element of criminality, namely that, its implementation embodied a sufficient risk that, if events follow the ordinary course, a crime will be committed'.[53] The Appeals Chamber found that the 'reference to "risk" should have been avoided when interpreting article 30 (2) of the Statute'.[54]

DEFINITION OF CERTAIN CRIMES

In relation to the definition of crimes, the *Lubanga* judgment clarified the 'active participation of hostilities' contained in Article 8-2-e-vii of the Rome Statute ('Conscripting or enlisting children under the age of fifteen years into armed forces or groups or using them to participate actively in hostilities'). This sentence is distinguished by the 'direct participation of hostilities' used by the international humanitarian law. The Trial Chamber decided that '[t]he decisive factor, therefore, in deciding if an "indirect" role is to be treated as active participation in hostilities is whether the support provided by the child to the combatants exposed him or her to real danger as a potential target'.[55] It means that 'active participation' is broader than 'direct participation'. The Appeals Chamber first stated that Article 8-2-e-vii should not have been interpreted 'so as to only refer to forms of direct participation in armed hostilities, as understood in the context of the principle of distinction and Common Article 3'.[56] However, it has concluded that the element of the 'potential target' is not a good one. The main element is the 'link between the activity and the hostilities'.[57] Here, 'although the extent to which the child was exposed to risk due to the activity in which he or she was engaged may well be an indicator of the existence of a sufficiently close relationship between the activity of the child and the hostilities, an assessment of such risk cannot replace an assessment of the relationship itself'.[58]

According to Judge Sang-Hyun Song,[59] it is worth noting that in the same decision, the Appeals Chamber did not clarify the question concerning the elements contained in Article 8-2-e-vii. Does the article identify three crimes (conscription, enlistment, and use) or three behaviours relating to one crime? The Trial Chamber stated that 'the use of the word "or" in Article 8(2)(e)(vii)' means the three behaviours 'are separate

[52] ICC, *The Prosecutor v Thomas Lubanga Dyilo,* Jugement rendu en application de l'article 74 du Statut, Trial Chamber, ICC-01/04-01/06-2842, 14 March 2012.

[53] Ibid., §984.

[54] ICC, *The Prosecutor v Thomas Lubanga Dyilo,* Judgment on the appeal of Mr Thomas Lubanga Dyilo against his conviction, Appeals Chamber, ICC-01/04-01/06A 5, 1 December 2014, §449.

[55] Ibid.

[56] Ibid., §328.

[57] Ibid., §333.

[58] Ibid.

[59] Ibid. Partly Dissenting Opinion of Judge Sang-Hyun Song.

offences'.[60] According to Judge Sang-Huyn Song, the Appeals Chamber could have taken the opportunity to overturn the Trial Chamber Decision.[61]

D. **Penalties**

In conclusion, this chapter will make some comments on the penalties pronounced in the *Katanga* judgment. The judgment pronounces the second penalty issued by the ICC (the first one was pronounced in the *Lubanga* case in 2012). M. Katanga was condemned to twelve years of imprisonment by a decision issued on 23 May 2014.[62] It is worth noting that Judges made a clear and instructive decision. First of all, the decision recalls principles taken into consideration to choose the tariff of penalties: gravity of crimes, aggravating and mitigating circumstances, etc.[63] Related to the gravity of crimes, the judges explained that all crimes under the jurisdiction of the court have not the same gravity: crimes against goods should be less punished than crimes against people.[64]

More important is the fact that judges have explained the purposes of the penalties.[65] The Trial Chamber stated that penalties pursued two important goals: retribution ('*c'est-à-dire l'expression de la réprobation sociale qui entoure l'acte criminel et son auteur et qui est aussi une manière de reconnaître le préjudice et les souffrances causées aux victimes*' [66]) and general deterrence ('*dont l'objectif est de détourner de leur projet d'éventuels candidats à la perpétration de crimes similaires*'[67]). Moreover, for the judges, the punishment should target the restoration of peace and reconciliation of people. Finally, the rehabilitation of condemned people has to be taken into consideration '*même si, en particulier en droit pénal international, cet objectif ne saurait être considéré comme prédominant car la peine ne peut, à elle seule, assurer la réinsertion du coupable*'.[68] Although these elements are well known by academics, international criminal law judgments forget them all too often. Furthermore, judges stated that fundamental principles of criminal law (legality, proportionality, and individualization) have to be respected.[69] This is unusual in international criminal law. One could hope that this pedagogic judgment is the first of many to come.

[60] ICC, *The Prosecutor v Thomas Lubanga Dyilo,* Jugement rendu en application de l'article 74 du Statut, Trial Chamber, ICC-01/04-01/06-2842, 14 March 2012, §609.

[61] Ibid. Partly Dissenting Opinion of Judge Sang-Hyun Song.

[62] ICC, *The Prosecutor v Germain Katanga,* Décision relative à la peine (article 76 du Statut), Trial Chamber, ICC-01/04-01/07, 23 May 2014.

[63] Ibid., §§33–34. [64] Ibid., §43.

[65] They did not do the same in the first decision on penalties in the *Lubanga* case.

[66] Ibid., §38.

[67] Ibid., §38. [68] Ibid., §38. [69] Ibid., §39.

16 Transitional justice mechanisms: challenges and opportunities

Valentina Cadelo[1]

Introduction

There is currently wider acknowledgment that it is preferable for societies emerging from armed conflict[2] to tap into a rich repertoire of transitional justice initiatives[3] rather than to rely upon a single mechanism. Reflecting on the United Nations (UN) experience in post conflict settings, the UN Secretary-General stressed that 'strategies must be holistic, incorporating integrated attention to individual prosecutions, reparations, truth seeking, institutional reform, vetting or dismissals, or an appropriately conceived combination thereof'.[4] He also underlined that 'the United Nations must consider

[1] Valentina Cadelo is a researcher at the Geneva Academy of International Humanitarian Law and Human Rights and a PhD candidate at the Faculty of Law, University of Geneva. Her main area of research is reparation for gross violations of human rights and serious violations of international humanitarian law.

[2] The expression 'societies emerging from armed conflict' is understood here as comprising situations in which armed conflict is still ongoing as well as post conflict situations.

[3] Transitional justice is commonly described as comprising the mechanisms and processes associated with a society's attempts to come to terms with a legacy of large-scale past abuses, in order to ensure accountability, serve justice, and achieve reconciliation. These may include both judicial and non-judicial mechanisms, with differing levels of international involvement (or none at all) and individual prosecutions, reparations, truth seeking, institutional reform, vetting and dismissals, or a combination thereof. See UN Secretary-General, 'The rule of law and transitional justice in conflict and post-conflict societies', 23 August 2004, UN doc. S/2004/616, §8 (hereafter, UNSG, Report 2004). The field of transitional justice has grown greatly in the past three decades. For an overview of its historical development and conception see, for example: Roht-Arriaza, N., Mariezcurrena, J. (eds.), 2006, *Transitional Justice in the Twenty-First Century: Beyond Truth Versus Justice*, Cambridge: Cambridge University Press.

[4] UNSG, Report 2004, §26. The importance of adopting a comprehensive strategy to address gross violations of human rights and serious violations of international humanitarian law has also been stressed by the Special Rapporteur on the promotion of truth, justice, reparation and guarantees of non-recurrence in his first annual report to the Human Rights Council. See 'Report of the Special Rapporteur on the promotion of truth, justice, reparation and guarantees of non-recurrence, Pablo de Greiff', 9 August 2012, A/HRC/21/46, §§22–27 (hereafter SR, Annual Report 2012).

through advance planning and consultation how different transitional justice mechanisms will interact to ensure that they do not conflict with one another'.[5]

The rationale behind adopting a holistic approach has a pragmatic beginning and a conceptual end.[6] At the outset, it is necessary to bear in mind the context in which transitional justice measures operate. Weak judicial and security institutions usually characterize societies emerging from armed conflict. Likewise, socio-economic and political challenges often prevent or hinder the recovery process.[7] As armed conflict and post conflict societies are very complex environments, accountability efforts cannot but include a coherent set of measures that will seek to address the justice needs of conflict-affected communities, including victims, while at the same time saving resources and promoting political stability. The second argument in favour of adopting a holistic approach relates to the limited reach of each of the measures that are part of a transitional justice policy. Today, there is no country that can legitimately claim complete success in this field.[8] Clearly, the multiplicity of goals, challenges, and constituencies present in the wake of armed conflict are unlikely to be satisfied by a single initiative.[9] Thus, the weakness of each of these measures cannot but provide a powerful incentive to seek ways in which each can interact with the others in order to overcome their respective constraints.[10] This holds even more true if we consider the interrelationship that exists among the different transitional justice measures.[11] As stated above, however, implementing a holistic

[5] UNSG, Report 2004, §26.

[6] de Greiff, P., 2012, 'Theorizing Transitional Justice'. In *Transitional Justice*, edited by Williams, M., Nagy, R., and Elster J., New York: New York University Press, pp. 32–3. See also Boraine, A. L., 2006, 'Transitional Justice: A Holistic Interpretation', *Journal of International Affairs*, vol. 60 no. 1: p. 17.

[7] See UN Secretary-General, 'The rule of law and transitional justice in conflict and post-conflict societies, 12 October 2011, UN doc. S/2011/634, §7 (hereafter, UNSG, Report 2011). In particular, the Secretary-General noted that in the aftermath of armed conflict '[i]nstitutional actors may prove to be incapable or unwilling to pursue accountability for serious crimes of the past. Civil society is not yet in a position to hold institutions accountable. In the absence of responsive Government, large swathes of the population may turn to belligerents for their justice and security needs, lending legitimacy to terrorist organizations and warlords. Civic trust is at a nadir, undermining collective efforts to meet rule of law challenges. The risk of relapse into violent conflict only increases with time'.

[8] de Greiff, P., 'Theorizing Transitional Justice', p. 35.

[9] Interestingly, field research suggest that implementing only one type of transitional justice mechanism does not strengthen human rights protections and, in some cases, has a reverse correlation. See for instance Olsen, T., Payne, L., Reiter, A., and Wiebelhaus-Brahm, E., 2010, 'When Truth Commissions Improve Human Rights', International Journal of Transitional Justice, vol. 4, no. 3: 457, at p. 463.

[10] de Greiff, P., 'Theorizing Transitional Justice', 35. See also Sirleaf, M., 2013, 'Beyond Truth and Punishment in Transitional Justice', *Virginia Journal of International Law* vol. 54 no. 2: p. 223.

[11] By way of example, let us think about the relationship between reparation and truth telling. It is generally understood that providing reparations in the absence of truth telling could give victims a reason to think that the benefits that they get are an attempt to buy their acquiescence. However, just as reparations seem to call for truth telling if the benefits are interpreted as a justice measure, truth-telling seems to call for reparations if words are seen, in the end, as a form or reparation. See de Greiff, P., 'Theorizing Transitional Justice', p. 37.

approach is not only reasonable for practical reasons. There are also some theoretical arguments to take into account. The UN Special Rapporteur on the promotion of truth, justice, reparation and guarantees of non-recurrence, for example, pointed out that combining a set of different measures is likely to best address transitional settings, including post conflict societies, given the two mediate goals—providing recognition to victims and fostering civic trust—and two ultimate objectives—reconciliation and democratization—that all of these mechanisms share.[12]

Against this background, this chapter seeks to examine the value of adopting a holistic approach in the wake of armed conflict. Given that much attention is already devoted to prosecution mechanisms, this chapter will instead look at how other components of transitional justice—truth seeking, reparation, and institutional reform, or a combination thereof—may contribute to the promotion of accountability and, at the same time, offer comprehensive responses to the justice and reconciliation needs of the victims and communities affected by armed conflict. The chapter is divided into three parts. Section A opens with an overview of the contribution and limits of prosecution in the wake of armed conflict. Section B looks at the other three transitional justice pillars, namely truth seeking, reparation, and institutional reform. In so doing, attention is given in particular to the various mechanisms and measures through which these principles are implemented. Section C concludes with an overview of transitional justice practice in 2014.

A. The contribution and limits of prosecution

The investigation and prosecution of international crimes is a critical component of any transitional justice effort. Prosecutions help strengthen the rule of law, reflect a new set of social norms, and begin the process of reforming and building trust in government institutions. Trials can also be a source of comfort for victims. When conducted in ways that reflect victims' needs and expectations, for instance, they can play a vital role in restoring their dignity and delivering justice. But prosecutions cannot achieve justice in isolation. This is due to two main reasons. On the one hand, when violations are widespread and systematic—as it is often the case in armed conflict situations—criminal justice systems simply cannot cope.[13] The large-scale nature of these crimes means that

[12] SR, Annual Report 2012, §§28–46. Many scholars have recently attempted to articulate the goals of transitional justice. See, for example Elster J., 2012 'Justice, Truth, Peace', in Williams M., Nagy R., Elster J. (eds.), *Transitional Justice*, New York: New York University Press, pp. 78–97.

[13] This is because the criminal justice process must demonstrate a scrupulous commitment to fairness and due process and this necessarily entails a significant commitment of time and resources. See van Zyl P., 'Promoting Transitional Justice in Post-Conflict Societies', in Bryden A., Hänggi H. (eds.), 2005, *Security Governance in Post-Conflict Peacebuilding*, Geneva: DCAF, p. 211.

they cannot be processed through the ordinary criminal justice system. It is a matter of fact that effective prosecution strategies for large-scale crimes often focus on the planners and organizers of these crimes, rather than on those that have a lower rank or level of responsibility. On the other hand, it is important to note that, from the victims' perspective, justice carries multiple meanings, criminal accountability is not necessarily the highest priority, and attitudes often change over time.[14] Indeed, empirical research over the past fifteen years regarding the attitudes of victims and communities suggests a more complex understanding of the meaning of justice for those living in the aftermath of armed conflict.[15]

To be clear, to recognize the limits of criminal justice systems should not be understood as a delegitimization of the role of prosecution. The establishment of different criminal tribunals worldwide has greatly helped bring justice and hope to victims, combat the impunity of perpetrators, and enrich the jurisprudence of international criminal law. Moreover, the importance of the Nuremberg trials, the prosecutions at the two ad hoc tribunals for the former Yugoslavia and Rwanda, and the more recent steps undertaken by the International Criminal Court (ICC) should not be diminished solely on the basis that they represent a small fraction of the total number of criminally responsible individuals.

Nevertheless, it is important to recognize that criminal justice can only ever be a partial response in situations of transition from armed conflict to peace. As stated above, different mechanisms may strengthen or compensate for the limited mandates of, and contextual constraints placed upon, prosecution. Truth commissions, for instance, are likely to bring a degree of clarity and accountability in those cases where it is institutionally and politically impossible to prosecute more than a small portion of the alleged perpetrators of crime.[16] Similarly, providing reparations—even in the form of memorials—may contribute to addressing the harm caused by the violations, as well as to respond in a more adequate manner to victims' justice claims.[17] Last, but not least,

[14] Weinstein H. M., et al., 2010, 'Stay the Hand of Justice: Whose Priorities Take Priority?', in Shaw R., Waldorf L., Hazan P. (eds.), Localizing Transitional Justice: Interventions and Priorities After Mass Violence, Stanford: Stanford University Press, pp. 37–46.

[15] See, for example, Yakintou C., 2014, 'Living with the Shadows of the Past. The Impact of Disappearance on Wives of the Missing in Lebanon', New York: International Center of Transitional Justice (ICTJ), at pp. 24–5, <https://www.ictj.org/publication/living-shadows-past-impact-disappearance-wives-missing-lebanon>; ICTJ Briefing 'Confronting Impunity and Engendering Transitional Justice Processes in Northern Uganda', June 2014, <https://www.ictj.org/sites/default/files/ICTJ-Uganda-GenderBriefing-New-2014.pdf>. See also the series of empirical studies on conflict-affected communities carried out by the Human Rights Center at the University of California, Berkeley. The studies focused on different countries, including Liberia, Cambodia, Uganda, Central African Republic, Democratic Republic of Congo, and Iraq, <https://www.law.berkeley.edu/centers/human-rights-center/publications/reports/>.

[16] Lawry-White M., 2015, 'The Reparative Effect of Truth Seeking in Transitional Justice', *International and Comparative Law Quarterly* Vol. 64(1): p. 141.

[17] See for instance de Greiff P., 2008, 'Justice and Reparations', in de Greiff P. (ed.) *The Handbook of Reparations*, Oxford: Oxford University Press, pp. 455–66.

vetting can play a role in establishing non-criminal accountability for certain violations, particularly in contexts where it is impossible to prosecute all those responsible.[18] Broader institutional capacity building, in turn, can provide a safer environment for authorities to conduct investigations.[19]

Ultimately, it is important to recall that societies emerging from armed conflict pursue a richer and broader definition of justice, which seeks not only to confront perpetrators, but also to address the needs of victims and assist the beginning of a process of reconciliation and transformation.[20] This means that, throughout the entire transition process, accountability efforts must be balanced with the need to build a stable society and a sustainable peace, in which both the rule of law and reconciliation can flourish. In that context, only a combination of complementary mechanisms can promote all these goals comprehensively.

B. Toward a comprehensive approach: truth seeking, reparation, and institutional reform

TRUTH SEEKING

The past years have seen a steady increase in the establishment and use of various truth seeking mechanisms ranging from State-sanctioned truth commissions to 'unofficial' truth-seeking processes, which are carried out by civil society groups, including victims' organizations.[21] Truth seeking has also been pursued at the international level by establishing commissions of inquiry and fact-finding missions.[22]

[18] See Mayer-Rieckh A., 2007, 'On Preventing Abuse: Vetting and Other Transitional Reforms', in de Greiff P., Mayer-Rieckh A. (eds.), *Justice as Prevention: Vetting Public Employees in Transitional Societies*, New York: Social Science Research Council, pp. 484–5. See also Kritz N. J., 1996, 'Coming to Terms with Atrocities: A Review of Accountability Mechanisms for Mass Violations of Human Rights', *Law and Contemporary Problems* Vol. 59 (4): 127, p. 139.

[19] UNSG, Report 2011, §20.

[20] Boraine A. L., 'Transitional Justice: A Holistic Interpretation', pp. 17–18.

[21] Some of them have produced important reports, including Brazil's Nunca Mais, Guatemala's Proyecto Interdiocesano de Recuperación de la Memoria Histórica (REHMI), Uruguay's Nunca Más, Northern Ireland's Ardoyne: the Untold Truth, and Greenbsoro's Truth and Reconciliation Commission's Final Report.

[22] See for example, the Independent International Commission of Inquiry on the Syrian Arab Republic, which was established on 22 August 2011 by the UN Human Rights Council (HRC) through resolution A/HRC/RES/S-17/1 with a mandate to investigate all alleged violations of international human rights law since March 2011 in the Syrian Arab Republic. See also the United Nations Independent Commission of Inquiry on the 2014 Gaza Conflict, which was established on 23 July 2014 by the HRC pursuant to resolution A/HRC/RES/S-21/1, with the mandate to investigate all violations of international humanitarian law and

Despite the increasing recourse to truth-seeking mechanisms, the notion of 'truth' remains rather complex. As highlighted by some scholars, a number of assumptions—such as the positive interaction between truth and reconciliation—currently contribute to oversimplifying what truth really means.[23] The understanding of the notion of truth with regards to serious violations of human rights and international humanitarian law (IHL) varies depending on the beneficiaries, be they individuals, the community, or the society as a whole. Ultimately, truth seeking now also has a legal dimension given the emergence of a right to know the truth. In a similar way, establishing the truth has some important legal implications, especially when it comes to ascertaining facts of a certain gravity or scale and specificity.[24]

Truth seeking: a multifaceted notion

Establishing the truth primarily means to ascertain what really happened. In armed conflict and post conflict situations, each side tends to claim that abuses were committed or to deny responsibility. This reinforces the need to determine the factual truth to distinguish between alleged violations that turn out to be unfounded and proven acts.[25]

Determining that violations have occurred, however, is only one element of truth seeking. As noted in the OHCHR Study on the right to truth, seeking the truth implies knowing 'the full and complete truth as to the events that transpired, their specific circumstances, and who participated in them, including knowing the circumstances in which the violations took place, as well as the reasons for them'.[26]

international human rights law in the Occupied Palestinian Territory, including East Jerusalem, particularly in the occupied Gaza Strip, in the context of the military operations conducted since 13 June 2014. A few months before, on 27 March 2014, pursuant to resolution A/HRC/25/1, the HRC also requested the UN High Commissioner for Human Rights (OHCHR) to 'undertake a comprehensive investigation into alleged serious violations and abuses of human rights and related crimes by both parties in Sri Lanka during the period covered by the Lessons Learnt and Reconciliation Commission, and to establish the facts and circumstances of such alleged violations and of the crimes perpetrated with a view to avoiding impunity and ensuring accountability, with assistance from relevant experts and special procedures mandate holders'.

[23] See Boutruche T., 2013, 'Seeking the Truth About Serious International Human Rights and Humanitarian Law Violations: The Various Facets of a Cardinal Notion of Transitional Justice', in Matthee M., Toebes B., Brus M. (eds.) *Armed Conflict and International Law: In Search of the Human Face*, The Hague: Springer, p. 305; Clark J., 2011, 'Transitional Justice, truth, and reconciliation: an under-explored relationship', *International Criminal Law Review* Vol.11: 241, p. 248. The Special Rapporteur on the promotion of truth, justice, reparation and guarantees of non-recurrence also noted that reconciliation is not a function that a truth commission can bring about on its own. See 'Report of the Special Rapporteur on the promotion of truth, justice, reparation and guarantees of non-recurrence, Pablo de Greiff', 28 August 2013, A/HRC/24/42, §102 (d) (hereafter, SR, Annual Report 2013).

[24] Boutruche T., 'Seeking the Truth About Serious International Human Rights and Humanitarian Law Violations', p. 305.

[25] Boutruche T., 'Seeking the Truth About Serious International Human Rights and Humanitarian Law Violations', p. 306.

[26] OHCHR, Promotion and Protection of Human Rights—Study on the Right to the Truth, UN doc E/CN.4/2006/91, 8 February 2006, §59.

In the context of societies addressing the scores of violations committed, this is of particular significance. First, by establishing the circumstances of the violations, truth seeking allows governments, victims, and perpetrators to acknowledge the wrongfulness of a given act. Providing the victims with a voice in the public discourse, for instance, can help to rebut official lies and myths regarding human rights and humanitarian law violations and thus help to restore the rule of law. Second, as knowing the identity of the perpetrators is part of the general process of truth seeking, truth seeking significantly contributes to promoting criminal accountability. Third, by determining the causes for the violations, truth seeking enhances the prospects of dealing constructively with historical grievances and, at the same time, helps future generations to inoculate against revisionism and return to violence.

The value of truth seeking is also exemplified by its healing function in restoring personal dignity to victims, often after years of stigmatization. At the end of hostilities, or after a peaceful settlement, societies affected by armed conflict may be tempted to just turn the page, to forget, and move on.[27] At first this does not sound surprising. Indeed, repressing bad memories seems a rather natural reaction for human beings.[28] What is problematic, however, is the fact that, although memory can be repressed for a while, this cannot be done forever. Victims, in particular, cannot forget. Giving victims an official truth may thus help to reduce their sense of outrage and suffering. In fact, not knowing the truth is intrinsically related to the trauma suffered by the victims. The most significant example in armed conflict situations is the case of the relatives of missing persons, people whose fate or whereabouts is unknown.[29] The problems that family members of missing persons face are complex and can be overwhelming. Relatives often spend years searching for their loved ones, suffer from symptoms of complicated grief, and often find it hard to cope with necessary activities at work and at home. Most importantly, this uncertainty prevents relatives from engaging in the mourning process and healing.[30]

While knowing the truth plays a primary role for victims, truth seeking also has a collective dimension. Very often, armed conflicts result in massive violations and collective traumas, which affect entire communities and society as a whole. In similar contexts,

[27] Michel N. and del Mar K., 2014, 'Transitional Justice', in Clapham A. and Gaeta P. (eds.), *The Oxford Handbook of International Law in Armed Conflict*, Oxford: Oxford University Press, p. 849.

[28] See Michel N. and del Mar K., 'Transitional Justice', at 849, quoting nobel peace prize laureate Elie Weisel who in 1986, reflecting upon human beings' ability to both forget and remember, stated that '[o]f course we could try to forget the past. Why not? Is it not natural for a human being to repress what causes him pain, what causes him shame? Like the body, memory protects its wounds... [However] [r]emembering is a noble and necessary act'.

[29] See Martin S., 2002, 'The Missing', *International Review of the Red Cross* Vol. 84 No. 848: 723, p. 724.

[30] Blaauw M., Lähteenmäk V., 2002, 'Denial and silence or acknowledgement and disclosure', *International Review of the Red Cross* Vol. 84 No. 848: 767, pp. 767–72.

seeking the truth about such massive violations becomes a necessary condition for the affected communities and society to recover.[31]

Truth seeking under international law

Two additional elements of truth seeking that are worth noting concern its legal implications—i.e., the impact that truth seeking might have on the legal qualifications of specific categories of acts—and its legal character—as an individual and a collective right—under international law.

Starting from the former, it is important to note that there is a close link between truth seeking and the legal qualification of certain acts. In some cases, truth seeking significantly contributes to determining the gravity or the specificity of a particular act.[32] Let us think, for example, about crimes against humanity. In some contexts, in the absence of truth telling, it is particularly difficult to determine the necessary elements required for that international crime to exist. The same holds true, for instance, for other international crimes, such as genocide and war crimes. In these contexts, thus, truth seeking can be of particular importance as it could help to shed some light when it is impossible to get all the necessary information.

The right to know the truth finds its origins in IHL, in particular in regard to the right of families to know the fate of their relatives together with the obligation of parties to armed conflict to search for missing persons.[33] Today, the right to the truth is explicitly recognized in a number of international law instruments and by intergovernmental mechanisms. The existence of this right is accepted by State practice consisting in both jurisprudential precedent and by the establishment of various truth-seeking mechanisms.[34]

Considering the truth as a right has some relevant implications. On the one hand, in as much as it concerns the victims, it constitutes great progress as it provides a normative framework for the protection of individuals in the context of violations

[31] A psychiatrist, for instance, noted that 'remembering and telling the truth about terrible events are prerequisites both for the restoration of the social order and for the healing of the individual victims'. See Herman J., 2001, *Trauma and Recovery: the aftermath of violence from domestic abuse to political terror*, London: Pandora, p. 1.

[32] Boutruche T., 'Seeking the Truth About Serious International Human Rights and Humanitarian Law Violations', pp. 313–5.

[33] In 2006 the OHCHR released a study on the right to truth that concluded 'the right to truth about gross human rights violations and serious violations of humanitarian law is an inalienable and autonomous right'. The study traced the development of the right to its origins in 1949 as part of the Geneva Conventions, described the historical and legal basis for such a right, and noted its expression in the 2005 Updated Set of Principles for the protection and promotion of human rights through action to combat impunity. See OHCHR, 'Study on the right to the truth', 8 February 2006, E/CN.4/2006/91, §5 (hereafter, OHCHR, Study 2006).

[34] OHCHR, Study 2006, §§9–24.

of human rights and humanitarian law. On the other hand, it raises some issues, taking into account the complexity of the notion of truth at the individual and collective level, as well as the different perceptions—and expectations—of the truth that victims have. Without going further into the debate, it is sufficient here to note that, while the core elements of the right to truth are well established, international law is still in a phase of development with respect to its broader scope of application and content.[35]

Truth commissions

Truth commissions are commonly defined as 'official, temporary, non-judicial fact-finding bodies that investigate a pattern of abuses of human rights or humanitarian law committed over a number of years'.[36] Over the past three decades, some forty official truth commissions have been created to provide an account of past abuse.[37]

The core activities of many truth commissions include the collecting of statements from victims, witnesses, and perpetrators; researching and investigating the root causes of an armed conflict; holding public hearings; engaging in outreach programmes; and issuing a final report that summarizes the truth commission's findings and recommendations.[38]

As noted by the UN Special Rapporteur on the promotion of truth, justice, reparation, and guarantees of non-recurrence, truth commissions have proven to be capable of making significant contributions, including by providing recognition to victims as rights-holders, fostering civic trust, and strengthening the rule of law.[39] Given the perceived potential of truth commissions, they have become a habitual response to the challenges posed by post conflict situations. Interestingly, some countries have even implemented similar mechanisms in the absence of a political transition and while

[35] See Boutruche T., 'Seeking the Truth About Serious International Human Rights and Humanitarian Law Violations', pp. 311–3, highlighting some of the concerns that this right raises when it is addressed in the framework of criminal justice and, for instance, when perpetrators are named pursuant to an extrajudicial mechanism. It is also important to note that the right to the truth is now commonly interpreted as encompassing a large array of subsumed rights. For example, these include: the right of relatives and communities to commemorate and mourn human loss in forms that are culturally appropriate and dignified; the State's duties to preserve documentary evidence for commemoration, to guarantee adequate access to archives with information on violations. The right to the truth can also be seen as an extension of freedom of information and freedom of expression. See González E., Varney H., 2013, *Truth Seeking: Elements of Creating an Effective Truth Commission*, New York: International Center for Transitional Justice, p. 3.

[36] UNSG, Report 2004, §50.

[37] Truth commissions have been the object of extensive study in the past years. See, for example, Hayner P., 2011, *Unspeakable Truths. Transitional Justice and the Challenge of Truth Commissions*, 2nd edn, Oxon: Routledge; Guematcha E., 2014, 'Les commissions vérité et les violations des droits de l'homme et du droit international humanitaire, Paris: Pedone.

[38] OHCHR, Truth Commissions 2006, pp. 17–20.

[39] See SR, Annual Report 2013, §24.

conflict is still ongoing. As a result, the mandates of truth commissions now frequently include investigating serious violations of IHL.[40]

While results depend in large part on the way truth commissions are designed and resourced, these mechanisms may face particular challenges in post-conflict settings. Obstacles include for instance the fact that truth commissions must provide an account of violations often perpetrated by a 'multiplicity of agents of violence',[41] ethnic cleavages, and security concerns.[42]

COMMISSIONS OF INQUIRY AND FACT-FINDING MISSIONS

Commissions of inquiry and fact-finding missions have been described as 'ad hoc investigative mechanisms tasked with ascertaining relevant facts and information relating to a situation of human rights or humanitarian concern, by means of which it is determined whether or not the relevant international [norms] have been violated by states or non-state actors'.[43]

Fact-finding mechanisms may constitute a preliminary step to the establishment of transitional justice mechanisms, and involve the collection of first-hand information. While the outcome of their work is also a report that includes conclusions and recommendations, as opposed to truth commissions, fact-finding mechanisms often operate within tighter time constraints. Consequently, they place less emphasis on the participation of victims, and more emphasis on providing a general overview of the events that took place.[44] Fact-finding mechanisms can be established at the international level, typically under the auspices of the United Nations or another international organization, or at the domestic level.[45]

Fact-finding mechanisms can have very narrow scopes of inquiry. In some cases they may only inquire into one particular event that occurred within the broader context of an armed conflict that took place over the course of many months, or even years.[46] The most critical example in this respect is the Bloody Sunday Inquiry, which was established by the House of Commons to inquire into the events of one day—30 January 1972—when

[40] SR, Annual Report 2013, §27. [41] SR, Annual Report 2013, §29.

[42] SR, Annual Report 2013, §29.

[43] Wilkinson S., 2011, *Standards of Proof in International Humanitarian and Human Rights Fact-Finding and Inquiry Missions*, Geneva: Geneva Academy of International Humanitarian Law and Human Rights, p. 11. For another definition of fact-finding mechanisms, see for instance Boutrouche T., 2011, 'Credible fact-finding and allegations of international humanitarian law violations: challenges in theory and practice', *Journal of Conflict and Security Law* Vol. 16 No.1: 105, p. 106.

[44] Michel N. and del Mar K., 'Transitional Justice', p. 854. [45] Ibid. [46] Ibid.

thirteen people were killed by military forces in Londonderry, Northern Ireland.[47] In other cases, these mechanisms may have broader mandates either in terms of temporal or spatial scope. By way of example, the Independent International Fact-Finding Mission on the Conflict in Georgia, which was established by the Council of the European Union, focused its investigations on 'the origins and the course of the conflict in Georgia'.[48]

Like truth commissions, fact-finding mechanisms may contribute significantly to revealing the truth. Many international actors increasingly resort to these mechanisms to address alleged violations that took place in the context of armed conflict or when the hostilities come to an end. However, while fact-finding mechanisms usually verify patterns of violations, in some cases they also have to choose among certain facts, thereby limiting their truth-seeking function.[49] This happened, for instance, to the International Commission of Inquiry in Darfur, which in light of the hundreds of incidents documented had to select the ones that were most representative for the determination of violations of human rights and IHL.[50]

REPARATION

Reparation is a central tenet of transitional justice. It is commonly contemplated in two different ways. On the one hand, reparation is a fundamental obligation placed upon States—and a basic human right—under international law. As such, reparation may take different forms, depending on its scope and beneficiaries. On the other hand, reparation relates to specific administrative programmes that can be implemented in order to provide benefits to victims directly.

Reparation under international law

Reparation is premised on 'a principle of international law, that a breach of an engagement involves an obligation to make reparation in an adequate form'.[51] Accordingly,

[47] See 'Report of The Bloody Sunday Inquiry', 15 June 2010, at <http://webarchive.nationalarchives.gov.uk/20101017060814/http://www.bloody-sunday-inquiry.org/index.html>.

[48] See 'Report of the Independent International Fact-Finding Mission on the Conflict in Georgia', 30 September 2009, at <http://www.refworld.org/docid/4ac45cd22.html>.

[49] Boutruche T., 'Seeking the Truth About Serious International Human Rights and Humanitarian Law Violations', pp. 320–1.

[50] See 'Report of the International Commission of Inquiry on Darfur to the United Nations Secretary-General, pursuant to Security Council Resolution 1564 of 18 September 2004', 25 January 2005, at p. 157, <http://www.un.org/news/dh/sudan/com_inq_darfur.pdf>.

[51] Permanent Court of International Justice (PCIJ), Factory at Chorzów Case (*Germany v Poland*), Jurisdiction, 1927, Ser. A, No. 9, p. 21. See also Art. 31, International Law Commission (ILC) Arts on the Responsibility of States for Internationally Wrongful Acts, UN doc. A/CN.4/L.602/Rev.1, 26 July 2001.

reparation shall comprise all measures aimed at 'restoring justice' through 'wiping out all the consequences' of the harm suffered by the individuals and communities concerned as result of a wrong, and at 're-establishing the situation which would have existed if the wrong had not been produced'.[52]

Despite the fact that reparation is traditionally considered a matter of State responsibility,[53] international law has progressively recognized the right of victims of human rights and humanitarian law violations to pursue their claims for redress and reparation before national judicial mechanisms and international courts. Today, many international and regional instruments confer on victims a right to domestic and international remedies if their rights under these instruments are violated, and States are bound to specific obligations, especially with regard to reparation.[54] Regional human rights mechanisms have also contributed to expanding the concept of reparation.[55] Likewise, recent UN practice and soft law documents have increasingly recognized the existence of such a right.[56] Finally, there is a growing tendency

[52] PCIJ, Factory at Chorzów Case, Judgment (Merits), Ser. A, No. 17, 1928, p. 47. See also commentary to Art. 31, ILC Commentaries on the Draft Articles on Responsibility of States for Internationally Wrongfully Acts, §3.

[53] See for example, Anzillotti D., 1906, 'La responsabilité international des Etats à raison des dommages soufferts par des étrangers', *Revue Générale de Droit International Public*, Vol. 13: 5; Domingo R., 2011, 'Gaius, Vattel and the New Global Law Paradigm', *European Journal of International Law*, Vol. 22, No. 3: 627, p. 634.

[54] See Art. 8, 1948 Universal Declaration of Human Rights. Many human rights instruments stipulate the general obligation of states to provide for—or the right of an individual to receive—an effective remedy. See for example: Art. 2(3) 1966 Covenant on Civil and Political Rights; Art. 13, 1984 Convention Against Torture; Arts 9 and 13, 2006 Convention for the Protection of All Persons from Enforced Disappearances; Art. 13, 1950 European Convention on Human Rights; Arts 7(1)(a) and 25, 1969 American Convention on Human Rights; Art. III(1), 1994 Inter-American Convention on Forced Disappearance of Persons; Art. 8(1), 1985 Inter-American Convention to Prevent and Punish Torture; Art. 7(1)(a), 1981 African Charter on Human and Peoples' Rights; and Art. 9, 2004 Arab Charter on Human Rights. However, it was only with the entry into force of treaties such as the 1984 Convention against Torture, Art. 14, the 1989 Convention on the Rights of the Child, Art. 39, and the 2006 International Convention for the Protection of All Persons from Enforced Disappearances, Art. 24 (4) and (5), that the duty to provide for reparation has been recognized per se in its different forms.

[55] The most advanced case law has been developed by the Inter-American Court of Human Rights, see, among others, *Velásquez Rodríguez v Honduras*, Judgment (Merits), 29 July 1988; *Moiwana Community v Suriname*, Judgment (Preliminary Objections, Merits, Reparations and Costs), 15 June 2005. In contrast, the European Court of Human Rights has for a long time adopted a rather conservative stance focusing solely on pecuniary compensation, and has only recently started to broaden its approach on reparation. Within the African human rights system, reparation has so far received insufficient attention.

[56] See UN Basic Principles on the Right to a Remedy and Reparation for Victims of Gross Violations of International Human Rights Law and Serious Violations of International Humanitarian Law, UN General Assembly Resolution 60/147, 16 December 2005, §1. (hereafter, 2005 UN Basic Principles on the Right to a Remedy and Reparation); and UN Updated Set of principles for the protection and promotion of human rights through action to combat impunity, in 'Report of the independent expert to update the Set of principles to combat impunity, Diane Orentlicher', 8 February 2005, E/CN.4/2005/102/Add.1,

within international and domestic judicial mechanisms to examine individual—and collective—reparation claims for serious violations of human rights and IHL.[57]

Types of reparation

Reparation may take different forms, including restitution, rehabilitation, compensation, satisfaction, and guarantees of non-repetition. These remedies can be implemented separately or in combination in response to the concerned violation.[58]

Restitution may include 'restoration of liberty, enjoyment of human rights, identity, family life and citizenship, return to one's place of residence, restoration of employment and return of property'.[59] Re-establishing the victims' *status quo ante*, however, is often not possible, especially in the context of serious and massive violations of human rights law and IHL. In contrast, restitution may be crucial in the context of violations of a continuing character, for example, in case of unlawful detention, where the authorities must end the breach by producing the victim.[60]

Compensation entails monetary payment for any economically assessable damage. As the legal obligation is to repair in full, compensation should cover both material and moral damage resulting from the violation.[61] Practice shows, however, that pecuniary measures may be difficult to achieve, particularly when the number of victims overwhelms the administrative and financial capacities of the responsible State. Furthermore, even when compensation programmes exist, victims might not accept them since, in their eyes, compensation cannot adequately repair the damage inflicted upon their lives.

Principle 31 (hereafter, 2005 Updated Set of principles to combat impunity). See also Resolution No. 2/2010, Reparation for Victims of Armed Conflict, adopted by the 74th Conference of the International Law Association, held at The Hague, 15–20 August 2010, at <http://www.ila-hq.org/en/committees/index.cfm/cid/1018>.

[57] As for the international level, it is important to recall that most recently the Appeal Chamber of the ICC issued its first judgment on the principles and procedures of reparation. See ICC, *Prosecutor v Lubanga*, Judgment on the appeals against the 'Decision establishing the principles and procedures to be applied to reparations' of 7 August 2012 with Amended order for reparations (Annex A) and public annexes 1 and 2 (Case No. ICC-01/04-01/06), 3 March 2015. For an overview of the most significant cases at the domestic level see the Reparations Legal Database of the Nuhanovic Foundation (NF), <http://www.nuhanovicfoundation.org/>.

[58] 2005 UN Basic Principles on the Right to a Remedy and Reparation, §§18–23. See also Arts 31–4, ILC Articles on Responsibility of States for Internationally Wrongful Acts.

[59] 2005 UN Basic Principles on the Right to a Remedy and Reparation, §19.

[60] Redress, *Implementing Victims' Rights. A Handbook on the Basic Principles on the Right to a Remedy and Reparation*, March 2006, <http://www.redress.org/reports/reports>.

[61] 2005 UN Basic Principles on the Right to a Remedy and Reparation, §20. See also Commentary to Art. 36, ILC Commentaries on the Draft Articles on Responsibility of States for Internationally Wrongful Acts.

Rehabilitation is a form of reparation that includes 'medical and psychological care as well as legal services'.[62] Services may be given in kind or the responsible party must cover their cost.[63]

Satisfaction covers any measure that repairs immaterial harm. Examples of satisfaction are: effective measures ensuring the cessation of the violation; public and full disclosure of the truth; search for the whereabouts of the disappeared; assistance in recovering, identifying, and reburying the bodies; an official declaration or judicial decision restoring the dignity, reputation, and rights of the victim; public apologies, including acknowledgments and acceptance of responsibility, legal and administrative sanctions against the person liable for the violations; commemorations and tributes to the victims; and inclusion of an account of the violations in teaching materials.[64]

Guarantees of non-repetition comprise an array of legal, administrative, and social measures, such as: review and reforms of laws; human rights and IHL training for police, armed, and security forces; as well as protection mechanisms for human rights defenders, and monitoring mechanisms for civil servants and law enforcement personnel.[65] Guarantees of non-repetition are distinct from other forms of reparation mainly by virtue of their preventive function.

Individual and collective reparation

Reparation can be awarded on an individual and collective basis. Individual reparations aim at remedying the harm caused to specific persons. The primary advantage of such reparations is to acknowledge victims' suffering and to provide them with appropriate redress. By focusing on the suffering of an individual, these forms of reparation recognize a person's distinct status as a victim, and acknowledge the harm from which they personally suffered. As a result, victims are more likely to have a sense of justice being achieved.[66]

Despite the above, individual reparations can be problematic. First, adopting an individualistic approach to reparation presents important limits in the case of massive violations of human rights and humanitarian law. In these circumstances, victims may face a number of challenges, including unequal access to courts, disparities in the magnitude of awards received, and ultimately absence of sufficient coordination between the

[62] 2005 UN Basic Principles on the Right to a Remedy and Reparation, §21.

[63] For an overview of rehabilitation measures, see Redress, Rehabilitation as a Form of Reparation: Opportunities and Challenges, Workshop Report, September 2010, <http://www.redress.org/reports/reports>.

[64] Redress, *Rehabilitation as a Form of Reparation: Opportunities and Challenges*, §22.

[65] 2005 UN Basic Principles on the Right to a Remedy and Reparation, §23.

[66] de Greiff P., 'Justice and Reparations', pp. 455–6.

benefits distributed and other measures that are also important. At the same time, the nature of massive violations may lead to insurmountable implementation challenges, mainly due to financial considerations but also to other practical problems.[67] Second, while individual reparation may privilege redress for harms caused to the individuals, it can obscure other important needs, such as structural reform, redress for the broad effects of violence, and preventing its recurrence.[68]

Given the various problems inherent in individual reparations, it is often suggested that a collective approach would better facilitate restorative justice. Collective reparations have become an important tool in transitional settings.[69] Collective reparations involve a wide range of benefits. Two aspects of these benefits deserve particular attention. First, these reparations provide a remedy for the harm of communities as a whole. As a result, they reach a greater number of victims, facilitating the healing and restoration of transitional societies. Second, collective reparations may take different forms, including public apologies, truth-seeking mechanisms, construction of memorials, and other projects that benefit victims as a group.[70]

However, collective reparations can also have some disadvantages. Among them is the concern that they are impersonal, and thus overlook the particular suffering of the victims. By focusing on the needs of the community as a whole, collective reparation risks distorting the importance of acknowledging victims and remedying their specific harm. This can create a sense among victims that justice has not been served.[71] Using reparation funds to provide non-exclusive goods or services can also result in the marginalization of vulnerable groups and minority groups who have additional or different needs. In addition, by focusing primarily on collective reparations, governments may feel allowed that they can get off with their obligations too easily.[72] Ultimately, in some

[67] de Greiff P., 'Justice and Reparations', pp. 458–9. See also Falk R., 2008, 'Reparations, International Law, and Global Justice: A New Frontier', in de Greiff P., *The Handbook of Reparations*, pp. 494–5.

[68] Roht-Arriaza N., Orlovsky K., 2009, 'A Complementary Relationship: Reparations and Development', in Duthie R., de Greiff P. (eds.), *Transitional Justice and Development: Making Connections*, New York: Social Science Research Council, p. 193.

[69] It is important to note that under international law there is no single definition of collective reparation. Over the past years, however, the idea that reparations can be distributed to collectivities has garnered interest and support. See: 2005 UN Basic Principles on the Right to a Remedy and Reparation, §13; and 2005 Updated Set of principles to combat impunity, Principle 32. For a definition of collective reparation see Rosenfeld F., 2010, 'Collective Reparations for victims of armed conflicts', *International Review of the Red Cross* Vol. 92 No. 879: 731, p. 732.

[70] Collective reparations have been conceptualized as either modalities of distribution of public goods—such as schools, health clinics, roads—tied to specific communities or as extra funds for the regions that have suffered most during the period of conflict, as in Peru or Morocco.

[71] By way of example, collective reparations may also potentially benefit perpetrators in the case of the construction of hospitals and schools.

[72] Roht-Arriaza N., Orlovsky K, 'A Complementary Relationship: Reparations and Development', pp. 192–5.

cases, it may be difficult to draw the line between collective reparations and general social services.

Clearly, the most effective and legitimate reparation programme will be one that combines individual and collective reparations of some kind, and in which the reparative value of both types is paramount.[73]

Reparation programmes

Reparation programmes are typically administrative procedures intended to address large-scale violations at the domestic level. Reparation programmes can play a significant role in the aftermath of massive violations, both in and out of conflict. To start with, given the rather large universe of beneficiaries that these programmes have, they are capable of addressing victims that have suffered various and multiple forms of abuse.[74] Moreover, administrative programmes compare more than favourably to judicial procedures. Part of that is because they offer 'faster results, lower costs, relaxed standards of evidence, non-adversarial procedures and a higher likelihood of receiving benefits'.[75] Besides that, reparation programmes are considered particularly suited in the context of mass violence as they focus on violations that come about in 'systematic ways', either as 'a consequence of the deliberate adoption of abusive policies or as a predictable consequence of other choices'.[76]

Over the past years, numerous countries facing armed conflict have implemented reparation programmes.[77] While the importance of these experiences should not be diminished, there is a certain reluctance of governments to establish such programmes. One of the main reasons that is usually invoked relates to the costs that such programmes involve. However, financial constraints only play a small role with respect to the effectiveness of these procedures. In most of the cases, indeed, other factors—i.e., lack of political will and/or reluctance to admit responsibility—prevent their establishment, or alternatively critically affect their correct implementation.[78]

[73] See OHCHR 'Rule-of-Law Tools for Post-Conflict States. Reparations Programmes', 2008, HR/PUB/08/1, pp. 22–27 (hereafter, OHCHR, Reparations Programmes 2008).

[74] OHCHR, Reparation Programmes 2008, p. 10.

[75] See 'Report of the Special Rapporteur on the promotion of truth, justice, reparation and guarantees of non-recurrence, Pablo de Greiff', 14 October 2014, A/69/518, §4 (hereafter, SR Annual Report 2014).

[76] OHCHR, Reparation Programmes 2008, p. 10.

[77] For example, Colombia, Ecuador, El Salvador, Germany, Ghana, Guatemala, Haiti, Iraq, Morocco, Nepal, Paraguay, Peru, the Philippines, Sierra Leone, Spain, Tunisia, and Uruguay.

[78] SR, Annual Report 2014, §§51–63.

INSTITUTIONAL REFORM

Institutional reform is commonly described as 'the process of reviewing and restructuring state institutions so that they respect human rights, preserve the rule of law, and are accountable to their constituents'.[79]

Reforming public institutions is a crucial task in countries emerging from armed conflict. Public institutions that perpetuated a conflict need to be transformed into institutions that support the transition, promote reconciliation, and preserve the rule of law.[80]

The importance of institutional reform can be subsumed in three principal points. First, fair and efficient public institutions play a critical role in preventing future violations. At the end of an armed conflict, preventing its recurrence constitutes the primary goal of any transitional justice strategy. Second, institutional reform contributes to addressing victims' needs as it enables public institutions, in particular in the security and justice sectors, to provide criminal accountability for the violations committed. A reformed police service, for example, can professionally investigate the abuses committed during the conflict; a reformed prosecutor's office can effectively issue indictments; and a reformed court can impartially render judgments about the alleged violations.[81] Institutional reform may, therefore, be a precondition to providing accountability for individual perpetrators and at the same time help to disable the structures that allowed violations to occur. Third, institutional reform contributes to acknowledging victims as citizens and as rights holders, and to build trust between them and their public institutions.[82]

Institutional reform may include a wide range of measures, such as: vetting, structural reform, oversight, legislative reforms, disarmament, demobilization and reintegration, training and education. An emphasis is placed here on vetting.

VETTING

Vetting is commonly defined as the process of 'assessing integrity to determine suitability for public employment'.[83] Notably, the term 'integrity' refers to 'an employee's adherence to international standards of human rights and professional conduct, including a person's financial propriety'.[84]

[79] See ICTJ website at <https://www.ictj.org/our-work/transitional-justice-issues/institutional-reform>.

[80] See OHCHR 'Rule-of-Law Tools for Post-Conflict States. Vetting: an operational framework', 2006, HR/PUB/06/5, p. 3 (hereafter, OHCHR, Vetting 2006).

[81] OHCHR, Vetting 2006, p. 3. [82] See ICTJ website.

[83] OHCHR, Vetting 2006, p. 4.

[84] See ICTJ, *Vetting Public Employees in Post-Conflict Settings: Operational Guidelines* (2006), pp. 20–1. See also OHCHR, Vetting 2006, p. 4.

A principal rationale for putting in place vetting processes in societies emerging from armed conflict is to transform abusive institutions in order to prevent the recurrence of the violations.[85] While some have argued that vetting processes are a form of sanction,[86] it is now widely accepted that vetting and the exclusion from public service of persons who committed serious violations are an essential measure in the context of transition.[87] Citizens, and in particular victims, are unlikely to trust and rely on a public institution that retains or hires individuals with serious integrity deficits. Vetting processes contribute to overcoming this lack of trust and, at the same time, legitimize public institutions.

Vetting is also important because of another reason. In the wake of armed conflict, public employees may well continue to use informal networks within which they carried out violations. Such organized networks may destabilize weak public institutions, resist the institutional reform process, and in some cases even undermine the transition process. Vetting and other exclusion processes, particularly from senior management positions, contribute to disabling such structures, thus enhancing accountability and, at the same time, strengthening the rule of law.

C. **Transitional justice in 2014**

In 2014, several countries around the world pursued agendas for transitional justice. Emphasis is here placed on the cases of Bosnia and Herzegovina and Colombia.

BOSNIA AND HERZEGOVINA

From 1992 to 1995, as Yugoslavia broke apart, the territory of Bosnia and Herzegovina (BiH) was the battleground for the most horrific crimes and serious violations of human rights and IHL. The armed conflict was characterized by atrocities: civilians were killed, concentration camps were set up, more than 2 million human beings were forced to internally displace or to seek refuge abroad, thousands of people disappeared without

[85] Mayer-Rieckh A., 2007, 'On Preventing Abuse: Vetting and Other Transitional Reforms', p. 484.

[86] See: Naarden G. L., 2003, 'Non-Prosecutorial Sanctions for Grave Violations of International Humanitarian Law: Wartime Conduct of Bosnian Police Officials', *American Journal of International Law* Vol. 97: p. 342; Ratner S. R. and. Abrams J. S, 2001, *Accountability for Human Rights Atrocities in International Law*, 2nd. ed., Oxford: Oxford University Press, p. 156.

[87] Mayer-Rieckh A., 'On Preventing Abuse: Vetting and Other Transitional Reforms', p. 485.

leaving a trace, and thousands of people were subjected to rape or otherwise sexually abused.[88]

On 14 December 1995 the General Framework Agreement for Peace in BiH—also known as the 'Dayton Peace Agreement'—put an end to the hostilities. Despite the progress that has followed since,[89] the agreement lacked a comprehensive approach and strategy in the area of transitional justice. This has significantly affected the recovery process of the BiH society, and in particular of the victims, who continued to suffer from a deep sense of frustration and exclusion.[90]

Although in the past years' trials have been carried out before the International Tribunal for the Former Yugoslavia (ICTY), transitional justice efforts undertaken in BiH have been incomplete and not in line with international standards. Unfortunately, the situation has not particularly changed in 2014.

The National Strategy on Transitional Justice

Discussions on drafting and adopting a holistic transitional justice strategy started in 2010. In the following two years, the United Nations Development Programme (UNDP) provided technical, administrative, and logistical support to an experts' working group charged with the drafting of a National Strategy on Transitional Justice. Both the working document of the strategy and the related action plan for its implementation were

[88] See 'General Allegation on the situation in Bosnia and Herzegovina to the Special Rapporteur on Truth, Justice, Reparations and Guarantees of Non-Recurrence', submitted by Track Impunity Always (TRIAL), Women's International League for Peace and Freedom, The Association of Genocide Victims and Witnesses, The Association Movement of Mothers of Srebrenica and Žepa Enclaves, February 2014, §10, <http://www.trial-ch.org/fileadmin/user_upload/documents/CAJ/BH/TRIAL_BiH_GA_SRTJ_Feb2014.pdf>. Over the past two decades, the atrocities committed in BiH have been extensively documented and addressed in legal forums by numerous NGOs and institutions. See, for example the work of: the Balkan Investigative Reporting Network Bosnia and Herzegovina (BIRN BiH), <http://birn.eu.com/en/network/birn-bosnia-and-herzegovina-home>; the Post Conflict Research Center (PCRC), <http://www.p-crc.org/>; TRIAL, <http://www.trial-ch.org/>.

[89] See International Crisis Group (ICG), 'Bosnia's Future', Europe Report No. 232, 10 July 2014, pp. 1–2. Notwithstanding these positive remarks on the current situation in BiH, the report highlights that its three communities' conflicting goals and interests are a permanent source of crisis, exacerbated by a constitution that meets no group's needs. See pp. 17–34.

[90] This was particularly evident during May 2014, when floods devastated parts of BiH leaving thousands of people—many of whom were refugees or internally-displaced during the armed conflict—once again homeless and losing almost everything they possessed. As noted by some observers, in those circumstances, the local authorities' response was belated and inadequate, revealing its impotence and lack of willingness to act responsibly. Another clear signal of the overwhelming sense of frustration of the population have been the civic protests that spread throughout the country in early February 2014, which resulted in citizens' plenums in Tuzla, Sarajevo and Mostar demanding the resignation of the current political elite. See Kosic M., 'Sarajevo, one hundred years later', 9 July 2014, <http://www.insightonconflict.org/2014/07/sarajevo-one-hundred-years-later/>.

finalized in late 2011. The draft Transitional Justice Strategy was then submitted to the two semi-autonomous entities of BiH—the Federation of Bosnia and Herzegovina (FBiH) and Republika Srpska (RS). As noted by some observers, the Strategy represents a comprehensive plan to combat impunity, provide redress for injustice, establish facts about the past, regain trust of citizens towards institutions, and deter future human rights violations.[91] Reflecting an ongoing political impasse, however, 2014 has not seen any concrete steps being undertaken toward its adoption. At the time of writing, the process is still paralysed.[92]

Truth seeking

Over the past years, there have been only a few attempts to put in place a national fact-finding and truth-seeking process in BiH.[93] Although some of these efforts have been supported by a number of organizations such as the UNDP, the United States Institute of Peace (USIP), and the International Federation of Human Rights, they have rarely demonstrated a tangible impact. Two initiatives were launched to form a truth and reconciliation commission, but with no concrete results.[94] Besides that, three fact-finding mechanisms were actually established to address violations committed in particular locations.[95] None

[91] See Šimić G., 'Transitional Justice Strategy for Bosnia and Herzegovina: an overview', 7 May 2013, <http://www.insightonconflict.org/2013/05/transitional-justice-strategy-bosnia-herzegovina/>. Notably, the draft Strategy covers non-judicial transitional justice mechanisms—truth seeking and truth telling, reparations, memorialization and institutional reforms.

[92] As it has been stressed in the 'General Allegation on the situation in Bosnia and Herzegovina to the Special Rapporteur on Truth, Justice, Reparations and Guarantees of Non-Recurrence', §19, this paralysis seems mainly due to a lack of political will by the FBiH and the RS.

[93] The importance of implementing a truth seeking national strategy was included already in the Dayton Peace Agreement, which made explicit reference to the establishment of a commission of inquiry with the purpose of promoting 'fact-finding and other necessary studies into the causes, conduct and consequences of the recent conflict on as broad and objective a basis as possible, and to issue a report thereon, to be made available to all interested countries and organizations. See the Side Letters to the Dayton Peace Agreement, 1996, reproduced in *International Legal Materials* Vol. 35: 75, pp. 160–2.

[94] In February 2000, after a conference held in Sarajevo where about 120 NGOs gathered and agreed on coordinating their efforts, the Association of Citizens Truth and Reconciliation (ATR) launched an initiative to achieve the establishment of the Truth and Reconciliation Commission of BiH. A draft law was presented in 2002 but it was never adopted. A second initiative was launched in 2005 by the NGOs Dayton Project and the USIP and supported by several national political parties but it did not succeed either.

[95] In December 2003, the government of Republika Srpska, in response to a decision by the Human Rights Chamber, created the Commission for Investigation of the Events in and around Srebrenica between 10 July and 19 July 1995. The commission was active for six months from January to June 2004 and submitted a final report in June 2004. See ICTJ, 'Bosnia and Herzegovina: Selected Developments in Transitional Justice', October 2004, p. 9, <https://www.ictj.org/publication/bosnia-and-herzegovina-selected-developments-transitional-justice>. In 2006, the Council of Ministers, in response to demands by Serb parties in the Parliamentary Assembly that the suffering of Bosnian Serbs in Sarajevo be investigated, created a Commission for Investigating the Truth Regarding Sufferings of the Serbs, Croats, Bosniaks,

of these, however, have managed to bring any visible long-term results for the BiH society, particularly for the victims.[96]

In 2014, the only State level fact-finding mechanism active in BiH was the Missing Persons Institute (MPI).[97] The MPI was created by the Law on Missing People (LMP) in 2004 to investigate the fate of the thousands of persons that went missing during the armed conflict, improve the process of tracing missing persons, and expedite the identification of mortal remains of missing persons. Today, the effectiveness of both the LMP and the MPI is unfortunately questionable. Indeed, the MPI is frequently criticized for being partial and unrepresentative.[98] Moreover, several provisions of the LMP are not yet fully implemented.[99]

Nevertheless, 2014 has seen a persistent demand in BiH for truth seeking, especially at the community level.[100] This need has prompted a number of initiatives by the civil society.[101] For example, in June 2014 the Post Conflict Research Center (PCRC) launched the 'Breaking the Stigma and Silence' campaign. The project, which was launched by PCRC in partnership with the British Embassy in Sarajevo, provided women—who had until now been forced to suffer in silence—an equal platform to present, discuss, and share their experiences of sexual violence during the armed conflict, as well as the social stigmas and lack of

Jews, and Others in Sarajevo in the period between 1992 and 1995. It, however, failed to produce a report. Lastly, in mid-2008, the Truth and Reconciliation Commission of the Municipal Assembly of Bijeljina was created. The Commission submitted its report to the Municipal Assembly for its consideration, but the report was not adopted. The report, which contains useful information on the violations that occurred in Srebrenica, can be accessed at <http://trial-ch.org/fileadmin/user_upload/documents/trialwatch/Srebrenica_Report2004.pdf>.

[96] Indeed, these mechanisms have been heavily criticized for the lack of involvement of the associations of victims in their creation and operation. See Pervanic K., 'Bosnia: Building a Shared Future, Facing the Past', Insights Newsletter—Reconciliation, 25 November 2014, <http://www.usip.org/bosnia-building-shared-future-facing-the-past>.

[97] See LMP, Official Gazette of BiH No. 50/04.

[98] See 'General Allegation on the situation in Bosnia and Herzegovina to the Special Rapporteur on Truth, Justice, Reparations and Guarantees of Non-Recurrence', §§31–3.

[99] Among the tasks that have yet to be completed are the finalization of the verification of the data inserted in the Central Record of Missing Persons (CEN) and the establishment of a Fund for the Families of the Missing. See 'General Allegation on the situation in Bosnia and Herzegovina to the Special Rapporteur on Truth, Justice, Reparations and Guarantees of Non-Recurrence', §§34–5. See also International Commission on Missing Persons (ICMP), at <http://www.ic-mp.org/where-we-work/europe/western-balkans/bosnia-and-herzegovina/>.

[100] The issue of the missing in particular continues to haunt BiH. At the end of the conflict, approximately 31,500 missing persons were unaccounted for. According to some recent figures, almost 70% of persons reported missing have been identified, but approximately 8,000 are still missing. See the interview with the ICMP Director, dated 21 March 2015, <http://www.ic-mp.org/uncategorized/one-director-of-the-missing-persons-institute-of-bosnia-and-herzegovina-issufficient/>.

[101] Civil society plays a key role in BiH with respect to transitional justice. For an exhaustive list of the NGOs and associations today operating in BiH see <http://www.insightonconflict.org/conflicts/western-balkans/>.

support that they have since endured.[102] Along the same lines, throughout 2014, the Balkan Investigative Reporting Network in BiH (BIRN BiH) launched a series of documentaries in an effort to encourage all victims to speak up and report the violations from which they suffered, as well as to promote the disclosure of the truth for all missing persons.[103] Finally, important steps were undertaken with respect to RECOM, a regional initiative aimed at establishing a regional truth commission, which today includes a large number of NGOs and associations, and has received wider support from many quarters, including the BiH authorities and the European Union.[104]

Reparation

Reparation for victims of armed conflict continued to be fragmented and insufficient in BiH during 2014.[105] To start with, despite the numerous recommendations to establish a comprehensive national reparation scheme, the BiH authorities have not yet upheld these suggestions.[106] In the absence of an adequate State response, NGOs and victims' organizations have often filled some of these gaps by providing humanitarian assistance to those victims they feel need it most.[107]

[102] Interestingly, the project provided a new perspective, as for the first time the experiences of female victims from Bosnia's three constituent ethnic groups were explored simultaneously. A photographic exhibition entitled 'Legacy of Rape' complemented the project in an effort to increase awareness of the 2014 'Global Summit to End Sexual Violence in Conflict' that was held in London.

[103] In November 2014 the BIRN BiH launched 'The Silent Scream', a documentary dedicated to the victims of sexual abuse in armed conflict, <http://birn.eu.com/en/news-and-events/birn-documentary-silent-scream-shown-in-sarajevo>. In July 2014 it presented the film 'Missing you…', dealing with the issue of missing persons, <http://birn.eu.com/en/news-and-events/birn-premieres-missing-persons-documentary>.

[104] On 14 November 2014, the Coalition held its Seventh Assembly, this time in Belgrade (Serbia), with 104 delegates, representing 1950 members, taking part in it. With one vote against and two abstentions, the delegates supported the Changes to the RECOM Statute, compiled by the envoys of the Presidents of Montenegro, Serbia, Croatia and Kosovo, and the Bosniak and Croatian members of the Presidency of BiH, in conjunction with the task of examining the constitutional and legal options for the establishment of RECOM in each country. See 'RECOM Initiative!VOICE', Vol. 20, February 2015, <http://www.zarekom.org/RECOM-Initiative-Voice/RECOM-Initiative-VOICE-No_20-2015.en.html>.

[105] For an exhaustive overview of the current reparations framework in BiH see Nuhanovic Foundation, 'War Reparations and Litigation: the case of Bosnia', 2014, pp. 17–38, <http://www.nuhanovicfoundation.org/en/news/new-report-on-war-reparations-and-litigation-in-bosnia/>.

[106] Many studies have stressed the need for BiH to establish a comprehensive reparation strategy. See for instance, 'Reparations for Wartime Victims in the Former Yugoslavia: In Search of the Way Forward', International Organization for Migration (IOM), June 2013, <http://iom.int/cms/en/sites/iom/home/what-we-do/reparation-programmes.html>. See also Popić L. Panjeta B., 'Compensation, transitional justice and conditional international credit in Bosnia and Herzegovina: Attempts to reform government payments to victims and veterans of the 1992-1995 war', June 2010, <http://www.justice-report.com/en/publications/reforming-war-related-compensation-as-part-of-transitional-justice-in-bosnia-and-herzegovina>.

[107] IOM, 'Reparations for Wartime Victims in the Former Yugoslavia: In Search of the Way Forward', p. 13, highlighting that most organizations have specialized in one particular category of victims, frequently related to what their founders went through during the armed conflict.

Besides these difficulties, victims continued to face a number of challenges in presenting their reparation claims, especially before domestic courts.[108] In 2014, many NGOs and civil society organizations complained of the inconsistent application of existing victims' legislation and the outright discrimination that some victims face, often in the context of continuing ethnic divisions.[109] In particular, victims of sexual violence continued to face great difficulties, both in accessing assistance and in obtaining some form of redress.[110] In a similar vein, the relatives of the missing continued to be largely excluded from reparation.[111] Along with discrimination, a multitude of further barriers continued to prevent victims from obtaining redress through the courts. These included, for instance, the lack of financial means for court and lawyers' fees, the psychological and physical burdens that the invariably long trials pose on victims, the unavailability of sufficient documentary evidence, and a continued lack of awareness amongst victims about the extent of their rights in this respect.[112] While these hurdles primarily affect the access of victims to redress at the domestic level, similar problems exist with respect to the victim's access to international/regional mechanisms. By way of example, in 2014 only a few reparation claims were examined by international and regional mechanisms. Notably, despite the fact that many of these claims concerned enforced disappearance cases that happened during the conflict, different bodies ended up adopting contradictory decisions.[113]

[108] For a comprehensive analysis of the current situation regarding the enforcement of property claims of victims of war crimes in particular, see TRIAL, 'Enforcement of damage compensation claims of victims of war crimes in criminal proceedings in Bosnia and Herzegovina—situation, challenges and perspectives', March 2015, <http://trial-ch.org/fileadmin/user_upload/documents/CAJ/BH/CompensationClaimsReport_March2015/TRIAL_CompensationClaim-analysisENG.pdf>. While the text puts a special emphasis on the compensation of non-pecuniary damages and specific needs and problems of the particularly vulnerable category of victims of war-related sexual violence, it also contains a review of international standards and comparative practices in relation to this issue, as well as an analysis of advantages and disadvantages of decision-making on compensation claims in criminal proceedings.

[109] See 'General Allegation on the situation in Bosnia and Herzegovina to the Special Rapporteur on Truth, Justice, Reparations and Guarantees of Non-Recurrence', §103. See also Nuhanovic Foundation, 'War Reparations and Litigation: the case of Bosnia', p. 53.

[110] As stated above, the fund to compensate missing people's families has never been set up because of continuing disagreements between the two entities about who was responsible for the conflict. See 'General Allegation on the situation in Bosnia and Herzegovina to the Special Rapporteur on Truth, Justice, Reparations and Guarantees of Non-Recurrence', §§113–15. See also Hronesova J., 'Bosnia's Search for Bones and Truth', in Balkan Insight, 17 October 2014, <http://www.balkaninsight.com/en/article/bosnia-s-search-for-bones-and-truth>.

[111] See 'General Allegation on the situation in Bosnia and Herzegovina to the Special Rapporteur on Truth, Justice, Reparations and Guarantees of Non-Recurrence', §§116–18.

[112] See Nuhanovic Foundation, 'War Reparations and Litigation: the case of Bosnia', pp. 55–6.

[113] See UN Human Rights Committee, *Communications by E. Kožljak* et al. before the Human Rights Council for the International Covenant on Civil and Political Rights, 28 October 2014; *Communications by T. Hero* et al. before the Human Rights Council for the International Covenant on Civil and Political Rights, 28 October 2014. In both cases, the Committee concluded that the events reported constituted a violation of Arts 6, 7, and 9 (2) (3) of the Covenant with regard to the victim, and Art 7 (2) (3) of the Covenant with regard to the claimants. Accordingly, applicants were entitled to redress and the State was

Institutional reform

The 1995 Dayton Peace Agreement essentially had two objectives: to end the fighting and to build a viable, democratic state of BiH. Despite the fact that the agreement managed to successfully put an end to the hostilities, the road to democracy and institutional reform has been more problematic. The agreement provided for weak State institutions. The new State of BiH was formed by two entities, the FBiH and SR, each controlling its own law enforcement, judicial, and prosecutorial functions, leading to highly fragmented sectors vulnerable to interference by local leaders with nationalist agendas.[114]

While much progress has been made during the past years to overcome such fragmentation, the institutional reform process in BiH is not yet over. Among others, two reforms in particular are needed in BiH. First of all, there is a strong need for a new constitution, involving 'a normal federation, territorially defined, without a special role for constituent peoples, but responsive to the interests of its three communities and the rights of all citizens'.[115] Over the past years, the fact that BiH was conceived as a State of two entities, but also of three constituent peoples (Bosniaks, Croats, Serbs) led to numerous problems. As noted by many observers, in 2014 BiH was still gripped in a vicious circle, including an endemic absence of political will on the part of ethnocentric leaders,[116] a cumbersome institutional framework, and a prevalent denial of responsibility for war crimes committed during the 1990s. The EU has attempted to effect change in the region as a condition of future membership. In November 2014, the United Kingdom and Germany launched a joint initiative offering an opportunity to make progress toward EU membership, if BiH authorities would sign up to substantive reforms.[117] This call has fortunately not failed. In a welcome move, in February 2015 the BiH Parliament endorsed a written commitment to critical reform addressing, among

given 180 days to inform the Committee on the measures that it would take to provide for an effective remedy to give effect to the views adopted by the Committee. The European Court of Human Rights (ECtHR) in the case of *Munira Mujkanović et al. v Bosnia and Herzegovina*, Application no. 47063/08, 3 June 2014, has instead taken an opposite view. Indeed, the Court concluded that, notwithstanding the failure to actually implement some essential provisions of the BiH Law on Missing Persons, the State had not been inactive and had taken important steps within its powers under the circumstances. Therefore there had been no violation of Arts 2, 3, 5, 8, or 13 of the European Convention of Human Rights.

[114] Mayer-Rieckh A., 2007, 'Vetting to Prevent future Abuses: Reforming the Police, Courts, and Prosecutor's Offices in Bosnia and Herzegovina'. In *Justice as Prevention. Vetting Public Employees in Transitional Societies*, edited by Mayer-Rieckh A. and de Greiff P., p. 185.

[115] See ICG, 'Bosnia's Future', at i. It is important to note that the state administration's need to reform is made acute by a 2009 decision of the ECtHR that in effect requires BiH to change the ethnicity-based way it chooses its chief executive and part of its legislature.

[116] Indeed, there are continuing tensions particularly when it comes to amending its constitution to allow minorities such as Roma and Jews to run for the highest offices. See Human Rights Watch, *World Report 2015*, p. 110, <http://www.hrw.org/world-report/2015>.

[117] See Jukic E. M., 'UK, Germany Launch Joint Initiative in Bosnia', 5 November 2014, <http://www.balkaninsight.com/en/article/uk-germany-propose-bosnia-s-renewed-eu-perspective>.

others, all the ethnic divisions that still languish almost twenty years since the end of the conflict.[118]

The second aspect deserving further attention is vetting, particularly in the law enforcement sector. Over the past years, considerable efforts and resources have been deployed to foster the vetting process in BiH. Taking into account that 'the police did not enforce the law impartially and the courts did not fairly render justice', and consequently 'public confidence in the rule of law remained low',[119] vetting processes focused mainly on the police and the judiciary. A firm reappointment process was thus put in place for the judiciary and courts, in which all judges and prosecutors were removed from their positions and had to reapply in an open competition.[120] Along the same lines, a police certification programme was established to exclude officers who had committed 'acts and/or omissions, and/or functions from the period of April 1992 to December 1995', and demonstrated 'the inability or unwillingness to uphold internationally recognized human rights standards'.[121] Despite these reforms, vetting, particularly of police, was far from being complete in 2014. Many obstacles can be cited in this respect, including above all the financial sustainability of the police framework, the continued fragmentation of the police system and the lack of independence of the police from politics.[122]

COLOMBIA

The armed conflict in Colombia is one of the longest running in the world. Over fifty years of conflict has generated a massive number of violations of human rights and humanitarian law, including the forced displacement of millions of people, more than 100,000 killings, thousands of cases of forced disappearances, sexual crimes and gender-based violence, and the forced recruitment of minors.

While efforts seeking to demobilize fighters and seek truth, justice, and reparations for victims have been going on for over ten years, 2014 represented a turning point for

[118] See Sito-Sucic D., 'Bosnia endorses reform pledge, potentially unblocking EU bid', 23 February 2015, <http://blogs.reuters.com/dariasito-sucic/>.

[119] Mayer-Rieckh A., 'Vetting to Prevent future Abuses: Reforming the Police, Courts, and Prosecutor's Offices in Bosnia and Herzegovina', p. 181.

[120] Mayer-Rieckh A., 'Vetting to Prevent future Abuses: Reforming the Police, Courts, and Prosecutor's Offices in Bosnia and Herzegovina', pp. 199–200.

[121] International Police Task Force Policy P10/2002, para. 2(h). See Mayer-Rieckh A., 'Vetting to Prevent future Abuses: Reforming the Police, Courts, and Prosecutor's Offices in Bosnia and Herzegovina', pp. 189–91.

[122] See for example Padurariu A., 2014, 'The Implementation of Police Reform in Bosnia and Herzegovina: Analysing UN and EU Efforts', International Journal of Security & Development Vol. 3 No. 4: 1.

transitional justice. Re-elected in June 2014 on a platform of continuing negotiations with the Revolutionary Armed Forces of Colombia (FARC), President Santos' administration has since entered into additional talks with the National Liberation Army (ELN).[123] Meanwhile, the Colombian Government–FARC peace talks have made significant progress. In July 2014, the parties started discussing transitional justice and, in August, a working group was established to begin looking at the 'end of the conflict', the last of five substantive agenda points.[124]

Although peace talks are increasingly raising hope that a comprehensive transitional justice strategy will soon be put in place, in 2014 responses in Colombia continued to be fragmented. Against this background, the following pages offer a brief overview of the most significant developments—and challenges—of the past months, with a particular emphasis on reparation and truth seeking.[125]

Peace talks

Peace talks achieved significant progress with respect to the transitional justice agenda during 2014. While discussions initiated with a series of landmark moves,[126] the parties have addressed many crucial aspects since.[127]

[123] See the joint press release 'Comunicado Conjunto Gobierno-ELN', 10 June 2014, <http://wsp.presidencia.gov.co/Prensa/2014/Junio/Paginas/20140610_01-Comunicado-Gobierno-ELN.aspx>. The talks began behind closed doors in Ecuador in January 2014 after a series of meetings held the previous year. See M. Gómez Giraldo, 'Los detalles de cómo se gestó el diálogo con el Eln', in *El Tiempo*, 14 June 2014, <http://www.eltiempo.com/politica/proceso-de-paz/asi-se-llego-a-los-dialogos-con-el-eln/14103015>.

[124] See ICG, 'The Day after Tomorrow: Colombia's FARC and the End of the Conflict', Latin America Report No. 53, 11 December 2014, p. 1, <http://www.crisisgroup.org/~/media/Files/latin-america/colombia/053-the-day-after-tomorrow-colombia-s-farc-and-the-end-of-the-conflict>. For an exhaustive overview of the Colombian peace talks timeline see also Colombia Reports, <http://colombiareports.co/category/colombia-news/peace-talks/>.

[125] As for institutional reform, limited measures have been undertaken thus far. The only significant exception is the current Colombian policy of disarmament, demobilization and reinsertion, which for reasons of space it is not possible to analyse here.

[126] On 7 June 2014, parties agreed on a 'Declaration of Principles' to guide discussions on transitional justice. Amid highly polarized political debate, the declaration clarified that parties would not mutually grant themselves impunity. Parties also recognized the victims' rights to truth, justice, reparation and guarantees of non-repetition. Further, in exchange for ruling out impunity, the government agreed to set up a truth commission to look into historical narrative of conflict. See Ciurlizza J., 'Paz y víctimas: en el camino correcto', in El Colombiano, 13 June 2014, <http://www.elcolombiano.com/historico/paz_y_victimas_en_el_camino_correcto-LXEC_298627>. Another important event took place on 16 August 2014, when peace talks resumed in Cuba and twelve victims of the conflict addressed the two teams of negotiators. Following the start of this new round of talks, on 22 August, General Javier Flórez, the second-in-command of Colombia's armed forces, sat down with the FARC's negotiators in Cuba, thus signalling that the talks were eventually moving into their hoped final phase. See 'The moment of truth', in *The Economist*, 30 August 2014, <http://www.economist.com/news/americas/21614157-government-and-farc-grapple-victims-truth-justice-and-mechanics-ending>.

[127] Arguably, the position undertaken by the FARC with respect to victims' rights played an important role. In this respect the FARC delegation presented ten proposals: (1) Clarification of the historical

First of all, some important steps have been undertaken with respect to truth seeking. On 21 August 2014, the Historical Commission on the Conflict and Victims (CHCV) was created to study the roots of the conflict, as well as the factors that have stood in the way of bringing it to an end.[128] On 11 February 2015, the CHCV, which is composed of twelve historians, released its report.[129] Notably, the report did not reveal one 'historic truth' or one 'official history' but clarified, at least in part, the causes of the conflict, highlighting at the same time where there is yet no consensus.[130] Along with this important achievement, it is also important to note that, in October 2014, the FARC proposed to create a 'national census of victims' of the armed conflict. The proposed census would aim to determine the number of victims from the armed conflict.[131] While a truth commission will emerge only once a peace agreement is signed, these two efforts cannot but be welcome as a further step toward this direction.

Second, critical proposals have been made with respect to victims' reparations. In early September 2014, the FARC proposed to create a compensation fund for victims of the conflict consisting of 3% of the country's Gross Domestic Product (GDP), which translates into US$11.3 billion.[132] Reportedly, the fund should guarantee the direct participation of representatives of victims' organizations, re-establish the situation of individual and collective victims as it was before the victimizing events took place, and

truth of the conflict and its impact on the population; (2) Recognition of the victims of the conflict; (3) Special recognition of collective victims; political and social organizations, trade unions and peasant and afro-descendant communities, and indigenous peoples; (4) Systemic responsibility, primary responsibility of the state and multiple responsibilities, including responsibilities of the guerrilla, towards the victims of the conflict; (5) Full recognition and real and effective materialization of the rights of the victims of the conflict, with particular attention to women's rights; (6) Full compensation for the victims of conflict and creation of the Special Fund for Comprehensive Compensation; (7) Direct participation of the victims of the conflict and their organizations in the definition of policies for the effective protection of their rights; (8) Agreed definition of legal mechanisms and tools to ensure the rights of the victims of the conflict; (9) Provision of real and material guarantees of non-repetition; (10) Political and social pardon as a foundation for a national reconciliation process. See FARC-EP, 'Comprehensive rights of victims for peace and national reconciliation', <http://farc-epeace.org/index.php/communiques/communiques-peace-delegation/item/521-comprehensive-rights-of-victims-for-peace-and-national-reconciliation.html>.

[128] See Vieira C., 'Breakthroughs and Hurdles in Colombia's Peace Talks', 25 August 2014, <http://www.ipsnews.net/2014/08/breakthroughs-and-hurdles-in-colombias-peace-talks/>.

[129] See Colombia Reports, 'Historic Commission releases report on causes of Colombia conflict', 11 February 2015, <http://colombiareports.co/historic-commission-releases-report-causes-colombia-conflict/>. The executive summary of the 800 pages report can be accessed at <http://www.eltiempo.com/contenido/politica/proceso-de-paz/ARCHIVO/ARCHIVO-15228175-0.pdf>.

[130] See Colombia Reports, 'Historic Commission releases report on causes of Colombia conflict'.

[131] See TeleSUR, 'FARC Proposes 'Census of Victims' in Colombia, 26 October 2014, <http://www.telesurtv.net/english/news/FARC-Proposes-Census-of-Victims-in-Colombia-20141026-0034.html>.

[132] See Colombia Reports, 'FARC proposes $11B fund for Colombia conflict victims', 8 September 2014, <http://colombiareports.co/colombias-guerrilla-group-farc-proposes-victims-compensation-fund/>.

compensate the impact on their lives, according to international standards.[133] The fund should additionally focus on social, territorial, and gender justice.

Third, much discussion has been devoted to accountability related questions. Not surprisingly, discussions have been more difficult in this respect. Indeed, while parties generally agree on the necessity to address the needs of the victims affected by the conflict, positions differ with respect to respective responsibilities for the violations committed during the conflict,[134] as well as regarding the conditions under which eventual prosecutions might take place.[135]

Truth seeking

Demands for truth seeking increased dramatically in Colombia during 2014, especially from the relatives of the missing. Notwithstanding the urgency of these calls, Colombian responses to truth seeking remained largely insufficient.[136]

A major obstacle that emerged relates to the fact that, while demobilization has been slowly making progress, so far only a limited number of former members of the guerrillas have agreed to contribute to truth seeking.[137] Arguably, such reluctance might be

[133] See FARC-EP, 'FARC propose fund for comprehensive victim's compensation', 7 September 2014, <http://farc-epeace.org/index.php/blogs/guests/item/525-farc-propose-fund-for-comprehensive-victim-s-compensation.html>.

[134] Thus far, the FARC position has not included an official admission of responsibility for the violations committed during the armed conflict. On 30 October 2014, for example, the FARC admitted that their actions have adversely affected the civilian population, but stated that they did not target civilians or commit war crimes. See ICG, Crisis Watch no. 136, 1 December 2014, <http://www.crisisgroup.org/~/media/Files/CrisisWatch/2014/cw136.ashx>.

[135] Indeed, the most contentious issue concerns the prosecution—and punishment—of those responsible for serious international crimes and other gross violations of human rights. So far, discussions seem to have been leaning toward more lenient punishments for those involved, such as non-prison sanctions, or reduced terms in jail. The condition, however, would be a firm commitment by the parties regarding reparation and other forms of assistance for the victims. In February 2015, however, the debate took another turn. Former President Gaviria suggested requiring not just guerrillas and soldiers, but also politicians, business people, landowners, and civilian officials, to confess their involvement in the most serious human rights abuses committed during the conflict. In exchange for such confessions and efforts to make amends to victims, Gaviria's proposal would exempt non-combatants from serving prison sentences. Among the Colombian military, the proposal would exempt lower-ranking officers, as well as those who committed crimes by 'omission'. For an overview of the surrounding debate see for instance: Washington Office on Latin America (WOLA), 'The Transitional Justice Debate Heats Up', posted on Colombia.org, 2 March 2015, <http://colombiapeace.org/2015/03/02/the-transitional-justice-debate-heats-up/>; Goi L., 'No peace with impunity for Colombia', posted on New Internationalist Blog, 31 March 2015.

[136] Meanwhile, exhumations continued to be carried out in Colombia. Recent figures indicated, for instance, that in 2014 more than 5,300 bodies were found, but more than 3,000 of these remains had not been identified.

[137] It has been reported that only the 8% of the members of armed groups who have decided to lay down their arms is willing to participate to truth seeking efforts. Most of them deny having any sort of information either on the whereabouts and fate of the missing or on the location of the mass graves. See Verdad

explained by the fact that most of the individuals involved in these violations persist in denying responsibility. However, this situation is also the result of some gaps in the current demobilization programme, particularly where it does not require participation in truth seeking as a condition for demobilized members of armed groups.[138]

Reparation

By contrast, reparation became increasingly a reality for victims in Colombia during 2014. As is well known, Colombia is a unique case in the universe of reparation. First of all, the process of reparation started while the conflict was still not over.[139] Second, the Victims and Land Restitution Law, passed in 2011,[140] is by far the most comprehensive and detailed piece of legislation that has ever been adopted in the world to redress victims of armed conflict.[141] Third, reparation efforts made huge progress not only in a quite restricted time frame, but also from the perspective of many categories of vulnerable people, including women, internally displaced persons (IDPs) and indigenous groups. As reparation covered a wide range of aspects in 2014, what follows is a brief overview of a few significant developments and challenges registered in the past months.

Abierta, 'Las deudas de Justicia y Paz con las víctimas', 9 April 2015, <http://www.verdadabierta.com/justicia-y-paz/reparaciones-a-victimas/5702-las-deudas-de-justicia-y-paz-con-las-victimas>. Notably, the implementation of the Justice and Peace law, which offers dramatically reduced sentences to demobilized paramilitaries who confess their crimes, has been very slow. As of September 2014, only thirty-seven of the more than 30,000 paramilitaries who officially demobilized had been convicted of crimes under the Justice and Peace law—nine years after it was approved. The convictions cover a small portion of the nearly 70,000 crimes confessed by defendants seeking the law's benefits. See Human Rights Watch, World Report 2015, pp. 168–9.

[138] See Verdad Abierta, 'Las deudas de Justicia y Paz con las víctimas'.

[139] The process of victim reparation in Colombia started already in 2005 with the adoption of the Law of Peace and Justice. See L. 975 D.O. art. 1. The law declared perpetrators responsible for providing reparations and offered reduced penalties in exchange. In order to receive reparations, victims first had to come forward and report the crime, and then go through a legal proceeding to establish the legal culpability of that particular crime's perpetrator. Once these steps were completed, the victim could subsequently seek damages and restitution from the guilty party. Despite its novelty, effective implementation of the Law of Peace and Justice faced a number of problems. See Summers N., 2012, 'Colombia's Victims' Law: Transitional Justice in a Time of Violent Conflict?', *Harvard Human Rights Law Journal*, Vol. 25: 219, pp. 223–4.

[140] Ley 1448 Diario Oficial (L.1448 DO). The law was approved and signed by President Juan Manuel Santos Calderón on 10 June 2011.

[141] L. 1448 DO, Arts 28, 31, 49, 51–4, and 132–33. The law provides a number of guarantees for the victims of the armed conflict: (1) it establishes an administrative program that allows victims massive access to comprehensive reparations, and places the burden of proof on the State; (2) it creates new institutions only and exclusively dedicated to guaranteeing victims' rights: the Land Restitution Unit, the Historical Memory Center, and the Unit for Attention and Reparation of Victims; (3) it creates the National System of Attention and Comprehensive Reparation of Victims, which gathers fifty-three national entities,

Women. Since the Colombian armed conflict has had a disproportionate impact on women's lives, over the past months there has been increasing attention to implement reparation from a gender and women's rights perspective.[142] Despite these efforts, the effective access to reparation by women continued to be prevented by a number of obstacles, including lack of awareness and adequate information on their rights and reparation mechanisms, socio-economic disparities, and persistent discriminatory attitudes among public officials.[143]

Victims of sexual violence. Special measures were taken with regard to victims of sexual abuse in the context of the conflict. Crimes against sexual freedom and integrity were set as one of the gradualness and progressiveness criteria established by the State to be able to access comprehensive reparation. As per the compensation measures, it was calculated that, as of August 2014, the government invested 2.4 trillion Colombian pesos (around US$1.3 billion) for 400,000 victims (specifically 2,300 victims whose victimizing event was a 'crime against sexual freedom and integrity'). The government also decided to contribute to the construction of a new life with the victims. As part of this programme, figures indicate that a total of 46,057 victims (65% of them women) have participated in financial education days that aim to provide victims guidance on their investments.

Indigenous groups. Access to reparation by indigenous communities increased significantly during 2014. The most notable developments have been registered in the context of land restitution claims, where indigenous groups most successfully asserted their rights, pressing for land claims, defining their own plans for land use and environmental management in their territories, and developing strategies to promote peace and economic and cultural development.[144]

monitoring bodies, mayors' offices, governorates, and the roundtables for the effective participation of victims; (4) it consolidates the Single Registry of Victims, both individual and collective ones, as a trusted source of information on the scale of victims caused by the internal armed conflict, disaggregated by all the differential approaches; (5) it creates environments and effective tools for the victims to directly influence the institutional bodies where the implementation of the public policy that benefits them is defined; (6) it includes measures to comprehensively repair victims of forced displacement, dispossession or forced abandonment of lands, homicide, kidnapping, torture, forced disappearance, recruitment of children and youth, landmines, and sexual violence in the context of the armed conflict; (7) prior-consultation proceedings are established as a mechanism and a tool to guarantee the rights of ethnic communities.

[142] According to some recent figures, women represent almost 50% of the total number of victims of the armed conflict. See the Statement by Ms Paula Gaviria Betancur, Head Director of the Unit for Attention and Reparation of Victims of Colombia, at the official presentation of the Guidance Note of the Secretary General: 'Reparations for Conflict-Related Sexual Violence', Permanent Mission of Colombia to the UN, 1 August 2014, <http://www.colombiaun.org/English/Recent%20Events/august_1_2014_Gaviria.html>.

[143] See ICTJ, 'Queremos ser oídas. Obstáculos para la participación de las mujeres en los mecanismos de participación para la atención a víctimas del conflicto armado interno', June 2014, <https://www.ictj.org/es/publication/queremos-ser-oidas-mujeres-reparaciones-colombia>.

[144] Particularly successful was the case of the Curvaradó and Jiguamiandó communities, which resulted in three eviction notices on occupiers of the land. See ABColombia, 'Civil Society Speaking Out: Agendas for a Sustainable Peace in Colombia', November 2014, <http://www.abcolombia.org.uk/subpage.asp?subid=454&mainid=23>.

Other communities. Sadly, access to reparation remained more difficult for communities who suffered from massive violations. In some cases, bureaucracy was at the origins of the problems, thus preventing access to courts by victims.[145] In other cases, existing reparation schemes faced numerous challenges in addressing large-scale reparation claims, mainly because of the extensive number of communities that suffered from these violations during the conflict and are today waiting for redress.[146]

Concluding remarks

Societies emerging from armed conflict face a number of complex challenges. Among these, there is primarily the need to address victims' demands for justice for the violations from which they suffered. However, from a victims' perspective, the pursuit of justice is not limited to prosecution. For some victims, justice is about learning the truth, knowing what happened to their relatives. Others see justice as tied to their recognition as right holders, entitled to remedies and social support. Similarly, other victims describe justice more broadly as a process of healing, building trust and reconciliation in a new society. What is thus indispensable, and what transitional justice measures seek to accomplish, is to recognize all these victims' needs in a comprehensive and integrated manner.

Today, transitional justice plays a predominant role in the wake of armed conflict. Along with Colombia and BiH, the two countries here studied, a significant number of countries have started implementing transitional justice strategies. It is sufficient here to recall, for example, the cases of Guatemala, Nepal, Peru, Sierra Leone, where major efforts have been put in place to establish truth commissions, prosecution mechanisms, reparations, and institutional reforms, either as stand-alone initiatives or in parallel

[145] See for example the case of the village of Santa Cecilia in Astrea, theatre of a cruel slaughter perpetrated by paramilitary North Block on January 28, 2000, which left 12 people dead and more than 800 inhabitants displaced. Today, after 15 years, the victims are still facing difficulties in getting access to the courts. See Verdad Abierta, 'Entanglement in the reparation of victims of Salvatore Mancuso', 9 February 2015, <http://www.verdadabierta.com/justicia-y-paz/reparaciones-a-victimas/5608-reparacion-victimas-mancuso>. Likewise the victims of the so-called Bloque Catatumbo, a paramilitary group, are still waiting to receive redress after more than a decade. See Verdad Abrierta, 'El largo camino para reparar a las víctimas de "El Iguano"', 25 June 2014, <http://www.verdadabierta.com/justicia-y-paz/reparaciones-a-victimas/5366-el-largo-camino-para-reparar-a-las-victimas-de-el-iguano>.

[146] This is especially true for communities that were internally displaced as a result of the conflict. See Verdad Abierta, 'How to repair damage from the war in the Pacific nariñense', 2 March 2014, <http://www.verdadabierta.com/justicia-y-paz/reparaciones-a-victimas/5271-como-reparar-los-danos-de-la-guerra-en-el-pacifico-narinense>.

with others.[147] While some of these initiatives continued throughout 2014, the past months witnessed important steps being undertaken in a few countries in an effort to start discussions on adopting a holistic transitional justice approach. In South Sudan, for example, a coalition of law and civil society groups has presented guidelines for achieving transitional justice in the country, including the establishment of a hybrid court.[148] Similarly, encouraging moves toward a comprehensive transitional justice strategy have been undertaken in Burundi, including the establishment of the Truth and Reconciliation Commission, initiatives to address land restitution and other forms of reparation, as well as some initial discussions on institutional reforms.[149]

Despite these welcome developments, many challenges remain when it comes to putting in place transitional justice mechanisms. As noted above, transitional justice efforts are often confronted with a number of obstacles, including lengthy negotiations and proceedings, politicization of the transitional process, financial and practical hurdles in addressing massive violations of human rights and IHL, different victims' perspectives and expectations, and reluctance by national authorities to fully engage in the transformation and reconciliation process.

Arguably, two main reflections can be drawn from these experiences. The first is that any transitional justice response must be primarily context based. Each country experience is indeed unique, given the different levels of armed violence involved, the type and magnitude of the harm suffered by the victims, and the various levels of responsibility therein involved. This does not mean that best practices cannot be identified. On the contrary, some initiatives like the ones currently under revision in BiH with respect to truth seeking and vetting, or the reparation programme provided by the Victims Law in Colombia, constitute certainly important experiences from which it is possible to draw some lessons for the future. Besides that, what perhaps emerges is that both victims and others—i.e., civil society, authorities, and other actors, including perpetrators and those responsible for the violations—must be involved in any discussion and implementation of transitional justice initiatives. Indeed, it is only by listening and giving voice to victims and to all the actors involved in the conflict that any transitional justice effort will perhaps achieve real justice for the victims and communities affected by armed conflict and, at the same time, bring hope and pave the way to a new society.

[147] For an exhaustive overview of the most recent developments see the countries profiles on the ICTJ website.

[148] The guidelines for South Sudan, linked for download below and titled 'Transitional Justice Strategy for South Sudan', emerged from an August 2014 conference held in Nairobi that included more than sixty national and international participants. See Radio Tamazuj, 'S Sudan lawyers offer transitional justice strategy', 16 October 2014, <https://radiotamazuj.org/en/article/s-sudan-lawyers-offer-transitional-justice-strategy>.

[149] See the Preliminary observations and recommendations by Special Rapporteur on the promotion of truth, justice, reparation and guarantees of non-recurrence, following his visit to Burundi on 8–16 December 2014, <http://www.ohchr.org/EN/NewsEvents/Pages/DisplayNews.aspx?NewsID=15426&LangID=E>.

INDEX

The manufacturer's authorised representative in the EU for product safety is Oxford University Press España S.A. of El Parque Empresarial San Fernando de Henares, Avenida de Castilla, 2 - 28830 Madrid (www.oup.es/en or product.safety@oup.com). OUP España S.A. also acts as importer into Spain of products made by the manufacturer.
Printed and bound by CPI Group (UK) Ltd, Croydon, CR0 4YY
22/09/2026
02220718-0001